KV-511-405

Contents

Acknowledgements

The authors would like to thank everyone who helped and assisted them with the creation of this second edition – including friends, colleagues and readers of the first edition whose positive and constructive comments were taken into account when the new format was devised.

Special thanks are due to our publisher, Margaret Berriman, for her invaluable advice and constant encouragement and to Jan Nikolic, her development editor, who had the unenviable job of processing an endless amount of paper in record time. We would also like to thank Paul Carysforth and Rebecca Hargreaves who willingly (we think!) helped us with some of the more routine and tedious aspects of book creation!

The authors and publishers would also like to thank the following individuals and organisations for permission to reproduce photographs and other copyright material:

Action Images Sports Photography, British School of Motoring Limited, Cap and Gown Services, Charities Aid Foundation (Direct Donor Services), Disneyland Paris, Employment Service Disability Services Branch, Ford Motor Company Limited, Girobank plc, The Guardian, John Lewis Partnership, The Leith Agency, Microsoft Limited, National Power, Pictor International, Popperfoto/Reuters, Prudential Assurance Company, Radio Advertising Bureau, Rover Cars, Sage Accounting Software, The Samaritans, Tesco plc, TSB Retail Banking and Insurance.

HEINEMANN
GNVQ

INTERMEDIATE
USINESS

SECOND EDITION

CAROL CARYSFORTH
MAUREEN RAWLINSON
MIKE NEILD

Heinemann

Heinemann Educational Publishers,
Halley Court, Jordan Hill, Oxford OX2 8EJ
a division of Reed Educational & Professional Publishing Ltd

MELBOURNE AUCKLAND FLORENCE
PRAGUE MADRID ATHENS SINGAPORE
TOKYO SAO PAULO CHICAGO PORTSMOUTH (NH)
MEXICO IBADAN GABORONE JOHANNESBURG
KAMPALA NAIROBI

First Published 1995

99 98 97 96
10 9 8 7 6 5 4 3

A catalogue record for this book is available from the
British Library on request

ISBN 0 435 45254 1

Designed by Roger Denning and typeset by TechType, Abingdon
Printed in Great Britain by Bath Press Ltd, Bath

Tutor introduction to new edition

When the first edition of this book was written, GNVQ schemes were still in their infancy, particularly in relation to grading, assessment and evidence collection. Since then, the schemes have been adjusted, amended and consolidated. Greater clarification has been given on the areas to be studied and the depth of knowledge required by students. At the same time, constant feedback from external verifiers and advisers has revealed a tendency on the part of teachers and tutors to over-assess candidates. Although this was understandable, given the original requirement to cover each of the performance criteria and all the range statements, it did result in loss of motivation for students. Many of them have experienced great difficulty in completing the amount of work that was necessary. In addition, too much of the assessable evidence was required in written format. The Evidence Indicators included in the scheme now give clear guidance as to the amount of assessment required.

This does give rise to a conflict for teachers whose students need regular practical activities to retain interest and involvement. Pages of text, and information with relatively few activities, are discouraging at this level of study.

These developments and observations, plus the comments and feedback received from tutors who used the first edition, have been taken into consideration when devising the format of this second edition. The aim has been to retain the student's active interest and participation – without overburdening either the student or the tutor with a mass of assessable activities – yet still cover the scheme in its entirety. At the same time, it is desirable that individual tutors have the scope to redesign or introduce specific projects and assignments to incorporate local industry, new initiatives and developments and the student's own practical experience.

The book has therefore been designed in the following way to meet these objectives.

- The main text is divided into four sections – one for each unit of the scheme.
- Each sub-section covers one element of the scheme. Therefore the first sub-section covers Element 1.1, and so on.
- The main text displays headings which relate directly to the performance criteria and the range statements. Practical and up-to-date examples from the real world of business are included throughout to enhance student understanding and retain interest.
- **Non-assessed activities** are provided at regular intervals to stimulate discussion and debate and to consolidate learning.
- **Optional evidence assignments** are included, which tutors may set for students to carry out. These help the students to develop their creativity, as well as skills in researching, analysing, and seeking information. The evidence produced is not always in written form, thereby reducing the amount of writing (and marking!) required and enhancing verbal and presentation skills.

Each evidence assignment lists the appropriate performance criteria and range for recording purposes. Many are ideal as homework or consolidation exercises. They are also invaluable for obtaining additional evidence of different aspects of the range statement which may not be incorporated into the Evidence Indicator project.

Tutors who do not wish to use these assignments as supplementary evidence can use them with groups of students to consolidate learning.

- In most elements, sections entitled '**Evidence Indicator project**' appear in the text when students should have completed criteria linked to one or two specified evidence indicators. At this point it may be suitable for students to start working towards their major project. In this case the project can be undertaken in stages, so that students can work towards completion as they cover different sections of the course. Tutors who are devising their own major project, or an integrated project to cover several elements or units, or who wish their students to do the main project *only* when the element has been completed, can instruct their students to ignore these prompts. Note that if there is only one evidence indicator for an element, this is stated at the start of the element.
- At the end of each element there is an **Evidence Indicator project**, which has been written so that it can easily be amended, adjusted or tailored to suit the individual needs of a student or institution. These pages are also photocopiable so that they can be included in the student's portfolio for reference by the internal and external verifiers.

v

From Element 1.1 it is suggested that students may benefit from adopting one company for an in-depth study throughout the course. The option to return to this same organisation to obtain additional evidence is given whenever possible throughout the book.

- Although the Evidence Indicator projects suggest that the students produce written evidence for their portfolios, there is no reason why, *equivalent* evidence, in another medium, should not be included. Reports can be oral and recorded on audio – or video cassette; they can comprise a poster presentation. Your students do not need to be constrained by the written word. Let them use their imaginations to put fun back into learning!
- Do note that assessment is now at element level and not at the level of individual performance criteria. This should simplify recording documentation and tracking quite considerably.

Tutors should note that for both optional evidence assignments and the evidence indicator project, general core skills areas are indicated but precise coverage is not. This is because it would be inappropriate to add this if tutors are being given the flexibility to adjust and adapt any assignment or project to suit their own needs and those of their students.

It is strongly recommended that individual tutors liaise over project submission dates to ensure these are staggered to prevent students being over-burdened at any stage of the course.

It is hoped that these adjustments will make this edition more readily usable for tutors and yet still retain the informative and friendly style of the first book which, we understand, was enjoyed by students and tutors alike.

Carol Carysforth
Maureen Rawlinson
Mike Neild
May 1995

Student information

This book has been written to help you to achieve your GNVQ Intermediate award in Business. To be successful you will have to produce a portfolio of evidence that proves you have covered and understood the full range of topics specified for each unit of the award.

- **Four** of the units are **mandatory**. This means they are compulsory.
- **Two** units are **optional**.
- In addition, you have to cover **three core skills.** Finally, you also have to pass an **external test** for each unit, which is set and marked by your awarding body. The pass mark for this test is 80 per cent.

You have the opportunity of achieving a Merit or Distinction provided that **at least one third** of the work in your portfolio meets the criteria for that grade (see under *Grading* in the *Student guide*).

You are strongly advised to read the *Student guide,* which follows this introduction, very carefully. This explains:

- the layout of the book and how it has been designed to help you
- the methods you can use to collect evidence (and some ideas for practising them)
- how you can achieve a Merit or a Distinction
- what is meant by 'Core skills' and 'Personal skills'.

Your tutor will give you the remaining information you need, which will include:

- the name of your awarding body
- the course content you have to cover, including your option units
- how you must record and store your evidence.

It is likely that you will have to complete a number of major projects and some minor assignments. Some assignments and projects are given in this book. Your tutor may decide to use some – or all – of these or to give you separate assignments and projects written with a local flavour, to reflect organisations in your own locality.

You may find some of the information overwhelming – or even confusing – at first. Remember that your tutor is there to help and advise you on any particular points. As you get used to the scheme, you will soon find that everything starts to fit into place.

We hope that you will enjoy your GNVQ course and learn much that is interesting and will be of help to you in the future.

Carol Carysforth
Maureen Rawlinson
Mike Neild
May 1995

Student guide

The layout of this book

The four main sections in this book relate to the four mandatory units in the award. Each unit is clearly divided into the individual elements you need to cover.

Within each section you will find:

- the **main text**, which covers all the topics you have to know about – the headings and sub-headings link to the performance criteria and range of topics you have to cover
- **activities** designed to help you to think for yourself and work with your fellow students – these activities have been designed to give you practice and develop your learning. They are not assessed as part of your award.
- **optional assignments** which your tutor may ask you to complete – these will help you to develop skills to carry out some of the main projects you will have to complete, and the activities may contribute towards your **supplementary evidence**, which you can show to your verifier
- **evidence indicator prompts** which will lead towards a main project at the end of each element – your tutor may ask you to work towards and complete this project, or may have written a special project for you to complete. This may link with other elements and units in the award, in which case it may be called an **integrated project.**

All assessable activities include details of the performance criteria and range covered, so that you can record this information accurately. The core skills areas are also indicated but specific coverage is not given, as your tutor may adjust these requirements before giving you the work to do. You will need to record all the areas you have covered accurately, so that you can show that, by the end of your course, you have covered all the parts of the scheme.

Understanding GNVQ and GNVQ terms

If you have progressed to your *GNVQ Intermediate* award by achieving a *GNVQ Foundation* award, you can probably skip this section. However, if you are new to GNVQ then many of the terms you hear will be very strange at first. This section is written to help you to understand them and to act as a reference section in the early stages of your course.

What is GNVQ and what is 'Intermediate' level?

The abbreviation 'GNVQ' stands for General National Vocational Qualification. An Intermediate level award is the same as four GCSEs, grade C or above (depending upon the final grade of your portfolio).

When you have achieved an Intermediate level GNVQ you can progress to Advanced level (which is equivalent to two A-levels). Alternatively, if you start work you may prefer to continue by studying an NVQ course at level 3. The abbreviation 'NVQ' stands for National Vocational Qualification.

What do I study?

All students on a GNVQ Intermediate course study:

- **four** mandatory – or compulsory – units
- **two** option units
- **three** core skills areas.

In addition, you may have the opportunity to study additional units or GCSEs alongside your Intermediate award.

Mandatory units

The mandatory units have been chosen for you. 'Mandatory' means compulsory. For Business, the mandatory units are:

1 Business organisations and employment
2 People in business organisations
3 Consumers and customers
4 Financial and administrative support for business.

Option units

There are **four** different option units you can choose from, but your school or college may not offer all of them. The choice available will also depend upon the awarding body with whom you are registered. City and Guilds, BTEC and RSA all offer different option units. You will have to discuss with your tutor which are available.

Some schools and colleges start their courses by concentrating only on the mandatory units and add the option units later. Talk to your tutor and find out if this occurs on your course.

Core skills

There are **three** core skills areas which are studied in all GNVQ courses at all levels. However, the skills you need to demonstrate are obviously different for the different levels of the award. The higher the level, the more skills you need.

The core skills areas are:

- Communication
- Application of number
- Information technology.

You may have separate lessons in these subjects, so that you can gain the skills required, and you may be asked to do a range of tasks or exercises in these subjects. However, for a GNVQ award you **demonstrate** that you can do them by **using** them in a practical way when you are doing assignments and projects related to the mandatory units and your chosen option units. This means that the core skills are **integrated** into your other assessments.

Don't, therefore, be surprised to find core skills areas coming up again and again in different projects!

Additional units

You can also achieve additional units to add to your GNVQ award. These may be special units offered by your awarding body, or extra GCSEs you decide to take, or GCSEs you decide to resit. These will help to convince either a prospective employer or an admissions tutor that you are capable of achieving more than the basic award. However, it is important that you don't try to do too much in one year – and jeopardise your main award.

Whereas additional units may not be necessary to progress to GNVQ Advanced level, if you are thinking about moving on to a degree course at some time in the future, you may need GCSE Mathematics and English at grade C or above. *Now* may be the perfect time to improve your grades in these subjects!

At Advanced level, additional units or an A-level as an extra qualification may considerably improve your chances of being accepted on the degree course of your choice.

Understanding the words used in GNVQs

Some special words are used in GNVQs and you *must* know what they mean. You have already met one GNVQ word – **mandatory**. Others are given below.

- **Units** – A unit is an area of study. For Intermediate GNVQ you have to complete six units, i.e. six areas of study.

- **Element** – Each unit is made up of elements. At Intermediate level there are **three** or **four** elements in every unit, e.g. Element 1.1 is *Explain the purposes and types of business organisations*. The first figure shows the unit number (1) and the second the element number (1). This is therefore the first element in the first unit of your Business course.

- **Performance criteria or 'must' statements** – For each element there are several statements that say what you must be able to do to prove you have studied the element. For instance, the first statement in Element 1.1 says that you must '*describe developments in industrial sectors*'. You *must* be able to do this to gain your award.

- **Range** – Range statements describe the specific areas you must cover in relation to each 'must' statement. For instance, in the performance criteria mentioned above, two statements are shown in bold type – **developments** and **industrial sectors**. These are repeated in the range statements, which explain what must be covered under 'developments' and what must be covered under 'industrial sectors'. These statements act as a guide, both for you *and* your tutor, to show exactly what you need to understand and be able to explain.

- **Evidence indicator** – This gives information on the evidence you need to provide, at the end of each element, to prove that you have covered all the key areas on which you will be assessed.

- **Portfolio** – Your portfolio is a folder or ring binder which, by the end of your course, will contain all your completed assignments. You will need to keep your work neatly filed and well-organised all year! Your portfolio must be locked away *safely* – if you lose it, report the fact to your tutor *immediately*.

- **Supplementary evidence** – Additional tasks and activities that do not form part of your main evidence should be filed neatly in a separate file. These provide extra proof of the work you have done during the year.

- **Verifier** – The role of a verifier is to check that you have provided evidence for each area of the course. The verifier checks this by looking through your portfolio to see the work which you have completed. The verifier may also study your supplementary evidence file to look at other activities or tasks you have carried out. There are two types of verifier:
  - the **internal verifier** is a member of your college or school staff who checks your portfolio
  - the **external verifier** is appointed by the awarding body who will give you your award – City and Guilds, BTEC or RSA. The external verifier will visit your school or college twice throughout the year to check the work that you are doing.

- **End tests** – These are short, one-hour tests that are set for three of the mandatory units. Only the mandatory unit *Financial and Administrative support for business* is not end-tested. Do not panic about end tests! Your tutor will explain them and give you practice before you take any. Quite simply, you will have to answer a number of objective questions (where you choose one option from several possible answers) to prove your knowledge in a particular unit. If you fail an end test then you can resit at a later date – as many times as your school or college will allow.

How do I gain the award?

You gain the award when you have proved you have completed your studies in all these areas. You do this by:

- passing the end tests for the *Intermediate Business* award
- completing all your projects and assignments and putting them in your portfolio of evidence
- providing additional or supplementary evidence to show the coursework you have done.

How do I obtain a Distinction or a Merit grade?

Each assignment you complete for your portfolio will be graded by your tutor and the grade will be entered on a special grading form. Information about grading is given on page xiv.

To obtain a Distinction or Merit grade, **at least one third** of your work *throughout your portfolio* must be at this grade. Individual units are not graded.

You will be able to see what grade you are achieving by looking at your grading form. It will be easy to see whether you are managing to achieve Distinction or Merit grades consistently across all the different grading themes.

Collecting evidence

There are many ways in which you can collect evidence. The following is therefore only a guide to the main methods used in this book. If you have never used some of these methods before, you may be uncertain what some of the terms mean. Read the explanations below *carefully* and return to this section to refresh your memory whenever you wish.

If you need to practise any of these methods, you can try the 'trial run' exercise(s) mentioned after some of these explanations. This will help you to understand the method described before you actually use it.

Brainstorming

This is a good way of generating new ideas within a group.

- Nominate a group leader.
- For a limited period (about ten minutes) the group leader should ask for as many ideas as possible.
- Write *all* of these down, no matter how wild some of them may seem to be! Don't criticise anyone's ideas at this stage.
- Group ideas together where they overlap and see if there are any 'themes'.
- Rate them in one of three ways – S (sensible), P (possible), F (far-fetched).
- Look at your themes and see how many sensible (or possible) ideas would fit. You should find that as you do this:
  - you discover ways in which some of the ideas could be adapted
  - you realise that some of the more far-fetched suggestions *could* be linked to the more sensible ones to give usable suggestions.

Trial run

1 Suppose your group wishes to raise money for a charity. In ten minutes write down as many ideas for fund-raising as you can for the group's nominated charity.
2 In fifteen minutes, how many uses can your group find for a paperclip?

Debating

If you have been involved in a debating society at school, you will know that, in a debate, there are two 'sides'. One side is *for* the issue being debated, the other side is *against*. A chairperson is in charge of the session, who should be impartial (i.e. not take sides). In the early days this role may be taken by your tutor.

- Prepare your case well – this will mean researching additional information to support your arguments and making sure these are up to date.
- Nominate your speaker(s). They should be people who can present the argument well, but during your course everyone should have a turn.
- The main speaker for each side should present the team's case without interruption for a limited, pre-set time. The speaker should stick to the facts but *use* them to try to persuade the 'audience' to agree with what is being said. The chairperson will bring the speech to a close if the speaker over-runs. Because this may mean that important points are omitted, it is important that the speakers time their speeches well.
- After the two main speakers have finished, each side has the right of reply. This may be the main speaker again, or someone else in the team who can respond quickly to the arguments that have been given by the opposing team.
- The issue is then thrown open for everyone to discuss, with the chairperson saying who should speak, and when.
- After a limited time a vote is taken, either for or against the issue (or 'motion' as it is often called).
- You should record the result of the vote taken by the group yourself, and say whether this agreed with your own vote. You should note whether the group was persuaded more by the arguments than the facts – and note down the main points which were raised.

Trial run

1 At present you can only vote in local or national government elections if you are over 18. Debate the motion 'People should be able to vote at the age of 16.'
2 Debate the motion 'Women are safer drivers than men.'

Interviewing

Interviewing means talking to people to find out information. A good interviewer:

- starts by thinking about all the information he or she would like to find out
- prepares the questions thoroughly and makes sure each point is covered
- asks 'open' questions (which require an explanation), rather than 'closed' questions (which only need a yes or no answer).
- asks the questions and *listens* to the answers!
- asks extra questions to clarify certain points or to find out more about an interesting topic
- makes a careful note of the answers
- thanks the person who was interviewed for his or her help.

In the early stages you may wish to check your draft list of questions with your tutor. It is also helpful to divide your notepad into two columns for interviews – one side for your questions and the other side for the answers.

Be careful – don't stick rigidly to your prepared questions if the interviewee obviously can give far more useful information in another area. Try to think on your feet! And remember – a good interviewer always lets the person being interviewed do most of the talking.

Trial run

1 Interview one of your fellow students. Find out all you can about what he or she watches on television.
2 Interview a parent or older relative. Find out how he or she spent leisure time at your age.

Presentations

Usually you will be asked to do a presentation as a member of a team. If the whole team work together, and support each other, this is far less of an ordeal than it may seem! Don't be surprised or worried if you are nervous – this is perfectly normal and, provided you are not too badly affected, it can actually *improve* your performance!

- Divide up the work of researching for the presentation *fairly* among the team.
- Work out how long each person must speak so that you don't over-run – either individually or as a group.
- It can be useful to nominate a leader who will co-ordinate the actual presentation and introduce individual members. Everyone should have their turn at this role at some stage.
- Prepare some good visual aids – use an overhead projector, or a model, or booklet or even a

handout. Anything is preferable to nothing!

- Dress smartly, in a business-like way – no jeans, trainers or T-shirts!
- Be prepared to answer questions, on your particular topic, from those who are watching you.
- Be prepared to help someone else who is asked a question and has difficulty thinking of an answer!

(See also *Core Skills Communication* chapter, page 534).

Trial run

As a class, hold a 'What the Papers Say' session. Each group chooses a separate newspaper published on the same day. The topic of the presentation is the content of the paper. You could include:

- a summary of the main three stories
- an overview of the different type of information and how much there is on different subjects, e.g. home news, foreign news, business, sport etc.
- the type of diagrams, charts and other graphics which are used
- the type of people who might buy or read that paper.

Researching

The first time you do this you may wonder where to start. Guidance is given in this book early in each section as to where you should look. There are a few basic rules.

- Get to know your library well – both the one at school or college and the central one in your area. Find out how it works, how the information is stored and the alternative methods of finding out about material than looking at books. This may, for instance, include searching through a CD-ROM on computer.
- Always be polite and friendly to the library staff. They can be an invaluable source of help if you don't know where to start.
- Remember that some reference material can only be used when you are in the library, so take a paper and pen with you! And beware of becoming so engrossed in other items of interest you take twice as long as necessary to find anything out!
- Other sources of 'research' include your friends, relatives and other people you know, plus local organisations in your area (e.g. banks, town hall, Citizens' Advice Bureau etc.).
- If you have to write away for information, make sure your letter is correctly worded, set out in a

professional way and prepared on a word processor or typewriter. Remember to enclose a stamped, addressed envelope for the reply.

- If you go on a work experience placement this gives you an ideal opportunity to gain valuable information about the company for which you are working. Remember that you should never take any documents or quote any company information without permission.

Trial run

Choose a famous personality and find out as much as you can about him or her. Ask a librarian which books would be useful. Talk to **five** people to find out what they know about the person you have chosen. Write a short report and show this to your tutor.

Surveys

How to design a questionnaire and carry out a survey is discussed in the the *Core Skills – Application of Number* unit, pages 569 and 570.

Remember that facts on their own may not be very useful. They may need to be carefully analysed and summarised to extract the maximum meaning.

Writing a letter or a report

This is covered as part of your Business course in Element 4.3 page 484 and in the *Core Skills – Communication* unit, page 551.

Writing a project

The project at the end of each element is the most substantial piece of work you will do for that particular element. It both tests your ability to find out information across the whole range of that element on your own *and* gives you the opportunity to achieve a Distinction grade.

You should make sure that your project is well researched, presented professionally using proper sections and headings (use the way the questions are grouped or worded as a guide), prepared on a word processor or typewriter, and bound properly. The front cover should give the project title, your name and group and the date. A back cover should be added (preferably on card).

Your tutor may give you a special submission date for each project. You must make a careful note of this and make sure you hand it in on time. It's a good idea to buy a diary – and use it!

Assessed activities

Your tutor may assess you during other activities, for instance, by observing you during a role play exercise or when you are doing 'real' work, e.g. dealing with visitors to your school or college. You may be shown a video and asked to prepare a summary. You may be questioned orally from time to time, especially after a presentation.

Assessing yourself

On other occasions you may have to assess yourself *before* your tutor makes a final assessment. For instance, you may be asked to take a tape recording of a conversation and then assess your own performance. Try to do this **objectively**, by listening to yourself as a stranger would. Start by commenting on your performance, then say what you would change – and why – if you repeated the exercise.

Grading

One of the important features of a GNVQ course is that *you* have to take responsibility for collecting your own evidence and keeping track of it. The more you can prove you are capable of working independently, the more likely you are to achieve a good grade.

When you first start your GNVQ course, grading may seem very complicated. However, when you start to see how this actually works it becomes much simpler to understand. Below are the main points of grading, but your tutor will explain these to you in more detail. In addition, the practice exercises included in this section should help you understand grading more clearly.

1 Each time you carry out a main project you will be assessed in seven areas.
2 These areas relate to four themes:
    Theme 1   Planning
    Theme 2   Information seeking/handling
    Theme 3   Evaluation
    Theme 4   Quality of outcomes
3 The number of grades you will be awarded is currently under review but is expected to be one grade for themes 1–3 (i.e. the preparation for the project) and one grade for theme 4 (i.e. the

content of the project). Check with your tutor if this is the case when you are studying for your award.
4 You may be awarded a Merit or a Distinction grade in each case, but this will often be determined by the level of difficulty of the task you have been asked to carry out. A simple list of jobs may only be worth a Merit grade even if you have done everything completely on your own.

Theme 1 – Planning

This is divided into **two** separate sections:

1 Drawing up plans of action
2 Monitoring courses of action.

For each section you can be awarded a grade.

What is an action plan?

An action plan is a list of activities you have to undertake to do a job. You can make an action plan for any job – from getting ready to go out, to making a cup of tea! The action plan is a list of all the stages involved and also gives an indication of the time likely to be taken at each stage.

Imagine you were getting ready to go on holiday. A coach is collecting you at 8.30 am to take you to the airport. Your action plan might read:

6.00 am	Get out of bed
6.05 am	Have shower, wash hair
6.15 am	Dry hair
6.30 am	Get dressed
6.35 am	Make breakfast
6.45 am	Eat breakfast
7.00 am	Wash-up and tidy kitchen
7.15 am	Pack case
8.00 am	Pack flight bag
8.10 am	Check tickets, currency and passport
8.20 am	Final check nothing is forgotten
8.30 am	Coach arrives – leave home and lock up.

By working out an action plan you would know what time you had to get out of bed to be organised and ready in plenty of time. In the same way, if you produce a good action plan for an assignment you will find it much easier to meet any deadlines you are given. You are also less likely to forget anything – provided you have remembered to list it in your plan!

You should note that a good action plan prioritises tasks in order of importance. In the example above the list is relatively easy as it is in time order – you wouldn't be able to do anything until you had first got out of bed! Planning for assignments, however, often means prioritising tasks in a slightly different way. You may need a key piece of information before you start, or to ensure that you have booked a computer for a specific day. Therefore prioritising may not just mean listing tasks in time order!

Monitoring an action plan

Action plans are ideal if nothing goes wrong. In the example above, what would happen if your alarm clock didn't go off until 6.30 am or 7 am? Or if you couldn't find your passport? Or your hairdrier had broken? Or you had an urgent telephone call at 8.25 am? All these problems would disrupt your plan and mean you are less likely to meet your deadline. For that reason, at regular intervals you need to 'monitor' or check that your plans are going to schedule.

If you were really going on holiday you would check by frequently looking at your watch and seeing if you were doing everything to the time you had stated. The same goes for an assignment. At regular periods you must check that everything you are doing is working out as you planned. If it is not, then you would have to revise your plan so that you could still meet your deadline. This may mean cutting out some stages or working more quickly.

Test yourself – exercise 1

A Imagine that you are going on holiday, using the action plan above and your alarm clock does not go off until 7 am! Draw up a revised action plan to cope with this situation.

B Draw up your own action plan for eating your evening meal and getting ready to go out within one hour of getting home from college.

C Imagine that your bus home is delayed and you now only have 45 minutes. Revise your action plan to cope with this situation.

D Below are seven tasks, again related to holidays. Prioritise these by putting them into the order in which you would sensibly do them, rather than the order in which they are given.
  a collect tickets
  b pack suitcase
  c select holiday
  d obtain passport
  e pay for holiday
  f obtain brochures
  g book holiday

Discuss all your work **with your tutor.**

Tutor input

To obtain a Distinction you need to be able to revise your plans **on your own.** This means that, when you are preparing an assignment, you have to identify regular times when you should check you are 'working to plan' and revise your plan if you are not.

Working independently does not mean you cannot discuss anything at all with your tutor. You can explain what you have done, and why. If you can justify your revisions then you will not be down-graded. However, if you actively need your tutor's help and guidance to revise your plan, you are more likely to be awarded a Merit grade.

Theme 2 – Information seeking and information handling

This, again, is divided into two separate sections:

1 Identifying information needs
2 Identifying and using sources to obtain information.

For each of these you can obtain a grade.

Identifying the information you need

For every assignment you will need to obtain information. What you need will vary, depending upon what you have been asked to do. As an example, if you were asked to make a list comparing different types of bank accounts and then to produce this using a word processor you would need:

- a list of the organisations offering bank accounts in your area
- information on the bank accounts themselves
- your own list comparing these accounts
- your computer, word processing and printer manuals.

Sources of information

Where and how you obtain your information may vary from writing or telephoning official organisations to using your local, school or college library. Don't forget that people, as well as places, can be good sources of information.

Identifying your sources of information before you start is important. It enables you obtain the maximum amount of information with the minimum of effort! You should always have a good reason for mentioning a source of information – this is called **justifying** your choice – and your tutor may ask you why you have included certain sources in your list.

Test yourself – exercise 2

A Write down the sources you would use to obtain the information listed above about bank accounts. Check your list with your tutor and try to **justify** each source you have identified.

B Suppose you have been asked to help with a project that involves comparing jobs in business now with those that were common 25 years ago. As a group, brainstorm as many types of information as you can that you think would be useful for this project.

C As a group, try to identify **at least one** source for each type of information. Ask your tutor to help you if you have a problem with this. In each case, discuss with your tutor what the justification would be.

Tutor input

As already mentioned, don't think that you cannot discuss anything with your tutor if you want to achieve a Distinction. Remember that it is one thing to have a discussion *with* your tutor and quite another to ask your tutor to list your sources *for* you!

You will usually find that throughout an assignment your tutor will wish to have regular discussions with you about your action plan and your information handling.

Theme 3 – Evaluation

The word 'evaluation' may be new to you. It means thinking about the value of something. In this case, you are asked to consider how valuable your action plan and your information were in helping you to produce that particular assignment.

Evaluation is **retrospective**. This means you do it *afterwards*. You have to look back at your plan, the activities you undertook, the information you obtained and the decisions you made and say if you could have done any of it any better. In other words, you are asked to learn from the experience!

Everyone knows that the first time you do something you might *try your best* but not be very successful. If you think back over what you did, you can probably think of ways to do it better next time. This is really what evaluation is about – it helps you to learn from your own mistakes.

The easiest way to do an evaluation is to look back at

everything you did and decide what the advantages and disadvantages were at all stages. Then decide what you could do next time to improve matters – think about alternative things you could have done.

Think about the assignment above which asks for details of different bank accounts. Look at an extract from the evaluation given below on the action taken.

Information required	Obtained by	Advantages	Disadvantages	Suggested improvements
List of banks	Walk round town	Made out list	Missed some Took time	Use *Yellow Pages*

Test yourself – exercise 3

A Look back at the action plan on page xiv which was written for someone going on holiday. **In a group of three or four**, criticise it and decide how it could be improved. Compare your list of criticisms with the other groups in your class and obtain your tutor's opinion.

B Look back at the work you did in parts B and C of exercise 2. See if you can improve on the ideas you had in any way.

C Identify **one** experience you have had in the last two weeks, where you would do things differently if you had another chance. Write down what you did, how you did it, what you would improve next time, and why. Be prepared to read out your statement and discuss it with the rest of your class.

Tutor input

Your tutor will be only too pleased to discuss how to evaluate your work with you, and will probably give you a form to complete that will help you to consider each point properly. Don't be tempted to criticise everything you did just for the sake of it – even if it went well! This will not get you a better grade! However, it is rare that *nothing* can be improved upon. Give an honest view of how you think things went and discuss what you are going to write with your tutor beforehand. In the early days, you may need some assistance before you can evaluate something completely on your own.

Remember that it is the depth of your evaluation which helps to determine your grade. The fact you have had some discussions with your tutor will not affect it.

Theme 4 – Quality of outcomes

This is divided into two sections:

1 Synthesis
2 Language.

What is synthesis?

Synthesis relates to the content of your assignment and the way in which it is put together. It is pointless doing an excellent action plan and then producing an awful or incorrect assignment – even if it does meet a deadline. Obviously, you obtain a grade that reflects the amount of knowledge and understanding you have **demonstrated** in your assignment and the skills you have used.

You will **not** obtain a grade for synthesis if:

■ you miss out important information
■ you ignore part of the question
■ your information is incorrect, inaccurate or cannot be understood by the reader.

Command of language

This concentrates even more upon your communication skills. Your sentences need to be clearly written and, when you use a term, you need to make it clear that you understand what it means.

Remember these key points.

■ Keep your sentences short and to the point.
■ Don't include words or phrases you do not understand.
■ Don't use slang expressions or 'trendy' words you hope your tutor will understand.
■ Don't hand in an assignment that is scruffy or very poorly presented.

The presentation of your work is important and demonstrates the core skills of communication and, frequently, information technology. You are therefore not using either of these skills if your assignment has no clear headings, is completely muddled or looks unprofessional!

Test yourself – exercise 4

A Write two paragraphs explaining what you like to do on a favourite night out. Don't include any slang expressions or phrases your tutor wouldn't understand (or like to read!). Ask your tutor to give you his or her view of this in terms of your 'language' skills.

B Look back at the work you have produced so far on this course (or on your course last year). Write a paragraph stating your strengths and weaknesses in relation to both written work and presentation. Are you always neat and tidy, or usually sloppy? Is your writing easy to read or illegible? Do you have difficulty with written English? If so, discuss your problems with your tutor to see what help is available.

Tutor input

Discuss with your tutor the standard of work expected for your assignments. It is useful, the first time, to draft out your first page and discuss it with your tutor. Then you can see if you are going into enough detail (or too much), or misunderstanding any of the questions. Don't be afraid to ask if you are unsure, especially at the start of your course.

Personal skills

On some GNVQ courses you will also be involved in additional personal skills. Personal skills may include your ability to:

■ take responsibility for yourself and your own development
■ work and co-operate with other people
■ solve problems when they occur.

Ask your tutor if personal skills are part of your particular course, and how you will record them for your verifier.

Joint projects and assignments

You should note that if you are asked to undertake a project or an assignment as a member of a group, then it must be absolutely clear which parts of the final work are *your* contribution. Many tutors will ask you to include a special page with such a piece of work, which clearly states the contribution of each member and is signed by everyone in the group. This is important so that your work can be graded accurately.

A final note

We hope you have not tried to work through this Guide in one session! The new terms used, the way in which you have to produce evidence and the grading procedures will be very strange to you at first, and may be very confusing. Slowly things will become clearer, and your tutor is there to help. Look back at this section throughout the first few months to refresh your memory – and to see how much more you understand!

On GNVQ courses, you are expected to take responsibility *yourself* for acquiring evidence and storing it neatly, and for keeping track of where you are and what still needs to be done. If you do this properly, at the end of the course you will have a portfolio of work of which you can be justly proud. Because of your personal involvement, you will also be able to remember most of the information in it – which will be invaluable for your external tests.

Explain the purposes and types of business organisations

■ This element covers the purposes of different types of business organisations, the industrial sectors in which they operate and the differences between the various types of business ownership.

After studying this chapter you should be able to:

1 describe *developments* in *industrial sectors*
2 explain the *purposes* of *business organisations*
3 explain the *differences* between *types* of *business ownership*
4 explain the *operation* of one business organisation.

Industrial sectors

In every industrialised country in the world, most of the population go out to work to earn their living. As you travel to school or college in the morning you pass people on their way to work – in cars and buses and on trains. Your parents or your sisters and brothers may go out to work, or be studying for a qualification, like you, so that they can earn their living in the future.

The jobs that people do are very varied. If you tried to list every type of job there is you would end up with hundreds of different occupations. People work on the land, at sea and in the air. They may be employed outside or inside, in factories or in offices. They may build roads, bridges or computers. They may write newspapers, design clothes or paint houses. They may sell food, washing machines, advertising or finance. They may work alone or with other people, teaching, nursing or entertaining them.

Traditionally, it is usual to divide all types of industrial activity into three sectors of production (see Figure 1.1):

■ primary
■ secondary
■ tertiary

The **primary** sector is concerned with extracting natural resources from the environment. Drilling for oil and mining for coal are obvious examples, as are forestry and fishing. Farming – from raising dairy cows or growing wheat in cold climates to producing wine or olive oil in warmer regions – is also included in the primary sector.

The **secondary** sector is concerned with manufacturing, processing and assembling finished goods, as well as construction work. These goods

Primary sector

Secondary sector

Tertiary sector

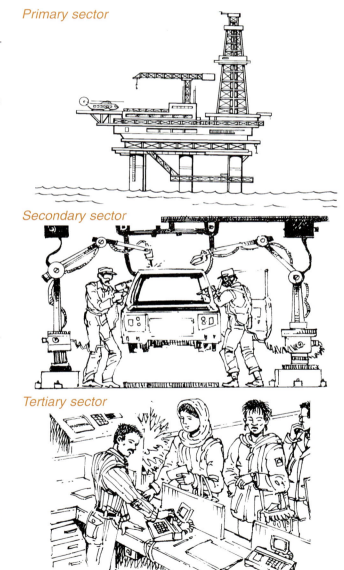

Figure 1.1 Industrial sectors

1

include things that are produced both for consumers and for industry, such as cars and cranes, furniture and books, tins of beans and electronic components. Motorway construction and building work are also included in this sector.

The **tertiary** sector is concerned with the provision of services either to members of the public (tourism, health, education and entertainment) or to other industries and businesses. Service industries which provide assistance for business include banks, insurance companies, freight services and advertising agencies. The communications industry is also included in this sector and includes radio, telecommunications and television.

Did you know?

Global communications are moving ahead very fast with the coming of the **information superhighway.** This is the rapid transfer of information by fibre optic cable – from telephone messages to cable television transmissions. It also includes the **Internet** system – a powerful world-wide computer network which now links more than 30 million people and 20 000 organisations and is growing rapidly. Electronic mail messages can be sent and data and programs exchanged via Internet all over the world. In time, the system is likely to be developed further and faster and other features introduced. One day you may be able to visit a virtual reality shopping mall and pay all your bills from your own home via Internet. One couple, communicating between the USA and Australia via Internet, decided to marry after a nine-month digital romance!

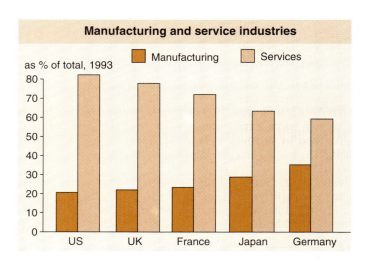

Figure 1.3 Manufacturing and service industries

Developments in industrial sectors

There are several reasons why industrial sectors do not remain the same for very long. If you are interested in history or geography then you may know that the profile of the United Kingdom as an industrial country has changed over time. In the middle ages and Tudor times, the UK was almost totally agricultural. The chief export was wool. Industry only started to develop in the middle of the eighteenth century. In Victorian times the UK grew rich as the 'workshop of the world', producing thousands of manufactured goods which were sold abroad – from chemicals to

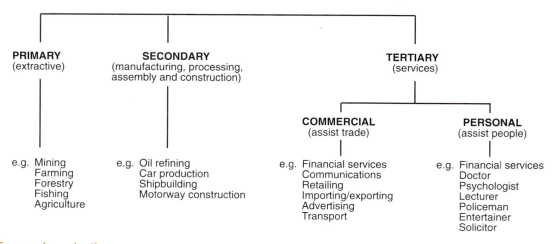

Figure 1.2 Types of production

cotton and from machinery to metal goods. In this century, manufacturing industry has declined and the services, or tertiary sector, has increased. This is now the largest sector in the UK.

This is not the case in some other countries of the world, or even in some countries in the European Union (EU). Countries such as Greece, Portugal and Eire still have a high level of agriculture so are more involved in primary production than the United Kingdom. In Germany, the Ruhr is a famous industrial area well known for its manufacturing industry. In Germany, as a whole, more than 30 per cent of employment is still in manufacturing, which is higher than any other European country, Japan or the United States (see Figure 1.3).

Recent past, present, likely future

Sectors change for many reasons. One sector may decline and another may grow. New discoveries, technological developments, changing tastes and lifestyles, consumer income and demands, government policies and changes in fashion all affect the type of goods and services provided by business organisations. Foreign investment can directly affect the output of a sector.

The primary sector

In 1993 only 1.1 per cent of the population of the UK were employed in agriculture – a much lower percentage than in many other countries. However, the output produced by farming has consistently risen, so that today Britain is more self-sufficient than it was ten or even twenty years ago. The prices of many agricultural products are determined by the Common Agricultural Policy (CAP) of the European Union and cannot be changed by individual farmers.

The UK has very good energy resources. North Sea oil production, which began in 1975, has meant that the UK is now a net exporter of oil. (Some oil still has to be imported because UK oil is not suitable for all types of use.) Natural gas is also available from the North Sea, although production is scheduled to decline in the 1990s as supplies start to dwindle.

Britain has large coal reserves but the amount of mining carried out has declined sharply (see Optional Evidence Assignment below). Supply of energy and water has been a key area in which the Government has concentrated its privatisation policy. British Petroleum, British Gas, British Coal, the electricity and water companies have all been privatised in the past ten years.

Did you know?

Privatisation is the term used when an organisation that has been owned wholly or partly by the Government on behalf of the public is transferred into private ownership. Examples include British Coal, British Telecom, British Gas and British Airways (see page 31).

The secondary sector

The 'heavy' industries of the UK – metals, mechanical engineering, textiles, shipping and motor production – have been in decline since the 1960s. Other important industries – tobacco, brewing and food manufacture – are all producing less today than they used to do. In 1981, 28 per cent of employees worked in manufacturing; today this figure is nearer 20 per cent. Until 1983 Britain was a net exporter of manufactured goods. This meant that exports were higher than imports. Today the situation is reversed; we import more than we export. In 1950 Britain produced over 25 per cent of the world's manufactured goods. In 1992 this had fallen to 8.4 per cent.

The main reason for the decline was the inability of British industry to compete with cheaper goods being manufactured abroad, because of its own high production costs and a slowness to recognise the new opportunities available. These are in areas such as electronics, new types of food production, household goods, electrical and advanced engineering products. Today production costs have fallen because of changes in working practices and lower real wage costs. Foreign investment has also assisted this sector. There are now over 120 Japanese manufacturing plants in the UK, producing a variety of goods from television sets to motor cars.

The future is therefore not all bleak. Existing organisations are actively trying to identify opportunities for the future. However, technological developments such as robotics are likely to mean that the numbers employed in this sector are unlikely to increase dramatically in the future.

Did you know?

The term 'real costs' is used to show the difference between amounts of money and the actual value of something, bearing in mind inflation. For instance, if you had bought a new Rover Mini in 1983 it would have cost you about £3000. Today the same car would cost nearer £6000. Does this mean that it is *really* twice as expensive?

In money terms the answer is obviously yes. In real terms the answer is no. This is because the average weekly earnings in 1983 were about £160 a week (for men) whereas they were about £350 a week in 1994. Therefore, in real terms the car is actually cheaper because the number of weeks you would have to save up to buy it is now seventeen, not nearly nineteen as it was in 1983.

Note: Women's average wages were nearly £100 in 1983 and in 1994 they were over £220. Whose wages have increased more in the last decade – men's or women's?

The service sector

Over the past 30 years there has been a steady movement of workers from agriculture and industry into the service sector. The main growth areas have been business and financial services, retailing and distribution and the communications industries. The sector has grown steadily each year from 1983 to 1994, by which time 15.4 million people were employed in this type of work, producing two-thirds of the nation's output.

Business and financial services include both banking and insurance. This area grew quickly in the 1980s because of the increase in consumer spending and, at the time, the rise in house prices. House prices have been static for several years now and consumer spending has fallen. Since 1990 employment in postal services and telecommunications, banking and finance, amongst estate agents and on the railways has fallen. However, major growth areas include the leisure industry and the public sector. Employment has increased in education as well as in medical and health services.

Did you know?

By now you should have realised that some types of business encompass more than one industrial sector. If not, you may realise it later when you have problems 'categorising' certain types of businesses. Typical 'product' examples include:

- oil, coal, gas and water, which have to be extracted (*primary*), refined (*secondary*) and distributed/sold to customers (*tertiary*)
- alcoholic drinks such as whisky and beer, which have to be distilled or brewed (*secondary*) and then distributed and sold to customers (*tertiary*)

- computers or software (*secondary*) are manufactured by companies like Microsoft, which are also involved in communications developments (*tertiary*).

These are just a few examples. If, for your project, you are investigating an organisation which covers more than one area, don't be surprised – and remember to include all the relevant sectors in your investigations!

Non-assessed activity

Each of the following events or trends has resulted in a change in a particular sector in the recent past. Explain:

a which sector was affected in each case, and

b whether the event or trend contributed towards the growth or decline of the sector as a whole.

- the introduction of the personal computer
- the discovery of North Sea oil
- a reduction in the number of real coal fires
- the increasing popularity of take-away food
- an increase in the number of people giving up smoking
- the introduction of cable television
- the discovery of North Sea gas
- the fact that fewer people now eat red meat
- a decrease in the number of people moving house
- the introduction of the mobile phone
- a reduction in the number of new roads built
- an increase in the number of people wanting to keep fit

Optional evidence assignment

*This activity can be carried out verbally in class **in a group** as a non-assessed activity to consolidate learning. Alternatively, if you do it **on your own,** it can count as supplementary evidence towards the following parts of the scheme.*

PC 1: Describe developments in industrial sectors

Range: Developments: recent past, present, likely future; decrease of the sector

Industrial sectors: primary

Core skills: Communication, application of number

Read the case study below and answer the questions which follow.

Case study on British Coal

In December 1994, after nearly 50 years of public ownership, British Coal was privatised. This followed nearly twenty years of friction between the miners and the Government, made worse by the decline in demand for British coal.

In the post-war years, coal was the major fuel burned by households throughout Britain. Two factors changed that – the desire for clean air and the rising price of coal in comparison with other (cleaner and easier to use) forms of fuel, particularly gas. Domestic consumption of coal fell. The power stations were still high users of coal and, until the electricity industry was privatised, had to buy their supplies from British Coal. Since privatisation, the electricity industry has concentrated on building cheaper gas-fired power stations and looking at cheaper alternatives to British coal, including imported coal and oil.

This has reduced the demand for British coal and the number of people employed in mining. When the pits were nationalised in 1946 there were 700 000 miners. In 1989 66 000 were employed. By the end of 1994 this figure had fallen to 7000. However, over this period output per miner per shift increased through flexible shift working, the closure of pits where extraction was expensive and the modernisation of those which were left (see Figure 1.4).

In October 1992 the Government announced that British Coal should be privatised, with up to 30 of the remaining 50 pits closing and leaving only about 20 'super-pits' in operation. By the end of 1994 this operation was complete. RJB Mining paid £815 million to purchase most of the English mines. Mining Scotland has purchased most of the Scottish assets. Celtic Mining, which has bought £94.5 million of the Welsh assets, is a management buyout – where managers and workers joined together to buy and run the pits themselves.

Until 1998 British mines have contracts to supply 30 million tonnes of coal a year for the power stations. The future of the coal industry of Britain may depend upon the renewal of these contracts.

1 State *two* factors which have contributed towards the fall in demand for British coal.

2 British coal is now produced more cheaply than it was before. Give *three* reasons why.

3 What percentage of jobs was lost in mining between 1946 and 1994?

4 What do *you* think was the effect on communities which depended upon coal for their livelihood during that period?

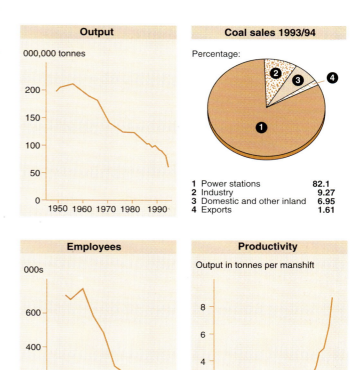

1	Power stations	82.1
2	Industry	9.27
3	Domestic and other inland	6.95
4	Exports	1.61

Source: British Coal Corporation

Figure 1.4 British Coal – a case study

5 **As a class**, debate the statement: 'Power stations should be forced to buy British coal, even if this results in more expensive electricity, in order to protect jobs.' Summarise the views both for and against this statement.

6 **In your own words**, write a short report saying what has happened to British Coal over the last few years and what you think might happen in the future. If possible, read other articles on the coal industry before you write your report.

Changes in sector size

You have already seen that sectors can change. If a sector is growing then the amount of output increases. Conversely, a sector which is decreasing produces a smaller amount of the country's total output each year.

The amount of output is measured each year and shown as a percentage of the nation's total output. Looking at these figures from one year to another shows which sectors are growing and which are declining.

Non-assessed activity

The following table shows the percentage value of each sector of production for the years 1989–1992. Study the table carefully.

	Primary	Secondary	Tertiary
1989	9%	30%	61%
1990	7%	30%	63%
1991	7%	28%	65%
1992	6%	29%	65%

As a group, try to answer the following questions.

1 Which sector decreased the most between 1989 and 1992?

2 The manufacturing sector in Britain has been in constant decline since 1989. True or false? (Give a reason for your answer).

3 If the total value of the items produced by **all** the industries was £497 billion in 1991, what must have been the value of services produced by the tertiary sector in that year?

4 In 1992 the total was approximately £515 billion. Calculate the value of each sector that year.

Employment in industrial sectors

Employment in industrial sectors has also changed over the years, as we have seen in mining. However, because of increases in technology, growth in a sector does not necessarily mean increases in employment. In banking and telecommunications, for instance, there have been large losses in employment, so the rate of increase in employment in the tertiary sector has not matched its growth rate as a sector. This topic is covered more comprehensively in Element 1.3.

Did you know?

The numbers of people employed in mechanical engineering, office machinery, electrical engineering and instruments have nearly halved since 1971. At that time there were 2.1 million people employed; in 1993 this had fallen to 1.2 million.

Non-assessed activity

Employment in each industry in 1993 was calculated to be:

primary	4%
manufacturing	19%
construction	6%
business services	19%
public administration, health, education	25%
other services (retailing, distribution, transport etc.)	27%

Illustrate these findings on a pie chart, preferably using a computer.

Typical activities in the sectors

You can easily work out the activities which typify each sector if you think of the type of work which is carried out and the jobs people do.

Non-assessed activity

1 Draw a simple chart with the headings 'Primary production', 'Secondary production' and 'Tertiary production', using the same sub-divisions as in the chart on page 2. Enter the following people in the correct categories, according to the job they do.

carpenter stockbroker nurse oil driller priest

musician engineer journalist bank clerk builder

fisherman teacher travel agent hotel manager

farmer

2 Now identify **at least 12** more occupations and categorise them. Try to make them as varied as you can, for example, from a Mafia boss to a baby minder! (Make sure you add **at least two** under each heading on your chart.)

Optional evidence assignment

*This activity can be carried out verbally in class **in a group** as a non-assessed activity to consolidate learning. Alternatively, if you do it **on your own**, it can count as supplementary evidence towards the following parts of the scheme.*

PC 1: Describe developments in industrial sectors

Range: Developments: recent past, present, likely future; growth of the sector, decrease of the sector; typical activities in the sector

Industrial sectors: primary, secondary, tertiary

Core skills: Communication, application of number (IT optional)

1 Read the two case studies below and then answer the questions which follow.

Case study A

Bryant and May closed down in Liverpool on 22 December 1994 after 151 years of making matches. From now on all matches sold in Britain will be imported – mainly from Sweden. When the factory closed the last 124 workers left – many in tears – it was a drastic decline from the heyday of the match works, when over 1000 people were employed. In those days 65 billion matches a year were produced but by 1994 demand for matches had fallen to 16 billion. This was mainly because fewer people smoke and those who do can buy cheap, disposable lighters. Automatic ignition devices are now common on cookers and fires. So now match production is to be concentrated in Sweden. Why there and not Liverpool? Quite simply, because there are plenty of trees in Sweden, whereas the Liverpool factory would have been dependent on imported wood from Canada.

a In which industrial sector was the match factory?
b What **four** reasons are given for its closure?
c Was its decline typical of the sector as a whole or not? Give reasons for your answer.
d How many jobs were lost when the match factory closed?
e Does this mean matches are no longer available? Give a reason for your answer.

Case study B

When Mrs Perween Warsi moved to Britain from India in 1975 she certainly didn't expect to be opening a £6 million factory in Derby and creating 400 jobs! Mrs Warsi's husband is a GP and, in common with many housewives, she frequently shopped for food which would suit her family. However, she was constantly disappointed with the quality of local ethnic food on offer and knew it was nowhere near as good as the food she could make herself. She began cooking onion bhajis and samosas in her own kitchen and selling them to shops and ethnic restaurants in the area. One day she sent some samples to the supermarket giant Asda who promptly placed an order for more. Today she sells a wide variety of exotic dishes to various supermarket chains including Safeway and Tesco under the name of S & A Foods – the company she formed when Asda first placed their order. Next year she is predicted to sell food worth about £12 million. All of it will be produced in the new factory which will have the most sophisticated cook-chill food processing facilities in Europe – a far cry from the days of Mrs Warsi's kitchen!

f In which sector is Mrs Warsi's business?
g In general, is this sector growing or declining?
h How many people will Mrs Warsi employ?
i What features of modern lifestyles have contributed towards the growth of her company?
j What do you consider will be the likely future of Mrs Warsi's company?

2 Below are seven examples of large UK companies and their main areas of activity. In which sector(s) does each of them operate?

British Telecom (communications)
British Gas (oil, gas and nuclear fuels)
Grand Metropolitan (brewers and distillers)
RTZ Corporation (mines)
Marks & Spencer (retail stores)
General Electric Company (electronics)
BTR (construction)

Evidence assignment

At this point your tutor may wish you to start work on the project which will prove to your verifiers that you understand this section of the element. If so, turn to page 42 and do Section 1 of the project. This covers the first evidence indicator for this element.

The purposes of business organisations

There are very many business organisations in Britain. As we have seen already, some produce goods, others offer services. Some are large and employ thousands of people, others may be very small or even sole trader businesses. Some people are in business to make a profit, others to help other people. Some organisations are owned privately and others are operated by the Government. Why are there so many different types of business organisation and what are the differences between them?

As a first step towards answering this question it is useful to look at the purposes or reasons why business organisations exist.

Non-assessed activity

1 The list below shows six different organisations. What do you consider to be the purpose of each?

a a building society
b the Samaritans
c local government
d a hospital
e Marks and Spencer plc
f a solicitor's office.

2 Below are statements made by six people who work for these organisations. From these, can you identify which one each person works for?

i   I've worked in the store for nearly five years but always part-time. At present I'm mainly on the Customer Service Desk but we do move around. The food section is very busy – and if you're on too long it can be hard to concentrate. The pay's quite good and there are lots of facilities for staff, including a hairdresser and chiropodist and subsidised meals.

ii I joined because I wanted to help other people and I work one evening a week. We are only known by our first names and aren't allowed to discuss our calls with anyone outside the organisation. Sometimes some of the calls can be upsetting but if you feel at least one person has benefited it makes it all worthwhile.

iii I started training four years ago and qualified last year. I now specialise in working with children, which I always wanted to do. Although I don't earn a fortune and sometimes have to work

Figure 1.5 Can you identify the different jobs they do?

unsocial hours or at Christmas, I do quite enjoy working alternate weekends, with free time during the week. I enjoy my job very much – which isn't something everyone can claim to do!

iv I started work in the organisation five years ago and even in that short time the way we work has changed beyond recognition. There are fewer staff involved, most transactions are now done by computer and we offer far more services than we used to do. We are very keen on customer service – the industry is very profitable but we always try to be the best in the business so that we can have more customers than anyone else. If a customer closes his or her account with a competitor and moves to us we consider that a real achievement. Only last year this organisation merged with another one and we ended up with twice as many customers to deal with in this area alone – but we only took on two more staff to cope with them!

v I like working for a small organisation though it's sometimes hectic. There are four senior partners and five junior partners in the practice and they all specialise in one way or another. Our clients come for a variety of reasons – for example, because they are buying a house, making a will or need specialist advice.

vi I work in our local tourist information office. I enjoy this as we get many enquiries every day both from visitors and over the telephone. I've been here for the past year. Before that I worked in the business rates section. That department is responsible for collecting rates from all business premises in this area and sending the total amount collected to the Government.

Businesses can exist for a variety of purposes. These include:

- to make a profit
- to increase market share
- to provide a commercial service for customers
- to provide a public service
- to help others or promote a special cause.

Other factors, such as providing good working conditions for employees or an interest for the owner may also be important. Indeed, most businesses have several aims or goals although there may only be one **main** purpose for their existence.

Profit

This is usually the main purpose of businesses which are owned privately. It is essential for the owner(s) to be able to make a living. Someone who starts a small business, invests his or her own money and takes the risk of losing this if the business doesn't do well is called an **entrepreneur.** However, many people set up a business not so much to make a fortune, but because they want to be their own boss, or they have redundancy money to invest. Often it may be because they have a good idea and feel that if they can supply consumers with something they need, and keep their customers happy, then they will have the opportunity to do well.

The amount of profit a business makes is influenced by the number of sales it makes, the price of the goods sold and the cost of each sale. This includes the cost of producing or buying the goods (or service) and the overheads (or running costs) of the business.

Quite simply, the final profit is the amount remaining after all the bills have been paid, including the cost of all purchases, the business expenses, and tax. Companies pay Government corporation tax on their net profit figure. Private individuals, sole traders and partners (see page 17) pay income tax.

A business person can increase profit by

- selling more goods
- increasing the selling price of the goods
- reducing the cost of making the goods
- reducing the costs of running the business.

However, some of these options may be difficult or impossible to take up. A business person may not be able to sell any more goods if sales are limited for some reason – think of demand for ice cream in January! – or if there is fierce competition in the area. Increasing the selling price may make the goods too expensive and cheaper options may be available to customers if they go elsewhere. It may be almost impossible to reduce the cost of making the goods, although technological developments can often help to reduce production costs. Sometimes organisations reduce the costs of running the business by reducing the number of staff employed. Banks, for instance, have replaced many cashiers with service tills and computerised deposit machines. In a small firm, reducing the number of staff is less likely to be an option than it is in a large organisation.

Did you know?

A percentage fall in costs will have a greater effect on profits than the same percentage increase in sales. Test it for yourself below!

Non-assessed activity

Bob's bikes cost £40 each to make and he sells them for £60. This makes him £20 profit on each sale. If he sells 1000 bikes a year he makes £20 000.

Bob decides this is not enough. He has three options:

a   Increase his selling price (but if he does, people will buy a cheaper bike elsewhere so he will lose sales)

b   Sell more bikes

c   Reduce the cost of making the bikes. Bob could use cheaper components to do this.

Bob works out that he could possibly increase his sales by 10 per cent if he works longer hours **or** reduce his costs by 10 per cent.

1   If he increases his sales by 10 per cent, how many bikes will he now sell in a year?

2   If each bike still sells for £60, how much money will he receive?

3   If his costs remain the same (i.e. £40 per bike), what will be his profit?

4   By how much (in money) has his profit increased?

5   If he reduces his costs by 10 per cent, what will it now cost him to make each bike?

6   What will be his new profit on each bike if the selling price stays at £60?

7   What will his profit be if he sells 1000 bikes?

8   Which course of action should he take? Why?

Did you know?

The amount of money received from sales, less the cost of the goods, gives a business's **gross profit. Net profit** (before tax) is the surplus which is remaining when all the expenses of running the business are deducted – heating, lighting, rent etc. In the example above, you have been calculating Bob's gross profit – not his net profit!

Profit and the creation of wealth

If a company is profitable it can afford to employ more people. It can also afford to pay higher wages. Both these factors increase the wealth of individuals and the community (because people will spend their wages buying goods and services in the area). High profits will also increase the wealth of the business owners.

The owners of the business vary depending upon the type of business (see page 14). Some businesses are owned by just one person. Some are run by partners. Limited companies have **directors** to run the business and **shareholders** who invest money in the company.

The owners can decide what to do with the profits. A sole trader could keep all the profits – but this may be unwise. It might be more sensible to plough some back into the business as **investment** for the future. For example, a sole trader retailer may expand the shop, buy new display units or a larger van. The trader is investing this money in the hope that, as the business increases in size, profits will be even larger in the years to come.

In a partnership, the partners have to agree what to do with the profits and how to distribute them. In a limited company, the directors propose a course of action but the shareholders have to vote on their decisions. Normally there isn't a dispute and in a small limited company the directors and the shareholders are often the same people – as we shall see later in this element!

All shareholders want a return for lending the company money. They receive this in the form of a dividend. The size of the **dividend** proposed by the directors will be determined by:

■   the amount of profit remaining after tax
■   the amount of money required for future investment
■   the amount of money to be paid back on loans and interest in the forthcoming year (which must be set aside)
■   the number of shareholders.

Did you know?

In Britain, many large organisations have been criticised for not keeping back enough money to invest for the future. They have therefore not been able to afford new machinery designed to take advantage of new technological developments. Why? Because the directors are worried that if they do not pay high enough dividends to shareholders, the shareholders will sell their shares and reinvest in a company which gives them a better return. If too many shares are sold at the same time, the value of the shares falls and the company is worth less money. It may then look 'cheap' to someone else, who promptly buys it up and takes it over. Then the directors may lose their jobs!

Non-assessed activity

1 Why do you think shareholders don't vote against this policy, on the basis that it isn't in the company's interest?

2 If you, as a group, were directors of a company, what would you do in this situation? Discuss your ideas with your tutor.

Market share

Market share is the number of sales made by a company compared with its competitors. Many companies aim to increase their market share year by year. They can do this:

- by providing a better service than their competitors
- by providing a cheaper service than their competitors
- by opening offices or factories in other areas or countries
- by expanding and growing as much as possible. This may mean 'taking over' (buying out) or merging with a competitor so that one organisation now has far more customers than before.

Advantages of taking over another company include:

a growing large very quickly
b having far more customers than before
c having economies of scale. These are savings made because the company operates on a large scale. For example, it may be able to buy its raw materials more cheaply because it will be able to negotiate discounts on large orders.

Taking over another organisation is one way in which a company can quickly increase its market share as – almost overnight – the number of customers may increase dramatically.

Market share is dealt with in more detail in Element 1.2.

Did you know?

The term used in business to describe the total amount of sales revenue a company receives in a year is **turnover**. The company with the largest market share will usually have the highest turnover of all organisations operating in a particular industry.

A case study in mergers and takeovers

In some industries, particularly where mass production methods are used, the market is dominated by a few giants. Smaller businesses often go out of business unless they produce specialised items on a smaller scale.

The car industry is one example. The market is dominated by the giants. In 1992 the leading companies were Ford (with the highest market share), General Motors/Vauxhall, Nissan, Peugeot and Rover. In the main, foreign companies were increasing their market share to a greater extent than Rover – the only *British* company with a sizeable market share.

The British car industry had been subject to a whole series of mergers and takeovers throughout its history, in an attempt to produce a giant to compete with the big American producers (and later the Japanese). The British Motor Corporation, formed in 1952, was an amalgam of Wolseley, Austin and Morris Motors. Further mergers with Jaguar and Leyland Motors (including Rover) resulted in the British Leyland Motor Corporation in 1968. This was nationalised in 1975 and renamed BL in 1978. In 1984 Jaguar/Daimler production was separated from BL and floated on the stock market. In 1986 BL was renamed as the Rover Group and sold to British Aerospace by the British Government in 1989.

In February 1994 Rover – by then the last major British car company – was sold to the German car giant BMW. The takeover of Rover cost BMW £800 million and enabled it to boost its market share to almost 7 per cent of the European car market and quickly expand its production of

Figure 1.6 A new Rover – a British car with German connections

cars at the lower end of the market. The total sales of BMW are now estimated to be nearly one million a year and the company will employ 100 000 people in total. Next time you watch an advert for Rover cars it may be interesting to remember the German connection!

Customer service

All organisations are keen to give good customer service. This means responding quickly to requests and enquiries, giving accurate and truthful information, employing polite and personable staff and, above all, putting the customer *first* when decisions are being made about opening hours, the layout of the building and so on. Very often a customer service pledge or promise is displayed on a large board near a special customer service desk. Customers visit this desk when they are on the premises if they have any specific enquiries or want to complain about something.

In other organisations there may be a special customer service unit which handles customer problems, suggestions and complaints. The organisation will be keen to obtain customers' views on its current style of operation and their suggestions for the future.

There is much more about customer service in Unit 3 on Consumers and Customers.

Public service

Public services are provided by organisations such as schools and hospitals, as well as by the police, fire and prison services, army, navy and so on. In all these cases, the public do not pay directly for the service they receive. Because these services are provided for the good of society as a whole, the money to finance them is collected by the Government through taxes. The service is then available freely to everyone. This is totally different from the provision of private services (such as those of an estate agent or bank) which customers pay for.

However, public service organisations still need to be aware of their obligations in terms of 'customer service'. This has become an important feature in organisations which are in the public sector (see page 29) such as local authorities, tax offices and hospitals. Their policy is usually printed in a **charter** which states the aims of the organisation. For instance, your local authority will have a charter which gives information on everything from the number of leisure centres in the area to how often the rubbish will be collected.

Did you know?

The aims and style of operation of public service organisations can change if there is a change of Government, because the way different politicians perceive the needs of the public may vary. For instance, we could argue that the water authorities should exist to provide a public service because everyone needs clean water and some poor people may not be able to afford to pay. A Conservative Government would disagree – it would argue that water is expensive to deliver and pipes need regular replacement. The water authorities must therefore make a profit, just like any commercial organisation, to raise the money for this type of investment. Otherwise taxpayers would have to pay more tax. This has been the thinking behind the privatisation of many public sector companies (see page 31).

Non-assessed activity

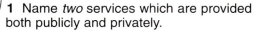

1 Name *two* services which are provided both publicly and privately.

2 **As a group,** discuss what you think would happen if people had to pay on delivery for services such as police assistance or calling out the fire brigade – and do you think this would be a good idea. Be prepared to present your arguments to the rest of your class.

Charitable organisations

Charitable organisations are in business for the purposes of helping other people and promoting special causes. They don't exist to make a profit in the true sense of the word. Their aim is to raise money for their own particular cause. From this is deducted their own expenditure on administration costs. Traditionally money was raised by a variety of fund-raising activities including:

- selling goods
- finding **sponsors** or people willing to make regular gifts
- holding special events.

Today, however, many charities are run on a more sophisticated basis, with professional public relations staff and fund-raising directors. They advertise in the national press, become involved with telethon appeals, operate computer mailing lists and send regular direct mail shots to try to persuade people to support them.

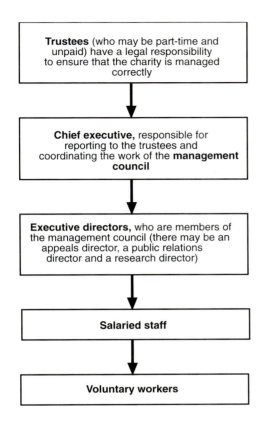

Trustees (who may be part-time and unpaid) have a legal responsibility to ensure that the charity is managed correctly

Chief executive, responsible for reporting to the trustees and coordinating the work of the **management council**

Executive directors, who are members of the management council (there may be an appeals director, a public relations director and a research director)

Salaried staff

Voluntary workers

Figure 1.7 Organisational structure of a large charity

There are over 170 000 charities in Britain that have **trust** status. A trust is a relationship in which a person called a **trustee** is responsible for holding funds or other assets which have been given for the benefit of other people. A charitable or public trust can be set up for one of four purposes:

- for the relief of poverty e.g. Oxfam
- for the advancement of education, e.g. an examinations board or a public school
- for the advancement of religion, e.g. maintenance of a church or other place of worship
- for other purposes, e.g. conservation or environmental charities such as Nature Conservancy Trusts and Greenpeace.

Most charities have to be registered with the Charity Commissioners who, under the Charities Act 1992, have general powers of supervision over their administration and the power to investigate if there is any suspicion about fraud or bogus fund-raising.

The structure of a large charity may be as in Figure 1.7.

It is important to remember that voluntary organisations must be properly governed and regulated, and keep accurate records, just like companies. If a charity went bankrupt because of incompetence, or if funds were used for non-charitable purposes, the trustees may find that they are both legally and financially liable.

Did you know?

1 Voluntary organisations handled more than £17 billion during 1992.
2 A manager in a large charity may have a budget of more than £50 million each year.
3 Under the Give As You Earn scheme employees can donate a percentage of their salary to a nominated charity. The giver pays only the net amount of the donation **after tax** but the charity receives the gross amount.
4 A percentage from the National Lottery is given to arts, sport, national heritage projects, charities and the Millennium Fund (which is concerned with proposals to celebrate the year 2000). In the first seven weeks of the lottery £96.5 million was raised for charity (see also Element 1.2).
5 There are more than 5500 charity shops in Britain and over £200 million a year is spent in them. In many cases a local authority or landlord would rather let a charity have an empty shop for nothing or at a reduced rent r than leave it empty.
6 Working for a charity is a professional career with salaries paid at similar levels to those paid by the civil service or local government.
7 Some charities are very up to date! For example, you can now reach the Samaritans via Internet by E-mailing them on joo@smaritans.org. To date they are responding to four or five Email messages every day, received from around the world!

Optional evidence assignment

*This activity can be carried out verbally in class **in a group** as a non-assessed activity to consolidate learning. Alternatively, if you do it **on your own**, it can count as supplementary evidence towards the following parts of the scheme.*

PC 2:	Explain the purposes of business organisations
Range:	Purposes: charitable
Core skills:	Communication, application of number, information technology

Charities are ranked each year by the Charities Aid Foundation in relation to the funds they have raised. Figure 1.8 shows the league table for 1993.

1 What was the total amount of income for all the charities in 1993?

2 Explain clearly the main purpose of charitable organisations.

3 Suggest reasons why a charity may increase or decrease in popularity and then give examples of actions charities can take to retain public interest.

4 a Calculate the percentage income of the total amount you calculated in question 1 earned by each of the top ten charities.

   b Design a pie chart, preferably using a computer, to show the percentage received by each of the top ten charities.

Charity	Income (£m)
1 National Trust (2)	78.7
2 Oxfam (4)	59.0
3 RNLI (lifeboats) (3)	56.2
4 Save the Children (1)	53.9
5 Imperial Cancer Research (5)	48.4
6 Cancer Research Campaign (6)	45.4
7 Barnardos (7)	36.5
8 Help the Aged (10)	33.1
9 Salvation Army (9)	32.3
10 NSPCC (12)	30.8
11 RSPCA (5)	28.3
12 Christian Aid (13)	28.1
13 Cancer R Macmillan (17)	27.6
14 British Heart Foundation (14)	27.5
15 British Red Cross (11)	26.9
16 RNIB (16)	25.7
17 Guide Dogs (15)	25.6
18 Inst Cancer Research (25)	22.3
19 Scope/Spastics Society (20)	22.2

Figure 1.8 The charities league table for 1993 (figures in brackets show the position for 1992)

Business organisations – ownership and size

Ownership – private and public sector

In Britain most organisations are owned privately. However, some are run by the Government on behalf of the public. This mix of ownership means that Britain has a **mixed** economy. The arguments for having both types of organisation are mainly as summarised below.

Private ownership

This encourages people to start up in business and work hard. The aim of the people running these businesses is to supply what their customers want so that they will make a profit. Unless they sell their goods or services at a competitive price customers will not buy from them. Therefore private ownership encourages people to work hard and means that they will supply what consumers want to buy and that the price of goods is usually competitive, which also benefits the consumer.

Public ownership

This is needed to provide those services which:

- people would find unprofitable to provide privately (e.g. education on a national scale)
- are considered essential for the well-being of the community (e.g. health care)
- are impossible to deliver to only those who pay (e.g. street lighting or defence).

In all these cases there is a social, rather than a profit-making purpose for their existence.

Large organisations

The largest organisations in the world are the **multinationals** or **transnationals**, so called because they own or control production facilities in more than one country in the world. Examples include the oil companies, drug companies, car producers and computer giants (e.g. IBM) which both produce and sell their goods on a world-wide basis.

If they are based in Britain they will be known as **public limited companies** (plc) – not to be confused with public ownership (see page 29). If they are based abroad then they will be called something different. For example, in America you would see 'Corp' or 'Inc' after a company's name, in Australia you would see 'Pty' and on the Continent 'SA'.

Large companies usually have a national or international market. This means they can produce the same product (or offer the same service) with little or no change, and sell it to a vast number of people. They are usually household names and are often operational in several areas of the country.

It is estimated that by the year 2000 the world's largest 250 multinationals will produce about half the world's goods.

Non-assessed activity

Benetton, Tate and Lyle, Nestlé and Pilkington Brothers are all multinational companies. **As a group**, do you know:

a what each company produces
b whether these products fit the description of typical multinational products given above
c which *two* companies are British
d in which countries in the EU do the other two companies have their headquarters?

Did you know?

You can buy Wispa, Picnic and Cadbury's Fruit & Nut in Russia? Cadbury/Schweppes has deliberately had a policy of reinvesting its profits by expanding across the world. In 1994 it invested £10 million in a Chinese chocolate factory, £15 million in Poland, £12 million in Argentina. It also made sizeable investments in India and in Mexico, where it bought a mineral water company. The result? Cadbury's sales world-wide were more than £4 billion for the first time – with £1.7 billion of sales in the UK. With UK profits of £231 million Cadbury has a few pounds more in the bank to expand still further!

Percentage of trading profit

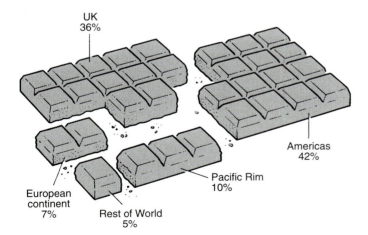

UK
36%

Americas
42%

Pacific Rim
10%

European
continent
7%

Rest of World
5%

Figure 1.9 Cadbury Scheppes – where the profit is earned

Medium-sized organisations

Britain has a large number of medium-sized organisations, each of which employs between 50 and 200 people. Most of these will be **private limited companies** (see page 22). Whilst some of these may operate on a national basis, most of them are more restricted geographically or produce a product which is more specialist in nature or design. They will have identified a **niche** in the market and try to fill it. This is a segment of an established branded market which can be filled by a specialist product. Therefore, whilst Ford and Vauxhall are large car manufacturers which produce the same model over and over again, a specialist car firm such as Morgan, TVR or Reliant will produce fewer cars for people who want a different type of product. Such organisations may not use the mass production methods favoured by large car producers. They will operate on a smaller scale, and this can even help to make their product more desirable. Niche producers operate in many large markets. Terry's and Thorntons are both producers of chocolate but they do not openly compete with the giants – Cadbury, Mars and Rowntree. Instead they produce their own specialist types of chocolates.

In some cases a company may be limited geographically because of competition outside a certain area. A group of retail shops may operate in a certain region, e.g. the north east or the south west, but not be found outside this area. This is because the demand for goods (and services) may vary from one part of the country to another – or because the owner does not want to expand any more.

Did you know?

In the UK today the only British-owned car producers are specialist companies who serve a niche market. Look at the car companies mentioned above and see if you can decide the type of market each of them serves.

Small organisations

Small organisations are those which are owned by one person (a **sole trader**) or by a few people (usually a **partnership** or **private limited company**). Although they may have some employees there are usually fewer than 30.

Most organisations start small and may then grow. Richard Branson, head of Virgin Enterprises, started in a small way, producing a magazine with a few helpers! In many cases, small organisations provide a personal or specialist service, such as a hairdresser, window cleaner, plumber, solicitor, accountant and estate agent's. Even in cases where small organisa-tions have the opportunity to grow and expand they may not do so. There are several reasons for this.

■ Many entrepreneurs prefer to be independent and avoid the legislation and restrictions involved in operating a large organisation. In 1988, out of nearly 800 000 organisations interviewed, nearly 55 per cent said they had no plans to grow beyond their present size, 35 per cent expected to grow slowly and only 10 per cent expected to grow rapidly.

■ The Government usually tries to encourage small enterprises because of the economic benefits. In Britain there are actually twice as many large companies for the size of the country as in any other European country. However, there is a definite lack of small and medium-sized companies. Economic evidence shows that these enterprises are more likely to provide new ideas, future leaders and greater job opportunities than large organisations. For that reason, in successive budgets, various organisations have lobbied the Government to assist the formation and growth of small businesses – especially to help them obtain finance.

■ Consumers like variety, so there are limits to mass production. Few of us like to spend money on new clothes, for example, and to see everyone else in the same outfit! Jewellery and furniture are other markets where people will pay more for something that is individual or hand-made.

■ Large organisations often require the services of many small companies. For instance, in the textile industry, the dyeing and finishing of cloth is often done by small, specialist companies who serve the market as a whole. Japanese car producers who have set up business in the north east of England have attracted around them a whole host of small suppliers of specialist components.

■ Small firms can join together to gain internal economies of scale. Typical examples are those of grocer combines, such as Spar, VG and Mace. Small grocers can gain from their association with a larger organisation which buys in bulk and markets the goods on their behalf.

■ Luxury goods cannot be mass produced. People want to pay for the name and gain status by owning something which is expensive and exclusive. Therefore the organisations which have a reputation for making prestigious goods will be small-scale and may even be choosy about their customers!

Did you know?

The most successful businesses are those where the type of ownership is the most suitable, bearing in mind the activities carried out, the type of product or service being provided and the scale (or size) of the operation. Organisations which require large amounts of finance or who want to operate on a national or global scale could not possibly do this if they were owned by a sole trader or a partnership. Similarly, it would be silly for your local butcher or newsagent to try to operate on a very large scale.

Types of business ownership

Business ownership can be divided into the following categories:

■ private enterprises (which comprise the private sector)
■ public enterprises (which comprise the public sector)
■ those which are either non-profit making or do not distribute their profits in the usual way (and therefore don't really fit either sector).

Figure 1.10 Small businesses may specialise in expensive and exclusive products

PRIVATE ENTERPRISES

1 **Sole trader** – a person is in business on his or her own behalf. The business is usually small, although the sole trader may employ other people as well.

2 **Partnerships** – two or more people own the business between them. Again they may employ other people.

3 **Private limited companies** – have the letters 'Ltd' after the name of the company. Private companies are often family businesses.

4 **Public limited companies** – have the letters 'plc' after their name. These are the largest type of company and the company shares are quoted on the Stock Exchange.

Note: A **franchise** is a small business run with the permission of a larger organisation – see page 24.

STATE-OWNED ENTERPRISES

1 **Local authorities** – enterprises organised and operated through the local town hall or council offices.

2 **Central government departments** – public enterprises run by the government and administered by government departments (e.g. Department of Health and the National Health Service, Department of Employment and Job Centres).

3 **Public corporations** – run in the same way as large private firms but owned and controlled by the government (e.g. the Post Office, British Rail). Remember that in recent years many public corporations have been privatised (i.e. moved into the private sector).

OTHER ORGANISATIONS

1 **Clubs** of many types – usually run by volunteers for the benefit of all members (e.g. your local squash or golf club).

2 **Charitable organisation**s – where the money raised, less administration costs, is spent on a particular cause (e.g. Greenpeace, NSPCC, RSPCA, Oxfam, etc.)

3 **Co-operatives** – some of these are organised for the benefit of the consumer and some (called producer co-operatives) are run for the benefit of the workers. Any surpluses are shared equally among the members.

Note: Building societies used to be run on a non-profit making basis – as Friendly Societies – but now some have become public limited companies and exist primarily to make a profit.

Figure 1.11 Main types of business organisations

Did you know?

Small businesses are usually **non-corporate organisations.** This basically means that:

- if anything happens to the owner(s) of the business then the business would cease to exist
- the owner can decide, at any time, to stop trading.

There are two types of non-corporate organisations – **sole traders** and **partnerships.**

Small businesses

Sole traders

A sole trader is a person who enters business working on his or her own. He or she puts in the capital to start the enterprise, works alone either or with employees and, as a reward, receives all the profits.

Sole traders are mainly found in those areas of business where a personal service is desirable, e.g. some retail shops such as a newsagent or a grocer, window cleaner, hairdresser, decorator etc.

Non-assessed activity

Read the following case study and, **as a group**, discuss the questions which follow.

Case study on Tony Sinclair

When he left school, Tony Sinclair trained to be a hairdresser. He has worked in three salons since, the latest being the most prestigious and expensive hairdressers in the town. He has built up his own list of clients who refuse to have their hair done by anyone else and he is now chief stylist where he works. He earns a good salary and excellent tips and gets on well, both with his boss and with the other employees.

Last month Tony's aunt died and left him £50 000. At the same time he found out that a suitable premises for a hairdressing business is for sale on a prime town-centre site. He is very tempted to leave his job and start up on his own – especially as he knows many of his customers will follow him.

Tony's friend, Neil, is in favour of this idea and they have talked nearly every night of the advantages of Tony setting up on his own. However, his sister, Paula, who is two years older, is more wary. She has told Tony to think carefully about the scheme. She has warned Tony of several disadvantages which could occur if he goes it alone.

1 What advantages do you think Tony has put forward in favour of the change?

2 What disadvantages do you think Paula has put forward?

3 If you were Tony what would you do – and why?

Compare your answers with Figure 1.12, which shows the advantages and disadvantages of being a sole trader. Note that your answer to question **3** will very much depend on whether you are a gambler – and prepared to risk your inheritance – or prefer to play safe and invest it. If you would be prepared to gamble then perhaps you would be good as an entrepreneur – someone who is prepared to risk their own money in the expectation of making a profit.

Partnerships

Most partnerships in Great Britain are **ordinary partnerships.** This means that they also have unlimited liability. An ordinary partnership is easy to set up. Each partner signs a Deed of Partnership which sets out the important details of the future business relationship. This is likely to include:

- the salary of each partner
- the share of the profits of each partner
- the name of the firm.

There are usually between two and twenty partners in most firms. You will find partnerships amongst the **professions**, e.g. accountants, solicitors, estate agents, doctors, dentists. In some cases more partners are allowed.

Did you know?

The term 'firm' is usually used for partnerships whereas the term 'company' or 'organisation' refers only to corporate organisations (see below).

Non-assessed activity

Imagine that you and a friend go into business as partners. You both invest £10 000. Ten years later you are doing well and your investment in the company has risen to £45 000

ADVANTAGES FOR SOLE TRADERS

- Easy to set up – no formal procedures if he/she is using his/her own name (apart from informing the Inland Revenue).

- Can make quick decisions and put plans into effect rapidly.

- Is independent.

- Can keep all the profit.

- Has no-one telling him/her what to do.

- Can provide a personal service to customers.

- Can avoid bad debts (unpaid debts) because he/she knows the customers well.

- Minimum of paperwork (but more if registered for VAT).

DISADVANTAGES FOR SOLE TRADERS

- Long working hours – little time off.

- Earns no money if business closed (e.g. if on holiday or off sick).

- Difficult to raise capital – borrowing is expensive and many banks don't like lending money to sole traders because of the risk involved.

- May be no room for expansion – or part of the house may have to be used for equipment or storage.

- The business may have to be sold on the death of the sole trader and the heirs may be liable for inheritance tax.

- Small-scale enterprises usually have high costs – no economies of scale (compare the amount a small grocer will pay for his stock in comparison with Sainsburys!).

- The flair of the owner may be for the job he did. He may have little, if any, financial expertise or management skills.

- **UNLIMITED LIABILITY**
  The biggest disadvantage for sole traders is the fact that they have **unlimited liability**. This means that if they lose a substantial amount of money and are declared bankrupt, then they may have to sell off their personal possessions (e.g. house, car, furniture and jewellery) to pay off their debts. In other words, their liability for their debts is not limited to a specific amount.

Figure 1.12 Advantages and disadvantages of sole traders each. Your partner, who has recently married, then dies and you find that he has left everything he owns to his wife. She therefore claims his share – £45 000.

As a group, decide your answers to the following.

1   What would be the effect on you, and your business, if you paid the money you owe?

2   Is there any action either you and your partner(s) could have taken to prevent this happening?

See if you can decide what really happens before you read it later!

Advantages of partnerships

1   Because each partner is expected to bring some money into the business, the partnership as a whole has more capital with which to operate.

2   Problems can be shared and discussed by everyone – and a variety of solutions may then be put forward.

3   New ideas and skills can be introduced.

4   The business affairs are still private.

5   The responsibility no longer rests with one person. It is therefore possible for the partners to take holidays and have free weekends – or even be ill – without worrying about the business.

6   Partners can specialise in their own field, e.g. a solicitor's office can have different partners specialising in conveyancing (buying and selling houses), divorce, criminal law, business law etc.

Did you know?

The term **specialisation** is used when a person concentrates on a particular aspect of their job. Another term you may see is **division of labour.** This means each person is responsible for a particular job, process or even a part of a process. The aim is to develop and use a person's skill and talent to the full to increase both quality and volume of production. It doesn't always work – people may get very bored with a repetitive job and cut corners.

Non-assessed activity

Read the following case study then, **as a group**, discuss the questions which follow.

Case study on an employment agency partnership

Jane, David and Saika became partners six months ago when they opened an employment agency. Each of them knew human resources officers in various companies in the area and felt sure that they could use these contacts to get to know about job vacancies in the area. They advertised in the local paper so that people who wanted jobs would also contact them. In the early months everything went well. Several people were found permanent jobs and a register of temporary staff was set up. These were people willing to work for companies at short notice for a few days or weeks.

Lately, however, there have been problems. The business has been struggling as many companies have been making employees redundant, rather than taking them on, and both the number of vacancies and the number of callers into the office have dwindled. At the weekly meeting there have been more and more disagreements.

- Jane and Saika wanted to spend more money on advertising their business, by sending leaflets to companies and putting adverts in the local paper. David said they couldn't afford this.
- Saika had recently purchased a fax machine without consulting either of the others. While the cost of this was not great – and the fax would be invaluable – Jane objected on principle to the fact that she was not consulted beforehand.
- David, who was learning how to drive, had started arranging his lessons during office hours. Both of the others objected to this.

At the last meeting they agreed that the business was desperately short of capital. Jane had said that her father was prepared to invest £5000 in the business – but only if he could be a sleeping partner. Neither of the others knew what this meant.

1   Should the partners spend more on advertising? Think of both the advantages and disadvantages of doing this.

2   What are your views on Saika's action in buying the fax machine?

3   Should David be allowed to take his driving lessons during office hours?

On a more general level, consider:

4   What could partners do if they began to disagree about how to run the business?

5   What could they do if a partner became unreliable – or took actions without consulting the others?

19

Figure 1.13 Jane, David and Saika's employment agency partnership

6 What should they do if a partner was lazy or incompetent?

7 What is the difference between an active partner and a sleeping partner? (If you don't know, see below.)

Partnership agreements

Because partners are all jointly responsible for the business, the actions of each of them affects the others. Therefore if one partner acts irresponsibly, this could jeopardise the business and bring the other partners into debt (remember they all have unlimited liability). Other problems can include disagreements, death of a partner or bankruptcy. Any of these may mean the termination of the partnership.

To prevent problems in case this happens, many partners draw up a **partnership agreement** to clarify matters which may cause a disagreement later. Although this document is not legally necessary, its existence may prevent problems occurring during difficult times. It is likely to include such points as:

- how the profits (or losses) should be shared
- what will happen to any assets if the partnership is dissolved
- the circumstances under which a partner could be

asked to leave (e.g. what would be considered to be professional misconduct).

Did you know?

The reason most partnerships are to be found in the professions is that, in many cases, the rules of a professional association may demand that the partners have unlimited liability. This is because it is believed that certain professional people, e.g. doctors, solicitors and accountants, should be seen to be fully committed to their clients (even including their own personal finances) – usually because the results of negligence could be very severe.

Death or retirement of a partner

The death or retirement of a partner can cause severe financial problems for the continuing partner(s) as they may have to find the money to buy out the other partner or anyone who would receive their share on death. It is therefore usual for the partnership to take out life assurance on each partner, which can be used to pay the family in the case of a partner's death. Some policies will pay out an amount when the partner has reached a certain age, and this money can be used to buy out a partner who is retiring.

Did you know?

Most partners in a business are **active** partners, which means they take an active part in the running of the business. A different type of partner is a **sleeping** partner. This is someone who invests money in the business but does not take an active part. Usually a sleeping partner will receive a smaller share of the profits than the active partner(s).

Limited partnerships

These are quite rare in Great Britain. In this case, as well as ordinary partners (who have unlimited liability) there are one or more partners who have limited liability. This means that their liability for the debts is limited to the amount they have invested in the business.

Having this option can be useful for people who want to participate in a partnership but are unwilling to risk their personal possessions. However:

- there must be at least one ordinary partner with unlimited liability
- the limited partner must be a sleeping partner.

Did you know?

John Lewis, which owns 22 department stores and 111 Waitrose supermarkets, is a **partnership!** Its 34 000 staff are officially described as partners and, although they don't actually control the company, they elect half the board. John Lewis also has a Partnership rule book which makes it clear that the members' happiness is very important. Because the group does not have outside shareholders, all the profit is available for reinvestment and the payment of an annual staff bonus. In 1994 the company made a profit of nearly £93.5 million – and allocated £43 million (46 per cent) to paying a bonus to all staff of 12 per cent of salary or six weeks' pay. Before you look for a job in a similar organisation be warned – the John Lewis Partnership is a very rare bird – in fact, in Britain it's the only one of its kind!

Figure 1.14 The John Lewis Partnership store in London's Oxford Street

Medium sized businesses

Non-assessed activity

Read the case study which follows and prepare your answers to the questions in Section 1. Then read the information given on private limited companies on page 22 before attempting Section 2.

Case study on Paul Makin and Andrea Wright – a partnership

Paul Makin and Andrea Wright have worked together for several years as computer consultants. They are both employed by a large national computer company and are based in Bristol. However, over the last twelve months they have both been concerned that their career prospects are very limited and they can see several opportunities for their services in the area which they feel their present employer is ignoring.

After much consideration they have decided to go into business together. They have each saved £6000. They think this may be enough capital for them to rent an office and start up on a small scale. They now have to decide what form of business would be the most appropriate, i.e. whether to become a partnership or to form a private limited company.

Section 1

1 What other expenses do you think Paul and Andrea will have to meet besides their rent? Write down what you consider would be a realistic figure for each expense for a year. (You may need to interview one or two people who regularly pay bills before you can do this!) Add the figures to find the total amount required.

2 Do you think £12 000 capital will be enough? If not, where do you think they can go for additional money and how much do you think they will need?

3 What will be the main disadvantages to them if they go into business as a partnership?

4 Do you think there would be any advantages to them if they formed a private limited company?

Did you know?

The term **capital** is used for the money the owner(s) put into the business. This can then be divided into:

- **fixed capital** (used for assets which last a long time, e.g. office furniture and equipment), and
- **working capital** (the money used for day to day expenditure and buying stock).

If a company spends too much on fixed assets and leaves itself short of working capital, it is rather like buying an expensive car and not being able to afford any petrol – or buying an expensive house and having nothing left to pay for food!

Section 2

5 If you were Paul and Andrea what would you call the company?

6 Why will they not be allowed to choose the same name as another organisation?

7 Who do you think will be the directors of their company?

8 If their authorised (allowed) capital, with their savings and the money they borrow, is £15 000, and they each hold 50 per cent of the shares, what is the maximum amount each of them could lose if the company went into liquidation?

9 What would happen to their company if a major disaster occurred in six months' time and both Paul and Andrea were killed in a car crash?

10 If Paul had saved more than Andrea, and owned 60 per cent of the shares what difference, if any, would this make?

Private limited company (Ltd)

A company differs from a partnership or a sole trader in two ways.

1 All shareholders in companies are protected by **limited liability.** A shareholder is someone who invests money in a company by buying a share in it. The company can be sued for its debts but the amount the shareholders owe is limited to the amount they spent when they bought their shares.

2 A company is known as a **corporate body** – this means that it has a separate legal identity. It can:

- employ staff
- sue people and be sued (if you hurt yourself in your local newsagent's you would sue the shopkeeper; if you hurt yourself in Debenhams you would sue the *company,* not the manager!)
- own property.

In addition, if all the shareholders died the company would still exist until it was formally wound up.

A company is run by the directors, who are usually the major shareholders. There is no limit to the number of shareholders but in a small organisation

these may be just the members of a family. At a meeting, each shareholder has **one vote per share.** Large shareholders can therefore outvote those with fewer shares. For that reason, the balance of shares (and the balance of power) in a small company can be important.

In a private company, shareholders must remember that:

- shares can only be transferred to someone else with the agreement of *all* the shareholders
- shares cannot be sold to the general public.

Did you know?

1 A new business is not allowed to trade under the same name as an existing company if there is likely to be any confusion to suppliers or customers. This is to stop a rogue organisation trading under false pretences by using the name of a reputable organisation.

2 Companies always give their registered office address on their company letter headed paper (often at the foot of the page). Note that no matter how many regional branches an organisation may have, one address will be its registered address.

3 The letters 'Ltd', which are found at the end of the name of a private limited company, stand for 'Limited'. Originally this was intended to be a warning to creditors (people to whom the company owes money). Because liability is limited, **creditors** are being warned that if the company goes into liquidation, they may not get their money back!

Large businesses

Public limited company (plc)

Non-assessed activity

Read the case study below then **as a group** discuss the questions which follow.

Case study on a computer consultancy partnership – continued

Five years later Paul and Andrea are doing very well indeed. They have four offices and employ 52 staff. There are five directors. Paul and Andrea still retain control with 35 per cent of the shares each. The other three directors each own 10 per cent of the shares.

Over the years they have ploughed back the profits into the business and borrowed money from the bank to finance their growth. Their total capital is now £120 000. All of the directors have ambitious plans to expand the organisation even further, and preferably quite quickly. However, to do this they would need to borrow even more money. At this week's Board Meeting they are discussing the advantages of asking the bank for a further loan or going public. This means they would apply to become a public limited company so that they could sell shares to the general public – and raise a lot more capital.

Paul is worried about the idea of becoming a public company as this will mean issuing and selling shares outside the company and therefore, to some extent, losing control. Large investment companies could buy up shares in their company and therefore be able to vote and have a say in how it is run. The company will have to publish its accounts every year, there will be more formal procedures to be followed, and the shares will be quoted on the Stock Exchange.

Andrea is against the idea of borrowing from a bank. She thinks that interest rates may go up, so that they have to pay a lot of money to the bank on top of the money they have borrowed. She also knows that the bank won't lend them more than £20 000, and this is not enough to finance the planned expansion programme. She gives the meeting several examples of small, successful companies which have become public companies to attract the capital they need to expand, e.g. The Body Shop and Richard Branson's organisation, Virgin.

The meeting adjourns for one week, during which time all the directors must consider how they will vote on the issue.

1   Draw up a list of advantages and disadvantages of going public. Read other books besides this one to help you to compile your list!

2   Why do you think large institutions (e.g. banks and investment companies) and members of the public might be willing to buy shares in the company?

3   Look in the financial pages of a daily newspaper. Prepare a line graph to show the share movements of **four** large organisations for a week (preferably using a spreadsheet package).

   ■ Are the share values going up or down?

   ■ Are they all moving in the same direction? If so, discuss with your tutor why this is the case.
   ■ List as many reasons as you can think of why shares fluctuate in value.

4   If Paul and Andrea go public, what letters will their company now have after its name?

5   Assume your group is the Board of Directors. Debate the issue of whether to go public or not. Summarise both the conclusion of the debate and your own views.

Did you know?

■ Not every company can 'go public'. There are certain requirements of companies which must be met before their shares can be traded on the Stock Exchange. For instance, they must have a minimum of £50 000 in capital.
■ **Flotation** is the term used to describe a private company becoming a public limited company.

Case study in flotation

Cablecomms is one of Britain's biggest cable systems operators and is owned by the New York firm Nynex. Nynex decided to float Cablecomms on the Stock Exchange with the aim of raising £400 million to pay for new developments in the UK cable market and to build up its cable television and telecommunications activity in the UK. Nynex will still retain a majority of the shares.

CableComms holds the franchise to supply cable to homes in Greater Manchester, parts of London and Derby, altogether 2.7 million homes. The company also wants to use the cash from the flotation to bid for more franchises as they come up for sale.

Note: Franchises are discussed below.

Who owns a company?

Limited companies are owned by their **shareholders** – those people (individuals and institutions) who invest their money in shares issued by the company. The total amount of those investments provides the capital to finance the different business activities which the company undertakes, although additional capital may be borrowed. As we saw earlier in this element, a proportion of the profits is distributed to shareholders in the form of a **dividend** – usually paid every six months (see also page 00).

Shareholders buy shares:

- in the hope that the shares will increase in value
- to receive the dividend.

Each shareholder has one vote for each ordinary share they own. This right to vote may be used at the Annual General Meeting but, in reality, unless a great number of shares are owned there is little hope of a shareholder influencing the activities of the directors and then the managers who actually control the company on a day-to-day basis.

Did you know?

In private limited companies – which are often family businesses – the directors are usually members of the family or have been closely involved in building up the company. They are *also* the shareholders. In a public limited company the shareholders are normally large institutional investors with large amounts of money to invest (e.g. pension funds and insurance companies). Even after the Government's privatisation campaigns, shareholders who are ordinary members of the public are still in a minority in Britain.

Mixing small and large businesses

Franchises

Did you know?

The Body Shop, Benetton, Kentucky Fried Chicken, Wimpy and Pizza Hut have something in common. They are all **franchise** operations, run by individual owners who are allowed to use the trade name and business appearance of a larger organisation.

Franchise operations

Franchises are a relatively new form of business and have grown enormously in Britain over the past ten years. The aim is to enable a person to run their own small business and yet have the security and expertise of a large, national (or international) organisation behind them.

The person who operates the business is known as the **franchisee.** The franchisee has to organise and carry out the business in the way determined by the **franchisor** – the organisation which controls the product or service being sold. Most of the capital has to be raised by the franchisee who will then be keen to work hard and make a success of the business. The franchisee has to pay an initial licensing fee *plus* a share of the profits to the franchisor for the use of the trade name. In return the franchisee often has exclusive rights to a specified area (e.g. only one shop per town) as well as expert advice and help from the franchisor.

In some operations franchisees may sell directly to the public (e.g. Tupperware reps) *or* be allocated the franchise by an organisation which provides its own service to the public (e.g. a hospital, hotel or leisure centre). In the latter case the franchisee is given permission to run a shop on the site of the main organisation, e.g. a hotel may have a florist, hairdresser, newsagent and coffee shop in its main foyer. The hotel will be the franchisor and will charge the franchisees for the right to operate their businesses on its premises.

Franchises in Britain are overseen by the British Franchise Association (BFA) which operates a code of conduct for its members.

In 1992 there were nearly 19 000 retail franchise outlets employing nearly 190 000 people. Their annual sales were more than £5 billion and are expected to be nearer £20 billion by the year 2000. Their continued growth has been forecast because of the world-wide decline in employment in manufacturing and the increase in service sector activities, together with the growth in the popularity of self-employment.

Did you know?

Franchise operations are not restricted to the retail trade. Some are operated by manufacturers. The most well known example is in the soft drinks trade. Coca-Cola, Pepsi-Cola and Seven-Up all franchise the bottling and canning of their drinks to independent companies. And as mentioned above, CableComms, the cable company also holds franchises to supply cable to homes in certain areas.

Another kind of franchise is that run by the British School of Motoring, whose professionally qualified driving instructors run individual franchise operations. They are supplied with duel-control tuition cars and business support.

International franchises

With the growth of the Single Market many European companies are setting up franchise operations in Britain. An example is Delifrance, which specialises in French pastries and bread. The pastries are prepared and frozen in France and then transported to franchisee outlets for baking. Foreign franchisor organisations are nothing new. The Spar operation is based in the Netherlands and yet there are nearly 2500 retail Spar shops in the UK – and have been for many years.

Non-assessed activity

1 The failure rate for franchise operations is less than half that for ordinary small businesses. Why do you think this is the case?

2 Discuss as a group and then list the advantages to

a a hospital, and

b a large organisation, e.g. Prontaprint or Tie Rack, of operating as a franchisor.

Working together

Co-operatives

All co-operatives exist to provide mutual benefits for their members. There are several different types of co-operatives, including:

- **retail co-operatives** – which are owned by the consumer
- **producer co-operatives** – which are owned and controlled by the people who work there. The enterprise provides them with employment.

Retail co-operatives

The co-operative movement was founded in the mid-1840s by a group of textile workers in Rochdale. Their aim was to buy foods and other necessities and sell them as cheaply as they could. At that time mill owners could operate shops in or near their mills and charge high prices on the basis that the workers had no choice but to buy from them. The Rochdale Pioneers (as they were called) had the idea of joining together, buying goods and then selling them to members of their movement without adding on any profit. At the end of the year any surplus was to be distributed among the members (i.e. those who had bought from them all year).

Non-assessed activity

Before you read any further – imagine you had been one of the Rochdale Pioneers. How would you have distributed the surplus? Equal shares to everyone or a different system? Discuss your ideas with the rest of your group.

The principles of co-operation

The principles of co-operation are the same for all co-operative institutions.

- Anyone can be a member.
- Each member has only one vote (compare this with the shareholder of a public limited company).
- A fixed interest rate is paid on capital invested.
- The members decide how any profits are distributed. Distribution should be fair and reasonable, for the benefit of the business, the members or the community.
- The organisation should also be concerned with educational and social issues, e.g. members' personal development.
- All co-operatives should work and co-operate with each other.

Did you know?

The Rochdale Pioneers decided to distribute any end of year surplus to the members in proportion to the amount they had spent on goods that year. In this way, those who spent the most money would receive the largest return.

The retail co-operative movement today

The retail co-operative movement went from strength to strength until the late 1960s. Goods were supplied by the Co-operative Wholesale Society to the retail shops which ensured constant supplies at reasonable prices. However, after a while problems were encountered.

■ When resale price maintenance ended, instead of goods having to be sold at a price specified by the manufacturer, there could be price wars between supermarkets. The co-ops found it difficult to compete *and* pay their members dividends.

■ Most retail co-operatives were corner shops and managing dozens of these from an area office proved difficult – especially by managers who had received little professional training.

■ Because the profits were given back to the members at the end of each year there was insufficient money to finance expansion or change.

■ Social changes occurred which altered people's life styles and shopping habits.

Optional evidence assignment

*This activity can be carried out verbally in class in **a group** as a non-assessed activity to consolidate learning. Alternatively, if you do it **on your own**, it can count as supplementary evidence towards the following parts of the scheme.*

PC 2: Explain the purposes of business organisations

PC 3: Explain the differences between types of business ownership

Range: Purposes: profit, market share, customer, public service, charitable

Types of business ownership: public limited company, co-operative

Core skills: Communication, IT

Read the two stories below and examine the charts which follow. Then carry out the following tasks.

1 List all the social changes you can find which are illustrated in the two stories below. Prepare a summary of these, using a word processor.

2 Indicate which social trends may have contributed to the downfall of small, corner shops, and in what way.

3 Identify the main purpose of the old co-operative and contrast this with the main purpose of a modern supermarket.

4 Identify the main type of business ownership of large modern supermarkets and state how this differs from the ownership of both small local shops and co-operative societies.

Note: You may wish to re-read pages 17–25 before you complete this question.

March 1954

Sarah rushed out of the house holding the ten-shilling note carefully. She recited the list of things she needed to herself as she ran to the co-op on the corner. Her mother bought all their groceries from the local co-op so that they could benefit from the dividend. Because prices were the same in every shop the co-op actually worked out cheaper because all the customers received some money back at the end of every six months. It was also essential that they shopped locally as they couldn't afford a car. Sarah's mother also shopped very frequently as otherwise perishable food would go off.

Sarah knew their dividend number off by heart – 54381. When she bought the things her mother wanted and said the number it was written on a special form, with the amount she had spent. She took a copy of this form

Figure 1.15 Sarah – then and now

home and the 'master' went to the main Emporium in town so they could calculate how much dividend was due for the goods her mother had bought. Normally the money was used for special things. This year Sarah was eleven and the money had gone to help to buy her uniform for her new school. Really it was her mother's way of saving. This was important as her mother didn't go out to work and they only had her father's wage to live on.

Sarah opened the door of the co-op and was immediately greeted by Mr Skinner, the friendly manager. He had been with the co-op since he left school and knew all his customers well. He took pride in the fact that all his customers regularly left their weekly orders with him and that he made them up personally and had the delivery boy get them out the same day. He lifted the cheese from the special cheese slicer and carefully put it under cover – then he turned to Sarah to see how he could help her.

March 1994

Sarah rushed out of work at 5 pm aware that she had very little food in the house and six people coming for supper. She had searched both the fridge and the freezer that morning, but without any luck. Usually she only shopped in bulk, once a month, as – like many other mothers – she also worked full-time so had little time to spare for shopping.

She drove as quickly as she could to the supermarket she used regularly. Although it was about five miles out of her way she liked the range of goods they stocked, thought their prices were competitive and knew where everything was – which saved precious time.

She grabbed a trolley and quickly collected the things she needed – virtually everything was pre-packed and easy to find. She had to queue for a while at the check-out as the girl was new and rather slow. Sarah's turn eventually came and she decided to pay by Access, as her bank account was running rather low that month.

At the supper party, later that evening, the conversation turned to shopping. One person, Mark, was quite keen on the co-op supermarket in another part of town, though he remarked that it was a pity they didn't offer dividends any more, but agreed people had more sophisticated ways of saving their money these days.

Producer co-operatives

Imagine a situation where you and a group of your friends want to set up in business together. You all

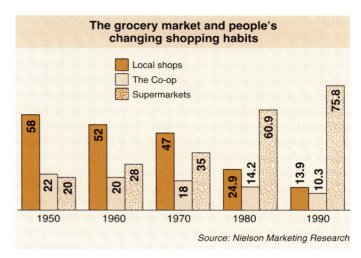

Figure 1.16 The decline of small shops

want to work hard and make money but no one wants to take charge. You all want to be equals, with an equal share of any profits you make. What do you do?

One answer would be to start a producer's or worker's co-operative with the same principles of co-operation as shown on page 25. When you investigate you find that:

■ there are several producer co-operatives in existence – and some very successful ones indeed in Europe
■ you can form a limited company – and have the protection of limited liability
■ all the workers can be involved in decision making
■ jobs can even be rotated, so that everyone takes their turn at work that is pleasant and work that is dirty or boring
■ it does not matter if all the workers are not members – it is up to you to decide.

You therefore find it rather puzzling when you find out that in Britain worker co-operatives have never been as successful as those abroad and decide you need to find out more.

Did you know?

Some worker co-operatives are the result of a **worker buyout**. This is when the owner wants to sell the business and the enterprise is bought by the employees. In some cases, if a business is in difficulties, the employees may buy it to save their jobs – especially if they think they can run it better. They may decide to run this as a co-operative, or as an ordinary private limited company.

Even more common are **management buyouts** where the managers of a business, which is under threat of closure, buy it from the existing owner. This may happen if a large company decides to sell or close down small subsidiary companies which have not been particularly successful. The managers may feel that they know enough to turn the business around and make it successful, if they can run it in their own way.

Test your memory. Do you remember that in the case study on British Coal you read about some of the Welsh mines being saved by a management buyout? If not, look back at page 5.

Optional evidence assignment

*This activity can be carried out verbally in class **in a group** as a non-assessed activity to consolidate learning. Alternatively, if you do it **on your own,** it can count as supplementary evidence towards the following parts of the scheme.*

PC 2:	Explain the purposes of business organisations
PC 3:	Explain the differences between types of business ownership
Range:	Purposes: profit, market share, customer, public service, charitable
	Types of business ownership: private limited company, co-operative
Core skills:	Communication, IT

Imagine you work for the producer co-operative described below. Read the questions and then prepare your answers as a report on producer co-operatives. If possible, use a word processor.

Case study on Workers United – a producer co-operative

Workers United was formed in 1990 by a group of ten women who either had been made redundant in the last two years or were trying to find jobs after being at home with their children. They had decided to form a producer co-operative with no one in overall charge so that the profits could be shared by them all. They decided this would make everyone work harder, as they all had an interest in how much money was made. The co-operative had been quite

successful, despite a few setbacks, and now sixteen people worked there.

In the beginning the co-operative had struggled for recognition. The local banks hadn't wanted to lend it any money and all the suppliers had wanted to be paid before they would make a delivery, mainly because they distrusted the set-up of a co-operative and didn't want to deal with a company which didn't have a manager. Eventually the women had obtained a loan from a special fund after obtaining help and advice from their local authority (see page 37) but knew they may have serious problems raising additional finance in the future.

Actually the co-op seemed to work quite well, apart from one or two internal disputes. A system of job rotation was in operation, so that everyone had the chance to do both the boring and the interesting jobs. The problem was that some people were better at some things than others, especially in relation to the office work and book-keeping. The same difficulties arose when a decision had to be made. Some members were forceful, intelligent and decisive and tended to dominate the others at the regular weekly meetings. In some cases it had taken several weeks before everyone was roughly in agreement. Even then there were often complaints afterwards by those who felt that their views had not been considered.

Another problem was that no one felt they had the right to tell other people what to do. When someone was thought to be slacking or was persistently late, there were no formal disciplinary procedures to be followed.

However, last week a serious problem had arisen. A group of workers had been investigating the idea of buying a new type of machine which would produce goods more cheaply and more quickly. The enterprise could benefit from technological development and stay competitive. However, others feared that this machine might put some members out of work, especially as there was a limited market for their goods. There seemed to be a clear split between those who thought the machine should be bought and those who wanted to protect jobs.

1 What advantages and disadvantages do you feel there are in being a member of a worker co-operative as opposed to being an employee in an ordinary private limited company?

2 List all the reasons you can why worker co-operatives may fail.

3 What are the main purposes of a worker co-operative? How do these differ from those of most private limited companies?

4 If you were a member of Workers United, what would you suggest to help them overcome each of their problems and yet still retain the principles of co-operative membership?

5 Divide into two groups. Group A should prepare arguments to defend the purchase of the new machine. Group B should prepare arguments to defend jobs. Debate the issue and reach a conclusion. Write up both arguments and the conclusion neatly.

State-owned organisations

Organisations which are state-owned are those which provide goods or services and are owned by the Government. These may be:

- run by central government departments, (e.g. hospitals which may be run by the Department of Health or Job Centres which are run by the Department of Employment)
- owned by local government and administered through your local town hall or county hall (e.g. leisure centres and libraries)
- public corporations or nationalised organisations which are owned by central government but run like private organisations to make a profit (e.g. the Post Office).

The cost of the goods and services provided by the public sector varies. They may be:

- free (e.g. borrowing library books, asking for advice in the Job Centre)
- offered at a reduced price (e.g. the entrance fee to a swimming pool may be subsidised by the local authority)

Services provided by the State

Probably the most famous State service is the National Health Service, which provides free medical care for the people of Britain through hospitals, health centres and family doctors. However, this is not the only service provided by the State. Indeed it has a wide range of responsibilities and provides a great number of services to both private citizens and businesses. Some of these are provided by **central government** (administered by Whitehall) and others by **local government** (administered by the local town hall).

Central government services

The policies of central government are determined by the political party currently elected to run the country. Since 1979 Britain has had a Conservative Government.

The **Cabinet** consists of the Prime Minister and their chosen ministers. It usually has about 21 members. Many of the Cabinet ministers are responsible for the activities which take place within their own departments, e.g. the Home Secretary is responsible for the Home Office, the Secretary of State for Trade and Industry is responsible for the Department of Trade and Industry (DTI) and so on.

Each department has its own budget and has to submit its spending plans to the **Treasury** each year. Each department is responsible for providing a range of services.

Through their policies and activities some departments have direct influence on business organisations, others concentrate mainly on providing services to the general public.

 ### Non-assessed activity

Examine Figure 1.17 and state, for each department, whether the services are mainly provided for the Government itself, businesses, the general public – or a mixture of these.

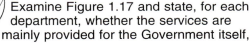 ### Did you know?

- The letters HM stand for Her Majesty.

- The First Lord of the Treasury is the Prime Minister – although he or she does not take part in the day-to-day activities of the Department.

Raising the money and spending the money

The money to provide government services is raised in two ways.

- Taxation – both **direct** taxes (e.g. income tax or corporation tax) and **indirect** tax (e.g. VAT)
- Government borrowing – from the general public (e.g. the sale of National Savings certificates and Premium Bonds) and from financial institutions. The term used for government borrowing (from

DEPARTMENT	RESPONSIBILITIES
HM Treasury	Plans and supervises the spending of all government departments, local authorities and public corporations. Advises the government on economic policy and puts this into effect.
Ministry of Defence	Administers the armed forces and implements of defence policy.
Department for Education	Coordinates full-time education up to the age of 16, plus further and higher education for those over that age.
Department of the Environment	Links with local authorities on local planning and inner cities. Responsible for conservation and environmental protection, including energy efficiency.
Export Credits Guarantee Department	Assists UK exports by providing export credit insurance to British exporters as well as guaranteeing repayment to British banks which provide finance for exports.
Employment Department Group	Employee rights, Health and Safety (by liaison with the Health and Safety Commission), pay and equal opportunities, Training and Enterprise Councils, local and regional employment policies.
Department of Transport	Airports, coastguards, motorways and trunk roads, road safety legislation, and licensing of vehicles.
Department of Trade and Industry	Promotes UK exports, gives information and advice to small firms, responsible for company legislation, consumer safety and protection and competition policy. Promotes the use of new technology.
Foreign and Commonwealth Office	Operates diplomatic missions and embassies worldwide to promote British interests and protect British citizens abroad.
Department of Health	Responsible for the operation of the National Health Service and the supervision of social services provided by local authorities.
Department of Social Security	Responsible for the operation of the social security and benefits system (e.g. child benefit, family credit, income support and the social fund).
Home Office	Responsible for the police, probation and prison services and immigration policy.
Ministry of Agriculture, Fisheries and Food (MAFF)	Responsible for policies on agriculture (including EC policies), plants, fisheries and forestry as well as food regulations.
HM Customs and Excise	The collection and administration of customs and excise duties and Value Added Tax.
Board of Inland Revenue	Administers and collects direct taxes – mainly income tax and corporation tax (paid by companies).
Department of National Heritage	Responsible for broadcasting, films, libraries, sport and tourism. Oversees the National Lottery

Figure 1.17   Government departments

whatever source) is **Public Sector Borrowing Requirement** (PSBR).

The November Budget

Each November the Government produces its Budget and the Chancellor of the Exchequer announces this in the House of Commons. The Budget Statement includes:

a the government spending forecast for the following year and its plans for the three subsequent years

b how much it intends to spend on each service or area of expenditure

c how much money the Government will raise through taxation over this period

d how much money the Government will raise through borrowing. This amount – the PSBR – is the **difference** between government spending and income (i.e. between **a** and **c**.

The way in which the Government raises and spends its money affects you – firstly as a taxpayer when you go to work and secondly as a user of government services.

Non-assessed activity

1 The pie chart in Figure 1.18 shows how the Government plans to raise its money in 1995–6.

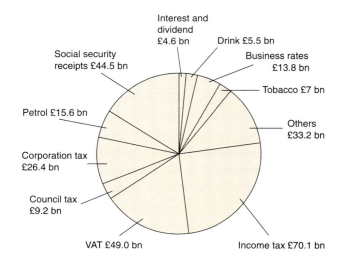

Figure 1.18   Sources of government finance, 1995–6

a List these sources of revenue in order i.e. with the highest one at the top of your list.

b Revise with your tutor the difference between corporation tax and income tax (see page 9).

c What is the total projected revenue of the Government for 1995–6?

d If the Government wanted to raise more money and decided to increase income tax by 10 per cent, what do you think would be the reaction of voters?

2 During 1995–6, the Government plans to spend its money as follows:

Social security	£87.1 billion
Health	£33 bn
Defence	£21.7 bn
Scotland, Wales and N Ireland	£28.9 bn
Local authorities	£30.3 bn
Education	£11 bn
The Home Office	£6.4 bn
Employment	£3.5 bn
Housing	£7 bn
Transport	£4.4 bn
Agriculture	£3 bn
Trade and industry	£1.4 bn
Environment	£2 bn
Other £62.3 bn	

a Prepare a pie chart (similar to the one on page 30) showing how the money will be spent, preferably using a spreadsheet package.

b Do you, **as a group,** agree with the Government's priorities?

c Form a government for a day. **As a group**, decide your own priorities and how much money you would spend in each area. Be prepared to explain your decisions to your tutor.

d How much will the Chancellor have to borrow (i.e. the value of the PSBR) to make up the difference between planned receipts and planned expenditure?

Did you know?

In November 1994, the Chancellor of the Exchequer, Kenneth Clarke, had to think again when his Budget proposal to increase VAT on fuel bills was not passed by Parliament. This meant he was £1 billion short. To make up the difference he increased National Insurance contributions and tax/excise duties on petrol, diesel, alcohol and tobacco.

The privatisation issue

Since 1979–80 the Government has had a policy of selling off industries which were publicly owned to private shareholders. Many have now been sold, including British Telecom, British Aerospace, British Gas, British Steel, British Airways, Rolls Royce, British Coal and the electricity generating companies – National Power and PowerGen. The money raised has meant that the Government has been able to reduce its own borrowing necessary to finance its expenditure – over £35 billion has been raised so far from privatisations.

Plans for further privatisations include British Rail and the Post Office. This will leave only the nuclear industries, the Civil Aviation Authority and London Transport as 'nationalised industries'.

Figure 1.19   National Power is one of the organisations recently privatised by the Government

Why privatise?

The belief of the Government was that public sector companies were frequently inefficient as they were 'protected' in two ways:

- they could not go bankrupt (if they made losses the Government gave them more money)
- they were frequently monopolies (i.e. the only supplier) – so they could dictate supply and price.

The idea was that if the companies were in the private sector they would have to become more efficient to cope with the increased competition.

A typical example was transport. If buses were privatised then competition would mean there were increased services and lower fares. Reducing the restrictions on taxis has had a similar result.

Advantages

Those in favour of privatisation claim that:

- Industries must lower their costs to remain competitive – which is better for consumers.
- The consumers will be able to choose from a wider variety of goods sold at lower prices – again because of competition. For instance, the choice of telephones on the market has increased dramatically since British Telecom was privatised.
- Privatisation will make managers and staff more efficient and give better service. If customers are lost because of inefficiency then the company may go out of business and both managers and staff would lose their jobs. This fear will encourage them to give good service.
- Government finance in supporting loss making industries is reduced – so there is less burden on taxpayers.
- Private individuals are encouraged to buy shares.

Disadvantages

Those who disagree with privatisation claim that:

- In many cases there are no 'real' competitors so the customer is worse off. In this case the company which was a public monopoly is now just a private monopoly. For instance, who will supply you with water if you fall out with your local water company?
- Standards of service do not always improve. A Mori survey carried out about British Telecom revealed that customers thought that standards of service were worse after privatisation than before.
- Unprofitable parts of an industry cannot be subsidised by profitable parts. For instance, the *real* cost of delivering a letter in the Scottish Highlands is much greater than in Inner London. What will happen to remote services if the Post Office is privatised?
- The Government is at present using the money it raises to reduce its own borrowing – but when everything has been sold off there will be nothing else left.

Did you know?

The proposed privatisation of the Post Office is already taking place by **franchising** Crown post offices and their operation to other retail outlets. Although the Post Office has not yet been officially privatised, over half of the 1500 original Crown post offices have been closed and their operation transferred to other outlets since 1989.

Non-assessed activity

Major job losses have occurred in many privatised industries, especially British Airways, British Steel and British Telecom as they have 'slimmed down' to reduce their operating costs and become more efficient. Critics blame the privatisation programme. Others argue that many other companies have had to reduce their staff levels to stay competitive during the recession – the privatised companies have only done the same thing. Another opinion is that many jobs have been lost because of new technology.

1 **As a group**, decide how you would define a recession. Check your answer with your tutor.

2 Work out how a company can improve its profits if it decides to reduce the number of staff. Translink is a delivery company which employs 50 staff. Last year its total revenue was £3 000 000 and its costs were £1 750 000. Last year the average pay for each employee was £20 000.

   a What was the total wage bill for the year?
   b How much profit did Translink make?
   c What is the total wage bill as a percentage of the total costs?
   d How much would the company save, on average, if twenty staff were made redundant?
   e If revenue remained the same next year, what would be the new profit figure?

3 **As a group,** decide why a company would be more likely to reduce staff in a recession, rather than increase the price of its products.

Did you know?

Because many privatised industries do not have many (or any) competitors and are therefore virtually monopoly suppliers, the Government has set up watchdog or regulatory bodies who will pursue customer complaints and oversee the profits (to make sure these have not risen too much).

Non-assessed activity

Oftel, Ofgas and Ofwat are the titles of three watchdog bodies. The industries they represent are listed below. Can you decide which belongs to which?

a British Gas
b The water industry
c British Telecom

Local authorities

Local authorities are responsible for providing a wide range of services on a local basis. This is because it would be both impossible and impractical for the Government to administer these services on a central basis for the following reasons.

- Areas in the country vary in what they need. For instance, the types of services required in an inner city will be different from those needed in a country area. The way in which money is spent locally can therefore reflect the needs of the area.
- Local politicians are more aware of the needs of the local people.
- The size of England and Wales is too great (over 20 million hectares) for it to be administered properly from London.

Local government structure

In most of England and Wales there are two tiers of local government.

- **County councils** provide services which need either considerable resources or planning and administration over a wide area.
- **District councils** provide local services to their area. In some cases these are known as Borough Councils.

In Scotland county councils are known as **regional councils.**

In London and some heavily populated areas the situation is slightly different.

- London is administered by the **London boroughs** which provide nearly all the services. The fire service is an exception. This is run by Joint Authorities to serve the whole of the rea.
- The six heavily populated areas of West Midlands, Greater Manchester, Merseyside, South Yorkshire, West Yorkshire and Tyne and Wear are known as **metropolitan areas.** In this case services apart from transport, police and fire are run by **district councils.** These three services are run by **joint authorities** which consist of representatives of all authorities using the service.

Local government review

The Local Government Commission completed a review of England's local authorities early in 1995. The Government had wanted more unitary authorities, i.e. authorities which offered *all* local government services rather than the 'two-tier' system.

Non-assessed activity

1 Find out the name of the council(s) which are responsible for the area in which you live. Unless you live in a city area then **two** councils will be involved – a county council and a district (or borough) council.

2 Below is a list of services provided by local authorities. Decide which you think will be provided on a local basis (e.g. by a district council) and which

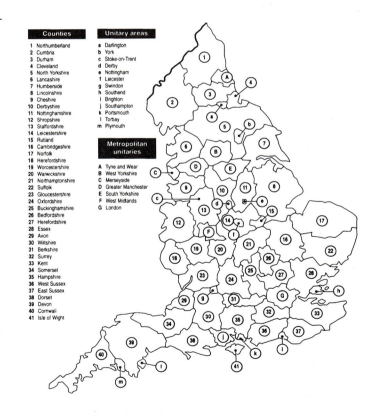

Counties	Unitary areas
1 Northumberland	a Darlington
2 Cumbria	b York
3 Durham	c Stoke-on-Trent
4 Cleveland	d Derby
5 North Yorkshire	e Nottingham
6 Lancashire	f Leicester
7 Humberside	g Swindon
8 Lincolnshire	h Southend
9 Cheshire	i Brighton
10 Derbyshire	j Southampton
11 Nottinghamshire	k Portsmouth
12 Shropshire	l Torbay
13 Staffordshire	m Plymouth
14 Leicestershire	
15 Rutland	
16 Cambridgeshire	**Metropolitan unitaries**
17 Norfolk	
18 Herefordshire	
19 Worcestershire	A Tyne and Wear
20 Warwickshire	B West Yorkshire
21 Northamptonshire	C Merseyside
22 Suffolk	D Greater Manchester
23 Gloucestershire	E South Yorkshire
24 Oxfordshire	F West Midlands
25 Buckinghamshire	G London
26 Bedfordshire	
27 Herefordshire	
28 Essex	
29 Avon	
30 Wiltshire	
31 Berkshire	
32 Surrey	
33 Kent	
34 Somerset	
35 Hampshire	
36 West Sussex	
37 East Sussex	
38 Dorset	
39 Devon	
40 Cornwall	
41 Isle of Wight	

Figure 1.20 The recommended structure of local government

33

on a wider basis (e.g. by a county council). If possible, refer to your local council's literature on how it spends its money.

Strategic planning   Fire service

Housing   Police

Education   Social services

Environmental health   Leisure services

Consumer protection   Local planning

Transport   Tourism

Libraries   Refuse collection and

Economic development   disposal

3 The map in Figure 1.20 shows the proposed new structure. Check your own area and discuss with your tutor whether the structure of your local authority may change in the future.

Organisation and control

Local people elect their own representatives in council elections each year. Most representatives (called **councillors**) are members of a political party, so the town or county may have an overall Labour or Conservative majority (which may – or may not – be the same as the political party in power in central government). If there is no overall majority it is called a **hung** council and the balance of power may be held by a minority party. The **mayor** is a councillor who has had long service on the council and the major parties usually take it in turns to 'provide' a mayor.

Local policy is decided by councillors during council meetings, e.g. of the Transport Committee, the Education Committee. Their decisions, and the day-to-day running of the council offices, are carried out by paid employees, known as **local government officers.**

Theoretically, local people can have a say in the actions of their council. If they do not agree with what their council is doing then they can show their disapproval when they vote in the next local elections.

Did you know?

The organisation of local government is similar to that of central government. Both MPs and local councillors are:

- elected by the people

- responsible for making decisions on behalf of the people

In the same way, both civil servants and local government officers are:

- paid employees
- responsible for carrying out policy and the day-to-day running of central or local government offices.

Local government finance

In order to spend money on the services it provides, a local authority must raise money. The amount required varies from one area to another depending on:

- the services offered
- the number of employees
- the efficiency of the council.

The Government provides the largest amount to councils (an estimated £68 billion in 1992–3) and is therefore very concerned with the efficiency of local authorities and the way in which they spend their money. In some cases, such as refuse collection, the Government has made councils **buy** in the service from outside providers if this would reduce the cost.

The councils raise money in six ways. The first two are the most important and raise the most money.

1 The Government Revenue Support grant.

2 Council tax.

3 Loans.

4 Rents from council houses.

5 Sale of services (e.g. swimming pools, leisure centres etc.).

6 Sale of council houses to tenants.

Did you know?

All council spending can be divided into two types – **capital expenditure** (on items such as schools or roads which last a long time) and **revenue spending** (on running council services, e.g. wages, cleaning and fuel). Each council is issued with a Standard Spending Assessment which states how much the Government has calculated it should spend to provide a standard level of service.

The council tax

The council tax was introduced on 1 April 1993 and replaced the community charge (or poll tax). The council tax is a local tax, set by local councils, and each household receives one bill based on the value of their property relative to others in the area. Discounts or benefits are available for some home owners. For instance, if there is only one adult living in the property the bill is reduced by 25 per cent. If people are on low incomes or are disabled they can claim a reduction.

Each house has been placed in one of eight council tax valuation bands according to its value. Changes in house prices will not affect the value, but if the state of a local area changes for the worse, e.g. if a motorway is built nearby, then houses in that area may be revalued and put into a lower band.

The amount of the council tax is set by the local council and the amount to be paid will depend on the valuation band each home is in.

Did you know?

Businesses don't pay council tax – they pay **business rates.** These are collected by the local council and paid into a national pool. They are then redistributed to each area on the basis of the size of the local population.

Differences between types of business ownership

You may think you have already identified dozens of differences between different types of business ownership. After all, there is little that a hospital and a solicitor or a plumber and a large retail store have in common – except, possibly, customer services! However, when you are identifying **key** differences, this means looking at more than the jobs people do or where they work.

The *main* differences you must note are:

- **type of liability** – whether or not the organisation has limited or unlimited liability
- **use of profit** – who receives the surplus and why, the owners, the shareholders or the Government.

However, you also need to consider:

- **the owners** – how many are there in different

businesses, what is their status and who actually controls the business.
- **sources of finance** – from whom the organisation receives its money, both to start with and on a day-to-day basis.

Type of liability

This term only applies to privately owned organisations and relates to what happens if an organisation cannot pay its debts. **Unlimited liability** is a feature of sole traders and partnerships. In both these cases the owners' liability for debts is unlimited – even to the extent of their having to sell their personal possessions to pay their debts.

Private and public limited companies and producer co-operatives all have **limited liability.** This means that their liability for their debts is limited to the amount they have invested in the enterprise. The personal possessions of owners or shareholders cannot be touched.

All large franchise organisations (franchisors) have limited liability, as do most franchisees, particularly when the operation is from a retail outlet. However, the situation may be different for small-scale operators. Tupperware salespeople are more like sole traders whose stock is supplied from one source. However, because of the nature of the business and the fact that they would not be allowed to amass large debts with the franchisor, the total liability they could incur is restricted.

Use of profit

Most people start a business because they want to make a profit. What happens to this profit or surplus?

Owners of a business

A sole trader or the owners of a partnership are free to decide themselves what to do with any profit they make. They may decide to reinvest some of it in the business, for instance, to expand the business premises or buy modern equipment or machinery. Sole traders can decide what to do with the money themselves – partners have to agree between them. Any remaining surplus after reinvestment may be enjoyed by the owners in any way they wish.

Remember that the owners of a producer co-operative would always share the profits 'fairly and

reasonably' (though not necessarily equally), as this is one of the basic principles of co-operative ownership.

Shareholders

The directors of a private or public limited company will decide how much profit should be paid to shareholders as a reward for their investment. Remember that in a private limited company the shareholders and the directors are often the same people!

The chart below shows the link between companies, shareholders and profit.

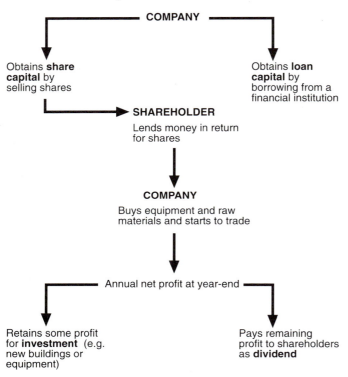

Figure 1.21 The capital of public limited companies

This aspect of businesses was discussed on page 10.

Government

Traditionally, for all state-owned enterprises, the Government was responsible for meeting any outstanding debts. This is one argument the Government used in favour of its privatisation

programme. Many organisations such as British Rail made a loss every year which was a burden to the Government and tax-payers alike. Once an enterprise is privatised the Government is no longer responsible for any losses.

However, the Government also benefits by taking the profits from state-owned enterprises which are successful. At the beginning of 1995 it was estimated that the Post Office was paying £4 million a week to the Treasury, which could be one reason the Post Office has not yet been privatised!

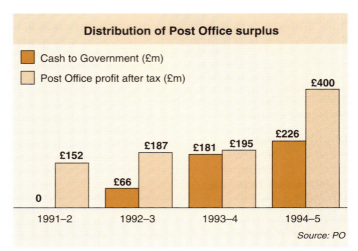

Figure 1.22 Post Office profits

Other organisations in the public sector, such as local authorities, hospitals, colleges and universities, are responsible for 'balancing their books' each year and are carefully monitored by Government. For instance, a Trust hospital is run by a Trust Board and the accounts are monitored by the NHS executive at periods from every three months to every year. If losses were incurred the hospital would have to put things in order quickly. If it did not, the Board could be sacked and replaced. Any surpluses are reinvested by the Trust each year in new buildings and equipment. Only a small percentage of the budget (less than 1 per cent) can be carried forward as profit to the next year.

Non-assessed activity

From the work you have done already, you should be able to determine who are the owners of a business, how these differ in terms of number and status and who actually controls the business. At the end of this element is a comparison chart to help you. In the meantime, try to draw up a chart of your own. Use the headings below to guide you and ask your tutor for help if necessary. Look back at previous pages for clues if you get stuck!

Type of organisation	No. of owners	Status of owners	Controller(s)
Sole trader			
Partnership			
Private limited company			
Public limited company			
Franchise			
Co-operative			
State-owned			

Sources of finance

Most businesses need to borrow money from one or more sources. However, the sources used and the amount of money which can be borrowed will vary considerably, depending upon the size of the business, how long it has traded and its reputation.

Small organisations

The main sources of finance for starting a small business include:

- personal savings
- redundancy money
- finance from friends and family
- bank loans
- bank overdrafts
- inheritances.

However, once the business is operating it may be necessary to raise additional finance – £5000 inherited from Aunt Winifred will not go very far if you are starting up in business! However, most small businesses do have problems raising money from banks and other financial institutions because they lack security and cannot afford the repayments – especially if interest rates are high.

Schemes designed to help small businesses include:

- the Business Start-Up Scheme, which gives people who have been unemployed for over six months the opportunity of a grant of £40 a week for up to twelve months

- the Prince's Youth Business Trust (PYBT), designed to provide grants and low interest loans to young people starting up a business and unable to raise money from other sources
- Livewire, sponsored by Shell (UK) Ltd and again offering assistance to young people
- Regional Area Development Associations, funded through local authorities to give grants to businesses in their area.

In addition many companies set up in **enterprise zones**. These are areas which allow organisations to locate in business parks or on industrial estates rate free, and sometimes rent free, for a certain amount of time.

Did you know?

A **grant** is a sum of money given to someone who needs it. Grants don't have to be paid back. They are available from various sources including local authorities and charitable trusts such as the PYBT.

A **loan** is money which must be paid back. In addition, interest on the loan is usually added. This is the lender's charge for making the loan. Fixed interest payments are better because the borrower knows exactly how much to repay and the amount cannot vary if interest rates change.

Medium sized businesses

Medium sized businesses or those which have been established for some time have a greater number of options for obtaining finance. They may:

- apply to a bank for a loan (the bank may wish to offer this under the **Loan Guarantee Scheme** where the Government guarantees 70 per cent of the amount borrowed)
- buy goods and services on credit, only to be paid for when they have been sold on to customers
- lease equipment or buy it on hire purchase, rather than have to pay large amounts of money at the outset (the main difference is that you never become the owner of something you lease, such as a car)
- arrange for their debts to be collected by a factoring agent, who will pay the amount which is owed to them immediately in return for a service charge on the amounts later collected

- sell shares in the business to friends and relatives (the Government's Business Expansion Scheme was devised to make it easier for business to expand by selling shares to an outside investor).

Did you know?

The difference between a **bank loan** and an **overdraft** is quite simple. A bank loan is a set amount borrowed for a fixed length of time. Repayments are normally made at regular intervals and will include the interest charge.

An overdraft is the term used when a customer overspends on their current account. The amount overdrawn is the amount overspent and this may vary during the month, depending upon the money paid into and out of the account. The bank charges a fixed rate for an agreed overdraft – but the amount agreed must not be exceeded. Charges are *very* high for an overdraft which has not been agreed beforehand and the bank has the right to refuse any payments out of the account. For all overdrafts, the bank has the right to insist on repayment on demand.

Large businesses

Because nearly all large businesses are public limited companies they will nearly always raise money by selling additional shares or debentures.

- Shares can be sold to the general public on the stock exchange. The company may decide to sell additional shares as a **rights issue**. This means the shares are offered first to existing shareholders at a discount.
- Debentures are a type of loan. Investors who buy debentures are lending their money to an organisation for a certain length of time. In return they receive interest until the loan is repaid. Debentures are a very safe form of investment.

All the money for the privatisation of large public sector organisations was obtained by selling shares to the general public.

Large businesses may apply to a bank or other financial institution for a loan. A much wider range of loans is available to large companies, often at lower interest rates, especially for those companies which have a successful record of doing business over many years.

State-owned organisations

The ways in which the public sector raises money are dealt with on pages 29 and 34.

Optional evidence assignment

This activity can be carried out to count as supplementary evidence towards the following parts of the scheme. In addition, the information obtained can also be used in relation to the project for Element 1.3.

PC 3: Explain the differences between types of business ownership

Range: Types of business ownership: sole trader, public limited company, state-owned

Differences: type of liability (limited, unlimited), use of profit (owners, shareholders, Government)

Core skills: Communication, IT

Read the case study below and answer the questions which follow.

Case study – starting work

Harminda, Joel and Rebecca are all about to start work. Harminda is starting work for a large public company, Joel will be working at the post office and Rebecca has obtained employment with a young computer whiz-kid who has just set up his own business. Yesterday you heard each of them make a remark which worried you.

Harminda: 'I don't know whether conditions at the company will be very good, the directors own the company and they keep all the profit, you know.'

Joel: 'Well, I'm looking forward to a good job with good prospects. The post office made good profits last year so everyone will get huge pay rises.'

Rebecca: 'My boss is very daring and progressive – he's just spent thousands of pounds on new stock. He says he can't go wrong. I'm sure my job will be secure for years.'

1 Write your comments about each of the three statements, saying where you think the speakers are incorrect in their assumptions.

2 Write brief notes on the liability of each of the three types of organisation and the way in which profits are distributed.

Evidence assignment

At this point your tutor may wish you to start or continue work on the project which will prove to your verifiers that you understand this section of the element. If you are starting the project then turn to page 42 and do Section 1 of the project. If you have already completed Section 1 of the project now start Section 2. This covers the second evidence indicator for this element.

The operation of business organisations

We have seen that businesses differ in terms of the products they supply, the purposes for which they exist and their type of ownership. They also differ in the way in which they operate – a fact you will soon learn once you start work. They operate in different markets with different types of customers. They have different policies and procedures. This is why it can take you a few weeks to settle down in a new job, no matter how experienced you are.

What they have in common is the simple fact that none of them operates in isolation. All organisations relate to and trade with other types of businesses every day. The area in which businesses operate is sometimes referred to as the **business environment** and this is dealt with in more detail in Element 2.2.

The major areas of operation you need to consider are discussed separately below.

Location

The location of a company can vary from a busy city centre to a rural area, from a site adjacent to a motorway to an industrial estate. The reasons for location are sometimes fairly obvious – but sometimes they are not. Location is dealt with in more detail in Element 1.2.

Product

The organisation may produce **goods** or **services.** This means it may operate in the secondary or tertiary sector. It may offer a commercial service, such as a solicitor or accountant, or a public service, such as a local authority or a government office (e.g. the Inland Revenue or Job Centre).

The range of goods or services it offers may also differ. It may have a broad product range (such as Heinz) or just manufacture one product (e.g. a paper mill). Normally, organisations offering a service have one specialist area in which they operate, e.g. law, finance, travel etc.

Links with other businesses

All organisations have regular routine contact with their customers and other business organisations with whom they trade, i.e. their suppliers. These organisations may provide raw materials for manufacturing processes or services – from distribution to finance. Remember that businesses are also consumers. Therefore one business may be the supplier of another business. A tyre manufacturer may provide goods directly to car owners but will also probably sell most of its goods to a car production company.

Did you know?

The Government is also a consumer – prisons, hospitals, schools and State offices all use a variety of goods and products every day. In addition, the State provides a variety of services – from the Post Office to the Job Centre. Some of these are advisory and aimed to assist businesses, e.g. the work of the Department of Trade and Industry. Finally, the State acts to regulate and control the action of both businesses and individuals in its capacity as a law enforcement agency. This includes the work of the police, the Inland Revenue and the VAT Office and the Department for the Environment.

Non-assessed activity

As a group, brainstorm the number of business contacts your school or college has in the course of an average month. Think of all the goods and services it buys and the service it provides. When you have finished, check your list with your tutor.

Purpose

You have already seen on page 8 that the purposes of business organisations may differ. Commercial organisations – from sole traders to public limited companies – are in business to make a profit.

Without this they could not survive. All other purposes will be secondary to this one main aim.

Only in the State sector will you find organisations whose aim is primarily to provide a public service. The charitable sector is in business to make a surplus (rather than a profit).

Did you know?

One owner of a thriving business used to ask at interviews, 'Why am I in business?' Any job applicant who answered, 'To provide a service,' was instantly written off – the only ones who survived were those who answered, 'To make a profit.' His reasoning was that only those people could understand why he was working so hard!

Type of ownership

You have already seen how ownership can vary from one organisation to another. If you have forgotten, look at the comparison chart in Figure 1.23. It has been designed to give you useful information to help with revision for your end test.

Evidence assignment

At this point your tutor may wish you to start or continue work on the project which will prove to your verifiers that you understand this section of the element. If you have already been working on the project then you may only have Section 3 to complete. Make sure you check with your tutor exactly what you have to do. Section 3 covers the third evidence indicator for this element.

Revision test

True or false?

1 The main purpose of most public sector organisations is to make a profit.

2 The managing director is the person who decides what should happen to the profits of a public limited company.

3 A person who operates a franchise operation on a day-to-day basis is called a franchisor.

4 A member of a co-operative organisation has one vote per share.

5 The maximum number of members in a partnership is 50.

Complete the blanks

6 The type of business organisation whose shares are quoted on the Stock Exchange is called a _____ _____ _____ .

7 A _____ _____ is someone who relies on his or her own capital to run a business.

8 The business organisation where those who invest have limited liability and yet shares are not publicly available is called a _____ _____ _____ .

9 Some of the profit made by a public limited company may be retained for investment in new buildings or machinery. The rest will be divided among the _____ and paid out to them as a _____ .

10 A bank is a service industry and is therefore in the _____ sector.

Short answer questions

11 Explain briefly why a hairdresser would be unlikely to form a public limited company.

12 State clearly the difference between limited liability and unlimited liability.

13 State **two** advantages and **two** disadvantages of forming a partnership.

14 Name **three** occupations in each of the primary, secondary and tertiary sectors of industry.

15 Name **four** other types of organisation with which a business may have regular contact.

Write a short paragraph to show you clearly understand each of the following terms.

16 Use of profit

17 Market share

18 Franchising

19 State owned

20 Secondary sector

COMPARISON CHART OF BUSINESS ORGANISATIONS

Type of organisation	No. of owners	Type of liability	Control	Capital	Sources of finance	Profits
Sole trader	1	Unlimited liability means owner personally responsible for debts to limits of personal wealth	Owner has full control	Little required at start. May be difficult to fund expansion	■ Personal savings ■ Redundancy money ■ Inheritances ■ Loan from family/friends ■ Loan/overdraft from bank	Kept by owner
Franchise	1 +	Decided by franchisor; franchisor has limited liability	Owner, under direction from franchisor	Provided by owner	■ As above ■ Franchisor may give guidance on sources of finance	Owner pays percentage of profits to franchisor
Partnership	2–20	Joint unlimited liability to limits of personal wealth	Shared by partners	Provided by all partners	As above but total amount achievable is greater	Shared according to partnership agreement
Limited Partnership	2–20	General partner(s) has unlimited liability, limited partner *only* liable to amount of capital invested	Only general partner(s) can manage	Provided by all partners	As above	As above
Co-operative	2 +	Limited liability by worker owners	Shared by workers	Provided by worker owners	■ As above ■ Special finance often available to co-operatives (e.g. from LAs) ■ Banks often reluctant to lend to co-operatives	Shared 'fairly and reasonably' and by agreement of all worker owners
Private limited company	2 or more only	Limited liability means shareholders liable up to amount invested	Directors have control. Directors are often shareholders	Provided by shareholders	■ Sale of shares restricted to owners/family/friends/employees ■ Bank loan/overdraft ■ Regional grants/loans ■ Lease equipment ■ Buy on credit	Shared by shareholders
Public limited company	2 or more	Limited liability for all shareholders	Directors, appointed by shareholders, control day-to-day running of the business	Must have minimum of £50 000 on formation – provided by shareholders	■ Sale of shares ■ on Stock Exchange ■ Rights Issues ■ Debenture Issues ■ Loans from bank or specialist financial institution	Profits paid as dividends to shareholders
State-owned	1 (the State)	Not applicable	Senior officials, responsible to Government ministers, must comply with Government instructions	Provided by State	■ Revenue raised by charging for certain services ■ Remainder may be by State grant, taxation or borrowing	State has the right to claim to any profit made

Figure 1.23 A comparison chart of business organisations

Evidence indicator project

Unit 1   Element 1.1

This project has been designed to cover all the evidence indicators related to Element 1.1. It is divided into three sections. Your tutor may ask you to complete the sections at the appropriate points marked in the text. Alternatively your tutor may prefer you to do the entire project at the end of the element.

Performance criteria: 1–4

Core skills: Communication
Application of number
Information technology

Section 1

This section concentrates on the first evidence indicator for this element. When you have completed the work store it safely as it will contribute towards your final project for this element.

Make sure you complete this section of the project by the deadline date given to you by your tutor.

Write a summary, in your own words, describing the developments in the primary, secondary and tertiary sectors. Concentrate on the recent past and present status of each sector. Explain the present growth or decrease which has occurred and illustrate your summary by giving examples of typical activities in each sector. Type out your summary neatly using a word processor.

Section 2

This section concentrates on the second evidence indicator for this element. When you have completed the work store it safely as it will contribute towards your final project for this element.

Make sure you complete this section of the project by the deadline date given to you by your tutor.

1 **On your own** decide on **seven** different businesses which have different types of ownership. Your list should include:

- at least one public sector business
- at least one small business
- at least one medium business
- at least one large private sector business.

Check your list with your tutor to make sure that the organisations you have chosen are suitable.

2 Write a brief description of each business which includes:

a   the name and address
b   the type of goods or services which it produces
c   the main purposes of the business
d   how it is owned and the principles of ownership which apply
e   whether it is in the private or public sector
f   if it is in the private sector, whether it has limited or unlimited liability
g   who will benefit if it makes a profit (see below)
h   typical sources of finance for this type of business.

Note: To discuss what happens to the profit does not mean that you need to know exactly how much profit was made or who actually received it! This information will be confidential for all privately owned organisations except public limited companies. What you have to do is to apply what you have learned about profit to the organisation you are describing.

3 Type up your notes neatly using a word processor. Start a new page for each business you are describing.

Section 3

This section concentrates on the final evidence indicator for this element. When you have completed the work store it safely as it will contribute towards your final project for this element.

This section also concentrates on the first part of an ongoing project which links your work in this element with those in subsequent elements and units.

Make sure you complete this section of the project by the deadline date given to you by your tutor.

Identify **one** business organisation with which you have regular contact for an ongoing project. This may, or may not, be one of the organisations you chose for your previous study. It may be an organisation where you have a part-time job, or a contact through friends or family or where you are spending time on work experience. Bear in mind that your study of this organisation may take place over a period of time. This may be the first stage in a much longer project.

1 Prepare a report on the organisation explaining each of the following aspects of its operation clearly and in as much detail as you can provide. This will probably involve interviewing someone at the company. Give examples so that it is clear to the reader that you have thought about each area carefully.

    a State the name and address of the organisation.

    b Clearly explain the main purpose of the business and any other purposes it has.

    c State the goods and/or services it produces and give examples.

    d Find out why the organisation chose to locate where it did.

    e Explain the type of ownership and state whether, in your opinion, this is the most suitable, bearing in mind the business carried out and the scale of operation. Give reasons for your decision.

    f List its major links with other businesses and individuals i.e. its routine contacts with other people and organisations.

2 Prepare your finished report on a word processor with a clear title page giving your name and the date the report was completed. Title your report: **Investigation into the Purpose and Ownership of** ....…………… (name of organisation).

Examine business location, environment, markets and products

This element covers the location of business organisations and the environment within which they operate. It considers the markets for different products, the type of products provided and the activities that businesses undertake to try to meet market demand. It also examines the potential for introducing new products or developing existing products.

After studying this element you should be able to:

1 explain the *reasons for location* of businesses

2 explain the *influences of the business environment* on business organisations

3 describe *markets* for businesses' products based on *demand*

4 identify *products provided* by business organisations

5 explain *activities undertaken by businesses* to improve their market position

6 propose products which would meet market demand.

The location of businesses

No matter where you live in the British Isles, the types of industries in your area have probably changed considerably over the past 50 years. Traditionally, the north was renowned for the heavy industries – steel, shipbuilding, coal mining – and for cotton and wool manufacture. The Midlands was famous for car production, pottery and engineering. The south east had a range of manufacturing companies plus canneries, refineries, tobacco companies and warehouses near the docks (e.g. in 'old' London docklands). Cornwall and South Wales had mining communities – the first for tin and the second for coal. Today few of these industries survive.

■ The cotton industry failed to cope with newer, synthetic textiles and cheap imported cotton from abroad.

■ Newer forms of energy production have reduced the demand for coal – again, when it is required it is usually cheaper to import it.

■ Too much capacity world-wide – and declining demand – saw the end of the shipbuilding industry and the decline of steel.

■ Japanese imports of cars threatened British car production – the UK motorcycle industry has now virtually gone out of existence for the same reason.

The trend today is for newer industries to emerge, e.g. in computers and electronics, light engineering and telecommunications, together with a growth in the service sector (see also Element 1.1, page 4). Automation has reduced the numbers of people employed and the size of factories and in virtually all areas, industries have moved out of towns and inner city areas to new industrial areas and parks on the outskirts – away from residential areas.

What causes industries to set up in certain areas? To what extent are some of them 'footloose', able to operate anywhere? What can the Government do to help areas which have been badly affected by industry closing?

Reasons for location

There are several reasons why businesses are located in one place rather than another. The most important factor will vary from one business to another, depending upon its main requirement(s).

Labour supply

All organisations need a labour force. A pool of skilled labour in a particular area will often attract industry. The most famous example is Silicon Valley in California where all the computer firms are located – because of the production specialists and programmers who live there. In Britain the M4 corridor has often been called England's Silicon Valley and Scotland has its own Silicon Glen. By locating in a region where the labour force is already trained in the type of work available, an organisation can reduce the time and money it would have to spend training new staff. It is also likely to have a greater number of potential employees from which it can choose.

Firms will also be tempted to start up where there is a ready supply of labour (often female part-time assembly workers). This is the case in many new towns, where light engineering factories are to be found, and in 'old' industrial areas, where there is large-scale unemployment and a labour force which is ready to adapt quickly and is desperate for jobs. Generally, the greater the supply of labour, the less likely it is that the organisation will have to offer high wages to attract workers.

Natural resources

Traditionally, many industries chose their location because of natural factors and resources, such as:

- the availability of raw materials
- the availability of power supplies
- the availability of water supplies
- the suitability of the local climate
- the nature of the local soil.

Availability of raw materials

Industries with a need for large quantities of heavy and bulky raw materials tended to locate close to the source of those materials. Examples of such industries include iron and steel making, which were established around Sheffield because of the availability of iron ore and limestone, and cement making which used the chalk from the hills of the south of England.

Availability of power supplies

Iron smelting required huge quantities of coal to fuel the furnaces. Sheffield had plentiful coal supplies, in addition to iron ore and limestone. Water power and then coal provided the power supplies for the Yorkshire and Lancashire textile industries.

Availability of water supplies

Water can provide power, but it is more important as part of some industrial processes. It is particularly important in the production of chemicals, in paper-

making, brewing and the textile industries. These industries grew where water was plentiful, for example by large rivers.

Suitability of the local climate

The climate of the Bordeaux region of France is well suited to the production of grapes for wine, and has for long been one of the world's leading wine-producing areas.

Nature of the local soil

The rich soils of Lincolnshire and East Anglia favour agriculture. This area has large cereal farms, and much of the UK's sugar beet is grown here. Peas and beans are also important crops. As food processing has developed, freezing and canning factories have moved to the area because of the availability of fresh produce.

Despite modern technological advances, some industries are still very dependent on natural factors.

- The quality of water supplies is still important for whisky production in Scotland, and climate considerations still control most agricultural activity, even with the use of glasshouses.
- Although many of Britain's mineral resources, such as iron ore, are now too expensive to exploit, industries such as steel-making still survive here, but have tended to move to coastal locations where cheap imported raw materials are readily available by sea.
- Industries such as brick-making in Bedfordshire still rely on local clay to provide the raw materials. **Bulk reducing** industries such as slate quarrying, coal mining and gravel extraction are still tied to areas where the resources are available,

because it is too expensive to transport such raw materials for any great distances.

Proximity of other businesses

Companies are usually grouped together in regions. For instance, the area around Stoke-on-Trent is still famous for its pottery industry, the area around Leicester is renowned for the boot and shoe trade, and so on. Why are organisations attracted to an area where *similar* companies are to be found nearby – bearing in mind that many of these will be its competitors? The answer is because they will benefit from **external economies of scale**. These are advantages to all firms from the growth of an industry in a particular area, such as:

■ a skilled local labour force

■ local courses at colleges (e.g. catering courses in Blackpool)

■ a range of small supplier companies which are attracted to the region as they can serve many larger organisations

■ co-operation between companies, e.g. in the establishment of research facilities which are set up as joint ventures to share the cost

■ formal contact at business meetings and informal contact locally (e.g. at the golf club!)

■ local service industries which develop a good knowledge of the needs of the industry and can therefore offer specialist advice and service (e.g. special insurance cover).

Did you know?

In Japan, business organisations do not carry large supplies of stocks. Instead, they encourage suppliers to locate nearby and guarantee them all of the host company's business if they will supply goods on a **just-in-time** basis. This means that the supplier works closely with the host company, always keeping stocks available and delivering them promptly on request.

Japanese organisations locating in Britain brought this practice with them. In the north east of England, for example, a wide range of car suppliers have located as satellite companies to car giants who would rather have the correct goods delivered quickly than to shop around or keep expensive supplies on the premises.

Access to customers

Nearness to markets has always been important – especially for goods which are imported or exported. Probably the best example of this is Rotterdam in the Netherlands, which has giant terminals for the storage of imported grain, oil, iron ore and sulphur which are then distributed (sometimes by river and canal) to the vast markets of West Germany.

Being close to the market reduces the costs companies have to bear – especially when they are involved in a **bulk increasing** industry. This means that they receive small components and assemble them into larger products (e.g. refrigerators, computers, furniture). In this case it is cheaper for the company to be located near its markets than to its source of supply. In Britain the largest market for goods is the south east, which is one reason for the diverse range of companies to be found in that area.

Companies which have a national market (such as large supermarkets) are likely to have distribution centres all around the country where their goods are stored. This reduces the time and cost of moving the goods to the stores which want them.

Transport services

Many 'new towns' in Britain have been developed since the 1950s. These have been most successful when they are situated with rapid motorway links close by, so that goods can be brought into the area and distributed from the area quickly and easily, e.g. Milton Keynes and Warrington New Town.

Industries which need to move large, bulky goods (e.g. cement or cars) have traditionally located as

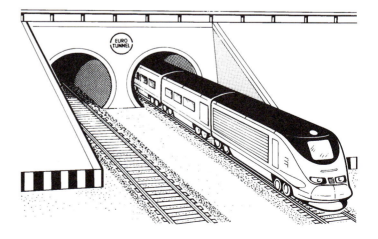

near as possible to good rail links. In some cases the company may even have its own rail sidings linked to the main network.

Did you know?

In Britain many companies which intend exporting to Europe have located their factories in the south of England to be near the Channel ports and the Channel tunnel.

Incentives

Local and national government

Both local and national government may offer financial incentives to companies to tempt them to locate in particular areas, e.g. a region where there is a high level of unemployment. These incentives may range from the allowance of special grants to reducing the amount of money companies have to pay in business rates in a particular area (see Figure 1.24). Organisations which are willing to locate in inner city areas can often obtain financial assistance through the City Challenge scheme or through an Industrial Improvement grant.

For the sake of large-scale foreign investment, the Government is often willing to assist the organisation to locate in Britain. Japanese car producers, such as Nissan, were able to obtain financial incentives from the Government to locate in regions with high unemployment. In some cases unemployment had been caused by the closure of traditional industries such as shipbuilding and mining. In these cases the areas are also attractive to new companies because there is likely to be strong competition for jobs – they can therefore hire the best people more cheaply than they could if labour was scarce.

European Union

Grants are available through the European Structural Funds – mainly the Regional Development Fund, which is designed to help rural areas and regions which are declining or lagging behind in industrial development, and the European Social Fund, which concentrates on training and the problems of young people in areas of high unemployment. Member governments of the EU doubled the amount of money available to the Structural Funds in 1993

bringing the budget for 1994–9 to 160 billion ECU (approximately £130.5 billion).

Figure 1.24 Urban priority areas in England

Optional evidence assignment

*This activity can be carried out verbally in class **in a group** as a non-assessed activity to consolidate learning. Alternatively, if you do it **on your own**, it can count as supplementary evidence towards the following parts of the scheme.*

PC 1: Explain the reasons for location of businesses

Range: Labour supply, natural resources, proximity of other businesses, access to customers, transport services, incentives

Core skills: Application of number, communication

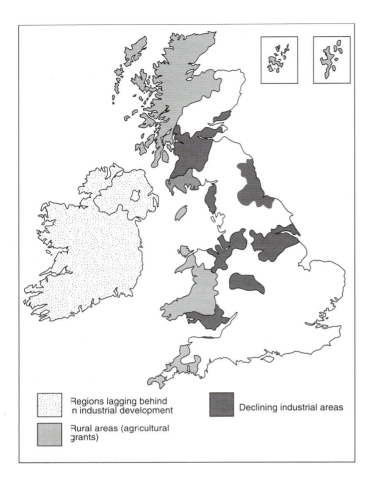

Figure 1.25 Eligible regions under EU grants

Legend:
- Regions lagging behind in industrial development
- Rural areas (agricultural grants)
- Declining industrial areas

Read the case study below and answer the questions which follow.

Case study – Alton Towers

Alton Towers is a famous theme park situated near Alton in Staffordshire. Initially this may seem to be a remote rural area with poor transport links, which would obviously affect the number of visitors who could obtain easy access to the park. However, the reality is that its situation is ideal for attracting people from all over Britain – rather than from just one area. In addition, there is no immediate competition in the area from other theme parks. The main disadvantage of setting up in a remote location may be shortage of labour but, in the same way as staff are 'bussed in' to motorway service areas, a large organisation will make its own arrangements to transport staff to and from nearby towns. However, the rural area itself will also benefit as the needs of the organisation will attract smaller satellite industries to set up nearby. A laundry, an electrical contractor, a bakery and a dairy may operate successfully by becoming the supplier to a theme park such as Alton Towers. However, rural residents may be less pleased with the increase in traffic, noise and litter in the area!

Other theme parks have been set up because of natural resources, e.g. nearness to water for an Aquapark, or nearness to a large market and labour supply, e.g. Blackpool Pleasure Beach. In many cases, these are clear examples of businesses in the leisure industry choosing their location on a similar basis to businesses in other types of industry.

1   a   Find Alton Towers on a map. Calculate its distance from both the M6 and M1 motorways.
    b   Look at a large-scale map of England. Roughly calculate the distance of Alton Towers from a northern town (e.g. Carlisle) and a southern town (e.g. Brighton).
    c   Identify **four** towns in the area where Alton Towers may recruit staff and offer transport provision.
    d   Write a brief conclusion of your opinion of the location of Alton Towers, bearing in mind the type of business it is.

2   Choose **one other** theme park in Britain – either small or large. Find out about the attractions it offers and draw a map showing its location. Summarise why you think this location has been chosen and its advantages and disadvantages.

3   Identify **four** organisations in your own region, state the product they make or service they offer, and give reasons for their choice of location.

Evidence assignment

A
B
C

At this point your tutor may wish you to start work on the project which will prove to your verifiers that you understand this section of the element. If so, turn to page 79 and do Section 1 of the project. This covers the first evidence indicator for this element.

Influences of the business environment

All businesses are affected by the environment in which they operate. What is this environment, how does it work and what does it do to influence the actions and decisions made in business organisations?

The business environment consists of other organisations, institutions and groups of people who – collectively or individually – undertake actions to further their own interests. In some cases they have a small effect on the actions of business, in other cases they have a profound or dramatic effect.

The chart in Figure 1.26 shows the range of bodies involved and their potential influence. Their main areas of influence can be divided into those of:

- competition
- legal
- environmental
- public.

Competition

To increase its market share it is often the case that one organisation has to take business away from another. This is because companies described as competitors are *competing* for the same customers. Most business organisations are very aware of the potential threat posed by the competition. This is especially true if the organisation operates in a competitive market, in which there are many organisations offering a similar service or product.

In this case, organisations may spend a lot of money investing in research and development to be 'one step ahead' of their competitors. They might be very keen on advertising and promotion to make sure customers are aware of the products or services they sell. A typical example is the car industry. In 1989, new car sales were high, but since then they have

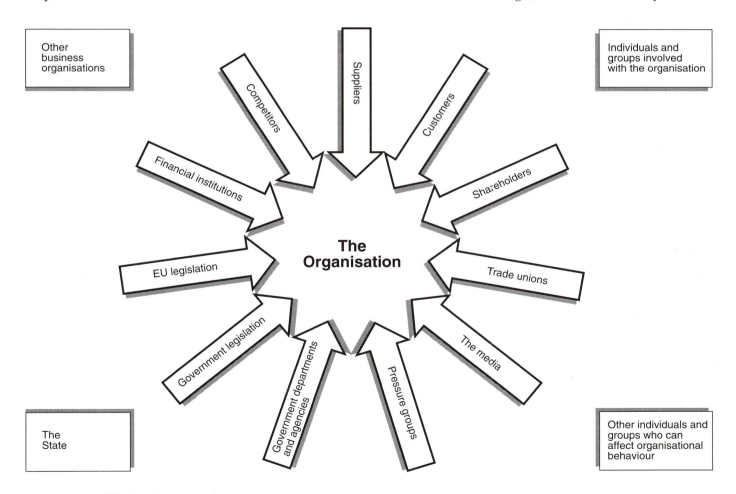

Figure 1.26 The business environment

been falling. This means that companies must work much harder to sell the same number of cars. A large number of car producers sell mass-produced cars on a global basis. You can probably name at least ten very easily! For this reason, car manufacturers are keen to introduce new refinements to their cars and keep new models and new ideas under conditions of tight security, until the official launch date. A glance at any newspaper, Sunday supplement or commercial television channel will give you a fairly good idea of the amount of money spent by manufacturers on promoting different models.

Some companies operate in a totally different type of market, where they are not as free to add refinements, bring out new products or change the prices very dramatically. This is usually the case if there are very few organisations that can be classed as competitors. Two examples are banking and petrol. In both cases there are only a few organisations providing exactly the same goods or services and the actions of one firm are often quickly copied by the others. Think of how often, when one petrol company changes its prices, the others follow suit almost immediately. If prices cannot easily be lowered to attract customers, the company must offer a better service or improve its image. For this reason banking advertisements, for instance, concentrate on attributes such as 'helpfulness', 'courtesy', 'speed of response' and 'range of services', rather than the cost of their services.

Companies are also always very keen that special terms and conditions which apply to their competitors also apply to them, so that competition is seen to be fair. On occasion they may lobby the Government on these issues. Fair trading and competition are important aspects of the work of the Office of Fair Trading and the Monopolies Commission (see page 52).

Did you know?

When the National Lottery started, football pool companies were at a disadvantage because they were not allowed to advertise. Takings fell by 17 per cent in the first two months. The Government had to take rapid action to remove restrictions on advertising which affected the pools companies, so that they could compete openly and fairly for business.

Legal requirements

All companies must comply with the law of the land. In addition, they have to take serious note of their social obligations – to the environment, the community, the general public and to the customer. If they do not, pressure groups and activists may bring the situation to the attention of the media, or seriously damage the image and reputation of the company.

Although the Government is keen to encourage competition and freedom of action by organisations it also has a major responsibility to stop or prevent undesirable behaviour in society. For this reason companies, as well as individuals, are restricted by many laws and regulations which constrain the way in which they operate. The main types of legislation you should know about are described below.

Did you know?

One of the most successful pressure groups of all time has been Action against Smoking for Health (ASH) – the anti-smoking lobby. Despite the fact that the tobacco giants are rich and powerful, ASH has systematically set about changing social attitudes to smoking. Cigarette smoking has fallen and is still doing so – considerably reducing the profits made by tobacco companies. Why do you think ASH has been successful in combatting the tobacco companies?

Health and safety legislation

The most important Act relating to **Health and Safety** is the **Health and Safety at Work Act 1974** (HASAWA). This places a legal responsibility on employers *and* employees in relation to health and safety issues. It has been designed to protect employees *and* the public from unsafe or dangerous work practices.

It is the employer's duty to provide:

- safe entry and exit routes in and out of the workplace
- a safe working environment and adequate welfare facilities
- safe equipment and systems of work
- arrangements for ensuring the safe use, handling, storage and transport of articles and substances
- information on health and safety, instruction, training and supervision
- investigation of any accidents.

Employees have a duty to:

- take reasonable care for their own health and safety
- take reasonable care for the health and safety of other people who may be affected by their actions
- co-operate with their employer or any other person carrying out duties under the Act.

In addition, if there are more than five employees, the employer must prepare a written document which states company policy on health and safety, and circulate this to all employees. The Act also allows for the appointment of safety representatives selected by a recognised trade union.

There are many other regulations which control different aspects of health and safety, and which have been introduced to keep the law up-to-date, including:

- the Reporting of Injuries, Diseases and Dangerous Occurrences Regulations (RIDDOR)
- the Control of Substances Hazardous to Health (COSHH)
- Electricity at Work Regulations
- Noise at Work Regulations
- Health and Safety (First Aid) Regulations
- Fire Precautions Regulations
- Display Screen Equipment Regulations
- Personal Protective Equipment at Work Regulations.

Non-assessed activity

1 Look at each of the statements below and identify the part(s) of the Health and Safety at Work Act under which they would categorised as an offence.

a An employee refuses to stay for roll call after an emergency evacuation.

b An emergency escape door has been blocked by a filing cabinet.

c No safety stools are provided for employees to reach files from high shelves.

d Toxic cleaning fluid is stored in an unlabelled bottle.

e A guillotine is kept in use even though the guard has broken.

f An employee wedges open a fire door.

2 Discuss with your tutor the specific aspects of work which relate to the different Regulations which have been introduced.

3 All of the following are examples of personal protective clothing. Can you state the type of work the wearers might be doing?

a a hard helmet
b safety shoes
c ear muffs
d safety goggles or mask
e gloves or gauntlets
f overalls or coveralls

Consumer protection legislation

This has been designed to safeguard customers from being sold shoddy goods, being misled over details of the product or price, or being sold dangerous goods. This therefore constrains the actions of both manufacturers and sellers. There are three main Acts which control the sale of goods:

- the Sale of Goods Act
- the Trades Description Act
- the Consumer Protection Act.

These are covered in full in Unit 3, Consumers and Customers (see pages 320–1).

Other legislation

Three other types of legislation also constrain the operation of business organisations and the actions of employers:

- employment legislation – designed to protect employees from unscrupulous employers, e.g. the Employment Protection Acts (see Element 2.2)
- environmental legislation – designed to prevent business organisations and individuals undertaking actions which put the environment at risk, e.g. the Environmental Protection Act
- company law – designed to protect shareholders and investors from unfair practices or fraud, e.g. the Companies Acts.

Did you know?

Today the word of the British Government is not necessarily final. The European Court of Justice has the right to over-rule government decisions, actions and even laws. If a directive is issued by the European Court then the British Government must obey.

Other methods of control and enforcement

There are government departments, agencies and bodies which are specifically involved with checking that companies comply with other laws and regulations. These include:

- HM Customs and Excise (which oversees VAT collection)
- the Inland Revenue (which oversees the collection of tax payments)
- the Department of Social Security (to whom companies pay their employees' National Insurance contributions)
- the Monopolies Commission which has the power to investigate any companies whose market share is thought to be above 25 per cent, as this may give the organisation a **monopoly** in the market. The company may then have an undesirable degree of control over prices and supply of the goods (see page 66).

Environmental influences

The welfare of future generations and concern for the environment has become a major issue for many people. Ecological and pressure groups such as Greenpeace and Friends of the Earth frequently have their views and activities reported in the media. Other groups lobby for particular types of action, e.g. the British Asthma Group (for cleaner air), Transport 2000 and the Council for the Protection of Rural England.

Their combined efforts have resulted in business organisations and the Government having to rethink certain actions they may have taken. These may have made sound economic sense in terms of making profits or saving money but were not in the interests of the environment. In some cases, business organisations have been criticised for not being pro-active enough. The electric car is one example of an environmentally friendly product that has never really been developed to its full potential – because of the commercial interests held by the large petroleum companies in the internal combustion engine. An example of action being taken is that after pressure by environmental groups the Government acknowledged that road building actually worsens the amount of traffic, pollution and congestion. Subsequently, several major road schemes were postponed, some of which had been planned in areas of outstanding natural beauty.

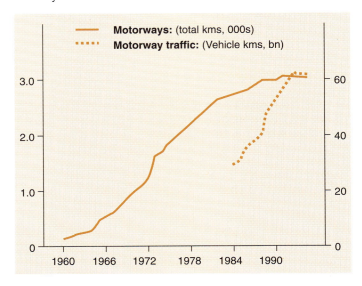

Figure 1.27 Motorways and motorway traffic

The European Union is extremely pro-active in environmental matters. The slogan 'pollution knows no boundaries' explains the importance of joint action by all governments and organisations. Forests dying through acid rain which may have been carried vast distances, polluted air and poisoned water are shared by all the inhabitants of the EU. For that reason, key EU policies include strict standards of protection and high environmental standards.

Today most businesses consider very carefully aspects such as noise and pollution of the air, rivers and waterways and land. They actively try to combat pollution through measures such as waste treatment, pollution free combustion, disposable or re-cyclable packaging materials, location of industrial buildings to avoid spoiling the countryside, landscaping and so on.

Did you know?

1. In April 1995, representatives from 100 countries met in Berlin to try to find agreement on cutting world greenhouse

gas emissions after the year 2000. Gases which cause the greenhouse effect include carbon dioxide (especially from coal-burning power stations) and methane (from landfill sites).

2 In collaboration with the European oil and car industries and the European Commission, 35 oil companies are contributing to a £7.4 million research programme. It aims to study fuel and engine technology and their effect on air quality. One possibility for the future is a reformulated fuel which results in less harmful fumes.

Public expectations

Ethical companies and those concerned with their image and reputation don't just comply with the law in terms of their actions and responsibilities – they go beyond it. They consider the effect of their actions on all sectors of the public – their customers, other individuals, people who live in the local community and those who may be influenced by their actions. They do not need to be forced by new laws or by the action of pressure groups (such as those mentioned above) or consumer groups to comply with environmental legislation or to offer goods and services which are in the public interest.

It is said that the highest level of business organisation does not just meet public expectations and respond to public opinion, but actually creates new expectations by voluntarily setting and following very high standards of social and moral responsibility. They blaze a trail for others to follow.

In some cases, the organisations do not simply try to please the public. They try to set new standards which are often revolutionary – and may sometimes result in a fall in profits. Examples are:

- car manufacturers who include – as standard – safety features which are charged for as extras on other cars
- insurance companies which operate 'no quibble' policies when a claim is made
- cosmetics companies which voluntarily adopt a 'not tested on animals' policy
- companies which donate a proportion of their profits to charity or environmental causes
- food companies which operated strict 'use by' coding *before* it was a legal requirement
- companies which do not risk public or customer safety by reducing safety testing of products to reduce costs

- companies which do not invest in or buy from countries with poor human rights records.

Considering the community

In addition, many organisations try to work with the local community and involve representatives with their plans. Such companies would not:

- 'flirt with the law', e.g. by emitting noise levels which are just below those that are legally permissible
- take advantage of employees by paying the minimum amount possible (regardless of company profits)
- disregard the needs or safety of the community, e.g. by allowing heavy or dirty vehicles through housing estates or near local primary schools.

Business organisations which are active in co-operating with the community take actions such as:

- encouraging members of staff to join local bodies, e.g. as school governors and giving them leave of absence to do so
- reacting promptly to complaints or queries raised by people in the neighbourhood
- being truthful about their future plans – and discussing them with community leaders to obtain their views
- linking with local educational institutions, e.g. by participating in the schools Compact scheme or offering work experience to college students, offering to visit schools and colleges and providing guest speakers
- operating an affirmative action policy for minority groups, e.g. employing registered disabled persons and operating an active equal opportunities policy
- giving donations to local charities.

They are often rewarded by a stable and committed workforce, a good name within the community and a strong customer base.

Non-assessed activity

Under the privatisation policy for British Rail several rail services are likely to be cut. These are services which often serve remote communities and do not make a profit. One such service in Scotland is the West Highland Line which provides a crucial link for the passengers who use it but which runs at a loss.

As a group, debate the motion: 'The main responsibility of Railtrack is to make a profit, not provide a public service.' Remember one side must speak for and one speak against the motion. Record the result of the debate.

Considering the customer

Under consumer protection legislation all organisations have several legal obligations to their customers. These are dealt with in Unit 3. Again an ethical company will go beyond this in several ways, for example:

- by printing an accurate and truthful description of the product on the packaging
- by not advertising in a way which is misleading or verges on the indecent
- by not implying that the product is larger than it is (either in its advertisements or choice of packaging)
- by date stamping all products
- by investigating and responding promptly to customer observations, enquiries and complaints
- by having strict safety standards and controls
- by not employing high pressure sales people
- by having a responsible and efficient after-sales service
- by never deliberately misleading customers about the product itself or to their rights as consumers
- by taking account of the needs of different customers and minority groups (e.g. the disabled)
- by having a properly trained staff who operate high levels of customer service.

Many companies operate consumer panels or carry out market research surveys so that they are aware of what their customers want. All organisations are aware of the dangers of falling foul of consumer watchdogs and pressure groups, such as television programmes on consumer rights and investigative magazines such as *Which?* Bad publicity about the product – particularly linked to safety – can destroy in a moment months of image building and advertising.

Optional evidence assignment

*This activity can be carried out verbally in class **in a group** as a non-assessed activity to consolidate learning. Alternatively, if you do it **on your own**, it can count as supplementary evidence towards the following parts of the scheme.*

PC 2:   Explain influences of the business environment on business organisations

Range: Competition, legal, environmental, public

Core skills: Communication

Read the case study below and answer the questions which follow.

Case study – Manchester Airport's second runway

After 101 days of hearings, and expenditure of over £1.25 million, the public enquiry into Manchester Airport's proposed second runway moved to Westminster where, after the completion of the inspector's report, the Secretary of State for the Environment will make a decision.

The case put by the airport is that its single existing runway will be full by 1998. A second runway would enable the airport to double the number of passengers it handles and this would have benefits for everyone in the north west of England – from private individuals to business organisations. By 2005 the airport would be capable of handling 30 million passengers a year. This would create up to 50 000 new jobs at the airport. Road traffic could be kept down by the provision of new road, rail and supertram links in an effort to ensure that 25 per cent of passengers use public transport. Unless the expansion goes ahead, the introduction of new routes to different cities in the world would not be possible and potential new passengers would have to use other congested airports. The Second Runway Support Group backed these proposals by sending more than 10 000 letters in favour of the runway to the Department of the Environment.

Protesters against the runway include the Manchester Airport Joint Action Group (MAJAG) and local village and community groups who have raised money to fight their campaign, through a variety of local fund-raising events. They are concerned about the loss of open countryside and historic homes and the 'intolerable' noise which will affect local communities over a wide area. They consider that airport expansion is not required for either business travel or the economic regeneration of the area and insist that additional passengers could be handled through other airports in the region – particularly Liverpool. This argument is supported by Liverpool Airport – which can modernise its facilities to cope with increased demand. This is hotly opposed by Manchester Airport, and is the subject of a separate inquiry being carried on at the same time.

To complicate matters even further at the airport, pilots and other members of the flight crew are actively campaigning against proposed new EU legislation which would increase their working hours. This is being drafted with the aim of harmonising standards throughout the EU but would result in an increase in time on duty for British flight crews. The pilots, through their union, BALPA, have joined forces with other European unions to try to block the new regulations, pointing out that pilot or crew error is the biggest single cause of international airline accidents and that higher levels of fatigue would increase the risk of such accidents.

1 **a** Two main pressure groups are opposed in the proposal for the second runway. Who are these pressure groups and what is *each* of them trying to do?

   b The pilots' pressure group is their union, BALPA. Can you try to identify what these letters stand for?

2 **a** To what degree do you consider Manchester Airport operates in a competitive environment? Why?

   b Liverpool Airport is the main regional competitor to Manchester Airport. What is its stance on the subject of the second runway?

   c Why do you think it has taken this view?

   d What is it trying to do to influence the Secretary of State?

3 The pilots are concerned about proposed new legislation which will affect their hours of employment.

   a In what way do they see this as a health and safety issue?

   b Do you agree with the concerns of the flight crews or not? Give reasons for your argument.

4 The runway inquiry is being dealt with by the Secretary of State for the Environment.

   a Why is this department involved?

   b What are the environmental arguments being put by *both* sides?

5 Both the airport and those opposed to the second runway have discussed the implications for the public – as employees at the airport, as members of the local business community, as holidaymakers, visitors and members of the local community.

   a How could **each** of these groups be affected by the building of the new runway?

   b If you lived in the north west of England, what would be your views?

6 Form **two** groups, one representing the airport and one the local community groups. Research the matter further if you can. If you undertake this assignment after 1996 you should be able to look up the final report and the decision of the Secretary of State.

Prepare sound arguments to support your position, and visual aids to illustrate your arguments. Nominate a good speaker and someone who will later reply to the debate (see Student Guide for additional information if you are not certain what to do). Then put the issue to the vote.

Record the outcome of the debate and attach this to any information you have researched or materials you, personally, have prepared.

Evidence assignment

At this point your tutor may wish you to start work on the project which will prove to your verifiers that you understand this section of the element. If so, turn to page 79 and do Section 2 of the project. This covers the second evidence indicator for this element.

Markets for businesses' products

How do business organisations know what to produce or how much to produce? The answer is quite simple. They respond to **signals** they receive from the marketplace.

Take a simple example and think of Mike the milkman. He operates by delivering milk to householders in a particular area. His 'market' for milk is limited to:

■ those people who like milk in the area

■ those people who want milk delivered

■ those people who are not away from home for some reason

■ the number of houses to which Mike can deliver milk in a certain period of time.

All these factors will help Mike to work out how much milk to supply. People who want more or less milk will usually leave a note on the doorstep, with their empty milk bottles. If the demand for milk is increasing, Mike will supply more. If the demand for milk is falling, he will supply less. In addition, if the demand falls permanently he may try to expand his area to retain his previous level of business.

You should note that one milk round's market for milk is not the same as the national market for milk – which is the total of all the people and organisations in the country who buy milk – either from a delivery person or from a retailer. From time to time the major dairy companies may try to influence the demand for milk by mounting an advertising campaign or issuing recipe leaflets containing milk-based dishes.

The basic principles are therefore as follows:

- producers will aim to supply goods to meet the needs of the market
- the needs of the market are indicated by the level of demand for certain goods and services
- producers may try to influence the level of demand by undertaking various activities, such as advertising.

To help you to understand this better, this section concentrates on:

- the different types of markets for goods and services
- the factors which influence the demand for goods and services
- the products which organisations produce to try to meet demand
- the activities in which organisations are involved to try to create or influence demand.

Markets

All products are created to satisfy the needs of a particular market. The 'market' is the total number of consumers who might buy the product. The characteristics of these consumers will be well-known to the supplier. For instance, the market for disposable nappies will be the parents of babies and young children, the market for low calorie foods will be people who are overweight, the market for cat food will be pet owners and so on.

Markets differ in various ways. They differ in terms of their geographical boundaries, their size and their value.

Domestic market

This is the market in the producing country. It does not include possible or actual exports. Some goods are restricted to a local domestic market for various reasons.

- They are a local or national delicacy which is mainly enjoyed in a particular region, e.g. frogs' legs in France, sauerkraut in Germany, raw fish in Japan, black puddings in the north of England, jellied eels in the south.
- They are made to conform with domestic regulations and they would have to be converted before they could be exported abroad, e.g. a British three-pin plug, television sets or mobile phones made to British standards.
- They are usually unsuitable for sale in many countries abroad, e.g. English newspapers, magazines and books.
- There are regulations which restrict their export, e.g. drugs and other medicines.

International market

Today, many products are sold all over the world because they appeal to consumers, regardless of their nationality. Typical examples are fizzy drinks (e.g. Coke), clothes (e.g. jeans and T-shirts), electronic goods (e.g. computers), cars and chocolate.

Products which are sold abroad earn revenue for Britain. This is especially good if exports are greater than imports – as this means that Britain has a trade surplus.

Did you know?

The music industry is one of Britain's top earners in the international market – in 1993 its total overseas earnings were more than £1 billion.

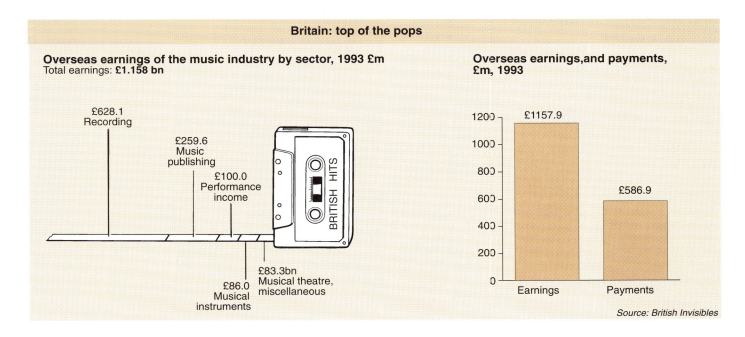

Figure 1.28 Overseas earnings of the music industry

Non-assessed activity

1 **As a group**, think of **30** items which are produced every day. If you are stuck, use a catalogue to help you. Identify whether the potential market for each product is domestic or international.

2 Think back to the last time you travelled abroad, or talk to someone who has recently travelled. Can you identify:

 a the type of British goods you could buy abroad
 b the items which weren't available?

3 Overseas earnings from British music exports in 1993 are shown as £1157.9 million in the chart above. In the same year, people spent £586 million on imported music. What was the net benefit to the British economy?

Did you know?

Exports are divided into two categories – visible and invisible.

- Visible exports are goods you can touch and feel, e.g. a record, cassette or musical instrument.
- Invisible exports are services, e.g. theatre performances in other countries.

You will meet these two categories again if you continue your studies to Advanced level.

Value of total market

The value of the market refers to the total value of all sales. Obviously the value will be greater:

- if the goods are sold internationally
- if a large number is sold each year.

As an example of a very large international market, the world-wide sales of fizzy drinks are valued at $160 billion of which $50 billion is taken in the United States. In contrast the large national market for chocolate was worth £3.1 billion in 1994 – a 79 per cent increase on ten years ago!

Did you know?

Some markets are very small, and are often a specialist sub-division of a larger market. This is often called a market **niche**. Identifying such a niche and producing a product for this type of market is often undertaken by smaller organisations. It gives them a chance to compete against the giants. Therefore, whereas a small company couldn't hope to compete with the car giants, specialist niche producers such as Reliant with its three-wheeler and TVR with its kit-form sports cars continue to do well.

Market share of businesses' products

Organisations often concentrate on increasing their market share. This was given as one of the purposes of organisations in Element 1.1 – and one of the reasons why one company may take over another. If you know the total value of the market and the market share of a particular company, it is easy to calculate the value of their market share.

Equally, if you know the size of the market in terms of the total number of sales, and the average price of the item, then you can calculate the value of the market as a whole. You can also calculate the market share of each company by finding out what percentage of sales relates to each organisation.

In many industries the trend has been towards fewer, large-scale businesses operating on a world-wide basis rather than a large number of smaller organisations selling on a national basis. A typical example is car production, which was discussed in Element 1.1.

In cases like this, a few firms share most of the market between them.

The chocolate industry

The UK market is dominated by Cadbury's, Mars and Nestlé/Rowntree.

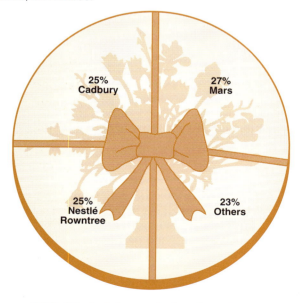

Figure 1.29 Market shares in the chocolate industry

The brewing industry

The UK market is dominated by Bass, Courage and Carlsberg/Tetley.

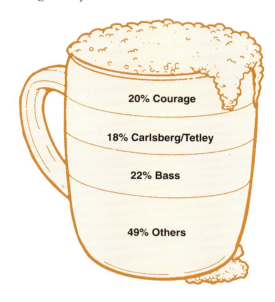

Figure 1.30 Market shares in the brewing industry

In both these industries the larger companies may choose to export their goods *or* to concentrate on selling purely in the UK. In the same way, foreign producers may decide to operate internationally and sell their products in Britain (e.g. Swiss chocolate and Australian lager).

Optional evidence assignment

This activity can be carried out verbally in class **in a group** as a non-assessed activity to consolidate learning. Alternatively, if you do it **on your own,** it can count as supplementary evidence towards the following parts of the scheme.

PC 3: Describe markets for businesses' products based on demand

Range: Domestic market, international market; value of total market, market share of businesses' products

Core skills: Application of number, Communication

1 The bar chart below shows the total value of the UK cinema market over the past few years. The market

share of the three major cinema chains was as follows in 1993.

MGM – 25.5%
UCI – 20.6%
Odeon – 19.6%

a What was the approximate total value of the market in 1993?

b What was the increase in value between 1992 and 1994?

c How would you account for this increase? (Before you answer this you may wish to read the rest of this element.)

d What was the approximate value of sales of cinema tickets to each of the chains above in 1994?

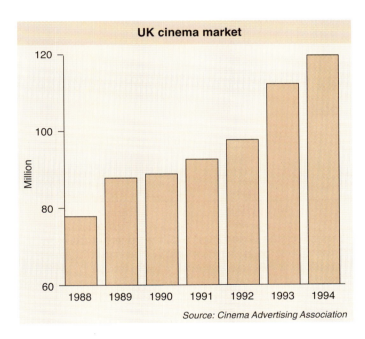

UK cinema market

Source: Cinema Advertising Association

Figure 1.31 The UK cinema market

2 The total value of the market for fizzy drinks world-wide, estimated for 1995, was $160 billion.

a If Coca-Cola have 40 per cent of the market and Pepsi Cola have 31 per cent of the market, what is the value of each company's sales world-wide during 1995?

b What activities does each company undertake to try to increase its market share? You may wish to read ahead to pages 70 to 73 before you answer this question.

c Cadbury Schweppes spent £1.1 billion taking over the American Dr Pepper group – which markets the 7-Up range. This has increased its market share in America from 3.5 per cent to 15 per cent. The American drinks market is worth $50 billion.

   i What will Cadbury's **new** share be worth?
   ii What is the increase in revenue compared to its old market share?
   ii Is the deal a profitable one? Give a reason for your answer.

d In recent years demand has fallen for Coke-type fizzy drinks. Some people have switched to low-calorie tonics and health drinks.

   i Can you suggest **two** reasons for the change?
   ii What new products have Pepsi and Coke introduced to counter the threat?

3 The circulation figures of Sunday newspapers for December 1994 are given in Figure 1.32.

a What was the total number of Sunday newspapers sold?

b Which paper is the market leader?

c Calculate the market share of each newspaper and illustrate this on a pie chart.

d Find out the average price of a Sunday newspaper and calculate the approximate value of the market.

e The newspaper industry is extremely competitive. If you owned a Sunday newspaper and wanted to increase sales, what would you do?

Newspaper	Sales
News of the World	4 716 391
Sunday Mirror	2 505 207
People	2 125 184
Mail on Sunday	1 924 432
Sunday Express	1 402 902
Sunday Times	1 227 838
Sunday Telegraph	657 317
Observer	467 969
Independent on Sunday	300 406

Figure 1.32 Sunday newspaper sales, December 1994

Demand

Very few markets remain constant over a period of time, although some are more **volatile**, or changeable, than others. Some change quickly – fads and fashions like skateboards and Doc Martens can be high sellers one year and low sellers the next.

The number of sales is determined by demand. The more customers demand an item, the more sales increase. In the exercise above, you saw that cinema attendances are increasing and you may have some ideas why that is the case – watching video films on a small screen has lost its appeal; people have more leisure time; better films are being released; going to the cinema is regarded as a pleasant evening out, and so on.

For a better understanding of demand, it is necessary to move on a stage and to look at how demand works in certain markets.

Special note

The section which follows has been designed to give you a basic understanding of demand and supply and the economic concepts involved in relation to specific markets. It will be a useful foundation if you progress to Advanced level as well as helping you to learn why markets work in the way they do – and when and how they can go wrong!

The meaning of demand

The demand for any good or service is the amount which will be bought at a given price at a certain time. The concept of price is crucial to any theory of demand – as business organisations are well aware. They know that for most normal goods and services, the lower the price of the product or service the greater the demand.

Non-assessed activity

Imagine that you are out for the day and you want to buy a souvenir for your friends and relatives. On sale are some special bars of chocolate which you know everyone would enjoy. Copy the table below and write how many bars you would buy, given that you have a limited amount of money to spend on presents – say £10 – at **each** of the prices shown. For example, if chocolate bars were £1, I might buy only one for my little sister and one for my mum and spend the rest of my money on something else!

Price	Quantity
£1	
80p	
60p	
40p	
20p	

Now draw a graph, by plotting your answers against the price and joining up your dots, on an outline like the one shown below.

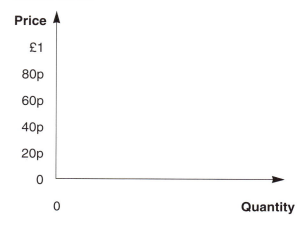

A demand curve

You have just completed a demand schedule and drawn your own demand curve for chocolate. The schedule states the amount which would be purchased at each price. The demand curve shows this diagrammatically. The curve normally slopes downwards from left to right, proving the **law of demand,** which says that **the lower the price, the greater the demand.** This is because a fall in price results in:

- an income effect – you can buy more with the same amount of money
- a substitution effect – a fall in the price of one product means that the prices of other similar goods are relatively higher, so you will buy the cheaper alternative instead.

You can trace a change in price by moving your finger along the line and reading off the quantity which would be purchased at each and every price. Do this on the demand curve below and read off the quantity which would be demanded if the price was 60p, doubled to £1.20 or fell to 30p.

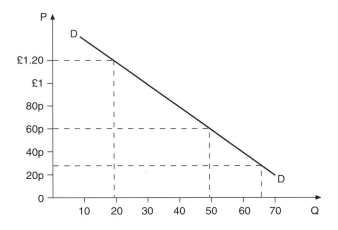

Figure 1.33 A demand curve

The conditions of demand

Other conditions which affect demand as well as price include:

a the **price of other commodities** – particularly substitute goods (e.g. bags of sweets or, in our example above, other presents you could take home)

b **income** (which affects the amount you have to spend)

c the **number of buyers** in the market – the total demand curve for chocolate would, of course, be everyone's individual demand added together

d your **individual preferences**. Everyone has individual likes and dislikes – the more you like something the higher it will be on your scale of preferences. Advertising is aimed at making you put a particular product high on your list of preferences!

Non-assessed activity

1 Find out your group's individual preferences for chocolate by asking people which type of chocolate bar they prefer. Then consider how advertisements play on this to change consumers' preferences.

2 Now create a demand schedule for chocolate for your group by adding together the demand schedules produced by each person. Represent this graphically on a demand curve. Remember to alter

the scale on your quantity line! Read off the quantities which would be bought at different prices.

Did you know?

Economists often talk about utility. This refers to the fact that people will buy something so long as it gives satisfaction. The more of a product you buy the less utility is gained. Think about being very thirsty and buying some cans of Coke. The first glass gives you maximum utility, the second a bit less, and so on. The amount of satisfaction you gained from the last glass you poured is known as the **marginal utility.** Eventually you would get no utility at all – in fact, you'd probably make yourself sick!

Exceptions to the law of demand

There are some goods where – believe it or not – more is demanded if the price goes up, and some for which demand goes down if our income goes up! These include:

- goods with a 'snob' value, e.g. 'designer' clothes or bags, or certain items of jewellery

- 'inferior' goods – which are items we buy when we are short of money, e.g. cheap margarine! As our income rises we buy less of it and substitute a better product e.g. butter.

Increases and decreases in demand

When more of a product is demanded at each and every price, there has obviously been an increase in demand. Conversely, when less is demanded at every price, there has been a decrease in demand.

These are shown graphically by a new demand curve, as shown in Figure 1.34. The increase in demand has resulted in a shift in the curve to the right from D to D^1, a decrease results in a shift to the left, i.e. from D to D^2.

Did you know?

When you draw demand (and supply) diagrams you should always label them; then you can refer to them easily. You should also make sure that your vertical line always represents prices and your horizontal line always represents **quantity.** You can either refer to exact **prices** or quantities or 'represent' these – as shown in Figure 1.39

on page 65. These are all useful tips for if you continue your studies to higher level!

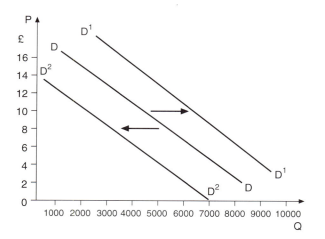

Figure 1.34   Changes in demand for CDs

Non-assessed activity

1   Can you identify:
- **three** products which people buy to impress other people and which they would **not** buy if they were mass produced cheaply
- **three** products which people buy when they have very little money and of which they would buy less if their incomes increased?

2   On Figure 1.34, which demand curve represents the following situations?

  a   Many people who had previously bought vinyl records buy CDs instead.

  b   CDs are replaced by an even better form of recording media.

3   How many CDs would be sold at a price of £8:

  a   now

  b   if demand increased

  c   if demand decreased?

Did you know?

Demand for some goods is more responsive to a change in price than others. Think of salt and lemons. If the price of salt doubled overnight then you would probably still buy some because:

- you think food cooked without salt tastes awful
- you only use a small amount at a time – so salt is only a tiny part of your budget
- salt isn't ridiculously expensive.

However, if the price of lemons doubled overnight you would probably not buy them. Rather than make a lemon meringue pie you could make an apple pie, and rather than put lemon juice on your pancakes you could use syrup. In other words, there are plenty of substitutes for lemons, but none for salt!

Demand for salt is therefore less affected by changes in price than demand for lemons. Economists would say that demand for salt is **inelastic** (it doesn't change very much when the price changes) and demand for lemons is **elastic** (it changes quite considerably when the price changes).

Oil companies are well aware that demand for petrol and diesel is fairly inelastic because people still want to travel and goods still have to be moved by lorry. Therefore they can put up their prices without it affecting demand too much.

Did you know?

The Government used to think that demand for cigarettes was relatively inelastic – increases in tax would not stop people smoking. Smokers would be prepared to pay the extra money, as they were addicted. Therefore the extra revenue gained would not be offset by a fall in sales. One year they were proved wrong. They raised the tax on cigarettes considerably, many people gave up smoking and the additional revenue they had hoped to receive was drastically reduced.

Non-assessed activity

1   As a group, try to identify **three** products which have a relatively elastic demand, and **three** which have a relatively inelastic demand.

2   Some people argue that the only type of goods which are perfectly inelastic are severely addictive, hard drugs such as heroin, because demand does not change with price. Look at the demand curve for a perfectly inelastic product shown in Figure 1.35. The line is vertical. On this diagram our user is going to want 8 grams every day regardless of the price.

  a   Do you agree that hard drugs are perfectly inelastic?

b What are the effects of this feature of the drugs market on society?

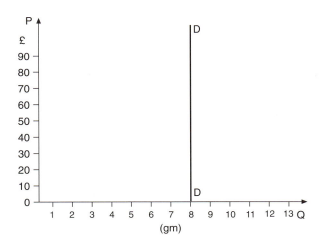

Figure 1.35 Demand curve for hard drugs

3 Government revenues were not as high as predicted, despite a tax increase, when people gave up smoking rather than pay more for cigarettes.

   a What other factors were also encouraging people to stop smoking besides the high price?

   b Do you think that demand for cigarettes is increasing or falling?

   c Can you show this on two demand curves – one for 20 years ago and one for today?

Did you know?

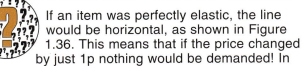 If an item was perfectly elastic, the line would be horizontal, as shown in Figure 1.36. This means that if the price changed by just 1p nothing would be demanded! In the diagram, the only price at which the good is demanded is £6. Nothing is demanded above or below this price. In reality, however, no products are *perfectly* elastic.

Supply

Supply is the total quantity of goods or services that individual firms offer for sale at a particular time.

Suppliers face various problems. They need to be able to receive sufficient revenues to cover their costs if they are going to stay in business. Some of these costs will increase as output increases: more raw

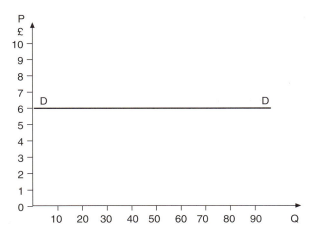

Figure 1.36 Perfectly elastic demand

materials will have to be purchased, more machines bought and more workers employed.

The conditions of supply

Before a company will make a decision to supply a product it will calculate the costs involved. It will also consider:

- the price of the product – as the price rises production becomes more profitable
- the price of alternative products – which may be more profitable to produce
- the amount of profit it wishes to make
- the state of technology – which may influence its costs of production
- the number of competitors in the market.

Because a high price would make production more profitable, the firm is prepared to supply a greater quantity if prices are high than if they are low. This can also be shown on a schedule.

Price of product (p)	Quantity supplied
0	0
20	100
40	200
60	400
80	800
100	1600

Non-assessed activity

Plot the schedule above on a graph, using the framework below, and then join your points together.

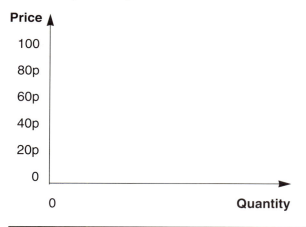

Supply curves

You have just drawn the supply curve for the firm. You will note that this slopes upwards from left to right. It shows the quantity which the supplier would be prepared to produce at each and every price. If the price increased, more suppliers would enter the market because it would be profitable for them to do so. Similarly, if the price fell, production would be less profitable and suppliers would leave the market. Total supply is represented on a curve which adds together the supplies of all the firms in the market. An example is shown in Figure 1.37. Can you read off the quantities which would be supplied at £80, £60 and £30?

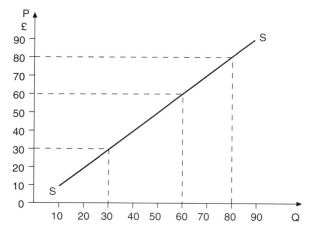

Figure 1.37 A supply curve

Did you know?

Mass production techniques reduce the costs of supplying a product. This is why 'new inventions' are in short supply when they are first introduced – because they are often very expensive to make. As technology develops, the product becomes cheaper to produce, more suppliers see the opportunities and move into the market. Probably the best example is colour televisions, which cost about £350 when they were first developed in Britain (in about 1967). Their price was equivalent to that of a small car! Compare that with prices today.

Increases and decreases in supply

An increase in supply means that more will be supplied at each and every price. A decrease in supply means that less would be produced at every price. An increase in supply could be caused by the introduction of new technology making goods cheaper to produce – as in the example of colour televisions above. As you can see from Figure 1.38, which shows a dairy farm's supply of milk, this would shift the supply curve to the right. A decrease in supply could be caused by an addition to the costs of production.

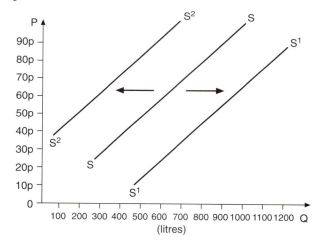

Figure 1.38 Increases and decreases in the supply of milk from a dairy farm

Non-assessed activity

1 Study Figure 1.38. Decide which supply curve would represent each of the following situations.

a The Government gives financial incentives to farmers to produce milk.
b The Government imposes a tax on all dairy herds.

2 How much would be supplied if the price of milk was 60p a litre:

  a now
  b if supply increased
  c if supply decreased?

3 Can you identify **three** products where supply has increased in recent years, and **three** products where supply has decreased? Brainstorm this **as a group** and see how many ideas you can come up with!

Putting the two together – the laws of supply and demand

Goods are sold at a price where demand and supply are equal – this is at the **equilibrium** price. At this price (P on Figure 1.39), the quantity suppliers are providing is just equal to the amount buyers want to buy. Everyone is happy and there is no pressure on the price to change.

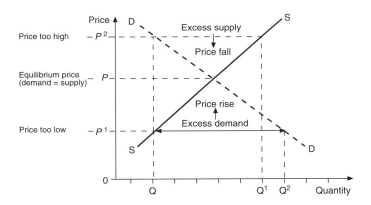

Figure 1.39 Demand and supply in a competitive market

If, on the other hand, prices were too high at P^2, demand would fall, stocks would accumulate and suppliers would lower the price of their goods.

Conversely, if prices were too low at P^1 and there was excess demand, suppliers would be aware of this and raise their prices.

Only where supply and demand intersect on Figure 1.39 are supply and demand equal bringing price

stability. The diagram not only illustrates this but enables you to read off the excess quantities which would be supplied (Q to Q^1) or demanded (Q to Q^2) at different prices.

Non-assessed activity

1 When car protection systems – mainly alarms – were first developed, they were costly to produce and could only be sold at a high price, if profits were to be made. However, some suppliers felt that the owners of expensive cars might be willing to buy them, so a few were prepared to offer them for sale.

  a Draw a supply curve for expensive car alarms (i.e. position it towards the left). Ask your tutor for advice on your price and quantity range.
  b Now draw a demand curve for expensive car alarms on the same diagram.

    i What is the equilibrium price?
    ii How many were sold?

2 A wide range of car protection equipment is available – ranging from cheap basic alarms to elaborate immobiliser and tracking systems. In addition the number of car thefts has increased and insurance companies are frequently offering reductions in premiums for cars fitted with a protection system.

  a Draw a second supply curve for car protection systems, alongside your original supply curve, showing that supply has increased at each and every price.
  b Say why you think more suppliers have entered the market.
  c Draw a second demand curve, alongside your original curve, which illustrates people's greater need for alarms as car thefts increase.

    Now read off the difference in:

    i equilibrium price
    ii quantity sold at that price.

3 What do your diagrams tell you about the market for car alarms?

Markets not working

If a market works properly, theoretically no suppliers can make excess profits. This is because very high profits will tempt other suppliers to enter the market as competitors and this will force the price down. Therefore goods which are demanded by consumers will be supplied at competitive and reasonable prices.

However, this can only happen if the market is free to operate. Anything which prevents this is likely to result in a worse deal for consumers.

In a **competitive market** there must be many buyers and sellers. People can make their own decisions about what to buy and sell without restrictions. Anything which restricts this activity will stop the market working properly.

- Buyers must be able to choose from a variety of sources and suppliers. If a village is a long way from the nearest town and villagers can only shop at one store, this store would be in a position to charge higher prices than it would if it had several competitors nearby. A few years ago, spectacles and contact lenses could only be purchased from specialist opticians and house conveyances could only be undertaken by solicitors. Now spectacles are freely available and house conveyancing (i.e. completing the documents for transfer of ownership) can be undertaken by estate agents and banks. The price of both has fallen because of the increased competition.
- There must be no restrictions on suppliers who want to enter the market. If government regulations protect a single supplier, or if a few large and powerful suppliers can act together to prevent new firms entering the market, then prices will be higher than necessary.

If the market is dominated by one company it is called a **monopoly.** This market dominance would enable the company to engage in practices which are against the public interest, such as setting a high price because people have no other source of supply. British Gas is one company which has been criticised for not having friendly policies, and maintaining a pricing structure which discriminates against those who are poor by allowing only customers who have a bank account and can pay by direct debit to benefit from certain discounts.

A market dominated by a few large companies is called an **oligopoly.** Examples include banks and oil companies.

Monopoly suppliers (or oligopoly suppliers acting together) can more effectively ignore market signals about what to produce, and can set the price themselves. Although there is nothing to stop buyers refusing to buy at a high price, if the monopoly supplies an essential or unique product, buyers will have no choice. Large organisations may operate restrictive practices to stop other organisations from entering the market. An example would be if a leading manufacturing organisation threatened a retailer that, if he stocked a competitor's product, they would stop supply. This is illegal, but some other practices are more difficult to prevent. A large organisation spotting a new entrant (who, initially, will have higher costs of production) might deliberately lower prices to a level at which the new firm cannot compete. Then, having put the new firm out of business, the large organisation simply raises its prices again.

For these reasons, the Monopolies Commission investigates cases where the market share of one supplier has risen above 25 per cent, as this represents market power which may be 'against the public interest'.

Did you know?

1 Richard Branson is taking legal action in both the UK and the US against British Airways for its alleged 'dirty tricks' campaign against Virgin.

2 If a market is dominated by two companies it is called a **duopoly.** The video games and consoles market in Britain is worth £550 million, of which Sega takes 38 per cent and Nintendo nearly 25 per cent. According to an investigation carried out by the Monopolies Commission, this market power has enabled both companies to make excessive profits from the supply of cartridges which were priced higher than necessary. The Commission has threatened to impose price controls if the practice does not change.

Non-assessed activity

1 Why do you think British Airways did not want Virgin to enter the market as a competitor, providing cheap flights from London to America?

2 Barclays announced profits of £1.8 billion for 1994 – a 180 per cent increase on the previous year. Discuss with your tutor why this increase may not have been possible in a more competitive market.

3 What is your opinion of the price of computer games? Sega and Nintendo both argue that the price is a result of high development costs. To what extent

do you think this argument could be proved wrong? In what way?

Defining and comparing markets

When you are considering markets, you must limit your comparisons to homogeneous products – i.e. those which are the same. You can only compare like with like. If you are considering the footwear market, for instance, you cannot compare sales of boots with sales of trainers, sandals or safety shoes because the features of each of these markets are different. Think of the difference between the type of people who buy trainers and those who buy safety shoes!

Dividing up a product market into different segments is important to many large organisations. As an example, the market for cars can be segmented or divided into different markets, e.g. small cars, hatchbacks, company cars, four-wheel-drive cars, sports cars and luxury cars. All of these will have different types of buyers with different needs, and vastly different incomes!

The features of different markets mean that the price can sometimes be varied – even for the same product. This is called **discriminatory pricing** – when an organisation takes advantage of the fact that one part of its market is willing to pay a higher price for something than another part will.

■ A book shop will be concerned about the total market for fiction and non-fiction books – whereas the publishers of this book are more interested in the total GNVQ market in Business.

■ Rover are interested in the mass car market, but this can be segmented or divided into different areas – and so on. Rolls Royce are interested in a completely different market segment – that for luxury cars.

The features of the different market segments will mean that they can charge distinct prices because demand operates in a different way.

Non-assessed activity

1 A publisher may consider carefully the market for a particular type of book. How many market segments can you think of for the book market? Brainstorm your ideas **as a group**.

2 British Rail discriminates between different types of markets – e.g. business users and students. How is this reflected in its prices? Discuss with your tutor how the elasticity of demand operating in both markets enabled British Rail to do this.

3 Discuss how the prices of different types of chocolate are related to the following:

■ the laws of demand and supply in the mass chocolate market
■ the elasticity of demand
■ the cost of production
■ 'snob' value.

4 From what you have read previously, state whether you think the laws of demand and supply operate effectively in the market for:

a newspapers
b gas
c computer games
d banking services
e fizzy drinks
f videos.

In each case give a reason for your views. In which cases do you think the customer gets more value for money? Why?

Needs and wants

What consumers **want** and what they **need** are two different things. You *need* to eat every day, and basic items such as bread, potatoes, meat, fruit and vegetables would keep you healthy. However, tonight you might *want* to eat a pizza – tomorrow you might like the idea of fish and chips. Again, you need to be clean and fresh if you want to stay healthy (and have any friends!). However, the idea of using a bar of soap may be less appealing than shower gel or bubble bath!

To a large extent, your wants have been developed by producers of goods who persuade you that life is far more interesting, pleasurable or easy if you buy their goods.

On a different level, when you are buying a particular product you can sub-divide your requirements into needs and wants. You may *need* a new sweater to keep you warm. You may *want* a green one with a round neck and long sleeves – but these are 'extras' rather than essentials.

Organisations which want to be successful will spend a considerable amount of time and money trying to assess the needs and wants of their consumers – and often undertake market research to establish these (see page 71).

Non-assessed activity

You are buying a computer.

1 List **five** features which you **need** and five features which you would **want.**

Upon which type of features do you think computer manufacturers concentrate in trying to sell their product, and why? Discuss your answers with your tutor.

2 Collect **five** computer advertisements from magazines or the national press. **As a group,** analyse whether the companies are appealing to customers' needs or wants and give examples to justify your decision.

3 Use your new-found knowledge of economics to explain why computer manufacturers spend so much on advertising!

Wish to buy, ability to buy

What five items would you buy if you won the National Lottery? Your answer should give you a good idea of the difference between wishing to buy something and having the resources or ability to buy it!

As you have learned, one of the conditions of demand is **income.** The **ability** to buy means having the time, opportunity and money available to buy the product. You may wish to buy a round-the-world cruise. But if you can't take time off work or haven't enough money to pay for such an expensive holiday, then you haven't the ability to buy it, no matter how much you may wish to do so. Having the opportunity to buy means that the item is available. If you want a good paperback book to read, but you are abroad and there are no English books on sale, then you have no opportunity to purchase what you want.

As you have seen, the more expensive a product or service, the fewer the people who have the ability to buy it. In some cases producers of luxury goods prefer this because it means their product retains its image and 'snob value'. For instance, a few years ago Porsche stopped manufacturing the model at the bottom of its range. Even though the car cost many thousands of pounds, it was selling too well! Porsche was worried that if too many of its cars were seen on the road, and thought to be commonplace, they would lose their customers to Lamborghini or Ferrari!

Usually a fall in 'spending power' by consumers will result in a fall in the sales of many products – apart from inferior goods. If you only have a limited amount of money to spend you are likely to buy

essential goods, such as food, before luxury items, such as a magazine or night out.

The fact that people today have more time available for leisure activities has increased demand for many products – from golf clubs to package holidays.

Producers will always try to ensure that people have the opportunity to buy goods by selling them at as many outlets as possible and ensuring that a large supply is available at times of heavy demand, such as Christmas.

Did you know?

Your 'spending power' is determined by the size of your disposable income. This is the amount of money you have left to spend when your essential bills, such as rent and council tax. have been paid. Therefore, if you received a 10 per cent wage increase, but your electricity went up by 20 per cent, the size of your disposable income might, in fact, have fallen.

Created by consumers

In business, a successful company does not just stay in touch with the market but tries to keep one step ahead. If it then identifies a 'gap' in the market which it can fill, it becomes a market leader. Sir Clive Sinclair revolutionised the home computer market with his Spectrum ZX. He was the first to invent a cheap, mass-produced games computer. However, when he tried to repeat this success with his single-seat, battery and pedal-powered tricycle – the C5 – it was a disastrous flop. Sir Clive had lost touch with what the consumers wanted.

Identifying what consumers want by listening to what people say and analysing consumer behaviour is the key to **marketing.** An organisation which produces a product to fill a consumer need (whether consumers actually realise they have this need or not) will find it easy to sell. It is not a good idea to think of a product, make it and then look around for someone to buy it!

If the demand exists, selling is easy. Think of the National Lottery as an obvious example. The total demand for this type of gambling was obviously not met by the football pools. People liked the idea of winning millions of pounds just by guessing six numbers correctly and placing their bet in the local shop. When the lottery was launched, demand was very high indeed.

Other examples of products developed to fill a consumer need include laptop computers ('portable' computers for travellers), trainers (a comfortable shoe to be worn during leisure time) and jeans (sturdy trousers which will withstand a lot of wear and tear).

Did you know?

Levi jeans were first invented in America during the Gold Rush. Levi was a New Yorker who had heard about the wealth to be made in California. He had a novel idea. He bought some rough, semi-waterproof cloth which could be used to provide shelters for the gold prospectors – thinking they were camping out and would need protection from the weather. When he arrived in California he realised it was hot and sunny, and shelter was not in demand. However, the prospectors' clothes were taking a terrible hammering. He made his material into trousers, sold them as Levis, and the rest is history!

Created by customers

Many products and services have been launched to meet customer demand, which has often been identified by market research surveys. In many cases these 'new' goods are an improvement on the basic product or service which was available for customers – and many were introduced after listening to comments from existing customers. These include:

- self-catering holidays
- double-sided sticky tape
- vegetarian ready meals
- cash machines
- non-drip paint

- sun roofs in cars
- removable car radios
- mobile phones.

Sometimes organisations get it wrong when they try to out-think their customers. Coke altered its formula a few years ago but had to change it back again when customers complained. They liked the original version too much!

Did you know?

Saturation is the term used for a market where everyone who is likely to buy is doing so. If one particular brand or type of good increases its sales then another will fall. Can you think of an example?

Non-assessed activity

1 Look back at the list of new products and services shown above. In each case:

a identify the basic product
b identify the additional needs and wants which are filled by the new product

2 Add **at least five** products to the list yourself. In each case state the needs or wants that are being catered for.

3 Identify **one** product (e.g. a course) or service (e.g. the refectory) in your own school or college which you think could be improved. Make suggestions which could be adopted for future students.

The products provided

Business organisations provide a wide range of products and services to different individuals.

Consumable goods

Consumable goods are items which are bought frequently and used quite soon afterwards, such as food and toiletries. They are the typical items sold by large supermarkets – often called in the trade 'FMCGs' for 'fast-moving consumer goods'. However, businesses also buy consumables – and not just the food which is sold in the canteen! Business consumables include office stationery and raw materials.

Durable goods

Durable goods are items which last a long time and are only purchased infrequently. Household items include cars, furniture and electrical goods. Business items include computers, machinery and vehicles.

Did you know?

Household kitchen durables are often known in the trade as 'white goods'. Can you think why?

Services

Some organisations concentrate on offering a **service**, to individuals, businesses or both.

- Services are bought by individual consumers who will benefit in some way. Examples are hairdressing, car repairs and entertainment.
- Services are also provided by specialists who carry out specific tasks for organisations, e.g. road haulage and distribution companies, advertising agencies and accountants.
- Services provided both for private individuals and for businesses include banking, insurance and legal advice.

For whom are products provided?

The different types of individuals for whom products are provided therefore include:

- **individual consumers** – i.e. private customers and households who buy goods and services for their own personal use
- **the Government** – e.g. hospitals, schools, government offices and local authorities – all of which buy goods and services
- **other businesses** – the **industrial market**, i.e. organisations which buy products or services that will be used in manufacturing other goods, in running the business or to be resold to other customers.

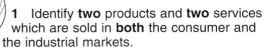

Non-assessed activity

1 Identify **two** products and **two** services which are sold in **both** the consumer and the industrial markets.

2 For **each** of the products listed below, state:

   a whether it is a consumable or durable good

   b whether it would be sold **mainly** to consumers or mainly to other businesses or the Government.

lubricating oil	X-ray machines
toothpaste	paper clips
hairdriers	vending machines
filing cabinets	shoes
sterile dressings	excavators

Activities undertaken by businesses

If a business is in touch with what its customers require, selling a new product or service may seem to be relatively simple. However, the fact that some markets are very competitive means that business organisations have to examine their products and services continually to see if they can be improved. They also have to advertise to make sure that their products have a high profile with customers. In addition, they will aim to supply the number of goods which will meet existing customer demand and **increase** customer demand by making their own product appear more desirable than their competitors'. They also need to keep in touch with the price their customers are prepared and able to pay.

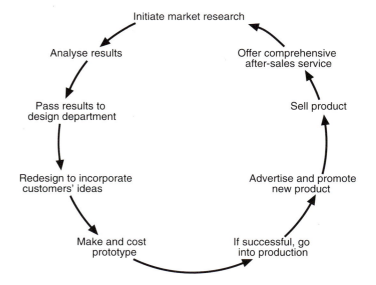

If the organisation is involved in technological developments which result in dramatically new innovations, it may be involved in actually creating market demand for the product.

Marketing-oriented companies will have a continuous cycle of improvement and development.

Did you know?

Very large companies can afford to have very large marketing budgets. The 1995 draught Guinness marketing budget is £35 million – more than enough to buy every male British drinker a free pint! They can afford to spend so much because the price added on to each pint of Guinness in marketing costs works out to quite a low figure since so much is sold.

Non-assessed activity

Discuss with your tutor why Guinness is prepared to spend so much on marketing when it already holds the giant's share of the market for stout.

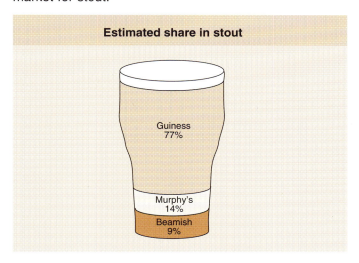

Estimated share in stout

Guiness 77%

Murphy's 14%

Beamish 9%

Figure 1.40 The market in stout

Market research

Market research involves analysing the market to find out what customers want and the amount they would be prepared to pay for a product or service. There are several ways of doing this, including:

- looking at statistics about the population, current levels of income and the sales of competitors' products
- contacting **potential** customers (consumers) to find out if they would be interested in the product or service on offer
- contacting **existing** customers to find out what improvements they can suggest.

Contact is made by direct mail (e.g. a questionnaire sent through the post with a prize as an incentive), by interviewing people face-to-face, by issuing questionnaires (e.g. to customers in a retail store) or by telephone.

The responses of consumers have to be analysed. This is more easily done if the questionnaires are designed to give a limited number of choices which can be counted and totalled by computer, using an optical mark reader. This is the way in which your end tests are designed and marked!

Design

Suggestions received from market research surveys, representatives and other sources should be passed to the design department to see if they are workable and how much they would cost. In some cases ideas can actually save money (e.g. leaving out a feature no-one uses!).

The design department may work on the design of the product itself, whilst the promotions department is working on the design of the sales literature. Companies are keen to alter the look of the packaging and advertising materials if the product has been improved or modernised in any way.

Finally, the design department will cost the changes and give the new price of the redesigned product. If this is acceptable and allows a suitable profit margin then the organisation may go into full production.

Did you know?

Designers can get it wrong! The McLaren Formula One racing car designers were forced back to the drawing board after complaints from Nigel Mansell and his fellow driver Mika Hakkinen that there wasn't enough room for them in the cockpit of their new cars. They described the test drives as being like 'trying to run a marathon in shoes that are too small' – and consequently they drove more slowly than their rivals. The cars, valued at £50 million, had to be readjusted to allow enough space for the drivers!

Production

The number of goods produced will have to be sufficient to meet the demand, otherwise customers will not have the opportunity to buy. However, no company wants to see goods left unsold. The number of potential sales therefore has to be carefully calculated and weighed against the loss of sales if customers have to wait for the product. As an example, the number of copies of this book which will be printed is based on:

- sales in previous years
- the total market of GNVQ Business Intermediate students
- the number of books on the market written by other authors.

The publishers have to estimate total demand and allow sufficient time to order reprints if demand is higher than expected. Otherwise you may decide not to wait, and buy a competitor's product instead!

Marketing communications

The organisation has to make certain that its consumers know the product exists. This is done in several ways.

Advertising

The type of advertising will depend on the product. It may mean a national television campaign, adverts in newspapers and magazines, on the cinema or radio, or a poster campaign.

The amount of the advertising budget and the size of the market will influence the amount of money spent on advertising.

Promotion

Promotional methods include special offers, competitions, point-of-sale displays, special packaging, logos and emblems on items such as clothing, showing the product at exhibitions and trade fairs, etc.

Sponsorship

This is often an economical way of advertising and is particularly suitable for products which can be used by famous personalities. Well-known tennis players, for example, may be paid large amounts of money to wear a particular brand of clothes or use certain racquets. Football teams are usually sponsored by a commercial company and wear the name on their strip. The name is therefore prominent to all their fans – and may be shown nationwide if the game is televised.

Sales literature

Many organisations produce leaflets and brochures about the products they sell or the services they offer. Often these are highly coloured and professionally produced to impress potential customers. Your school or college probably issues a prospectus each year which it hopes will persuade potential students to study there.

Sales

Some organisations employ a specific sales force to help to sell the product to customers. A typical example is a car showroom which will have salespeople on duty every day to explain the various features of different cars to potential customers.

Representatives are normally employed for trade or industrial markets. For instance, businesses do not buy a new lift, or farmers a new tractor, or large retailers a new line in chocolates until they have been convinced of the benefits. Therefore manufacturers of these products, such as Otis, Massey Ferguson and Mars, will employ representatives to keep in touch with potential customers, discuss the cost of the product, possible discounts and delivery details and try to obtain a firm order.

Did you know?

Merchandisers are a new type of salesperson. Merchandisers were originally employed to visit supermarkets, to check the displays of their products and ensure any special promotions were in place. They would also obtain feedback from customers and sales staff. They did not actively promote the goods, as this was done by the sales representative who visited to collect the order. Today many large supermarkets do all their ordering by computer using Electronic Data Interchange (EDI – see Element 4.1). There is therefore no need for any sales representative to visit. Orders and discounts are negotiated at a high level and then the order is dealt with electronically. The merchandiser is then the only person from the supplier who is regularly in touch with the seller – and has a more prominent marketing role.

After-sales service

Today, after-sales service is a feature of all durable products. If something goes wrong with the product then the manufacturer or supplier will make every effort to put it right. If you buy a washing machine you expect it to be mended if it breaks. If a business buys a fork lift truck it has the same requirement. Most durables are sold with a **warranty** or **guarantee** that can be extended by taking out special insurance cover.

Enterprising organisations also offer good customer service and response times in relation to all the goods they sell. Therefore, if you bought a tin of soup which had a peculiar taste you could contact the company for an instant response to your problem.

Bear in mind that **basic** after-sales service relating to faulty goods is required under the Sales of Goods and Services Act.

Note: The functions of a marketing department are dealt with in more detail in Element 2.1. Marketing communications, after-sales service and consumer legislation are dealt with in Unit 3.

Optional evidence assignment

*This activity can be carried out verbally in class **in a group** as a non-assessed activity to consolidate learning. Alternatively, if you do it **on your own**, it can count as supplementary evidence towards the following parts of the scheme.*

PC 3: Describe markets for businesses' products based on demand

PC 4: Identify products provided by business organisations

PC 5: Explain activities undertaken by businesses to improve their market position

Range: Markets: domestic market, value of total market

Demand: needs, wants; wish to buy, ability to buy; created by consumers, created by customers

Products: consumable, services

Activities: marketing research, marketing communications, sales

Read the case study below and answer the questions which follow.

Case study – the National Lottery

When the National Lottery was introduced in Britain in 1994 its aim was:

- to give the British public the opportunity to win large amounts of money each week simply by picking six lucky numbers
- to raise money for the Government
- to raise money for the arts, sports, national heritage, charities and the Millennium Fund.

Sales of lottery tickets average £50 million a week. However these aren't high enough for Camelot, the organiser, to meet its targets. Camelot had estimated yearly sales of £4.6 billion – the equivalent of each household spending £4 a week on lottery tickets. Camelot was not worried about these figures. A spokesman said that at present there were only 12 000 retail outlets, whereas by 1996 there would be 40 000. In addition, the scratch card game *Instants* had still to be introduced, in response to customer demand for an 'instant win', and possibly a mid-week or superdraw will be started in the future.

The lottery is seen as fun by many people but has not been without its critics. The impact of the lottery cost the jobs of some people in the football pools business, as takings fell by over 17 per cent. Even higher was the fall in entries to 'spot the ball' competitions, which plunged by 25 per cent. Some are predicting the end of small charity scratch-card competitions as they consider the market is not large enough to sustain them.

Concern was voiced that certain charities would not benefit from the lottery – for instance those concerned with animal welfare and protection. Only 6p in each pound spent on a lottery ticket goes to charities, so there could be better ways to support good causes. In addition, the National Council for Voluntary Organisations warned that over £200 million may be lost to the charitable sector as a whole if people changed their normal pattern of spending on charities and turned to the lottery instead.

However, for some the lottery was seen as an inspiration and an opportunity. A variety of books on 'how to win the lottery' hit the book shops in time for the Christmas market; one publisher quickly brought out issue one of the National Lottery magazine with 'tips to make you rich'; and an insurance broker in Leeds came up with a policy to protect companies who might lose a large number of workers overnight if a workers' syndicate had a jackpot win.

1 How did Camelot estimate the value of its potential market?

2 Who are Camelot's competitors?

3 What techniques has Camelot used to gain a high market share?

4 Why is the National Lottery suitable only for the domestic market?

5 a In what ways does the market for the national lottery overlap with that for football pools and 'spot the ball' promotions?
   b What was the effect of the introduction of the lottery on other, similar, gambling activities?

6 What factors do you consider influence the demand for lottery tickets?

7 Why do charities fear that the lottery may divert funds from other forms of charitable giving?

8 Briefly analyse the lottery under each of the following headings and explain its success.

   a Customers' needs and wants
   b Customers' wish to buy
   c Customers' ability to buy
   d Created by consumers
   e Created by customers

9 a What activities did Camelot (the organisers) undertake to make sure that:

   i   as many people as possible knew about the National Lottery before it was launched
   ii as many people as possible would have the opportunity to buy a ticket?

   b How do Camelot hope to increase sales in the future?

10 In the first week, the lottery raised £49 million and £12.65 million was allocated to the lottery's 'good causes'. What percentage of the money raised was given to charity?

11 a Give **two** examples of 'spin-offs' from the lottery which have benefited people with good ideas.
    b Why do you think these ideas have been successful?
    c Can you think of any good ideas for future spin-offs yourself?

Evidence assignment

At this point your tutor may wish you to start or continue work on the project which will prove to your verifiers that you understand this section of the element. If you are starting the project then turn to page 79 and do Section 1. If you already working through the project, now start Section 3. This covers the third evidence indicator for this element.

Proposing products

There are dozens of products and services on the market today which did not exist ten or twenty years ago. Most have been introduced because:

- they were developed as a result of technological breakthrough, e.g. silicon chips, lasers and videos
- they have evolved from other products, e.g. personal stereos, laptop computers and mobile phones
- they were a new invention and the result of someone's very bright idea (the best-known example of this is 'cat's eyes' in the road – although they were introduced far more than twenty years ago!)

In some cases, inventions and innovations can mean that existing products become obsolete. Slide rules are no longer used because pocket calculators have taken over. Typewriters were first of all manual, then electric, finally electronic and have now largely been replaced by word processors.

These products have catered for the needs of individuals and businesses to make calculations and process documents more quickly and easily. As standards of living rise (so consumers have more money to spend) and the pace of living gets even faster, people are likely to spend more money on items which save them work, time or both.

Did you know?

Innovation need not be confined just to products. It can also be applied to services. In Britain, you check-in at an airport by queuing up with your heavy luggage at a check-in desk – sometimes for up to an hour. You are then handed your boarding card, go to the departure lounge and finally proceed to the departure gate. In America the system is different. Your luggage is taken away from you immediately upon arrival at the airport (on the pavement outside!) and weighed. You receive your boarding card near to the gate itself. In the meantime you are free to wander around the airport, visit the shops and have something to eat – without worrying about your luggage.

Change and its effects

It is no use a company developing a new product and then assuming it will meet the needs and wants of consumers forever! Our needs and wants change because of various factors – social trends, fashion and new legal requirements, to name but a few.

Changing social trends have included the following features.

- More women work and have less time to shop (and therefore buy microwave meals or takeaways!).
- People work fewer hours and have more time for leisure.
- Fewer people go to church on Sunday or belong to an organised religion which discourages them from shopping on that day.
- More people are health conscious – and therefore buy diet meals, low calorie drinks, visit exercise clubs and try to stop smoking (hence the success of non-smoking patches).

Fashion trends also affect our needs and wants. Clothes – in particular – change from one year to the next. Therefore although, for instance, most people wear jeans, the colour and the style will vary from one year to another. Other trends can become crazes which just last for a short time, e.g. roller skates and BMX bicycles.

Finally, **legal requirements** can affect our needs and wants. Seat belts were seen by the Government as essential to reduce the scale of injuries sustained in vehicle collisions. Many people did not want them but were forced to wear them when the law made this compulsory. The current concern with the environment has led to most cars being fitted with catalytic converters, which convert toxic gases from the engine exhausts of cars into less harmful emissions.

Note: Consumer wants and needs and how these change are dealt with more fully in Unit 3.

Did you know?

Since April 1995, when legal restrictions in England and Wales on where a couple can marry were relaxed, dozens of historic buildings and stately home proprietors have been seeking licences so that couples can tie the knot on their premises!

Market changes and innovations

Because markets vary in whether they are **expanding**, **stagnant** (not moving very much) or **contracting,** each organisation has to keep a close eye on the sales of *all* its products. If a market is contracting, companies have *either* to reduce their operations (e.g. by closing down factories) or to diversify and make different products.

An example of reducing operations is Mercury Communications. The increased ownership of mobile phones and telephone credit cards reduced the demand for public pay telephones. This resulted in Mercury making the decision to scrap its involvement in the public phone box business from spring 1995 and to concentrate on business and international telecommunications.

Probably the best example of diversification is Richard Branson's Virgin Group, which is involved – at the present time – in markets as diverse as music, cola, vodka, radio broadcasting, airline travel, retailing and investments. Not one to rest for a minute, Richard Branson is currently bidding to build the Channel tunnel high-speed rail link.

Some companies pride themselves on being 'ahead of the market' and introducing a range of new products or ideas – many with help from their employees. Many organisations operate suggestion schemes so that staff can contribute ideas for new products or new ways of doing things. In many cases employees can win monetary prizes if an idea is implemented. Hewlett Packard, the computer company, is reputed to think up ideas for eight new products a week – even though they may not be used.

In some cases ideas need not be radical but can be developed from an existing product. For example, 3M designed the Post-It note – which is simply a development from ordinary small pads of paper but has a sticky top part for keeping the note firmly on a vertical or horizontal surface. The idea was simple, but the organisation saw its profits increase rapidly after the idea caught on.

New products and developments from existing products

Some people argue that nothing is really new – everything is based on a previous idea and is a development of something which has gone before. Make your own mind up about the following:

- non-stick Teflon trousers, made by Farah, which repel anything spilled on them
- an ironing board shaped like a bottle which is claimed to increase ironing 'output' by 25 per cent – called the Bottle Board
- the Data Link wristwatch – the result of a collaboration between Timex and Microsoft – which acts something like a mini personal computer
- the first 24-hour UK supermarket chain store quickly opened after the Government relaxed restrictions on shop opening hours – do you live near Asda in Clapham, London?

- in-car computerised maps and information systems (just introduced in Europe by BMW)
- the idea of a basic car with interchangeable roof structures – to convert it into an estate car, convertible or pick-up just by taking it back to the dealer to swap tops (being developed by Mercedes and named the Vario)
- a Dream Machine which helps people have lucid and controllable dreams, invented by Dr Keith Hearne, formerly of Liverpool University and the Medical Research Council
- an electronic 'nose' developed at Manchester Institute of Science and Technology (UMIST). The noses, which cost £25 000 each, are in demand by hospitals, food manufacturers, car makers and can also be used in space travel. What for? Examples include assisting in product development (e.g. which type of upholstery in a car smells best) and detecting infection at an early stage. The name of the company? Aromascan!
- an electronic cash card called Mondex – being piloted in Swindon this year by NatWest, Midland and British Telecom. The card is scheduled to be nationally available from 1996 and by the year 2000 over 900 million electronic cash transactions a year are forecast. It is also envisaged that the card will eventually be compatible with the Internet.

- Sharp, the Japanese company, has just produced a 20-minute video showing its technological predictions for the year 2000, including a domestic computer network through which the washing machine can contact the electricity company to find out the cheapest time to switch itself on!

Did you know?

1 Tom Baccei is an ex-hippie who stared at beansprouts one day and thought he saw them make a picture. His idea of hidden pictures has now grown into the £130 million Magic Eye industry that has made him a rich man – and driven everyone else mad!

2 Each year the UK Innovations and Inventions Exhibition is held. At this exhibition are displayed a wide range of inventions and creations – some of them sensible and some less so. Bright recent ideas included flashing indicators for cyclists, special pads to keep ladders secure and a device to stop children turning on hot water taps. More wacky ideas included a dog seat belt – the Hollyjack – a decorative wheelie bin and a lockable briefcase for the executive cyclist.

Non-assessed activity

1 How many products among those listed above are completely new and how many were developed from existing products?

2 For how many of them do you think there is a market demand?

3 Imagine that friends of your parents own a country pub. You have just read that the Government has extended licensing laws on a Sunday so that alcohol can be served all day. In addition the Government has relaxed restrictions on children in pubs so that under-fourteen-year-olds are allowed in pubs with a 'suitable family atmosphere' until 9 pm.

You know that things have been difficult for your parents' friends. **As a group**, brainstorm the opportunities which the changes in licensing laws would give them to improve their business.

4 Look at how the electronic cashcard mentioned on page 76 will work. Choose one of the ideas mentioned on page 76 and, **as a group**, discuss whether you think it will catch on and the advantages and disadvantages of the idea.

Optional evidence assignment

*This activity is meant to start **as a group** activity. If you work **on your own** from point **2** onwards then you can count it as supplementary evidence towards the following part of the scheme.*

PC 6: Propose products which would meet market demand

Range: Propose products: new, developed from existing product

Core skills: Communication

1 **As a group**, hold a brain-storming session to see how many new products you can think of which would fulfil the needs or wants of a member of your family or group. For instance, your mother may want clothes to be made out of a fabric which never needs ironing, your father may want grass which doesn't grow, an unstealable car and a cure for baldness, and you may like the idea of a computer which teaches you to use the keyboard perfectly in an hour! Your tutor may prefer a computer which automatically scans, marks and corrects all your work!

The ideas suggested by your group (if you brainstorm properly) should range from the fanciful and ridiculous to the practical and sensible. Sometimes a silly idea can lead you on to something which has more potential.

Write all the ideas down, on the blackboard, whiteboard or a flip chart.

2 Choose **one or two** ideas which appeal to you and think about how they could be adapted.

3 Develop **one** idea to the point where you can prepare a sketch and notes on what the product would look like and how it would work. Try to think of a suitable name.

4 Present your idea to the rest of your group. Answer any questions they may have on how your product would work and what it would be used for. See if they can come up with suggestions which would improve your idea, rather than criticise it.

5 Finally write a summary of the session and your final conclusion to add to your supplementary evidence file.

Evidence assignment

At this point your tutor may wish you to start or continue work on the project which will prove to your verifiers that you understand this section of the element. If you are starting the project then turn to page 79 and do Section 1. Alternatively you may now be up to Section 4. This covers the fourth evidence indicator for this element.

Revision test

True or false?

1 Companies which assemble large products, e.g. freezers, prefer to locate near their markets.

2 The law of demand states that the lower the price, the greater the quantity which will be demanded.

3 Consumable products are those which last a long time.

4 The Government is a large buyer of goods and services.

5 The more profitable goods are to produce and the greater the demand, the more suppliers will move into a market.

Complete the blanks

6 A firm will undertake a _____ _____ survey to find out what customers think about their products.

7 A product where more is demanded as incomes fall is known as an _____ _____ .

8 The international market is larger than the _____ market.

9 Protection from unsafe working practices is a key feature of an Act entitled the _____ _____ _____ _____ _____ _____ .

10 The results of a survey are often passed to the _____ department, who then produce a prototype of the new product.

Short answer questions

11 State **four** products which are sold internationally.

12 Briefly explain the difference between consumer wants and needs.

13 State **four** products which have been introduced in recent years to fulfil a market want or need.

14 Give **three** reasons why a company may choose to locate near to other businesses.

15 Figure 1.41 relates to the market share of DIY companies in 1993 and the average sales per store.

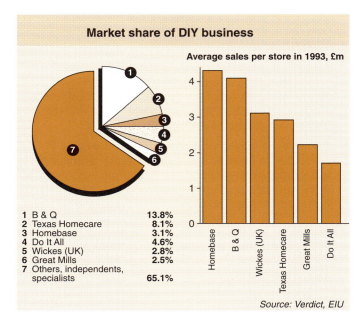

Market share of DIY business

1	B & Q	13.8%
2	Texas Homecare	8.1%
3	Homebase	3.1%
4	Do It All	4.6%
5	Wickes (UK)	2.8%
6	Great Mills	2.5%
7	Others, independents, specialists	65.1%

Average sales per store in 1993, £m

Source: Verdict, EIU

Figure 1.41 The DIY business

a Which company has the highest market share?

b Which company has the highest average sales per store?

c Can you suggest one reason why the two answers are different?

Write a short paragraph to show you clearly understand each of the following terms:

16 Business environment

17 Sponsorship

18 Ability to buy

19 Value of total market

20 After-sales service

Evidence indicator project

Unit 1 Element 1.2

This project has been designed to cover all the evidence indicators related to Element 1.2. It is divided into four sections. Tutors may wish students to complete the sections at the appropriate points marked in the text. Alternatively, tutors may prefer their students to do the entire project at the end of the element.

Performance criteria: 1–6

Core skills: Communication
Application of number
Information technology

Section 1

Select one business organisation which operates in your own area. This may be either a traditional or a new industry. If you wish, you may use the organisation you identified for your major project study in Element 1.1.

Draw a map which identifies its location and show any relevant natural resources, the proximity of other businesses and customers' and transport services.

Attach a brief explanation giving the reasons for its location.

Make sure you complete this section of the project by the deadline date given you by your tutor.

Section 2

Write a summary which explains the competitive business environment in which all businesses operate. Include in your notes reference to the legal, environmental and public influences on business organisations.

Make sure you complete this section of the project by the deadline date given you by your tutor.

Section 3

1 For this section you can either use the same organisation you studied in Section 1, the organisation you have chosen for your major project study or a different organisation altogether. You should select a large business with a sizeable advertising budget which undertakes a large number of activities to improve its market position. You may obtain some ideas from your readings in this chapter of products with a large international or domestic market.

2 Investigate the range of goods (or services) provided by the organisation. If possible, obtain examples of advertising and promotional literature which give information on these in more detail. State whether the products are consumable or durable and for whom the products are provided.

Select one product or service for further investigation.

3 Research the main market in which the organisation operates. Find out

   a if this is domestic, international or both
   b the value of the total market for the product or service you have selected
   c the market share held by the organisation.

4 Interview one person in the marketing department who is willing to discuss with you

   ■ the typical customer profile
   ■ how his/her needs and wants are assessed
   ■ the type of market research carried out
   ■ how goods are distributed
   ■ the range of advertising and promotional activities undertaken
   ■ the activities the company undertakes to improve sales and market share
   ■ how after-sales service or customer service is organised
   ■ the extent to which the marketing communications used have affected market share.

If the organisation is too far away to be visited then you could write to the marketing department for information. You could also collect examples of promotional materials and advertisements and research its market share (past and present) in your library.

Make sure you complete this section of the project by the deadline date given you by your tutor.

Section 4

Either refine your notes from the optional evidence assignment on page 77 or think of an original idea for a new or developed product. Produce notes and sketches that support your proposal which make it clear what your product would look like and how it would work. Include suggested costs of production and profit margins. Estimate potential demand which includes a suggested suitable price and calculate possible profits. Hold an 'in-class' Innovations and Inventions Exhibition and sell your idea to your tutor and any other visitors.

Make sure you complete this section of the project by the deadline date given you by your tutor.

Final stage

Type up all the written documents you have produced neatly and clearly on a word processor. Put these into a folder with the map you produced in Section 1 and the sketches produced in Section 4. Design a title page with the heading: **Investigation into Business Location, Environment, Markets and Products**. Don't forget to include your name and the date.

Present results of investigations into employment

This element covers different types of employment and opportunities in both the United Kingdom (UK) and the European Union (EU). It also examines different kinds of working conditions.

After studying this element you should be able to:

1 describe and give examples of *types of employment*

2 collect, *analyse* and explain *information* about employment in different regions

3 *compare working conditions* for employees in different organisations

4 present results of an investigation into employment or comparison of working conditions.

Types of employment

At one time it was standard practice for many people to leave school, find a full-time job – starting at trainee or apprentice level – and then, once fully skilled, stay in the same type of job until they retired. Those who had **capital** to invest (and the courage to go it alone) might have decided to start a business and become self-employed, or they might have worked in a family business and inherited it at some stage in their lives.

Today the pattern of employment is far more varied and unemployment is far more widespread. There are no longer jobs 'for life' – many people have two or more careers during their working life. No longer are all jobs full-time. No longer is it the case that once you find a job you will be secure for ever – or required by your employer to do only the specific job for which you trained. No longer is it the case that few people have either the opportunity or the finances to start in business for themselves.

In this element we examine the different types of employment you may encounter.

Full-time or part-time

The number of people working part-time has increased dramatically over the past ten years, not just in Britain but also throughout the European Union. This is one of the consequences of the growth in the **service industries** discussed later in this element, on page 88. In retailing, catering, hotel work, health care, banking and education many jobs are now part-time. Indeed many British companies employ far greater numbers of production, administrative and clerical staff on a part-time basis than ever before.

The main difference between working part-time and working full-time is in the number of hours worked. A part-time employee will work fewer than the standard operating hours of the company. In some cases, two part-time employees might **job-share** one full-time job, and do the work between them.

 Did you know?

There are many different types of job sharing. Typical shares are:

■ one partner working mornings and the other afternoons
■ alternate day working
■ shares of two and a half days each
■ one partner working a three-day week, the other a two-day week and then alternating.

In some cases, however, the split may be unequal. For example, one partner may always work two days and the other three days.

See Unit 2, Element 2.1, page 147 for more information on different types of working arrangements.

Employers may prefer part-time staff for several reasons.

1 The company's wage bill is reduced. If part-time staff are employed for evening or weekend work

Figure 1.42 Some people share jobs

they are not eligible for the overtime rates which would be paid to full-time staff. The employer also saves on National Insurance payments if part-time staff earn less than the lower earnings limit.

2 Part-time staff are more flexible – they can be used to cover for absent staff and work extra hours when the company is busy or wants to open longer hours.

3 There may be more people willing to work part-time in areas where there is a skills shortage. Therefore a company prepared to offer part-time jobs can recruit the people it needs.

Did you know?

One argument in favour of part-time workers used to be that employers could pay them less per hour and refuse to offer them fringe benefits such as profit sharing or subsidised mortgages. They also had less job security as they had fewer legal rights. The situation has now changed and the European Court has ruled that most part-time workers have the same rights as full-time workers.

Preferences for working full- or part-time

Employees may prefer to work part-time for several reasons.

1 They can have a greater say in the days and hours they work. This is often important for mothers of school children, for example.

2 Part-time work enables a person to earn some money and still have more time for leisure.

3 It is better than being unemployed.

4 It is a useful way of earning some money, for those who cannot work full time, e.g. students, those who are disabled or ill, or pensioners who want to supplement their pension.

Non-assessed activity

Read the following case study and then answer the questions which follow.

Case study – Karen Mitchell

Karen Mitchell is 19 years old and has worked in the Administration section of Taylor Electronics for the past six months. She is employed full-time as a wages clerk. Two other women also work in the same section – Betty, the section supervisor and Kathleen, the second wages clerk. Kathleen is 26, has two young children and has worked in the wages office for nearly a year.

Taylor Electronics have just introduced a computerised payroll system. All the employees are now paid directly via their bank accounts at the end of each month. Last Friday, the Chief Accountant interviewed all the wages staff and informed them that, as of the beginning of next month, only Betty would be able to remain as a member of the full-time staff.

He pointed out that neither Karen nor Kathleen had employment protection as they have worked for the company for less two years. However, in good faith, the company is prepared to offer them the following options:

a they could each work part-time independently
b they could job-share
c they could offer their services freelance and charge their own fees to the company (and use their spare hours to hire their services to other organisations).

Kathleen prefers the idea of job sharing but Karen doesn't agree. She likes the idea of working freelance as this will give her more flexibility and possibly enable her to earn more money. The two of them have until Monday morning to make a decision.

1 If you were Karen, what would you suggest to Kathleen and why?

Note: Use the advantages and disadvantages of each method of work to each person to support your argument.

2 Find out how the situation might have been different if the two women had both worked for the company for more than two years. To do this, you will have to research how a full-time employee is protected by the Employment Protection (Consolidation) Act 1978. This is covered in Element 2.2 on page 166.

Optional evidence assignment

*This activity can be carried out verbally in class **in a group** as a non-assessed activity to consolidate learning. Alternatively, if you do it **on your own**, it can count as supplementary evidence towards the following parts of the scheme.*

PC 1: Describe and give examples of types of employment

Range: Types of employment: full-time, part-time

Core skills: Communication, application of number (IT optional)

1 Look in your local paper and local Job Centre and note down the numbers of full-time and part-time jobs on offer in offices and retail stores. Work out the ratio of full-time to part-time jobs. If you don't know how to do this, refer to the Core Skills Numeracy section.

2 Carry out a survey of:

- your fellow students
- your friends and relatives
- at least 20 other people

to find out whether they have part-time jobs and, if so, their reason for working part-time. For instance, is it because they do not want a full-time job or cannot find one, because they are still at school, are disabled, or is there some other reason?

Analyse your findings. Then sub-divide your results into male and female and see if this shows any difference. Summarise your findings neatly in a short report, preferably typed on a word processor.

Permanent or temporary

Temporary staff are used by many companies to cope with very busy times or to cover for absent staff. In most industries there is always *some* temporary working – in others such as construction, temporary or **casual work** is normal.

The main difference between a permanent member of staff and a temporary worker is that the latter is hired for a limited period of time, usually for a specific reason. Examples include:

- seasonal workers, e.g. clerks employed over a holiday season in a tourist centre or additional Post Office delivery staff hired for the Christmas period
- 'temps' provided by employment agencies to fill staff gaps caused by holidays or sickness, or to deal with emergency workloads
- casual workers whose days and times of working may depend on day-to-day demand
- fixed-term contract workers who are employed for a specified period of time
- temporary workers, employed for an unspecified period of time.

Temporary workers may be employed on a full-time or part-time basis. They may even be eligible for overtime pay. They can be laid off at any time or leave automatically at the end of their contract. There is no difference in British employment law between temporary and permanent employees – everything depends on the number of hours worked and the length of service.

Temporary workers who are provided by employment agencies are paid an hourly rate *by the agency*. The agency receives a higher rate from the employer and deducts an amount for administration. Many clerical workers in large cities start out 'temping' to gain experience. Students may also 'temp' in a gap year to earn additional money. In addition to their wages they can also claim travelling expenses. Some employment agencies pay their regular 'temps' sick pay and holiday pay, and even give them specialised training, e.g. on word processors and computers. See also Element 2.1.

Non-assessed activity

Research has shown that some industries are more likely than others to use part-time and temporary workers. Look at the chart in Figure 1.43.

1 Put the information in a bar graph to show the extent to which different industries employ such workers.

2 Write a short paragraph (using a word processor) stating:

a the **two** industries which employ the largest percentage of part-time workers. Give at least one reason why you think they do.

Industry	Average part-time workforce* %	Average temporary workforce* %
Chemical	3.1	0.8
Electricity, gas, water	7.5	3.6
Engineering	2.4	4.3
Finance	11.1	3.5
Food, drink, tobacco	7.3	1.5
General manufacturing	3.5	7.0
General services	5.2	15.9
Hotels and catering	24.9	11.7
Public services	18.0	11.0
Retail and wholesale	18.7	1.2
Textiles	7.2	0.0
Transport and communication	1.5	1.2

*As a proportion of the total workforce.

Figure 1.43 Part-time and temporary workers

b the two industries which employ the lowest percentage of temporary workers. Give **at least one** reason why you think they don't employ more.

Optional evidence assignment

*This activity can be carried out verbally in class **in a group** as a non-assessed activity to consolidate learning. Alternatively, if you do it* **on your own***, it can count as supplementary evidence towards the following parts of the scheme.*

PC 1: Describe and give examples of types of employment

Range: Types of employment: permanent, temporary

Core skills: Communication

1 Try to arrange an interview with someone who works for a local employment agency. Obtain as many details as possible on their 'temp' scheme, e.g.

■ whether holiday or sick pay is given
■ what training is given

■ whether 'temps' can arrange time off (e.g. for hospital appointments)
■ whether there are any other benefits.

2 Try to interview **at least one** person who has worked as a 'temp'. List the advantages and disadvantages of this method of working.

3 Do you think temporary working is more suitable for some people than others? Think about the type of person who would prefer it and the type of person who would not (e.g. in terms of age, qualifications, marital and family status, etc.).

4 Look in your local newspaper and/or Job Centre and collect **three** examples of temporary jobs. In each case state why you think the job is not a permanent one.

Skilled or unskilled

Nowadays most workers have a variety of skills.

Core skills

Workers can read, write and calculate. They also normally have some information technology skills.

Personal skills

People can manage their own work and their own learning, and they can control their emotions. They can work with other people, they can talk to them, persuade them, they can follow instructions, and solve most of their own problems.

Job skills

Workers have a particular skill which is used on a particular job. If they work in a restaurant, they have to know how to cook, if they work in an office they be able to keyboard, and so on. In many cases they have a qualification which shows the level of skill they have in a particular area.

(See Element 2.4 for more information about the way in which you need to develop these skills for your own benefit to increase your chances of getting a job.)

Did you know?

The *level* of skill needed by existing employees is rising according to 63 per cent of employers interviewed in a recent survey.

Skilled workers

One problem, however, is that as modern industries change and develop, so too do the skills needed.

Multi-skilling

Nowadays most workers have to develop more than one skill. They may, for instance, be expected to use a number of different job skills if they are part of a production team. They may also be expected to combine job skills with personal skills.

Did you know?

One carpet manufacturing firm now expects its drivers to deliver the goods to the customers *and* to be skilled in customer care – on the grounds that the customers will have more regular contact with the drivers than with the sales force!

Upskilling

The level of skills required is now increasing. A typical example would be the machine operator who becomes responsible for a range of computerised equipment and must therefore be trained to supervisory level. In an office, an example would be the former invoice typist who, with a microcomputer, can produce documents much more quickly and is therefore trained as a word-processor operator and made responsible for a wider range of jobs.

De-skilling

This term is used to describe the situation when technology has led to decline in the need of traditional craft skills. For example, if all computers had speech input, the days of the keyboard operator would rapidly be drawing to a close. The operator would be required merely to switch on the machine, give it instructions and data vocally, monitor its progress, load the printer and distribute the print-outs. That is a typical example of de-skilling.

De-skilling has affected a wide range of occupations. The traditional television engineer needed to know exactly what could go wrong with a television and where to find the fault. Today it is simply a case of replacing printed circuit boards. A television engineer may spend more time travelling from call to call than on mending television sets! In industry, maintenance workers may be similarly affected. Indeed in some cases, computers are not only used to operate machinery but also to diagnose faults.

A final example can be taken from the retail trade. Ask your parents or an elderly relative about the skills required to run a retail shop 30 years ago. They would probably include a good memory (to remember prices) and numeracy (to total the goods). Neither of these skills is required today – the automated cash register does both! However, others may argue that this frees staff to look after customers and find out more about the product range they have in stock, and about new developments.

Did you know?

De-skilling can be used as a reason to reduce wages. By employing unskilled or lower-skilled workers for such jobs, companies can pay lower wages.

Skill shortages

Even in these days of high unemployment there are skill shortages, as the following table shows.

Percentage of employers with current vacancies that are hard to fill

	%
Hotel and catering	27
Textiles, clothing & footwear	21
Medical and other ehalth services	16
Mechanical engineering	14
Electical/electronic engineering	12
Motor verhicles/transport equipmeny engineering	11

This can result in a situation where:

- the number of job vacancies in certain occupational areas rises
- employers, knowing that they cannot find a person with the exact skills required, employ someone less skilled.

Non-assessed activity

As a group, discuss the dangers of employing people who do not have the appropriate skills.

Discuss also the ways in which employers might overcome any problems caused.

Did you know?

In a recent survey, 53 per cent of the employers felt that a skills gap exists, not only in specific job skills and core skills such as information technology and computer literacy, but also in personal skills such as motivation, the willingness to work in a team and general communication skills.

Unskilled workers

Whatever the problems you may have as a skilled worker, they are still fewer than those you will have if you have no job skills at all – and are therefore regarded as unskilled. 20 years ago there were still jobs which needed few or no skills. People could be employed on assembly lines or on general labouring jobs and, although the pay may not have been very good, at least the work was there. Nowadays the rise in unemployment and the impact of modern technology – by which machines have gradually been replacing jobs (see page 114) – have resulted in a fall in the number of jobs for which no skills are required. It is surprising therefore that, even in 1995, between 25 per cent and 30 per cent of the population of working age has no formal qualifications or skills.

Non-assessed activity

Imagine that you and a group of friends have left school and are in the process of learning various skills.

- David is at college studying for a teaching qualification.

- Marilyn wants to become an engineer and is planning to take an engineering degree.

- Rachel has enrolled for a secretarial administration course.

- Trevor is studying to be a physiotherapist.

Projected change in employment by standard occupational classification: 1993–2001 (UK)		
Occupation		%
Managers and administrators	Corporate managers and administrators	24
	Managers/proprietors in agriculture and services	11
Professional occupations	Health professionals	13
	Teaching professionals	14
	Other professional occupations	43
Associate professional and technical	Science and engineering associate professions	15
	Health associate professionals	0
	Other associate professionals	30
Clerical and secretarial	Clerical	−4
	Secretarial	−2
Craft and skilled manual	Skilled construction trades	15
	Skilled engineering trades	−13
	Other skilled trades	−5
Personal and protective	Protective service occupations	15
	Personal service occupations	28
Sales	Buyers, brokers and sales representatives	0
	Other sales occupations	4
Plant and machine operatives	Drivers and mobile machine operators	−4
	Industrial plant and machine operators	−5
Other	Other occupations in agriculture, etc.	−11
	Other elementary occupations	−13
All occupations		**7**

Source: Institute for Employment Research 1994

Figure 1.43 Projected change in employment

- Barbara wants a company car and is undergoing some training to be a sales representative for a cosmetics company.

- Emilio wants to obtain a HGV licence.

Look at the table in Figure 1.44 listing the projected changes in various types of employment. From the information given, list in order which of these friends is the most likely and which the least likely to be given a chance of using their skills.

Employed or self-employed?

It is easy to think that you are employed if you work for somebody else and you are self-employed if you work for yourself! But life isn't quite so simple. For example, what would be your status if you applied for and accepted the job advertised opposite?

Keyboard operators

required urgently

Must be capable of inputting data at minimum of 40 keystrokes per minute. Only freelance operators should apply. Ring Claire Southern for details on

01891-930849

Data Processing Services Ltd

Marsh Lane

Hightown

In this case you would actually be classified as **self-employed** – and your rights, responsibilities and obligations, so far as tax and National Insurance are concerned, would be different from those of someone with employee status. The rights and responsibilities of an employee are covered in Element 2.2.

Self-employment

Being self-employed is not a status restricted to people who run their own business in the sense of owning property and stock and perhaps employing their own staff. Millions of people work from home in a wide range of occupations, and many of them are classed as self-employed, e.g. the hairdresser who has set up shop in one room of the house (or visits clients in their own homes), the freelance book-keeper who does the accounts for other small businesses, the woman who holds clothing or Tupperware parties, and the artist who takes on freelance work from various publishing companies.

People who work on a freelance basis hire out their skills to anyone who will pay them – a freelance photographer, for instance, might be contracted to do a specific job for a newspaper, or may take photographs of events on the chance that he can sell them.

Did you know?

The number of people in the UK who are classed as self-employed rose by 52 per cent between 1979 and 1990, from 2.2 million

to 3.3 million, and most of them work on their own, i.e. they do not employ other people. Although there has been a slight decrease in the past few years, numbers are now beginning to increase again and by 2001 it has been estimated that self-employed people will make up over 13 per cent of the workforce. In many cases these are people who have set up in business by using their savings or their redundancy payments, or have taken advantage of one of the government funding schemes (see page 37).

More men than women are self-employed (76 per cent men, 24 per cent women) although between 1991 and 1993 the percentage of self-employed women increased. Self-employment becomes more popular as people grow older – young people under the age of 25 are the least likely to be self-employed.

(For more information on the self-employed look at Element 2.4 page 245.)

Evidence assignment

At this point your tutor may wish you to start work on the project which will prove to your verifiers that you understand this section of the element. If so, turn to page 118 and do Section 1 of the project. This covers the first Evidence Indicator for this element.

Analysing information

Before you start to analyse any information, you need to collect it! This section covers the types of information available about employment in different regions. Once you have obtained the information then you need to be able to analyse it:

- in terms of factors contributing to numbers of people employed
- in terms of the growth and decline of manufacturing and service sectors.

Did you know?

The term **analyse** means to examine in detail. This means that you need to look at data and information for trends and indications about the factors which may apply. You may have made some assumptions, but you need hard evidence to confirm them. This is not always evident just by glancing at a page of information! Sometimes you will have to

87

think about it carefully and see what patterns emerge. The best way is to think of yourself as a detective looking for clues.

Start by analysing information from different points of view – your tutor will help you to do this in the early stages. Remember that you may make lots of random notes. You will need to put these into a sensible order before your reader can understand them!

Factors contributing to the number of people employed

Your job opportunities can depend on a number of different factors. They can depend on **you** – your skills, your qualifications, your experience. However, they can also depend upon the area in which you live or want to live, or the type of industry in which you want to work. Factors which can influence employment opportunities include:

- historical considerations, i.e. events that have happened in the past to lead a particular industry to become established in one particular area

- geographical considerations, e.g. industries being set up in regions near a port, near the canals, in an area with a lot of natural resources etc.

- cultural considerations, e.g. in some areas there is a tradition of family-run businesses and it may be difficult for an 'outsider' to obtain employment in one of them.

In addition, there are certain factors that affect employment opportunities no matter where you live.

- Industry-wide changes (such as the overall decline of the manufacturing industries and growth of the service industries and/or the introduction of new technology) have taken place throughout the UK.

- The political and economic policies of whichever government is in power also have the power to affect the availability of jobs. If the Government tries to stimulate the economy by giving financial incentives to small businesses, then jobs in that area will grow. If, on the other hand, it encourages growth in the public sector, employment opportunities will increase in areas such health, education and social work.

The information given on the following pages is designed to help you to find out where the greatest job opportunities occur, not just for you but for anyone looking for work.

Growth and decline of manufacturing and services sectors

Start by looking back at Element 1.1 to remind yourself of the difference between manufacturing and service industries, if you have forgotten! A considerable amount of information on the growth and decline of these sectors was included in that element. You will probably find it helpful to read pages 1 to 6 again, before you start this section.

During the 1980s most of the employment growth took place in the service sectors; between 1981 and 1991, service industries increased their employment by over 2.3 million. However, during the recession of the early 1990s the numbers of jobs in the service sector decreased slightly.

As technological changes and pressure to reduce labour costs continue, employment in manufacturing industries is likely to decrease even further, and it has been forecast that between 1993 and 2001:

- jobs in manufacturing will fall by 8 per cent

- jobs in the **private** services sector will rise by 23 per cent.

Did you know?

The **public** services sector covers jobs in areas such as health, education and public administration. During the 1980s employment in this sector grew by 1.3 per cent. However, prospects for further growth depend on government policy, as any cuts in public spending can lead to cuts in employment. Even so, one research team has estimated that about 500 000 jobs will be created between 1993 and 2001, although most of these will be in the health and education areas, not in public administration and defence.

Non-assessed activity

As a group, discuss the possible reasons for the estimated **increase** in jobs in health and education, and the **decrease** in those in public administration and defence.

Information about employment

After all the media coverage about unemployment figures, it may come as a surprise that the number of people in employment has actually increased by about 3.5 million between 1983 and 1990. Despite a slight downturn in numbers between 1990 and 1994, the growth is set to continue.

Did you know?

The Institute for Employment Research at Warwick University has predicted that:

■ between 1993 and 1997 employment will grow by 0.6 per cent per year on average

■ by 2001 an extra 1.6 million jobs will have been created.

Male and female

In recent years, some sections of the workforce have done better than others in finding employment! For instance, the number of women in employment increased between 1983 and 1990 whilst, during the same period, the number of men fell.

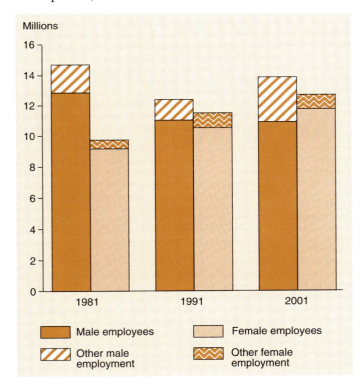

Figure 1.45 Trends in employment in the UK, 1981–2001

Non-assessed activity

1 Display the following information on a pie chart. Remember to use a heading.

In the UK in 1994 there were:

9.6 million male full-time workers
1.1 million male part-time workers
2.5 million male self-employed workers
5.7 million female full-time workers
4.9 million female part-time workers
0.8 million female self-employed workers

2 Read the following extract about the differences in male and female employment and answer the questions below.

Since the early 1960s women's employment has risen almost continuously apart from the recessions of the early 1980s and early 1990s. Conversely, men's employment has fallen during most of that period, apart from a period in the late 1980s.

Over the 1993–2001 period the number of female employees is expected to rise by over 1.2 million, whereas the number of male employees is likely to see a slight fall of something approaching 0.2 million.

In 1981, 42 per cent of employees were women. By 1993 this had increased to 49 per cent. If the further increase goes as predicted, the percentage in 2001 will be just under 52 per cent.

However, given that there will still be a larger number of men who are self-employed, men will still outnumber women in the workforce.

a Has the increase in female employment and the decrease in male employment been continuous (i.e. without any break) throughout the past 20 years?

b What is the significance of the change in percentage of male and female employees by 2001? Will it be a female-dominated workforce?

By age

A lot of research has taken place about the **age** of the workforce.

Non-assessed activity

1 Look at the table in Figure 1.46 and, **as a group**, discuss why:

a the age groups for men and women

differ once they reach 50. (Those for men cover 50–64 and for women 50–59.)

b there are fewer women than men in the 25–49 age group.

	16–24	25–49	50–64 (men) 50–59 (women)
Men	2693	9599	3133
Women	2230	7522	1914

Source: Summer 1994 Labour Force Survey

Figure 1.46 Age of the workforce in Great Britain (thousands)

2 The workforce is gradually growing older.

The number of workers who are over 35 is expected to increase by 1.6 million between 1994 and 2000, which contrasts with a projected fall of 0.9 million in the number of those under 35. The patterns are similar for men and women. In 1994 there were over 800 000 people over retirement age who were still in employment.

As a group, discuss:

a what effect you think this trend may have on **your** job prospects

b what advantages and disadvantages there are – for **everyone** concerned – in having an older workforce. (Think, for instance, about the experience the older worker may have and the fewer claims there may be on the social services if more people continue in work for a longer period of time.)

Write a short paragraph giving your views. Use a word processor if you can.

Percentage employed in manufacturing sectors and service sectors

Recent statistics show that:

■ 18.6 per cent of UK employees work in manufacturing industries

■ 46.9 per cent work in the private services sector

■ 25 per cent work in the public services sector.

In addition:

■ 3.7 per cent work in primary industries and utilities (i.e. in agriculture, mining, electricity, gas or water)

■ 5.8 per cent work in construction.

You should remember from Element 1.1 that the private services sector is often sub-divided into:

distribution, transport and communications	retailing, distribution, hotels and catering, transport and communications
business and other services	banking, finance, insurance, computing and other professional services such as legal services, leisure, recreation and tourism
the public services sector	health, education, public administration and defence.

You might choose a job which can be carried out either within the manufacturing or within the services sector. For example, an accountant might be employed in an engineering firm, a hospital, a large store or a hotel, and a cleaner can clean anywhere. Other jobs, however, tend to be limited to one particular sector. If you want to work in a shop, you will be looking for a job in retail and wholesale, which forms part of the services sector. If you want to be a production engineer you will be looking for a job in the manufacturing sector and so on.

Non-assessed activity

Look at the pie chart in Figure 1.47, which shows a further breakdown of the percentage of jobs in each of the areas and list the following jobs:

a under *either* Manufacturing, Primary and Utilities, Private Services, Public Services or

b under the heading 'All sectors'.

Human resources (Personnel) manager
Waiter
Sales assistant
Quality controller
Warehouse manager
Long distance lorry driver

Public relations officer
Air freight controller
Actor
Cleaner
Production manager
Farmer

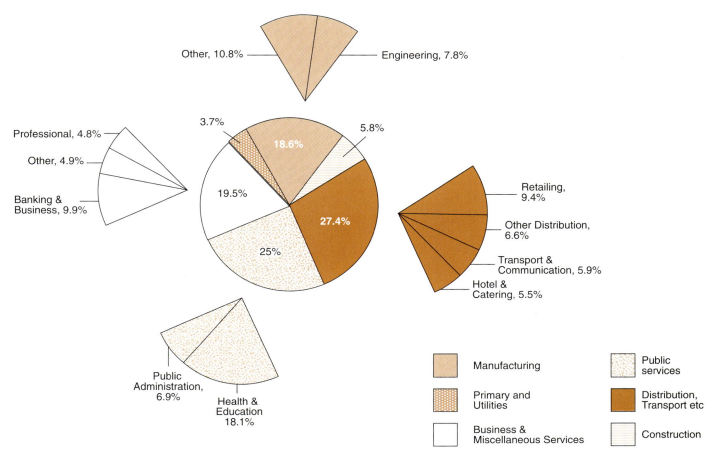

Figure 1.47 Where the jobs are – employees by industry, 1993 (UK)

Information about different regions

The three types of information you can obtain which relate to geographical areas are:

- local information on your own area
- national information on the UK as a whole
- information on the European Union as a whole.

Local information

It is sometimes useful to start by considering the **region** you are in, rather than a specific locality. As you can see from the **regional** statistics in Figure 1.47, there are not many differences in trends from region to region.

Non-assessed activity

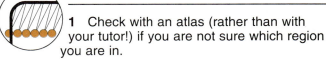

1   Check with an atlas (rather than with your tutor!) if you are not sure which region you are in.

2   There is a marked difference in one area. Can you spot it? Discuss with your tutor possible reasons for it.

Focusing on your own locality

It is probably useful for you to look at your own area in more detail. There are several sources of reference which you can use to check on:

- the number of people who are employed in your area

	Manufacturing %	Private services %	Public services %
Northern Ireland	16	37	33
Scotland	17	45	27
Wales	20	41	27
North West	21	47	25
North	22	41	26
Yorkshire/Humberside	22	43	25
East Midlands	26	41	29
W. Midlands	26	42	23
South West	16	46	26
East Anglia	19	44	24
Greater London	11	60	23
Rest of South East	16	49	25

Figure 1.48 Regional percentage of those working in manufacturing and service sectors

■ the industries in which they are employed.

Your sources include:

■ your school, college or local library
■ your local Training and Enterprise Council (TEC)
■ your local Chamber of Commerce
■ the Economic Development Unit at your town (or county) hall
■ the local Job Centre.

National information

Many of the statistics you will find in reference books and reports relate to the number of people in employment in the UK as a whole. You can look back at this type of information in this element. For instance, if you look at the charts on pages 89 and 90 – which have been subdivided into male and female employment and employment by age – you have the picture for the whole of the UK. If you add the figures together this gives you the overall national picture!

EU information

One of the reasons for the UK entering the European Union was to create more job opportunities both by increasing trade links with other countries and by allowing workers more freedom to work anywhere in the EU.

Throughout this element you will find additional information on the European Union – on unemployment rates, pay, hours of work etc. You can use this as reference for any of your assignments or projects. Your library will also have a range of information on Europe and European business. Try not to get side-tracked into reading about tourism and holiday information when you are looking through it!

Did you know?

Article 48 of the Treaty of Rome (the agreement entered into by the UK when it joined the EU) gave workers the right to look for work anywhere in the EU. However, the Treaty did not provide for the differences in education between countries and it has proved very difficult to compare the qualifications of, say, a worker in Germany with those of a worker in France, etc.

Job opportunities in the EU

Before you pack your bags and set off for Germany, France or wherever takes your fancy, it may be as well if you have some idea of what the job opportunities are in those countries. If unemployment is high, earnings very low or opportunities for one section of the workforce – such as women or part-timers – are limited, that might influence your choice. Since 1985 the number of jobs available has increased in most **Member States** (i.e. countries belonging to the EU) and the number of unemployed has fallen. However, most of the new jobs have been filled not by those who are officially unemployed, but by newcomers to the job market, e.g. women who had never declared themselves officially unemployed and who were therefore never included in the unemployment figures. Many of the new jobs are part-time jobs which don't appeal to everyone. (Look back to page 82 to remind yourself of reasons for wanting to take up part-time work.)

The **active population**, i.e. the number of people who are **either** employed or looking for employment, differs from country to country. It is lowest in Ireland and Spain (at around 38 per cent) and highest in Denmark (at over 56 per cent).

Did you know?

The percentage of the working population in the EU *as a whole* is 45 per cent – lower than in the US or Japan, where it is about 50 per cent.

Non-assessed activity

There are fifteen countries which are members of the European Union – can you name them? To help you, below is a map which shows all the countries. There is also a short quiz for you to try. A brief business summary of each country is given, together with some geographical information and a few hints to help you. Your task is to:

a name the country in each case
b state its capital city.

You should note that the three latest signatories only joined the EU in January 1995. For that reason, on some tables, you may find these countries are not included. Check the dates on your sources.

1 This country has a high population density of 237.8 people per square kilometre. It is a leading industrial

Figure 1.46 Countries in the EU

nation but there has been a broad shift from manufacturing industries to service industries since 1980. At one time it was known as the 'workplace of the world' but its trading position has declined since then. Today its main exports include oil, electronics and financial services. This country is an island so fishing is important but only a small percentage of people are employed in this area. American tourists enjoy visiting here – often because of its history and monarchy.

2 A northern country of Europe, this country is a relative newcomer to the EU. It has an advanced industrial economy and high standards of social welfare – some would say these are very progressive. Much of the country is wooded so paper and furniture account for much of its export. The country also has large deposits of uranium and iron ore.

3 This country borders the North Sea and many of its inhabitants are renowned for being able to speak three languages – English, French and German – as well as their mother tongue. It is a low-lying country with few natural resources but is a high exporter of dairy products, meat, vegetables and flowers. Most industry is concentrated in the Randstad which is only a small area. The country is developing a firm base in computing, telecommunications and biotechnology industries. It has a very famous port which is a major oil terminal.

4 This country is bordered by the sea on its long west and its short south coasts and most of its people are Roman Catholic. Most inhabitants are employed in agriculture, and the main manufacturing industries are textiles and footwear. The north is more prosperous than the south although the country's road links have been modernised since it joined the EU. Tourists are welcomed and often enjoy a cheap and tasty speciality of the area – freshly caught sardines!

5 This member state is bordered by four other European countries and has a very high population density – 328.4 people per square kilometre. Traditional industries include steel, iron, vehicles, textiles and coal mining, although difficulties have been experienced since the recession. This has been serious because the country relies heavily on its export earnings; this country is notable because 70 per cent of all the goods it produces are sold abroad. The centre of the EU is sited here.

6 This country can boast some of the most varied and unspoilt scenery in Europe – from quiet sandy beaches to rugged cliffs. Glorious views are to be found in the south west. It was never industrialised

as much as other countries in Europe and agriculture was the main focus until recent years. It still remains a key industry. Foreign textile, chemical and electronics companies have now invested here. The people are friendly and informal and the proportion of their income spent on food, drink and tobacco is among the highest in the European Union – especially on a dark drink with a creamy top!

7 Another relative newcomer to the EU, this country also lies in the northern reaches of Europe. Its capital is situated to the south of the country, which is not surprising given the climate in the north. The country is highly industrialised; timber and related industries account for 40 per cent of all exports. Agriculture is important despite the very short growing season. This is also the land of the midnight sun in summer! Paper, chemicals, woodworking, metal ores and textiles are other major export industries.

8 This is a popular country for holidaymakers, who first discovered it in the 1970s. It has a major industrialised economy with a large agricultural sector. It joined the EU in 1986. It is famous for its olive oil and wine; its processed foods industry is also important. Many of its traditional industries – shipbuilding, steel and textiles – have declined, but tourism still contributes substantially to the economy.

9 A tiny country with only 390 000 people, this place is still famous for its radio services! It is a prosperous country with a high standard of living and is surrounded by three other European countries. Unemployment is very low – virtually non-existent. Financial services (banking and insurance) are the major features of the economy. Steel was also a key industry, but the Government is encouraging investment from audio-visual equipment and construction companies. Its location at the heart of the EU means it is one of the most popular destinations for conferences and conventions!

10 This country is surrounded by the sea on three sides and has a famous island only three kilometres from its south-east point. It also boasts two famous volcanoes. Its economy is industrialised in the north and agricultural to the south, where its inhabitants are substantially poorer. Exports include industrial machinery, vehicles, aircraft, chemicals, electronics, textiles and clothing. This is Benetton's home ground. The tourism industry is also important; many people visit because of its rich history.

11 One fifth of this country consists of islands – most of which are high on any tourist's agenda. Again rich in historical importance, the country also has many famous buildings. The economy is traditionally agricultural though the industrial sectors of textiles, clothing and shoes, cement, metals, steel and processed agricultural products have developed since it joined the EU. Wheat, barley, maize, tobacco and fruit are also exported. Several famous wealthy shipping magnates come from here!

12 This country is the largest in Europe with nearly 3000 kilometres of coastline. It has the fourth strongest economy in the world after the USA, Japan and Germany. Its industries range from agriculture to advanced technology – it also has a good service sector. Over half the country is devoted to farming, so it is self-sufficient in most foods with enough to export, too. Its nuclear power industry can meet over half its energy requirements. It was a founder member of the EU.

13 This is the smallest Scandinavian country – comprising a peninsula and over 500 islands, some linked to the mainland by ferry or bridge. It has a high standard of living as two-thirds of its produce – mainly cheese, beef and bacon – is exported. Its manufacturing industries include iron, steel, electronics and bio-technology. Food processing and drinks are also important. Most people speak English, which is helpful as its language is very difficult to pronounce!

14 Another newcomer to the EU, this country is land-locked in the middle of Europe. The country consists mainly of mountains so it is popular with tourists – particularly winter-sports lovers. It has low inflation and unemployment rates. Both agriculture and manufacturing are important. Iron and steel, chemicals, metal working and engineering are all important industries. Crops include sugar beet, potatoes, grain, grapes, tobacco and wine.

15 This country has a relatively high population density of 227 people per square kilometres and the strongest economy in Europe. It was a founder member of the EU in 1957. The economy is mainly industrial, with large chemical and car manufacturing plants, mechanical, electrical and electronic engineering and a service sector which includes computing, bio-technology, information processing and the media. It is more prosperous in the west than the east, and the two have only recently been unified. The cost of increasing prosperity in the east will be a decline in the overall economy for at least a decade.

Note: The answers to this quiz are given at the end of the unit.

Optional evidence assignment

*This activity can be carried out, verbally in class **in a group** as a non-assessed activity to consolidate learning. Alternatively, if you do it **on your own**, it can count as supplementary evidence towards the following parts of the scheme.*

PC 2: Collect, analyse and explain information about employment in different regions

Range: Information: percentage employed in manufacturing and service sectors, local

Core skills: Communication

1 **As a class,** divide into **five** groups. Each group must undertake one of the following activities.

  a Visit the college or local library to check the databases for local information.
  b Write to your local TEC.
  c Write to your local Chamber of Commerce.
  d Write to the Economic Development Unit of your town hall or local authority.
  e Contact your local Job Centre.

  Try to find out:

  ■ the percentage of people in employment in your region
  ■ their sex and age
  ■ whether they work in the manufacturing or services sectors.

  Combine all your information into a short report.

2 Carry out a survey of **at least ten** of your friends and relatives to find out:

  a whether they are self-employed, employed or unemployed
  b if employed, whether they are employed full-time or part-time
  c the type of business they work in – and the sector it is in
  d how many people work for their employer (accept an approximate answer, e.g. 'about 200', 'between 20 and 30'.)
  e whether the numbers have increased or decreased during the past two years. Again accept an approximate answer – the people you are asking may only have a rough idea. Examples might be 'We've been laying people off during the past few months', 'We're doing OK – we've been advertising for new staff recently'.

3 Combine your findings as a class. Draw up a simple chart headed 'Employment Trends in ... [your particular area]'. Use the following headings.

  a Number of firms (broken down into firms in the manufacturing and firms in the service sector).
  b Number of people employed in each firm.
  c The employment trend – upward or downward.

4 **On your own**, write a short paragraph describing what you think the overall employment trend is in your area – whether it is declining or growing.

Evidence assignment

At this point your tutor may wish you to start or continue work on the project which will prove to your verifiers that you understand this section of the element. If so, turn to page 118 and do Section 2 of the project. This covers the second Evidence Indicator for this element.

Working conditions

Travel to work

Nowadays a very common seventeenth birthday present is a course of driving lessons. Although 40 years ago it was unusual for anyone who wasn't very well off (and normally middle aged!) to have a car, today a 'set of wheels' is of great importance to almost anyone over seventeen. Not only is it important for social reasons, it can also have a big effect on your job opportunities. If you live in a city you should have access to a number of jobs which might all be within your reach by means of public transport (although you might not like the thought of travelling on a crowded tube during rush hour). If you live in a small town or in the country, your job opportunities might be limited by the transport available to you, although your quality of life may be better. If you have your own car, job opportunities may improve, although you still have to take into account the cost of the petrol, depreciation and maintenance of the vehicle.

Did you know?

Many Training Enterprise Councils (TECs) and colleges now take into account the 'travel to work' area when setting up new training provision, as people who are unemployed cannot be expected to travel great distances to undertake a course of study. One alternative is for them to arrange for classes to be held at out-centres, away from the main campus.

Time

One reason why colleges may set up out-centres is because people cannot afford the time to travel far. Mothers with young children, for example, often have to take them to school and collect them. Therefore they need to be working – or studying – close to home.

Time may influence your choice of transport. Rather than spend hours in a traffic jam you may prefer to travel by public transport and go from one city centre to another relatively quickly by train. Until, of course, there is a breakdown on the line or a strike!

Your domestic commitments are likely to influence the time you are prepared to allow for travelling. An hour travelling to and from work every day adds up to ten extra hours in a week. You may think that it is worth this, however, if you have a super job with great prospects.

Cost

Time and cost are interlinked in that the greater the distance you travel, the higher your travelling costs are likely to be. You may want to work out the difference in costs between different forms of travel – e.g. bus, train and private car (remember to add parking). Probably the cheapest method is to share a car with a colleague who would be going your way anyway!

The cost of travel must be considered in relation to your proposed salary. If you had a job at home which paid £8000 a year (within walking distance or a short bus journey) or one which paid £10 000 but was 30 kilometres away, you need to consider your options carefully. If transport links are good and relatively cheap – and prospects excellent – you may decide to take the more distant job. If the expenditure on travel would be more than the difference in **take-home** pay and prospects were dubious, you may decide not to bother.

Did you know?

Most organisations operate a system of paying travel expenses if cars are used for business purposes, but very few are prepared to pay for travel to and from home. Some organisations will include a company car as part of an overall pay package – although normally you would have to be in a fairly senior position or need the car for business purposes to be entitled to this.

Non-assessed activity

Obviously the cost of travelling a long distance to and from work will influence you in deciding whether to apply for a job in a particular area. There can be other problems, though, affecting whether you choose to work near home or some distance away. Read the script below and, **as a group,** discuss the questions which follow.

Des: I'd love to work in the city like you – it's like being buried alive out here in this place.

Andy: It's OK. I like my job and I wouldn't get a similar one round here – but there are snags. I have to be up at half-past six and don't get home until seven at night. My girlfriend is going mad.

Des: Do you travel by car or by train?

Andy: I've tried both. Car is better – for obvious reasons – but the traffic is impossible at rush hours, and I'm not sure how healthy it is, sitting hour after hour, breathing in all those exhaust fumes.

Des: Why not go by train then?

Andy: You can't always be sure of a seat – and in winter there are problems caused by the weather. In any case I have to take the car to the station, and it costs a fair bit to park in the official car park. What's also difficult is that I've got to keep an eye on the clock towards the end

of the day to see that I get to the station on time. If my boss calls me in to speak to me late in the afternoon I can hardly concentrate because I'm afraid I'll miss the train.

Des: We've both got our problems, then! I don't have to worry about travel but I do have to worry about money – and promotion prospects. You earn more now and you're bound to earn more in the future. I'm stuck.

1 What are the advantages and disadvantages of:

   a working in your home town (however small)
   b having to travel to work?

2 What might be done to resolve the disadvantages of having to travel? See further information on **flexitime** in Element 2.1, page 00 for one possible solution!

Job mobility

One difficulty, even if you do find a job near home or within your travel-to-work area, is that at some time in the future you may be expected to transfer to another branch of the organisation, some distance away. You may not want to do this.

Much depends on whether you have agreed that you would move as and when required. You may have signed an agreement which contains a **job mobility** clause, in which you agree to work anywhere in the UK – or even anywhere in the world if you happen to work for an international organisation! In that case you may find it difficult to refuse to move. However, even without such an agreement you must be careful not to agree **implicitly** (by implication) to a move.

Suppose, for instance, you once went to work on a building site with a group of workers who were employed to build a housing estate. When the work was completed you moved with them to another site, and so on. There may come a time when you don't feel like moving around any more and you refuse to do so. Even if you have not expressly agreed in your contract to move, you might find that you are judged to have implicitly agreed because you have always moved before, and because the very nature of your job suggests that you will have to move to stay in work.

Physical conditions

Even when you actually get to work – by whatever means – you will find that different places of employment have different physical conditions.

There is a vast difference between the physical conditions experienced by a bank clerk and a farmer. The first works in a clean, heated and – probably – attractively decorated and carpeted building, and he or she deals with other members of staff and customers, so there is a 'social' aspect to the work. The hours are probably relatively predictable and standard, e.g. 9 am to 5.30 pm. Holidays can be planned in advance and can be arranged, within reason, to suit the employee. The work is clean and safe and employees will therefore wear quite formal, smart clothes.

Contrast this with the farmer who works outdoors in all weathers, may have little or no contact with other people for much of the day, has to work a long day – especially if there is a dairy herd needing to be milked – and at certain times, such as harvest time, may work almost around the clock. Holidays are difficult if not impossible to organise. The work may be dirty and sometimes involve the use of dangerous chemicals. Old clothes would be standard wear – with special protective clothing when necessary.

Did you know?

The term **working conditions** is sometimes used to describe physical conditions. However, it is also used to describe the particular benefits of certain jobs, e.g. rates of pay, hours, holidays, eligibility for sick pay, pension schemes and redundancy pay. As you can see, hours and holidays can be included in both. However, in the case of physical conditions we are concerned more with *extremes*, e.g. having to work long or unsocial hours. Working conditions are dealt with in full on page 99.

Physical conditions can vary tremendously:

- between industries
- within industries, and
- within one organisation!

Between industries

For a moment, think about the difference in physical conditions experienced by a motorway construction worker and an electronics engineer. You might know very little about electronics companies or electronic engineering – but you should realise, at the very least, that one worker will be working outside, exposed to the elements, and the other will not! The motorway worker is doing a job which is strenuous and dirty, and will wear clothes which reflect this. In contrast, in parts of the electronics industry people work in special 'clean' rooms where dust is kept to a minimum. The operators wear nylon suits to prevent dust from their clothes contaminating the components, and they have to pass through a changing room to get to their work.

In some industries the work is particularly arduous and conditions may even be hot and dangerous, e.g. in an iron foundry or steel mill.

Did you know?

■ Protective clothing is widespread in all types of industries and is not just restricted to safety hats or safety shoes.
Male workers in drug companies producing the contraceptive pill have to wear special overalls to prevent them being affected by the female hormones in the pill itself.

■ People who work in very hot conditions – or operate welding equipment or work near high temperature gas-fired ovens – sometimes have special 'relaxation periods' built into their job, so that they can cool down at regular intervals.

Within industries

In manufacturing, probably more than in any other sector, physical conditions between different organisations may vary. One factory may be modern and airy and situated on a new industrial estate, another may be in a run-down area, possibly in an old converted mill with several storeys.

Did you know?

The Health and Safety Executive (HSE) is responsible for standards of safety in factories and for appointing inspectors to check that *all* organisations comply with safety legislation such as the Health and Safety at Work Act 1974 and the Control of Substances Hazardous to Health (1988). Health and Safety legislation is covered in more detail in Element 1.2 and on page 105.

Within organisations

If you have never been in a factory, you may have only a very hazy idea of what it is like. The first thing you would probably notice is that either different buildings – or different areas of the same building – are used for different purposes.

Production is carried out in large rooms usually called the 'shop floor'. The size of the shop floor will depend on the product being made and the scale of operations. A large car factory may have an enormous assembly area, a small plastics factory – which makes items such as the outer casing for ball point pens – may have a much smaller area. Some assembly areas are noisy, others are quiet and streamlined. Some have individual workers operating different machines, others have a continuous or automated process.

In contrast, the administration work will be carried out in offices which may be situated in a different block, away from the production areas. These may be small and cramped or large, spacious and airy. They may be purely functional, with a basic desk and filing cabinet, or designed to impress important clients, with carpets, 'executive' furniture and paintings on the walls. There might be a mixture: it is doubtful that the main offices and the managing director's office will be decorated and furnished in exactly the same style!

Some jobs require people to move around both within and between different buildings. A maintenance engineer would go to different departments to deal with machine breakdowns. A salesperson may travel 300 kilometres or more in a day visiting customers.

Optional evidence assignment

This activity can be carried out verbally, in class in a group as a non-assessed activity to consolidate learning. Alternatively, if you do it on your own, it can count as supplementary evidence towards the following parts of the scheme.

PC 3: Compare working conditions for employees in different organisations

Range: Working conditions: physical conditions

Core skills: Communication

During your course try to arrange to go on visits to **two** factories. If possible, these should be in totally different industries.

Whilst you are there make notes about the areas you visit, the work carried out there and the physical conditions in each case.

Use a word processor to produce a report which compares and contrasts the different areas in each factory and also compares both organisations. Try to link your findings to the type of product made by each company and the stages required in its manufacture.

Service industries

If you look back at the chart on page 91, you will see that this sector contains a wide variety of occupations and therefore incorporates very different physical conditions. Transport drivers, postmen and policemen often work outdoors, insurance workers, teachers and those in the medical profession usually work indoors. Retail work is probably the most varied – from a market stall to a department store.

Non-assessed activity

Select *either* **two** contrasting occupations in commercial services *or* **two** contrasting occupations in personal services.

1 Evaluate the physical conditions which apply for each occupation.

2 *Either*

   a State how these may change if a job holder gains promotion (e.g. from police constable to inspector or from student nurse to nurse manager).

   or

   b State how these can vary *within* the occupation you have chosen (e.g. the various jobs within the postal or telecommunications industry).

Hours of work

Whatever the nature of the work, you will almost certainly be expected to work an agreed number of hours. In most cases these are agreed between you and your employer. So, too, is the way in which you work them. See Element 2.1, page 147 for details of various working arrangements.

However, this freedom is affected to a certain extent by:

social pressures	– employees like to have a say in what hours they work and the times they work them.
economic pressures	– employers want to remain competitive and have therefore to be able to respond quickly to a demand for longer opening hours or increased productivity by means of the introduction of shifts, etc.

Obviously these two pressure... conflict. Trade unions have ne... reduction in the length of the w... years. In the past, limitations on ...mes cause hours worked – particularly those ... and young people – were imposed b...ual in recent years many of these restricti...the repealed and regulation of working tim...the normally negotiated through the unions... collective agreements (see Element 2.2).

Non-assessed activity

Evidence suggests that recent reductions in the working week have, in many places, had no effect on the actual working hours of individuals, as overtime working has been increased to make up the reductions. **As a group,** discuss the possible harm this may cause to both employer and employee.

EU Working Time Directive

The European Union has issued a Working Time Directive which proposes a maximum 48-hour week. As the table below indicates the average total weekly hours of employees tends to be lower than that, in every EU country.

Average working hours per week of full-time employees

	Average weekly hours
Belgium	38.0
Denmark	39.0
France	39.6
Germany	39.9
Greece	40.1
Ireland	40.4
Luxembourg	39.9
Netherlands	39.0
Portugal	41.9
Spain	40.7
UK	43.7

Note that full-time UK employees work the *longest* average weekly hours of all employees throughout the community!

People in the UK work the longest hours

The picture is not the same for one section of the working population. In 1990 approximately 25 million people in the EU were either self-employed or family workers (nearly one fifth of all employed people), and most of these people tended to work much longer than 48 hours a week.

Average working hours per week of self-employed people in the EU

	Average weekly hours
Belgium	54.6
Denmark	54.5
France	54.9
Germany	55.4
Greece	50.3
Ireland	60.5
Italy	46.2
Luxembourg	54.2
Netherlands	58.3
Portugal	52.6
Spain	46.7
UK	52.6

Part-time employment

Obviously those people working under arrangements which are not regarded as full-time will work a varying number of hours, and a lot depends on the individual working arrangements.

Did you know?

One reason for some workers wishing to work fewer hours is the National Insurance (NI) system. If your weekly pay falls below what is known as the Lower Earnings Limit (LEL) neither you nor your employer pays NI. Again, in some cases it is better for tax reasons that a person works short hours (so that he or she pays no income tax or a very small amount) rather than work extra hours and pay more tax on the additional income.

Non-assessed activity

Look at the table on page 101, which gives a list of 23 UK organisations which employ part-time workers and the ways in which they do so. Then answer the questions which follow.

1 List the total number of organisations which employ part-timers:

   a over 16 hours per week
   b 8–15 hours per week
   c less than 8 hours
   d during term time
   e as job sharers.

2 Write a short paragraph giving **at least one** reason (in your opinion) for the **most** popular type of part-time arrangement used by employers and **one** reason for the **least** popular.

3 As a student, you may be working in a part time job – or looking for one. Write a short paragraph saying which type of part time work you would personally prefer – and why it would suit you best.

Did you know?

Not all workers work a five-day week. One recent survey showed that in the UK 8.6 per cent of all people in employment (about 2.2 million people) work seven days per week.

	Job share	16 hrs or more	8–15 hrs	Under 8 hrs	Term time
Chemicals Co.					
1		*			
2	*	*			
3		*			
4				*	
Building Co.					
1	*	*		*	
2	*		*		
Electricity, gas & water Co.					
1	*	*	*	*	
2		*	*	*	
3		*	*		
4	*	*	*		
Engineering Co.					
1		*			
2		*	*		
3		*			
4		*			
5		*	*		
6		*	*	*	
Finance Co.					
1	*	*	*	*	*
2	*	*			*
3	*	*			
4		*	*		
Food, drink & tobacco Co.					
1		*	*	*	
2		*			
3		*	*		

Figure 1.50 Survey of part-time working practices in 23 UK organisations

Non-assessed activity

The percentage of people working seven days a week rises to about 25 per cent in the case of the self-employed. **As a group,** discuss the possible reasons for this.

Did you know?

1 The EU Working Time Directive proposes that a minimum of one day's rest per week be averaged over two weeks.

2 Sunday working in the UK is already quite common. Four-fifths of establishments across all industries open in some capacity on a Sunday. Even the banks have plans for Sunday openings, although the

NWSA – one of the bank unions – claiming that there should be staff and negotiations over spec... in favour, with

Holiday entitlement

Most EU states have legislation which se... the minimum levels of paid holiday entit... The exceptions are the UK, which has none... Italy, which specifies the right to a holiday b... gives no minimum entitlement. However, in m... most workers *are* given paid holidays, particularly if they are full-time workers. Typically, they receive four to five weeks' (25 days) annual leave; this tends to increase the longer they work for a particular organisation. The following table shows the holiday entitlement of workers in many of the EU countries.

	Annual leave (days)	Public holidays
Belgium	20	13.5
Denmark	25	10
France	25	11
Germany	15	11
Greece	20–22	13
Ireland	15	9
Italy	–	11
Luxembourg	25	12
Netherlands	20	9
Portugal	15–21	13
Spain	25	13
UK	–	8

Figure 1.51 Holiday entitlement in the EU

Non-assessed activity

Imagine that, over the past few years, you have written regularly to two friends – one living in Denmark and one in Greece. Both are now interested in working in the UK if possible. Your Greek friend wants to open his own business and your Danish friend wants to find a job. They have heard that working life in the UK is very easy when compared to work in Denmark and Greece. Write a paragraph to be included

...each of them. Tell them why they ...set about the hours they may have to ...holidays they can expect.

When you first start work you may think that this is the most important feature of the job! There are two ways in which you can calculate pay – firstly in terms of your wages, and secondly in terms of any extra payments you might receive.

Wages

The terms **wages** and **salaries** are sometimes used to mean the same thing. The most common way of distinguishing between them used to be as follows.

- **Wage** is the term usually used for the money paid to manual workers who are paid every week, normally on a Friday. Wages can vary from week to week, since manual workers can be paid according to how hard or long they work. Manual workers can also be asked to work on Saturdays and/or Sundays and be paid overtime. Wages consist of a basic rate or flat rate with additions for overtime or bonus payments.
- **Salary** is the term usually used for the money paid to clerical and managerial staff who are paid once a month. Some companies pay every four weeks (thirteen times a year); others pay every calendar month (twelve times a year). Salaried staff may be expected to work late *without* being paid overtime.

Today, the distinction between wages and salaries is becoming more blurred. For instance, how would you define a clerk in the administration section who receives a weekly payment?

The average weekly earnings of all full-time adult employees are at present approximately £325 per week, but there are some differences in the earnings paid to men and women and to those working in different occupations and industries.

Non-assessed activity

Look at Figure 1.52, which shows the average earnings of men and women in manual and non-manual occupations.

	£
All men	362.1
Men in manual occupations	280.7
Men in non-manual occupations	428.2
All women	261.5
Women in manual occupations	181.9
Women in non-manual occupations	278.4

Figure 1.52 Average gross weekly earnings

As a group, discuss why:

- men still earn more money than women
- manual workers earn less than non-manual workers.

Did you know?

It has been claimed by one researcher that the gap in pay between male and female workers is closing more slowly in the UK than in almost any other EU country (with the exception of Luxembourg).

Regional pay rates

In the UK, the highest earners are concentrated in the south east, particularly in Greater London where the average weekly wage is £415. The lowest paying part of the country is Cornwall, where the average weekly wage is just £265. Earnings in Wales and Scotland are also low – in seven out of the eight Welsh counties and six out of the nine Scottish regions, average earnings are below £300 a week.

However, according to some experts the north–south wage gap is beginning to narrow and it is forecast that both male and female earnings in Greater London – which raced ahead of the rest of the country in the 1980s – will rise more slowly than in any other region until 1999!

High earnings

What is worrying some people is the growing gap between the rich and the poor, as the two following examples indicate.

- The weekly earnings of a doctor rose from £499 in 1971 to £746 in 1994.
- The weekly earnings of a waiter rose from £105 in 1971 to £157 in 1994.

Some concern has been expressed about the very high salaries which have recently been paid to top managing directors of both private and public-sector organisations. A City task force (backed by the Confederation of British Industry, the Stock Exchange, the Association of British Insurers and the Institute of Directors) has been formed to draw up a code of practice. It will try to ensure that pay levels are set by independent directors, that the firms make their policy public, and that directors are seen actually to be working for their money.

Non-assessed activity

1   Divide into **two groups.** In the first group, spend five minutes deciding on an argument in favour of imposing a top limit on any salary (so that even the most important managing director could not receive above a certain amount). In the second group, spend the same amount of time deciding on an argument in favour of allowing organisations to pay their top people any sum they wish (to keep them in the company, to improve profits, etc.). Choose a spokesperson from each group to present each argument (using a flipchart where possible). Ask the course tutor to decide which argument is the more convincing!

2   Read the following extract from an article about the gap between high and low wage earners. Then answer the questions which follow.

'The gap between rich and poor is now very wide and there are no signs of it lessening. Since 1977 the proportion of the population with less than half the average income has more than trebled. The poorest 20–30 per cent of the population have failed to share in economic growth since 1979, with the experience of poverty much higher in the non-white population.

'Reasons for this rise include:

- growing unemployment – more people are on income support
- growth in the number of single parents
- difference in wage rises for the poor, for middle-income earners and richer members of society.

'There is also a growing difference between the "work rich" and 'work poor" households. Between 1975 and 1993 the number of two-adult households where both adults work has jumped from 51 per cent to 60 per cent, while the proportion with no earner increased from 3 per cent to 11 per cent. This was because it has become progressively harder to find work, leading to longer periods of unemployment, particularly for people without a working partner.

'One of the groups most affected by these changes is the young. While those working in the upper and middle part of the wage scale can expect to earn more than those in earlier generations at the same stage in their career, those in the bottom 10 per cent who were born after 1960 earn real wages below those earned by their predecessors.'

a   List the reasons for the growing difference in the wage rates for the rich and for the poor.
b   Write a sentence explaining what is meant by 'work rich' and 'work poor' households.
c   Write a paragraph identifying the **two** groups most affected by the difference in wage rates. Try to give a reason for this.

Minimum wage

Many European countries try to look after their lower wage earners by insisting on a minimum wage limit. The UK does not.

Did you know?

Until recently the Wages Councils, which covered 2.3 million low-paid workers, had the right to impose a minimum wage rate. However, these councils have now been abolished.

Non-assessed activity

Read the following extract from an article about the minimum wage and draw up a list of the advantages and disadvantages of insisting that employers pay a minimum wage rate. Type out your answers using a word processor.

A national minimum wage

'The most usual arguments in favour of a national minimum wage are that it addresses the issue of low pay directly and ensures that everyone in work at least gets a basic level of pay, that poverty is reduced and that there is a fairer balance between employer and employee with little or no effect on jobs.

'In support of this argument some people point to other developed countries which have minimum wage structures without any ill effect on jobs.

'However, there are problems. European countries such as France, Belgium and the Netherlands have minimum wages which are high relative to average earnings. But Britain achieved a faster rate of employment growth than those countries – and those countries have a higher rate of youth unemployment than the UK (in France the rate is nearly twice as high). One research body has concluded that minimum wages hit the young particularly hard. In a free labour market, employers may choose to take them on at lower wages to compensate for the fact that they are less productive and need training. Faced with an across-the-board minimum wage, the scope to do so is reduced.'

Earnings in the EU

The amount you can earn differs enormously between member states. However, you may find it difficult to compare how much you would earn as an office worker in various countries simply because you would be paid in different currencies – francs, guilders etc. To help you, a formula called the purchasing power standard (PPS) has been established which can, for instance, tell you that the hourly earnings of a manual worker in Denmark are at present 11.90 PPS but only 3.76 PPS in Portugal (almost a third of the Danish figure).

Non-assessed activity

Look at the table in Figure 1.55 which gives the comparative earning rates of some of the EU Member States.

As a group, discuss:

1 where you would look for the best paid jobs as:

   a an assembly worker
   b a production manager
   c an office manager.

2 where you would perhaps avoid if you were:

   a a secretary
   b a purchasing officer
   c a garage mechanic.

Check with your tutor if you are not sure what is meant by manual or white-collar work.

	Assembly workers workers (per hour)	Industrial white collar workers (per month)	Commerial white collar workers (per month)
Belgium	9.30	2 360	1 779
Denmark	10.63	1 928	–
Germany	10.41	2 538	1 793
Greece	4.80	1 315	712
Spain	7.48	1 725	1 129
France	7..13	2 062	1 553
Ireland	8.62	2 333	–
Italy	–	–	–
Luxembourg	8.31	–	–
Netherlands	9.30	2 120	1 685
Portugal	3.37	1 029	722
UK	9.03	2 418	2 052

Figure 1.53 Comparative earning rates of the EU member states in 1992 – all figures in PPS per month

Your pay

No matter what anyone else is paid, when you start work you will be interested first and foremost in what **you** are to be paid. You will want to know:

- how much you are going to be paid
- whether you will be paid hourly, weekly or monthly
- the 'perks' or additional benefits you may get
- the National Insurance and income tax you will have to pay out of your salary (unless you earn a very small amount each week).

Unless you understand how these systems operate you cannot check your own pay or know what to do if something is wrong. It is therefore in your own interest that you understand how both National Insurance and the PAYE income tax system operate.

Did you know?

One of the jobs of a trade union is to negotiate rates of pay (see Element 2.2, page 166 for other duties of trade union officials). However, during the second half of the 1980s 'collective bargaining', as it is called, decreased in importance and less than half of all employees now have their pay determined in such a way. Collective bargaining is more likely to be used for public-sector employees than for the private sector.

Extra payments

Usually, the higher up the organisational ladder you climb the more likely it is that you will be paid a fixed salary. However, additional payments which may be made to employees include:

- **commission**, which may be paid on top of a basic salary (the method often used to pay sales staff, so that the more they sell, the higher their commission); or at a high rate *instead* of a wage or salary; so that in a bad week nothing will be earned
- **bonus payments** paid to staff as a reward for higher productivity or extra effort at a busy time of year
- **profit-sharing** schemes, organised by some companies, in which employees receive a share in any profits made and announced at the end of the year
- **expenses** – strictly speaking these are not really an additional payment, as the employee might only be being reimbursed for money he or she has already spent (e.g. on petrol or entertaining).

Other ways of linking your pay to the work you actually do include:

- extra payment if you have been appraised or assessed by a senior member of staff as deserving rewards for working extra hard
- payment for being a member of a group where certain targets have been achieved, such as when a selling team meets its sales targets, and every member of the team receives some extra pay.

Did you know?

British Gas have recently reorganised their pay system so that their employees have a lower rate of basic pay but are expected to earn more through commission.

Deductions

The total amount an employee earns from all sources is known as **gross** pay. Unfortunately for the employee, however, the total wage or salary has to have various amounts taken out. These are known as **deductions.** The pay which is then taken home (i.e. gross pay *minus* deductions) is known as **net** pay.

For further information about deductions see Element 2.2, page 198.

Safety

The basics about the Health and Safety at Work Act were covered in Element 1.2. Check to make sure you understand the rules.

You may like the idea of working:

- in a factory
- in a manufacturing organisation in a job involving the use of heavy machinery
- on a North Sea Gas rig
- in a garage
- in the parks and gardens department of the local council
- in a restaurant
- in a bank
- in an office.

Whatever area you choose, when you start work you will be given quite a lot of information about health and safety rules and regulations. If you have found work in one of the first four areas (or even the fifth or sixth) you should certainly be very interested in what these rules are, since if you don't pay attention to them you could be injured or even killed. If you work in a bank or an office, however, you might feel inclined to be less interested – after all, what's dangerous about working in a bank or office? If you later find yourself lying in a hospital bed with a broken leg, a scalded arm or a strained back, however, caused by an accident at work, you might wish you had paid a bit more attention.

Any workplace can be dangerous. The law recognises this and has placed a big responsibility on employers to make sure that their premises are safe. However, the law also imposes an obligation upon you as the employee to look after yourself and the people you work with (see also elements 1.2 and 2.2).

Did you know?

1   Fatal accidents to the public in supermarkets, DIY stores, hotels, launderettes and other service sector premises have doubled in the past three years. The number of serious injuries has also risen.

2 Even your lunch break may be hazardous. The National Consumer Council says that diet-related diseases kill more people each year than smoking, alcohol, accidents and AIDS all put together. Apart from the obvious dangers of overeating and of eating fatty foods, there are other dangers – the Consumers' Association magazine *Which?* has found that 31 out of 36 takeaway salads bought from six restaurants with self-service bars in and around London were contaminated in some way.

Potential hazards

What exactly is there to worry about if you work in an office or similar place of work?

Office furniture and equipment

Experts in **ergonomics** – the science of designing 'people-friendly' workplaces – think that the manufacturers of office furniture and equipment quite often do not take into account the needs of the people who will be using them. For instance, it is now thought unhealthy for workers to sit in front of a keyboard and computer screen all day – if they do so, they might suffer from back problems, wrist injuries or eyestrain. Other concerns relate to:

- headaches and migraine
- using VDUs when pregnant.

See Information Technology Core Skills chapter.

Did you know?

1 According to experts, typing on a traditional typewriter does not cause the same problems as keying on a computer. No matter how good a typist you are, you cannot normally type as fast as you would be expected to key data into a computer – and with a typewriter you are not tempted to stare at a screen for hours on end.

2 A recent study at the University of California showed that the average keyboard user performs 10 000–80 000 mouse clicks a week, with users of more mouse-intensive applications such as graphics software being most at risk.

3 A paper published by the Swedish Work Environment Fund states that emissions from computer monitors can affect not only eyes but also tooth fillings! Those working in computing departments were also found to be more likely to develop skin problems.

Repetitive strain injury (RSI)

Sometimes the term RSI is used to describe wrist injuries suffered by users of computer keyboards. Some sufferers have sued their employers for compensation, on the grounds that it is an industrial injury. However, in a recent case a judge held that RSI was not 'in itself a condition known to medical science'.

Did you know?

The condition known as RSI is not a new disease. Doctor Bernadino Ramazzini first described it 280 years ago.

Back strain

Computer keyboard operators can suffer back trouble if they spend too long at the keyboard. However, there can be other reasons for bad backs. A considerable number of workers each year injure their backs by carrying objects which are too heavy for them or which they have lifted in the wrong way. It has been estimated that in 1994 81.3 million working days were lost because of absences through back injuries, compared with 67 million the year before and 59 million the year before that!

Did you know?

Bad backs are not confined to adults. The National Back Pain Association has set up a working party to look into the problem of pupils at school injuring their backs through having to carry books around all day at school, rather than being given a locker or desk in which to keep them.

Falls

Many injuries are caused by workers tripping over and falling. Few workers have to face as high a risk as construction workers – who stand a 1 in 500 chance of falling to their deaths if they stay in the job throughout their working lives! However, other workers – including office workers – have found themselves suffering broken arms or legs caused by tripping over uneven surfaces, open drawers of filing cabinets, etc.

Faulty equipment

When you switch on your computer at work you probably don't realise that you might be carrying out quite a risky action. The Electricity at Work Regulations say that a company must check its electrical equipment – but they don't say how the equipment should be checked or what tests should be carried out. Employers know, however, that if there is an accident at work, the first question that will be asked is when the equipment was last checked. (For details of employers' responsibilities towards their employees see Element 2.2.) Large organisations have their own health and safety officers and specially trained maintenance staff to carry out such work. Smaller organisations can struggle.

Did you know?

To help smaller organisations, a computer software package has been devised to check all portable electrical equipment, from electric fans and kettles to modern high-tech equipment. It consists of a machine which reads bar codes, an instrument for testing electrical equipment and a laptop computer. A bar code is fixed to each item of a client's electrical equipment. Details, including the type of equipment, are fed on to a disc. The equipment is then passed as safe or the system explains where it is at fault. All the information can be downloaded on to the client's own computer to give a full record, including the value of each item of equipment.

Sick building syndrome

Today most organisations look very carefully at the way in which any new buildings are designed or new work areas are laid out. If, for instance, a new reception area is being planned to which both staff and members of the general public have access, the architects and designers will have to take care to build in every type of fire precaution – smoke alarms, fire alarms, sprinkler systems, fire extinguishers, fire-resistant self-closing doors, fireproof furnishings, fire door notices etc. Other safety precautions will be needed, such as good lighting (with provision for emergency lighting if the main lighting fails), anti-slip floor coverings and stair treads, handrails, wide double doors, solid safety rails etc.

In addition, increasing attention is paid nowadays to certain safety hazards which, in the past, might have been ignored. **Sick building syndrome** is a term used to describe buildings which are considered to cause illness in staff. In some buildings, for instance, staff have complained about headaches, dizziness, tiredness, nausea, skin rashes and eye irritations. The following possible causes have been suggested:

- poor air conditioning
- poor ventilation
- fumes from photocopiers or other equipment
- dust from carpets and furnishings
- ineffective lighting
- lack of control for staff over their own comfort level.

Health and safety legislation

Some (although by no means all) of these problems have been addressed by the Health and Safety at Work Act 1974 (and subsequent legislation) and also by EU Health and Safety Directives which lay down certain standards on equipment, seating and lighting.

- All chairs must be capable of swivelling up and down to varying levels and be on a movable base (i.e. castors). They should be comfortable and have adjustable back rests to give support.
- VDU desks must not reflect light, must be 68 cm high and large enough to hold all the equipment plus any paperwork.
- Keyboards must be separate from VDUs and adjustable to lie flat or slope upwards at an angle

between 10° and 15°. The keys should have a matt finish. Good keyboard design is essential to reduce of prevent the chance or RSI. Keys should be concave to reduce the risk of fingers slipping off them and to reduce the shock on the fingertips, fingers, wrists and arms.

■ VDU screens must be adjustable in terms of the angle at which they are positioned and the brightness and contrast of the screen. The screen should be non-reflective and flicker-free.

The directives also include the right for VDU operators to:

■ have a free eye test prior to VDU work and regularly thereafter
■ have regular rest breaks
■ be involved in discussions about the design of workstations.

In addition employers must comply with:

■ the Manual Handling Operations Regulations 1992, which requires employers to take a variety of measures to avoid or reduce the dangers of back injury related to heavy lifting
■ the Management of Health and Safety at Work Regulations 1992, which requires employers to assess the possibility of risks to the health and safety of their employees.

Did you know?

In 1995 Microsoft launched its new natural keyboard. The new keyboard looks and feels quite different from the standard

Figure 1.54 Microsoft's natural keyboard

keyboard. The keys are divided into two distinct groups, one resting under each hand. The space bar and command keys are far larger than on a standard keyboard. The layout is supposed to help the user to adopt a more natural and comfortable posture. It encourages the typist to type properly rather than pecking at the keys with one or two fingers. The keyboard's front can be raised or lowered to allow for differing desk heights, and it incorporates a sloping wrist rest to support the hands when not typing. Other companies are offering the same sort of facility.

Non-assessed activity

1   The new EU legislation only applies where computer screens are 'habitually used'. There have been protests about this, particularly by some unions. **As a group**, discuss why they aren't happy about this restriction.

2   Imagine you are employed as an assistant in the Human Resources Department of Quantum Electronics. The Human Resources Manager is Ms Margery Stevens. The company employs several staff as VDU operators and has recently changed its policy in line with the EU directives. In future all operators will:

■ receive a free eye test at regular periods
■ have regular breaks away from their machines.

In addition, the main office areas where VDUs are sited have been redecorated and new lighting and new workstations have been installed.

To make sure that all employees know why these measures have been taken, and understand other important aspects of working with VDUs and health and safety, Ms Stevens has decided to hold a short training session for all VDU staff tomorrow afternoon. She has asked you and your colleagues to help with the following tasks.

a   Carry out your own research on this subject, both from the information provided and from that available in the library. She has suggested that you might like to obtain additional information by contacting your local Health and Safety Executive (HSE) office. The address is in your phone book.
b   Prepare a short (ten minute) presentation to highlight the main points. Use visual aids such as overhead transparencies to make your main points.

Tiredness

There's quite a difference between feeling tired because you haven't gone to bed early enough the night before and feeling exhausted because the job has become too much for you. One reason for your tiredness may simply be the hours you work. Many people work a set number of hours per day or week (remind yourself about the general pattern in the UK by looking back to page 99). Others work shifts – some people entirely on night shifts. All these are common working patterns and generally cause no difficulties. Problems can occur, however, where:

- the hours of work are very long – in recent months there has been a lot of publicity given to the hours worked by junior hospital doctors. A train crash in Clapham also highlighted the long hours worked by many transport employees. The large number of hours worked by many lorry drivers has resulted in lorries being fitted with equipment to check how many hours they are actually on the road – and a legal limit is placed on this.
- the pattern of work is irregular, i.e. not a standard working day – leading to disrupted sleep patterns. If you are working from 6 am to 2 pm every day one week, 2 pm to 10 pm the next and 10 pm to 6 am the next, your body is going to have to adjust to sleeping at different times – and sometimes this is difficult.

Non-assessed activity

The interest in the hours worked by the doctors, transport workers and lorry drivers has arisen not only because of concern for their personal welfare. What other reason can you, as a group, suggest for this anxiety?

Did you know?

A House of Lords Select Committee has looked into the question of working time and has suggested that the law should be changed to ban staff from working very long hours when health and safety is at risk. It placed special emphasis on jobs where the workers' tiredness puts not only them, but also the public at risk – pilots, doctors, security staff, bus and train drivers, etc.

Stress

Some workers face the problem not only of physical but of mental tiredness – now normally referred to as **work related** or **occupational** stress. In one US survey 72 per cent of 600 full-time workers said that they suffered from stress related symptoms such as anxiety, sleeplessness, and headaches, and the situation is much the same in the UK according to experts at Manchester Institute of Science and Technology.

Non-assessed activity

Mariam, Ahmed, Marie, Martin and Lawrence all work in the same large store.

- Mariam works on the check-out till. There is little variety in the work she does and – apart from short breaks morning and afternoon and her lunch break – she does not move from her working area all day.
- Ahmed is a trainee manager. He had to undergo a very stiff selection procedure to get the job and he knows he is very lucky to have been among the fifteen out of one hundred applicants to have been offered a job. He is very anxious to keep it.
- Marie works in the Complaints Department and her supervisor often leaves her to work on her own for long periods. She has to deal with dissatisfied customers all day long.
- Martin works in the warehouse. It is very warm and the noise from the delivery vehicles is deafening, making it difficult for him to concentrate. He has to shout to make himself heard.
- Lawrence is employed on a fixed-term contract which comes up for renewal at the end of the year.

1 List the pressures you think may be affecting each of these five people.

2 **As a group**, discuss some possible solutions, other than going off sick! Bear in mind the development of new skills to increase job opportunities, the need to discuss problems with other people, and possible solutions to those problems, the need for leisure interests etc.

Did you know?

Research has shown that stress counselling works. A study of Post Office employees in the North showed a 66 per cent reduction in staff absences after counselling sessions had taken place.

Job security

When your grandparents first began work they faced the possibility of either:

a learning a skill and staying with one employer virtually all their working lives or

b losing their jobs because of high unemployment.

Your parents were probably luckier in that they may have started work at a time when employment was quite easy to get. They might have learned a skill or gained a professional qualification which they hoped would be of use to them (and probably was) for a long time.

Nowadays, however, the position has changed. There is no guarantee that you will find a job for life or that one skill or one qualification will last you for ever. You should be prepared therefore constantly to update your skills (see Element 2.4).

Unemployment

Many people have to face the prospect of unemployment at some stage in their working life.

Employment levels

The total number of people who work in Britain is called the **working population.** This does not include everyone – some people are too old, too young or too infirm to go out to work. In other cases people want to stay at home, for example, some mothers of young children do not go out to work. Look back to page 89 to remind yourself of the number of people at present employed in the UK.

If you subtract from the total working population the total of people who are employed, you end up with the total number unemployed.

The level of unemployment will increase if firms are laying off people more quickly than these people can find alternative employment. The level of unemployment will stick if there are not enough unfilled vacancies for those who want jobs. If the level increases beyond a figure which is politically acceptable, the Government has to take action to try to reduce the numbers unemployed – or risk losing the next election.

The ratio of the working population to those who do not work is important because the Government can only raise tax from people in work. As this money goes towards paying unemployment benefit, family allowance and pensions, those in work are responsible, through their taxes, for supporting those who do not work.

Non-assessed activity

Look at the profiles of the following people.

- Pauline is a married woman. She has been unemployed for only three weeks. She is looking for a job as a VDU operator.
- Jack has no qualifications but has worked for many years as a labourer on a building site. He has been out of work for six months. He is wondering about self-employment.
- Sophie has been made redundant from her previous job. She has a degree in accountancy and wants to work for a stockbroker.

Read the following key findings about unemployed people and then write a short paragraph about Pauline, Jack and Sophie, saying why you think they may or may not soon find employment.

Key findings about unemployment

- Men's share of total unemployment has grown steadily in recent years: 68 per cent of the total were men in 1993 as compared with only 60 per cent in 1984.
- The unemployment rate for married women was less than half that for men and non-married women; this gap has widened considerably in recent years.
- People who had lost or left their previous jobs made up a bigger proportion of the total unemployed.
- Some 13 per cent of the unemployed were returners to the labour market.
- New entrants to the labour market (mostly young people) formed about 9 per cent of the unemployed total – down from 13 per cent in 1984.
- Self-employment is losing its popularity as an option for unemployed people – only 3 per cent were seeking to become self-employed, 10 per cent down on the year before.
- Long-term unemployment as a proportion of the total unemployed was 42 per cent – up from 34 per cent in 1990.

- Unemployment rates were three times higher for those previously in manual jobs than for those in non-manual jobs.
- Unemployment rates were highest in construction and lowest in banking and finance.
- Unemployment rates rose faster for those with no or lower levels of qualifications – 3 per cent as compared with 1.1 per cent for people with qualifications above 'A' level.

Unemployment in the EU

If you are looking for a job abroad it might be useful if you know what the unemployment situation is like in the country you are considering. Unemployment rates differ widely in the EU – Luxembourg has the lowest rate and Spain and Ireland the highest.

Did you know?

In all EU countries, not just the UK, unemployment rates can vary from region to region. Those with the highest rates tend to be underdeveloped or to have traditional industries in decline.

Non-assessed activity

Read the following article and, **as a group,** discuss the answers to the questions given below.

Unemployment in the EU

'In the EU unemployment amongst women was 11.1 per cent in 1990 compared with only 6.5 per cent for men. Out of every 100 individuals out of work, 53 were women who accounted for over 50 per cent of the unemployed in every Member State except Ireland (36.2 per cent) and the UK (38.7 per cent). In Portugal, Belgium and Greece the level was 60 per cent or more.

'The unemployment rate amongst the under 25s was higher than the overall rate, with 14 per cent of men under 25 out of work compared with 6.5 per cent of the active male population as a whole. The rate for young women was as high as 18.4 per cent – over 4 per cent higher than for their male equivalents.

'The average age of the EU's unemployed was 31.7 years. People out of work tended to be younger in Italy,

Portugal, Spain and Greece than in Denmark, Germany or the UK.

'Some 10 per cent of households in the EU had one member unemployed and in a further 4 per cent, several members were unemployed. Over 20 per cent of Spanish households had at least one member out of work compared with only 2 per cent in Luxembourg.

'Of the male unemployed, 52.7 per cent were heads of a household and 1.2 per cent were partners to the head of a household.'

1 Generally speaking, are more women than men unemployed?

2 If you are under 25, are your chances of being unemployed higher or lower than if you are over 25? Does it make a difference which country you are in?

3 What percentage of households have at least one member unemployed? Which country is in the worst position? Which country is in the best? Why do you think it is considered very important to find out about whether heads of households are unemployed?

Did you know?

You are NOT classed as unemployed if you

- register for work at a Job Centre but do not claim unemployment benefit.
- are on an employment or training programme.
- are a housewife or married woman looking for work.
- are a man over 60 without a job (because you would receive income support not unemployment benefit)
- are not available for work or actively seeking work (e.g. because you are currently on a full-time course)

Economic policy and unemployment

If you read the newspapers or listen to the news then you will find that many people either blame the Government or expect the Government to do something about unemployment – or both. What can the Government do to promote employment and reduce unemployment?

Economic policy refers to the measures taken by the Government to run the British economy. Usually *any* Government has several economic objectives when it comes into power, including:

- stable currency
- minimum unemployment
- a stable balance of payments
- increasing economic growth
- low inflation.

The problem is that policies to improve one objective often have the opposite effect on others! In the case of unemployment, this is usually made worse when economic policies are used which aim to reduce inflation – and this has been the main objective of the present British Government.

The problems caused by unemployment

- People who are unemployed no longer pay income tax. Instead they claim benefit.
- The unemployed can no longer afford to buy many consumer goods.
- Demand for goods falls, so businesses sell less.
- More businesses have to close, making even more people unemployed.
- Businesses which have closed down no longer pay corporation tax to the Government.

Government measures to increase employment

These include:

- reducing benefits (or making them more difficult to obtain) to try to reduce the number of people preferring to remain unemployed rather than to find work
- reducing trade union power, as it was claimed that trade union activities resulted in higher wages, and if a company had to meet a high pay settlement for its workers then it might lay some workers off to reduce its total wage bill – or not take on additional workers
- providing incentives for companies to move to Assisted Areas or inner cities with severe unemployment levels
- administering schemes to encourage unemployed people to start in business themselves
- introducing training schemes such as Youth Training and Modern Apprenticeships.

Career opportunities

The best way of finding out about careers is to see what other people do, and how they have moved up within an organisation. When they first start work, most people begin at the bottom of the career ladder, work hard and carry on to gain additional qualifications. As they gain qualifications and experience they apply for more senior jobs, either in the same organisation or in a different one. Slowly they move up, usually one level at a time, undertaking progressively more senior job roles. Needless to say, some people are more ambitious than others and try to get to the very top, whilst others are content to stay in an easier job lower down in the organisation.

You might want to think about the *type* of organisation which would suit you best. This is closely related to the working environment which operates both in terms of the organisation as a whole and the departments within it.

In some organisations there may be a range of career opportunities open to you if you work hard. This is likely to be the case if you work for a large organisation with a **hierarchical** structure (see Element 2.1). This means that you can aim for your boss's job – and after that his or her boss's job and so on! If the organisation has a **flat** structure – or is very small – the opportunities may not be as great to move 'onwards and upwards'. You are also likely to be stuck if your immediate supervisor is not much older than you and likely to be in the job for several years yet! In this case, you may have to look outside your organisation for progression, assuming, of course, that you are suitably qualified to move on!

Non-assessed activity

1 Look at the list of addresses of the various professional institutes given at the end of this unit. As a group, discuss the type of employment each organisation represents and list these.

2 Choose **two** jobs in which you think you may be interested and write to the relevant institute to ask for details about both the employment prospects and the qualifications required.

Did you know?

It is surprising how many new jobs are being created all the time to meet the changing needs of the working world.

Non-assessed activity

Read the following descriptions of jobs which are in related areas. In each case decide:

a which is a 'new' job
b which is a well-established job.

Give reasons for your answers.

1 Andy is a care manager for a small charity. He is in charge of a half-way house for ex-psychiatric patients moving from hospital to the 'real world'.

Nazana is a psychiatric nurse. She is a ward manager supervising twelve patients.

2 Lesley is a BT operator. She now works as a 100 operator, i.e. giving help to customers making a UK call, and before that she worked on directory enquiries.

Tony works for a company he started himself two years ago. He is an Internet support manager and connects people to the Internet, a global network of computer networks.

3 Julie washes car windscreens at traffic lights, accepting any money people can give her. She is unemployed and hasn't had a regular job since working in a pub three years ago.

Tom has a window-cleaning business with a partner. They usually keep to private houses but occasionally clean windows for local businesses and shops.

Training opportunities

The type of qualifications required obviously varies tremendously from one job to another. Therefore, when you start work it is likely that you will be offered training to:

- learn specific aspects of the job
- understand health and safety practices related to your job
- obtain higher-level qualifications.

Some large organisations encourage their staff to continue to study on a day-release basis at college. They may pay for them to study for a part-time degree or a professional qualification, such as the qualification for management accountants.

Sometimes these courses are available only in the evening, which can mean being fairly dedicated when you are tired from a full day at work and have to go on to study at night!

This sort of training is known as **off-the-job training** – employees study away from work.

An alternative is **on-the-job training**. In this case the employee learns at the workplace. This is often related to a skill aspect of the job, e.g. learning how to operate a switchboard or a particular type of equipment, learning a software package or how to use fire extinguishers.

You may also be given the opportunity to attend short courses – to keep you up to date or to learn new skills, such as first aid.

If ever you can take advantage of training – paid for by your employer – to develop your skills then you should seize the chance with both hands! Generally the range of opportunities is greater if you work for a large organisation than for a small one, because they will have a training budget especially for this purpose. However, there is nothing to stop you talking to the bosses of a small firm and persuading them that it will benefit both you and the company if you continue to study!

Non-assessed activity

People can study NVQs and GNVQs in certain **occupational areas.** You have chosen to study in Business. Alternatively you could have selected Art and Design or Leisure and Tourism.

1 Find out the different occupational routes which offer *both* NVQ and GNVQ qualifications. List these neatly.

2 Select **two** occupational routes in which you may be personally interested and find out the qualifications which are available at *each level*, the length of study for each of these and whether they are available on a full-time or part-time basis, or both. Design a chart on which you can show this information.

3 Make out for yourself **two** proposed career routes:

   a assuming you leave *full-time* education at eighteen or nineteen and obtain a job

   b assuming you remain in full-time education until your early twenties.

Use of new technology

Many jobs have changed dramatically over the last twenty years or so because of the effect of technological developments. Technology can affect jobs in one of four ways:

- it can create them
- it can destroy them
- it can change their content
- it can change their location.

In some of the larger organisations a vast amount of technological equipment is now used. You may be linked by computer network to everyone else in your organisation – and perhaps outside of it by Internet. You can communicate with the world by electronic mail! The company may communicate with its suppliers by Electronic Data Interchange (see page 116 and Element 4.1) and the items it produces may be produced by robot. Most of the sales staff may work from home and communicate with the office by notebook computer (and modem) or by fax or mobile phone. Sales presentations may be put together by means of computer. Products may be designed on computer and the warehouse may have a computerised picking and distribution system. Your telephone might be linked through a digital switchboard to give you a range of facilities including 'voice mail', which stores messages for you when you are out.

Alternatively, in a small service organisation, there may be one person using an electronic typewriter, telephone and photocopier!

When you are comparing working conditions you need to look at the amount and the extent to which new technology is employed. You may also wish to note whether it has been used to *assist* employees or to *replace* them!

Recent developments in technology

1 Miniaturisation of all electronic items is ongoing. Today camcorders are hand-held, computers are the size of notebooks and mobile phones can fit into your pocket! The latest computers are a fraction of the size of the earlier ones – with far more memory and higher processing speed. The latest microcomputers are faster and more powerful than the original mainframe computers were years ago.

2 In industry there is computer integrated manufacturing (CIM), computer aided design (CAD), computer aided manufacture (CAM) and robotics.

3 In the future, flexible manufacturing system (FMS) technology could mean that the design and drawing of components will be produced in the office by a CAD package and, programmed directly into a computer which oversees the operation of the machinery and robots in the plant!

4 Communications have been revolutionised with fax machines, digital switchboards, communications satellites and computer networks. BT already make a video telephone.

5 Self-service has been greatly facilitated by electronic devices such as tagging (to prevent shop-lifting) and automated tills where a checkout operator can deal quickly and accurately with a range of purchases. Bar codes on products are read automatically by a bar code reader attached to a cash register, which also automatically prints cheques and processes debit and credit cards. Both in industry and retail, computers are used for automated stock control procedures. Each sale in a supermarket, for instance, is logged by the cash register and used automatically to adjust the number of goods in stock. If stocks fall below a pre-set figure, an order is automatically produced to send to the supplier.

6 Scientists are working on even more powerful, even smaller and even cheaper computers with an even greater range of applications. 'Pen' computers – with touch sensitive screens that recognise handwriting – are available and those which recognise basic spoken commands are now available (e.g. 'open file' or 'delete').

7 Interactive telephones – again using voice recognition – have been developed in the United States. A pilot project in Colorado introduced Voice Dialling. In Britain, BT has developed CallMinder – an automatic telephone-answering service which uses a computer to take calls. It is also developing a computerised voice recognition system to allow users to call a computer and pay their bills by credit or debit card.

8 Multimedia systems will be available on which users can watch videos, use computer software, play interactive games and do electronic shopping. In the future you will not ask your boss for half a day off to study for your next award or to attend a training course – you will interact with your local college tutor by means of your computer!

Did you know?

A computer network consists of cables which link personal computers so that they can exchange information. Other equipment can be included on the network, e.g. fax machines and photocopiers. Networks can operate over a small or large geographical area and can be used to transmit information large distances over satellite links.

New jobs and old jobs

Many types of employment have changed as a result of new technology, as well as because of new opportunities. Today you could find work in a virtual reality studio! You could create text for teletext and commercial databases or work for an IT journal or computer magazine.

You would be less likely to be employed producing pay slips or invoices – as these can be generated easily by microcomputer – unless you worked for a very small or old-fashioned firm.

Did you know?

Over 70 000 jobs were lost in the banking industry over a two-year period – many because of developments in banking technology. This included the introduction of automatic teller machines (ATMs) which are now used for over 60 per cent of personal cash withdrawals, centralising cheque processing, telephone and computer banking and the increased use of debit cards (see Element 4.1) rather than cheques.

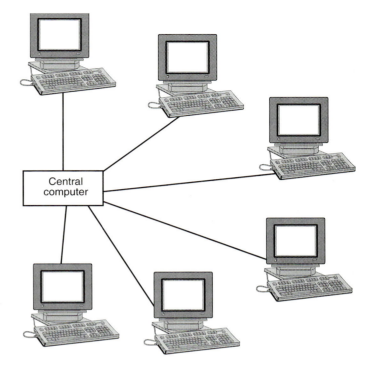

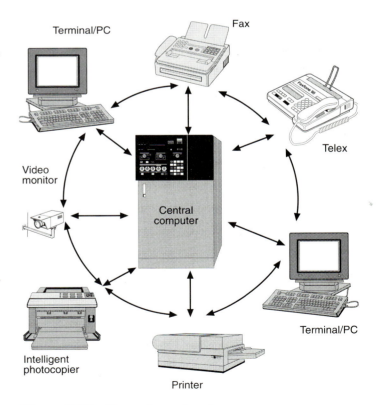

Figure 1.55   Computer networks

Non-assessed activity

1 Visit your local bank and find out about both telephone banking and computer banking or contact a 'specialist' telephone bank such as First Direct. List the type of transactions which can be carried out in this way.

2 Interview **at least one** person who can tell you about banking roughly fifteen years ago. Try to find out the number of branches in your area, the hours the bank opened, the range of services etc. Write a brief report on the interview which includes the questions you asked and the answers you received.

3 Summarise how technology has changed banking and the implications for bank employees.

Did you know?

The abbreviation EDI stands for Electronic Data Interchange between companies. By this means a retailer can place an electronic order with a supplier who can also send the advice note to the customer electronically when the goods have been despatched – and then follow this with an electronic invoice! Retailers already using EDI include B & Q and the Sears group – which includes Selfridges, Olympus, and footwear shops such as Dolcis, Saxone, Freeman Hardy & Willis and Lilley & Skinner. Tesco and Boots trade electronically with their European suppliers.

In industry more and more companies are using EDI to process orders more quickly and more accurately – including British Telecom and British Aerospace. It is envisaged that within the next two or three years EDI will be used by more than 50 000 organisations world-wide. The topic of EDI is covered in more detail in Element 4.1.

Non-assessed activity

1 Interview *either* someone who worked in retailing *or* someone who worked in an office several years ago. Find out the range of manual operations which are now done by computer and list these.

Write a short report on how you think jobs have altered because of these changes and the advantages and disadvantages for employees.

2 Write a paragraph about the future you envisage for office workers in the 21st century. Research current information on technological developments to help you.

Evidence assignment

At this point your tutor may wish you to start or continue work on the project which will prove to your verifiers that you understand this section of the element. If so, turn to page 118 and do Section 3 of the project. This covers the third evidence indicator for this element.

Presentation of results of investigations into employment or working conditions

Making a presentation

Make sure you have read, understood and completed the exercises relating to the preparation for a presentation (see page 534).

Evidence assignment

At this point your tutor may wish you to start or continue work on the project which will prove to your verifiers that you understand this section of the element. If you are starting the project then turn to page 118 and do Section 1 of the project. If you have already completed Sections 1, 2 and 3 of the project now start Section 4. This covers the fourth evidence indicator for this element.

Answers to EU member states quiz (page 93)

1 United Kingdom	2 Sweden	3 Netherlands
4 Portugal	5 Belgium	6 Ireland
7 Finland	8 Spain	9 Luxembourg
10 Italy	11 Greece	12 France
13 Denmark	14 Austria	15 Germany

Revision test

True or false?

1 Workers in the UK have longer holidays than workers in most other EU countries.

2 Protective clothing refers only to safety hats and shoes.

3 The more qualifications you have the less chance there is that you will be unemployed.

4 The longer you have been unemployed the more difficult it is to get a job.

5 There are more self-employed women than men in the UK.

Complete the blanks

6 The _____ _____ _____ _____ sets standards of safety in factories.

7 _____ occurs when technology has replaced some of the traditional craft skills.

8 Two people who divide the duties and pay of one job between them are known as _____ _____ .

9 Temporary staff who are hired as they are needed, often on a daily basis, are known as _____ _____ .

10 The European Union has issued a _____ _____ Directive to try to limit the number of hours worked each week.

Short answer questions

11 Give **two** possible health problems caused by using a VDU.

12 State **three** disadvantages of unemployment.

13 Give **three** reasons why employers like to employ part-time workers

14 Give **four** examples of areas where jobs have been created as a result of technology.

15 Give **three** skills which most workers must possess.

Write a short paragraph to show you clearly understand each of the following terms:

16 Multi-skilling

17 Physical conditions

18 Job security

19 Part time employment

20 Commission

Evidence indicator project

Unit 1 Element 1.3

This project has been designed to cover all the evidence indicators related to Element 1.3. It is divided into four sections. Your tutor may ask you to complete the sections at the appropriate points marked in the text. Alternatively, your tutor may prefer you to do the entire project at the end of the element.

Performance criteria: 1–4

Core skills: Communication
                                              Application of number
                                              Information technology

Section 1

This section concentrates on the first evidence indicator for this element. When you have completed the work, store it safely as it will contribute towards your final project for this element.

Make sure you complete this section of the project by the deadline date given to you by your tutor.

1   If possible, find **seven** people (friends, relatives, other students) who are engaged in the following types of employment.

   ■ a full-time worker
   ■ a part-time worker
   ■ a permanent employee
   ■ a temporary employee
   ■ a skilled worker
   ■ an unskilled worker
   ■ a self-employed worker

2   Prepare a list of questions to find out:

   a   their job title, e.g. a waitress, an office manager, a shop assistant etc.
   b   what they actually do, i.e. a description of their duties
   c   what they like and what they dislike about being a full-time/part-time/permanent/temporary/skilled/unskilled/self-employed worker

3   Write a short report containing a paragraph about each of the people you have interviewed.

4   If there are any types of employment for which you cannot find someone to interview, write a description of the type of employment such a worker might be involved in.

Section 2

This section concentrates on the second evidence indicator for this element. When you have completed the work store it safely as it will contribute towards your final project for this element.

Make sure you complete this section of the project by the deadline date given to you by your tutor.

1   Choose **two** EU Regions (one of which should be in the UK – you might want to choose the region where you live).

2   Collect information on:

   a   the percentage of people in employment
   b   their gender and age
   c   whether they work in a manufacturing or services sector.

   Note: If you have already done the Optional Evidence Assignment on page 95 you will find that you can use some of the information you gathered together for that activity.

3   Write a summary explaining the differences in the number of people employed in both regions and also the growth or decline of one manufacturing and one service sector in each region.

Section 3

This section concentrates on the third evidence indicator for this element. When you have completed the work store it safely as it will contribute towards your final project for this element.

Make sure you complete this section of the project by the deadline date given to you by your tutor.

1   Try to find **two** people from **two different organisations** (preferably one from the private sector and one from the public sector – or one from a manufacturing industry and one from a service industry) and ask them if you can interview them about their working conditions. Before you begin the interview draw up a list of questions which should include:

a *Hours of work*
what are their hours of work?
how many days a week do they work?
do they work overtime?
what holidays do they have?

b *Career opportunities*
have they ever been promoted at work, or are they hoping to be promoted?

c *Training opportunities*
does the organisation have a training officer/department?
does it let employees have time off for training?
does it run its own training programmes?

d *Use of new technology*
has the organisation introduced any new technology over the past five years – if so, what?

2 On a word processor draw up a form (one for each person interviewed) giving:

- his/her name
- his/her organisation
- his/her job title.

Use a heading and leave a space for the date.

3 List the questions down the left-hand side of the page and leave plenty of space for the reply. Make sure that both you and the person you are interviewing have a copy of the form. Write out the answers as clearly as possible – don't scribble. Read the answers back to make sure you both agree what has been said.

4 When both interviews have been completed, compare what each person has said and write a short report about your findings section by section. Make certain you point out any differences between the two sets of working conditions and try, if possible, to give reasons for these.

Section 4

This section concentrates on the fourth and final evidence indicator for this element. When you have completed the work store it safely as it will contribute towards your final project for this element.

Make sure you complete this section of the project by the deadline date given to you by your tutor.

Refer to the Student Guide to make sure that you know how to make a presentation and also that you know how to prepare suitable visual aids.

Discuss this with your tutor before you start as he or she will probably want the class to work together in groups on this section. Look back at the information you

gathered together to complete Evidence Indicator 2 and, this time as a member of a group, decide:

1 whether you wish to make a presentation about the percentages of people employed and employment opportunities across **at least two** EU regions *or* a presentation comparing working conditions of **two** individuals

2 who is to do the additional research

who is to write up the script

who is to prepare the visual aids (and what these aids are going to be)

who is going to co-ordinate all the work, plan the rehearsals, book the room etc.

who is to deliver the various parts of the presentation.

Be sure to leave yourself enough preparation time – don't leave this part of your project until the last minute!

Keep a record of your script and copies of the visual aids you have used.

Prepare your finished report on a word processor with a clear title page giving your name and the date your report was completed. Entitle your report either:

- An investigation into employment and working conditions in ... *or*
- An investigation into working conditions of ... .

Addresses for non-assessed activity, page 112

Association of Accounting Technicians,
154 Clerkenwell Road,
London EC1R 5AD

Chartered Institute of Certified Accountants,
29 Lincoln's Inn Fields,
London WC2A 3EE

Chartered Institute of Management Accountants,
63 Portland Place,
London WIN 4AB

CAM Foundation Ltd,
Abford House,
15 Wilton Road,
London SW1V 1NJ

Chartered Institute of Marketing (CIM)
Moor Hall, Cookham,
Maidenhead,
Berkshire SL6 9QH

Engineering Training Authority (EnTra),
Vector House,
41 Clarendon Road,
Watford,
Hertfordshire WD1 1HS

Institute of Chartered Secretaries and Administrators,
The Careers Department,
16 Park Crescent,
London W1N 4AH

Institute of Logistics and Distribution Management,
Douglas House,
Queens Square,
Corby,
Northants NN17 1PL

Institute of Management,
Management House,
Cottingham Road,
Corby,
Northants NN17 1TT

Institute of Management Services,
1 Cecil Court,
London Road,
Enfield,
Middlesex EN2 6DD

The Education Office,
The Market Research Society,
15 Northburgh Street,
London EC1V 0AH

Institute of Personnel Development,
IPD House,
Camp Road,
Wimbledon,
London SW19 4UX

Institute of Public Relations,
The Old Trading Houses,
15 Northburgh Street,
London EC1V OPR

Institute of Practitioners in Advertising,
44 Belgrave Square,
London SW1X 8QS

Institute of Purchasing and Supply and the Association
of Supervisors in Purchasing and Supply,
Easton House,
Easton on the Hill,
Stamford,
Lincolnshire PE9 3NZ

Institute of Quality Assurance,
PO Box 712,
61 Southwark Street,
London SE1 1SB

Institute of Sales and Marketing Management,
31 Upper George Street,
Luton,
Bedfordshire LU1 2RD

Trades Union Congress,
Congress House,
Great Russell Street,
London WC1B 3ES

Examine and compare structures and working arrangements in organisations

This element covers the way in which business organisations are structured, the work carried out by the different departments in an organisation, the different working arrangements in various organisations and why these may change.

After studying this element you should be able to:

1 describe *organisational structures*

2 produce organisational charts showing *departments*

3 describe the work and explain the interdependence of *departments* within business organisations

4 identify and explain *differences in working arrangements*

5 explain and give examples of *reasons for change* in working arrangements in one business organisation.

Organisational structures

The structure of an organisation refers to the way in which its activities are grouped or arranged. In any organisation it is sensible for people who do similar types of work to be grouped together, so that they can communicate more easily and the work can be divided among them effectively.

In a small organisation this happens quite informally. If you worked in a business which had only two or three staff, you would probably find that the work was divided among everyone, depending on their skills, qualifications and experience. If there were managers, they would be responsible for making the decisions about allocating the work. In a crisis, everyone would be expected to help out.

As an organisation grows in size it will become completely unmanageable unless it is structured more formally. If you worked in a business which employed 30 people, you would need to know which jobs were carried out by which members of staff – otherwise you could waste hours looking for the right person to contact about a particular item. In the same way, the managers of the enterprise need to know who is responsible for each aspect of the work, so that they can check everything is being done properly and know who to blame if it isn't! In an organisation with a large number of employees, a proper structure is crucial to its efficiency.

Variations in structure

The structure of an organisation will not only depend on its size and number of employees. It will also depend on other factors such as:

- whether it is in the manufacturing or service sector
- whether it is a local, national or international organisation
- the type of work with which it is involved.

Therefore all companies are different! There is no right or wrong structure – provided that the way in which the company is organised helps people to do their work more efficiently, communicate with each other easily and assists the business to achieve its objectives.

Did you know?

In a large organisation there will be more **specialisation**, i.e. each person will concentrate on his or her own specific job. For instance, accounts staff will only deal with financial matters. In a small organisation, finance may simply be a part of a manager's job.

The organisation chart

The structure of an organisation can be shown most easily by means of an organisation chart. (See page 128 for the ways in which the departments in an organisation can be displayed in chart form.) The

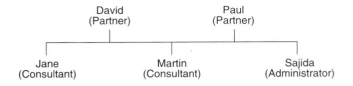

Figure 2.1 A flat organisation chart (two levels)

chart usually gives the job titles of employees and how these jobs relate to each other. Sometimes the job holder's name is shown. Those at the top of the chart are more important, have more responsibility (and are paid more) than those lower down. They can also give instructions to people below them who have a duty to carry out these instructions.

As an example, DPTS is a small computer consultancy. There are two partners, David and Paul and they employ two consultants, Jane and Martin, and an administrator, Sajida.

On an organisation chart, the structure of DPTS would be as shown in Figure 2.1.

This shows that David and Paul are of equal status (they are on the same level on the chart) and they are *equally* responsible for the consultants and for Sajida. At the same time, all the staff are on the same level.

If David was responsible for Jane and Martin, and Paul was responsible for Sajida then the chart would be drawn differently. If Sajida was less senior than the two consultants this would also be shown by her position on the chart.

The arrows on the chart in Figure 2.2 show that managers or supervisors are *responsible* for staff who report to them, and that, in return these staff are *accountable* to the manager for their actions.

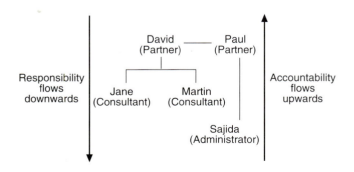

Figure 2.2 A flat organisation chart (three levels)

Did you know?

The phrase 'passing it down the line' can refer to jobs and information passed down an organisation from one level to another – as shown by the lines on the organisation chart.

Hierarchical structures

A hierarchical structure is one in which there are many levels. It looks 'tall'. Each person has a number of people for whom he or she is responsible. Jobs are specialised, for example a manager may be appointed for a specific area – sales, finance, human resources, etc., and staff employed in this area will concentrate on this type of work.

Usually, the more hierarchical an organisation the more 'formal' it is. There will be official procedures to be followed and a number of written rules and regulations, e.g.:

- official job titles and a specified salary scale for each 'level' of job
- a formal health and safety policy
- standard procedures laid down on hours of work, holidays, personal days off, punctuality, disciplinary procedures and so on
- an official interview procedure
- guidelines (or rules) on dress, customer service, layout of documents, methods of working etc.

Why is all this necessary? The two main reasons are:

1 to ensure that the standards throughout the organisation will be the same – for customers and for employees
2 to ensure that there is fairness to all employees – because they are all treated the same.

With a large number of employees this would be impossible unless some standards were laid down as different managers would respond to situations in different ways – and this would lead to problems.

Did you know?

Hierarchical structures are often called pyramid structures. This is because the shape is like a pyramid if you take into account the fact that at each level downwards in the organisation there will be more employees. The more hierarchical, the steeper the pyramid.

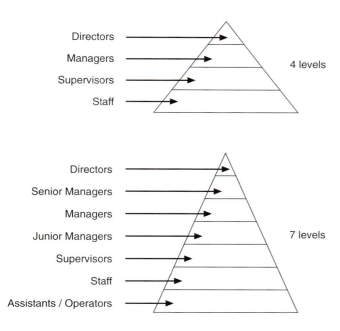

Figure 2.3   Two examples of pyramid structures

Flat structures

An organisation with only two or three levels is known as a **flat** structure. The business is likely to be run relatively informally, as everyone will know everyone else. There will probably be good communication between bosses and employees. This should mean that they can respond quickly to changing situations and specific customer requests.

Non-assessed activity

1 Draw an organisation chart for a doctors' practice which has three partners, Dr Gilbert, Dr Ahmed and Dr Ashe. They employ four receptionists, Anne, Pat, Marion and Lorraine, for whom they are jointly responsible.

2 Now draw the chart again, showing how it would look if they employed a nurse, Bridget, who was at a higher level than the four receptionists.

3 Bearing in mind the type of work carried out, why do you think it is important that a doctors' practice has a flat organisational structure? **As a group**, discuss the reasons and make a list of as many advantages as possible.

Changing the structure

As an organisation grows, keeping a 'flat' structure can be more difficult. If DPTS employed another ten consultants then David and Paul would be in charge of thirteen people altogether. They would also need office staff. If five more office staff were employed, then the directors would be in charge of eighteen people! They would then spend more time supervising the work done by other people than they would on doing their own job.

A special term for the number of people each manager can oversee is **span of control**. If David and Paul divided the staff into two equal groups, they would each have a span of control of nine people. Whilst this may be possible if employees are undertaking very routine or similar work (e.g. assemblers on a production line) it is almost impossible to supervise a large number of staff properly if they are involved in complicated work or very different types of jobs.

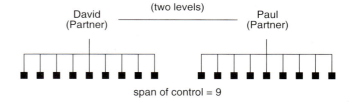

Figure 2.4   Span of control

There would also be another problem – officially David could not give instructions to Paul's staff, nor could Paul give orders to those who report to David. In a small office this would be unworkable – and would reduce flexibility and response times dramatically.

One solution is to introduce another 'level' into DPTS. Assume that twelve months later DPTS is a limited company and David and Paul are now the two directors – and have reorganised the company.

Stage 1

David and Paul again take joint responsibility for Martin, Jane and Sajida. They promote Martin and Jane to the position of senior consultant. Each is responsible for the work of five other consultants. All the office staff report to Sajida, who has been

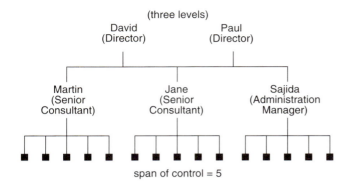

Figure 2.5 Span of control after reorganisation

promoted to administration manager. The organisation chart of the company now looks like Figure 2.5.

Stage 2

As time goes by, DPTS Ltd continues to expand. Four consultants have left and David and Paul decide that they now want to recruit *trainee* consultants who they can train in their own ways of working. They also appoint a financial manager, Gerry, and a sales and marketing manager, Brian. These managers are at the same level as the senior consultants.

At the same time they reorganise the office staff, who now number six. In addition Paul appoints his own

secretary/PA – Vivien. Because she does not report to anyone else, she is shown as linked to him by a dotted line. The new organisation chart is shown in Figure 2.6, and it is far more hierarchical.

Did you know?

Hierarchical organisations are also called **bureaucracies** – a name given to them by Max Weber, a German sociologist, who was one of the first people to look at the advantages and disadvantages of this type of organisation structure. Typical bureaucracies are the civil service and local government, as well as large-scale private companies.

One problem with bureaucracies can be that, because everyone has to follow rules and procedures, decision-making can be slow. In addition there might be a desire to impress the boss – and tell him what he wants to hear, rather than the truth!

Non-assessed activity

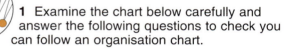

1 Examine the chart below carefully and answer the following questions to check you can follow an organisation chart.

a How many levels are there in DPTS now?
b Who is responsible for the trainee accountant?
c If Damien has a problem with the trainee consultant for whom he is responsible, who should he go to?

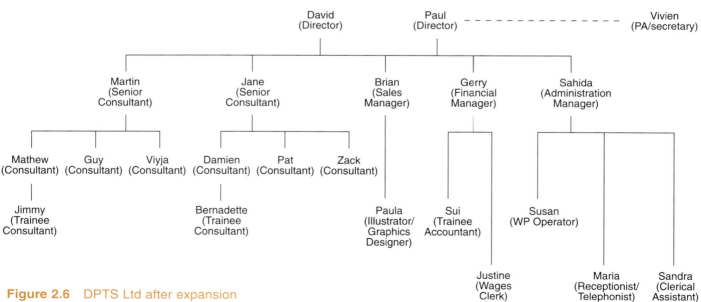

Figure 2.6 DPTS Ltd after expansion

d Can Susan, the WP operator, give instructions to the receptionist/telephonist?

e To whom is Viyja responsible on a day-to-day basis? Who should she see if her immediate boss is absent through illness and a serious problem arises?

f At what level is Sui in relation to:
  i Bernadette
  ii Sandra
  iii Sahida?

2 Re-draw the chart, assuming the following changes are made.

  a Jimmy is promoted to consultant and reports directly to Martin.

  b Another trainee consultant, Yvonne, is appointed in his place.

  c Paula gains a clerical assistant, Michela.

  d A second WP operator is appointed, Naomi.

  e An office junior, Ben, is appointed. Although he reports to Sahida he is at a lower level than anyone else in the organisation.

  f David also appoints his own secretary/PA, Cathie.

3 **As a group**, discuss the advantages and disadvantages there will be for staff working in an organisation of this size, rather than in the original DPTS structure.

4 An organisation chart only shows the formal structure of an organisation, not the informal relationships. What difference do you think it would make to Martin if David played golf with Guy every Sunday morning?

Did you know?

A deputy is higher than an assistant, and therefore has a different position on the organisation chart.

Examine the chart in Figure 2.7. The deputy is directly below the manager, which means that if the manager leaves, the deputy could move 'up the line' and take his place. He or she would certainly be eligible to apply for the job.

The assistant, on the other hand, is to one side. This means he is literally 'not in line for the job'.

Figure 2.7   Deputies and assistants

Matrix structure

The matrix structure is a different type of organisational structure. It is less common than a hierarchical or flat structure but is becoming more popular. The aim is to group people by skill or key area rather than by their position in the organisation. This is because a key area may often cross several departments. If you take your college or school as an example you may find that it is structured in one of two ways.

It may have a hierarchical structure in which a number of related courses and staff are grouped into separate departments. They are supported by departments which are concerned with the operation

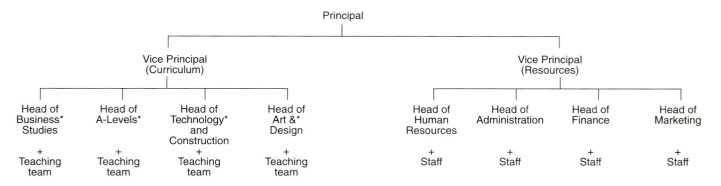

*Teachers in each department in the main teach on courses in that department, e.g. Business Studies staff would teach accounts, law, business studies etc. to students on business studies courses

Figure 2.8   Hierarchical structure in a school or college and maintenance of your college or school, such as finance, administration, human resources (personnel) and marketing (see Figure 2.8).

Although this works quite well, there are sometimes problems, for instance, in double staffing. You may find that accounts on a business studies course is taught by a member of staff in the Business Studies department and that accounts on an A-level course is taught by a member of the A-level department, when it might be more efficient for all accounts to be taught by a small team of accounts staff, no matter what the course may be. In this case, accounts is being identified as a key area. Therefore your school or college may use the matrix system which groups all staff together according to their key areas – i.e. the main subjects they teach. The other departments would be organised to support these groups so that, for instance, there would be separate groups of staff in the Administration, Finance, Human Resources and Marketing departments specifically allocated to work with the separate teaching groups.

This would be represented on an organisation chart as shown in Figure 2.9 below.

The matrix structure in business

In the business world the matrix structure is becoming quite common. It is frequently found in organisations which deal with specialised one-off projects, such as in civil engineering companies. A civil engineering company will bid for different contracts, such as motorway construction in the UK, building a bridge abroad or a high-rise banking building in London. A team of people will be put together to work on one project. As well as the experts in the teams, support will be required from the main functions of the organisation – finance, human resources, design and development – and the heads of all the projects will be in constant contact with the major function heads about costings, staffing and design. The project teams will continue to work on the project until completion, when the team will be disbanded. A new team would be formed to work on a different project when the next bid was won.

This can be shown on an organisation chart as in Figure 2.10. Trace the dotted lines to see which person each project manager contacts regularly.

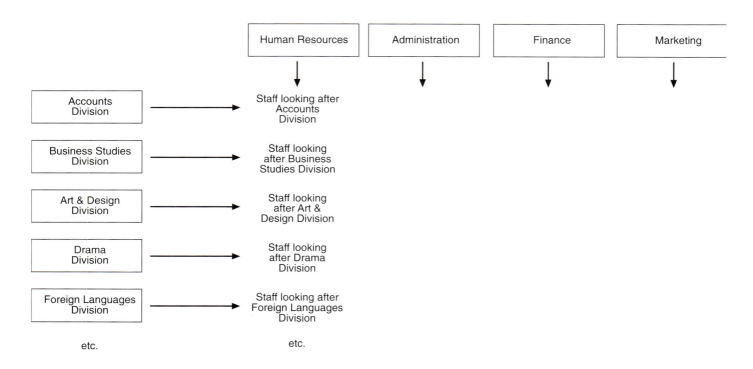

Figure 2.9 The matrix structure in a school or college

Many businesses now choose to work in this way, so that staff can focus on the product and its market rather than on their particular role. A publishing company may employ a team of editors, designers, production people and sales and marketing staff who all focus on, say, primary school books or library books for adults. A more old-fashioned company may just have editors or sales and marketing staff who work on a range of different types of books and who can't possibly understand all the needs of various customers. You can read more about teamworking on page 148.

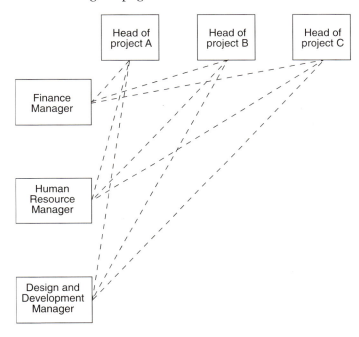

Note: The dotted lines show that these are temporary relationships. In other words the heads of projects are 'in charge' for the duration of the project.

Figure 2.10   The matrix structure in business

The advantages of a matrix structure

The advantages of a matrix system are that:

- everyone is making the best possible use of his or her specialist skills
- service departments such as Finance can have specialist staff to support the main teams
- new teams can be formed and easily included in the structure
- old teams can easily be removed from the structure.

Non-assessed activity

1 As a group, discuss the **disadvantages** of the structure. Think of:

a   Possible problems of communications between staff in all the various areas. (Think of your own course – suppose the staff who teach you communication never talked to the staff who teach you numeracy, and so on.)

b   The drawbacks of specialising in just one area – with no opportunity for staff to get any wider experience.

2   Imagine you are employed by a small television production company which, you are told, has a matrix structure.

a   Why do you think such a structure has been chosen for this type of company?

b   Make a rough sketch, showing what it may look like.

Organisational charts showing departments

Organisational charts are not only used to show where **individuals** fit into an organisation (see page 121) but also the **departmental** structure within the organisation. Whilst the number and type of departments in an organisation may vary (see page 129), the way in which the charts are drawn is identical to the way in which they were drawn for individuals.

Non-assessed activity

Imagine you are working in the human resources section of a family business which makes and sells confectionery. Recently the managing director has retired and a new managing director has taken over. The organisation has always had a **flat** structure.

However, the new managing director feels that the time has come for a change in structure. He discusses with his senior staff the idea of either changing the structure to a **hierarchical** or a **matrix** structure and shows them an example of what the organisation would look like in each case.

1   Look at the **three** charts below. Can you identify which chart belongs to which structure?

2   Which do you think would be:

a most suitable for a small company

b most suitable for a large company

c most suitable for a company with specialised areas?

3 Today many companies are moving away from a hierarchical structure towards a flatter or matrix structure. In many cases this is to do with 'streamlining' the organisation and reducing bureaucratic procedures.

a Discuss with your tutor why a change of structure may help to increase the speed at which paperwork is dealt with and decisions are made.

b Discuss how such changes may affect the staff who work in different departments.

The work and interdependence of departments

On page 124 you read that DPTS Ltd had created three functional areas – Finance, Sales and Marketing, and Administration. You may now also have identified these areas in your own school or college. Establishing specialist areas like this is normal. As a company increases in size, the most obvious way in which to group people is according to their **function** – i.e. the job they carry out. It is likely that:

■ some people are involved in producing the goods

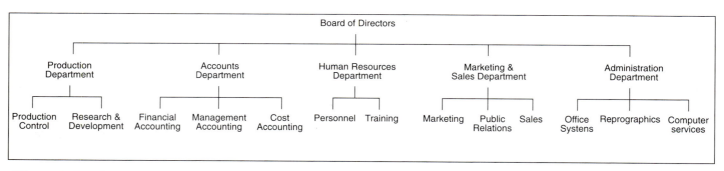

Figure 2.11 Structure A

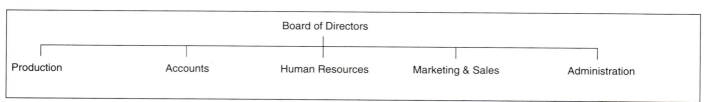

Figure 2.12 Structure B

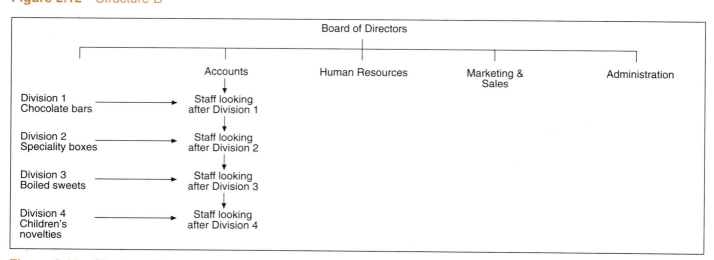

Figure 2.13 Structure C

- some people are responsible for selling the goods
- other people provide support services – in general administration, finance or human resources.

The company may then be structured into departments which reflect these functions as shown in Figure 2.14.

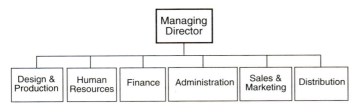

Figure 2.14   Functional departments of an organisation

Departments in business organisations

There is no such thing as a typical business organisation. Obviously, an organisation which is concerned with providing a **service** would not have a production department. For instance, a mail order company which buys goods from elsewhere, stores them and distributes them to its customers may have a large distribution department (which includes warehousing) but no production department.

Therefore the titles of the departments, and their number, will depend very much on the work carried out by the organisation.

Departments in the public sector

In the public sector, virtually all organisations provide a service. However, these services may not be suitable for sub-division in the same way as in the private sector. Therefore the names of the departments – or the way in which they have been selected – may be very different.

- A local authority may have departments such as Housing, Finance, Operations, Economic Development, Leisure Services and Development.
- A hospital is likely to be divided into specialist areas, e.g. paediatrics, orthopaedic, maternity, psychiatric, etc.
- A college or university has departments based on subject specialisations, e.g.
  - Engineering, Computing and Mathematics
  - Physics and Material Sciences
  - Biology
  - Performing Arts
  - Information Technology
  - Humanities

Organisations which are structured on specialist lines, such as hospitals, colleges and universities, usually have general support services which are used by every department.

- A borough council or hospital may have a Human Resources department, a Legal department and an Administration department.
- A college or university may have a Finance department, a Buildings department, a Human Resources department and a Student Services department.

To differentiate these support services from the main departments they may be called by another name, e.g. unit or section.

Non-assessed activity

1 **As a group**, *either*
   a Find out the names of the departments which exist at your local council offices. Write a brief paragraph on the work done by each one and make sure you clearly distinguish those which provide a support service, *or*
   b Find out the structure of your local hospital, the names of each department and the type of work carried out there. List separately those departments (or sections) which provide a support service.

2 Obtain a prospectus from a university and discuss the different departments which are shown. Under each department, list **at least three** subjects you could study.

   As a group, make a separate note of those departments which provide a service – either to students, staff or to other departments.

Optional evidence assignment

*This activity can be carried out verbally in class **in a group** as a non-assessed activity to consolidate learning. Alternatively, if you do it **on your own**, it can count as supplementary evidence towards the following parts of the scheme.*

PC 1:   Describe organisational structures

PC 2:   Produce organisational charts showing departments

Range: Organisational structures: hierarchical, flat, matrix

Departments: purchasing, accounting, human resources (personnel), marketing, computer (IT) services, customer services

Core skills: Communication

Read the assignment below and then answer the questions which follow.

1 Find out the structure of your own school or college.
   a Draw an organisation chart which shows the *main* job titles (there is no need to include the names of the job holders) and who is responsible for whom.
   b Compose a short paragraph stating whether you consider this to be a hierarchical, flat or matrix structure and the reasons for your decision.
   c Write a second paragraph which summarises the advantages and disadvantages of this particular structure for an educational establishment.

2 a List any departments (or sections) in your school or college which provide a support service for the rest of the organisation. State clearly what each one does. You should particularly identify areas such as accounts (or finance), human resources (personnel), marketing, administration, computer services and customer (or student) services.
   b Redraw the organisation structure, showing how the departments relate to each other (rather than in terms of job holders).
   c Change the organisation of your school or college to see what it would look like. If it is now hierarchical you could make it flat or matrix. If it is a matrix structure then you could design a flat or hierarchical structure.
   d **In a short paragraph**, briefly state the advantages and disadvantages of changing to this new structure.

Departments in the private sector

You have already seen that in the private sector the majority of organisations are sub-divided according to **functions**. There are several advantages of doing this.

- Specialists can work together.
- Staff can become more experienced.
- There are opportunities for promotion and career development.
- The manager will be an expert in that particular area.

There are, however, disadvantages, as departments can become competitive rather than having the benefits and aims of the organisation as a whole in mind. If, for instance, staff cuts have to be made, all the managers will try to defend their own departments.

It is quite common for employees to stay in a particular department for most – if not all – of their working lives, although they may move from one organisation to another. Before you can make any decisions about which area you would prefer to work in, it is important that you understand the type of function carried out by the main departments.

Did you know?

The **scope** of each department – and the type of work it carries out – will not be identical in any two organisations. There will be similarities, but you should also expect to find differences. You are therefore not wrong if you find that in an organisation you are investigating there are several functions for a department which you didn't expect – or several missing which you *did* expect.

To help you, the descriptions below contain virtually everything you may find during your investigations, but don't be surprised if your eventual list is rather different!

Research and Development

Typical job titles	Departmental functions
Chief designer	Design and product development
Designers	
Clerks	

The Research and Development department is more commonly known as 'R and D'. The aim of R and D is to stay one step ahead of the competitors in devising new products and systems and redesigning old ones.

The two types of design are basically:

- **industrial design** – concerned with appearance and product use
- **engineering design** – concerned with performance.

For instance, when a car is being developed the **industrial** designers will be concerned with the shape and features on the car, whereas the **engineering** designers will be concerned with engine size, fuel consumption and acceleration.

New products are being developed all the time – and existing ones re-designed. For instance, the design of household appliances, furniture, carpets and office equipment is changing all the time. Today, for example, we use lightweight plastic jug kettles which can boil one cup of water at a time, rather than the traditional heavy metal kettles which had to be half-full before they could be used. The design of consumer electric goods – videos, camcorders, televisions and computers – is changing all the time. In many cases they are getting smaller or, as in the case of televisions, thinner. In the fashion trade, new designs for clothes are a main feature of the industry. The packaging industry is another area where design is important – although you may not think so if you have ever struggled to open a packet of sandwiches quickly during your lunch hour! The design of a can, tin or box (and the colours used) can influence us – as consumers – to buy or not to buy.

Did you know?

Research and development is not just restricted to private sector organisations. Universities have been involved in the development of a CD-ROM package which will enable potential students to view the courses and have a 'walk-round' tour of the facilities on a computer – rather than plough through a prospectus or watch a boring film!

The job of the designers

The job of the design department is to create a design which:

- will appeal to consumers
- reflects the image of the product
- costs as little as possible to manufacture
- fulfils safety standards and regulations
- is as easy as possible for production to manufacture
- is constructed so that it will last over the intended life of the product
- will enable product maintenance to be carried out easily.

Did you know?

Sometimes the ideas for new developments have to be refined before they are 'marketable' – that is, before they can be produced at a price customers are willing to pay. Porsche have been involved in developing a cruise-control function which enables its cars to travel at a pre-set speed more safely. Infra-red sensors monitor the

speed and distance of the vehicle ahead plus road friction and braking distance. If the car is going too fast for the conditions, a warning light shows on the dashboard and the accelerator rises.

What are the difficulties? The sensors are still too expensive for commercial use – even in a Porsche – and, as yet, they don't work in fog. Porsche research and development specialists are still working on these problems.

Non-assessed activity

1 Divide into groups. Each group should discuss **one** of the articles below and decide which features are part of industrial design and which are part of engineering design.

- an electric razor
- a hairdrier
- a portable CD player
- a computer printer
- a camera
- a calculator

2 Railtrack, the government body responsible for Britain's rail network, is proposing a new generation of 160 mph tilt trains which will reduce the time of a five-hour journey to four hours. An alternative is a double-decker train which will run at 186 mph. However, the shock waves which can be caused by such trains could mean a massive rebuilding project of Victorian tunnels and bridges, and special shields may have to be erected in stations to prevent passengers being sucked onto the tracks.

   a As a group, decide which of the two types of train you would choose if you were the management of Railtrack, and give reasons why.

   b List the ways in which research and development has changed the design and performance of trains over the years.

   c Discuss with your tutor why old tunnels and bridges may have to be rebuilt and shields erected in stations.

   d Given the precautions required, why do you think Railtrack are still interested in these new trains?

Did you know?

Many products are designed using computers. A **computer-aided design (CAD)** package enables designers to sketch basic shapes and then vary the dimensions, angles and size of certain parts as they wish. The product can even undergo stress testing by computer.

131

In some industries CAD packages are linked to **computer-aided manufacturing** (**CAM**). In the carpet industry, a new design can be planned on computer and the tufting machine which actually makes the carpet (and looks something like a giant knitting machine!) can be pre-set and controlled to produce the design by computer.

Production

Typical job titles	Departmental functions
Works manager	Production of goods
Chief engineer	Maintenance of equipment
Factory operatives	Quality control
Production control clerks	Stock control
Quality controllers	Work study
Production planners	Production planning and control
Order clerks	Stores control
Storemen	Despatch
Draughtsmen	
Foremen	
Despatch clerks	
Engineers	

Production departments are found in manufacturing industries rather than in those industries which are engaged in providing services.

The method of production you will see in an organisation will depend upon the type of product being made and the size of the average order. Aeroplanes are not manufactured in the same way as ballpoint pens!

The four main types of production process are:

- **job production** – concerned with small orders or luxury goods. Each product is virtually a 'one-off', e.g. designer fashions, designer jewellery, shipbuilding and the aerospace industry (such as satellites).
- **batch production** – where whole batches of products are made. A typical example is a small bakery where the baker would make batches of meat pies, loaves, fruit tarts etc. before the shop opened.
- **mass production** – where large quantities of identical products are made on a production line.

This is the case with cars, many household appliances and consumer electronics.
- **flow production** – where the product is produced continuously using a technological process, e.g. gas or oil.

Did you know?

Japanese car manufacturers use a system known as **lean production**. This is a variation on the traditional mass production system whereby workers are arranged in groups and take responsibility for *all* aspects of the process they are undertaking, including quality control checks. A car passes from one bay of workers to another, rather than moving on a continuous production line. This means changes can be made to certain cars, or different models can be made. Therefore the system is far more flexible than the traditional production line. (For further examples of different types of teamwork see Element 2.3, page 221.)

The production function

Production can be divided into the two areas of:

- **planning** and
- **control**.

Although these obviously overlap, it is easier to understand them if you think of each area separately at the beginning.

Production planning

After a product has been designed, its manufacture must be carefully planned, e.g.

- what raw materials will be needed and in what quantities
- how many of these should be stored and how many bought as required
- what machines will be required
- what personnel will be needed and whether existing personnel have the necessary skills
- how the product will be assembled
- the average time needed to manufacture each item
- what packaging materials will be required.

Some of these factors may influence the final price of the product, e.g. the cost of the raw materials and the time and skills needed to make the product. For this reason there will be close liaison between the production planners and the cost accountant (see page 135). There will also be close links with sales and marketing – it is no good producing hundreds of products which sales cannot sell! (See page 141.)

Non-assessed activity

Working out how many machines or operators are required for a process is a key part of production planning. It is no use having ten people working on the first part and only five on the second if this would create a bottleneck (or hold-up) between the two stages. The same applies to machines – as some work faster than others.

Test your numeracy skills on the following problem. You are about to go into production making chocolate Easter eggs. For this you will need four machines.

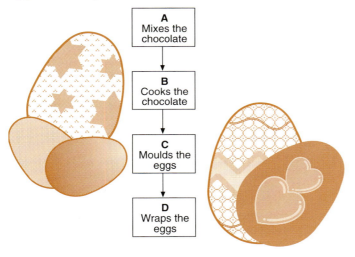

A
Mixes the chocolate

↓

B
Cooks the chocolate

↓

C
Moulds the eggs

↓

D
Wraps the eggs

The problem is that they all work at different speeds. In one hour, machine A will mix the chocolate for 400 eggs, machine B will cook the chocolate for 1200 eggs, machine C will mould 800 eggs and machine D will wrap 600 eggs. If, therefore, you buy one of each machine, you can only produce 400 eggs every hour (i.e. the speed of the slowest machine) *and* you have idle capacity on all the other machines.

Assuming money is no problem, how many of each machine must you buy to ensure you have no bottlenecks or spare capacity? And how many eggs will you be making every hour?

Did you know?

The layout of the production area is carefully planned to minimise time wasted by people having to walk backwards and

forwards. Normally, assembly of the product will start at one end and finish at the other.

Production control

Once the plans have been made and the manufacturing process started, it is vital that controls are in place to make sure that what was planned really happens. Otherwise production targets may not be met and nobody will know why. For this reason, there are several controls, including:

- **Progress control** – progress chasing means checking that planned output is as scheduled. If it is not, the cause of the problem has to be found, e.g. machine breakdown, substandard materials or labour problems. The problem needs to be solved *and* production schedules have to be readjusted to try to make up for lost time.
- **Quality control** – quality controllers check the standard of the finished product. They may do this by examining each article or by random sampling, e.g. selecting certain items for inspection on a random basis. Many companies today operate a TQM or total quality management system.
- **Stock control** – ensures that supplies of raw materials and components are always available so that production schedules are not interrupted.
- **Machine utilisation control** – this controls the use of the machines – to ensure none are overloaded or overused without being checked and maintained. Because machine breakdowns can be critical, many organisations have a maintenance plan which shows the dates on which machines will be out of operation for inspection and servicing.

Did you know?

Automation and computers have changed many of the functions of production workers. Not only can the products themselves now be made by a completely automated process and controlled by computer (known as **computer-integrated manufacturing** (**CIM**), but traditional jobs may now be done very differently, e.g.

- Quality control may be done automatically by machine. For instance, a machine which makes hacksaw blades of a certain length will have a computerised checkpoint at the end, so that the length and thickness of each blade is automatically checked. The machine will stop if faults are detected.
- Progress chasers may now receive much of their information either on computer VDU or computer

print-out. They do not need, therefore, to run around a large factory checking on progress. In days gone by, some chasers in large factories, e.g. at British Aerospace, used a bicycle to get round the area they needed to cover!

Optional evidence assignment

*This activity can be carried out verbally in class **in a group** as a non-assessed activity to consolidate learning. Alternatively, if you do it **on your own**, it can count as supplementary evidence towards the following parts of the scheme.*

PC 3:	Describe the work and explain the interdependence of departments within business organisations
Range:	Departments: research & development, production
Core skills:	Communication, application of number, Information technology

During your course you should arrange to visit *at least* one manufacturing organisation. Revise the notes you have just read before your visit. Whilst you are there make notes on what you see in relation to their production processes. Prepare some questions to ask to add to your knowledge of how different departments operate.

The key information to find out is:

- the type of product(s) being made
- the research and development which takes place – whether this is a separate department or part of production
- how research and development links to production
- the scale of production (e.g. small, medium or large)
- the type of production process being used
- the degree to which the process was automated or computerised
- the layout of the production area
- the way in which production is scheduled and controlled.

Using your word processor, write a brief report of your findings. Include a paragraph which states how the departments you have covered are interlinked in relation to the production of goods.

Purchasing

It is essential that the people in the purchasing (or buying) department are skilled at buying the raw materials at the right quantity and price. If they buy at too high a price the whole cost of the product is

Typical job titles	Departmental functions
Purchasing manager Purchasing assistants Buyers	The buying of goods and services for the organisation as a whole

affected. If they buy too much, valuable storage space is used up and money, which could be earning interest, is tied up.

Buying for the organisation as a whole, rather than each department buying what it wants on its own, usually saves money. This is because orders can be co-ordinated so that bulk orders can be placed. More discount is usually allowed on large orders from suppliers. In addition, the buyers become specialists and know what is available and from which supplier. They can then give advice to particular departments.

Specialist buyers are particularly important for retail organisations. Marks & Spencer, for example, employs buyers who research what customers want, who know the latest fashions and can adapt these to suit typical customers.

Did you know?

Many companies today use what is known as the **just in time** (**JIT**) system of purchasing supplies. This means that they do not have to hold large stocks of materials (which saves both money and storage space) but instead they expect suppliers to deliver the raw materials as and when they are needed. The system is obviously most suitable for large organisations who, because of the size of their orders, have a degree of control over their suppliers.

Accounting

Many managers consider the Accounting department the most important one in any organisation – and the most unpopular! This is because the Accounting department is responsible for obtaining the capital required and keeping a check on expenditure, including checking incoming and outgoing payments. Since few of us like to be told to reduce our spending, it is unlikely that any department will be pleased at being told by Accounting that it is spending too much.

The basic job of the Accounting department is to record and analyse all the different financial

Typical job titles	Departmental functions
Chief accountant	Obtaining finance
Cost accountant	Recording financial transactions
Management accountant	Preparing wages and salaries
Credit controller	Costings
Chief cashier	Preparing final accounts
Wages clerks	Producing continuous financial information for management
Cost clerks	
Ledger clerks	Debt management
Credit control clerks	

transactions taking place in the organisation. However, there are various reasons why this is done, and various ways in which the resulting figures can be used. For this reason, finance is usually divided into the three main areas of:

- **financial accounting**
- **management accounting** and
- **cost accounting**.

In addition, the wages and salaries section will normally be a sub-division of the finance department.

Financial accounting

The financial accountant is responsible for producing the monthly and yearly accounts for the organisation. These will include the trading and profit-and-loss accounts and the balance sheet. A small organisation is likely to use an outside firm of accountants to do this, rather than employ its own accountant. A large company – particularly a public limited company whose accounts must be published each year – will have its own financial accountant.

The problem with end-of-year accounts is that they give **historic** (i.e. old) information. It is of little use if the managing director finds out in April that in January the company was in debt! For that reason, although financial returns are produced as a legal requirement, other accountants are employed to give different types of information.

Did you know?

It is the job of an accounting manager to obtain finance for new projects and to calculate if they are worth undertaking. This is

done by calculating the potential return on the investment. If this is greater than the cost of obtaining the finance then the project will go ahead.

Management accounting

It is the management accountant's job to provide management with up-to-date financial information, virtually on a daily basis. This is so that corrections and adjustments can be made as they are needed. If, for instance, the Sales and Marketing department are spending more than they should, the management accountant will bring this to their attention.

Did you know?

Many companies obtain much of their financial information by computer. Many large retail stores, with computerised cash registers, operate a system whereby daily sales information from them is transmitted to head office each evening and analysed by computer overnight. The following morning, management can see how much each store is selling, which lines are sticking and which lines are selling well – and react accordingly.

Non-assessed activity

You are part of the management team of a large chain of department stores. This morning you have received the following information.

- Two stores are selling far less than the others.
- One store is performing very well indeed.
- Garden furniture is sticking in every store.
- There is a shortage of electrical goods in three stores and a surplus in another two.

What action could you take to improve sales throughout the chain?

Cost accounting

In a manufacturing company some of the most important financial information is to do with the cost of making a product, because this will affect the price.

The accountant divides all costs into **direct** or **indirect** costs. Direct costs are easy to identify and include labour and materials. Indirect costs are more difficult, as they include the overall costs of heating, lighting and rent. These have to be added together

135

and divided or **apportioned** for each product. Obviously, as costs increase the figures must be updated and the selling price must be increased or profits will fall.

Non-assessed activity

Try to calculate the cost of one hour of your lessons. You need an idea of the labour (the cost of your tutor) and the materials involved. You then need to think about the indirect costs of running and maintaining the building you are in – and how these should be apportioned between classes. You may be surprised at your answer!

Did you know?

Another way of looking at costs is to classify them as fixed costs and variable costs. Fixed costs stay the same and don't change with volume of output. They include rates, machinery, insurance, etc. which have to be paid even if no goods are produced. Variable costs change with volume of output, e.g. raw materials, electricity and overtime payments. Labour can be either a fixed or a variable cost. Labour which is employed all the time, such as office staff, are a fixed cost. Labour which is hired just for a specific purpose, e.g. casual workers, are a variable cost.

Non-assessed activity

You are about to move into a flat with a friend. List all the expenditure you are likely to encounter and divide it into fixed and variable costs. If you want to save money, which will be the easier to reduce? Why?

Did you know?

Another function sometimes carried out by the accounts department is to keep a check on those customers who have not paid their bills! There is normally a company policy about how long customers should be allowed to continue to buy goods on credit and how big a debt they should be allowed to amass. Because this is a rather unpleasant (although essential) job, some companies employ outside debt collection (or credit control) agencies to carry out this work for them.

Human Resources (Personnel)

Did you know?

Some organisations (and some books) refer to human resources under the title personnel. Therefore if you see someone with the job title of 'Personnel Manager' then this means the same thing as 'Human Resources Manager'.

Typical job titles	Departmental functions
Personnel or HR manager	Recruitment and employment of staff
Training officer	Keeping staff records
Welfare officer	Education and training
Employment officer	Industrial relations and trade union negotiations
Personnel assistants	
Record clerks	Staff welfare
Canteen staff	Health and safety
Welfare/nursing staff	Wages and salary administration
Security staff	Manpower planning
	Security

Your first contact with an organisation is likely to be with the Personnel or Human Resources department as, amongst other things, they are involved with recruitment and selection. Therefore if you apply for a job you will be in contact with this department. However, this is only one part of their work.

Did you know?

The importance of the Human Resources department varies from one organisation to another. In some companies it may be a large department with highly qualified staff. In others it may be much smaller. This often shows the importance the company attaches to its staff!

Peter Drucker, a management writer, considered that people were the most important of all resources. His view was that if you buy any other resource, such as land, a building or a machine, then it is inflexible. What you see is what you get. People are different. They have the ability to work hard and achieve great things, if they are encouraged and given the opportunity to do so.

Companies which believe this often invest a considerable amount in their Human Resources department. It is also likely that they have a Human Resources Director (rather than a Human Resources Manager). This means that the head of Human Resources is often a member of the board of directors and, as such, will be involved in all the future plans of the organisation. He or she can then look at the future staffing needs of the company concerned and make sure that these are met.

Recruitment

All organisations regularly need new staff – to replace those who are leaving or to fill new vacancies if the company is expanding. Other departments in the company will notify the Human Resources department, who will then try to fill the vacancy.

They will usually do this by a set process.

The recruitment process

When a vacancy occurs in any department, the Human Resources department is required to:

- obtain a full job description – a summary of the job which lists the duties to be carried out and the areas for which the job holder is responsible
- look at various ways of filling the vacancy
- send out application forms and other details to those who apply
- look at all the job applications received
- arrange a shortlisting meeting, i.e. where a group of people – normally including a senior manager and a member of the Human Resources department – select a number of candidates for interview
- arrange the interview – on a one to one basis, with a panel of interviewers, or by means of a series of interviews.

Non-assessed activity

As a group, discuss how many methods of recruitment you think may be used. A list of these is given at the end of the element.

Did you know?

Sometimes candidates are given a test – either an aptitude test (generally to test speed of reaction, etc.), an intelligence test, a personality test

or a practical test such as a keyboarding exercise. If you are going for an interview, it is worth remembering this!

The selection process

If great care has been taken, the right candidate *should* have been selected, although that is not always the case. Nevertheless there are certain guidelines interviewers normally follow to try to reduce the chances of making a wrong choice.

- They will check carefully that the job applicant has the right qualifications and experience.
- They will also want to check on the candidate's personal qualities, which are more difficult to identify. Someone who is good at an interview may not necessarily be good at the job!

Experience is more difficult to identify, particularly **relevant** experience. Someone who has had a lot of experience in making and serving sandwiches in a sandwich bar might have a suitable catering qualification and 'experience' in catering but might be hopeless at making and serving canteen meals for 150 people!

Non-assessed activity

Imagine you work as an administrative assistant in a Human Resources department. You are asked to check on the experience of the following job applicants. Why do you think they may not be suitable for the jobs for which they have applied?

1 For a job as a HGV driver

   'I've had a full driving licence since I was 17 – and I've driven my boss all over the place – he hates driving.'

2 For a job as a private secretary

   'I'm an excellent typist – I spend at least three days a week typing out orders and invoices.'

3 For a job as a sales representative

   'Everyone says I can be very persuasive . I'm always the one who's sent round to collect for Children in Need.'

4 For a job as a security guard

   'I don't stand any nonsense – any cheek from anyone and they're out. I learned that when I was a bouncer at a night club.'

leaving date, qualifications and experience and works number. There is usually space to record additional training courses and qualifications obtained.

If the company operates a system of **appraisal** interviews, where existing staff are interviewed annually by their supervisors and their current performance is noted, these interview forms may also be attached.

It is important to note that *all* personnel records are confidential, especially comments on attendance, punctuality and personal circumstances.

Did you know?

New staff usually take part in an **induction** programme. This is designed to help newcomers get to know their way around quite quickly. An induction programme usually covers the work carried out by the company in general and the newcomer's own department in particular, and general points they need to know, e.g. regarding company policy on pay, safety, fire regulations, staff facilities and so on. You probably took part in a similar programme for students when you started your course.

Training

It is sensible for any organisation to encourage its staff to take further qualifications or to participate in training programmes. This means they will be capable of taking on different types of work or doing their existing job more efficiently. Training is usually necessary:

- to enable junior employees to develop their skills and obtain higher level qualifications
- to enable existing employees to cope with changes to their jobs, e.g. the introduction of computers or word processors
- to enable promoted employees to cope with new responsibilities, e.g. managerial or supervisory training
- to improve efficiency, e.g. till training by retail stores, health and safety training to reduce accidents in factories, telephone training for sales staff.

You can find out more about training in Element 2.2.

Industrial relations

It is the job of the Human Resources department to negotiate with trade unions and their representatives in relation to:

Did you know?

Some organisations have a policy of advertising all vacancies first to existing staff, so that people who want to apply for promotion are given the first opportunity to apply. If there are sufficient applications, the company may not advertise outside at all.

Other companies advertise all vacancies both inside and outside the company, so that existing employees who want promotion have to take their chances alongside outsiders who apply.

Non-assessed activity

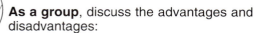

As a group, discuss the advantages and disadvantages:

   a to existing employees
b to the organisation

of having a policy whereby all vacancies are advertised inside and outside the company at the same time.

Staff records

The Human Resources department will keep a record of every employee – past and present. This is usually kept on a computer database. The record will include details of the employee's name and address, date of birth, current job title and salary, starting and

- redundancies
- health and safety procedures
- training
- wages
- disciplinary procedures
- grievance procedures.

The Human Resources Manager of an organisation will liaise with shop stewards and/or local union officials, at either branch or district level, over issues with which the union would be concerned. Trade unions are covered in more detail on page 166 and more information about grievance and disciplinary procedures are outlined on page 178.

Redundancies

One of the most difficult jobs for a Human Resources Manager is to deal with **redundancies** when the company finds that it has too many employees for the work available. Redundancy occurs when:

- the company stops trading altogether – so that everyone is out of work
- the company stops trading in one area but continues to trade in others
- the company continues to trade but no longer requires the services of some of its employees because the need for their particular job has disappeared.

(See Element 2.2, page 184, for individual employee rights in relation to redundancy.)

Did you know?

- The European Commission has issued a **Directive on Collective Redundancies** which aims to standardise the treatment of redundant workers across Europe.

- The sale of a business from one owner to another may result in some workers being made redundant, because the new owner may require fewer workers. It used to mean that since the workers' contracts of employment with the first owner had ceased, they had to enter into new contracts with the second owner. This might mean they lose some of the legal rights which depend on the number of years they have worked (including the right to redundancy pay). However, the European Community has passed an **Acquired Rights Directive** which protects workers in this situation.

- If you are told that you are going to be made redundant you have the right to be given paid time off to look for work. However, the maximum payment is for two days and you have to have been employed for at least two years to be entitled to this.

Wages and salary administration

All large companies have a specified wage structure for their employees, based on a job grading or job evaluation scheme. This ensures that those with the greatest responsibility are paid accordingly. It also ensures that there is fairness for employees.

When rates are about to change, they must be considered in terms of their effects on all employees. Any changes must also be carefully considered in relation to the company's profits, future business prospects, pay rates of other firms in the area and so on.

Fringe benefits are also the responsibility of the Human Resources department.

Staff welfare

Employees of a large organisation may benefit from a whole range of social facilities, e.g. a social club, sports facilities and regular social activities. Welfare also covers the provision of canteen facilities and pension schemes as well as providing a counselling service for employees who are having personal problems.

Did you know?

Some large companies arrange for professional counsellors to interview their staff. As an example, Relate counsellors – who specialise in marriage guidance – may visit companies by appointment to see members of staff. The view of the organisation is that this costs less than losing employees through absence because of personal worries or because they need time to see a counsellor privately.

Health

Many companies routinely arrange medical examinations for new staff. Their initial appointment to the job may even be dependent on the medical report being satisfactory. Health checks and screening may be offered to employees, and large firms will have their own nurse to whom employees can go if they are ill or injured. The organisation may even contract the services of a doctor to visit the company on a regular basis.

Safety

All companies must comply with current safety legislation (see pages 50 and 206), and this will be monitored by safety representatives who are also trade union members. They will usually meet as a safety committee on a regular basis, and at least one member of the Human Resources department will also attend. It is their responsibility to:

- follow up complaints about hazards
- ensure that accident prevention and reporting systems are followed
- investigate all accidents that occur
- deal with accident claims.

Security

In many organisations the security staff are also members of the Human Resources department. In some organisations an outside firm of security guards may be contracted to provide a security service. This may include:

- vetting visitors at the main gate
- patrolling the premises
- checking doors and windows are locked
- accompanying staff carrying money from one building to another
- protecting those involved in handling cash (either cash received or paid out – e.g. wages).

Marketing and Sales

The scale and range of jobs carried out by the Marketing and Sales department will vary greatly from one organisation to another, but will normally include selling, promoting, advertising and public relations. In some companies many specialist agencies are used, e.g:

- market research agencies
- public relations consultants
- advertising agencies.

Other organisations may be large enough to employ their own specialist staff to cover many of these areas.

Typical job titles	Departmental functions
Marketing manager	Market research
Sales manager – home sales	Promotions and advertising, public relations
Export manager	Home and export sales
Advertising manager	Preparing sales documentation
Market researchers	Attending trade fairs
Public relations officer	Keeping customer records
Sales co-ordinator	
Sales representatives	
Order clerks	
Telephone sales staff	

Market research

Market research involves finding out what the consumer thinks and what he or she wants from a product. This may be a proposed new product or an existing product. Market research may be carried out:

- by post
- by interviewing
- by telephone.

The postal method is the cheapest but has the lowest success rate. An organisation will send a questionnaire to selected customers or households and ask them to complete it. Most do not!

Interviews are common. You will often see market researchers in your own town centre asking people questions. Much depends on the skill of the interviewer. Again, only suitable people will be chosen – there is little point in asking a woman what she thinks about an electric razor or a pensioner what he thinks about jeans!

The telephone method is growing in popularity. Specialist agencies 'collect' a number of volunteers by asking them to take part in periodic surveys.

Then they telephone the volunteers at intervals and ask them to reply to a series of questions. These could be on anything from newspapers to pension schemes. The agency summarises the results for the client. The cost is reasonable and the results are rapid.

Most questionnaires are designed to be analysed by computer, for speed. The result will reveal the predicted market demand for the product. This information (plus any advance orders) will be given to the production department and will determine the size of production 'runs' which will take place.

Further information on how to design a questionnaire, carry out and analyse a survey is given in the Core Skills Element on Application of Number, page 569.

Did you know?

Some organisations use their own staff as market researchers! Food companies may test a new product on their canteen menu. It will be free to those who try it but they have to complete a questionnaire saying how much they liked it. Companies making hosiery (tights and stockings) may test new colours and new styles by giving samples to their female staff to try.

Selling

The difference between sales and marketing is that sales is just *one small part* of the marketing operation. Traditionally, people first made a product and then someone had to try to sell it! Henry Ford was a prime example of this. When he made the model T Ford, he said that customers could have it 'in any colour so long as it's black!'

Today no organisation can afford to operate in that way. Instead companies try to find out what the customer wants – and then make it. Selling is therefore easy! In the words of Peter Drucker, a famous management writer, marketing is 'looking at the company through the customer's eyes'.

Promoting and advertising

Deciding on the best type of advertising and promotion for a particular product, at a particular

stage in its life cycle, is a job for an expert. Advertising and promotional campaigns are expensive and money can easily be wasted.

Companies have a choice of promotional methods for each product which will include:

- relying on word-of-mouth recommendation
- paying for advertising in the mass media, e.g. on television and in newspapers
- sales promotion, e.g. exhibitions, sponsorship, special offers, competitions etc.
- personal selling, which relies on persuasiveness by the sales person
- publicity for the company and a good corporate image (known as public relations).

Few companies are likely to rely on the first. Virtually all companies will try to achieve the last (mainly because a good story will mean free coverage by the press).

Whether to choose advertising, promotion or personal selling will depend on the product itself. You will cover this topic more thoroughly in Unit 3.

Non-assessed activity

As a group, identify **four** products where the selling is done by representatives (frequently called reps). Suggest reasons why reps are employed to sell these goods and not others.

Public relations

'Public relations' is the term for maintaining good 'relations' with those outside the organisation. The idea is simple. If people think well of the company – and believe it is trustworthy, reliable and honest – they will buy its products. A good example is Marks & Spencer. In various ways, such as support for local charities and the arts, good customer service, a generous exchange policy and so on, they have been able to form a strong corporate image. Marks & Spencer rarely advertise – to some extent they rely on their name and reputation to sell their goods.

A Public Relations Manager will represent the company to the outside world. This will include the media, visitors to the organisation, interest groups (e.g. environmentalists), the business community, other organisations and even politicians. It is the

141

Public Relations Manager's job to make sure that the company is well-known by the public for all the right reasons, and one way in which this can be done is by free publicity in newspapers and on TV.

Letting the media know when something important is about to happen is a much cheaper way of getting press coverage than paying for advertising. The media are informed on a special **press release** which gives details of the story. Each release may have a special **embargo date**, which means the story mustn't be published before then.

The local papers and local radio and television companies are looking for stories about local organisations all the time. For a story to be printed in the national papers it must be very eye-catching and different. The 'serious' papers all carry on their business pages reports about companies, including new developments, details of the financial results for the year and so on. However, these pages are mainly read by other business people and investors. For *consumers* to read the story it needs to appear on the main pages of the paper.

Non-assessed activity

1 Look in your local papers and a selection of national papers over a period of one week. Cut out **six** articles that 'tell a story' about different companies.
2 Assess each one and decide whether it will give a good or a bad impression of the company to consumers.
3 Imagine you and your fellow students are starting a charity appeal to raise money for a good cause. You are holding a special indoor charity football match with guest appearances of two famous football players.
   a Decide which cause you would like to support.
   b Decide on your promotional methods.
   c Prepare a brief press release to send to your local paper. Invent the other details which you think would be important to tell readers.

Administration

Administration can encompass a large or small number of areas – depending upon the company and the way it is organised. Basically it refers to all the service operations required by the organisation. The people working within administration may be:

- reprographics staff (photocopying and duplicating)

Typical job titles	Departmental functions
Company secretary	Legal affairs
Office manager	Insurance
Secretarial supervisor	Dealing with shareholders
Reprographics supervisor	Organising meetings
Clerical, office and secretarial staff	Office planning
Cleaning staff	Office systems and services including mail handling, reception, telecommunications
	Cleaning

- reception staff
- telecommunications and switchboard staff
- word processing staff
- mailroom staff
- filing clerks
- general clerical assistants.

In a large organisation with **centralised** services, these areas will be overseen by an office manager, even though some departments also have clerical staff of their own. In an organisation where such jobs are decentralised (i.e. each department does its own photocopying, filing etc.) the office manager will control fewer staff (see also page 148).

Did you know?

The **company secretary** may oversee the administration section, or report directly to the managing director (and would therefore be shown with a dotted line on the organisation chart). It is a legal requirement of all UK companies to have a company secretary who is responsible for:

- arranging and keeping records of meetings of the board of directors
- overseeing the administration of pensions and insurance
- making sure that the company always operates within the law
- keeping the register of shareholders and communicating with them about meetings, dividends etc.

Reception

When you first walk into an organisation and go up to the reception desk you will notice:

- the area in which it is situated and
- the people who staff it,

and you will probably find that the way in which the staff treat you is more important than the way in which the area is laid out. Even so a good manager will always make certain that the reception area creates a good first impression of the organisation.

Did you know?

Nowadays there are companies which specialise in the planning and furnishing of reception areas to meet specific client needs. Before they make any suggestions, they will want to know whether the reception area is at street level – in which case the floor covering must be able to cope with dirt and the windows may need blinds. Additional heating may be required for staff because of draughts.

Mail handling

The Administration Manager **must** make sure that mail is dealt with promptly and efficiently. Otherwise the organisation is likely to come to a halt. If the mail is part of a centralised system – and in most larger organisations it is – then certain procedures can be put into operation to make sure all goes well (particularly at the beginning and end of each day).

Every company is likely to have its own mailroom procedures which administrative staff must follow. Staff employed in this area must also know how to operate mailroom equipment and understand the range of postal services which the organisation can use.

Telecommunications

A modern Administration department will probably be responsible for the communication systems within the organisation as a whole, which can include:

- a modern telephone system
- a fax machine or machines
- electronic mail
- paging equipment, bleepers and mobile phones.

Fax and E-mail are discussed in detail in Element 4.3, pages 510 and 514.

Telephone equipment

Today most large businesses have an automated switchboard which is operated by a designated switchboard operator. Smaller firms may have a key telephone system where each telephone contains a microchip. All modern systems offer a wide range of facilities for users including call diversion, music on hold and call logging – where all calls from extensions are noted together with the time and cost.

Paging equipment

Today most people are used to the idea that a communications system does not have to be fixed to the wall, as old-fashioned telephones were! Mobile communication systems are used by representatives and by security staff – or anyone else who may move around a building or area in the course of their job. They make it easy for anyone to be contacted at any time, which can be invaluable in an emergency.

Non-assessed activity

1 Imagine you work for an organisation where electronic mail is available to all staff. You have discovered that there are some disadvantages. Sometimes staff can't be bothered to switch on their machine and to check their E-mail. Some staff 'hog' the system or use it for personal matters such as selling cars, household goods or wedding dresses. Some staff won't use it at all.

As a group, list any suggestions you may have for overcoming these problems.

2 Discuss the type of emergencies and other situations

which may occur when a mobile communications system would be indispensable.

3 Try to see a fax machine in operation. Discuss with your tutor why a fax to Australia takes virtually the same length of time to transmit as a fax to a nearby town!

Computer (IT) Services

Typical job titles	Departmental functions
Computer services manager	Designing computer systems
Data processing manager	Programming computers
Computer programmers	Providing computer services
Computer operators	
Technical staff	

Keeping computers operational, and assisting users, is a vital service. In some organisations it may be part of the administration section. However, these days it is more likely that computer support will be a separate section on its own. It is usually headed by a Computer Services Manager who heads specialist staff.

The way in which computer services operate may depend, to some extent, on whether a mainframe computer or a set of linked personal computers – known as a network – is installed (see Core Skills, Information Technology section). If a mainframe computer is installed, the Computer Services department is likely to be located in one particular area. If a network is in operation, then Computer Services staff will visit different departments to assist users.

Usually, a company with a large mainframe system will employ specialist programmers who will write programs to give computer users the services they require. This may include a program to print delivery notes and invoices and remind late payers of unpaid debts. A company with a network is likely to buy commercial software and – possibly – information on CD ROMs which can be made available for all users on the system. For this, a **site licence** must be obtained from the manufacturer of the software. This means the program can be made available to all network users.

The Computer Services department will be responsible for the maintenance and upgrading of all the hardware (equipment) as well as the installation of all the software. Staff will be involved in one or more of the following duties:

- repairing faults on the system and with individual computers
- installing security systems
- purchasing new equipment and software
- testing and installing new equipment and software on the system
- giving general advice to users
- organising training programmes for users (in conjunction with the Human Resources Department)
- keeping up-to-date with new developments
- making recommendations to management for upgrading of equipment and systems.

Further information on Information Technology hardware and software is given in the Core Skills chapter on page 610.

Did you know?

Sometimes problems can occur which are no fault of Computer Services staff. Hewlett Packard 'improved' their Deskjet printer but the wheels that gripped the paper didn't work properly on the new models. HP then issued all users with a special device for roughening the wheels so they would grip the paper properly. In a centralised organisation it would be the job of Computer Services staff to make sure all HP Deskjet printers were modified.

Customer Services

Typical job titles	Departmental functions
Customer services manager	Customer service and liaison
Administration staff	

Today, customer service or support is not just the responsibility of the Sales and Marketing department, even though staff in this department may deal with customers more often than other people working for the organisation. More usually, putting the customer first is seen as important for *all* members of staff, from the switchboard operator to the car park attendant. In some cases there is a Customer Service department or section which is linked with a quality control group within the organisation. Its major role is to deal with any complaints and to provide information to the rest of the organisation about how customer care can be improved. (See page 156 for information on customers' demand for quality.) Customer service is also dealt with fully in Element 3.4.

Distribution (logistics)

Typical job titles	Departmental functions
Distribution manager	Scheduling the distribution of goods
Warehouse supervisor	
Transport/shipping clerks	Arranging transport
Despatch clerks	Preparing documentation
Stock control clerks	Checking stocks
Warehouse staff	Fulfilling customer orders
Drivers	Maintaining vehicles
Mechanics	Logistics

It is an old saying that a product has to be in the right place, at the right time, and in the right condition, to be sold. The goods have been packed by Production and sold by Sales and Marketing, but someone has to get them from the manufacturer to the customer, on time and in good condition. This is the responsibility of the Distribution department. The department has obvious links with the Purchasing department as regards the storage of raw materials before production and of the finished products before distribution. (See page 134.)

Channels of distribution and transport methods have already been covered in Element 1.2. This element looks at the work done within the organisation in relation to distribution.

Major responsibilities include:

■ the maintenance of the vehicles
■ safety precautions both in relation to the vehicles and to the drivers
■ the security of the goods – protection from theft, damage etc.

The size of the distribution function can vary. It may be:

■ a small transport section which arranges for outside haulage companies or distributors to deliver the goods
■ part of the Sales and Marketing department
■ a medium-sized operation where goods are delivered in the company's own lorries or wagons

■ a large and important function, with depots or warehouses all over the UK controlled by a central distribution facility. In such cases you may find that one employee specialises in **logistics**, i.e. in working out the most economical and cost-effective routes etc.

Did you know?

Logistics is the science of moving and storing goods. The term originated in America and came into general use in World War II in connection with the supply and storage of all the items required by the armed forces, including storage, transport and distribution of ammunition, fuel, food etc.

Non-assessed activity

You and a group of your friends want to go to a local disco. You haven't much money for petrol but – a bit rashly – you have promised to give everybody a lift in your car. Look at Figure 2.15 and discuss as a group the most economic route you could take both to and from the disco. It shows how difficult the job of a logistics manager can be!

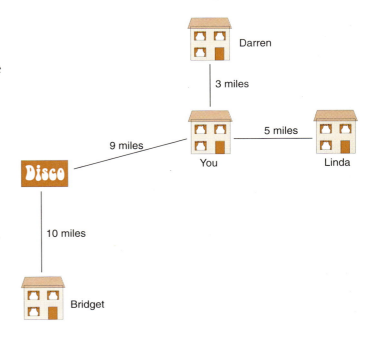

Figure 2.15 Looking for the best route

Specialist distribution staff

In addition, companies who export will have specialist staff – often known as shipping clerks – who will complete the paperwork required by customs authorities and either the airline or shipping line which is transporting the goods.

Did you know?

Information technology is used extensively by distribution centres to:

- plan and schedule loading and delivery routes
- keep stock records
- allow for major customers to order direct by computer using **Electronic Data Interchange** (see Element 4.1).

Non-assessed activity

You work for a company which manufactures biscuits. Until now your organisation has employed outside distributors to take the biscuits to your customers – who range from large stores to small retailers. Your boss is considering buying a fleet of lorries and having an in-house distribution department to deliver the biscuits as from next March.

As a group, discuss the advantages and disadvantages of this proposal.

Evidence assignment

At this point your tutor may wish you to start work on the project which will prove to your verifiers that you understand this section of the element. If so, turn to page 161 and do Section 1 of the project. This covers the first evidence indicator for this element.

The interdependence of departments

Even though you have just been reading about individual departments and their various functions, remind yourself – by looking back at the organisational charts on pages 124–127 – just how interlinked these departments are! There is no point

having a Sales department if there is nothing to sell. A Research and Development department would be redundant if the organisation stopped manufacturing products. If there were no workers, there would be no job for the Human Resources department, and so on. That's where the job of the managers is so important. They must make certain that their departments are running smoothly and also liaise with all the other departments. A good organisational structure can help – that's why so much emphasis has been put on it in this section – but the success of the structure depends very much on the people within it and whether or not they are sufficiently well informed, trained and motivated to make the system work!

Non-assessed activity

Give **two** ways in which you think each of the following departments **could** interlink, e.g. the Research and Development department could link with Marketing over (a) market research and (b) design of a particular new product.

1 Production and Distribution (logistics)
2 Production and Purchasing
3 Purchasing and Marketing or Sales
4 Administration and Computer (IT) Services
5 Human Resources and Accounting
6 Customer Services and Administration
7 Marketing or Sales and Human Resources

Optional evidence assignment

*This activity can be carried out verbally in class **in a group** as a non-assessed activity to consolidate learning. Alternatively, if you do it **on your own**, it can count as supplementary evidence towards the following parts of the scheme.*

PC 3:   Describe the work and explain the interdependence of departments within business organisations

Range: Departments: purchasing, accounting, human resources (personnel), marketing, sales, administration, computer (IT) services, customer services, distribution (logistics)

Core: Communication, information technology

Read the case study below and then undertake the tasks which follow.

Case study – Giftware Direct

You have recently started work in the Human Resources department at Giftware Direct. This is a large mail order company which sells a wide range of goods directly to the customer. Catalogues are produced twice a year for customers. Customers can place orders by post or by ringing a special customer services line. They can pay by credit card or by cheque (with order). Some customers are registered as agents and receive 10 per cent discount on all purchases. Agents are invoiced for the goods they order each month.

The company does not produce any goods itself. Instead it purchases items from a wide range of suppliers and stores them in a large warehouse. Stock is controlled by computer. When customers place an order, Customer Services staff key this in on computer. The order is automatically passed to the warehouse and the staff there pack the boxes with the goods including a copy of the order. Any invoices are automatically generated by computer the following day and reminders are sent if the invoice isn't paid within fourteen days. All packages are despatched by parcel post.

The company has recently opened ten shops in nearby towns to take customer orders face-to-face. The shops sell a smaller range than the complete catalogue. Shop orders receive top priority and are delivered by company van the following day.

1 List **six** categories of staff you think will be employed by Giftware Direct.
2 Obtain a copy of a mail order catalogue, e.g. Next Directory, Benetton Direct, Express Gifts, Argos etc. Discuss, **with your tutor** and **as a group**:
   a how goods can be ordered
   b how orders are handled when they are received by the organisation.

   If there is a mail order company near your school or college, find out if your tutor can arrange a visit for your class.

   Make notes on all your findings.

3 **In groups of two or three**, prepare an induction booklet to be given to new staff which states the role of each of the following departments in the company.
   a Purchasing
   b Accounting
   c Human Resources
   d Marketing
   e Sales (e.g. staff in the shops)
   f Administration
   g Computer (IT) Services
   h Customer Services
   i Distribution

Use the information in this book to help you to expand on the case study, together with the notes you made in part 2, above.

4 Write a brief report explaining how each department relates to the others. In particular, stress the links between:
   a Purchasing and Accounting
   b Computer Services and Accounting
   c Administration and Distribution
   d Marketing and Customer Services
   e Human Resources and Sales.
5 **As a group**, prepare a five-minute talk to give to new employees, explaining the information in your booklet and the way in which the organisation operates.

Evidence assignment

At this point your tutor may wish you to start or continue work on the project which will prove to your verifiers that you understand this section of the element. If so, turn to page 161 and do Section 2 of the project. This covers the second evidence indicator for this element.

Differences in working arrangements

When you and a group of friends leave college, you might agree to have yearly reunions. At the first reunion you would probably discover that although all of you have now got jobs you don't all work under the same conditions. Some of you work as a member of a team, some of you work more independently. One or two of you work in a

centralised department which services all the rest of the departments. You all work different hours and at different times. Even the places where you work differ. Some of you are allowed to work from home: one of the group is 'mobile' and moves from place to place.

Teamworking

No matter where you work you will have a particular job to do. What you do depends on your individual skills. However, you may also be expected to work as part of a team.

Some jobs are designed to be carried out by an individual – the type of job may almost demand it. Others are designed to be carried out by members of a team.

Non-assessed activity

Write **two** headings: 'Individual work' and 'Work as a member of a team'. Now place each of the following jobs under the heading which you think more accurately describes the job.

- district nurse
- small shopkeeper
- car assembly worker
- commercial traveller
- staff nurse in a hospital
- sewing machinist in a factory
- shop assistant in a department store
- petrol pump attendant
- dressmaker

Teamwork in particular structures

Generally speaking, more people are expected to work in a team than completely on their own. What can affect the issue, however, is the type of organisational structure that is in place. If you are employed in a workers' co-operative, by definition you will have to work as a member of a group. A doctor, working in a medical practice which has a flat structure, would be more likely to work as an individual. In a hierarchical structure, much depends on your actual job. In a matrix structure most people may work in teams. Teamworking is popular for several reasons. Many people prefer to work with other people rather than completely alone as this adds a social aspect to the job. Managers prefer it for several reasons, including the following.

- A **good** team consists of people with different strengths. These can be utilised for the benefit of everyone.
- The team will 'pull together' and help each other out in a crisis. If one member is absent the others can compensate.
- The productivity of a good team, collectively, is usually higher than the each person's individual efforts added together.

Even within teams, there will be a team leader. For further details of teamwork see Element 2.3 page 221.

Centralised/decentralised arrangements

You have already met the term centralisation on page 142. This simply means that main services of an organisation are grouped together in one place. For instance, if you worked in the Printing department of your local council this would be a **centralised** service because it does the printing work for all the rest of the departments. People who require printing would complete a special request form and send the order to the Printing section. The printing would be done by people who knew the equipment well and were professionals at their job. The finished items would then be sent back to the different departments.

This is different to a non-centralised organisation, where each department is responsible for virtually all its administrative activities, as well as for the work in which it specialises, e.g. Finance, Sales and Marketing etc.

Optional evidence assignment

*This activity can be carried out verbally in class **in a group** as a non-assessed activity to consolidate learning. Alternatively, if you do it **on your own**, it can count as supplementary evidence towards the following parts of the scheme.*

PC 4: Identify and explain differences in working arrangements

Range: Working arrangements: team working, centralised, de-centralised

Core skills: Communication, Information technology

Read the case study below and answer the questions which follow.

Case study – evaluating central services

You move from your job working in the centralised filing section of the local council to working as a filing clerk in the administration department in a large manufacturing company. You miss the company of other members of staff doing the same type of work as yourself, as you are the only person in charge of filing for that department.

The company has another six departments – all of a similar size to the Administration department. Each has its own filing clerk. Your manager is keen to introduce some centralised services throughout the organisation – particularly in areas such as filing, printing and reprographics. Although some of the other managers are very interested, others are not as enthusiastic. The managing director asks your manager to prepare a short report for the next managers' meeting. Because of your previous job, your manager asks you to prepare a brief list of the advantages and disadvantages of such a system.

You decide to ask the other managers for their views and are given the following comments:

Figure 2.16 Different points of view

1 **As a group**, discuss what you think are:
   a the advantages of a centralised system
   b the disadvantages.
2 What advantages do you think there will be both to the staff and the company if there are a **team** of filing clerks working together in one section?

Word process your answers.

Flexible hours (shifts/flexitime)

At your student reunion, another difference you find is that you are all expected to work different hours including:

■ shift work – full- or part-time work carried out at different times over a twenty-four-hour period
■ flexi work – work which is carried out at times fixed by agreement between the employer and employee.

If you compare the hours worked by your grandparents, your parents or an older friend or relative with the hours worked by you or friends of the same age, you will probably find that nowadays hours of work are shorter and more variable than they used to be.

You may be expected to work:

■ a regular number of hours a day (either with or without overtime)
■ at nights
■ on shifts (e.g. 6 am–2 pm, 2 pm–10 pm or 10 pm–6 am).

What you might also find, however, is that you are allowed some choice in what hours you work and when you work them.

Your employer may, for instance, operate a flexitime system. In such a case, as the following table shows, you would probably be expected to work some set hours, e.g. between 10 am and 4 pm – known as **core time**. The time before 10 am and after 4 pm, (e.g. between 8 am and 10 am and between 4 pm and 6 pm) is known as **flexitime**.

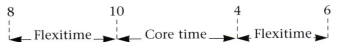

When you choose to work your flexitime hours depends on you, and whether you are a 'lark' or an 'owl'. Some organisations allow you to build up some credit hours by working all the flexitime as well as the core time hours and taking a day off in lieu, but they normally put some limits on this. You can't work flat out for six months and then demand three months off!

Advantages of flexitime working

- Travelling problems are eased by letting staff travel outside peak travelling hours.
- Employees with families are allowed to work around school times, etc.
- Time-keeping is improved as there can be fewer excuses about being 'caught in the traffic', having to leave early to catch the only convenient bus, etc.
- Morale can be improved by allowing staff some say over their working hours.
- Efficiency (and customer care) can be improved by allowing the workplace to be covered for longer periods of time. Some staff might find it easier to work in the quieter periods of the day such as first thing in the morning or last thing in the evening.
- Overtime may be reduced.

Disadvantages of flexitime

- The checking of individual work hours can cause an increase in administration (and therefore an increase in costs).
- There can be problems with having to schedule all important meetings within the core time hours to make sure that all staff can attend.

Did you know?

Some organisations use a 'flexi year' system, in which employees are asked to work a certain number of hours per year rather than per week. The advantages to the employer include a reduction in overtime payments, less need to employ temporary workers in traditionally short-staffed times such as the summer months, and fewer employee absences. The employee has more opportunity for planning other leisure or work activities. However, disadvantages include the difficulty in combining normal and flexitime systems of work and in forecasting exactly what time is to be worked and what time is to be taken off over a full-year period.

Non-assessed activity

1 You have been offered a temporary job packing for a Christmas card company. The company operates a three-shift system at busy times (6 am–2 pm, 2 pm–10 pm or 10 pm–6 am). **As a group**, discuss:

a which shifts you would most like to work and why
b which shift(s) you would least like to work and why

2 From your discussions, list the advantages and disadvantages of shift-work from the point of view of:
a the employer
b the employee.

3 Dan and Katy work in an office which does not operate a flexitime system. The hours are from 9 am to 5 pm. Dan lives 12 miles away and travels in each day during the rush hour. He is nearly always in at the last minute, particularly since he is not good at getting up early. He has asked if he can start a bit later and work on, but the office manager is not willing to let him do so.

Katy has a small daughter who goes to nursery school and is then looked after by a child minder. The child minder's hours are from 8 am to 5.15 pm, and Katy is always anxious not to be late in collecting her little girl. Her job requires a lot of attention to detail and she often finds it difficult to concentrate during the day when the office is full of people.

As a group, discuss the advantages that a change to flexitime would have for both Dan and Katy.

Casual work

Casual workers also have flexible working hours. However, in this case, it is normally the employer who dictates what the hours are, and the casual workers are offered work only when the employer needs them – not necessarily on a regular basis.

Did you know?

A recent development has been the introduction of **zero hour contracts,** under which employees are kept on the books but are not guaranteed any specific hours of work. One example is the fire service, where 'retained firefighters' are often used to provide additional cover in emergencies. Several universities have the same arrangement with some of their teaching staff. Hotels also often keep lists of catering staff who can be used to fill staffing gaps at short notice during busy seasons.

Contracts – fixed term/permanent

Nowadays fewer and fewer people are working under permanent contracts of employment. Many people are now temporary workers or work under a fixed-term contract.

Permanent full-time employment

These employees work for a set number of hours per week under a contract which has a start date but no definite end date. The contract will end when the employee leaves, retires or is dismissed.

Temporary work

In this case, employees are given full- or part-time work for a limited number of weeks, months or years.

Work under a fixed term contract

Fixed-term contracts give employees full- or part-time work which has both a definite start date and a definite end date.

Non-assessed activity

Your friend, Stavros, writes to you asking for your advice. He is lucky enough to have two job offers in computing. One is a permanent job with a local firm. The firm is long established but is looking for new recruits to help to bring a bit of new life into the place. Many of the staff in the Computing department are nearing retirement age, which means that there may be an opportunity for promotion when the older staff retire, although he doesn't know exactly when this will be. The salary is OK and so are the hours of work. The physical conditions are a bit grim; the firm is situated between the canal and the railway station! The staff he has met so far are very pleasant and he thinks he will be made to feel welcome.

The other job is in France. Stavros can't speak French but he has been told that the rest of the staff speak good English – and anyway he is young enough to learn a new language. He's not so sure! He didn't make much progress in French at school! The contract is only for two years and there is no guarantee that it will be renewed. The money is excellent but the hours are long and the holidays poor. He is not sure about any prospects of promotion even if his contract is renewed. His girlfriend is very doubtful about whether he will settle down. He is a bit doubtful about how he will feel at the end of the two years and whether his job opportunities will be better or worse if he then wants to come back to the UK.

As a group, discuss the advantages and disadvantages of each type of contract and summarise your views in a short note to your friend.

Workbase

Office, factory, shop, outdoors

When you go for an interview you will probably have the opportunity to meet your future boss and to have a look around the establishment. If you have applied for a job in an office, shop or factory you may also be shown where you will be working, and possibly be introduced to some of the existing staff. By then you will probably have formed some impression of what it will be like to work there. If the job is an outdoor job, the same procedure may be followed.

You may have more difficulty in finding out what the work will be like, however, if the job for which you have applied is a home-based job or one which is mobile.

Mobile work

This is work carried out on different sites or at different workplaces, either as an employee of an organisation or as a self-employed person. Examples of people who are mobile include sales representatives, merchandisers, plumbers, electricians, service engineers and hairdressers who visit customers in their own homes. Being mobile can be a cheaper alternative to setting up 'shop', as there are fewer overheads. However, the time taken in travelling must be taken into account, as must the fact that only one customer can be seen at a time.

Homeworking

This is work carried out at home. This can include **teleworking**, involving the use of information technology equipment and communications systems.

Non-assessed activity

1 Your friend, Sarah, has just been made redundant, as the hairdresser for whom she was working has closed his business. Her customers have said that they will continue to use her services if she stays in business. She cannot decide whether to use her front room as a salon, open a shop herself or visit her customers at home. She can drive and has a small car.

a List the advantages and disadvantages of all **three** courses of action.

b If you were Sarah, what would you choose to do? Why?

2 Read the following conversation between two friends who live next door to one another.

Val: I hope I pass my driving test next month. I've just heard that they are making even further cuts in the bus service.

Jan: Well, I've looked in the local paper every night for the past month and I haven't found any vacancies within a fifteen-kilometre radius. My trouble is that I *can* drive – I just can't afford a car.

Val: I've asked Margaret if she knows anywhere I can apply but she says she hasn't really been looking for jobs because she can't get her children into a nursery and there's no-one else to look after them.

Jan: Mike isn't looking for a job either. Since his accident he can't face the hassle of getting his wheelchair on and off public transport.

As a group, discuss why the four people mentioned might like to be offered a job where they can work from home.

Working from home

In the 1800s almost everyone worked at or from home in various 'cottage' industries and the family formed the main working group. The Industrial Revolution – which moved work from the home into the factory – changed all that. It has become the custom for people to 'go out to work', i.e. to travel from home to the workplace each day. However, for some people, this can prove very difficult (as the above activity shows). They may have to look after a young family or an elderly relative, they may live in a rural area some distance from a town, or they may have some form of disability which makes it less easy for them to travel to and from work each day. In such circumstances they need the opportunity to be able to work from home.

A recent survey suggests that in the UK there are at present 645 000 homeworkers, 179 000 men and 466 000 women. The majority are self employed or work in a family business, although 113 000 are employed by an outside organisation.

Non-assessed activity

As a group, discuss why more self-employed people than employees tend to work from home.

Types of homeworking

In some cases manual skills are needed – for packing, assembling, painting, or hand-finishing garments. In others, clerical or selling skills can be used. One engineering company employs three home-based sales staff: a firm supplying library books has its entire workforce of 30 staff based at home.

There have been developments in homeworking, particularly in relation to new technology, and a recent survey found that, of a random sample of 1000 employers, one in twenty employ staff who work at home using information technology. They are generally known as **teleworkers**. The highest percentage is that of management and computer consultants and secretarial or administrative staff, closely followed by data entry clerks and training and education specialists. Other teleworkers include researchers and sales or marketing staff, accountants and finance workers and writers, journalists and designers.

Did you know?

1 There is obviously an overlap between homeworking and teleworking and it is likely that, in a lot of cases, teleworking may have developed from earlier forms of home-based employment. A filing clerk working from home, for instance, could be 'transformed' into a teleworker if he or she was provided with a computer and could carry out the work by using a database rather than a filing cabinet.

2 However, teleworking is different from homeworking in that teleworkers are often better qualified and better paid: homeworkers are often regarded as unskilled manual workers and are therefore poorly paid.

Non-assessed activity

Your friend, Anita, is lively and vivacious and has been working as a word-processor operator for the last two years in a large company situated three miles away. Because of increasing costs the company is relocating to a more remote area approximately sixteen miles away. Anita has three choices. She can:

a travel every day (she has no car)
b resign and get a job nearer home
c become a teleworker – as the company has offered to provide her with the equipment to work from home if she wishes.

She has two weeks to make a decision. At the moment she is quite tempted by the idea of teleworking. You don't know if this would be such a good idea.

Summarise the advantages and disadvantages of each option and come to a conclusion about the action you think she should take.

Optional evidence assignment

*This activity can be carried out verbally in class **in a group** as a non-assessed activity to consolidate learning. Alternatively, if you do it **on your own**, it can count as supplementary evidence towards the following parts of the scheme.*

PC 4: Identify and explain differences in working arrangements

Range: Working arrangements: flexible (shifts, flexi-hours), contracts (fixed term, permanent), workbase (office, factory, shop, outdoors, home, mobile)

Core skills: Communication, Information technology

At your school reunion you found that you have all got jobs – but they are very different!

Your letter of appointment from the Administration department stated the date when you were to start work and also your weekly hours of work – 9 am to 5 pm, Monday to Friday. There is no stated end date.

Patrick has found a job as a security guard with a large electronics firm. One week he works from 6 am to 2 pm, the following week from 2 pm to 10 pm and the third week from 10 pm to 6 am. His job requires him to patrol the grounds of the factory on a regular basis.

	Permanent work	Temporary work	Shift work	Fixed term	Casual work	Homeworking	Teleworking	Mobile work
You								
Patrick								
Suzanne								
Jaroslav								
Melissa								
Tahiya								
Simon								
Sharon								
Marie								

Figure 2.17 Outline chart

Suzanne was keen to work in the media and she was delighted when she was offered a job with the local radio station to cover for one of the staff who was on maternity leave.

Jaroslav was always interested in computing. After leaving college he was offered the chance to work from home use the latest IT equipment.

Melissa eventually wants to open her own restaurant. At the moment she is learning the trade by working as a waitress at a local hotel. Although she works long hours, they are not fixed and they vary from week to week.

Tahiya has found work as an office administrator at the hospital for a two-year period beginning in January 1995 and ending in December 1997.

Simon has completed his engineering course and obtained work in a factory, but he didn't like being indoors all day. He has just obtained a job as a service engineer for a household appliance firm. He will have the use of the firm's van and will repair machines in customers' homes.

Sharon has a few domestic problems and has therefore found a job which she can do at home. The firm which employs her sends her some materials each week which she makes up into baby clothes and returns the following week.

Marie is studying for a degree, but her student grant doesn't go far. She earns some extra money by working every Saturday and Sunday in a supermarket.

1   Design a chart like the one in Figure 2.17 on the previous page. Tick the working arrangements which apply to you and your friends from the descriptions given above. Note: you may be able to tick more than one box.
2   Each of these working arrangements has advantages and disadvantages (both for you and for your employer). These are summarised in Figure 2.18.

Use these points, design a second table, using the format of Figure 2.19 on page 155, and complete it with what you think are the advantages and disadvantages of each working arrangement (the first one has been completed for you).

Evidence assignment

At this point your tutor may wish you to start or continue work on the project which will prove to your verifiers that you understand this section of the element. If so, turn to page 161 and do Section 3 of the project. This covers the third evidence indicator for this element.

Advantages

1   Allows continuous production over a twenty-four hour period (or continuous staffing in service areas such as hospitals, the police, etc.)
2   More job security.
3   Possible increase in productivity because of lack of interruptions.
4   Useful if a worker is employed for a particular project after which he or she is no longer required.
5   The employee can often fit the work around other responsibilities or at times when he or she needs some extra money – like Christmas.
6   Employees do not have to travel to work each day and can combine work with home responsibilities.
7   Employers can reduce overheads particularly in the case of expensive office space in large cities.
8   Good for recruitment in specialist areas as employers can look country-wide for their staff.
9   Fewer changes in staff and therefore greater continuity.
10   Greater commitment by staff.
11   Better prospects of promotion.
12   Useful if someone wants to work abroad but doesn't want to be committed to a permanent post.
13   Often higher rates of pay.
14   Easier to promote teamwork.
15   Employer can employ staff only when needed.
16   Flexibility fo the employer (particularly those who want to respond to public demand by extending opening hours).
17   Flexibility for the employee (if they have other commitments such as looking after a family).
18   Useful for employers to fill gaps caused by someone away sick, on holiday, on a training course, on maternity leave, etc.
19   Useful for certain workers, e.g. students who want to work during the holidays, people who are using it as a stopgap until they find permanent employment, etc.

Disadvantages

A   Generally less money will be earned.
B   Employees can feel very isolated – there is little personal contact.
C   Little job security – and few legal rights.
D   Limited in use – not much good for a doctor or nurse!
E   Problems of tiredness.
F   Few career prospects.
G   Difficult to get full attendance at meetings, staff training sessions, etc.
H   More difficult to deal with a group of people who are constantly changing than with a group who have worked with each other for some time.
I   As the contract comes to an end, the employee might become anxious about finding another job and might therefore be more concerned about that than concentrating on his or her existing job.
J   Staff may be less willing to adapt to any change in working methods.
K   Supervision can be difficult.
L   Possibly less commitment (if an employee knows that he or she is going to be moving on shortly, there may not be the same interest in the job).
M   Less mobile and therefore possibly ageing staff.
N   Unsocial hours.

Figure 2.18   Advantages and disadvantages of working arrangements

	Advantages	Disadvantages
Full-time employment	2, 9, 10, 11, 13, 14	J, M
Temporary employment		
Shift work		
Work on a fixed term contract		
Casual work		
Homeworking		
Teleworking		
Mobile work		

Figure 2.19 Comparison chart

Reasons for change in working arrangements

Figure 2.20 Different attitudes

As a general rule people don't like changes, particularly changes over which they have little control. There is a very big difference, for instance, between looking for a job because you fancy a change and looking for a job because you have just been made redundant. But even if the move was forced upon you, it might turn out to be the best move you have ever made.

The same can be true of organisational changes. Those organisations which refused to accept the fact that the motor car was likely to replace the need for a horse and cart went bankrupt! Those who recognised the need for change made a lot of money.

Productivity

One of the major reasons for changes in working arrangements has been to increase productivity, i.e. to allow the business to produce more *without increasing the costs of production to the same extent*. This will increase the profitability of the business, as more goods are available to be sold – yet production costs have not risen by the same amount. Service organisations can also increase productivity – for example, with each hairdresser in a salon styling more clients' hair each day.

Changing working arrangements to increase productivity

Organisations are constantly looking at ways of increasing productivity. Their options may include:

- paying existing staff bonuses to produce more than a basic number of goods
- re-organising the work of teams so that they work more efficiently
- employing more permanent staff on the basis that they will become experienced operatives
- centralising operations so that people become specialists at one job
- buying new machinery which will produce items more rapidly. This may mean employing fewer permanent staff.

Measuring productivity

Measuring productivity is relatively easy in a production environment because targets can be set for each person. Output can easily be measured each day for each worker or team. Any workers who consistently fail to meet targets are likely to lose their jobs.

155

Targets can also be set for sales staff and performance can be measured against these. Sales staff may be offered additional commission or bonuses to encourage them to sell more. In some jobs, a sales person's *only* income comes from commission.

Productivity is more difficult to measure if people work in an office or provide a service. For instance, how would you measure the productivity of your doctor or your tutor? Some people may say that the number of patients seen per hour or pupils taught per hour would give an indication. However, if none of the patients recovered from their illnesses or none of the students passed their courses, the effectiveness of the doctor or tutor would be very questionable indeed! For that reason, pushing for greater productivity – regardless of other factors – can be very risky. If the **quality** of the goods decreases and customers become dissatisfied, sales fall no matter how much is produced. The same applies to services. If the quality of the service starts to fall, then sales will also fall.

Non-assessed activity

Four people are working as a team – but with difficulty. Each is paid £4 an hour for an eight-hour day. They produce 75 usable widgets a day, with an average of five spoiled widgets a day. A fifth person joins the team on the same amount of pay and the work is re-organised. The team now works more effectively and produces 120 usable widgets a day and no spoiled widgets.

a How much did the original team earn each day?
b What was the staff cost of making each widget originally?
c How much does the team now earn each day?
d What is the new cost of making each widget?
e Has productivity increased or decreased?
f What would be the effect on costs if the number of spoiled widgets had increased to 25 per day?

Quality assurance

The most successful organisations have often achieved success by concentrating primarily on improving the **quality** of the products or services they offer.

Much attention has been paid to quality in recent years and – in particular – to the ways in which it can be achieved. However, it is not as easy as it may sound. If you asked a Production Manager what they thought quality management meant the answer might be:

- the setting of a number of standards against which the finished products should be measured
- a reduction in the amount of wastage caused by products not reaching those standards.

The Production Manager would know that high-quality products lead to satisfied customers and to increased profits for the company.

If, however, you asked a Human Resources Manager the same question the answer might be:

- greater employee commitment and involvement
- a happy and motivated staff.

The Human Resources Manager would know that a contented workforce is an effective workforce – which should also lead to an increase in the profits made by the company!

Both answers are right, of course.

Did you know?

Some organisations, including both manufacturing companies and public service organisations, take a lot of trouble to make sure that all their procedures are carried out in accordance with a certain set of standards known as BS 5750 (now renamed BS EN ISO 9000 to conform to international standards). Although firms who work to these standards use them as proof that they are offering a high-quality service, there have been criticisms on the grounds that there is too much concentration on following correct written-down procedures rather than on improving the actual quality of the goods or service.

Non-assessed activity

As a group, discuss why you think the following organisations wanted to improve the quality of their product or service.

1 In the late 1980s and early 1990s Rolls Royce saw a fall in its sales.
2 Throughout the 1980s one London borough was always referred to in the popular press as 'Barmy Brent'.
3 The Royal Mail was facing what it regarded as the 'threat' of privatisation, particularly in respect of its monopoly to deliver letters.

Changing working arrangements to improve quality

Many methods are used in quality management programmes. Many of them concern the use of teamwork to help the company to meet its quality objectives.

- Forming quality improvement teams, quality councils or quality departments. One London borough gives *all* its employees the right to meet for two hours every month in workplace teams which are run by trained quality experts.
- Operating a **cellular** production model where each team is responsible for the quality of the product it makes.
- Employing specialist staff – either in centralised sections or as permanent workers so that they are experienced employees who are committed to quality.
- Ensuring that employees are well trained and supervised on company premises.
- Ensuring that mobile employees follow standard company procedures.

A company with a high commitment to quality will have more reservations about employing people as casual workers or homeworkers – in case the quality of their service or output cannot be checked.

Did you know?

The term **quality circle** is often used to describe any group of employees from the same work areas who meet regularly to agree ways of improving aspects of their day-to-day working routine.

Checking on quality

How can an organisation tell if its quality has been improved? In most cases it does so by setting **targets** and checking to see if they have been achieved. The type of targets used include:

- delivery on time
- less waste
- 'right first time' assembly
- 'internal customer' satisfaction, i.e. how satisfied the production staff are with the work carried out by the Administration department etc.
- external customer satisfaction (and a reduction in complaints!).

Did you know?

Some organisations use **benchmarking** as a check on quality by testing their products

and procedures against those of other organisations which have already been identified as high quality. The Department of Trade and Industry promotes benchmarking through its 'Managing in the 90s' programme to help companies to improve their competitiveness by following the example of firms which have established good practices.

Non-assessed activity

As a group, discuss the targets most likely to be set to measure quality in the following organisations:

- a company manufacturing light bulbs
- a firm of solicitors
- a Job Centre.

Did you know?

The UK Quality Award looks at quality improvements by assessing company performance in nine areas:

- leadership
- people management
- policy and strategy
- resources
- processes
- people satisfaction
- customer satisfaction
- impact on society
- business results.

It was launched at the beginning of 1994 by the British Quality Foundation with the support of the Department of Trade and Industry, and mirrors the European Quality Award given by the European Foundation of Quality Management.

Letting staff know about quality issues

Every employee has to be aware of the importance of quality assurance and therefore most organisations spend a lot of time to keep them informed about what is going on.

Methods include:

- **information packs** – some organisations produce quality information packs or handbooks for their employees
- **news sheets** or newsletters devoted to quality issues (plus audio tapes for employees working outside the main organisation)

- **team briefings** on a regular weekly basis
- the **sharing of ideas** through a number of teamwork 'events' during the year
- **in-house training** covering specific areas such as customer care, etc.

Competition

Sometimes changes occur simply because management feel that they might benefit the company or the workforce. Other changes are forced upon the company because of outside pressures. In the past ten years, for instance, these pressures have included increased competition both at home and abroad.

Organisations **must** be aware of **direct** competition – where they have competitors which produce similar products and appeal to the same group of consumers. They should also be aware of **indirect** competition – where customers have a choice of different products on which to spend their spare money. You might want to go to the cinema, or a football match or buy a pair of shoes. You have some money but not enough to do all three, and you therefore have to make a choice. The owners of the cinema have to be aware that there is competition for that money – so too do the owners of the football stadium and shoe shop! (See also Element 1.2.)

All of them have to adopt certain measures to ensure that they get their share of the market.

Did you know?

During the 1980s imports to the UK grew from 43 per cent of total trade to 51 per cent: it was also the time when competition from the Far East started to increase. More recently the opening up of the Eastern European markets has created further competition.

Changing working arrangements to cope with increased competition

Increased competition normally puts pressure on organisations in one of the following two ways:

- competitors offer a similar product or service at a lower price
- competitors offer a better service. This may, for instance, be longer opening hours.

A rival firm will try to match the competition and will possibly change their working arrangements to allow for this, e.g.:

- by increasing productivity to reduce production costs (see page 00)
- by reducing the number of permanent employees to reduce staff costs
- by introducing flexitime to increase the number of hours the organisation is open
- by employing people at a cheaper rate to work in their own homes.

Non-assessed activity

1 Imagine you and a group of your friends from college decide to set up a mobile catering service to provide a range of sandwiches to office workers during their lunch breaks. Your market research shows that there is at least one other firm offering the same service in the area.

As a group, discuss what actions you would take to make sure that your product and service is better than that of your competitors.

2 You have managed to keep ahead of the existing competition and then, to your dismay, you find that a new firm has started up which offers not only a lunchtime but also a breakfast service. **As a group**, discuss how you could alter your working arrangements to cope with this challenge.

Technology

New technology has affected working arrangements quite dramatically in many different organisations. You have already seen (pages 151–2) how homeworking has been changed by the advent of teleworking. On page 114 in Element 1.3 you can see how technology has caused changes to the skill level of jobs. In some cases job skills have been increased because people have to do a wider range of jobs

Figure 2.21 A computerised news room at Reuters, equipped with an electronic picture desk

using new technology. In other cases the skills required have changed or decreased. Newspapers, for instance, used to be produced by skilled typesetters – today the text is keyed in on computer, often by the journalists themselves. In some cases jobs have been created, in others they have been lost altogether.

Technology has affected jobs in all areas. In offices, people are rarely employed as invoice typists or wage clerks. Invoicing and payroll processing is more usually handled by computer. In factories, industrial robots can be used to repair and maintain equipment as well as to do routine or dangerous production tasks. In shops you will rarely see people putting price labels on goods – bar code readers are used to scan the items at the checkout and produce an itemised receipt.

People who work outdoors or who are mobile can stay in touch with their base by means of a mobile phone or even a mobile fax! And, as you have already seen, homeworkers can be connected to their workplace by means of a computer link.

Changes to working arrangements because of technology

In many cases technology has increased flexibility of employment. This has resulted in:

- de-centralisation as people can do a wider range of operations on their own
- fixed-term contracts for people to undertake routine work involving computers or electronic equipment
- a change in workbase – more people can work from their cars or their homes.

Optional evidence assignment

*This activity can be carried out verbally in class **in a group** as a non-assessed activity to consolidate learning. Alternatively, if you do it **on your own**, it can count as supplementary evidence towards the following parts of the scheme.*

PC 5: Explain and give examples of reasons for change in working arrangements in one business organisation

Range: Working arrangements: flexible (shifts, flexi-hours), contracts (fixed term, permanent), workbase (office, factory, shop, outdoors, home, mobile)
Reasons for change: productivity, quality assurance, competition, technology

Core skills: Communication, Information technology

Read the following case study and answer the questions which follow.

Case study

The role and services offered by banks in Great Britain have changed dramatically over the past fifteen years. Competition increased when building societies were allowed to offer current account services to their customers. Because building societies opened longer hours during the week and on a Saturday as well, banks were forced to reconsider their style of operation. A traditional bank used to be open from 10 am to 3.30 pm, five days a week!

Technology helped banks to increase profits as staff costs could be reduced. **Automatic teller machines** (ATMs or cash machines) are cheaper than bank cashiers – and reduce queues enormously. They are also open seven days a week, 24 hours a day! An extension of the 'high-tech' bank is First Direct, which offers a full banking service by telephone or computer. Why bother visiting the bank or writing a cheque when you can simply pick up the telephone to transfer money from your account to someone else, quickly and easily?

Some banks have been quick to react to claims that their service is not all it should be. The Midland Bank has introduced a high-quality programme called 'Customer Focus', through which it hopes to become 'Britain's most respected and successful bank'. One of its aims is to keep customers for life. It wants to focus on four key areas including staff attitudes, knowledge and helpfulness to customers and it needs staff co-operation to achieve its targets. Barclays Bank has introduced its own telephone banking service.

1 a In what way did competition affect the opening hours of banks?
  b How would this alter working arrangements for employees?
2 a If you were a bank manager and wanted to measure productivity what would you do?
  b In what way have the introduction of ATMs increased productivity?
  c What has been their effect on the jobs of full-time bank cashiers?
3 Visit your local bank and find out about both telephone banking and computer banking *or* contact a 'specialist' telephone bank such as First Direct. State the differences you think there would be for staff working in such a bank rather than for a 'traditional' bank.

4 **a** Why is the Midland Bank now interested in quality?

b Suggest **two** ways in which this may affect working arrangements for staff.

Evidence assignment

At this point your tutor may wish you to start or continue work on the project which will prove to your verifiers that you understand this section of the element. If so, turn to page 161 and do Section 4 of the project. This covers the fourth and final Evidence Indicator for this element.

Sources of recruitment – key to activity on page 137

Methods of finding suitable candidates include:

1 checking whether someone in the organisation might be suitable – and may want a transfer or promotion
2 notifying the job centres, private employment agencies, schools, colleges and professional associations
3 putting advertisements in the local and national press and also specialised trade journals, if appropriate
4 checking through personnel files to see if there are any possible candidates amongst those who have made a general enquiry about work in your organisation.

Revision test

True or false?

1 An assistant manager is higher than a deputy.
2 Small companies often have a hierarchical structure.
3 Dealing with trade unions is the job of the Accounts department.

4 All organisations employ sales representatives.
5 There are more rules in a hierarchical organisation.

Complete the blanks

6 The executive responsible for dealing with shareholders, insurance and making sure the company always operates within the law is called the _____ _____ .
7 Machine maintenance is one of the jobs carried out by the _____ department.
8 Finding out what customers think about a product is called _____ _____ .
9 The structure of a company is drawn on an _____ _____ .
10 The word used to describe the storage and supply of goods is _____ .

Short answer questions

11 State **four** functions carried out by the Human Resources department.
12 Give **three** decisions which would be made by the manager of a small organisation but *not* by the manager in a large one.
13 State **three** reasons why rules and procedures are necessary in a large organisation.
14 Give **two** reasons why computers may be used by the Distribution department.
15 State **four** areas of operation which may be controlled by the Administration department.

Write a short paragraph to show you clearly understand each of the following terms.

16 Hierarchy
17 Design
18 Production control
19 Public relations
20 Flat structure

Evidence indicator project

Unit 2 Element 2.1

This project has been designed to cover all the evidence indicators related to Element 2.1. It is divided into four sections. Tutors may wish students to complete the sections at the appropriate points marked in the text. Alternatively, tutors may prefer their students to do the entire project at the end of the element.

Performance criteria: 1–5

Core Skills: Communication
Application of number
Information technology

Section 1

This section concentrates on the first evidence indicator for this element. When you have completed the work, store it safely as it will contribute towards your final project for this element.

Make sure you complete this section of the project by the deadline date given to you by your tutor.

Select **two** local business organisations of different size and of different structures. One should be a traditional hierarchical departmental structure and the other should be a flat or matrix structure.

Arrange to visit each organisation. Before your visit, prepare a list of questions which will enable you to find out:

a   the size of the organisation
b   the number of employees
c   the number of levels and average span of control of the organisation
d   the departments/sections of the organisations
e   the functions each department carries out
f   how each department interlinks with the other departments
g   how teamworking operates within each organisation
h   why teamworking was introduced and the benefits of this style of working to the organisation.

Find out how **each** organisation is structured and draw a simple organisation chart in each case to illustrate the difference between the two structures.

Keep the rest of your notes safely filed.

The completed organisation charts will form your first Evidence Indicator.

Section 2

This section concentrates on the second evidence indicator for this element. When you have completed the work store it safely as it will contribute towards your final project for this element.

Make sure you complete this section of the project by the deadline date given to you by your tutor.

Refer back to the notes you made. Select the organisation for which you have the fullest set of notes on the work of different departments. This is most likely to be the largest organisation you visited.

a   Write brief notes about each of the departments.
b   Indicate how these departments link up (i.e. show their interdependence on one another). Think, for instance, of the way in which the Production department may be dependent on the Purchasing department, the Distribution and Transport department on the Production department and so on.

Section 3

This section concentrates on the third evidence indicator for this element. When you have completed the work, store it safely as it will contribute towards your final project for this element.

Make sure you complete this section of the project by the deadline date given to you by your tutor.

From what you have found out at the organisations you have visited, write a short account of any differences in working arrangements between the two organisations e.g. the way in which people work – either as individuals or as members of a team. Give some examples of the teams which operate in both organisations.

For at least **one** of your organisation state why teamworking was introduced and the benefits to the organisation of this type of working arrangement.

(You may want to look at the information about teamwork given in Element 2.3 before you complete this part of the project.)

Section 4

This section concentrates on the fourth evidence indicator for this element. When you have completed the work store it safely as it will contribute towards your final project for this element.

Make sure you complete this section of the project by the deadline date given to you by your tutor.

Give a short account of any changes to working arrangements which have occurred in **one** of the organisations you visited because of **one** of the following:

- the need for an increase in productivity, *or*
- quality assurance, *or*
- competition, *or*
- the need to keep up with new technology.

Concentrate on just **one** example.

Final stage

Type out your findings on a word processor, using suitable headings. Don't forget to include your organisation chart. Make a front cover for your project which gives your name, the date and the title **Structures and Working Arrangements in Two Organisations** (then insert their names).

...n that she doesn't check her work

...ter Ms Martin calls a meeting of all staff ...., for some reason, business isn't good and ... will have to make some redundancies. Liz is ...ed. She is the newest member of staff and if the ... in first out' rule is followed she will lose her job and she probably won't be the only one!

Non-assessed activity

There could be a lot of reasons for the reduction in sales of the company. However, one of them could be the lack of co-operation between management and staff (and among the staff themselves).

1 List the ways in which staff and management do not co-operate with one another.
2 Assume that everyone in the company **does** co-operate with one another. Re-write each of the above incidents to show how Liz and her colleagues **should** have behaved.
3 One difficulty you might meet at work is when you see another employee who is not obeying company rules or following company procedures (one example being Faizal's refusal to wear safety goggles). Describe what would you do if you found yourself in such a position.

Did you know?

An employee who reports a company or a colleague for not following rules or regulations is said to be 'whistle blowing'!

Employer-employee co-operation

Employers and employees need to co-operate with one another for several reasons. Firstly, the atmosphere in the workplace is likely to be much better if people have mutual respect for each other and consider each other's needs. Secondly, the potential for the performance of the business is increased dramatically if people work together – and that includes management and staff as well as colleagues at the same level.

It may help to think of an engine which is tuned so that everything runs smoothly. All the separate parts are correctly connected and playing their parts in making the engine work. The output from the engine will be greater than if it was neglected or rusty or if

Figure 2.22 Whistle-blowing

one part was spoiling the functioning of several others. A business organisation can be seen as an engine or power house containing different people in different jobs all with various views of the world. If these 'components' are looked after in terms of training, consultation and communication processes then there is a far better chance that fewer breakdowns will occur!

In the business world there are several key benefits to maintaining employer and employee co-operation.

The survival of the business

Employees who are discontented or take collective action against their employer may not just injure the company – they could bring it to its knees.

Liz's failure to tell Ian or Malcolm that the suppliers **could** find the spare part could have resulted in an unhappy customer who had to wait longer for his or her car to be repaired – and deciding not to give any more business to the company! If she did this on several occasions or – even worse – if everyone on the sales team was very casual about selling parts or cars, then the organisation might go out of business.

Improved employee commitment to the business

If the Managing Director had been a bit more reasonable with Liz over the telephone call, Liz would probably have done the work more willingly – and more carefully.

Managers who fail to take account of employee's concerns cannot expect the employees to be prepared to work hard for them or to stay late when required. Equally, employees who refuse to do anything extra can expect little co-operation from the management if they want time off or any special favour.

Improved efficiency

If the problem of payment of commission to Terry and Rob had been sorted out, then they would both have been keen to sell more cars and would therefore have taken time to improve their selling skills.

Co-operation here may imply identifying training needs and assisting employees to develop. It does not encourage anyone to work harder if they are continually criticised or belittled, especially in front of other people. Managers should be loyal to their staff – and should be able to expect loyalty from their employees. Hard work and effort should be rewarded. If both employer and employee work together then the employee will gain more job satisfaction as they become more efficient at the job. This has mutual benefits as the employee then becomes more promotable to a higher level position with a better salary.

The breakdown of co-operation

Unfortunately, there are occasions on which co-operation is not forthcoming. This may be because of a breakdown in communications, a misunderstanding or a deliberate act on the part of the employer or employee. It is important for the well-being of the staff and the organisation that any disagreements or disputes are resolved as quickly as possible.

Ways to resolve disagreements

The following case describes a disagreement at work and the various attempts made to resolve it, i.e. by means of:

- trade union negotiation
- legal representation
- an industrial tribunal
- the Appeal Courts and the European Court of Justice.

Case study – part 1

Emily works as a packer in a mail order firm. She has worked there for several years and has always liked the job. However, things change when a new supervisor, Don, is appointed. Don is ambitious and is anxious to please his boss, the Distribution Manager, who has asked him to improve productivity. He is concerned about meeting the new production targets and feels that Emily is too old and too slow to cope.

Emily does struggle with the new targets and fails to meet them two weeks running. At the end of the second week, Don warns her that her work isn't up to standard. She is so worried that she panics and doesn't meet the targets on either the third or the fourth week. Don gives her a second warning – this time in writing. He also criticises her in front of the rest of the staff, which upsets Emily even more. She asks to speak to him privately to discuss some domestic problems she is having but Don refuses to listen.

Emily eventually decides to ask someone for help and she contacts her trade union representative.

Did you know?

Emily has a set route to follow if she wishes. The table below gives an indication of what she can do if she feels she has a genuine legal grievance. The steps involved in legal proceedings are as follows:

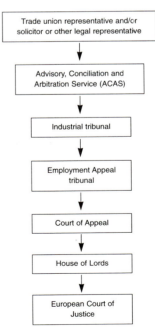

| Trade union representative and/or solicitor or other legal representative |
| Advisory, Conciliation and Arbitration Service (ACAS) |
| Industrial tribunal |
| Employment Appeal tribunal |
| Court of Appeal |
| House of Lords |
| European Court of Justice |

Trade union negotiation

A trade union consists of a group of people who work in similar jobs or types of jobs and who join together with common aims and objectives. These are usually concerned with the protection of members' working conditions and employee rights and welfare. There have been several laws covering trade union matters, the most important of which are the **Employment Protection (Consolidation) Act 1978** and the **Trades Union and Labour Relations (Consolidation) Act 1992** (as amended by the **Trade Union and Reform and Employment Rights Act 1993**). Under this legislation employees have the right:

- to choose whether or not to be a member of a trade union
- to take part in trade union activities
- to take time off for trade union duties or activities.

They must also be allowed to take part in trade union activities 'at an appropriate time'.

If they become a trade union representative or official the employer must also allow them reasonable time off – with pay – during working hours to let them carry out their duties, e.g. attendance at meetings, training courses etc.

They must not be harassed or victimised by the employer because they are or are not a trade union member, e.g. by withholding promotion or by not giving them the same fringe benefits as other employees.

Non-assessed activity

As a group, decide which of the following times would be regarded as 'appropriate' for trade union activities.

- before work starts in the morning
- at the end of the working day
- during the lunch period
- during a tea break
- during a time when there is no work to do.

Union officials

If a union is operational where you are employed, you will probably be approached to join fairly quickly after you start work. A **shop steward** is the elected worker representative who voluntarily represents the members of the union to management, and who would tell you about the benefits of being a member. In a large company there may be several shop stewards with a **convenor** – the chief shop steward who co-ordinates union activity.

Did you know?

Shop stewards are called different names in different industries. In **white collar** (clerical and professional) unions they are often known as **staff representatives.** In the printing trade they have a more unusual name. A male shop steward is known as father of the chapel, and a female shop steward is called the mother of the chapel!

Union membership

Joining a union will help to protect an employee in relation to:

- security of employment
- protection against unfair practices and discrimination in areas such as recruitment, training, discipline, redundancy and dismissals
- conditions of employment, e.g. hours, holidays etc.
- rights under the **Health and Safety at Work Act** and other safety regulations.

In addition the union will continually negotiate for improvements in pay and working conditions. If the union wants its members to take any type of industrial action then it must **ballot** them first (i.e. allow them to vote in secret). This is because the union is, in effect, asking employees to break their contract of employment and they risk dismissal by their employer. If some employees decide not to take part in the action then the union has to respect their wishes.

Did you know?

1 There are various types of industrial action. A **work to rule** means that you only do what is expressly required of you under your contract of employment. Other forms of action include an **overtime ban** or a **go slow** – where workers do the work properly – but deliberately work at less than their normal speed.
2 There has been a steady decline in union membership since the late 1970s. This has come about partly because of a fall in the number of people employed in manufacturing (members of **blue collar** unions) and a rise in part-time employment.

Non-assessed activity

Talk to **two** people who are members of a union – if possible, try to find one person who is a blue collar worker and one who is a white collar worker. Find out why they joined the union, the benefits of membership, how much they pay to be a member and any disadvantages they have experienced.

Grievance procedures

Your contract of employment should make reference to what you can do if you feel you have been treated unfairly. If you feel that this is the case, your first step should normally be to talk to your immediate supervisor to see if some solution can be reached. If a solution cannot be found or if it is your relationship with your supervisor which is the problem, you may decide instead to talk to someone in the Human Resources department (possibly someone who is appointed specifically to look after staff welfare) or even to your supervisor's manager. You can also discuss the matter with your union representative. If your problem cannot be sorted out informally you may have to use a more formal procedure known as a **grievance procedure.**

Most grievance procedures cover two broad areas:

- **money** – e.g. mistakes in the calculation of payments or loss of pay because of a change in the basis of payment, e.g. the introduction of performance-related pay
- **work issues** – e.g. the way in which different jobs are allocated, the transfer of employees from one type of job to another, changes as a result of job grading schemes, physical conditions, allocation of overtime, time off, holidays etc.

Non-assessed activity

Discuss, **as a group** and **with your tutor,** the advantages and disadvantages of making a complaint to your supervisor's own manager, rather than asking someone in the Human Resources department for advice.

Did you know?

If a particular problem concerns not only you but also a number of other people in the organisation, the union might bring what is known as a **collective grievance** on the group's behalf.

Non-assessed activity

Many organisations have a **grievance policy** such as that illustrated below. **As a group**, discuss what is meant by the terms 'duress', 'status quo' and 'precedent'.

1	Management accepts the rights of employees, individually or collectively through their recognised unions, to present complaints to it.
2	It is in the interests of all concerned to establish and maintain formal procedures for dealing with such complaints.
3	Any differences which may arise should, wherever possible, be resolved quickly and without the use of industrial action.
4	Management is not prepared to discuss or consider any complaint under duress whether actual or threatened.
5	Whenever there is a difference in respect of a change in terms and conditions of employment, the status quo will apply until the matter is resolved.
6	Management will ensure that even though a decision is reached in one particular case, it will not necessarily set a precedent which might subsequently be claimed to apply throughout the organisation

Figure 2.23   A typical grievance policy

Did you know?

Over 95 per cent of establishments with more than 200 employees and 70 per cent of those with between 25 and 49 employees have individual grievance procedures.

Stages in an individual grievance procedure

There are normally three stages in a grievance procedure.

1 **Within the department** – the department manager should first of all check the facts and, if necessary, alter the decision of the supervisor or other member of the management team. If he or she does so the grievance procedure will usually come to an end. If not, it goes on to Stage 2.
2 **Outside the department** – the dispute is taken to the next level of management who have to check the facts, listen to the evidence and reach a decision. Sometimes a joint committee of both union and management representatives is involved at this stage. (See page 206 for details of **joint consultative committees.**)
3 **Outside the organisation** – in some organisations the grievance procedure may allow for a 'third party' such as ACAS (see page 169 for further details) to judge whether the management's decision is fair.

The grievance interview

1 The manager must establish what the grievance procedure is all about and must decide whether to make an immediate response or whether time is needed to gather more information or to consult with other members of management.
2 The manager must then explain the organisation's position.
3 The manager should try to identify alternative courses of action to arrive at a joint agreement.
4 The final stage is the decision, details of which should be given in a letter of confirmation to the employee.

Case study – part 2

Emily's trade union representative makes little progress with Don, who says he is only following company rules and that it is up to Emily to work a bit harder. Emily then decides to think about asking advice from a solicitor or other legal adviser.

Legal representation

Most people think of a solicitor if they want any legal advice. People who are on low incomes may find that they are entitled to legal aid, as under the **Legal Aid Acts** a person whose income and savings are below a certain limit may get some legal help at a reduced price. However, it is not available to anyone who wants to take a case to an industrial tribunal.

Law centres

Other ways of getting legal advice include going to a law centre which may offer a legal service at very small cost, or even free.

Did you know?

The UK has followed the American lead of setting up neighbourhood law centres which are intended to make a legal service available to people with not much money. They are staffed by qualified solicitors and their main areas of work tend to be housing, social security, employment, race relations, immigration and consumer problems. In recent years, however, local authority cutbacks in funding have reduced the services these centres can offer.

The Citizens' Advice Bureau (CAB)

In addition, Citizens' Advice Bureaux may have solicitors or other experienced lay helpers who can assist. These are people with no formal legal training.

Non-assessed activity

The annual report and accounts of one Citizens' Advice Bureau contained the following table showing the numbers of people who have consulted the bureau over various issues.

Help wanted	Number of clients
Communication	103
Travel, transport, holidays	283
Immigration and nationality	227
Administration of justice	636
Education	157
Employment	1465
National and international	238
Local information enquiries	618
Family and personal	1499
Social security	4373
Health	271
Housing, property and land	1280
Taxes and duties	672
Consumer, trade and business	3264
Leisure	17
Enquiries about CAB	5

Figure 2.24 Clients consulting a Citizens' Advice Bureau on different topics

It also gives examples of the types of problems which occur under each of the headings.

1 Draw up a bar chart to show the number of enquiries received under each heading. Use a suitable heading and key if necessary. Write a short paragraph about the **two** categories which had the highest number of enquiries and try to give reasons for this.

2 Look at the following questions and state the category into which you think they fit.

Why have I been refused credit by this firm?
How can I emigrate to Australia?
How do I change my doctor?
Have I got to do jury service?
Can I get a grant to study?
I'm off work sick – can I get sickness benefit?
What's the geographical difference between the UK and Great Britain?
The hotel wasn't built when I got there.
Can I become a British citizen?
Which days are market days?
How do I make a complaint about a newspaper?
Where can I learn about bee-keeping?
My tenants are wrecking the place – can I get rid of them?
How do I become a CAB adviser?
I'm always late for work – can I be sacked?
If we get divorced, who will get the house?

Case study – part 3

Emily speaks to someone in the CAB who discusses her problem with her and gives her some information about what she could do should she be dismissed.

The situation does not improve at work and Emily constantly fails to meet her targets. She also starts to make mistakes and Don receives several complaints from customers about the wrong goods having been sent. Don reports the matter to the Distribution Manager who calls Emily into his office and dismisses her with a month's notice.

Emily feels that her dismissal was unfair and decides to take her case to the industrial tribunal.

She asks the CAB for an application form (she could also have got one from the Job Centre), fills it in and sends it off to the Central Office of Industrial Tribunals. A copy of that form is sent to ACAS.

Advisory, Conciliation and Arbitration Service (ACAS)

The Advisory, Conciliation and Arbitration Service was set up to assist in industrial disputes. It publishes **codes of practice**. These codes are not legally binding on employers but if they are not followed, employers may find that they have difficulty in winning a case at an industrial tribunal.

It also has a duty to try to settle disputes between employer and employee and when a claim is sent to a tribunal, an ACAS official must be consulted. This official has to try to find out whether both sides are interested in solving the dispute and reaching an agreement out of court. If they are willing to do so then the matter is settled and the complaint never reaches the tribunal. If either the employer or the employee refuses to agree, however, the ACAS official can't insist that they do so.

Non-assessed activity

Emily is now serving her notice. Relations between her and Don are so bad at this point that they are not speaking to each other. Don is convinced that Emily is too slow and that if he ignores it and the department's targets as a whole go down, not only is his job in danger but so is everyone else's. Emily is equally convinced that Don is picking on her and making it difficult for her to concentrate on making her targets. She is also upset that he won't talk to her about her personal problems, nor will he let her have any re-training.

They are therefore in great need of someone who will listen to both sides of the argument!

1 Split into **two groups** – one to prepare a list of questions the official should ask Don and one a list to ask Emily (in separate interviews).

2 Ask **three** members of your group to act the part of the ACAS official, Don and Emily and to carry out the interviews in front of the group.

3 Take a vote on who is the most convincing, and who is likely to win the case if agreement can't be reached and the case has to go to an industrial tribunal!

Industrial tribunals

An industrial tribunal is a court set up to deal with employment disputes. It is more informal than a normal court – no-one wears a wig or gown and the atmosphere is slightly more relaxed – but it is still a court! A legally qualified chairperson is in charge but sits with two non-legal people – one representing the Trades Union Congress and the other the management organisations. The panel listens to both sides of the argument and then comes to a decision. If Emily wins her case the tribunal can order that she gets her old job back, that she is given another similar job or that she is given some compensation.

Non-assessed activity

As a group, discuss why an industrial tribunal needs these people without legal qualifications.

Case study – part 4

Emily and Don cannot agree and the case then goes to the industrial tribunal.

Procedure at a tribunal

Emily is asked by the tribunal chairperson to explain her side of the case (her trade union representative is there to help her). She has asked one of her friends to be a witness and is allowed to ask her some questions. The company solicitor is also allowed to ask the witness some questions. Don then gives his side of the case (helped by the solicitor) and brings a witness along to support him.

The tribunal panel then has to make a decision. In this case it makes the decision on the same day although if the case had been very complicated it may need a longer time to arrive at its decision.

Remedies

If the tribunal decides Emily has been dismissed unfairly it can:

■ tell her employer to give her job back or to offer her another one (re-instatement or re-engagement)

■ order her employer to pay her some compensation which is made up of:

a a basic award up to a maximum amount – the amount is normally based on the amount of redundancy pay to which Emily would have been entitled if she had been made redundant

b a 'compensatory' award (up to a maximum amount which is changed each year) to compensate Emily for any economic loss, e.g. any period of unemployment, loss of prospects, loss of pension rights etc. Note that this amount may be reduced if, for instance, Emily was found guilty of some misconduct which nevertheless didn't justify dismissal. Emily will also be expected to minimise her loss as far as possible, e.g. by looking for another job.

Tribunal decision

The panel decides that the dismissal was fair because Emily was not capable of carrying out the work she was supposed to do. Emily, of course, is not pleased!

European Court of Justice

Emily decides not to take the case any further. She has found another job which she likes and she puts the whole episode behind her.

However, if she had wanted to proceed further she could, under certain circumstances, have asked for her case to be heard at a higher level court – either one of the Appeal Courts or even the European Court of Justice.

When the UK agreed to become a member of the European Community it signed the Treaty of Rome under which it agreed to be bound by a number of rules and regulations. One of these rules was that it would recognise the authority of the European Court.

The Court consists of thirteen judges appointed by agreement between the Member States, i.e. the countries in the EU. It has to legislate in respect of:

■ **regulations** which are immediately binding on all the Member States (i.e. all countries must obey them)

- **directives** which are binding – but the individual Member State can choose when and how to introduce them
- **decisions** which are binding on the State to which they directly apply (not necessarily to all States).

A UK court therefore has to obey the European Court, and there have been a number of Directives which have been passed relating to employment, i.e:

- equal pay for men and women
- equal pay for work of equal value
- employees' rights when the business for which they have been working has been transferred to a new owner
- protection of employees who have been made redundant or whose organisation has become bankrupt
- freedom of movement of workers from country to country
- health and safety.

Did you know?

In recent years the European Court of Justice has decided that a woman who worked for SW Hampshire Area Health Authority was discriminated against by being made to retire at 60 when her male colleagues could work on until they were 65. This has resulted in most firms reviewing their pension schemes and the Government reviewing when state pensions should be paid!

Optional evidence assignment

*This activity can be carried out verbally in class **in a group** as a non-assessed activity to consolidate learning. Alternatively, if you do it **on your own**, it can count as supplementary evidence towards the following parts of the scheme.*

PC 1: Explain the benefits of employer and employee co-operation

PC 2: Describe ways to resolve disagreements

Range: Benefits of employer and employee co-operation: survival of the business, improved employee commitment to the business, improved efficiency.
Ways to resolve disagreements: trades union negotiation, legal representation (ACAS), industrial tribunals, European Court of Justice

Core skills: Communication, information technology

1 Divide into small groups of three or four. Select **two or three** of the unions listed in the table below and find out their addresses from the library.

   a Draft out a letter, using a word processor, asking each union for some information on any guidelines it gives to its union representatives about what they should do if asked to help a member with a grievance procedure.

   b Collect together your findings in a short report and then present these to the rest of your class.

Unison

Union of Shop, Distributive and Allied Workers (USDAW)

Transport and General Workers' Union (T & GWU)

Union of Construction, Allied Trades and Technicians (UCATT)

Banking, Insurance and Finance Union

GMB (formerly General, Municipal, Boilermakers and Allied Trades Union)

Graphical, Paper and Media Union

Manufacturing, Science and Finance Union

National Union of Civil and Public Servants

National Union of Teachers

Figure 2.25 Major unions

2 Find out about the grievance procedures, if any, which exist in your school or college for students who have a complaint. See how these compare with the information you obtained from the unions. Write a summary of the action you should take if you have a complaint.

3 Read the case study below and undertake the activities that follow.

Case study – Tracey's training

Tracey has worked for a local organisation as a telephone sales representative for the past four years. She is expected to sell the company's products over the telephone to customers, some of whom have bought goods before and some of whom have not. She has met the targets set in relation to goods sold to existing customers but not in relation to those sold to new customers.

Tracey thinks this is because of increased competition from two new firms in the area. She also feels that she has not had sufficient training in modern selling techniques. She was hoping to get a performance-related pay increment this year but has just found out that she has not received one. She protests but her supervisor remains firm.

At the interview with the departmental manager she outlines her case. The manager, having talked to the supervisor, says that the other telephone sales representatives have met their targets. He also says that Tracey's numbers of sales have decreased steadily over the past 6 months. Tracey says that she has been under pressure because she has just had to move house and has also had to nurse her mother through a serious illness.

a The manager has now to come to a decision. Decide what you think he should do and give reasons for your answer. Remember that it is better for him (and Tracey) at this stage to think of a compromise.

b Set out clearly the steps Tracey could take if she did not agree with the decision.

c Assume **several** telephone sales representatives have failed to meet their targets. All these staff are annoyed because they think their manager has deliberately set the targets very high to prevent them being awarded any performance related pay.

What effect could such as dispute have on:

i the future survival of the business
ii employee commitment to the business
iii employee efficiency?

Employer rights

When you start work you will have several expectations of your employer.

Equally, your employer will have expectations of *you*. They will expect you to arrive on time, be a willing and co-operative worker, be prepared to learn new skills or tasks, be sociable with other employees and relate well to customers. You will be expected to obey company rules and regulations and to follow standard procedures (e.g. notifying your boss if you are off sick).

In many of these areas both you and your employer are affected by legislation. This means that in some of these areas you have a legal right to have your expectations met. And so does your employer! The two main areas of legislation which affect employee and employer rights and responsibilities are:

- employment law
- health and safety legislation.

In these areas the law imposes certain obligations on both of you which must be followed.

Your employer has certain **rights**, i.e:

- to expect you to work to the terms of your contract
- to be able to take disciplinary action against you if you do not
- to expect you to co-operate with measures taken to comply with the Health and Safety at Work Act.

Employees' compliance with terms of contract

A **contract of employment** is a written document which sets out the terms and conditions of employment in a job.

Most of your rights and obligations are usually made clear to you during your interview or period of induction – and many of them will be *expressly* stated in your contract of employment (see Figure 2.26 and page 201).

However, there are other rights and obligations which may not be written down or even expressly stated. These are known as **implied** conditions, simply because they are regarded as being so obvious that nothing more need be said – 'it goes without saying' that you have agreed to accept these obligations. They are nevertheless as much part of your contract as the terms which are written down.

When you agree to work for an employer you are agreeing to five conditions. You must:

- be ready and willing to work
- use reasonable care and skill
- obey reasonable orders
- take care of your employer's property
- act in good faith.

Each of these is covered separately below.

Non-assessed activity

Figure 2.26 (on page 174) is a letter sent to Sarah Hayes when she was offered a job as a Saturday sales assistant. All the items mentioned are **express** conditions. List the key areas these cover.

What do you think will be the **implied** conditions of such a job? Discuss your answers with the rest of your group and your tutor.

Ready and willing to work

If you agree to work for someone as an employee, you must be able and willing to do that work. Look at the following two profiles.

Gillian	Fred
is clean and tidy	looks awful
smiles	is sulky
is willing and enthusiastic	thinks it silly to show enthusiasm
tries hard	can't be bothered
tries to get on with everybody	hates everybody

Which of the two would you say is 'ready and willing to work'?

What you should also note, however, is that you must be able and willing to do the work *yourself*. You owe your employer what is known as 'personal service'. If therefore you feel like having a morning in bed after a late night and persuade your mother to turn up in your place, your employer is not obliged to accept her as substitute!

Did you know?

This is one of the major differences between being an employee and being self-employed. If you were running your own window-cleaning business, for instance, you *could* send someone else in your place. (See Element 2.4, page 244.).

Use reasonable care and skill

When you accept the offer of a job you have agreed:

- not to be negligent (i.e. careless)
- to be competent.

If, therefore, you agree to work as a driver, you must be able to drive (and have a full driving licence). You must also be able to drive safely. In one case, a driver carelessly reversed his lorry and injured a fellow employee. The employers had to pay damages to the injured employee.

Even if you are not negligent you may still be held to be in breach of this part of the contract if you don't possess the skills necessary for the job. If you accept a job inputting data on a computer, you must be able to key in quickly and accurately. If you accept a job as a painter and decorator, you must be willing and able to climb stepladders.

In reality, of course, much depends on just how capable you are. You may think you can key in information on a computer satisfactorily if you manage ten words a minute. Your employer might want you to input at 50 words a minute!

Did you know?

When an employer employs someone, that employer accepts responsibility for actions carried out by that employee during the course of employment. If, therefore, you accidentally injure another employee, your employer must pay damages to that employee. However, your employer may be able to claim compensation from you because you have broken the term in your contract not to be negligent. That's what happened to the lorry driver in the example above.

Obey reasonable orders

If your employer asks you to carry out a particular job you must be prepared to do so, provided that it

ZENITH COMPUTER STORES
Lindale Road
HIGHTOWN
HG1 2PM

Tel: 01829 585859
Fax: 01829 377261

12 October 199X

Miss Sarah Hayes
22 Abbey Close
HIGHTOWN
HG6 3KM

Dear Sarah

SATURDAY SALES ASSISTANT

I have pleasure in writing to you to confirm your appointment to the above position at this store.

The terms and conditions of your employment are set out below:

1 Your appointment will commence with effect from Saturday, 16 October 199-
2 Your salary on appointment will be £3.50 per hour, payable monthly in arrears, direct to the bank.
   It is normal practice for the Company to review all salaries annually.
3 Your appointment will be subject to one week's notice in writing on either side.
4 Your hours of work will be 8 hours, Saturdays, but you may be required to work extra hours to meet
   the needs of the business. Your hours of work, however, cannot be permanently guaranteed because
   these will depend, again, on the needs of the business. If a change needs to be made your
   supervisor will inform you as far in advance as possible. If no advance notification is possible you
   will be offered a minimum of three hours' work.
5 All employees who work on a day designated as a bank holiday will be paid double time for actual
   hours worked.
6 You will responsible to the Store Manager.
7 Your first 21 days is your probationary period, during which time your performance will be evaluated.
   If your performance is rated as satisfactory during this time you will be taken off your
   probationary status.
8 In the event of sickness you must telephone your Supervisor within one hour of the time you were
   due to commence work, on the day in question, or arrange for someone to do so on your behalf. Any
   period of sickness in excess of 3 days requires the submission of a self-certification form. Any
   period of sickness in excess of one week requires the submission of a doctor's certificate. Payment
   for any self-certificated period of sickness will be at the discretion of the Company. You will
   receive statutory sick pay if appropriate which is payable up to twenty eight weeks in any year. Any
   entitlements after that time are paid by the DSS.
9 From the commencement of your employment you will start to accumulate paid holiday entitlement. This
   entitlement starts to operate when you have been in continuous employment for 26 weeks. Any holiday
   taken within the first 26 weeks will be unpaid. Between 26 weeks and 1 year you are entitled to one
   Saturday with holiday pay. After 1 year you are entitled to two Saturdays with holiday pay.
10 If you have any grievance relating to your employment you should approach your immediate supervisor
   and try to reach a satisfactory conclusion. If there is a failure to agree, the matter should be
   referred, in writing, to Mrs T Marshall, Human Resources Manager. Thereafter, if there is still a
   failure to agree you have the right of appeal, in writing only, to Mr G Brent, Managing Director.

I should be obliged if you would please sign and return the enclosed copy indicating your acceptance of
these terms.

Finally, I should like to welcome you to the Zenith team and hope that we will both benefit from a long
and happy working relationship.

Yours sincerely

Teresa Marshall

Teresa Marshall
Human Resources Manager

Figure 2.26 Sarah's job appointment letter

from working as a sales representative for another organisation either within a certain period of time (say two years) or within a certain distance (say 30 miles). The courts normally allow such a clause to be included *provided it is reasonable*. If you were banned for a period of 50 years or for a distance of 500 miles, the courts may not be willing to allow such a clause.

Non-assessed activity

As a group, discuss why some organisations make use of such a clause. Which organisations do you think are the most likely to use it?

Did you know?

George Michael has had a long-running fight with his record company Sony – who have claimed that he was contracted to work exclusively for them and that they could therefore retain his services as a recording artist for another ten years, even though George claimed that the contract was unreasonable. The High Court decided in favour of Sony, but it is likely that there will be an appeal against the decision.

Optional evidence assignment

This activity can be carried out verbally in class in a group as a non-assessed activity to consolidate learning. Alternatively, if you do it on your own, it can count as supplementary evidence towards the following parts of the scheme.

PC 3: Explain employer rights and responsibilities

Range: Employer rights: employees' compliance with terms of contract

Core skills: Communication

Read the following case study and then answer the questions which follow, in each case giving a **reason** for your answer. Prepare your final answers using a word processor.

Case study

Naomi and Kirti have started work in different departments of the same company and have met during the company's induction training programme. They agree to have lunch each week to discuss how they are getting on. After a few weeks it is apparent that they are both having some problems.

Naomi works as a clerical assistant in the Human Resources department. Her job description says that she will be expected to prepare and update personnel records of all members of staff, send out letters asking job applicants to attend for interview and make all the interviewing arrangements.

However, in the course of her work, she has had to deal with certain situations, some of which she feels she hasn't dealt with very well.

- She is not computer minded, and when the personnel record system became computerised she felt she would not be able to cope and refused to do the work.
- She mentioned to one of the other clerical assistants in the accounts department that one of the members of staff in his department would be off for at least six months with a nervous breakdown.
- She went for lunch one day and left unlocked a filing cabinet containing some confidential papers. When she returned she found that some papers had disappeared.
- A desperate job applicant telephoned her and promised her two Cup Final tickets if she could get him an interview. She agreed to see what she could do.

Kirti has a different problem. He works in the Accounts department but feels he is being asked to carry out jobs he doesn't think he is obliged to do. In the past week he has been asked to do several tasks he considers are beneath him.

- On Monday he was asked to collect his boss's suit from the dry cleaners.
- Later that day he was asked to clean his boss's car.
- On Tuesday he had to answer the telephone and re-direct calls when the switchboard operator was at lunch or on a break.
- On Wednesday and Thursday he had to make tea for the other members of the department.

a   Consider Naomi's problems carefully. For **each** situation compose a short paragraph about:
  i   where you think she may have made a mistake and why
  ii what you would have done in the same circumstances.

b   State which duties you think Kirti is obliged to carry out and which he is not. In cases where you think he is not obliged to do so, suggest what he should do to avoid annoying his boss too much by an outright refusal!

Figure 2.28 Which jobs should Kirti do?

Employees' compliance with health and safety regulations

Although your employer cannot delegate his responsibility for health, safety and welfare, under the **Health and Safety at Work Act** *you* also have an obligation to make sure that you:

- take care of your own health and safety
- take reasonable care of the health and safety of other people who may be injured by your careless actions
- co-operate with your employer or any other person carrying out duties under the Act.

Did you know?

In some circumstances, if you are injured, your employer may be able to claim that:

- you *voluntarily* took the risk of being injured (if, for instance, you knew you were undertaking some

dangerous work) – although the courts are not very impressed with this argument
- you *contributed* towards the injury – by not wearing safety goggles, by not following set safety procedures, etc. If this is the case then the amount of damages you can claim if an accident does occur will be reduced.

Safe working environment

Whilst it is up to the employer to make sure that working areas are cleaned regularly, that there are adequate storage areas and safe equipment, there is a duty on employees as well. If you have a desk like a bomb-site and never put anything away then you are hardly co-operating with your employer. Safe working practices can be divided into:

- good housekeeping
- the provision of suitable equipment and training in use of it
- the provision of suitable furniture and proper care and use of it
- suitable accommodation
- reduction in noise
- safe working habits
- provision of information.

Health and Safety at Work is also covered in Elements 1.2 and 2.1.

Disciplinary action

Your employer has the right to expect that you will carry out your side of the contract of employment and that you will behave reasonably. If you do not, your employer may be entitled to take some action against you.

Most organisations have a clearly stated **disciplinary policy** which sets down guidelines of the ways in which they are going to handle any disciplinary problems. See Figure 2.29 for an example.

Non-assessed activity

As a group, discuss:

1   The difference between 'informal' and 'formal' procedures.
2   The occasions on which you might suggest that informal counselling would not be appropriate.

1. It is the employee's responsibility to follow all the company's rules and working procedures.
2. If an employee is performing or behaving badly, the first step management will take will be **informal** counselling.
3. **Formal** disciplinary procedures will be put into operation only when informal counselling has been unsuccessful or where the actions of the employee show that informal counselling is inappropriate.
4. No employee will be formally disciplined without a fair hearing and an opportunity to put his or her case.
5. Management will seek to act fairly and consistently when carrying out any disciplinary action.

Figure 2.29 A typical disciplinary policy

Disciplinary procedures

As well as a disciplinary policy, organisations should also have a set of **disciplinary procedures**, details of which should be made available to all employees (see page 202). If an organisation wishes to draw up its own procedures it can do so, but most organisations follow a common set of procedures recommended by ACAS in its code of practice, **Disciplinary Practice and Procedures in Employment**.

Look back to page 169 to remind yourself of what other duties ACAS has.

Code of practice

The code of practice recommends that disciplinary procedures should:

■ be formal and in writing
■ state to whom they apply
■ ensure that everyone has access to a copy of them.

They must also specify:

■ what disciplinary action may be taken
■ which level of management has the authority to take such action
■ that if a complaint is made, the employee concerned is notified of the complaint and is

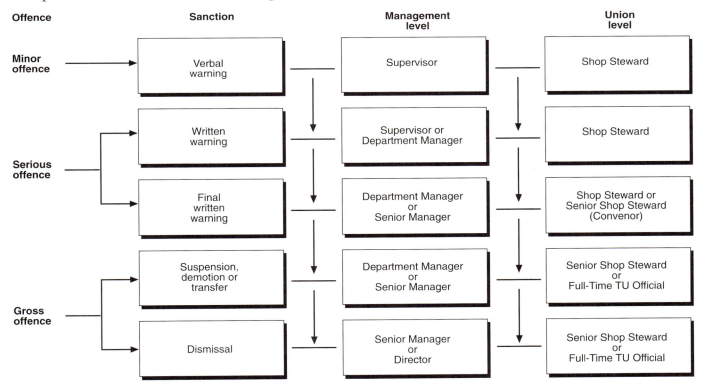

In some organisations the Human Resources department will be involved at a very early stage and the Human Resources Manager may take the place of or act with the department manager

Figure 2.30 Stages in the disciplinary procedure

given the opportunity to state his or her case and is represented, if desired, by a union representative or fellow employee
- that no disciplinary action is taken without full investigation
- that an employee is not dismissed for a single incident *unless* it is **gross**, i.e. very serious, misconduct
- that the employee should be provided with a right of appeal against any disciplinary action.

Non-assessed activity

From what you have already read in relation to the implied terms in your contract of employment, suggest what type of behaviour could be included in a list of disciplinary offences. See how many you can think of before you read any further.

Types of misconduct

Each organisation must decide what offences are going to result in disciplinary measures being taken. Normally, provided the same rules are applied to everyone, the industrial tribunal will not interfere. Common examples of what are normally regarded as disciplinary offences include:

- frequent absence
- frequent lateness
- fighting
- swearing
- drunkenness
- giving out confidential information
- sexual harassment
- stealing
- clocking or signing in or out for someone else
- using company equipment/tools for a private job.

Types of sanction (punishment)

As you can see in Figure 2.30, there are normally at least five stages in any disciplinary procedure. Each stage is progressively more severe, so an employer has the opportunity merely to warn an employee who has been guilty of a minor offence, e.g. by means of a verbal warning before any more serious action need be taken. A very serious offence, however, might be dealt with more severely, even though it may be the first offence the employee has committed.

Non-assessed activity

Look at the types of misconduct listed above. Try to decide which might be regarded as minor, unless repeated frequently, and which might be regarded as more serious, even if only done once.

Verbal warning

This is the most frequent and least severe penalty. Remember, quite often an employee will be 'told off' by a supervisor on a very informal basis which will normally be the end of the matter. You therefore need to distinguish between those verbal warnings which are **not** part of the formal procedure and those which are – although an employee should be left in no doubt as to whether or not the warning is formal!

Non-assessed activity

Decide in which of the following situations the warning should form part of the formal disciplinary procedure. Give reasons. Note – you may like to discuss these in a group first.

1 You miss the bus two days running and come in late. Your supervisor asks you why you are late and, when you explain, asks you to be a bit more careful about your time-keeping in future.
2 You pretend to feel ill one afternoon so that you can go to the Job Centre to look for another job. Unfortunately someone sees you and tells your supervisor. He calls you into his office and tells you that sort of behaviour is unacceptable.
3 Your supervisor asks you to change your lunch hour from noon to one o'clock. You don't like this idea and say that you prefer to lunch at noon. He insists and you have a slight argument about it. He tells you to be careful about your attitude.
4 You find out that your company is interested in buying some property owned by the local brewery where your friend works. You tell him and he tells his boss. Word gets back to your company and your supervisor tells you that you have committed a serious offence.

Did you know?

Even though a formal *verbal* warning is verbal, i.e. spoken, an employee should be given *written* confirmation of it – and a note to this effect will be put on their file – in case, at a later date, there are any disagreements about what was really said.

Written warning

If you repeat an offence despite being given a warning **or** if your misconduct is more serious you may be given a written warning. In it you will be told:

- the offence for which you have been disciplined
- where relevant – any previous warnings you have been given
- what your future conduct is expected to be.

You may also be asked to sign that you have received and understood it.

Depending on the nature of the offence, you may be given a 'first' or a 'final' written warning.

Did you know?

If you have been given a formal warning you may be concerned at the effect it may have on your future prospects. Most organisations, however, will give you a fresh start after a certain time. Depending on how serious your misconduct has been, you may find that a record of it will be removed from your file any time between a period of three months to two years.

Suspension

The two types of suspension are:

- suspension **with pay** pending a disciplinary investigation
- suspension **without pay** as a punishment within the formal disciplinary procedure.

Transfer or demotion

Sometimes employees may be transferred to another job or even moved to a more junior position (i.e. **demoted**) as an alternative to being dismissed.

Did you know?

In the nineteenth century it was common for an employer to fine an employee for any breach of company rules. The problem there, however, was that if the fine was too small it had no effect. If it was too large it could be regarded as what is known as a 'penalty' and thus be considered illegal. Nowadays the **Wages Act 1986** restricts the right to impose fines to cases where it is actually stated in the contract of employment and the employee agrees in writing to such an arrangement.

Dismissal

In most cases, dismissal takes place only where all other options have been exhausted. If an employee is dismissed he or she normally has the right of appeal to a top level of management. The procedure should specify the period of time within which the appeal must be lodged and a further period of time within which it must be heard. If the appeal is dismissed the employee is left with the alternative of accepting the dismissal or of taking his or her case to an industrial tribunal on the grounds that the dismissal was unfair. (See page 185.)

Non-assessed activity

The appeal must be heard by a level of management not previously involved and of a higher level than the level of management involved in the initial procedures. Suggest why this should be the case.

The disciplinary interview

A manager who is asked to conduct a disciplinary interview generally has to:

- hold it within a reasonable period of time of the offence having been committed
- make sure that the employee knows that it is a disciplinary interview
- establish the facts
- impose a sanction (if justified).

The manager therefore needs to be satisfied that the employee has been guilty of some misconduct by:

- checking on what rule has been broken
- looking at the evidence
- deciding whether or not there is a case to answer.

It is also advisable that the interview is held in private and that sufficient time, free from any interruption, is allowed for it.

During the interview the manager should:

- allow the employee to state his or her case

- behave calmly and not get angry, sarcastic or rude
- suggest ways in which the employee could improve and listen also to the employee's suggestions
- summarise the facts and make sure the employee knows he or she has been disciplined (if this is the case) and knows about the right of appeal
- send written confirmation to the employee after the interview, with a copy to the trade union representative.

The right to dismiss

Ultimately the employer does have the right to dismiss the employee if all other disciplinary procedures have failed or if the misconduct has been so serious that it warrants dismissal without the need for any other disciplinary action.

The employee may claim that he or she has been unfairly dismissed and take the claim to an industrial tribunal.

Proof of dismissal

It is up to the employee to prove unfair dismissal. In most cases this is quite easy to do! In some cases, however, particularly if there has been an argument or series of arguments, it is difficult for the tribunal to decide whether the employer has actually dismissed the employee or just lost patience. If, for example, in the course of an argument, a manager tells an employee to leave, does it mean leave the office or leave the company?

Employees have to be careful also that they don't resign by mistake. Saying that they've had enough of the place could be quite dangerous!

Non-assessed activity

Look at the following statements.

1 From a sales manager to a sales representative:

'If you don't like the way we work, there's the door.'

2 From a manager to a cleaner:

'It looks as though we might have to part company.'

In what ways could you argue:
- **a** that a dismissal has occurred in both these cases
- **b** that it has not?

As a group, discuss what other factors the tribunal may take into account when reaching such a decision. Consider, for instance, the status of the two people concerned and whether or not the incident was a one-off or part of a series of arguments.

Unfair dismissal

Once the fact of dismissal has been proved, employers have the right to defend their decision by using one of the following defences:

- the employee was incapable of carrying out the work
- the employee was guilty of some type of misconduct
- the employee was redundant, i.e. the need for the job has disappeared (or the firm has closed down!)
- an Act of Parliament prevented the employee from continuing to be employed
- there was 'some other substantial reason' (SOSR) to justify the dismissal.

Capability

Remember the implied duty in the contract of employment that the employee provides the skills needed to do the job. If the employee doesn't have these skills, theoretically the employer can dismiss the employee and claim that they have done so fairly. However, nowadays tribunals are more sympathetic to incompetent employees. They will expect the employer to have made it clear that the employee is not reaching the required standard – it mustn't come as a surprise to the employee to be called into the manager's office and dismissed.

As an example, suppose that you are employed in the accounts department and just cannot get to grips with the computerised accounts system. *You* know you haven't grasped it and it makes no difference, therefore, that your manager keeps telling you that you haven't. What your employers are expected to do in such circumstances is to show that they have tried to *help* you – by arranging extra training sessions, for example.

Two cases show the right and the wrong way to deal with such a situation. In one case an employee who had worked for the same garage for many years was, as the result of a re-organisation, asked to undertake some clerical duties in addition to his other work. He found it difficult to cope and the firm dismissed him. The tribunal was not pleased to discover that although he had been told that he wasn't doing his job properly, no attempt had been made to help him.

By contrast the manager of a dress shop, who was dismissed for inefficiency, was held to have been fairly dismissed because the company could show that they had tried to help her in many ways – by giving her training in window display, in book-keeping and in maintaining good staff relationships.

Did you know?

If you are ill for a long period, this could eventually justify your employer in dismissing you on the grounds that you are incapable of work. As you might expect, however, the tribunal is normally reluctant to hold that such a dismissal is fair unless the employer has taken measures to find an alternative solution. It will want to know, for instance, that:

- all reasonable efforts have been taken to check on your state of health – including consulting a doctor – and that you have been made aware that further or continued absence could result in dismissal
- that the dismissal was reasonable because of the nature of your work and the effect your ill health has had on the organisation.

Factors to be taken into account include:

- the nature of the illness
- your age
- the length of time you have been employed
- your nearness to retirement
- the need for your job to be done and the need for a replacement to do it.

Non-assessed activity

As a group, discuss what factors the tribunal will consider in the case of each of the following people who have been dismissed on ill-health grounds.

- a 63-year-old man with chronic bronchitis
- a 20-year-old drummer with a pop group which is currently touring the UK, who has had a nervous breakdown
- a 40-year-old production manager responsible for meeting the company's production targets who has had a minor heart attack.

Misconduct

In most cases an employee is dismissed for misconduct only after all other disciplinary measures have been taken. If an employer cannot prove that these procedures have been followed the tribunal will not usually hold the dismissal fair.

Did you know?

The most common **criminal** act carried out in the workplace is stealing. In such cases the employer can only dismiss if they have good reason for believing that an employee is guilty of theft – at the time of dismissal. If they merely suspect the employee of theft, dismiss him or her and then find out afterwards (e.g. because of a police investigation) that theft has been proved, this does not necessarily make the dismissal fair. However, if an employer has carried out a thorough investigation they need only have 'good reason to believe' that employees have been stealing and not proof 'beyond reasonable doubt'. Note, too, that in one case in which it was almost certain that one of two employees had stolen some cash from their employer's safe, the employer was held entitled to dismiss both of them!

Did you know?

A supermarket worker who claimed he was too hungry to pay for a current bun before eating it was accused of stealing by the store manager of the Safeway store where he worked. The manager took the bun from his mouth and froze it to use as evidence and sacked the employee. The employee claimed unfair dismissal but lost his case because of the strict rules which operate in the retail trade about such matters.

Conduct outside working hours

Normally what you do in your own time is your own concern. If, therefore, someone gets very drunk one evening and ends up in the police cells charged with drunk and disorderly conduct, his or her employer, even though disapproving of this behaviour, will not normally be able to dismiss the employee because of it – although his or her chances of promotion might have vanished! However, if an employee's conduct outside work is such that it could have an effect on what he or she does at work, then the situation changes.

Non-assessed activity

Consider the following cases and decide in each case whether the employee's conduct

Did you know?

The most common criteria in redundancy selection agreements refer to:

- volunteers
- sub-contractors
- last in first out (LIFO).

However, some organisations also have a set of 'efficiency' criteria by which employees are judged on absence, time-keeping, work performance, disciplinary record, etc.

Statutory restrictions

Not many employees are dismissed under this heading. On some occasions, however, employees are dismissed because a statute or Act of Parliament forbids the employer to employ them. Suppose, for instance, a teenage girl has been employed to work a night shift in a factory and then the employer discovers that by law she is not old enough to do so. Unless the employer can find the teenager another job, he has no choice but to dismiss her.

Some other substantial reason

This is a catch-all phrase which allows an employer to claim that a dismissal is fair even though the reason for it doesn't fit into any of the other categories. In one case, for example, an employee who was already working in an organisation refused to sign a 'restraint of trade' clause which the company wanted to include in his existing contract of employment. He was good at his job and it would have been difficult for the employer to claim that he was guilty of any misconduct – given that he had initially been employed on different terms. However, because of the genuine fear the company had that they would lose customers to rival firms if their ex-employees left them to work for these firms, the tribunal held the dismissal to be fair.

Summary dismissal

Being dismissed is a severe enough penalty – even if you are given notice! However, in some circumstances an employer has the right to dismiss an employee instantly, i.e. without any notice or without following any disciplinary procedures. Normally this punishment is reserved:

- for very serious offences (possibly involving breaches of health and safety rules) or

will affect his or her work. In each case give reasons for your decision.

1 A sales representative is found guilty of a drink driving offence and his driving licence is revoked.
2 A company accountant is found guilty of embezzling funds from the social club of which she is the treasurer.
3 A teacher, who is also a football fan, is involved in a riot and found guilty of assault and battery.
4 An RSPCA officer is found guilty of ill-treating his dog.
5 A clerk is convicted of shop lifting.
6 A human resources manager is found guilty of obstructing the police at a trades union rally.

Redundancy

If a company closes down altogether and all the employees are made redundant because there is no work for them to do, then they are regarded as being dismissed because of redundancy. In most cases this dismissal will be regarded as fair because the employer has little choice. Even if some only of the employees are dismissed because of redundancy this is normally regarded as fair (if the proper consultation has taken place) unless they can show that the employer has ignored a redundancy selection agreement negotiated with the union (stating, for example, that those with the shortest amount of service have to be made redundant first).

■ for offences which are less serious but which are very common in a particular organisation and which the employer wants to stop.

Non-assessed activity

Given below is a list of offences upon which some employers have imposed the penalty of summary dismissal. Re-order them into:

a offences which you think have health and safety implications

b offences which you think an employer wants to prevent simply because they are occurring too often.

1 clocking in or signing in for someone else
2 not being able to balance the till when cashing up
3 fighting on the shop floor
4 being found taking tools out of the workplace
5 smoking in an area where flammable liquids are stored
6 not wearing safety goggles
7 taking time off without permission
8 not wearing an identity badge
9 removing money without authority
10 deliberately assaulting or injuring any employee or customer.

Employers' right to legal representation

A large company may have a legal department staffed by solicitors and other legally trained people who will be responsible for all aspects of the organisation's legal affairs. One section may concentrate on the law relating to buildings and property, another on the drawing up of commercial contracts, another on local authority legislation and so on. In addition, one section will be expected to take responsibility for all employment law issues in relation to the contract of employment, trade union membership, dismissal, redundancy and discrimination.

Smaller companies may have legally qualified persons in their administration department or they may rely – for employment law matters – on their human resources staff. Many employers pay a firm of solicitors a **retainer** (normally a fixed yearly fee) in case they need any legal advice or representation.

Advisory, Conciliation and Arbitration Service (ACAS)

An employer has the same right as an employee to approach ACAS if there is a dispute with an

employee. (See page 169 for further details.) ACAS is also expected to act as a 'peacemaker' between employer and union – if asked to do so.

That is part of its **conciliation** and **arbitration** role.

■ **Conciliation** – ACAS can try to act as the intermediary in a dispute, i.e. an ACAS representative might meet an employer and union separately and act as a channel of communication between them.
■ **Arbitration** – if both parties in a dispute agree, ACAS can act as an arbitrator – which means that once a decision is made, both parties have to accept it.

Non-assessed activity

1 Why do you think more use is made of ACAS as a conciliator rather than as an arbitrator?

2 Imagine you are an ACAS official and have been asked to act as the go-between in a dispute between an employer and a trade union over the suspension of two workers who were found leaving the premises with some company equipment. Discuss as a group what additional information you would need, from both employer and trade union officials, before you could start to try and help them to reach an agreement.

Industrial tribunals

Employers are allowed to make the same use of industrial tribunals as employees. If they lose a case they face the prospect of being asked to re-engage or re-instate an employee. In most cases, however, they would have to pay compensation.

Did you know?

By far the most common remedy is compensation. In 1992–3, 5587 cases were not upheld. Of the cases that were upheld, only 73 led to re-instatement or re-engagement as opposed to 2636 awards of compensation.

Non-assessed activity

As a group, discuss why the tribunal is reluctant to make an employer take back an employee who has been dismissed – and the advantages and disadvantages to the employee.

European Court of Justice

Traditionally the European Court of Justice has been a forum for addressing **employee** rights. However, since the Court is responsible for interpreting EU law, employers do get the advantage of knowing exactly what their rights and obligations are over a wide range of employment issues. (To remind yourself of what these are look back to page 170.)

Optional evidence assignment

*This activity can be carried out verbally in class **in a group** as a non-assessed activity to consolidate learning. Alternatively, if you do it **on your own**, it can count as supplementary evidence towards the following parts of the scheme.*

PC 3:   Explain employer rights and responsibilities

Range: Employer rights: employees' compliance with terms of contract, health and safety regulations, disciplinary action, legal representation

Core skills: Communication

1   Contact your local ACAS branch and obtain a copy of the code of practice on Disciplinary Practice and Procedures. Ask also for details of the other codes of practice which are available. (You can get the address of your local ACAS from the Department of Employment.)

2   Obtain a copy of the student disciplinary policy and procedure of your college or school.
   a   **As a group**, discuss how these affect you as students. Write down your comments, and add any items you think should be changed. Give reasons.
   b   Read carefully the type of offences for which you can be disciplined. Do you think everything important has been included – or can you add anything extra?
   c   Read carefully the way in which you can be disciplined and the system which is used. How does this compare with the system used in industry?

3   Imagine that your friend, Rob, has always been anti-authority and hates rules and regulations. Although you are a friend of his you are surprised one day when the fire bell goes and he ignores it, saying 'only a drill again'. When you make him leave the room he runs up the corridor, wedges open the fire doors and deliberately sets off two fire extinguishers. Then he takes the lift to the ground floor laughing at you. The next day you find he is being disciplined for actions which contravene the Health and Safety at Work Act.

   a   List the actions Rob took which were wrong.
   b   Which requirements of the Health and Safety at Work Act did Rob contravene?
   c   Rob was sent for by the Human Resources manager. He was summarily dismissed for 'failing to obey an instruction designed to protect the safety of any employee'. He is shocked to find that he has been dismissed without notice, without payment in lieu of notice and will lose all his holiday pay.

   State whether you think the dismissal is fair or unfair and give reasons for your decision.

   d   Rob tells you that he considers his dismissal is unfair because he knows someone else in the company who was disciplined for the same type of offence and only received a written warning.

      i   Write down the action Rob *could* take if he feels he has a strong case.
      ii   What is your advice to Rob?

Employer responsibilities

To explain business objectives

Many organisations now have what they call a **mission statement** which sets out in simple terms what the organisation wants to achieve, e.g.

■   'The company aims to become the fastest growing company with the highest profit margins in the retail sector.'
■   'This college exists to serve the educational, cultural, social and economic needs of the local community.'

What the mission statement does is to summarise the goals or objectives of a particular organisation. For practical purposes, however, an employer needs much more precise objectives which can be understood by both management and workforce.

Different types of organisations have different types of objectives. A manufacturing firm may have as its main objective the need to make a profit. A non-profit making organisation may have a very different objective.

Non-assessed activity

Read the following list of objectives.

1 To ensure the safety of the funds entrusted to us by our customers.

2 To maximise the number of successful treatments.

3 To provide a satisfactory service to the local community.

Match each one to one of the following organisations.

a a hospital

b a bank or building society

c a local authority.

The strategic development plan

Many organisations now include all the objectives they hope to achieve in a **strategic development plan,** which is normally prepared by the senior management of the organisation and which covers a specified period of time – usually from three to five years. Each department or area will normally state what its objectives are over the period in question and will be expected to monitor progress towards those objectives at periodic intervals.

Many employers go a stage further and break down their objectives into:

- company objectives
- departmental objectives.

Obviously many departmental objectives will depend on the work of the department itself. For example, one of the objectives of a sales department may be to beat last year's sales targets. One of the objectives of a marketing department will be to launch a successful marketing initiative, and so on. However, some objectives will be the same for all departments. Departmental managers will be concerned to:

- run the department as economically as possible (and may be expected to keep within a certain budget)
- look after staff (objectives here may include, for instance, the number of staff trained or the number who have undergone a staff appraisal interview)
- co-operate with other departments (the Human Resources department may be expected to show that it has assisted in setting up a certain number of training programmes each year, etc.)

Non-assessed activity

1 Write down **one** specific objective that you think each of the following departments might have.

- Research and Development
- Accounts
- Purchasing
- Human Resources.

2 Obviously, to be able to work towards the employer's objectives, employees have to know what they are. **As a group,** discuss what methods of communication an employer might use to make sure that all the workforce is aware of what the company objectives are. Write a summary of your discussions.

To offer and facilitate training

Staff training is normally within the terms of reference of the Human Resources department (see also page 138), although in smaller organisations it may be undertaken by each department separately.

Training can be divided into:

- **on the job** – where employees learn skills at the workplace, e.g. how to operate a particular machine or piece of equipment
- **off the job** – where employees learn their skills through attendance on courses outside the organisation, e.g. management training or studying for a professional qualification.

In the first case, the advantages are that the employee can learn specific job skills without leaving the place of work. However, there is the disadvantage that there may be little time available for training and the instruction may not be carried out by a qualified trainer. In the second case, time off may be available (known as **day-release**) or the employees may be expected to attend the course in their own time, e.g. in the evening.

Did you know?

Staff who pay for their own NVQ training programmes can claim tax relief on the course fee.

Training today

According to the *Industrial Society,* employers are spending less on staff training. In 1993 employers spent on average £492 per employee, but by 1994 this had fallen to £384. In 1994 24 per cent of companies spent less than £100 per person, and only four per cent spent more than £1000 per person.

In many cases this is because employers are putting more responsibility for training on the employee. They acknowledge that, today, people may change jobs several times in their careers, and may even encourage them to take any course which will improve their personal or professional skills. However, most employers think that responsibility for training and staff development is 60 per cent that of the staff and 40 per cent that of the company. Some consider that employees' responsibility for their own training and development will be as high as 80 per cent in future. This means that it is up to employees to identify courses they wish to take and, in many cases, contribute towards the fees. This is because training is seen to benefit the individual as much as – if not more than – the company.

Did you know?

1 Ford and Rover are two companies which offer training, as a perk, on almost any subject the employee chooses – from holiday French to pottery painting. In five years over 100 000 employees have opted for training projects and 80 have completed degree courses.
2 McDonald's operate education, books, scholarship and junior business management programmes for the benefit of their part-time and full-time staff. They

offer student awards of up to £250 towards course fees and up to £50 towards books. The Scholarship Award is for employees taking part-time courses in Business Studies or a related area (at HND or degree level). The Junior Business Management Programme is open to 18–19-year-old employees who want to link a management skills training programme with a specific FE course.

Figure 2.31 Some staff are highly qualified thanks to training schemes

Non-assessed activity

Read the following extract from an article on training and answer the questions given below.

The importance of training

Any country which has a highly trained labour force has a great advantage over others. In the UK there has been a shortage of skilled workers since the Second World War, and this situation has contributed to the slow rate of economic growth.

This is not a new situation. In 1884 the Royal Commission of Training Instruction reported that the main reason for Britain being unable to compete with the rest of the world was because of its lack of attention to training.

Training should be 'lifetime' training, i.e. it should start when an employee first enters the firm and should continue until he or she leaves. The advantages to the employer are enormous – increased proficiency, increased productivity and increased safety.

1 **As a group**, discuss why lack of training creates problems for British industry.
2 The advantages of training to the employer are set out in the extract. What are the advantages to the employee?
3 Suppose you have the opportunity of either:

   a undergoing some training which could eventually lead to promotion in the firm where you are working but which is useful to you **only** if you remained with that firm, or
   b undergoing some training (perhaps in your own time) which would not lead to immediate promotion in your firm but **may** give you a greater chance of getting another job.

   Which would you choose? Why?

4 As a group, debate the idea that 'it is the responsibility of employees to identify their own training needs as it is more in their own long term interests than that of the employer.' Argue for and against this statement and summarise the result of the debate.

Did you know?

The Training and Enterprise Councils (TECs) were set up in the 1990s to encourage training in particular skills. They are employer led, independent local bodies which arrange training and enterprise programmes in local areas to meet the needs of the local business community. Although they receive start-up funds from central government, they are expected to become increasingly financed by local businesses.

Implementing equal opportunities legislation at work

The Sex Discrimination Act

The **Sex Discrimination Act 1975** (as amended by the **Sex Discrimination Act 1980**) forbids discrimination – i.e. treating men and women differently from each other, in areas such as employment. It also specifically forbids discrimination against married women. Amongst other things it covers:

- selection for jobs
- promotion
- job training
- dismissal
- fringe benefits.

Did you know?

Although the majority of sex discrimination cases are brought by women, men can also claim that they have been discriminated against. In one case a male delicatessen assistant claimed unfair dismissal from his job at Safeway. He lost his job because he had grown his hair long and had a ponytail. He claimed that a female employee with hair of the same length and style would not have been dismissed. His claim was upheld.

Types of discrimination

There are two types of discrimination:

- **direct discrimination**, e.g. 'I am never going to employ a woman,' or 'I don't want a male secretary'
- **indirect discrimination**, i.e. where it is far more difficult for members of one sex than the other to meet the requirements e.g. 'I am only going to employ someone who is over six feet tall and who has a beard.'

Did you know?

An employer may be allowed to prefer an employee of one particular sex if it can be justified on other grounds, such as:

- because it might be too expensive to do otherwise (although this defence is not very popular with the court)
- because of a 'genuine occupational qualification' (GOQ) where the nature of the job requires a man or woman, e.g. modelling or acting
- where the work is to be carried out in a private home or requires the employee to live in
- where the job is outside the UK and in a country whose laws and customs prevent the work being undertaken by a woman
- where the job is one of two to be held by a married couple
- where personal services are required which are most effectively provided by a man, e.g. work in a boy's hostel.

Non-assessed activity

Imagine you are working in the advertising section of your local paper, accepting and checking text for job vacancies. Several advertisements you have received today are worrying you. **On your own**, write down your comment about the following and then compare your answers with the rest of your group.

1 Two advertisements, one of which asks for a 'barman' and one for a 'Girl Friday'.
2 One advert which asks for a building site worker who is willing to work topless in the summer.
3 The following copy of a job advertisement received earlier by another member of staff.

Word Processor Operators

urgently required!

Only white females under the age of 35 need apply.

Ring 0389 3879198 for details.

---

4 An advert which asks for a local girl to play Cinderella in the Christmas pantomime.

Race Relations Act

The **Race Relations Act 1976** forbids discrimination on grounds of 'colour, race, nationality or ethnic or racial origin'.

It contains much the same provisions as the **Sex Discrimination Act** – it forbids both direct and indirect discrimination unless there is a need for a GOQ or if the employer can justify it on grounds other than race. Therefore, one employer who told a job centre he didn't want to be sent any more Pakistani job applicants because of customer complaints, was held to be guilty of *direct* discrimination.

A condition placed on applicants for management training that they should have had certain previous managerial experience was held to be a more difficult requirement for overseas applicants to meet and was therefore regarded as *indirect* discrimination.

Did you know?

Some companies have gone one stage further than having equal opportunities policies and have introduced a positive action programme. This means that they set targets for the

---

Equal opportunities information chart

You are being **sexually harassed** if someone:

- touches you unnecessarily, repeatedly or intimately
- makes sexual comments or innuendoes about your appearance or actions
- plays jokes or pranks on you which are offensive
- shows you (or circulates) sexually offensive or explicit photographs or documents
- asks you for sexual favours
- threatens you (e.g. with dismissal or a lower grade job) if you don't comply

You are being **racially harassed** if someone:

- mocks you or tells racist jokes
- uses abusive language with a racial content
- calls you a racist name
- shows you (or circulates) racially offensive material
- persistently questions you about your private life, culture, ethnic origin or religion
- gives you more work than the rest of the staff or more menial jobs
- unreasonably excludes you from normal conversation or events

What to do

If you are being sexually or racially harassed, tell the person or persons concerned that you find their attitude unacceptable and that they must stop this behaviour. If this has no effect, then report the matter to your supervisor immediately and in confidence. If, for some reason, you cannot confide in your supervisor, then see another senior person or a trusted colleague who has worked for the company some time.

But ...

Never bring such a complaint falsely or maliciously, or disciplinary action is likely to be taken against you.

Figure 2.32 Equal opportunities

number of women or ethnic minority workers they aim to employ by a certain date. You will sometimes see this mentioned in advertisements. The BBC is one organisation which has set specific targets for future recruitment.

Victimisation

The law tries to protect people who have claimed racial or sex discrimination from being victimised when they return to work. If, for instance, they are made redundant or are transferred to a less well-paid or pleasant job, they can complain to an industrial tribunal.

Did you know?

Sexual or racial harassment is against the law and both the harasser *and* the organisation could be held liable if nothing is done. If you think you are a victim, look at Figure 232.

Did you know?

A black barmaid was sacked for walking out of a bar because she objected to a Jim Davidson video which was being shown in the pub where she worked. The audience of 30 customers were all white. She found Davidson's jokes about black people racist and offensive. However, the landlady sacked her when she complained about having to work in these conditions. Her claim for unfair dismissal was upheld because racially offensive jokes in the workplace can be both hurtful and humiliating.

Equal Pay Act

Under EU law 'men and women should receive equal pay for equal work'. The **Equal Pay Act 1970,** amended by the **Equal Pay (Amendment) Regulations 1983,** also provides for equal pay for men and women. In Northern Ireland, the Act which applies is the **Fair Employment (NI) Act.** These acts state that a woman must get the same pay as a man (or vice versa):

- If she is employed on the same work as a man. Minor differences don't count. If she works next to a man in a packing department, she must get the same rate of pay. It won't matter if she is packing chocolate biscuits and he is packing plain biscuits.

- If a woman's job is rated as the same as that of a man under a job grading scheme.
- If a woman's work is regarded as being of 'equal value'. In one case, a woman who worked as a cook in a shipyard canteen claimed that her work was of equal value to the organisation as that of a man who was a shipyard worker.

Figure 2.33 Dissimilar jobs can be equally important

Did you know?

This last provision is particularly important in cases where women are 'segregated' into women-only jobs. If, for instance, a group of women are working on an assembly line and there is no man doing the same work, the women have no-one with whom they can compare themselves. Their only solution, therefore, is to take the same route as the shipyard cook and to try to compare themselves with a man doing a *different* job, but one which they can claim is of no greater value than theirs.

Employer defences

An employer may be able to use one of two defences.

1 There is an *important* difference between the two

jobs (if, for example, the man in the packing department is expected to carry out other duties such as lifting heavy weights or to work in more unpleasant conditions). In one case some female cleaners claimed equal pay with male cleaners. The work involved cleaning newly built houses. However, the men did the heavy work such as removing excess plaster; the women did the lighter cleaning jobs. The men were held to be entitled to a higher rate of pay. If a man takes more responsibility than a woman (or vice versa) this would also entitle him to be paid more – although he must really assume that responsibility. In one case it was found that a male wages clerk who was paid more than a female wages clerk because he took responsibility for the accuracy of the figures, was actually relying on the woman to check his work.

2 The second defence is that there is an important difference between the man and the woman (e.g. the man is better qualified, older, more experienced, etc.). Again this must be a real difference. If, for instance, the man has only had a couple more years' experience than the woman he would not be entitled to be paid very much more.

Optional evidence assignment

*This activity can be carried out verbally in class **in a group** as a non-assessed activity to consolidate learning. Alternatively, if you do it* **on your own**, *it can count as supplementary evidence towards the following parts of the scheme.*

PC 3: Explain employer rights and responsibilities

Range: Employer responsibilities: to implement equal opportunities legislation at work

Core skills: Communication

1 Salma works as an assembler alongside John but does not get the same pay. John has been working in the factory for many years.

Marian works as an office supervisor but thinks her job is just as important as that of Frank, who is the Safety Officer and who gets more money than she does.

Alison and Michael work together in the payroll section but Michael is responsible for checking the work.

a Do you think Salma should receive the same pay as John, Marian the same pay as Frank, and Alison the same pay as Michael? Give reasons in each case for your decision.

b Salma decides she has a grievance. From what you have read previously, what steps do you think she should take?

2 Read the following extracts of some conversations between work colleagues and write a short paragraph stating whether or not you think each woman is entitled to equal pay – and if so, why.

Conversation 1

Norman What's the problem?

Katie I've just found out that I'm getting less pay than Peter and I don't think it's fair.

Norman Why isn't it fair? You're getting a better rate of pay than most other administrative assistants you know. Go down to the Job Centre and look at all the job vacancies on display if you don't believe me.

Katie I'm not arguing about that. All I'm saying is that my work is just as important as Peter's but he gets more money than I do.

Norman Well, you'll just have to apply to be an accounts clerk like him then.

Katie But I don't want to be an accounts clerk ... .

Norman Well, that's the only way you'll get the same pay as he does.

Conversation 2

Farouk You don't do the same work as I do you know. It's a very different job. I have to sort through a mass of information, key it into a computer terminal, index it, update it and recall it when required. It takes a lot of time and effort.

Brenda I agree – but I collect together information, I word process it, I store it and update it, retrieve it when wanted. You use a computer. I use a filing cabinet. Where's the difference? I should be paid the same as you.

Conversation 3

Manager It's like speaking to the wall – how often do I have to tell you that you can't have any more pay?

Robina Why not?

Manager Because although you and Jack work together he has to work in the outside office. Workpeople are coming in and out all day long and it's very difficult to keep the place

warm. You work in a very much more comfortable place.

Robina It isn't all that comfortable. People are pushing past me all day long to get to the drinks machine.

Manager Well, I know where I'd rather work.

3 In 1994 Harrods faced more than 20 industrial tribunal cases, including fifteen from ethnic minority workers. All were claiming they had been unfairly dismissed, and five were claiming racial discrimination. Others claimed race was a factor in the decision to sack them.

Case 1 – One black woman from the stationery department had worked for Harrods for six years. She was sacked for breaching the company dress code but claimed no-one told her anything was wrong with her appearance.

Case 2 – A black worker claimed he lost his job because he wore a short goatee beard. He claimed many white people working for Harrods had full beards.

Case 3 – A Hindu worker claimed discrimination because the company ordered her to remove a nose stud which she said was the equivalent of a wedding ring.

a If you were defending these workers what evidence would you look for to support their claims?

b If you were defending the employer, what evidence would you look for to support the company's claims that:
   i it is a fair equal opportunities employer with 50 nationalities represented among the 4000 staff
   ii the high number of dismissals of black workers was simply 'coincidence'
   iii the correct procedures were carried out.

c Give your opinion on **each** case separately, saying whether you think the claim will be upheld or dismissed and why.

d **As a group,** look in your college or local library to find out what happened.

Did you know?

A special body known as the **Equal Opportunities Commission** (EOC) was formed to check that the **Sex Discrimination** and **Equal Pay** acts are working. The **Commission for Racial Equality** (CRE) does the same in respect of the **Race Relations Act.**

Complying with health and safety regulations

Under the **Health and Safety at Work Act 1974** the employer has a major responsibility for making sure that employees work in a safe place. The employer has a duty to check that the people working for the company are competent. If, therefore, someone is injured because of the actions of another employee, the employer will have to take responsibility for that injury (see page 173).

The employer must also provide:

- safe entrances and exits
- a safe working environment and adequate welfare facilities
- safe equipment and systems
- means of ensuring the safe use, handling, storage and transport of articles and substances
- information, instruction, training and supervision
- investigation of any accidents.

Safe working environment

Almost any safety hazard can come under this heading and most organisations now look very carefully at the way in which any new buildings are designed or work areas laid out.

If, for instance, a new reception area is being planned to which both staff and members of the general public have access, the architects and designers will have to take care to build in such features as:

- adequate fire precautions – fire alarms; fire extinguishers; fire resistant, self closing doors; fire-proof furnishings; fire door notices, etc.
- other safety precautions such as good lighting (with provision for emergency lighting if the main lighting fails); anti-slip floor coverings and stair treads; handrails; wide, two-way doors; solid safety rails, etc.

Element 1.3, page 107, covers the 'sick building syndrome'. You may find it useful to read through it again.

Non-assessed activity

Read the following suggestions for the sort of safe working practices which should be carried out by both employer and employee. Divide the information into what you think an employer should do and what an employee should do and include it in a table containing two columns, one headed 'Employer responsibility' and one 'Employee responsibility'. Add any other suggestions you can think of in relation to each of the items.

- **Good housekeeping** – tidiness and cleanliness of working areas and safe storage of dangerous or inflammable substances
- **Equipment** – no electrical hazards through trailing leads or broken sockets. Any equipment which can give out dangerous fumes (e.g. a photocopier) should be kept in a well ventilated, preferably separate, room. Safety filing cabinets should be installed where only one drawer can open at once to prevent tilting. Equipment should only be used in accordance with correct operating procedures.
- **furniture** – safety stools provided for reaching items stored on high shelves, adjustable chairs for keyboard operators to reduce backache.
- **accommodation** – no overcrowding, offices above 16°C (61°F) but not too hot, good ventilation and blinds for windows in direct sunlight. Good lighting, safe floor surfaces (not worn or slippery) and adequate toilet facilities.
- **Noise** – kept to reasonable limits, e.g. acoustic hoods on computer printers
- **Safe work habits** – e.g. not running down corridors, not carrying heavy objects, not carrying so many items that vision is obscured.
- **Provision of information** – all employees to know the correct procedure in case of fire, where extinguishers are situated, who are first-aiders and safety representatives, how to report an accident, etc.

Look back to Element 1.3, pages 107–108, to remind yourself of the employer's responsibilities in relation to VDU equipment.

Violence

One increasing threat to some staff – particularly those who deal with the general public or work in areas which are open to the general public – is that of violence. Many employers, therefore, now make sure that the environment in which they work is made as safe as possible by:

- improving communication systems, e.g. by installing panic buttons
- installing glass screens in reception areas
- re-organising work schedules so that no-one has to be alone in a high risk area.

Did you know?

Under the **Employers' Liability (Compulsory Insurance) Act 1982** every employer carrying on a business in the UK must be insured against any injury to an employee during the course of his employment.

Non-assessed activity

1 As a group, visit three buildings in your town which have public access and assess them for health and safety. List all the relevant items you can find.

2 Assess the same buildings for staff security. What precautions have been taken to protect staff from customer violence?

3 If you go on work experience during your course, what provision is made for you to be insured against injury?

Health and safety policy

Your employer should produce a written statement of the organisation's health and safety policy together with details of the arrangements for carrying out that policy.

It should include details of:

- how accidents should be reported
- those who are trained in first aid
- those who are safety representatives (and the duties they must undertake)
- the person responsible overall for the health and safety policy
- safe working practices.

Safety committees

Every large organisation should have a safety committee which discusses safety issues and supervises the health and safety policy.

The committee must:

- look carefully at any accidents which have occurred and suggest any action to prevent their happening again
- look at statistical information about accidents and other safety issues and recommend changes to company working practices where relevant
- consider any suggestions or reports made about safety matters and recommend whether or not they should be adopted

■ try to make sure that employers and employees are constantly aware of the need for safe working practices.

Non-assessed activity

Imagine that the Safety Committee at the organisation where you work sends a memo to all employees asking for any ideas they may have for a 'Health and Safety at Work' promotional week which is scheduled to take place the following month. Prepare a memo to the chair person of the Safety Committee outlining your suggestions:

1 for any activities which could take place during that week
2 any promotional material which could be prepared.

Safety representatives

In many organisations – particularly larger ones – there will normally be a number of trade-union-appointed safety representatives who check on the day-to-day working of the safety policy. Their duties include:

■ looking into any possible hazards, e.g. unguarded machinery or badly stored chemicals
■ investigating accidents
■ investigating employee complaints
■ reporting back to management
■ carrying out inspections (at least every three months)
■ talking to the Health and Safety Executive inspectors or Environmental Health Officers.

Did you know?

The **Health and Safety Executive,** set up by the **Health and Safety at Work Act**, controls the activities of inspectors who are authorised to visit any premises without warning, either to investigate an accident or complaint or simply to make a general inspection. If they are dissatisfied with what they see or hear they can issue:

■ an **improvement notice** requiring the employer to put matters right within a specified period of time
■ a **prohibition notice** to stop operations immediately if there is immediate danger.

Non-assessed activity

Obtain a copy of the health and safety at work policy in the college or school where you are studying or at your work experience placement. Make a note of how it covers the points listed on page 194.

Remuneration

One of the main reasons anyone works is to get paid. 'Remuneration' is just a term used to describe the amount they are paid.

Pay

When you start work you may find either that you are paid a wage on a weekly basis or you receive a salary on a monthly basis. If you are paid a salary you may find that your pay will increase at regular intervals (normally yearly), if you work in an organisation which operates a salary scale system. If you accepted a job as a bank clerk, for instance, you may find there is a salary scale which has a starting point of £8850 and a finishing point of £12190, with various stages or **increments** in between.

In a salary scale each rise is known as a **point in the scale**, and is also referred to as an increment. If you are given one increment at the end of the year, that is normal practice. If you receive more than one, this usually means you have worked exceptionally well.

In some cases you will begin right at the bottom of the salary scale 'ladder'. In other cases your employer might start you at a higher point on the scale after taking into account factors such as:

- your age
- your qualifications
- your past experience.

Note: Wages are also discussed in Element 1.3 on page 102.

Payment by age

Young workers are normally paid at lower rates than the adult workforce. In most cases their pay will be a percentage of the adult rate. For instance, the Automobile Association pays its sixteen-year-olds 80 per cent of the adult rate and its nineteen-year-olds 90 per cent.

However, the actual amount of pay normally depends on the type of work and the area in which it will be undertaken. An apprentice may only receive 30–50 per cent of the adult rate. For a junior worker in another area the percentage might be higher.

The role of the union

One of the major roles of union representatives is to negotiate increases in pay for their members by means of **collective agreements.** These agreements normally apply to both union members and non-union members, and are normally incorporated – that is, included into individual contracts.

Non-assessed activity

Why do you think that non-union (as well as union) members benefit from collective agreements?

Additional payments

Many employers allow you to increase your basic pay by working overtime or by being on some type of bonus scheme.

Overtime

The higher up the organisation you climb, the less likely it is that you will receive extra money for any additional time you work. However, at the beginning of your career, you will probably find that you will be paid for overtime.

The time counted as overtime varies. Although the 'normal' working week is usually defined as Monday to Friday, in some organisations Saturday (or at least Saturday morning) is also included, so that you would only be paid the basic rate during that period. Most organisations treat Sundays as outside the normal working week.

In most organisations 'time and a half' is the norm, i.e. one and a half hour's pay for one hour's work, but some are now prepared to pay only time and a third or even time and a quarter.

In some cases, you may even be expected to work a certain number of hours of overtime before you become entitled to the extra pay. For example, if your normal working day is from 9 am to 5 pm, you may be expected to work an extra half hour or hour for the basic rate of pay before you can start being paid the overtime rate.

You may be *obliged* to work overtime whether you want to or not – so read your contract of employment carefully. If overtime is compulsory this must be made clear.

Bonus schemes

You may receive a bonus if you:

- are paid on a piecework basis
- receive commission for sales
- are paid a productivity bonus
- receive performance related pay
- are employed in a company which operates a profit-sharing scheme.

All these schemes are designed to reward people who work hard. Obviously it is in the company's interests for its employees to be hard-working as, normally, higher profits will be made at the end of the year.

Piecework is the oldest type of incentive scheme. Employees are paid according to the number of 'pieces' produced, e.g. a packer might be paid so much for each full crate produced. Sales people are often paid commission to encourage them to sell more. Both the company and the employee benefit. Today, it is rare to find people being paid only on a piecework or a commission scheme. In most cases employees receive a 'minimum earnings guarantee', so that they are entitled to a certain weekly sum no matter what their output or sales.

A **productivity bonus** is paid in certain jobs if employees do more work in a certain time than is normal. A data-processing clerk might be paid at a basic rate for inputting 40 orders an hour and a bonus payment for any additional orders keyed in within that time.

Performance-related pay schemes may be linked to quality as well as quantity of work. Some organisations interview their employees at the end of each year in a staff appraisal interview. People who have performed well, and receive a high appraisal score, receive a pay award.

In some organisations, all employees receive bonuses at the end of the year if the company does well, because they participate in a profit-sharing scheme. In some schemes anyone can join; in others the right to participate may be confined to those who have worked for the organisation for a period of time (normally five years). Again, the aim is to motivate the employees to work hard, as this will then be in the interests of both employer and employee.

Non-assessed activity

1 Visit your local careers office or Job Centre. Select **three** jobs in business and write down the current rates of pay.
2 Collect advertisements from your local paper which advertise similar jobs and note down:
    a the rates of pay
    b any salary scales given.
3 Interview **at least three** working people you know and find out what bonus systems (if any) operate within their organisation. Don't ask them how much they are paid!

Did you know?

Some organisations will encourage you to join a **Save As You Earn** (SAYE) scheme under which you invest a certain sum of money into the scheme for five years. At the end of this time you will have accumulated some savings, plus the bonus paid by the financial institution which is administering the scheme.

Fringe benefits

Many organisations offer their employees **fringe benefits**. Probably the most important of these are:

- **an occupational pension scheme** – which is paid in addition to any state pension

- **an occupational sick pay scheme**. All employees who pay sufficient National Insurance contributions are entitled to **statutory sick pay** (SSP) if they are ill (see chart below). In some cases, employers will also pay the difference between SSP and the normal weekly wage or even offer a **private health insurance scheme** – so that their employees can obtain treatment privately if they are ill

Eligibility
To be eligible, your average total pay in the eight weeks before the start of sickness must be above a certain limit (if you earn below a certain sum you will not pay NI contributions but neither will you get SSP).

Payment
There are two rates of SSP. One rate is paid to lower-earning employees and one to higher-earning employees.

Qualifying days
SSP is paid only for periods of sickness of four days or more. These days must be days when an employee is supposed to work (e.g. a Sunday will not count if you do not normally work on a Sunday).

Waiting days
The first three qualifying days of sickness are unpaid. If, however, you are ill again less than eight weeks after the first period of sickness, you will not need to serve any further waiting days.

Maximum entitlement
SSP is payable for a maximum of 28 weeks in any period of sickness.

Notification procedure
If you are ill for at least four days but no more than seven, your employer can ask you to fill in a **self certification form**. If you are ill for longer than seven days then you must get a medical certificate from your doctor.

Figure 2.34 Current statutory sick pay provisions

- **holiday pay** – most employers allow employees some paid time off for holidays. The number of days normally depends on length of service and the seniority of the employee.

Did you know?

Some organisations go much further in providing benefits for their employees. Staff who work in Marks & Spencer stores can have their hair done, visit a chiropodist and eat a good meal – all subsidised by their employer!

Non-assessed activity

As a group, hold a brainstorming session to see how many fringe benefits you can think of in ten minutes.

Did you know?

It could be quite easy to lose track of all the payments to which you are entitled. For that reason, the law says that you must be given an **itemised pay statement** which provides most of that information. (For details of what it should contain see Element 4.2, page 458.) If you don't, then you are entitled to complain to an industrial tribunal.

Deduction of income tax

Unfortunately, your weekly wage or monthly salary is not all yours to keep. Your employer has a duty to take out from it various amounts – known as deductions.

The two types of deductions are:

- **statutory** – required by law
- **voluntary** – agreed or requested by the employee; examples are union contributions and charitable contributions.

The main statutory deductions are:

- income tax
- National Insurance.

Income tax

Most people have income tax deducted from their wage or salary by their employer who then sends the money to the Inland Revenue. The amount due is calculated in relation to how much an employee earns in each tax year (from 6 April one year to 5 April the next). This is known as PAYE (the Pay As You Earn system).

Income tax isn't paid on all your earnings. Everyone is entitled to certain allowances, which vary according to their personal circumstances. If you stop work you must inform your tax office immediately – otherwise they will still go on trying to deduct tax.

Did you know?

If you are a student and have any savings, you can register with your bank or building society to receive interest on your savings without tax being deducted. If you registered before you were sixteen, you must re-register after that date if you want this to continue. When you start work, you will no longer be eligible and must inform your bank or building society immediately that in future they must deduct tax from any interest you are paid.

Self-employed people

Self-employed people or those who run small businesses pay their tax in a completely different way. Their accountants send their end-of-year accounts (i.e. their profit and loss account and their balance sheet) to the Inland Revenue, which then calculates the amount of tax. Payment is then made in two instalments during the following year – usually one in January and a second in July. There will be some changes to this system in 1996/7, when self-employed people will be assessed over a two-year period and have their earnings averaged out over that period.

Did you know?

Most self-employed people have accountants to help them to arrange their affairs and to keep the tax they pay to a minimum each year. This is quite legal and is known as tax avoidance. It is totally different from tax evasion, which means trying to get out of paying tax by making false statements. This is illegal.

Payment of National Insurance

National Insurance (NI) is paid every week by both employed and self-employed people. In the case of employees, the company will calculate and deduct National Insurance on a weekly or monthly basis. Those who are self-employed will arrange for the money to be paid automatically each month, usually by direct debit. This means the amount is automatically claimed from the person's bank account by the Department of Social Security (DSS) each month. If the amount changes then the DSS simply claims more or less – but must notify the person concerned at the same time.

Did you know?

1 Just before their sixteenth birthday everyone is sent a National Insurance

card by the DSS which gives their National Insurance number. This stays the same all their working life.

Figure 2.35   A sixteenth birthday card from the DSS

2 Even if you only have a temporary job in the holidays, but work long hours, you could find yourself paying a considerable amount of income tax. If your earnings then stop you should contact your tax office as you will be owed a tax refund.

Pension deductions

When you are starting work for the first time, you may find that you need to come to some decision about your occupational pension. You will be asked if you are going to contribute towards the government pension scheme (called the **State Earnings Related Pension Scheme** – SERPS) or join a private or company pension scheme. Those who pay towards SERPS pay a higher rate of National Insurance than those who are in private schemes – but everyone pays some National Insurance as these contributions pay for a number of cash benefits including:

- unemployment benefit
- statutory sick pay
- statutory maternity pay
- the basic state retirement pension
- industrial disablement benefit
- child benefit
- widow's benefit
- death grant.

National Insurance contributions are payable by both **employees** and **employers**, although under the deductions column of the pay slip only the employees' contribution is listed.

Did you know?

1 You are not allowed to opt out of SERPS without joining a private or company pension scheme. Whilst you should take advice on this for your own personal circumstances, it is usually true that if you are young and starting work you will be much better off eventually if you join a private or company scheme.

2 Even if you contract out of SERPS and join a company or private pension scheme, your payslip will still show National Insurance deductions at the full rate. This is because the DSS still receives the full payments and then they pay it into any personal scheme you have. You can check the correct amount has been paid in at the end of the year by asking your pension scheme manager for a list of all the contributions made by the DSS during the year.

Optional evidence assignment

*This activity can be carried out verbally in class **in a group** as a non-assessed activity to consolidate learning. Alternatively, if you do it **on your own**, it can count as supplementary evidence towards the following parts of the scheme.*

PC 3: Explain employer rights and responsibilities

Range: Employer responsibilities: to explain business objectives, to offer and facilitate training, to implement equal opportunities legislation at work, to comply with health and safety regulations, remuneration.

Core skills: Communication

Read the case study below and answer the questions which follow.

Case study – Elaine Walker

Elaine Walker was a student on a business course. She desperately needed a part-time job to provide her with basic spending money and was delighted to be offered a part-time job at a local sandwich bar. The manageress, Mrs Phillips, explained at the interview that Elaine would have to wear special overalls, tie back her long hair and wear a hair net and hat. She would have to keep her uniform on the premises at all times and would have to wash her hands before commencing duty, after a break or undertaking any activity away from the kitchen or food area. Any cuts, grazes or tummy upsets had to be reported immediately. Only light make-up was allowed and no jewellery. Her starting pay would be £3.25 an hour. Elaine was given a booklet to read which explained all these requirements in more detail.

On her first day she worked alongside another employee, Mark Jones, who had been at the sandwich bar for over a year. He showed Elaine how the sandwiches were made and wrapped using special equipment. He also explained how cleaning duties were carried out, but added that the cleaning and stripping down of heavy equipment each night was done by himself and another employee, Steve.

For the first few weeks Elaine worked hard, although she was rather annoyed when she found out that Steve was on £4 an hour. She particularly enjoyed working on the days a young man called Martin called. She thought he looked very attractive, but felt that she looked a sight in her hat and hairnet. She worked out that Mrs Phillips went to lunch on Saturdays at 1 pm – just before the time Martin usually arrived. That Saturday, just after Mrs Phillips left, Elaine took off her hat and hairnet and put on plenty of make-up. She was so excited she slipped with the knife when she was making sandwiches and cut her finger quite badly. She didn't bother to put on

one of the special plasters she was supposed to use, as she was rushing to be on the counter by the time Martin came. He usually waited to be served at the far end of the counter, nearest the door. Elaine moved up to that position expectantly – ignoring warnings from her colleagues about her appearance.

When Martin walked in Elaine rushed to serve him. Whilst she was handling his order, her head was down so she didn't look towards the door and see Mrs Phillips return for a parcel she had forgotten to take to the post. In two minutes Mrs Phillips realised what was happening and ordered Elaine away from the food counter. In front of everyone she sacked Elaine for gross misconduct and ordered her from the shop. Elaine was furious at being shown up in front of the very person she was trying to impress. She held her head high and said that she would probably claim unfair dismissal and discrimination – as Mrs Phillips paid the male workers at the shop a higher rate of pay than the female workers.

1 a What do you consider are the main objectives of a food shop?
   b Why do you consider that such shops are so strict about hygiene regulations?
   c Do you think it is fair that employees can be sacked for gross misconduct if they 'deliberately endanger the health of any other employee or customer'?
2 Do you consider that Mrs Phillips fulfilled her employer responsibilities in relation to:
   a explaining business objectives
   b offering and facilitating training
   c complying with health and safety regulations
   d remuneration?
3 What is your opinion of Elaine's claim that Mrs Phillips discriminates against her female employees in relation to pay? Give reasons for your answer.
4 a What is your opinion of Elaine's behaviour?
   b Do you think Mrs Phillips was within her rights to sack Elaine in the way she did?
   c Do you think she could bring a claim of unfair dismissal? Give a reason for your answer.

Employee rights

Remuneration

You have a right to be paid for the work you do. In the past you had an **implied** right to be paid even if nothing had been expressly agreed. (See also page 195.) Now, however, you are protected by a statute which requires that, amongst other things, your pay is **expressly** agreed between you and your employer.

Did you know?

1 If you are not paid anything at all, there is no contract of employment between you and your employer. However, provided you are paid some money the law will not generally concern itself about how much! That is normally a matter for you or your trade union to negotiate.

2 If your employer pays you, generally speaking he or she need not give you any work to do. Although that might sound wonderful, you may find that in reality if that happens to you for some reason, you will either be worried about your career prospects or about being made redundant. Your employer must, however, provide you with work if:

- you work on a piecework or commission only basis
- your future career prospects depend on your reputation. If, for instance, you are a well-known journalist, whose work appears regularly under your own name in a paper or magazine, your prospects of any future work will be harmed if you are not allowed to write anything – even though you are still being paid.

3 Before 1986, employees who worked in a shop or other retail establishment could have some of their pay deducted if there were any cash shortages in the till or stock discrepancies (e.g. the disappearance or loss of goods) in areas for which they were responsible. Today employers must limit this to one-tenth of the gross amount of that day's wages.

Non-assessed activity

Why do you think an employer must provide work for someone being paid on a piecework or a commission only basis?

Employer compliance with terms of contract

At one time, whatever agreement you and your employer reached, whether relating to pay or anything else, was up to you. If you agreed to a contract which later caused you some hardship, that was your misfortune.

However, the law has now made it clear that both employer and employee have certain *specified* legal rights and responsibilities, whatever else they may agree to. These rights and obligations are contained in the **Employment Protection (Consolidation) Act**

1978 (EPCA, updated by the **Trade Union Reform and Employment Rights Act 1993**) which covers:

- the right to be given a written statement of terms and conditions of employment
- the right to an itemised pay statement
- the right to a statutory period of notice
- the right to choose whether or not to be a member of a trade union
- the right to maternity pay and to return to work after a pregnancy
- the right not to be unfairly dismissed
- the right to a redundancy payment.

One of the terms covered by the legislation is the **contract of employment** and what must be expressly contained in it.

Did you know?

If an employer wants to give *more* information than that required by the Act, they can do so. McDonald's, for instance, take the opportunity of giving their employees a complete handbook of information about the company in addition to the bare details of their contract.

Terms and conditions in the contract

When you are offered a job by a company, this will be subject to certain **terms and conditions** which will be specified at the interview and may also be repeated in the letter which offers you the job. When you agree to accept the job then you are also considered to have agreed to those terms and conditions. Within two months of starting work, you will then receive your contract of employment which sets these out in writing. As with all contracts, both parties (i.e. you and your employer) then have a legal obligation to comply with the terms laid down.

In any contract there must be the three basic elements:

- **the offer** – your employer offers you the job
- **the acceptance** – you accept it
- **payment** – you agree to do some work in return for some pay.

You should also *intend* to enter into the agreement – if you misheard what the interviewer said and thought you were only being offered a work experience placement then you would not be held to the agreement.

Under the EPCA the major terms and conditions which must be put in writing are:

- **your name and the name of your employer** – 'to whom it may concern' is not enough
- **the date you began work** – this is important because many of your rights under the Acts depend on how long you have worked for a particular organisation. If, for instance, you wanted to claim that you had been unfairly dismissed you would have to prove that you had worked for your employer for at least two years
- **your pay** – this can be the actual amount or the relevant point on a pay scale (see page 195)
- **when you are paid** – every week, every month etc.
- **your hours of work**
- **your holiday entitlement (if any)** – your employer is normally not obliged to give you any holiday
- **your entitlement to holiday pay**
- **your entitlement to time off** because of sickness or injury and any provisions regarding sick pay
- **your pension rights**
- the **length of notice** you or your employer must give when either of you want to end the contract – there's a *minimum* entitlement although your employers may give you a longer entitlement if they wish (see also page 204)
- whether or not your terms and conditions of employment are the subject of a **collective agreement** (see page 196 for the trade union official's role in negotiating such agreements)
- the **place** where you work
- your **job title** or a brief job description.

Did you know?

Employers are not obliged to give a full job description, so potential employees should be careful. One woman agreed to a contract in which her job title was stated to be 'cleaner'. She thought she was going to be an office cleaner when in fact she was expected to do heavy industrial cleaning in the loading bays of a factory.

Additional items

Your statement must also include reference to:

- any **disciplinary** rules
- any **grievance procedures.**

See pages 167 and 168 for more details.

Because the documents outlining the disciplinary and grievance procedures tend to be very long, your contract need not contain everything they cover, provided it tells you where you can obtain a copy of them.

Did you know?

A Blackpool dustman was sacked for arriving at work too early! He was fired for gross misconduct after starting his 7 am shift ten minutes early. He claimed unfair dismissal and was awarded £2742 in compensation by the industrial tribunal. His employers – a private refuse company – claimed they were following council time-keeping regulations!

Non-assessed activity

Check back to the letter sent to Sarah Hayes on page 174.

1 Did Sarah's letter contain information on all the key items mentioned above?
2 If any information has been omitted, discuss with your tutor why this may be the case.

Did you know?

Details contained in a job advertisement and a job description *may* form part of a contract of employment. If you were asked to undertake duties which were totally different from those advertised, you might be able to refer back to the advertisement and complain to your supervisor.

Continuous employment

Your contract of employment must give the date when you first start work. This is important because many of your employment rights depend upon the length of time you have worked with one particular organisation. If you look at the table below you will see that, although you have some rights immediately you start work, for other rights you need to have been working for the organisation for some time.

Note: Not every right has been included here – just the major ones.

Qualifying period			
Claim	Nil	2 months	2 years
Equal pay	✓		
The right not to be discriminated against	✓		
Unfair dismissal for trade union reasons	✓		
Action short of dismissal for trade union reasons	✓		
Time off for ante-natal care	✓		
Contract of employment		✓	
Unfair dismissal			✓
Maternity pay			✓
Right to return to work after pregnancy			✓
Redundancy payment*			✓

*Starting on eighteenth birthday if employee began work before that date

Figure 2.36   The length of employment needed to be eligible for certain employee rights

Did you know?

Your period of employment is counted in *weeks* not in *years* – therefore two years' employment is counted as 104 weeks.

Non-assessed activity

Suppose that your friends know you have been studying basic employment law. They have asked for your help with several queries. Refer to the table above and then decide what your answers will be to their problems.

1 Sam has been working for the same firm for nine months. He wants to know the legal rights he has acquired.
2 Your elder sister is pregnant. After what period of time is she eligible for time off for ante-natal care – and when does she have the right to return after pregnancy?
3 Ahmed has worked in an organisation for only one month but thinks he has been racially discriminated against in several ways. Can he do anything about it?

Statutory period of notice

Under the legislation an employer must give an employee a certain period of **statutory** notice depending on how long he or she has worked for the organisation.

Length of continuous employment	Period of notice
Less than 1 month	No period necessary
1 month but less than 2 years	1 week
2 years or more	1 week for each completed year up to a maximum of 12 weeks

Figure 2.37   Statutory periods of notice

Non-assessed activity

1 Imagine you have just started work for EC Electronics plc. You like your job and intend to stay with the company for some time. What will be the statutory period of notice to which you will be entitled if you work for them for:

a one year
b eighteen months
c two years
d eight years
e fifteen years?

2 Under the legislation, an employee also now has to give a *minimum* period of one week's notice – but some do not! What do you think an employer would offer you if they wanted you to leave immediately – instead of allowing you to work your notice period?

Did you know?

Although the legislation gives the statutory minimum amount of notice you should be given, it does not prevent an employer from giving you a *longer* period of notice. Normally the more senior a person is in an organisation the longer will be the period of notice.

Implied terms of the contract

Just as your employer has two types of contractual rights – express and implied – so too do you. Your **express** contractual rights have already been dealt with. However, you are also entitled to expect your employer to:

- treat you reasonably
- give you the opportunity (although not necessarily the right) to participate in and be consulted on certain company matters.

Reasonable treatment

Legally, if your employer treats you so unreasonably that the court considers it to be a breach of your contract, you may be able to leave and yet still claim that you have been dismissed. This is known as **constructive dismissal.** Remember, though, that the treatment must be serious – minor changes to your contract or personal irritations don't count!

Suppose, for instance, your employer is in some financial difficulty. In order to try to save your job he asks you to continue doing the same work but for a lower rate of pay. If you agree to this because you want to keep your job – fine! If you don't, and your employer insists on paying you less, you could leave and claim that you have been constructively dismissed. You would not *actually* have been dismissed but your employer's action would probably be regarded as a breach of the contract under which you were to be paid a certain sum. The same situation might arise if you were moved from one job to another with fewer promotion prospects, or if you were expected to work in a different physical working environment – outside rather than inside, standing up rather than sitting down, etc.

In some cases, too, if your employer acts so unreasonably that you feel he or she is making your life a misery and possibly affecting your health, this might be regarded as a breach of contract – but remember, just being told off for coming back late from lunch is not likely to be considered a sufficient

reason for claiming constructive dismissal, even if you think everyone else is getting away with it! The courts don't usually interfere in such cases.

Note that it doesn't normally matter whether you resent any changes *unless* you can show that your efficiency or health is being affected.

It is important to remember that you, too, have a duty to behave reasonably and if, therefore, your employer asks you to accept a minor change in your job description or to co-operate in another way, the industrial tribunal isn't going to be too sympathetic if you leave and then try to claim constructive dismissal!

Did you know?

The TSB was chastised by an industrial tribunal for listening to office gossip and sacking two workers – a clerk and a manager – because a cleaner thought she saw them in a compromising position in the office. The clerk was sacked for gross misconduct and the manager walked out, claiming constructive dismissal. Both protested their innocence but their pleas were ignored.

The tribunal ruled that the TSB should have investigated the rumours more carefully and taken note of conflicts in the evidence. It therefore did not act as a reasonable employer should.

Non-assessed activity

Look at the facts of the cases given below. **As a group**, decide – giving reasons – whether the employee could claim constructive dismissal. Type up your answers, preferably using a word processor.

1 Your employer moves Mildred from a day job to a night job which makes it difficult for her to deal with her domestic commitments.
2 Paul really enjoyed his job working on the counter of the bank. But he has been moved to a backroom job and neither likes it or feels that he is any good at it.
3 Audrey has been moved from the main office to a branch office, where there are only two other employees. Both have been there for years and are not likely to leave until they retire.
4 Your employer seems to pick on you all the time. You are constantly criticised, although the rest of the employees are not. You are not sleeping very well and have been to see the doctor because you are so depressed.

5 Frank's employer asks him to have his holidays in July rather than August.

6 Frank's employer then asks him to postpone his holidays until next year.

Employee participation and consultation

In the past the employer was expected to make *all* the decisions relating to what went on at work. All the employee had to do was to obey instructions. Nowadays, however, many managers recognise that their employees might have some very good ideas that could be used to the benefit of the company. They also realise that employees who are consulted about major changes to company practices, procedures or working conditions are more likely to co-operate than those who are not. This has led to an increase in **employee participation.** There are two forms of participation – direct and indirect.

Direct	Indirect
Regular team briefings between employees and supervisors	Worker directors
	Works councils
Re-design of work to focus on employee needs and opinions	
Transfer of some work-related decisions from management to employees	

Worker councils

Worker councils are principally consultative, i.e. they give advice and assistance rather than make decisions. They consist of worker representatives. They tend to run in parallel to any union/management bodies set up for the purpose of negotiating terms and conditions of employment. (See the next page for details of **joint consultative committees.**)

Their terms of reference vary widely among different organisations. Most concentrate on staff welfare issues, although Cadbury Schweppes and Bulmers have both established what they call 'employee councils', which act as the central point for all their communication and consultation arrangements.

Did you know?

The EU has adopted a directive requiring multinationals operating in Europe to set up European Works Councils. These will be entitled to information and consultation but to few other powers. The UK has opted out of the provisions, so they will not cover UK employees directly, but some British companies will be affected if they have branches in Europe. Moreover, the Labour Party says that it is committed to ending Britain's opt out if it comes to power.

Non-assessed activity

Why do you think the Labour Party is in favour of works councils and therefore of this directive?

Worker directors

The idea of having an employee as a director who sits on the board and attends board meetings is well established in many European countries – and is a legal requirement. In the UK, however, not many organisations have adopted this idea. Two exceptions are the British Steel Corporation and the Post Office.

Figure 2.38   A worker director is an employee who sits on the board to represent workers' views

The advantages of having such directors are that they should be able to:

- improve the quality of board decisions and discussion by giving the workers' views first hand
- secure greater employee commitment to board decisions
- reduce conflict, by making employees aware of the problems management have to face.

Employee consultation

Many organisations now have **joint consultative committees.** In most cases these are union based and tend to consist of a number of trade union and management representatives. Normally, at such meetings:

- management decisions are notified and discussed **and**
- negotiations take place on all major industrial relations issues such as pay, working conditions, grievance and disciplinary matters, redundancy issues and so on.

Much depends, however, on whether the committee is merely an **advisory** or **consultative** body, or whether it has **negotiating** powers. If the latter is the case, then the decisions made are normally binding on the company.

Non-assessed activity

Imagine you have been appointed to be a member of the Workers' Council and looked forward eagerly to attending the first meeting. Afterwards you returned to the office to tell your colleagues about the issues which were discussed – those that weren't confidential.

You attend the meetings each week, and are flattered to think that you are highly thought of, both by management and by your friends. However, after six weeks your supervisor is complaining because of your continued absences from your desk and your colleagues have started to claim that you only tell them what you want them to know and don't really represent their interests. You don't feel they understand the problems of working with senior management.

Things came to a head yesterday. Several workers were indignant about changes to the canteen opening hours. They think you should have told management how they feel – and now won't include you in any of their discussions.

1 From the above passage, list the advantages and disadvantages of being a member of a workers' council.
2 **As a group,** decide how you think these could be overcome.

Did you know?

One specific type of consultation required by law is when an employer is proposing to make some employees redundant. In such cases the employer must give the union a **minimum statutory period of notice** before the redundancies are scheduled to occur, to allow the union time to consult with them about any alternative courses of action which might be considered. (See also the role of the Human Resources department in this respect, Element 2.1, page 139.)

Non-assessed activity

Arrange for each member of your group to write to **at least two** organisations in your area to ask them whether they have a joint consultative committee and, if they do, whether they will provide you with some information about it. Using a word processor, write a short report on your findings.

Health and safety at work

The main right of an employee is that the employer should comply with the health and safety legislation – just as the main right of the employer in this respect is that the employee should co-operate in complying with any health and safety procedures laid down. (Look back to the sections on employer rights and responsibilities to remind yourself of what these are.)

Non-assessed activity

Imagine you are asked to operate some printing equipment with an automatic guillotine. You are not given much training and are therefore a bit nervous about using it. You also think – though you are unsure – that it should have a safety guard on it, but you don't want to be thought of as a nuisance or as stupid by persisting in asking about it.

Your supervisor has told you that your long hair could get caught in the equipment and asks you to have it cut or to tie your hair back. You don't want to do this.

In a group, discuss the following points. If an accident occurs:

1 Would your employer would be considered negligent in any way? Look back to page 193 for your employer's responsibilities.
2 How far could you be held responsible? Look back to page 178 for details of *your* responsibilities.

Equal opportunities at work

The law states that you have the right not to be discriminated against on the grounds of sex or race. (Look back to page 00 for details about what the Sex Discrimination Act, Race Relations Act and the Equal Pay Act have to say about discrimination.) However, many employers go further than the law and publish their own equal opportunity statements. This may say something like 'this organisation will not discriminate against anyone on grounds of sex, race, age, creed, colour, religion or disability.'

Non-assessed activity

Ask your tutor to show you a copy of the equal opportunities policy in operation at your school or college.

Did you know?

Age discrimination is not unlawful – although many people consider it to be unfair. But the law does take some measures to try to help disabled workers, e.g.

- the **Disabled Persons (Employment) Acts 1944/58**, which place a statutory duty on all employers employing 20 or more full-time workers to employ a quota of registered disabled people based on a percentage of the total workforce
- the **Companies (Directors' Report) Employment of Disabled Persons Regulations 1980,** which requires that every annual company report to which the regulations apply should contain a statement outlining what the company has done to give fair consideration to applications for employment by disabled persons, and to arrange for appropriate training for them.

Did you know?

The symbol in Figure 2.39 has been introduced by the Employment Department

to be used by organisations which employ people for their abilities rather than their disabilities. What they mean by this is that a huge number of people can be excellent employees, despite being disabled, provided they are given the chance.

Figure 2.39 The Employment Department symbol

Legal representation

There is little use in your being given a series of legal rights if you are not able to enforce any of them. Therefore, at about the same time that most of the major employment legislation was passed, measures were also introduced to give employees an official body to complain to if they felt that they were being denied a right. Consequently, **ACAS**, the **industrial tribunals** and the **European Court of Justice** were established. This means that employees can now look for assistance at the highest possible level. (Look back to pages 169–171 for more details of these three bodies.)

Optional evidence assignment

*This activity can be carried out verbally in class **in a group** as a non-assessed activity to consolidate learning. Alternatively, if you do* it **on your own**, it can count as supplementary evidence towards the following parts of the scheme.

PC 4: Explain employee rights and responsibilities

Range: Employee rights: remuneration, employer compliance with terms of contract, equal opportunities at work, legal representation

Core skills: Communication, application of number

Read the case study below and answer the questions which follow.

Case study – Christine Hill and the AA

An AA employee lost her job despite having won an award in 1992 for being the senior shop manager of the year. Christine Hill claimed unfair dismissal when the regional sales manager made her redundant in June 1994 and then almost immediately replaced her with a woman believed to be his mistress – who, it was claimed, had always wanted Mrs Hill's job.

Mrs Hill, who earned nearly £20 000 a year, was paid £31 500 redundancy pay by the AA, her employers for the previous twelve years. She had been a shop manager for more than seven years and was in charge of sixteen staff. In 1993 Mrs Hill had applied for the post of area sales manager but the job went to a friend and male colleague of the regional sales manager.

At the industrial tribunal, the AA settled the case after legal discussion. The AA admitted Mrs Hill had been unfairly dismissed, agreed to give her a signed reference and agreed to pay her an additional £10 000 as compensation for the way in which she has been treated. The organisation said that there had been a 'regrettable breach of its redundancy procedures' but said that this had nothing to do with the unsubstantiated allegations against the regional sales manager, which had been investigated in a separate enquiry.

1   What remuneration did Mrs Hill receive in her job as shop manager?
2   What evidence is there in the story that she had been a good employee?
3   a   How long had Mrs Hill been working for the company when she became shop manager?
    b   How long had she been shop manager when she applied for promotion to area sales manager?
    c   Is there any evidence that her failure to become area sales manager was because of sex discrimination?

4   When Mrs Hill was made 'redundant' her contract of employment was terminated.
    a   The letter to Mrs Hill informing her of this said that 'your position is redundant from 30 June 1994'. Was this true? Give a reason for your answer.
    b   The AA admitted there had been a 'breach of its redundancy procedures'. What does this mean?
5   Although the case went to an industrial tribunal the matter was settled 'after legal discussion'.
    a   What do you think this means?
    b   Why do you think the AA was prepared to settle before the full tribunal hearing?

Employee responsibilities

You have already learned much about employer rights and responsibilities and the rights of an employee. The responsibilities of an employee should be fairly obvious by now. Basically these are:

■   to meet the terms of the contract
■   to meet health and safety regulations
■   to meet the objectives of the business
■   to meet customers' needs
■   to maintain quality standards.

You have undertaken an in-depth study of the first three of these on previous pages. If you have undertaken any studies in Unit 1 or 3, you will already know how vital customers are to the success of business organisations. It is obviously important that employees try to co-operate with their employer in this respect to maintain and, if possible, increase the amount of business undertaken by the company. Apart from anything else, this increases their own job security!

Quality was covered in full in Element 2.1, page 156. It is pointless for an organisation to have quality standards if employees do not co-operate, and allow slipshod products to be made, or a poor service to be offered. Again customers will be lost and this puts everyone's job at risk.

Because you have already covered all these areas, this final section is designed as a case study/optional evidence assignment. You can put all the knowledge you have gained so far to good use and produce further evidence for your portfolio as you work through this part of the element.

Optional evidence assignment

*This activity can be carried out verbally in class **in a group** as a non-assessed activity to consolidate learning. Alternatively, if you do it **on your own**, it can count as supplementary evidence towards the following parts of the scheme.*

PC 1: Explain the benefits of employer and employee co-operation

PC 4: Explain employee rights and responsibilities

Range: Benefits of employer and employee co-operation: survival of the business; improved employee commitment to the business, improved efficiency

Employee responsibilities: to meet the terms of contract, to meet health and safety regulations, to meet the objectives of the business, to meet customers' needs, to maintain quality standards

Core skills: Communication

The case study below is divided into five sections. Read each section separately and then answer the questions which follow.

Case study

Section 1

Francis works as a waiter in a café bar. He has been given his written statement of terms and conditions which tells him (amongst other things) his hours of work, his pay, his right to holiday pay, sick pay and pension. It also gives him details of the company's disciplinary and grievance procedures. He is quite a good worker but he is not particularly interested in making a career as a waiter – secretly he fancies being a DJ and this is what he is already doing on a part-time basis on his nights off. Unfortunately a DJ's hours mean that he is not getting to bed until 2 am and consequently he is having great difficulty in getting up early enough in the morning to get to work on time (even though he only starts at 11 am). Sometimes, too, he sneaks off early when he knows the manager is away.

Section 2

Francis has to do a lot of running about when he is on duty. Customers demand attention – and so do the

kitchen staff who don't like the food they have cooked getting cold. He therefore wedges open a fire door, which makes life easier for him when he is dashing about from kitchen to dining area.

He has been told that he is supposed to carry only so much at one time. He ignores that advice and argues that he is strong enough to carry more. He also encourages the rest of the staff to do so – even though some of them are older and smaller than he is. One afternoon a new waitress, whom Francis was supposed to be training, falls when carrying a very heavy tray and breaks her ankle.

Training sessions on health and safety issues are held once a month. Francis tries to dodge them whenever he can. He doesn't have the first idea who the safety representative is, or what the company's safety policy is.

Section 3

The owners of the café bar know that there is very great competition for customers in the area where they operate. Apart from making a profit and staying in business, one of their objectives is to provide a relaxed atmosphere for their customers and one in which they get first-class service from the staff. At one of the regular staff meetings, the manager asks the staff for their views on how that objective can be achieved.

Section 4

The café bar works almost on a self-service basis. If customers want to order food they go to one serving area. If all they want is coffee or tea they are served by the staff in that area. If they want food they have to hand in an order and wait for someone to come to serve them. If they want a soft drink or alcohol they have to go to the bar which is in another part of the room. The manager has introduced this system because she thinks that there are two different groups of customers – those who come in for a drink and those who come in for something to eat. Francis and the rest of the staff are not so sure. They know that at busy times customers have to queue up a long time at the food counter because the staff often have to spend time serving coffee or tea before they can take anyone else's orders. They also know that some customers like an alcoholic drink with their meal and aren't keen on the idea of queuing up in one place for their food and in another place for a drink. A new café bar has opened up across the street and it is obvious that some trade is going that way.

Section 5

Francis is always the one who gets the complaints! If the food is cold or not what the customer ordered, he is in trouble. If a customer is too hot or too cold, Francis is the one who is expected to do something about it – and so on. He does deal with the complaints as they arise but recently he has become aware that the number of complaints is increasing. When he talks to the rest of the staff he finds out that they feel the same. Francis thinks that the main grumble is about the food – it is a bit expensive and the portions served aren't very large. Nor is the menu very varied. He wonders about telling the manager but he is friendly with the kitchen staff and feels that if he does so, they might get into trouble.

1 Section 1 is about Francis' requirement to meet the terms of his contract. From what you have read he could be failing to comply with this. What **express** obligation and what **implied** obligation is he breaking?
2 a Which section is concerned with health and safety?
  b In what ways is Francis failing to meet his responsibilities in respect of health and safety regulations?
  c If you were his manager, what would you do to try to make him see how important safety was to him personally and also to the people with whom he works?
3 a What do you consider are the objectives of the café bar business?
  b List **your** suggestions for:
  i   creating a relaxed atmosphere
  ii improving service.

4 Section 4 is about meeting customers' needs.
  a In what ways do Francis and his colleagues feel that the café bar is failing to meet customer needs?
  b What do you think they could do to convince the manager to change the working arrangements?
5 Francis is concerned about the quality of food served and the effect upon customers.
  a What will be the result for the café bar if customers go elsewhere?
  b What could be result for Francis?
  c What would you do if you were Francis?
6 In several places in this case study it would appear that Francis is apprehensive about talking to the manager of the cafe bar.
  a Give **two** examples where Francis is not co-operating with his employer.
  b Give **two** examples where the employer does not appear to have a good relationship with staff.
  c What would be the benefit for both parties if there was an open, friendly atmosphere and co-operation on both sides?

Revision test

True or false?

1 An employee has the right to be given some work to do.
2 Health and safety is the sole responsibility of the employer.
3 An employee must be given a written statement of the terms and conditions of employment within two months of starting work.
4 An employee can insist on being paid in cash.
5 Statutory Sick Pay is paid only for periods of sickness of four days or more.

Fill in the blanks

6 For a first offence an employee is normally given a _____ warning
7 If you are told you cannot have the job because you are a woman this is an example of _____ .
8 An elected union representative who represents the members of a union is called a _____ .
9 If you accept a bribe or disclose confidential information about your company you may be in breach of your obligation to act _____ .
10 Advice to employers and unions about how to resolve a dispute can be obtained from the _____ _____ _____ Service.

Short answer questions

11 List the **five** main defences an employer can use if an employee claims unfair dismissal.

12 State how long a statutory period of notice should be given by an employee.

13 List the major health and safety responsibilities of an employer.

14 List **three** ways in which you might earn a bonus payment.

15 List **four** of the main items covered by the Sex Discrimination Act.

Write a short paragraph to show you clearly understand each of the following terms

16 Disciplinary procedures

17 Equal opportunities

18 Contract of employment

19 Employee consultation

20 Remuneration.

Evidence indicator project

Unit 2 Element 2.2

This project has been designed to cover the evidence indicator related to Element 2.2.

Performance criteria: 1–4

Core skills: Communication
Application of number
Information technology

Make sure you complete the project by the deadline date given to you by your tutor.

Special note

There is a choice of two projects for this element. The first project closely matches the evidence indicators given and requires the investigation of an actual business organisation. However, because business organisations may be reluctant to discuss or give examples of disagreements and their resolutions, an optional second choice is included. This is based on a case study and gives students the opportunity to undertake the requirements of the project and produce a report without having to ask an organisation for confidential information.

Option A

Stage 1

Arrange to interview the Human Resources manager at an organisation with which you have regular contact. This could be an organisation where you work on a part-time basis, one which you visit as part of your work experience placement or one where you are undertaking an in-depth project in other areas (e.g. for Unit 1).

Explain to the manager concerned that you wish to discuss employee/employer co-operation and disagreements but you are not asking for access to confidential information and are happy to discuss general issues rather than specific events involving certain people.

Prepare for the interview by making out a list of questions which includes asking about:

1 the objectives of the business
2 the contract of employment issued to staff
3 induction and health and safety training

4 the benefits which the Human Resources manager feels ensue from employee and employer co-operation in the company
5 an example of at least one disagreement and how this was resolved.

Undertake the interview and write a report on your findings. Prepare a final version of the report on a word processor.

Stage 2

1 *Either* use the example of the disagreement given to you at the interview *or* find an example of an employer/employee disagreement in the national press. State clearly the steps an employee could take if he or she could not resolve the problem amicably with his or her manager(s).
2 a Give **at least two** examples of employers' and employees' rights and responsibilities.
   b State clearly how these are affected by equal opportunities legislation.

Type up your findings neatly on a word processor. Prepare a front cover with your name and the date. Insert the title: **Employee and Employer Responsibilities and Rights** at (insert the name of the company). Put your report neatly into a project folder with the title page at the front.

Option B

Read the case study below and undertake the tasks which follow.

Case study

Imagine you work in the Human Resources department of a large departmental store as the personnel assistant to Mr Drysdale, the Human Resources manager. One of the responsibilities of the Human Resources department is to deal with industrial relations issues and, in particular, with grievance and disciplinary procedures. It also has to ensure that the store's equal opportunities policy is implemented.

One of the stated objectives of the department is to record all industrial relations issues together with a note of how they were dealt with and suggestions for any improvements. You meet with Mr Drysdale every three months to prepare the quarterly report together.

There have been a number of issues raised during the previous three-month period.

- The managing director wanted to change the existing opening hours of the store (at present 9 am to 5.30 pm Monday to Friday and 9 am to 6 pm on Saturday) to 10 am to 6.30 pm Monday to Saturday, and on Sunday 10 am to 4 pm.
- Mr Drysdale has been having problems with Theresa Chang, one of the word processor operators in the department. She has been producing work which is not accurate, even though it has been taking her twice as long as the other operators to produce. She has been warned but there has been no improvement.

- Derek House, a member of staff in the hardware department, has had a number of differences of opinion with his supervisor. The supervisor claims that Derek is being deliberately awkward.: Derek claims that the supervisor is picking on him and treats him much more strictly than he treats the other staff.
- The storeroom staff have been unsettled for some time because they feel that their pay rate should be higher than that of the care-taking and cleaning staff.
- A very difficult situation has arisen in the ladies' fashion department. An advertisement for Saturday assistants, which was placed in the local newspaper, included a statement that the firm was an equal opportunities employer. An Asian girl applied for the job but was told by the departmental supervisor that all the vacancies had been filled. However, a day later a white girl was offered a job. Both girls had the

same qualifications and experience. The Asian girl is now taking legal action.
- Sally Lomax, a member of staff in the kitchenware department, was slightly burned when demonstrating a gas-fired barbecue. She had been shown how to use the equipment on the morning of the demonstration but had forgotten to follow one of the safety precautions when she actually gave the demonstration.

You check to see what progress has been made over each of the issues.

1 The managing director and union have agreed on the longer opening hours provided that there is a deal reached about overtime and time off in lieu.
2 Mr Drysdale has now arranged for Theresa to attend the open learning centre at her local college to see if her skills can be improved.
3 The Human Resources department has become involved in the dispute involving Derek House. The supervisor wishes to discipline him and Derek wishes to register a grievance against the supervisor. The procedures have begun in both cases.
4 There have been extensive negotiations with the company's trade union officials over the pay claim. Nothing has as yet been resolved and the situation is becoming very tense. ACAS is set to become involved.
5 The race discrimination claim is now at the stage of being dealt with by an industrial tribunal.
6 Sally wants to bring a claim against the store under the Health and Safety at Work Act. Her supervisor says that she was adequately trained: she says she was not.

Tasks

1 Prepare a draft report for Mr Drysdale to submit to the board of directors which indicates which issues have been resolved, and which issues are still proceeding. Present this using a word processor.

2 A new personnel assistant has just started work. Mr Drysdale asks you to do some on-the-job training with him. As a general overview to industrial relations issues, he asks you to go through the draft report written in Task 1 and to explain each item in more detail.

You decide that you will be able to explain things more clearly if, before you start the training session, you write a short paragraph about each item. You draft out some notes to remind you of what you want to say, i.e:

a Hours of work case – emphasise the benefits of co-operation between employer and employee and the advantages to the company of that co-operation.

b The word processor operator case – point out where Theresa was failing to comply with her obligations: explain also why Mr Drysdale was correct in doing what he did.

c Derek House's case – describe what is meant by:
   i a disciplinary procedure
   ii a grievance procedure.

d The pay claim dispute – explain the role of the trade union and the trade union representative – and also what part ACAS might play.

e The equal opportunities case – explain what is meant by an equal opportunities policy (and mention the relevant Acts). Explain also the role of and procedure at the industrial tribunal – and what might happen if either the company or the girl concerned lose the case and yet want to take the matter further.

f The health and safety case – outline what is said in the Health and Safety at Work Act about employer and employee duties.

Expand your notes into a report. Use a word processor to prepare it.

3 To help the new assistant even further you decide to try to explain to him the rights and responsibilities of both employer and employee. Prepare a summary giving two examples of:
   a employer rights
   b employer responsibilities
   c employee rights
   d employee responsibilities.

Give a short description of how employers and employees are affected by legislation, in particular equal opportunities legislation.

Present results of investigations into job roles

This element covers the main job roles to be found in business organisations and the tasks which different role holders undertake. It identifies how these may vary depending upon the level of the role holder and emphasises the benefits of team membership. After studying this element you should be able to:

1 identify and describe individuals' *job roles* at different *levels* within organisations

2 explain the *benefits of team membership* in performing job roles

3 identify *activities* performed by individuals at different *levels* within organisations

4 identify *tasks* in job roles

5 present results of investigation into job roles.

Special note

Although two evidence indicators are given for this element, students are unlikely to be able to do the project justice until they have completed the element. For that reason the project incorporating both evidence indicators is given at the end of the element, on page 243.

Job roles at different levels within organisations

When you first start work you will want to know what you are expected to do (i.e. your job role), but you will also want to know what others around you are expected to do.

Within the private sector the roles of those in charge differ, depending on the size of the organisation. In a large organisation there will be opportunities for **specialisation**; employees may have quite clearly defined and specific roles. In a small organisation or one-man business, the roles are less defined. The manager might be doing virtually everything!

Non-assessed activity

As a group, discuss how the role of a manager may differ in each of the following types of organisation. Think in terms of how much freedom each of them has to operate, the variety of their work, the number of people to whom they are responsible and the number for whom they are responsible.

1 A sole trader who runs a retail business and employs two part-time staff.
2 A junior partner in a firm of solicitors which has four senior partners, six junior partners, six section heads/legal executives, and twelve clerical staff.
3 A director in a small, family-run motor vehicle repair garage, which is a private limited company; the two directors are brothers, there is one foreman, four mechanics and two part-time office staff.
4 The Human Resources manager in a large retail store which is a public limited company, who reports directly to the Human Resources Director at head office and is responsible for the branch's recruitment of full and part-time staff.
5 The training officer at the local town hall,

Figure 2.40 In a small organisation the manager might be doing virtually everything!

responsible for organising and planning training for all staff and operating within a specified budget
6 A nurse manager in a large hospital, responsible for six wards and the staff on each of them.

Did you know?

In general terms, the major roles in an organisation can be shown in the shape of a pyramid.

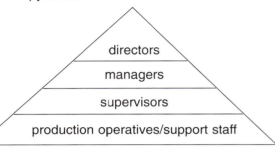

directors
managers
supervisors
production operatives/support staff

Non-assessed activity

Why do you think these roles are shown like this – bearing in mind the *shape* of a pyramid? Discuss your answer with your tutor. (See also Element 2.1, page 122.)

Did you know?

These roles can be undertaken by people in all parts of the organisation – whichever department they work in.

Directors

In the private sector the chief executive would normally be called the managing director and be assisted by a team of other executives who would normally be on the board of directors. In the public sector, an equivalent structure is for the principal of a college, the head teacher of a school or the general manager of a hospital to be the 'chief' and to be assisted by a board of governors.

The chairman of the board of directors is elected by the other directors. In some companies this job is also undertaken by the managing director.

The board of directors may consist of two types of directors.

Executive directors

- They work for the organisation on a full-time basis.
- They are members of the board of directors.

Non-executive directors

- They are not employees of the organisation.
- They are asked to take a seat on the board because of their knowledge, experience and ability to take a 'wider view' than the executive directors.

Did you know?

Many Members of Parliament, leading industrialists (e.g. Sir John Harvey Jones, who was Chairman of ICI), and financial experts often hold seats on the boards of several companies.

Non-assessed activity

Visit your library and find a reference book which lists the directors of large organisations.

1 Select **three** large companies and note down the number of executive and non-executive directors. (If the book in which you are looking for the information doesn't sub-divide them in this way, then write down a complete list.)
2 Look up information on **two** famous personalities (e.g. MPs past or present, or well-known people in the business world) and find out for which companies they are non-executive directors.

Did you know?

The term 'managing director' is given to the chief executive because he or she wears two 'hats' – one as a director and the other as a manager – with the job of co-ordinating the work of all the other managers and directors.

Duties of the board of directors

The board of directors are expected to:

- set appropriate targets
- establish the policies and strategies of the organisation

Figure 2.41 The person with two hats

- decide long-term plans
- make important financial decisions (e.g. regarding future investment and large-scale capital expenditure)
- ensure the organisation always acts within the law
- control all the organisation's activities
- look after major human resource functions – the recruitment and promotion of senior managers and the dismissal and redundancy of any staff.

Did you know?

The board of directors will normally meet at regular intervals. Board meetings are normally held in a special room, called a board room, often used just for this purpose.

Duties of individual executive directors

The duties of the individual directors fall into two areas. They have overall responsibility for the development of the organisation, which is exercised at the board meetings they attend. Each executive director will also be in charge of a *particular* functional area, e.g. the Human Resources director or the Sales and Marketing director will have specific responsibilities. These will include:

- deciding the long-term plans of the department
- setting targets for the department and checking that these are being met
- telling the departmental managers of any policy decisions made by the board of directors (if these are not confidential)

- reporting back to the managing director or board of directors when necessary
- overseeing the activities of the managers, keeping them informed of all developments and receiving information from them
- delegating duties to the management teams.

Did you know?

There are two main differences between a director and a manager.

1 A director has a seat on the board; a manager does not.
2 A director is more concerned with the long-term affairs of the company and how resources should be obtained. A manager is more concerned with the day-to-day affairs and how resources should actually be allocated.

Non-assessed activity

Directors and managers are often expected by their organisations to undertake activities outside that organisation and to become JPs, governors of schools or colleges, advisory members of local government committees, etc. Why do you think they are encouraged to do so? Discuss your ideas with your tutor.

Managers

The role of manager can be undertaken by many people in an organisation. Senior managers can be heads of departments and be assisted by 'middle' or 'junior' managers who each run their own section or unit. Some managers look after people, others look after tasks.

Duties of managers

Managers are expected to::

- carry out the instructions of the director to whom they are responsible
- schedule and allocate work between the people they manage
- ensure that the staff do the work effectively
- make operational decisions which relate to the work of the department
- check that staff are meeting pre-agreed targets
- solve day-to-day problems

217

- carry out the administrative and personnel duties relating to their area of work, including identifying training needs
- inform the director of developments, progress or problems
- keep their own staff informed of non-confidential organisational developments.

Supervisors

A supervisor, sometimes known as a **first-line manager**, normally fits into one of two categories:

- an experienced skilled worker who has been promoted after a number of years' experience as a team member, either on the shop floor or as a team member in another department
- a new recruit who has gained a qualification or a skill and comes to the company directly from college or university, or after a short period of working elsewhere.

Supervisors carry out **some** but not all of the duties of a manager. Look back at page 217 to remind yourself of the duties of a manager. In most cases they are also the duties expected of a supervisor. The only differences are:

a the supervisor will generally report to a manager who, in turn, reports to a director
b a supervisor's span of control, i.e. the number of people he or she supervises, tends to be narrower than that of a manager
c the manager may be involved in important strategic decisions which affect the future plans of the organisation. A supervisor is more likely to be concerned with making operational decisions related to the work to be done. (See page 236 for additional information on decision-making.)

Non-assessed activity

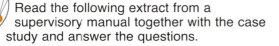

Read the following extract from a supervisory manual together with the case study and answer the questions.

Case study

Kevin is an experienced supervisor of a section of the production department for a firm of office furniture manufacturers. During the past week he has:

1 checked that the weekly production targets have been met
2 attended the production supervisors' weekly meeting
3 telephoned the maintenance section when one of the machines went down
4 talked to one of the operatives about his untidy workplace
5 talked to another operative about his poor attendance record
6 checked that the raw materials for next month's production have been ordered
7 planned the hours of work so that no-one is working excessive overtime.

Write down in each case which supervisory responsibility he is carrying out.

Production operatives

Kevin was a production operative until he was promoted to supervisor two years ago. When he was an operative he:

Figure 2.42 Kevin at work on a woodworking machine

Responsibilities of a supervisor

A supervisor is responsible for:

staff	morale, consultation, discipline, welfare, safety, training
work	quantity, quality

cost	maximum economy
machines	operation, maintenance and equipment
materials	supplies, waste, suitability
workplace	layout, tidiness, good housekeeping
links with other departments	– co-operation

- used his skills to complete the job assigned to him, i.e. assembling dining room tables and chairs
- worked to the targets set by the supervisor
- worked as a member of the production team in that section.

He was paid to carry out a certain job and to make decisions only concerning that job. He worked with a group of people and took part in discussions, but was not expected to take charge of the group. He was a qualified woodworking machinist: other people who worked with him were semi-skilled or unskilled.

Did you know?

The role of production operative isn't limited to someone who makes or assembles goods and equipment. Think a little more broadly; someone who keys in text for a newspaper, puts up scaffolding or is involved in cooking French fries in a fast food restaurant would also be classed as a production operative!

Support staff

Kevin and his colleagues have a role which is clearly linked with **one** area of work, i.e. production. As you already know, production – although an extremely important part of the organisation – is only one of a number of departments. All the other departments are staffed by managers and supervisors but the people who work at more junior levels in those departments are often known as support staff, because they support or assist other people to do their work. Office staff carry out all the administrative work in an organisation, customer service staff deal with customer enquiries and complaints, security guards are responsible for protecting both staff and property throughout the organisation, cleaners are involved in keeping the place neat and tidy, and so on.

You can compare the distinction between production and support staff with the differences you have already noticed between production departments and service departments – the service departments such as Human Resources support the work of departments such as Production.

Non-assessed activity

There is sometimes conflict between production staff and support staff. The production staff feel that they have a more important role in the organisation because if they did not produce the goods, the company would go out of existence. The support staff disagree.

Spend ten minutes **in two groups**, one group preparing arguments to support what the production staff are saying and the other preparing arguments for the support staff. Debate the issue and summarise the outcome.

Levels within organisations

Most people go to three different levels of school – infant, junior and secondary. In business terms this can be translated into junior, middle and senior levels, although much depends on the organisational structure. (Look back to Element 2.1, pages 121–8 to remind yourself of the different structures.) The different levels are easier to see in a hierarchical structure than in a flat or matrix structure.

Senior level

The managing director is normally the most senior member of staff in a private organisation. In the public sector the most senior member is normally referred to as the chief executive.

Directors are obviously members of the senior staff and so – in some organisations – are managers. However, this can vary. Sometimes the title of 'manager' is given quite loosely in an organisation; a printshop manager is a member of staff who would be more likely to be working at middle management level.

A good clue to the manager's level is the word before the word 'manager'! If the word denotes one of the main departments in the organisation, then it is likely the manager is a member of the senior staff.

Middle level

This is usually the supervisory or 'first-line' management level. It can be a difficult position to hold, since it is sandwiched between a senior manager and more junior staff. A major job role is receiving instructions and then transmitting them to staff below in such a way that they will be accepted. If the sales director blew her top about targets not being met and told the telesales supervisor to 'tell them to buck up or they're all out', this may not be the best way for the supervisor to express the message to his staff!

Junior level

This is the role undertaken by production operatives and support staff – i.e. anyone below the rank of supervisor. You know you are in a junior level position when people give you orders but you have no-one to whom you can pass them on!

Did you know?

There is one structure deliberately designed so that there aren't any different levels at all. In a workers' co-operative, no-one is anyone else's boss and decisions are taken by agreement. It sounds marvellous and there are some advantages. Equally, however, there are some disadvantages!

Non-assessed activity

Read the following script of a conversation among a group of friends wishing to set up a small co-operative market garden, growing and selling flowers and plants.

Mike: Look, Frank and I have both worked in market gardens during the holidays and on work experience. Yasmin is good at accounts and can also run the office and Malcolm always says he is a super salesman. Jan can handle the purchasing side. We've all the skills we need.

Yasmin: Isn't it a bit risky setting up our own business?

Mike: What have we got to lose? We can't find other jobs.

Malcolm: How will we be paid?

Mike: Every week we can work out what profit we have made, and then we'll divide the money equally amongst us.

Jan: Suppose we don't make any money?

Mike: Then no-one gets paid that week.

Yasmin: Who's going to be the boss then?

Mike: No-one – we'll all have an equal say in what goes on.

Frank: What happens if we fall out with one another – if we can't agree on something, for instance?

Mike: We'll decide by majority vote.

Jan: Suppose one of us isn't working as hard as the others?

Mike: If we all get together and discuss it, it won't be very easy for that person to hold out. It's not like a normal workplace where someone can get away with doing very little.

Malcolm: I'm not sure about equal pay for everyone – if I can't sell our goods, no-one gets paid.

Frank: If I don't grow the goods, no-one gets paid.

Yasmin: If I don't ...

Mike: Hang on – that's the point of the exercise – we all contribute equally and we all get paid the same.

Figure 2.43 The seeds of a market gardening business

As a group, discuss what you have just read and list what you think are the advantages and disadvantages of this one-level structure.

Note: workers' cooperatives are described more fully in Element 1.1, page 27.

Levels within departments

Most organisations place staff at different levels and link those levels with the amount of money they are paid. If you start work in a particular department you should know from the beginning who the boss is. Normally he or she would be at a middle level in the department (assuming that you begin at a junior level) and his or her own boss would be at a senior level. It might take you longer to find out at which level everyone in the organisation is placed, although you may be given that information (possibly in the form of an organisation chart) as part of your induction training.

Did you know?

You are well advised to find out who is who in an organisation very quickly – otherwise you can put your foot in it. Age isn't a good guide to seniority – neither is appearance. The quiet young man you see in jeans and a T-shirt wandering down the corridor could be the managing director of a modern software company. Treating him as if he were the teaboy would not do much for your career prospects.

Non-assessed activity

Draw two pyramids, each divided into senior, middle and junior. Look back to pages 134 and 140 which described the work of:

a the Accounting department and
b the Marketing and Sales department

Write in the boxes on your pyramid the job titles of those people you think are at senior, at middle and those at junior level within each department.

Optional evidence assignment

*This activity can be carried out verbally in class **in a group** as a non-assessed activity to consolidate learning. Alternatively, if you do it **on your own**, it can count as supplementary evidence towards the following parts of the scheme.*

PC 1:	Identify and describe individuals' job roles and different levels within organisations
Range:	Job roles: director, manager, supervisor, production operative, support staff
	Levels: senior, middle, junior
Core skills:	Communication, Information technology

Ask your tutor to arrange for your class to be given a short talk by **three** members of your college or school. One should have a senior position (e.g. the head or deputy head in a school, or the principal, vice-principal, head of a department or dean of a faculty). Another speaker should be at the middle level. This may be a head of section or the head of a department in a sixth form college. The third should be at junior level. This may be a new tutor or a member of the support staff. However – a word of warning. Be careful how you use the word 'junior'! Your caretaker is a member of your support staff but he is unlikely to take very kindly to being called a junior member of staff – especially if he has worked in the same job for the past twenty years!

The talk should be on the individual's job role in the organisation. Before it is scheduled to start, make out a list of questions, as a group, to use as a checklist. Then

if the person speaking to you misses out anything important you can ask him or her about it later.

Finally, prepare a summary on your word processor which states:

1 the job role of each individual you met
2 how job roles differ from one level to another.

The benefits of team membership in performing job roles

People aren't often expected to work completely on their own with no contact at all with anyone else. (See Element 2.1, page 148.) Both at work and in leisure time you will probably expect to be in a group of people.

However, being a member of a group isn't quite the same thing as being a member of a team. You can be a member of a **group** of friends when you go to a disco or to watch a football match. You will be a member of a **team** if you are actually playing in the football match.

Even so, when someone says that you are a good 'team player' they might not necessarily mean that you are good at football! In work terms it means that you are able to work with other people to try to achieve a common aim or objective.

Although team members need not always be at the most junior level in the organisation, it is likely that when you start work you will start as a team member, such as a clerk in the wages section or an administrative assistant in a solicitor's office.

Your duties will include these responsibilities:

- to carry out the duties as specified on the job description and as required by the manager or supervisor
- to obey reasonable instructions (remember your legal obligations – see Element 2.2, page 173)
- to co-operate with other team members.

Work teams

Different departments have different types of 'work teams'. The Sales department, for instance, may have a sales team which will be brought together for sales training days, to exchange information on customers and so on. However, for the most part each member may work alone – perhaps responsible for a specific geographical area.

Other teams may work more closely together in the same area. For instance, many people who work in production are involved in assembly work. This involves putting together the parts of a machine or article to make the final product. In car manufacturing, for example, originally a car travelled along a production line with each assembly worker adding a 'part' to the final product, such as the wheels, the windscreen wipers, or the lights. Each worker worked alone. Today, more and more assembly workers operate as a member of a **team.** They will be concerned with the output of the team as a whole and the quality of their part of the production process, and they may even undertake **job rotation** – i.e. members of the team switch jobs – to give them more variety and help them understand the work of other people.

Figure 2.44 A car assembly line

Did you know?

One pharmaceutical company has restructured its organisation so that:

- all its production workers are in teams of 4–20
- each team is supervised by a team leader
- each team plans and organises its own work and is responsible for the standard of the work.

Achievement of objectives and targets

Most organisations create work teams to make it easier to achieve the objectives and targets they have set themselves in their strategic development plans. (See page 235.) They think that if a group of people can take ownership of a particular job the results will be better than if the responsibility were left to an individual. In the case of the production workers,

they hope that productivity will be improved; in the case of support staff, they hope that the quality of the service will improve. Much depends on the make-up of the team itself – if it is effective then the strengths of all members of the team can be used to support one another. (For further information about the setting and achieving of targets see page 239.)

Non-assessed activity

Suppose that five of you work in the Computer Services department. You all work on different jobs but you are sometimes expected to work as a team, especially at busy times of the year when a large amount of information has to be input in a short period and there is a lot of pressure to get the work done quickly and accurately. Four of you get on well and work happily together to meet departmental targets. You go out together after work, and often discuss work problems and try to solve them. Brian, the fifth member of your group, doesn't seem to fit in. He isn't interested in football like the rest of you, and he doesn't approve of going to discos or clubs. He works hard but it is difficult to get him to relax with you, and if things go wrong he either panics or loses his temper. Your manager notices that he is being isolated and that although four of you are co-operating in meeting departmental targets, he isn't. She calls you all together to discuss the problem. No-one is willing to say anything to her, but afterwards the four of you meet at lunchtime and try to decide what to do.

As a group, discuss whether you should:

a meet as a full group with Brian to talk things over
b appoint one member of the group to talk to him on a one-to-one basis to see what he feels about the situation
c decide to start including him more when you go out together after work or at lunchtimes
d ask the manager to see if Brian can be transferred
e ask the manager if there is anyone in the Human Resources department who is responsible for staff welfare and who could give you some help and advice.

Awareness of the needs of team members

To be an effective team member you have to be good at:

- listening to other people and not interrupting or criticising their ideas
- taking account of other people's views and beliefs

- thinking before you speak
- offering help, support and suggestions when they are needed
- being prepared to accept *constructive* criticism from other people gracefully
- putting your own views in a calm manner
- acting as a peacemaker if necessary.

Non-assessed activity

Some people are better than others at being good team players.

Nadia is quiet. When she has a problem or worry she keeps it to herself and won't even talk about it to her closest friend.

Faiyaz is always willing to ask for help and advice if he has a problem.

Darren prides himself on being able to carry a job through from start to finish. He is a very independent type.

Kamran always thinks he's right – and he's not slow to tell other people when he thinks they're wrong.

Alistair is thoughtful. He always thanks people who have helped him in some way.

Cheryl is good at picking up on someone's suggestion and developing it further. She is a good listener.

Francis isn't very generous. When he buys any crisps or sweets he hides them in his desk drawer in case he has to offer them round.

Lance is an ideas man – he has hundreds of them. They're good, but he doesn't often carry them through.

As a group, discuss:

a which of these people would make a good member of a team – and give reasons for your answers
b what could be done to make those people you think **may not** be very good at working in a team into good team members.

Team roles

In order to get the best out of a team everyone must be playing to their strengths. The best teams have a mixture of personalities including:

- those who are born leaders
- those who like getting on with things
- the thinkers who come up with ideas
- the supporters who are good at keeping the peace, getting people to work together and so on
- the followers – who do what they are asked.

Non-assessed activity

1 **As a group**, discuss which of the people mentioned above fit into these categories.
2 Work in **pairs**. Write down which category best describes you and which describes your partner. Compare notes with the rest of the group to see how many people fit into the various categories and if, as a whole group, there are enough of you in each category to make a good team.
3 If you don't have a good balance discuss ways in which you think you could overcome the problem.

Did you know?

A very effective way of getting people to work together as a team is to carry out a series of team-building activities. There are several organisations which offer all sorts of courses in team-building – some of them indoor activities and some of them outdoor. Many courses, for instance, get course members to build rafts, to canoe, to abseil and to go rock climbing. The idea is that you can develop not only **individual** qualities such as self-reliance, assertiveness and the ability to think quickly, but also a **group** entity through mutual support and co-operation with each other – at the same time as having a lot of fun!

Figure 2.45 Team-building activities

The role of team leader

A good team leader is obviously vital if the team itself is going to succeed.

Non-assessed activity

Ahmed is highly critical of some members of his team and he makes certain that they know about it – sometimes in public. He is only interested in what some members of the team have to say – he ignores the rest. He sits back and lets discussions go on for hours and doesn't mind if the group start to fall out. At the end of each meeting no-one is ever sure about what – if anything – has been decided. He is obviously not very good as a team leader!

Assume Naomi is going to take over as the leader and that she knows what she is doing. Write a paragraph to show how differently she will treat the team.

Did you know?

Many organisations use team briefings to make sure that their employees are kept informed about what is happening. In smaller organisations all the employees meet together once a week or once a month. In larger organisations, information is passed down the line – from the managing director to the departmental manager – and from the departmental manager to the staff.

Improved commitment to the job role

The ability of a team to work together well, help one another and to be sensitive to the needs of each other is critical to how well they work because:

- people who work in a good atmosphere will work harder – and produce better work
- a team which works co-operatively can achieve far more in a short space of time than a team which does not.

Non-assessed activity

Your tutor will divide you into teams of **four** and provide you with white A4 paper, red and black sticky paper and scissors. **As a team** you are going into production making paper aeroplanes, and competing with other teams to see how many saleable aeroplanes you can produce. Much will depend on the quality of your planning, how well you organise yourselves and your ability to co-operate as a team.

At the end of the exercise you should prepare an account of the process which includes:

- how well you consider the team operated together
- the value of your own contribution (in your opinion!)
- what improvements or adjustments you would make if you did the exercise again
- what you consider the role of a team member was in this exercise.

Details for aeroplane construction

Your organisation makes four kinds of aeroplanes:

- black stripe – with a black stripe on each wing – worth 10 points
- red stripe – with a red stripe 5 cm long on each wing – worth 15 points
- multi-stripe – with a 2.5 cm black and a red stripe 4 cm long on each wing – worth 25 points
- star series – with a black star on one wing and a red star on the other – worth 50 points.

Your task is to plan your production schedule and divide up your team to achieve this. You have **20 minutes** for planning, during which time you can practise making aeroplanes, but these cannot be counted towards the final score and must be thrown away at the end of the planning time. You then have **15 minutes** to produce *and display* as many high quality aeroplanes as you can. The team which achieves the highest number of points wins. Bear in mind that:

- there should be some quality control built in to your production line, as any faulty aeroplanes will be rejected by the final consumer (your tutor!)
- your final aeroplanes must be displayed in a tidy area. This means that you have to clear up your production debris at some stage. Any team which has a poor 'sales area' will have its two highest value aeroplanes discounted.

Optional evidence assignment

*This activity can be carried out verbally in class **in a group** as a non-assessed activity to consolidate learning. Alternatively, if you do it **on your own**, it can count as supplementary evidence towards the following parts of the scheme.*

PC 2: Explain the benefits of team membership in performing job roles

Range: Benefits of team membership: achievement of objectives and targets, awareness of the needs of team members, improved commitment to job role

Core skills: Communication, Information technology

Read the following case study and undertake the tasks which follow.

Case study

Chris receives a letter from a friend of his whom he hasn't seen for some time. When they left college, they both got jobs in the Sales Department of different organisations.

12 Leith Street,
Farnborough

22 March 199-

Dear Chris

I keep ringing you - but with no success. You must have a much better social life than I do! I've just broken up with Rachel so I'm not feeling too great at the moment.

Work doesn't help either. I'm beginning to hate the place. I've been set certain sales targets which I don't mind but it means that I'm in competition with all the other salesmen and that doesn't exactly lead to a lot of staff co-operation. You've no idea how many messages go 'missing' and when I try to follow up a call I find someone else has got there before me.

I haven't a clue about what is going on - we have meetings now and then but they are awful. The manager takes every opportunity to set us against one another - he praises those who have reached their targets and screams at those who haven't, always in front of everyone else. Even with all that pressure we don't ever seem able to meet the overall departmental target. I'm terrified when I make a mistake - I daren't admit it and just hope no-one finds out. I thought things might improve when I got to know one or two people but there are so many people leaving that it is difficult to get friendly with anyone.

I've started applying for other jobs so keep your fingers crossed for me.

Give me a ring some time - I need to hear a friendly voice.

Simon

Figure 2.46 A letter to Chris

Chris is more fortunate – he works in a sales **team** where, although targets are set and there is pressure on everyone to achieve them, the team supports one another and the Sales manager encourages them to think of a team target rather than an individual target. They very rarely fail to meet their targets. Chris doesn't hate his work – in fact he enjoys it. He likes the rest of the team and they have started going out together outside working hours. Staff turnover is very low and so there is the opportunity for everyone to get to know each other really well. The manager, although firm, is supportive, and Chris hopes to get a job like his in the not too distant future.

Chris is committed to his job – poor Simon is not!

1 In **two or three sentences,** say why Chris is happy at work and Simon is not.
2 Why is the team in which Chris is working so good at achieving objectives and targets whilst Simon's is not?
3 Give examples of the way Chris's manager is obviously aware of the needs of team members.
4 Which person – Chris or Simon – is more committed to his job role? Give evidence to support your answer.
5 You find out unexpectedly that Simon's boss is an old friend of your parents. Your parents claim that Philip (Simon's boss) is a 'great guy'. They think that Simon may be taking everything too personally – sales is a high powered environment and perhaps Simon isn't tough enough to cope.

   With your tutor playing the role of your father or mother and you playing the role of Chris, discuss this further. Try to persuade your parents to have a word with Philip, using the benefits of team membership as the main focus of your argument.
6 Write back to Simon following this discussion. Don't mention the relationship between your parents and his boss. Do give him some hints and tips on how to improve matters – or how to cope until he finds a new job.

Activities performed by individuals at different levels within organisations

We are going to follow nine of the people who work in different departments of a typical manufacturing organisation through a fairly average day to find out what activities they carry out by looking at the **key events** in their day. You should be able to link these fairly easily with the work of each department which you studied in Element 2.1.

Human resourcing – Paul Evans, Human Resources Director

Producing (goods or services) – Ronan O'Brian, Production Operative

Accounting – Barbara Woodhead, Accounts Manager

Administration – Cheryl Wright, Administration Clerk

Sales and marketing – Martin Gold, Advertising Manager

Distributing – Malcolm Obindi, Shipping Clerk

Providing customer service – Corinne Holding, Customer Services Manager

Cleaning Peter Davro, Cleaning Supervisor

Security – Terence Limbrick, Security Guard

Optional evidence assignment

*This activity can be carried out verbally in class **in a group** as a non assessed activity to consolidate learning. Alternatively, if you do it **on your own**, it can count as supplementary evidence towards the following parts of the scheme.*

PC 3: Identify activities performed by individuals at different levels within organisations

Range: Activities: human resourcing, producing (goods or services), accounting, administration, selling, marketing, distributing, providing customer service, cleaning, security

Core skills: Communication

Part 1

As you read below about the work each person carries out, you will be asked various questions. Then you will be asked to produce a short list summarising their main activities. Keep each list safely until you have finished the section and reach Part 2 of this assignment.

Human resourcing

Paul Evans – Human Resources Director

Paul begins the day with a meeting with the Human Resources manager and his deputy. It is held every week and involves a discussion on routine matters such as:

- number of vacancies
- a check on interview schedules organised
- a check on staff absences.

This week the group are concerned with the results of a recent survey which shows that in the Administration department staff are leaving the company after an average of only ten months, whereas the retention target for the organisation as a whole is two years per employee. Paul argues that it is expensive to recruit and train staff and then to lose them quickly, as all this money is wasted. He authorises the Human Resources manager to carry out a further investigation and to check the figures carefully before they discuss the matter further. He also informs him that from now on it will be company policy for staff leaving the company to attend a short interview with Human Resources staff so that their reasons for leaving can be assessed and recorded. The Human Resources manager agrees to put the necessary procedures into operation immediately.

Paul then attends the first interview for the replacement Purchasing manager. It is part of the recruitment policy of the company that he attends all interviews for both manager and director positions.

Paul then has a discussion with the Human Resources manager and the Training manager about their plans for putting on in-house training courses – for all staff – in stress management, assertiveness and personal effectiveness. He asks the Human Resources manager to find out how much this will cost before he agrees to put the plans into operation.

After lunch Paul is faced with a rather awkward situation. A cleaner has been caught twice trying to smuggle out some cleaning materials. On the first occasion she was given a verbal warning and on the second a written warning. She is protesting that her supervisor told her that she could have the cleaning materials and is threatening to go to the press about what she says is harassment by the firm. Paul and the Human Resources manager meet her and her trade union representative to try to sort matters out. Paul refuses to make any decision until he speaks to the supervisor.

In mid-afternoon Paul attends a meeting of the Board of Directors and outlines a proposed new scheme for employees wanting to take early retirement. His paper is accepted and he is asked to take steps to put the plan into operation.

Activity 1

Remember that Paul is a director of the organisation. From the information you have just read, give examples where Paul has:

a made a policy decision
b been involved in recruitment
c been involved in disciplining a member of staff
d been involved in problem-solving
e been involved in monitoring targets.

Now list the main activities with which Paul is involved, under the heading 'Human Resourcing'. Keep your list safely for presentation as part of your Optional Evidence Assignment.

Non-assessed activity

How many reasons can you think of for the high turnover of staff in the Administration department – and what solutions can you offer? Discuss your ideas with your tutor.

Producing (goods or services)

Ronan O'Brian – Production Operative

Ronan is on night shift this week. He reports to his supervisor at 10 pm, has a chat with Dave, who was on the 2–10 pm shift, and asks him if everything is all right. Dave says he has had no problems. Ronan begins work on producing parts for the cameras and camcorders manufactured by the company. When he has completed his part of the job, the goods are passed on to the packing section. Ronan knows he has a target to meet but he is an experienced worker and knows that normally he has no problem in doing this. However, he notices that Shabbir, who only started last month, is having some difficulty. He gives him some advice while he works on, but he can see that Shabbir is still struggling. He eventually stops his own work and gives Shabbir some help. He has to speed up a bit when he returns to his own job. About half an hour later, his machine breaks down. He looks round for his supervisor, but he has been called into the Production manager's office. He therefore telephones the Maintenance department but is told that there is no-one available to see to the machine. Luckily at this point the supervisor returns and puts pressure on the Maintenance supervisor to send over one of his staff. The fault is repaired and Ronan starts work yet again. Just before his shift finishes his supervisor comes over and returns two of the parts he has just completed. Apparently they have not passed quality control. Ronan is so fed up that on the very minute of 6 am he leaves, without talking to Phil, who is coming in for the 6 am to 2 pm shift.

Activity 2

As a production operative Ronan is responsible for completing the work he is given to a certain standard. Find examples in the extract above where he:

a made a decision
b supported a team member
c didn't support a team member
d solved one problem but created another.

Now list the main activities with which Ronan is involved, under the heading 'Producing'. Keep your list safely for presentation as part of your Optional Evidence Assignment.

Non-assessed activity

As a group, discuss how good a supervisor Ronan has.

Accounting

Barbara Woodhead – Accounts Manager

Barbara has a feeling that she has a hard day ahead. One of the wages clerks has been persistently late over the past few weeks. The Chief Cashier has spoken to him on several occasions but this has not solved the problem. The Chief Cashier has now reported the matter to Barbara. She calls the clerk into her room to find out if there are any special reasons she should know about. There are not. She tells the clerk that disciplinary action will be taken if his lateness continues.

Barbara then has a meeting with her Accounts director to talk about the suggested change from a manual to a computerised payroll system. She has prepared a report for him outlining the advantages that such a system will bring, and emphasises in particular the amount of time the computerised system will save, both because it could produce figures accurately and quickly, and because updating of the figures could be done easily.

She is concerned, however, about possible staff reaction. Staff have already said that they are worried about coping with the new skills involved, and are even more worried about the possibility of losing their jobs.

She therefore wants to arrange for a meeting at which all staff can be given full information about the plans and reassured that their job security will not be affected. She also decides to meet her team leaders first, to discuss how and when the new system could be installed and the training which would be required.

After lunch Barbara has a difficult decision to make. She has been anxious for some time about unpaid bills particularly as the Finance director has been under pressure from the managing director to do something about it. She spends some time looking at the sales ledgers which record customers' paid accounts, and finds her suspicions confirmed that too many customers are being allowed high levels of credit. She has a meeting with the Credit Controller and discusses the existing policy with him. At present all customers are allowed to run up bills to a maximum of £3000 before any stop is placed on their purchases.

Barbara feels that customers fall into different categories, i.e:

- new and existing customers
- 'good' and 'slow' payers.

She also wants new cash limits to be imposed. She therefore prepares a report to the Accounts director proposing that:

- new customers should be allowed to run up bills of no more than £500
- existing customers of at least 6 months should be allowed a higher credit limit of up to £1500 if their past record shows them to be good payers. 'Slow' payers would be held to the £500 limit.

Activity 3

Barbara's role is that of a manager. From what you have just read, give **at least one** example in each case of where she:

a   reported a decision she had made to her own boss
b   was supporting a member of her staff
c   was involved in problem-solving
d   was disciplining a member of staff
e   was setting targets.

Now list the main activities with which Barbara is involved, under the heading Accounting. Keep your list safely for presentation as part of your Optional Evidence Assignment.

Non-assessed activity

Why would staff be worried about losing their jobs if a computerised payroll system was installed? What advantages would there be in Barbara giving them full information about the proposed changes – both from *her* point of view and that of the staff? Discuss your ideas with your tutor.

Administration

Cheryl Wright – Administration Clerk

Cheryl started work in the Administration department two weeks ago after leaving college. She finds the directors rather frightening but the rest of the staff are very friendly and her own supervisor, Joan Glover, is very helpful and understanding. Joan Glover is the office manager.

Cheryl's first job every morning is to see to the incoming mail for the Administration department. She follows Joan's instructions and:

- opens all correspondence with a letter opening machine (other than those marked 'personal' or 'private and confidential')
- date stamps it
- checks the enclosures and staples or pins them to the main document
- sorts out the mail marked 'urgent', 'private and confidential', 'personal'
- checks the envelopes to make sure they are empty
- delivers the mail to the right people.

She has been instructed that all the mail has to be delivered no later than 10.30 am each day. Cheryl is also responsible for doing most of the photocopying for the department. She has learned most of the functions, and how to correct a paper jam. In case she forgets what to do there is a manual in a side pocket of the machine. Sometimes she finds some of the instructions written by the staff almost impossible to read. She knows it is important to check what they want first – rather than waste dozens of copies.

Cheryl then sees that one of her colleagues, Mark, is overwhelmed with a tremendous amount of filing to do. Mark was off sick earlier in the week and is trying to catch up a backlog of work. Because Cheryl hasn't as much photocopying to do as usual, she decides to help Mark. The files are stored in filing cabinets and are in alphabetical order. There is a folder in which to record the dates when any files are borrowed and also the dates when they are returned. Cheryl copes quite well until the Marketing director's secretary arrives in a hurry and demands a file quickly. When Cheryl looks in the cabinets the file is missing! She checks the book quickly and discovers that it was borrowed this morning by the Marketing director himself. She quickly tells his secretary who goes off to track it down herself.

After lunch Cheryl undertakes some routine tasks. On several occasions the telephone rings. Cheryl knows how to answer correctly and how to pass calls on promptly or take a message if the person isn't available. She knows this is important to give a good impression of the company. She also knows how important it is to follow up messages. Last week a junior member of staff had placed an important message on the office manager's desk, telling her that a meeting that evening was cancelled. The junior didn't check before he went home that the office manager had seen the message. The following day he was in serious trouble. Joan Glover had gone straight from a meeting in the managing director's office to the second meeting – 20 miles away – only to find out that it had been cancelled.

Activity 4

Cheryl's role is that of a member of the support staff. From what you have read, find **at least one** example in each case of where Cheryl has:

a made a decision
b solved a problem
c supported a colleague
d checked before taking action
e been involved in customer service.

Now list the main activities with which Cheryl is involved, under the heading 'Administration'. Keep your list safely for presentation as part of your Optional Evidence Assignment.

Non-assessed activity

1 Was Cheryl right to volunteer to help Mark when she found she had some spare time – or should she have checked with her supervisor first? Discuss **with your tutor** occasions when *each* type of action would be suitable and when it would not.
2 If you made a serious error, such as not checking that an important message had been received, how would you feel about being reprimanded by your supervisor or manager? How would you respond? Discuss your answers **as a group** and **with your tutor**. What action should the junior employee have taken in this situation?

Selling and marketing

Martin Gold – Advertising Manager

At 12 noon Martin arrives in the office, having just got back from attending a conference in London on the latest developments in video presentations. He has dictated some notes onto his cassette on his way back from the conference and gives them to his secretary to sort out into a report for the Marketing director.

He has to deal with a crisis almost immediately. The Quality Assurance officer has just discovered that a batch of 500 cameras despatched a month ago is faulty. Some of these will be in retailers' shops and some will have been sold. Martin decides to place adverts in the local press and the trade press to recall as many as possible. Anyone who returns a camera is to be given a replacement, plus free film for six months, to compensate them for the inconvenience.

Martin then has a working lunch with his advertising assistant plus the Public Relations officers from two large stores to discuss arrangements for in-store promotions of the company's new camcorder and camera range. After lunch, Martin asks his assistant to check the current advertisement rates being charged by the national newspapers and the relevant trade journals. He is worried that the department will overspend on advertising this quarter.

Early in the afternoon Martin discusses with his team some quotations he has received from a new firm of printers. Their prices are far lower than those of the printers normally used by the department. The team discuss whether or not to try out the new firm, although some anxiety is expressed about possible reduction in quality and reliability. Martin suggests that a representative from the printers be asked to come to one of the team meetings to make a presentation to them.

Martin then checks through some draft advertisements prepared by members of his team. He also reads a report prepared by the market research officer, who has been asked to investigate customer reaction to the television commercial advertising the organisation's new range of cameras. First reaction is favourable and Martin therefore lets his advertising team know the good news.

Finally Martin has to spend some time with a member of his team who is upset because her son is ill in hospital. The woman is a very hard worker and Martin realises that she is under stress. He tells her he will lighten her workload so that she can cope more easily, and to take the next two days off to get her personal life more in order.

Activity 5

Martin is also a manager. From what you have read, find **at least one** example in each case of where he:

a made a decision
b solved a problem
c gave information to his staff
d was involved in achieving targets

e was involved in dealing with people from outside the organisation

Now list the main activities with which Martin is involved, under the heading Selling and Marketing. Keep your list safely for inputting as part of your Optional Evidence Assignment.

Distributing

Malcolm Obindi – Shipping Clerk

Malcolm has worked for the organisation for the past five years. He started in the administration section and moved to distribution two years ago. His job is complex and only now does he feel confident of all the procedures he has to follow. Basically, because the company exports many of its goods, Malcolm has to arrange the transport for these to their overseas destinations. Most go by sea, but some urgent items are sent by air. There are complicated documents to complete to satisfy the customs authorities, and Malcolm also has to insure all the items so that the company will receive payment if they are damaged in transit.

If a large consignment is due to leave then Malcolm may even work on Sundays – when the lorries leave for the docks – to ensure that everything is in order and the paperwork is correct. He knows that if a delivery is late this can cause severe problems for the company.

The morning's work is fairly routine. However, near lunchtime a crisis occurs. A film company have agreed to purchase a large number of specialist cameras provided that they can be shipped to North Africa, where they are filming, no later than next Wednesday. A large order is at stake and Malcolm sets to work to try all his contacts to see what can be done. He rings around his contacts – his cheapest shipping agent cannot help until Wednesday morning – which is cutting it too fine. By 2 pm he has solved the problem and arranged for the cameras to be air-freighted to their destination on Tuesday afternoon. Even though the cost is rather more, at least the goods will arrive on time.

However, when he rings one of the production staff he is told that, as the goods won't be packed until Tuesday lunchtime they won't be ready in time. Desperate, he refers the problem to the Distribution manager. Just before he leaves, he is told that the problem is solved. The Distribution manager talked to the Production manager and, because of the importance of this consignment, overtime will be worked so that the goods will be ready for collection on Monday afternoon.

Activity 6

Malcolm is a member of the support staff in the Distribution department, but mainly works on his own as he operates in a specialised area.

Give **at least one** example in each case of where he:

a was involved in problem-solving
b was involved in decision-making
c helped to achieve targets.

Now list the main activities with which Malcolm is involved, under the heading 'Distributing'. Keep your list safely for presentation as part of your Optional Evidence Assignment.

Non-assessed activity

1 Can you say why Malcolm did not try to solve the production problem himself but decided to refer it to his boss instead?
2 Add **two** more examples of where it would be unwise for a junior employee to try to solve a problem on his or her own.

Figure 2.47 Malcolm is a member of the support staff

Providing customer service

Corinne Holding – Customer Services Manager

Corinne has a job which can be stressful. She manages the Customer Services department and she knows that her role is vitally important – a dissatisfied customer is an ex-customer! She is very keen that her staff handle queries for information quickly and efficiently and therefore her first job this morning is to hold a team briefing session to update them on the new type of camera which the company is launching.

She notices that two of the staff, Frank and Paula, are sitting apart from each other and are pointedly not speaking – which is very surprising since they are known to be going out with one another. At the end of the meeting one of the other members of staff tells her that they have had a row and the relationship has ended. Since they work next to one another all day, Corinne feels she may have a problem. She makes a note to keep an eye on them to see if their work is going to be affected. If it is, she will have to do something about it.

Over a cup of coffee with her PA, Corinne discusses the draft of the departmental report which she is preparing for the company strategic development plan. She is concerned that two out of the five staff she agreed would go on a telesales course have not yet done so and she asks her PA to check with the Human Resources department to see if there are sufficient funds in the training budget to cover this.

After lunch she is approached by one of the sales force who is very annoyed. He says that Fiona, one of her staff, has been rude to him because he hadn't returned her phone call. Corinne speaks to Fiona who says that it isn't the first time he hasn't returned her calls. Whatever she does she cannot get any information out of him and this makes it difficult for her to handle customer enquiries. Corinne agrees to talk to the salesman but reminds Fiona that in her job in particular she must remain calm and polite no matter how much she is provoked.

Corinne's staff wear uniforms to promote the company image. Some of the staff have been complaining that no matter what the weather or temperature they cannot take off their jackets, and a representative comes to see Corinne about this. Corinne agrees that jackets need not be worn provided that everyone is wearing the uniform shirt or blouse.

Activity 7

Corinne is a manager. From what you have read give at least one example in each case of where she has:

a made a decision
b monitored a target she had set
c solved a problem
d communicated with staff.

Now list the main activities with which Corinne is involved, under the heading 'Providing Customer Service'. Keep your list safely for presentation as part of your Optional Evidence Assignment.

Non-assessed activity

Frank and Paula are in a predicament (unless they make up!). **As a group**, discuss whether you think people should form close relationships at work and, if so, how they should deal with the sort of problem Frank and Paula are now facing.

Cleaning

Peter Davro – Cleaning Supervisor

Peter has just joined the organisation as a cleaning supervisor after several years' experience working as a cleaning sub-contractor, hiring his services and those of his staff to a number of different organisations. He begins his day checking to see that all the cleaners have turned up for work. He finds that one of them has telephoned to say she is ill. Peter, however, has a stand-by list of cleaners who live nearby and will come in at a moment's notice. He rings one of them and she agrees to come in straight away.

As part of his quality control system he inspects two areas of the organisation each day to see that the cleaning meets the standards he has laid down. In one area everything is fine and he compliments the staff on their work. In the other area the standards are not nearly as good. He talks to the cleaner concerned, who says that she has never been told to carry out some of the work Peter says she should be doing. Peter points out that he has put her with one of the more experienced staff and that she should have copied what that cleaner did. He says that he will check again tomorrow to see if the standards have improved.

Each week Peter checks the stocks of cleaning materials and re-orders where necessary. He does the ordering through the Administration department and, at his request, one of the clerks does a periodic check of a number of suppliers' price lists to see that he is getting the best deal possible. Because he is worried about an increasing number of thefts in this area, he spends some time talking to the staff who have his authority to take items from the stores, to see that they are following agreed security procedures.

He attends a weekly meeting of Administration staff and makes a note of certain items to pass on to his staff. He then has a further meeting with a representative of a firm of cleaning material suppliers who is trying to persuade him to buy a new type of soap dispenser. Peter is interested and makes an appointment to see the Administration manager to discuss whether or not there is money available to purchase the dispensers.

Activity 8

Peter is a supervisor. From what you have just read, give **at least one** example in each case of where he:

a   was supportive of his staff
b   disciplined his staff
c   reported to his senior manager
d   solved a problem
e   monitored a target
f   planned ahead.

Now list the main activities with which Peter is involved, under the heading 'Cleaning'. Keep your list safely for presentation as part of your Optional Evidence Assignment.

Non-assessed activity

1   What targets do you think Peter could have set his staff in respect of the cleaning of the various areas for which they were responsible?

2   Do you think he was effective in handling the interview with the cleaner who did not meet the standards he required. If not, what should he have done?

Security

Terence Limbrick – Security Guard

Terence is on day shifts this week. He attends the normal daily briefing of all security guards and is reminded that there is some concern at the moment about the amount of pilfering that is going on. There have also been a lot of complaints about cars being broken into in the car park.

With a colleague he sets off on one of the six tours of duty round the premises he is expected to complete during the course of the shift. He notices that there are

some valuable items being left in full view in a number of cars in the car park, and wonders if that is one of the causes for the increased number of thefts. He also notices that one part of the fence around the car park has been kicked down. He makes a note to include both items on the report sheet he will have to complete before the end of his shift.

He receives a call from the receptionist on duty asking him to come to the main entrance as quickly as possible. When he gets there he finds that she is trying to deal with a tramp who has been demanding money and who refuses to leave the premises. Terence has been trained to deal with such situations and he manages to get the tramp to leave the building quietly. He has a chat with the receptionist and tells her to use the panic button beneath her desk if the tramp should re-appear.

He gets another call, this time from the cleaning supervisor who has discovered a cleaner trying to leave the premises with some goods she is suspected of having stolen. Terence escorts her to the Human Resources manager's office. He is careful not to lock her in or to give her the impression she is being detained against her will – otherwise the company may face a charge of false imprisonment.

Just before the end of his shift Terence is called into his supervisor's office who tells him that his application to go on a course about modern developments in security alarm systems has been accepted.

Figure 2.48 Terence the Security Guard

Activity 9

Terence is a member of the support staff. Give **at least one** example in each case of where he:

a helped another member of staff
b was successful in carrying out a particular task
c used his initiative.

Now list the main activities with which Terence is involved, under the heading 'Security'. Keep your list safely for presentation as part of your Optional Evidence Assignment.

Non-assessed activity

Imagine you have three friends who are all hoping to be security guards.

Denis is good at sport and is 'one of the lads'. He wanted to join the police but wasn't accepted because he hadn't got the necessary academic qualifications. He was very disappointed but is now thinking of security work as an alternative. He is a very forceful and impulsive character and no-one will take him on in a hurry. He tends to act first and to think later.

Nathan has just left the army and is used to fairly disciplined work. He enjoyed his experience in the army and is very used to taking orders and doing what he is told. Surprisingly he is a bit of a loner, and one thing he didn't particularly like about the army was being with a group of people all the time. He is quietly spoken but can be assertive when necessary.

Amy is outgoing and confident. She doesn't want to be tied to a desk and she gets on very well with people. However, she can be a bit lazy at times and really needs quite close supervision.

All three have strengths and weaknesses. **In a group**, discuss the different difficulties an employer may have in employing them as part of the security staff.

Optional evidence assignment

Part 2

1 Assemble all your answers and, using a word processor, produce a final version which clearly shows the type of activities carried out by each job holder in each area.
2 Discuss **with your tutor** and **other members of your group** how the activities undertaken by job holders in each of the areas studied may vary:
   a according to different organisations
   b according to different job levels.

Summarise the main points of the discussion in two or three paragraphs.

Tasks in job roles

Everyone who goes to work carries out a range of tasks in their day-to-day work – but the scope varies. Some people will be involved in thinking about problems, considering alternatives and making decisions. Others will be concerned with operating a machine, filing documents or inputting information to a computer. The tasks with which people are involved will differ considerably, depending on their role in the organisation.

Non-assessed activity

There is a considerable difference between the work of a director, a manager or supervisor, and support staff. Below are three extracts from interviews with people in three of these roles.

Read these carefully and then answer the questions which follow.

A We have a large centralised reprographics section in our company and my job is to do the photocopying for all the departments. I need to sort this into urgent and non-urgent jobs. Often I have to explain to people why there might be a delay – such as if the machine breaks down. My supervisor is very good, though, and supports me if there are any problems with other staff. Minor problems I can sort out myself, but sometimes I have to send for the technician. I need to decide what to do in these situations. I like my job – I can plan my own day, though sometimes it does get very busy and I have to bear in mind the pressures on the other staff in this section.

B I sometimes miss having very little contact with my staff on a day-to-day basis. Sometimes I seem to go from one meeting to another all day. A lot of my time is spent planning for the future of the organisation – often over the next five years. This involves looking at both the opportunities available to us as an organisation, and the type of problems we may encounter. I also deal with people from outside the organisation quite frequently, and have to represent the company in an official capacity. Although I was trained to be an accountant I do very little of that type of work now – most of my job is looking at the company as a whole to see which would be the best course of action to take in the future.

C Although I have a considerable number of staff for whom I am responsible, and like to see most of them regularly, I don't have time to see them all every day. I would expect to be told if there were problems on which I need to take action. These may involve difficulties with people, either staff in my own department or elsewhere in the organisation, or with work scheduling and how our sales targets can be achieved. Customers, too, can be a problem if they want something quickly that we cannot supply. No matter what problems we face, I think it's my responsibility to create a good working atmosphere – otherwise I wouldn't get to know what was going on. A major aspect of my job is representing the staff to my own boss – and making sure those at the top understand how we operate and what we need.

1 One extract was by a director, one by a manager and one by a member of the support staff. From the descriptions of their jobs, can you say who said which?
2 From the extracts can you say:
   ■ who spends the most time planning
   ■ who spends the most time supervising
   ■ what activities are common to all?
3 The type of problems faced by each person are different. Under the headings of director, manager and member of the support staff, write a brief account of the type of problems they encounter.
4 From what you read in Element 2.1 can you say in which functional area the speaker of extract C works? Give reasons for your choice.

Different tasks linked to different roles

There have been many famous studies to find out if people's tasks change as they move up into higher positions in an organisation. Certain tasks are common to directors, manager and supervisors. These may be routine or non-routine tasks.

Routine tasks include:

■ **planning** – what must be done in the future, how it is to be done, and what will be needed to do it in terms of staff and other resources
■ **decision-making** – choosing between alternative courses of action, often closely linked to planning
■ **problem-solving** – problems may be simple or complex, involve people or tasks and require immediate solutions or a considerable amount of thought. One theory says that people respond to problems on a priority basis (i.e. the most urgent, not the most important) and that those which involve other people are more difficult than those which involve tasks.

■ **setting and achieving targets** – all organisations today set targets in relation to what they want to achieve. It is important that managers check whether these are being achieved. Targets are dealt with in more detail on page 239.

Non-routine tasks include:

■ **dealing with the unforeseen** – if emergencies or accidents occur in a department a number of people can become involved. The responsibility for taking a decision about what to do in such circumstances is normally that of a senior member of staff or his or her deputy.

Production operatives and support staff may also be involved in some of these tasks – but they will be specifically related to their own particular job. For instance, an operator working a machine will have to check that the settings are correct, that safety precautions are being taken and that the goods produced are of the right quality. A clerk in an Administration department may have to plan his or her work for the day – making sure that urgent jobs are done first. This will obviously involve a certain amount of decision-making, If anything goes wrong, e.g. a machine develops a fault, or a crisis occurs in Administration because three people are away with 'flu, then these problems will have to be solved before work can continue.

Did you know?

Some tasks are carried out by *all* staff, no matter what their role. A typical example is that of **customer service**. Today most organisations are very aware of the importance of the customer (see also Element 3.1) and putting the customer *first* is considered a priority for all staff, no matter what their job.

Figure 2.49 The customer may not always be right, but *is* always a priority!

Routine tasks

Planning

Almost all the individuals whose work you have just been studying have to **plan** their work. Directors have to take part in preparing the overall strategic development plan of the organisation and managers and supervisors have to plan not only their work but also the work of the rest of their staff. Other members of staff have the responsibility for planning out the work assigned to them.

There are three types of planning.

1 **Long-term planning** – where a plan is prepared to take effect over a long period of time, such as where the Sales director of a superstore is examining customer trends and working out the sales plan for the next five years.
2 **Medium-term planning** – where the store buyers and managers are looking at the ranges to be stocked in the store over the next twelve months.
3 **Short-term planning** – where the store supervisors are checking which items are selling best, refilling the shelves, and moving stock around to best advantage.

There are also different **levels** of planning.

- **Top level planning** is carried out by top level management such as the board of directors. The company strategic development plan would be an example of this type of planning.
- **Second level planning** is carried out by senior managers who would be expected, for instance, to plan a departmental re-organisation.
- **Third level planning** is carried out by almost everyone in an organisation on a monthly, weekly or daily basis.

Preparing a plan

When you first leave college you may be involved in preparing:

a a **business** plan if you want to set up your own business (for further information see Element 2.4 page 265)
b a **personal** action plan. These are used by people who are employed to help them carry out the work given to them by a supervisor.

Suppose, for instance, you work as an assistant manager at a Job Centre and have been asked by the departmental manager to look into a complaint made by a member of the general public that one of

the staff had been rude to her when she came in to ask if there were any office vacancies.

You will need to prepare a plan of action, i.e:

a find out what your deadline is for replying to your manager
b make certain that you know **exactly** what you have been asked to do – whether you have to draw any conclusions such as who is to blame, or if are you merely reporting facts
c collect all the information – who spoke to the woman concerned, what exactly was said, how long it took, etc.
d decide whether to write a report or to report back verbally to your supervisor
e having made the decision, carry it out.

What you have done in this case is to follow the steps set out in the planning chart below.

1	Establish your objectives, i.e. what you have been asked to plan or to do.
2	Clear up any possible confusion, i.e. are you sure you know **exactly** what you have been asked to do?
3	Collect and sort out all the relevant information.
4	Look at other possible courses of action.
5	Choose what seems to you to be the best course of action.

Carrying out the plan

Once you have prepared the plan you will then have to try and carry it out. It is a good idea to prepare a checklist of all the jobs you have to do and to tick them off one by one as you do them. You then always know how near you are to completing what you have set out to do.

Did you know?

You should find a great deal of similarity in this section between the action planning, information seeking and evaluation tasks you are graded on for your assignments and the planning procedures in organisations! If you don't, then it is time you had a serious word with your tutor.

You may think planning is tedious in relation to projects – but it is good practice for the future!

235

An example of a planning checklist

Look at the following example relating to preparations you might need to make for an internal departmental meeting held once a week.

BOWERS PLC
Administration Department

Checklist

Departmental meeting   2 pm   21 May

Action to be taken	Date	Date completed
Send out agenda		
Book room		
Order coffee		
Check on other papers required		
Check to see room tidy/warm etc.		
Check to see room tidy at end of meeting		
Send out notes of meeting		

Figure 2.50 A planning checklist

Non-assessed activity

John has been asked to arrange interviews for a job vacancy in his department. His manager knows John isn't used to arranging interviews and tells him to have a word with Joanne, who has a lot of experience in this area. John forgets. In fact, he is so busy with other work he only remembers a week before the interviews that he hasn't contacted any of the interview candidates. He puts pressure on one of the clerical staff to telephone all the candidates to let them know the interview date. A day before the actual interviews he starts getting together an information pack about the company but realises that some of it is missing and some of it is out of date.

On the day of the interview he suddenly remembers that he should have booked an interview room and made arrangements for the candidates to have coffee and lunch. He manages to talk the canteen manager into doing this but he forgets altogether to let the receptionist know that the some visitors are arriving. When they arrive, she hasn't arranged for them to have visitor's passes or car parking spaces. She is not at all pleased.

Neither is his manager pleased when he asks for the interviewees' application forms so that he can read them through, and John has to spend half an hour looking for them.

When the interviews are over, John heaves a sigh of relief. That's that over with! Two weeks later one of the candidates rings up and asks if he has got the job. He is quite annoyed when John tells him he hasn't and asks why he hasn't been told before.

John has obviously forgotten that in order to plan effectively he should have:

  a prepared well in advance
  b planned in as much detail as possible
  c tried not to inconvenience other people who were involved in the plan
  d asked for help where he had a problem.
1 Give **one** example in each case of where he failed to achieve these four things.
2 Draw up a checklist for John which would have helped him to avoid the mistakes he made. Try to work out how long you think John should have given himself to make the arrangements.

Decision-making

How much or how little opportunity you have for making decisions can depend not only on the level of your job but also on the type of organisation in which you work. In small organisations the owners will be responsible for most of the decisions. In a larger organisation many of these decisions will be taken by other people, which will then free senior management from having to make day-to-day operational decisions and allow them to concentrate on decisions which affect the long-term prospects of the organisation. This is a more effective and economical use of everyone's time. Senior staff aren't paid to worry about the number of photocopies being made!

Non-assessed activity

1 Bill Jones owns a shoe shop. He employs two assistants. Below are ten decisions which were made yesterday. Identify those that only Bill could make, as the owner, and those that could be made by the assistants.
  a new opening hours for the shop
  b the style of the new window display

c the style of the new uniforms for the assistants
d which customer to serve first
e when to unpack some new stock
f whether to hold a sale next month
g whether to buy a new computerised cash register
h whether to start to accept credit cards
i whether to ask a mother to control an unruly child
j whether to tidy up a messy area of the shop.

2 If Bill employed an additional member of staff, as a supervisor, which decisions could the supervisor make instead of Bill?

3 The two assistants have been arguing recently about who should take early lunch and who should take late lunch. What advantages are there in Bill telling them to make up their minds themselves, rather than dictating the times to them?

Figure 2.51   Bill Jones' shoe shop

Did you know?

The term **delegation** is used when responsibility for undertaking a task is passed down from a manager to a subordinate. This helps to develop staff, makes their work more interesting and enables the managers to concentrate more on the type of work only they can do.

Managerial decisions

Normally managers make the final decisions in areas such as:

■ staffing and overall salary levels

■ raising additional finance
■ plans for the future
■ company organisation
■ overall expenditure levels
■ company policy.

Operational decisions

These decisions normally relate to the area of responsibility of each member of staff. For instance, the Accounting manager would be responsible for making decisions about:

■ the authorisation level for petty cash expenditure
■ whether to extend a customer's credit
■ whether the organisation can afford to take on an additional member of staff.

The Sales and Marketing manager could decide:

■ where to advertise the company's products
■ how to run a sales campaign
■ which printing firm would be the best to produce a new leaflet.

The Administration manager would be able to decide:

■ whether a new photocopier was required
■ how the filing system should be organised.

Equally the staff for whom they are responsible would also be making their own day-to-day decisions.

You make decisions every day of your life – what you want to eat for breakfast, where you want to go in the evening – even though there may be some limitations placed on your decisions. You may decide not to hand in an assignment; your tutor might decide to insist that you do so.

Many of the decisions that you make are simple and do not carry much risk – if you choose to buy a cup of tea rather than a cup of coffee and the tea is cold you haven't made a major error. You either drink it cold or ask for another cup. Some decisions, however, are much more important. At sixteen you normally have to decide to try to find a job or to remain in full-time education. That's a crucial decision for you to make. So, too, is whether or not you are going to marry a particular person – and so on.

In the business world the decisions you are called upon to make can be classified in a similar way. They may be low, medium or high risk, and they may be major or minor.

237

Non-assessed activity

The following decisions need to be taken. **As a group**, discuss which are low, which medium and which high risk.

1 A manager has to decide which of two members of staff to promote to a senior post.
2 A supervisor has to decide on a weekly work rota for staff.
3 A managing director has to decide whether to finance the production of a new product.
4 The Staff Welfare committee has to decide where to hold the office Christmas party.

Did you know?

Group decision-making can often be helpful. A good manager or team leader will include all members of the team in most of the decisions. In that way staff should feel 'ownership' of any decision made and may be more willing to stick by it.

Other guidelines concentrate on helping you to avoid too many mistakes in making decisions, e.g.

- try not to make a decision under stress or on the spur of the moment (although this isn't always possible)
- remember, however, that generally speaking you will feel better when you do make a decision – if you keep delaying a decision, you will feel worse and worse about it
- accept the fact that sometimes you will make the wrong decision – everyone does
- once a decision is made, it's made – don't keep changing your mind (although there are occasions when you can be persuaded to change your mind, and that's not always a bad thing).

Problem-solving

Obviously decision-making and problem-solving are closely related – if you think carefully before you make a decision, you have often solved a problem at the same time.

When you are at work you are being *paid* to solve problems – whatever role you have. It is therefore important for you to know what guidelines to use.

Remember, of course, that the higher you climb in any organisation, the more problems you will have to solve and the more likely it is that they will be important.

- Think carefully about the situation – if you are worried, write down your concerns clearly, e.g. I can't understand the new ordering system.
- Analyse the problem more carefully – what is it exactly that you can't understand – is it the procedure to be followed, is it the information on the order itself, is it inputting it to the new computer system?
- Consider as many solutions to the problem as possible – read through the instruction manual again (if there is one), asking a friend or your supervisor to help you.
- Select the solution which you think is most likely to work.
- If this doesn't work, try the second one on your list. Keep trying until you succeed – and don't be afraid to ask for help.

Problems with people

It is often said that problems involving people are always more difficult to solve than those involving tasks. You can test this for yourself. If you buy a new gadget and have a problem getting it to work the answer is relatively straightforward. You read the instruction leaflet carefully and, if it still doesn't work, you take it back to the shop where you bought it. People are more problematical – because they all have views of their own. If you are trying to decide where you should go with six friends next Saturday night, you may find that getting total agreement is nearly impossible. If some people are particularly difficult you could end up never making a decision at all.

Non-assessed activity

1 The Administration manager in a large organisation has decided to dispense with all the electronic typewriters and to replace these with word processors. He has two basic problems:
a to decide which computers to buy and which word processing software to purchase
b how to convince the typists that the change will be for the best.
   i Which, in your opinion, could be the most difficult problem area, **a** or **b**? Why?
   ii What information will the manager need before he can make the best decision about which computers and software to buy? Make a list of everything you can think of.
As a group, discuss all the objections which might

be raised by staff who are having to change from typewriters to word processors. For each objection, try to think of something positive the manager could do or suggest to help to solve the problem.

2 Look back to pages 226–233, in which the people whose working day was described faced certain problems. Some of them were solved immediately. Others were not. Practise your own decision-making skills by deciding what steps you think should now be taken to solve the particular problems outlined below.

a Paul receives a phone call from a reporter on the local newspaper who says that he has heard that one of the female cleaning staff is being victimised. How do you think Paul should deal with him?

b Barbara receives a phone call from an irate customer who is protesting very strongly about not being allowed a higher limit of credit. He has not dealt with the firm before but – according to him – he was prepared to give a very large order. He gives the names of several other firms with whom he has done business in the past and asks Barbara to check with them whether or not he is a good payer. However, if Barbara allows him the higher limit she realises she may be opening the door for similar requests from other new customers who might not be such good payers. What should she do?

c Martin and his team listen to a presentation made by the firm of printers anxious to be given some business. They are quite impressed with what they hear as the prices are lower, but are a bit reluctant to stop dealing with their existing firm of printers who have given them good service in the past. What should Martin do?

d Cheryl's biggest problem is when she is involved with the filing system. She knows that no-one should be allowed to borrow a file without having it recorded, but one or two senior members of the staff insist on doing so and she is too nervous to stop them. Is there anything she can do?

e Malcolm is used to claiming overtime at double time when he has to work on a Sunday for one or two hours to supervise a shipment. However, the company is now trying to cut costs and a memo has been received from the Accounts manager to say that all weekend working has been suspended for the time being. An important shipment is due to leave next Sunday. What should he do?

Setting targets, achieving targets

You and some friends are going on a car journey of 200 miles to catch a cross-Channel ferry at the start of your holidays. If you miss the ferry then it is doubtful you will be able to catch one later, as during the summer the ferries are booked up several months in advance. It is therefore important that you arrive at the ferryport at the correct time for check-in or earlier.

Figure 2.51 Don't miss the boat!

You cannot set off aimlessly at whatever time you want. You will need to have a plan or schedule to follow so that you can achieve your objective of arriving on time. You need to decide what time to leave. This will depend on various factors – weather, traffic, speed of your car etc. This will be your first target – to ensure everyone meets at the specified time, with everything done, so that you leave punctually.

However, during the journey things can go wrong. Unexpected road works, a puncture, queues at the service station – all these can disrupt your plan. You would then have to make adjustments to ensure that you can still arrive on time. If you were sensible, you would have plotted **target** times throughout the journey. If you found that you were falling behind at any particular stage, then you could try to put things right. You would also be able to recognise if your plan was disintegrating completely! For instance, if a real emergency developed, and you had no hope of arriving on time, then you might have to abandon your plan altogether, and telephone the ferryport to see if an alternative could be arranged.

In business, similar plans are made and **targets** are set to ensure that progress towards the final objective can be achieved. If the final objective is to make a profit at the end of the year, then the steps towards this need to be worked out and set down. They can then be monitored regularly – and adjustments made if the plan is falling behind. Achieving the targets needs everyone's co-operation (in the same way that you would depend on the other people going with you on holiday to leave their homes on time).

Targets, costs and budgets

All organisations compile a budget for the year. This gives details of the planned revenue and the expected costs. The difference will be the projected profit for the year. Obviously, if revenue falls and costs increase then the profit could be zero – or the company might even make a loss. It is therefore important that the budget plan is followed.

To do this, the budget is broken down into departmental budgets. Each department knows its own contribution, e.g. the Sales department knows how much it has to sell to achieve the revenue required – and the Production department knows how many goods will have to be made. All departments are told the maximum amount of money they are allowed to spend.

A manager may then divide the targets up among staff, e.g. each sales representative is given an individual sales target. The manager's job would then be to check, at regular intervals, that the target is being achieved. If it is not, then it is the manager's job to find out why, and see if something can be done to remedy the situation.

Many organisations offer financial incentives to help people achieve targets. Production workers may receive a productivity bonus or sales people may receive commission. The employees as a whole may participate in a profit-sharing scheme. (Types of bonus payments were dealt with in Element 2.2, page 196 and budgets are also covered in Element 4.2, page 469.)

Setting and achieving targets

A manager has two roles in relation to targets. As well as monitoring progress he or she is normally involved in setting targets in the first place – and will often consult staff beforehand.

Setting realistic targets is important. Targets which are too high will depress everybody; targets which are too low will mean the organisation isn't as profitable as it could be. It will be the manager's job to obtain accurate information on the current

situation and other details which may affect the future. For instance, a sales manager setting sales targets for the year will need to know:

- the level of current sales
- the sales made by competitors
- whether the market is increasing or decreasing
- how much can be spent on advertising and promotion
- what customers think of current products
- what new products are being developed.

The manager will probably consult the sales representatives as they will have a better idea of what customers think and what can be achieved. If the sales representatives are actively involved in setting the targets then they will be more motivated to try to achieve them. Therefore, both the setting and achieving of targets is undertaken by people in a variety of job roles – from senior management to team members.

Non-assessed activity

The type of targets varies from one department to another. In addition, some targets are **positive** (e.g. to meet or increase the number of sales), whilst some will be **negative** (e.g. to reduce the number of customer complaints).

The chart in Figure 2.52 shows the type of targets which operate in different departments.

1 In each case, identify which would be positive and which would be negative targets.
2 From what you learned in Element 2.1 about the functions of each department, add one target of your own in each case.
3 **As a group**, discuss the information a manager would need to set realistic targets in each of the following areas:
   - projected staff turnover for the year
   - speed of delivery service
   - quality control on goods produced.
   Summarise your answers.
4 You have recently been employed as a clerk in the Administration department. Your manager wants you to improve your performance in three areas and has given you your own targets of:
   - improved quality of photocopying
   - better telephone manner with customers
   - more accurate keying-in of data on computer.

   What action would you take to achieve each of them?

Department	Type of target
Sales and Marketing	number of sales number of new customers number of complaints
Production	number of goods produced number of faulty goods amount of time machines being repaired
Human Resources	speed of filling vacancies rate of staff turnover
Accounting	total of outstanding debts by customers speed of processing accounts
Administration	speed of mail distribution speed of answering by switchboard operator
Distribution	speed of deliveries damage to goods

Figure 2.52 Types of targets

Non-routine tasks

Planning ahead and setting targets are skills which can be learned and normally become easier the more experienced you are and the more senior the position you reach. What is always difficult to deal with, however, wherever you are in an organisation is the **non-routine** task – such as an emergency or accident. Many organisations have plans ready to be put into operation at a moment's notice should a **major** emergency occur. One mineral water firm had to use such a plan, for instance, when it was alleged that their product was polluted. It could have used the same plan if another different emergency had arisen.

At a lower level the departmental manager or supervisor has to be prepared to deal with the unexpected – and to make sure that the rest of the staff are similarly prepared. Some non-routine tasks are easier to prepare for than others, of course. For instance, all organisations have standard procedures which must be followed in case of the building having to be evacuated or an accident having occurred.

Some emergencies, however, are more difficult to deal with than others – no matter how well you have planned for them.

Non-assessed activity

You work in the booking office of a railway station. Given below are a number of incidents which have occurred during the week. **As a group** discuss:

a how you would deal with them
b what, if anything, you would plan to do if the same emergency occurred again.

1 A man complains that you have given him the wrong change. He gave you a £20 note and you have given him the change for a £10 note. You know that he only gave you a £10 note. He threatens to stand there all night if you don't give him the correct money. The people in the queue behind him are getting restless because they don't want to miss their trains.
2 You are on your own in the office because everyone else is on their break. A little girl runs up to you and says that her mother has just fallen down some steps. She is getting very upset and you are having difficulty in calming her down.
3 You are handing over a ticket to a passenger when she faints.
4 You see one of the railway staff trying to get a passenger, who has had one too many drinks, to leave the area. The passenger is becoming abusive and you can see that your colleague is having some trouble. You are alarmed that he might be hurt.

Optional evidence assignment

*This activity can be carried out verbally in class **in a group** as a non assessed activity to consolidate learning. Alternatively, if you do it **on your own**, it can count as supplementary evidence towards the following parts of the scheme.*

PC 1:	Identify and describe individual's job roles at different levels within organisations
PC 2:	Explain the benefits of team membership in performing job roles
PC 4:	Identify tasks in job roles
Range:	Job roles: director, manager, supervisor, production operative, support staff
	Levels: senior, middle and junior
	Benefits of team membership: achievement of objectives and targets, awareness of the needs of team members, improved commitment to job role

Tasks: routine (planning, decision-making, problem-solving, setting targets, achieving targets): non-routine (dealing with emergencies or accidents)

Core skills: Communication, Information technology

You can undertake this assignment during your time on work experience. Alternatively, if you work part-time in the evenings or on Saturday the focus of your study can be your place of employment.

1 Describe your job role either on work experience or in your part-time job. State the activities with which you are involved and the level at which you operate. Give an example of how your job role varies fromthat of a member of staff who operates at a more senior level.
2 Describe the nature of the team in which you work. Describe its objectives and targets and how these are met, the other team members and their strengths and weaknesses (you do not need to give their names) and the commitment of the team (and yourself!) to their job roles.
3 a Make a list of the activities with which you are involved.
  b Give examples of routine tasks you undertake in relation to:
    i   planning
    ii decision-making
    iii problem-solving
    iv setting targets (even if only your own)
    v achieving targets.
4 a Find out the procedures which must be followed if there is an emergency such as a fire or bomb alert and the building has to be evacuated. Include examples of any notices or lists of instructions which are used and also – if you can – a description of one practice evacuation in which you took part (including comments on how well or badly it went).
  b Carry out the same exercise in respect of the first aid facilities. Check to see what the procedures are (where the first aid boxes are, who are the members of staff trained in first aid, where the first aid room is, what should happen if someone is ill or has an accident).
Type out your report neatly on a word processor.

Revision test

True or false?

1 All directors have a seat on the board of directors.
2 Managers are more senior than directors

3 All staff, no matter what their role, have to make decisions.
4 A good manager will involve his or her staff in setting targets that affect them.
5 Non-executive directors are employed full-time by the organisation.

Fill in the blanks

6 Two targets which could be set for the Sales and Marketing department are _____ and _____ .
7 The most senior role in a private organisation is usually occupied by the _____ _____ .
8 Two differences between managers and directors are _____ and _____ .
9 An advantage of group decision making is that _____ .
10 Two functions of the Board of Directors are _____ and _____ .

Short answer questions

11 Imagine you work in the Sales and Marketing department processing orders. Give **two** examples of problems you might face – one of which you would need to refer to your manager.
12 Give **three** ways in which you could improve your performance as a team member.
13 State **three** decisions a Human Resources manager may make in the course of a day.
14 Why do you think it is important for a manager to be supportive of his/her staff? Give two examples of occasions when this might be necessary.
15 State **three** targets which might have to be achieved by a Production manager and his staff.

Write a short paragraph to show you clearly understand each of the following terms.

16 Support staff
17 Targets
18 Director
19 Planning
20 Manager

Evidence indicator project

Unit 2   Element 2.3

This project has been designed to cover both the evidence indicators related to Element 2.3. It is divided into two sections. As stated at the beginning of this element, because of the content it is felt more appropriate if the project is commenced after the element has been studied.

Performance criteria   1–5

Core skills   Communication, Application of number, Information technology

Section 1

This section concentrates on the first evidence indicator for this element. When you have completed the work, store it safely as it will contribute towards your final project for this element.

Make sure you complete this section of the project by the deadline date given to you by your tutor.

Arrange to interview **three** people who work in different job roles and undertake different functions in a commercial organisation. These may be people you know personally, or people known by your family – or you could undertake this project whilst you are on work experience.

Note: It may be a good idea for you to link work on this project with the work you have already carried out in Element 2.1 and to use the same organisation(s) in your investigation.

Prepare a list of questions which will enable you to:

1 Write a description of the key activities and tasks they carry out in an average day.
2 State clearly how they are involved in:
   a planning
   b decision-making
   c problem-solving
   d setting and achieving targets.

3 Explain how they work as a member of a team (or as a leader of the team) and what benefits they get from working in a team.

Using your word processor, prepare a summary of each interview using clear headings.

Section 2

This section concentrates on the second evidence indicator for this element. When you have completed the work, store it safely as it will contribute towards your final project for this element.

Make sure you complete this section of the project by the deadline date given to you by your tutor.

Choose **one** of the three people you interviewed and prepare a presentation which describes:

a his or her activities and tasks
b a routine problem he or she has to deal with (e.g. if you choose to interview someone in the Purchasing department he or she may have to solve the routine problem of always having sufficient stock to meet the company's needs)
c a non-routine task such as dealing with the evacuation of a building if fire breaks out (if you have carried out the optional evidence assignment on page 242 you will be able to compare those procedures with the ones your interviewee describes).

Remember:

a to look at the Core Skills chapter on Communication, page 534, to remind yourself of how to prepare an effective presentation and
b to make use of good visual aids – OHTs, posters etc.

Keep a record of what you have prepared including examples of the visual aids.

Final part

Make a front cover for your project which gives your name, the date and the title: **Results of an Investigation into the Job Roles of** (then insert the names).

Prepare for employment or self-employment

This element covers the types of and opportunities for employment and self-employment. It gives relevant sources of information and allows you to analyse the skills needed for employment or self-employment and to discuss your own strengths and weaknesses in relation to the skills required in each of these areas. Some useful job application and interview tips are given at the end of the element.

After studying this element you should be able to:

- identify *types of employment and self-employment*
- identify *opportunities* for employment and self-employment
- select *information* from relevant sources which applies to identified employment opportunities
- *analyse skills* for employment or self-employment
- discuss own strengths and weaknesses in relation to skills for employment or self-employment.

Non-assessed activity

Read the following extract from a newspaper article about the attitudes of college leavers towards getting a job.

'Anxiety about never finding jobs, or losing them, is causing young people to adopt devil-may-care behaviour according to a recently published lifestyle survey. The number of 15–24 year olds wishing to appear sensible and responsible is falling, while those who think of themselves as 'wild and unpredictable' is growing. Many of those are affluent young people born into the A and B social classes.

'Four out of ten of those under 25 who are in work worry about losing their jobs over the next five years, while seven in ten of those who do not have jobs worry about not finding one.

'After worries about jobs come concerns about personal health (30 per cent), not having enough money to live on (47 per cent) and not having enough money for a comfortable lifestyle (45 per cent).'

As a group, discuss:

a whether, from your experience, you think that what is said in this extract is true
b what steps can be taken to improve the situation – both by others and by you.

Types of employment and self-employment

In the group discussion suggested above, you probably decided that you need to keep thinking positively. If you convince yourself that you are not going to get a job, you're not likely to find one. If you are determined to get employment, you probably will.

Employment can be classified in many different ways. Look back to Element 2.1 to remind yourself of the different **occupational areas** into which jobs can be divided.

Paid or voluntary

Employment can be divided into:

- work in the **paid** sector (whether in the public or private sector)
- work in the **voluntary** sector (normally for a charitable organisation).

Obviously most people will be looking for **paid** work unless:

- they have enough money from other sources
- they are retired
- they are between jobs.

In this case they may be able to afford to work for a charity or other voluntary organisation on an unpaid basis. In addition, many people find the time to work a few hours extra each week or each month doing something to help others.

Non-assessed activity

1 Contact:
   a the Citizens' Advice Bureau
   b the local hospital
   c the town hall
   d the library
   for details of local organisations staffed by volunteers which try to help various sections of the community. It may be a good idea if you work **as a group** to collect this information, otherwise the staff are going to be handing out the same information over and over again, which might not please them too much!
2 Choose **one** organisation to investigate in more detail. (If any of you are involved in any kind of voluntary work, use that as an example.)
3 Write a short report describing the activities of this organisation and how many people are employed there, both paid and unpaid. In each case try to find details of how many hours they work, their ages, how many are male and how many female etc.

Did you know?

Voluntary work can be carried out abroad as well as at home. Organisations such as Voluntary Service Overseas (VSO) recruit people to work overseas in developing countries, normally over a two-year period. Volunteers are expected to have skills in areas such as agriculture, construction, nursing, teaching etc. (See page 251.)

Other opportunities for working abroad as a volunteer can be found in books such as *The Directory of Work and Study in Developing Countries* (Vacation Work Publications). This is a guide to voluntary work for those who wish to experience life there as more than a tourist. It lists thousands of opportunities for work or study, with over 400 organisations in over 100 countries throughout the developing world. It includes short and long-term openings in Africa, the Middle East, Asia, the Far East, the Pacific, Latin America and the Caribbean.

Own business

Before you start the next section make sure you remember the difference between:

Figure 2.53 Opportunities exist for voluntary work abroad

- sole traders
- partnerships
- private and public limited companies
- franchisess
- worker co-operatives.

Look back to Element 1.1, pages 17–29 if you are not sure.

What would you say if you were asked what type of job you would like to do? Your response might be:

- I want to run a hotel.
- I want to be a sports teacher.
- I like the idea of accountancy.

In all these cases you are looking for **employment.** If, however, you had said:

- I want to own a hotel.
- I want to open a sports equipment shop.
- I want to be a partner in a firm of accountants.

you are looking for is **self-employment.**

There are several different types of self-employment.

Non-assessed activity

All the following people are self-employed. Read what they have to say about their jobs.

1 When I left school I found a job with the local newspaper as a trainee reporter. I eventually became

a sub-editor but then I fancied a move to the country. Obviously I couldn't stay in my full-time job so I left and offered my services as a freelance writer to a number of newspapers and magazines. I can research from home easily enough and, provided I meet editors' deadlines, I'm OK.

2   I suppose I got my interest in the law from a friend of mine who is now a solicitor. I'm at university at the moment but when I've finished there and passed the solicitors' finals, I want to join a law firm. Eventually I want to be a partner.

3   I just drifted into this job by chance. I was employed as office manager in a firm of accountants for a few years but then an elderly aunt died and left me some money. Through a friend I got to hear of the idea of franchising and, after a lot of thought, I bought a franchise for a fast food takeaway. It's been quite a change!

4   When a group of us left drama school none of us could get jobs, so we got together and set up a small touring company going round schools and putting on plays for children. We pooled all our resources and got off to a successful start. However, after a few months, even though business was good, we found that we needed to buy some extra stage equipment and also a new van. We applied to the local Training and Enterprise Council for a grant.

5   I did a media studies course at college, enjoyed it and then went in for sound engineering. Luckily my dad had spotted a gap in the market for the production of health and safety training videos and he set up a small company a few years ago to produce some. He offered me a job so I'm now in the process of learning the business from him.

6   I've always wanted to own my own business but I've never had the money. I wandered into a bank one day and saw a booklet on the business start-up scheme they offered. I had a chat with one of the advisers and started to work through a training manual the bank had devised for anyone interested in setting up their own business. I've now taken the plunge and started my own printing workshop.

Although all these people are self-employed, the first one is an independent or 'freelance' self-employed person. The others have all decided to enter different forms of self-employment.

Working **on your own,** try to identify:

a   the family business
b   the business set up under a business start-up scheme
c   the business set up with help from an enterprise scheme
d   the partnership
e   the franchise.

The family business

A family business is often (although not always) quite small and is, as its name implies, a business in which most if not all of the senior positions are held by the members of a family. The family are the owners of the business and are therefore classified as self-employed. Non-members of the family are normally regarded as employees and work either at lower level positions or in jobs where a special expertise is required.

Figure 2.54   A family business

 Non-assessed activity

As a group, decide what are the advantages and disadvantages of joining a family business

a   if you are an outsider
b   if you are one of the family.

The business start-up

Many newcomers to the business world need financial help in starting up their own business. There are several ways in which they can get that help. They can:

■   visit their local bank manager to see if they can get a loan or an overdraft

■ contact the Economic Development Department of their local authority to see if they can get a grant

■ check with their local job centre for information on various funding schemes. (See below for the section on enterprise schemes.)

■ check with their local TEC (see page 257) to see if they are eligible for a business start-up grant.

Did you know?

1 Most people wishing to set up their own business are advised to read:

■ *Services for Small Businesses* (published free by the Small Firms Service)
■ *The Structure and Financing of Your Small Business* (published by Business in the Community, 227a City Road, London EC1V 1LX)
■ *Small Business Guides* published by all major banks.

2 If you are aged between 16 and 25, an organisation called Livewire will link you to a local business advisor who will help you to produce your business plan. You can submit your plan for the annual start-up awards competition which provides you with cash and publicity to help you get started.

Enterprise scheme

Several organisations offer funding and advice to people involved in some type of business enterprise – including starting up their own business.

Non-assessed activity

Read Figure 2.55, which is an extract from a leaflet issued by an Enterprise Trust organisation in Lancashire, set up to offer financial support both for start up and existing businesses. It operates in association with the local chamber of commerce and also with the Borough Council Economic Development Department.

As a group, decide your answers to the following questions.

1 Describe what you think may be meant by:
  a a **viable** business proposition
  b a repayment holiday
  c a cash flow forecast
  d a Trading/Profit and Loss Account
  e a bank loan guaranteed by the Borough.

Support funding available for commercial enterprises

Given below is a list of some sources of funding open to you in the local area. Funding is available for viable business ideas, both as non-repayable grants and loans. Some loans may enjoy a repayment holiday.

In every case lenders will require to see a comprehensive business plan based on adequate market research which is supported by a cash flow forecast and a Trading/Profit and Loss Account. Some lenders may require these to cover up to three years and incorporate a balance sheet for the end of each trading year.

FirmBase (supported by the local East Lancashire TEC)

The successor to the Enterprise Allowance Scheme in East Lancashire, the FirmBase programme offers an optional free training course to develop your business plan together with business support from qualified business counsellors. There is also financial support over the first 6 months in the form of a weekly allowance and stage bonus payments.

Borough Loan Guarantee Scheme

This scheme is available for businesses setting up within the Borough essentially in the manufacturing or productive service industries – not retail enterprises. Maximum funding is £10 000 of which £1500 or 30 per cent of the total package, whichever is the lower, could be available as a grant at the discretion of the Council and the balance as a bank loan fully guaranteed by the Borough.

Lancashire Enterprises Rosebud Fund

Funding is available for businesses based in Lancashire which must be incorporated companies. Loans of up to £50 000 are repayable usually over 3 years, interest is payable monthly and capital repayments quarterly after a possible 6 month repayment holiday.

Regional Selective Assistance

RSA grants are negotiated as the minimum to ensure a project goes ahead. You may apply more than once provided that each application is for a new project. No action should be taken in setting up your business before contacting the Department of Trade and Industry as, if you have done so, they are not likely to consider your proposition.

British Coal Enterprises

Loans can be made of up to 25 per cent of your project costs with a ceiling of £5000 per job created. Loans are usually for 5 years with a repayment holiday. You are offered a FastTrack decision within 21 days of a satisfactory business plan.

Figure 2.55 Support funding

2 Under the Borough Loan Guarantee Scheme you could be lent £10 000 of which £1500 or 30 per cent of the total package, **whichever is the lower,** is available as a grant. How much would you receive as a grant if you borrowed:
  a £4000
  b £8500?
3 The Borough scheme is available to manufacturing and productive service industries but not to retail enterprises.
  a Why do you think this is the case? (Think about why the Borough is prepared to offer loans to certain businesses to attract them to the area.)
  b Do you think this policy is fair?
4 You have set up a small car valeting business and want some additional funding. Is there any funding which is not likely to be available to you?

Check all your answers with your tutor.

Did you know?

You may already be finding out how enterprising you are if you are taking part in a Young Enterprise Scheme at your school or college. The scheme provides you with the opportunity to learn about the world of work by running your own company whilst still in full-time education. There is a voluntary examination which recognises the valuable skills you have acquired (which is helpful additional evidence for you to use either at job interviews or when applying for a college or university place).

Partnerships

You already know what a partnership is. (If you can't remember, look back to Element 1.1 page 18.) It is a form of self-employment but is normally used mainly by professional people, e.g. groups of solicitors, accountants, doctors etc.

Non-assessed activity

Some partnerships are dissolved (i.e. come to an end) because of personal disagreements between the partners. Discuss **with your tutor** the most common types of disagreements which may arise amongst partners.

Franchises

You already know something about franchises (see Element 1.1, page 24). Franchising allows you to be self-employed and to deal with a known product or service without having to take the risk of launching something new on to the market.

Did you know?

Each year the British Franchise Exhibition is held. This advertises a range of franchise opportunities. Exhibitors at a recent exhibition included Holiday Inn, Rover Cars, Wimpy, Cape Classic Wines, Card Connection, Coffee Man, Molly Maid, PDC Copyprint, Business Post, Countrywide Gardens, Garage Door Associates, Just Wills, Master Brew, Motabitz, Northern Dairies, Rent-A-Wreck, Stop-A-Thief and VA Signs.

Non-assessed activity

Discuss **with your tutor** the type of business opportunity offered by **at least six** of the companies listed above.

Identify opportunities for employment or self-employment

When you investigated the opportunities for employment in Element 1.3 you looked at various employment trends. You noted the differences between male and female employment and between employment in the manufacturing and services sectors. You might now be interested to know about the job opportunities which exist for an employed person and for one who is self-employed. Nowadays, you don't just need to know what opportunities there are in your own area or even in the UK. As a UK citizen you are entitled to work anywhere in the EU. Job opportunities in other parts of the world may also be open to you.

Local

You might first want to know where job opportunities are most likely to occur in your local area (unless you are determined to become a professional footballer or a ballet dancer no matter what!) Later on in this element you can read about the various people and organisations who can help you find a job in your area. In the meantime, look out for job advertisements in your local paper to see what types of jobs are being advertised, and the types of organisations which are doing the advertising.

Non-assessed activity

If you constantly see the same organisations advertising for staff in the papers, it could mean one of two things. What do you think these could be?

National

If you want to move around the UK, maybe you have a definite place in mind. London always sounds like a good idea until you think about the cost of accommodation and the distance you would have to travel to work. The same applies to other big cities. Blackpool might sound fun, until you spend a January day there trying to keep warm and looking at all the shops, stalls and boarding houses which are shut down until the summer months, and which may suggest your chances of all-year-round employment are a bit limited! You may fancy the idea of life in the country until you discover that you are miles away from the nearest railway station and the local bus company offers one bus a day in and out of the village.

It is much wiser to think of an area where you want to work rather than just one town or city, and decide what type of work you want to do. You can use the same sources of information as for local job opportunities. Check, though, in which area of the UK the type of work you want is most likely to be available, whether you want to find a job or to start up your own business.

Non-assessed activity

1   Look at the pie charts in Figure 2.57, which give percentages of the people employed in various industrial sectors in different parts of the UK.
a   Draw a bar chart to show the different percentages of people employed in manufacturing industries, region by region. Draw up a second chart to show the different percentages of people employed in the Business and Miscellaneous Services sector.
b   Discuss with your tutor some of the differences between the regions and the reasons for these.
2   Look at the map of the UK given in Figure 2.56

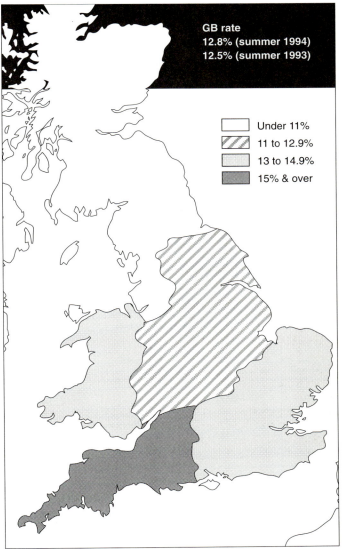

GB rate
12.8% (summer 1994)
12.5% (summer 1993)

Under 11%
11 to 12.9%
13 to 14.9%
15% & over

Source: *Employment Gazette*

Figure 2.56 Self-employment shown as a percentage of the total employed population in each region

which shows the regional variations in the number of people who are **self-employed.**

List which of the following people are the most likely – statistically at least – to set up their own business, in order of their potential success.

- Darren who lives in Glasgow
- Ahmed who lives in Bristol
- Jeanette who lives in London
- Grace who lives in Nottingham
- Phil who lives in Cardiff.

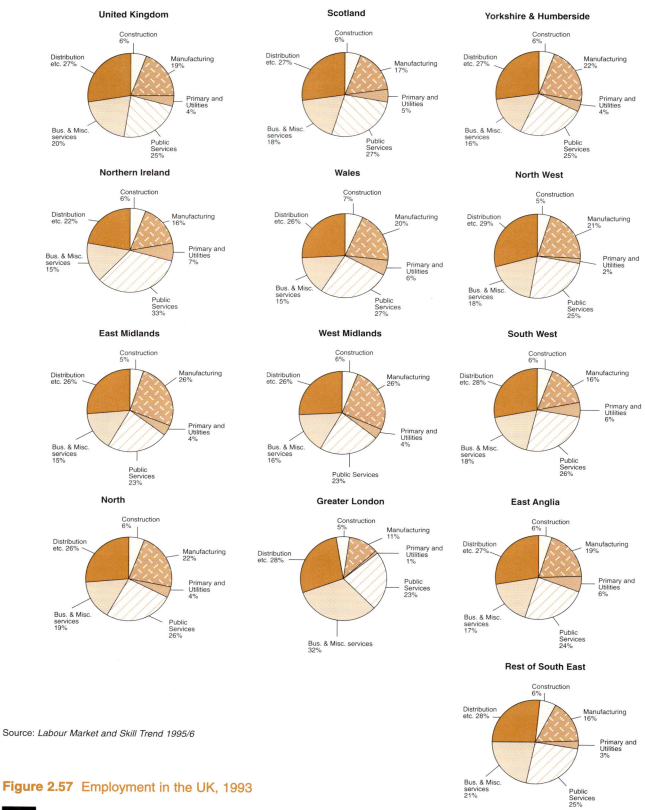

Source: *Labour Market and Skill Trend 1995/6*

Figure 2.57 Employment in the UK, 1993

Do you want to work overseas?

The Commission of the European Communities can give you information on all aspects of what it actually means to live in a Member State of the EU - including information about the right to work in Member States, Young People and Europe and Disabled People in the Community.

Want to know more? Then write to one of the following addresses.

Regional addresses:
England: 8 Storey's Gate, London SW1P 3AT
Scotland: 9 Alva Street, Edinburgh EH2 4PH
Wales: 4 Cathedral Street, Cardiff CF1 1SG
Northern Ireland: 9/15 Bedford Street, Belfast BT2 7EG

Figure 2.58a Do you want to work abroad?

Overseas Placing Unit

The OPU, through Job Centres, can give advice and guidance to anyone who wants to take up employment overseas. You can obtain information (a vacancy application if you are 18+, an information pack if you are 16+) by either calling into your local Job Centre or writing to the address below.

Overseas Placing Unit (Employment
Service) (OPU)
c/o Rockingham House
13 West Street
Sheffield
S1 4ER

Figure 2.58b Do you still want to work abroad?

International

Opportunities for both employment and self-employment can vary from country to country. From Element 1.3 you will know something about employment conditions in the EU countries. If you actually want to work there – or even further afield – you need to have as much information as possible before you make any decisions. There are various organisations which can help, and also several books which you can read for background information.

Non-assessed activity

1 Two notices, as shown in Figure 2.58, are pinned up on your college notice board.

a Write to the Commission at one of the addresses given on the notice, asking for a copy of the information sheets.
b Either call in at the local Job Centre and ask for an Overseas Planning Unit Information Pack or write to the Unit at their Sheffield address.
2 You find the outline information in Figure 2.59 on the database in your college library. As a group, decide your answers to the following questions.
a The title of the first book distinguishes between jobs and careers. What do you think is the difference?
b **As a group,** discuss why it is very important to read

Directory of Jobs and Careers Abroad
Vacation Work Publications
A guide to permanent career opportunities abroad. It explains the most successful methods of finding work abroad for people of all ages from the school leaver onwards. It gives facts on careers abroad.

Travellers' Survival Kit Series
Vacation Work Publications
A range of books covering various countries which covers areas such as accommodation, food and drink, transport, health precautions, personal safety as well as background information on the people, culture, history and language.

Countries covered include South America, Europe, Russia, the CIS and Eastern Europe, The East, Australia and New Zealand, USA & Canada, Central America, Cuba.

Figure 2.59 Jobs and careers abroad

books such as *The Travellers' Survival Kit*, which contain much information about the country where you want to visit or in which you want to work, **before** you apply for a job there.

Did you know?

One way of finding out whether you would like to live abroad is to go on a working holiday first. There are several organisations which can make arrangements for you to do so. One example is **Working Holidays** (Central Bureau for Educational Visits and Exchanges) which describes various holiday jobs abroad including:

- picking pears in Australia
- teaching in a summer camp in North America
- cutting trails through a rain forest in Costa Rica
- being a holiday courier in Spain
- picking grapes in France
- crewing a yacht in the Mediterranean etc.

Full information is given on each job, together with details on work/residence permits, travel, insurance, accommodation and other sources of information.

Remember, though, that your age, experience and qualifications will affect the sort of jobs you can be offered. So too, probably, will what your parents have to say about it!

What questions do you need to ask?

If you do want to work abroad, not only do you need to find out all the relevant information in the same way that you would if looking for a job nearer home (see below), you should also think about other of questions you need to ask! There's a bit of a difference between applying for a job in the next town and applying for one in Australia or Finland.

Non-assessed activity

As a group, spend **ten** minutes in a brainstorming session thinking of all the additional information you may need if you want to find a job in France rather than the UK.

Select information from relevant sources

Elise and Mark met when they were studying at college and have gone out together for the past two years. They each have different ideas about what they want to do when they leave college.

Elise hopes to leave with a GNVQ Advanced in Leisure and Tourism and an A level in Physical

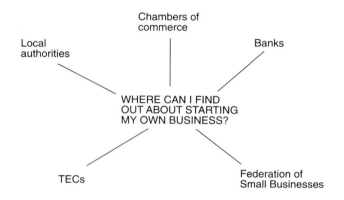

Figure 2.60 Sources of reference for employment

Education and she would like, if possible, to find work in a Leisure Centre.

Mark took a GNVQ in Business at Intermediate level, progressed to Advanced level and is now just about to complete his Business Administration degree. He didn't work very hard at school and doing GNVQs gave him the opportunity he needed to do well. He has always wanted to open his own business and feels that his degree has given him enough background knowledge to do so.

As a first step, they both visit the college careers adviser who talks to them and gives them some information about the various sources of reference open to them (see Figure 2.60).

Job Centres

Mark, who is older than Elise, visits the Job Centre. He has a look at the vacancies which are displayed

Figure 2.61 Mark and Elise

on the notice boards and which give details of local vacancies and also vacancies throughout the country and overseas. However, he is still keen to find out about starting his own business. One of the specialist advisers talks to him about the various steps he should take.

He has read about the 'five-point' job help package which the Employment Service operates through its Job Centres and the adviser tells him this means that:

a   every newly unemployed person must receive an in-depth interview during which a 'back to work' plan is discussed and followed up at subsequent interviews

b   the same adviser must be available every time the person is interviewed

c   there are special advisory interviews available after thirteen weeks of unemployment for people whose skills are in demand locally

d   extra help is given to the long-term unemployed who do not take up places in Employment Training or Job Clubs

e   intensive help with job search from trained advisers over a period of several weeks is now available for those who reach two years' unemployment.

Did you know?

1 The Employment Service has introduced a number of job help schemes including:

- **Job Review Workshops** which are aimed at helping unemployed managers and executives back to work
- **Jobplan Workshops** which are a measure designed to help those who have been out of work for twelve months or more
- the **Restart Programme** which offers similar help to a Jobplan Workshop for those who have been out of work for less than twelve months
- **Community Action Programmes** which encourage the long-term unemployed to keep in touch with the world of work by undertaking work which is of benefit to the community for a period of up to six months
- **Learning for Work** which is designed to encourage people back into education without loss of any financial benefits – programmes can be run by the TECs or colleges of further education.

2 Job Clubs or Job Search Seminars are also run by the Employment Service through the Job Clubs and are intended to help people to find work by giving them some tuition in writing letters of application, interview techniques and compiling a curriculum vitae (CV). A CV is a list of experience and qualifications (see page 274). Job Clubs also offer an opportunity for people who are looking for work to get together as a group.

Non-assessed activity

1 Mark is surprised when he is told that one of the benefits of a Job Club is that people who are looking for work can all meet together. He argues that since they are all looking for work and are therefore in competition with one another, there is bound to be some friction. The Job Centre adviser strongly disagrees with him. **As a group,** discuss why meeting together can be a help to you if you are looking for work.

2 The Employment Service has launched a **Jobseekers' Charter** which is shown in Figure 2.62.

Find out where your nearest Job Centre is situated. **As a group**, decide:

a   who will visit it to check on:
   i   whether or not local targets are displayed (or available on request)
   ii   how many people have been helped into jobs
   iii whether all staff are wearing name badges and the names of the managers are displayed in each office

b   who will telephone the Job Centre to ask for:
   i   a copy of the complaints procedure

253

National targets for the delivery of services must be published each year.

Local targets must be displayed in each local office on:

a waiting time (up to a national limit of 10 minutes)
b time to answer telephone calls
c promptness and accuracy of benefit payments
d numbers of people helped into jobs.

Name badges should be worn by staff who will give their name in writing and on the telephone. The name of local and area managers must be displayed in each office.

Customer satisfaction surveys must be carried out at a national and local level.

An easy-to-use complaints procedure must be set up and publicised in each office.

Details of help available from the Employment Service must be displayed in each local office and supplemented with widely available leaflets.

Figure 2.62 The Jobseekers' Charter

ii a copy of the general information leaflet 'Details of the extensive range of Employment Department employment and training programmes and business help' No. EMPL41

and **at the same time** check whether the person answering gives his or her name!

Write a report of your findings, using suitable headings. Use a word processor if possible.

Media (radio, TV, newspapers)

Mark and Elise don't have much time to read the papers or watch TV, nor do they listen to the radio other than late at night when they want some relaxing music. However, one day as they are driving to college, Mark switches on the car radio and hears an advertisement by a local firm with some job vacancies. None of them is for jobs he or Elise particularly want, but it makes them both realise that the local radio is one source of reference open to them.

They also start thinking about the way in which TV can assist them. Obviously there are few TV job advertisements but there are several schools and college programmes which are normally broadcast at off-peak times, which they think may be of interest. Fortunately Elise has a video recorder and can video any programmes which sound useful but which are broadcast whilst they are both out.

They also start checking the local newspapers regularly. They note that most of the local job advertisements are published on the same day each week, so they make sure that they always buy the paper on that particular day. Elise starts making it a habit to go to the local library to check the national newspapers for any job opportunities and she photocopies any articles about jobs – or self employment – which she thinks may be interesting for her and Mark to read. At the same time she checks journals such as *Leisure Management* for any job vacancies.

In a recent edition she sees an advertisement in which a large leisure centre is asking for applications from suitably qualified college leavers who want to be considered for trainee management positions in the centre. She is quite interested in this opportunity, but it is 200 miles away from where she lives. When she tells Mark about it, he is not very pleased at the thought of Elise moving so far away. Even so she completes an application form, sends it off and is asked to attend for an interview. She is unlucky in that she is up against a number of better qualified people, and she doesn't get the job. She comforts herself that at least it has given her some valuable interview experience, especially since the interviewer who talked to her after the interview had told her that she had interviewed very well.

Non-assessed activity

1 Elise is in love with Mark. She wants to be with him but she also needs to find work. If she had been offered the job 200 miles away she might have had to make a choice between accepting it and risking ending her relationship with Mark, or refusing it and remaining out of work. **As a group,** discuss what decision you think Elise should have made. Discuss also how you think Mark should have behaved in this situation and whether any compromise could have been reached.

2 On one of her visits to the library Elise discovers an article on a specialised form of self-employment and she copies it for Mark (see Figure 2.63).

A chance to soar in the slump

For Emjet Hassan, a systems consultant, the recession has produced new opportunities and a way of life most people could only dream of. He is part of an elite band of professionals, all of them top quality freelance computer staff, who have continued to be in demand despite the slump.

One large employment agency places its computer staff on a variety of long- or short-term contracts. Placements vary from between four and 52 weeks, the average being 17 weeks, although some staff can work for the same companies for several years on a freelance basis.

There are many reasons why companies take on temporary computer staff – freezes on staff numbers, increased pressures from early deadlines on specific developments, etc. The freelance computer staff prefer contract work because they can earn double the salary of an equivalent worker in a permanent position, and a small minority can earn much more. For example, one team leader in charge of a group of analyst programmers in the south of England claims to be earning a rate of pay which

will enable her to retire comfortably in three years. She is 27.

On the other hand contracting out can produce an uncertain lifestyle because work is never guaranteed outside a specified contract. Most of Emjet's contracts last two to three months, although short contracts can be extended several times. He can expect to earn anything between 70 per cent and 130 per cent more than permanent employees doing similar jobs but that, however, is not clear profit. He has overheads to pay - he had to set up his own company and has to pay accountancy and administrative costs.

An important asset for successful contractors is the ability to market themselves, which includes the necessity for keeping their skills up to date. Emjet budgets for up to six weeks' training a year.

He is married with no children and is very happy with what he is doing. He gets a 'buzz' out of not knowing where he will be in six months. He admits, however, that if he had children his attitude could change completely.

Figure 2.63 A special sort of self-employment

As a group, decide your answers to the questions given below.

a List the reasons why:
  i companies like to employ computer staff on a freelance short-term basis
  ii the staff themselves prefer it.
  From what you have read, do you think that the attitude of the computer staff would remain the same no matter what their personal circumstances were?

b Do you think there are any **disadvantages** in being able to retire at 30? If so, what could they be?

c If a company employed both permanent and short-term contract computer staff on the same project, what problems do you think could arise? How might they be resolved?

Careers offices

Elise visits the local careers office to find out about local vacancies and other courses and training which may be available. The adviser scans the vacancy database for her and also offers to compile a profile of her strengths and weaknesses, in case she has a hidden talent!

Whilst she is there, Elise looks through the large number of careers leaflets and brochures the careers office stocks and notices all the files which are kept on every university and college course throughout the UK. She picks up a large reference book called 'Occupations' and skims through the index. Over 600 jobs are listed, from unskilled work to the professional occupations. Each entry describes:

- the type of work involved
- the working environment
- pay and conditions
- job opportunities and prospects
- personal characteristics required
- entry requirements and training available
- where to go to find out more information.

Elise looks at the entry for leisure and is surprised at the range of jobs in that area.

Employment agencies

One evening Elise meets up with a girl friend and they go to see a film. Just before the main feature some advertisements are shown, including one for a local employment agency. It reminds Elise that there are several employment agencies in the area and the next day she looks in *Yellow Pages* to check on them. She soon discovers that some of them are agencies which specialise in certain jobs: one specialises purely in secretarial and clerical work, another in nannies and au pairs, another in computer staff and one in accountancy personnel. She rings one or two of them and is asked to call in for a chat. When she arrives she is interviewed and is asked a number of questions including:

- whether she wishes to work full or part-time, or how many hours she is available to work each week
- whether she is looking for temporary or permanent work (Elise tells them she is a student and they want to know whether she is only interested in working during the holidays or until she goes off on to another training course)
- what skills and qualifications she has to offer.

Elise completes an application form and the interviewer tells her he will contact her if any suitable jobs occur, although he can't guarantee that anything specifically in the leisure area will come up. Elise agrees to consider a clerical or administrative job as an alternative – fortunately her leisure studies course covered fairly advanced word processing and other information technology skills.

Did you know?

1 Employment agencies have to comply with the requirements of the **Employment Agencies Act.** They must charge the employer *and not you* if they find you a job, unless you are an actor, a musician, or an entertainer, in which case the theatrical agency **can** charge you commission on any work it finds for you.

2 You are not likely to be considered an **employee** of the agency, so even if you register with an agency and carry out a series of jobs for them, with different employers over a long period of time, you will not be able to enforce any legal employment rights. (Look back to Element 2.2 page 200 to remind yourself of the legal rights you do have as an employee.)

Federation of Small Businesses

Mark spots a reference to the Federation of Small Businesses in a newspaper article. He finds the following details of the organisation in his college library and he writes to them for some information.

The Federation of Small Businesses

140 Lower Marsh
London SE1 7AE

Founded:	1974
No. of members:	50 000
Publications:	*First Voice*, bimonthly
Member profile:	Small businesses
Aims:	To speak for small businesses and to ensure that government, opposition parties and civil servants are aware of the problems and needs of Britain's small business sectors.

Figure 2.64   A useful source of information.

Banks

The Federation gives Mark some useful advice. It also suggests that he visits the local branches of all the major banks to see what information they can offer him about starting his own business. He finds that most of them have very comprehensive packs on the subject. Lloyds Bank, for instance, in collaboration with Shell and the National Extension College, has prepared a complete folder covering every step which should be taken by anyone wishing to set up in business for the first time i.e:

- Considering self employment
- Where to find business ideas
- Testing out that idea
- Turning the idea into a business
- Putting together a business plan
- Obtaining finance
- Deciding on a business structure
- Legal requirements
- Place of business
- Costing and pricing
- Ways of obtaining customers
- Finding suppliers.

It's hardly light reading but Mark is interested enough to make the effort and he spends a long time working his way through the various packs.

Non-assessed activity

In most cases Mark found the banks either eager to help him or at least willing to talk to him. Why do you think he may have received such a warm welcome?

Training and Enterprise Councils (TECs)

When Mark reaches the section on 'obtaining finance' in one of the packs he is reading, he notices that a reference is made to Training and Enterprise Councils or TECs. By chance, that evening he is reading the local paper and he sees a photograph of a group of local businessmen, with a brief account of a breakfast seminar they attended run by the local TEC. He checks with his college careers adviser who tells him that in December 1989 a network of Training and Enterprise Councils was set up in England and Wales (in Scotland they are known as Local Enterprise Companies or LECs). They are required to:

- promote more effective training
- provide practical help to employers to improve their training
- deliver and develop youth training
- stimulate business/education partnerships
- stimulate enterprise and economic growth through the enterprise allowance scheme, by which help is given to those setting up in business (look back to page 247 to remind yourself of the type of financial assistance a TEC can offer).

Mark finds the address in the telephone directory and sends a letter asking for details of any financial assistance he might be able to get if he started up his own business.

Charitable organisations

Mark and Elise have been on two working holidays: one, grape-picking in France, which they enjoyed but which tired them out even though they are both keep-fit enthusiasts, and one in the UK where they worked at a summer holiday camp run especially for disabled children. Whilst they were at the camp they met other students who were also nearing the end of their course and were looking for work.

One evening Mark gets a call from Pat, one of the students they met at the camp, who mentions, during the course of the conversation, that he is going into business with a friend and has been given some money to do so by the Prince's Youth Business Trust. He gives Mark the address to write to, for further information, and tells him that the Trust is a registered charity which aims to help young people achieve financial independence through self-employment. Loans are made on easy repayment terms and grants are awarded to young people who have a good business idea but no adequate means to finance it. A special scheme is in operation to help the disabled.

Because they both enjoyed their time abroad, Elise undertakes to find out more details of work with Voluntary Service Overseas (VSO), although they both realise that such work would be for a limited period and that they may not have the skills required. (Look back to page 245 for information about work abroad with charitable institutions.)

Optional evidence assignment

*This activity can be carried out verbally in class **in a group** as a non-assessed activity to consolidate learning. Alternatively, if you do it **on your own**, it can count as supplementary evidence towards the following parts of the scheme.*

PC 1: Identify types of employment and self-employment

PC 2: Identify opportunities for employment or self-employment

PC 3: Select information from relevant sources which applies to identified employment opportunities

Range: Types of employment and self-employment: paid, voluntary, own business

Opportunities: local, national, international

Information sources: Job Centres, media, careers offices, employment agencies, Federation of Small Businesses, banks, Training and Enterprise Councils, charitable organisations.

Core skills: Communication, Information technology

As a group, you have decided to set up a library of information on employment and self-employment.

1 List all the types of employment and self-employment in which you personally may be interested. Put all your lists together and create a master list.
2 Nominate **eight** people to be involved in collecting information from the local and national press. Each person has to collect advertisements for jobs in which members of the group are interested in one of the following areas:
- national business jobs for young people
- international business opportunities
- local jobs in the private sector

257

■ local jobs in the public sector
■ voluntary work in the UK
■ voluntary work overseas
■ franchise opportunities
■ advertisements placed by local employment agencies

3 Nominate different people to write to the following organisations for information:

 a your nearest TEC (write for the same information Mark requested from his local TEC)

 b the Prince's Youth Business Trust, 5 Cleveland Place, London SW1Y 6JJ (for further information on the way in which the trust operates)

 c Voluntary Service Overseas, 317 Putney Bridge Road, London SW15 2PN (for further details about work with them)

 d the Federation of Small Businesses (the address is on page 256) asking for fuller details of its aims and objectives.

4 Collect the information which members of your group obtained, as a result of the non-assessed activity on page 251, from the Commission of European Communities and the Overseas Placing Unit.

5 Nominate **two** members of your group to visit the Job Centre and summarise the type of jobs on offer.

6 Nominate a further **two** people to visit the careers office to check if there is any information the careers advisers can offer which will be of use for your library.

7 Nominate **one** or **two** people to visit banks in your area and collect information on self-employment and start-up information.

Categorise all your information and file it so that it is readily accessible for every member of your group.

Write a short report which gives details of the work everyone carried out and your own contribution to the project. Use a word processor if possible.

Analysing skills for employment or self-employment

Own skills achievement

The careers adviser Elise saw when she visited the careers office made her think more closely about herself, particularly when he talked to her about her strengths and weaknesses. She asks Mark to tell her honestly what **he** thinks are her good and bad points, but as he is obviously a bit biased in her favour (and wants to avoid a row!) he doesn't tell her what he thinks she **isn't** very good at doing. The

same thing happens when he asks her to analyse his strengths and weaknesses. What they both need is some independent advice.

Figure 2.65 Mark and Elise want to remain in harmony ...

They go back yet again to their college careers adviser who lets them have a **skills checklist** to complete.

Non-assessed activity

1 Look at the skills checklist in Figure 2.66 and write a short paragraph about:

 a which of those skills you think you have
 b which you do not have
 c which you are not sure about.

Add a final paragraph in which you list any skills which you think you have but which are not included in the list.

2 Divide into **pairs,** preferably with someone you know quite well. Write a similar paragraph about each other and then compare notes. If you agree – fine. If not, discuss why you disagree. Suppose, for instance, you have said that you are good at organising people and your partner thinks differently. Try to find out why he or she thinks that. Similarly, if you think you are not very good at problem-solving and your partner thinks you are, try to find out why. Your tutor may have to act as a consultant in some cases!

3 Elise and Mark should be checking their **work** skills

Skills check audit

Answer the following questions by ticking the correct box.

I am good at:	True	False	Not sure
using the telephone	☐	☐	☐
speaking to people	☐	☐	☐
speaking in public	☐	☐	☐
answering queries	☐	☐	☐
writing letters or reports	☐	☐	☐
taking notes	☐	☐	☐
correcting mistakes	☐	☐	☐
working accurately	☐	☐	☐
working with details	☐	☐	☐
writing neatly	☐	☐	☐
keeping files	☐	☐	☐
finding what I've put away	☐	☐	☐
organising systems	☐	☐	☐
organising people	☐	☐	☐
doing accounts	☐	☐	☐
handling cash	☐	☐	☐
dealing with numbers	☐	☐	☐
solving problems	☐	☐	☐
thinking up new ideas	☐	☐	☐
thinking things through and planning carefully	☐	☐	☐
operating machines, e.g. word processing equipment	☐	☐	☐
maintaining machines	☐	☐	☐
repairing machines	☐	☐	☐

Figure 2.66 A skills checklist

and their **personal** skills. It is little use Elise being an absolutely first class swimming instructor if:

a she hates children
b she can't express herself clearly.

Use the quiz in Figure 2.67 to give yourself some idea of what your personal strengths and

weaknesses are. Then talk to your tutor to see whether he or she agrees. Draw up an action plan to show how you intend to develop any areas that need improvement (and use it, if relevant, in your National Record of Achievement).

Quiz – assess your personal skills

Achievement profile
1 Are you competitive or laid back?
2 Are you willing to accept responsibility for your own actions - or do you expect someone else to 'rescue' you when you encounter problems?
3 Are you always looking for new challenges or are you prepared to rest on past glories?
4 Are the targets and goals you set yourself realistic and well thought out?
5 How do you react to failure?
6 Do you stay with a job until it is finished - or give up if the going gets tough?
7 Do you ever put the blame on someone else when you have made a mistake?
8 Would you cheat to get what you want?

Emotional profile
1 Do you get upset easily?
2 Are you easily bored - if so, do you show it?
3 Are you easily depressed?
4 Do you enjoy arguing or are you nervous when you are with someone in authority (e.g. a boss or your tutor)?
5 Are you ever aggressive?
6 Do you jump onto the defensive if someone comments on something you have done?
7 Do you think you are tactful?
8 Can you compromise with other people when necessary?
9 Do you sulk or bear grudges?
10 Have you got a temper - if so, can you control it?
11 Do you think before you speak?
12 Are you a good listener?

Social profile
1 Do you make friends easily?
2 Do you like a busy social life?
3 Do you like being 'in' with the crowd?
4 Do you like being on your own?
5 Are you always friendly?
6 Can you keep a secret easily?
7 How do you react if you find out someone doesn't like you?
8 Are you easily impressed?
9 Do you respect other people's opinions - even if they differ from your own?

Life profile
1 Are you always in a rush?
2 Do you burn the candle at both ends?
3 Do you like to keep fit?
4 Do you work quickly?
5 Can you cope with - and meet - deadlines?
6 Are you a worrier - or does nothing bother you?
7 Do you quickly grasp what to do or need it spelled out for you?
8 Do you find it difficult to relax - or very hard to get going?

Figure 2.67 Skills quiz

Work style

The careers adviser tells Elise and Mark that not only should they analyse their skills but also what they *want* from work. Is money the only requirement, or is an interesting job or a job where they can help people in some way equally important? Do they work best alone, or with other people? Do they want to be in charge, or are they happy to work as a member of a team? – and so on.

Non-assessed activity

Look at the questions listed on the job profile chart in Figure 2.68 and write a short paragraph headed with your own name. List the items which apply to you, e.g:

I want a job which is – secure, has regular hours etc.

Job profile

I want a job which:

- pays me a lot of money even though it may not be paid on a regular basis
- brings me in a regular income
- pays me by performance, i.e. the more successful I am the more money I get: the less successful, the less money I get
- has regular hours
- has flexible hours
- is secure
- offers promotion prospects
- is near home
- is based near home but involves living somewhere else
- is miles away from home
- is outdoors
- is indoors
- involves working with other people
- involves working alone
- involves dealing with members of the public
- requires me to use my own initiative
- requires me to be a member of a team
- will give me a lot of status
- allows me to help others.

Figure 2.68 Make a personal job profile

You should now have your own **personal profile** which you can use as a reference guide in your job search.

Ways to develop and improve skills

By now Mark and Elise have a good idea of their existing skills. They also know what they aren't yet able to do. They have two choices. They can continue to look for work based on their existing skills, and if these are good enough they will probably find a job. Alternatively they can try to improve the skills they have and also to develop new ones if possible.

Did you know?

Many employers now think in terms of 'lifetime learning'. They encourage their employees to develop their existing skills and to learn new ones, no matter how experienced or qualified they may be. In a recent survey for the Employment Department, over 90 per cent of the employers interviewed agreed that 'people should be encouraged to participate in education and training throughout their working lives.'

Further training

The careers adviser at the careers office rings Elise one day and tells her that there is a vacancy at the local leisure centre for an administrative assistant. Elise isn't certain that this is exactly the job she wants but the careers adviser tells her that it might be a good idea to go along for the interview, to find out what the job entails and also what the job prospects are. When she arrives at the centre she is rather impressed with what she sees and starts to hope that she has a chance. She has prepared herself well for the interview and thinks she has made a good impression. When she is asked whether she wants any further information she remembers what she has been told during her college course, and asks the interviewer if there are any opportunities to develop her skills and improve on her qualifications. The interviewer tells her that it is the policy of the local authority (which runs the leisure centre) to encourage staff wherever possible to improve and update their skills. Opportunities include:

- **off-the-job training** – the leisure centre encourages part-time day-release courses at the local college for staff to improve their qualifications. Every year members of the college staff visit the centre and discuss various possibilities with the staff. A recent development has been the provision by the college of distance learning, where leisure centre employees work at home from prepared packs and videos. College tutors come to the centre each month to check on progress and to give individual tutorials. Every few weeks the students all meet together for group activities.

Some employees are encouraged to improve their skills by attending the college drop-in skills centre to update their skills in areas such as information technology. The advantage of such centres is that people are not limited to one specific time each week but can attend at the hours most convenient to them, until they have reached the level of skill they require.

■ **on-the-job training** – another way in which Elise would be able to maintain and improve her skills would simply be by working with an experienced member of staff in the leisure centre. If, for instance, she was unsure about using a new word processing package, it would be useful for her to be able to ask a member of the staff for help, rather than plodding through a complicated manual.

She would also be eligible to attend any training courses put on at the centre itself. She might, for instance, be required to attend an 'in-house' course on how to organise an evacuation of the building in the event of a fire, or the latest techniques in supervisory management etc.

Elise gets the job! She is thrilled. She feels that one of the reasons for her success has been the care she has taken in preparing for the interview. (If you want to know what she did, look on page 271 at the end of this element on how to apply for a job, and how to avoid the pitfalls!) Mark is pleased for her but it makes him even more anxious to find work for himself. He still plans to start his own business but he feels it might take some time to do it. In the meantime he wants to make sure that his current skills do not deteriorate, and he feels that his prospects of success will depend upon his keeping up to date. He remembers the newspaper article he read about Emjet Hassan, the self-employed computer expert, who constantly re-trains in order to improve his skills. He therefore returns to the Job Centre and, after his in-depth interview, decides that he will enrol on a part-time management course at the local college to learn more about areas which his business studies course did not cover.

Evidence assignment

At this point your tutor may wish you to start on the project which will prove to your

verifiers that you understand this part of the element. If so, turn to page 279 and do Sections 1 and 2. These sections of the project cover the first two evidence indicators for this element. Make sure that you check with your tutor exactly what you have to do.

Strengths and weaknesses in relation to skills for employment or self-employment

At the Job Centre adviser's suggestion, Mark starts to re-analyse his skills (both work and personal). As Elise now has a job, he tries to compare the skills she needs as an employee with the skills he needs as a self-employed worker.

From the information he has already obtained from various sources he decides to compile a list of what he thinks are the main skill requirements for both employment and self-employment.

He draws up the following chart.

Self employment skills	
Use of initiative	Good self-starter
Independent	Persuasive
Employment skills	
Ability to work as a member of a team	
Co-operative	
Sociable	
Loyal	
Dependable	

At this point Mark starts to hesitate. He can think of many other **work** skills needed in the workplace but most of them are common to both employment and self-employment. He therefore draws up a second list of skills which he thinks all workers should have.

Employment skills
Ability to:
■ manage time
■ make decisions
■ solve problems
■ plan ahead
■ find out and evaluate information
■ communicate clearly
■ deal with numbers
■ use information technology

Working with others or working independently

Mark likes to be part of a group. He is a member of the local cycling club and he and Elise have a lot of friends. However, unlike Elise, he feels quite comfortable working on his own, making his own decisions and planning what he wants to do without feeling the need to consult other people. As an employee, it is very likely that he would have to work as a team member before proving himself capable of becoming a team leader, and although he *could* do that, he would feel a bit frustrated at not being able to be his own boss. In this respect he is ideally suited to becoming self-employed. (Look back to Element 2.3, page 221, which discusses the value of teamwork.)

Self reliance

Being a good self starter is a useful skill for both employees and the self employed. However it is particularly useful for those wanting to be their own boss, whether right away or at a future date.

By now you should have a good idea of the personal strengths and weaknesses of members in your group.

Non-assessed activity

1 Mark *is* quite sociable and can get along with people. Suppose, however, that he was a complete loner. What problems do you think there may be even if he intended to work for himself and not for others?

2 Most successful business people are good 'self-starters', i.e. they can motivate and organise themselves without assistance from anyone else. Read the extract from a magazine article in Figure 2.69 and answer the following questions:

   a **As a group,** discuss which of you fits the profile most closely.

   b What does each of you need to do to improve your self-starting profile?

Time management

Mark has lost count of the number of times he has heard the following remarks:

■ I just don't have the time!
■ Is that the time already?
■ Sorry, you'll have to wait – I haven't got round to it.

Do you need a push or can you run on your own!

Check if you are a self-starter with our checklist below!

Most successful self-starters are able to:

■ arrive at work well before everyone else – and start work right away!
■ be totally organised in working habits and arrangements
■ use a number of memory aids, e.g. checklists, electronic diaries etc.
■ always keep to time
■ set and meet their own deadlines
■ check the progress of a time-constrained task on a regular basis without having to be reminded
■ make the best use of the information available
■ make a difficult decision.

Figure 2.69 Are you a self-starter?

He is a bit unsympathetic – he doesn't realise that a lot of people really do feel that they don't have enough time to get through the work they are expected to do. In some cases this is because they genuinely have too heavy a workload. In other cases, it may have little to do with the workload; it may be because the people concerned can't organise themselves – or their time – effectively.

One of the first things Mark will have to learn if he is interested in becoming a good time manager is to know himself and what makes him operate at his best. What he should do, therefore, is to ask himself the following questions.

■ Do I work best early or late in the day?
■ Do I like to pace my work, or do I prefer to concentrate my efforts into short sharp bursts?
■ Do I like dealing with one issue at a time, or can I juggle with several jobs at once?
■ Do I like dealing with tasks or with people? (Remember that dealing with people can take up a lot of your time!)
■ Do I like delegating work to others –- or am I better carrying out a job from start to finish?

As Mark intends to be self-employed he can answer those questions right away and try to organise his work around them. If Elise had been answering those questions she would have had to bear in mind the way in which her organisation wanted her to work. It's no use her saying that she can't get started in the morning if her employer expects her to be ready for work on the dot of 8.30 am!

Time wasting!

Mark learns that in order to be able to manage time, he must not waste it!

Non-assessed activity

Read the following case study and answer the questions given below.

Case study

Alex works as an administrative assistant in a sales department. His manager is very pleasant and helpful but she has an annoying habit of giving Alex a job to do and checking up every half hour to see how he is getting on. He sits next to a couple of friends who spend the first hour each morning chatting about what they did the night before. They have a friend in another department who comes in now and then to join in the discussion.

Figure 2.70 Alex works in the sales department

Every morning Alex works steadily through his in-tray, starting with the first item in the basket and working through it, item by item, until it is time to go home. The next day he starts again.

The sales department is organised on an open-plan basis and Alex sits near to the door, next to the drinks vending machine. The photocopier is two floors down and Alex shares a telephone with three other people.

As a group, list:

1 the ways in which time is being wasted in the sales department
2 some improvements which could be made.

Read on for some possible suggestions!

Improving the use of time

On the management course Mark is taking to update his skills he is pleased to note that there is a session on time management. During that session the tutor gives the group a number of helpful suggestions.

a Plan ahead – however hard you may work, you may still waste your time if you don't spend part of it **planning** what you should do. (Look back to Element 2.3, page 235 to remind yourself of the basic principles of planning your work.)
b Set targets – you can soon learn to set yourself realistic **targets** either in terms of the amount of work you want to get through or the amount of time you will spend on one particular job. (Again look back to Element 2.3, page 239 to remind yourself how to set targets.)
c Negotiate with people – if other people are disturbing you, tell them so, nicely but firmly. You don't have to be aggressive or rude, merely assertive!

Non-assessed activity

1 Discuss the difference between aggressiveness and assertiveness. Ask your tutor afterwards to say which members of the group put their views aggressively and which put their views assertively, and to summarise the difference.
2 **As a group:**
   a Plan what Alex should say to his manager to let her know that she was disturbing him, and that he cannot work as effectively when interrupted.
   b Plan what Alex should say to his work colleagues.
   c Ask one member of the group to be Alex and others to take the part of the manager and Alex's colleagues. Act out the conversations in which Alex tries to convince the others that he doesn't like all the interruptions.

3 Test yourself to see whether or not *you* ever waste time! Look back at what you did yesterday (or on your last working day) and decide how many of the following time wasting activities apply to you.
- chatting to a friend when you should have been completing an assignment
- disturbing a friend who is trying to complete an assignment
- looking out of the window/at the clock
- coming back late from breaks/lunch
- re-doing a job which you didn't do well enough the first time
- trying to find something on an untidy desk or in an untidy bag
- forgetting to plan ahead and therefore taking twice as long over a job as you need to do.

4 Ask your tutor for his or her opinion of your time-management skills! If every assignment for the past three months has been handed in one minute before the deadline, be prepared to be told some hard facts!

Did you know?

Some specialist skills can be important in time management. For instance, if you are expected to read a large number of papers every day there are ways of cutting down the time you spend doing this by being **selective** about your reading. Ask yourself:

- what is essential
- what is essential and urgent
- what is essential but not immediate
- what is not essential (although interesting).

Non-assessed activity

Imagine you have the following documents to read. **As a group,** discuss which of these documents can be classified under each of the headings given above:

a a report which is to be discussed at a meeting in an hour's time
b a magazine article about a new development in office systems
c a letter of complaint to which you must reply today
d the staff newsletter
e your new terms and conditions of employment
f the company's annual report.

Did you know?

Even managers can be guilty of time-wasting and many organisations run training sessions to help them improve their time management.

Non-assessed activity

One organisation has given its executives tips to help them to manage their time better. Look at the following list and answer the questions below.

Time management hints and tips

- Never allow days or weeks at work just to happen – think ahead and make out daily and weekly schedules to help you.
- Do not have too many meetings – they are great time wasters.
- Do not let appointments overrun – ration your time.
- Encourage your staff to filter out unimportant phone calls or visits by handling them personally or delegating them to others.
- Allocate daily blocks of time to:
  - uninterrupted personal work
  - discussions with staff
  - meetings with clients or senior managers
  - taking and making telephone calls
  - reading job-related documents
  - external appointments with customers etc.

Figure 2.71 Tips on time management

1 Give **one** example where managers are told to:
a plan ahead
b set targets for themselves
c negotiate with other people.
2 Managers are advised not to have too many meetings. **As a group,** discuss other time saving ways in which managers can communicate information.

Decision-making and problem-solving

Look back to Unit 2.3, pages 236 and 238 to remind yourself of the different types of decisions you may be expected to make and the different types of problems you may have to solve.

Elise and Mark don't often have arguments, but they do have one when Mark tells her not to worry about her new job – she'll only be expected to do as she is told so she won't have any decisions to make or problems to solve! She argues that even as a new employee she will have some decisions to make and that *everyone* has to solve problems. The only difference is what those problems and decisions are. Mark disagrees and says that only self-employed people face real decisions and *real* problems, because they are not in such a protected environment as employees.

Non-assessed activity

1 Spend **ten** minutes thinking of examples of decisions and problems which:

a Elise faces as an employee
b Mark might face as a self-employed worker.

2 Draw up a list divided into employment and self-employment and put under each section examples of:

a the type of problems
b the types of decisions

appropriate to each type of employment.

Planning

At college, Mark and Elise have been reminded frequently about the need to plan ahead, both in respect of their college work and also in relation to their future careers. Both are now quite good at preparing plans and keeping to them. (Look back to Element 2.3 to remind yourself of how you should go about planning ahead.) Elise feels that this skill helped her to get the job at the leisure centre. When she drew up her plan of action she considered the following questions.

a What is the purpose of the plan?
b What time period is involved?
c What resources will I need?
d Where will I obtain them?
e How will I monitor my plan?
f How can I evaluate my plan afterwards?

Elise followed her plan quite rigidly. The purpose of her plan was to find a job. She allowed herself a three-month period initially, although she checked each month to see whether the timescale was still suitable or whether she had been a bit unrealistic in her expectations. She also checked her aims regularly to see whether she still wanted to work in the leisure field even though, as time went on, she

was learning more and more about other jobs. She consulted the careers advisers at college and in the careers office. She was quite lucky. Just when she had begun to think that she would have to modify her plan of action, she was offered a job.

Non-assessed activity

When Elise actually starts work she will have to use the same planning skills she used in getting the job. Read the following scenario which illustrates the need for planning in whatever job you may have.

You work in a solicitor's office. You and your boss, Louise Tranmer, have both just come back from holiday and a number of messages have been left on your desk for your attention. **As a group,** discuss the order in which you will deal with all these messages and why.

- Mrs Lawson wants to make an appointment to see Mrs Tranmer about altering her will.
- Nadia Lancaster, from the Citizens' Advice Bureau, is in the process of updating the legal aid information booklet and wants to check one or two points with Mrs Tranmer. The printers are waiting for the copy and must have it by the end of today.
- Mrs Tranmer has to appear in court at 11 am and some documents have to be lodged with the magistrate's clerk before then.
- Mrs Tranmer has come back from holiday with raging toothache. She wants a dental appointment at the earliest possible moment.
- The senior partner wants to see her as soon as possible.

Business planning

Mark has a different form of planning to carry out. All the organisations he has contacted about funding for his business have asked him to provide a **business plan.** Fortunately he has learned how to do this during his business studies course. If he hadn't he could have attended one of a number of business start-up seminars organised by the local TEC or Chamber of Commerce.

By now, and after some considerable research, he has decided that he would like to start up his own office cleaning service and he starts to prepare his plan. He follows the steps in the chart outlined in Figure 2.72.

Preparing a business plan

1 Give a brief description of what you want to do.
2 Describe yourself – your age, qualifications, experience and also anyone who is working with you or for you.
3 Set out what you propose to achieve over the next 3–5 years.
4 Give information about your potential customers (together with any market research findings).
5 State what you need to organise your business and how you are going to obtain it, e.g. premises, equipment etc.
6 Include information about start-up costs, e.g. purchase of equipment or goods; sales forecast – how much you expect to sell each month over the first year; cash flow projections – how much working capital is needed over the year: profit and loss projections – how much profit you expect to make.
7 Indicate how much financial support you need and where it will come from, e.g. personal savings, bank loans or grants.

Figure 2.72 Hints and tips on business planning

Did you know?

In most cases a business plan will refer to a SWOT analysis. This is an acronym for a report on the **s**trengths, **w**eaknesses, **o**pportunities and **t**hreats to the plan. Mark, for instance, may draw up the following list in relation to his plan to set up an office cleaning business.

Strengths

- Low start-up and running costs
- Plenty of ideas for future development
- Good range of contacts available through his father (who has his own office equipment firm)
- Mark's energy and enthusiasm!

Weaknesses

- Mark's lack of business experience
- Start-up money needed for equipment, staffing, advertising
- Lack of proper premises.

Opportunities

- Growing number of small to medium-sized firms in the area – two new industrial estates established within a 20 mile radius.

Threats

- A number of other competitors in the area
- The continuing recession and closure of many small businesses.

Information seeking and evaluating

The amount of information which you will acquire each day is amazing, and you will be acquiring it almost without realising that you are doing so e.g. every time you ask a question and get an answer. Mark and Elise have taken information-seeking a stage further in their efforts to find employment. They have discovered a number of sources of reference and have used them. When they start work they will have to continue that process.

At work, being able to gather together information is vitally important, even for something as simple as a telephone number. Elise's first job when she starts work will be to try to find out where everything is (helped by her induction training)! She should have access to at least five different types of information, all of which are shown on the following chart.

1 **Number**-based information in chart form – such as tables, graphs, pie charts.
2 **Oral** information – from colleagues, managers, meetings and so on.
3 **Written** information – such as reports, factsheets, briefings, summaries, letters, memoranda, notices, minutes of meetings.
4 **Audio-visual** information – videos, cassettes, slides, charts, photographs.
5 **Persuasive** information – advertisements, sales literature, posters, newsletters, presentations and so on.

Figure 2.73 Types of information

Seeking information

Elise will also need to know what external sources of information are available to her when she starts work. She might need to consult reference books on a regular basis, she might also need to know about external organisations such as the departments of the local authority with whom she might need to be in contact.

Non-assessed activity

1 Elise's new job is administrative assistant to the assistant manager at the leisure centre. She is going to begin work in the large reception area where, as part of her initial training, she will be expected to answer the telephone and carry out various clerical duties, including word processing documents such as the centre's annual report and statistics about centre usage.

She will also be expected to speak to and advise customers about the various leisure facilities available to them. She will take part in team meetings and attend team briefings and she has also volunteered to be part of the centre's marketing group. She is quite keen to be part of the group that visits local schools to tell the pupils about the centre.

List which types of information given on the above chart she may have to use.

2 When Elise arrives at work she will probably have no idea where to find anything, and certainly she may not know which external sources of information will be useful to her. **As a group,** discuss how her colleagues and her manager can help her.

Evaluating information

Finding the information is only the first step. What you do with it is the second – and more important step. To be of any use information must be:

- up to date
- accurate
- relevant.

Therefore, each time you hear or read a piece of information, you must try to decide whether you can **rely** upon it. Checking whether it is up to date or relevant is normally straightforward. Checking whether it is accurate is more difficult.

Non-assessed activity

Nowadays most people have access to computer-based information, i.e. databases. (See Core Skills, Information technology, page 610 for details of the advantages of such databases.) A very common complaint in offices is that these databases are out of date and inaccurate and that the computer staff – who are often not part of the departmental staff but form part of a centralised service – are not making the necessary improvements. This can result in staff refusing to use the system, which causes obvious problems for the departmental manager.

As a group, discuss what measures a manager should take if this problem arises. Draw up a plan of action for the manager to carry out.

Communication, application of number, information technology

In your Core Skills work you will learn more about how to communicate, how to use numbers and the importance of information technology, but you will probably have realised already that these are the three basic skills needed at work, whether you are intending to be employed or self-employed.

Occupational skills

Mark and Elise would have had even greater difficulty in finding employment if they had been completely unskilled. Their personal skills have proved to be very important in the way in which they went about looking for employment. However, if they had nothing else to offer they may have faced problems.

Elise, would have depended on her skills-related qualifications to get her a job. Mark was less dependent on his skills-related qualifications, because of the kind of business he decided on. However, if he had decided to become a self-employed accountant, he would have needed accountancy skills, and if he had wanted to open a business in which he made and sold furniture, he would probably have needed some training leading to a qualification.

Non-assessed activity

1 When you visit a job centre you will see a number of vacancies displayed on notice boards. Nearly all of them give some details of what occupational skills are necessary for the job advertised. See Figure 2.74.

Running short training courses in a variety of subjects. Supervising other forms of training – part-time day-release courses at local colleges, apprenticeship schemes etc. Qualifications required are normally a minimum of 2 A levels or a degree. The Institute of Personnel Management also offers relevant qualifications

Buying materials, manufactured goods with services for the organisation. Liaison with suppliers, monitoring of progress, checking of delivery. Obtaining quotations and making out contracts. Qualifications vary. Advisable to have the Institute of Purchasing Certificate or Diploma.

Analysing, interpreting and presenting information about an organisation's existing and potential customers. Degree normally required and there are short courses run by the Chartered Institute of Marketing.

Making manufactured goods involving working alone at a bench or on an assembly line. No formal qualifications required.

Maintaining and preparing documents such as share registers, reports and accounts. Preparing the documentation relating to Board meetings. Writing the company annual report. Normally a degree or professional qualification required such as that awarded by the Institute of Chartered Secretaries and Administrators.

Keyboarding, taking minutes of meetings, arranging events, running an office, undertaking some research duties. Qualifications normally good GCSEs, A levels or degree plus secretarial skills

Responsibility for the movement and storage of goods and materials, co-ordination of warehousing, transport, materials handling, inventory control, order processing and packing. Qualifications normally HNC/D in Distribution or Business Studies plus Institute of Logistics and Distribution Management's Diploma in Distribution Studies.

Producing plans and drawings from which a range of products can be manufactured. Normally a minimum of 5 GCSEs required including Maths, English and a science or technology subject. An engineering qualification may be taken on a part-time basis.

Taking orders from customers over the telephone and giving information about various products before an order is taken. Normally no formal qualifications required.

Applying logical and analytical methods to the solution of problems. Advising on how to improve productivity and use of resources. Degree or relevant experience normally required. Institute of Management Services offers a number of relevant qualifications. City and Guilds offer a Certificate in Work Study.

Making sure that the customers receive the goods or services they want, when and where they want them, at a price that suits both the customers and the company. Dealing with the planning and co-ordination of all stages of marketing, market research, product development, promotion, pricing, sales and distribution. Normally a degree required or HND in Business and Finance. Institute of Marketing run part-time courses at various levels.

Writing computer programs to perform specific tasks, e.g. stock control, payroll. GCSEs including English and Maths normally required although nowadays degree important. British Computer Society and Institute of Data Processing Management offer professional qualifications.

Making sure that the customers receive the goods or services they want, when and where they want them, at a price that suits both the customers and the company. Dealing with the planning and co-ordination of all stages of marketing, market research, product development, promotion, pricing, sales and distribution. Normally a degree required or HND in Business and Finance. Institute of Marketing run part-time courses at various levels.

Organising and arranging trade fairs, writing press releases, making use of market research, countering bad publicity, promoting positive view of the company. GCSEs or A levels required, preferably followed by the Communication Advertising and Marketing Education Foundation Diploma covering Management and Strategy and Public Relations Practice.

Working at switchboards and handling incoming and outgoing telephone calls. No formal qualifications normally required.

Protecting property, goods, money and people. Preventing theft and vandalism, minimising the danger of fire, flood etc. No formal qualifications normally required.

Translating the objectives of the marketing plan into sales targets for individual representatives. Reporting back to management on how well the goods or services are received and on the activities of competitor firms. Normally a degree is required and/or an Institute of Marketing or Institute of Sales and Marketing Management qualification.

Overseeing activities associated with production. Ensuring production targets are met. Planning and controlling resources. An engineering qualification required. A supervisory management qualification such as NEBSM (National Examination Board in Supervisory Management) also useful.

Dealing with members of the public, answering enquiries, organising appointment systems, using the telephone, handling petty cash. No formal qualifications required, but GNVQ Intermediate in Business useful.

Figure 2.74 Job descriptions giving occupational skills

Test yourself by looking at Figure 2.74 which gives the job descriptions. Draw up a list in which you match up the descriptions with the job titles in Figure 2.75.

Job titles	
computer applications programmer	public relations officer
company secretary	purchasing officer/buyer
distribution manager	receptionist
draughtsman/woman	sales manager
market research executive	security officer
personal secretary	telephonist
product designer	telephone order clerk
production manager	training officer
production worker	works study/organisation and methods officer

Figure 2.75 Job titles

2 From Figure 2.76, which qualities would you attach to each job? (Note that you can use any quality more than once.)

Qualities	
accuracy	numeracy skills
creativity	patience
discretion	persistence
good judgement	persuasiveness
honesty	speaking skills
imagination	tact
leadership skills	writing skills
logic	

Figure 2.76 Personal qualities

Your own occupational skills

The very fact that you are reading this element means that you are probably undertaking a business studies course and are hoping to be able to use the qualification as a means of finding employment in the business world. It might be useful for you to see how your qualifications compare with other qualifications.

Academic qualifications

These include GCSEs and GCE A levels, which are an entry qualification for Higher Education and are tested mainly by examination. GCE A/S levels were introduced in 1987 and are the same standard as 'A' levels but with about half the content.

Vocational qualifications

General National Vocational Qualifications (GNVQs) are a work-related alternative to GCSEs and A and AS levels for full-time students. There are three levels – Foundation, Intermediate and Advanced – which are tested by both examinations and assessment of work done during the course.

Other qualifications include:

■ BTEC First – a one-year programme of initial work-related education for those students aged 16+
■ BTEC National – a two- or three-year course related to broad occupational areas ranging from agriculture to zoological studies. (Note: BTEC First Certificates and National qualifications will all eventually be replaced by GNVQs.)
■ BTEC Higher National Diplomas and Certificates (HNDs and HNCs) – two-year vocational higher education programmes. Generally accepted as being equivalent to a pass degree.

Occupational qualifications

National Vocational Qualifications (NVQs) – partly competence-based for a specific job, meeting standards agreed by employers in that particular industry. People are assessed in workplace conditions and by practical, oral or written examinations.

Non-assessed activity

As a group, discuss the answers to the following questions.

1 What is the difference between an **academic** and a **vocational** qualification?
2 Do you agree that there need to be two types of qualification?

3 Why do you think that some courses are tested only by examination and others by examination and course work?

4 What's the point of having an AS level?

5 Find out where you are on the chart (Figure 2.77). Do you want to stay at that point? If so, why? Do you want to move on? If so, why?

Give your answers in a short report using a suitable heading. Prepare it using a word processor. Draw a ladder which indicates the qualification route you intend to take and mark where you are at present.

	Occupational	Vocational	Academic
5	NVQ5	Professional	Postgraduate
4	NVQ4	BTEC Higher National	Degree
3	NVQ3	Advanced GNVQ or BTEC National	2 GCE A Levels or 1 GCE A Level & 2 AS qualifications, or 4 AS levels
2	NVQ 2	Intermediate GNVQ or BTEC First	5 GCSEs at Grades A to C
1	NVQ 1	Foundation GNVQ	4 GCSEs at Grades D to G

Figure 2.77 Qualifications and how they fit together

Optional evidence activity

*This activity can be carried out verbally in class **in a group** as a non-assessed activity to consolidate learning. Alternatively, if you do it **on your own**, it can count as supplementary evidence towards the following parts of the scheme.*

PC 4:   Analyse skills for employment or self-employment

PC 5:   Discuss own strengths and weaknesses in relation to skills for employment or self-employment

Range: Analyse: in terms of own skills achievement; ways to develop and improve skills

Skills: working with others, working independently, time management, decision-making, problem-solving, planning, information seeking, evaluating, communication, application of number, information technology, occupational skills

Core skills: Communication
Application of number
Information technology

Read the case study below and answer the questions which follow.

Case study

Mark decides to go ahead with his idea for opening his own office cleaning business. He made his decision after following the advice of the bank adviser to consider a number of ideas which he could get from:

- looking through *Yellow Pages* to see what types of small businesses are located in the area
- asking friends or relatives if they know of any possible gaps in the market
- making use of a leisure interest or hobby, e.g. a sports enthusiast might consider opening a sporting goods shop
- using particular skills or abilities, e.g. an accountant could open up his or her accounting practice: a management graduate could think of becoming a management consultant etc.

After Mark has made his decision he has to try to find a USP: this is a **u**nique **s**elling **p**oint which makes his business different from the other office cleaning businesses. He knows already, from looking in *Yellow Pages,* that he has at least four competitors and he therefore has to think of a way of making his business 'unique'. He can do so by:

a thinking up an eye-catching name or design for his business
b concentrating on the speed and efficiency of his service
c offering a slightly different service to anyone else
d emphasising his competitive prices
e highlighting the quality of his service
f emphasising any additional services.

Mark decides to emphasise personal service and flexibility – he will offer the services of a few hand-picked people who will come to clean the offices at whatever time the customer wants (including weekends).

He then carries out a SWOT analysis and prepares a business plan. (Look back to page 266 to remind yourself of how he should do this.)

The hardest part of the plan, Mark finds, is working out his cost. He bases his estimates on the following information:

- he intends to work from home
- he wants to employ two cleaners at first, to be paid on an hourly rate
- he needs cleaning materials and equipment
- he needs computing equipment
- he needs a van
- he needs to do some advertising.

He checks on the legal requirements he will have to satisfy.

a If he intends to give his customers credit he will have to apply for a licence under the Consumer Credit Act.
b As he intends to keep the names and addresses of all his customers on a database he will need to register under the Data Protection Act.
c He will have to take out the appropriate insurance in respect of the van and possibly also in respect of:
  - public liability – for protection against claims brought by the public who, for instance, are injured by some careless act by one of his employees
  - goods in transit – if, for example, he wants to insure against cleaning equipment being stolen from his van
d He will also have to contact the Local Authority Planning Department to see if he is entitled to work from home.
e He also checks up on his duties and responsibilities as an employer. (To remind yourself of what they are, look back to Element 2.2, page 186).

Having obtained some funding to make a start – and having informed the Inland Revenue that he is now self-employed – Mark is in a position to go ahead.

1 Decide in what ways he has had to use:
  a his communication skills – whether verbal or written
  b his application of number skills
  c his information technology skills
  d his research skills.

Present your findings in a word-processed report.

2 Mark decides that he must now:
  - advertise for and interview staff
  - advertise his services to his potential customers
  - buy or hire his equipment (including transport)
  - organise his room at home into an office.

Ask your tutor to divide you into **four groups.** Each group should undertake one of the four tasks given below and should be prepared to make a presentation of their findings, backed up with visual aids.

  a Check in your local Job Centre and in the local paper for advertisements for cleaning staff, to see what rates of pay are being offered, and then draw up a job description which should include their hours of work, rates of pay and the duties they are expected to carry out.
  b Contact **at least two** firms of printers to see what they would charge for printing 100–200 leaflets suitable for posting through letter boxes (your tutor may ask one of you to carry out that job for the full group). Compare their prices with your estimate of the cost of desk top publishing and photocopying. Draw up a draft leaflet advertising the new business.
  c Draw up a list of what type of cleaning materials and equipment are required and cost them out. (Your tutor may be able to borrow a catalogue for you – if not, you may have to visit a supermarket or other store to check on prices.)
  d Decide how the office should be organised and equipped and draw up a plan indicating the layout of the furniture. Make a list of equipment needed and its cost – both individually and as a total sum. Give **at least two** estimates from two different firms.
3 Analyse your own skills and prepare a word-processed report saying where you consider you have the skills to enable you to do what Mark did, and where you think your skills are lacking. Identify how you think these skills could be improved.

Applying for the job – and avoiding the pitfalls

If you find out about a job which you think you might like, there are two different ways of applying for it – the right way and the wrong way!

Non-assessed activity

Read the following scenario and undertake the activity which follows.

Kurt Eriksen has read in his local newspaper that a firm of office equipment suppliers is looking for a trainee office manager. He rings them and is put through to the Human Resources department, where the following conversation takes place.

Secretary Good morning, this is the Human Resources Manager's secretary. Can I help you?

Kurt Who did you say you were?

Secretary The Human Resources Manager's secretary – how can I help you?

Kurt I don't want to speak to you – it's the Human Resources Manager I want.

Secretary I'm sorry but he's not available – can I take a message?

Kurt Is there anyone more important than you to speak to?

Secretary Well who had you in mind – the Prime Minister, Madonna, Damon Hill?

Kurt How about the Office Manager?

Secretary He's busy too – what do you want?

Kurt I want a job.

Secretary Any job? Managing director, window cleaner ...?

Kurt Now don't start that again – I want the job of trainee office manager. Is it still open?

Secretary Could you hold on and I'll check for you .... (after a few minutes) Hello?

Kurt You took your time!

Secretary I'm sorry but we have a number of vacancies at the moment and I was checking through the computer records. The job is still open but the Office Manager wants all applications to be in writing and to be sent in before the end of this week. Do you want me to send you an application form?

Kurt I suppose so, but it seems a lot of trouble to go to for a job I might not get – make sure it's in the post tonight!

Kurt gives the secretary his name and address and rings off. The secretary looks at the notes she has made and then throws them in the waste paper basket. Kurt waits in vain for the application form to arrive.

Discuss with your tutor why the secretary didn't seem to like Kurt's approach. Rewrite the conversation to give Kurt a better chance of at least being given the application form! (You might also like to rewrite the secretary's replies!)

Methods of application

In most cases, when you apply for a job you will be asked either to:

■ complete an application form, sometimes with a covering letter, or
■ write a letter of application together with a curriculum vitae, i.e. a description of your qualifications and experience (see page 274).

Non-assessed activity

Discuss **with your tutor** the advantages and disadvantages of each of these. Think about:

■ the need to have specific answers to specific questions
■ the difference between a handwritten and a word-processed document
■ allowing someone to give a complete picture of what he or she can do
■ checking on spelling, punctuation, grammar and the way in which someone can compose a continuous piece of writing
■ the advantage of having the information given by each candidate displayed in the same way in the same order.

Application forms

One problem about an application form is that it is difficult to use a word processor or even a typewriter to fill it in. You may have to complete it by hand. If you do, be careful to:

■ Collect all the information you need before you start to fill in the form, otherwise you will be stopping and starting each time you want to find your examination results, the date when you left college, etc. The Record of Achievement you have been compiling during your time at school/college will help – provided you keep it up to date!

- Take a photocopy (or copies) of the form before you write anything at all.
- Practise on the photocopy to make sure that you can display all the information in the best way.
- Check that the pen you are going to use is blotch-free (and make sure it contains blue or black ink).
- Ask someone to check your copy *before* you begin to transfer over the information, especially the spelling, punctuation and grammar.
- Keep a photocopy of the completed form so that you can read it again before you attend for interview. If you have forgotten that you have said that your leisure interests include visiting art galleries, the interviewer might be a bit surprised if you suddenly change your mind and say that you spend most of your time outside college playing snooker!

Remember, however, there is a difference between presenting yourself in the best possible light and telling downright lies! You might be justified in glossing over the fact that you have taken a particular examination five times. You wouldn't be justified in saying that you had passed it first time. Most interviewers are trained to spot gaps in application forms, so come clean if you have been out of work for a time.

Did you know?

'Clangers' on an application form can include:

- your date of birth written with *this year* as the year of your birth
- completing the part which says 'for office use only' by mistake
- not realising what is meant by the term 'next of kin' and writing something silly.

Make sure you avoid *all* of these traps!

Non-assessed activity

Probably the worst part of an application you may have to complete is a small section which may say, '*Write a short paragraph in support of your application*'. In this part you are really having to sell yourself. In three or four sentences you must say why the company should employ *you*.

Assume you are applying for a job and have received an application form with a space for you to complete. Write a short paragraph saying why *you* are an ideal candidate, using the Personal Statement and Other Achievements sections in your Record of Achievement. Check your finished work with your tutor.

Letter of application

Even if you are asked to write a letter of application rather than completing an application form, a similar process should be followed. Gather together all the information you need, make sure the letter is well put together and that grammar, punctuation and spelling are correct. If you have difficulty in writing letters look at Element 4.3 for suggested ways of going about it.

In the case of a letter, *you* have to decide what to put in it. Remember that staff in the Human Resources department might be reading a large number of letters each day, so you need to make your letter brief and to the point. Normally three or four short simple paragraphs are sufficient;

- An opening paragraph says where you saw the advertisement (or how you found out about the job) and that you would like to apply for the post.
- The second paragraph gives general background information about yourself – at college and at work (where and for how long).

  At this stage you would normally refer to your attached **curriculum vitae** (see page 274). This states all the details about you – which makes life a lot simpler

- The third paragraph gives the particular reasons you have for wanting either this type of job or to work for this particular organisation – or anything you can think of to make your application a little bit different and a little bit special.
- The final paragraph says you are available for interview at any time (or says when you are *not* available for interview).

273

2 Manor Road
Wallingford
Oxon
OX3 4BR
9 April 199-

Dear Sir,

I should like to apply for the post of Sales Administrator advertised in the Evening Post on 8 April. I am in Year 12 at Woodcote High School where I am studying for a GNVQ in Intermediate Business which I will complete at the end of May. I am particularly interested in Sales and Marketing and for my optional subjects I have chosen marketing together with European studies and administration. I attach my curriculum vitae with this letter which gives full details of my educational achievements.

I would particularly like to work for your company because I believe the sportswear you manufacture is the best on the market. I have bought your trainers since they first appeared in the shops. The company also has an excellent reputation for training staff and I should like to work hard and improve my qualifications.

If called, I should be pleased to attend an interview at any time that is convenient for you.

Yours faithfully

Ashe Wilson

Ashe Wilson

Figure 2.78 A letter of application

Curriculum vitae

A curriculum vitae is best prepared on a word processor so that you can keep it on disk, update it whenever you wish and send out an original (not a copy) each time you apply for a job. Normally you would include the following information.

Personal details

- name, title and address
- telephone number
- date of birth.

Educational details

- school(s) attended (not primary) and dates
- GCSE results
- other awards at school/positions of responsibility held, etc.
- further education details – college, dates and course
- examinations/awards taken or being taken and results, if known
- any other details, e.g. member of student union or committee
- work experience details.

Employment details

- current job held if working (a brief description of duties)
- previous jobs and areas of responsibility (if applicable)
- details of any part-time or Saturday jobs you have done if you are a full-time student.

Other useful information

- details of any hobbies, interests or sports
- details of any organisations to which you belong
- any other useful information, e.g. driving licence.

Referees

It is usual to give two names (but ask permission first). If you don't want your present employers to know that you are applying for other jobs you can say that you don't want them to be contacted until you have been offered the job.

Did you know?

If you are about to leave school or college, one of your tutors would make a suitable referee – but remember it is always courteous to **ask first,** not to let your tutor to find out when he or she receives a formal request from the company!

CURRICULUM VITAE

Name: Mr Ashe Wilson
Address 2 Manor Road
Wallingford
Oxon OX3 4BR
Telephone: 01491 87263
Date of birth: 23.10.1978

Education: Woodcote High School Sept 1990–May 1996
GCSE Passes: English (B)
Maths (D)
Business Studies (C)
Science (D)
Physical Education (A)
History (F)

I have passed all my external tests for my GNVQ Intermediate in Business and expect to achieve a merit award.

Employment Details: I have worked regularly at our local supermarket for the last 2 years. At first I just stacked shelves but for the last 12 months I have checked in deliveries on Friday evenings and monitored stock levels: on Saturdays I work at the checkout.

Hobbies: I have played for the School XI football team for the last 2 years and have played in the County Under-18 team this year. I have run 2 half marathons in the last year coming 10th in the Youth Section of the Tidmarsh one in March.

I also enjoy reading science fiction and going to the cinema.

Referees:

Mr J Hutton
Head of Business Studies
Woodcote School
Woodcote Hill
Oxon RG8 3XP

Ms A Sikorski
General Manager
Waitrose Limited
Benson
Oxon OX2 8DT

Figure 2.79 A curriculum vitae

Non-assessed activity

From the example given in Figure 2.79, draft out a CV for yourself and check it with your tutor before inputting it to a word processor.

The interview

No matter how confident you are, you aren't likely to look forward to an interview – very few people do. It is annoying – but a fact of life – that some people are naturally very good at interviews, even though they might not be quite as good at doing the job. Unless you are one of these people, take comfort from the fact that:

- most interviewers are trained to ask the right questions and to assess the personality and ability of each candidate
- you can *improve* your own interviewing skills.

The main rule is to be prepared. Even if you are noted for your witty, off-the-cuff remarks at college, you might not be able to use that approach so easily when the interviewers ask you to give two good reasons why they should offer you the job. Nor is it a good idea to arrive 30 seconds before (or worse, 30 seconds after) the stated time of interview, because you have had to run all the way from the car park or bus stop. It goes without saying that you will find out beforehand as much information as possible about what the firm actually does.

Did you know?

You shouldn't forget to take your Record of Achievement with you to the interview. Not only will it tell the interviewer something about you, but it can be used as the focus of several questions. This will mean you will be asked about things you know and have done, which will help you relax at the start of an interview when you are at your most nervous.

Non-assessed activity

1 Discuss with your tutor how you would go about finding information on an organisation in your area.
2 Ask your tutor for the name of a well-known company in the area and then find out as much as you can about it. Prepare **two** questions you could sensibly ask at an interview, based on your research, and check these with your tutor.

275

Ten golden rules for the interview

1 Make sure you know where the firm is situated and the best way of getting there – have a trial run if necessary.

2 Check on your appearance – what goes down well at the local disco might not impress an interviewer. Wear what you think you would be expected to wear if you had been offered the job and were actually working in the firm. It may be dreaded advice, but it is a good idea to ask your parents what they think. Despite your views of their fashion sense, the chances are that the interviewer will be nearer their age than yours, and hold similar opinions!

3 Make sure you know the interviewer's name. Ask him or her to repeat it if you haven't heard it the first time. Don't snigger if it's a name like Shufflebotham or Smellie!

4 *Smile* when you are first introduced and then follow the interviewer's lead. Sit down when asked, shake hands if the interviewer wants you to do so. Remain **pleasant** and try to look interested and enthusiastic. Look at the interviewer, not at the floor.

5 Expect to be nervous at the beginning of the interview. The interviewer will take this into account and should try to put you at your ease. If not, that's a sign of a poor interviewer and you just have to cope.

6 Try to answer each question as fully as possible. Most interviewers will help you by asking questions which require more than a 'yes' or 'no' answer. If they do not, you have to try to find a way round the problem. If, for instance, the interviewer asks you whether you have enjoyed being at college, don't just answer 'yes' or 'no'. Try something like, 'Yes, I have – I didn't realise that computer studies were so interesting. I've got a PC at home now … .' The interviewer should be able to pick up that lead and that will give you the opportunity of talking about something you're good at.

7 If you don't know the answer to a question, say so. Don't bluster.

8 At the end of the interview the interviewer may ask you whether you have any questions. If your mind goes blank at this point, don't worry, but it may be as well if you have a list of possible questions at the back of your mind in case you are asked. It is an even better idea to have it written down, so you can't forget your questions.

9 When the interviewer indicates that the interview is over, thank him or her and remember to gather up all your belongings before you leave the room.

10 If you are offered the job there and then, accept it, if it is what you want. If you are not sure, however, ask for a day in which to think it over. You can always say that you would like to have a word with your parents, your girlfriend or boyfriend or your tutor. You take the risk that the job will be offered to someone else, but that's better than accepting a job you are unhappy about, or accepting a job and going back on your word at a later stage. You never know when another job will come up with the same company, and you don't want to spoil your chances of applying for that one.

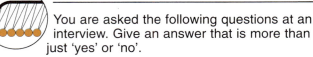

Non-assessed activity

You are asked the following questions at an interview. Give an answer that is more than just 'yes' or 'no'.

- Have you had any part-time jobs since you left school?
- Did you like your course at college?
- Do you like working with people?
- Are you good at figures?
- I see that you like swimming. Are you interested in all sports?
- Have you a full driving licence?

Did you know?

It's sometimes useful to try to 'second guess' your interviewer and to try to think how they are judging you. Most interviewers have a checklist that they use to judge whether or not someone is suitable for a particular job. Most lists include:

- your appearance – the way you dress and the way you speak
- your qualifications and previous experience – whether you have actually done what you claim on the application form, or can explain some points in more detail
- your general intelligence – do you answer the questions correctly, do you understand what is being said, can you follow an argument, etc.
- any special skills – are you bilingual, etc.
- your personality – are you friendly or quiet, confident or nervous, quick or slow on the uptake etc.
- your background – where do you live, how do you propose to get to work, have you a car, are you 'mobile', i.e. able to work in all parts of the country.

Non-assessed activity

Don't attempt this exercise if you know that afterwards you won't be on speaking terms with your partner. It's not worth it. However, if you think you can both cope with and give *positive* feedback about your skills as an interviewee, then:

- find a partner
- look in the local newspaper for two suitable job vacancies
- get together to discuss the possible questions to ask
- interview each other for the job advertised
- assess each other using the checklist given above
- give feedback, but don't let it develop into a fist fight!

Where possible ask your tutor to observe what you are doing. He or she may be able to give you some additional feedback.

Non-assessed activity

Your best friend, Nicki, just can't seem to get a job. She is getting a bit fed up so you suggest that you try out the exercise given above and that you give her a mock interview. You look in the local newspaper and spot the following advertisement.

CLERICAL ASSISTANT

Clerical assistant required for the sales department of a small engineering firm. Candidates should be able to use a keyboard and input information at about 50 wpm. They should also have a sound knowledge of English and be able to cope with basic business calculations. A pleasant personality is essential as is the ability to use initiative. A good telephone manner is also desirable.

You prepare a list of questions and decide to record the interview on cassette so that you can play it back if necessary. After the interview you go home, replay the cassette and have to decide how you are going to break the bad news to her. A transcript of the interview is given below. Write down what you will say to Nicki about where you think she is going wrong. Discuss your answers with the rest of the group.

Nicki I've come about the job you advertised.
You Let me go through your application form for some details. Why did you apply for this job?

Nicki I were out of work.
You Anything which appealed to you about it?
Nicki (shrugs) Nothing special.
You You've just left college haven't you? What did you like best about college life?
Nicki (long pause)
You You've done quite a bit of work with computers haven't you? How did you get on?
Nicki Well I didn't like the teacher for a start. If it hadn't been for him I'd have done all right. He has favourites you know – and I wasn't one of them.
You Can we get down to hard facts – what examinations did you pass?
Nicki Well I took the test for the CLAIT certificate.
You Did you pass?
Nicki No, but I'm very good on a computer really. I just panic when I have to have a test.
You What about English?
Nicki What about it?
You Did you like it?
Nicki Not much! I did English at school. I don't know why we had to waste our time at college. It were called communications anyway.
You What does that mean exactly?
Nicki I never found out.
You Have you passed any examinations in it?
Nicki No.
You Have you any business qualifications at all?
Nicki No.
You Shall I tell you a bit about the job?
Nicki (leans back in the chair) If you like.
You You'll be expected to do a number of clerical duties – answering the telephone, dealing with customers, keeping the petty cash, using the electronic filing system. How do you feel about that sort of work?
Nicki It's a job I suppose.
You Are you used to speaking on the telephone?
Nicki Never off it at home.
You No, that's not quite what I meant. Did you learn telephone techniques at college?
Nicki They never taught us anything there – it were a right waste of time.
You I don't think there's much point in going any further. You don't seem to know too much about this job do you?
Nicki I've read the ad.
You Have you any questions to ask me?
Nicki (pause) How much do I get?
You (passing her a paper) Here are the details.
Nicki Is that all?

You Are there any other questions?

Nicki No.

You Thank you very much. I think that's it for the moment.

Nicki Have I got the job then?

You don't give any reply – you're speechless.

Evidence assignment

At this point your tutor may wish you to start or continue work on the project which will prove to your verifier that you understand this section of the element. If so, turn to page 278. If you have already started work on the project you may be up to Section 3. Sections 3 and 4 cover the last two evidence indicators for this element. Make sure that you check with your tutor exactly what you have to do.

Revision test

True or false?

1 If you work for an employment agency you will be an employee of that agency.
2 The Prince's Youth Business Trust is only open to adults.
3 Television is useless as a source of reference if you want to find out about jobs.
4 If you pay a sum of money for a licence to run a particular business it is known as a franchise.
5 It is more important for an employee than a self-employed worker to be able to work independently.

Fill in the blanks

6 Some self-employed people such as solicitors or accountants work together in a _____ .
7 If you have a good idea for starting up a new business or improving an existing one you can apply for funding under an _____ scheme.
8 If anyone applies to a bank or other source for funding to start up a business they may be asked to prepare a _____ _____ .
9 In order not to waste your time at work, you should be aware of the importance of _____ _____ .
10 If you work for no pay you are said to be undertaking _____ work.

Short answer questions

11 Give **three** sources of funding for anyone wishing to start up their own business.
12 Name **four** sources of reference for people looking for employment.
13 Name **two** sources of reference for people looking for self employment.
14 Name **one** charitable organisation offering job opportunities abroad.
15 List **four** personal skills self-employed workers need to have.

Write a short paragraph to show you clearly understand each of the following terms

16 Occupational skills
17 International job opportunities
18 Working holidays
19 TECs
20 Job Centres

Evidence indicator project

Unit 2 Element 2.4

This project has been designed to cover the four evidence Indicators related to Element 2.4. It is divided into four sections.

Performance criteria: 1–5

Core skills: Communication, Application of number, Information technology

Section 1

Ask **three** people – they could be friends or relatives – who are in different types of employment, if you can interview them. Before you start the interview make sure that you prepare a list of questions including:

■ how the people interviewed came to be in their current employment – you might want to ask them about their previous jobs

■ what their skills and qualifications are, both personal and occupational

■ how they use those skills in their present jobs.

Using your word processor, prepare a summary of your findings (not forgetting to include the name of each person interviewed).

Make sure you complete this section of the project by the deadline given to you by your tutor.

Section 2

Collect together examples of **three** local, national and international employment or self-employment opportunities. You can find out the information from:

■ job advertisements in both local and national newspapers

■ articles in newspapers, magazines or journals

■ information obtained from Careers Offices or Job Centres

On your word processor prepare a summary of your findings, giving details of where you found the information and also any other relevant information. If you select a job opportunity in an EU country, for instance, you may want to give some information about employment opportunities in the EU. If you choose a local job opportunity you may be able to give some additional information about the firm concerned. You might also want to comment about the qualifications and skills asked for.

Make sure you complete this section of the project by the deadline given to you by your tutor.

Section 3

Draw up a chart showing:

a the skills needed for employment and self-employment

b an analysis of what you have achieved and how you intend to improve and develop your skills.

You may, for instance, identify a personal skill that you have, such as verbal communication. You may want to develop that skill, however, by taking a major part in any presentations which are going to be made. On the other hand, you may identify an occupational skill such as word processing and be able to say how you intend to become even more proficient.

Make sure you complete this section of the project by the deadline given to you by your tutor.

Section 4

Prepare an analysis of your strengths and weaknesses in relation to your skills for employment or self-employment, and arrange a time to discuss this with your tutor. If you have completed the relevant activities between pages 258 and 270 you will already have a basis for this. Check with your tutors whether they intend to hold a group discussion in which you summarise your analysis and deal with questions from the rest of the group, or whether they prefer to speak to you on an individual basis. After the discussion, summarise when it took place, who was involved and what was said.

Make sure you complete this section of the project by the deadline given to you by your tutor.

Final stage

Make a front cover for your project which gives your name, the date and the title: **Preparation for Employment or Self-Employment.**

Explain the importance of consumers and customers

This element starts by examining the way in which consumers affect the supply and sales of different products. It then goes on to look at the characteristics of consumers and how these affect buying habits. Past trends and possible future trends of consumer behaviour are discussed as well as causes of change. Finally, the importance of customers to business organisations is examined. After studying this element you should be able to:

1   describe the *effect of consumers* on sales of goods and services

2   identify and explain the *buying habits of consumers* with different *characteristics*

3   identify *trends in consumer demand*

4   produce graphics to illustrate the trends

5   explain *causes of change in consumer demand* for consumer goods and services

6   explain and give examples of the *importance of customers* to business organisations.

The effect of consumers on sales

Consumers of goods and services include individuals, business organisations and the Government. Throughout Britain, a huge number of goods and services are purchased by consumers every day. However, the type of goods and services on which money is spent, and the frequency with which they are bought, varies considerably.

Manufacturers and suppliers spend millions of pounds advertising and promoting their products, employing sales staff and trying to influence the buying behaviour of consumers to increase sales. They will try to encourage consumers to become regular customers by providing a good and reliable service. However, the power of producers is limited. They may try to tempt people to buy with lower prices, special offers and persuasive advertising, but if consumers are not interested in the product, or still cannot afford it, it will not sell. Equally, if a product suddenly becomes very fashionable or desirable, producers may struggle to make enough goods to meet a sudden surge in demand, and there will be a shortage. This may be overcome by raising the price, so that fewer people can afford to purchase the goods.

It can be said, therefore, that the buying behaviour of consumers influences:

■   the type of goods and services which are produced
■   the quantity which are produced and
■   the price at which they are sold.

Creating demand – weak and strong

The ability of consumers to create demand depends on:

■   their buying power
■   the type of supplier from whom they are buying.

Buying power

Demand for goods is measured by the sales, or potential sales, for particular goods and services. If sales increase and are sustained over a period of time, and the consumers who are buying the goods are those who have money to spend, demand is **strong.** If demand fluctuates and total sales potential is only low, demand may be **weak.**

Not all consumers have the same power in the marketplace. The ability of consumers to create demand is closely linked to the amount of money they have to spend – not individually, but as a group.

Because most organisations are in business to make a profit (see Element 1.1) they will always try to provide those goods and services which will make the highest profit. This means they will produce the items required by the people who have the most money to spend, and this may actually **disadvantage** those who have very little to spend.

Producers will concentrate on providing goods and services for those who can afford to buy them. These are people who can turn their plans into reality – which is why actual demand (as opposed to planned demand) is often called **realised demand**.

This is why Harrods stock cuddly toys for children which sell for nearly £2000, and overcoats for dogs at nearly £50. It is also the reason why there are dozens of luxury holidays to exotic destinations on sale at your local travel agent and very few holidays especially designed for lower income groups such as lone parents and their children. Lone parents are unlikely to have much money to spend on luxury items such as holidays, so although many may wish to go on holiday, few have the ability to do so. Even if they do go, once on holiday they are unlikely to have a large amount of money to spend. And the fact there is only one adult means that any hotel would lose additional income from the bars, restaurants and other areas. So the market power of lone parents is weak and their potential to create realised demand is low. Hotels and tour companies prefer to concentrate on providing holidays for people with more money to spend.

Figure 3.1 A luxury lapdog

The type of supplier

Suppliers which operate in a competitive market *must* react to consumer demand if they are to stay in business. If holidays do not sell well in the first few months of the year, tour operators will reduce their prices and try to tempt people with bargains. If a local shop does not stock the goods people wish to buy it will quickly go out of business – so it must react quickly to consumer demand.

However, if there are only a few suppliers of an essential product (e.g. petrol), there is less need for the organisation to react quickly to pressure from consumers, because there is nowhere else for them to go! Banks have been criticised for not reacting promptly to what their customers want, or giving accurate information about their services. According to reports from the Consumers' Association and Manchester Business School, the big four banks offer the worst service, and only Lloyds was classed as 'average'. As a group banks can afford to be less responsive because, if people want to open a bank account, they have to accept the services which are on offer.

Did you know?

A recent report has suggested that the population of Britain can be divided into three sectors.

- The **privileged** are those whose market power has increased since 1979. They are in secure jobs or have been self-employed for over two years. They represent 40 per cent of the consumer market.
- The **marginalised** or **insecure** are those who are in temporary employment, low-paid part-time employment or unprotected full-time jobs. They account for 30 per cent of the market.
- The last category are the **disadvantaged.** This sector includes those who are out of work – whether or not they are receiving benefits. This 30 per cent of the population have little money to spend even on essential items, let alone luxuries.

Non-assessed activity

1 **As a class**, list 20 products which you regularly see on sale in shops and stores which can only be bought by people on high incomes.

2 Examine the following statements.
   - 'People have the right to decide how to spend their own money.'
   - 'It is immoral that some people are spending £50 on coats for their dogs in Harrods when other people are sleeping in doorways.'

With which statement do you agree more? Why? **As a group**, debate this and discuss your findings with your tutor.

3 Read page 66 in Element 1.2, where the differences between monopoly, oligopoly and competitive organisations are discussed. Discuss with your tutor

how these terms link with the type of suppliers mentioned above.

Causing changes in demand

Consumer demand can change in two main ways.

1 It can be greater or lesser than expected.
2 It may switch from one product to another as consumers are influenced by fashion and advertising.

Increases and decreases in demand

This topic is covered in detail in Element 1.2. In this element you should realise why demand increases and decreases. Demand is influenced by:

- unemployment rates
- the cost of borrowing money (i.e. interest rates)
- disposable income (the amount of money left to spend after paying essential bills)
- the price of goods
- consumers' confidence to spend.

Obviously if unemployment is high, a large number of people have less money to spend. If interest rates are high, anyone who has borrowed money or who has a mortgage has to allow for an increase in interest payments. Both these factors will affect the amount of money people have to spend, i.e. their **disposable income**.

From Element 1.2, it is clear that the price of goods is critical to demand. The law of demand states that with normal goods, the lower the price, the greater the quantity demanded. The final factor which affects demand is consumer confidence.

Confidence to spend is linked to people's expectations of the future. If they are in a secure job, earn a good salary and have few worries, they may plan to spend quite a high proportion of their income satisfying their needs. Conversely, if they are worried about being made redundant or the price of essential services (e.g. electricity) rising, they are likely to reduce their spending and save their money. In this case the demand for all goods and services across the economy will fall. (Consumer confidence is dealt with again on page 303.)

Changes in demand

This is discussed in detail on pages 302–304. Organisations are not in business to produce goods or services for which demand is low. If they did so they would not make a profit and would rapidly go out of business.

If a large number of consumers change their behaviour, total demand for a product will be affected – sometimes temporarily and sometimes permanently. Recent examples include:

- the closure of many bowling alleys because young people prefer disco dancing
- a fall in video rentals as cinema attendances increase and more people buy films on impulse from supermarkets
- a fall in the demand for sun beds as more people worry about the effects of tanning and turn to fake tanning creams instead.

Trends in consumer demand and the reasons for these are discussed in more detail on pages 296 and 305.

Did you know?

If demand rises sharply and people's confidence to spend is high, this is called a **consumer boom.** If the opposite occurs it is called a **slump.**

The danger with a slump is that firms who are not selling their goods will reduce the number of goods they produce and make some of their workers redundant. This will reduce more people's spending power and increase their worries about the future. They will therefore spend even less. Even more firms will reduce production and so on. When this happens over a period of time the economy is said to be in a **recession.**

Non-assessed activity

1 As a class, discuss what actions you think the government could take to increase consumer demand if there is a recession.
2 Investigate the state of the economy at the time you are studying this book by reading newspaper headlines, and discuss your findings with your tutor.

Stimulating supply of goods and services to meet demand

The collective decisions of consumers, in terms of the goods and services they wish to buy, affect demand and the decisions of suppliers to produce goods. The Government, rather than individuals, is the largest **potential** consumer of goods and services and therefore has considerable market power. Each year it plans its spending priorities and publishes them in the November budget (see page 30, Element 1.1). If the Government plans to reduce spending on large projects (e.g. motorway, school or hospital building), demand will fall. If the Government plans to increase spending, demand will increase.

If this year the Government decided to increase the amount of money spent on building new hospitals, this would have several results.

- More construction workers would be employed building the hospitals. They would earn wages which would increase their ability to buy.
- Suppliers of building materials, e.g. bricks, cement, window panes and wood would all increase supplies of their products.
- Suppliers of hospital fittings and fixtures would also increase their supplies, e.g. hospital beds, operating tables, bedside tables etc.
- Suppliers of consumables would produce more bed linen, bandages, crutches, etc.
- The suppliers of all these items may employ additional workers to meet the surge in demand.
- More people would decide to train to be nurses and doctors because employment prospects would have improved.

Figure 3.2 Building the economy

One decision to increase demand can have a spin-off effect in many different directions. The decision can benefit most people and disadvantage few, if any. Unfortunately not all decisions about demand have that effect.

- Because most people prefer to watch quiz shows, soaps and popular films on television, there has been a decline in the number of films made for minority interest groups.
- Because many consumers prefer to buy pre-wrapped goods – often in large quantities – there has been a decline in the number of items which can be bought singly. A good example is batteries. This can disadvantage old people or those who live alone, who perhaps only want to buy a small quantity.
- Because young people like playing on arcade machines, amusement arcades may be opened near schools and colleges regardless of the fact that this may encourage truancy.

Figure 3.3 These games aren't on the curriculum!

This is one disadvantage of the market economy – the fact that goods and services will be provided purely with the profit motive in mind. For that reason the Government itself provides goods and services which are essential for social reasons (e.g. education and health) and regulates the provision of some goods and services which could be harmful if generally available, e.g. cigarettes, alcohol and films which show excessive violence.

Non-assessed activity

Discuss **with your tutor** the factors which influence Government demand for goods and services. (Refer to Element 1.1, pages 30 and 31, for information on how the Government raises money and spends its money.)

Optional evidence assignment

*This activity can be carried out verbally in class **in a group** as a non-assessed activity to consolidate learning. Alternatively, if you do it **on your own**, it can count as supplementary evidence towards the following parts of the scheme.*

PC 1: Describe the effect of consumers on sales of goods and services

PC 3: Identify trends in consumer demand

PC 4: Produce graphics to illustrate the trends

Range: Effect of consumers: create demand (weak, strong), cause changes in demand, stimulate supply of goods and services to meet demand

Trends in consumer demand: past (long-term), future (long-term), increasing consumer demand

Core skills: Communication, Information technology, Application of number

Read the article below and then answer the questions which follow.

'In two separate reports, one produced by the Food Commission and another produced by the Institute for Public Policy Research (IPPR), supermarkets have been accused of promoting fatty junk foods, such as burgers, chips, crisps and biscuits instead of healthier fruits and vegetables. This is because the cheaper discounted goods are often those which are the least nutritious when compared with the ideal diet recommended in the Department of Health's National Food Guide. In addition, low prices on these goods are offset by higher prices on other items – including fresh fruit and vegetables. Therefore those customers who have the least money to spend will struggle to be able to afford a good diet.

'Supermarkets have objected, saying they simply "give customers what they want" and that this has been a key feature of their success. Larger stores now offer more than 17 000 different products – many from all over the world. In addition, because they compete with each other they have to sell goods cheaply – hence their "price wars" which benefit all customers.

'The writers of the IPPR report, entitled "Off Our Trolleys", claim that supermarkets have become too powerful. So many small shops have closed, because they couldn't compete with the cut-price policies of supermarkets, that many customers today have nowhere else to shop. Two thirds of the food

sales in a town are likely to be at the big supermarkets – Sainsbury, Safeway, Tesco or Kwik Save. Therefore customers – especially those who are poor – have little choice but to accept what they are given.'

1 Supermarkets argue that they offer a large range of goods and give customers what they want.
   a In what way do the reports claim that this variety is only on offer to those with high buying power?
   b In which way do the writers think supermarkets discriminate against those who have less money to spend?

2 Explain why consumers with low buying power have less effect on the sales of goods and services than those with high buying power.

3 Visit a large supermarket in your area and obtain examples of the way in which the supply of goods has changed because of increasing consumer demand for:
   a foreign food and exotic dishes
   b vegetarian food
   c ready prepared meals
   d 'one-stop shopping'.

4 Look at the current trend in unemployment below. If this trend continues, what will be the effect on the total demand for goods and services and why?

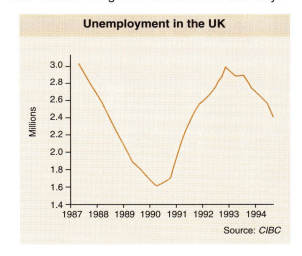

Unemployment in the UK

Source: *CIBC*

Figure 3.4 Trends in unemployment

5 The growth in UK superstores is shown on the chart on page 286.
   a Calculate the percentage growth in the number of superstores:
      i from 1980 to 1994
      ii from 1993 to 1994.
   b Assume that the trend will continue at the same

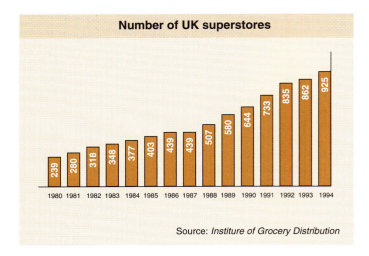

Number of UK superstores

Year	Number
1980	239
1981	280
1982	318
1983	348
1984	377
1985	403
1986	439
1987	439
1988	507
1989	580
1990	644
1991	733
1992	835
1993	862
1994	925

Source: *Institure of Grocery Distribution*

Figure 3.5 Growth of superstores

rate as in (ii) above, and calculate how many UK superstores there will be in the year 2000. You may find this easier to do if you use a spreadsheet.

c Preferably using a computer, show this trend graphically by extending the bar chart to the year 2000.

d Do you think that the growth of supermarkets will continue at the rate you have projected? Give reasons for your views.

Evidence assignment

At this point your tutor may wish you to start work on the project which will prove to your verifiers that you understand this section of the element. If so, turn to page 310 and do Section 1 of the project. This covers the first Evidence Indicator for this element.

The buying habits of consumers with different characteristics

Every organisation needs to know which consumers buy their product or service (and which do not, and why not). We are *all* consumers, as everyone buys goods or services or receives them 'free' from the Government (e.g. library services or police protection). People in employment pay for these 'free' services through taxation. However, we are only customers if we pay a supplier for a specific product or service. Knowing which consumers are their customers – and how to increase the number of

customers – is an important goal for most organisations.

Organisations also need to be able to find out when consumers are changing their buying habits – and why – so they can adapt their product (or make new ones) to cope with changing demand. Studies are usually undertaken by the Marketing department, and special market research agencies may be employed (see elements 1.2 and 2.1). Computer databases are also extensively used for targeting potential customers according to their characteristics. Specialist agencies record details of people including their name, age, income, number of children, assets and possessions and provide address lists to companies, on request, which highlight relevant factors. For instance, a company selling cheap motor insurance for the over-50s would not want to send mailshots to people in their 30s!

Non-assessed activity

A novel form of targeting was carried out by Porsche – the luxury sports car firm. One year it stopped advertising altogether and sent a glossy video pack on its new £70 000 car to 1000 image-conscious top earners in the country.

1 Why do you think Porsche changed its approach?
2 How would you identify a typical Porsche driver in terms of:
   ■ age
   ■ gender
   ■ income
   ■ taste
   ■ lifestyle?

As a group, discuss this and write down your ideas.

Figure 3.6 Who drives a Porsche?

The buying habits of consumers

We all have different buying habits, because the way we prefer to lead our lives and the money we have to spend on goods and services differs from one person to another. People on high incomes do not necessarily spend a lot of money – some may prefer to invest it. The couple you see in a caravan may, therefore, be millionaires – but this is rare. People on high incomes are *more likely* to buy luxury goods – which is why organisations selling this type of product will aim their advertising at the people who can afford it.

Our buying habits vary in:

- the types of goods and services we buy
- our level of buying
- our frequency of buying.

These habits are often broadly predictable when they are linked to individual characteristics of consumers such as age, gender, where they live and their lifestyle.

The type of goods and service we buy

The fact that we differ in our buying habits is the main reason why such a wide variety of goods and

Classification/grade	Occupation	Percentage of population
A	Upper/upper middle class	Top managers and professionals	4%
B	Middle class	Senior managers, professionals and administrators	19.5%
C1	Lower middle class	Supervisors, junior managers and clerical staff	21%
C2	Skilled working class	Skilled manual workers	30.5%
D	Working class	Semi-skilled and unskilled manual workers	17%
E	Lowest level of subsistence	State pensioners, disabled, casual workers and unemployed	8%

Figure 3.7 UK classification of social class

services is offered for sale. You only have to visit a large shopping mall or supermarket with an older member of your family and ask him or her how the range compares with goods on offer 30 years ago, to find there is a considerable difference!

Organisations often refer to the UK classification of social class to give them an indication of their potential customers. This ranks people according to their occupations and gives quite a reliable guide to the relationship between a person's job and their income. It also gives an indication of different patterns of buying. For instance, those in the top income groups are more likely to pay for private health insurance, private education and expensive cars. Those in the lower income groups are likely to have a greater need for other items, from public transport to cut-price groceries. This information is used by the Marketing departments of organisations to help them decide what to produce and even where to locate their sales outlets. Aldi and Netto, for example, the cut-price supermarkets, always open shops in areas with greater numbers of low-income households, as these people are more likely to be their customers.

Level of buying

Our level of buying relates to our **propensity to spend**. We all have some friends who spend every penny they earn immediately they receive it, and others who (almost magically) always have something left at the end of the month! Investment companies and banks and building societies which offer savings accounts try to encourage us to **save** our money. Producers of consumable and durable goods try to encourage us to **spend** as much as possible – and even offer cheap loans to encourage us to spend more than we can really afford.

Interestingly, lower income groups usually have a higher propensity to spend than high income groups. This is because they need to spend virtually all their money on essentials so there is very little left over to save. For that reason, investment companies will usually target high income groups when they are trying to increase their customers.

Frequency of buying

Some goods and services, such as bread, potatoes and milk, are bought regularly by virtually everyone because they are essential items. Others, such as business computers or vegetarian food, are bought regularly only by certain types of consumers. Some items, such as a new car or house, are only purchased very infrequently.

To complicate matters even further, some goods are seasonal whilst others are in demand all year round. Obvious seasonal goods include Easter eggs, fireworks and Christmas crackers. There is a complete marketing cycle which takes place throughout the year and which is easy to spot in supermarkets and card shops. You will all have heard people groaning that no sooner is Christmas over than shops are full of Easter eggs, and then barbecues and sun-tan lotion, and then – about the end of September – Christmas goods start appearing again.

Finally, there are people who are shopaholics and those who detest shopping. Shopaholics get their kicks out of going shopping – and usually buy something. They prefer to buy daily rather than to stock up for a fortnight. They are easily tempted by tantalising displays of goods and may run up large debts with credit card companies through buying goods they don't even need. At the opposite extreme are those who detest shopping – the queues, the hordes of people and the rush and bustle. They may either be quite miserly and only buy when they really need it, or they may prefer to buy from a mail order catalogue in the comfort of their own home.

Figure 3.8 Shopaholic!

Did you know?

Our buying habits can change for a variety of reasons. Think of some of the factors which could affect your buying habits before you move on to the next section!

Non-assessed activity

1 a You have talked to six people and asked what they do for a living. The answers are below. List them in order of income, putting the one you think would earn the most first.

- head teacher
- pensioner
- police sergeant
- labourer
- plumber
- hospital consultant

b Each of them buys one of the following daily newspapers. Which one do you think each buys? If you are not familiar with the content of the papers then, as a group, collect a 'set' to help you.

- *The Times*
- *The Daily Mirror*
- *The Guardian*
- *The Daily Express*
- *The Sun*
- *The Daily Mail*

Note: There is no absolute answer to this question – only a *probable* answer. Our most probable answer is given on page 309.

2 Assume you work for a travel agent. You have the following brochures to send to potential customers. Which classification (see Figure 3.7) would you choose for each brochure?

- A caravanning holiday in Wales
- An inclusive package holiday to Ibiza
- Self-catering holidays in French villas
- Two week fly-drive holidays to the USA
- World cruises on the QE2
- Hotels and boarding houses in Blackpool

Note: Again there is no definite answer – an unemployed teenager might like the idea of going to Ibiza for two weeks, but is unlikely to be able to afford it! You are *likely*, therefore, to be more successful if you target your brochures according to income.

3 Greeting card manufacturers make certain standard cards which are good sellers all year. They then increase demand for their product by producing cards to celebrate minor occasions which occur throughout the year. Many people allege that

Father's Day was the invention of greeting card manufacturers who had a lull in sales in June!

a Name **three** types of cards which are bought all year round.

b Identify **four** other types of cards which celebrate specific occasions during the year.

Characteristics of consumers

For the answer to the question on page 286 you may have said that the average Porsche driver is male, in his 30s, has a taste for luxury and fast cars and a fairly flashy lifestyle, e.g. a well-paid job and an active social life. Therefore Porsche marketing will be targeted at this group. There would seem to be little point in sending the information to a 76-year-old female pensioner – although there are exceptions to every rule!

Think about the goods which are bought by you and your family. The chances are that you don't buy the same type of goods as your parents, neither do you (or they) buy the same goods as your grandparents. If you have brothers or sisters, again, the type of goods each of you buys will vary. This is because the type of goods we buy is influenced by **demographic differences**, such as our age and gender (i.e. whether we are male or female). However, our lifestyle also influences our decisions about what to buy. People keen on health and fitness or who have particular hobbies will buy goods and services to reflect their interests and preferences.

Some goods have a specific market (e.g. sports cars, caravans, sports equipment). Others, which may be basic necessities such as food and clothing, are bought by nearly everyone. Consumer characteristics are still important here, however, as they affect buying habits. **Brand names** may be promoted by an organisation to try to sub-divide the market. In this case, the characteristics of people who buy the individual brands are often different.

 Did you know?

The population of Britain is getting older. In the early 1950s there were:

- 5.6 million people over 65
- 1.6 million people over 75
- 234 000 people over 85.

By the 1990s this had risen to:

- 9 million people over 65
- 4 million people over 75
- 892 000 people over 85.

The same pattern is true for all European countries, mainly because of improvements in diet and health care, which mean that people can expect to live longer.

 Did you know?

It is forecast that in Europe, whereas just under a fifth of its population are already 60 plus, this will rise to over a third by 2020.

A book called *A Social Portrait of Europe* gives facts and statistics on consumer behaviour throughout Europe. The version which concentrates on the UK is called *Social Trends*. There is probably a copy of this in your library.

Age

Our age often determines the type of products we buy. In any shopping centre you will see different age-groups in different types of shops – record and computer games shops will have more young customers, as will fashion boutiques and chain stores such as Next. Marks & Spencer will attract older customers and so will men's tailors and exclusive dress shops. The range of goods carried by these retail stores and the decor of the shops are likely to be influenced by the age of the customers they expect to serve – and will be quite different from the atmosphere in Next or River Island.

Manufacturers are also influenced by age groups and make different versions of the same type of product for different age groups. A good example of this is in the market for toiletry products. If you visit Boots, you will see different age groups buying different types of toiletry products. Mothers will buy baby powder for infants and Matey bubble bath for young children. You may buy hair gel or fixing spray. All your family may use shower gel – yet your grandparents might think that this is an extravagance, and simply buy soap.

Remember that as people grow older their buying habits change. This may be because they:

- are more set in their ways
- are less mobile
- have less money to spend after retirement. This is especially true if people are totally dependent on the state old age pension.

289

Non-assessed activity

1 Walk around your own shopping centre. List **six** retail outlets which are regularly used by young people and **six** which are used by older people. State the goods which are sold in each case. Give **one** example, in each case, of how this has affected the style and decor of the shop.

2 A friend of yours, Matthew Baker, who lives some distance away, belongs to a family in which there are two young children under ten, two teenagers, parents in their early 40s and an elderly grandparent in his 60s. They are visiting your area on a shopping trip and have asked you to suggest where they could have something to eat around mid-day. Where would you suggest if:

 a you wanted to please the young children
 b you wanted to please the teenagers
 c you wanted to suggest somewhere which would appeal to the parents
 d you had the grandfather in mind?

Give a reason for each of your suggestions.

Did you know?

Producers of goods for particular age groups are very interested in population trends because this gives them an idea of future demand for their products. Mothercare, for instance, will want to know whether the birth rate is rising or falling and whether more boy babies than girl babies are being born.

Other producers will be more interested in the figures relating to elderly people, i.e. suppliers of products and services targeted at older people, e.g. Saga holidays, lower car insurance premiums for the over 50s, those who operate old people's homes and sheltered accommodation.

Gender

People are living longer. However, the figures for males and females, in terms of life expectancy, are different. A baby boy, born in 1986, can expect to live until he is 71 years and 9 months old. A baby girl can be expected to reach 77 years and 6 months. For this reason, more products and services aimed at elderly people are likely to be bought or used by women than men.

Whilst there would appear to be some very obvious differences between the products bought by men and women, manufacturers have to be careful. In many cases, items which are used by one sex may be bought by the other – e.g. women buying after-shave and ties, men buying perfume. It is therefore pointless for a manufacturer of, say, shaving foam to target all its marketing at men if shaving foam is bought by women doing the weekly shopping at the supermarket!

In the car market, manufacturers have started to become aware of the influence of women on men's buying behaviour, and in the more progressive motor dealers, salespeople have been less inclined to dismiss the views of any women present! However, it is still the case that car advertisements for men are likely to emphasise engine performance whilst those for women will emphasise storage space for shopping, and economy!

Figure 3.9 Car salespeople have to work harder now!

Non-assessed activity

1 Obtain **six** car advertisements from different sources, e.g. Sunday colour supplements and women's magazines. Compare the models advertised and the ways in which the advertisements are worded. Write a summary of the differences between those targeted at men and those for women.

2 Identify **one other** product which is bought by both men and women but which is advertised differently in each case, and obtain examples of advertisements.

3 Obtain a general magazine which which is designed to be read by men, e.g. *Maxim* and examine the type of goods advertised. Compare these

advertisements with those found in typical women's magazines and state the differences you find, both in terms of products advertised and style of advertisement.

Did you know?

There is one toy on the market which is identical, in terms of its composition, when it is bought by girls and boys. Yet the packaging is entirely different. Indeed, if you bought a boy the 'girl's box' and a girl the 'boy's box' as a present, you may find you have a riot on your hands! Can you name the toy? (The answer is given at the end of this element!)

Geographical

There are considerable differences in buying habits in the various regions of the UK, let alone in the different countries in Europe. Tastes and preferences are different, as the charts on page 293 show. People in different regions choose to spend their money in different ways. Sometimes this is through no fault of their own. If rents are high, for instance, they will have less disposable income to spend on leisure. In other cases tastes and preferences are more clearly defined. In some regions a higher proportion of income is spent on clothing than in others, in some areas people would rather spend any spare income on household goods.

The geographical features of different regions can influence consumer demand. Obviously, regions where there are high numbers of tourists each year will sell more souvenir goods; areas next to the sea or a lake will have a demand for boating equipment; mountainous areas will have camping or mountaineering shops and so on.

In addition, lifestyles in each region may be different. This will depend on a variety of factors including the number of large towns or cities or, conversely, on whether parts of the region are comparatively isolated.

Non-assessed activity

1   Visit your nearest library and ask for the latest edition of *Social Trends.* Use this to find out how:
- income from employment, and
- household disposable income

varies between all the regions of Great Britain and Northern Ireland.

2   Find **three** other tables in either *Social Trends*, or the *Household Expenditure Survey* which gives information per region. State how each of these tables would be useful for a particular manufacturer.

3   Find **three** products which are popular in your particular region but may be difficult to find if you travel out of the area. How can you account for their popularity?

Did you know?

If a company wants to test market a product it may choose to sell it in only one region to start with. It would therefore choose its region carefully – based on previous patterns of expenditure for that type of product in that area. It would also advertise its product on regional television programmes. From the sales figures, the company could assess the success (or otherwise) of the test marketing campaign.

The international aspect

Consumer demand also varies from one nation to another – sometimes quite considerably. This is because tastes and lifestyles are even more different from one nation to another than they are between regions. In addition, because wealthy nations will spend more on household appliances (known as consumer durables), more of these goods will be sold in some countries than in others.

However, despite national differences in terms of taste, lifestyle and income, there is also a great number of similarities. People in the western world dress similarly – so clothes can be sold internationally (think of jeans!). In many cases, people's tastes are actually becoming more similar, especially in areas such as music, films and cars. It is believed that this is because communications and travel between countries are easier than ever before. We are therefore all assimilating the ideas of other people – and our tastes and preferences are changing.

Did you know?

Within the European Union there are several differences in terms of consumer demand and the type of goods supplied.
- Germany is the largest consumer of fruit juices and mineral water.
- The Belgians are famous for their chocolates.

- The Spanish buy most of their televisions in out-of-town hypermarkets.
- The range of tinned cooked meats available in Portuguese supermarkets is only a fraction of those to be found in the UK.
- Although French hypermarkets stock a very wide choice of fresh foods, bread and cakes are still produced by a large number of family-owned small bakeries and patisseries.
- Italy is not only famous for its pasta but also for its ice cream and knitwear.
- In the UK, consumer preferences for ethnic and convenience foods have resulted in the availability of far more 'cook-in' sauces.

Figure 3.10 There are regional variations in taste

Optional evidence assignment

*This activity can be carried out verbally in class **in a group** as a non-assessed activity to consolidate learning. Alternatively, if you do it **on your own**, it can count as supplementary evidence towards the following parts of the scheme.*

PC 2: Identify and explain the buying habits of consumers with different characteristics

Range: Characteristics of consumers: geographical, lifestyle

Core skills: Communication, Application of number

Figure 3.11 shows the percentage of income spent by the residents of different UK regions in 1992 on different items. Figure 3.12 shows the percentage of income spent by residents of different countries in the European Union in 1990 on these items. (The 1992 European table was not available at the time of going to print.) Study the tables carefully and then answer the questions below.

1 Start by finding your own region. How representative of your family is the pattern of expenditure shown?
2 The actual money spent per household on fuel, light and power in the UK is about £13.00 a week *in all regions*. Can you suggest any reason for this similarity? How, then, can you explain the differences in the percentage figures for this item?
3 In one region of England the percentage of income spent on travel is noticeably higher than in any other. Can you suggest why?
4 People talk about the north/south divide. What evidence in terms of lifestyle and expenditure can you find to illustrate this?
5 Which countries in the EU spend the most on leisure and recreation? Which country *also* spends a lot on food, beverages and tobacco? What does this indicate about the possible types of entertainment its inhabitants enjoy?
6 In which countries would it be best to
  a open a clothing store
  b sell household goods
  c buy property to rent out?
7 Medical care and health is a separate category on the European chart but ignored altogether on the English chart. Why?
8 The Netherlands is notable for low expenditure on transport. What is there about the geographical features of the country which can make very cheap transport an alternative for many people?
9 Choose a country you would like to visit. From the comparative figures given for that country and your own region, summarise the differences you would expect to find.

Global marketing

Today more and more companies market their goods across continents. A typical example is the film industry; films made in Hollywood are distributed around the world. Some people claim that this breaks down barriers between nations; others disagree.

In reality, social customs, traditions and lifestyles affect consumer choice – therefore what will sell in one country won't sell in another. As an example, it is only in the last few years that Smarties packets in

% of weekly expenditure

Community or service	North	Yorkshire and Humberside	North West	East Midlands	West Midlands	East Anglia	South East	Greater London	Rest of South East	South West
Housing	17.0	19.0	18.6	18.8	19.6	18.3	20.7	22.7	19.6	20.6
Fuel, light and power	5.4	5.6	5.1	4.8	5.3	4.4	4.0	4.0	4.0	4.4
Food	18.3	18.0	17.5	16.6	18.7	17.6	15.8	17.0	15.3	16.7
Drink and tobacco	8.1	7.3	6.6	5.9	6.3	5.4	4.8	5.1	4.6	5.5
Clothing and footwear	6.5	6.5	6.6	6.2	6.2	5.8	5.0	5.7	4.7	5.0
Household goods	8.9	7.0	7.7	8.7	7.5	8.8	7.3	7.1	7.4	8.2
Household services	3.6	4.0	4.8	4.3	4.2	6.8	5.2	5.2	5.2	5.3
Personal goods and services	3.9	3.8	3.6	4.1	3.8	4.0	3.6	3.8	3.5	3.4
Motoring and travel	15.4	13.2	14.5	16.4	16.0	15.7	16.3	14.5	17.2	14.7
Leisure goods and services	12.5	14.9	14.2	13.6	11.8	12.6	16.7	14.4	17.9	15.5
Miscellaneous	0.4	0.7	0.8	0.6	0.6	0.6	0.6	0.5	0.6	0.7
Total	100.0	100.0	100.0	100.0	100.0	100.0	100.0	100.0	100.0	100.0

Adapted from *Household Expenditure Survey 1992*

Figure 3.11 Expenditure of households by English regions, 1992

% of weekly expenditure

Community or service	Austria	Belgium	Denmark	Finland	France	Germany	Greece	Ireland	Italy	Luxembourg	Netherlands	Portugal	Spain	Sweden	United Kingdom	Total
Rent, fuel and power	17.7	16.7	27.8	18.2	18.9	18.3	11.6	10.3	14.8	19.8	18.7	5.0	12.6	25.7	18.5	100
Food, beverages and tobacco	20.2	19.0	21.2	23.1	19.1	16.8	37.9	35.0	20.7	19.4	18.1	37.1	21.8	22.0	21.8	100
Clothing and footwear	9.5	7.8	5.3	5.4	6.4	7.4	8.7	6.9	10.1	6.1	6.9	10.3	8.9	7.2	6.2	100
Household goods	7.9	10.8	6.5	6.8	7.8	8.4	8.2	7.7	9.4	10.8	8.5	8.6	6.6	6.4	6.7	100
Medical care and health	5.1	11.2	2.1	4.1	9.3	14.2	3.8	3.8	6.6	7.5	12.5	4.5	3.8	2.6	1.4	100
Transport	16.5	13.6	16.3	18.4	16.7	15.9	14.3	12.9	12.2	17.5	11.0	15.4	15.4	18.1	17.9	100
Leisure and recreation	6.9	6.6	9.8	10.7	7.6	9.2	5.6	10.7	9.2	4.3	9.9	5.7	6.5	9.7	9.7	100
Miscellaneous	16.3	15.5	10.8	13.2	14.1	9.9	9.9	9.2	16.9	14.5	14.5	13.4	24.4	8.3	18.0	100

Note: Although Austria, Finland and Sweden were not member states in 1990, the table has been adapted to include them.
Adapted from Basic Statistics of the Community – Eurostat – 1993

Figure 3.12 Expenditure of households in the European Union, 1990

Britain contained blue Smarties – as the British traditionally don't like blue sweets! The car market is particularly changeable in terms of models, colours and size from one country to another. In America, for instance, the average size of cars is much larger than in Europe. In addition, regulations on pollution and safety are stricter. A company which sells its products worldwide needs to be aware of all these facts.

Did you know?

In China a new invention currently being advertised is a high voltage 'self-defence vest' which will overpower attackers by giving them an electric shock! What do you think would be the reaction if these were sold in Britain? Why?

Lifestyle characteristics

Lifestyle is the way in which people live and how they spend our time. Our lifestyle is often determined by our job – which dictates our income, the amount of leisure time we have, the people we mix with and their interests. Lifestyles can also be affected by what is fashionable and what is not. Today more people are health conscious – which has reduced tobacco consumption and increased demand for wholefood products and vegetarian meals. There are also more 'working' mothers today – so that the lifestyle of many families has changed, with husbands now helping with the shopping and doing more of the household chores than before.

Non-assessed activity

1 What type of lifestyle would you associate with each of the following people?
- a company director
- a shop assistant
- a person who is unemployed

Think in terms of income, leisure time, entertainment and hobbies, goods and services each would buy, etc.

2 In what way do you consider lifestyle changes in relation to:
- **a** age
- **b** income
- **c** the place where people live?

Discuss these issues as a group and then summarise your answers.

Taste

You may have heard phrases before such as 'that's in poor taste' or 'he has no taste at all'. What do these phrases mean and what is this elusive thing called 'taste'?

Taste is defined as the ability to distinguish between those things which are good and beautiful and those which are not. However, many people would argue that taste is a personal thing. It is not necessarily 'tasteless' to have a car full of chrome or a cabinet full of souvenirs from seaside towns if that's what you like. Frequently, however, taste is associated with items which are well-designed, under-stated, timeless – and often expensive.

Your taste is influenced by a variety of factors, including what you personally find attractive and what you do not. Your taste is likely to change as you grow older, learn more about the world and are influenced by the views of people other than your immediate family and friends. It is for this reason that education, rather than money, is often seen as having a major bearing on taste. The phrase *'nouveau riche'* is often used to describe people who have moved from poverty to riches very quickly but have not acquired the taste to go with their newfound wealth. They may be out-of-step with the people with whom they are now associating on a social level.

Taste can also be associated with snobbery. Once you have achieved enough of an education not to put your foot in it, by thinking that Rembrandt painted

Figure 3.13 Tastes can change as you grow older

houses or Chippendale had quite a nice line in kitchen cabinets, you should have faith in your own judgement. It is also worth knowing that many business organisations deliberately play on people's muddled ideas of snobbery, taste and exclusivity to sell very expensive 'designer' goods, e.g. Gucci luggage, Patek Phillipe wristwatches and Armani suits. If you know someone who regularly tells you the designer name of everything they buy, you may come to the conclusion they have no taste at all!

Fashion

Fashionable goods have a very short **life cycle.** This is how long it takes for a product to become obsolete from the time it was introduced. It can be illustrated graphically as in Figure 3.14. The life cycle of the average pop record, for instance, is much shorter than that of classical records, which are sold over a much longer period.

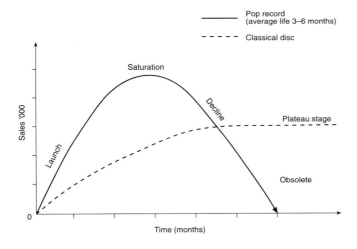

Figure 3.14   Life cycles

Everyone is influenced by what is in fashion and what is not, but teenagers are probably the most responsive group. Whereas father might wear last year's wider leg trousers because they are still a good fit, the teenage son in the family wouldn't be seen dead in them. Mother may still be wearing stiletto heels because she likes them whilst her daughter only has two pairs of boots in her wardrobe, and so on.

Even in more subtle ways most consumers show they wish to follow fashion in one way or another – whether it is by joining an aerobics class or by

buying a conservatory because it is the 'in thing' to do. In this respect consumers are very influenced by the media – and magazines and Sunday supplements are frequently full of ideas and photographs of the clothes to wear, the places to visit and the way to redecorate your house. Organisations can use this consumer characteristic to keep sales buoyant. A good example of this is men's ties. It is quite arguable that if a man has a range of ties in different colours, to match different suits and jackets, these will last him all his life. For that reason, fashion dictates that the *width* of the tie should be correct – so that all the 'kipper' ties bought in the 1970s are discarded in the dustbin and replaced by those which are much narrower – even by the older generations.

Preference

Imagine a world where we all liked exactly the same things. Everyone would wear identical clothes, have the same hairstyle, drive the same cars, read the same books, furnish and decorate their houses in the same way and so on.

But we all have different preferences – in music, clothes, shoes, food and drink, cars – and almost anything else you like to think about! Our individual preferences are more lasting than taste but can also change with age, fashion and opinions. Preferences also vary between men and women (as anyone who has ever worked in a pub or bar will tell you!). Preference is the reason why, given two identical products at a similar price, you might choose one brand and your friend might choose the other – or why she may order coffee whilst you always drink tea.

Did you know?

One type of vehicle rapidly growing in popularity is the (expensive) 4 × 4 'off the road' car, such as Range Rovers, Land Rovers and Jeeps! Men who buy them say they like the outdoor, adventurous image, but these cars are apparently very popular with women too! Women don't want to take them 'off the road', but say they are suitable for large families and heaps of shopping. Is this true or is it just a fashion fad for those who want to ride higher than their neighbours? What do you think?

Non-assessed activity

1   a Look through an expensive magazine, such as *Lady, Country Life,*

Vogue or *House and Garden.* Try to find **four** examples of advertisements or features which are written to influence or appeal to consumers' tastes rather than their desire to be fashionable.

   b Compare your findings with the type of articles and advertisements you will find in a more mainstream magazine, such as *Cosmopolitan* or *Options.*

2 **As a group**, select a type of clothing where fashion has dictated several changes and trends over the years. (A good example is footwear.) Discuss **with your tutor** the changes that have taken place, how fashion influences buying behaviour and the type of consumers who are most influenced by different fashions.

3 You have recently made friends with someone who is very much against using animals to test products. He will only buy toiletries from Body Shop or which are clearly labelled as not being tested on animals and is aghast that you have never considered this issue. How may his opinions change your own personal preference? If more people took this view, how might this change manufacturers' behaviour?

4 **As an individual**, write out your own answers to the points below. Then compare your answers with everyone else in your group. Ask each person to try to say *why* they have made the choices they have. What do their reasons tell you about how people develop their individual preferences?
   a your top five TV programmes
   b your top five groups or singers
   c your two favourite soft drinks
   d your five favourite foods

Optional evidence assignment

*This activity can be carried out verbally in class **in a group** as a non-assessed activity to consolidate learning. Alternatively, if you do it **on your own**, it can count as supplementary evidence towards the following parts of the scheme.*

PC 2:   Identify and explain the buying habits of consumers with different characteristics

Range: Characteristics of consumers: age, gender, lifestyle (taste, fashion, preferences)

Core skills: Communication

A typical area where brand names are used to sub-divide a market according to consumer characteristics is make-up and beauty products. Whilst cosmetic companies will obviously all target their marketing at women, brands do differ in their appeal to different *types*

of women – in terms of age, taste, income and lifestyle. In addition, all producers of beauty products are very interested in keeping up with fashion.

1 Visit a local shop and find out about the type of goods produced by Rimmel, Max Factor and Estee Lauder. Write down a sample of their prices and make a note of the design of their packaging.

2 From this information, decide what you think are the characteristics of each of their average customers in terms of age, income, taste, desire to be in fashion and personal preferences.

3 Identify **three** other well-known manufacturers of beauty products and describe the type of customers to which they would appeal. From this you should be able to identify which manufacturers are in direct competition with each other – and which are not!

4 Obtain an example of an advertisement from each of the cosmetic manufacturers mentioned above (and those which you identified). Explain in each case to what extent you think the content and style of the advertisement is aimed at the target market.

5 When Body Shop opened as a distinct outlet for its own beauty products, many people wrongly thought it could not survive against the competition from large producers such as Max Factor and Boots. However, Body Shop founder Anita Roddick argued that she was appealing to a different type of consumer.
   a What do you consider are the typical characteristics of a Body Shop customer?
   b How is this reflected in:
      i the range of products sold
      ii the way in which the goods are advertised?

Evidence assignment

At this point your tutor may wish you to start or continue work on the project which will prove to your verifiers that you understand this section of the element. If you are starting the project then turn to page 310 and do Section 1 of the project. If you have already completed Section 1 of the project, now start Section 2. This covers the second Evidence Indicator for this element.

Trends in consumer demand

We live in a rapidly changing world. No organisation can ignore this – products which were popular twenty, ten or even five years ago may be unsaleable today. Companies which make or sell products or services must keep up with the times – or fail. Some trends affect a whole range of goods and services, others relate only to specific products. In some cases trends are short-term and short-lived. In other areas there are long-term changes to our patterns of expenditure. Some changes are in the past and others have yet to come. The task of organisations is to try to forecast future trends so that they can be one step ahead of their competitors in meeting the demands of consumers.

Did you know?

Changes in Government legislation can affect the demand for products. Since the drink-driving laws were introduced fewer people go out to have a drink and more alcohol is consumed in the home. This has increased the sales of alcohol in supermarkets and stores. Another example is reading glasses. Until 1984 registered opticians had a virtual monopoly in dispensing glasses. Today ready-to-wear reading glasses can be bought at a range of outlets – and sales have increased dramatically. For short-sighted people the big trend is now towards contact lenses. In 1991 2.9 million single lenses were sold compared with 803 000 in 1982.

Figure 3.15 Seeing things in a new light!

Past trends

Changes that have taken place in the past can be ascribed to various causes, some of which have already been mentioned, including lifestyle and changing preferences. Consumer attitudes and new technology also affect demand. If you look around your home, it is likely that very few consumer durables have *not* changed over the past ten years. Televisions now have remote controls, stereo sound and teletext. Video recorders can be programmed using codes from TV listing magazines. Microwave ovens have pre-programmable settings to defrost or cook different types of food. Even toasters contain microchips to enable them to toast frozen bread. In addition, many products are getting smaller – computers, telephones and cameras are typical examples.

Probably the biggest influence on demand are changes in attitudes, tastes and lifestyles.

- Today we are more health-conscious. We smoke fewer cigarettes, eat more calorie-reduced foods, buy fewer animal fats and drink more fruit juice. More people are becoming vegetarians and less meat is being eaten each year.
- People's lifestyles are changing. An important event in the life of any family is if the mother starts work as this can have a variety of effects. The type of food bought and the ways in which it is prepared will change. Today more women work than ever before and there has been a surge in the sales of convenience foods and household appliances (especially microwave ovens) – and the demand for child minders and creches.
- Social attitudes are also changing – more people use credit cards today. Thirty years ago being in debt was considered to be awful! Fewer people go to church. More and more people shop on Sundays, and fewer and fewer people think this is wrong.
- People in Britain as a whole have more disposable income than ever before and work fewer hours. This has led to an increase in leisure time which has resulted in increased participation in leisure activities and holidays and increased sales of sports goods, DIY products and magazines and equipment for people pursuing a hobby.

All these changes influence the type of products which people demand. If the change is sustained so that it can be charted graphically, this is a **trend.** For instance, the number of drink-driving accidents and offences has fallen considerably since 1983 because

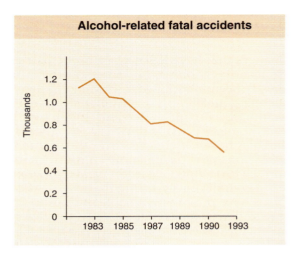

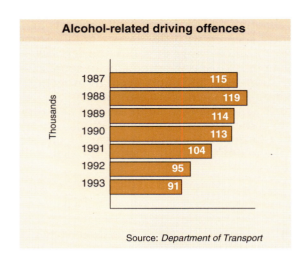

Source: *Department of Transport*

Figure 3.16 Drinking and driving

of changing attitudes to drinking and driving, Government advertising and legal deterrents for offenders. Figure 3.16 shows these trends illustrated graphically – first as a graph and secondly as a bar chart.

Did you know?

In 1990 the people of Britain spent about eight times as much *in real terms* on consumer goods as they did in the early 1950s. If you have forgotten what the phrase 'in real terms' means (or do not know) then look back to pages 3 and 4 to find out!

Non-assessed activity

1 As a group, hold a brainstorming session. Try to think of at least 30 products or services which are sold today which weren't available 20 years ago. In each case, try to identify whether their introduction can be attributed to advances in technology, changing social attitudes, or fashion and current trends (or a combination of these).

2 The number of households owning cars or vans between 1972 and 1992 is shown in Figure 3.17.
  a Is the number of households with no car or van increasing, decreasing or static?
  b Is the number of households which own one car or van increasing, decreasing or static?
  c Is the number of households owning two cars or more increasing or decreasing?

3 a Draw a graph to illustrate **one** of these trends.
  b State whether you think it is likely to continue and why.
4 Look at Figure 3.18 and, **as a group,** discuss the ways in which this illustrates the low buying power of poor people in the car market. What will be the response of car manufacturers?

Short-term and long-term trends

Only trends which are sustained over two to three years can be called long-term trends. In other cases there may be a trend which is more short-term, say over about six months. This may be because the item which is selling is fashionable (and short-lived), a one-off event or seasonal. You should be able to think quite easily of examples where a short-term trend is identifiable, e.g.:

- visitors to Blackpool pleasure beach
- the sale of a Christmas record
- tickets to a football final
- the sale of a particular computer game
- the sale of a special edition of a magazine or newspaper.

Short-term trends often relate to a particular product, rather than the market as a whole. Therefore the sales of newspapers may be falling overall, but there may be a sudden surge of demand for editions which contain a special discount offer or competition tokens.

Short-term trends can be identified on graphs because the line rises and falls separately from the overall movement of the graph.

Housholds										Great Britain
Cars or vans	1972 %	1975 %	1979 %	1982 %	1985 %	1987 %	1989 %	1990 %	1991 %	1992 %
Households with:										
no car or van	48	44	43	41	38	36	33	33	32	31
one car or van	43	45	44	43	45	44	43	44	44	44
two cars or vans	8	10	12	14	14	16	19	19	19	20
three or more cars or vans	1	1	2	2	3	3	4	4	4	4
Base = 100%	*11624*	*11929*	*11459*	*10303*	*9963*	*10334*	*10085*	*9604*	*9910*	*10031*

Figure 3.17 Cars or vans, 1972–92

Households								Great Britain: 1992
Number of cars or vans available to household	Socio-economic group of head of household*							
	Economically active heads							
	Professional	Employers and managers	Intermediate non-manual	Junior non-manual	Skilled manual and own account non-professional	Semi-skilled manual and personal service	Unskilled manual	Economically Total heads
	%	%	%	%	%	%	%	% %
None	6	4	13	28	14	30	48	55 31
1	43	40	54	51	53	52	41	38 44
2 or more	51	56	32	21	32	18	12	7 24
Base = 100%	*510*	*1274*	*791*	*518*	*1879*	*763*	*263*	*3873 9871*

* *Excluding members of the Armed Forces, and economically active full-time students and those who were unemployed and had never worked.*

Source: *General Household Survey 1992 OPCS*

Figure 3.18 Availability of a car or van by socio-economic group of head of household

Non-assessed activity

Figure 3.19 illustrates retail sales growth between 1992 and 1994.

1 Discuss **with your tutor**:
   a the short-term trends in consumer expenditure illustrated over that period – and how they have changed
   b the overall long-term trend which is illustrated.
2 Describe the graph in your own words, in **one paragraph.**

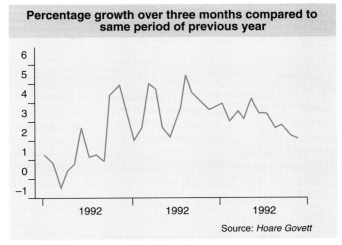

Percentage growth over three months compared to same period of previous year

Source: *Hoare Govett*

Figure 3.19 Retail sales growth

Future trends

It is one thing to find the statistics for past trends and quite another to be able to predict what is going to happen in the future! Yet this is important for organisations who are more interested in forecasts which will help them plan for the future than historical information.

To help them to predict future trends organisations will refer to statistics showing past trends, identify why the trend has occurred and the factors which contributed towards it and then try to calculate whether the trend will be short-term or long-term.

In some cases this is fairly easy to estimate, on other occasions consumer behaviour is less predictable.

Increasing demand, decreasing demand

Trends can operate in both directions. Demand may be increasing or decreasing. To make matters even worse, short-term trends may not accurately reflect long-term demand. Therefore, examining only the short-term trend may give a false picture of the market as a whole or even that particular product. The longer the period over which you base a study, and the more data you can obtain, the more accurate your final forecast is likely to be.

You need to take into account both external and internal factors which can affect future demand. Fashions may change or related events may make a product more popular (e.g. rising crime has resulted in higher sales of car and burglar alarms). The manufacturers are also likely to be taking action. If demand is falling they will try to change this trend – by increasing advertising or even redesigning the product.

Non-assessed activity

1 As a group, consider each of the following products which was sold during 1994/5 and give your views on the following.
a whether you think demand is increasing or decreasing
b whether the trend is short-term or long-term
c if you think the trend will continue.

Give reasons for your answers in each case and discuss these with your tutor.

i Power Rangers toys
ii Sega Mega CDs
iii The Gladiators television programme
iv National Lottery tickets
v Mobile phones
vi Barbie dolls
vii Low-priced 'throw-away' jewellery from high street chain store retailers
viii Red meat
ix Laptop or notebook computers
x Theme parks

2 Trends in alcohol consumption have resulted in a fall in demand for traditional dark beers sold in pubs and a rise in demand for lager.
a **As a group**, can you suggest reasons for this trend? As a clue, think of changes in attitudes, lifestyles and legislation.
b Look at Figure 3.20. If sales fall by the same percentage over the next five years as they did over the last five years, how much ale and stout do you estimate will be sold in 1999?

3 Figure 3.21 shows the trend affecting Radio 1. Do you think this trend will continue, and to what extent? If you ran the radio station, what would you do to increase numbers of listeners? **As a group**, discuss your answers.

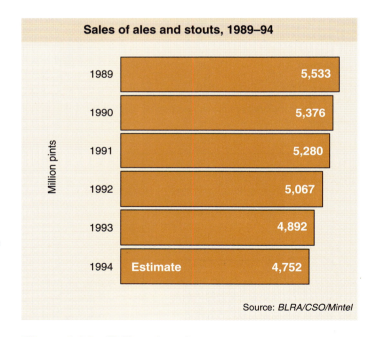

Figure 3.20 Falling ale sales

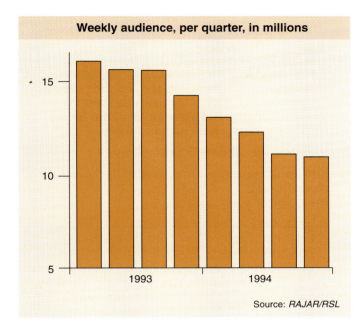

Figure 3.21 Radio 1's falling numbers

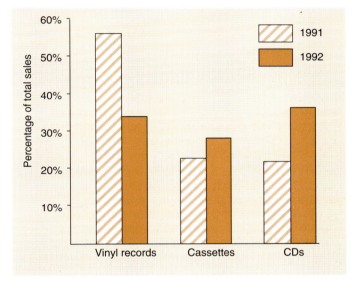

Optional evidence assignment

*This activity can be carried out verbally in class **in a group** as a non-assessed activity to consolidate learning. Alternatively, if you do it **on your own**, it can count as supplementary evidence towards the following parts of the scheme.*

PC 3: Identify trends in consumer demand

PC 4: Produce graphics to illustrate the trends

Range: Trends in consumer demand: past (short-term, long-term), future (short-term, long-term), increasing consumer demand, decreasing consumer demand

Core skills: Communication, Information technology, Application of number

Record companies have been seriously considering stopping the manufacture of single vinyl records. In 1992 the industry lost around £25 million on singles. Today cassette and compact disc singles are more popular.

Statistics show that in 1986 singles were in the charts for an average of 6.5 weeks. By 1992 this had dropped to 4.2 weeks. In the 1960s groups were in the charts for as long as thirteen weeks or more! In addition, the average age of the record-buying public has increased.

Teenagers buy far fewer records than ever before – the greatest number of sales are to those aged between 24 and 35.

However, ageing rockers have refused to accept defeat. In 1994, after thirteen years of decline, the sales of twelve-inch vinyl LPs increased by 80 per cent in the United States. A spin-off was the increase in the sale of traditional record players – up by over 50 per cent.

Those who prefer vinyl argue it produces a better sound. In addition, club disc jockeys rely on twelve-inch discs for live mixes and 'indie' labels still use vinyl to promote new bands. Artists prefer LPs because cover art looks better on a twelve-inch sleeve. Producers of CDs are not fazed. They cannot see a day dawning when those who have bought CD players go back to vinyl.

Figure 3.22 How the market for recorded entertainment is changing

1 How would you account for the decrease in the sale of single vinyl records?
2 Why do you consider consumer demand by teenagers for records is lower than ever before?
3 a Enter the data in Figure 3.22 into a spreadsheet. Although the figures cover only two years try to predict the situation in the year 2000 if the trend shown in the table continues. Produce graphics to show what you consider the market for vinyl records, cassettes and CDs will be at that time.
  b In what way does the information received from the United States (above) affect your analysis of the trend for vinyl records?

301

c What is your personal prediction for the future of vinyl records? Give a reason for your answer.

4 Record shops are now selling other products as well as records, CDs and tapes. Visit at least one shop in your area and investigate what other goods are being sold.

5 The record industry and its performers have both short-term and long-term trends. Bands and singers can either last a long time or be 'here today and gone tomorrow'. Singers like Phil Collins, Elton John and Sting are all 'old-timers' who are getting richer year by year. Bands like Oasis may do well – or may not.

    a Identify two records or CDs made by bands or singers which have sold well on a long-term basis. Give a reason why you think this has occurred.

    b Identify two records or CDs which have only had short-term success.

    c Record producers constantly look for a formula to convert a one-off success by a band into a long-term success. If you did their job, what features would you look for and why?

Causes of change in consumer demand

We have already seen why long-term changes take place. However, both short- and long-term changes in demand can occur if people have less money to spend. Throughout this element we have concentrated on various reasons for consumer demand, but we have never directly mentioned the price of goods! The way in which price influences buyer behaviour is complicated, and depends very much on the type of goods (or service) being provided. As an example, you may try to buy the cheapest can of beans on a shelf but are unlikely to select a foreign holiday by the same method! Equally, the woman who buys Estee Lauder cosmetics (think back to page 296), and the Porsche owner have not had a low price in mind when they made their decision to buy. In some cases, a low price can actually have a negative effect on buyer demand. A sweater at £5 may be considered rubbish, whereas the same one at £20 is considered good value for money!

You can apply two rules to consumer behaviour.

- With most normal goods, the lower the price, the more goods are sold.
- The more people earn, the more money they spend (and vice versa).

(See also Element 1.2, pages 60–66.)

Money to spend

One of the key considerations in how much anyone spends is their **income** – not their gross income but their **disposable income**, i.e. the amount they have left to spend after they have paid income tax, National Insurance and all their essential living expenses, e.g. rent, rates, fuel and food.

Your disposable income is affected by:

- how much you need to spend to live – called the cost of living
- the amount you earn.

The cost of living

The cost of living is measured by the Retail Prices Index (RPI). Quite simply, the RPI is calculated by taking a 'basketful of goods' and then, month on month, finding out how much these cost. In January 1987 the RPI stood at 100. In December 1994 it was 146.0. This means that a basketful of goods which cost £100 in 1987 would cost £146 in December 1994. In other words, between 1987 and 1994 the inflation rate had been 46 per cent – an average of nearly seven per cent per year.

Earnings

Increases in the cost of living would have been perfectly acceptable if, in those seven years, rises in salary had been above the level of inflation. Otherwise, people would have had less money to spend in real terms.

Inflation can be beneficial if you have borrowed money (because there is less, *in real terms*, to repay). However, inflation makes life very difficult for people on fixed or low incomes – such as pensioners – and for people who are trying to save to buy an expensive item, as it may go up in price faster than they can save the additional money.

 ### Did you know?

Economists believe there are two possible reasons for inflation.

1 Organisations put up their prices because their costs have risen and they need more revenue to keep their profit margins.

2 People have too much money to spend on too few goods. If all your group went to an auction and each person had £10 to spend then the most any item could cost is £10. If each person had £40 then the most any item could cost is £40 and so on. In this case, increases in income result in increases in demand for goods. Because producers cannot instantly meet this increased demand the number of goods on the market is reduced. Suppliers therefore put up the price of those remaining.

Confidence to spend

This has already been discussed on page 283. Remember that it is not only *actual* increases or decreases which affect people's behaviour but their *expectations* of the future. If you think you are going to lose your job you will reduce your spending and start to save. Equally if you expect to do well in the next few years then you may be less cautious. In other words you have *confidence* in the future. Your confidence may also be affected by the actions of the Government.

Non-assessed activity

1 Name **at least two** products which you would buy, if either the price was lower or your income was higher.

2 Can you name **at least one** item which you buy now but which you would not buy if your income increased?

Did you know?

The Government may tax some goods to make them more expensive and directly reduce demand, e.g. excise duties make alcohol and cigarettes more expensive.

Changing needs

Your needs can change for several reasons – the main one being a dramatic change to your lifestyle. The most fundamental of these are setting up home with a partner (or getting married) and having children.

As you get older your needs also change (as you saw on page 289). As a teenager you are not normally concerned about the cost of new carpets or washing machines. At 50 you will be past the age when you have to think about buying disposable nappies or baby food.

Your health, family responsibilities, where you live and your job may also affect your needs. If you suffer from asthma you will probably know all there is to know about buying inhalers. If you have elderly parents you will need to look after their requirements. If you move away from home you will have different needs – one of which may be your own transport. If you get a job you may need a bank account, if you don't already have one, so that your salary can be paid in each month. You may also need to buy some clothes which are suitable for working in an office – rather than a new pair of jeans, a T-shirt or some trainers!

Figure 3.23 Your first car?

Changing wants

Your consumer 'wants' are more fickle than your 'needs'. If you *need* something, then you really do *have* to buy it. What you want, on the other hand, is not an essential item. You may 'want' a completely new wardrobe of clothes – but unless you have absolutely nothing to wear, you certainly don't need one!

Commercial organisations are well aware of the importance of making people 'want' something. This is why you will see wonderful displays of goods in the shops – all set out attractively to make people want them. It is also why some supermarkets put chocolates and sweets near the check-outs so that children waiting in the queue will want some. 'Wanting' leads us to 'impulse buying' of goods we probably don't need. How many times have you been out and spent more than you intended because you saw something and bought it – if only a bar of chocolate or a bag of crisps?

Did you know?

Camelot, the organisers of the National Lottery, are cashing in on impulse buying with their scratch card 'Instants'. Because people will know immediately whether they have won something, people will buy a card on impulse – whereas they may think more carefully about entering the lottery where the results won't be announced until Saturday.

Advertising

Organisations advertise their products to persuade us to buy them (see Element 3.2) and to keep the name of their goods in our mind. This is why they usually advertise so often – and why you may see the same new car advertised four times in one evening on television. The last thing the manufacturer wants you to do is to forget the name of the car before the night is over!

The aim of many advertisements is to persuade you that you want something – even if you've never heard of it before. A good example is fabric softener. People washed clothes quite satisfactorily for many years without using fabric softeners. However, when the advertisements persuaded them how comfortable softer clothes would be, thousands of people decided they wanted to buy the product. Today fabric softener is a familiar sight in many homes and is no longer regarded as unusual or a luxury item.

If you flick through any magazine or watch television for any length of time you will find several items being advertised which you may think you want. Television shopping channels and many record adverts try to persuade people to act on their impulses by phoning in immediately to place an order. If you restrain yourself, you might find that after a few days you have forgotten about the desire for the product altogether.

Did you know?

Advertising is restricted by the Government for certain products such as cigarettes and spirits so that young people will not be as tempted to buy them. Cigarette advertising is banned on television and in the cinema; advertisements for spirits are banned on television but they can be advertised in the cinema. Both can be advertised freely in the press.

Optional evidence assignment

*This activity can be carried out verbally in class **in a group** as a non-assessed activity to consolidate learning. Alternatively, if you do it **on your own**, it can count as supplementary evidence towards the following parts of the scheme.*

PC 2: Identify and explain the buying habits of consumers with different characteristics

PC 3: Identify trends in consumer demand

PC 4: Produce graphics to illustrate the trends

PC 5: Explain causes of change in consumer demand for consumer goods and services

Range: Buying habits of consumers: types of goods and services, level of buying, frequency of buying

Characteristics: age, gender, geographical, lifestyle (fashion, preferences)

Trends in consumer demand: past (short-term, long-term), future (short-term, long-term) increasing consumer demand

Causes of change in consumer demand: money to spend (cost of living, earnings); confidence to spend; changing needs, changing wants, advertising

Core skills: Communication, Application of number, Information technology

Read the following case study, then answer the questions that follow.

Case study – Old Spice and after

After-shave first came to Britain during the Second World War along with the Americans. The GIs regularly used Old Spice aftershave, which they thought would make them more appealing to the opposite sex. The British, however, frowned upon such fripperies; men considered them sissy and ignored them.

In 1957 Old Spice was officially launched in Britain. Business was booming in the United States so the company forecast a market value of over £12 million by the mid-1960s. They were wrong. By 1965 the market was only worth a paltry £6 million.

Today all this has changed. In 1993 men's toiletry sales were worth over £340 million and over £212 million was spent on aftershave alone. What has made the difference? Some people blame the adverts for the slow growth in sales. In the 1970s aftershave adverts depicted 'outdoor' man in a range of sporting activities – skiing, mountaineering, sailing. Names like 12-Bore and Sabre abounded. In the 1980s advertisers woke up to the fact that most men wear aftershave to attract women and promoted the sexy, tough guy image in their adverts. Today the tough guy has gone even though the sensual allure has not.

Over 200 different varieties of aftershave are now on the shelves – from basic brands such as Lynx and Insignia to designer names such as Lagerfeld and Armani. Perhaps the advertisers have taken 40 years to get it right, or British men may be slow to change – but eventually the transformation has taken place.

1 Give as many reasons as you can why men's toiletries were not successful when they were first launched. (Don't forget to consider the characteristics of consumers and the attitudes of British men at the time.)

2 a In what way were advertisers blamed for the slow growth in sales of aftershave?

 b In what ways have advertisers changed the image of both men and aftershave in the last 30 years?

 c What reasons can you put forward for the success of 'tough guy' adverts in the United States when they were unsuccessful in Britain?

3 a Do you consider that men's toiletries are an essential or a luxury item today? Give reasons for your answer.

 b In what way do you think men would alter their buying habits of toiletry products if they had either less or more money to spend?

 c In what way do you consider men's needs in relation to toiletry products change over time and with age? Try to interview three or four men of different ages before you answer this question.

4 a From the figures given, project the amount of money which will be spent on men's toiletries in the year 2000, assuming the same rate of growth.

 b In 1993 actual spending on toiletries was as follows.

Aftershave	£212 million
Fragrance	£145 million
Body spray	£39 million
Deodorant	£49 million
Shaving preparations	£36 million
Hairdressing	£22 million
Bath and shower products	£16 million
Talc	£11 million
Shampoo	£2 million

i Work out the percentage of the total amount sold for each type of product.

ii Represent this in a pie chart, preferably created on a computer.

Evidence assignment

At this point your tutor may wish you to start or continue work on the project which will prove to your verifiers that you understand this section of the element. If you have already been working on the project then you may only have Section 3 to complete. Make sure you check with your tutor exactly what you have to do. Section 3, on page 310, covers the third Evidence Indicator for this element.

The importance of customers

In the last ten years, more and more businesses have become 'consumer-led' – in other words, they have produced their goods or offered a service primarily with the customer in mind. Their aim is to:

■ increase their market share over their competitors
■ obtain new customers
■ keep their existing customers.

Seeing the customer as the most important person means the company has a **marketing** approach to its business. The differences between a company which concentrates on marketing, and one which simply sells its goods or service are that:

■ A company which is market-led will try to find out what the customer wants and do everything it can to provide this, not just during the sale but both before and afterwards. It will also take account of changes in consumer tastes, fashion, social attitudes and technology.
■ The company which is sales-led will make its goods – then go out to try to sell them.

Did you know?

Companies frequently change their image to keep up to date – this can mean altering the design of their premises or the packaging of their products or the style of their advertising.

■ Our Price music stores were redesigned with modernised cash counters which made it easier for customers to sign documents in more places around the store. This was to meet the increased use of credit cards where vouchers have to be signed when goods are purchased.

- NatWest bank is transforming its branches so that customers will have more space than the staff. Currently staff have 80 per cent and customers 20 per cent. Banks will be open-plan with more automatic cash machines and new sophisticated communications systems to deal with problems and enquiries.

The importance of customers to income

The number of customers directly affects the income of every business. This is because, as a rule, the more customers there are the greater the number of goods sold. The number of goods sold is translated by the accounts department into the **value of sales** or **turnover** of the organisation. This is so important that, in the retail trade, large organisations calculate the value of sales per square metre of the premises. They may even sub-divide this for different sections so that Marks & Spencer, for example, will know how much it earns from each area of the store. If a particular line (e.g. household furnishings) has a poor sales value in a particular store, this line may be dropped and replaced with another which is more profitable.

By dividing the value of sales by the number of customers, it is possible for organisations to calculate the average amount spent by each person. In a supermarket, for instance, the average customer spends about £50 per week. Because there are limitations on trying to make people spend more each week (e.g. through impulse buying), the best way to increase income from sales is to increase the number of customers who visit the store.

However, note that the amount of income earned on sales depends upon the profit margin. On item A the organisation may make 40p profit, on item B it may make £4 profit. However, if the company sells 5000 of item A each day and only 10 of item B, overall more income is made from item A.

Did you know?

The price of the product is not just determined by the cost of making it. It is also limited by the price which people are prepared to pay – and the cost of competitors' products. This is why, in a highly competitive market, goods may be sold which only have small profit margins.

The importance of customers to repeat business

Whilst every customer who spends money is a source of income to the organisation, it is sometimes easy to forget that the customer who spends £5 is as important as the one who spends £50 or £500, firstly because several five pound notes easily add up to a much larger amount and secondly because the customer who spends £5 today, if satisfied, may return and spend a much larger amount tomorrow.

Not only are satisfied customers likely to return to organisations they like time and again, they are also likely to have friends and relatives who may want the type of product or service your organisation sells. A few good recommendations are usually worth more than an expensive advert, as they ensure a considerable amount of new business.

Many companies actively stay in contact with their past customers and notify them of special offers and sales which will interest them. They may even include bonus offers if customers introduce a friend who also buys a product.

The importance of customers to the survival of the business

Quite obviously, for all organisations, customers are essential for their survival. The day the last customer walks out of the door is the day the business closes for good.

No business would ever want to come anywhere near getting down to its very last customer. Indeed, long before that it would have gone out of business. However, it is often the case that busy staff may forget how important customers are to survival and sometimes treat them less courteously than they should. The question in your own mind should always be – would you act the same if it was your own business? If you can answer 'yes', you are usually doing quite a good job!

The importance of customers as a source of information

All commercial organisations are well aware of the importance of customers as a source of information. Regular analyses and surveys of customers will be undertaken to find out:

- what they are buying

- what they are not buying – and why
- what they would like to buy but cannot – because it is not available
- their general likes and dislikes about the organisation, the staff and the layout
- other suggestions and recommendations they may have.

Information can be obtained in one of two ways. Sales can be analysed by management accountants who then give their recommendations to management. Computerised cash registers have greatly helped this process. Goods can be entered with a specific code so that frequency of purchase is identified. This tells managers the lines which are the most and least popular – and the most and least profitable.

In addition, question and answer surveys can be designed by the Marketing department. Customers may be questioned on the premises or a survey may be sent to their homes. The results of the survey will be carefully analysed to find out the changes which could be made to increase customer satisfaction and the number of possible sales which can be made.

The contribution to profit by customers

The vast majority of organisations are in business to make a profit. Usually the greater the number of customers, the more goods (or the more of their service) they will sell. If more goods are sold, more income is received and, normally, more profit is made. Each customer, therefore, is individually contributing to the total amount of profit made by the company at the end of the year.

Did you know?

Profit is calculated by taking the total value of all sales and deducting the cost of all purchases. This is the cost of the goods that have been sold plus the value of any unsold stock. This results in the **gross profit** of the organisation. From the gross profit are deducted all the expenses – staff costs, rent, heating, advertising and so on. This results in the **net profit** or the **pre-tax profit.** Organisations pay corporation tax on their profit and this final figure is the amount they have left to reinvest in the business and to pay dividends to shareholders.

Optional evidence assignment

*This activity can be carried out verbally in class **in a group** as a non-assessed activity to consolidate learning. Alternatively, if you do it **on your own**, it can count as supplementary evidence towards the following parts of the scheme.*

PC 3:	Identify trends in consumer demand
PC 5:	Explain causes of change in consumer demand for consumer goods and services
PC 6:	Explain and give examples of the importance of customers to business organisations
Range:	Trends in consumer demand: past (long-term), decreasing consumer demand
	Causes of change in consumer demand: money to spend (cost of living, earnings); confidence to spend, changing needs, changing wants, advertising
	Importance of customers: to income, to repeat business, to survival of business, for information, to contribute to profit
Core skills:	Communication, Application of number

Read the case study below and then answer the questions which follow.

Case study – MFI

MFI are well known to most people for their cheap-and-cheerful, build-it-yourself furniture. During the property boom of the 1980s MFI did well – sales were high as people rushed to spend money on their new homes. Unhappily, the depressed housing market of the 1990s – with fewer people buying and selling – badly affected MFI. Interestingly, sales were not reduced by recent interest rate increases – even though these lowered householders' disposable incomes because of increased borrowing charges and generally affected people's confidence to spend.

The group makes about 50 per cent of the goods it sells and has been severely affected by increases in raw material prices on such items as paper, chipboard, chemicals and plastics. The company made a conscious decision to absorb these increases and reduce profit margins – rather than pass on the increases to the customer. Instead it looked to save money on staff costs

– by increased productivity (i.e. higher sales per staff member). In addition it opened a number of new stores and spent an extra £3 million refitting existing stores to make them more attractive to customers. It also opened nearly 70 stores in France to make the group less vulnerable to the effects of the British economy.

The result of these strategies was an increase in the value of sales over six months by 13 per cent to £363.1 million. Its pre-tax profits for the half year were £29 million – an 18 per cent increase on the previous figures. The chairman, Derek Hunt, hopes to sustain this by increasing the sales of high-margin items through staff training and new sales techniques. However, he is aware that, regardless of the range of goods on offer, if people prefer to buy Swedish-made bedroom furniture rather than goods made by MFI themselves, then overall profit margins will be lower.

Figure 3.24 Another satisfied customer!

1 Has the trend in consumer demand for MFI goods been increasing or decreasing over the past ten years? Give reasons for your answer.
2 **a** State **two** strategies used by the company to increase sales of all MFI goods.
   b State **two** strategies used to increase the sales of the more profitable items.
3 How have these strategies contributed to an increase in profits?
4 What evidence is there that the chairman is well aware of the importance of customers in relation to income, survival of the business and contribution to profit?
5 If you were the chairman of MFI, what would you do to:
   a increase the amount of repeat business
   b obtain information on future requirements from your customers?
6 **a** MFI's sales are given as £363.1 million – an increase of 13 per cent on the previous six months. What would the sales figure for six months ago have been?
   b Five per cent of sales occurred in France in the current period.
      i   What was the value of French sales?
      ii What was the value of British sales?
   c MFI has 6.08 million square feet of retail space in Britain. What was the value of sales per square foot?
   d MFI pre-tax profit increased by 18 per cent to £29 million. What was the profit in the previous period?
   e Explain why there is such a large difference between the value of sales from customers and the profit figure.
7 MFI has opened in France so that it is no longer so dependent on the British economy.
   a Give one example from the text of a change in the British economy which affected the amount of money people had to spend.
   b In what ways do you think people's decision to move house is linked to their confidence to spend? Give reasons for your answer.
   c Why did a slow-down in house sales change customer demand for MFI goods?

Evidence assignment

At this point your tutor may wish you to start or continue work on the project which will prove to your verifiers that you understand this section of the element. If you have already been working on the project then you may only have Section 4 and the final stage to complete. Make sure you check with your tutor exactly what you have to do. Section 4, on page 310, covers the final evidence indicator for this element.

Answer to children's toy (page 291)

The children's toy which is identical for both boys and girls is **Lego.** Only the packaging (and details of what to build) are different!

Key to newspapers (page 288)

According to statistics, the newspapers most likely to be bought by our readers on the previous page are as follows:

The Times – Hospital consultant (A)

The Guardian – Head teacher (B)

The Daily Express/Daily Mail – Police sergeant (C1) and plumber (C2)

The Daily Mirror/Sun – Labourer/pensioner (D/E)

Note: Of course, if our pensioner is a retired hospital consultant this confuses the picture! Therefore, it is important to remember that the table can only be used as a *guide* – other factors also have a bearing on buyer behaviour.

Revision test

True or false?

1 Poor people have high buying power.
2 People in different regions have different preferences for goods.
3 Past trends in consumer demand always give a clear indication of what will happen in the future.
4 People's tastes and preferences change as they get older.
5 The amount of people's income affects the type of goods they buy.

Fill in the blanks

6 Another phrase for differences in age and gender between consumers is _____ differences.

7 The letters RPI stand for _____ _____ _____ .
8 It is possible for manufacturers to change people's perceptions of what they want to buy by _____ .
9 The amount of income remaining to spend after tax, National Insurance and essential living expenses have been paid is known as _____ income.
10 Another name for value of sales is _____ .

Short answer questions

11 State **three** reasons why demand for a product may change.
12 Give **four** examples of products or services for which there has been greater demand in the last ten years.
13 Give **two** examples of changes in consumers' lifestyles in the last few years.
14 State **three** ways in which age can affect buying habits.
15 State **five** different characteristics of consumers.

Write a short paragraph to show you clearly understand each of the following terms

16 Consumer demand
17 Cost of living
18 Lifestyle
19 Taste
20 Confidence to spend

Evidence indicator project

Unit 3 Element 3.1

This project has been designed to cover the evidence indicator related to Element 3.1.

Performance criteria: 1–6

Core skills: Communication
Application of number
Information technology

Section 1

Select **one** type of product and **one** service. Describe clearly, in a summary, the way in which:

■ consumers have created demand for these items
■ consumers have caused changes in demand for these items
■ consumers have stimulated supply.

Type up your summary using a word processor.

Make sure you complete this section of the project by the deadline date given to you by your tutor.

Section 2

Prepare a summary which:

1 identifies **three** changes in buying habits which have occurred over the past two to three years
2 explains how these buying habits are linked to consumers' characteristics
3 makes suggestions why these changes in buying habits may have occurred.

Make sure you complete this section of the project by the deadline date given to you by your tutor.

Section 3

1 Select from **four to six** products or services which are currently offered for sale. Try to choose well-known products or services for which demand has changed over the years and which you can investigate without too much difficulty. Some of the products and services mentioned in this element may help you make your choice. Alternatively, look through newspapers and magazines for ideas.

2 Visit your college, school or local library and investigate trends in sales of these goods and services over the past 2–3 years. Your librarian will help you select useful reference books. If you have access to a CD-ROM containing recent newspaper reports then this will be very helpful indeed.

3 Examine each of these trends carefully. Then write **two or three** paragraphs on each product or service
 a describing the trend which has occurred
 b suggesting why the trend occurred.

4 Use the trend to predict what you consider will happen over the next 2–3 years and produce graphics showing your prediction, preferably using a computer.
 Write **two or three** paragraphs either supporting your graphics or modifying the trend line because of other factors (e.g. legislative changes, new technology) which you think should be taken into account.

5 Write a memo to the sales manager of your organisation stating what you consider demand for each of these products will be in the future, giving your reasons. State what you consider the supply of goods (or services) should be over the next 2–3 years to meet this predicted demand.

Make sure you complete this section of the project by the deadline date given to you by your tutor.

Section 4

Your friend is about to start work in a retail store but has little appreciation of the importance of customers. Write notes for your friend which explain why customers are an important source of income, repeat business and information. Include examples from actual businesses as evidence for your views.

Make sure you complete this section of the project by the deadline date given to you by your tutor.

Final stage

Make certain that all your documents are neatly typed and displayed. Put them neatly into a folder with a front sheet showing your name and the date of submission. Give your report the title: **Information on the Importance of Consumers and Customers.**

Plan, design and produce promotional material

This element covers the types of promotional materials used in marketing, the constraints on their content and the ways in which promotional materials may be produced. The purpose of producing such materials is explained, together with the type of plans which are required. Methods of evaluation to find out if the materials were successful in achieving their particular purpose are also discussed. After studying this element you should be able to:

1 identify and give examples of *types of promotions* used in marketing goods and services
2 describe *constraints* on the content of promotional materials
3 *plan* to produce *promotional materials* to promote particular goods or services
4 explain the *purpose* of the planned promotional material
5 design and produce promotional materials and use them to promote goods or services
6 *evaluate* how successful the promotional materials were in achieving the stated purpose.

Introduction to promotions

Virtually every organisation, whether large or small, undertakes promotional activities of some kind – otherwise nobody would know of their existence, let alone buy their goods and services. Stop for a moment and think about all the local organisations you know about (let alone the national ones!). You will soon realise that the way you found out about them was not through your friends and family telling you about them! You have been subjected to a constant stream of information about them on posters, leaflets, advertisements and on radio and television over quite a long period of time. The messages you have received have been sent to you with the specific purpose of influencing your behaviour, especially when you are buying goods or deciding where to go – whether for an evening out or a holiday.

Your college or school will promote its goods and services (i.e. its courses) to the area it serves. Advertisements will be placed in the press, a prospectus and course leaflets will be produced for enquirers, in summer there may be a special advertising campaign on the local radio. All these activities have one aim – to increase the number of students who enrol next year by telling them:

■ what is available
■ the benefits of taking part
■ what potential students need to do next to join a course.

These messages are the main focus of all promotional materials. In some cases the emphasis is more on

information and in other cases more on **persuasion** (see page 336). In all promotions, people who are interested are given full details of what they need to do next – to buy the product, attend the event or enrol on a course.

To produce promotional materials you need to know and understand various aspects concerned with the range of materials available, the constraints there are on the 'messages' you can send and how to plan, design and evaluate your materials so that you can achieve maximum publicity and learn from your mistakes (so that you don't repeat them next time!)

Case studies in promotion

In July 1985, Bob Geldof's Live Aid concerts in Philadelphia and London raised £35 million for famine relief. Ten months later, in May 1986, the Sport Aid event, which took place in 277 cities in 78 countries, raised over £67 million for the same cause. These were the first two major events to use publicity to raise money for charity. On a slightly lesser scale this is replicated once a year for Children in Need and once every two years for Red Nose Day. In all these cases, money is raised because a tremendous number of people participate in a variety of events. They join in because:

■ they want to help people less fortunate than themselves
■ there is a tremendous amount of publicity telling them how they can help.

This includes:

- logos and distinctive reminders e.g. red noses on cars, Pudsey Bear pictures for Children in Need
- advertising – through poster campaigns, special radio and TV programmes and Press features
- promotions – e.g. sponsorship of special events by famous celebrities and organisations.

Figure 3.25 Red Nose Day raises a lot of money for good causes

Did you know?

The record 'Do They Know It's Christmas', written by Bob Geldof and Midge Ure to raise money for famine relief, had the highest sales of any single record in the UK. Approximately 12 million copies were sold worldwide to raise a total amount of £110 million.

Types of promotions

The type of promotional material produced to advertise Children in Need or Red Nose Day is not unlike that produced by commercial organisations to promote their goods and services. The exact choice of promotion will depend upon several factors, e.g.:

- whether the product or service is being offered locally or nationally
- whether it will appeal to the consumer market or to a specialist industrial market
- the amount of money which can be spent on the promotion.

Four types of promotions are commonly used to make the public aware of the range of goods and services on offer:

- point-of-sale advertising and displays
- advertisements – on posters, radio, TV and in newspapers and magazines
- sponsorship
- competitions.

Point-of-sale

'Point-of-sale' includes the promotional literature and displays to be found at the place where the goods or service are purchased by the consumer. This material is specifically designed to attract people's attention and encourage people to buy. It often identifies a particular outlet as a place where something can be bought (e.g. 'on sale here' notices).

Figure 3.26 Point-of-sale displays

Examples of point-of-sale displays include:

- posters for shop windows and walls – often in bright, attractive colours
- show cards which can be set up on sales or reception counters (e.g. those advertising credit cards)
- dummy packs – empty display cases, packets and bottles which can be stacked attractively
- dump bins – which are filled to overflowing with a product and placed at the end of aisles in supermarkets to encourage consumers to impulse buy
- illuminated signs and displays – today these can

include video or LED displays which flash or change the message (think of Piccadilly Circus in London)

- public announcements – which often include special offers in supermarkets
- mobiles and models – mobiles are created out of cut-out displays and suspended on strings from the ceiling. Models can be cardboard cut-outs or even working models. These are often used for toys when a particular character is well known to children.
- stickers, transfers and badges containing the name of a product
- mats and ashtrays – usually found in bars and restaurants to advertise drinks on sale on the premises
- dispenser cards and packs – these hang up on special stands or fix to the wall, e.g. for nuts, confectionery, small toys, small personal items (e.g. combs and nail scissors)
- free samples and tastings – often used to promote new types of food and drink in supermarkets.

In addition, either in a central location or near to the products themselves, there may be a range of holders containing literature on different goods and services. These may be small leaflets or quite elaborate brochures and booklets.

Non-assessed activity

1 How do the National Lottery organisers enable you to spot their sales outlets instantly?

Figure 3.27 National Lottery tickets on sale here!

2 **As a class**, divide into groups of **two or three**. Each group should visit one of the following types of establishment and make notes on the type of point-of-sale promotions they find. The test is to imagine you have entered the premises to make one specific purchase and see how many other things 'catch your eye' or tempt you to buy. Make notes on your findings and compare these with other groups on your return.

- a supermarket
- a large chemist's shop
- a bookshop
- a travel agency
- a bank
- a large toy shop
- a record shop.

Advertisements

The most popular method of promotion is by advertising – on posters, on radio and in the press (e.g. newspapers and magazines). There are advantages and disadvantages to using each of these. The particular features which apply often influence the content and style of the advertisement.

Posters

Advantages

1 A poster can remain in place for a long time to gain the attention of people who pass by.
2 Posters can be big, bold and colourful. Many have messages with considerable impact.
3 Campaigns can be targeted at specific towns or regions. Conversely, a national campaign can be planned with just a few posters in main towns and cities.
4 In places where people have nothing to do, e.g. railway stations, on trains and buses, travelling on the Underground, many people read the adverts for entertainment!
5 Bus adverts can be specially targeted for local readers – it is even possible to decorate a whole bus so that it is eye-catching and memorable!
6 Local traders can often be persuaded to put posters in their windows – provided the poster is not too big.

Disadvantages

1 Posters can be damaged by vandals – or the weather.

313

2 Messages *must* be brief – the travelling public and motorists have little time to read. Any detail is therefore completely out of the question.

3 Environmentalists may object to posters as detrimental to the area.

4 Posters and billboards can distract drivers.

5 If a lot of small posters are concentrated in one area (e.g. on a bus or in an underground station) the impact of each one may be lost – and few (if any) remembered.

Non-assessed activity

1 Look around your own area and find examples of **four** posters or billboards which attract your attention. Look for those with strong, clever or witty headlines or very eye-catching designs.

2 What differences do you find between the type of goods advertised on hoardings and those advertised on buses? Give examples of **two** bus adverts you have seen recently which have caught your attention.

3 The positioning of posters can be critical. For instance, hoardings and poster sites near supermarkets carry food advertisements, those near a bank may advertise financial services, those in airports may advertise goods and services related to travel and so on.

Find **three** different poster sites in your own area and give examples of the types of goods advertised.

Did you know?

Many organisations pay an advertising agency to produce the artwork and make all the arrangements necessary for a combined media campaign. In this case, adverts on television will be shown at the same time as they appear in the press and posters are placed on hoardings. This means that the public is bombarded with information on a particular product or service over a certain period of time.

Commercial radio

Advantages

1 Radio advertising is much less expensive than either the press and television – both to produce and to buy air time. Spot announcements are even cheaper.

2 If the signal is strong, quite a large audience may be reached. Many of these can be classed as a 'captive audience', e.g. car drivers – but many other people put the radio on while they work, e.g. in factories, hairdressing salons and in the home.

3 The advert can be repeated many times a day to catch different people.

4 The voice which delivers the advert can be persuasive – a feature which is impossible with a press advert.

5 Radio is ideal for local traders – because of its price and the fact most commercial radio stations operate on a local network basis.

Disadvantages

1 Sound is not as memorable as pictures. Therefore a radio advert will soon be forgotten.

2 If the signal quality is poor, the listener may not be able to hear clearly what is said.

3 Repetitive adverts on radio (e.g. jingles) may annoy rather than attract the listener.

4 The listener may 'station hop' whilst the adverts are on.

The press – newspapers and magazines

Advantages

1 Magazines and business journals are often kept for a few days or weeks, so the advert may be seen several times, or by several people. The reader can cut it out for reference.

2 Special interest magazines and newspaper readership can be categorised by social class (see Element 3.1). This means that particular readers can be targeted.

3 Local newspapers can be used to publicise local events very effectively. Sometimes there are special features in which certain types of advertisements are included at a cheaper rate to benefit particular organisations (e.g. a 'dining out' feature in a Bank Holiday edition).

4 Advertisers can use tear-off coupons so that readers can reply to the advert. By coding these so that they can be identified by the organisation when they are received, it is possible to assess the effectiveness of each particular advert. In Figure 3.28, can you spot the reference number?

5 Newspapers and magazines are frequently read by people other than the buyers, e.g. in waiting rooms, in libraries etc.

6 Colour printing is now possible because of modern technology.

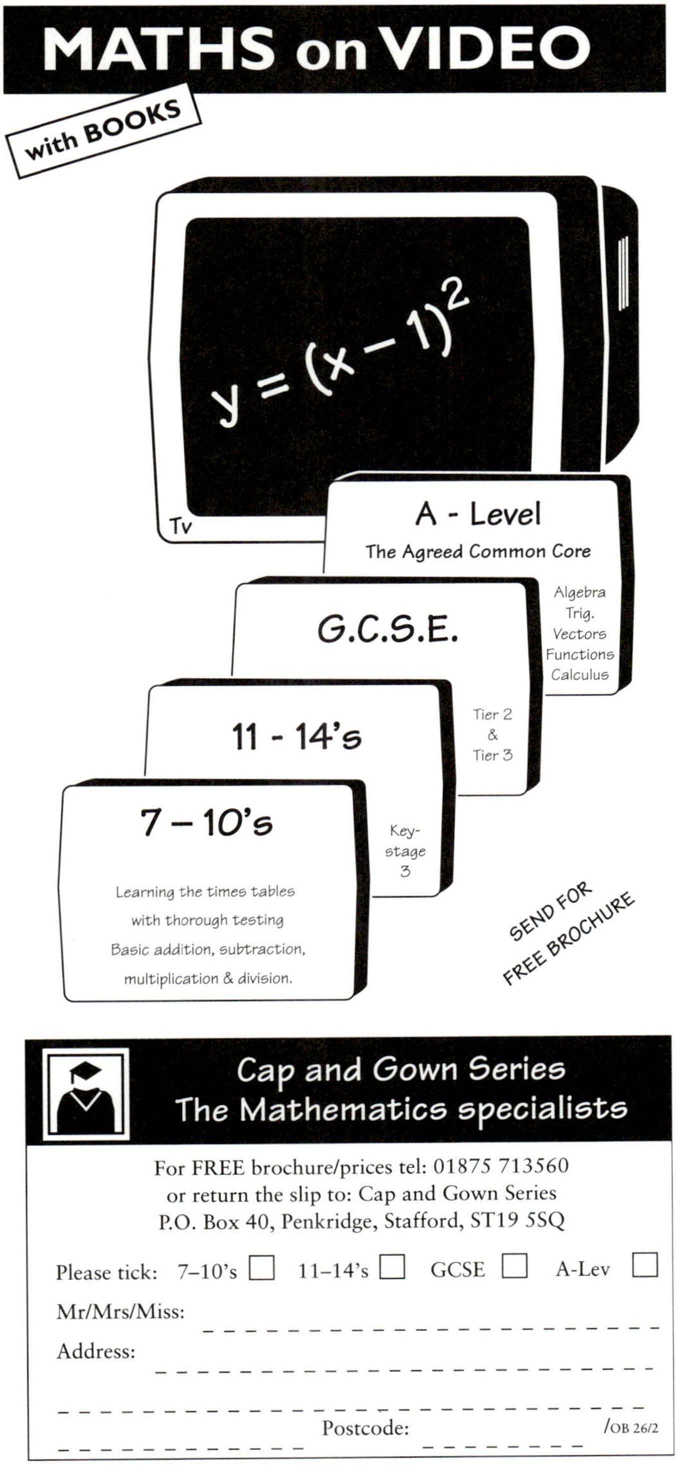

MATHS on VIDEO

with BOOKS

$$y = (x - 1)^2$$

Tv

A - Level
The Agreed Common Core

Algebra
Trig.
Vectors
Functions
Calculus

G.C.S.E.

Tier 2
&
Tier 3

11 - 14's

7 – 10's

Key-
stage
3

Learning the times tables
with thorough testing
Basic addition, subtraction,
multiplication & division.

SEND FOR FREE BROCHURE

Cap and Gown Series
The Mathematics specialists

For FREE brochure/prices tel: 01875 713560
or return the slip to: Cap and Gown Series
P.O. Box 40, Penkridge, Stafford, ST19 5SQ

Please tick: 7–10's ☐   11–14's ☐   GCSE ☐   A-Lev ☐

Mr/Mrs/Miss: _ _ _ _ _ _ _ _ _ _ _ _ _ _ _ _ _

Address: _ _ _ _ _ _ _ _ _ _ _ _ _ _ _ _ _

_ _

Postcode: _ _ _ _ _ _ _ _ _   /OB 26/2

Figure 3.28   Spot the reference number!

Disadvantages

1   The reader may skim through quickly and either miss or ignore the advert.
2   The language used must be easy to understand, take account of the readership of the paper or magazine, and must attract the reader's attention.
3   An advert for one type of paper or magazine may be unsuitable for another – and have to be rewritten.
4   Most daily newspapers are thrown away after being read.
5   Newspaper adverts generally suffer from poor quality reproduction – especially those containing photographs.
6   Adverts may be grouped together so that each loses impact because they are crowded. It is therefore better if each has 'white space' around the text so that it is easily distinguished from its neighbours.

You will, of course, also find advertisements on television and in the cinema. Whilst you could not use this form of promotion for any college or school campaign with which you are involved, because of the necessary organisation and expense, it is important that you realise that commercial organisations can use both to good effect to promote their goods and services.

Non-assessed activity

1   Look through about **four** magazines and newspapers. Select **ten** advertisements which attract your attention and make you want to read further.

Analyse what it was that caught your eye, made you interested and the features of the advertisement which have been deliberately included to create desire for the product or service.

2   **As a group,** discuss adverts you have heard on the radio and decide which ones attract your attention and why. Try to time the length of some of the more frequent radio commercials.

Other methods of promotion

Leaflets and brochures

Many organisations produce leaflets and brochures about their products or services, to give additional information to consumers and customers. Both your local Trading Standards Department and the Advertising Standards Authority (see page 323) issue leaflets explaining their services. If you visit your local tourist information office you will find other examples. Travel companies are an obvious example of organisations which produce glossy brochures. Your school or college may have a glossy brochure too, which it uses for promotion purposes, though it will probably call this a prospectus. It may also have leaflets available about individual courses.

If the leaflet is mainly informational it is likely to contain more text and fewer illustrations. Compare this with a travel leaflet, which has much less text and more photographs – to persuade you to visit the place being advertised.

Direct marketing

Direct marketing has been growing in importance since the 1970s and describes any type of marketing which enables customers to buy products or services without visiting a shop. It includes:

- adverts on television where you can ring up and buy the product using a credit card
- teletext advertisements
- advertisements where you can cut out a coupon and order directly from the manufacturer
- direct mail.

Direct mail is the most commonly used, and it generally arrives unannounced through your door. It is usually of two types.

1 Letters may be written, addressing you by name. This approach is often used by financial organisations (trying to persuade you to borrow money) and charities (trying to persuade you to give them money).

Today these documents are easily produced and individually named, using a computer or word processor. Because they are cheap to produce, and many people like receiving and opening mail, direct mailshots are often a very effective method of promotion. If the company is selective about the addresses to which it sends its mailshots, it cuts down the cost of the promotion.

The message may be just text (e.g. a letter) or include pictures. Charities such as the RSPCA, NSPCC and Help the Aged usually illustrate their appeal literature. They always include a donation form and may even arrange to follow up the mailshot with a telephone call at a later date if no reply has been received.

2 An alternative to personalised literature sent by post are the leaflets and booklets which are delivered through your door. These may include money-off coupons or trial-size offers. Perfume manufacturers often include a sealed section which has been impregnated with the perfume, to give the potential customer a sample with the mailshot. In many cases you can buy goods direct from the seller simply by completing a coupon.

With both types of mailshot it is possible to target customers by postcode, by TV area or demographically (so that potential customers are identified by age, address, status, profession, income etc.).

Did you know?

Many organisations with a large computer mailing list (e.g. credit card companies, local authorities etc.) sell their mailing lists to other companies wishing to set up their own database for direct mailshots.

Sponsorship

Sponsorship is obtained with the objective of raising money. Commercial sponsorship is concentrated mainly in sports and the arts. About £2 million a year is spent by large companies on sports sponsorship alone. As an example, Coca Cola have sponsored swimming events, athletics and the Olympic Games and Carling currently sponsors the Football Premier League. An alternative form of sports sponsorship is when a clothing or equipment manufacturer pays a famous personality to wear or use their products – tennis player Andre Agassi is paid large sums to wear Nike clothing and footwear. Sports sponsorship has therefore the highest profile – which means you will probably know quite a bit about it even before you read this section!

Did you know?

If a sponsorship deal between the food and drinks company Allied Domecq (previously Allied Lyons) and Coronation Street is finalised, not only will you see Allied food products appearing on the opening and closing credits of the programme but you will also see Tetley tea bags on the shelves of BettaBuys supermarket and Tetley beer and Castlemaine lager being sold at the Rovers Return! The three-year deal is estimated as costing Allied Domecq £30 million.

The advantages of sponsorship

1 There is constant promotion of the sponsor's brand or name in relation to:
   - publicity for the event
   - the holding of the event
   - constant association with the sport.

   Bear in mind that audiences are large and that some sports seasons last a long time (e.g. the football season).

2 It provides a route by which manufacturers of goods which must not be advertised on television, such as cigarette companies, can have their names visible in programme coverage, e.g. hoardings and posters.

3 Television commentators may mention the company as they discuss the sport (e.g. the Lombard UK car rally or the Milk race) – or a winning team will be associated with their sponsor. This is particularly true in the case of sports such as motor racing and yachting – where different companies sponsor different drivers or crews. A winner at any sport can increase sales. The sales of Puma rackets rose by about $50 million after Boris Becker first won at Wimbledon in 1985.

4 It may prove more cost-effective for a company to sponsor an event (in terms of publicity, television coverage, etc.) than to pay for advertisements. Whitbread (who sponsor the Round The World Yacht Race) estimated that for an investment of approximately £8 million the company achieved advertising worth £30 million worldwide.

5 The company can take customers to watch the event or even participate in the sport. One organisation involved in sponsoring show jumping at the Barcelona Olympics – Henderson Administration – claimed it was cheaper to charter a plane to Barcelona than it was to take customers for a day out at Wimbledon.

6 The company image is promoted – and often enhanced – among those potential customers to whom it most wants to appeal. The image given to a product or company sponsoring a sport is often one of grace, style, fitness and the ability to meet a challenge. In many cases masculine products are linked to masculine sports (see the information about the sponsor of the Rugby Union at the end of this element).

Other companies use sponsorship to promote a caring image, especially in a related area.
For example, Mothercare sponsors research at Great Ormond Street Children's Hospital. This is also true for organisations which sponsor a charity event.

Note that a company will only sponsor an event which matches the image it is trying to project and/or one to which its customers (and potential customers) are likely to go. For instance, the *Financial Times* might sponsor an opera, ballet or play – but would be extremely unlikely to sponsor a pop concert or a wrestling match! *The Sun* newspaper might make exactly the opposite decision.

The Opera Factory at Glyndebourne have a novel approach to sponsorship. They persuaded Haagen-Daz to provide ice-cream to be eaten during the banquet scene of *Don Giovanni*. For an opera about two shepherds they were asking for sponsorship from the International Wool Secretariat, the Sheep Shop in London and the Nationwide Building Society (because the latter includes sheep in its adverts)!

Figure 3.29 Sponsorship can take some surprising forms

Did you know?

Because of 'company image', companies do not want to sponsor famous personalities who may bring them into disrepute. An example was when Pepsi dropped Michael Jackson when he admitted he was addicted to pain-killing drugs.

Non-assessed activity

As a group, answer as many of these questions as you can.

1 Which whisky producer sponsors the Scottish League Premier Division?
2 Which brand of cigarettes is linked to Rugby League?
3 Which soft drink was promoted on ITV in conjunction with premieres of Hollywood Films?
4 Which brewery sponsors the Rugby Union championships?
5 Which electronics company spent £4 million sponsoring the World Cup in 1994?
6 Which organisation sponsors your local football team?

Answers, apart from number 6, are at the end of this chapter.

Competition

Most people, at some time in their lives, have entered a competition. It may have been a promotion by a manufacturer or by a publisher, e.g. in a magazine or newspaper. Sometimes, to enter, it is necessary to buy the product several times, either because clues are given over a period of time or because tokens have to be collected. The aim in both cases is to turn the occasional customer into a regular buyer of the product.

To fulfil legal requirements, the competition has to have an element of skill so that there is an outright winner. For this reason, most competitions have a tie-breaker, where a slogan or reason for entering has to be written. Results must be published so that anyone who entered can see who were the winners.

The success of competitions can vary enormously, depending upon the prize. Most people prefer cash (or a car) rather than other goods (which they may already have) or a holiday (which might be difficult to take).

The National Lottery is successful because it takes advantage of people's liking for competitions and for winning something for nothing (or very little!). The scratch card game was launched because it is a popular form of 'instant' competition and the organisers, Camelot, consider that they will raise an extra £1 billion a year from sales.

Did you know?

Some promotions which aim at giving people something for nothing can run into trouble. To increase sales of their One-2-One phones at the end of 1994, Mercury offered subscribers who bought their phones after 8 November the opportunity to 'call the world for free' on Christmas Day. Thousands of people bought Mercury One-2-One mobile phones because of this promise but, because of excessive demand on the day, many people couldn't make their calls as the lines became congested. Twenty people spent more than twelve hours on the phone and another twenty made more than 2000 calls between them. This resulted in hundreds of complaints by those who couldn't take advantage of the free offer.

Figure 3.30 Not an instant winner!

Figure 3.31 Call the world ...

Non-assessed activity

1 Look through some newspapers and magazines at home over the next few days and try to find **three** examples of competitions. Cut them out.

2 Compare the competitions you have found with those found by other members of your class in terms of:

- the skills required
- the prize(s) offered
- whether there are any conditions to entry (e.g. collecting tokens, being over a certain age etc.)
- how an outright winner is selected
- how winners are notified.

3 Specific magazines are on the market to help people who regularly enter competitions to win more prizes. What sort of articles do you think these contain? If possible, try to find a copy and look through it for ideas.

Optional evidence assignment

*This activity can be carried out verbally in class **in a group** as a non-assessed activity to consolidate learning. Alternatively, if you do it **on your own**, it can count as supplementary evidence towards the following parts of the scheme.*

PC 1:   Identify and give examples of types of promotions used in marketing goods and services

Range: Types of promotions: point-of-sale, advertisements (posters, radio, newspaper, magazine), sponsorship, competition

Core skills: Communication, information technology

Imagine you and five of your friends have formed an Enterprise group linked to your Business Studies course. Your idea is to clean and valet cars which are parked in and around the town whilst the owners are shopping. You obviously need hot running water to do this so you may be limited to the type of car parks you can use (e.g. supermarket ones rather than multi-storey). You would also need the permission of the owners of the car parks before you can approach their customers. Your aim is to charge a reasonable rate and give 80 per cent of the proceeds to a charity (of your choice). The remaining 20 per cent is to meet your costs. However, you have calculated that if you could obtain sponsorship for your venture, you may be able to give all the money you raise to charity.

1 Assess your local area and make a list of possible car parks which would be suitable – if the owners agreed.

2 Which supermarkets and other car park owners would you approach to support your scheme? List the *additional* help you could ask for if they were willing to sponsor your idea.

3 Note down any other possible sponsors in the area. These could include companies you know well or companies linked to the materials you will be using to clean the cars, or the suppliers of these materials.

4 Note down:
  a how you would approach these companies to 'sell' your scheme
  b what you would ask for.
  Bear in mind that sponsors want some return for their support. What would your sponsors gain from being involved with you?

5 Assume that you now have several sponsors. **As a group**, hold a brainstorming session to decide the ways in which you could promote your scheme so that the general public knows about it.

6 Describe **three** examples of each of the following which you think could help you with ideas when you are designing your promotional materials. Better still, where possible, obtain actual examples.
  a point-of-sale displays
  b press advertisements
  c posters or leaflets
  d catchy radio slogans/messages
  e competition entry forms

Figure 3.32   Sponsored shampooing

319

Evidence assignment

At this point your tutor may wish you to start work on the project which will prove to your verifiers that you understand this section of the element. If you are starting the project then turn to page 342 and do Section 1.

Constraints on promotions

When you are trying to attract attention and create interest with promotional materials, you may be tempted to make wild or exaggerated claims about the benefits of a product or service! You may not be telling a deliberate lie, but it may be that you have not quite told the whole story – for your own reasons! If this is the case, you could be in trouble. Every organisation which promotes its products or services must be aware of the controls that exist on advertising in Britain. Some of these are **legal** constraints, others relate to the maintenance of certain **standards.** In the advertising world, many standards are voluntary codes which have been agreed by those organisations which are involved in promotions, to avoid giving offence or misleading people.

Legal constraints

The main Acts which affect both the promotion *and* the sale of goods and services are the **Trades Description Act, Sale of Goods Act** and the **Consumer Protection Act.** You do not have to know all the details of each Act, but it is important that you know how they are designed to protect consumers.

Note: The following Acts all apply to England and Wales – the situation in Scotland and Northern Ireland is broadly similar, though some Acts have different names and dates. The Office of Fair Trading issues special leaflets on consumer rights in Scotland and Northern Ireland and these can be obtained by writing to the OFT, Field House, Bream Building, London EC4A 1PR.

Trade Descriptions Act 1968

The main purpose of this Act is to prevent the **false description of goods.** Any seller who gives a false description of goods or supplies or offers to supply goods which are falsely described is guilty of an offence. This includes:

- selling goods which are wrongly described by the manufacturer e.g. 'made of real leather' when they are not
- implied descriptions, e.g. a picture or illustration giving a false impression
- other aspects of the goods, including quantity, size, composition, method of manufacture etc.

Usually the spoken word of the seller overrides the written description of the goods as the buyer can rely on the expertise of the salesperson.

Complaints under this Act are investigated by local Trading Standards Officers (see page 322). In one case, Boots were fined £250 for selling a diet chocolate bar, called Shaper, which actually contained as many calories as an ordinary brand of chocolate.

The Sale of Goods Act 1979

This is probably the most important piece of legislation as far as the customer and the supplier are concerned. The main purpose of the Act is to prevent buyers from being deceived into buying goods which are not fit to be sold. Under this Act, goods for sale must be:

- as described
- of merchantable quality
- fit for the purpose for which they are intended.

As described

Where there is a contract for the sale of goods there is an implied condition that the goods will correspond with the description. If you bought some scissors labelled 'stainless steel' and then found out they weren't, you could claim your money back. The Trade Descriptions Act deals even more fully with the question of description (see above).

Of merchantable quality

This means the goods must work and includes goods sold at sale prices. However, various points should be noted.

- If a defect is specifically drawn to the buyer's attention before the sale is completed then this is acceptable.
- If the buyer examines the goods before the sale and should have been able to see the defect easily

(e.g. a scratch on the paintwork of a car) this is also acceptable.

- The seller must be a business seller – private sales are exempt.
- The seller can be a manufacturer, wholesaler or retailer.
- A person cannot reasonably expect the same standard of quality and durability from cheap goods as expensive goods, although if the goods were bought in a sale the price would probably not be relevant.
- Goods described as 'shop soiled', 'seconds' or 'manufacturers' rejects' cannot be expected to be of the same quality as a new or perfect product.

Fit for the purpose for which they are intended

Most goods have an implicit purpose for which they are intended, e.g. a hole punch should punch holes in paper. If it will not, the seller is contravening the Sale of Goods Act.

Consumers often place considerable reliance on the advice and experience of the seller or sales representative. If the seller indicates that the goods will do a particular task and they fail to do so, the seller will be liable.

If the goods do not conform to any one of these three criteria then the buyer is entitled to a **refund.**

- Buyers *may* accept a replacement or repair, but the seller is not obliged to offer anything except cash compensation.
- Buyers do *not* have to accept a credit note – if they do, they may have difficulty getting their money back later if they find nothing else they like.
- Notices such as 'No money refunded' are illegal and should be reported to the local Trading Standards Officer.
- Secondhand goods are also covered by the Act but the buyer's right to compensation will depend on many factors, e.g. price paid, age of the article, how it was described etc.
- Sale items are also covered by the Act but if the price is reduced *because* the item is damaged the buyer cannot complain later about that particular fault.
- There is no legal obligation on the buyer to produce a receipt and signs such as 'No refunds without a receipt' have no legal standing. However, the buyer can be asked for proof of purchase, e.g. cheque counterfoil, credit card copy sales voucher, etc.

Did you know?

Buyers are *not* entitled to anything if they:

- change their minds
- decide that something does not fit
- damage the item themselves
- were aware of the fault or should have seen it
- did not purchase the item themselves (e.g. received it as a gift).

Did you know?

Under the **Supply of Goods and Services Act 1982** consumer protection is extended to include goods supplied as part of a service, on hire or in part exchange. These, too, must be as described, of merchantable quality and fit for the purpose made known to the supplier. Therefore if a garage fits rear seat belts to a car, a woman hires a carpet cleaning machine (and especially asks if it can cope with long-pile rugs) and a couple trade in their old gas fire for a new one at the gas showrooms, these 'goods' are all covered under the Act.

The standard of services offered to a consumer is also covered by this Act – such as those provided by builders, plumbers, TV repairers, hairdressers, garages, etc. It protects the buyer against shoddy workmanship, delays and exorbitant charges. The Act states that all services should be carried out:

- for a reasonable charge
- within a reasonable time
- with reasonable care and skill.

Consumer Protection Act 1987

This Act introduced two new areas to consumer protection in general.

- A person is guilty of an offence by giving consumers an indication which is misleading as to the price at which any goods, services, accommodation or facilities are available, e.g.
  - false comparisons with recommended prices (e.g. saying the goods are £20 less than the recommended price when they are not)
  - indications that the price is less than the real price (e.g. where hidden extras are added to the advertised price, or VAT has been deliberately omitted)
  - false comparisons with a previous price (e.g.

false statement that the goods were £50 and are now £25)

- where the stated method of determining the price is different to the method actually used.

■ The Act also states that it is an offence to supply consumer goods which are not reasonably safe. An offence is also committed by offering or agreeing to supply unsafe goods or possessing them for supply.

Standards

In Britain, most advertising is self-regulating. This means that the advertising industry *itself* acts as its own 'policeman'. An organisation which instructed an advertising agency to create an unethical advertisement would normally be told by the agency that this would be unacceptable. Similarly, a newspaper would refuse to accept an advertisement which may offend its readers.

The two main watchdog bodies which check that standards (both legal and voluntary) are maintained are the Trading Standards Office and the Advertising Standards Authority.

Did you know?

The British Code of Advertising Practice states that all advertisements should be 'legal, decent, honest and truthful'. It particularly covers areas such as:

■ testimonials and recommendations by famous personalities
■ advertising aimed at children
■ advertisements for cigarettes, alcohol, slimming and medical products
■ comparative advertising (where one advertiser compares his product with another).

No advertiser is allowed to make a claim which cannot be proved.

Trading Standards Office

Your local Trading Standards Department will be run by your nearest County, Regional or Borough Council. In Northern Ireland it will be run by the Department of Economic Development. You can look up the telephone number and the address in your phone book.

The Trading Standards Department enforces consumer laws and advises consumers on their legal

rights and how to make and pursue complaints. Trading Standards Officers visit shops and other commercial premises and advise traders how to comply with the law. In addition they will:

■ investigate claims that traders are selling, or offering for sale, goods which are unsafe to use
■ check that any weighing and measuring equipment on the premises has been regularly tested and is showing accurate and correct quantities
■ ensure that all items on sale are accurately labelled and described and that food items are of a certain standard quality
■ check that prices are clearly displayed and that no misleading claims are being made about price reductions. Food traders must show the price per pound of certain foods such as fruit, vegetables and meat. Pubs and restaurants must display a clear price list outside the premises.
■ ensure that organisations offering credit are licensed to do so
■ check that organisations are not displaying signs which appear to take away a consumer's right to complain (e.g. 'no refunds given').

Consumers can contact the Trading Standards Department to check that they have a valid complaint. They will then be advised to try to settle the matter with the retailer (or person from whom they purchased the goods or service) directly. If they are unsuccessful, the Trading Standards Department may help them to pursue their claim through the County Courts.

Figure 3.33 A roadside check

Did you know?

Trading Standards Officers are also responsible for enforcing the law preventing the overloading of goods vehicles. Sometimes they set up checkpoints by the side of the road. Heavy goods vehicles may be stopped and the load checked to make sure that it complies with the law and is securely fastened.

The Advertising Standards Authority

This is an independent organisation which investigates complaints from the public about the content of advertisements. Sometimes advertisers may send a copy of the advertisement to the ASA for checking before it is put into print.

Each year the ASA receives about 8000 complaints and each month publishes a Case Report which gives details of the complaints investigated and the action taken. If a complaint is upheld, the advertiser will be asked to withdraw or change the advert. The ASA may also ask the media not to accept any more adverts on the same theme.

The standards for advertisements are currently undergoing a major review and the ASA will introduce a tougher code regulating advertisements in newspapers, magazines and on billboards during 1995. In many cases, concern has been expressed at the type of posters and advertisements being designed to advertise some items such as films and videos – the argument is simply that to watch some films you have to be over eighteen, but there is no age limit on seeing a poster or advert. Similarly, many people objected to the range of Benetton adverts which were designed with the object of 'raising social consciousness' (according to Benetton) but offended people by portraying war, famine and someone dying from AIDS. It is likely that the new regulations will give the ASA the power to be more proactive in relation to the type of advertisements allowed – rather than concentrating on reviewing those which have already been produced.

Did you know?

It is not only the ASA who can act quickly to have offending posters removed. In Liverpool, Merseyside Transport insisted that posters advertising the film Disclosure, which showed Demi Moore and Michael Douglas in a compromising position, were removed after several drivers had accidents on the way to work because of staring at the posters!

Optional evidence assignment

*This activity can be carried out verbally in class **in a group** as a non-assessed activity to consolidate learning. Alternatively, if you do it **on your own**, it can count as supplementary evidence towards the following parts of the scheme.*

PC 2: Describe constraints on the content of promotional materials

Range: Constraints: legal (Trades Description Act, Sale of Goods Act, Consumer Protection Act); standards (Trading Standards Office, Advertising Standards Authority)

Core skills: Communication, Information technology

You have started work for a retail shop which sells a wide variety of toys. The owner, Mr Price, is concerned because there have been several reports in the press of unsafe toys being sold and he has just been offered a large quantity of items made abroad at very low prices. He is unsure whether he will be liable to prosecution if he sells these goods. He is also worried because, on two occasions recently, people have complained about advertisements he has placed in the local press. He has asked you to research the problem for him and produce a short report which will give him guidance on the subject.

1 Write (or telephone) your local Trading Standards Department and ask them for leaflets on the services it offers, both to consumers and retailers.
   Mr Price has heard something about a lion symbol which guarantees quality and safety and has asked you to find out details.

2 Write to the Advertising Standards Authority at Brook House, 2–16 Torrington Place, London WC1E 7HN and ask for literature on its work and a copy of a recent Case Report.
   Find out about the regulations which apply to advertisements aimed at children. Compare these with the effects adverts have on children you know (or had on you *yourself* when you were young). Write brief notes on how effective you think the controls are.

3 Comment on each of the following events which took place in the shop over the last month and write down what you think should have taken place and why.
   a Mr Price refused to give a refund when someone wanted to exchange a toy because it wouldn't work, even though the customer produced a receipt as proof of purchase. He insisted that the boy had to choose another toy in the shop.

b The shop placed an advert in the local paper with the slogan 'If your mum really loves you, she'll bring you to Price's toy shop.'

c Mr Price held a sale. The notice said that all goods were reduced by ten per cent but some had only been reduced by five per cent.

d A parent complained that a teddy bear was unsafe because the eyes were loose and could easily be pulled out – a child might swallow them. Mr Price said the parent should write a letter to the manufacturer.

e Mr Price exaggerated the size of a toy truck in an advertisement by putting an enlarged photograph next to a small boy.

f Mr Price reduced the price of a dolls' house because it was slightly damaged and pointed this out to the buyer. He refused to change this when the buyer later returned saying he had changed his mind about the purchase.

Plan to produce promotional materials

The aim of this element is not just to give you information on promotional materials but to enable you to produce them yourself. You should find that, having learned something about promotion, you will have some ideas about the methods to use and what can be achieved. However, it is one thing calling in specialists to design the campaign for you – and quite another to do it yourself! What are you likely to need and how can you go about obtaining them?

Time

Any promotional campaign has different stages. Normally these fall into four categories:

a the planning stage
b the production stage
c the post-event stage
d the evaluation stage.

The amount of time you can allocate to each stage will depend on the total amount of time between deciding on the promotion – and the deadline for the product launch or event.

Planning

This is a key part of any campaign and should never be skimped. A good plan is the bedrock upon which

you build your campaign. If you hurry this stage then nobody – including you – will have a clear idea about what they are doing!

Your plan should include:

- what you aim to achieve
- the methods you will use
- the people who will be involved
- the timing of each part of the campaign
- the materials and equipment you will need and how these will be acquired
- deciding the theme of your campaign
- deciding how the tasks should be allocated between members of the team.

Production

This is when the real work begins – creating posters, writing to people to obtain sponsorship, taking photographs, printing leaflets, making films and videos. You must allow time for people to be creative, to correct mistakes, to reply to letters and to edit films and videos.

It is always a good idea to end a promotional campaign with something important, rather than letting it fade out like a damp squib. If you are running a competition, it is a good idea to make a presentation to the winner. If you have been publicising an event, the date of the event is critical – and you would want to arrange publicity coverage on the day.

Post-event

Usually after the main event, you can follow it up to obtain post-event publicity, e.g. films or videos of the actual event, presentation or launch, and articles about it in the Press or staff magazines. It is important that this is done promptly – before everyone forgets what actually happened and it becomes history rather than news!

Evaluation

This is critical if you want to learn from the experience. It involves reviewing everything that was done, thinking about how successful it was and whether it could have been improved upon. Evaluation is dealt with in detail on page 338.

People

If you are involved in promotional activities you will probably be expected to work as a member of a team.

Each person on the team will have different strengths and weaknesses and possess a variety of skills. A good team uses these to its advantage. In addition, some people may have more time to spare than others, or more access to equipment. All these factors should be taken into account when deciding which person should undertake which part of the promotion.

The type of skills required for a promotional team will include:

- the ability to deal with people
- the ability to listen to other people's points of view
- the ability to write good, clear 'copy'
- graphic design skills
- the ability to sell the idea and persuade other people to help (e.g. by placing an advertisement in their shop or becoming a sponsor)
- the ability to use different media and equipment, e.g. cameras, camcorders, computers and reprographic equipment.

In addition, *all* members of the group should support one another and show consideration for each other when things aren't going too well. A sense of humour (at the right time) can be an invaluable asset.

Hints and tips on copywriting and graphic design are given on pages 329 and 330.

Materials

The range of materials at your disposal will determine the type of work you can produce.

Below is a list of the range of materials which are useful for promotional work.

Figure 3.34   The basics

Basic essentials

- Cutting equipment – knives, scissors, a guillotine and/or a rotary trimmer
- An eraser!
- A pencil sharpener – the softer the pencil you use the more you will need to sharpen it. Don't sharpen pencils over a desk and don't put the shavings anywhere but in the bin!

Pencils and markers

- Black pencils with different leads. Use a soft lead to sketch ideas you will want to erase later. B pencils are soft, 9B are the softest – and H pencils are hard, 10H being the hardest.
- Coloured pencils, felt tips and/or wax crayons. Each achieves a different effect.
- Marker pens of different thicknesses –fine line and thick line. If you use marker pens bear in mind that water-based markers can be 'layered' for different effects. Marker pens dry up quickly so keep the caps on when they are not in use.

Paint and brushes

- Paint – acrylic paints are very popular today and can be used on almost any surface. Another alternative is gouache. If you use the latter and want to cover a large area, mix it with Chinese white to make it easier. Water-colours are available in two standards – artists' quality and students' quality. Choose the latter – they are cheaper and quite adequate to practise with.
- Brushes are hard and soft, are sold in different shapes and sizes. They can be flat, round or oval-shaped. Sizes start at 00 (very small) and go to about size 14 (quite large). Brushes must be washed after use and stored dry, either standing with the bristles upwards or lying flat and kept in the fresh air.

Stationery items

- Paper and board. Many different types of papers are available. Layout paper is the cheapest and gives you the chance to try out your ideas without spending much money. Tracing paper is useful if you want to copy a design or illustration. Cartridge paper is heavier weight and often used for drawing. Board is simply high quality drawing paper put on to a stiff backing board. Different weights of board are available and many graphic design shops will cut these to the required size. Both paper and board are available in a variety of colours.

- TV layout pads are packs of pre-printed paper with TV-screen-shaped masks. They are ideal if you are preparing a storyboard prior to making a video.
- Film or acetate transparencies are useful if you are preparing a promotion which will involve the use of an overhead projector.
- Masking film – to cover up areas you don't want to paint. You can make a mask of letters for your headline, paint or spray around it and when you peel the film away your headline will be the only area not covered and will therefore stand out.
- Dry transfers, e.g. Letraset. These give instant lettering in a variety of typefaces but are expensive!

Equipment

In a professional studio you would find adjustable drawing boards and a visualiser (which enlarges illustrations). Special copying and printing machines would be available. It is doubtful if you have this type of equipment at your disposal. The equipment which would be helpful, however, includes the following.

- A copying machine – either a photocopier or offset litho machine. The former is easier to use, especially if you have a modern colour copier. If you have an older colour photocopier, you may have to produce your artwork in stages. Each stage would give the text and graphics for a particular colour. The paper must be passed through the machine once for each colour and the text/graphics are overlaid, one on top of another. The critical factor is **registration**. This is the placing of each piece of text or graphic exactly in position, so all the colours fit in with each other. If you get it wrong your footballer with the red shirt and blue pants could have a muddy waistband in the middle and may even have red arms!
- A computer and laser printer – this enables you to produce a variety of graphics and typefaces with ease (see page 327 and Element 4.3).
- A film camera or, even better, a Polaroid. This means that you can remedy any disasters immediately without having to wait until your film is developed.
- A camcorder – to produce your own videos – and a video machine on which to play them. Plus video tape!

Did you know?

A **scanner** converts an image on a drawing, photograph or video still into a series of digital impulses which produces the image on a computer screen. These enable sophisticated graphics to be created and printed. You may have seen one in operation if you have ever seen designs on T-shirts being produced from people's photographs.

Computer-generated material

Today computers are used for a wide range of graphic material and promotional literature. In professional studios computer illustration is becoming a specialisation in itself. Graphic packages offer the artist the choice between drawing and painting modes. Very sophisticated software packages are available, such as Aldus Freehand, Adobe Illustrator and Photoshop – which can be used even to change the colours in a photograph. The most popular choice of computer with artists and designers is the Apple Macintosh. The benefits of using computer graphics are that:

- each stage of the illustration can be stored and recalled as necessary
- illustrations can be manipulated as desired, or copied at the touch of a key
- 'clip art' – pre-drawn art, stored on disk, which can be selected, modified as required and included in other documents – is available for amateurs and professionals alike.

Did you know?

Many of the graphics you see at the beginning of television programmes and the special effects you see on films are produced on computer. See if you can find at least two examples.

Desk-top publishing

This enables you to bring text and graphics together in a document, which could be a poster, newsletter or advert. Text is keyed in using a compatible word processing package. Graphics are usually scanned in, using a flatbed document scanner or a hand scanner. The package enables you to:

- choose different fonts, or typefaces, for your text
- position your text where you wish – in columns if you are producing a newsletter
- create headings of different sizes

- move, cut, trim, enlarge or reduce your graphics to fit your page
- draw different borders around illustrations by varying the type of box you use, e.g. square or rounded corners, and the line thickness.

You really need a laser printer to get the best from a desk-top publishing package. If it is a *Postscript* printer, which has an additional processor for complex fonts and graphics, you may have a wider range of typefaces to choose from. Check with your tutor what type of printer you will be using.

Desk-top publishing packages are ideal for designing the title page of your projects. Simply draw two or three boxes on your page and insert the main text. The secret of success is to keep the design simple until you know what you are doing! Don't be tempted to use too many different fonts on a page.

Figure 3.35 Produce professional-looking titles for your reports.

Did you know?

You can't just copy text and illustrations from magazines, or you could be in danger of breaking the law on copyright! If you are worried about what you can use, have a word with your tutor.

Alternatively, use the clip art page we have included at the back of this book. You can scan any image from this page *without* breaking copyright.

Non-assessed activity

Go through the lists of materials and equipment given above carefully, with the rest of your group and your tutor. Identify how many items:

a you can provide
b other members of your group can provide
c your school or college can provide.

Remember that in acquiring additional items you have sometimes to be quite resourceful! If you can borrow a Stanley knife, this is ideal for cutting board. Someone you know may be prepared to lend you a camera if you don't own one yourself. You may be able to beg or borrow items from students in the art department, and so on.

Bearing this in mind, **as a group,** consider how many *legal* ideas you can come up with for acquiring items which you don't own at the moment.

Cost

You may find that, no matter how hard you try, you still have certain items missing. You now have two choices: you either manage without them or you find the money to pay for them! It might be the case that, if you are organising a special promotion, you need items which *can't* be produced in-house. As an example, many charity campaigns make use of printed stick-on badges (or even proper printed badges) and you would need a professional to make these for you.

You may find that there is money available in your school or college (e.g. through the petty cash system) to pay for small requirements such as paper, board or marker pens. If you want to aim higher, you may have to raise the money yourself. Rather than starting from scratch, it is sensible to cost out what you need and then use this cost as a target. You then have to decide how to raise the money – don't forget that you could use money raised in advance from corporate sponsors to have some items printed professionally.

Remember that in any promotional campaign you have to keep track of the cost involved. Even the largest companies have a fixed budget for advertising and promotion which the Marketing manager must keep within! Once you have decided what is available and the size of your budget, *don't* suddenly make a decision which will drastically increase the cost. You wouldn't be able to do this in business, so don't do it now!

Did you know?

You actually save money if you look after the materials you use (see above on storing brushes, using marker pens properly and so on). This means they need replacing less often and there is more money available for other things to be bought! Try to find a lockable cupboard you can use, as a group, for storage.

Optional evidence assignment

*This activity can be carried out in class **in a group** as a non-assessed activity to consolidate learning. Alternatively, if you do it **on your own**, it can count as supplementary evidence towards the following parts of the scheme.*

PC 3:   Plan to produce promotion materials to promote particular goods or services

PC 5:   Design and produce promotional materials and use them to promote goods or services

Range: Plan: time, people, materials, equipment, cost

Promotional materials: advertisement, sponsorship, competition

Core skills: Communication, Application of number

1 a Visit a local art shop and cost the following materials.
- two good-quality paint brushes
- a large piece of coloured board, size A1
- spraymount adhesive
- six dry markers in different colours and widths

b If your group wasted the equivalent of the above materials four times a year, how much would that cost your school or college?

c Suppose you have a friend who is careless and untidy. He spends a fortune on stationery each year. Write down four hints or tips to help him save money.

2 Suppose your school or college is holding a Christmas Fayre on the second Saturday before Christmas. All proceeds will go to a local children's charity. You have been asked to help promote the event to parents and local organisations.

a What methods of promotion will you use to advertise this event? Why?

b Make suggestions for:
i   sponsorship you could ask for
ii a competition you could organise to raise additional money.

c Divide into teams of **three or four.** Draft a plan of action which shows the dates when you aim to start planning your campaign, the time-scale for planning and producing your materials, and the date on which you want to start advertising, for maximum impact. Bear in mind that if this is too early it will lose impact, but if it is too late people won't be able to make arrangements to come. Your plan should show who is responsible for different activities (according to their talents and strengths) and state the materials and equipment you think you will need and an estimate of how much they will cost.

Figure 3.36 *Original designs have more impact*

d Design a poster which is eye-catching and original to advertise the event.

e Calculate the materials you have used and how long it took you. Compare your actual usage of materials and time with your plan and give reasons for any differences.

Promotional materials

The purpose and type of promotion will affect the range and style of the promotional materials which are produced. As an example, a university may produce quite formal brochures and booklets with photographs of the campus, facilities and student accommodation. A promotional leaflet from MacDonald's is likely to be far more informal, with a different style of wording and more informal illustrations.

The style of promotional materials is strongly influenced by their purpose, the creativity of the team producing them and the total budget. The purpose of promotions is covered on page 334. This section concentrates on giving hints and tips so that you can produce materials yourself.

Promotional materials are designed to:

- attract the **attention** of consumers, e.g. by the use of colour, good layout, a 'punchy' headline or slogan and by being used in the right time and in the right place
- gain consumers' **interest**, e.g. by including a special offer, eye-catching pictures or illustrations or text which makes the reader want to know more
- create a **desire** to own the product or buy the service, e.g. by persuading consumers that they will gain pleasure and satisfaction from the purchase
- explain to consumers how they can take **action** e.g. where the goods are on sale, what they must do next.

These four aims are known by the acronym **AIDA**. They apply to every type of promotional campaign.

Did you know?

In 1994 Pepsi signed up supermodel Cindy Crawford to make a total of 17 adverts promoting the drink in an attempt to increase its market share over Coke. It is easy to see how Pepsi aim to attract attention, gain interest and create desire!

Advertisements

It is useless spending money promoting a product or service if the message is:

- unclear
- ambiguous
- too long to be remembered.

Organisations often employ specialist advertising agencies to design an advertising campaign, think up slogans, produce artwork etc. The type of campaign – and the message – will depend on:

- the product or service being promoted
- the method of advertising being used
- whether the aim is to *persuade* or *inform* people (see page 336).

Before you start to write an advertisement it is important that you:

- check that you have all the main details in front of you
- clearly understand how much space you have available
- know the purpose of your promotion (see page 334).

Now think about the advertisement from the point of view of the customers. How much information do they really need? Is there a catchy headline you can use to attract attention? How can you make them continue to read to the end?

The two skills which you can develop to help you to design and create attractive advertisements are **copywriting skills** (writing the text) and **graphic design skills** (creating the design and graphics). Hints and tips on both of these, given below, are just as useful whether you are designing an advertisement, a poster or a leaflet.

Did you know?

If you have a good story to tell or an 'angle' which would interest people, your local press will cover an event free of charge. You may also find that your local radio station will invite you on a programme to talk about it. This is free publicity which can be very useful in helping your promotion.

Copywriting skills

Copywriting is writing a message which will sell a product or event. Even if the copy will be supported by illustrations, the wording is critical. The copywriter must work closely with anyone involved in visual aspects of the work, so that the two parts join together and don't clash. If the copy is going to be typed, this also needs to be discussed so that the font size and weight of the text is correct.

Some important rules to remember

- People don't *read* advertisements – they scan them. The message must therefore use the minimum number of words.
- Every word must be easily understood – so the language used must be simple and appropriate.
- Buzz words attract, e.g. 'free', 'new', 'now'.
- Action words hold the reader's attention, e.g. 'try', 'watch', 'come', 'enjoy', 'take', 'buy', 'do', 'remember', 'consider', 'explore'.
- Adjectives create an image in the reader's mind, e.g. 'wonderful', 'beautiful', 'super', 'exciting', 'amazing', 'time-saving', 'mouth-watering', 'economical'.
- Alliteration or rhyme makes a phrase memorable. An alliterative sentence is one in which a sound is repeated several times – e.g. 'Cuddles – the complete caring cat food'.

Examples of alliteration and rhyme from actual advertisements include

- We're going well, we're going Shell
- A Mars a day helps you work, rest and play
- Don't be vague, ask for Haig
- Nissan – Hot Hatch of the Year
- The Canon copier gives copies round the clock.

- Think of a bold headline which attracts attention (remember the ones you found on posters). Look through magazines for examples.
- Many adverts appeal to people's emotions. A burglar alarm advertisement would appeal to people's need for security, a dating agency for people's need for companionship and love, a health product for people's need for self-preservation. Find examples of charity adverts which appeal to the emotions in a range of different ways.
- Make sure all the key information is included so that the reader knows what to do next, e.g. the date, time and place where an event will be held. If you miss this off there is very little point doing an advert in the first place.

Non-assessed activity

Your school or college social committee are holding a Hallowe'en Disco on Friday, 31 October. It will be held in a local club – Barney's Place – and run from 8 pm until 1 pm. Tickets are £4 each. You have been asked to design a poster to advertise the event. Before you start, read the section on graphic design (below) to help you.

Did you know?

Most people who work creatively – artists, musicians, designers, architects (and even best-selling authors!) – find a blank page of paper daunting at first. Don't let it frighten you. Have a go at something – even if it is in pencil and you rub it out later. At least you've broken through that awful 'don't know where to start' feeling!

Graphic design

You may find some of these skills rather daunting and/or lacking in your team. After all, if you were all potential designers you would presumably be taking a GNVQ in Art and Design! However, understanding that you don't have to cover a page in text for effect is crucial – in fact this would be counter-productive. Many adverts can gain from a few words which say a lot – often from the way the text is positioned. A good example is shown in Figure 3.37.

Some basic hints and tips to help you with this type of technique are given below.

- The average focal point for most people on a poster is about a third of the way down from the

Figure 3.37   Positioning the text imaginatively can help

top of the page, not half way down. You will therefore often achieve a better effect by dividing a poster or advert into thirds.

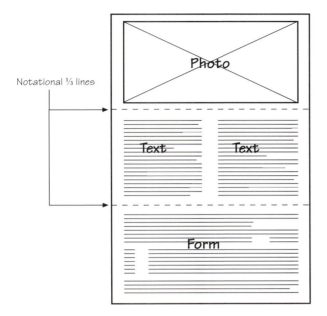

Figure 3.38 Imagine the depth divided into thirds for best effect.

■ A headline can be positioned in a variety of ways – not just across the top, left to right! Its size can also vary. Don't be scared to think big! Generally, it is better **not** to use a mixture of colours in one headline – it is apt to look childish.

Figure 3.39 Where to place the headline?

■ Position illustrations and text in unusual ways and unusual places for different effects. Keeping plenty of white space (empty space) means the poster or advert has more impact and is easier to read.

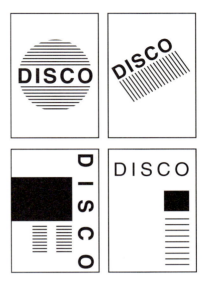

Figure 3.40 Achieving interesting effects

■ Remember you don't have to show the whole of something to indicate it is there – part of an illustration will often be enough, especially if it is enlarged.

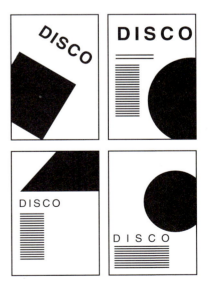

Figure 3.41 Images dropping off the page

331

- Combinations of lines and shapes can give dramatic effects.

Figure 3.42 Combinations of lines and shapes

- Use colour to indicate mood – yellow and blue give the impression of a bright, sunny day (look at travel posters), black is dramatic, and so on. Think about buying paper or card of a suitable background colour – but make sure the colour of text you choose shows up well.
- Choose a typeface (text size or shape) which is appropriate for the type of poster you are designing. You are safer keeping to the same one throughout.

Figure 3.43 Choosing an appropriate typeface

- Be *very* careful about using a border – sometimes it could spoil your work. Whatever you do, *never* use a fancy one!

You may find it is useful to start by drawing up a thumbnail sketch, similar to most of the illustrations shown above. You can practise your skills by cutting text and illustrations in different shapes and sizes out of a newspaper and moving these around an A4 page. Vary the layout and see what effects you can achieve!

An easy way to create a dramatic poster is to build up a montage. There is also less danger of a disaster near the end. Cut out letters, illustrations and text and mount them on card. You can overlay some, write on top of others and make some stand out from the paper more than the rest. A coloured montage on black paper can be extremely effective.

Did you know?

If you use a Spraymount adhesive (available from art shops) you can move and reposition items before you finally press them into place. If you do, though, it is a good tip to use it inside a large cardboard box, to limit over-spray.

Sponsorship

Most people have tried to obtain sponsors at one time or another to support them when they are taking part in an event to raise money for charity. You may have done this yourself at school. In the business world there are two types of sponsors – **corporate sponsors** (i.e. businesses) and **private sponsors**. Most people try to obtain private sponsors who have plenty of money to spend.

Corporate sponsors can help your cause in several ways. If you obtain official sponsorship, it will help the 'image' of your campaign because it will appear more respectable and 'official'. People are likely to be more impressed by what you are doing and will be more inclined to take notice.

It is always easier to ask for sponsorship from companies and people you know. If you were undertaking a charity campaign at school or college, and wanted corporate sponsors, you would be well advised to start by making a list of companies who are connected to your organisation, i.e. firms who accept students on work experience, suppliers of goods and services, businesses owned by school governors or parents and so on. You can then write to each of them asking for help. Be very clear about what you want them to contribute – and how you will publicise the fact that they are helping (which is sometimes their main reason for doing it!). Here are two hints which may help.

- Be prepared for some disappointments – many organisations get hundreds of requests in the course of a year and are forced to turn many of them down, or they would go bankrupt!
- Don't keep returning to the same people again and again for help, because they may get annoyed. You are better going for one big campaign than lots of little ones.

One advantage of obtaining corporate sponsors at the start is that any money you raise can help you to produce better quality leaflets and advertisements to publicise the rest of your campaign. This matter has already been referred to on page 327, under 'Cost'.

Private sponsors are usually obtained by designing a sponsorship form which can easily be completed, listing each sponsor and their contribution. The pain is often in going around collecting the money after the event! One tip is to ask people to donate a specific amount of money, rather than an amount which must be calculated later. This way most people pay 'up front' and it saves having to go around again afterwards.

Did you know?

Many organisations have specific policies for assisting people with sponsorship requests. Some, such as MacDonald's, have special 'packages' which they can make available for special events – such as a visit from Ronald MacDonald for the kids, a bran tub and other 'goodies'. Others, such as Marks & Spencer, have a committee at each store which examines local requests and decides which to support.

Competitions

Holding a competition can be tricky. You have to make sure that you have a one clear winner at the end. The main danger to avoid is having 25 winners (all sharing £5 for example!) or no winners at all – which is worse! You also want a competition which is easy to 'mark' – setting everyone a 1000-word essay to write on 'the classroom of the future' would be a nightmare. It would take hours and hours to assess all the entries and the 'judgement' might always be questionable. A competition like that would need a panel of experts whose judgement couldn't be questioned afterwards.

It is far easier to design something simple and to help people as much as possible by having easy-to-complete competition forms. Don't make the competition too hard or too elaborate. Make it clear how much 'luck' is involved, e.g. 'first correct entry picked out of the box'. Remember that if you want to hold a raffle or charge for entries to a wide audience, you may need a licence. You can obtain an application form from your local town hall but will need official help in completing it. You also need to beware of using any copyright materials (e.g. pictures of famous people). Think carefully about any legal restrictions which may apply. Ask your tutor for guidance if you are not sure what you will be allowed to do.

Bear in mind that people *like* the element of chance in a competition but *want* to be able to put in sensible entries. You can always make things easier by giving the answers, but in such a way that competitors have to use their skill to arrive at the correct sequence of answers. Even if they get stuck, they can guess at the correct answer. Make sure that the competition forms clearly state what the prizes are, what entrants have to do, how winners will be selected and how they will be notified. If you make special arrangements to present the prizes then you can obtain press coverage and publicity to cover this, too!

Did you know?

1 You can combine a competition with sponsorship by asking local organisations to donate prizes. Often these are in the form of vouchers, e.g. from MacDonald's or Pizza Hut, or as tickets, e.g. to the local cinema.

2 Unless you are very clever, or know a mathematics genius, steer well clear of anything like the National Lottery! You would have to calculate the number of options very carefully indeed against the number of possible entries to make sure you had a winner! Even Camelot rolls over the jackpot on some weeks because no-one has won! Holding a raffle is far less complicated. (See Application of Number chapter, page 600.)

Optional evidence assignment

*This activity can be carried out in class **in a group** as a non-assessed activity to consolidate learning. Alternatively, if you do it* *on your own*, it can count as supplementary evidence towards the following parts of the scheme.

PC 5: Design and produce promotion materials and use them to promote goods or services

Range: Promotional materials: advertisement, sponsorship, competition

Core skills: Communication, information technology. application of number

1 If you advertise a possession in your local paper you have to give the reader information. However, too much detail will cost you money – as you will probably pay 'per word'. The skill is in keeping to the main selling points and saying these in as few words as possible.

   a Look through your local newspaper to see how other advertisers have achieved this. Make notes of those words and phrases you think would be effective.

   b Choose any one of the following. Invent any details you want and write out an advert to try to sell the item in your local newspaper. Try to keep the number of words you use to fewer than 20.
   - a personal stereo
   - a portable compact disc player
   - an expensive tennis racquet

   c **As a group**, contact your local newspaper and find out their rates for advertising – both for classified and personal advertisements and for display adverts. You will find that, whereas the former is charged for by the number of words used, display adverts are costed by size, i.e. height by column widths.

Figure 3.44 Marching for Shelter

On your own, design a chart which clearly shows the cost of different types of adverts. Illustrate this by cutting out a selection of display adverts, calculating their size and working out the estimated cost of each one.

2 You are going on a 20 mile charity walk a week on Sunday, to raise money for Shelter, a charity which helps the homeless. You want your friends and relatives to sponsor you. Write a letter, using your word processor, asking for their help. Make this as persuasive as possible. Save your document and then enter the names and addresses of six of your friends or relatives. Use the mail-merge function on your word processor to produce an individual letter for each person.

3 Your friend is a member of the local youth club. They are holding a summer fair to raise money to refurbish the premises, and she has decided to hold a simple competition which people can pay to enter. Think of an idea which will raise money. The competition must be easy to enter and to judge, so that the winner can be announced at the end of the fair. Write a brief description of your idea in a letter to your friend (invent the name and address yourself).

The purpose of promotions

All organisations are regularly involved in promotional activities to make sure that customers do not forget about the products they produce or the services they supply.

The two main purposes of producing most promotional materials are:

- to communicate a message to an audience
- to create sales.

To communicate a message to an audience

It is arguable that all promotions communicate a message. The type of message will depend on the organisation – a bank will try to indicate it is secure and stable and a theme park will want to indicate it is a 'fun' place to visit. Organisations will allude to this in all their promotional materials, from the style of their letter heading, to the style of their packaging and logo, their corporate colours and the style of their advertisements.

Subliminal messages

If you have never heard of this word before, then look it up! A subliminal message is one which you don't really think about because you receive it subconsciously. Professional promotions give us both obvious and subliminal messages by a variety of techniques.

Colour is often used to give a subliminal message – perfumes are packaged in gold or black containers to give the message that they are luxury items. Bright primary colours (e.g. blue, yellow and red) signify that an organisation is modern and up to date. Subtle colours, e.g. dark green and navy, are used to indicate high-quality or sophistication. Masculine products are usually packaged in dark colours with silver – not pale pink! Natural food products (e.g. muesli) often have brown packaging because the colour is associated with nature.

The name of a campaign or a product also gives a message to consumers. Many household cleaning products bear names associated with speed, e.g. Jif and Flash. Romantic or exotic names are often chosen for chocolates e.g. Moonlight and Black Magic. Comfort is an obvious choice for a fabric softener, and so on.

Figure 3.45 Whiz through that cleaning!

Many messages are not just linked with the use of the product! For instance, it is often implied that by buying a particular product – from fast cars to hair shampoos – the customer will become more attractive to the opposite sex.

Logos are symbols and designs used by a company so that its adverts and products are instantly recognisable. Both logos and trademarks are protected by law once they have been registered by a company. No-one else can use or reproduce them without that company's permission.

Slogans are often used because they are memorable. 'Put a tiger in your tank' was a famous Esso slogan for many years. Nintendo developed the slogan 'Will you ever reach the end?' to promote their software products. The benefit of a short, punchy slogan is that it is easily remembered, becomes associated with the product (or company) and can be used on posters and billboards – which are generally viewed only fleetingly.

Did you know?

There have been some disasters with product names in the past. Henry Ford named a new car Edsel (after his son). It flopped. So did Fiat's car called Rustica (can you think why?). Part of the problem lies in the fact that names might not translate well into other languages. A specialist company will check a proposed name in every country where the product may be sold. Vauxhall found out that they couldn't sell cars called Nova in Spain because this translates into 'no go' in Spanish – hence the car became the Corsa.

Obvious messages

We are all used to receiving obvious messages as part of promotional campaigns. These range from being told how much we will save if we buy something to a list of benefits we will gain.

In some cases, however, a promotional campaign is launched with the sole purpose of giving us a certain message. A good example was the campaign related to Phone Day which concentrated on telling us to amend the dialling code of most town and cities by inserting an additional '1'. Campaigns concerned with road safety and the firework code – and of course, the AIDS campaign – are other notable examples.

Non-assessed activity

1 Many logos and trademarks are so well known that you can instantly recognise the company – e.g. can you say:
- which bank has a prancing horse as its symbol
- which car has a lion symbol
- which driving school has a red map of Britain in a triangular sign?
2 Find out the logo for each of the following.
- British Rail
- Barclays Bank

- Audi cars
- British Telecom
- Lacoste clothes
- Kentucky Fried Chicken.

3 Which companies use the following slogans?
- Play time
- Everything we do is driven by you!
- It's the real thing!
- Helps you work, rest and play
- The ultimate driving machine.

4 Collect a **minimum of six** adverts from newspapers or magazines and try to analyse them for 'messages' – both obvious and subliminal. Compare your answers with other members of the group – you may be surprised to find that different people see different things in a variety of adverts.

Creating sales

The aim of the majority of promotions is to create or increase sales. This can be achieved by:

- informing people about where and how they can obtain the product or service
- building up customer loyalty to a brand or organisation
- persuading consumers that this particular product or service is better than those offered by competitors
- persuading customers that they will benefit from buying the product or service
- creating consumer awareness of a range of products.

The way in which the organisation slants its promotion can either be **persuasive** or **informational**.

Persuasive promotions – influencing customers' perceptions

The idea of a persuasive promotion is that it **influences customers** and changes their perception or attitude towards a product or service and therefore alters their buying behaviour. They will also be tempted to buy if:

- the brand name sticks in their mind (so they will remember it next time they are shopping)
- there is a logo or trademark which means they can instantly recognise the company or the item
- benefits are suggested or implied in the message or slogan.

Another way of making adverts memorable is to make them humorous. One of the most famous –

and successful – campaigns has been the PG Tips chimpanzee adverts. Gordon's Gin cinema adverts and Heineken adverts are both well known for their humour.

Providing information

The press or direct marketing are the main media used for informational promotions. Because informational promotions contain a considerable amount of detail, any other form of the mass media would be unsuitable – as it would be quickly forgotten.

The skill of the copywriter is to get people's attention – so that they will continue to read a quite wordy advert or leaflet to the end. To do this the copywriter will probably use an eye-catching heading, bold print, dramatic pictures or other visual effects, and careful use of space.

Informational promotions are typically used for financial investments, cars (to give information about engine size etc.) and computers. They are also used for charity appeals. Some advertisers combine persuasive and informational advertising, as in the Disneyland advert in Figure 3.46.

Figure 3.46 An advert for Disneyland

Did you know?

1 The basic difference between informational adverts and persuasive promotions is that the first are used when there are definite advantages or features to the product or service which make it different from its competitors. Persuasion is used when there are not.

2 One of the most successful financial advertising campaigns has used persuasion in the form of slogans and adapted these for use on TV, in the press or for outdoor adverts. This was the Prudential's 'Wanna Be' campaign – which used persuasion rather than information to promote its financial services. So there appear to be no hard and fast rules to follow – provided you have a good idea!

Figure 3.47 Prudential advertisement: a strong message and wide use of all media have proved a winning combination

Non-assessed activity

1 Your college or school wants to increase the number of students on its courses. Two advertisements are prepared.
The first says that your institution achieved the best examination results in the area. The second gives a list of courses available.
a Which advert is persuasive and which is informational?
b Which would appeal to you the most as a parent, and why?

2 Figure 3.48 shows many different aims of promotional material. Study it carefully.
a At first sight, does it look as if educational institutions would become involved in persuasive advertising?
b Do you think this is true? If not, why not?
c A further purpose of promotions is simply to give a message without creating sales. Which organisation does this?
d If 'creating sales' is taken in its widest sense, how does this apply to:
  i political parties
  ii charities
  iii pressure groups?

Promoter	Aims of promotion
Industry	To sell industrial goods, to persuade retailers and wholesalers to stock goods, to attract investors to buy shares, to recruit staff, to give information about their products.
Retail stores	To promote their store, to inform the public about sales, special offers, product ranges and services, to inform the public of new stores opening
Political party	To win votes, to change attitudes on a specific issue (e.g. unemployment)
Pressure groups (e.g. Greenpeace, Friends of the Earth)	To win support for a cause, to lobby government, to attract donations
Charity	To attract support, raise money, attract volunteers, gain sympathy for their cause
Entertainment and sports industries	To increase attendance, to attract people to the event
Educational establishment	To give information about courses, to give information about the establishment itself, to attract students or pupils
Local government	To give important information on local services and relevant changes (e.g. road closures in the area), to give information on planning applications
Central government	To give information on new laws, to promote health and safety, to discourage antisocial or unlawful behaviour
The media (e.g. radio, television, newspapers, magazines)	To increase their readership or viewing/listening figures, to encourage advertising

Figure 3.48 The different aims of promotion

3 Figure 3.49 shows an advertisement for commercial radio.
a Who is the advert aimed at?
b Is it persuasive or informational?
c What does the headline imply about the benefits of commercial radio – in only three words?

337

Figure 3.49   An advertisement for commercial radio

Figure 3.50   An advertisement for a charity card

4   Figure 3.50 is an advertisement which is both
    informational and persuasive.
    a   What aspects of the advert are informational?
    b   What aspects of the advert are persuasive?
    c   Why do you think the copywriter designed the
        advertisement this way?
    d   How can the advertisers check the success of
        that particular advert?
5   Job adverts can also attract our attention and be
    persuasive because of their wording and the different
    'angle' that has been used.
    a   Can you guess the advertisers of the following
        job? (The answer is given on page 341.)
    b   To which of our emotions is the advertisement
        intended to appeal?

Evidence assignment

At this point your tutor may wish you to start
or continue work on the project which will
prove to your verifiers that you understand
this section of the element. If you are starting the project
then turn to page 342 and do Section 1. If you have
already completed Section 1 of the project, now start
Section 2.

Evaluating success

Evaluation takes place when the production team
meets together afterwards to judge the success of the
campaign. What went well and what did not? What
could be improved upon next time? The evaluation
meeting should take place fairly soon after the

campaign has ended, while people still have it in mind and are still talking about it!

The aim of all evaluation sessions is to make sure that lessons are learned from the previous experience and that these are put into practice next time – otherwise the team will simply make the same mistakes over and over again. Even experienced and professional teams have evaluation sessions – and sometimes some of the best and brightest ideas for the next campaign are the result!

If you are new to evaluation sessions it is useful to prepare a checklist (which can be added to or amended later) which focuses attention on the main points. Your first – key – item of information is the degree of **response** to your promotion. This is often gauged by taking a tally of the people who attended an event or the number of sales of a product or the number of enquiries from an advertisement. If there has been a poor response, the evaluation may turn into something more like an inquest – where everyone tries to find out what went wrong. If the promotion has been successful, there still may be some key factors to be taken into account. Rarely is anything so perfect that it can never be improved upon!

It is useful to evaluate the promotion under the following headings and under each of these a series of questions has been drawn up to help you.

Did you know?

You should remember from what you read earlier that many organisations code response forms on advertisements and response cards sent by direct mail, so they can accurately assess the effectiveness, not just of the campaign as a whole but of each individual part of it.

Effectiveness in communicating to an audience

- How well did you communicate the message to your audience?
- Who was your audience and did you reach everybody?
- Were the messages you used appropriate? Did any cause unnecessary offence?
- Were any words or phrases used that your audience wouldn't understand?
- Was the message muddled or clear?
- Did your promotions attract attention?
- How do your findings influence your plans for future promotions?

Effectiveness in creating sales

Remember that 'sales' means the same as 'response' in this situation. Therefore the number of people who attended an event relates directly to how well you 'sold' the idea of attending, just as the total number of items sold refers to how well you 'sold' the idea of buying the product.

- How many types of promotion were used?
- Why were these chosen?
- Were there good reasons for omitting any?
- Was response to all types of promotion monitored – if so, how?
- Were any areas not monitored – if so, why?
- Which promotions were the most successful? How do you know? What reasons can you suggest for this?
- Which promotions were the least successful? How do you know? What reasons can you suggest for this?
- How do your findings influence your plans for future promotions?

Influence on customers' perceptions

- Were the messages the most suitable for the purpose of the promotion?
- If informational, was the amount of information given about right, too detailed or too skimped?
- If persuasive, would the 'angle' have influenced customers?
- Was the best image projected? Could this have been improved and how?
- Did the promotional materials look as professional as possible? Could the cost have been reduced?
- How do your findings influence your plans for future promotions?

Effectiveness in providing information

- Was all the necessary information included?
- Were all the details accurate?
- Was important information easy to see?
- Were all the claims made accurate – or were any misleading or exaggerated?
- Did customers know how to respond?
- Were the people handling enquiries well equipped to deal with them?
- Were any customer complaints received because of a misunderstanding?
- How do your findings influence your plans for future promotions?

General

- Was the promotion properly planned and co-ordinated, or was time and energy wasted because some people didn't know what they were doing or duplicated work done by others?
- Did you use all the methods of production available to you or not? If not, was there good reason for missing any (e.g. lack of time or excessive cost)?
- Were all possible opportunities taken to obtain publicity, or were some chances missed? If so, why?
- How do your findings influence your plans for future promotions?

Did you know?

Evaluation sessions can be difficult unless they are handled properly, mainly because people will naturally try to defend their own ideas and actions. Try, therefore, not to attack specific points of the campaign or to put blame on anyone for having an idea which, at the end of the day, didn't work out very well. Be sensitive to other people's feelings and try to examine each aspect of the promotion objectively. Gather evidence to support your views.

Optional evidence assignment

*This activity can be carried out in class **in a group** as a non-assessed activity to consolidate learning. Alternatively, if you do it **on your own**, it can count as supplementary evidence towards the following parts of the scheme.*

PC 3:   Plan to produce promotion materials to promote particular goods or services

PC 4:   Explain the purpose of the planned promotional material

PC 5:   Design and produce promotional materials and use them to promote goods or services

PC 6:   Evaluate how successful the promotional materials were in achieving the stated purpose

Range: Plan: time, people, materials, equipment, cost

Promotional materials: advertisement, sponsorship, competition

Purpose: to communicate a message to an audience, to create sales; to influence customers' perception, to provide information

Evaluate: effectiveness in communicating to audience, effectiveness in creating sales, influence on customers' perceptions, effectiveness in providing information

Core skills: Communication, Application of number, Information technology

As a group, you are going to create one item of promotional material and have it assessed by your colleagues. You are then going to write your own evaluation report on your material with suggestions on how you could improve it next time.

1. Choose **one** of the following ideas (or think of one yourself!).
   a an advertisement or leaflet for your own course of study
   b an advertisement for something quite valuable that you own
   c a poster for a special event
   d a letter requesting sponsorship or a sponsorship form
   e a simple competition with an appropriate entry form
2. Write an action plan which gives:
   a full details of the item of promotional material you are going to create
   b reasons why you have chosen this idea (which should link to your own particular talents and abilities!)
   c a target completion date
   d a list of materials you will need and their approximate cost
   e a note about the equipment you will be using.
3. Decide whether you are aiming for persuasion or information, then design and produce your promotional material.
   Write a brief explanation which states your reason for the purpose you chose and how this is reflected in your completed work.
4. Submit your material for 'judgement' by your tutor and your colleagues. Ask them to make comments on:
   a the effectiveness in communicating to your audience
   b how effective they think it would be in creating sales
   c its influence on customers' perceptions
   d its effectiveness in providing information.
5. Write a final evaluative report yourself, which

incorporates their comments, saying what you would do differently next time and why. Type this out neatly, using a word processor.

Evidence assignment

At this point your tutor may wish you to start or complete work on the project which will prove that you have understood this element. This project is printed on pages 342 to 343. If you have already started the project then you may only need to complete it by undertaking Section 3.

Answer to advertisement puzzle

The remainder of the advertisement on page 378 is shown below.

If you'd like to find out what rewards there are for Samaritans, and can spare a few hours, give us a ring - we're in the phone book. But please don't ring unless you are serious. Someone else may be trying to get through.

Revision test

True or false?

1 Only large organisations promote their goods and services.
2 The ASA is the Advertising Standards Association.
3 Competitions must contain some element of skill to be legal.
4 Every promotion only has one main purpose.
5 Planning is usually the most important stage in a promotional campaign.

Fill in the blanks

6 The two types of adverts are _____ and _____ .
7 The local Consumer Protection agency which assists consumers is known as the _____ _____ .
8 The requirements that goods must be 'as described' is contained in the _____ _____ _____ Act

9 Newsletters, adverts and posters can be produced on computer using a _____ _____ package.
10 If a commercial organisation decides to give backing or financial assistance to a promotion it becomes a _____ _____ .

Short answer questions

11 Think of **six** suitable questions for a team to consider during an evaluation session.
12 Write down **six** tips on effective poster design.
13 State **three** advantages of obtaining sponsorship for an event.
14 Give **four** disadvantages of advertising in the press.
15 State **three** purposes of producing promotional materials.

Write a short paragraph to show you clearly understand each of the following terms.

16 Point-of-sale
17 Financial resources
18 Trading standards
19 Physical resources
20 Sponsorship

Answers to sponsorship questions on page 318

1 Bells
2 Silk Cut
3 Diet Coke
4 Courage, Heineken and McEwans
5 Panasonic

Evidence indicator project

Unit 3   Element 3.2

This project has been designed to cover all the evidence indicators related to Element 3.2. It is divided into three sections. Tutors may wish students to complete the sections at the appropriate points marked in the text. Alternatively, tutors may prefer their students to do the entire project at the end of the element.

Performance criteria: 1–6

Core skills: Communication, Application of number Information technology

Section 1

This section concentrates on the first evidence indicator for this element. When you have completed the work store it safely as it will contribute towards your final project.

Obtain examples of three types of promotion, including a sponsorship and an advertisement. Write a brief report on each item which describes

- the product being promoted
- the content of the promotion
- any constraints on the content, bearing in mind the terms of the Consumer Protection Act and the standards of the Advertising Standards Authority. (It may help you if you think about what the content might have been without these constraints!)

Make sure you complete this section of the project by the deadline date given to you by your tutor.

Section 2

This activity concentrates on the second and third evidence indicators for this element.

Make sure you complete this section of the project by the deadline date given to you by your tutor.

1   **As a class**, hold a preliminary meeting to discuss a venture which you can promote during the year of your course. This could be related to any of the following:

a   the sale of goods or services under a Business Enterprise scheme

b   an event or series of activities designed to raise money for charity

c   an event being undertaken by your school or college, e.g. a Christmas or Easter Fayre or an Open Night for potential students

d   an event connected to a business or voluntary organisation with which some of the group are involved.

These ideas are not exclusive. You and your tutor may have other thoughts on this topic. You may wish to talk through various options at the first meeting and then take a break to think about the advantages and disadvantages of different ideas.

Write brief notes on the meeting which summarise the ideas which were considered. Type these out neatly on a word processor.

2   Hold a second meeting to discuss the ideas further and vote on which venture should be pursued. At this meeting you should aim to decide:

a   the nature of the event

b   the time-scale over which the promotion and the event(s) will take place

c   outline plans on the type of promotional materials which are likely to be suitable and their cost.

Again write out notes summarising your discussions and type these out neatly on a word processor.

3   Arrange the date of a planning meeting. Before this date:

a   undertake some preliminary research of promotional activities in your own area which will help you to gain ideas for your own campaign

b   make a list which states the range of promotional materials which you think you should produce for your campaign

c   for each of your suggestions, state the purpose of the promotional materials you have identified. Give an approximate cost of the materials which you think you will need and state how these could be provided.

4   At the planning meeting, undertake the following tasks.

a   Combine your ideas and decide which are and which are not feasible.

b   Make out a plan which explains the purpose of all the promotional materials which have been selected and estimates the time, people, materials, equipment and costs involved in producing them.

c Divide up the work so that everyone is producing an item which:

   i advertises the product, service or event or

   ii outlines a sponsorship scheme or

   iii details a competition.

The material could include a poster, leaflet, video or audio tape and could be produced using a computer.

Highlight your own name on the plan wherever it appears.

5 Before you start to produce any materials, it is important that you check that you are familiar with the legal constraints on promotions and the standards which must be maintained. To do this, refresh your memory by re-reading pages 320–323 carefully!

6 Produce the materials which have been assigned to you and obtain a spare copy of each for your portfolio. Type up all your other notes carefully on a word processor.

Section 3

This activity concentrates on the fourth evidence indicator for this element.

Make sure you complete this section of the project by the deadline date given to you by your tutor.

1 Before the promotion or actual event takes place, work out as a group how you will measure its success in **quantifiable** ways. You could do this by designing a questionnaire or by keeping a tally of visitors or responses or by adding up the money you receive and working out the profit from the event. (Note: questionnaires and surveys are dealt with in the Core Skills chapter Application of number).

2 Launch the promotion and/or hold the event and then measure its success in line with the decision you came to in (1) above. This will mean analysing your questionnaires or tally sheets to spot any trends or patterns, and obtaining useful information.

3 Prepare for an evaluation meeting to discuss the success of your campaign by studying the questions given on page 339 and preparing **your own** list. This should include those questions you have copied because they apply to your campaign, and those you have thought of yourself.

4 Evaluate your promotional materials in terms of how well they achieved their stated purpose and the response of the targeted audience.

Type up your findings neatly on a word processor.

Final stage

Make sure that your work from each section of the project is neatly filed in a binder. Prepare a title page with your name and the date. Give your project the title: **The Production of Promotional Material for** and insert the name of the venture or event.

Providing customer service

This element covers the needs of customers and the methods by which organisations try to meet these needs. This includes different types of communications, how enquiries and complaints are handled and the legal requirements which underpin all customer relationships. After studying this element you should be able to:

1 identify an organisation's customers and its *customer needs*
2 identify and describe *customer service* in an organisation
3 identify *business communications* which meet *customer needs*
4 demonstrate business communications which meet customers' needs

5 describe procedures in one business organisation for dealing with customer complaints
6 identify relevant *legislation* to protect customers.

Special note

Some of the written business communications included in this element overlap with those listed for Element 4.3. You will therefore find that the Optional Evidence Assignment which covers these topics includes cross-references for the performance criteria and range you will cover in both elements.

The organisation's customers

Before you even begin to think about customer needs, you need to decide exactly who are your customers. You can then think more clearly about what they are likely to want when they contact you and the actions you can take to meet their needs.

If you have spent any time on work experience in business – or in a part-time or temporary job – you may realise quite quickly that your 'customers' are not just people outside the organisation. Staff and colleagues in other departments may contact you for help, information or consumables. People may visit the organisation to look around – these may be students, prospective customers or VIPs on official visits. Some organisations even have 'visitor centres' attached to them because they have such a large number of visitors each year. Some of your customers may have special needs: foreign visitors may need an interpreter, those with mobility difficulties may need a wheelchair, others may be hard of hearing or have a visual impairment.

So, throughout this element, try to think about customers as more than simply those people who arrive to buy and pay for goods and services. 'Consumer-led' organisations are very aware of the fact that **everybody** is a potential customer – or knows of someone who is. The image of the organisation to all outside organisations and groups of people is therefore considered to be all-important.

Customer needs

Customers may contact you:

- to buy the goods or services on offer
- to obtain information on goods and/or services
- to place an order
- to enquire about the progress of their order
- to clarify details
- to query details
- to query their accounts
- to obtain a refund
- to exchange goods
- to complain, if they are dissatisfied with the service they have received or the product they have purchased
- to ask if they can return goods, or have them repaired
- to ask for assistance if they have particular needs.

Whether they call in person or telephone the organisation, basically they are likely to need:

- **information**, e.g. on the range of goods you stock, prices, discounts and delivery times
- **help or assistance**, e.g. to find a product which suits their needs or to answer a query

- **after-sales service**, e.g. to obtain a refund or replacement
- **care and attention** – there is nothing more annoying than to feel that neither an organisation nor its staff care one jot whether you buy something or not!

There are many jobs where you may have to deal with both external and internal customers on a daily basis. External customers range from members of the public (if you work in a bank, the local town hall or a shop) to foreign visitors or specialist industrial buyers (if you work for a manufacturing company). In the first case you would be probably expected to know enough about the products or services your organisation provides to assist the customer yourself. In the second, you would have to act professionally in your dealings with customers and clients – even if it was not your job to assist them specifically.

Internal customers are likely to be people from other sections or departments. You are very likely to have such customers if you work in a centralised section of a large company. For example, the Printing department will provide printed material for its internal customers. The Human Resources department may issue protective clothing and the stores section may book out spare parts or stationery supplies. A centralised filing section will issue files, on request, to different departments. A switchboard operator is a good example of a person who has to cope with a stream of enquiries from internal and external 'customers' all day long.

Figure 3.51   On the telephone to customers all day

Did you know?

We all remember 'first occasions' very vividly, like the first day we started secondary school or the first time we met someone important. For some reason, these occasions often assume more importance than subsequent visits or meetings. No matter what our first impressions are in our social lives, however, we may change our minds about people if we get to know them well. Unfortunately in business, a poor first impression is likely to lead to losing an external customer for ever, as someone who forms a poor opinion of an organisation is unlikely to return to give it a second chance.

Therefore, the way you greet people who visit your organisation or office is very important. Although it may not seem fair, if you are the first person they meet, *you* are the person who will influence their opinion of the whole company. What you say, and what you do, can therefore be critical.

Customers wishing to make a purchase

It is far easier to sell a packet of sweets or a newspaper than it is to sell a car or a computer, because so much less **product knowledge** is required. In addition, customers who buy sweets and newspapers pay in cash, whereas those who buy expensive items may need information on the types of credit available.

It is never advisable to persuade customers to buy a product just because you want to get rid of it (or them!). Trying to help a customer who is not certain what to buy means knowing what is available and thinking about what would be best for that particular person. This may mean asking some basic questions – which can be difficult if you are shy or new to the job.

Information on goods and products

In some organisations your main role will be to ensure that customers are put in touch with an appropriate salesperson who can give them detailed information. In some cases, a representative may visit a potential customer at home to talk about their requirements in more detail. In others, there may be salespeople who specialise in particular types of products – in this case, you need to find out who knows about what!

There are times when *you* will be expected to know enough about products to describe them properly to customers and give them basic technical information. To do this you should:

- *read* about the product from the literature available and note down the main features and selling points
- *ask* your supervisor to clarify any points which you do not understand
- *practise* explaining how the product functions (and how to demonstrate it in operation, if this is applicable)
- *find out* the price
- *think about* any questions you may be asked
- *be prepared* to compare one make of product with others in a range (e.g. one make of calculator with another).

Non-assessed activity

Choose *either* an item of equipment you have at home which you could easily bring to class (e.g. a personal stereo or calculator) *or* a suitable item of equipment in school or college (e.g. a photocopier).

Follow the instructions above to familiarise yourself with how it works and its main features.

Then prepare a short demonstration to the rest of your group – one of whom should play the role of the customer and ask you questions (just as they would if they were thinking of purchasing the product).

Record your demonstration on tape and then write up a commentary on your own performance – and the areas you think you still need to improve.

Did you know?

'Product' knowledge is still important if you work in the tertiary sector or services industry as the services you sell are your 'products', whether these are banking facilities or types of insurance.

In many cases, in these industries, a good knowledge of the product range is vital. You know this yourself. If you visit your local travel agent and are thinking of spending your carefully saved money on the holiday of a lifetime, you want sound, professional advice – not someone simply waving an arm towards a stack of brochures.

Related services

Customers don't just want to know about the products they can buy. Your organisation may also be judged on the additional services it provides, e.g:

- free delivery
- extended warranties or guarantees
- special offers
- free help desk or phone line for customers
- ordering goods which are currently out-of-stock
- different methods of payment and credit terms.

If you forget to mention any of these, you may lose a sale for your company. Bear in mind also that you need to keep up-to-date – in particular on special offers, as these may change regularly.

Most organisations usually have a considerable amount of literature available on their products and services to which you can refer (see page 366). Always check difficult queries with your supervisor rather than give the wrong answer.

Non-assessed activity

In the case of each of these enquiries, discuss as a group and then write down:

- the type of procedures which would be followed
- the type of forms which would be completed
- what could go wrong through staff inefficiency.

1 an order for a CD not in stock at a record shop
2 an application to open a bank account
3 an enquiry to replace existing window frames with PVC plastic frames
4 an application from a potential student to attend a college course
5 a telephone request from an existing customer for an insurance quotation for his son
6 a hurried visit from a young couple to a solicitor's office one lunchtime because they have just bought their first house. All the people who could see them are out at lunch

Customers wishing to obtain information

Information can range from that relating to specific products or services to general enquiries or even questions relating to your organisation. It is likely that you will only be in a position to answer all the different types of enquiries when you have worked for a company for some time. The type of general information you need to know includes:

- basic facts – such as the correct address and postcode of your organisation, the telephone number and fax number, its opening hours
- your company structure and organisation – who deals with what type of queries

- the range of products/services your company offers – not just a broad appreciation but details of what you can and can't offer. The expertise you can gain in this area will depend very much on the type of company you work for, e.g.
    - in a retail organisation sales assistants should know their stock well, its uses, the range, what can be ordered and so on.
    - in a service industry, e.g. an insurance company or solicitors, staff should know the full range of services offered and who to contact in the organisation for further information if required.
    - in a manufacturing industry the technical details of some products may be too intricate to be known by anyone other than the technical specialists. In this case you should have a good knowledge of the range of products manufactured and know who to contact in relation to the particular query you are asked.
- which goods have guarantees and warranties and for how long – and whether special insurance can be taken out to prolong cover
- your company procedures and the main methods of communication between and within departments
- basic facts about consumer law in relation to its aim of protecting customers, e.g. the Sale of Goods Act, the Trades Descriptions Act and the Consumer Protection Act (see Element 3.2, page 320)

- what literature is available, e.g. brochures, leaflets, price lists, reference books, etc.
- company policy on refunds and replacements
- the after-sales service offered by your organisation
- the correct procedure for dealing with customer complaints
- where to go for more information, help or advice.

Did you know?

It is perfectly natural for anyone in a new job to feel lost and rather useless when they first have to deal with a customer enquiry. You become effective much more quickly if you:

- read all the information available
- look at the products sold (if possible)
- listen to (and watch) experienced colleagues
- ask questions
- **remember the answers!**

Non-assessed activity

1 **As a group**, discuss the occasions when:

- you have contacted a shop or other organisation and received very poor service
- you have asked about products or services but the person you spoke to didn't know (or care!) enough to help you.

Write down your comments about how this affected your opinion of these organisations.

2 Have you, or any other member of your group, ever worked for an organisation (full-time or part-time) where you have received specific training on customer service?

Did the company have any type of merit system for service, e.g. the McDonald's 'star' badge system? If so, compare notes and write a **brief** report.

3 Think of all the things that have happened to you in shops and stores (and ask your parents or friends for examples) which have annoyed you or put you off returning to that shop. List as many things as you can.

Figure 3.52 Customers need information

General enquiries

At a basic level, people may approach you with a general query either about the goods that you stock or the services you provide. You might not always know the answer but you can still appear helpful – if

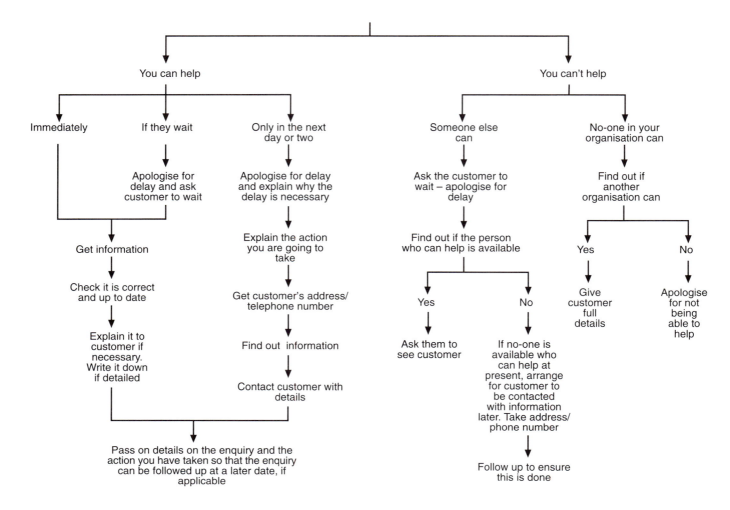

Figure 3.53 Answering general calls and enquiries

necessary by finding another member of staff who *could* help them. Over time, you can store up the answers to the general enquiries you receive and soon become a mine of information! You will know you are succeeding when you find you are able to answer more and more queries on your own.

Use Figure 3.53 to see how you should handle general enquiries. Make sure you know or can find out:

- *where* to get the information you need and *what* type of information is available – leaflets, catalogues, brochures etc. Don't forget people will always want to know about the price – and the ways in which they can pay, e.g. by cheque, credit card, or instalments. (See Element 4.1.)
- *who* to ask for help or further information, if that is required. Don't 'overstep' your area of

responsibility by promising anything to a customer which is outside your area of authority.
- *enough* about the customer to be able to recommend the right product or service for him or her. You should not be so keen to recommend a product or service that you 'lumber' customers with something that will not suit them as:
  - they will probably come back to complain later, and/or
  - they will go elsewhere next time
  - in some financial service industries this is illegal!
- *how* to follow up the enquiry. This means taking full details of the enquiry and making any special notes which will be useful or relevant to colleagues who may have to follow it up. Most organisations have standard procedures for dealing with enquiries, and standard forms to

complete. If there are any *additional* details which do not seem to fit anywhere on the form, write these out neatly and clip your notes *securely* to the form. Make sure you process the enquiry on to its 'next stage' without undue delay.

■ *how to keep the customer informed*! Tell the customer the procedure that is to be followed, how long it will take, what delays (if any) may be expected – and why. Promise to keep him or her informed if the situation changes in any way. This type of assurance would be essential, of course, if your company is out of stock of the product required and it has to be ordered. It is far more professional to tell customers that *you* will inform *them* when it is available, rather than asking them to ring you!

Did you know?

If ever you feel you need help and assistance from a more senior member of staff, you should always *ask*. It is far better to do this than to make a bad mistake and lose a customer for ever.

Non-assessed activity

You have worked in a local book shop each Saturday for several months. A new Saturday girl has just been employed and, for the first few weeks, you have been asked to keep your eye on her. The first morning you are very busy unpacking some new stock. When you come out of the stockroom you are horrified to see a queue of customers forming at the sales desk and the new employee standing at one end of the shop, obviously chatting to a friend who has called in. When you have a word with her she says she couldn't help anyone as she doesn't know where anything is and no-one has shown her how the till works.

a Was the new employee correct in saying that she couldn't help anyone? What do you think she *should* have done in this situation?
b To what extent were you and the other bookshop staff at fault that morning?
c If your boss now decides to spend the first hour with new staff on basic training, what items do you think should be included? Why?

Customers wishing to obtain a refund or exchange goods

Most organisations have a policy on what staff should do if a customer returns goods – either because they are faulty or because the customer has changed his or her mind. You must be aware of the following facts.

■ The organisation has to comply with the requirements of consumer legislation, e.g. the **Trades Description Act** and the **Sale of Goods Acts** (see Element 3.2 page 320 and this element, page 370). The main point to note is that customers who return faulty goods have a **legal right** to a refund – they do not have to accept a credit note, gift vouchers or alternative item. However, the person who actually bought the goods should return them – because the legal contract is between the buyer and seller and not with any third party.

■ Some organisations have policies which go beyond their legal requirements – for instance they will exchange goods without a receipt even if customers have only returned them because they have changed their mind. They may also change unwanted presents even though the person returning the goods is not the original purchaser (see Figure 3.54).

BHS and Mothercare
Will accept unwanted presents or goods about which purchasers have changed their minds but will only give a cash refund or allow an exchange if the customer has a receipt. Otherwise any exchange is at the discretion of the branch manager.

Marks & Spencer
Usually a cash refund is only given if the customer has a receipt, otherwise the customer is offered vouchers.

The Burton Group (Dorothy Perkins, Top Shop, Debenhams, Burtons, Principles, Evans)
Have a very generous policy. They will exchange or refund any items at the customer's request and do not insist on proof of purchase.

Comet
Goods can only be exchanged for a different product or for gift vouchers if they are returned within 14 days of purchase. After that time any exchanges are at the manager's discretion.

B & Q
Goods can be exchanged up to 28 days after purchase and will qualify for a cash refund if the customer has a receipt. Any refunds without a receipt are at the manager's discretion.

Superdrug
Cash refunds are allowed against a receipt but refund applications over £15 must be sent to head office. Only the lowest price is paid when refunds are made without a receipt – in some cases this may mean the customer has to accept a sale price even though the full price was originally paid.

Woolworths
Will not exchange computer hardware or software. Goods can be exchanged without a receipt or the customer is offered gift vouchers as an alternative. The goods must be in their original packing.

Figure 3.54 Returns policies at different High Street stores

There should be a clear procedure laid down for dealing with faulty goods – the badly-printed poster, the dress with the stitching undone or the cracked plate. In some stores, customers returning goods are referred to a special customer service desk where refunds are made. In some cases, nominated staff are allowed to give refunds. In others, permission has to be obtained from the supervisor. The customer may simply wish to exchange the damaged item for a perfect one, but has the right to insist on a refund (there might be no other suitable alternative in stock).

Policies on exchanging goods which are *not* damaged vary tremendously from one organisation to another. Because they are so varied the golden rule is not to assume *anything*. **Check** the policy of the organisation for which you are working – often it is clearly displayed behind a customer service desk for everyone to see, or is printed on the back of receipts!

Non-assessed activity

As a group, suggest a reason for each of the following policies which are in operation in many organisations. Discuss your answers with your tutor.

1 If a customer has paid by credit card a cash return is not usually given. Instead a voucher is made out to credit the card account by the due amount.
2 Most retailers who sell computer software will not exchange it or give a refund unless it can be proved to be faulty.
3 Cinemas and theatres which allow you to book tickets in advance using a credit card will not allow you a refund if you change your mind and decide not to go.
4 Travel agents and airline companies will not give a refund if you change your mind about going on holiday after you have made the booking. All bookings must be covered by holiday insurance to be legal.
5 Your dentist will reserve the right to charge you if you do not turn up for your appointment.

Customers wishing to make a complaint

Satisfied customers are usually easy to deal with. They are pleased with the service they have received and will probably call again when they want something else.

Dissatisfied customers are different. They may be dissatisfied because:

- they want a service you cannot provide
- they consider the service they have received to date is unsatisfactory and want to make a complaint
- they have a query which no-one seems to be able to answer
- they are annoyed at something you have told them (e.g. they cannot have credit)
- a product they bought is faulty.

Whether you have to deal with a difficult customer face-to-face or over the telephone, the way to handle the situation is the same (see below).

Most large organisations have specific procedures for dealing with and monitoring complaints (see also Element 3.4, page 385). In others you may be on your own! It is usual for complaints which can't be solved quickly and easily to be referred to a supervisor or manager, so they can keep a watchful eye on the way the business is run, and take steps to rectify problem areas.

Non-assessed activity

Figure 3.55 shows an example of the procedure for dealing with complaints, in operation in a large retail store.

1 Study the diagram carefully and trace what happens when a customer complains.
2 Discuss with your tutor the type of complaints which
   a could be rectified immediately
   b would have to be investigated by the Customer Services Manager.
3 Why is the Store Manager involved and at what stage?
4 Why are all complaints acknowledged immediately even if they cannot be rectified straight away?
5 Draw up a written description which matches the diagram to explain the complaints procedure in operation.

Did you know?

The boss of Dixons, Stanley Kalms, regularly works on the switchboard answering complaints to see what customers don't like about his organisation. If you worked for Dixons, how would you feel about this? Do you have the same feelings as a consumer?

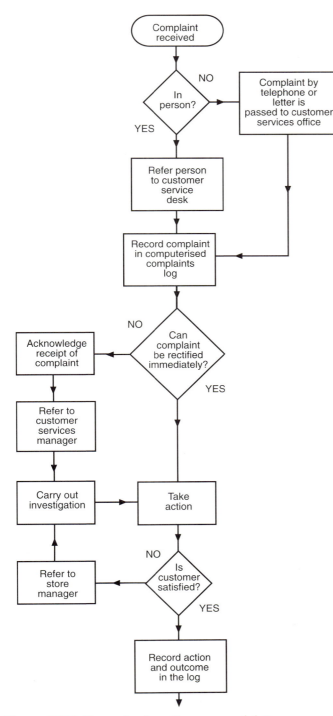

Example of customer complaints procedure in a large retail store

Figure 3.55 Example of customer complaints procedure in a large retail store

Dealing with complaints

You may be the 'first stage' of someone making a complaint – even though you are not the last. The way in which people make complaints will vary depending upon their personality and how well they know their consumer rights. They may be hesitant and apologetic, or they may be angry. The way you respond can make all the difference to their reaction.

Listen sympathetically.	**Don't** interrupt in the early stages of the conversation.
Take down all the facts.	**Don't** give vague excuses.
Check you have these down correctly by repeating them to the customer.	**Don't** put the blame on anyone.
Remain polite, patient and reasonable.	**Don't** get annoyed yourself.
Refer the problem to your supervisor if you cannot solve the problem or if the customer is very rude or aggressive.	**Don't** try to pretend the problem doesn't exist.
If necessary, explain that the problem will be investigated and give the customera specific time when he or she will hear from your company.	**Don't** make promises you can't keep.

Did you know?

You do not have to put up with abuse or threats from a customer who is annoyed. If this happens, get help immediately.

Non-assessed activity

You work for a large company which manufacturers household appliances and sells them through a range of retail outlets. All machines are covered by a one-year guarantee and the company operates its own regional service centres for faulty appliances – whatever their age. Therefore, when an appliance is faulty the customer telephones the regional service centre, not the manufacturer or retailer.

In the last few weeks your office has received several complaints on the service it gives, including:

- telephone line constantly engaged

- telephone line not answered during working hours
- unhelpful staff, e.g. won't book a service call unless the caller knows everything about the machine, including the model number
- restricted hours of repair staff which are incompatible with customers who go out to work all day
- long delays between calls being received and the visit of the repairman
- few parts carried by repairers – often a second call has to be booked when the part is available, which may be several days later.

1 Write down how you consider a customer will react to this situation – both immediately and in the long term.

2 List your suggestions to correct *each* problem.

3 Play the role of employee at the service centre, with one of your fellow students in the role of a householder whose washing machine has broken and who is annoyed because no-one has called, although she first telephoned your organisation four days ago. Record your conversation and write a brief report on your performance.

Customers who have special needs

As well as their different requirements you will find that customers are different in age, temperament and personality. Some will be obliging and patient, others ill-tempered or impatient. Some are confident – and know what they want – others are uncertain or even shy and tongue-tied.

Some may have special needs which require particular attention. A person with impaired vision, wanting a microwave oven, is likely to be unimpressed with the state-of-the-art LED display panel and want something with buttons and knobs which can be adjusted by touch. The mother with three young children may be more keen to become a customer of your organisation if the waiting area contains toys as distractions, and a lift – which will hold a pram – to the third floor.

Today most organisations are very keen to look after people with special needs. Vegetarian food is an option in most establishments, wheelchair access has been considered in relation to aisle widths in shops and stores, special play areas for children are to be found in most toy shops and virtually all shops and stores will allow guide dogs – even though other animals are prohibited.

It is impossible to give specific advice on every situation you are likely to meet. However, you have a responsibility both to your employer and to your customers to know what facilities are available, and to report requests for those which are not. It is also relatively easy for all staff to acquire some basic skills and knowledge which they can then *adapt,* according to the person and the situation.

Individuals with special needs are likely to belong to one of the following categories.

The handicapped

If you deal with people regularly then you will obviously meet people who are handicapped in one way or another. Many people feel awkward if they have to deal with handicapped customers. Whilst this may be understandable – especially if you have no experience of dealing with handicapped people – there really is no need to see this as a problem. The important thing is *not* to be patronising or treat people as if they are less intelligent, just because they have a physical handicap. Remember that *they* are used to coping with their disability, and don't feel embarrassed. Think about how their disability may affect their choice of products or services – the profoundly deaf don't usually buy audio tapes, and the blind do not buy books or newspapers (unless as a present). Thinking ahead will not only stop you making thoughtless remarks, but will help you to make some useful suggestions for that particular person.

- **The deaf** – you won't know that someone is deaf (unless he or she tells you) as there are no visible signs. If you think this might be the case make sure you *look* at the person when you speak (in case he or she lip-reads) and speak *relatively* slowly and clearly. *Don't* shout!
- **The blind or partially-sighted** – speak as you approach them – to avoid startling them. Your voice will also guide them towards you. Someone who is completely blind may have a white stick and/or a guide dog. If you want a blind person to follow you then *find out* if they wish you to lead them – don't just grab hold of them. If you approach any steps then say whether these are *up* or *down* and how many there are. Bear in mind that the worst thing a shop or store can do for a partially sighted person is move things around! Be prepared to take them to something they need – rather than give meaningless directions.
- **The disabled** – life will be much easier for any disabled customers if there are ramps, rather than steps, in your building – especially for those confined to a wheelchair. In addition, direct people away from narrow areas or places where

the wheelchair couldn't be turned around easily. Be ready to open doors if necessary. *Don't* try to rush them or appear impatient. Apart from being attentive and thoughtful and prepared to offer help when necessary, concentrate on the *person* rather than the disability.

Those with mobility difficulties

Some people have mobility difficulties even though they are not disabled. Obvious examples are the elderly, people with arthritis who cannot climb lots of stairs, and anyone who has a leg in plaster! Many organisations have collapsible wheelchairs on offer, particularly when the premises are very large. Lifts are a feature in most buildings today but if there is not one available, it may be possible to reserve a ground floor office for a meeting, rather than one upstairs. Don't try to rush people around if they find difficulty in walking – go at their pace and allow extra space for a walking stick, a walking frame or crutches.

The elderly

Many elderly people have very sharp minds so don't think that being old means being unable to think properly! However, elderly people are often slower to make decisions and may be overwhelmed by a vast amount of information, particularly if the product or service is something which hasn't been around very long!

Figure 3.56 Sometimes an elderly customer may need a little extra attention

Always allow elderly people more time (they often have plenty!). They may want to discuss the finer points of a product carefully before they buy it – often because they have two main needs when they shop. The first is to buy whatever it is you are selling. The second is to find someone to talk to for a while!

The mentally handicapped

Mentally handicapped customers may have difficulty in saying what they want or in making you understand them, as their vocabulary may be limited. Be patient. They normally know what they want, but just need *time* to cope with the situation.

Young children

Young children have special needs because they easily become bored and fretful. Babies and toddlers are likely to arrive in prams or buggies which require plenty of space and are difficult to get upstairs. Difficulties are encountered by the parents if there are no toilet facilities they can use, the waiting room is beautifully set out with expensive vases at knee height or if everyone always speaks with hushed voices. Places which deal with young children regularly, such as clinics and hospitals, doctors and dentists and even some large stores, have a range of 'distracters' available – from a fish tank to a toy box. Today many restaurants have 'colouring' place mats and crayons on the table. They also have special areas set aside in which mothers can feed and change their babies. Other organisations provide a creche where children can be looked after. Many creches are restricted to children of two years and over. Under this age, far more specially trained staff have to be on duty and this can make operating the creche very expensive.

If you have a younger brother or sister then you won't be too worried if you have to help distract a young child for a short time. Acknowledging a child's existence is better than trying to ignore him or her – and sometimes results in instant shyness! Be careful what you give very small children and babies to play with. Sharp or small objects are totally unsuitable – a large bunch of jingly keys is often much better, even if not very hygienic!

Foreign visitors

Another caller with a special need is the customer who does not speak English very well. In this case you might struggle to find out what it is he or she really wants. Assuming there is no-one on the premises who can act as interpreter then it might help if you

Listen carefully.	**Don't** speak quickly.
Use simple English.	**Don't** use long sentences.
Repeat carefully what you think is meant, to check you are right.	**Don't** shout!
Ask for help if you cannot understand the customer at all.	**Don't** become impatient.

Shy and nervous customers

These customers can be of either sex and of any age. You may be able to identify them because their 'body language' will usually show that they are hesitant or ill at ease. They may try to avoid eye contact if they speak to you. They may move backwards as you approach them.

Make sure you appear friendly without over-whelming them.	**Don't** be pushy or impatient.
Offer to help and speak gently, calmly and deliberately (nervous people don't 'take things in' quickly).	**Don't** try to rush them or finish off sentences for them.
If they want to take their time then agree and keep a watchful eye on them.	**Don't** neglect them or forget all about them.

Emergencies

The final category of customers with special needs are those who need assistance in an emergency. The type of emergency with which you may be involved will vary, depending upon the place where you work. If you worked in a doctor's surgery, for example, you would have been told exactly what to do if someone collapsed on the premises. You are less likely to have been trained properly if you work in a retail shop on a Saturday.

Emergencies can range from health or security problems to people in a hurry who need assistance quickly. Key points to remember are that you should:

- know your organisation's standard procedures for evacuation thoroughly
- know how to find the first-aider on duty – many

large organisations have an emergency extension number you can ring

- realise that at times you may have to drop everything to deal with an urgent request, whether this is being made from an external or internal customer. There is nothing more annoying for someone in a hurry than coming across another person who appears to have two speeds – dead slow and stop! If you are worried about cutting corners or rushing something through then find your supervisor and ask for help.

Non-assessed activity

1 Assess your school or college for access and facilities provided for handicapped customers and compare it with **three** other public buildings or shops in your town.

a What features do architects and builders incorporate into buildings to help handicapped people and those with mobility difficulties?

b How does your building score in relation to the others you have assessed?

c What **additional** help can organisations offer to handicapped or disabled customers or those with mobility difficulties?

2 As a group, check, that you know the emergency procedures to follow if:
- the fire bell rings
- someone collapses in the corridor.

Ethical standards

Business ethics are the personal and professional standards of people who work in an organisation. Sometimes there can be a conflict between ethics and other considerations – such as sales targets. An organisation which has high ethical standards would never condone an employee misleading a potential customer in order to make a sale. Telling someone that an outfit suits them when it obviously doesn't (to increase your commission) or asking the problem customer to call back tomorrow (because it's your day off) are examples of being unethical. You have not been honest and fair with the customer. It is also unforgivable to tell a deliberate lie rather than admit you don't know the answer to something. In some cases, not being completely honest can be illegal, e.g. deliberately misleading a customer about the capabilities of an item or its price (see Element 3.2, page 320).

In addition to honesty, ethical standards also relate to confidential issues. You are showing no integrity at all if, after leaving a client who has given you personal information, you gossip about it to everyone else in the office. In many organisations you could be handling the personal or financial details of clients and customers. You need to be sensitive to the type of enquiries where the content is such that it should not be discussed in a public area, e.g.:

■ **financial** discussions on loans, income, expenditure, payment difficulties etc.
■ **medical** discussions about personal health or the health of close family, serious illnesses etc.
■ **personal** discussions when information is relevant to past/future behaviour, criminal records, marital relations etc.

All organisations which have these types of discussions with customers will have private offices where interviews can be held. Every company will have a room where clients and customers can be taken if they need to pass on restricted information or discuss a particular problem.

The standard procedures and forms will still be completed with the relevant details – and often full, separate details of the visit are summarised for the benefit of other staff dealing with the customer later. Any such documents are usually kept in a customer file, marked confidential, and should *never* be the topic of open discussions with other staff or discussed outside the company.

Did you know?

No matter what job you do, there will also be facts and information about your company and other staff that you should not discuss with customers. Sometimes this can be difficult, especially if you are asked a question outright.

■ In any organisation you work for, make sure you are aware, of the type of information which must *not* be given to customers.
■ Deal with outright questions, if necessary, by implying that you don't know the answer, then refer the matter to someone else, e.g. 'I'm sorry, I'm not sure about that. If you wish, you can ask the supervisor, Mr Bates.' It is much more diplomatic to take this approach than to admit to knowing while saying that you *won't* tell!

Non-assessed activity

1 **a** Discuss **with your group and your tutor** the type of enquiries and occasions when your school or college might need to see parents in private and keep information confidential. (Bear in mind that for an educational establishment the parents and students are the customers!) Write down your ideas and keep them safe.

b How would you feel, as a customer of your school or college, if you found that personal information about your educational history or your family were known by all the staff?

2 Identify which of the following discussions should be held in private and why. In **each** of the cases you identify note down **why** you think it is important that a record of the discussion is kept in the relevant file.

a travel agent – discussion with client regarding a holiday in Malta
b building society – discussion about extending a mortgage repayment period
c estate agent – discussion with client about buying a property
d accountant – discussion regarding tax payable on additional earnings.

Customer service

Customer service is a very important feature in most organisations because of the advantages it brings. An organisation which makes a specific effort to meet its customers' needs will benefit in several ways.

1 **a** It will retain existing customers.
   b Word will get around – and new customers will be attracted.
   These factors will improve company performance as sales will increase and, therefore, so will profitability.
2 Service will be improved as the company (and staff) will learn from mistakes made in the past and put the best of their 'good practice' into everyday use.
3 It will improve the morale of staff and customers. If you *know* that you will be encouraged to give good service to customers, this will improve your own morale. We all get a 'buzz' out of helping people. Equally the person you help will also be grateful – and think well both of you and the company.

Non-assessed activity

You work in a hotel. A couple arrive in reception complaining that, although they ordered a room with shower, they have been given a room with a bath. You tell them you will see what you can do. Five minutes later another couple appear in reception. They have been given a room with bath when they ordered a room with a shower. You decide the obvious solution is to switch them around. When you do so, both are delighted and thank you profusely.

How would you feel at this stage? Would this give you a 'buzz' or would you be unaffected? **As a group**, discuss your reactions.

Figure 3.57 Four more satisfied customers

Did you know?

Companies that concentrate on giving excellent customer service can often rely on word of mouth to boost the number of customers, rather than advertising. Marks & Spencer is a good example. You will rarely see an M & S advert in the press or on television, so their advertising costs are relatively low. Instead, they rely on their good name and promote this by good customer service and helping the community and local charities.

Non-assessed activity

1 Visit **three** large stores in your own area. Assess customer service in relation to:
    a   speed of assistance
b staff appearance
c staff knowledge of goods and products

    d attitude of staff
    e policy on refunds.
2 Find **at least one** example of a store which has its 'customer service pledge' in a prominent position. Copy out the main points of this and comment on how these would help the customer.
3 Some organisations show a list of staff and give their titles. How do you think this might assist the customer?

Meeting the needs of internal and external customers

The ways in which organisations meet the needs of their customers depend upon:

- the type of business they are in
- their size
- the *type* of customers they have
- the *range* of customers they deal with
- the needs of these customers.

Remember that 'customer' in this context means anyone who needs information, help, assistance or advice. Some of these will be external customers and others will be internal customers (see page 344). To help, we are going to look at one particular type of organisation – a bank. We are going to try to:

- identify its external customers
- identify their needs
- identify possible internal customers
- identify their needs
- identify the range of other individuals and organisations that may contact the bank for help or information
- look at how the organisation tries to meet all these needs.

External customers

The external customers of a bank are those private individuals and business organisations who hold bank accounts at the bank. These may be savings, investment, loan or current accounts. Some customers will hold private accounts, others will hold business accounts. All will require sound financial advice, accurate and prompt service and the knowledge that their money is secure.

The bank will be well aware of the importance of potential customers, mainly because people rarely change their bank accounts. They will therefore go to considerable lengths to persuade young people and students to open an account with them, such as offering free gifts or vouchers to young savers and special loan terms to students. Banks frequently have special stands at colleges and universities during enrolment week. This is also why banks spend large amounts of money advertising in the press and on television. They also support educational initiatives, by backing Young Enterprise projects and other schemes and producing materials which can be used by tutors.

Internal customers

A large bank will have many different branches throughout the country. All of these will be 'internal customers' to the regional or 'head office' bank. Branches will require:

- information or assistance on employment law in relation to personnel problems
- regular stocks of advertising leaflets and booklets
- regular stocks of printed bank forms
- rapid processing of transactions through the inter-bank computer system
- information and assistance in relation to difficult or obscure queries
- the ability to make appointments for customers to see specialist advisers from the regional bank about specific issues.

Staff working at the regional bank or head office will also have their own external customers to deal with. Their daily workload will comprise servicing the needs of *both* types of customer.

Providing help or information for individuals

Banks have a large number of individual callers each day. They also receive requests by telephone and in writing. Their customers range from the young to the old, the rich to the relatively poor. Parents may want to open a savings account for their child, someone else may wish to take out a personal loan for a new car. Some people will need specialist advice or confidential counselling about financial matters. Holidaymakers will want to change their sterling into foreign currency. Another person may wish to sell some shares or make an arrangement for a bill to be paid automatically. Dozens of people a day want to pay money into their accounts or withdraw money from their accounts. Another person may wish to use a bank safe to deposit valuable items or to borrow money to start a business. A young couple may want to take out a mortgage on a house they want to buy. All day long

people are making requests in relation to investing, borrowing or transferring money. Every customer will want access to his or her money 24 hours a day and seven days a week. They will all want regular information on their financial position.

Banks meet the needs of these individuals by providing information leaflets on their services, sending out regular statements to account holders and providing a range of facilities and services to transfer money quickly and easily. This includes automatic cash machines and computer links with the main banking system. They have bank clerks on duty to deal with standard transactions, specialist staff to deal with other queries, a foreign exchange clerk to deal with requests for foreign currency and financial advisers who can see customers by appointment.

They also train their staff very thoroughly in customer service techniques. This includes their ability to answer the telephone promptly and deal effectively with all enquiries, and the way in which they handle personal callers.

Providing help or information for business organisations

Banks are also used to providing a wide range of help and information to various business organisations – not all of whom may be account holders.

Business account holders often want a different type of service from a bank – they may want their wages to be paid automatically or large amounts of money transferred overseas. The manager will need to know the specialist needs of local industry (see Element 1.2) and current economic trends which are affecting local business people. He or she will also need to give sound financial advice to people considering expanding their business or wanting to borrow large sums of money to finance an export deal. Business customers will expect the bank to be aware of economic trends and to advise them accordingly.

The bank will also be contacted by local organisations such as solicitors, estate agents and building societies. A solicitor may contact a bank if a client has died and the account must be closed. An estate agent or building society may be in contact with a bank if a large amount of money has to be transferred to pay for a house. Organisations may contact the bank for a reference on a local trader who holds an account there, before they will start to sell this person goods on credit.

The bank will appoint staff in different job roles to deal with the types of requests it receives and the specialist information it must provide. The bank manager is likely to be a member of the local Chamber of Commerce and have informal contacts with many business customers.

Non-assessed activity

1 Many organisations concentrate on fulfilling the primary or main needs of their customers. We have already seen that the customers of a bank value security very highly. Think of **one or two** key words to identify the primary needs of the customers of the following organisations. (Start by thinking about who their customers **are**!)
   a a video shop
   b a children's playground
   c a dentist's practice
   d a fish and chip shop
   e a clothes shop
   f a car dealership
   g a secondary school
2 A newspaper is another good example of an organisation which is contacted by private individuals and by business organisations. Discuss **with your tutor:**
   a why individuals would want to contact your local newspaper and the help and information they may require
   b why business organisations would contact the paper and how their requests may differ from those of private individuals.
3 Ethical standards are often a key issue in the way some papers report news stories. Discuss, **as a group** and **with your tutor,** the type of ethical standards individuals and organisations should be able to expect:
   a from a newspaper
   b from a bank.

Optional evidence assignment

*This activity can be carried out verbally in class **in a group** as a non-assessed activity to consolidate learning. Alternatively, if you do it **on your own,** it can count as supplementary evidence towards the following parts of the scheme.*

PC 1: Identify an organisation's customers and its customer needs

PC 2: Identify and describe customer service in an organisation

PC 5: Describe procedures in one business organisation for dealing with customer complaints

Range: Customer needs: wishing to make a purchase, to obtain information, to obtain a refund, to exchange goods, to make a complaint, for special needs, ethical standards

Customer service: meeting the needs of internal and external customers; providing help or information for individuals and for business organisations

Core skills: Communication, Information technology

1 Think carefully about an organisation you have visited on holiday or on an evening out. This could be a hotel, theme park, cinema or restaurant. Think of somewhere you remember quite well, rather than somewhere you last visited ten years ago!
   a Name the organisation and state the type of business it is.
   b List all the different types of customers who use the facilities and identify their needs.
   c Give details of how the organisation met the needs of:
      i external customers wishing to make a purchase (remember, a 'purchase' can mean buying a cinema ticket or booking a hotel room)
      ii people needing information – either before or during a visit
      iii people with special needs.
2 Talk to someone you know who is in business or ask the owner of a local shop to spend a few minutes talking to you.
   a Find out the policy on refunds and exchanges.
   b Make notes on the type of complaints which have been received recently and how these have been dealt with.
   c Discuss the needs of individuals and/or business organisations who contact the shop and obtain examples of occasions when help or information has been requested.
3 Talk to someone you know who works for a large organisation.
   a Ask for details of the internal 'customers' dealt with in the course of a week, their requirements and how these are met.
   b Find out his or her views on ethical standards and how these affect conduct in that organisation.
Type up all your findings neatly, using a word processor.

Evidence assignment

At this point your tutor may wish you to start work on the project which will prove to your verifiers that you understand this section of the element. If you are starting the project then turn to page 374 and do Section 1. This relates to the first evidence indicator for this element.

Business communications

When you communicate with customers you give an impression, not just of yourself but of the organisation you represent. This is true whether you speak to them face-to-face, over the telephone or send them a letter or memo. For the customer you *are* the organisation. There are basically two ways in which you communicate with customers: by speaking to them (oral communications) and by writing to them.

Did you know?

Some people consider that a third important way in which we communicate is by body language. This includes our facial expressions, gestures and posture. It is useless saying or doing the right thing if your **body language** says the opposite! If you *look* bored and are slouching, the words you say are irrelevant – customers will form their

impression of you from what you look like. Therefore your body language *must* match your words. Stand up straight and look interested – even if you aren't!

Oral communication

You speak to people every day – your parents, relatives, friends and even total strangers. How many of them find you 'easy to talk to', how many of them understand you easily? Or do you create confusion and irritation as people try to work out what you mean? A good oral communicator:

- has a clear speaking voice
- speaks at the right pace (too slow and you bore people, too fast and they may not follow what you are saying)
- is a good listener
- chooses the correct words and 'tone' for the situation
- puts people at their ease
- has the confidence to talk to strangers
- understands how non-verbal communication gestures can affect people.

What do you sound like?

Many people are horrified the first time they hear their voice on a tape recorder. It is a nasty shock to find that you don't sound the same to other people as you sound to yourself!

There are two aspects to your voice which affect what you sound like. The first is **timbre** – or quality of sound – and the second is your **accent** and the way you pronounce words.

If you think your voice is squeaky or sharp then try to lower the pitch just a little. Try not to get excited or rush too much as this can make you sound harsh.

Regional accents and dialects can be *very* attractive but if you have a very broad regional accent, this may be almost unintelligible to someone from another part of the country or from abroad. The situation will be even worse if you use regional or slang expressions as well!

Figure 3.58   Some people can tell a lot from body language

Non-assessed activity

1 a As a group, make a list of words which you use which may not be easily understood by a listener from another part of the country or of another age group! Your list should include regional words and slang expressions which are in vogue at the moment.

b Make a second list of slang expressions which just don't sound appropriate when you are involved in a business discussion. The most obvious is 'OK'!

2 a Prepare a three- to five-minute talk on your favourite interest or hobby or a place you know well. *Tape* your talk – preferably without reading from your notes.

b Play back the tape and write down your own criticisms of it from the point of view of how you *sounded* (rather than what you said). You should lose a mark every time you said 'er' or 'um' and when you used words or expressions that would not be understood by someone else (either because they are slang or jargon). Check the pace of your speech – was it gabbled or hesitant and slow? Did you say the words clearly (and pronounce the *ends* of words? Was the volume too low, too loud or just right?

c Now tape your talk again – and see if you can improve on your first attempt.

Listening skills

Most people are actually poor listeners. They listen to the first part of a conversation, then think of a reply and wait impatiently for the speaker to be quiet so that they can start their own response. During this time they are not listening to a word that is being said!

You should try to concentrate on:

- listening until someone has *finished* speaking
- stopping yourself from interrupting in mid-sentence!

Remember that if *you* go on speaking for too long, people will have stopped listening to you, too!

Tone

Tone is a skill which is important for all types of communications. It is so important that it should be one of the main factors that determines the words and phrases you choose. The tone of what you are saying will make it acceptable or unacceptable to the receiver.

Non-assessed activity

You take a telephone message for a colleague to say that a dental appointment, originally made for tomorrow at 2 pm, has had to be cancelled as the dentist is ill. The patient should ring next week to make another appointment.

Write down what you would say if you were passing this message to:

a Mr Sharpe, the managing director of the company for which you work

b Mrs Browne, your colleague in customer services, who is ten years older than you

c Your best friend.

Analyse the difference in tone in each message.

Face-to-face communication

This means that the person to whom you are talking is actually in front of you. You have all the clues in the voice to tell you how he or she feels *and* the body language as well.

Unless you work in a very large store, most organisations have 'regular' customers. Although all customers are important to an organisation, regular customers are *vital*. It can take years, and a considerable amount of hard work (and money spent on advertising), to build up a good customer relationship. Yet this can be ruined in minutes with poor service or back-up, or surly staff.

Greeting the customer

Golden rule – always greet regular customers *by name*. We all react favourably to this type of treatment as it makes us feel important. If you *should* know someone's name but have forgotten it, don't bluff. Admit, at the outset, that you don't know, e.g. 'I'm sorry, I know I should remember your name but . . .' – if you pause at the right moment you will find that the customer will happily give you the information you want. The trick to remembering someone's name is to repeat it several times within the next few minutes during your conversation with them. At the same time, try to memorise what they look like – the experts on memory tests suggest that you should look for some feature you can link to the name (e.g. Mr Brown has brown hair) – but this isn't always as easy as it sounds.

In addition to the name, you will always be more effective if you can remember some details about your 'regulars', e.g. their likes and dislikes, who they deal with and other details. This will enable you to give them a far more personal service which will be noticed and appreciated. If nothing else, try to remember the last time you dealt with them and what it was about.

Virtually all organisations train staff to welcome customers with a smile and a greeting, e.g. 'Good morning, may I help you?' Try to make customers feel that you are there if you are needed but will not harass them (for instance, if they are just looking around). Casual callers may prefer to be left alone for a while and you should respect their wishes. You can judge if this is the case by watching for their first reaction. Do they mirror your smile or look hesitant and avert their eyes?

The type of organisation for which you work will affect the number of casual callers you are expected to deal with. Casual callers are far more likely in a retail establishment than in any other type of organisation. You can hardly imagine many casual visitors roaming around the main branch of a bank each day!

Establishing the customer's needs

Even if you are not able to give customers specific information, you can still help them effectively. To do this you need to be able to convince them that, after contact with you, progress has been made in the area of their concern. Customers should feel that by seeing you they have achieved something. If you leave customers feeling that they have made little – if any – progress, they will probably take their business elsewhere in future. At the very least, they will be annoyed that their time has been wasted as nothing has been achieved.

The first step to doing this is to find out what they need. You may have to ask some customers, while others will spell it out for you! When they are saying what they want, listen carefully. If you have to repeat their requirements to someone else later your information will be useless if you have missed out most of the details.

Attempting to meet the customer's needs

It may be that you can assist the customer yourself. In this case you should do so (provided what you would be doing is not outside your authority). If you can't, your job is to put customers in touch with someone who *can* assist them, or take a message regarding their requirements and arrange for someone else to call them later.

Here are some other golden rules to remember.

- Remain polite and helpful throughout the conversation.
- *Never* do anything which will annoy customers and distract them from the conversation, e.g. chew, sniff or scratch!
- If you know it, use the customer's name at frequent intervals.
- Don't try to be clever or witty – it doesn't work.
- If you take a message for someone then make sure you pass it on promptly.

Finishing the conversation

This is easier with some customers than others! You can aim to bring the conversation to a close with a few carefully chosen phrases, such as 'Fine, thank you Mr ... , we will be in touch with you on Thursday.' If that doesn't work, you may have to employ body language to help you – try walking to the door with a customer.

Remember to say goodbye *properly*. In a business situation it is not appropriate to shout 'See you' as the customer reaches the door.

Figure 3.59 Sometimes it is polite to see your customers to the door.

Non-assessed activity

Practise your social skills by role playing, with either another member of your group or your tutor. Make sure that you practise:

- greeting customers
- establishing their needs
- trying to meet those needs
- finishing the communication.

Start with an easy role play – such as a customer who knows what he or she want and knows when to say goodbye! From this you can progress to trying to cope with people who don't know what they want, have special needs or never know when to leave!

Using the telephone

The main difference between face-to-face communications and using a telephone is that you have no non-verbal clues to help you. In addition, you may only be used to using a telephone at home – and speaking to your friends. Now, the tone – and the words you use – must be different.

Non-assessed activity

As a group, discuss:

- how you first greet a telephone caller on your own phone
- how you end a telephone call
- the type of slang words and expressions you use
- what should be different in a business call!

Did you know?

Many organisations have strict rules on how customer service staff answer the telephone. Staff are trained to identify themselves by their first name and to answer within a certain number of rings. On very busy phone systems, a taped queuing system will be in operation – together with accompanying music!

Hints and tips

- *Never* answer a telephone without a pen or pencil in your hand and a piece of paper (or preferably a message pad) nearby.
- Answer *promptly* – the caller can't see how busy you are!
- *Never* eat or drink when using the telephone.
- *Always* sound pleasant and helpful.
- If the call is for someone who is available:
  - ask who is calling
  - ask the caller to hold the line a moment (*please*!). *Don't* say 'hang on'.

  - tell the person being called they are wanted and give them the name of the caller.
- If the call is for someone who is not available:
  - ask if he or she would like to speak to someone else
  - see if you can help
  - offer to take a message
  - suggest the caller rings back later or suggest the person wanted rings back later. This may depend on the policy of your organisation.
- If the caller wants information which will take you a while to find, don't keep him or her holding on – offer to ring back when you have it to hand.
- *Never* promise to ring callers back and then let them down.
- *Always* check with your supervisor if you are being asked for information which you think may be confidential.
- Be aware that a receiver left lying on a desk picks up the general office conversation and casual remarks!
- Treat important information you receive over the telephone as confidential.

Did you know?

Sometimes callers with an enquiry need transferring to another extension. It is important that all employees know how to do this correctly on their telephone system so that they don't cut anyone off by mistake. You should also know how to divert your calls to another extension if you are going to leave your telephone unattended.

The professional touch

People who sound really effective on the telephone usually know one or two things that other people don't – such as:

- Using a person's name during a conversation makes them feel important.
- Concluding a call by saying 'thank you for calling' has the same effect.
- If you are cut off in the middle of a conversation, the person who made the call should attempt the reconnection.
- Figures said in *pairs* are always easier to understand, e.g. '45' '62' '34' *not* '456' '234'.
- It is always better (if possible) to let the person who made the call conclude it.
- A 'smile' in the voice is identified as being friendly on the other end of a telephone.
- There is nothing wrong in asking people to repeat

a name or a figure to check you have written it correctly. People with an unusual name are quite used to having to spell it out over the telephone and you should *always* read back a telephone number to make sure it is correct.

- It is far better to check all the details *before* ringing off than to have to ring back later.
- If you are making a call then make sure you have all the relevant facts and figures before you ring. If you prepare well you sound more efficient.

Did you know?

In a new job most people don't like answering the telephone in case they won't be able to cope with the call. In fact it is perfectly possible to sound competent and efficient and give a good impression *without* being able to give someone specific help.

Optional evidence assignment

*This activity can be carried out verbally in class **in a group** as a non-assessed activity to consolidate learning. Alternatively, if you do it **on your own**, it can count as supplementary evidence towards the following parts of the scheme.*

PC 3:	Identify business communications which meet customer needs
PC 4:	Demonstrate business communications which meet customers' needs
Range:	Business communications: oral: face-to-face, telephone
Core skills:	Communication, Information technology

1 Arrange with your tutor to be on duty to assist visitors on at least **one** of the following occasions held at your school or college.
   a Open Day
   b Parents' evening
   c Interviewing sessions
   Alternatively, identify an alternative suitable event you can attend. Deal with potential customers and enquirers by greeting them courteously and helping to give relevant information.

   Write up a report after the event stating your role and giving details of the people you dealt with and how you helped them.

2 Read the case study and answer the questions which follow.

Case study – video rental shop

You have obtained a part-time job in your local video rental shop and work there one evening a week and all day Saturday. The shop is open from 9.30 am to 9.30 pm each day. Films must be returned by 8 pm the following day or a daily fine is levied. Customers must be members and a list of these is kept on a computer database, together with the membership number. This also gives the date of hire of each film and any fines not paid. Customers who owe more than £5 are not allowed to rent any more films unless the manageress, Mrs Karen Robbins, gives her permission. Films can be ordered over the telephone and will be saved for up to three hours.

a Today you are working on the counter and answering the telephone. You receive the following telephone calls. Either role play these and record your conversations (which is better) *or* write down what you would say in each case. Then discuss your responses **with your tutor** and state how these could be improved (or role play them again).
   i A call from a Mr Benson who wants to reserve the film *Rough Justice*. When you look on the shelf you see there are three copies in stock. He quotes his membership number as 3160.
   ii A call from a Miss Paula Saunders. She wants to hire two films for that evening. When you check the database record you find that she owes £10 in fines and still has one film out on hire.
   iii A call from a Mr Zaheer Ahmed. He has just borrowed the film *Ultra Hijack*. When he started to watch it he found it was totally blank. You have no more copies of this film in stock.
   iv A young child telephones and asks if he can reserve a cartoon film.
   v The regional manager telephones and asks to speak to Mrs Robbins about a confidential matter. You know that she has gone to a nearby shop for a minute to buy a birthday card for her son.
   vi A young man phones and asks if he can reserve a film which is for over-eighteens only. From his voice, you are fairly sure that he is only about thirteen or fourteen.
   vii A Mr Samuels telephones. He is very upset. He has just returned from three weeks' holiday and found a video film which he thought had been returned to you. When you check your database you find that the fines have amounted to £28. He says he will not pay as he has been a customer for years and never been a day late returning a film. He thinks you should let him off on this occasion.

363

viii You receive a call from a regular, elderly customer, Miss Threlfall. She gives you the title of quite an old film she wants to hire. You think you might have a copy upstairs, where some old stock is kept, but it will take you some time to find out if you are right.

b On your day off you want to telephone the shop yourself. Mrs Robbins has asked if you can work an extra evening for the next two weeks. You can't manage next week as you have already made arrangements to go out that night. You can, however, work the following week. Write down what you would say to Mrs Robbins.

c Design a database record card which could be used for recording customer information at the shop. Include all the sections which would be useful for staff.

d How do you think having a database of customers might improve customer service in the shop? In what way could it assist the shop to meet customer needs and handle enquiries?

e The manageress notices that several customers have overdue films but are not bringing them back – presumably because they are frightened about having to pay large fines. What could the shop do to try to get the films returned? If possible, the manageress does not want to take legal action against anybody as the size of the fines would not warrant the cost.

When you have completed all the work for this assignment, type up the answers neatly, using your word processor.

Figure 3.60 Working in the video shop

Evidence assignment

At this point your tutor may wish you to start or continue work on the project which will prove to your verifiers that you understand this section of the element. If you are starting the project then turn to page 374 and do Section 1. If you have already completed Section 1 of the project now start Section 2. This covers the third evidence indicator for this element.

Written business communications

Letter

All organisations write business letters to their customers, suppliers and other organisations with whom they have dealings. Writing and composing business letters is covered in more detail in Element 4.3, page 484, and is reviewed in the Core Skills chapter on Communication.

Because you may cover business letters in this element first, the main components of a letter are included, but generally this section examines the types of letters written to customers, primarily by customer service units or departments.

Business letters are not written in the same way as personal letters. There are several differences.

■ They are usually produced on a typewriter or word processor.
■ They are printed on letter-headed paper.
■ They contain certain items, such as a reference and the recipient's name and address, which are not usually included in personal letters.
■ The language used is more formal.
■ They are usually only signed by staff who have specific authority to send out letters on the organisation's behalf.

All these features are illustrated in the letter in Figure 3.61.

Standard letters and responses

A customer service section may have certain 'standard' letters, which have been pre-printed with gaps left for the details. These may be written in, but it is better if any specific information is typed to match the letter itself. On a computer this is easy to do. You simply recall the saved 'master' document and edit it. If you have several letters to send and you know how to use mail-merge, the details can be

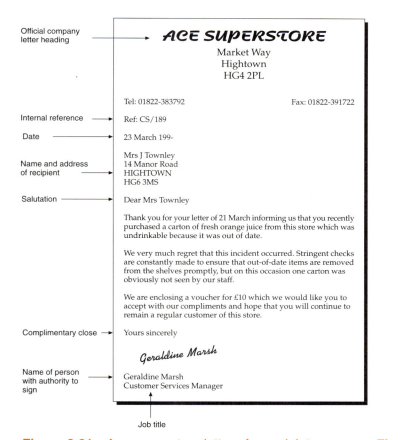

Official company letter heading →

ACE SUPERSTORE
Market Way
Hightown
HG4 2PL

Tel: 01822-383792   Fax: 01822-391722

Internal reference → Ref: CS/189

Date → 23 March 199-

Name and address of recipient → Mrs J Townley
14 Manor Road
HIGHTOWN
HG6 3MS

Salutation → Dear Mrs Townley

Thank you for your letter of 21 March informing us that you recently purchased a carton of fresh orange juice from this store which was undrinkable because it was out of date.

We very much regret that this incident occurred. Stringent checks are constantly made to ensure that out-of-date items are removed from the shelves promptly, but on this occasion one carton was obviously not seen by our staff.

We are enclosing a voucher for £10 which we would like you to accept with our compliments and hope that you will continue to remain a regular customer of this store.

Complimentary close → Yours sincerely

Geraldine Marsh

Name of person with authority to sign → Geraldine Marsh
Customer Services Manager

Job title

Figure 3.61   A response to a letter of complaint

ACE SUPERSTORE
Market Way
Hightown
HG4 2PL

Tel: 01822-383792   Fax: 01822-391722

Ref: CS/1/Std

Dear

We thank you for your recent letter complaining about a faulty item you purchased from this store.

Because of the nature of the complaint it is necessary for us to make a more detailed investigation.

We should be grateful if you could return the goods to us as soon as possible for testing. We will then be in a position to comment further.

Yours sincerely

Geraldine Marsh
Customer Services Manager

Figure 3.62 An alternative letter

inserted automatically and the letters can then be printed.

Non-assessed activity

1 Above is shown an example of a typical standard letter. Discuss with your tutor
   a the main components which are illustrated
   b the layout of the letter
2 Compare this letter with Figure 3.62. Which details will be added before the letter is sent?

Did you know?

Letters which start 'Dear Sir' or 'Dear Madam' always end with 'Yours faithfully'. Those which start with the person's name, e.g. 'Dear Mr Brown', *always* end with 'Yours sincerely'. Both 'faithfully' and 'sincerely' are *always* written with a small first letter.

Circular letters

These are letters which are very similar to standard letters but are produced to be sent to a large number of people. They usually start with a general phrase, e.g. Dear customer or Dear colleague. If your school or college sends such letters it will probably start them 'Dear parent'.

Circular letters are usually mass produced and may be used as a method of advertising.

Producing letters yourself

If you are asked to write a letter yourself, you must be certain that your spelling, grammar and punctuation are 100 per cent accurate! There are exercises to help you to perfect this in Element 4.3 (pages 496–500) and in the Core Skills chapter on Communication (pages 539–548).

At first, keep your letters simple and to the point. The secret is to practise! Make certain that you know the 'message' you have to say, concentrate on getting your 'tone' right and think about your communication from the point of view of the person who will be reading it.

Never send out a letter unless you have had it checked carefully by a supervisor and never sign a letter unless you have received specific permission to do so.

Did you know?

The Crystal Mark is a special mark which can be placed on literature whose clarity is approved by the Plain English campaign. This means that the text is easy to follow and understand – and doesn't contain jargon or specialist words the average person wouldn't know about.

Crystal Mark

Clarity approved by Plain English Campaign

Figure 3.63 The Crystal Mark

Memo

Memos are written communications which are sent from one person to another *within* an organisation. They are less formal than business letters and there is no salutation or complimentary close. Neither are memos signed by the sender, although they may be initialled. Memos are also covered in more detail in Element 4.3, page 488

You will probably find yourself in the situation where you are writing a memo to someone earlier in your career than writing a business letter. Care and attention must be paid to spelling, grammar and punctuation.

MEMO

TO	Geoff Pearson, Fresh Provisions Supervisor
FROM	Geraldine Marsh, Customer Services Manager
DATE	23 March 199-
REF	GM/TL

We have recently had two complaints about the condition in which our oven ready chickens are sold. Customers are alleging that fresh chickens are almost frozen when they are unwrapped.

Could you please check the temperature of the cooler unit in which they are stored immediately and let me know your findings.

GM

Figure 3.64 An internal response to two complaints

Customer/product information

A wide range of information is produced by organisations in relation to their goods and services. This is usually pre-printed by professional printing firms. The most obvious time to see this is if you visit an exhibition, when nearly everyone with a display stand will have brochures and leaflets for you to take away and read. These can range from elaborately printed colour booklets to simple A5 pages. The aim is the same – to provide customers with material to which they can refer in the future.

Product information

Don't think of 'products' as simply 'goods'. Argos may produce a catalogue full of goods but a bank's brochure on its services, your college or school's prospectus and a holiday brochure all contain 'products' too!

For product information to be of any use it must be up to date and easy to read. In some cases supplementary information may be available. Your school or college may have additional leaflets giving details of specific courses, and hotels mentioned in a travel brochure will each produce their own leaflets giving more details.

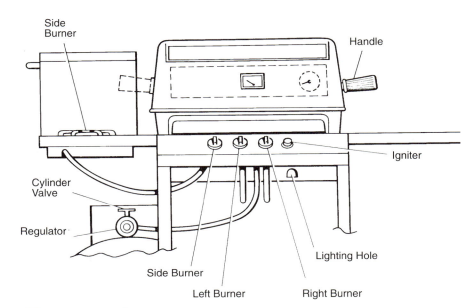

1. The appliance must be fully assembled as per the detailed assembly instructions.

2. Make sure your gas cylinder is filled with gas.

3. Check that there are no gas leaks in the gas supply system. See leak Testing.

4. Check that the venturis are properly located over the gas valve outlets.

5. Read carefully all instructions contained on the information plate attached to the barbeque.

6. **WARNING: Raise lid before lighting.**

Figure 3.65 Part of the instruction manual from a gas appliance

The style of the leaflets will vary depending upon the type of organisation and its 'product'. You have already seen in Element 3.2 how the materials produced vary with the image and the message the company is trying to convey.

When you buy a particular item there may be additional product information telling you how to use it. Customers are notoriously poor at reading these so it is as well to keep them short and simple. One survey found that people only use, on average, about 20 per cent of the controls found on elaborate video recorders! If you try this with the commands on a software package you may get into a mess! Illustrations are often used to make the operation easier to understand, or schematic diagrams can show the stages to be undertaken one at a time (see Figure 3.65).

Statement of account

Statements of account are sent to customers at the end of each month summarising all the transactions which have taken place during the month. This includes goods which have been purchased and for which the customer owes money, and any payments which have been received during that time. Statements of account are illustrated and covered in more detail in Element 4.1, page 422.

Prices

Product information – particularly in the form of illustrated, colour brochures and catalogues – can be very expensive to produce. Such material is therefore revised as infrequently as possible. However, within the 'life' of the average catalogue, prices may change several times. For this reason organisations often print separate price lists which are inserted into the catalogue. This means they can be revised whenever necessary without costing very much. In some cases, price lists will even be printed 'in-house' as they are usually just black and white, and are simple pages with two or three columns.

Guarantees

Guarantees and warranties are sold with many types of durable goods – from washing machines to computers. Often there is a registration card for the purchaser to complete. However, very often this merely registers the purchaser as a customer (which means the organisation can then send mailshots about other products in the future) – if buyers forget to post the card their statutory (legal) rights are not affected. Guarantees and warranties usually cover labour and parts for repairing the item over a certain period. They cover faults which develop through usage but do not cover accidental damage.

Many organisations also offer additional cover in the form of insurance to cover repairs after the guarantee period has ended. Some of these have been criticised as being far too expensive.

The printed guarantee will state the customer's rights under the terms of the agreement. The small print will often state the occasions on which a claim will not be met. Some retail stores issue a certificate of purchase at the time of the sale which means that the product does not have to be unpacked for the guarantee to be stamped – Boots is one example. This certificate is made out by the sales assistant and stamped with the date of purchase. It is then given to the buyer who must return it, with the goods, if a replacement is required.

Safety notices

A vast number of safety notices and signs can be purchased from specialist companies – ranging from simple 'No Smoking' signs to those which show which areas are dangerous or have restricted access. Some notices merely give information, such as what to do in the case of fire.

Under the **Safety Signs Regulations 1980**, all signs must be issued in one of four colours and one of four shapes.

- red, blue, yellow or green
- rectangular, triangular, a bold circle or a circle with a cross bar.

One shape/colour denotes a **prohibition** i.e. *don't do*. Another is a **mandatory sign** i.e. what you *must do*. A third is a **warning** to indicate *danger* and the fourth shows a safe condition.

You should note that any signs which act as disclaimers stating that accidents are nothing to do with the management have no meaning in law. This is covered in more detail below, under legislation.

Did you know?

If you are getting together literature to give to a customer you should never take the last copy without making sure that either:

- you have ordered some more
- you get some more from stock to replace what you have taken.

There is nothing more infuriating for other staff to find that they have run out of essential information because someone has used the last copy without telling anyone!

Non-assessed activity

1 **On your own,** obtain a sample of leaflets or some brochures from a local organisation. Compare the set you have obtained with those obtained by other members of the group. Note how they vary in terms of:

- size
- colour
- use of illustrations
- language and jargon.

See if you can decide **why** certain leaflets and brochures are produced in the way they are and how their style reflects the organisation which produced them, the goods or services they sell and the needs of their particular customers.

2 Ask your parents to show you a statement of account they have received from an organisation (a credit card statement will do if necessary). Otherwise, refer to Element 4.1, page 422.

3 Ask your parents if they will lend you a guarantee or warranty for a household appliance. Try to read the terms through to the end! Then compare the conditions you have read with those contained in the guarantees or warranties studied by other members of your group.

4 Look around your school or college for examples of safety notices. You should already know where the 'in case of fire' notices are! In the text above, you read that certain colours and shapes are used.
- **a** Identify which colour and shape has which meaning.
- **b** Find **at least two** examples of each type of sign and say what each one means.

Optional evidence assignment

*This activity can be carried out verbally in class **in a group** as a non-assessed activity to consolidate learning. Alternatively, if you do it **on your own**, it can count as supplementary evidence towards the following parts of the scheme.*

Element 3.3

PC 3:	Identify business communications which meet customer needs
PC 4:	Demonstrate business communications which meet customers' needs
Range:	Business communications: written: letter, memo; customer/product information (statement of account, prices, guarantees, safety notices)

Element 4.3

PC 1: Produce examples and explain the purpose of routine business documents

Range: Business documents: letters (dealing with a customer complaint), memo

Core skills: Communication, Information technology, Application of number

You work for Mary Tomkins, Customer Service Manager of Watson & Reid Ltd. The company supplies computer hardware and software to private individuals and local business organisations.

Mary Tomkins has asked you to help her today by undertaking the following activities:

1 On a word processor, using plain paper, *draft* a letter to Mr T Brooks, Chapel Street, Hightown, HG2 7ED. Use the following notes to help you.
   - Thank him for his recent letter and the disks he returned.
   - Apologise for the latest box of disks he bought which proved to be faulty.
   - Say that we are currently out of stock of high density disks.
   - Say that we have credited his account with the amount of the disks.
   - Tell him that we will give him a free supply of two boxes of disks as soon as our new stocks are received.

   Make sure you display the letter correctly and that you carefully check your spelling, punctuation and grammar.

2 Prepare a statement of account for Mr Brooks to send with his letter. A blank form on which you can enter the information is given at the back of the book. Your tutor can photocopy this for you.

   His opening balance this month was zero. He purchased goods on the 10th and the 15th of the month. Those bought on the 10th were listed on invoice 2081 and cost £67.50 and those bought on the 15th (which included the disks) were detailed on invoice 2147 and cost £27.60. Add his credit of £15 for the disks he returned on the 19th. Don't forget to check that his balance is correct.

3 Write a memo from Mary Tomkins, Customer Services Manager to Gerald Stevens, Purchasing Manager. Use today's date. Say that you have recently received a fourth complaint about the latest batch of disks, all of which proved to be faulty. Ask Gerald Stevens to contact the supplier immediately for a refund and to make arrangements to buy disks elsewhere in the future.

4 The price of some items sold by Watson & Reid have to be adjusted. Some are increased and some are decreased. An extract from the existing price list is shown below with Mrs Tomkins' comments. Prepare a new price list with the correct prices on your word processor.

5 A new member of staff started at Watson & Reid last week. He has no idea why guarantees or warranties are issued. Write some brief notes to explain their purpose. If possible, refer to an actual guarantee you have obtained and give examples of typical terms and conditions which are stated.

6 There have been problems during the last week with office staff trying to unjam the photocopier and not realising that the toner unit gets very hot. Yesterday a junior member of staff burnt his arm quite badly.

Mrs Tomkins has asked you to design a suitable safety notice to be positioned above the machine, warning people about this problem and saying that they must report any faults or paper jams to the office supervisor.

WATSON & REID
Computer Supplies

EXTRACT FROM PRICE LIST

Floppy Disks

Stock No	Size	Type	Price per box of 10	
1827	3½	DS/HD	4.80	
1828	3½	DS/DD	3.60	*increase by 5% – round prices if necessary*
1829	3½	DS/HD	3.85	
2501	5¼	DS/HD	4.60	
2502	5¼	DS/DD	2.70	
2503	5¼	DS/QD	4.95	

Floptical disks

Stock No	Type	Disks per box	Price per box	
3090	21 MB	2	23.90	*Reduce by 2½%*
3091	21 MB	5	51.50	

Padded disk pouches

Stock No	Disk capacity	Price	
1011	8	6.45	*increase by 6%*
1012	16	9.96	

Note – I hope you know what all the abbreviations mean – if not, ask me!

Figure 3.66 The extract from the price list of Watson & Reid

Legislation

All customers have a legal right to be protected from:

- dangerous goods
- faulty and damaged goods
- poor service
- accidents occurring through the negligence of employees
- being deliberately misled by company staff
- being quoted a misleading price.

All consumer have certain legal rights when they enter, as a buyer, into a contract with a seller. They also have the right to **redress** (or **compensation**) in law if the company which supplied them with the product or service is at fault.

However, it is important to note that in some cases a customer may be dissatisfied and yet not be able to get compensation in law. This is because basic customer requirements are covered by consumer protection laws, but some aspects of service (e.g. polite and friendly staff) are not.

Three Acts, covered in Element 3.2 on pages 320–322, were all designed to protect consumers. They are:

- The Trades Description Act
- The Sale of Goods Act
- The Consumer Protection Act.

Non-assessed activity

Turn back to those pages now and refresh your memory.

- Under which Act would be it be an offence to sell a pen which didn't write?
- Which Act states that selling dangerous goods is unsafe?
- Which Act is concerned with the way in which advertising material and salespeople describe goods?

Did you know?

Some organisations may try to evade their responsibility by using exclusion clauses or disclaimers on their premises, tickets or booking forms (e.g. 'all articles are left at the owner's risk').

Under the **Unfair Contract Terms Act 1977** none of these disclaimers is valid unless the organisation can prove that their terms are fair and responsible. Therefore, if they lose or damage an article through their own negligence, the owner is probably entitled to compensation. This will not be the case if the organisation can prove they took reasonable care of the goods and could not be held responsible for what occurred.

Notices and disclaimers can *never* absolve an organisation from its liability to either staff or customers if personal injury or death is caused through its negligence.

Health and Safety at Work Act

As you saw in Unit 2, The Health and Safety at Work Act covers employees – but what about customers or visitors to a company? What could you do if you slipped and broke your ankle because a cleaner had mopped the floor and forgotten to put up any warning signs?

Any organisation which deals with or admits members of the public on to its premises can find it is liable to claims in law, e.g.:

- if a customer (or service engineer) is injured, through negligence on the part of an employee, unsafe premises or fittings, etc.
- if a customer is injured because a product is faulty
- if a customer suffers personal financial loss or distress through professional negligence, faulty workmanship, etc.

For this reason most firms take out insurance to cover themselves against such claims. Typical policies include:

- **public liability insurance** – this is a legal requirement for some businesses such as builders and hairdressers, and it covers the business against claims because of personal injury caused by negligence, defects on the premises, etc.
- **product liability insurance** – this covers claims for injury caused by faulty goods
- **professional indemnity** – this covers claims for damages caused by professional negligence. This type of policy is usually taken out by architects, accountants, solicitors, etc.

Most **trade associations** offer policies for their members. Trade associations are bodies associated with specific trades, e.g. the Building Employers Federation, the Association of British Travel Agents, etc. They provide advice, assistance and information to their members and frequently have a voluntary code of practice to which their members subscribe. A code of practice is a guide to all members on how customers should be treated and how complaints should be handled. Trading associations will also deal with complaints from members of the public about companies in their industry, though they obviously have more influence over companies who are members, rather than those who are not.

Did you know?

Many insurance policies have a condition attached that the insurance company may, if it wishes, defend any claim on behalf of the insured. They also insist that the company shall not make any admission of liability to the person who has been injured.

Non-assessed activity

1 As a group, discuss the different types of public liability claims which might be received by:

- a dentist
- a hotel
- a builder.

2 How do you think staff in an organisation will be affected in their dealings with a customer who has been injured on the premises, bearing in mind the condition made by insurance companies that they must not make any admission of liability to the injured person? Discuss your answer with your tutor.

Did you know?

All companies must *by law* insure their employees against accidents at work. This type of insurance is called Employer's Liability Insurance and it covers employees against bodily injury or diseases contracted as a result of their work.

Optional evidence assignment

*This activity can be carried out verbally in class **in a group** as a non-assessed activity to consolidate learning. Alternatively, if you do it **on your own**, it can count as supplementary evidence towards the following parts of the scheme.*

PC 6:   Identify relevant legislation to protect customers

Range: Trades Description Act, Sale of Goods Act, Consumer Protection Act, Health and Safety At Work Act

Core skills: Communication, information technology

You are about to have one of the worst days of your life! However, with your knowledge of consumer legislation you should be able to cope! Read both case studies below and answer the questions on each which follow.

Case study 1

You have been saving up for months to buy a computer. You want it to be able to play games *and* run basic business packages, e.g. word processing, database and spreadsheet. A friend of yours recommends a new shop which has just opened. You go there and buy from them the model which is recommended by the salesman, plus a couple of computer games.

When you arrive home you find that:

a the VDU is half the size of the one illustrated in the brochure
b when you touch the screen you get a nasty shock
c the disk drive won't work
d the computer is not suitable as a games machine.

When you take it back to the shop the salesman points to a large sign in the shop which says 'No refunds given'.

Questions

Your knowledge of consumer legislation should enable you to make a claim for **each** of the faults plus the refund notice under different Acts.

1 Match up each different fault with the Act which covers that particular problem.
2 What would you say to the salesman about the refunds policy?

Case study 2

After leaving the computer shop you visit a local hairdresser to have your hair coloured and permed. The person who runs the shop is ill and you are asked if a trainee can do your hair. You agree. The end result is a disaster and your scalp is badly burned because some solution was left on too long. You decide to claim a refund plus compensation for the pain and discomfort you suffered.

Figure 3.67 A hair-raising day!

Questions

1 Does the hairdresser have a **legal** responsibility to take care of you as a customer?
2 Legally, should you win your claim?
3 The hairdresser has taken out insurance for protection against claims such as yours. What is the name of this type of insurance?
4 Could you take out a claim if you had done your own hair at home and not used the product according to the instructions?
5 Would it make any difference if you *had* followed the instructions? If so, who would you claim against?
6 During your visit, the owner also told you that:
   ■ the trainee was in her third year of training, when she was really in her first
   ■ she had done this work before, when she hadn't
   ■ it was impossible to arrange your appointment for a week later as the shop would be closed.
   a Which of these statements would be likely to *help* your claim – and why?
   b Which would not?

 ### Did you know?

The **Property Misdescriptions Act** now makes it an offence for estate agents to give

misleading or dishonest descriptions of properties. No longer can they write:

■ interesting town view (when it really overlooks the gas works)
■ neat compact garden (for a plot of land three metres square)
■ interesting original features (when this means nothing has been done to the house for 50 years!).

Even casual remarks by junior members of staff can mean the agent is liable under the Act. In future, estate agents may have to be rather more careful with adjectives such as 'quiet', 'pleasant' and 'rural' – and stick to the facts!

Evidence assignment

At this point your tutor may wish you to start or continue work on the project which will prove to your verifiers that you understand this section of the element. If you are starting the project then turn to page 374 and do Section 1. If you have already completed Section 1 and 2 of the project then you can complete it easily by doing Section 3 and the final stage. Section 3 covers the second evidence indicator for this element.

Revision test

True or false?

1 It is impossible to sound efficient over the telephone unless you can give a caller specific help.
2 Product knowledge is unnecessary if you work for an organisation which provides a service.
3 Only paying customers receive good service, internal 'customers' don't count.
4 If someone is annoyed, make sure you state your own point of view immediately.
5 Organisations have a legal responsibility to provide a safe environment for customers.

Fill in the blanks

6 Figures said in _____ are always easier to remember.
7 Three types of enquiries which should be dealt with in private involve _____ _____ and _____ matters.
8 It is an offence under the _____ _____ Act to exaggerate the size of a product.
9 If a product is faulty, then the customer has a legal right to be given a _____ .

10 If you have telephoned a customer and then been cut off, you should _____ .

Short answer questions

11 Identify the **six** main needs of customers.

12 State **two** types of handicapped customers and how you would deal with them.

13 Give **five** characteristics of a good verbal communicator.

14 Identify **four** types of business communications which relate to goods a customer has bought and provide information.

15 State **six** ways in which a telephone user can sound more professional.

Write a short paragraph to show you clearly understand each of the following terms.

16 Special needs of customers.
17 Face-to-face communication.
18 Customer service.
19 After-sales service.
20 Legislation.

373

Evidence indicator project

Unit 3 Element 3.3

This project has been designed to cover all the evidence indicators related to Element 3.3. It is divided into three sections. Tutors may wish students to complete the sections at the appropriate points marked in the text. Alternatively, tutors may prefer their students to do the entire project at the end of the element.

Performance criteria: 1–6

Core skills: Communication
Application of number
Information technology

Section 1

You are about to conduct an in-depth study of customer service in one organisation. This may be:

- the organisation you have selected in Unit 1 for your ongoing project
- the organisation which you visit on work experience
- an organisation in which you are employed on a part-time basis
- an organisation to which you have access through a friend or member of your family
- your own school or college.

1 Identify the most suitable organisation for your purpose. Discuss your choice with your tutor.

2 Write a brief introduction to your project which gives:

- the name of the organisation
- its address
- the business activities it undertakes
- your reason(s) for choosing it.

3 Arrange to visit the organisation and to interview someone who can give you details of its customer services and allow you to observe staff dealing with customers.

4 Prepare a list of questions to ask at the interview. Your job is find out:

a the range of external and internal customers staff deal with
b the type of requests they receive for help or information
c the complaints procedure in operation
d the refunds/exchange policy of the company.

Write a brief report summarising your findings.

5 Ask politely if you can obtain an example of a written business communication. This may only be possible if the word 'SAMPLE' is written across in large letters. Don't be too worried if this request is turned down – many organisations are very concerned about the possible consequences of communications going outside the premises. Your tutor should be able to give you an example of a letter produced by your college or school which is not confidential.

6 Ask if you can observe staff on the customer service desk or on the telephone in the customer services section. Make notes on at least one conversation you overhear. Again, if this request is denied, your tutor may be able to help by allowing you to observe school or college staff dealing with customers or visitors.

Type up all your notes carefully, using a word processor, and keep them safely.

Make sure you complete this section of the project by the deadline date given to you by your tutor.

Section 2

When you are working either on a Saturday or part-time or during your work placement, start a diary which gives details of your oral conversations with customers under each of the following headings. If you have no opportunity to deal with actual customers then ask your tutor for the opportunity to help out on school or college Open Days or interview sessions – or even on the college reception desk or in the school office. Alternatively, if you have arranged an event to take place or to sell goods for your project in Element 3.2, you could use your dealings for customers in this context.

You should note that your conversations with customers must be observed by a responsible person who can confirm that you performed the task satisfactorily. They will want to observe you greeting a customer, establishing his or her needs, attempting to meet these needs and finishing the communication.

If you undertook task 1 on page 363 then you will have already made some notes to help you.

Make sure you complete this section of the project by the deadline date given to you by your tutor.

Headings for notes

a the type of customers with whom you dealt

b the requests they made for information

c how you dealt with customers who wished to make a purchase

d any requests you had for refunds (and how you handled these)

e any requests you had for goods to be exchanged – and what you did

f how you handled any complaints

g how you dealt with any customer who had a special need.

Type up all your notes neatly on a word processor and attach documentary evidence from the person who observed you and has stated that you performed the job well.

Notes

1 If, during the time you keep your diary, you do not have any dealing with customers with special needs then write a description of how you *would* deal with someone who had mobility difficulties, young children in a pushchair or who had a visual or hearing impairment.

2 If you are unable to find any opportunities to deal with customers 'for real', then you will have to arrange to undertake a simulation with your tutor.

Section 3

Your friend has recently started work in a large store but knows nothing about consumer legislation or health and safety. Write a brief summary which identifies the three Acts which protect consumers when they are buying goods, and the Act which protects them in terms of their health and safety.

Type up your summary neatly, using a word processor.

Make sure you complete this section of the project by the deadline date given to you by your tutor.

Final stages

Make sure that your work from each stage of the project is neatly filed in a binder. Prepare a title page with your name and the date. Give your project the title: **Investigation into Customer Services at ...** and add the name of the organisation.

Present proposals for improvement to customer service

This element covers the importance of customer service in business organisations, in both the private and the public sector. It examines how these affect customers and how they can be monitored and improved. It also gives guidance on presenting proposals for possible improvements. After studying this element you should be able to:

1 explain the *importance of customer service* in business organisations
2 identify how business organisations *monitor*

customer satisfaction
3 identify *improvements to customer service*
4 present proposals for improvements to customer services in one organisation.

Special note

There is only one evidence indicator for this element. The evidence indicator project is therefore given at the end of the element, on page 398.

What is customer service?

If a member of staff in a large store stopped you suddenly and asked for your opinion of their customer service, what would you say? You might jump to the wrong conclusion – that they were merely referring to their customer service desk, where people called with queries and complaints. You might not think of other aspects of service, including staff attitudes and knowledge, the layout and safety features of the premises, the ease with which you could find out about company policies in relation to complaints, exchanged or faulty goods. These are a few aspects of **complete** customer service.

Figure 3.68 Finding out about customer relations

Today customer service involves a wide range of activities, all designed with one purpose: to keep the customers satisfied so that they will return, again and again. Some companies are better at this than others, as you will see as you read on.

Some of the factors relating to customer service were covered in the preceding element, particularly those involving communications with customers and dealing with queries and complaints. In this element you will see how customer satisfaction can be monitored and suggestions made for improvements. In addition, several other important areas of customer service are covered. To help you, there is a checklist on the next page, for you to use as a guide.

Non-assessed activity

Turn to this page now and discuss these headings, and the areas under each of them, **with your tutor**. Discuss how you would rank your college or school under each area. How would you interpret questions about goods/services in an educational establishment? How would you change this sample checklist so that it would be more appropriate for a school or college?

The importance of customer service

In the last ten years, more and more businesses have become 'consumer-led' – in other words, they have produced their goods or offered a service primarily

Feature	Yes	No	Don't know	Not applicable
Staff Helpful Knowledgeable about product/service Friendly Polite Clean and smart				
Service Prompt Efficient				
Goods/service Good quality Wide range Value for money Safety features Ordering service				
After-sales service Complaints answered promptly Procedure for exchanges/dealing with complaints Repair service Reasonable charges/turn round for repaired goods				
Access/layout Clear signs Logical layout Wide doors Ramps for disabled Safety features, e.g. handrails, wide steps etc.				
Delivery Reasonable charges Rapid delivery service				
Other Clean premises Clear information leaflets				

Figure 3.69 Sample checklist for customer service

with the customer in mind. The four main reasons for this are:

- to gain new customers and retain old customers
- to gain customer satisfaction
- to obtain customer loyalty
- to enhance the image of the organisation.

This is true of organisations in both the private and the public sector.

The private sector

Quite obviously, to organisations in the private sector, customers are essential for their survival. Such organisations are in business to make a profit; this is only possible if they can sell their goods or services. For this, they need customers – not just new, casual customers but regular customers who return every week.

As you already know, seeing the customer as the most important person means the company has a marketing approach to its business.

Did you know?

Companies frequently change their image to keep up to date. This can mean continually amending the type of service they offer.

- Tesco Stores has made a pledge to its customers to open another till if there is more than one person in front of them in a queue for the check-out.
- Marks & Spencer now offer an ordering service in all stores – so that if your size isn't on the rack when you call they will obtain it from one of their other stores and have it delivered to your local branch in a matter of days.

The public sector

It is not clear why an organisation in the public sector should be market-led or put the customer first, until you consider that:

- many public sector organisations have competitors in the private sector (e.g. a National Health hospital and a private hospital)
- many organisations in the public sector also depend on people using their services to survive (e.g. your local college can only exist whilst people enrol on courses)
- because we all pay to maintain the public sector through taxes (e.g. income tax and VAT), we can argue that we have just the same right to a

Figure 3.70   The Tesco pledge

courteous and efficient service as when we are dealing with a commercial organisation.

Did you know?

1   Many public sector organisations publish a charter which sets out their main aims and the service they intend to provide for their clients. Hospitals produce a Patients' Charter, the Inland Revenue have issued a Taxpayers' Charter and HM Customs and Excise abide by a Travellers' Charter. There is also a Students' Charter which concerns you. Have you seen a copy?

2   The Government is planning to introduce a new complaints line – Charterline – at the end of 1995. Callers can get instant information on who to contact if they have a complaint about a public service – from refuse collection to road works. All calls will be charged at local rate.

Gain and retain customers

Most of the goods and services we buy are offered for sale by a wide range of suppliers. We therefore have a choice whether to give our custom to one organisation or another. What influences that decision? In many cases the goods (or services) are identical. One supplier may be closer than another, a third may be cheaper, but generally – given that in a large shopping centre several suppliers may be within easy reach and all competitively priced – it will be other factors which will influence the decision. These may include the range and quality of goods on offer, the layout of the store and ease of access, how helpful the staff are, whether they can serve you quickly in your lunch-hour and so on. Many of these features are listed in the chart on page 377.

If you visit a supplier and these factors impress you, you are likely to return again and again. Equally, you will stop going to places which offer a poor service.

Did you know?

The quality of service becomes even more important if you are spending a lot of money. A can of Coke is not a major purchase, so the local shop seems the obvious choice. If, however, you were spending your hard-earned savings on a personal CD player, you would expect a lot of help and advice from the seller.

Gaining customer satisfaction

Customer satisfaction describes the feeling a customer has after contacting a supplier. However, there is quite a difference between being completely satisfied and actively dissatisfied. It could be argued that no supplier can *always* give exactly what you want – possibly because what you want to buy is not available or cannot be obtained within the time limit you specify, or at the price you want to pay.

However, the supplier will try to achieve a situation where the majority of customers are satisfied most of the time and it is likely to measure this by undertaking a range of surveys to obtain customer opinions of the service offered. This is covered in more detail on page 381.

Gaining customer loyalty

There are various strategies used by suppliers to gain customer loyalty. One of the most common is to develop a good-quality brand with a distinctive image. Food items are an obvious example. Customers can recognise the brand instantly on a supermarket shelf and know that they can rely on it to taste the same, time and again.

It is not just food products which are branded. So too are holidays, computers, household goods and cars – to name but a few. Manufacturers and suppliers are well aware that a customer who has a good experience will be more likely to buy the same brand again. This is why some people always replace one Ford car with another, say they can't exist without their Zanussi washers or always take a Thomsons holiday. Building up brand loyalty is a very important part of a company's marketing strategy.

Another method used to gain customer loyalty is to introduce a promotion based on repeat business. Examples include Airmiles and Profile Points – offered to Access credit card holders and Barclaycard holders respectively. Continued use of the card builds up miles, which can be turned into airline tickets or points which can be redeemed against various goods. Vouchers which can be used on a return visit or a discount card for regular customers are other common ways of securing repeat business.

In the business world, many suppliers of raw materials and office consumables offer better credit terms to regular customers and higher rates of discounts.

However, no matter how many tempting offers are put their way, a consumer is unlikely to take advantage of them if the basic product and service is poor or mediocre. Today most customers automatically expect a reliable, high-quality product or service, friendly and knowledgeable staff and prompt service. If these are not forthcoming, then the customers are unlikely to return.

Did you know?

Microsoft boss Bill Gates refused for years to market Microsoft as a brand name. He considered that the product was good enough to sell itself. Today he has abandoned that idea. Microsoft products are now sold with the name clearly shown and with the slogan 'Where do you want to go today?'

Non-assessed activity

Test the loyalty of your family to brands. **As a group**, make out a list of **twelve** common products every family buys on a regular basis, e.g. washing powder, tea, coffee, baked beans, tomato ketchup etc. Then put the brand name alongside each item bought by your family. At this point you can test brand popularity by seeing which are the most popular brands used by members of your class.

Then stun your mother or father by offering to do some shopping. When you do, buy a different brand and watch the reaction! If you feel this might be a bit extreme, just try asking why a certain brand is always bought and see if you get a logical reaction!

Did you know?

A lot of fuss has been made recently by the manufacturers of branded goods about 'copycat' own-label brands with similar names or colours. 'Own label' brands are those produced by the major supermarket chains. Have you noticed, though, that nearly all tomato ketchup bottles look very similar to Heinz, and many own-label coffee jars have the word 'Gold' somewhere in the title? Whilst the makers of the original products are annoyed by this, shoppers aren't confused. A survey found only three per cent are misled into buying the wrong brand.

Enhancing the organisation's image

'Word of mouth' promotion is a very important part of marketing. It is pointless for a company to spend thousands of pounds a year on advertising if, once someone has tried to buy the product or service, they promptly tell all their acquaintances never to set foot in the place!

Equally, bad publicity in the national press, on television or in a consumer magazine such as *Which?* can undo several promotional campaigns in one day. This is especially true if many complaints have been received about a product being unsafe and if customers have the opportunity to buy alternatives from dozens of other suppliers.

However, just as bad publicity can be harmful, good publicity helps to enhance the image. Favourable comments from one person to another are likely to increase the number of customers who will try the supplier or the product. If they agree with the recommendation they received then the organisation is likely to have gained another regular customer.

Selling the 'image' of the organisation is often the job of a Public Relations department or an outside firm of PR consultants. They concentrate on people's perception of the organisation rather than selling actual products or services. They attempt to link the

name of the organisation with favourable themes – quality, reliability, honesty. Some people consider this is a positive thing to do, others do not. They claim that PR gives some companies the excuse to concentrate on their image rather than improving the product or service they offer. (Public relations is also discussed in Element 2.1, page 141.)

Non-assessed activity

Read the case study below and then, as a group, discuss your answers to the questions which follow.

Case study

When *The People* newspaper awarded the Happy Eater chain of restaurants its Worst Hamburger award, the organisation appointed a PR adviser to turn its disaster into a triumph. Jane Smith, the consultant they employed, did just this. She advised Happy Eater to respond by offering a free hamburger to any reader who took a copy of *The People* into one of its restaurants. Readers could sample a hamburger themselves and complete the Happy Eater's own survey.

The offer increased both sales of the newspaper and the number of customers at Happy Eater restaurants. In addition, response to the new survey was positive – after all people usually like a free meal. The results of this survey were then published in the paper.

The only twist to the story is that the management of Happy Eater did nothing to improve the basic product – the hamburger *The People* had complained about in the first place. Instead they simply concentrated on restoring the image of the organisation.

1 Why were Happy Eater anxious to respond to *The People*'s survey?
2 Why did the challenge they issued restore people's confidence in their food?
3 Divide into **two groups** – one arguing in favour of the management's decision to restore their image and one in favour of improving the product. Decide who has the best argument.
4 Carry out a survey of hamburgers offered by fast food chains near your school or college. Choose up to **five** outlets and visit them in teams. Decide on how you will assess the hamburgers so that the view of each team can be measured against those of the other teams. (If you can afford it, you could visit each place independently!)
5 Before your visit, decide the customer service

aspects of fast food outlets which are important to you. Use the checklist on page 377 as a guide – but draft out one of your own which links more closely with this type of organisation.

6 Make your visits and keep clear records. Compare your results and type up a summary chart, using your word processor, giving a score to each organisation you visited.

Figure 3.71 Survey a burger

Did you know?

In February 1995 Toby Manning from *The Guardian* reviewed the seven major food stores operating in the UK. His results are shown in Figure 3.72. To what extent do you agree with the headings he chose? Which headings would be your choice if you were visiting a supermarket?

Monitoring customer satisfaction

How does an organisation know if its customers are satisfied with the service they receive? There are several methods they can use, besides reading national surveys in newspapers or articles about their products in consumer magazines.

Numbers of customers

The simplest way to check whether the organisation is attracting customers is to count the number of people who contact the organisation:

- to make an enquiry
- to buy the product or service
- to complain.

If a company receives a high number of enquiries but only a small number turn into sales, this can be analysed to find out why. It may be that the staff who answer the enquiries put people off or don't know enough to help them. It may be that prices are too high or delivery takes too long.

If a high number of enquiries are converted into sales, this indicates that the staff who deal with enquiries are efficient at their job, that the product is popular and competitively priced. If a large number of first-time customers are converted into regular customers, it is likely that the service is very good indeed.

Customers can be counted in various ways, depending upon the type of organisation.

- Your college or school will count the number of application forms it receives, the number of people who attend open evenings and the number of students who stay on to do a further course of study.
- A holiday company will log the number of brochures it issues and often code these to check who has replied with a firm holiday order. Mail order companies often do the same with their catalogues.
- A theatre, cinema or hotel can easily check its customers by seeing how many seats or rooms have been booked over a particular period.
- Retail shops and stores can log sales through their electronic cash registers. As well as analysing the number of sales, these also enable managers to see which products are selling most, and in which stores. In a large chain this can be useful, as it means a shortage in one store can be met by moving a surplus from another.
- An organisation which relies on telephone or computerised dealing can use the system itself to log callers. An example is First Direct bank, which does all its business over the telephone or by computer.

An organisation may classify its customers into various types. For instance, a large college will look at the number of adults and school-leavers who attend. A hotel may differentiate between business users and private individuals. A bank may analyse its customers by age range and income. It would become worried if it only attracted elderly people to open new accounts.

Name	No. of stores	Parking	Aesthetic	Aisles	Sign quality	Prices	Have you any saffron?	Payment	Special facilities	Future technology	Celebrity shoppers
Asda/ Dales	200	Free, extensive, though not always easily accessible.	Black and white, very spacious, although difficult to see past high shelving. Clean.	Wide, but shelves are piled very high, and are often difficult to reach.	Poor. Even staff seem confused.	420g can baked beans: 21p (Heinz 26p) Bread: 35p Orange juice/ litre: 52p Milk: 24p 100g jar instant coffee: 99p (Nescafé £1.69)	Initially unhelpful, then after explanation unable to explain where dried herbs were.	All kinds accepted.	Lottery ✓ Coffee bar; change point.	Automatic "Checkout save" money-off vouchers with receipt.	Kenneth, Clarke, Robbie from Take That!
Kwik Save	874	Only outside city centres.	Red, blue and white, yellow tiles. Slightly shabby looking. High shelving.	Reasonably wide but in overall cramped space.	Poor, no prices on some items.	Beans: "No frills" 7p (Heinz 26p) Bread: "No frills" 22p white, 29p brown Orange juice:45p Milk: 27p Coffee: 59p (Nescafé £1.75)	Directed to herbs and spices, but not stocked.	Credit cards not accepted; Switch accepted in newer shops (heavily flagged in student areas).	Lottery ✓ Free phone for taxis.	"We keep abreast of changes which will benefit our customers."	Helen Mirren
Marks & Spencer	282	None, except in 17 edge of town stores.	Cream and green. Very clean.	Wide around fruit and veg, narrow elsewhere. Cramped feel to volume of shoppers.	Poor (you should know your way around Marks, it seems).	Beans: 29p Sliced loaf: 39p Orange juice: freshly squeezed £1.09 Milk: 39p Coffee: £1.99	No saffron, I was told unapologetically.	Accept neither credit cards nor Switch.	Lottery ✗ Free phone for taxis in some stores.	"We never tell people what our future plans are."	Margaret Thatcher, Princess Diana, Thora Hird
Safeway	376	Free, extensive. Parent with child parking near entrance.	The ubiquitous cream and green. Attractively laid out and very clean.	Wide aisles. Acknowledged as the best for supermarket flirting. But beware – one's availability is judged by the contents of one's trolley.	Very clear, including prices.	Beans: 21p (Heinz 29p) Bread: 35p white, 39p brown Orange juice: 52p Milk: 28p Coffee: £1.87 (Nescafé £1.92)	Vague directions to dried spices, where they had freeze-dried saffron.	All kinds accepted. Cash-back facilities available.	Lottery ✓ Free taxi phone. Bottle/can banks; some baby changing rooms; eight stores have creches.	"We don't discuss our plans for reasons of commercial sensitivity."	Catherine Zeta Jones, Keith Chegwin
Sainsbury's	354	Free, extensive. Some areas have two-hour limit and ticket that needs stamping at counter.	White, with blue and yellow tiles. Attractively laid out and very clean.	Wide.	Good, clear, except for prices.	Beans: 21p (Heinz 29p) Bread: 35p white, 45p brown Orange juice: 69p Milk: 29p Coffee: £1.48 (£1.76 for Nescafé)	Helpful assistant took me to dried spices where they had freeze-dried saffron.	All kinds accepted. Cash-back available.	Lottery ✓ Bottle/ plastic/paper banks. Coffee shop. Free taxi phone. Toilets/baby changing facilities in many stores.	Doesn't disclose future plans.	Joanna Lumley
Tesco	443	Free and extensive. Parent with child parking available.	Cream and green again. Functional rather than appealing.	Most not wide enough, bad jams throughout.	Good.	Beans: 21p (Heinz 29p) Bread: 35p white, 54p brown Orange juice: 57p Milk: 28p Coffee: £1.88 (£1.92 for Nescafé)	"Saffron? Not in here there isn't!" (Wrong – they had it freeze-dried).	All kinds accepted.	Lottery ✓ Coffee shop; paper, bottle plastic, can banks. Baby changing facilities. Free phone for taxis in many stores.	No response.	Richard Branson, Germaine Jackson, Norma Major, Princess Diana (again)
Waitrose	111	Free for two hours.	Cream-tiled floors, walls with a green border. Benches and potted plants in entrance. Very clean.	Very broad. Low shelving.	Clear, large signs, but price signs in italics hard either to find or read.	Beans: 21p (Heinz 29p) Bread: 49p Orange juice: 89p Milk: 28p Coffee: £1.87 (Nescafé £1.92)	Friendly staff directed me to freeze-dried saffron.	All kinds accepted in majority of branches.	Lottery ✓ Carry to car service. Toilets/baby changing facilities in 12 newest branches. Some free phones for taxis.	Currently refurbishing tills to introduce scanners in all branches (others already have them).	"I'm sorry, we don't talk about our customers."

Figure 3.72 How the supermarkets compare

Often an organisation will keep a database of its customers, so that it can contact them by post to inform them about special offers and sales. Banks, for instance, frequently contact their good customers to offer them special loans or investment advice. A mail order or holiday company may continue to issue its brochures to ex-customers for two or three years, in the hope that they will buy from them again.

Did you know?

Most organisations teach staff answering enquirers by telephone to answer by identifying themselves with their first name. A usual greeting may be 'Good morning, Direct Mail Order, Karen speaking. How may I help you?' The aim is that the name 'Karen' registers with the customer who knows who to contact with any further enquiries or any subsequent complaints.

Non-assessed activity

Figures 3.74a and b show the number of people visiting British cinemas in four years 1984, 1988, 1990 and 1994 and the frequency of attendance.

Figure 3.73 Personalising service over the telephone

As a group, discuss:

a how the figures might have been compiled
b how the compilers found out the age of customers
c how the compilers might have measured frequency of attendance
d why the figures may be useful to cinema chains (as a clue, think of additional facilities they could provide and adverts which might be popular).

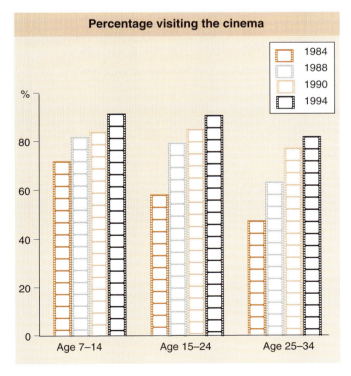

Figure 3.74a Cinema attendance in the UK

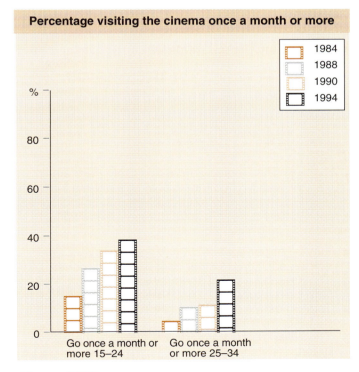

Figure 3.74b

Level of sales

If sales increase steadily, either the company has several new customers or their existing customers are buying more from them.

Sales will increase if the number of enquiries which are converted into sales increases or if more new customers are attracted to the organisation. Sales may also increase if the organisation has a special promotion or reduced price offer, or seasonally at certain times of the year, e.g. Christmas. However, this will increase sales on a temporary basis only. It is far harder to increase sales on a permanent basis.

The level of sales is worked out by calculating the income from sales and dividing this by the number of customers, to give the average amount spent by each customer. The organisation must adjust its figures for inflation if it compares the level of sales this year with those in previous years. It can do this by making adjustments in line with the retail price index, which was discussed in Element 3.3.

Levels of sales in a store can also be estimated by seeing how many people are queuing at the tills, how much they have in their baskets or trolleys and how many people appear to be leaving empty-handed. If you visualise the same store in the Christmas rush you will understand the differences which occur in level of sales over a year.

Manufacturing organisations will find that their sales levels will rise and fall in line with their products' **life cycles** (see Element 3.2). This is why such organisations will be investing in new products to take the place of those where sales are falling.

Did you know?

The Henley Centre and GAH Partnership researched the level of sales of the National Lottery. They have published their findings in a report called Lottery Fallout. Some of their findings include the following information.

■ Fifty-eight per cent of UK citizens play every week and an additional six per cent play each month.
■ The average amount spent by each person on the National Lottery is £2.08.
■ Total sales will reach £3.1 billion in the first year and £4 billion by 1997.
■ The sales of scratch cards will raise another £1 billion.
■ Sales in shops with lottery terminals have increased by 20 per cent.

■ Supermarkets have gained an extra 5000 customers per week and smaller shops an additional 2700.
■ The lottery has increased the number of regular gamblers in the UK from 15 million to 25 million.
■ People often buy treats such as sweets, chocolates and magazines, on impulse, whilst queuing for their tickets.

Non-assessed activity

1 Imagine your family own a small newsagents shop but don't agree with gambling. So far they have refused to have a lottery terminal installed. However, they are interested in increasing the level of sales in the shop. How might the findings above influence their decision in the future?

2 What do you consider was the 'level of sales' at your own school or college for your course? How do you know?

3 Figure 3.75 shows level of sales of different aspects of the film market. **As a group,** identify:
   a those areas where level of sales is increasing
   b those where it is falling.

What additional services could you offer to customers if you owned a video rental shop to counter the threat of increasing video sales?

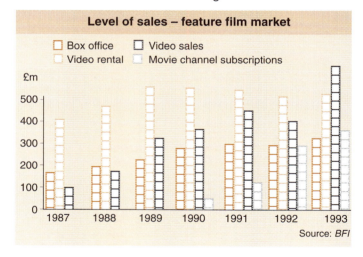

Figure 3.75 Levels of sales – feature film market

Feedback

There are various ways in which feedback can be obtained from customers. Some of these are quite informal and others are more structured and formal. The method used may depend on the type of organisation and the business it carries out.

■ **On-the-spot questions from staff** – the best example of an informal feedback method is a waiter coming up to you in a restaurant and checking that you are satisfied that everything is all right. Another example is the sales representative who gives verbal feedback to the boss from customers.

Figure 3.76 A waiter obtains feedback from customers

■ **Under-cover customers** – an unknown executive or rep from head office sometimes visits a branch as a make-believe customer and rates the branch on the service they receive. Vauxhall do this regularly by sending out 'mystery buyers' to their dealers. Each dealer then receives a feedback report.
■ **Consumer panels** are organised in some companies. Members of staff and the public meet regularly to discuss products, service, and new ideas. Boots plc has operated this system for some time in all its stores. This is a typical example of a more formal method of obtaining feedback.

Repeat business

The number of repeat purchases each customer makes is easier to track for companies supplying industrial customers than for retail outlets. An industrial customer would expect to buy the goods **on credit** (i.e. buy now and pay after receiving the invoice). Each customer would therefore have their own account which would show the number (and value) of transactions in each accounting year.

However, repeat business can be easier to track if a system of logging regular customers is introduced. Methods used include:

■ membership, bonus or discount cards
■ keeping customer records on a database and matching new orders placed against these records
■ special offers or competitions which require the customer to make a set number of purchases (in the hope that he or she will become a regular buyer).

Did you know?

Organisations will often attempt to find out the names and addresses of their customers by means of special offers. Every customer who fills in a request has to enter their name and address; these details can be recorded on a computer database. The company can then contact them to ask them to complete questionnaires, send them details of future special offers, new products etc.

Complaints

Most organisations record the complaints they have received and the action that was taken in each case. If many complaints are received about one particular aspect of the business then this is investigated thoroughly. Minor complaints which can be solved quickly may be dealt with through informal systems – a quick chat to a member of staff, for instance. A serious complaint should always be handled formally in case there was the possibility of legal action being taken. This would mean keeping a written record of everything which took place.

In addition the company may keep a record of **returned goods.** Returned goods not only indicate that the goods being sold are not up to standard but also that at least one customer has been inconvenienced and will be dissatisfied with the company. If the goods have been purchased from one particular supplier, this supplier may be cautioned or even stopped from supplying any more goods.

The BBC set up a special Programme Complaints Unit in January 1995 after Government pressure that it should become more accountable, and because the public wasn't satisfied with the effectiveness of programmes such as *Points of View* and *Feedback*. In its first eight months the unit investigated 590 complaints and upheld 102 of them. Three complaints resulted in apologies being made over the air. Thirty-two per cent of the complaints related to entertainments programmes and 28 per cent related to current affairs. Most of the complaints (143) related to bias (mainly political) and 115 complaints came under the heading 'poor taste'.

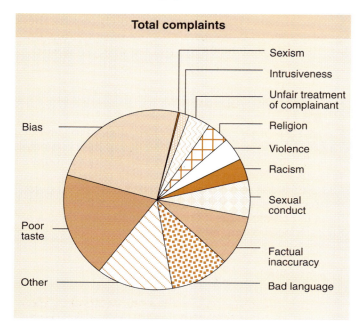

Figure 3.77 Complaints against BBC television programmes

Complaints against public sector organisations are usually dealt with by 'watchdog' organisations (e.g. OFTEL which oversees British Telecom, or OFLOT which oversees the National Lottery) or else by senior staff. If there are too many complaints about an organisation, regulations could be introduced by the Government to control the way in which they operate.

Did you know?

Some companies make compensatory offers to customers who complain or return goods, as a gesture of goodwill and to try to prevent the customer from thinking badly of them in the future. For example, a fast food chain may offer a free meal to anyone who has to wait more than 20 minutes to be served.

Marketing research

The role of marketing was discussed in Unit 2, and market research was also covered in Element 3.1. Market research sections are frequently involved in finding out what customers think of existing products and carrying out surveys on spending patterns. They are also very concerned with customer opinions of the company as a whole.

Market researchers will usually compile a questionnaire for customers or users of a service to complete, in order to give their views. As an example, if you go away on a package holiday you will probably find that on your return you will be asked to complete a questionnaire which asks you to rate certain aspects of the flight, the hotel facilities and services of the representative as excellent, very good, good, satisfactory or poor. The responses are analysed and the company will take action about those areas which can be improved.

Market research is never carried out in a haphazard or casual way. It is carefully structured so that the information obtained can be easily analysed. The people surveyed are specially targeted to give a representative sample of the average view of a customer or a potential customer. There is little point in asking 65-year-olds what they think of Levi jeans or Nintendo computer games, or fourteen-year-olds about brown bread or *News at Ten!*

Did you know?

In a survey undertaken by the Consumers Association, people were asked to choose from a list of public services and rank these in terms of which they felt provided the worst value for money and quality of service. British Rail ranked highest with 27 per cent. Water companies were a close second, with many people complaining about the quality of the service and inaccurate bills.

Non-assessed activity

Today many colleges and schools carry out surveys of students to find out their opinions of their courses and other aspects of the organisation. This may range from the advice and customer service given at interview, to the quality and value of food in the refectory. Find out about the type of surveys carried out by your school or college, the questions that are asked and how the questionnaires

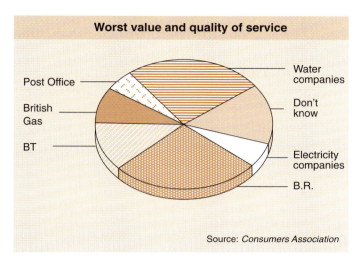

Figure 3.78 Consumers' opinions on which organisations provided the worst service and value

are analysed and evaluated. How do you think the questions may differ in relation to full-time and part-time students? Why?

Optional evidence assignment

*This activity can be carried out verbally in class **in a group** as a non-assessed activity to consolidate learning. Alternatively, if you do it **on your own**, it can count as supplementary evidence towards the following parts of the scheme.*

PC 1: Explain the importance of customer service in business organisations

PC 2: Identify how business organisations monitor customer satisfaction

Range: Importance of customer service: to gain and retain customers, to gain customer satisfaction, customer loyalty, to enhance organisation's image

How businesses monitor customer satisfaction: numbers of customers, level of sales, feedback (repeat business, complaints), marketing research

Core skills: Communication, Information technology

Read the article below and then answer the questions which follow.

'The big banks are frequently in the spotlight and have been criticised for poor service and information. In 1994 a survey of banks and building societies was carried out by the Consumers Association and ranked Barclays, Midland and NatWest the worst in overall customer satisfaction. According to the Consumers Association, their poor customer service made a mockery of slogans and advertisements such as "the listening bank". The association polled 8000 members and nearly 4000 replied. In addition, researchers were sent into banks and building societies posing as customers to check the accuracy of information given. This was frequently poor even on basic questions such as the number of days it takes for cash to clear into an account.

'This is somewhat ironic, since the Midland Bank has introduced a new Customer Focus programme aimed at:

■ putting people and quality first by developing internal service quality and employee satisfaction
■ keeping customers for life by customer recruitment, repeat sales and customer recommendation.

'The bank launched an Action Pack which it sent to all 1750 branches containing information on:

■ running quality service action teams
■ carrying out local customer surveys
■ establishing customer focus groups
■ sharing best practice ideas
■ organising in house training.

'It uses a number of methods to assess improvement in its quality of service including quarterly postal surveys of a representative sample of 10 000 customers, and carrying out "mystery shopping"\ visits to assess service at most of its branches. After each visit by a mystery shopper, the branch receives the results in the form of a score and a written report.

'However, in 1995 the Midland aims to cut over 2000 jobs – mainly at management level – despite profits of £905 million. Senior executives argue that removing excess managerial layers will give local managers more power and discretion and improve links with local communities. Banking unions have a different view and cannot see how improved service can be achieved or sustained with fewer employees.'

1 a What is the organisational image the big banks like to portray in their advertisements?
b Why have the Consumers Association claimed this image is false?
c What effect do reports such as that by the Consumers Association have on 'organisational image'?
2 What evidence is there in the article that the Midland Bank considers customer service to be important?

3 a How did the Consumers Association monitor customer satisfaction with the banks?

   b What methods do Midland use to monitor customer satisfaction?

4 a To what degree is staff expertise and morale important in providing customer service? Give a reason for your views.

   b What methods is the Midland using to involve its employees in improving customer service?

   c How might the announcements about recent job cuts affect staff morale and commitment to service?

5 Prepare **three** simple questions in relation to banking procedures. (You may wish to do this with help from your Financial Transactions tutor.) Write down the correct answer to each question.

   Arrange with your tutor for each person in your class to visit **one** major bank or building society in your area. Assess the service you receive (use the checklist on page 377 as a guide). Then ask your questions and note down the replies. See how many are correct.

   As a group, score each place you visited both for customer service and staff knowledge and expertise and see which organisation is the best – and which the worst.

Figure 3.79 Carrying out a survey of major banks

Improvements to customer services

No matter how good the result of customer surveys, there are few organisations (if any!) which can honestly boast that no improvements are possible. Most organisations actually publish the fact that they have an ongoing commitment to improving customer service. Indeed, if you measured the facilities and service available only a few years ago against those which we are starting to expect today, you would find quite a difference.

Improvements can be introduced in many areas. The key ones are described in more detail below.

Reliability

Reliability is an important aspect of customer service because it implies that the organisation can be relied upon or trusted to fulfil its promises or pledges. This means that you won't have a fruitless journey to the newsagent to collect a magazine which you were assured would arrive yesterday, neither will you sit around drumming your fingers waiting for the taxi you ordered which never appears.

There are several aspects of reliability which are important – including that of the product you buy. Product reliability is very important both to purchasers and suppliers. Purchasers are keen that the goods they buy can be relied upon to work properly for some time. Suppliers also want the goods they manufacture or sell to be reliable. Otherwise they will receive a high number of complaints, a large number of returned goods, and they are likely to see sales plummet. A retailer who stocks a 'bad line' is likely to refuse to stock any more in case customers start blaming him for their problems!

The Consumers Association publishes a monthly magazine *Which?* that reports on products which they have tested. In addition to giving information on the best value products, they also take reliability into account wherever possible. In 1995 they published a survey giving the reliability of a wide range of products, from washing machines and faxes to colour TVs and microwave ovens – saying which brands were the best for reliability.

Reliability isn't important only when you are buying goods. It is also a major consideration when you are buying a service. You wouldn't use a dry cleaners if, nine times out of ten, the clothes you had left were never ready when they were supposed to be, or they had forgotten to mend the hem when you asked them to, or hadn't taken note that you wanted a stain removed. Neither would you use a florist who never delivered the flowers as promised or took them to the wrong house. However, these are *known* services where you can quickly and accurately judge the quality. Reliability becomes even more important when you have to trust someone because of your lack of knowledge. Garages, appliance repairers, plumbers and electricians are all examples of service people we often need to trust because our knowledge of the situation isn't good enough to use our own judgement. Therefore, if the local garage quotes you £150 to mend your car, you want to be able to rely on it to give you an accurate and knowledgeable diagnosis of the fault and the repair required. You would get a shock afterwards if your car-mad next-door neighbour told you that the fault could have been repaired quite simply for under £25!

Transport companies are another example of an organisation where reliability is a key aspect of the service. Holidays can be ruined if there are long delays at airports. British Rail have become the target of many jokes because of trains being delayed for a variety of reasons – from leaves on the track in autumn, to train drivers not knowing their way around some routes! Bus companies come under fire when buses are expected but don't turn up, or are so late that passengers miss an important appointment.

Did you know?

Many home repairers have a code of practice for dealing with customers. This may include items such as:

- setting service targets for repaired goods
- making home visits out of normal working hours

- making all visits within three days of being called
- giving value for money
- repairing 80 per cent of items on the first visit
- obtaining new parts within fourteen working days of the fault being identified
- leaving the working area clean and tidy afterwards.

Non-assessed activity

Visit your school, college or local library and look up the *Which?* report on appliance reliability (March 1995). Check any appliances you own at home and see how they rate. Find out which make of television and fax machine you should buy – and which products are the most reliable and which the least.

Suggestions for improving reliability

Decide whether you would like to recommend improving the reliability of a service, a product or both. Product reliability would normally have to be referred back to research and development (see Element 2.1) if improvements to the design or technical construction are required.

It is more likely that you will be concentrating on improving the reliability of customer service. You may find, for instance, that service is good when the main staff, who have been properly trained, are on duty. It may be less good when people are undertaking these duties in an emergency or to cover for breaks. Training is often a key aspect, together with adequate information about the systems in use. This helps people who are new to the job to cope with the range of queries they will meet. Alternatively, you may recommend that the reliability of the service will be improved if the number of staff working in this area is restricted to those who have been through an official training scheme or are properly qualified.

One basic recommendation you may be tempted to make is that staff don't make promises that they can't keep!

Friendliness

It is unfortunate that some people mistake efficiency with being abrupt or rude. They are so busy proving how good they are that they haven't time for the common courtesies, which include 'Good morning', 'please' and 'thank you'!

We judge whether someone is friendly *not* just by the words they use but by the expression on their face, the way they stand and the amount of interest they show. Someone who deals with your query in five seconds flat, to get you out of the way, can hardly be described as being friendly! Equally, you don't expect someone you are contacting on business to talk to you like an old friend! Somewhere in the middle there is a balance. It is *quite* possible to be efficient *and* business-like *and* friendly *and* welcoming, all at the same time. This holds for staff dealing with customers face-to-face *and* over the telephone.

Staff working on a customer services desk are trained to greet people with a smile, to look interested and to be helpful – and to have *time* for people. It is less easy for staff who are actually very busy with another job to appear friendly, when they are rudely interrupted, in the middle, by a customer. However, given that the customer sees that member of staff not as an individual, but as a representative of the organisation, it really is crucial that staff appear not to mind being interrupted. The customer *must* come first – without the customer the member of staff is unlikely to have any job to do!

Suggestions for improving friendliness

It is impossible only to employ staff who are always outgoing and cheerful! However, staff who are on 'the front line' in terms of customer service must have the right image. It helps enormously if they have a friendly 'open' face and appear approachable. Staff who hate dealing with people, or are very shy or nervous, are better kept behind the scenes!

Supervisors need to be able to keep an eye on staff during their dealings with customers. If any member of staff is acting in an unfriendly way or has a particularly harsh manner, it is the job of the supervisor to talk to him or her and arrange training, if necessary – or a change of job.

Availability of goods and services

No organisation can stock every item which may be required by customers – although many large superstores try very hard. If you are after barbecue lighters at Christmas or Christmas wrapping paper in July you may have problems!

It can be very frustrating for customers to find that, no matter where they go, they cannot buy a routine item, or that their neighbourhood shops have stopped selling an item they use regularly.

Customers' needs to buy a wide variety of goods can conflict with the retailers' need to stock fast-moving goods – because these are the most profitable lines. However, a good retailer should be able to cater for most people's needs, especially if an ordering service is available. A typical example of a retail outlet where a good ordering service can make all the difference to customer service is the record trade. People's tastes in music vary considerably. Whilst 80 per cent of the public might want standard popular and classical music, a further 20 per cent will not. They may prefer the type of music produced by independents or on 'white' labels, rather than the major record companies. A small shop which provides a comprehensive information and ordering service can increase its takings considerably and often prove more popular with customers than a chain store which only stocks the top-selling records and CDs.

Suggestions for improving availability of goods or services

Any suggestions have to be reasonable, and not threaten to bankrupt the owner of the business! Remember that there are some lines which wouldn't be profitable. Neither is it feasible to suggest that the organisation should order almost anything, on demand, from anywhere! It is far easier for a giant superstore – with a substantial amount of money to invest in stock and EDI links – to carry a wide range of stock, and obtain goods quickly, than it is for a small local shop.

The points to consider include:

- the range of stock on offer
- how well this meets, say, 80 per cent of the requests made by regular customers
- how often re-stocking takes place
- how many **actual** sales are lost because items aren't available
- the length of time it takes for ordered goods to be received (and the degree to which this can be controlled by the organisation itself)
- whether the organisation offers any additional services, e.g. telephoning customers (or sending them a card) when something has arrived in stock.

Non-assessed activity

Visit a local bookshop and assess it for availability of goods. Look at the range of books on offer and see whether this is very comprehensive, quite comprehensive or awful! Find out about their ordering system and how long it takes for books to be delivered. While you are asking about this, you can also make some mental notes about the friendliness of the staff.

When you return to class, compare your findings with the rest of your group. Imagine how you would react to the comments if you were the owner of the bookshop – and then decide on the improvements which could be made.

Did you know?

Rumbelows, the High Street electrical retailers, only held limited stock and asked customers to wait three weeks for delivery. This chainstore collapsed in February 1995! This gives you some idea of the expectations of customers today, both in relation to the availability of goods and services *and* speed of delivery.

Speed of delivery

How many times have you ordered something at the last minute as a present – especially by post – and then seen the words 'allow 28 days for delivery'? Why does it take so long?

In many cases, organisations use phrases like this to protect themselves from hundreds of customers contacting them after about five days asking them about delivery. In actual fact, in today's high-speed world when many items can be ordered by phone, fax or EDI and paid for electronically, the rate of turn-round of an order can be speeded up quite considerably, and this may be crucial in attracting new customers (see also EDI, Element 4.1). Think how impressed you would be if you ordered an item by phone and found it on your doorstep three days later!

It isn't just the customer who benefits from a rapid response. The more quickly items can be obtained, the less need there is for large organisations to keep massive stocks of goods. This reduces the amount of money tied up in stock *and* the cost of storage space. It is therefore both in the organisation's interests *and* in the customer's interests if goods can be obtained quickly.

Did you know?

The Royal Mail publishes targets in relation to the speed of delivery of first-class and second-class letters. It aims to deliver first-class letters by the next working day and second-class letters by the third working day. Latest figures show that this is achieved for 92 per cent of first-class letters and 98 per cent of second-class letters. Parcelforce fares less well. It delivers 87 per cent of parcels within three working days. It aims to increase this to 90 per cent.

Figure 3.80 The Royal Mail tries to meet its targets

Suggestions for improving speed of delivery

Some organisations are dependent on their own suppliers and, unless they are very powerful buyers, may not be able to influence the delivery time. Basically, speed of delivery is based on the turn-round time of an order. If it sits on someone's desk for three days, delivery is bound to be slow. If a clear system is in operation so that orders always receive top priority treatment, then delivery is likely to be much quicker.

Electronic communications systems are obviously more rapid than old-fashioned paper and postal systems. However, the telephone is useful too! Many chemists phone their wholesalers each evening to place orders, which are delivered the following morning, so the company doesn't have to spend a fortune installing expensive computer equipment to provide items quickly. What it does need to do is to 'shop around' for suppliers who will respond promptly.

It is not wise for an organisation to try to improve its speed of delivery to an impossible extent. This would force the business to make promises it couldn't keep. In some cases, speeding up the process costs money. One answer may be to have an 'express' service available for an additional charge – such as that operated by many dry cleaning firms, laundries and some florists.

Optional evidence assignment

*This activity can be carried out verbally in class **in a group** as a non-assessed activity to consolidate learning. Alternatively, if you do it **on your own,** it can count as supplementary evidence towards the following parts of the scheme.*

PC 1: Explain the importance of customer service in business organisations

PC 2: Identify how business organisations monitor customer satisfaction

PC 3: Identify improvements to customer service

PC 4: Present proposals for improvements to customer services in one organisation

Range: Importance of customer service: to gain and retain customers, to gain customer satisfaction, customer loyalty, to enhance organisation's image

How businesses monitor customer satisfaction: numbers of customers, level of sales, feedback (repeat business, complaints), marketing research

Improvements to customer service: reliability, friendliness, availability of goods or services, speed of delivery

Core skills: Communication, Information technology, Application of number

Read the case study below and then answer the questions which follow.

Case study

Your friend Steve has been looking for a job for over a year. You are pleased when you hear he has been offered the opportunity of obtaining a milk franchise from Daily Dairies. You start to worry when you read a newspaper report that says many large dairies are cutting back staff because they are being squeezed out of business by the supermarkets. According to the press report,

supermarkets use milk as loss-leaders and often sell it as cheaply as 20p a pint, whereas doorstep milk can cost up to 40p a pint. The market share of milk rounds fell from 83 per cent in 1984 to only 50 per cent in 1994.

Then you start to think about your own milkman, Tom. You know he works very hard, but you remember that last week he was telling someone about a new car he has bought. You reckon his business can't be all that bad. When you chat to him, you find out that he starts his deliveries at 2 am – *after* collecting the milk from the dairy – and then races around to deliver to 750 customers before 8 am. He reckons that's essential, because otherwise people wouldn't have their milk in time for breakfast. Tom also keeps his eyes on his elderly customers – only last week he called the police when he noticed an old lady's milk hadn't been taken in for two days. The old lady was found collapsed on the floor and was rushed to hospital. He also tells you that on occasions he has pushed front door keys through the letterbox, when someone has left them in the lock! Over the years he has gained more and more customers over a larger area.

Tom also works as a franchisee for a dairy. In addition to selling milk he delivers bacon, eggs, cheese, potatoes, butter, yoghurt and bread. A phone call can be made to the dairy, and a special order made before 9 pm is guaranteed to be delivered the next day. If any part of the service goes wrong, the dairy gives a 30p voucher to compensate customers for any inconvenience caused. Tom says these additional items are very popular and his sales have increased considerably. This is important because the more he sells, the more he earns. He keeps 15 per cent of all his takings.

Figure 3.81 Making a milkround a success

You know that your friend thought he could give quite a good service if he started his rounds at 6 am and just delivered milk and cream. You have a feeling that his business won't do very well unless you discuss how he can improve his ideas on customer service. Given that, as a franchisee, his earnings will also depend on his sales, your advice could be critical to his future success.

1 Give examples from the text which show that Tom is very aware of the importance of customer service to:
   a gain and retain customers
   b gain customer satisfaction
   c gain customer loyalty.

2 Explain briefly what you think Tom's image is to his customers.

3 Describe the two ways in which Tom's business has grown. How is this an indication of customer satisfaction?

4 Write your friend Steve a brief note which explains the importance of the following aspects of customer service to his business:
   a reliability
   b friendliness
   c availability of goods
   d speed of delivery.

   Then make suggestions for improving the ideas he has already.

5 A week later you receive a reply. Steve thinks that he can make life easy for himself by reducing his potential area from 600 houses to 300 – so he can get round quicker. He also feels that if he reduced the price of his milk from 40p a pint to 20p a pint he could compete with the supermarkets.
   a If every household buys an average of two pints of milk a day, how much will Steve's takings be each day if:
      i   he sells to 600 houses at the original price
      ii he makes his proposed changes?
   b How does this compare to the takings of your milkman Tom, if Tom sells the same amount of milk to each of his customers plus an average of 50p in other goods to each house on his round?
   c What is your advice to Steve based on these calculations?

Published policy for exchanges or refunds

This was discussed in full in Element 3.3. Turn back to page 349 and refresh your memory on this aspect of customer service.

Non-assessed activity

As a group, decide on the type of improvements which could sensibly be suggested in relation to policies for exchanges and refunds. What, in your view, is the ideal policy? What, if you are a small shopkeeper making a precarious living, might be the compromise position?

Access to buildings

For most of us, visiting different buildings, shops and offices isn't a problem. We may grumble if there are lots of stairs and the lift isn't working, but it isn't a catastrophe. We may get annoyed when we can't find our way around, but we can always ask someone. But what if you were 'disabled' in some way – e.g. reliant on a wheelchair, or deaf? In that case, lifts and clear signs would be absolutely essential, rather than an optional extra.

Since 1985 the law has dictated that public buildings must be accessible. New guidelines were issued by the Department of the Environment in 1992. Despite these, disabled people, including those whose sight is impaired or who have hearing difficulties, still have problems. They find ramps are too steep or too long, doors are heavy and unwieldy, there are no toilets specifically for their use, there is no car park close by, parking places reserved for disabled drivers are used by other drivers, lifts are too small for wheelchairs, there is a lack of clear signs, and handrails are missing or poorly maintained, as are steps and floor coverings.

Good access is also important for mothers with young children who may be pushing a pram or pushchair as well as trying to carry shopping and control a toddler! Organisations can help, not only by assessing their premises and *asking* shoppers with disabilities for their views, but also by offering additional services, e.g. taking heavy shopping loads to a car or placing the most essential and fast-moving sales items on the ground floor.

Suggestions for improving access

If you are making suggestions for a building you know well, you may have to look at this with 'fresh eyes'. You will have become so used to your surroundings that you might miss many features that would be obvious to someone visiting for the first time.

Remember that you can hardly suggest that a building is torn down and the architects start all over again! In some cases, particularly in 'listed' buildings which have special historical interest, it may be impossible to install a lift or escalator – or even to widen doorways. However, ramps are an easier alternative and, in any case, you could recommend that the most commonly used services are on the ground floor.

Figure 3.83 Entrance ramps make access possible for everyone

Non-assessed activity

Assess your own college or school in terms of access. Think back to when you were a new student. How easy was it to find your way around? If you broke your leg tomorrow and arrived in a wheelchair or on crutches, how would you cope? If there are any students with specific difficulties in your group, you will benefit enormously by asking them for their views.

Report back your suggestions for improvements to your tutor.

Care for the environment

Organisations in general are becoming more aware of environmental issues. They may produce goods in packaging which can be easily recycled and actively encourage customers to do this. They may advertise that their products are 'environmentally friendly' and, for example, produce items in pump-action sprays rather than aerosols to reduce the use of CFCs, which damage the environment.

Those organisations that are conscious of their *immediate* environment will have clean and tidy premises. Rubbish will be removed regularly and staff will take a pride in their workplace. Plenty of rubbish bins will be available so that customers who want to throw away receipts or other items can do so easily. Cleaners will be employed to make sure that the area is cleaned daily. Staff will pick up any rubbish dropped on the floor rather than just pass by and ignore it.

In a good organisation, the same standards will prevail behind the scenes. It won't just be the areas on public display that are kept immaculate but also the areas the public never sees. Proper procedures will also operate to remove rubbish from the premises on a regular basis.

Did you know?

In Germany a Green Dot system is in operation. This shows that the manufacturer is a member of the DSD – *Duales System Deutschland.* This is the German response to the European packaging directive which came into force in 1995. It means that the suppliers of goods have to be prepared to receive the packaging back from the customer. The packaging is put into special yellow bins and separated into paper, card, plastic and other materials – and then recycled. One result has been a reduction of approximately a million tonnes of packaging by suppliers who found it easier to reduce the amount of packaging used than take it all back again! The British version will be called Valpack. When it is operational perhaps, like the Germans, most British shoppers will be removing the pack and disposing of it at the checkout – to save taking it home and putting it in a special yellow bin!

Suggesting improvements in relation to care for the environment

The standard of cleanliness you can reasonably expect will depend on the type of organisation you are visiting, and the facilities inside the building. You should naturally expect that a hospital, restaurant or food shop is immaculately clean. You can lower your standards a little if you are visiting the library or railway station! However, you do have a right to expect the place to be cleaned and swept regularly, for there to be adequate litter bins and for the toilet areas to be spotlessly clean.

Assess how *easy* the area is to clean – is the flooring tiled or carpeted? Is the furniture fixed to the wall? If it is movable, is it too heavy for one person to manage alone? Are trolleys available for removing packaging and rubbish? Is the back area full of rubbish which should have been moved long ago, or is it clean and swept? Do the staff appear to be neat, clean and well-trained, or scruffy and sloppy in their work habits? Are there mounds of paper on every desk, or is each work surface clean and tidy?

Did you know?

You should never believe that desks and counters full of paper or other items denote efficiency. They don't. They look a mess, and the owner is more likely to lose an important piece of paper than find it. Quite apart from anything else, they are probably a serious fire hazard.

Non-assessed activity

Marks & Spencer stores undergoing a refit, or building alterations, operate a policy of giving away vouchers that will give customers money off on future trips to the store.

1 Why do you think M & S operate this policy?
2 Why do they issue vouchers rather than just reducing the price of the goods on offer?

Customer safety

Customers' safety can be considered from two points of view. The first is in relation to customers' personal safety when they visit the premises, the second is in relation to their safety when they buy a product. Both of these have been dealt with earlier in this unit and both are covered by specific legislation. The safety of visitors and customers is covered by the Health and Safety at Work Act and product safety is covered by the Sale of Goods Act, and the Consumer Protection Act.

Turn back to elements 3.2 and 3.3 now (pages 320 and 370) to refresh your memory on the points that were made.

Remember, too, that a person's legal rights cannot be taken away because a notice is put up on the premises. A sign which says 'Beware of Slipping' may act as a warning, but if someone has polished the floor so that it is like glass, the organisation will still be liable if someone has an accident.

When you visit an organisation, don't just think about the safety of adults. Think about children, old people and the disabled as well. If there are steep steps, a very high handrail or gaps between railings that a child could put his head through, then safety is still very questionable. Check what you would do if an emergency occurred – are emergency exits within reach and clearly marked? Are they wide enough to take a lot of people trying to get out in a panic? What would happen if the lights failed in a fire – can you spot the emergency lighting? How would you get out quickly if you were upstairs, disabled and in a wheelchair?

When you look at products, see how many have been approved by the British Standards Institute or carry the Kitemark to prove they are safe. Read instructions you receive to see if safety procedures are mentioned. Check there are no sharp edges or plastic bags (without holes) which could suffocate a small child. Check no areas become unpleasantly hot when an appliance is in use – unless it is logical for them to do so (e.g. a gas fire or electric cooker). If the item could be used by a child, check that nothing small could easily be removed – and then swallowed!

Suggesting improvements for customer safety

Unsafe practices are not just the result of a lack of suitable exits or proper emergency procedures. They are also likely to be caused by staff complacency. If several months go by and no-one has an accident, people become more casual in their approach. Fire doors may be left open, an emergency exit may be blocked by boxes, someone may use the lift in an emergency evacuation without thinking – or walk half way round *inside* the building to get out in a fire drill, near the assembly point (just because it is raining!)

You could make recommendations which include regular staff training or better warnings of emergency procedures, or signposting for casual visitors.

If you find a product that is unsafe you could write to the company or even report the fact to your local Trading Standards Officer (see Element 3.2, page 322).

Did you know?

Customer service is entering a new phase in the mid-1990s with large retail organisations entering an era of 'value added' incentives to persuade shoppers to visit them. In addition to giving customers good service and a clean environment many large organisations – particularly superstores – now add extras.

- Tesco has a Clubcard which adds up points for money spent and then gives money-back vouchers. Some stores have 'customer service centres' where customers are invited to sample any new brands.
- Sainsbury's offered £1 million worth of prizes in a recent free draw.
- In some Asda stores you can have a haircut, and in Bristol, Asda has 'singles nights' with special areas where people can find a partner (e.g. the ready meals area and wine racks)
- Safeway provides creches.

What ideas do you have for what the future might bring?

Optional evidence assignment

*This activity can be carried out verbally in class **in a group** as a non-assessed activity to consolidate learning. Alternatively, if you do it **on your own**, it can count as supplementary evidence towards the following parts of the scheme.*

PC 3: Identify improvements to customer service

PC 4: Present proposals for improvements to customer services in one organisation

Range: Improvements to customer service: friendliness, published policy for exchanges or refunds, access to buildings, care for the environment, customer safety

Core skills: Communication, Information technology

Compile a questionnaire to find out which of your local retail stores is the most customer friendly – especially to shoppers with young children, i.e. those with prams and pushchairs. As a start you may like to include such factors as:

- the length of queues
- the friendliness of staff
- whether there are steps or ramps
- whether there are automatic doors
- whether there are lifts between floors
- whether or not sweets are placed low down near cash points (so that children can grab them easily!)
- cleanliness (think of toddlers sitting on the floor!)
- safety aspects
- whether there is a **published** policy on goods which are returned.

As a group, think of as many relevant questions as possible (and check these with your tutor). Design your questionnaire then go out and score each store in your area. If you want to be even more objective, you should obtain the views of some of the mothers of small children you see entering or leaving the store.

Finally, evaluate your answers – and draw up a list of recommendations that the worst store on your list could implement if it wanted to improve sales!

Evidence indicator project

Your tutor may now wish you to start work on the Evidence Indicator Project which will prove to your external verifier that you have covered all the work for this element. This project is given on page 398 and covers the evidence indicator for this element.

Revision test

True or false?

1 Providers of public services aren't interested in customer service.
2 Questionnaires assessing consumer opinion are usually designed by the marketing research section.
3 A hire company that has a sign saying 'all equipment supplied at customer's own risk' is never liable for claims.
4 The safety of customers whilst on business premises is covered by the Health and Safety at Work Act.
5 Finding out details of complaints received is one way of obtaining feedback from customers.

Fill in the blanks

6 Easy access to a building is particularly important for anyone who is _____ .
7 Under the Green Dot system in Germany, packaging is collected, sorted and then _____ .
8 Organisations may set _____ which staff must meet to ensure that they provide a reliable service.
9 Marketing research staff may carry out a _____ to obtain the opinion of a particular group of people.
10 *Which?* reports are published by the _____ _____ .

Short answer questions

11 Briefly state how you would assess friendliness on the part of a sales assistant.
12 State **three** ways in which an organisation can monitor customer satisfaction.

13 State **two** ways in which organisations can demonstrate they care about the environment.

14 State **two** ways in which availability of goods or services may be improved.

15 State **two** ways in which feedback from customers may be obtained.

Write a short paragraph to show you clearly understand each of the following terms

16 Access to buildings

17 Customer loyalty

18 Organisational image

19 Policies for exchanges or refunds

20 Speed of delivery

Evidence indicator project

Unit 3 Element 3.4

This project has been designed to cover the evidence indicator related to Element 3.4. Because there is only one evidence indicator for this element, the project is designed to be carried out at the end of the element.

Performance criteria: 1–4

Core skills: Communication
Application of number
Information technology

1 **In a group of three or four** you are going to assess the customer services in one business organisation. Your tutor will divide you into suitable groups. You then need to decide which organisation you are going to visit. It is suggested that you choose one frequently used by members of the public. This could be a public building (e.g. a library or town hall) or a commercial organisation (e.g. a supermarket or chain store).

Check with your tutor that the organisation you have chosen is suitable.

2 Devise a checklist that will enable you to assess as many of the following as possible
   ■ the friendliness of staff
   ■ availability of goods or services
   ■ speed of delivery
   ■ policies for exchanges or refunds
   ■ access to buildings
   ■ customer safety
   ■ care for the environment.

Note that you must study **at least three** areas in detail.

3 Visit the organisation and make notes on what you find. Make arrangements for the visit beforehand with the assistance of your tutor, then staff will not keep stopping you to find out what you are doing! You should also ask if you can interview a member of staff whilst you are there, to find out how the organisation monitors its customers' satisfaction.

4 **As a team,** compare your findings. Then decide on the improvements which could be made. Decide, in each case, how your suggested improvements would help to
   ■ attract customers
   ■ secure customer satisfaction
   ■ develop customer loyalty
   ■ enhance the organisation's image.

5 Prepare a report which describes the customer services you have observed, which clearly states how the organisation monitors its customers' satisfaction and outlines your proposals for improvements to customer service. Make sure the report clearly shows the involvement of each member of the team.

6 Summarise the report on one sheet of A4 paper under a series of headings. Prepare an oral presentation to make to your tutor, who will be representing the management of the organisation you visited. Prepare some visual aids to support a brief ten-minute talk.

7 **As a group,** deliver your talk, under the following sections:
   a Introduction – the organisation you chose and why. Preparations before the visit.
   b Observations made and recorded on customer services
   c Results of interview with staff and summary of how the organisation monitors its customers' satisfaction
   d Your proposals for improvements and how these will benefit the organisation.

Be prepared to answer any questions put to you by your tutor at the end of the presentation.

Make sure you complete this project by the deadline date given to you by your tutor.

Identify and explain financial transactions and documents

This element explains the various types of financial transactions which regularly occur in business. It also describes the documents which are needed to record these transactions.

After studying this element you should be able to:

- explain *financial transactions* which take place regularly in organisations and explain

- why *records of transactions* are kept
- explain and give examples of *purchases* and *purchase documents*
- explain and give examples of *sales transactions* and *sales documents*
- explain and give examples of *payment methods* and *receipt documents*
- explain the *importance of security and security checks* for receipts and payments

What are financial transactions?

Although you may not realise it, you are probably involved in transactions every day! If you buy a can of Coke from a shop you complete a transaction because you *pay* some money and you *receive* the can. When you go to the cinema you *pay* the admission fee and are *allowed* to watch the film. A transaction occurs whenever a person pays some money in return for goods or services. Business organisations can be involved in two kinds of transactions:

- **outward transactions** when the organisation itself pays for the cost of goods and services it has

bought. Money from the firm flows outwards to suppliers of goods, services and labour.

- **inward transactions** when customers pay for goods or services the organisation has supplied. This is income received by the organisation. In this case money flows inwards to the organisation from people who buy the items it produces.

Another form of inward transaction is a loan where a business borrows money from a bank to help get started or for capital items (such as to buy new equipment or to build an extension).

Examples of the outwards and inwards transactions of a company manufacturing jeans is shown in Figure 4.1.

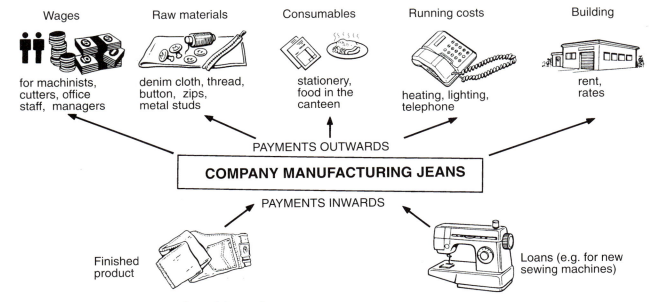

Wages — for machinists, cutters, office staff, managers

Raw materials — denim cloth, thread, button, zips, metal studs

Consumables — stationery, food in the canteen

Running costs — heating, lighting, telephone

Building — rent, rates

PAYMENTS OUTWARDS

COMPANY MANUFACTURING JEANS

PAYMENTS INWARDS

Finished product

Loans (e.g. for new sewing machines)

Figure 4.1 Transactions outwards and inwards

Outward transactions to pay for costs

When a newsagent pays the paper girl on a Saturday or sends a cheque to the newspaper supplier he is making an **outward transaction.** This means he is paying out money. He needs people to deliver the newspapers and he needs newspapers to deliver to keep his business going. So he has to pay for the service (delivery) and the goods (newspapers).

Larger businesses are involved in many outward transactions every day. Most of these can be listed under three main headings:

- wages
- materials
- overheads.

Wages

With the exception of those working for voluntary organisations, people who work are paid **wages** or **salaries.** Exactly how they often receive their money is explained later in this element.

The amount of wages people are paid can be as little as 50p per hour for homeworkers (people who work at home doing tasks such as packing), to as much as £500 per hour for a managing director of a large company. The most important thing is that the business gets value for money for the wages it pays. This means the employees who are paid must have enough skill, energy and enthusiasm to justify the money they earn. Equally, people have a right to expect a fair amount of money for the work that they do. (Wage rates are covered in more detail in Unit 2.)

Materials

On a particular day, a chip shop could order the following materials:

potatoes	detergent (for cleaning)
fish	new overalls for the staff
flour (for batter)	stationery

The items in the left-hand column are **direct materials** since they are sold directly to the customers after preparation and cooking. The materials in the right-hand column are ordered and used regularly but do not go directly to the customer. They are known as **consumables.** They are **consumed by the business**, not sold to the customer.

Both types of materials are purchased from suppliers. Just as with wages, it is important that the materials bought give value for money. A chip shop which sells high quality food will be prepared to pay a good price for fish in return for high quality.

Overheads

When a car is serviced at a garage, the customer could pay £15 per hour for the mechanic's time. You may think mechanics are doing very well, being paid this amount, but they are more likely to be paid between £4 and £5 per hour. So where does the extra £10 per hour go? The answer is in **overheads.** Think for a minute. In order to do the job, the mechanic needs many things, including:

- a heated building
- a ramp, tools and other equipment
- a supervisor
- administrative staff to place orders, collect payments and deal with customers.

The wages paid to the mechanic are only a fraction of the costs involved in providing a service to the customer.

Overheads are hidden costs that the customer does not see directly, but which are necessary to provide the goods or service. Because they are not linked directly to what the customer receives, overheads are more difficult to justify. Turning up the heating in the garage workshop may make the mechanic feel more comfortable, but does it make him work any harder?

Non-assessed activity

A consumer appliance service company may charge £35 per hour for a service engineer to visit a customer's home to repair his washing machine. The cost of any spare parts used will be added to this 'labour' charge to give the total bill. **As a group**, make out a list of all the extra costs that the business will have to pay out of the £35. Remember that the engineer will spend time travelling between customers' homes. Compare the list made by your group with those of other groups in your class.

Inward transactions to receive income

Payments

When a newsagent receives payment from a customer, his business is involved in **inward transactions.** He has **provided** goods (newspapers) and a service (delivery) and as his 'reward' he **receives** payments into his business.

Over a period of time, the inward transactions for a business should be higher than the outward transactions. Then the business makes a **profit.**

Payments can be made in many different ways, including cash, cheques, and credit cards. These will be described later, under 'Payment methods' – see page 424. The documents used to process and record inward transactions are described both in this element and in Element 4.2.

Loans

Virtually all businesses need to borrow money to start up in business. Many borrow later to pay for new equipment or to extend their premises. People may start a small business by borrowing money from a bank (a loan) or they may use their own savings. In this case they are 'borrowing' money from themselves.

Rebecca wants to open a small fashion shop. She takes advice from her bank manager and realises that, despite the fact she is confident in her ideas, she needs quite a lot of money to get started. She needs many things such as:

- shop premises – rent for three months in advance
- fittings – such as dress rails and changing rooms and a counter for serving customers
- stock – such as clothes to put on display and bags which have the name of the shop written on them.

She works out how much all this will cost and includes it in her **business plan.** This is a plan of how much she expects the business to spend and earn in the first period of trading (see Element 2.4, page 266). She presents her business plan to the bank and asks for a loan to help her get started.

The loan is agreed but, of course, she has to pay interest at quite a high rate, and promise to pay the money back within a certain time. In addition, the bank charges a fee for arranging the loan. Once the loan is agreed, the bank opens a **loan account** in Rebecca's name. The first bank statement shows how much money she has to repay in total. The bank manager has agreed that Rebecca should transfer a fixed amount from her ordinary bank account (called her **current account**) to the loan account each month. This transfer can be done automatically by the bank. Each month she will then receive a statement which shows the balance on her loan account reducing until all the money has been paid back.

Note that by taking out a loan (an **inward transaction**) Rebecca has committed herself to regular payments plus interest payments (an **outward transaction**).

Most companies, both large and small, take out loans. Some have to be repaid quite quickly, whilst others can be repaid over several years.

Figure 4.2 Rebecca has always dreamed of opening her own shop

Did you know?

Instead of taking out a loan, some businesses arrange to have an **overdraft** facility instead. This means that they can borrow money from the bank via their current account by spending more than they actually have in the bank. The limit – or maximum size – of the overdraft is agreed in advance and must not be exceeded. The problem is that the interest rate on overdrafts is higher than that on loans, but the size of the overdraft will vary as money is paid in and out of the account each month. The interest is only calculated on the overdraft on the actual days the account is overdrawn.

Records of transactions

When a transaction takes place in business, a record will nearly always be made. This may be on paper, on computer or both. The main reasons for this are so that the business can:

- produce accounts (both for internal and external use)
- ensure security
- monitor business performance (profit and loss).

Keeping accurate and up-to-date records is essential for all business organisations as they provide a permanent record which can be referred to in the future if anything needs to be checked. You can't rely on people's memories!

Without records of transactions, bills wouldn't get paid and the owner might even forget to collect money that people owe. In addition, there are several organisations, such as the Inland Revenue and the VAT office (see page 403), which are very interested in the financial affairs of businesses – both large and small. Public limited companies have a legal duty to publish their accounts, to demonstrate how the business has performed. Their shareholders will be particularly interested in this information.

Did you know?

Most people don't know how they spend their money. There is frequently a cry of 'I had £10 yesterday and I don't know where it's gone!' Could you write down now how much spending money you received last month? The answer is probably 'yes'. Could you also write down exactly what you spent it on and on which day? Probably not!

If you were a business you would *have* to record this type of information. The only way to do this is to record things *as they happen*.

Producing accounts

All accounts documents are a summary of certain types of transactions. These may be quite simple documents, such as a statement summarising the transactions that occurred in a month, or quite complicated accounts, such as the **balance sheet** or **profit and loss account.** It is possible to divide accounts into two types – those produced regularly for internal use and those provided each year for external use.

Accounts – internal for the business's own use

The owners or managers of a business need to keep accounts records which will give them the financial information they need to know on a regular basis. This will include the following.

- The purchases that have been made – and how much is owing to each supplier. Until the amount has been paid this person is known as a **creditor.** A creditor represents a debt which must be paid.
- The sales that have been made – and the debts owed by different customers. Until the money has been paid this person is known as a **debtor.** A debtor represents money owing to the company.
- The amount of money held in the bank.
- The amount of money kept in cash on the premises.
- How much is being spent on different types of expenses – from the telephone to the wage bill.

Did you know?

The accounts will be kept in a special set of books. The **cash book** records the money held on the premises and in the bank. It is also used to record cash payments. The **purchases ledger** records all the items which have been bought for resale where the goods have been bought on credit and the **sales ledger** is used to record the sales which have been made on credit. Buying and selling on credit is quite common in the business world. This means that the debt is settled a few weeks after the goods have been bought or sold. Any other financial transactions – such as expenses, and refunds on any items returned because they were faulty – are recorded in the **general ledger.**

Each month, the accounts section usually produces a **trial balance.** This is simply a list of all the balances in the different accounts books. This gives a snapshot of the business on the day it is prepared and enables the owner or manager to see various facts at a glance.

Did you know?

Companies which are liable to pay VAT must keep their internal accounts in order because they can be inspected at any time by Her Majesty's Customs and Excise Officers (VAT office). The sales, purchase and expenses transactions form the basis on which VAT is calculated. Companies that are not registered for VAT, simply because their annual sales figure (**turnover**) is below the VAT limit, need to keep a careful eye on the business – in case they do well enough to become liable to pay VAT.

Non-assessed activity

The trial balance for Rebecca's fashion shop after her first month of trading is shown in Figure 4.3. Discuss with your tutor:

a the different entries and the information these give to Rebecca

b how Rebecca can compare one month's trial balance with the next to spot important trends in her financial affairs.

Did you know?

Today many organisations record all their financial transactions on computer. A trial balance can then be printed out at any time, simply by pressing a few keys!

Trial balance for Rebecca's Fashions as at 30 June 199-

	Debit £	Credit £
Purchases	3 500	
Sales		5 500
Fashion Supplies Ltd (creditor)		1 300
J Taylor (debtor)	500	
Fixtures and fittings	1 000	
Bank	4 800	
Cash	200	
Capital		3 200
	10 000	10 000

Figure 4.3 Trial balance for Rebecca's fashion shop

External accounts to be published annually

All businesses produce two types of annual accounts each year – the **profit and loss account** and the **balance sheet.** The fact that they are called **annual** accounts means that they are produced for the same date every year. This date is called the end of the financial year. In practice they are produced much later. So, for example, if a business's financial year ends on 5th June, it may produce its accounts in August or September.

These accounts are used to provide the Inland Revenue with information, so they can assess the income tax for the owner(s) of small businesses (sole traders and partnerships) and corporation tax for limited companies.

Non-assessed activity

People who are involved in recording financial transactions in business use several special words which you will need to know. Look at Figure 4.4 to see how many you know already. Try to decide how many terms refer to external accounts before you read any further.

Terms used in finance

Asset This can be money held as cash or in the bank. The term is also used for anything of value such as stock, buildings or equipment. Finally, any money owed to the business by its customers is also an asset.

Balance sheet A summary of the assets and liabilities of the business at the end of a financial year.

Capital The money the owner of the business puts into the company.

Credit A situation where goods or services are provided and there is a delay before the account is paid.

Creditors People or organisations to which the company owes money. Creditors are a liability because they represent a debt which must be paid.

Debtors People or organisations which owe the company money. Debtors are an asset because they represent money owing to the business.

Financial year Businesses summarise their financial situation on the same date each year. The date is known as the end of the financial year.

Income and expenditure account The accounts drawn up by a non-profit-making business, which summarise all the inward and outward transactions. This shows whether there is a surplus at the end of the period or whether expenditure has been greater than income.

Inward transactions Transactions which involve money flowing into the business as income, e.g. from the sale of goods and/or services.

Liability This is money the business owes to its suppliers or other organisations. These are debts which must be repaid, e.g. a loan from the bank.

Outward transactions Transactions that involve money leaving the business as payments, e.g. to buy raw materials or consumables and to pay wages.

Overheads Payments for items that do not go into creating the final product or service, but are necessary to run the business. For example, consumables, heating and lighting are all business overheads.

Profit and loss account A summary of all the transactions that have taken place during the financial year, for both income and expenditure. The difference between the two is known as profit or loss.

Trial balance A summary of all the balances in the different account books. The trial balance provides useful information on the financial health of the business.

Figure 4.4 Terms used in financial accounting

Profit and loss account

A profit and loss account is a summary of all the financial transactions (outward and inward) which a business has made over a year, grouped under certain headings. The term 'profit and loss' is actually misleading since, in any given year, a company cannot make a profit *and* a loss! It would make sense to call it a profit or loss account.

When a business makes a profit, the owner or managers may decide to invest money back into the business to increase sales or profitability. So, for example, it could increase the amount of money it spends on advertising, or buy more efficient equipment.

If it makes a loss, decisions may have to be made to make people redundant, reduce overheads or increase the price of its products or service.

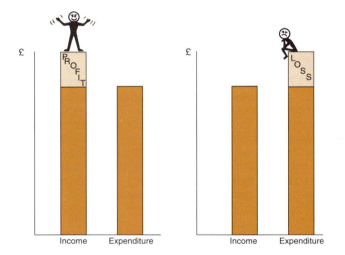

Figure 4.5 Profit or loss

Did you know?

A non-profit making organisation, such as a trade union or a sports club, will not produce a profit and loss account – for obvious reasons! Instead it produces an **income and expenditure account,** which is virtually the same thing. The word 'surplus' is substituted for the word 'profit' if income is higher than expenditure, in which case it means 'surplus of income over expenditure'. If there is a loss this is referred to as an excess, meaning 'excess of expenditure over income'. If the two are identical then the organisation is said to have **broken even.**

	£	£
Income		
Sales		1 559 000
Expenditure		
Wages	712 000	
Materials	420 000	
Overheads	370 000	
		1 502 000
Profit		57 000

Figure 4.6 Example of a simple profit and loss account

Balance sheet as at 31 May 199-	
Sources of funds (Liabilities)	£ (m)
Shareholders' investment	200
Retained profits	75
Loans	50
Creditors	20
	345
Use of Funds (Assets)	
Land and buildings	167
Machinery	80
Debtors	25
Stock	51
Cash in bank	22
	345

Figure 4.7 Example of a simplified balance sheet

Balance sheet

A profit and loss account is like a video, telling the story of what happened to a business during the financial year. In comparison, a balance sheet is like a photograph showing what a business was like on the last day of the financial year. The date is always clearly shown on a balance sheet.

All businesses need an amount of money to be invested when they are starting up. This money is called **capital**. A balance sheet shows what happens to that money at yearly intervals. If the business is doing well, the capital in the business will have grown because the profits can be added to the capital. Profits in one year may have been invested in additional **fixed assets** – such as more expensive equipment. This, too, will show on the balance sheet.

As an example, the simplified balance sheet of a public limited company is shown in Figure 4.7. Note that the total amount under Sources of Funds is equal to the total under Use of Funds, in other words the figures **balance**. Hence the term **balance** sheet. The business is showing what it has done with the money invested in it.

Did you know?

Stock includes any raw materials, work-in-progress or finished goods held by the company but not yet sold. The 'cash in bank' refers to the money in the company's **current** bank account.

Publishing external accounts

All businesses have to produce annual accounts so that tax can be assessed. Large businesses have accounts departments to look after all their financial records and reports. People in small businesses either do their own accounts or employ the services of professional accountants. All annual accounts have to be approved by a qualified registered accountant. **Limited** companies have a legal requirement to have their accounts **audited.** This means that all the transactions are checked in detail by an auditor. In addition, a **public limited company** has a legal requirement to publish (or make public) its financial affairs. This is why reports on the finances of large companies often appear in national newspapers.

Non-assessed activity

Look in a national newspaper – one which represents the 'serious' press, (e.g. *The Times, Independent* or the *Financial Times*) and find some examples of the financial information published by public limited companies.

Ensuring security

An important reason for recording transactions is **security.** When money or goods change hands, mistakes can be made and, unfortunately, there may be opportunities for unscrupulous people to steal. In addition, businesses may attempt to cheat the Inland

Revenue or other authorities out of money which ought to be paid.

The main reasons for security measures are:

■ to have information available for inspection by officials
■ to enable errors to be traced
■ to ensure that only people with authority carry out or authorise the transaction. This is particularly important when cash is involved.

If any problems occur, the records will be examined to discover exactly what happened. When cash is being handled this can be vital – as money cannot easily be traced. With cheques and credit cards it is usually easy to find out where the money has come from and where it has gone to.

Did you know?

The term 'theft' is used when people steal something which does not belong to them – whether goods or money. The term 'fraud' is used when there is a deliberate attempt to deceive somebody over money matters, e.g. by recording false transactions or altering the figures in a set of accounts.

Non-assessed activity

As a group, decide your answers to the following questions.

1 If you return faulty goods to a shop you will be asked to show your receipt. Why do you think this is so?
2 If you sent a cheque in payment for an item and the seller later said you hadn't paid, how could you prove he was wrong?

Monitoring business performance

If you read a local or national newspaper regularly, sooner or later you will find an article which tells of a business closing down. This is a sad occasion since, not only do people lose their jobs (owners/managers and employees) but the shareholders, banks and suppliers may lose money. The shareholders may include retired people who have invested their savings in the business.

The reason for the business closing will probably be that it has made a loss over a period of time. This means its expenditure has been greater than its income.

Businesses that **earn** more money than they **spend** make a **profit.** This means that employees' jobs are more secure and possibly more people can be employed. The company can invest in new equipment and develop new products or services.

Sometimes businesses that are not doing very well can take remedial action to try to help matters. These may include reducing overheads or even making people redundant. In time, business may improve and the organisation can start to expand again. If nothing was done or – even worse – the owner(s) carried on spending extravagantly, the business might go bankrupt very quickly indeed. Therefore it is vital that the owners or managers **monitor** the performance of the business as often as they can. This should include:

■ the debts owed to the company, by whom and for how long
■ the level of sales and the lines which are selling best (and worst)
■ the cost of purchases and whether prices are increasing from any particular suppliers
■ the amount of money being paid out, and whether this is increasing or decreasing.

Did you know?

Computerised accounts procedures have meant that the managers of many large organisations now have a breakdown of each day's trading on their desk the following morning, so that they can act on any problems immediately.

Monitoring profit

You may think that this is a silly thing to do: if a company is making a profit, there is nothing to worry about. If you employed an accountant, he or she would not agree with you! Profit lying idle is a waste of resources, especially if it is sitting in a bank account that doesn't pay interest, such as a current account. An accountant would instruct clients to use their profit to make even more money, e.g. by expanding the business.

Monitoring loss

Losses are a more serious problem. They are caused by expenditure being higher than income. If you owned the business you would have a basic choice – sell more (or collect all the debts you are owed) or spend less. Probably both would be ideal! As a last resort, companies will increase the price of their goods but, in a competitive market, this may mean that they lose business rather than gain it.

Did you know?

Businesses usually have budgets that set the level of planned expenditure in each area. Actual expenditure is then measured against planned expenditure. Budgets do not serve any purpose unless managers take **action** when things are not going according to plan, particularly if expenditure exceeds income. Businesses fail for two main reasons:

■ they do not have an adequate planning and monitoring system
■ they do not **act** on the information which a good system gives them.

Producing income and expenditure accounts

It is one thing to read about income and expenditure accounts, and quite another to produce them! Yet they are basically very easy – and also useful in your private life. They show a quick summary that tells you – in black and white – whether you have a surplus in the bank or owe money all over the place!

As an example, Martin is a young man who has just moved away from home. He rents a flat at £50 a week and pays a further £2.50 a week, for electricity and heating. His telephone bill is also £2.50 a week, and he spends an average of £35 a week on food. Costs of travel to work amount to £8 a week, and he likes going out with his friends and also likes buying new clothes. He spends about £50 a week on entertainment and an average of £25 a week on clothes. His income comes from two sources. His take-home pay from his regular job is £130 a week and he also works three nights a week in a bar and receives £3 an hour for five hours' work each night. He decides to draw up an income and expenditure account to assess his financial situation on a monthly basis. He knows that he will have to make adjustments depending on whether each month consists of four weeks or five weeks.

Non-assessed activity

Martin's friends want him to go on holiday with them in July. The cost will be £300 per person, with the balance due in the middle of May. Martin has ten weeks to save up the money. He decides to work one extra night in the bar and to reduce his

February 199- (4 weeks)		
	£	£
Income		
Regular job		520
Bar work		180
		700
Expenditure		
Rent	200	
Electric, heating	10	
Telephone	10	
Food	140	
Travel	32	
Entertainment	200	
Clothes	100	
		692
Surplus		8

Figure 4.8 Income and expenditure account – Martin Desai

expenditure on clothes to £50 a month. Draw up his income and expenditure account for March – a **five week month** – and find out whether he will have any surplus at the end of the month after making his holiday payments.

Optional evidence assignment

*This activity can be carried out verbally in class **in a group** as a non-assessed activity to consolidate learning. Alternatively, if you do it **on your own**, it can count as supplementary evidence towards the following parts of the scheme.*

PC 1: Explain financial transactions which take place regularly in an organisation and explain why records of transactions are kept

Range: Financial transactions: outward transactions to pay for costs, inward transactions to receive income

Records of transactions: to produce accounts (internal for the business's own use), to ensure security, to monitor business performance

Core skills: Communication, Information technology, Application of number

407

Read the case study below and then answer the questions which follow.

Case study

Tom Field is a plumber who works as a sole trader. As well as regular repair jobs which he undertakes for private customers and other customers – such as schools and businesses – he also installs new bathrooms. He buys all his plumbing materials from a local plumbers' merchant and bathroom suites, tiles and bathroom fittings from a large wholesale company on the outskirts of the town. He gets 20 per cent discount as a 'trader'.

Tom is often paid in cash by customers, particularly for small repair jobs, but very few people ask for a receipt. Also, when Tom buys materials from the plumbers' merchant, he pays in cash and sometimes loses the receipt. He usually pays by cheque for items from the bathroom supplier because the bill is much larger.

Recently Tom has taken on a young assistant, James. To save himself the bother of visiting the plumbers' merchant, Tom often gives James a few pounds and tells him to get what is needed. Yesterday Tom was wondering whether it would be worth setting up a shop and displaying bathroom fittings himself. He thought he could get a loan to do this from the bank. This would an extra commitment because he is still paying off a loan he took out last year for a new van.

Figure 4.9 Tom seems so disorganised …

Tom's wife has the job of doing the accounts. Whilst she wants Tom to do well, she is concerned about the idea of an additional loan, particularly as Tom seems so disorganised. She is also worried that at the end of the year there may be a problem giving the accountants all the information they need to prepare the final accounts for the tax authorities.

1   a   Give examples of **four** regular outward transactions Tom now makes to pay for his costs.
    b   Give examples of **four** additional outwards transactions he would have to make if he bought a shop.
2   State the inward transactions which have resulted in Tom receiving income.
3   State **three** reasons why Tom should keep accurate records of his transactions, with clear examples of what could go wrong if he does not.
4   Tom's wife has estimated that last year he spent £32 000 with the bathroom company and £12 000 at the plumbers' merchant. He repaid £3000 off his loan for the van including interest. Other costs of running the business amounted to £4000. He earned £50 000 from fitting bathrooms and £22 000 from general repairs.
    a   Draw up a simple income and expenditure account and say whether his expenditure was less than, equal to or more than his income.
    b   Calculate his profit or loss.
    c   Identify which part of the business – repairs or bathrooms – is the more profitable.
5   This month Tom's wife is concerned that:
    ■   unpaid debts from customers have increased
    ■   the amount of cash withdrawn from the bank to pay the plumbers' merchant has increased dramatically.
    Give reasons why these situations may have occurred and recommend the action Tom should take.
6   You know Tom well. Write him a letter to his home address – 24 Sutton Road, Hightown, HG4 9TG – using a word processor, and explain the importance of keeping records for all his transactions.

Evidence assignment

At this point your tutor may wish you to start work on the project which will prove to your verifiers that you understand this section of the element. If so, turn to page 448 and do Section 1 of the project. This covers the first evidence indicator for this element.

Special note – Qualprint

Some of the transactions and documents described in this element will be related to a fictitious business called Qualprint. This is a printing company which was set up four years ago by its owner, Chris Gaston. As well as printing posters, invitations, brochures etc. in response to customers', orders, Qualprint also has a retail counter selling stationery and similar items.

You will meet this company again in Element 4.2, where you will be asked to complete financial documents on behalf of Chris Gaston. The layout and design of Qualprint documents should therefore be familiar to you by the time you are actually asked to use them.

Figure 4.10 Chris Gaston of Qualprint

Purchases

Almost all businesses purchase materials, services and people's labour. They usually pay for materials and services on **credit.** This means they pay *after* they have taken delivery of the goods. They pay for people's labour by paying out **wages,** either once a week or once a month.

Materials

These may be items which go into a manufacturing process to be converted into products, in which case they are known as **raw materials.** They can also be

items such as stationery and cleaning products used in the running of the business. Such items are called **consumables.** All these goods are ordered using **order forms.**

Another type of item which a business can purchase is **capital equipment.** This category includes production equipment, buildings, office furniture, etc. These are known as **capital items** and special purchasing systems are used.

This section of the element is concerned with materials purchased and used on a regular basis.

Did you know?

If companies are buying an expensive item then they may ask for several **quotations** from different suppliers stating the price at which the goods can be purchased and any discounts which are offered. If a supplier gives a quotation, the price paid will be the same as the price quoted. Instead of a quotation a supplier *may* issue an **estimate.** This is less precise than a quotation as it only gives a total price – not an itemised list.

A buyer may advertise that certain goods or a particular service are wanted and ask people to submit **tenders** (offers) stating the price for which they are prepared to provide the service (or supply the goods). The buyer will have a closing date for tenders to be received and, on that day, will open them and choose the best one.

Non-assessed activity

1 **As a group**, discuss any occasions on which members of your family have asked for a quotation or an estimate. This is likely if they wanted special work to be done, e.g. building or repair jobs. See if you can also find out how near the final bill was to the quotation or estimate they first received. Your tutors may also be able to give you examples from their own experience. Remember, if it was a quotation, the price paid should have been the price quoted.
2 Look in your local paper and see if you can find any examples of advertisements for tenders. These are usually placed in or near the classified advertisement section.

Services

Sometimes a business asks another business or person to provide a specific service. Examples of services include window cleaning, machine maintenance and decorating. Services are normally 'ordered' by **contract**. This is a legal agreement in which details of the service are written down (e.g. how many windows should be cleaned and how often) as well as the amount to be paid. Normally both supplier and customer sign the contract.

Did you know?

Very expensive purchases of capital equipment may also be agreed in a contract. A contract may contain a **penalty clause,** which is a statement that normally says that if the goods are not delivered or the service is not performed by a certain date, the buyer has the right to pay less than the agreed amount. If a company was paying a building contractor to erect a new warehouse, for instance, it may be vital that the agreed completion date is met, in which case a penalty clause would put pressure on the builder to keep to schedule.

Wages

Employees of a business may be considered to provide a service. In return they are paid wages (see Unit 2 for employer and employee rights and responsibilities). In this case the document involved is the **contract of employment.** This is covered in Element 2.2, page 201. When an employer agrees to pay someone a wage, they also commit themselves to paying National Insurance contributions (if these apply) and probably pension contributions. National Insurance and pensions are also covered in Unit 2.

Non-assessed activity

1 **As a group**, compile **two** lists of materials that Qualprint *could* purchase. In the first list include as many items as possible that might be bought for use in production. The second list is for consumable items.

Try to think of as many items as you can. You could brainstorm for this exercise.

2 **On your own,** write down as many types of service as you can which a business might purchase. Compare your list with those of your fellow students and see if they have thought of anything you have not.

3 **As a group,** discuss why businesses might wish to buy in a service rather than do the work themselves. For instance, should Chris Gaston decorate his office or should he pay a decorator to do it? How many reasons can you think of?

Did you know?

Many companies offer discounts to businesses to persuade them to place an order.

■ **Trade discount** is given either as an allowance to people in the same type of business (because they will buy items regularly) or because the buyer is placing a large order. (You may remember this if you did the assignment about Tom Field.)
■ **Cash discount** is a percentage off the price given for prompt payment. The term 'five per cent *one month'* means that buyers can deduct five per cent from the price if they pay within one month.

The buyer can calculate how much he or she will have to pay by:

1 taking the total price and subtracting any discounts
2 adding VAT at the current rate to the *discounted* price (at present VAT is 17.5 per cent)
3 adding on VAT to the quoted delivery charge
4 adding together the totals obtained in stages 2 and 3. (This procedure is discussed in more detail in Element 4.2.)

Purchase documents

There may be up to four documents involved in the purchasing process.

■ First of all, when an order is placed the purchaser completes an **order form.** This is sent to the supplier, normally through the post.
■ The purchaser will receive a **purchase invoice** from the supplier requesting payment for the goods.
■ If some of the items sent are faulty, the purchaser will return these to the supplier. In return he or she will receive a **credit note** listing the faulty items and the amount of money the purchaser no longer needs to pay.
■ When the materials are received, a **goods received note** (GRN) is completed and passed to the accounts department.

Did you know?

When goods are delivered by the supplier then they are usually accompanied by a **delivery note.** If the goods are sent by another form of transport, e.g. by rail or by haulage company, the supplier will send the buyer an **advice note** so that the buyer knows that the goods are on their way.

Orders placed

Qualprint need to buy a special type of card on which to print wedding invitations. They have dealt with the supplier – Business Supplies Ltd – for some time and therefore know exactly what and how to order. The buyer places an order by completing a Qualprint order form and includes details of exactly what type of card is required. The price is checked against the catalogue. Although no money will change hands at this stage, the buyer needs to be sure of the cost of the materials being ordered.

All Qualprint's order forms are completed with a unique serial number for easy reference. The order is sent to the supplier and a copy is kept by Qualprint, in case there are any queries later.

When order forms are sent, this is taken as a firm commitment that the goods are required. Occasionally people send order forms to suppliers and then change their minds, but this is rare. Goods may also be ordered by telephone in an emergency, but an order form is then sent as soon as possible as confirmation. If a fax is used, orders can be sent immediately.

The latest system of ordering goods is by computer using **electronic data interchange** (EDI). This is discussed on page 428. Private individuals may use their credit cards to order goods by telephone and give the supplier their name, address, card number and its expiry date. This is a reasonably secure system, especially if the goods are sent to the address associated with the card. Credit cards are described in more detail on page 429.

Did you know?

Many businesses issue printed price lists *separately* from their catalogues. This means that a new catalogue will not have to be produced every time there are price changes, as this would be too expensive.

Most price lists are shown in page order to match the catalogue, but the buyer must be very careful to:

■ make sure that the current price list is being used
■ check the correct catalogue number in the price list against the one shown in the catalogue, as the

numbers will vary for different colours and sizes
■ write the number accurately when completing the order. Transposing the numbers will mean the wrong goods arrive, and the supplier is under no obligation to take them back!

Non-assessed activity

Figure 4.11 is an illustration of Qualprint's order form.

1 List the sections completed at Qualprint. **As a group,** discuss why each set of information is needed.
2 If the unit price is £10, calculate how much the order is worth in total.
3 Obtain a computer supplies catalogue and price list and a copy of a blank Qualprint order form. Practise completing an order form by ordering the following goods for Chris Gaston on order number 122/934:
1 disk box to contain at least 20 $3\frac{1}{2}$" disks
6 boxes of $3\frac{1}{2}$" high density disks
2 mouse mats

QUALPRINT LTD.

22 CARNEI WAY
GLENDALE
NEWSHIRE
FE1 8CA

Tel: 01323 745612

ORDER

VAT Reg No 680 73842 88

To: Business Supplies Ltd
14 Docklands Parade
GLENDALE
FE2 8DJ

Date: 15 October 199-
Order No: 121/934

Please supply

QUANTITY	DESCRIPTION	REF. NO.	UNIT PRICE
2 packs	A4 Superlux Card/. White	SL/7	£10

Delivery: AS SOON AS POSSIBLE
Signed: *C. Gaston*

Figure 4.11 Qualprint's order

Purchase invoice

After the goods have been delivered an invoice is sent to the purchaser, usually by post. The invoice will describe the goods sent and give the total amount of payment due. This should be checked by the buyer against the information on the order form. Many companies also wait until the goods received note (GRN) has been completed as this is also a useful check (see page 414). The invoice is, in effect, a bill saying how much money must be paid. It may also state a time period (e.g. 28 days) within which payment should be made. A copy of the invoice is always kept by the supplier for his own records.

Did you know?

All invoices are printed with the letters E & OE at the bottom. This stands for 'errors and omissions excepted'. It ensures that the supplier can send a further invoice if a mistake has been made and the buyer is undercharged.

Checking an invoice

All invoices which are received are carefully checked before they are passed for payment (see also page 420). The invoice in Figure 4.12 has been received by Qualprint from Business Supplies.

The accounts staff must check that:

- the invoice is meant for them (i.e. it has been sent to the correct address)
- the order number quoted is correct
- the goods listed match those listed on the goods received note, both in terms of description and quantity (see below)
- the price is the same as on the quotation or as shown in the catalogue (this can be checked by looking at the order)
- the calculations are accurate
- any discounts are as agreed.

If there are any discrepancies the accounts staff (or the owner of a small business) must be notified. If there is no record of delivery it is usual to telephone the supplier and ask for proof of delivery.

Did you know?

1 Only businesses that are registered for VAT are allowed to include VAT on their invoices. You can check if a

---

Business Supplies Ltd

14 Docklands Parade
Glendale
FE2 8DJ

TEL: 01323 782943

FAX: 01323 212314

VAT Reg No: 483/2837/75

INVOICE

To: Qualprint Ltd
22 Carnei Way
GLENDALE
Newshire
FE1 8CA

Deliver to:

Your order no.	Invoice date/tax point	Invoice no.	Despatch date
121/934	24.10.9-	1274	23.10.9-

Quantity	Description	Cat. no.	Unit price	Total price	VAT rate	VAT amount
2 packs	A4 Superlux Card. White	SL/7	£10	£20	17.5%	£3.50
	Delivery charges			£1.00	17.5%	£0.17
	Sub-total			£21.00		
	VAT			£3.67		
	Total amount due			£24.67		

Terms: 28 days
E & OE

Figure 4.12 An invoice from Business Supplies Ltd

company is VAT registered because their VAT registration number is printed on all their accounts documents.

2 If items have been delivered but are missing from the invoice, or the customer has been undercharged, it is usual for the supplier to send a **supplementary invoice** to cover the difference.

Non-assessed activity

Study the invoice Qualprint has received carefully, and then answer the following questions.

1 Are there any entries which are *different* from those shown on the order in Figure 4.11? If so, identify them.

2 Has Qualprint received any discount from the

supplier?

3   Is the amount Qualprint owes the same as the total you calculated for the order on page 411? If not, why not?
4   What do you think would happen if Qualprint did not pay the supplier within 28 days?
5   Check all the calculations on the invoice. Then tell your tutor if they are correct or not.

Did you know?

A different type of purchase invoice is sometimes issued when a business person buys an item from a private seller and needs to be able to prove to the tax authorities how the money was spent. An example would be a jeweller buying a valuable ring, or an antique dealer buying a painting from a private house. In both cases the business person would be paying out money – possibly cash – which could amount to thousands of pounds. The business accountant would not be pleased if there was no evidence to prove to the tax authorities that the transaction really took place.

As evidence, the jeweller or the antique dealer would make out an invoice and clearly label this **Purchase invoice.** The buyer would then list the goods bought and the price paid. The seller would sign the invoice to confirm the transaction.

Credit notes

A credit note is sent by a supplier to the purchaser if the latter has been over-charged on an invoice. This could happen if:

- faulty goods were supplied and are returned
- incorrect goods were supplied and are returned
- fewer goods were delivered than stated on the invoice and the customer does not want the outstanding items delivered
- the purchaser changes his or her mind, decides the goods are not required, and the seller agrees to take them back.

A credit note can be used as part-payment on future orders. However, this assumes that the purchaser will be placing more orders in the future. A customer who decides not to deal with the supplier again will insist that the amount showing on the credit note is repaid.

Did you know?

In the past, credit notes used to be printed in red to signify that money was owing from the seller to the buyer. Today they are printed in black – mainly because most computer printers only print in one colour!

Non-assessed activity

Look at the example of a credit note in Figure 4.13. Qualprint returned one pack of Superlux card which was badly packed and damaged on delivery. Business Supplies Ltd have accepted responsibility and sent a credit note. As well as the price of the card, the amount of VAT also has to be refunded. In some cases the organisation will also refund any delivery charges.

1   Check the credit note carefully. Do you agree with all the calculations?
2   How much does Qualprint now owe Business Supplies Ltd for the Superlux card they received in October?

Business Supplies Ltd

14 Docklands Parade
Glendale
FE2 8DJ

TEL: 01323 782943

FAX: 01323 212314

VAT Reg No: 483/2837/75

To: Qualprint Ltd
      22 Carnei Way
      GLENDALE
      Newshire
      FE1 8CA

CREDIT NOTE

Credit Note No.	Invoice no.	Date
CR8 379	1274	20 October 199-

Quantity	Description	Cat. no.	Unit price	Total price	VAT rate	VAT amount
1 pack	A4 Superlux Card. White	SL/7	£10	£10	17.5%	£1.75

Refunded charge	£1.00	17.5% £0.17
Sub-total	£11.00	
VAT	£1.92	
Total amount due	£12.92	

Terms: 28 days
E & OE

Figure 4.13 A credit note from Business Supplies Ltd

Goods received notes

The goods received note is completed by the person who receives the goods after they are delivered, when checking the description of the goods given on the packages or containers. The quantity delivered is also noted. If there is any doubt, the items may have to be counted. All the items are checked against the delivery note as the GRN is completed.

Goods received notes provide a record of what has *actually* been delivered. The person receiving them may not know what was on the original order. The GRN will be checked by the accounts staff against the order and also the invoice before payment is authorised.

Did you know?

Large businesses have a special point to receive goods. This is called 'Goods inwards'. See if you can see a sign next time you pass a factory or supermarket. It might just say 'deliveries'.

Today many large businesses produce their GRNs on computer. The GRNs can then be printed out and sent to the accounts department *or* the information can be accessed direct by the accounts department on their own computer screens. The accounts department checks the GRN against the invoice when this is received.

An illustration of a GRN produced on computer is shown in Figure 4.14.

Problems with deliveries

Problems might arise if goods are damaged or missing, or if the wrong goods have been sent in error. This is why it is important that goods are unpacked, counted and carefully checked.

Missing goods

Goods may be omitted because they were out of stock when ordered or because the firm forgot to send them. Out of stock goods will either be marked 'to follow' on the delivery note (i.e. they will be

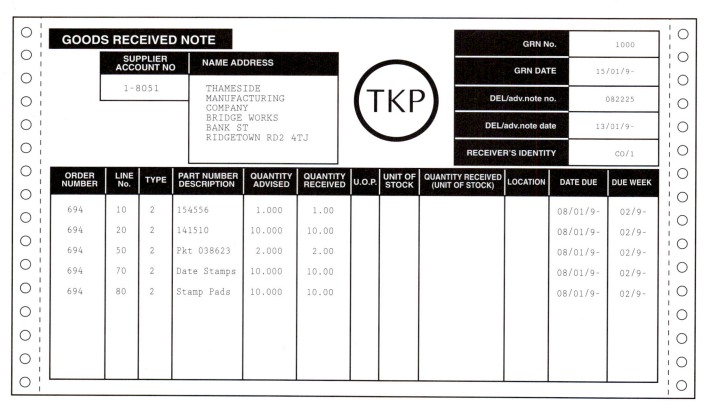

GOODS RECEIVED NOTE

SUPPLIER ACCOUNT NO	NAME ADDRESS
1-8051	THAMESIDE MANUFACTURING COMPANY BRIDGE WORKS BANK ST RIDGETOWN RD2 4TJ

TKP

GRN No.	1000
GRN DATE	15/01/9-
DEL/adv.note no.	082225
DEL/adv.note date	13/01/9-
RECEIVER'S IDENTITY	CO/1

ORDER NUMBER	LINE No.	TYPE	PART NUMBER DESCRIPTION	QUANTITY ADVISED	QUANTITY RECEIVED	U.O.P.	UNIT OF STOCK	QUANTITY RECEIVED (UNIT OF STOCK)	LOCATION	DATE DUE	DUE WEEK
694	10	2	154556	1.000	1.00					08/01/9-	02/9-
694	20	2	141510	10.000	10.00					08/01/9-	02/9-
694	50	2	Pkt 038623	2.000	2.00					08/01/9-	02/9-
694	70	2	Date Stamps	10.000	10.00					08/01/9-	02/9-
694	80	2	Stamp Pads	10.000	10.00					08/01/9-	02/9-

Figure 4.14 An example of a GRN produced on computer

delivered later) or noted as 'discontinued'. Sometimes a firm will substitute another similar item for a discontinued line.

If the omission is because of a mistake on the part of the supplier, there will normally be a discrepancy between the number listed on the delivery note (which will match the order) and the actual number received.

The fact that the GRN shows a difference between the order and the number delivered will enable the accounts department to ensure nothing is paid for which wasn't received. It will also mean that substitute items can be inspected to see if they are suitable. The supplier should be contacted to find out what has happened to any goods which are missing and not marked 'to follow'.

Additional goods

A mistake by a packer may mean goods are received which were not ordered. These should be returned to the supplier. They will show up on the GRN but *not* on the original order.

Sometimes a buyer may fax or telephone an order to the supplier for additional items in an emergency. However, the written records must be then be updated so that they match any verbal instructions.

Incorrect goods

If the wrong goods are received, they too must be returned unused. Again, these will be easy to identify because the description on the GRN will not match that on the order.

Damaged or faulty goods

The supplier should be notified immediately and there will normally be no problem exchanging these. On some GRN forms there is a space for the goods inwards clerk to note any damage found.

Goods ordered in error

These are the biggest problem, as the supplier is under no legal obligation to take them back! Much will depend on the relationship between the two companies – in many cases a supplier will exchange them rather than risk losing a customer.

Non-assessed activity

Figure 4.15 is a GRN form completed at Qualprint.

1 Identify the sections which have been completed by the person receiving the goods.
2 Why should all GRNs be signed?
3 Check the GRN against the order in Figure 4.11. You should identify several differences! Discuss **with your tutor** how these may have occurred and what should be done in each case.

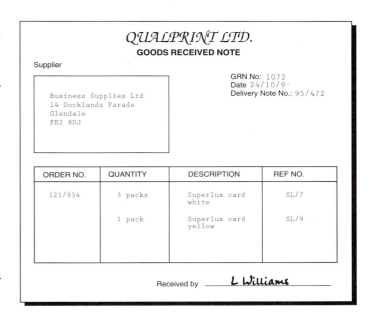

Figure 4.15 Qualprint's GRN

Optional evidence assignment

*This activity can be carried out verbally in class **in a group** as a non-assessed activity to consolidate learning. Alternatively, if you do it **on your own**, it can count as supplementary evidence towards the following parts of the scheme.*

PC 2:   Explain and give examples of purchases and purchase documents

Range: Purchases: materials, services, wages

Purchases documents: orders placed, purchase invoice, credit note, goods received note

Core skills: Communication, Application of number

Read the case study below and answer the questions which follow.

Case study

Mark Sandiford is an old school friend of yours who has been looking for a job since he left school. You bump into him unexpectedly during your lunch hour. He tells you that he has just been offered temporary work in the purchasing office of your local area health authority, which buys supplies for all the hospitals and clinics in your area. If all goes well, he is hoping for a permanent job.

He tells you that he thinks the work will be 'dead easy' because people buy health care from the National Health Service, so there can't be many orders to make out. You like Mark so think it is up to you to put him straight, before his temporary job is the shortest on record!

1   Mark is obviously wrong in his assumption that hospitals don't buy anything! Make a list of at least **four** examples of:
    a   the type of staff who would be employed and to whom wages would be paid
    b   the type of materials that would be bought
    c   the overheads involved in running the hospital.
2   Draw a quick sketch of an order form, to give Mark an idea what one looks like. Include all the key information required.
3   Write a brief explanation for Mark stating the procedure that is followed and the document that is issued:
    a   when the seller receives the order

Figure 4.16 Mark at work

b   when goods are delivered
c   if faulty goods are received.
4   Mark is puzzled that the total amount estimated on an order and the final amount on an invoice are different. Explain why this difference occurs, **giving an actual numerical example** so that Mark can understand this more clearly.
5   When you have completed your explanations to Mark he is pleased. He says he feels far more capable of coping with the job. However, he still can't see the point of completing goods received notes. He says it would be much simpler to miss these out and check the purchase invoice against the order. You disagree.

List **four** advantages of using GRNs rather than following Mark's idea.

Sales transactions

Every business organisation has to have a purpose for its existence – as was discussed in Element 1.1. For most organisations their primary purpose is to make a profit. They do this by selling goods and services – either to other business organisations or to private consumers. In some cases organisations provide both goods and services. Sales transactions are vitally important to the survival of the company because the quantity and type of sales determines the amount of income received.

Goods – business to business and business to consumer

Goods can take many forms, ranging from a box of matches to a multi-million pound aeroplane. These are classed as 'finished goods', since they are ready to be used by the customer as soon as they are delivered. They can be divided into consumable products (which are used quickly after purchase, such as paper) and durables (which are expected to last a long time, such as a car).

Consumable goods and durable goods are bought by both businesses and private individuals. However, the type of goods may differ. A private buyer is unlikely to buy a crane or a lorry!

Goods supplied from one business to another can be for direct use, e.g. stationery items, food for the canteen or office equipment. Alternatively, they can be raw materials that are not ready for final use but are used in the manufacture of the final product or a production process. For example, a company making an aeroplane purchases hundreds of components and fittings from its suppliers. Other examples include electrical components for a video recorder, sand for a glass factory or china clay for a paper-making company. Businesses also buy machinery and equipment used for administration purposes and for production, e.g. computers, lathes and grinders.

Goods supplied to consumers are finished products in the sense that they are for personal consumption and not for immediate resale. This applies whether the consumer is buying a tin of beans or a television. However, not all consumer goods are delivered in their completed form – think of kit-cars, model-building sets and build-it-yourself furniture!

Did you know?

A car manufacturer sells a range of models of cars to customers. All the models are virtually the same apart from engine sizes, trim etc. But each car contains thousands of different components provided by dozens of suppliers. Hence the purchasing department of the car manufacturer has to deal with the sales departments of many different organisations.

Services – business-to-business and business to consumer

When a business sells a service to its customers or clients it may be offering one or more of the following:

- **labour** – where physical effort and skills are supplied, for example window cleaners and security guards
- **specialist knowledge and expertise** – driving instructors and solicitors would come into this category
- **the use and operation of specialised equipment** – such as colour photocopiers or drain cleaners.

Some organisations provide a service that is used solely by private individuals (such as a hairdresser) and some provide services only for business organisations (such as an advertising agency). Others may provide a service for both, e.g. an electrician.

Did you know?

Some business organisations offer a combination of goods and services. For instance, a photocopier company not only sells the machine but also sells maintenance contracts under which they will repair it if it goes wrong. Companies that sell fire extinguishers not only install them but also inspect them and refill used extinguishers at regular intervals.

Non-assessed activity

Decide which of the business organisations listed below is selling:

- **a** only goods
- **b** only services
- **c** a combination of the two.

1. British Rail
2. an estate agent
3. a restaurant
4. a plumber
5. Heinz
6. Barclays Bank
7. a dry cleaners
8. a cinema
9. a milk delivery person
10. a newsagent

The difference between sales to businesses and sales to private consumers

There are several differences between selling goods and services to businesses and selling them to private individuals. Organisations which sell mainly to businesses are often said to be in the **industrial market,** while those which sell mainly to private individuals are classed as being in the consumer market. This can affect:

- the range and type of goods and services sold
- the way the goods and services are advertised and promoted
- the sales transaction itself – the procedure that is followed, the terms of the sales agreement and the paperwork.

You will be learning about the range and type of goods and services, and promotion methods, in other units. This unit concentrates on the sales transaction itself.

Sales transactions to private individuals

Normally these transactions are short and simple and involve the minimum of paperwork. The customer sees an article in a shop, and offers to pay the price shown. The shop-keeper accepts the offer, wraps up the item and takes the money. The customer receives a receipt in return, confirming that the goods have been paid for.

There may be slightly more paperwork involved if payment is by credit card or cheque but, again, there are only likely to be one or two pieces of paper involved.

If you buy an expensive item, such as a car, you may be offered a **credit agreement** – a means of buying the car now and paying for it in instalments. The credit agreement is unlikely to be with the retailer; it will probably be with a **finance company** used by the retailer. You are helped to complete the forms and understand the terms and conditions of the loan and must be given a copy of anything you sign.

If you buy an ongoing service, this may be done simply by verbal agreement – e.g. with the local window cleaner or milkman. If you were buying expensive goods or services, such as having new windows fitted, you might shop around quite a bit and obtain different quotations and estimates. You may then haggle about the price and find out if there any discounts available. You would negotiate a start date and the method of payment. This is the nearest you are likely to get to the type of negotiations that take place in sales transactions between businesses.

Sales transactions to businesses

Most business organisations operating in the industrial market employ specialist salespeople who may be involved in negotiating sales agreements all over the world. They will know that industrial buyers:

- 'shop around' for a reliable and competitive supplier
- expect discounts to be given on bulk orders
- often require detailed written information on the items to be supplied and the financial terms
- will expect credit – i.e. to be able to buy the goods now and be invoiced for them later
- will expect good after-sales service, and for any equipment supplied to be in working order upon installation and to be regularly maintained and serviced.

In some cases, particularly for export deals, sales transactions involve quite complicated financial arrangements about payment.

Sales staff will be prepared to put considerable time and energy into making the sale and obtaining a new customer. The deal itself could range from anything

from a few hundred pounds worth of stationery to a multi-million-pound aircraft order. As you have seen, in many cases there may be a service contract involved as well.

Figure 4.17 Sales staff sometimes work hard for a sale

There will be a range of documents involved. The chart in Figure 4.18 shows those which are issued by the seller and how these link to the purchases documents you have already read about. Each of these is also described in detail in the next section.

Non-assessed activity

Discuss **with your tutor** the procedure in operation in your school or college for buying stationery or other items. Try to see examples of the documents involved.

Sales documents

Sales documents are closely linked to purchasing documents – as you can see from Figure 4.18. Remember that every written order sent by a purchaser is a sale from the point of view of the supplier. All orders received are recorded and processed to ensure that customers receive the correct goods.

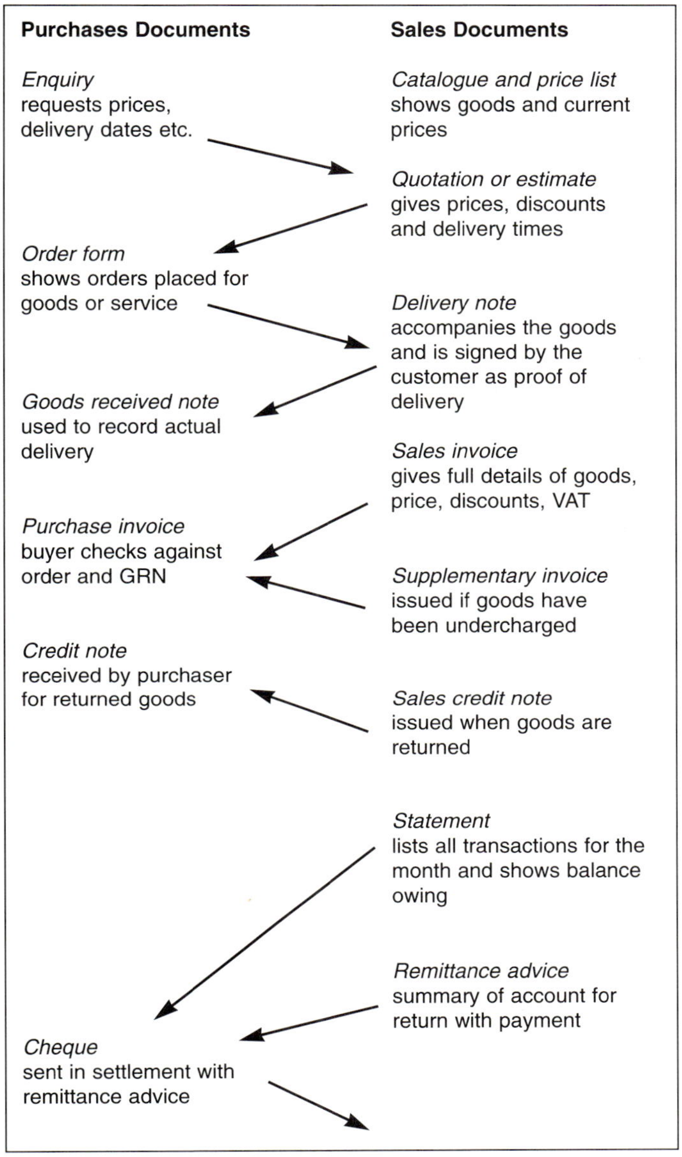
Purchases Documents
Sales Documents
Enquiry
requests prices, delivery dates etc.
Catalogue and price list
shows goods and current prices
Quotation or estimate
gives prices, discounts and delivery times
Order form
shows orders placed for goods or service
Delivery note
accompanies the goods and is signed by the customer as proof of delivery
Goods received note
used to record actual delivery
Sales invoice
gives full details of goods, price, discounts, VAT
Purchase invoice
buyer checks against order and GRN
Supplementary invoice
issued if goods have been undercharged
Credit note
received by purchaser for returned goods
Sales credit note
issued when goods are returned
Statement
lists all transactions for the month and shows balance owing
Remittance advice
summary of account for return with payment
Cheque
sent in settlement with remittance advice

Figure 4.18 Documents involved in sales and purchasing

Orders received

The order which Qualprint placed with Business Supplies Ltd was shown in Figure 4.11. Orders can take other forms – for example, computers are increasingly used to transmit orders electronically using **electronic data interchange** (EDI, see page 428). When you walk into a shop and ask for a magazine, in effect you are placing an order. In business, however, orders are usually received in written form and anyone placing an order by telephone is asked to confirm it in writing immediately *or* give their official order number. This protects the supplier from sending goods that have not been officially requested and which might therefore be returned.

When an order is received it must first be checked to ensure that the information is complete and correct.

- Does the description of the goods match the catalogue or serial number?
- Is the price given correct? If there has been a recent price change the customer may not know.
- Is the customer allowed credit (i.e. extended time to pay)? Most business to business transactions are done on a credit basis – see page 431.
- Is the customer allowed discount? If so, how much?
- Are there any special conditions which must be met, e.g. delivery by a certain date?

If there are any problems with the order then these must be resolved before any further action is taken.

If the order is acceptable, the supplier will take the necessary steps to meet the customer's requirements. This may mean that the production department has to be informed so that the goods can be manufactured. It may be, however, that the items are already in stock, in which case the goods can be supplied reasonably quickly. Alternatively, they may have to be ordered from another supplier before being resold to the customer.

Non-assessed activity

Qualprint receives an order from J & J Briggs, a regular customer in a nearby town. However, there are some problems with it.

- Qualprint no longer stocks blotting paper as there is very little demand for it.
- Another item, some clipboards, can be supplied but not by the required date.
- The organisation concerned has not paid its account for some time and is near its credit limit.

Assume that you are the salesperson handling the order. What would you do about it and why? Discuss your answers with your tutor.

Sales invoices

On page 412, we saw that Qualprint received a purchase invoice from Business Supplies Ltd. When Qualprint sells goods it will issue a **sales invoice** to its customers. However, not every sale requires an invoice. When people call in at Qualprint to buy stationery for cash they are not given an invoice because they are paying for the goods immediately. Invoices are a formal record that money needs to be paid and are therefore issued when the goods have been sold on credit. This means payment is made some time after the goods are delivered or the service has been performed.

It is important that invoices are *accurate* and sent *promptly*. Most customers don't pay immediately the invoice is received and if the invoice is delayed or is incorrect then payment will be made even later.

Did you know?

One of the biggest problems for small businesses is having to wait a long time to receive money they are owed. This obviously affects the amount of cash the company has to work with (known as its **working capital**). If the business also has to pay its own bills on time because it is pressurised by its own suppliers, the consequences can be disastrous – and include bankruptcy.

The components of an invoice

Invoices often differ in design but, basically, all of them contain:

- the name and address of the buyer
- the delivery address (in case this is different from the ordering address)
- the order number
- the invoice date and number
- the date the goods were despatched (and sometimes the method of despatch)
- the quantity of goods sold and a description and the catalogue number (if applicable)
- how much the goods cost each (their **unit price**)
- the total price for the goods, given the quantity ordered
- the amount of VAT due
- the discount allowed
- any delivery charges.

Non-assessed activity

1   Examine the invoice in Figure 4.19, which has been sent by Qualprint to Glendale Borough Council. Identify all the main components of an invoice, as listed above, on this example.
2   Discuss **with your tutor** why each type of information is important, for both the buyer and the seller.
3   How much discount has been allowed to the buyer?
4   Check the invoice – is the total correct?
5   Can you work out what the total amount due on the invoice would have been if no discount had been allowed? Check your answer with your tutor.

QUALPRINT LTD.

22 CARNEI WAY
GLENDALE
NEWSHIRE
FE1 8CA

TEL: 01323 745612   VAT Reg No: 680/73842/88

INVOICE

To: Glendale Borough Council   Deliver to:
      Town Hall
      GLENDALE
      Newshire

Your order no.	Invoice date tax point	Invoice no.	Despatch date
A/8720	27 Oct 199-	2624	20 Oct 199-

Quantity	Description	Cat. no.	Unit price	Total price	VAT rate	VAT amount
200	Black ball point pens	105	£0.12	£24.00		
20	Staplers	137	£2.00	£40.00		
				64.00		
	Less 10% trade discount			6.40		
				57.60	17.5%	10.08

Delivery charges	———	
Sub-total	57.60	
VAT	10.08	
Total amount due	67.68	

Terms: 28 days
E & OE

Figure 4.19   Qualprint's invoice to Glendale Borough Council

Delivery notes

When goods are sent to a customer they are often accompanied by a delivery note. When the customer is satisfied that the quantity and type of goods are correct they sign the delivery note. One copy is kept by the supplier and one by the customer. Therefore a delivery note is a formal record that the goods have been received. In effect, once the delivery note is signed, the goods belong to the customer.

Did you know?

When you receive goods yourself and are asked to sign a delivery note to acknowledge receipt it is possible that you won't have time to check the goods. You should therefore sign the delivery note but mark it 'goods received but not examined'.

Non-assessed activity

A copy of the delivery note sent by Qualprint to Glendale Borough Council is shown below.

Figure 4.20 Qualprint's delivery note to Glendale Borough Council

1 For each entry on the delivery note say why you think it has been included.
2 When the goods were unpacked by staff at the Council Offices they found that 200 red ballpoint pens had been delivered instead of 200 black pens and that two of the staplers didn't work. What should the person unpacking the goods do now?
3 What do you think Qualprint should do now to rectify the situation?

Did you know?

Delivery notes and invoices are sometimes almost identical and are printed at the same time. The two main differences are usually that:

■ delivery notes do not include prices
■ there is space on a delivery note for the signature of the person who receives the goods.

Sales documents can be hand-written or typed but today it is more usual for them to be produced by computer. Special stationery, which makes copies without having to use carbon paper, is used to produce up to six copies of the documents – each for a different purpose.

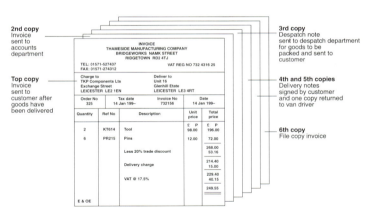

Figure 4.21 Multiple copy stationery

Sales credit notes

In the current situation, Qualprint should collect the incorrect goods from Glendale Borough Council and issue a **credit note.** You may wonder why the person who collects the incorrect goods can't just arrive with the correct goods and swap them. This is probably what you would do in a shop if you were sold the wrong item, but in business this rarely happens – mainly because it would be difficult for the accountants to trace the transaction properly. In a large organisation, the **sales department** would deal with the complaint about incorrect or faulty goods, whereas all the financial paperwork is dealt with by the **accounts department.**

Cash refunds cannot be given because the goods have been sold on credit – so as yet no money has changed hands. This is different from the procedure followed in retail shops, which cannot refuse to give a cash refund if faulty goods are returned. However, as you may also know from your own shopping experiences, organisations often prefer to give a credit note (or gift voucher in the case of shops) for goods which are returned because the buyer changes his or her mind. This encourages the customer to buy from the company again in the future.

Non-assessed activity

As discussed in Element 3.3, retail organisations vary in their policies on making exchanges where the buyer has simply made a mistake. However, given that business customers can spend thousands of pounds in a year, what do you think Qualprint's policy on exchanging goods is likely to be if, for example, the buyer at Glendale Borough Council had mistakenly ordered red pens instead of black?

Figure 4.22   What will Qualprint's policy be on exchanges for big customers?

Statements of account

At the end of each month, the supplier will usually send a **statement** to each customer. Qualprint will therefore send one to Glendale Borough Council.

Statements are summaries of transactions between two businesses or between a business and its bank. (Bank statements are dealt with on pages 436–7.) For example, a business may sell a customer several items at different times during the month. At the end of the month a statement is sent to the customer listing the totals shown on all the invoices. If any payments have been received these are also noted. The balance shown at the end of the statement is the amount of money still to be paid. This figure will be carried forward as a running total to the next statement – and printed at the top.

Statements allow businesses to check that each knows what the other owes them. They can also act as a tactful reminder that bills have not been paid.

Non-assessed activity

Figure 4.23 shows the statement issued by Qualprint to Glendale Borough Council.

1   Study the statement carefully. Note that a **running total** is shown down the right-hand side so that the balance after each transaction is clearly shown.
2   Now answer the following questions.
   a   How much did Glendale Borough Council owe Qualprint at the beginning of the month?
   b   How many times has Qualprint sold goods to Glendale Borough Council during the month of October?
   c   Have Glendale made any payments to Qualprint during the month?
   d   How much money did Glendale Borough Council owe Qualprint on the day the statement was issued?

Remittance advice

After Qualprint has issued statements at the end of the month, you may think that the staff can simply sit back and wait for payments to arrive. Normally these would be in the form of cheques, sent by post. Imagine what would happen if thousands of cheques simply appeared a few days later. Staff would have to spend hours trying to match them up against different invoices! To prevent this problem – and to save the buyer having to write a note to say which

QUALPRINT LTD.

22 CARNEI WAY
GLENDALE
NEWSHIRE
FE1 8CA

TEL: 01323 745612

FAX: 01323 849783

VAT Reg No: 680/73842/88

STATEMENT

To: Glendale Borough Council
Town Hall
GLENDALE
Newshire

Date 31 October 199-   Account no. 437

Date	Details	Debit	Credit	Balance
1 Oct	Balance			£10.00
21 Oct	Invoice 2623	£24.67		£34.67
23 Oct	Payment		£10.00	£24.67
27 Oct	Invoice 2624	£67.68		£92.35

Figure 4.23 A statement from Qualprint to Glendale Borough Council

---

REMITTANCE ADVICE

Please send this slip, together with your remittance, to

QUALPRINT LTD
22 Carnei Way
Glendale
Newshire
FE1 8CA

All cheques should be made payable to Qualprint Ltd

Invoice name and address:

Glendale Borough Council
Town Hall
Glendale
Newshire

Account No: 437   Date: 31 October 199-

Date of statement: 31 October 199-

Amount owing: £92.35

Payment enclosed:..

Cheque No.:..

Your ref: ....

Figure 4.24 A remittance advice slip from Qualprint to Glendale Borough Council

---

statement or invoice the cheque relates to – Qualprint will issue a **remittance advice**, usually at the same time as the invoice.

The remittance advice is a brief form that summarises the main points on an invoice or statement. Some organisations print invoices with the remittance advice attached as a tear-off form. The buyer simply returns this with the cheque and the payment is then easily matched to the correct transaction.

Non-assessed activity

1 Figure 4.24 is an illustration of a remittance advice form issued by Qualprint. Discuss with your tutor the main information given and why each item is required by staff at Qualprint.

2 If your parents (or your tutor!) pay any invoices by cheque find out how they make sure that the supplier can match their payment to the correct bill. (Some people send the invoice back with their cheque – asking for it to be 'receipted and returned').

3 Ask if your tutor can find any examples of remittance advice forms in the college or school office to show you as examples.

Optional evidence assignment

*This activity can be carried out verbally in class **in a group** as a non-assessed activity to consolidate learning. Alternatively, if you do it **on your own**, it can count as supplementary evidence towards the following parts of the scheme.*

PC 3:	Explain and give examples of sales transactions and sales documents
Range:	Sales transactions: goods, services, business-to-business, business-to-consumer
	Sales documents: orders received, sales invoice, delivery note, sales credit note, statement of account, remittance advice
Core skills:	Communication, Information technology

Read the case study below and answer the questions which follow.

Case study

You are employed in the sales office of Fortress Security Company, a large organisation in your home town. The Human Resources Manager at the company, Philip West, is revising the induction pack given to new employees and has decided to cover the sales procedures of the company, as many new staff are actively involved in selling. Your boss, the Accounts Manager, has asked you to prepare some information on the type of sales transactions carried out by the company and the documents involved. He has informed you that you can work with one or two colleagues preparing this, but he would like details afterwards of each person's contribution to the task.

1   Work in a **group of two or three.** Your tutor may form the group for you or suggest colleagues you should work with.

2   Prepare an information sheet entitled **Sales Transactions in the Security Industry**. Include in it examples of:
    a   the type of goods sold by the company
    b   the type of services sold by the company
    c   the type of goods and services sold to businesses
    d   the type of goods and services sold to private consumers.

    To help, you may wish to look ahead to the final sections of this element, pages 438–46, find examples of security company advertisements in the press and *Yellow Pages* or contact a local firm for information.

3   Prepare a second information sheet which:
    a   lists the sales documents used by the company and shows the relationship between each
    b   states the main components of **each** document and why these are included.

    Attach a sketched example of **three** of these documents.

4   Type up your written information, using a word processor. Prepare a summary sheet which you can use as a basis of a five-minute presentation on the topic 'Sales transactions and documents used by Fortress Security Company'.

5   Give your talk to your tutor, who will act the role of Philip West. Use your sketched examples as visual aids.

Payment methods

A customer who makes a purchase can pay:

■ by cheque
■ in cash
■ by BACS (automatically through the bank)
■ by EDI (automatically via a computer)
■ by credit card
■ by debit card
■ by credit (e.g. credit sale or hire purchase).

Customers who pay by cheque, in cash, by BACS, EDI or by debit card are paying *immediately* for the goods they purchase (these are generally termed as 'cash' payments). When customers pay by credit card the organisation receives the money quickly, but it is up to the customer whether or not to settle the account from the credit card company promptly, or over several months. A customer who buys an expensive item, and wants to pay over a period of time, may choose to take out a credit agreement. This section examines what each method entails and why a customer may choose one method of payment, rather than another.

Cheque

Cheques are probably still the most common method used by businesses to pay suppliers. When a company sends a cheque for the amount shown on an invoice or statement it is, in effect, instructing the bank to take the amount from its own bank account and pay this into the supplier's account. The way that this happens is quite complicated but is very efficient and rarely goes wrong.

Paying by cheque is better than paying in cash for the following reasons.

■ Cash can easily be lost or stolen and used by anyone who has it. A cheque is normally only of any use to the receiver. Therefore cheques are a more secure way of transferring money.
■ The system of processing cheques means that a **receipt** is not needed. Confirmation that the transaction has taken place is shown on both companies' **bank statements.** However, some businesses still send receipts when they get a cheque, to inform the sender that it has been received.
■ Cheques can be sent through the post because, unlike cash, they are of no use to anyone stealing them – provided they are crossed.

A cheque book is supplied by a bank when a **current bank account** is opened. As an extra record, there is a counterfoil attached to each cheque where information is recorded, including:

- the name of the person or business to whom it is made out
- the date
- the amount
- the reason for payment.

Every cheque has a unique serial number and this number is also printed on the counterfoil.

Did you know?

A crossed cheque has two lines printed down the centre. All cheques are printed like this automatically today and have the words 'Account Payee' written in this space for added security. This means that the person receiving it *must* pay it into his or her own bank account – the cheque cannot be exchanged for cash or passed on to someone else.

Cheque guarantee cards

When people open a current account the bank often issues them with a **cheque guarantee card.** If a cheque is presented to a retailer – for an amount no greater than the limit on the card – the recipient should write the number from the card on the back of the cheque. This *guarantees* that the bank will transfer the money, even if the cheque and card are stolen or if the purchaser does not have enough money in the bank. A cheque that is guaranteed cannot be stopped for any reason, e.g. if the buyer later changes his or her mind.

Items on a cheque

There are three parties to any cheque:

- the **payee** – the person or company named on the cheque to receive the money
- the **drawee** – the bank from which the money is drawn
- the **drawer** – the person making out the cheque, who will have the money taken out of his or her account.

Did you know?

If someone tells you that you forgot to pay for something when you know you sent them

a cheque two weeks ago, it is no use waving the cheque stub in their face as proof. This merely proves you are capable of writing out a cheque counterfoil! You would have to produce your bank statement, which showed that the transaction had taken place and the money had been removed from your account. This is legal proof that the supplier has been paid.

Non-assessed activity

1 Visit one of the main bank branches in your town and obtain one of their leaflets telling you about bank current accounts. Note the range of services offered by the bank and the information given about cheque books, cheque guarantee cards and bank statements.

Compare your information with that obtained by other members of your group who have visited different banks.

2 Study the cheque printed below and find the name of the drawee and the drawer and where the payee's name would be written. Identify the vertical lines that mean the cheque is crossed. Note the different numbers printed on the cheque and why they are used.

Why do you think the amount of money has to be written in words *and* in figures?

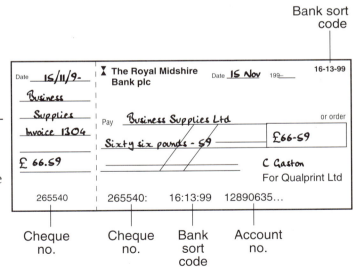

Figure 4.25 A correctly-written cheque

3 Find out if any members of your group work in the retail trade in the evenings or at weekends. Ask them to tell you what they have been trained to do when they are handed a cheque and a cheque guarantee card – and why they have to do it.

Did you know?

It is not unlikely that at some time you will have to write cheques yourself – in your private life if not in business. This aspect of cheques is covered in Element 4.2 on page 461.

Cash

Today very few people carry large sums of cash. Quite apart from the bulk, there is the worry of it being lost or stolen.

Did you know?

According to the law, no business *has* to give change if the customer cannot offer the exact amount. However, it is unlikely any business would survive for long if it insisted on all its customers offering an exact amount! Where restrictions can occur, however, is in terms of **legal tender** – i.e. the type of money that is legally acceptable in payment. A business has the right to refuse to accept, say, a hundred 2p coins in payment of a £2 account. Technically, large quantities of coins can be refused as not being legal tender. A supplier or retailer may refuse to accept:

- more than 20p worth of bronze coins
- more than £5 of 5p and 10p coins
- more than £10 worth of 20p and 50p coins.

You should note that Scottish bank notes and Northern Ireland notes are both legal tender in England, just as Bank of England notes are acceptable in those countries.

Figure 4.26 There are legal limits to how much coinage can be offered ...

Non-assessed activity

1 Suppose you have been saving your small change and have now decided to buy a new sweater. You have a jar full of bronze and small value silver coins. You know you can't take the jar to the shop as they may refuse to accept it. What would you do to change your savings into a more acceptable form?

2 Find out the largest denomination bank note issued by:
- the Bank of England
- the Bank of Scotland.

3 How strict do you think shops are about the type of coinage they will accept? Do you know any other services (e.g. bus transport) where only the exact amount is accepted? How do you think customers (or travellers) feel about this? Discuss your answers as a group.

Did you know?

Businesses are now so concerned about the number of fraudulent bank notes in use that most ask sales assistants to hold them to the light to check the metal strip is present. An alternative is to buy a small machine that automatically scans the note to check it.

Bank Automated Clearing System – BACS

The banks use the term BACS as a short way of saying Bank Automated Clearing System. It is a system by which money is transferred electronically, by banks, between bank accounts. It doesn't matter whether these are business accounts or private accounts. Neither does it matter which bank (or building society) you use. The basic principle is that any information that can be written on a piece of paper can also be transmitted electronically. In practice it means that money can be transferred from one bank account to another **instantly.**

Did you know?

The company called BACS Ltd is jointly owned by all the major High Street banks and building societies. It handles all the cashless and paperless transactions given below.

Standing orders

A standing order is an arrangement where a bank receives written authorisation to pay another person or business a fixed amount on fixed dates. For example, a student at university could receive £40 for living expenses from his parents each Thursday. The money would appear in his bank account each week as if by magic! Once the standing order has been signed by his parents the money is automatically transferred each week until the order is altered in some way or cancelled.

You should note that standing orders are used:

- where the amount to be paid rarely changes
- when the money is paid at regular intervals.

Direct debits

At first sight, direct debits may seem similar to standing orders, but there are some important differences. A supplier receives authorisation from a customer to deduct amounts of money from that customer's bank account and transfer it to his or her own account. The supplier passes this authorisation to the bank. The supplier can then later instruct the bank how much to transfer and when.

You may think this is a very casual method of allowing anyone to take money out of your account whenever they want. In reality there are strict controls on the system. You must receive an account clearly stating the amount being withdrawn *before* the withdrawal takes place. In addition, only authorised and reputable organisations are allowed to receive money by this system. The system is ideal when:

- the amounts to be paid vary from one time period to another
- the times when payment is required may also vary.

Direct debit is used to pay accounts such as electricity, gas and telephone bills where the usage – and therefore the amount owing – will vary from one payment period to another.

Credit transfer

Even if you don't have a bank account you can use BACS to transfer some of your money to someone who does have a bank account. You just visit any bank, complete a credit transfer form, and pay over the money you owe. The bank would then transfer this money to the person you specify, although they are likely to charge you for the service unless you have an account with them! Sometimes you can make payments through the Girobank system at post offices. Many organisations have bank accounts that enable them to collect payments through the post office network.

Figure 4.27 The Girobank system is part of the credit transfer network

Many of the bills you receive at home will have attached to them an optional credit transfer form you can take to the bank . The main details of the transaction are printed on the form.

A major use of credit transfer by businesses is for payment of salaries and wages. The company simply gives the bank a copy of its key payroll information, e.g. the names and addresses of its employees and their bank details. Each week or month the variable payroll information is passed to the bank. This states how much each person must receive. The bank then transfers the money from the company's account to the accounts of its employees. This is a much safer way of paying wages than giving people cash, as far less money needs to be kept on company premises. In addition, it saves having to employ staff to count the money and make up individual pay packets.

Did you know?

- Most BACS payments are transferred overnight, between 9 pm and 6 am when the systems are not busy.
- Information can be transferred by magnetic tapes which are delivered to the BACS centre at Edgeware in London.
- Another method of transfer is by wire via the Public Switched Telephone Network (PSTN).
- Over 90 per cent of monthly salaries are paid by BACS. By law, you can no longer insist on receiving your wages in cash!

427

Non-assessed activity

1 Visit your local bank or building society and obtain a leaflet which gives details of their standing order and direct debit services.

2 Check if any members of your group receive pay for any part-time jobs they do via BACS. Your tutor will almost certainly be paid by this method. Find out what information they had to provide to their employer so that this method of payment could take place.

3 **As a group**, discuss the advantages to the **employee** of receiving payment directly into a bank account rather than being paid in cash.

Electronic data interchange (EDI)

Electronic data interchange is a development of the basic principles of BACS. All the financial documents you have learned about so far are designed to **record** and **communicate** information. For example, a purchase order records the items required from the supplier and communicates this information when it is received. Electronic data interchange is concerned with the electronic transmission of documents and payments, for example, all the information involved in a sales transaction. Quite simply the buyer and seller communicate by computer rather than by telephone or by post.

Payments using EDI are made by means of 'smart cards', which can have information programmed into them. They contain chips, rather than magnetic stripes. The potential for smart cards is considerable and they have applications beyond the use of EDI (see below, and the information on the Mondex card in Element 1.2).

The system of EDI was initiated in the 1980s by the retail trade and the motor industries, both of which wanted fast communication systems with their suppliers. All orders and invoices are communicated by computer, to companies in the UK, in Europe and world-wide. Because orders can be processed very quickly, EDI reduces the amount of stock that needs to be held, and this reduces storage costs. Some users of EDI don't wait for invoices to arrive by computer from the supplier – they produce their own. They consider this to be more efficient because it reduces errors. It is then up to the supplier – rather than the buyer – to prove that payment is wrong!

Payment is made by specific computer terminals which are nominated as the payment terminals.

Access to the computer is available only by means of the smart card and a personal security code. The payment computer communicates with the banks so that money is taken out of the purchaser's bank and received by the supplier's bank simultaneously. A computerised acknowledgement is also sent to the supplier's computer.

Did you know?

1 The Government has been considering the introduction of a national database containing key information on all the citizens of the UK. This could be the first step to a national identity card system (such as those used in the United States and many European countries). Rather than a paper ID card, however, each person would carry a 'smart ID card'. Information – such as criminal convictions – could be programmed into the card and read by the police or other interested parties on request!

2 Two large UK companies who use EDI are Tesco and Rover. Tesco claims that 95 per cent of its orders and 60 per cent of its invoices are now transmitted as EDI messages. All its ordering systems are electronic – computerised terminals register the items being sold and this information is converted into orders sent to the supplier via EDI. Rover trades electronically with over 270 suppliers, each of which is given between twelve hours and one week's notice to deliver goods. However, in an emergency, delivery times have been known to be as short as

Figure 4.28 'Smart ID cards' – OK?

40 minutes. Rover is one company that raises its own electronic invoice once the goods have been received.

3 The Royal Mail provides an EDIPOST service for suppliers who are too small to install an EDI system. The Royal Mail prints the messages and despatches them by first class post.

Non-assessed activity

1 Consider the potential of all drivers carrying a smart card. Discuss the type of information it might contain and how this may be useful – and to whom!

2 Divide into **two groups.** One group should argue that the idea of everyone having to carry a 'smart ID card' is an infringement of personal liberty. The other group should argue that this information is necessary for the security of law-abiding citizens. See what issues are raised in the debate.

3 **As a group**, try to list the benefits to a large retail store such as Tesco of using EDI. Can you think of any disadvantages?

4 Ask your tutor to contact the Banking Information Service, 10 Lombard Street, London EC3V 9AT for information on Banking Technology. This will give you the latest information on EDI and other electronic developments in payment systems.

Credit cards

The most common credit cards in use today are Access and Visa cards (note that abroad Access is known as Mastercard). These cards are accepted by many organisations including garages, shops, restaurants and hotels, and this fact is normally advertised in the window or near the counter.

Figure 4.29 Some well-known credit cards

If businesses are offered a credit card in payment they must check that the card is acceptable and seek authorisation when necessary.

Authorisation – the traditional method

All organisations have a **floor limit.** This is the maximum amount they can accept before they make a special check. The agreed floor limit may be as low as zero or as high as £500.

If a transaction goes above the floor limit a telephone call is made to the credit card company who run an immediate check through their computer to ensure that the card hasn't been stolen and is not over its credit limit. If there are no problems, they issue an authorisation code which is entered onto the voucher. This guarantees the payment.

Authorisation – the new method

Electronic transmission of information has meant considerable changes in the handling of credit cards.

- The card number is keyed into a special terminal linked to the credit card companies.
- The card is swiped through the terminal and information is transmitted 'down the line' and automatically checked by computer.
- If the check runs smoothly, a sales voucher is automatically printed by the terminal. The customer signs this and takes the top copy.
- If the check shows a problem, e.g. that the card is stolen or the customer has exceeded his or her credit limit, a referral is made for further information and investigation. The method by which this is carried out may vary depending on the terminal used.

Did you know?

Many organisations – especially retail stores – have their own sales vouchers for use with the normal credit cards *as well as* their own store cards. The information from these vouchers is extracted by the store and then transmitted electronically, rather than the vouchers themselves being processed.

It used to be the case that people who couldn't pay for what they bought immediately were considered rather irresponsible. Today, you are as likely to see someone paying by credit card as by any other means. Therefore society has changed its views on people 'buying today and paying tomorrow'.

The major advantage of using a credit card is that *no* interest is charged if the holder pays the account in full each month. Depending on the date of purchase, a customer can gain up to about six weeks' *free* credit. However, many credit card companies charge an annual fee for the card, and there is the more serious problem that people may be tempted to spend beyond their means and then have difficulties paying off their account.

An important advantage of using credit cards is that if the purchaser has any problem in relation to faulty goods, non-delivery or poor service and is unable to get any satisfaction from the store itself, a claim can be made against the credit card company which provided the finance. Therefore, it may be advisable to pay for items such as holidays by credit card. Then if the tour operator 'fails to deliver' as promised, a claim can be made against the credit card company *as well as* the supplier.

Non-assessed activity

1 Credit card companies *deduct* a percentage from the payment they make to retail organisations as their commission. To compensate for this, organisations can charge different prices, if they so decide, for goods bought by cash and goods bought by credit card.
As a group, decide:

a why most companies have decided against the idea of having two prices on all the items they sell
b why the idea is more feasible for an organisation like a petrol station than a department store.

2 Discuss the advantages and disadvantages of using a credit card.

Debit cards

Debit cards are a relatively new method of paying for goods and are like 'electronic cheques'. The system saves the customer the trouble of writing out a cheque and the funds are transferred almost immediately from the customer's account to the supplier's account. Debit cards are marked as such and are issued under the Connect or Switch system. When the card is swiped through an electronic cash

register linked to the system, the customer's bank account is automatically checked (to make sure there are sufficient funds in the account) and the money is then transferred.

Because there will be no record of the transaction in the customer's cheque book (e.g. a counterfoil), when a customer pays by debit card a voucher (similar to a credit card voucher) is printed, which the customer must sign. A copy is then given to the customer for his or her records.

Not all businesses can accept debit cards. This is because their cash registers are not linked to the EFTPOS system. EFTPOS stands for **Electronic Funds Transfer at Point Of Sale.** For a business to be able to accept debit cards it must be linked to this system.

Processing a debit card

The process which takes place when a debit card is offered in payment is shown in the flow chart in Figure 4.31. In reality the transfer of funds takes place at night when all the transactions are processed by the debit card company. Within two days the bank accounts have been adjusted by the value of the purchase.

Some sales assistants are not sure how they should handle the situation if a message shows that the card is unacceptable. In many large stores the sales assistant will call for assistance from a supervisor at this point. It is important not to embarrass the customer as a mistake may have been made by the bank – not every person whose card is rejected should automatically be treated as a potential criminal!

Did you know?

Debit cards are rapidly increasing in popularity. The number of personal transactions per year – in millions – is shown below.

	1990	1993	By 2000 (forecast)
Cheque	1840	1700	1275
Credit card	740	800	1100
Debit card	200	657	1900

Figure 4.30 Personal transactions each year

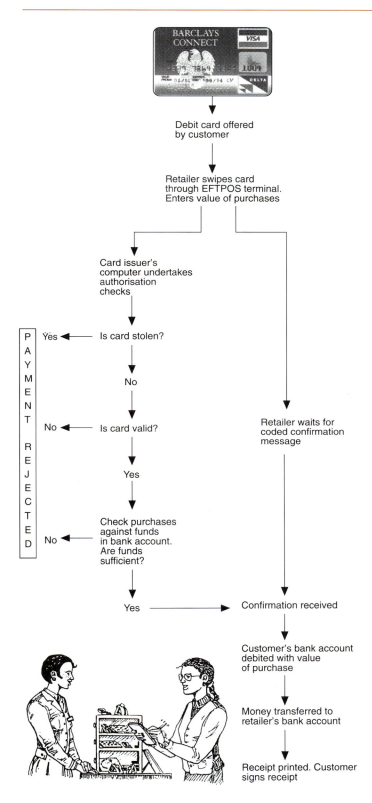

Figure 4.31 Debit card payments

Non-assessed activity

Study Figure 4.30 and answer the following questions.

1 How many transactions took place in 1993?
2 By what percentage are cheque transactions forecast to fall between 1993 and 2000?
3 a What reasons can you suggest for the increased use of debit cards?
  b What traditional method of payment are they replacing?
4 a In 1993, 3500 million cheques (for business and private use) were processed. A cheque measures approximately 200 mm by 74 mm. How much paper would have been used to produce these cheques?
  b The tallest building in the UK is the headquarters of the National Westminster Bank. It is 183 metres tall and has a floor area of 59 121 square metres.
    i How many cheques would it take to cover all the floors of the building?
    ii How many times would one year's worth of cheques cover the floor?

Note: Talk through these problems with your numeracy tutor if you do not know where to start!

Credit

There are occasions when a customer – whether a private individual or a business – wants to 'buy now and pay later'. Private individuals may want to spread the cost of payments on a large item (a house is the most obvious example!) and so might a business. Consumers may decide to use a credit card, but this is a very expensive method of obtaining credit because high interest charges are levied if the account isn't paid in full. In addition, all credit cards have a spending limit, and this would be too low for items such as a fitted kitchen or new car.

Businesses, too, may want credit *above and beyond* the terms they are normally allowed. Most goods are sold on credit terms, which mean they have to be paid for within a month or two at the most. A company buying a very expensive item, such as £1 million of computer equipment, may want a special finance deal, with special interest rates, as part of the 'sales package'. You will learn about these if you continue your studies to higher level. This element discusses the type of credit made available on a regular basis to consumers.

There are two types of credit agreements available to consumers – both are discussed on the next page.

Hire purchase

Under a hire purchase agreement, the customer does not become the legal owner of the goods until the last instalment is paid. If the customer defaults on the payment, the item can be **repossessed** (taken back). However, two factors that would be taken into consideration are:

- the amount that has already been paid
- whether or not the customer has offered to try to meet the payments (e.g. offered a reduced amount per month because of financial problems).

Usually, before a company will allow a customer to buy on hire purchase, staff have to check that his or her **credit rating** is acceptable. This is done by contacting a Credit Reference Agency, which will give information on existing credit and whether the potential customer is known as a good or bad payer. Only if the rating is satisfactory will the agreement be signed.

In some cases (e.g. large stores) the organisation itself provides the finance, and is therefore the legal owner of the goods until the final payment has been made. In others (e.g. car dealerships) the company has an agreement with a finance company, which provides the finance and then becomes the temporary legal owner.

Credit insurance

It is possible for customers to take out credit payment protection insurance to cover the possibility of their not being able to meet the payments because of illness or unemployment. However, these can be expensive and may have restrictive terms which mean that they are unsuitable for some buyers, e.g:

- the buyer must be employed full-time (and have been so for a specified period)
- there is no cover if a previous illness recurs
- there is an upper age limit.

If a customer enquires about insurance, staff should get expert help from a supervisor.

Credit sale

Many clothes shops and mail order firms offer this type of credit sale. The goods are sold to the customer, and the payments are spread over 20 weeks. The customer becomes the legal owner immediately the first payment has been made. If the customer defaults, the shop will take the customer to court and sue for the amount owing.

Calculating how much is owed

Calculating the amount the customer owes, and the amount of the monthly repayments, must be done with care. The amount will depend on:

- the total sum borrowed
- the interest rate
- the period of the loan
- the administrative charges.

Some organisations have special charts for staff to use. Provided the person using them knows what he or she is doing, and follows the instructions carefully, they give all the information needed.

The seller has a legal obligation to inform the customer about the **annual percentage rate of charge** (APR) of the loan. This is the true cost of borrowing the money (see below). It is therefore important to be aware of the law in relation to companies that provide credit facilities for their customers.

APR – annual percentage rate of charge

The APR *must* be calculated by all credit companies in a standard way, set down by law. All the interest and other charges for giving credit are added together and the total is expressed as an annual percentage rate. This gives the true cost of borrowing the money over one year, which monthly rates do not. From the point of view of the borrower, the lower the APR the better.

If *you* ever buy something on credit *always* shop around and compare the APRs of different companies. It is often given in advertisements, can always be obtained by asking for a written quotation, and *must* be clearly shown in all credit agreements.

Note that the monthly rate is no indication at all. A company quoting a *lower* monthly rate than another may have a *higher* APR!

Did you know?

1 It may be possible to obtain a personal loan from a bank at a lower APR than that quoted by a company. Sometimes, by borrowing the money from the bank and paying the organisation in *cash*, you can get the goods more cheaply. A typical example is a car – virtually all dealers will reduce the price if they are offered cash, so you would therefore be saving twice!

2 All credit transactions are covered by the **Consumer Credit Act.** Apart from stating that all buyers must be given full information about the money they owe in clear terms, this Act also allows a 'cooling-off' period if the agreement is signed anywhere but on the seller's business premises. This protects anyone who may have been bullied into buying something they don't need by someone who called at their home.

Non-assessed activity

1 Suppose a customer calls in at your store and buys a computer priced at £800. You have a special offer on at present for goods bought on credit – nothing to pay for three months then zero per cent APR. The customer starts to write out a cheque for the computer. Do you give any advice to the customer – and if so, what do you say?

2 You have been saving up to buy a car. You see one advertised which is £500 more than the amount of money you have saved. You think about borrowing the money so that you can be mobile as soon as possible. You want the loan for twelve months.

a The garage selling the car can lend you the money. Their APR is 32.5 per cent. How much would you repay in total if you took out a loan with the garage?

b Your bank's APR rate is 20 per cent. How much would you save if you borrowed the money from the bank instead?

Receipt documents

A receipt document is one which confirms that an amount of money has been paid from one person (or organisation) to another. These may take the form of:

- written or printed receipts
- cheques
- paying-in slips
- bank statements.

In all these cases the document will state the amount of money that has been paid and the date.

Three of the receipt documents listed above relate to banking transactions. Almost all business organisations process their financial transactions through a bank. Originally, banks were simply secure places for people to store their money. Banks still have large safes and strong-rooms for this purpose. Modern banks also provide a wide range of services for customers, both private and business. One of the main services is the provision of **current accounts.**

Money can be paid into a current account and withdrawn easily. Payments may be in the form of cheques and cash. Cheques can be written to pay other people or businesses, and cash can be withdrawn. Money can also be transferred from one current account to another by using debit cards and by credit transfer, e.g. the BACS system of paying wages.

The three main documents used in connection with a current account are cheques, paying-in slips and bank statements – three of the receipt documents listed above.

Receipt

Customers who pay in cash need a receipt as proof of payment. Organisations which do not use tills usually make out receipts on special forms. Customers may specifically request a receipt, particularly if they wish to claim the money back from someone else. Each receipt is numbered for ease of reference.

Receipts normally have the following items to be completed – and you can easily remember them since all the words begin with **w**:

- **who** has made the payment (name of payee)
- **when** payment was made (date)
- **what** amount was paid
- **why** the money was paid
- **who** received the money (on behalf of the organisation).

Hand-written receipts are always issued in *duplicate* and the company keeps a copy for its own records.

Did you know?

A ticket is a form of receipt, because it shows that you have paid to attend an event, or travel on a particular form of transport. It is important that you look after the ticket, particularly if you have paid in advance. You need to be extra careful if your ticket does not include the name of the purchaser, as it can be used by someone else very easily.

Raffle tickets are a special kind of ticket. They are used, for instance, by charities to raise money. It is important to keep the ticket safely, as it serves as proof of payment if you need to claim a prize.

Receipts can also be issued if goods are left at a shop, e.g. if you take clothes to be dry cleaned or a watch to be repaired. The receipt must be produced as proof of ownership when you collect the goods.

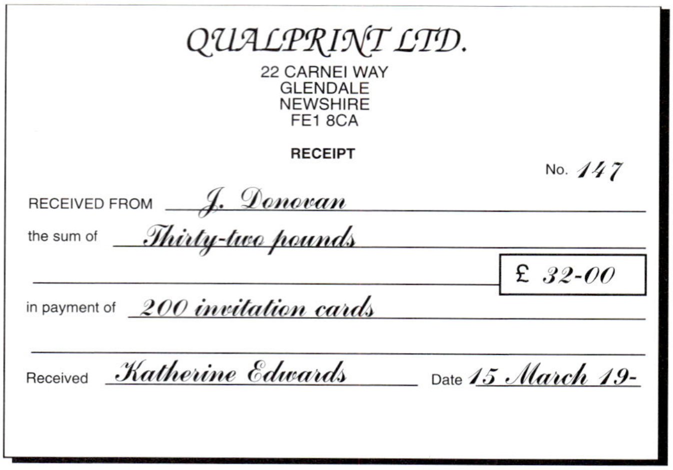

Non-assessed activity

1 Study the hand-written receipt in Figure 4.32 to see how the information it contains links with the five 'ws' given above.
2 Collect **at least five** receipts yourself. You may include till receipts, tickets, invoices marked 'received with thanks', cash deposit machine print-outs at a bank or hand-written receipts. Compare your collection with those of other members in your group.

Cheque

When a cheque is received by a business, staff would look at it carefully to see that all the information is correct. (See page 424 if you need to remind yourself about cheques.) If anything is wrong then the bank may refuse to accept the cheque, and return it to the payee. This will also occur if the drawer (the person

QUALPRINT LTD.
22 CARNEI WAY
GLENDALE
NEWSHIRE
FE1 8CA

RECEIPT   No. *147*

RECEIVED FROM   *J. Donovan*

the sum of   *Thirty-two pounds*

£ *32-00*

in payment of   *200 invitation cards*

Received   *Katherine Edwards*   Date *15 March 19-*

Figure 4.32   A hand-written receipt

who wrote the cheque) does not have enough money in the account, and the cheque has not been covered by a cheque guarantee card. Procedures for checking a cheque are covered in full in Element 4.2.

Written receipts are not usually issued when cheques are received, because the drawer has a record of the payment on the cheque counterfoil. In addition, when the cheque has been presented to the bank and the money has been transferred, a record of the transaction will appear on the **bank statement** of both the payee and the drawer. There will also be a record on the **paying-in slip** used by the payee.

Did you know?

Modern cash registers can automatically print all the details on a cheque. The sales assistant then usually asks the **customer** to check that all the details are correct, and sign it.

Clearing cheques

When a cheque is paid into a bank the money is not officially available to go into the account until is has been **cleared.** This means checking that the writer of the cheque has enough money in the account to pay. Only then is the money transferred. This process usually takes about three days and it is important that, during this time, the recipient does not depend on this money when making out other cheques!

Did you know?

Many banks issue the same card for a variety of purposes, e.g. cash card, cheque card, debit card. The words *cheque guarantee* may therefore *not* appear on the front of the card, but on the reverse.

Paying-in slips

To avoid keeping large sums of money on their premises, a company should bank their takings regularly. A very large organisation may employ a special security company, such as Securicor, to transfer the money. Even a small organisation should bank their takings quickly and use the bank's night safe if the bank has closed by the time they have cashed up. Any cash left on the premises must be locked away in the safe. (See also security, page 438.)

Figure 4.33 Security companies will take large amounts of cash to the bank

All bank account holders are issued with a paying-in book which has the account number printed on each slip, together with the name of the account holder. Each paying-in slip also has its own counterfoil or duplicate page for the account holder's own records. The person paying in the money records any cash received and totals it, then does the same for any cheques that are being put into the bank. The total amount being paid in, and the date, are written on the slip and the counterfoil is completed.

A *separate* list of all cheques should also be kept by the company, in case there are any queries. The accounts staff and, later, the company accountants will also require this information. (See also Element 4.2.)

Bank procedure

The bank will check the amount of money handed over – they count notes and weigh bags of coins.

They will tick each entry on the paying-in slip as they check it. If all is correct they will initial both the paying-in slip and the counterfoil (or duplicate paying-in slip) and date stamp both. The cashier keeps the top copy of the paying-in slip and returns the book.

Did you know?

Money can now be paid into the bank at automated deposit machines. Sometimes these are situated *inside* the bank and are useful if the counters are very busy. See if you can spot one in your local branch and watch it being used – but don't get too close or people might think you are trying to see their personal identification number (known as the PIN).

Non-assessed activity

The paying-in slip in Figure 4.34 has been completed by a new temporary worker at Qualprint. Note how all the cash has to be divided into denominations. The cash for banking was made up as:

2 × £50 notes	7 × 20p coins
7 × £20 notes	9 × 10p coins
6 × £10 notes	17 × 5p coins
23 × £5 notes	17 × 2p coins
7 × £1 coins	12 × 1p coins
11 × 50p coins.	

In addition the cheques have been listed on the reverse and the total carried forward. (Postal orders are also listed with cheques – in exactly the same way).

Check the entries carefully to see if you can find any errors.

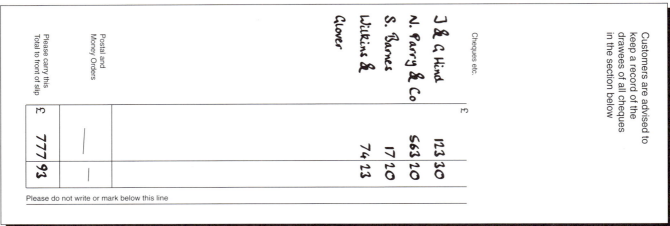

Figure 4.34 Qualprint's paying-in slip

Bank statements

Every so often, usually once a month, a bank sends out statements to its customers, listing all the transactions that have taken place since their previous statement. A bank statement is a receipt document because it shows details of all the money received into the account and paid out over a period of time. A statement should be checked to make sure that the entries are correct.

Statements include the following information.

Withdrawals

These are mainly cheques which have been written in payment to creditors. The number in the details column is the serial number of the cheque. The date shows the date on which the money was transferred out of the account, *not* the date on which the cheque was written.

Withdrawals also include standing orders and direct debits – you learnt about these on page 00.

Deposits

These are payments made into the bank account. They may be:

■ cash and cheques paid in on paying-in slips
■ electronic transfers, such as
   – salary payments made by BACS
   – any standing orders paid to a person (such as the student at university) or standing orders

and direct debits paid to a business organisation

- any other payments made to business organisations electronically, e.g. by debit card, credit card or EDI.

A balance figure

This shows the amount of money in the account on the date the statement was issued.

Did you know?

Traditionally, if a bank account holder was overdrawn (i.e. had taken out more money than he or she had deposited) the bank would print this amount in red. From this comes the expression 'in the red'. Today, bank statements are produced by computer and cannot be printed in red. The letters OD appear against any overdrawn amount, to draw the account holder's attention to the problem.

Non-assessed activity

Figure 4.35 shows Qualprint's latest bank statement.

1 Find **one** standing order and **one** direct debit on Qualprints' bank statement. What are each of these payments for?
2 Compare the sample paying-in slip in Figure 4.34 with the statement. Can you find the entry for the deposit? What does the number in the details column represent?

Did you know?

The amount shown as the balance on the bank statement may not be the amount of money which is really there! Why? If some cheques have not been presented, the amount shown will be too high; there may have been one or two payments into the account after the statement was prepared, so they would not be recorded. Therefore most companies **reconcile** their bank statements at the end of each month, by adding on any deposits which have not been included on the statement, and subtracting any withdrawals. Then they know exactly how much money they have in their account (see also Element 4.2, page 466).

The Royal Midshire Bank plc

14 Castle Way
Glendale
Newshire
FE1 9PT

ACCOUNT CURRENT
QUALPRINT LTD

A/c no. 12890635

Telephone 01323 837922

Statement date 30.4.199-

Confidential

Sheet No. 75

Date	Details	Withdrawals	Deposits	Balance £
	Balance from sheet 74			607.21
2 APR	001625	103.71		503.50
	001629	222.93		280.57
5 APR	161325 CC		194.31	474.88
10 APR	001626	53.24		421.64
15 APR	161326 CC		1209.04	1630.68
20 APR	001627	1003.20		627.48
21 APR	British Telecom DD	121.54		505.94
26 APR	Motor Insurance SO	57.41		448.53
29 APR	001628	571.24		122.71 OD

KEY	SO	Standing order	DD	Direct debit	OD	Overdrawn
	TR	Transfer	CC	Cash cheques	CM	Cash machine

Figure 4.35 Qualprint's bank statement

Optional evidence assignment

*This activity can be carried out verbally in class **in a group** as a non-assessed activity to consolidate learning. Alternatively, if you do it **on your own**, it can count as supplementary evidence towards the following parts of the scheme.*

PC 4: Explain and give examples of payment methods and receipt documents

Range: Payment methods: cheque, cash, BACS, EDI, credit card, debit card, credit

Receipt documents: receipt, cheque, paying-in slip, bank statement

Core skills: Communication

Read the case study on the next page and then answer the questions which follow.

Case study

Your parents have owned a toy shop for many years and operate this on a small scale. They want to retire and your sister and brother are taking over the business. When you have completed your course you hope to work with them.

Your brother has very big ideas. He wants to expand the business and considers this will be essential if it is to support all three of you. His ideas are not going down too well with your father and one night you walk in to find them involved in quite a heated argument.

Your father thinks that if people don't have the cash, they can't afford to buy. Your brother, on the other hand, wants to introduce new methods of payment into the business. He wants to buy a computer and an electronic cash register. He is also in the process of altering the way in which the business pays its own bills – so these are taken out of the shop's bank account automatically.

Your father is forecasting doom and gloom and you feel you should intervene to try to keep the peace.

1. Either explain **verbally** (to your tutor), *or* write brief notes, on the advantages to a business of receiving payment by each of the following methods:
   a cheque
   b credit card
   c debit card.
2. Write brief notes that clearly state the difference between a standing order and a direct debit. Give examples of the payments which may be made by **each** system.
3. Prepare a brief explanation for your brother of why installing EDI would be unsuitable for the business. Either give this explanation **verbally** to your tutor or write out short notes.
4. Your brother considers a greater number of expensive items can be sold if they are available on hire purchase. You think, but can't remember the details, that a credit sale would be more appropriate. Research this information and state which would be best and why.
5. How would you answer each of the following comments by your father?
   a 'There's no difference between a receipt from my old till and one from one of these new-fangled electronic tills.'
   b 'Cheques are hopeless. People will try to pay you with them when they've no money in their account.'
   c 'You've no way of knowing how much money you've given to the bank or how much you've really got.'

Figure 4.36 Security inside the toy shop

Evidence assignment

At this point your tutor may wish you to start work on the project which will prove to your verifiers that you understand this section of the element. If so, turn to page 448. If you have already started the project you may be ready to do Section 2. This covers the second evidence indicator for this element.

The importance of security

In the early part of this element there was a brief reference to security and the fact that business people could more easily be defrauded if records of transactions were not kept.

Now we look at security in more detail and consider both its importance and the type of checks which should be made when dealing with financial documents.

To prevent fraud

Fraud and theft are similar in the sense that someone steals money or goods from people or businesses. The difference is that fraud is more likely to involve systematic deception over a period of time. In other words, the person tries to cover up the fact that something is missing. In the case of theft, everyone knows that something has been stolen but the thief simply hopes that he or she will not be discovered.

To prevent fraud, businesses need to run very careful and thorough checks, at regular intervals, on all financial transactions. Checks will also be made by the company accountants and the auditors of limited companies, who follow each transaction through very carefully indeed. If they find any inconsistencies they will investigate further and will interview all the staff involved. Internal auditors are employed to undertake spot checks on documents and transactions, or systematically go through internal accounts. Suspected fraud can be reported to the police who have a special branch – the Fraud Squad – to investigate complicated transfers of funds and accounts documents.

Large banks have special departments set up to combat computer fraud. This type of fraud can range from people attempting to steal money from cash machines, to sophisticated criminals attempting to obtain large amounts of money by electronic transfer.

Fraud can be carried out on a small scale as well as on a large scale. Staff obtaining a petty cash voucher (see Element 4.2) against a receipt for goods which they have bought for themselves, or a representative fiddling an expense claim, are both defrauding the company just as much as an accountant who 'cooks the books'.

There are no quick solutions to fraud. Dishonest people can be ingenious, constantly thinking of new ways of defrauding businesses. Special care has to be taken when cash or cheques are being paid out. Senior managers need to check that payments are being made and recorded correctly. The golden rule is, the larger the payment, the more senior the person who needs to approve it.

Specific examples of checks which are made regularly are given in the next section.

Did you know?

Fraud costs businesses and governments billions of pounds every year. A report by a security consultancy stated that fraud by organised crime is one of the biggest threats to business.

However, new technology is helping the fight against crime. Two companies have recently invented machines that can detect a stolen credit card in seconds. The Cardcast and Card Clear systems both transmit stolen credit card numbers to a special system connected to the machines. When a credit card is swiped through the machine it instantly reads 'clear' or 'hot'.

Non-assessed activity

Examples of areas in which fraudulent activities occur include:

- social security payments
- the theft of mobile phones
- the use of colour photocopiers
- computer use.

As a group and **with your tutor,** discuss the way in which each of these may be misused by fraudsters.

To prevent theft

Each year, thousands of people steal money or goods from businesses. Cash is stolen; stock and equipment are stolen either for the thief's own personal use or to sell for cash. Items stolen may be business property or belong to employees. For that reason alone, all employees have a responsibility to co-operate with organisational security procedures and to help in identifying and preventing theft themselves.

The precautions taken will depend upon the item needing protection and the type of organisation.

Did you know?

Losses through theft affect company profits and, indirectly, the number of employees the company can afford and the salaries they can be paid. In 1992 Marks and Spencer plc lost £30 million because of crime – and spent £23 million improving security procedures designed to discourage theft and make staff areas more secure.

Protecting cash

Criminals will take more risks trying to steal cash than anything else. This means that organisations (and staff) who deal with cash need proper security procedures. If possible, the amount of cash on the

439

premises should be kept to a minimum, especially overnight. Cash to be transported should be handled by security staff and the times and routes followed should be varied. Organisations which receive large amounts of cash often have 'no return' slots where bank notes can be deposited, to keep the amount in the cash register as small as possible. Most businesses only allow authorised people, who have proved that they can be trusted, to handle cash.

The fact that no employees can insist on being paid in cash and most companies pay salaries by BACS reduces cash on the premises on pay-day. In addition, many companies have installed cashless vending machines and card pay phones, again to reduce the number of locations where cash is at risk.

Did you know?

The fact that the amount you have to pay in a shop is usually displayed on both sides of the cash register is one measure which has been introduced to try to prevent theft. A dishonest shop assistant could key in £2 for an item which costs £3 and keep the difference. The fact that the amount keyed in is displayed to both the customer and the shop assistant helps to stop this happening.

Stock and equipment

Stock and equipment can be protected by a variety of means. **Electronic tagging** means that the position of each tagged item can be checked by computer. **Security chains** and **anchoring devices** can be attached to valuable equipment to prevent it being moved, with the most valuable items being stored in the most secure buildings. These can also be security marked, often using an ultra-violet pen or a special security label showing the name of the company as the owner. Easily pilfered items are not kept in public buildings. A proper system of stock control is usually in operation, so items are only issued against official signed documents. In addition, all callers to the building have to register at a reception desk and be issued with special visitors' badges.

Retail stores have a special problem with theft. They really cannot keep all their goods locked away out of sight! However, having goods on display makes it easy for shoplifters to steal items, unless precautions are taken.

Valuable or confidential documents

You may be surprised at some of the documents which a thief would class as 'valuable'. All of the following have a value to a thief.

- cheque books (especially with guarantee cards)
- bank statements
- credit or cheque cards
- blank order forms and invoices
- letter-headed paper

All such documents should be kept locked away unless they are in use.

Non-assessed activity

1 **As a group**, brainstorm the methods you have seen in use in shops to prevent shoplifters from taking goods on display.
2 Can you suggest **at least one** use a thief would have for each of the documents given above? Discuss your ideas with your tutor.
3 Why is a cheque book more valuable to a thief if the guarantee card is with it?

Personal property belonging to staff

You are wise if you limit the type and value of personal property you take to work and never leave anything unattended. In addition, make sure that you:

- never lend your bank card to anyone and ask them to get cash on your behalf, as this would mean telling them your PIN number
- never take your passport to work (regarded as highly desirable by thieves)
- limit the amount of cash you carry
- keep your cheque book and cheque card in different places (if you need to take them at all)
- leave credit cards at home
- never leave a wallet in an unattended jacket, or a handbag open in a public area.

If your personal property is missing, don't panic or accuse anyone (as you would have to prove your allegation!). Look around carefully and methodically and retrace your steps to think where it might be. Try to think when you last had the property with you. *Make sure* the item is missing before you take action. Report the missing item, with a full description, to someone in authority. You may be advised to contact the police if the item is valuable.

Computer data

Computer security is important for several reasons. Valuable information may be stored on computer and could take months to replace. In addition, the confidentiality of personal data held on computers is covered by law – under the **Data Protection Act** (see Core Skills in Information Technology, page 628).

All computer users should be aware that:

- unauthorised print-outs must never be given to anyone
- print-outs containing personal or confidential information should not be left lying around – neither should any floppy disks containing such information
- precautions must be taken to prevent unauthorised people from being able to read confidential information on screen
- user IDs and computer passwords must be kept confidential and never told to anyone
- security systems in place to prevent the accidental erasure of information or the introduction of viruses must always be followed (see also Core Skills in Information Technology).

Vigilance

The best way to prevent theft is for all staff to be vigilant – and not just leave this to supervisors or security guards. It also means that you should:

- lock the doors of rooms when they are not in use
- obey all the rules about handling cash
- report to a manager anyone who is acting suspiciously, or anyone you don't recognise, to a manager
- lock away any valuable or desirable items after use
- not leave keys lying about (or hide them in an obvious place).

 ### Did you know?

Most thieves are known by police as 'opportunists'. This means that they do not plan to steal but will take the opportunity to do so when it arises. Vigilant staff actively reduce the number of opportunities for thieves every day of the year.

Non-assessed activity

Suppose that at a meeting between your boss and a security guard you hear them discussing the following security measures as a possible way of preventing theft. In each case, suggest why the measure may be employed.

- security fences
- bollards on a pavement in front of a plate glass window
- security guards
- staff identity badges
- security cameras
- alarms linked to doors, pressure pads and infra-red detectors
- working in pairs
- coded access doors
- emptying tills regularly
- personal ID numbers to log-in to the computer system.

Ensuring high standards of honesty

Unfortunately, businesses lose money not just through shoplifters and burglaries but because their staff steal from them as well. Most people are honest, but some are dishonest. For example, one person could find a postage stamp on the floor and hand it in to reception. Another could find a £10 note in the same place and quickly hide it in a pocket. A lot depends on an individual's own integrity.

People can also be honest or dishonest in different situations. For example, the person who handed in the stamp could use the office phone to ring several friends every day. On the other hand, the individual

Figure 4.37 Not all thieves come from outside the organisation

who took the £10 may *always* use the pay-phone in the reception foyer!

In the previous sections there has been a lot of information about measures which can be taken to prevent theft and fraud. If everyone was honest, these steps would not be necessary and industry and commerce would be saved the huge costs of security. Prices could even fall!

Did you know?

On average, every shopper in the UK pays an extra £120 a year to compensate for theft. Crime against retailers cost the retail industry £2.15 billion in 1993/4. The value of stolen goods amounted to £748.4 million and additional costs were incurred in trying to prevent thefts. However, not all theft was by customers – staff thefts were nearly as bad, as the table below shows.

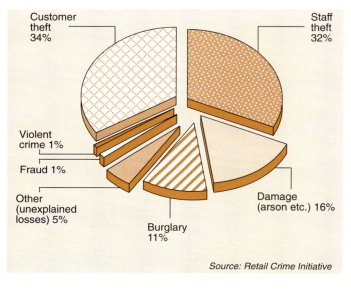

Source: Retail Crime Initiative

Figure 4.38 Percentage costs to retail outlets of various crimes

Non-assessed activity

What is your opinion of the views of each of the following people?

Sam I reckon it's OK to use the phone for private calls or to take home office stationery – everyone does it – but I'd never steal any money or anything valuable.

Jim It wouldn't bother me to fiddle some money out of the till if I thought I could get away with it. It's a big firm and they can afford it. They've more money than I have!

Tony I think dishonesty, in any form, is always wrong.

Compare your answers with those given by other members of the group and with your tutor. Can you suggest any reasons for the different opinions you may have found people hold?

Encouraging honesty

There are three main ways in which organisations can encourage honesty in their staff:

a by the recruitment methods they use
b by setting a good example
c by reducing the opportunities for dishonesty.

By recruitment

The best way to avoid having dishonest staff is not to employ them in the first place. It would be hard to detect dishonesty at an interview, but **references** can help. Referees do not always know the people they are writing about very well but if they *did* know that someone was dishonest then they should say so.

Organisations can take extra precautions when recruiting employees who will handle cash, particularly large amounts. They may check with *all* previous employers and agencies who keep records of bad debts. Sometimes businesses check the electoral roll to make sure that people live where they say they do!

Did you know?

If a referee consciously misled someone about the character of a potential employee with a deliberate lie, e.g. by saying an applicant was completely honest when he or she had a criminal conviction for theft which was known to the referee, then the referee could be sued for making a false statement.

By example

Many people behave dishonestly because they see other people doing it, so everyone who works in an organisation can influence everyone else. This is especially true when younger or junior staff see older or more senior staff acting dishonestly. This can range from discussing confidential information in public, to telling a deliberate lie to a customer, or using the office photocopier to do private work.

Did you know?

Special insurance can be taken out by an employer for protection in case an employee who is in a trusted position, and handles large amounts of cash, steals the money. Needless to say, the personal details of the person are carefully scrutinised by the insurance company before the policy comes into force. However, it is no use the person involved succumbing to temptation and then begging for forgiveness. The insurance company will only pay out on the policy if the employer agrees to prosecute the employee for theft, to prevent collusion between employer and thief.

By reducing opportunities

This relates to the organisation having sound security procedures and systems in operation so that it is extremely difficult for employees to be dishonest. Some of the more general types of security systems and checks have already been discussed. Those concerning financial documents are covered below.

Did you know?

Another form of employee theft is stealing **information.** Units 1 and 3 show that one way for businesses to be successful is to introduce better products than their competitors – or develop new ones. Sometimes employees may be tempted to sell information about a new product to a rival firm. If this is a possibility then the employee's conditions of employment may specifically ban this.

For similar reasons, government employees are often asked to sign the **Official Secrets Act.**

Security checks for receipts and payments

Authorisation of orders

When an order is sent to a supplier, the business sending it is almost always committed to accepting the goods and paying for them. Because sending an order is the same as spending money, it is very important that an order is sent when it is definite that the organisation needs the goods. Therefore it is also important that someone with the correct authority

authorises the order. This means that they will probably sign it and are responsible for making sure that it is appropriate for the business. The two main criteria for deciding who authorises an order are:

- the amount of money to be spent
- the type of goods being purchased.

The amount of money

The general rule is that the larger the amount of money involved, the more senior the person who has to authorise it. The actual amounts will vary between organisations but, usually, managers will be responsible for authorising general expenditure in their own areas. Therefore a training manager could authorise payment for £300 for a video recorder for use on courses. However, the board of directors would have to approve the building of a new training block costing half a million pounds.

Type of goods

People are normally only allowed to authorise orders for items which are appropriate for the work for which they are responsible. For example, a maintenance supervisor could order a spare part for a machine but could not order a new drinks vending machine! The catering manager *would* be allowed to order this type of equipment.

Non-assessed activity

Rachel Williams is the Administration Manager in a factory. She is allowed to authorise orders up to the value of £250 for any single item. One day the Purchasing department receives an order from her for a new carpet to be fitted in her office. The value of the order is £410. The Maintenance department is responsible for decorating and maintaining the buildings and this would normally include the purchase and installation of carpets and other fittings.

1 Assume you are the Purchasing Manager. Write a tactful note to Rachel, in your own name, explaining why the order cannot be allowed. Tell her what she should do if she needs a new carpet.
2 Why do you think the Purchasing Manager needs to take this action?

Invoices checked against orders and goods received notes

These three documents have different functions:

443

- **an order** gives details of goods required from a supplier
- **an invoice** is a request for payment for the goods once they have been delivered
- **a goods received note** (GRN) is completed by the person receiving and checking the goods when they arrive.

If you are not sure about any of these documents, refresh your memory by looking back at pages 411–5.

Invoices should not be processed for payment until someone with the appropriate authority has satisfied themselves that everything is correct. This means that the information on the invoice must be identical with that on the original order *and* with the details entered on the GRN. Once an invoice has been authorised, the Finance department will make the payment automatically.

Processing invoices for payment

Ideally a variety of people should be involved in checking the invoice. It should *not* just be the responsibility of one person, especially if it is for a very large amount of money. The procedure for checking invoices was covered on page 412.

Usually the document is stamped to show the stages it must pass through. As each person carries out the necessary function, he or she initials the appropriate box.

ACCOUNT VERIFICATION		
Item	Status	Verification
Goods received		
Invoice details as Order		
Invoice details as GRN		
Invoice correct		
Payment approved _____ (signed)		

Figure 4.39 A rubber stamp summarising the proper stages and procedures

Did you know?

In very large companies it may be uneconomic to employ someone to check every invoice, especially those for very small

amounts. In this case invoices over a certain figure, e.g. £100, would be checked and smaller totals would be batch checked, i.e. certain ones checked at random.

Types of discrepancy

Some reasons why an invoice would not be passed for payment immediately are that:

- the invoice may have been incorrectly completed, e.g. with the wrong goods, price or quantity
- items may have been delivered at different times (in a 'split' order) and so more than one GRN would have to be found and checked
- the GRN could have been incorrectly completed and contain inaccurate or insufficient information
- the person receiving the goods may not have checked them properly, e.g. some may have been reported damaged and returned at a later date
- invoices are often printed by computer or typed. GRNs are more likely to be completed by hand. If someone's handwriting is illegible it may be impossible to check the GRN against the invoice.

Problem-solving

If you find a mistake or discrepancy on an invoice you must know how to deal with it. The procedure is often different in small and large organisations. In a large organisation the problem would be referred to a supervisor. In a small organisation the clerks in the accounts department may have to sort it out.

- If the discrepancy is small and the organisation is one which is dealt with regularly, it is normal to telephone them to point out the error. They may issue a replacement invoice but are more likely to send a supplementary invoice or a credit note for the difference.
- If the discrepancy is large, it is better to write to the organisation, as any correspondence will then be on file and can be referred to later.
- If there are regular discrepancies from a particular organisation then a more formal letter of complaint may be sent by the manager.

Did you know?

A *reputable* company points out all errors, whether they are being overcharged or undercharged! Most companies would rather keep their reputation than save a few pounds by keeping quiet about a mistake which will probably be discovered by the supplier at a later date.

Paying the account

When the invoice has been authorised for payment the Accounting department will pay the supplier, usually by cheque. However, in many cases the company waits until a **statement** has been received from the supplier showing the balance owing to date. This document is also checked before the cheque is sent. Usually the cheque would be made out for the amount shown on the statement. However, if a company can take advantage of special cash discount terms by paying more promptly, it is more likely that payment will be made before the statement is due.

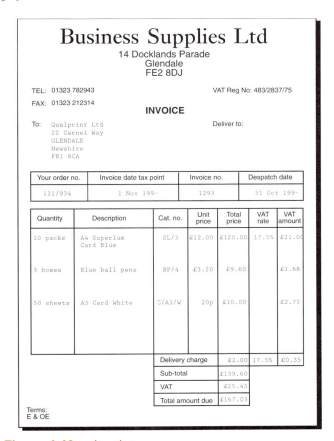

Figure 4.40a   Invoice

Non-assessed activity

1 Study the invoice, order and GRN in Figure 4.40 carefully and then write down your answer to the following questions.
a Can payment of the invoice be authorised? If not, list the discrepancies you have found.
b What action should now be taken?

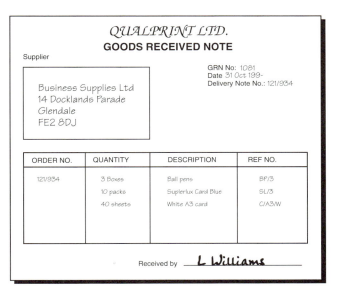

Figure 4.40b   Goods received note

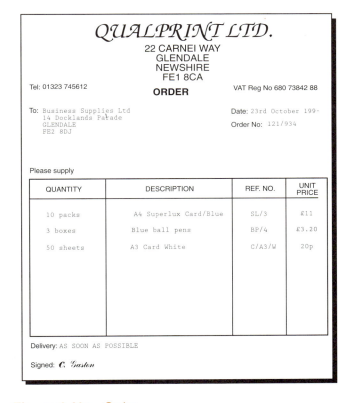

Figure 4.40c   Order

2 What other reasons can you think of why someone checking invoices against orders and GRNs may not be able to authorise payment? Compare your answers with other members of your group.

Cheques signed by authorised signatories

When a person or business opens a bank account with a cheque facility, the bank asks for a sample of a signature from everyone who will be allowed to sign cheques. Those people who provide the signature are those who must sign the cheques used to pay suppliers. The reason for this is that a signature can be very difficult to forge. Cheques can only be signed by those people who have the correct authority, each of whom is known as an **authorised cheque signatory.**

The bank keeps the sample signatures and, if there are any queries, checks them against those on the cheques which are presented for payments. In practice this happens very rarely for small amounts, but if a forged cheque is presented and the bank pays out the money, in law it is responsible and has to compensate for the loss.

Company signatories

A business can nominate whoever it likes to authorise cheques.

- Some organisations have rules that say how much a particular signatory can authorise. Normally, for large amounts of money the cheques are signed by a very senior person, e.g. the chief executive or managing director.
- Another organisation may insist that cheques need two signatures – especially if they are for large amounts of money, e.g. over £500.
- Some companies nominate three or four signatories with the agreement that any one or any two can sign.

These measures are designed:

- to prevent fraud
- to ensure that money is paid correctly, i.e. the right amount to the right person or business at the right time
- to protect those people who *are* allowed to sign cheques from allegations or doubt as to their actions. If two people are always involved then each person has another witness as to his or her actions.

Did you know?

On most occasions, people who sign cheques for businesses don't complete the other details. This is done by someone else or even by computer. It is also common practice to have pre-printed signatures when many similar cheques are to be paid out. These are stored in a cheque-printing machine which can automatically process the cheques very rapidly. Needless to say, the machine is locked when not in use. Without one of these the chief accountant of a county council would have a very sore hand each pay day!

Optional evidence assignment

*This activity can be carried out verbally in class **in a group** as a non-assessed activity to consolidate learning. Alternatively, if you do it **on your own**, it can count as supplementary evidence towards the following parts of the scheme.*

PC 5:	Explain the importance of security and security checks for receipts and payments
Range:	Importance: to prevent fraud, to prevent theft, to ensure high standards of honesty
	Security checks: authorisation of orders, invoices checked against orders, invoices checked against goods received notes, cheques signed by authorised signatories
Core skills:	Communication, Information technology, Application of number

Read the case study below and answer the questions which follow.

Case study

Ray Smith, the accountant at Billsborough Engineering, was a very careful man. Unfortunately, one day there was an exception. He was sitting at his desk signing cheques when the phone rang. His wife, who was very upset, told him that their young son had been involved in an accident and taken to hospital. Ray was obviously very alarmed and ran straight to his car to go and see his son.

Ray's son was quite seriously hurt and Ray decided to take a few days of his personal leave to be with his family. In the meantime, he told his assistant, James, to carry out any urgent tasks.

When Ray returned to work the following Monday, James was nowhere to be found. Ray checked the holiday rota but James wasn't listed as being away. No phone call was received to say he was ill. When Ray tried to contact him, there was no reply.

As the week wore on, however, various aspects of James' behaviour came to light. The storeman told Ray about deliveries of a variety of expensive items, including a computer, camcorder and mobile phone – all of which had then mysteriously disappeared. Some invoices for other items appeared to have been passed for payment even though there was no order on record and no goods received note on the file. When the firm's bank statement arrived on Friday a large cash withdrawal was recorded. The cheque number was the one cheque Ray had signed before he had dashed out of his office the week before. The cheque book itself was nowhere to be found.

1 Write a short report on what could happen to the stolen cheques. Also say what action Ray should take.
2 Summarise what you think James' activities were during the week that Ray was away.
3 What security systems and checks do you think the firm should have had in operation to prevent James being able to take advantage of Ray's absence?
4 To what extent do you think James was an 'opportunist' thief? Give reasons for your answer.
5 On investigation, the police conclude that James had been systematically ordering about £150 of goods a week for the past twelve months. However, during the time that James was on holiday for three weeks, no unauthorised purchases were made. What is the approximate value of the goods he obtained?
6 Ray appears to be an honest man. James was not.
  a What is your view of James' behaviour?
  b What precautions could Ray take when he hires a replacement for James, to try to reduce the possibility of this happening again?

Type up your answers using a word processor.

Evidence assignment

At this point your tutor may wish you to start work on the project which will prove to your verifiers that you understand this section of the element. If so, turn to page 448. If you have already started the project you may be ready to do Section 3. This covers the third evidence indicator for this element.

Revision test

True or false?

1 VAT inspectors regularly check the accounts of companies which are VAT registered.
2 Hand-written receipts are not usually given for payments made by cheque.
3 Cash discount is given to encourage companies to pay promptly.
4 All cheques must be signed by at least two people.
5 Faulty goods cannot be returned if they have been bought on hire purchase.

Fill in the blanks

6 EDI stands for _____ _____ _____ .
7 The two main types of annual accounts are the _____ _____ and the _____ _____ _____ _____ .
8 The amount on a cheque must be written in _____ and _____ .
9 Goods inwards are recorded on a _____ _____ _____ .
10 The document sent by a company to its customers, which shows all the transactions which have taken place that month, is called a_____ .

Short answer questions

11 Give **four** reasons why financial transactions must be recorded.
12 State **three** ways in which an organisation can try to ensure high standards of honesty in its staff.
13 Give **five** items which must be included on an invoice.
14 State **three** differences between debit cards and credit cards.
15 State **four** reasons why an invoice may not be passed for payment.

Write a short paragraph to show you clearly understand each of the following terms.

16 BACS
17 Authorisation of orders
18 Paying-in slip
19 Credit note
20 Delivery note

Evidence indicator project

Unit 4   Element 4.1

This project has been designed to cover all the evidence indicators related to Element 4.1. It is divided into three sections. Tutors may wish students to complete the sections at the appropriate points marked in the text. Alternatively, tutors may prefer their students to do the entire project at the end of the element.

Performance criteria: 1–5

Core skills: Communication
Application of number
Information technology

Section 1

This section concentrates on the first evidence indicator for this element. When you have completed the work, store it safely as it will contribute towards your final project for this element.

> **Make sure you complete this section of the project by the deadline date given to you by your tutor.**

For some years Sue Sharp has been the envy of her friends because of her ability to make beautiful hand-made chocolates. She gives these as presents for birthdays and at Christmas. A few months ago Sue's elderly aunt left her some money and Sue decided to set up in business herself.

She hunted around for suitable premises and bought the equipment she needed to make the chocolates. When you meet her, however, she is looking worried. Sue might be good at making chocolates but doesn't know anything about keeping accounts. She hasn't a clue whether her business is doing well or not. You tell her to give you the financial information relating to the last three months and you will draw up an income and expenditure account for each month, to show her whether her business is going forwards or backwards.

She hands you the notes below.

a   Use this information to produce **three** income and expenditure accounts, one for each month.

b   On each, say whether the expenditure of all purchases is less than, equal to, or more than income (all sales). For the first month, include Sue's capital as part of her 'income'.

c   Write a letter to Sue at her home address – 15 Chadburn Walk, Hightown, HG3 9KR – explaining why keeping and recording financial information is essential to a business. Enclose the accounts you have prepared.

<u>February</u>

Inherited £7000 from my aunt but spent £6000 on equipment, £400 on rent, £85 on a phone/answering machine, £300 on raw materials (chocolate etc!), £250 on chocolate boxes and wrapping paper, £100 on stationery, £200 on fittings (the place was bare when I rented it!) I also leased a small van. The payments are £200 per calendar month. Petrol cost me £25. Electricity is paid for on a budget account basis and costs me £25 a month.

However, I did sell 80 small boxes of chocolates at £3 each and 20 large boxes at £6 each. I also made a presentation pack which sold for £25 and did 40 Valentine's Day boxes which sold for £3.50 each.

<u>March</u>

I spent less this month! Paid my rent and for the van + the electric! Spent £500 on raw materials and another £250 on chocolate boxes and wrapping paper. My petrol costs were £29.
Sales were up! I sold 180 small boxes of chocolates but only 50 large ones. I sold one presentation pack but made some special chocolate boxes for Mother's Day – I made 100 and sold them for £5.50. I sold all but two – so I took them home, gave one to my mother and the other to the old lady next door!

<u>April</u>

Paid my usual monthly bills – rent, van and electric and received my first telephone bill for £42. Raw materials cost me £600 and chocolate boxes/wrapping paper £300. Petrol was £26 and I spent £12 on postage sending a special order to a friend in France. I also spent £27 on stationery.
I sold 260 small boxes of chocolates and 140 large

ones. I sold 10 presentation packs. All my special chocolate Easter eggs and Easter bunnies sold. The eggs sold for £4 each and the Easter bunnies for £1.25 each. I made 150 eggs and 100 Easter bunnies. I was quite glad when Easter was over! Oh, the order to France sold for £57!

Section 2

This section concentrates on the second evidence indicator for this element. When you have completed the work store it safely as it will contribute towards your final project for this element.

Make sure you complete this section of the project by the deadline date given to you by your tutor.

1 Collect **one** example of each of the following financial documents and label it clearly. Where possible obtain actual examples from home or from your work experience placement. Note that you may be restricted on the type of real examples you can obtain from business, and some companies will insist on marking these with the word 'sample'. If you are completely stuck for one or two, you could use examples photocopied from the back of this book – but these should be the **exception** – not the rule!

Purchase documents

a order placed
b purchase invoice
c credit note
d goods received note

Sales documents

e order received
f sales invoice
g delivery note

h sales credit note
i statement of account
j remittance advice

Receipt documents

k receipt
l cheque
m paying-in slip
n bank statement

2 Under each of the headings shown above, write a brief explanation of the purpose of each document.
3 Choose **any four** payment methods from those mentioned in this element and write a brief description of each one.

Type up your answers using a word processor.

Section 3

This section concentrates on the third evidence indicator for this element. When you have completed the work store it safely as it will contribute towards your final project for this element.

Make sure you complete this section of the project by the deadline date given to you by your tutor.

Type out a list of security checks which should be made by a business to protect financial documents and prevent fraud and theft. Include two or three paragraphs explaining the importance of security to a business organisation.

Final stage

Assemble all your accounts and typed documents together. Place these in a folder. Prepare a front sheet headed **Financial Transactions Project 1.** Add your name and the date. Add your front sheet to your folder. The work is now ready to give to your tutor.

Complete financial documents and explain financial recording

This element gives you practical experience in completing financial documents clearly and correctly, and calculating totals. It also covers budgets; it reviews why financial information must be recorded, and its links to both internal and external accounts are reinforced and expanded. A section is included that looks at the way in which information technology is used by businesses to record and monitor financial transactions.

After studying this element you should be able to:

- complete *purchase* and *sales documents* clearly and correctly, and calculate totals
- complete *payments* and *receipts documents* clearly and correctly, and calculate totals
- explain why *financial information* must be *recorded*

- identify and give examples of *information technology* which businesses use to record and monitor *financial information.*

Special note

Qualprint was the fictitious company discussed in the last element. You may remember that this is a small printing company which also sells stationery. In this element you will be asked to imagine you work at Qualprint and asked to complete financial documents for the owner, Chris Gaston. Throughout this element you will need copies of the blank financial documents included at the end of this book. *Do not mark or complete the original documents in this book – or you will not have enough to work with.* Your tutor will help you to photocopy the quantity you

Completing documents

Later in this element, and during the project which follows, you will be completing several types of document yourself. When you do, you must make sure that the information is *complete, accurate* and that you write as *neatly as possible.*

Ensuring documents are complete

A partly completed document is of no use to anyone. If someone else has to go back to do the rest of the work, they might as well have done it all in the first place! Most financial documents which are incomplete – a cheque without a signature or date, an invoice without all the items included, a paying-in slip with the cheques omitted – are useless. You may think this is obvious. Omissions that are less obvious include delivery charges and discounts, yet without them the document is both incomplete and inaccurate.

To help you, most financial documents have headings and spaces where information must be inserted. Always check carefully that nothing relevant has been missed out.

Accuracy

When you fill in financial documents, accuracy is vital. One incorrect figure, or even a decimal point in the wrong place, can cause a major problem. Think what would happen if a clerk processing an order for ready-mix concrete added an extra nought to the quantity ordered. There is a lot of difference between 10 cubic metres of concrete and 100 cubic metres! Similarly, if the clerk filled in the wrong address for a customer, the results could be very embarrassing!

Sometimes, documents are designed to provide duplicate information so that errors can be spotted. For example, when you write a cheque you have to write the amount of money in words *and* figures, and they must match. If they do not, the bank will not honour it. Orders often have space for a description of the goods required and a catalogue or serial number. Even though these safeguards exist, it does not mean that people who complete the documents can be any less careful.

Did you know?

A single postcode covers approximately fifteen houses, so if someone wrote your address completely wrongly the letter would probably still reach you, provided that the postman or neighbours know your name and house number. This is another example of how duplicating information can minimise problems!

Writing neatly

This may seem to be such a basic requirement that you wonder why it is mentioned now. After all, you have left school and are taking a qualification which will lead to either higher education or employment, so why are you being told to write clearly? The answer is simple: if you don't, people won't be able to read the information you record, and whilst they may be able to guess at the words, it is impossible to guess at figures as there are no clues to help!

If you write unclearly, and someone copies this information onto another document, a disaster could occur. Imagine the situation where you are asked to pass on a message about the balance in a friend's account. *You* write down £17.80 but it looks more like £77.80. Your friend happily writes out a cheque for £60 and then finds the account is overdrawn at the end of the month and the bank has charged £15 because of this!

Figure 4.41 An unexpected overdraft

Checking

When a document has been completed, it is important that the information which has been inserted is *checked*. Always go back over each item carefully and check it for accuracy. Some people find it difficult to check their own work because they are likely to assume that they did it properly the first time. A useful tip is to check the form in a different sequence to the way it was filled in, or check it out loud with someone else.

In some business situations, where large amounts of money are involved, several people may have to check that a document is correct. When you start work in business or are on work experience, people may ask you to complete a document and take it to them for checking. If you are nervous or uncertain, it is much better to ask someone to check your work rather than risk an embarrassing error. People will respect you for this, provided that you build up confidence to do things on your own.

Non-assessed activity

What do you think would happen if the following errors are made when documents are completed? Start by discussing the possibilities **as a group**, then **with your tutor.**

1 An order form is sent out with two items missing.
2 An invoice requesting payment is sent to the wrong customer.
3 A pay slip shows the wrong amount for overtime – £8 instead of £80.
4 A cheque is sent without being signed.
5 A receipt has the wrong year in the date.

Did you know?

If you start a document and make a mess of it you should start again. In business it would not be acceptable to send out anything which is illegible or crossed out and then corrected. If possible, try to type the majority of sales and purchases documents you produce, e.g. invoices, orders and statements. You are obviously expected to write those documents which are normally hand-written, e.g. cheques, petty cash vouchers and receipts.

Completing purchase documents

Element 4.1 described the four documents relating to purchase transactions:

- an order
- a purchase invoice
- a credit note
- a goods received note.

The **purchaser** would complete the order and the goods received note. Normally the purchase invoice and the credit note would be issued by the seller and **checked**, on receipt, by the purchaser.

The total amount of money spent on purchases during each month would be listed and then entered on the income and expenditure account.

Placing an order

1 Make sure you are allowed to order the goods in the first place!
2 Check that you have up-to-date information on the items you require – the catalogue number, price and the correct name and address of the supplier.
3 Find out the next order number.
4 Complete the form neatly and ask your supervisor for his or her signature as formal authorisation for the order.

Non-assessed activity

Practise completing a purchase order. Ask your tutor for a blank Qualprint order form. Chris Gaston wants to buy more Superlux card from Business Supplies. You can see the address of Business Supplies in Figure 4.42.

Write out an order, number 122/204, for six packs of white card (catalogue reference SL/7) and three packs of green card (catalogue reference SL/3). The unit price of the card is £10. Delivery should be as soon as possible. Use today's date.

Ask your tutor to check your purchase order and sign it, if it is correct. Put the order **in a safe place** – you can use it for reference when you complete your project.

Purchase invoices

When the purchase invoice arrives it must be correct in every detail. The items listed must be as ordered

and the prices should match those shown on the order and in the price list. No additional items should be included which had not been ordered, and even delivery charges should be known in advance. All totals must obviously be correct.

Non-assessed activity

Figure 4.42 is the purchase invoice received from Business Supplies. Ask your tutor for a photocopy and check that the invoice correct. If there are any errors then ring these **in pencil**. Check your finished work with your tutor.

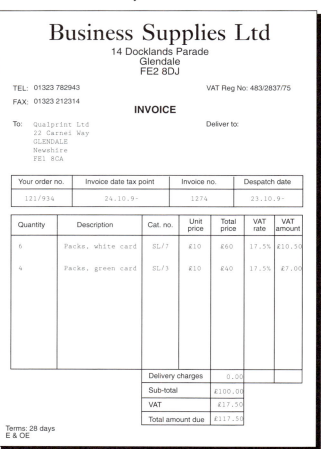

Figure 4.42 The invoice from Business Supplies Ltd

Credit notes

A credit note should contain the same information as the invoice. For instance, if VAT was levied on the goods, this must be shown on the credit note. The number of items listed should be checked against the number which were returned. The price must be the same.

Non-assessed activity

Business Supplies Ltd send you a credit note to compensate for the card for which you had been invoiced in error (above). Again, ask for a photocopy and ring any errors in **pencil.** Check your finished work with your tutor.

Business Supplies Ltd

14 Docklands Parade
Glendale
FE2 8DJ

TEL: 01323 782943   VAT Reg No: 483/2837/75

FAX: 01323 212314

To: Qualprint Ltd   **CREDIT NOTE**
     22 Carnei Way
     GLENDALE
     Newshire
     FE1 8CA

Credit Note No.	Invoice no.	Date
CR4862	1289	12 December 199-

Quantity	Description	Cat. no.	Unit price	Total price	VAT rate	VAT amount
1 pack	A4 Superlux Card. Green	SL/3	£10	£10	17.5%	£1.75
		Delivery charge	0.00			
		Sub-total	£10.00			
		VAT	£1.75			
		Total amount due	£11.75			

Terms: 28 days
E & OE

Figure 4.43 The credit note from Business Supplies Ltd

Goods received notes

When items are received they are booked in and a goods received note (GRN) is completed. This must

show all the items which were *actually* received – not necessarily those which were ordered! Sometimes they may include items delivered against *several* orders if these all arrive at the same time. On other occasions, when a delivery is split, two or more goods received notes may be issued against one order.

Non-assessed activity

Obtain a blank Qualprint goods received note from your tutor. Assume that today you received the following items from Business Supplies Ltd on delivery note 96/745.

9 packs Superlux card – red Ref SL/2, Order 122/186
6 packs Superlux card – white Ref SL/7, Order 122/204
3 packs Superlux card – green Ref SL/3, Order 122/204

None of the goods is damaged. Your next GRN number is 1105. Make out a GRN to show the goods which have been received.

Check your finished work with your tutor. If the document has no errors, file this safely for reference when you are doing your final project.

Did you know?

A record of all purchases made is entered in the **purchase ledger** under each particular supplier. It is possible to see at a glance how much is owing to each supplier. The **total** amount of purchases is shown in the **general ledger.** This book also records any returns which have been made – for which credit notes will have been received. The difference between the balances in the two is the net value of all goods bought over a certain period, usually each month.

Non-assessed activity

During March, purchase invoices were received by Qualprint for the following amounts: £271.20, £584.30, £22, £16.50, £840.50, £341. In addition two credit notes were received – one for £14 and one for £52.20. What was the net value of all purchases during March?

Completing sales documents

The sales documents you may be asked to complete or check include:

- orders received
- sales invoices
- delivery notes
- sales credit notes
- statements of account
- remittance advice.

You will usually **check** orders received and complete all the other documents.

Orders received

It is important that you check that:

- you can read and understand the order
- the catalogue references match the descriptions
- the descriptions are given in full and no essential information is missing
- the prices are current (i.e. up to date).

If you were involved in making up the order for despatch, your next job would be to check that the goods were in stock.

Non-assessed activity

The order shown in Figure 4.44 has been received from Hightown College. Assuming that the catalogue references are correct and the prices are up to date, can you find **two** items of essential information which are missing from the order?

Check your answers with your tutor.

Sales invoices

The main components of an invoice are covered in Element 4.1 (page 420). Completing most sections is quite easy. The part you still have to learn is how to calculate an invoice total.

Non-assessed activity

Look at the examples of invoices in Figure 4.45. Both are for student brochures printed for Hightown College. However, the total amount due in each case is different. Can you see why?

Calculating invoice totals

The difference is in the terms offered and therefore the amount of VAT. It is important that you

Figure 4.44 An order from Hightown College

remember that the total amount shown on an invoice will vary, depending on whether **cash discount** is allowed. Cash discount is an incentive offered by suppliers to encourage their customers to pay promptly. A certain amount is deducted if the buyer pays within a certain period.

Basic invoices

- Enter all the items.
- Total the goods.
- Calculate VAT owing at the current rate.
- Add on any delivery charges.
- Calculate VAT on delivery charges.

The total of these items – goods, VAT on goods, delivery charges and VAT on delivery – is the total amount due.

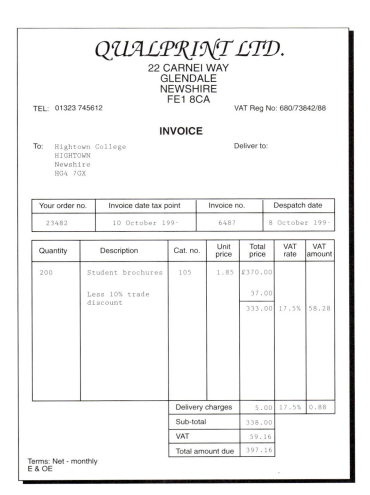

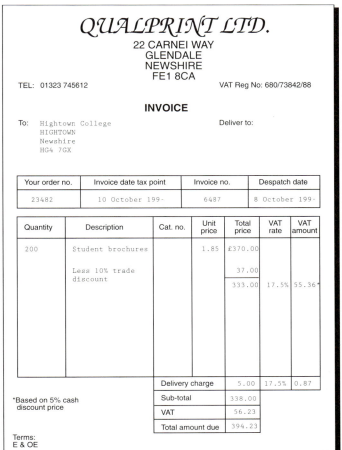

Figure 4.45 Sample invoices

Invoice with trade discount

See the first invoice in Figure 4.45.

- Enter all the items.
- Total the goods.
- Deduct trade discount.
- Calculate VAT owing at the current rate.
- Add on any delivery charges.
- Calculate VAT on delivery charges.

The total of these items – goods less discount, plus VAT, plus delivery charges, plus VAT on delivery – is the total amount due.

Invoice with cash discount

See the second invoice in Figure 4.45.

In this case it is assumed that the buyer will want to pay promptly to take advantage of the additional discount. VAT is therefore calculated on the price after all discounts have been deducted.

- Enter all the items.
- Total the goods.
- Deduct trade discount.
- Deduct cash discount.
- Calculate VAT on *this* figure.
- Add on any delivery charges.
- Calculate VAT on delivery charges.

The total of these items – goods less *all* discounts, plus VAT, plus delivery charges, plus VAT on delivery – is the total amount due.

455

Important points to note

- VAT is levied on the goods *and* any delivery charge.
- If the goods are supplied with cash discount available, it is assumed that the buyer will want to take advantage of this. In the second invoice shown above, if the buyer paid within ten days he would pay £333 – £16.65 (5 per cent) = £316.35 for the goods. The VAT is calculated on *this* figure – 17.5 per cent of £316.35 = £55.36 – even though the discounted figure is not shown on the invoice.
- The VAT for the delivery charge must then be added to the VAT for the goods to calculate the total amount of VAT.

You must remember that if the invoice is settled within ten days then the amount owing is:

- the discounted price of £316.35
- plus VAT of £55.36
- plus £5.87 for delivery and VAT.

Therefore the total due is £377.58.

If the invoice is settled *after* ten days then the full amount for the goods is due but the VAT figure *does not* change. The buyer therefore pays the total amount shown on the invoice of £394.23.

Non-assessed activity

For this activity you will need **four** blank Qualprint invoice forms.

Qualprint has undertaken the job of printing 2000 leaflets for the college at a price of 35p per leaflet. The college order number was 23502 and the invoice number is 6501. The invoice date and despatch date should both be tomorrow. The address of the college is shown in Figures 4.44 and 4.45.

1 Make out an invoice assuming no discount is allowed and no delivery charge is levied by Qualprint. However, VAT is charged on the goods sold.

   Check your work with your tutor.

2 Make out a second invoice assuming no discount is allowed but Qualprint charge £10 for delivery. Don't forget to add on the VAT for delivery as well as VAT for the goods.

   Check your work with your tutor.

3 Make out a third invoice assuming that Qualprint allow the college ten per cent trade discount. The delivery charge this time is £8.

4 Make out a final invoice assuming the terms are 'five per cent cash discount if the invoice is settled within ten days'. In this case don't forget that you will calculate VAT on the total discounted price (even though the cash discounted price isn't shown on the invoice). Delivery is £8.

   How much will Qualprint receive if Hightown College pays its account promptly?

Check all your invoices with your tutor. Label them clearly so that you can refer to them when you are undertaking your evidence project and file them safely.

Delivery notes

Remember that in business a delivery note is often made out at the same time as the invoice. Special multi-sets are used which simply blank out sections not required on some documents. Basically the only difference between a delivery note and an invoice is the inclusion of prices. No amounts of money are shown on a delivery note.

Non-assessed activity

The leaflets are ready to be delivered to the college. Look back at all the information you have already been given and refer to this to complete a blank Qualprint delivery note. Bear in mind that there is no catalogue number because the leaflets were a special order.

Figure 4.46 The order is delivered

Check your finished work with your tutor. Then file your example document safely for reference when you do your project.

Sales credit notes

Credit notes are sent to companies to re-adjust their account when they have been overcharged on an invoice. The basic rule is that the terms on the credit note must be identical to those on the original invoice. Therefore, if no discount was allowed on the original invoice, no discount is allowed on the credit note. If ten per cent trade discount was allowed on the invoice, this must be shown on the credit note. The same applies to cash discount.

'Carriage' or 'refunded delivery charges' may sometimes be shown. This means the supplier is refunding the delivery charges originally paid by the buyer. This is likely to be the case if the error was made by the supplier, or if the goods were faulty. A way round this is for the replacement goods to be sent free of charge.

Remember that VAT must also be refunded, both on the goods and on any delivery charges. Look back to the example credit note in Element 4.1 on page 413 which shows how this is included.

Non-assessed activity

Assume that Hightown College have returned 200 leaflets because they hadn't been printed properly. They want their account to be credited by the correct amount. Ask your tutor to provide you with some blank Qualprint credit notes.

Make out a credit note for the amount the college was overcharged. Use the same information as before. Your credit note number is CR 2910.

- The first time, assume there was no discount at all and no delivery charges.
- Now make out another credit note. Assume there was ten per cent trade discount and Chris Gaston has also told you to refund £2 of the delivery charge as a gesture of goodwill.
- Finally make out a credit note to match the terms given for cash discount, i.e. five per cent in ten days. This time Chris Gaston is refunding £4 of the delivery charge to the college. (Don't forget the VAT!)

Check your completed credit notes with your tutor. Then file them safely for later reference.

Statements of account

A statement of account is simply a list of all the transactions which have taken place in a month. Many students have problems with these because they do not remember to keep adjusting the balance figure on every line!

Look back at the statement in Figure 4.21 on page 423, which shows the transactions between Qualprint and Glendale Borough Council. The statement starts by showing the balance carried forward from the previous month. If there had been no money owing at the start of the month, this line would have been omitted. Then an entry follows for each transaction. Note how the balance figure changes on each line to take account of the latest transaction. The last entry is the balance owing.

Statements are usually sent at the end of the month, therefore the usual date on a statement is the last day of the month.

Non-assessed activity

Ask your tutor for a blank Qualprint statement. Make out a statement, dated for the last working day of this month, to Hightown College. The account number is 520.

- Assume the balance carried forward from last month is £65.
- Add the invoice for the leaflets. Use the one which showed ten per cent trade discount and a delivery charge of £8 (i.e. the third one you made out).
- Add the credit note you made out which also shows ten per cent trade discount and £2 of the delivery charge refunded (i.e. the second one you made out).
- Finally, Hightown College had a further 1500 leaflets printed yesterday at the same price. The invoice number was 6521.

Check your statement with your tutor. If it is correct, file it for reference.

Remittance advice

Some organisations issue a remittance advice to the customer so that it can be returned with their payment. Accounts staff can then see the reason for the payment because all the key information relating to the transaction is printed on the remittance advice form.

Look back at the remittance advice on Figure 4.24 on page 423 to refresh your memory about the information it contains. Remember that the last part is for the customer to complete.

Non-assessed activity

Qualprint issue remittance advice forms. Obtain a copy of the blank form at the back of this book. Make it out to Hightown College to link with the statement you have just completed.

Ask your tutor to check it, and then file it safely.

Did you know?

A record of all sales made is entered in the **sales ledger** under the names of individual customers. It is possible to see at a glance how much is owed by each person who is allowed to buy goods on credit. This is very important information because people who do not pay their bills promptly must be sent reminders. If they still fail to pay, legal action may be taken against them. Certainly they wouldn't be allowed any more goods.

The **total** amount of sales is shown in the **general ledger.** This book also records information on any items which have been returned to Qualprint and for which credit notes will have been issued. The difference between the balances in the two is the **net** value of all goods sold over a certain period, usually each month.

Non-assessed activity

During March, sales invoices sent by Qualprint were for the following amounts: £516, £243.15, £93, £22.50, £1295.40, £680. In addition two credit notes were issued – one for £12 and one for £35.20. What was the net value of all sales during March?

Optional evidence assignment

This activity can be used to help you assemble documents produced previously into a format where they can be used as additional evidence to your main project. They can then count as supplementary evidence towards the following parts of the scheme.

PC 1: Complete purchase and sales documents clearly and correctly and calculate totals

Range: Purchase documents: orders placed, purchase invoice, credit note, goods received note

Sales documents: orders received, sales invoice, delivery note, sales credit note, statement of account, remittance advice

Core skills: Communication, Application of number

1 Assemble copies of the sample documents you have either written or checked, in the order stated above in the range statements.
2 Write a brief paragraph clearly showing the link between all these documents and the internal accounts of the company.

Completing payments documents

You have already learnt about one type of payment document – a cheque – in Element 4.1. Two other types of documents are used in relation to making payments, so there are three you may have to complete. These are:

■ pay slips
■ cheques
■ petty cash vouchers.

It is unlikely that you will be asked to make out a pay slip, since they are usually printed by computer. However, you should certainly know how to check one – if only your own!

Petty cash vouchers can be completed by all staff, as they are used when someone has paid out a small amount of money on behalf of the organisation and wants to be reimbursed.

Pay slips

You may find some of the financial documents used in business a bit uninspiring or even boring! The one which you will *always* find interesting, however, is your **pay slip** – sometimes called a **pay advice note.**

This section explains how pay slips are made up. Element 2.2 covers wages, taxation and National Insurance. If you haven't already worked through that element, you could turn to pages 195–99 now, to note the main points before you continue to read this section.

You should know that:

■ people are normally paid either weekly or monthly

- the total amount people earn is known as **gross pay**
- **deductions** are made for income tax, National Insurance, pensions, charitable contributions, social clubs etc.
- the amount of money a person actually receives, after deductions, is known as **net pay.**

A pay slip is either enclosed in a pay packet, for people paid in cash or by cheque, or given to people whose money is paid directly into a bank account. Today, most people are paid by this method.

It is important that you can understand your pay slip – otherwise you won't be able to check it to see if a mistake has been made.

All pay slips contain the employee's name and usually an individual number. In most organisations, employees are given a unique pay reference number which is particularly useful for computer records. Large organisations will also include the name of the department, which may again be shortened to a simple reference number. The pay slip will also state the **pay period** – this may be a month or a week number. This is the week in the tax year in which payment is being made.

Figure 4.47 A pay slip can be a very exciting financial document!

Did you know?

The tax year is also known as the **fiscal year** and runs from 6 April one year to 5 April the following year.

Calculating income tax

Pay slips are made out by the wages department, which is also responsible for calculating the income tax and National Insurance payable by each employee. You will be pleased to know that income tax is not payable on all your earnings; the amount of your **taxable income** and your **free pay** (i.e. the amount you can earn before paying tax) will depend on your allowances. The Inland Revenue notifies taxpayers of their PAYE code number in a **notice of coding** and also informs their employers.

The wages department uses the code number to look up the amount of free pay for the employee each week or month by referring to **tax tables** issued by the Inland Revenue. This amount is then deducted from the total gross pay to date, to find the taxable pay. Another set of tables gives how much tax is due on the taxable pay to date, up to certain weekly or monthly limits.

The wages department records the information on a **tax deduction card** (called a P11) for each employee. If an employee changes jobs during the year the wages clerk prepares a P45 which gives details of the employee's code number, total pay to date, tax due and tax paid to date. This is given to the new employer so that tax can continue to be calculated correctly.

Did you know?

- An employee without a code number is put on emergency coding until everything is sorted out. On this code *more* tax is deducted than is necessary. It is therefore important that anyone on emergency coding completes a coding claim as soon as possible and sends this to the Inland Revenue so that the correct tax code can be allocated as soon as possible.
- If you start work and haven't got a P45, your new employer will ask you to complete the form P46. This gives the tax office vital information they need quickly to try to sort out your tax code.
- A tax code will change if an employee's circumstances change and these affect the allowances to which they are entitled. Because there may be some delay before the tax code is adjusted, this can mean a person receiving a tax rebate in one particular week or month. This will put things straight if too much tax has been deducted in previous weeks.

Calculating National Insurance

This is also done by referring to a set of tables. Contributions are payable by both employees and employers, and the tables state the correct amount to be deducted according to the gross pay. There are different tables if the employee has contracted out or not contracted out of the State Earnings Related Pension Scheme – SERPS. The deductions for National Insurance are also entered on the P11.

The job of the wages department

It is the responsibility of the wages department to prepare:

- the individual deductions working sheet for each employee (P11)
- the individual pay advice slip for each employee
- the payroll for the organisation.

They will also obtain money for cash payments and notify the bank about pay to be transferred directly to employees' bank accounts under the BACS system, which is discussed in Element 4.1.

Every month the tax and National Insurance collected is sent to the Inland Revenue. Once a year the wages department completes an **end of year return** for each employee. This gives details of all pay received, tax deductions, NI contributions and statutory sick pay or statutory maternity pay received during the last year. The employee receives a copy – known as the P60.

The P60 is really an alternative version of the final pay slip for the year. This is because, on *each* pay slip, there are details of current earnings *as well as* information on total pay received and total tax paid so far in that tax year.

Did you know?

- Some employees don't earn enough to be liable for either income tax or National Insurance. This would be the case, for instance, if you do a Saturday job whilst you are a student. In this case you must sign a **student exemption form** when you start work.
- Some organisations operate a **payroll giving scheme.** If you join this you can agree to donate a certain amount to charity each week or month, and this amount will not be taxed.
- Other employees may choose to save money every

pay period out of their salary by subscribing to a Save As You Earn (SAYE) scheme.

Non-assessed activity

1 Bill Gibson, a driver at Qualprint, is paid on an hourly basis. His standard rate is £5.20 an hour and he receives time and half for Saturday work (i.e. his hourly rate plus half as much again) and double time for Sunday work.
 a Last week he worked 38 hours at standard rate, four hours on Saturday and three hours on Sunday. What was his gross pay for the week?
 b His deductions for the week amounted to £72.50. What was his net pay for the week?

2 Karen Sharples is employed on the stationery counter at Qualprint. She is paid monthly directly into her bank account. Because this is a fixed amount there are no entries under 'hours and rate'. Her latest pay slip is shown below. Karen has the following queries. Can you help her?
 a Karen's tax code has recently changed and she has now discovered she is paying less tax than before. Can you suggest what may have happened?
 b Karen is thinking of joining the payroll giving scheme and contributing £5 to charity each week. She wants to know if this amount will be taxed.
 c Karen has heard that some organisations which operate a monthly scheme pay their employees twelve times a year and others pay them thirteen times a year (e.g. every four weeks). Her annual salary is £9300. How many times a year is she paid?
 d Karen has noticed that the difference between her total pay to date and her taxable pay to date is

PAY ADVICE			Pay period	May 199-	
Emp no.	Employee name		Dept	Tax code	
15	KAREN SHARPLES		A1	325 L	
Pay and allowances			NI no BD 301048C	Method of payment BACS	
Hrs	Rate (£)	Amount (£)	Deductions		Total pay to date 1550.00
			Item	Amt (£)	
			Tax	134.50	Tax to date 274.50
			NI	32.50	NI to date 64.40
			Social fund	2.00	
			SAYE	10.00	Taxable pay to date 1010.00
GROSS PAY	£775.00		Total deductions	£187.70	net pay £583.30

Figure 4.48 Karen Sharples' pay slip

over £500. What does this figure represent?

e Karen thinks that the wages department have made a mistake on her pay slip when they calculated her net pay. Do you agree? If so, obtain a blank Qualprint pay advice form, copy out the information neatly, but this time enter the **correct** net pay figure. File the pay slip safely for future reference.

Did you know?

Although you may be asked to complete a pay slip from information you have been given, actually calculating income tax and National Insurance is a specialist job for which you need to be trained. In most organisations today computers are used to calculate wages and salaries and the pay slips and payroll are printed automatically.

Cheques

Cheques are discussed in detail in Element 4.1. In this section you will learn how to write out cheques. However, remember that it is very unlikely that you will be asked to sign one on behalf of the company!

Needless to say, all the details on a cheque must be written clearly and accurately. In addition, most banks prefer them to be written in blue or black ink.

- Write the date in full, i.e. 30 January 199– rather than 30.1.199–.
- Write the payee's name clearly on the top line. If it is a long name then keep your writing small to fit it in! If the cheque is made out to a person rather than an organisation, most banks prefer the name to be written in full and do not require the title. Therefore 'Peter Stevens' is better than 'Mr P. Stevens'.
- Start writing the amount to the extreme left of the lines, to make alterations or additions difficult if not impossible.
- Some people add the word 'only' after writing the amount, especially if there are no pence, e.g. 'three hundred pounds only'.
- Note that you can write the amount of pence in figures throughout.
- Cancel any blank spaces remaining by drawing lines through them.
- Remember **not** to sign it.

Non-assessed activity

Using copies of the blank cheques at the end of this book, make out **four** cheques, ready for Chris Gaston to sign. Date them all with today's date. If you want to look back at an example of a completed cheque, one was shown in Element 4.1 on page 425.

1 Data Services Ltd – £247.25
2 Glendale Property Services – £600
3 Newshire County Council – £750
4 British Telecom – £154.70

Ask your tutor to sign each cheque **only** if it has been made out correctly. Then file them safely for reference.

Petty cash vouchers

Businesses normally keep a small amount of cash available to pay for small items such as milk bills, taxi fares, etc. The money is kept in a lockable petty cash tin and a receipt is obtained for each payment. In larger businesses someone in authority, e.g. a manager, may have to approve the expenditure to make sure that the system is not abused. The authorisation form – called a **petty cash voucher** – and the receipt are clipped together and kept safely.

In most organisations petty cash is used:

- to pay for small items which would not be paid for by cheque (e.g. magazines for reception, coffee, tea, sugar, etc.)
- to reimburse (pay back) members of staff who have paid for an item out of their own pockets (e.g. a taxi fare)
- to pay service people who prefer their accounts settling immediately in cash (e.g. the milkman and the window cleaner)
- to pay for emergency requirements where the goods are not normally kept in stock, e.g. a jiffy bag to protect a special parcel
- to pay for special items of postage, e.g. the fee for a registered letter.

Did you know?

A petty cash voucher is a receipt showing how money has been spent. Businesses normally have an upper limit on the amount of money that can be spent on any purchase through the petty cash system, e.g. £10. Anything above this amount must be bought using a purchase order form.

461

| PETTY CASH VOUCHER | NO | 53 | | Date | 12 Feb 199- |
| Name | | | | Dept | |

Purpose, attach all receipts & invoices	TOTAL incl. VAT	VAT	Net excl. VAT
Milk for office	3 75		
The sum of in words as far to the left as possible	£ 3 75	£	£

Approved by *A. Jones*   date *12 Feb 199-*
Received by *W Smith*   date *12 Feb 199-*

Figure 4.49 A petty cash voucher

At the end of a given period (usually each month) the petty cashier will add up the petty cash expenditure, using a special **analysis page.** This breaks down the expenditure into different categories, e.g. travel, stationery, office sundries etc. This enables the manager to see how much is being spent in each area. The total spent must be balanced against the totals on all the vouchers which have been issued.

The money spent is usually reimbursed by the company cashier, so that the **petty cash float** is back to its original total at the beginning of the next accounting period. This is known as the **imprest system.** The float can vary from as much as £500 to as little as £20, depending upon the size of the company and the type of expenditure allowed under the petty cash system.

The job of the petty cashier

There is usually a petty cashier in charge of petty cash, who is responsible for ensuring that:

- all expenditure from petty cash is only for authorised payments
- all expenditure is recorded accurately
- there are no discrepancies between recorded expenditure and the amount actually paid out
- security procedures for keeping petty cash are correctly followed
- the petty cash book balances at the end of the month.

The voucher system

To make sure that only correct amounts are paid out, petty cash vouchers are used to record the money spent. All vouchers are numbered and should be issued in *numerical* order.

- The vouchers are usually issued *before* the money is spent.
- Junior staff must obtain authorisation *before* spending any money on behalf of the company or claiming any money from petty cash. Senior members of staff may spend money first and then present the petty cash voucher for reimbursement.
- An official receipt should be attached to the voucher as proof of the amount of money spent.
- Vouchers for multiple items must be checked to ensure the addition is correct.
- Completed vouchers must be filed safely, in numerical or date order.
- Any claims for unauthorised expenditure or discrepancies should be referred to the petty cashier. No payment should be made until the matter has been sorted out.

Did you know?

When a company is VAT registered, any VAT paid on petty cash items *must* be listed separately on the vouchers. This is because the total amount of VAT which has been spent can be reclaimed from HM Customs and Excise at a later date.

Non-assessed activity

Complete **three** petty cash vouchers (using copies of forms at the back of this book) for the following items of expenditure. Number these consecutively starting at 301 and use today's date.

Remember that you must enter the VAT in its own column if it is shown separately.

1 Flowers for reception £13.50.
2 Taxi fare £3.50 plus train fare of £12.00.
3 Stationery £24.00 + £4.20 VAT = £28.20.

Sign the vouchers and ask your tutor to authorise them. Then file them safely.

Balancing petty cash

If you are responsible for keeping petty cash vouchers, at regular intervals you should add up the vouchers to find out the total amount paid out and *deduct* this from the amount of the petty cash float. You should then check that this figure agrees with the amount of money remaining in the petty cash tin.

At the end of a fixed period, e.g. a week or month, the petty cashier will record the items in the petty cash book, balance it and restore the **imprest**. This means that the amount held in petty cash will be brought back up to the full amount allocated for the petty cash float.

Did you know?

Occasionally, because of a large amount withdrawn or a few 'emergencies', the amount in petty cash may run low before the imprest is due to be restored. If this occurs, the petty cashier should be notified immediately.

Non-assessed activity

1 In each of the following cases, work out how much money should be remaining in the petty cash tin on the date given. Identify any case(s) where the amount remaining is too low and should be reported to the petty cashier.

a 16 November – imprest amount £100, vouchers paid out to date: £16.50, £4.85, £2.00, 85p, £18.32

b 12 December – imprest amount £50, vouchers paid out to date: £6.58, £3.20, 60p, 45p, £14.20, £3.48, 98p

c 16 January – imprest amount £350, vouchers paid out to date: £64.20, £22, 75p, £23.20, £16.80, £85.43, £22.97, 56p, £40, £28.30.

2 Paul is in charge of petty cash at Qualprint and has the key to the tin. Mary, who has just started work in the Sales department, asks for £15 to buy three ribbons for their computer printer. At Qualprint the petty cash limit is £10. **As a group,** discuss what Paul should say to Mary and what Mary should do to get her ribbons.

Did you know?

All payments are recorded in **books of account.** In the cases above, some entries would be recorded in the **cash book** because payments represent a deduction from the money in the bank or the money in cash at the company. The cash book is often divided into analysis columns so that expenditure on different items can be seen easily – so the total amount of money paid out on wages is easy to find out, as is the amount paid out on petty cash.

Payments by cheque may be for purchases which have previously been recorded in the **purchase ledger.** The total amount paid out for purchases during the month would be recorded in the **purchases·account** in the **general ledger.** Cheques made out for expenses such as heating, lighting, rent and so on will also be recorded in the general ledger.

Non-assessed activity

1 During March, Qualprint settled the following suppliers' accounts – £235, £60, £271.20, £16.50, £584.30.

a How much was paid out on purchases altogether?

b Discuss **with your tutor** why the total amount paid is not identical to the actual orders placed by Qualprint during March.

2 Three staff are employed at Qualprint besides Chris Gaston, the owner. Paul Turner runs the print room and Karen Sharples runs the stationery counter. Bill Gibson is the driver and also helps out in the print room.

Paul Turner receives a monthly salary of £1500, Karen Sharples earns £9300 a year and Bill Gibson receives £5.20 an hour for a standard 38-hour week. What is Qualprint's monthly wage bill?

Did you know?

Chris Gaston wants to take money out of the business for his own use. Because Qualprint is a limited company he will also be paid a salary. This is because the company also employs him – as well as the other staff. If Qualprint was not a limited company, any money drawn out by Chris Gaston would be called **drawings.** In both cases the money taken out obviously reduces the money at the bank.

Completing receipt documents

The four basic receipt documents related to financial transactions are:

- receipts (either issued by a till or hand-written)
- cheques received
- paying-in slips
- bank statements.

You may be expected to write out a receipt or complete a paying-in slip. Rarely will you be asked to make out a cheque you are receiving (although it is possible – see below)! The bank statement is pre-printed by the bank but has to be checked in several ways and is a very useful source of financial information.

Receipts

Cash registers and electronic tills produce receipts automatically. Occasionally, receipts need to be made out by hand. Look back at the receipt shown in Element 4.1, page 434, to see how this was completed.

Non-assessed activity

You have received the following payments in cash. Make out a receipt for each one, starting with number 101. Use copies of the receipt forms at the back of this book. Use today's date and don't forget to sign them.

1	Mr A McFarlane	£45.00
2	Miss A Petersen	£125.60
3	Mr H Resinger	£204.05
4	Ms V Nayyar	£74.80

Cheques

You won't usually be asked to complete a cheque you are receiving – although this could occur. An example is when the cheque is being printed automatically by an electronic till (so the keys you press determine the amount showing on the cheque). Another example would be if a customer asked you to make out the cheque on his or her behalf – for example a customer who has very poor sight or has an arm in plaster! All you would then do is to point to the line where they had to sign the cheque.

More usually you will be asked to go through incoming cheques to make sure there are no errors. A cheque will not be acceptable if:

■ the date is more than six months ago, or in the future
■ the name of the payee is wrong or misspelled
■ the amount in words is different from that in figures
■ the signature does not match that on the cheque guarantee card
■ alterations have been made and not initialled.

Figure 4.50 Some customers may ask you to help them make out a cheque

In addition, a cheque will only be covered by a guarantee card if the card has not expired (check the expiry date), the amount is within that specified on the guarantee card, and the bank sort code number is the same as that printed on the cheque.

It is up to the receiver to write the cheque card serial number on the back of the cheque. Most organisations would also expect you to initial the back of the cheque too, and some organisations also ask for the customer's address.

Did you know?

A post-dated cheque is one which is made out for a later date than the date on which payment is being made. Most companies refuse to accept them.

Non-assessed activity

You are helping out on the stationery counter at Qualprint today. What would you do in each of the following cases?

1 The cheque in Figure 4.51 has been handed to you by a girl of about 16. She is obviously not used to writing out cheques. Assuming the amount for which it is made out is correct, what advice would you give her for writing out cheques in future?

Figure 4.51 An incorrectly-completed cheque

2   When you ask her for her guarantee card you notice it is not signed. What would you tell her? Why?
3   Chris Gaston considers that the amount of £50 on most cheque guarantee cards is too low. He is therefore prepared to accept cheques made out for up to £100 provided that the customer can offer other adequate identification. List **three** forms of identification which you think would be acceptable and give your reasons in each case.
4   A customer offers you a cheque drawn on a 'special savings account'. On the bottom of the cheque are printed the words 'Minimum amount £100'. The customer has made out this cheque for £90 and has no other cheque book or credit cards with her. What would you do?

Paying-in slips

You may be asked to complete a paying-in slip if you are cashing up money received before it is taken to the bank. It is obviously important that the paying-in slip is correct. A minor error may be corrected by the bank cashier, but if you make a serious mistake the paying-in slip will not be acceptable. In this case the person who has taken the money to the bank will simply be given everything back so that the error can be corrected!

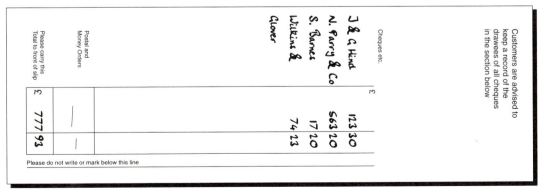

Figure 4.52 A correctly-completed paying-in slip

If someone has just walked for ten minutes through pouring rain to bank the money, you are unlikely to be popular if the error was yours!

Paying-in slips look much more complicated than they really are. The most important thing to remember is that any cash must be listed in denominations. Also it is the **amount** of money in each denomination you enter on the paying-in slip, **not** the quantity of notes. Therefore $8 \times £20 = £160$. Don't be tempted to write 8 or 80!

To help you while you make out your first paying-in slip, the paying-in slip you saw first in Element 4.1 is reprinted in Figure 4.52. Go through each stage of this with your tutor to refresh your memory.

Non-assessed activity

Complete a paying-in slip for Qualprint and date it today. Use a photocopy of the form at the back of this book. Your takings are:

Three cheques – £185.45 (Mr A Brand), £63.60 (Mr J Long) and £1060.00 (Vale Engineering Ltd)

Cash –

1 × £50 note	17 × 20p coins
15 × £20 notes	6 × 10p coins
5 × £10 notes	15 × 5p coins
16 × £5 notes	13 × 2p coins
13 × £1 coins	3 × 1p coins
22 × 50p coins	

After your tutor has checked it, file your completed paying-in slip for future reference.

Bank statements

It is safe to assume that you will never be asked to write out a bank statement. Even bank staff don't do this: all statements today are produced by computer. For that reason it may seem unnecessary even to check a statement – after all, computers cannot calculate things wrongly. Or can they? All computers can do is to follow instructions. If the instruction is wrong then there will be a mistake. For instance:

- an amount may have been keyed in wrongly
- an amount may have been missed off
- details may be included from somebody else's account, particularly if it is someone with the same name.

Checking a statement

When a business receives a statement, all the entries need to be checked.

- Deposits must be checked against the entries in the paying-in book. If some deposits have been made just before the statement was printed then they may not appear.
- Withdrawals should be checked against the cheque counterfoils. It is usual to tick each cheque counterfoil to denote the amount has been withdrawn. In some cases people do not pay cheques into their accounts immediately. In this case, there will be outstanding cheques which have not yet been presented.

Non-assessed activity

1 Without looking at the notes, study the sample statement given in Element 4.1, page 437. For each of the following entries, explain what each item represents and why it needs to be included on the statement.
a bank account number
b statement date
c withdrawals
d deposits
e balance
f date of transaction
g cheque number
h paying-in slip number
i the letters 'OD'.

2 Chris Gaston notes that on the 30 April he paid £1304.20 into the account but this is not shown on his statement. There are also two outstanding cheques for £30.26 and £74.18 which have still not been presented for payment.

How much money has Qualprint in its account on the day Chris **receives** the statement?

Did you know?

All payments into the bank are recorded in the **cash book.** Similarly all payments in cash made to the company will be recorded in the cash book. All organisations are reluctant to keep much cash on the premises for security reasons. Therefore, surplus cash will be banked. The cash book will show a transfer of money from cash to bank. Equally, if cash is withdrawn from the bank for any reason, the transfer will be shown in the opposite direction.

Optional evidence assignment

This activity can be used to help you assemble documents produced previously into a format where they can be used as additional evidence to your main project. They can then count as supplementary evidence towards the following parts of the scheme.

PC 2: Complete payments and receipts documents clearly and correctly and calculate totals

Range: Payments documents: pay slip, cheque, petty cash voucher

Receipt documents: receipt, cheque, paying-in slip, bank statement

Core skills: Communication, Application of number

1 Assemble copies of the sample documents you have either written or checked, in the order stated above in the range statements.
2 Write a brief paragraph which shows clearly the link between all these documents and the internal accounts of the company.

Evidence assignment

At this stage your tutor may wish you to start work on the first section of your final project. If so, turn to page 476. This will give you all the evidence you need to prove to the external verifier that you have undertaken the work required to fulfil the first evidence indicator for this element.

Financial information

The fact that financial information is transferred to internal accounts and then used to compile external annual accounts was discussed in Element 4.1. This section develops the information you were given there, to help you to see more clearly the relationship between the two, and the importance of financial recording.

Internal accounts

Many accounts books have been mentioned in this element, as well as in the previous one. The books or **ledgers** are prepared to show at a glance the following information.

Purchases

- the quantity and value of purchases
- the amount spent on purchases
- money outstanding to suppliers.

Sales

- the quantity and value of sales
- the amount received for goods sold
- money outstanding from customers.

Stock

- the quantity and value of unsold stock kept by the company.

Payments

- the amount of money paid out in wages
- the amount of money paid out on raw materials
- the amount of money paid out on overheads and consumables.

Receipts

- the amount of money received
- the reason it has been received.

Cash and bank

- the current bank balance
- the amount of money in cash held by the company.

All these internal account books give essential information to the owners of the business and enable them to keep a close eye on the financial health of the company and take immediate action if necessary.

Did you know?

The term **cash flow** means the flow of money in and out of the business. If more money is flowing out than in, then the company will get into difficulties. However, this might not be because it isn't doing any business. If customers were late paying Qualprint and yet suppliers were insisting on prompt payment, Qualprint may have a cash flow crisis. In the case of a small business which deals with one or two large customers, the business may be forced into bankruptcy if the customers fail to pay.

External annual accounts

As discussed in Element 4.1, these comprise the **profit and loss account** and the **balance sheet.** However, before the profit and loss account is worked out, the accountants will also prepare a **trading account.**

- The trading account shows the gross profit made by the company.
- The profit and loss account shows the net profit made by the company.
- The balance sheet gives a snapshot of the company's finances on the date it is prepared.

The trading account

At the end of the year, Qualprint will have sold some goods, bought goods and have some goods (stock) left over. The accountants will obtain the information they need on purchases and sales from the ledgers mentioned above. Qualprint will do a stock inventory to find out how much stock has not been sold. When everything has been counted its value is calculated – usually at the price the stock cost.

The formula for **gross profit** is

sales – (purchases – unsold stock) = gross profit

Remember that in any formula where there are brackets you must work out this part first. If Qualprint's purchases this year were £125 000 and the value of unsold stock was £25 000, then the cost of the goods they actually sold would be £100 000.

If Qualprint's sales had been £170 000 for the year, then the gross profit would be

£170 000 – £100 000 = £70 000.

The profit and loss account

This account starts with the gross profit figure. From this is deducted all the expenses incurred by Qualprint over the year. The difference is the net profit. Therefore, if expenses had been £45 000, the **net profit** would have been £25 000. This is the surplus at the end of the year, which can be distributed to shareholders and/or reinvested in the business.

It is this figure, not the gross profit, on which Income Tax (in the case of sole traders and partnerships) and Corporation Tax (in the case of limited companies) is calculated.

Non-assessed activity

Work out the gross profit for Qualprint if sales for the year are £248 000, purchases are £170 000 and the unsold stock had cost £22 000.

Now work out what the net profit would be if expenses were £60 000.

Did you know?

After the trading and profit and loss accounts have been calculated, the sales and purchases accounts are closed for the year. The balance of the closing stock is transferred to a new stock account, which is kept in the general ledger, and the value of the stock entered.

The balance sheet

This shows all the assets and the capital and liabilities of the company.

- Capital is the amount of money which was introduced into the company when it started. To this figure is added any surplus profit at the end of a year's trading.
- Liabilities are debts owed by the company, e.g. a bank loan and any other creditors.
- Assets are all the items owned by the company – the premises, furniture and fittings, motor vehicles, debtors, stock, cash at the bank, etc.

To be correct, the balance sheet **must** balance. That is:

capital + liabilities = assets.

Originally balance sheets were set out with the two columns alongside each other, but today they are usually shown vertically. However, the example in Figure 4.53 has been deliberately produced in the older format so that you can see how both sides balance.

Non-assessed activity

Qualprint's balance sheet at the end of the year is shown in Figure 4.53. Talk through the entries with your tutor. Then, if you have time, play with it a bit! Make a few alterations and notice how:

- every transaction affects two entries
- after **every** transaction (if you do it correctly) the balance sheet will still balance.

This basic principle will be very important if you go on to study accounts at a higher level.

Suggested alterations

1 Chris Gaston withdraws £8000 from the bank for another van.
2 Qualprint sell £2000 of stock and put the money in the bank.
3 Chris Gaston is paid £800 by people who owe him money (his debtors) and he banks the money.
4 Qualprint buys stock worth £5000 on credit.

Balance Sheet of Qualprint Ltd as at 31 March 199-			
Capital and liabilities	£	Assets	£
Capital	50 000	Premises	19 000
		Equipment	14 000
Bank Loan	5 000	Fixtures and	
Creditors	8 000	fittings	3 000
		Motor vehicles	9 000
		Stock	4 000
		Debtors	900
		Cash in Bank	12 500
		Cash in Hand	600
	63 000		63 000

Figure 4.53 Qualprint's balance sheet

Budgets

A **budget** is a financial plan. All companies make plans in relation to their sales and the amount of money they hope to receive. They also plan their expenditure and try not to exceed it. If their plans work out, the planned profit figure should also materialise!

Forecasts are made for income and expenditure on a weekly or monthly basis, and actual income and expenditure is checked against these forecasts. The budget states both the planned *and* actual income and expenditure over a certain period of time.

The income side of the budget will largely be the concern of the Marketing and the Production departments. Sales and production targets will be set in line with the income forecast and it will be the managers' job to try to ensure these are met, and to take remedial action if they are not.

Expenditure is the concern of all managers and all staff. Budgets are normally divided into **revenue** (or consumable) items and **capital** items. For example, the Catering Manager at a school or college may be allowed to spend £40 000 on food in a year and £5000 on capital items such as a microwave oven or a chilled food display rack.

It is the manager's job to keep expenditure for the department within the level set in the budget. If the total for a week or month exceeds the budgeted amount, less may have to be ordered the following week. If your school or college refectory serves beans on toast all next week, this may be the reason!

Did you know?

A **personal budget** is a good way of managing your own finances – particularly if you find it hard to save. Making it out is the easy part; sticking to it is much more difficult!

Non-assessed activity

Mark Jones is desperate to save for a holiday this summer. He hasn't been away for three years, his friends are all off to Greece and he wants to join them.

Mark is a student who lives away from home. He receives a grant of £50 a week and his parents top this up with a further £10 a week. Mark has two part-time jobs. He works in McDonalds for an average of twelve hours a week and earns £3.50 an hour. He also works as a DJ at a club one night a week and earns a further £30.

He pays £35 a week rent, £8 for electricity and heating, £12 on travel and £22 on food. Phone calls cost him an average of £3 a week. He spends £2 a day on lunches but eats in his room at weekends. He likes going out and buying new clothes. He has worked out he needs to save £30 a week to go on holiday.

Use the form overleaf to work out a budget for Mark. Advise him how much he can afford to spend on clothes and entertainment *and* go on holiday! Note that to make the budget work, Mark would have to record his actual expenditure in the correct columns and monitor this regularly to see if he was sticking to the amounts which were forecast!

PERSONAL BUDGET PLAN				
Date	Income		Expenditure	
	Planned	Actual	Planned	Actual
Mon				
Tues				
Wed				
Thur				
Fri				
Sat				
Sun				
TOTAL				

Figure 4.54 Will Mark make it to Greece?

Recording financial information

In Element 4.1 the main reasons why financial information must be recorded were discussed. Below is a summary of these reasons to refresh your memory.

For security

It is much easier for someone to steal from or defraud a company if information isn't recorded. Cash could be taken from the petty cash box and never noticed, cheques could be misappropriated (i.e. used for the wrong reasons) if bank statements were never checked. People could even pay themselves additional expenses or higher salaries if there was no check on the wages!

Look back at the assignment on Tom Field on page 408 and the section on security, page 438, and see how this links with the additional facts you have learned since then.

To monitor income and expenditure

If income is falling, action needs to be taken. It may be that sales have to be increased and additional advertising and promotions are required. There may have to be a change to the product line or to the service provided. Or it may be that some customers are just not paying their accounts on time and must be reminded or more forceful action taken.

Similarly, if expenditure is increasing for any reason then this needs to be controlled. If prices are rising with one supplier, it may be necessary to find another, more competitive, source. Cuts may have to be made and fewer consumables used or lower quality products bought.

Non-assessed activity

As a group, brainstorm both of the following and see how many ideas you can come up with.

1 How many ways could a dishonest person obtain funds illegally if a company was careless about recording financial information?
2 Qualprint is in trouble. Sales of stationery have been falling and the amount of money spent running the business is rising. What should Chris Gaston do?

To keep customer accounts up to date

Many customers buy goods on credit. If the goods they buy and the payments they make aren't recorded then several things can go wrong.

■ Customers may not receive invoices for the goods they buy.

- Customers who are poor payers would not receive reminders.
- Customers who have paid may receive a reminder to pay!

In the first two cases, the company would not receive the money it is owed. In the final case the customer may become annoyed and go elsewhere next time.

To keep the business accounts up to date

On page 467you saw the wide range of information which is kept in the internal accounts. All of this information is of critical importance to the owner or manager of the business. It is useless if it is out of date, as the correct decisions can only be made if they are based on the facts as they are today.

All businesses must submit their annual accounts to the Inland Revenue, whether they are large or small. If the accounts are not up to date they may be prepared late by the accountants. In the meantime the Inland Revenue will have prepared an estimate of the tax owed – which is likely to be much higher than the actual amount. Moreover, the owner has to pay it if the accounts haven't been submitted. Only later, when everything is sorted out, will the Inland Revenue refund the overpaid tax. This fact alone is enough to make most business people keep their accounts up to date!

To monitor performance

Keeping records of financial transactions enables income and expenditure to be assessed – almost on a daily basis. This means that each week or month the actual income and expenditure can be checked against the budget. Any discrepancies can be investigated. The more closely a company sticks to its budget, the better its chances of reaching its target profit for the year. And budgets are easier to control on a weekly or monthly basis. If things are allowed to slide for three to six months then it may be too late to rescue the situation.

Non-assessed activity

Look back at all the information kept in the internal accounts, listed on page 467. **As a group** and **with your tutor**, discuss how each type of information can help the business owner to:

- monitor income and expenditure
- monitor performance of the company.

In each case, discuss the type of remedial action that could be taken if things were going wrong.

Information technology and financial information

Today most organisations use computers to help them to record financial information and produce internal and annual accounts. You may wonder, therefore, why you have been asked to learn how to complete so many documents and to understand **manual** systems. The reason is that it is far more difficult to understand what all these packages can do – let alone how to use them – if you have no idea what financial transactions are or how they should be recorded. You will see what this means if you imagine that you had read this section at the beginning of the unit, rather than towards the end!

Two types of software are used to record financial information; both of these are described below.

Accounting software

Many packages on the market are designed to record financial transactions and produce accounts. Many of these are specifically designed for small businesses. A good accounts package will:

- keep a record of all sales made to each customer on credit
- keep a record of all cash sales
- produce invoices, credit notes and statements
- list amounts outstanding from customers (called an **aged debtors' report)**
- keep a record of all purchases (both by supplier and type of goods)
- either keep a record of stock or link to a stock control package
- either keep a record of wages paid as an expense or, better still, link to a payroll package so that the wages are calculated automatically and the pay slips are printed
- keep a record of all accounts paid/still to be paid to suppliers
- record all bank transactions
- undertake all the book-keeping tasks required
- print out a variety of 'reports', e.g. trial balance, profit and loss account, balance sheet, VAT returns, bank analysis and so on.

Starting up

The owner starts by making out a list of headings needed to record the accounts. If a manual accounting system has been used then the existing account headings can be transferred onto computer. Each account will be given a number automatically by the computer, and categorised under the following main headings:

- sales (different categories of sales can be listed under different numbers)
- other income
- purchases (i.e. purchases of stock)
- expenses and overheads
- capital
- liabilities (e.g. any money owed, such as a bank loan)
- fixed assets (e.g. the premises and fixtures and fittings)
- current assets (assets which keep changing, e.g. stock, cash, money in the bank etc.)
- current liabilities (money which must be paid quite quickly, e.g. the amount owed to the VAT authorities).

Certain numbers will *not* be used. These are ones which have been allocated by the computer, e.g. for total sales or total purchases. These totals will automatically be calculated by the computer from the information it is given.

The remaining task is to enter the opening balances for each account, e.g. the money in the bank at present, capital in the business etc.

Customer/supplier records

The owner now needs to record details of:

- all the customers, e.g. name and address, telephone number, discount allowed
- all the suppliers, e.g. name and address, telephone number

This is usually set up just like a database system, with record cards to complete.

There will usually be blank fields for items such as 'amount owing' or 'total amount outstanding'. These fields are automatically completed by the computer when a sale or purchase is made.

Cash and credit transactions

The computer divides all transactions into two types:

- **cash transactions** – where payment is instant (whether it is by cash, cheque, credit or debit card) as in a shop
- **credit transactions** – where a customer is given several weeks to pay and the transaction necessitates an invoice and a statement at the end of the month. Both these documents – as well as credit notes and remittance advices – are printed by computer.

Month end

At the end of each month the software will prompt the user to run the **month end reports.** It will print out a copy of all the accounts for the month which should be stored safely.

The **month end function** then usually tidies all the files by removing all the paid items and automatically moves to the next accounting month in the financial year.

Lists and reports

A variety of lists and reports can be produced, at any time, at the touch of a key. These can include:

- customer list with names and addresses
- aged debtors' or aged creditors' analysis
- lists of sales and purchases
- list of all money received or paid
- list of suppliers
- an audit list (showing every transaction that month).

In addition, the user can produce:

- trading and profit and loss account
- trial balance
- balance sheet
- a VAT return.

Integrated accounting software

Integrated packages are those which are linked together. For instance, accounting software can be linked with stock control software and payroll software. The more complicated or sophisticated the package, the more difficult it is to use. Unless you work with it every day you are likely to forget what to do. For that reason, many small business owners prefer simpler packages which they can use once or twice a week without any problem.

Did you know?

Advertisements for accounting software are given in computer and software magazines as well as in business magazines and some national newspapers.

Below is shown a typical advertisement for Sage accounting software showing some of the products available.

Figure 4.55 An advertisement for Sage software

Spreadsheets

You may have already discussed spreadsheets in your Core Skills lessons on Information Technology, and more detailed information on spreadsheets is given in the Core Skills chapter in this book.

Quite simply, a spreadsheet is a computer program that enables the user to input numerical information and analyse the results. A spreadsheet is ideal if a financial manager wants to enter actual or planned information on income and expenditure and see the possible effects on potential profit.

A large sheet of paper (which gives the spreadsheet its name) is ruled off into columns and rows. Headings can be given to both the **columns** and the **rows.** Figures can then be added to show income, expenditure, sales, profit etc. either on a weekly or monthly basis (see Figure 4.56).

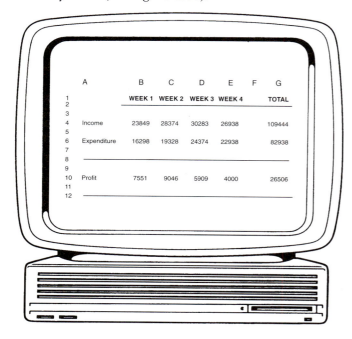

	A	B	C	D	E	F	G
		WEEK 1	WEEK 2	WEEK 3	WEEK 4		TOTAL
1							
2							
3							
4	Income	23849	28374	30283	26938		109444
5							
6	Expenditure	16298	19328	24374	22938		82938
7							
8							
9							
10	Profit	7551	9046	5909	4000		26506
11							
12							

Figure 4.56 A spreadsheet program

Spreadsheets are particularly useful for 'what if' calculations. Real problems can occur when alterations have to be made to past figures, or when predictions about the results of possible changes in the future have to be made. For instance, if Chris Gaston wanted to give a pay rise to the staff, but

wasn't sure how much he could afford and the effect of the increase on possible profits, he could enter the various percentage increases he was considering and, in each case, the spreadsheet would *immediately* tell him what the result of that decision would be.

Because figures can be entered easily and the result of different courses of action can be seen immediately, a spreadsheet is ideal for budgets. The planned figures are entered and these immediately give the projected results. Actual figures are then entered and this will show any deviation from the plan. If the company then decides to take action to resolve a possible problem, the results of different ideas can also be entered. For instance:

- Chris Gaston plans to sell £25 000 worth of stationery next year.
- Two months later, sales begin to fall because a cut-price stationery store has opened near Qualprint.
- Chris considers three possible courses of action:
  - a increase advertising
  - b reduce his prices
  - c move into selling micro-computers and business software.
- He works out the possible financial results of each of these actions by:
  - a entering the increase in advertising costs and balancing this against the potential increase in sales
  - b examining his profit margins on the goods he sells and seeing how these can be reduced – then using his spreadsheet to calculate the effect on total profit assuming sales increased by different percentage rates
  - c entering the cost of moving into this market and balancing this against the projected increase in revenue.

The spreadsheet will save Chris hours and hours of time, and sheets of paper, a pencil and an eraser! It will also help him to make a more informed decision because the possible results of his actions are calculated for him.

Did you know?

There are many different spreadsheets on the market – names to look for include Lotus 123, Microsoft Excel, Supercalc. Find out from your tutor which spreadsheet packages are used in your college and add to the list by looking at software and other business magazines.

Non-assessed activity

Use a spreadsheet package to enter a budget and find out how the 'what if' aspect of spreadsheets works.

Enter the budget you made out for Mark Jones (page 470) on a spreadsheet. See what happens to his savings if:

- Mark works four more hours at McDonalds
- Mark gets a pay rise of four per cent at McDonalds
- Mark loses his DJ job

and any other changes you like!

Now find out what happens if any of his expenses increase or decrease, for example, if Mark took sandwiches to work, or walked every day, or stopped going out or went out twice as often. You can enter any permutation of these events and, every time, the spreadsheet will show you the financial outcome.

You can then start to appreciate a little more, just how useful spreadsheets are to financial planning in business!

Evidence assignment

At this stage your tutor may wish you to start work on the second section of your final project. If so, turn to page 481. This will give you all the evidence you need to prove to the external verifier that you have undertaken the work required to fulfil the second evidence indicator for this element.

Review quiz

True or false?

1 All tills produce a printed receipt.
2 Cash discount is given to encourage companies to pay promptly.

3 A pay slip must list all deductions from the employee's wage.
4 The trading account shows the gross profit of the business.
5 Trade discount is never shown on credit notes.

Fill in the blanks

6 'What if' calculations can be done quickly and easily on _____ computer packages.
7 Tax is paid on the _____ profit figure of the company.
8 A balance sheet has three components – liabilities and capital on one side must match _____ on the other.
9 Gross profit minus _____ = net profit.
10 If a person needs reimbursing for money spent on the company's behalf, he or she will complete a _____ _____ _____ .

Short answer questions

11 State **four** main checks which must be made when a cheque is given in payment.
12 State **two** reasons why it is important to keep customer accounts up-to-date.
13 State **two** reasons why it is important to keep the business accounts up-to-date.
14 State **three** ways in which you could find out about accounting software on sale.
15 State **six** items of information to be found on a pay slip.

Write a short paragraph to show you clearly understand each of the following terms

16 External annual accounts
17 Accounting software
18 Remittance advice
19 Budgets
20 Monitor performance

Evidence indicator project

Unit 4   Element 4.2

This project has been designed to cover all the evidence indicators related to Element 4.2. It is divided into two sections. Tutors may wish students to complete the sections at the appropriate points marked in the text. Alternatively, tutors may prefer their students to do the entire project at the end of the element.

Performance criteria: 1–4

Core skills: Communication
Application of number
Information technology

Section 1

Student scenario

You are a new employee of Qualprint, the small printing business. You have been employed as assistant accounts clerk, having obtained a GNVQ Intermediate in Business. You are expected to have a good knowledge of the various types of financial documents used by the company.

Qualprint is a small organisation that produces various types of printed material to customers' orders. In addition, Qualprint supplies office and stationery goods and has a small retail/trade counter.

Make sure you complete this section of the project by the deadline date given to you by your tutor.

Your job

You start work for Qualprint on 1 June and work for Chris Gaston. Chris explains to you that copies of financial documents are used to provide information to compile an income and expenditure account each month. This account is very important because the total amounts of income and expenditure are used by Chris Gaston to monitor the performance of Qualprint.

Your job will include:

■ completing financial documents
■ calculating totals for the income and expenditure account

■ helping to draw up the income and expenditure account at the end of the month.

As a guide, Chris Gaston shows you last month's account which was prepared recently.

Chris suggests you use these headings as a guide for the information he will need from you at the end of each month. Therefore, for instance, if you total petty cash expenditure for a month you can give him the total amount spent, and so on.

QUALPRINT LTD TOTAL INCOME AND EXPENDITURE – MAY	
Income	
Printing	£9 500
Stationery sales – credit	£11 400
– cash	£2 100
	£23 000
Expenditure	
Purchases of stationery	£8 200
Raw materials (paper, ink etc)	£3 200
Consumables	500
Furniture and fittings	150
Travel and entertainment	100
Rent	400
Phone	65
Fax	50
Petty cash	50
Fuel and van repairs	80
Van repayments	250
Heating (gas)	35
Electricity	30
Advertising	100
Wages and salaries	£5 100
	£18 310

Figure 4.57 Last month's income and expenditure account for Qualprint

June 199-

During June you are asked to complete or check each of the documents listed below.

Undertake these tasks, in each case noting whether the document represents income or expenditure and noting down the value under your headings.

Purchase documents and payments

1 Make out an order to Super Office Ltd for an executive chair required by Chris Gaston. The address of the company is Shorrock Way, Prespool, Newshire, PR3 1QH. The reference number is EC27 and the price is £170 plus VAT. This company gives 5 per cent trade discount. The order number is 121/938.

2 Make out an order to Stationery Stores Ltd, 16–18 Hamilton Road, Glendale, FE7 8MS for 250 wallet folders (assorted colours) reference 3090 at 15p each and 500 manila folders reference 2080 at 10p each. This company gives 10 per cent trade discount. Use the next order number in sequence.

3 When the order from Stationery Stores is delivered you help to unpack the goods. The wallet folders are acceptable but 200 manilla folders are damaged and must be returned.

Make out an appropriate goods received note, number 1081.

4 The purchase invoice arrives for the executive chair. Check it carefully. If it is correct make out a cheque in payment but **do not sign it.**

5 Check the following invoices which have been received from the Delaware Hotel and from the firm which service Qualprint's vehicles. If they are correct make out cheques in payment, ready to be signed.

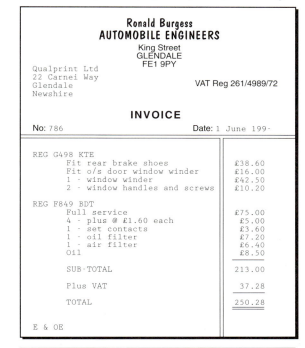

Figure 4.58 An invoice from Super Office Ltd

Figure 4.59 Invoices to be checked

Stationery Stores Ltd

16–18 Hamilton Road
GLENDALE
FE7 8MS

TEL: 01323 383977

FAX: 01323 487972

VAT Reg No: 294/18732/78

INVOICE

To: Qualprint Ltd
22 Carnei Way
GLENDALE
Newshire
FE1 8CA

Your order no.	Invoice no.	Despatch date
121/939	201189	10 June 199-

Quantity	Description	Cat. no.	Unit price	Total price	VAT rate	VAT amount
250	Wallet folders (assorted colours)	1062	15p	£37.50		
500	Manilla folders	2080	10p	£50.00		
	Total			£87.50		
	Less 10% trade discount			8.75		
				78.75	17.5%	£13.78

Delivery charge	—		
Sub-total	£78.75		
VAT	£13.78		
Total amount due	£92.53		

Terms: 28 days
E & OE

Stationery Stores Ltd

16–18 Hamilton Road
GLENDALE
FE7 8MS

TEL: 01323 383977

FAX: 01323 487972

VAT Reg No: 294/18732/78

CREDIT NOTE

To: Qualprint Ltd
22 Carnei Way
GLENDALE
Newshire
FE1 8CA

Your order no.	Invoice no.	Despatch date
3050	201189	14 June 199-

Quantity	Description	Cat. no.	Unit price	Total price	VAT rate	VAT amount
200	Manilla folders	2080	10p	£20.00		
	Less 10% trade discount			2.00		
				18.00	17.5%	£3.15

Delivery charge	—		
Sub-total	£18.00		
VAT	£3.15		
Total amount due	£21.15		

Terms: 28 days
E & OE

Figure 4.60 An invoice and a credit note from Stationery Stores

6 The invoice and credit note from Stationery Stores are both received. Check these carefully. If they are correct, make out a cheque for the **difference** owing to Stationery Stores.

7 Chris Gaston asks you to make out some other cheques for him

Glendale Lettings Ltd	£400 for rent
Midshire Electric	£35 for electricity
Marsh Corner Garage	£60 for petrol
Glendale Advertiser	£40 for advert
Printing Supplies Ltd	£2500 for raw materials

8 Petty cash vouchers need to be made out for several items. The float for petty cash is £100 and this is renewed at the end of every month. Your first voucher should be numbered 210.

£6.50 for tea and coffee
£12.20 for postage
£14.30 for train and taxi fare

£9.60 for sandwiches
£20.40 for replacement jug kettle

9 Chris Gaston hired a temporary worker called Bob O'Connell in the print shop for one week in June. He was paid at the rate of £3 an hour and worked for 39 hours and then worked 4.5 hours at time and a half. He finished work yesterday. Chris Gaston has asked you to make out his pay advice. Under employee number put TEMP. His NI number is KE483794D and his tax code is 344L. His deduction are as follows: tax £17.40, National Insurance £7.81. His taxable pay to date is £85.00.

Obviously, because this is the only week he has worked for Qualprint (he has been unemployed until recently) the figures in the other cumulative boxes will be identical to the figures for this week.

Make out the pay slip and a cheque for the amount he is owed.

Sales documents and receipts

1 The following orders shown in Figure 4.61a, b and c have been received by Qualprint and are due to be delivered this afternoon. Make out both delivery notes **and** sales invoices to match each one. The orders have already been checked by Chris Gaston and the unit prices for the goods are correct. Date all documents 10 June. Your first delivery note number is Q/1222. Your first invoice number is 2876 and all these companies are given ten per cent trade discount. Delivery charges are £5 in each case.

2 Blades Ice Arena contact you to say that Chris Gaston had agreed to produce the posters for nothing because they are required for a charity match. Chris Gaston agrees that a mistake has been made and asks you to complete a credit note to cancel the charge.

3 Chris Gaston tells you that a customer, Mrs T Ryan of 14 Tenby Walk, Glendale FE7 2HS, is calling in to collect her printing order. This comprises:
100 wedding invitations at 30p each + VAT
200 place cards 5p each + VAT
200 service sheets at 20p each + VAT

She wants to pay her bill at the same time in cash.

a Make out an invoice for the items shown above.
b You serve Mrs Ryan. Issue a receipt for the money you receive.

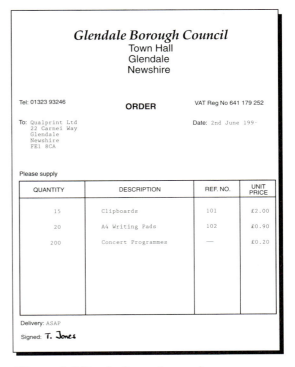

Figure 4.61b An incoming order

Figure 4.61a An incoming order

Figure 4.61c An incoming order

479

Figure 4.63 Four cheques were received

4 Four cheques were received yesterday in payment for stationery sold in the shop. Chris Gaston asks you to check these carefully and make notes if any mistakes mean they cannot be banked.

5 Chris Gaston passes you the cashing up sheet which was made out last night. It has only partially been completed. He asks you to complete this with the money received in the shop, add on the cheques which can be banked and complete a paying-in slip.

Qualprint Ltd – cashing up sheet		
Date **15 June 199-**		
Notes/coins	No. in till	Amount received
£50	1	£50.00
£20	6	£120.00
£10	8	£80.00
£5	5	
£1	24	
50p	17	
20p	12	
10p	16	
5p	2	
2p	13	
1p	7	
CASH TOTAL		
Cheques		
TOTAL		
Less £20 float		
TOTAL RECEIVED		
Signed _____		

Figure 4.62 The cashing-up sheet

6 **Two** statements of account and remittance advices need to be prepared. One is to Glendale Borough Council, Town Hall, Glendale, Newshire, account number 437. The other is to Blades Ice Arena, Philips Road, Glendale, Newshire, FE7 5PR, account number 270.

At the start of June, Glendale Borough Council owed Qualprint £65. Goods were sold to them on invoice 2850 for £150 on 2 June and you made out an invoice to them on 10 June. No payment has been received.

Blades Ice Arena had no opening balance. You had dealings with them on 10 June and issued an invoice and a credit note. On 25 June they asked for some more printing to be undertaken. This was billed on invoices 2885 for £260 and 2889 for £135.50.

Complete the statement of account and a remittance advice in each case.

7 At the end of June, Chris receives his bank statement which shows that there is £650 in the current account.

Chris says that this amount is not correct. Yesterday he banked £400 received as payment for printing. His standing order for £250 for van repayments is also not shown on the statement. Neither is this month's payments for phone and fax – £65 and £59 respectively.

How much money has Chris Gaston really got in the current account?

Total income and total expenditure

Throughout the month you have been involved in completing or checking a variety of financial documents. **In each case** you should have been making a record of the amount involved and keeping a note of this under the headings shown on the income and expenditure account.

1 Go back through your work and check that your information is correct.

2 List your information, in the form of a draft income and expenditure account, to which Chris Gaston can add other transactions with which different members of staff have been involved.

Section 2

Research the type of computer software which a business could use to record and monitor financial information.

You could divide this task up as a class so that different people research different sources.

- Obtain advertisements from business and IT publications, such as
  Byte
  CD-ROM World
  Computer Weekly
  PC Magazine
  PC Plus
  Software Magazine
  Windows International

  (Your school or college library may keep back copies of these. Alternatively your tutor or IT tutor may have other suggestions. Note that you will only need one copy of each journal for your group.)

- Write to software manufacturers for details of their products.
- Visit a computer software exhibition or contact suppliers in your own area.

Do divide these tasks up among you so that only one person contacts each place. Otherwise you may find that people stop being quite so helpful if they are swamped with different versions of the same enquiry.

When you have obtained the information you require, make out a list that names the supplier, the cost and the features of the software. Type this out neatly, using a word processor.

Make sure you complete this section of the project by the deadline date given to you by your tutor.

Final stage

Put all your documents from Section 1 plus your software list from Section 2 in a folder. Design a front sheet giving your name and the date. Give it the title: **Financial Transactions Project 2.**

Produce, evaluate and store business documents

This element covers the range of routine written documents which are produced by businesses every day. It looks at the ways these can be compared, produced, evaluated, sent and stored. In addition it examines how the different methods of transmission and retention can be assessed.

After studying this element you should be able to:

1 produce examples and explain the *purpose* of routine *business documents*

2 *evaluate* each business document produced

3 *compare the methods of processing* business documents

4 *reference*, correctly file and retrieve business documents

5 identify and *evaluate ways to send* and ways to *store* business documents.

Business documents

Many different types of business documents are produced every day. Earlier in this unit some of the many different financial documents were discussed. This element concentrates on the main documents written by people in business organisations, i.e:

- letters
- memos
- invitations
- notices
- messages.

The writer of any document is judged by the people who receive it. They are unlikely to think very much of either the writer *or* the organisation if the document is scruffy, poorly punctuated, difficult to follow or if the spelling and grammar are awful.

This element starts by discussing the purpose of such documents and when each of the different types of document is used. At all times it is important to remember that communication by means of effective and well-presented business documents is essential in the business world.

The purpose of business documents

All business documents are created to communicate a message to the recipient. You have already studied financial documents. These are designed to

Figure 4.64 Communications are essential in the business world

communicate information related to financial transactions.

- **Orders** communicate the specific items required.
- **Invoices** communicate the fact that money is owed.
- **Cheques** tell a bank to transfer money.
- **Accounts** record how much money the business is worth and describe its 'financial health'.

What messages do other business documents give, and to whom are the messages sent? Messages may be sent to:

- customers
- colleagues
- other businesses.

Communicating with customers

One of the major purposes of business documents is communication with customers. There are several messages a business may want to send to a customer. It could be information about products, contained in leaflets, brochures, catalogues and in advertisements (see Element 4.2). Businesses often need to communicate with individual customers to:

- answer an enquiry
- give detailed information about a product
- respond to a complaint
- ask them to attend an event
- query something unclear
- update them on a particular situation.

This is often done by letter. If the message has to be transmitted urgently, special postal services can be used to ensure it arrives promptly (see page 508) or fax machine may be used (see page 510).

Communicating with a colleague

Good communication among colleagues is vital if an organisation is to work effectively. If you don't know what is going on around you – or if someone else doesn't know what *you* are doing – you will not be able to work effectively. Accurate information is the lifeblood of any organisation. Huge amounts of information – both on paper and on electronic systems – are transmitted within organisations every day.

Colleagues working in the same office will usually communicate informally and verbally. However, there are occasions when it is better to write the information down, usually by means of an informal message or **memo.** There are several advantages in putting the information in writing.

- A written message is a permanent record that can be referred to repeatedly.
- There is less chance of it being forgotten, particularly if it is long or complicated.
- The information can be stored and retrieved in the future.

Many organisations operate an electronic mail system (E-mail) which speeds up internal (and some external) communications for both sender and recipient (see page 514).

Communicating with other businesses

All business organisations communicate on a regular basis with other businesses, e.g:

- contacting the bank about a loan
- providing a reference for an ex-employee
- querying a delivery from a supplier
- writing to the accountants with a tax query
- contacting an architect about proposed building alterations
- faxing the local newspaper with an urgent advertisement.

Every business organisation is part of a network which links it to the suppliers of all the goods and services it may need. Regular contact and communication are vital.

Non-assessed activity

In small groups, look through your local *Yellow Pages.* Select ten categories of businesses with which you think a business may communicate. In each case give a reason why communications may be made. Compare your list with those made by other groups in your class.

Business documents

There are five basic types of written communications – apart from electronic messages – which are used regularly by business organisations. Each of these is dealt with separately below. As you read about each one, take the opportunity to note the correct format or layout of each document from the illustration, so that you can copy it accurately.

Letters

Letters are normally sent when you want to communicate formally with people outside your organisation. It is therefore important that they are well presented.

Business letters may be sent for a variety of reasons, for example:

- to make or respond to an enquiry
- to ask for or provide information
- to make or answer a complaint
- to confirm or advise arrangements, e.g. for a meeting or interview
- to sell or promote goods or services.

There are standard rules which apply to all business letters and must be followed. These include the layout, style and type of phrasing used in business letters.

An example of a business letter is shown in Figure 4.65. It shows the layout used by most organisations today. However, this may vary slightly and it is worthwhile asking someone to show you an example of the 'house style' when you start work. Remember that it will be your job to conform to their layout – not their job to change to yours!

Key points to note

- The first items are usually the references. The internal reference, which comes first, relates to the originator of the letter and the typist or word-processor operator (giving the initials of the first followed by the initials of the second). In some cases this may be followed by the file number.

  The external reference is the one given on the letter to which you are responding and *must* be quoted in any reply.

- The date comes next. It is usual for this to be written in full, i.e. 14 February 199– *not* 14/2/199–. Today it is considered old-fashioned to use ordinal numbers, e.g. 1st, 2nd, 13th etc. The date does not usually contain any punctuation.

- The name and designation of the recipient should be shown above the company name. The town or city is typed in capitals and followed by the postcode.

- The salutation is the 'opening' – if you use 'Dear Sir' then you *must* close the letter with 'Yours faithfully'. If you start with a person's name then you must finish with 'Yours sincerely'.

- The complimentary close is given after the body of the letter and follows the rules above. Note the spelling of 'sincerely' and the fact that *neither* 'faithfully' *nor* 'sincerely' starts with a capital letter!

- Sometimes the name of the organisation is shown immediately below the complimentary close. This confirms the writer is sending the letter on behalf of the organisation.

- Finally, after the space for the signature, the name and official title of the writer are given.

- Sometimes the letters 'Enc.' may be included at the end of the document. This signifies there are some enclosures. Another method is to type a row of dots in the margin alongside the line where the enclosure is mentioned, but this practice is declining because it is more difficult to do on a word processor.

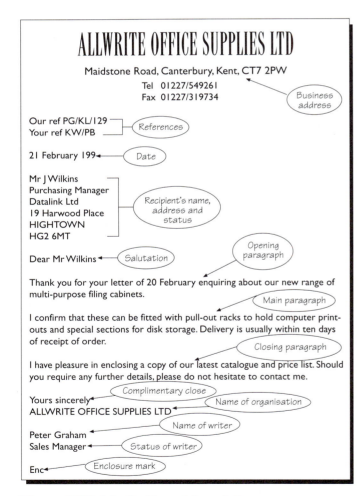

Figure 4.65 A typical layout for a letter

Did you know?

Business letters are *always* sent on specially printed letter headed paper. You must never send out a document on behalf of your organisation without using an official letter heading.

You should *never* include a person's initials in the salutation. 'Dear Mr T Wright' is *wrong*. If you have trouble remembering this, bear in mind the way you would speak. You would never say, 'Hello, Mr T Wright', and neither should you write to him like this.

Business style

The style of a business letter is different from the style used to write a letter to a friend and is more formal. For instance:

- Abbreviated forms of words are very rarely used in business letters. It is incorrect to write 'isn't', 'don't' and 'can't'. Instead you should write 'is not', 'do not' and 'cannot'.
- Slang phrases and expressions are never used. Imagine you were informing someone they should pay their account promptly. It would be totally inappropriate to say people like, 'Unless you pay up straight away we're going to have to do something about it.' A business phrase (which says the same thing!) would be: 'We regret that unless we receive payment shortly we shall have to take further action.'
- It is usual to have distinct paragraphs in a letter, each of which deals with a specific point.
  - The opening paragraph usually gives background information as to why the letter is being written.
  - The next paragraph usually gives further details (usually the information is too long to be given in full in the opening paragraph).
  - The third paragraph will 'round off' the letter.

If more than one topic has to be dealt with then there will obviously be more paragraphs.

- All the sentences you write must be *complete* sentences. This means they must have a subject and a verb. Note form is never used in business letters.
- A confidential letter has 'PERSONAL' or 'CONFIDENTIAL' typed clearly at the top (usually between the date and the name and address). The word is also clearly shown on the envelope, above the name and address.

- If any dates are referred to in the body of the letter then these must be given properly, preferably with the *day* as well, as a double-check. Your boss may have said to you 'I'm visiting them a week on Wednesday at 2 o'clock', but your job is to write 'Mr Blank will visit you on Wednesday, 13 March at 2 pm'.

Did you know?

Your writing and composition skills have a critical bearing on your ability to use *any* communications – not just business letters. Useful information to help you to develop those skills is given in the Core Skills unit on Communication, pages 539–48.

Non-assessed activity

Identify which of the following sentences are incorrect because they are in note form, are not complete sentences or contain a slang expression. Then write an acceptable alternative in each case.

1 Hope to hear from you.
2 Thank you for your letter of 18 June.
3 Can you call in to see us next week?
4 We can get over this obstacle if you pop in to see us for a chat when you are next in the area.
5 With reference to your recent letter.
6 Goods were sent Friday 23 March.
7 We can't prepare your accounts from the stuff you sent us as the papers didn't make sense.
8 Please let me know if you will be available to attend on that date.

Did you know?

- Very few letters are sent out today which start Dear Sir/Madam. Many organisations try to use the name of the person to whom the letter should be addressed, as this makes it more personal.
- If a woman signs her name but does not indicate whether or not she is married, you can solve the problem by using 'Ms' when you reply.
- Every letter contains certain **key facts** which must be included. Unless these are present you are only giving the recipient part of the required information. You can then build up your letter by adding certain standard phrases.

- You should never be tempted to sign a letter which has someone else's name at the bottom unless you have the authority to do so!

Composing business letters

Remember that a business letter must also be clear, concise and courteous and must not include any jargon or abbreviations that the reader would not understand.

Preparation stages

- Check that you have all the information to hand.
- Arrange the information in a logical order; always give background information or the reason for writing *first*.
- Decide on a suitable opening and conclusion.
- Draft out the letter.
- Read it through *as if you were the recipient*. Check:
  - the tone
  - the order
  - the terms and phrases you have used
  - that no key information has been omitted.
- Type it out using your organisation's house style.

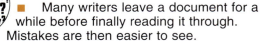

Did you know?

- Many writers leave a document for a while before finally reading it through. Mistakes are then easier to see.
- It is totally wrong to begin any letter with the phrase 'I am writing ... ' – because this is obvious!

Starting and concluding a letter

Starting and ending a letter can create more problems than anything else when you are not used to writing letters. The following points may help you.

- If you are replying to a letter you have received, start with 'Thank you for your letter of (date) regarding ... '
- If you are writing after speaking to someone on the telephone, start with 'further to our recent telephone conversation ... ' *but do make sure you complete the sentence!*
- There are several standard conclusions, e.g.

- We look forward to hearing from you.
- Please let us know if we can be of any further assistance.
- We look forward to receiving your confirmation.
- We hope this information will be helpful to you.
- If you have any further queries, please do not hesitate to contact us.

Again, do make sure you write in *complete* sentences.

Did you know?

In some organisations staff are instructed to write 'we' and not 'I' when they compose a letter. This is because the person concerned is writing for the company as a whole and not personally. Check if this is the case where you work by looking at existing letters in the files. What you should never do is change from one to the other in the middle!

Letters confirming a meeting

There are several key facts required in this type of letter. They include:

- **where** the meeting will be held
- **when** the meeting will be held (day, date and time)
- **why** it will be held.

Some letters also give an indication of **who** will be there.

Starting the letter is easy if you have previously made arrangements by telephone (see above). Your letter could then be worded as follows.

> Following our telephone conversation yesterday, I should like to confirm the arrangements for this month's advisory committee meeting. This will be held in this office at 4 pm on Tuesday, 30 October.
>
> As usual, a car parking space will be pre-booked for you and refreshments will be available on arrival.
>
> If you are unable to attend, I should be grateful if you could let me know.

Note that the letter is short and to the point *but* it is courteous – and relatively formal. It is not the kind of letter you would write to your best friend to confirm a meeting!

Did you know?

If you cannot think how to end a letter confirming a meeting, you could say 'I look forward to meeting you then' or 'I look forward to seeing you again'. If you are expecting the recipient to reply, the most useful ending is 'I look forward to hearing from you'.

Non-assessed activity

It is usual to include both the *day* and the *date* in a letter confirming a meeting. Can you think why?

Answering an enquiry

If you are **answering** an enquiry, you must respond to the issues raised by the enquirer. Normally, if you are replying to an enquiry the possibilities are:

- you can respond positively to *all* the issues raised
- you cannot respond positively to *any* of the issues raised
- you can give *some* help but cannot answer everything
- you can't help – but you can refer them to another organisation that can.

However, regardless of how you are responding, the key facts will include:

- a response to each point raised
- the provision of information (if available) *or* details of where the information can be obtained or a polite response saying that unfortunately you can't help.

As an example, imagine that a student has contacted your school or college for details about two courses – only one of which your institution provides. A reply may be sent as follows.

Thank you for your enquiry about GNVQ Leisure and Tourism courses and GNVQ Legal Studies courses.

We offer GNVQ Leisure and Tourism courses at three levels – Foundation, Intermediate and Advanced level. The level upon which you would start your studies would normally depend on your GCSE results. We have pleasure in enclosing leaflets on all three courses, giving the detailed information you require.

We regret that we do not offer GNVQ courses in Legal Studies. To our knowledge, such courses have not yet been introduced. However, you may wish to contact the National Council for Vocational Qualifications at ... to find out if there are any plans to offer this course.

Should you require any further information on the Leisure and Tourism courses, please do not hesitate to contact us.

Did you know?

An alternative phrase that can be used to end a letter responding to an enquiry is 'I hope you find this information helpful.'

Non-assessed activity

The company where you are undertaking your work experience has received **three** letters and asked you to draft a reply in each case. Prepare your draft and ask your tutor for comments on your work.

1 Your boss, James Evans, the Sales Manager, has arranged a meeting with Gerald Clark, the Purchasing Manager of Dugdale Electronics Ltd, Parry Court, Hightown, HG2 9DK. The meeting will take place in Mr Clark's office at 9 am a week on Tuesday. Mr Clark has asked your boss to confirm the meeting in writing.
2 An enquiry has been received from a young man – Mr Robert Westall, 14 Kelvin Avenue, Hightown, HG5 9SP. He would like to be considered for a Saturday job as he has just reached the age of sixteen. Write back thanking him for his enquiry and informing him that although there are no vacancies at present you will keep his letter on file and will notify him if one occurs in the near future.
3 Mr D Isherwood, 50 Rydall Close, Hightown, HG3 5ET has written asking if you hire out large garden mowers. Reply saying that you don't offer this service at present and suggest he contacts Barton's Garden Centre of Nixon Road.

Dealing with a customer complaint

Customer complaints should be acknowledged promptly, even if at that point you cannot actually deal with the complaint because it is being investigated. Keeping the customer waiting for a reply is hardly going to improve his or her opinion of your organisation (which is presumably not very good anyway!).

Usually, letters responding to a complaint are aimed at pacifying the customer and keeping his or her business. They may contain:

■ a **recognition** and **acknowledgement** of the original complaint
■ an **apology** for the fact the customer has been inconvenienced (**Note**: This is not the same as admitting it is all your fault!)
■ a **simple explanation** as to why any problem occured.

If the company accepts responsibility for all or part of the complaint, the letter usually ends with some reassurance it will not happen again. Sometimes organisations offer something in compensation – but not always!

It is more difficult to write a letter when the company does not accept responsibility for the problem. When you first start work, it is likely that such a letter would be written by your supervisor – or the least you could expect is some guidance on how to word it!

Did you know?

When you apologise in response to a complaint, you are *not* making a personal apology or accepting responsibility yourself. You are expressing regrets **on behalf of your organisation** that, on this occasion, the customer is less than satisfied.

Non-assessed activity

1 Compare the two letters in Figure 4.66, both sent in response to a complaint by a customer. One is sent acknowledging that it is the fault of the company; the other does not acknowledge this.

a Compare the way in which the letters are phrased, their similarities and their differences.
b Put yourself in the position of the recipient. Ask yourself, would you continue to take your clothes to those cleaners?
2 You work for a company that sells floppy disks. You have received a complaint from a customer that two boxes of disks purchased recently were both faulty. The disks have been returned by the customer, who is annoyed because he needed them urgently. Upon investigation you find that the disks were part of a faulty batch received from the supplier. Write to the customer, Tim Hawthorn, 45 Garside Road, Hightown, H26 9KM, apologising and offering a voucher for a free box of disks as compensation.

Memos

These are more informal than business letters but the degree of informality will depend on who is writing to whom! If you send a memo to someone at the same level as yourself in the organisation, you can be more informal than if you are sending it to someone senior to yourself. Remember this when you are writing a memo to your boss! It is also worth bearing in mind that as your memo may be filed for future reference, silly phrases and comments may keep staring back at you for years!

The usual functions of a memo are to:

■ give information
■ confirm arrangements
■ make a specific request or query
■ ask for or make comments or suggestions
■ state action that has been taken about a certain matter.

An example of a memo is shown in Figure 4.67 on page 490.

Key points to note

■ Most organisations use pre-printed memo forms which may, or may not, include the name of the company. Whereas the layout may vary from one company to another it nearly always includes the following printed headings:

– **To** (stating the name of the recipient)
– **From** (stating the name of sender)
– **Date** (recording the date it was sent)
– **Ref** (recording the internal reference – as for business letters).

■ Memos should always start with a clear subject heading. This helps the recipient to identify at a glance what the memo is about and find it

15 February 199–

Mrs T Hanson
15 Bradley Park
HIGHTOWN
HG4 8DM

Dear Mrs Hanson

Thank you for your letter of yesterday, informing us that the dress you left for dry cleaning recently was returned with the stain still showing.

We have checked our records and find that you did, indeed, inform our assistant that the stain was a bad grease mark. This should have enabled her to ensure that the correct solution was used to remove it.

If you would like to return your dress to the shop we will clean it for you again, obviously free of charge.

We apologise for any inconvenience you have been caused and hope you will continue to use our services.

Yours sincerely

Brenda Harrison

Brenda Harrison
Manager

---

15 February 199–

Mrs T Hanson
15 Bradley Park
HIGHTOWN
HG4 8DM

Dear Mrs Hanson

Thank you for your letter of yesterday, informing us that the dress you left for dry cleaning recently was returned with the stain still showing.

I have checked our records and talked to the assistant who received the article. It would appear that you did not mention the stain when you brought the dress into the shop. This is unfortunate because my assistant would have informed you that, because the stain is rust-based it is almost impossible to remove.

I am sorry that on this occasion you have been disappointed but do hope that you will continue to use our services in the future.

Yours sincerely

Brenda Harrison

Brenda Harrison
Manager

Figure 4.66 Compare these two letters

quickly when necessary.

It is therefore *not* usual to write a memo about more than one topic. Instead, separate memos would be written in each case. This also saves problems when they have to be filed.

- There is no salutation or complimentary close on a memo.
- Memos are never signed but may be initialled by the sender.
- If there is an enclosure this is indicated underneath the initials, with the abbreviation 'Enc.'.
- Confidential memos may be sent. These should have 'personal' or 'confidential' in a prominent place (usually at the top) and be sent out in an envelope addressed to the recipient.

Non-assessed activity

You work in a sales department for Karen Thorpe, the Sales Director. Write memos to cover each of the following situations.

1 Before she went out of the office early today she asked you to arrange a meeting for her with Chris Maitland, the Managing Director. The MD's secretary has just telephoned to confirm that the MD can see her for half an hour at 9.30 in the morning.
2 You had arranged to take a personal day off, two weeks from today, to go shopping with a friend. Your friend has now informed you that she can't get that day off and wants to make it a week later. You obviously need permission from Ms Thorpe before you can agree to this.

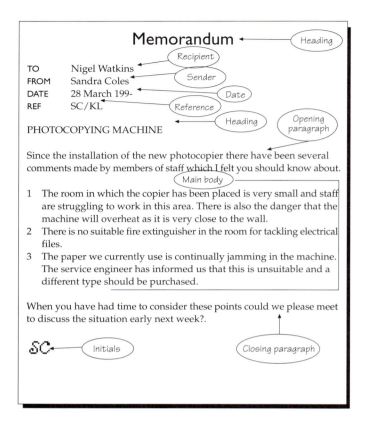

Figure 4.67 A typical memo

Invitations

Invitations may be in the form of a letter or on pre-printed cards. Pre-printed cards are normally used for more formal occasions (e.g. a wedding or special event) when the guests are 'hand-picked'. Letters are often used for informal invitations, especially when a large number of people are invited, for example, to attend an open day or parent's evening.

Non-assessed activity

Look at the example of a formal invitation and a formal reply given below and check the following features.

■ The language is usually formal. Instead of saying 'We should like to invite you to Rachel's 18th birthday party', the formal style is written in the third person and includes the names of the people issuing

the invitation and the name of the person receiving the invitation.

■ There is nearly always a request for a reply e.g. RSVP (*Répondez s'il vous plait* – a French phrase meaning 'please reply').

■ The date is normally given at the bottom of the invitation.

■ The layout gives the address at the top and the date the invitation is issued. The wording is usually centred on a relatively small card (about postcard size).

> *23 Wellesley Drive Midbury Lincolnshire*
> *14 May 199–*
> *Mr and Mrs F Abraham have pleasure in inviting*
> _James Roland_ _ _ _
> *to the 18th birthday party of their daughter, Rachel*
> *to be held at*
> *The Old King's Arms*
> *Dudesbury*
> *on*
> *Saturday 25 July*
> *from 7.30 pm until midnight*
> *RSVP*

.56 Harrow Grove
NESTON
Lincolnshire

1 June 199–

Mr James Roland thanks Mr and Mrs F Abraham for their kind invitation to the 18th birthday party of their daughter, Rachel and is delighted to accept.

Figure 4..68 A formal invitation and an acceptance

Did you know?

■ On very formal invitations a space is left for the name of the person being invited, which is then written by hand. This 'personalises' the invitation.

■ If you decline a formal invitation it is usual to give

some sort of reason! This doesn't mean a long explanation. Neither does it entail you saying where you are going instead! Look at Figure 4.69 for a useful phrase to use.

---

56 Harrow Grove
NESTON
Lincolnshire

1 June 199–

Mr James Roland thanks Mr and Mrs F Abraham for their kind invitation to the 18th birthday party of their daughter, Rachel. Unfortunately he is unable to attend because of a previous commitment.

Figure 4.69 A polite and formal refusal

Hightown College – Computer Shop

N E W !

From 1 October onwards the following new items will be available in the shop.

– Multiform Floppy Disk Filing
– Cabinets
– Diskette Storage boxes

Prices are very competitive - come along and see for yourself.

Opening hours: 12 noon to 5 pm

Monday to Friday

05.09.9–

Figure 4.70 A typical notice

Notices

A notice is a very quick and easy way of sending information to a large number of people, particularly if you want to send it to an unknown audience, for example if you want to sell your car.

In some organisations, **electronic mail** (E-mail, see page 514) can be used for this purpose instead of a notice board. However, since not all organisations have that facility, be prepared to use a paper-based system.

Did you know?

Notices are used:

- to convey the same information to a large number of people.
- to relay informal as well as formal information e.g. an organisation's notice board can contain a wide variety of information ranging from a change in the car parking procedures to arrangements for an inter-departmental trivia quiz competition.

Notices are usually displayed so that they are eye-catching – with the most important information prominently placed so that the reader can easily see it.

Did you know?

If you can use a desktop publishing package you will find that you can make a notice look very eye catching by the use of different fonts – but don't go over the top and use too many! You will make it look overdone and difficult to read.

Creating notices

- Write the notice so that *everyone* can understand it. You are not sending the information to one person, but to a whole group of people, many of whom you won't know – from the managing director to the newest employee in the maintenance section.
- Use clear and simple language. 'Attention please' is better than 'I should like to draw your attention to ... '
- Make it short – people won't stand for hours reading a notice on a notice board, particularly if they are reading it over somebody's shoulder.
- Use colour if you think it helps – but keep to one or two. Too many colours gives a childish effect.
- Always date it, so that you (or the person responsible for the notice board) will know how long it has been displayed and when its 'shelf life' is over.

491

Non-assessed activity

Trevor is a new trainee in the general office of a building firm. One of his jobs is to look after the departmental notice board, which he is expected to update each week. Last week the following items of information were left on his desk ready for him to sort out and put on the board. Put the information into a suitable form for the notice board. If you can use a word processor or desktop publishing package, try to make use of some of its functions – bold, italics etc.

15 November

Trevor – can you let staff know about the car park. Resurfacing will start next Monday and staff will have to use the temporary car park at the back of the annexe until it is finished. I'm not sure how long it will take – probably at least a week.

Frances

16 November

Trev – I'm desperate for some help for the children's Christmas party. As usual everyone is trying to back out at the last minute and I'm very short of volunteers. Can you try to 'persuade' one or two to help? If anyone is interested you can ask them to contact me direct. My new extension number is 5632.

Eileen

18 November

I'm the proud father of a new baby girl – and I want everyone to know about it! She's called Tamara, she has blonde hair – and she's great!

Cliff Derbyshire

Messages

There are many occasions on which you may be asked to take a message, e.g.

- following an internal or external telephone call
- after talking to a visitor
- after talking to a colleague.

Whenever anyone wants you to pass some information on to someone else, you will probably need to write out a message.

Non-assessed activity

Why it is better to write down messages than pass them on verbally? Look back at page 483 to refresh your memory!

Message taking

It is always helpful to use a standard message form to record a message, as the headings help you to remember all the information you need. A typical form is shown in Figure 4.71.

Remember that you should always:

- use simple, straightforward words
- keep your sentences short but vary the length a little so that your message reads well
- include all the key facts
- leave out irrelevant information
- if you are repeating a request to your boss to do something, make it a request *not* an order!
- be very specific about days, dates and times. If you must give a non-specific time, e.g. 'tomorrow', add the day and date in case your message isn't read immediately

---

```
MESSAGE FORM
TO ..................................  DEPT ................................
DATE ...............................  TIME ................................

CALLER'S NAME ..............................................................
ORGANISATION ..............................................................
TEL NO .............................  EXT NO ..........................
Telephoned                              ☐
Returned your call                      ☐
Called to see you                       ☐
Left a message                          ☐

Please return call                      ☐
Please arrange appointment              ☐

Message:
..................................................................................
..................................................................................
..................................................................................
..................................................................................
..................................................................................
..................................................................................
..................................................................................
Taken by: ..................................  Dept ..........................
```

Figure 4.71 A typical message form

■ mark urgent messages *clearly*.

Your responsibility doesn't end when you place the message on the right desk – it only ends when the person has read it and understood it! Check later that urgent messages have been seen by someone and tell your supervisor or someone senior if they have not, so that the correct action can be taken. *Never* take a message and then forget it – the results can be disastrous!

Identifying key facts

Every message contains key facts. If you miss them out the message will not make sense – or not make *complete* sense. Business callers are normally quite good at giving the key facts in an ordered way and checking them through afterwards. Private callers may be less helpful and some may like to chat so that it is difficult to sort out what is important from what is not. A good way to check that you have the message clear in your mind is to read back your summary to the caller at the end.

You may have to develop the skill of questioning people to find out additional information which you think is important, or facts they have forgotten to tell you, e.g. their telephone number! Use your message form as a guide to help you and don't be put off asking a question, even if the caller sounds abrupt or nervous.

Non-assessed activity

1 Identify the key facts in the following message.

2 Identify any additional information which would be helpful but which the caller hasn't offered, and for which you should ask.

3 Write the message clearly on a photocopy of the message form at the back of this book and check it with your tutor.

'Good morning. My name is Philip Bryant of the *Hightown Gazette*. I wonder if you could tell your sales manager, Margery Tyler, that we're doing a four-page feature soon on insurance and thought your company would like to advertise in it. The feature will include articles on house, motor and travel insurance for the general public. The last date for us to receive your advert would be a month today – but if she's interested I'd like to know what size advert she'd be thinking of, then I can book the space. Can you ask her to give me a ring on Hightown 405928, extension 3420? Thanks.'

Evidence assignment

At this point your tutor may wish you to start work on the project which will prove to your verifiers that you understand this section of the element. If so, turn to page 525 and do Section 1 of the project. This covers the first evidence indicator for this element.

Evaluating business documents

All the business documents you have produced so far have been **evaluated** by your tutor. This means that your tutor has assessed how good they are and whether they would be acceptable in a business environment. When you are at work, your supervisor will not expect to have to evaluate everything you produce – there is just not time! In addition, at work you are getting paid to do your own job, and to do it effectively. You will not be earning your wages properly if everything you do has to be checked carefully by someone else!

This means that you have to learn to evaluate documents *yourself*. You will know you are getting good at this when you start criticising letters and other documents you receive in the post!

You can evaluate a document in terms of:

- its appearance or presentation
- its language or content.

Each of these is discussed separately below.

Appearance

The appearance of a document is simply what it looks like. Everyone probably has a friend who is artistic and can even make doodles on a scrap of paper look good! Equally, you probably know someone else who is untidy, sloppy and makes every sheet of paper look appalling. If you stop thinking of business documents as boring or tedious and start thinking of yourself as something of an artist – creating a work of art on a sheet of paper – you will soon become fussy about the appearance of your documents.

Style

Many business organisations spend a lot of money on projecting their **image**. They may have letter-headed paper specially produced, using silver or gold lettering, or a company logo that is raised from the page. The paper may be quite thick, or embossed or a special colour. The envelopes may have been designed to match. In other words, the documents they send out of the organisation have a style that says 'we are professionals, we give a high quality service, we care about the work we produce.' The aim is that customers feel this concern with quality involves everything the company does – the goods it produces and the services it offers – and that this will help business.

Whilst you may not have the resources to produce documents with this sort of style, you can learn to recognise it. You can also learn to design your own documents with flair. Style and design are

interrelated – a stylish notice has good clear print, perhaps two colours for effect and maybe some quite discreet artwork. One without style may have a twiddly border, ten colours and a sketch at the bottom! Simplicity often goes hand-in-hand with style. Fancy lettering is *out* (unless you are absolutely marvellous at calligraphy!)

Non-assessed activity

1   Even a heading can be modern in terms of style – or old-fashioned. Look at the two headings below. Which do you think has been printed in the more modern style? Why?

a   Dear Student

HIGHER EDUCATION FAIR

On Tuesday, 19 May, a Higher Education Fair will be held in … .

b   Dear Student

Higher Education Fair

On Tuesday, 19 May, a Higher Education Fair will be held in … .

2   Opposite are two invitation cards. Which do you think has more style? Why? Discuss your answers with your colleagues and your tutor.

3   Look at the posters and notices in your school or college. Assess them for style yourself, then compare your opinions with those of the rest of your class.

Format

Format means the **layout** of a document. The layout should enable the information to be easily read. For instance, when typing a document:

- highlight headings and important words in **bold** (rather than underlining them)
- leave a line space after a heading
- leave a line space between paragraphs
- leave two letter spaces after a full stop and one after a comma
- use block paragraphs.

In addition to setting out the text correctly, you will also be expected to choose:

Portrait: paper
short side at top

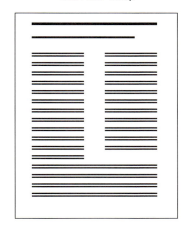

Landscape: paper
long side at top

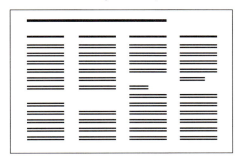

Figure 4.72 Which has style?

Figure 4.73 Portrait and landscape formats

- the paper size
- whether to use portrait or landscape format
- the size of your margins (left, right, top and bottom)
- line spacing
- whether or not to **justify** your right hand margin
- the type and size of characters to use.

Many organisations have standard settings for certain documents, which you need to check carefully if you work for them (look in the files!). This is called their **house style.**

Look back at the correct format for a business letter, memo, invitation, notice and message shown in this element to refresh your memory.

Did you know?

Style and format are closely linked. A document with a mixture of different type faces, uneven margins and with the text all crammed in the top third of the page not only proves the creator had little idea how to choose an effective layout but also shows a complete absence of style.

Language

If you are evaluating language, you are concentrating on the content of the document and how it is worded rather than how it is presented. Most people wince (or laugh!) if they see a spelling mistake or silly grammatical error in a business document – make sure that this doesn't happen with anything you produce!

495

Spelling

Generally, the more you read the better you become at spelling. This is because you constantly see the correct spelling of a word and will notice when it is written in any other way.

You should be able to spell basic words correctly all the time. You can check in a dictionary for longer words but it is a good idea to make a real effort to improve your spelling by consciously learning new words – and the best way to do this is to write out the word two or three times, concentrating on the spelling all the time.

If you *really* can't remember how to spell a word, choose an alternative instead!

Figure 4.74 You can always check in the dictionary!

Common errors

Errors often occur when words with different meanings sound the same and are spelt differently. The most common areas of confusion are given below.

There/their/they're

- there = a place (e.g. here and there). It is also used before a verb, e.g. there is.

- their = belonging to them (e.g. their coats)
- they're = a **contracted** word – short for 'they are'.

Where/wear/were

- where = a place (e.g. where are you?)
- wear = to put on (e.g. will you wear that coat?)
- were = a verb, a different form of 'was' (e.g. we were here).

To/too/two

- to = used as part of the infinitive of a verb, or before a pronoun (e.g. to go to them)
- too = as well (e.g. we will go too) or more than normal (e.g. too loud, too many)
- two = the number 2.

Be careful also of *know* and *no*, *of* and *off* and *your* and *you're*.

Did you know?

Although the spelling may be correct, words which should be written separately are sometimes written together in error. Typical examples include:

- thank you – which is *always* two words
- all right - *not* alright
- a lot – a poor phrase to use, but still two words.

Be careful, too, of words which are sometimes written together and sometimes separately, e.g:

- may be/maybe – 'maybe' written together means perhaps'.

Changes in spelling

This, too, can cause confusion and errors. The most common are

- forgetting to change a 'y' to an 'i' for the past tense, e.g.:
  pay becomes paid (*not* payed!)
  try becomes tried (*not* tryed!)
- adding 'full' to a word and forgetting to drop the final 'l', e.g.:
  beautiful, careful, forgetful, successful.
- not understanding the difference between a noun (spelt with a 'c') and a verb (spelt with an 's'), e.g.

Noun	Verb
practice	practise
licence	license
advice	advise

Remember! If you can put 'the' at the front, the word is a noun, e.g:
the doctor's practice, the driving licence, the solicitor's advice.

If you can put the word 'to' in front of it, the word is a verb, e.g:
to practise medicine, to license the car, to advise a client.

Did you know?

Probably the most common spelling errors involve mixing up 'i' and 'e'. A good general rule to follow is:

'i' before 'e' unless after 'c', or if the word says the sound 'a'. Therefore:

medieval (not after 'c') *but* receipt (after 'c')

relief (not after 'c') but deceive (after 'c')

rein, reign, vein, veil and weight – all words which say 'a'.

Even then there are exceptions, e.g. leisure, neither, either, weird and height – so be careful. Check in a dictionary if you're not sure.

Non-assessed activity

1   Below are some words used commonly in business documents. Twenty are spelled **incorrectly**. Can you identify which ones?

accomodation	liason
advertisment	manouvre
awfull	miniture
alledge	noticeable
benevolant	occurrance
colleages	ommitted
committee	predecesser
competant	prestigous
courteous	questionaire
conscientious	received
consistant	referred
definate	seperate

Figure 4.75 Try to remember whether the i or e comes first!

deficient	sincerly
development	underrate
enviroment	waive

2   Rewrite the following sentences, correcting all the spelling mistakes.
   a   The President gave a humourous speech yesterday, when he was the honorary guest at our centenery.
   b   She wanted to order fourty reams of paper from the stationary store but was told this was to much and the order had to be refered to the manager.
   c   She recieved two differant references – one said she was incompetant and unfit to join the permanant staff whilst the other described her as extremly conscientous.
   d   It was embarassing when the forein minister visited Parliment yesterday with all his advisors acompanying him.

Grammar

You may smile if you hear a young child say, 'I is tired' or 'He learned me to do that'. People don't smile when they hear adults make similar grammatical errors. In speech such mistakes sometimes pass relatively unnoticed. In writing, once you know they are wrong, such errors almost seem to leap out from the page!

Non-assessed activity

Try to identify what is wrong in each of the following sentences.

1 Which boy works the hardest – Tony or Dave?
2 Neither of the flats were suitable.
3 The Government are going to debate this tomorrow.
4 Do you know who you will be working for?
5 We haven't been nowhere near his house.
6 Neither the girl or her mother had visited the shop.
7 I shall be delighted if you would come to see me tomorrow.
8 He had to quickly run to meet his friend.
9 She asked if you and me could see her in the morning.
10 I understand you met Mr Sharp yesterday. How did you find him?

Common grammatical errors

Some of the errors above may have seemed obvious – others more difficult. Look through the explanations and answers below and study carefully those you *didn't* find in the list above.

Comparative and superlative

■ If you are comparing *two* objects, then add 'er'. If you are comparing more than two, add 'est'.

Therefore sentence 1 should read: 'Which boy works the harder – Tony or Dave?'

■ Some words cannot have 'er' or 'est' added to them, e.g. beautiful, handsome. If you are comparing *two* objects put the word 'more' in front, if more than two, use the word 'most', e.g: She is the most beautiful girl I have ever seen. She is certainly more beautiful than Sarah.

Agreeing singular and plural words

The verbs which follow singular words must also be singular, and those which follow plural words must be plural. This is simple and we follow this rule every time we speak, e.g.

■ I *am* going – we *are* going
■ He *was* leaving – they *were* leaving

Difficulties arise when we are given alternatives to the basic pronouns, e.g. each, every, all, none, either, neither and none. The test here is to see if you can put the word 'one' afterwards. If you can, the word is singular and takes a singular verb. Therefore:

■ each (one) and every (one) – both are singular
■ either (one) and neither (one) – singular again
■ none = not one – another singular

Therefore sentence 2 should read: 'Neither of the flats was suitable.' (Neither one of the flats was suitable.)

Confusion occurs more often because of the phrase in the middle. Try to make things easier for yourself by ignoring any words in the middle (as well as adding 'one' to help you), e.g.

■ None of the people on yesterday's boat trip ... over 65. = Not one of the people (....) *was* over 65.

Collective nouns also cause problems. These are used to describe a group, e.g. government, committee, society, board. Although there may be many people involved it is only *one* group and is therefore singular. Therefore sentence 3 should read: 'The Government is going to debate this tomorrow.'

Ending a sentence

When you are writing, try to avoid ending a sentence with a preposition, e.g. 'to', 'of', 'with', 'about' or 'for'. This may mean changing the sentence around e.g.

Which company are you referring to? *should* read

- To which company are you referring? (or)
- Which company do you mean?

You may have to alter 'who' to 'whom' when you change your sentence. For instance, sentence 4 should read: 'Do you know for whom you will be working?'

Although this seems very formal, it is really correct English. If you think it sounds too severe, you can reword the sentence entirely, e.g. 'Do you know the name of your manager?'

Double negatives

These cancel each other out! 'I am not going nowhere' means you must be going somewhere! If you use a double negative when you are speaking, the listener will probably ignore it – *don't* use one when you are writing. By now you should realise that sentence 5 should read: 'We haven't been anywhere near his house.'

"HONEST, I AIN'T GOT NONE!"

Word pairs

Some words always go together – particularly either/or and neither/nor. Sentence 6 should therefore read: 'Neither the girl nor her mother had visited the shop.'

Other matches include:

- shall and will
- should and would

Sentence 7 should read:

- I shall be delighted if you will come and see me tomorrow. *or*
- I should be delighted if you would come and see me tomorrow.

A pair of words which causes confusion is 'who' and 'whom'. The rule for this is rather complicated, so if you are unsure which is right and cannot check it with anyone, try to find a way round it by rewording your sentence, e.g:

Mr Baker is the person to who/whom you should write.

can become:

You should write to Mr Baker.

In other words, keep it simple!

Split infinitives

The *infinitive* is the root of a verb – 'to go', 'to run', 'to carry' etc. Wherever possible, try not to split an infinitive by putting another word in the middle. Some people still wince at the start of *Star Trek*, which includes the words 'to boldly go', because it is a split infinitive!

Simply change the words around in your sentence, so that sentence 8 reads: 'He had to run quickly to meet his friend.'

'I' and 'me'

It can sometimes be difficult to decide whether you should write 'you and I' or 'you and me'. The simple way to decide this is to try substituting 'we' or 'us'.

we = you and I
us = you and me

This means that the expression 'between you and I' is wrong; it should be 'between you and me'. Using the same test, sentence 9 would read: 'She asked if *we* could see her in the morning.' Therefore the correct version is: 'She asked if you and I could see her in the morning.'

Ambiguity

An ambiguous sentence is one that could mean two things. If you said to a friend 'you need your hair cutting badly' she may reply 'No, I need my hair cutting very well!'

In example 10 the second sentence is ambiguous – and also slang. We do not know if the writer meant 'How did you find' in a geographical sense (as you would find something that was lost) or as 'what did you think of him?'

Make sure what you write is precise and accurate so that the reader knows exactly what you mean.

Did you know?

Words to avoid (because they mean so little) are 'got' and 'nice'. Think of the sentence – The day got nicer and nicer. This is so imprecise it is hardly worth writing – even though you may have a vague idea what the writer meant!

Other bad errors

Word confusions which sound terrible include:

- learned and taught
- lend and borrow.

These words mean quite different things – check in a dictionary if you are unsure.

Did you know?

There are no such phrases in the English language as 'could of', 'would of' or 'should of'! If you find yourself writing any expressions like this you are wrong. You are using the conditional form of the verb to have, therefore you should write: could have, would have, should have etc.

Non-assessed activity

1 Retest your ability to spot grammatical errors by correcting the following sentences.

a The Safety Committee are using that room next week.

b She wanted to know where he was going to.

c She never has no time to talk about it.

d None of us were interested in his proposal.

e The car which developed the fault was a BMW which is unusual.

f She had to rapidly produce the memo he wanted.

g I would be pleased if you will send us the cheque immediately.

h Do you know whom Mr Taylor wants to see?

i He has asked to see you and I at noon.

j He is someone who I have never been able to get along with.

2 Rewrite the following passage without using the word 'got' once, and without changing the meaning. Think of a suitable alternative for the word 'nice' every time it appears and replace any slang expressions with more acceptable words.

Keith got ready early for his job interview yesterday. It was a nice day and the place wasn't far away. The guy who saw him looked quite nice and had a nice big office. They chatted for a bit then got involved discussing Keith's application form. Keith got a bit lost when the bloke asked what he had been up to between 16 and 17 as Keith had taken a year out but wanted to keep this quiet. He got over the problem by referring to the nice part-time job he'd had at the time. At the end of the interview Keith shook hands with the guy who promised to get back to him soon. After two weeks Keith got a nice letter telling him he'd landed the job but got a shock when he saw the salary. He thought he could have got more and wondered whether to hang on a bit longer and see if he could get fixed up somewhere else.

Figure 4.76 Keith got ready early for his job interview ..

Did you know?

Knowing how to punctuate properly and having a good vocabulary also help you to write business documents correctly. Hints and tips on punctuation and vocabulary – as well as additional practice on spelling and grammar – are given in the Core Skills unit on Communication.

Optional evidence assignment

*This activity can be carried out verbally in class **in a group** as a non-assessed activity to consolidate learning. Alternatively, if you do it **on your own**, it can count as supplementary evidence towards the following parts of the scheme.*

PC 1: Produce examples and explain the purpose of routine business documents

PC 2: Evaluate each business document produced

Range: Purpose: to communicate with customers, to communicate with a colleague, to communicate with other businesses

Business documents: letters, memo, invitation, notice, message

Evaluate each document: in terms of appearance, in terms of language

Core skills: Communication

1 You have been asked to produce **five** documents to help your tutor prepare for an open day. Your tutor may add additional details **verbally** to the ones given below.
   a Prepare a memo to all staff, saying that the Open Day has been arranged for 11 May from 2 pm to 4 pm. Students will be required for reception duties and to assist parents on arrival. Refreshments will be available. Tutors should each submit the names of two students, who are available to help, to *your* tutor by next Friday.
   b Prepare a notice, informing all students about the Open Day, and inviting them to bring their friends and members of their own family. Invent any other details to make your notice realistic.
   c Write a letter in response to an enquiry from Mr P Attwood, 15 Rosewood Gardens, Hightown, HG3 8DM, asking about the date and times on which the Open Day will be held.
   d Write a brief message to the secretary, saying that the local florist has telephoned and the flower

displays for the Open Day will be delivered at 11 am that morning.
   e Prepare an informal invitation to all parents, inviting them to attend.
2 When you have completed the documents, write a brief evaluation sheet stating your opinion of your own work in terms of appearance (style and format) and language (spelling and grammar).
3 Now exchange your work with that of another member of your class. Evaluate your colleague's work, under the same headings as in task 2.
4 **In pairs,** discuss with your tutor your evaluation sheets and the work you both produced, to see if he or she agrees with your comments.
5 Write a short paragraph to explain the main purpose of routine business documents.

Comparing methods of processing business documents

Business documents may be:

- hand-written
- typed
- word processed
- printed
- photocopied.

The method to choose will depend on several factors – not least is the type of equipment available at the time! If you are trying to prepare a draft report at home for your tutor, you may *have* to hand-write it, even though the final version has to be produced on a word processor to give it a business-like appearance.

In some businesses you will have a choice of methods. Which should you choose, and why? It is possible to compare different methods in terms of:

- legibility
- cost
- time taken to produce
- ability to make changes
- storage potential.

Hand-written documents

You may find it surprising that people produce anything by hand, these days. However, if you went to a meeting and had to make a few quick notes, people would be more than surprised if you pulled out a laptop computer rather than a notebook!

The principal type of hand-written document is the informal message – mainly because people haven't time to start keying in to a typewriter or word processor whenever they want to pass on a message. The other reason for writing messages is that no-one has yet designed a computer package which enables anyone to complete a **pre-printed** form without a lot of difficulty. Some software designers have tried to get round this by producing software in which formats for standard forms can be designed and saved, then recalled for completion. However, this may be time-consuming and simply isn't worth doing for short messages.

The benefits of producing documents by hand are the speed (provided it isn't a long document), the cost (it's cheap) and the fact you can keep the document safely to refer to later (e.g. documents in your portfolio!). The disadvantages may be legibility – if your handwriting is poor – and the difficulty you will have in changing the document around or amending things you see which are wrong. Covering the page in correction fluid is hardly likely to create a good impression!

Figure 4.77 It is often necessary to produce hand-written documents.

Did you know?

A summary of all the different methods of processing business documents is given in the chart on page 504. As you read about each method of processing documents, check how it rates on the chart.

Typed documents

Typewriters are still in existence in many business organisations – even though, in your school or college, they may have been totally replaced by computers. Most typewriters today are **electronic** – this means they have been programmed, by means of a silicon chip, to 'remember' certain commands. There is a vast difference between the features on a top-of-the-range electronic typewriter and a cheap portable. However, given a skilled operator, all can be used to produce very attractive documents which are easy to read (i.e. legible).

All electronic typewriters have some 'memory' which will enable simple corrections to be made quickly and easily. The more expensive versions have larger memory capacity, which means that:

- they can 'automatically' correct errors made anywhere on the page – rather than only in the last sentence or two
- standard sentences and paragraphs can be stored and recalled as required.

On some typewriters, there is a 'window' or small screen in which the text can be displayed before being committed to the paper. This means that alterations can be made quickly and easily.

Electronic typewriters are quite cheap (for businesses, anyway!) but the speed at which documents can be produced still depends on how good the operator is at keying in text quickly and accurately.

Word-processed documents

It is likely that you are involved in creating documents using a word processing package as part of your course. The main advantage of using a word processor is the ability to move text around and change it easily whenever you need to make alterations. When you become really skilled you can import text from one document to another, automatically insert names and addresses in standard letters and produce tables and other graphics (on some packages) quite easily. You can also use a spell check to help to reduce possible spelling or typing errors, although you still need to read your work through for sense!

The speed at which documents are produced depends upon your keyboard skills and your knowledge of the software you are using. An expert word processor operator will produce documents more cheaply than a beginner, because there are likely to be fewer draft versions of a document before the final 'perfect' copy is produced.

The word processor offers an additional advantage. Documents can be printed out and stored in a paper-based filing system and/or stored on disk for future retrieval. Storage systems are dealt with in more detail on page 517.

Printed documents

There are occasions when documents need to be produced by a skilled printer. Some organisations have their own internal printing department – but this may be used only for basic leaflets and posters. The services of a professional printer are likely to be needed for brochures and catalogues, particularly if colour illustrations and photographs are required. A professional printer would also be used if special notices or embossed invitations are required.

Printers are not cheap, although the greater the number of copies you require the cheaper (per copy) their services become. This is because they price each item they produce in terms of the artwork and design. Once the **printing plate** has been produced the actual **print run** costs are only calculated in terms of the operator's time and the amount of paper used.

If you send a document out of the company to be printed professionally, you will be sent a **proof**, which you need to check carefully for mistakes. You will be expected only to alter typographical errors, not to rewrite the document. If, at this stage, you want to add three paragraphs, the printer will charge you extra, so it is important to know what you want when you first place the order! You also need to allow enough time for the printer to design the document, send it back to you for proof-reading and then print it. Don't expect to be able to receive the finished version in three days' time!

Did you know?

Desktop publishing systems can produce documents to the same standards as those professionally printed – provided a skilled operator is doing the work! Text and graphics can be keyed or scanned in, moved around, placed in columns (like a newspaper) and shading and other effects can be added. The operator can also use a wide range of type fonts and styles for headings and special effects (see Core Skills Information Technology chapter).

Photocopied documents

Millions of business documents are photocopied every day. In fact, if you asked people who work in business what they did before photocopiers were invented, they would find it very difficult to tell you!

Because a photocopier produces a replica of the original document, there is no need to check the copies. However, it is important that the original document is of good quality and, preferably, on white paper. Black ink or print photocopies much better than coloured ink. Changes can be made to the original using correction fluid. There is a special kind of fluid for correcting photocopies, but this is not always very successful.

Modern photocopiers are very fast and easy to use. Many companies use a **key system.** Each authorised user has a special number to key in to the machine to make it operational. The machine records the number of copies made by key-number holder, to enable the accounts department to keep a check on usage.

Photocopiers are often rented or leased from a photocopier supplier, and then usage is charged per copy – so the more copies made the higher the bill. Normally copies will work out at about 1.5p. Paper is quite cheap – about 1p to 3p a sheet depending on quality. When you are charged 10p a page in the local library, the rest is profit for someone! In business, a critical factor is wastage. If the original is crooked when it is placed on the glass (or even worse, print-side up!) and then 200 copies are made, the firm's money is being wasted!

Figure 4.78 Photocopying is not difficult, if you follow the basics

Methods of processing business documents

	Hand-written	Typed	Word-processed	Printed	Photocopied
Legibility	Very good to poor	Excellent	Excellent	Excellent	Excellent
Cost	Cheap	Relatively inexpensive	Relatively inexpensive	Expensive	Relatively inexpensive
Time taken to produce	Quite fast	Depends on keyboard skills	Depends on keyboard skills	Quite slow	Fast
Ability to make changes	Difficult to do neatly	Depends on equipment	Good	Increases cost	Difficult but not impossible
Storage	Paper-based filing system	Paper-based filing system	Disk storage possible	Paper-based filing system	Paper-based filing system

Figure 4.79 Comparison chart for different methods of producing documents

Did you know?

Photocopied documents are usually only sent outside the company if the recipients *know* they are receiving copies. People normally expect to receive an original. This also applies when you are sending out your CV with a job application. Most Human Resources managers frown when they receive a photocopy, because it gives the impression that the writer is applying for jobs all over the place!

Non-assessed activity

1 Visit some local shops or stores that sell electronic typewriters and word processors. Obtain some leaflets on both types of machine and assess them for their features.
2 Ask your tutor to demonstrate a school or college photocopier to you and show you how to make copies perfectly at the first attempt!
3 Ask your IT tutor to assess your own keyboarding skills. How quickly could you produce a professional document using an electronic typewriter or word processor?

Optional evidence assignment

*This activity can be carried out verbally in class **in a group** as a non-assessed activity to consolidate learning. Alternatively, if you do it **on your own**, it can count as supplementary evidence towards the following parts of the scheme.*

PC 1: Produce examples and explain the purpose of routine business documents

PC 3: Compare the methods of processing business documents

Range: Business documents: notice

Compare: in terms of legibility, cost, time taken to produce, ability to make changes, storage

Methods of processing: hand-written, typed, word processed, printed, photocopied

Core skills: Communication, Information technology, Application of number

1 Prepare a chart which will enable you to compare the methods of processing a business document. If you wish, use the comparison chart in Figure 4.79 as a guide.

2 You have been asked to prepare a notice by your tutor to advertise the fact that your group is holding a penalty shoot-out in the sports hall for Children in Need at 2 pm on 15 November. Some local 'star' footballers have been invited, but as you are not sure who your local club will send, you daren't mention any names! The professionals will be in goal, whilst your teams try to shoot past them. Entry is 50p per person and a signed football will be raffled at the event. Sponsorship forms are also available for those who wish to sponsor the teams.
   a Draft the notice required by hand, clearly showing the format and layout you prefer.
   b Make a note of how long it took you to prepare the notice.

c Check your work **with your tutor** and make any suggested changes as neatly as you can.

3 Prepare a printed version of your notice using one of the following methods:
- a typewriter
- a computer and word processing package
- a computer and desktop publishing package

Again make a note of how long it takes you.

4 Ask your tutor to provide a sample notice if any of these methods are **not** chosen by at least one student.

5 Make **ten** photocopies of your notice. Just before you do, alter the time of the kick-off to 2.15 pm. Make the alteration as neatly as you can. Make a note of how long it takes you to make the photocopies.

6 Compare each of the documents you have produced and enter your findings on your chart. If your tutor has obtained examples of other methods of processing documents, enter comments about these as well.

To complete the section on cost, assume you are employed and paid £5 an hour. Use your records of time to calculate the cost of each document if paper is 3p a sheet and photocopies cost 1.5p a page.

7 Write a sentence describing how you would store a copy of the notice if you had produced it by each method.

Evidence assignment

At this point your tutor may wish you to continue work on the project which will prove to your verifiers that you understand this section of the element. If so, turn to page 525 and do Section 2 of the project. This covers the second evidence indicator for this element.

Reference, file and retrieve business documents

An important advantage of producing a **written** business document is that it can be referred to again, so it is a fairly pointless exercise to print out a document and then lose it. Therefore, it is usual in business to place everything *methodically* in a **filing system.** The aim is not just to store the document safely but also to enable *anybody* who needs it, and is authorised to do so, to retrieve it. The measure of a good filing system is the **speed of retrieval.** Anyone can store something – finding it again is the skilful part.

Non-assessed activity

Test yourself! How quickly can you find:
- a piece of work you completed last week
- a handout you received last month?
- your last school report?

Compare your responses with those of other members of your group.

Figure 4.79 How quickly can you find your last school report?

Referencing systems

The way in which paper files are grouped and stored will vary from one organisation to another depending upon its particular needs. However, the four main systems in use are:

- alphabetical – by name
- subject – by topic
- numerical – by number
- chronological – by date.

Each of these is covered separately below.

Alphabetical filing

In this system, the files are stored in alphabetical order under the name of the person – e.g. a customer or employee – or an organisation .

All alphabetical systems are simple to understand and easy to use because they are **direct**. This means you can go straight to a file without having to refer to an index first.

If there are not enough papers under any one heading to warrant a separate file, it is usual to create a miscellaneous file. A **miscellaneous** file could be opened for every letter of the alphabet and this would usually be placed at the front of the appropriate letter section.

If your organisation operates an alphabetical system, you must know the rules to follow to ensure you can locate and store files properly. These are given in the chart in Figure 4.81.

Did you know?

The best way to test if you understand the rules is to look in the *Phone Book* – this is simply a collection of names of people and organisations listed using these rules. However, individual companies may vary in the way these rules are interpreted, so your final check should be the company files.

Non-assessed activity

All the **organisations** on the chart in Figure 4.81 start with the letter 'S'. Rearrange these into one long list and add the following:

Social Services Department, Blackpool
The Samaritans
Serrick Marsden Ltd
Shorrock & Company, Solicitors
The Sahara Restaurant
Southampton District Council
St Mary's Rest Home
60 Plus Club
Sunway Travel Agency
SAS Tippers Ltd
John Schofield (Engineering) Ltd
Seventh Heaven Dress Designers

Rule to follow	Example
People	
Surname first	Clark Peter
Short names before long	Clark Peter
	Clarke Peter
If identical, follow first names or initials	Clark Peter Anthony
	Clark Peter Michael
	Clarke Peter
Nothing always comes before something	Clark P
	Clark Peter Anthony
	Clark Peter M
	Clark Peter Michael
Mac and Mc – all treated as Mac and filed before 'M'	MacDonald T
	McNulty J
	Marsden T
Ignore apostrophes	Obertelli J
	O'Brien D
	Oldfield C
Organisation	
Ignore the word 'the'	Sandwich Place, The
	Security Store, The
Numbers become words	Seven Miles Garage
	Seven Trees Hotel
If names are identical, follow street or town	Seven Trees Hotel, Kings road
	Seven Trees Hotel, Skye Place
Initials come before full names (ignore the word 'and')	SB Animal Feeds
	S & J Upholstery
	SRA Associates
	Saatchi and Saatchi
Saint and St – all treated Saint	Sainsbury J plc
	St John Ambulance
	Salford City Council
File public bodies under name of town	Social Security, Dept of
	Social Services Dept, Bradford
	Social Services Dept, Leeds

Figure 4.81 Rules for alphabetical filing

Filing by subject

This system is used when it is more appropriate to file under a topic than under a name. For example:

- a chain store may keep files under the **type of stock**
- an insurance company may keep files under the **type of insurance**
- a manager may keep files under topics such as **meetings, conferences, projects** etc.

Each file is clearly labelled with the name of the topic and then placed in alphabetical order.

Did you know?

If a topic is very broad it is usually sub-divided, e.g.

Meetings – Annual General
           Marketing
           Publicity
           Safety

Non-assessed activity

Rearrange the following into correct subject order.

Seminars	Personnel – Health and Safety
Publicity – Open Days	
Personnel – Training	Personnel – Appraisals
Publicity – Leaflets	Conferences
Travel	Publicity – Advertising
Publicity – Displays	Personnel – Welfare
Personnel – Staff Records	Personnel – Recruitment
Publicity – Exhibitions	

Filing by number

The main disadvantage with all alphabetical systems is that they are unsuitable for very large numbers of files. Imagine your local hospital keeping all its patient files in alphabetical order. Very soon there would be congestion under common letters of the alphabet and the whole system would then have to be rearranged to create additional space.

To prevent this problem, organisations often use a numerical system of filing. In a numerical system there *must* be a separate alphabetical index – otherwise the user would not know where to find the file. Often the number used for the file is quoted in all correspondence, which saves people having to look up the file number when they want to file a letter. They simply refer to the number in the reference. If the number is *not* quoted, then you would have to look in the index and copy the number *accurately* onto the document to be filed.

Did you know?

Transposing two figures can create havoc in a numerical system. If a document is placed in the wrong file – or a file in the wrong place – it can be almost impossible to find.

Non-assessed activity

Rearrange the following list twice. Firstly, put it into numerical order to show the order the files would be stored in a filing cabinet. Secondly, put it into alphabetical order to show the order in which the index cards would be filed.

Bryant M	482311	Gibbs P	413727
Jones R	478963	Berkovitz T	473218
Sanderson D	475712	Houldsworth S	473213
Kent G	462834	Hacking M	423314
Jallucci K	479836	Patel W	413292
Bolton T	477914	Heap S	477712

Filing by date

Some organisations file particular papers in **chronological** or **date** order for easy access. In a sense, this is a variation of a numerical system and is used when the date has a special significance. Examples include:

- travel agents – who usually file clients' travel documents under date of departure
- school departments – which store past examination papers according to the date on which the examination took place
- government departments – which store birth and death certificates
- accounts departments – to store petty cash vouchers.

Did you know?

- Correspondence received by a company is stored in date order in a file.
- The most recent document is always at the top.

- When writing out a list it is usual to
  - put the earliest date **first**
  - use a consistent date style – i.e. 24 March 199– or 24.03.199– but *not* both.

Non-assessed activity

Change the following list to date order using a consistent date style.

Name	Date of birth
James Baird	29.11.77
K Barnes	04.11.76
Peter Best	March 4th, 1977
Gemma Brooks	18 August 1978
Vincent Chang	December 3rd, 76
Janice Cruikshank	9 April 1977
Roberta Fletcher	13/3/76
P Ormerod	October 12 1977
John Taylor	01/06/75
Nicola Walker	23:07:78
F Williams	5 Nov 1977
K Yates	20.9.76

Did you know?

Computer print-outs are often stored by date, particularly when a large computer run is undertaken, e.g. for a payroll listing or for all invoices that have been sent in a month.

Evaluating ways to send and store business documents

You have already practised evaluating business documents in relation to their appearance and language. However, if you are producing business documents you must also make sure they reach the recipient, usually as quickly as possible. It is not normal to produce a business letter on Monday and post it some time on Thursday afternoon!

The three main options are:

- special delivery postal methods
- regular postal methods
- electronic transmission.

You also need to be able to identify and evaluate the following ways of storing business documents:

- paper filing
- computer files

- computer back-up files.

Ways to evaluate

The methods you use to evaluate ways of sending and storing documents can be classified under:

- ease of sending and storing
- ease of finding and retrieving
- cost
- document safety
- document security.

The section below covers each of these options.

Ways to send documents

Special delivery

Everyone knows about the services of the Royal Mail service because virtually everyone, at some time in their life, has put a stamp on an envelope and posted something. This is only one facet of the huge range of Royal Mail services available to businesses. One of these is the special delivery service, which enables urgent documents to be transported quickly.

The Royal Mail guarantees that any document sent by special delivery will be delivered by 12.30 pm the

Figure 4.83 Special delivery is just one service offered by the Royal Mail

next day, in return for a small fee. When you use special delivery a coloured sticker is placed on the envelope and your documents will receive priority treatment at the sorting office.

The service is very easy to use, provided your nearest post office is reasonably accessible! The cost is only small and there is some compensation paid if the item is lost or damaged. However, this isn't very much, so the service isn't appropriate (on its own) for any important documents such as a certificate or the deeds to a house.

Did you know?

■ · An equivalent service for documents being sent abroad is available – called **Swiftair.**

■ Important documents should also be sent by **recorded delivery** if additional security is required. Additional compensation is then payable if they are lost.

Non-assessed activity

Find out the current fee for sending documents by:

■ special delivery
■ recorded delivery.

Obtain a leaflet on each and look up the amount of compensation that is paid at present.

Post

The routine postal service offers the choice of first- and second-class delivery. Businesses often send routine mail by second-class mail to save money. If this is the case, but you want to send something first class, you should write this on the envelope (usually at the top left-hand corner). The Royal Mail service aims to deliver first-class items the next day and second-class items within three days.

The service is easier to use than special delivery as you don't have to go to a post office. You can simply post the correctly stamped and addressed envelope into your nearest post box! However, with the routine services you have no way of knowing whether your document is safe. There are ways round this. Recorded delivery can be used, but there is a fee. An alternative – free – method is to obtain a certificate of posting, though this is only available

over the post office counter. Once this certificate is issued, at least you have proof of when you posted the letter.

If you send a document by recorded delivery, the sticker on your envelope or package contains a bar code which is used to track the document. Your receipt tells you what to do if the item is not delivered. The Royal Mail service can use its tracking system to tell you if, where and why there are any hold-ups, for example, if you have written an incomplete address on the envelope.

Did you know?

No document is likely to arrive on time if the envelope is illegible, incorrectly addressed or doesn't include the postcode.

Addressing an envelope correctly is a skill you should already have, but many people make basic mistakes and do not follow the Royal Mail guidelines. Apart from anything else the address on the envelope should be *neatly* written if it has not been printed or typed. There are some other important points.

■ Start writing half way down the envelope.
■ Start with the name and title (e.g. Mr, Mrs, Ms, Miss, Dr) of the addressee.
■ Start a new line for each line of the address.
■ *Always* put the town or city in *capitals.*
■ Put the postcode as the last item, preferably on its own line, with **no** punctuation.
■ Special mailing instructions, e.g. by hand, or urgent, should be put at the top left-hand side.
■ Special addressee instructions should be put two lines before the rest of the address, e.g. personal, private and confidential, or for the attention of ... .
■ Letters going abroad should have *both* the city (or town) *and* the country in capitals.
■ The Royal Mail service prefer it if **no** punctuation is used in *any part* of the address.
■ If you don't know a postcode you can find it by phoning the Royal Mail Postcode enquiry line on 0345 111222 – you will be charged at the local rate for your telephone call.

Non-assessed activity

1 Look at the address label in Figure 4.83. There are **four** errors. Can you find them?
2 Address an envelope to a friend of yours. Include the postcode. If you don't know it, find it out! Ask your tutor to check it and give you his or her comments.

Mrs P Hanson, Personnel Manager
Briggs & Saunders Ltd
Fountain Road
Reading
<u>RD7 JXL</u>

Figure 4.83 Look at this address and find four errors

Figure 4.84 A standard fax machine

Electronic transmission

Many organisations transmit dozens of documents a day **electronically** – and this trend is likely to increase. The day may even come when the Royal Mail service handles mainly birthday and Christmas cards and a few personal letters.

In a modern business organisation there are often two electronic systems that can be used. Both are explained below.

Fax

Even in many very small businesses, one item of equipment considered essential is the fax machine. For virtually the price of a telephone call, documents containing text and graphics and even photographs can be sent easily to almost anywhere in the world.

A fax machine scans a document, converts the dark parts (the text/graphics) into digital pulses and transmits these pulses down a telephone line to another fax machine. The second machine then repeats the pulses it receives, to create a replica of the original document.

The process is quick and easy and the users can discuss the document on the telephone if necessary – usually immediately after it has been transmitted.

Fax machines have been falling in price and at the same time the features they offer have become more and more sophisticated. There is a wide range of machines on the market, ranging from simple desktop models to much larger machines designed for almost constant use.

Did you know?

The smallest fax machine on the market doubles as a telephone as well as a copier and is less than 30 cm by 18 cm! Measure that, if you're not sure of the size! The price is currently under £300.

Facts about fax

Most fax machines use specially coated paper, which is supplied on a roll, although one of the main developments is the increasing number of machines, including cheaper models, which use plain A4 paper.

All fax machines have some type of display panel which will prompt you, a key pad and, usually, a telephone handset. They can both transmit and receive messages automatically. Most large companies have a separate telephone line installed just for faxes, but many small businesses do not. It is quite to easy to switch between telephone and fax communications if the usage of either is only small. Modern fax machines will do this automatically for incoming calls.

Many features are now common to almost all fax machines and new developments are taking place all the time. However, there is still a difference between the features you will generally find on a small machine and those you will find on a high-volume machine.

Basic functions on most machines

Activity log – the machine automatically prints out a report on the document(s) sent/received and the result of each (e.g. OK or not OK).

Anti-curl device – straightens out the paper from a fax roll

Automatic dialling – automatic transmission once the connection has been made

Document carrier – a special holder for important or flimsy originals

Document feeder – the holder for originals yet to be transmitted

Fax header – automatically prints the company name, fax number, date and time on the top of all documents – plus the page number

Loudspeaker – so that you can hear what is happening as you try to make a connection *without* having to lift the handset

Number memory – stores the most frequently used fax numbers so that you can dial using a short numeric code

Paper-out warning – warns you to refill the paper tray or replace the fax roll

Repeat dialling – automatically keeps trying a number if the other fax is engaged

Transmission report – is printed out after each fax, gives details of time, date, sender, receiver, number of pages, duration and result (e.g. OK or not OK).

Verification mark – a small mark printed at the foot of each transmitted page

Voice contact – enables sender and receiver to discuss the fax. On cheaper machines you can only do this once transmission is complete.

More expensive machines can send several faxes automatically, transmit overnight, send two-sided documents and be linked to a computer network. The possibilities are almost endless!

Did you know?

■ Faxes of the future will work in colour. The technology already exists for this but, as yet, the machines are too expensive to be worth marketing.
■ In ten years many business people on the move will have fax machines in their cars. Fax machines may be integrated with PCs in special workstations and act as a printer and copier all in one!

Using a fax machine

The easiest way to learn how to use a fax machine is to watch someone else who knows how to do it. Instruction manuals vary from very good to very poor, and you may easily forget what to do if you don't use the machine regularly. Watch, take notes and ask questions if you are unsure. Then write out a 'help sheet' for yourself to remind you what to do next time. If you need to use a fax machine, you will need to know:

■ how to prepare material for transmission
■ how to send faxes
■ how to deal with incoming faxes.

You will also be more popular if you learn what to do to speed up your messages and reduce the costs of transmission.

Preparing material for transmission

The main factors to consider, whether you are sending faxes on your own behalf or for other people, are the following.

■ What type of paper is used in your organisation to send faxes? Some companies use letter-headed paper, others specially printed fax forms, some use plain paper and type the words **fax message** at the top.
■ Is there any particular format you should use? Often faxes are set out in a format similar to a memo (see Figure 4.85) but not always.
■ Are any important or original documents to be faxed? If so, and these are valuable, coloured, very small, very large *or* poorly printed, you will have to take a photocopy and make any size and print adjustments. Fax machines print only in black and white – so coloured print on an original comes out very poorly. Photocopy any doubtful documents first.
■ Word your message carefully – the shorter it is (without being too brief!) the more quickly it will transmit and the less this will cost. Normally fax messages are quite informal but, like most communications, this really depends upon the importance of the person you are faxing. Unlike memos, fax messages are often signed.
■ How many pages are you sending? Faxes are numbered differently from other documents, e.g. page 1 of 3, page 2 of 3 and so on. This tells the

receiver how many documents to expect so he or she can check at the end that all have been received.

J BAXTER & CO LTD
15 Bridge Street
HIGHTOWN

Tel: 01892 585728   Fax: 01892 449922

FAX MESSAGE

TO: Tony Barnes, Advertising Department

FROM: Sarah Goodison

DATE: 14 July 199-   **Page 1 of 3**

ADVERTISING PROOFS

The only error I can see is in the contact name on the last line of the advert. Name should be Sandra Gray, not Sarah Gray. We have also made some alterations to the chart on page 2 - amended text follows this message.

Please can you confirm the date the adverts will appear and, if possible, try to place them as near the front of the paper as possible.

Thanks

Sarah

Figure 4.85 A typical fax message

Did you know?

Some fax machines have the ability to store signatures and then print them on the appropriate documents. Obviously there must be a security system linked to this – or someone could easily send a message in someone else's name.

Sending faxes

Below are some general guidelines, but the most important thing to remember is – if in doubt, refer to the manual or ask somebody who knows!

- Check the document guide is set correctly for the width of your paper.

- Check you have the right number to call. If you are unsure then use the *UK Fax Book* to find out.
- Check which way your text should face – otherwise you will simply transmit blank pages!
- Check you know how to:
  - dial the number, check it is correct and cancel it if you make a mistake (normally this is shown on a small display)
  - remove the paper quickly if it is crooked or starts to jam in the machine
  - cancel a call if you can't get through, or set the machine to redial automatically
- Dial the number, check your display, and press 'send' or a similar designated key when you are connected (unless this procedure is automatic).
- If your fax machine feeds the paper *in*, leave the machine to push it *out* again – it doesn't need any help!
- The display screen will usually prompt you and inform you if there is any fault on the line or problem with the transmission (see page 513).
- Either the display screen or a bleeper will warn you if the other operator wants to speak to you.
- Check you have a verification mark on each page transmitted and that the transmission report says 'OK'.
- Fasten the transmission report to your fax and return it to the sender (or store it safely if it's your own document).
- Either file your fax immediately or, if you are waiting for a reply, put it in your pending tray to remind you.

Receiving faxes

On some machines, incoming faxes are automatically stacked in a special paper tray. On cheaper models they may come out as cut or uncut rolls of paper (very tightly rolled up if the roll is nearly at an end). Make sure you don't mistake any of these for rubbish if the fax is sited on a nearby desk – especially if the paper falls on the floor!

Check who should receive each fax and deliver it *quickly* – remember, faxes are used for urgent information! If the recipient is absent or away from the office, find someone else to deal with it. *Don't* just put it on someone's desk if you have no idea where he or she is.

Did you know?

- All fax machines can be used as copying machines when not in use for faxes.

■ The *UK Fax Book* is the fax directory for the UK. Directory enquiries for numbers not listed, and for overseas subscribers, can be contacted by dialling 153.

Fax faults and problems

Below are listed the main faults that can occur and what you should do. However, each fax machine is sold with a manual clearly stating the basic procedures to follow in the case of equipment problems. Do check this for your machine – especially the 'trouble-shooting' guide (probably near the back).

■ **Transmission failure part-way through** – check the verification marks to see where the transmission failed. Write a short note saying what happened. Go back one page and reconnect, faxing your note first.
■ **Blank sheets faxed** – paper was in the machine upside-down or printing ribbon/cartridge has run out.
■ **Machine cut off part-way through** – probably because paper ran out. Refill, and next time don't ignore the warnings that the paper is running out. The red stripe which appears towards the end of a fax roll is not a new type of design, it's telling you to replace the roll!
■ **Fax printing wrong day/date** – reset time and date.
■ **Display poor or dull** – batteries need changing (this may be shown on your screen).
■ **Overheating** – low-volume fax used too much, or for very long transmission, or when sending a page that is very black. Wait a short time and then try again.
■ **Paper jam** – instructions on how to solve this will be in your manual. Don't panic if an alarm sounds when you open the machine – there is usually a reset button to stop this.
■ **Message unreadable** – poor quality original. Photocopy it (preferably with ink density set higher) and/or enlarge it and try again.
■ **Dirty marks on messages** – machine needs cleaning – particularly the rollers. Use methylated spirits, *not* water!
■ **Top or bottom of document missing** – *either* text starts too high or low, or the operator did not feed in the original correctly or pulled out the original before transmission was finished.
■ **Fax sent to wrong company** – faulty dialling or wrong number.

Non-assessed activity

Discuss **with your tutor** the action you should take in each of the following situations.

■ You receive a fax meant for another organisation.
■ You receive a fax meant for you which becomes unreadable half-way through transmission.
■ You receive a fax with a page missing.
■ A manager in your company gives you a note to fax and asks you to type it out first. You can hardly read a word that he has written.
■ You cannot transmit an urgent fax within the deadline given to you because the line is constantly engaged.
■ You receive a fax marked 'urgent – to whom it may concern' but you don't know who to give it to.

Evaluating faxes

Despite everything you have read, fax machines are quite simple to use – especially if you use one regularly. If you use a complicated or elaborate machine infrequently, you may have to read the manual or your help sheet at regular intervals to refresh your memory!

Fax costs

The machines themselves are very cheap. Small machines start below £300 and even quite sophisticated machines are well under £1000. Transmission costs are the same as if you were making a telephone call. It is therefore cheaper if:

■ you send faxes overnight
■ transmission time is short.

The speed of transmission is determined by:

■ the type of machine you have
■ the resolution mode being used
■ the length of the message
■ the amount of detail and its density
■ its destination.

The average time taken to transmit an A4 page with a modern machine is about 20 seconds. If you are linked to ISDN (BT's high-speed digital dial-up system) the time is much shorter. Faxing in 'standard' resolution mode is much more rapid than if the machine is set on 'fine' or 'superfine'. Standard resolution is perfectly acceptable for most general documents.

Because the machine is 'reading' black lines, the fewer there are, the less it has to read and the more quickly the fax will be transmitted. Similarly, if you have a few lines of text top and bottom, and a line drawing in the middle, this will fax more quickly than a long printed document. A very dark or intricate diagram, or a lot of solid text, will take longest.

Non-assessed activity

1 Which of the faxes below would take the longest time to send? Which the shortest?

A   B   C

Figure 4.86 Which fax would go fastest?

2 See if you can explain to your tutor why a document sent to the company across the road will take (virtually) the same time to transmit as one to Australia!

Did you know?

It can cost less to fax a one-page document overseas than to post it by airmail. You can work this out by comparing the cost of an airmail letter to the USA (see Royal Mail Overseas Postal Rates leaflet) and the cost of a telephone call lasting 30 seconds at cheap rate. Remember that the cheap rate period in the USA is different from that in the UK!

Fax machines and security

You may think that because messages simply 'arrive' on a fax machine, there is no way in which confidential information can be sent by fax. On the smaller, desktop models this is usually true. However, the larger machines often have a range of security features, which may include passwords or pass codes. Incoming messages are stored in memory and only the person with the correct password can print out a copy.

Did you know?

Fax machines can be used to transmit messages to electronic mailboxes. See below.

Electronic mail

Electronic mail, usually called E-mail, is a system of sending messages from one computer to another by a system of mailboxes. All users have their own mailbox in which their electronic mail is stored until they are ready to read it. The user can reply, store or delete messages, print them out, redirect them and even check if a message sent previously has been read by the recipient.

The advantages of electronic mail are that:

- all types of data can be transmitted, including graphics, text, spreadsheets etc.
- there is a fairly high level of confidentiality, as only the user can access his or her own mailbox by using a password and ID
- E-mail messages can be sent and retrieved from virtually anywhere in the world
- messages can be sent to several mailboxes at the same time
- a recipient who wishes to incorporate the information received by E-mail into other computer files does not need to key it in for a second time.

Internal electronic mail

Many companies operate their own electronic mail system on computers which are linked by a network (see Core Skills in Information Technology). This saves people making telephone calls, sending memos or other internal messages. The network can be in just one building, in several buildings in one area, throughout the UK or even international! A network can link the head office of a company with all the branch offices and with other subsidiary companies.

External electronic mail

The two main commercial E-mail services are **Telecom Gold** and the **New Prestel Mailbox service.** Telecom Gold is the more popular of the two. However, both these services are declining in popularity as more and more computer users become linked to **Internet.** This is a global network of linked computers, sometimes referred to as the **superhighway.** Many companies are now linked via the Internet system and sending E-mail messages out of the company is no more difficult than sending them to someone in the next office – except that the 'address' line can be quite long!

All E-mail systems operate by means of a user ID (or mailbox ID) *plus* a password (which can be changed at any time).

E-mail features

Whether you are using an internal or external service, the following features are likely to be available.

Blind copy – the ability to send a copy of a message to other users without anyone else knowing that you have done so.

Carbon copy – sending a copy of a message to someone else.

Cancel – discontinues a message you were going to send.

Delete – erases messages you've read and don't need again.

Envelope – the line on a screen which summarises an incoming message – and which usually changes colour when the message has been read.

Forward – sending a message you have received to someone else – you can attach your own comments if you want.

Information – the usual command for finding out whether the recipient has read your message yet – and at what time on what day!

In mailbox – contains incoming messages in date/time order.

Message – the message screen on which you compose a message.

Out mailbox – the mailbox that stores outgoing mail.

Print – enables you to print the contents of messages.

Read – enables you to read a message.

Reply – the option chosen if you want to reply to a message you have received – both your name and the recipient's name are usually included automatically.

Scan – (external systems only) condenses information so that you can read several messages quickly.

Send – the command to transmit your message to the recipient's mailbox.

User group – a group of people, with a common title, which is set up so that you can send simultaneous messages to all members of that group.

Using electronic mail

If you have never used the system yourself, you will find it far easier if someone demonstrates it to you. Internal E-mail systems are usually easy to use. External E-mail systems are a little more complicated, and Telecom Gold can be quite difficult for a beginner.

- Concentrate on the commands you need to know *first,* i.e. read, delete, message, send and cancel.
- Learn to read your screen properly (many prompts are there if you know where to look!) and know how to use the 'help' facility
- If you are listed as a user, check your mailbox *daily.* People use E-mail for urgent messages, and it is annoying if someone hasn't read his or her mail three days later!
- Look at the files to check the layout (or ask someone) if you are sending a message for the first time. Usually the top of the message is pre-set (and will include your name as sender and the date and time automatically). You enter the name of the recipient and give your message a title (which will appear in the recipient's envelope). Keep this short and to the point.
- The message is usually informal. It is your choice whether or not to include any informal salutation (e.g. regards) or your name at the end (as it is printed on the top anyway – see example below).
- Check it first before you send it – don't risk sending an E-mail message to everyone on the network, then finding it includes a very obvious spelling error!
- Only print out a message if you know you are going to need to take action on it later or file it. The idea of the system is to save people using masses of paper!

- Regularly delete any unwanted messages in your In mailbox and Out mailbox, otherwise it will take you ages to search through everything if you want to find a specific message again.

From Alana McCabe (MCCABE.A)
To Simpson J
Date Tuesday, 14 June 199- 0935 am
Subject Furnishing Fabric

Simon Foster called quite late yesterday and left some samples for us to look at. Think these could be useful in relation to the Hudson job. I left them in your office and locked the door so no doubt you found them first thing this morning!

Could you take a look at these and also show them to Melinda for her opinion? If you're interested I'll work out quantity required and get a firm price from Simon later today.

Thanks

cc SHAW.M

Figure 4.87 An E-mail message

Did you know?

On all E-mail systems you can save or store messages you may want at a later date. You can then delete them from your mailbox, but will know that they haven't gone forever!

Faults and problems

If everything is functioning properly you should have few problems. However, some you may encounter are listed below.

- **Unknown user ID** – you are trying to send to an unlisted user. You may be able to list all users – check if your system does this. Then check the spelling of the name and that you have the correct initial. On most systems you can flag a user from the list and transfer this to your message so that you can be sure it is copied correctly.

- **No response** – it may be that the system failed during transmission. This isn't often known or signalled to the user. Check your information screen to see if the recipient has read the message. If not, send a reminder and/or telephone them.

- **Cannot read received message** – often due to a temporary system problem, e.g. maintenance work was being done on the system when the message was sent. If you can identify the sender, E-mail or ring them to tell them your problem. If it happens often, contact your internal computer service engineer or help desk.

- **System failure** – if this happens part-way through a message you may find your screen freezes on you, which can be extremely annoying if you are halfway through a very long message! On most systems you should phone your computer service engineer or help desk. If you are using New Prestel or Telecom Gold, remember that you are still *connected via the phone link* (so you are still being charged!). *Either* press the relevant button on your modem to cancel the call (if there is one) or switch off your PC (if you can't log off properly) and then re-enter. Then instruct your telephone to hang up. Both Telecom Gold and New Prestel operate a help line for users who are having problems.

Did you know?

On some internal systems, routine maintenance work or systems failure can mean that messages you have read are deleted – perhaps before you wanted them to be. On other systems this happens automatically after a certain time period to save space in the system.

Evaluating E-mail

Internal Email is almost as easy to use as a fax machine – especially when you get used to the system. Internet is also easy to use, because transmission out of the company is automatic and may take place at scheduled times each day. Using New Prestel and Telecom Gold can be more difficult – especially for a beginner. You really need to learn from someone who knows what he or she is doing.

E-mail costs

Internal electronic mail may be free – because the company already has the network and computers in place. E-mail may be simply an additional, useful facility on a local network. However, to communicate over a large area, or to company employees in remote locations (e.g. working from home) the basic internal system will have to be extended by one of the special services available. For this the company will pay a registration fee, plus a monthly standing charge, and then additional charges for usage and special services.

E-mail and security

There should be no problems unless someone guesses your password – or you tell someone what it is! Try to avoid doing this even in an emergency, because it means someone can send out messages in your name and read your mail!

Probably the biggest security problem is being distracted or interrupted whilst accessing E-mail and then leaving your computer on and walking away from it. At that point anyone can use it – and it will appear to be you.

Figure 4.88 Don't be distracted whilst connected to the E-mail network

Ways to store documents

Paper filing

Ways to reference documents before they are filed in a paper filing system are discussed on page 505. The convenience and ease of use of manual filing systems vary according to their type. You can analyse them according to:

- ease of storage
- ease of finding and retrieving.

Ease of storage

Most paper filing systems are easy to use, provided you recognise the system being used and stick to the rules! The important part is to make sure you identify the file in which the document should be placed, before you file it.

Most filing systems use a system of labelled tabs that stick up from the rack or the drawer, making the section for that file is easy to find. Make sure you know whether the files are kept in front of the tab or behind it!

Ease of finding and retrieving

If documents have been filed in the right place, they are easy to find. If they are in the wrong place you may not have a clue where to start looking! You could try files nearby, or those with similar titles. You could ask the person who filed the document – if you can establish who this was. If it is your own system then you have no-one to blame but yourself.

One problem arises when people want to borrow a document or file. Documents should never be lent out, as you will forget who borrowed them. By the time you need them again it may be too difficult to retrieve them. Normally only full files are lent and these are booked out in a special **absence book.** If they are not returned within a certain time the borrower is reminded and asked to bring them back promptly.

Did you know?

You will struggle to find paper documents if you don't file them regularly. If you are very busy and see a stack of paper starting to mount up, use a concertina file divided into lettered compartments. This is ideal if you are using an alphabetical reference system.

Pre-sort each document by writing the name under which it must be filed at the top right-hand corner and place it in the concertina file under the appropriate letter. You can then find the document in a hurry even if it isn't yet in the main system.

Cost of paper filing

Paper files may be filed in a vertical or horizontal filing cabinet. Vertical cabinets are the most common – usually containing either three or four drawers. Horizontal cabinets have shelves that are specially adapted to hold files (and even computer print-outs – see below) or a mixture of items such as files, computer supplies and reference books.

Cabinets vary in price depending upon quality. Their major disadvantage is the space they take up in an office. Therefore, rather than simply expanding the files indefinitely, it is usual to sort through the files, under supervision, at regular intervals and to **archive** or **destroy** documents which are no longer needed. Archived documents are placed in special holders and stored in a designated area – often in the basement where they are out of the way. Documents will be archived if they must be kept for some time according to the law, or if they may be needed again. Other documents, which will never be required again, can be destroyed.

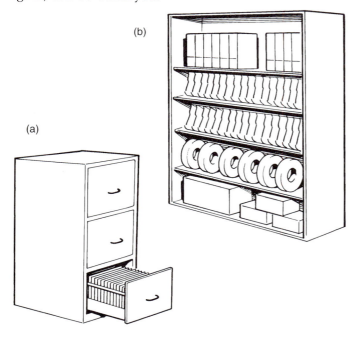

(b)

(a)

Figure 4.89 (a) A vertical filing cabinet (b) A lateral or horizontal filing cabinet

Non-assessed activity

■ Ask your tutor to let you see the type of filing equipment used in your college or school.

■ Look in an office supplies catalogue and find out the price of a good-quality, four-drawer vertical cabinet and a multi-purpose lateral cabinet.

Safety and security

Most cabinets have several in-built safety features. For instance, you can only open one drawer at a time in a vertical cabinet to prevent it tilting towards you. All cabinets are lockable; this is obviously necessary if the documents are personal or confidential. Very important confidential documents can be stored in a specially strengthened cabinet with the top drawer designed as a safe. Many modern filing cabinets are fire-resistant, waterproof and crash-proof. This means that if a fire breaks out the papers in the cabinet will not burn, *and* if the cabinet heats up and then is cooled quickly by water from a fire hose it will not split. Neither will it break open if someone throws it from a top floor window!

Document security can vanish, however, when you are destroying or archiving documents, unless you are very careful. Confidential documents should be destroyed in a **shredder.** Important archives should be kept in a locked room, and a list of key holders kept.

Computer files

Most computer operators save their work on disk – either on floppy disk or hard disk depending upon the facilities available on their computer.

Ease of storing

On most packages you simply press a key to save the document. At this point you will normally be prompted to give a name to the document you are saving. It is then that your organisational skills are tested! If you label your memos as memo1, memo2 etc. you will have few clues to help you to find which memo relates to what, if you need to retrieve one later.

All systems have some type of directory showing all the documents or files stored on a particular disk or system. Therefore the way in which you manage your disks and directory is very important.

If you are using floppy disks you need to label each one clearly. Keep all your documents relating to a particular topic on one disk – or more, if you need to. Make sure you use the same title for all disks relating to one topic, but number them, for example, Sales1, Sales2. Make sure you record what is on each disk. If you are lazy, and can't be bothered to switch disks to save a document, you will pay the price later. Set up a system for naming your documents so that you give yourself as many clues as possible when you are searching for them later.

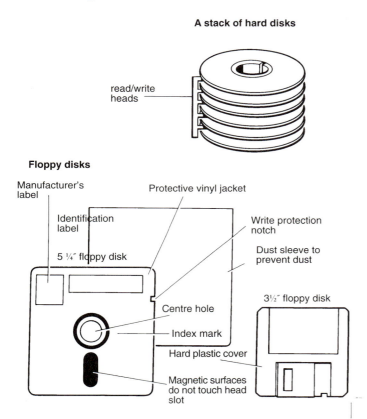

A stack of hard disks

read/write heads

Floppy disks

Manufacturer's label

Protective vinyl jacket

Identification label

Write protection notch

5 ¼″ floppy disk

Dust sleeve to prevent dust

3½″ floppy disk

Centre hole

Index mark

Hard plastic cover

Magnetic surfaces do not touch head slot

Figure 4.90 Hard disks and floppy disks

On a hard disk, computer users normally set up a system of main directories and sub-directories. You may have a main directory, sometimes called the **root directory**, e.g. WPLETTERS, for all the letters you type. In this you could have six sub-directories, for instance, if you produce work for six different people. These could be labelled by their surnames, e.g. WPLETKING, WPLETBROWN and so on. (You may have to abbreviate these names if your system restricts file and directory names to eight characters.) The directories

would then hold a smaller number of documents and each would be easy to find, no matter which method you use to search for it (see page 520).

Did you know?

This type of electronic filing is often called **tree and branch filing.** Think of the main or root directory as the tree and the sub-directories as separate branches off the main trunk. Each branch can have further divisions as necessary. In a similar way, the tree could be the filing cabinet, the branches would be the drawers and so on. The titles of your documents are your file labels, and so on. Taking a print-out of your directory can also be useful way of knowing what is on each file or disk.

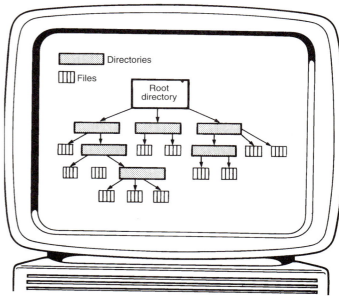

Directories

Files

Root directory

Figure 4.91 The tree-and-branch system of filing on a computer

Non-assessed activity

Suppose you use a word-processing package to produce letters, memos and monthly sales reports for two managers – Mrs Swann and Mr Pansetti.

You have just been given a new computer and want to set up a proper directory system on the hard disk so that you can find documents quickly and easily.

519

Devise a simple directory system that will enable you to save and retrieve all the different types of documents you create quickly and easily.

Did you know?

Good directory management means regularly going through all the documents and deleting those that are no longer needed.

Ease of retrieval

As with paper filing systems, this usually depends on how well the documents were filed in the first place! However, if you have a sensible directory system, many computer packages contain facilities to help you to retrieve documents quickly and easily. On the best systems you can do a search for a specific document if you know any part of its content, or even the date on which it was produced. For instance you may be able to:

- set up an automatic search in which you type in a key word or code and the computer does the rest
- search by key fields. This is often used for files stored on a database package, when you may be able to target the information you require during your search. For instance, the Vehicle Licensing Authority keeps a database of all drivers in the UK. By using multi-field searching it can immediately retrieve a list of all **male** drivers, **born before** 1940, with a **clean** licence, who live in **Cheshire** simply by searching under the categories in bold above.

If you cannot undertake any of these automatic searching techniques, you may have to scroll through all the titles of the documents yourself, which can be time-consuming, especially if half the documents are very old and should have been erased months ago!

Did you know?

Optical disks are growing in popularity as a storage medium, because they can store a vast amount of information and are less apt to be damaged than magnetic disks. A 5″ CD-ROM disk (where the data can be read but not erased or replaced) can hold up to 250 000 pages of text, and any page can be accessed in seconds simply by typing in a key or code word. However, access times are not yet as fast as for magnetic disks.

Cost

Floppy disks are available in two sizes – 5¼″ and 3½″, although the 5¼″ size is becoming obsolete. The amount that can be stored depends on whether the disk is single or double sided and whether it is single, double or high density. High-density disks are now becoming standard. Floppy disks aren't expensive, particularly when you consider that the documents can be deleted when they are no longer needed, to create additional storage space. However, the price does vary depending upon the size and type of disk (see above) and the quality.

Optical disks are far more expensive – particularly erasable optical disks. However, prices are falling and, as they do, it is likely that these disks will become the 'floppy disk' of the future.

Computers with hard disks vary in price, depending upon other facilities such as processing speed and memory size. Today, virtually all computers are sold with a hard disk.

Non-assessed activity

Obtain a computer supplies catalogue and look up the current prices of the different disks mentioned above. Find out the price of three different computers and assess why the prices vary. Compare your findings with those of the rest of your class.

Safety of documents

All floppy disks can be **write protected**, which means that no information can be added to or deleted from the disk. This can protect your documents and prevent anyone else from accidentally overwriting something you need. On a 5¼″ disk you must cover the **write protect notch** with a small piece of sticky paper (provided with the disk). On a 3½″ disk there is a small plastic clip which you slide into position. If you want to look after your documents it is important that you take good care of your floppy disks. Although 3½″ disks are more robust than 5¼″ disks, the same general rules still apply.

- Write the label for the disk *before* sticking it on. Never press on the disk itself with a pen.
- Always keep the disk in its dust jacket or box when it is not in use.
- Always store disks carefully in a special, purpose-made disk box.

- Never overfill a disk box so that the disks rub against each other.
- Keep the disks away from anything magnetic.
- Don't leave the disks near direct heat, e.g. radiators or sunlight.
- Don't touch the exposed recording surface.

Finally, a word of warning – think carefully before you start deleting files or documents. If you are careless you may find you have deleted the wrong one in error.

Documents stored on a hard disk can also be deleted in error – although on some programs you will receive an 'are you sure?' prompt. Fortunately, on many DOS and Windows systems there is an 'undelete' function which, with the help of a member of the computer services staff, *may* be used to find a document you deleted in error! Of course, if you have made a back-up file, this assistance won't be necessary (see below).

Security of documents

Most organisations have a system of **user identification** (ID) and **passwords** to prevent or restrict access to important or confidential information. Each user will have an ID which will determine the level of access for that particular person. For instance, a director of the company may have full access to all files, a supervisor to most files, but a junior employee to only certain files.

In addition, each user will have an individual password. This has to be used in conjunction with the ID and enables the computer to check whether the person logging on is the genuine user. All passwords should be:

- kept confidential
- changed frequently
- remembered – not written down
- original words rather than obvious ones (e.g. do not use 'Xmas' in December and 'holiday' in the middle of July).

A final precaution may be to make certain files completely inaccessible unless a specific password is used. This may only be known by high ranking people in the organisation or those in charge of computer maintenance who may need to be able to access operating files not available to anyone else.

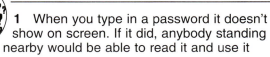

Did you know?

1 When you type in a password it doesn't show on screen. If it did, anybody standing nearby would be able to read it and use it later!
2 A 'hacker' is a person who tries to gain unauthorised entry into a computer system by working out the password.

Computers and disk security

One of the biggest headaches for computer maintenance staff is caused not by hackers or unauthorised access to information, but by **viruses.** A virus is a rogue program introduced into a computer system, and it can create untold damage. This may include blanking screens, wiping hard disks or even making the whole system inoperable. Floppy disks can 'carry' the virus – if a floppy disk becomes 'infected', it can pass on the virus to every other computer in which it is used.

Floppy disks suspected of carrying any virus should be 'swept' to check if a virus is present. If so, the disk must be wiped or discarded. This not only gets rid of the virus but also any other information on the disk – even if this is important or irretrievable.

You should therefore:

- always take back-up copies of your work (even if it is saved on hard disk) – see below
- store both these *and the original disks* in a secure place (and never leave them lying on your desk!)
- never take to work any borrowed programs or disks from an unknown source or outside computer and load them on your machine.

In many cases, the most *valuable* items in an organisation are not the most *expensive!* Whilst computer disks are very cheap to buy, the information they contain may cost a considerable amount of time and money to replace. For that reason, copy or back-up disks should be stored in special boxes inside heat resistant safes so that, in the case of fire, the contents will not be damaged.

As a final point, computer disks should never be thrown away without being wiped or damaged in some way to make them unreadable.

Figure 4.92 Disks must never be thrown away unless they have been wiped or damaged!

Did you know?

Disk manufacturers will only guarantee information on disks up to 52° Celsius. Beyond this it is probable all information will be lost. If such disks contained all the company's records and there were no back-ups stored in a separate place, it could be weeks or even months before the organisation is operational again.

Security and the Data Protection Act

The confidentiality of personal data held on computers is covered by law – under the **Data Protection Act.** If you leave disks with confidential documents on them lying around, and they fall into the wrong hands, you could be liable to prosecution under the Act.

The main requirements of the Act are that:

- all persons or companies who hold personal data on computer must be registered as data users with the **Data Protection Registrar**
- any information held on computer must have been acquired legally
- personal data must only be used and disclosed to others for reasons which are compatible with the purpose for which it is held

- the data must be relevant, accurate, kept up-to-date and not excessive for the purpose for which it is required
- records must not be kept for longer than necessary
- individuals must be given access to information held about them and this must be corrected or erased if it is shown to be incorrect
- proper security measures must be taken against unauthorised or accidental access to the data or alteration, disclosure, loss or destruction of the information held.

The last point is very important. All computer users should be aware that:

- unauthorised print-outs of information must never be given to anyone
- precautions must be taken to prevent unauthorised people from being able to read confidential information on screen
- user IDs and computer passwords must be kept confidential
- security systems in place to prevent accidental erasure of information on disk must always be followed.

Did you know?

All employees have a right to see all computerised information held about them. They may be able to claim compensation if this information is inaccurate.

Computer back-up files

If you save an important document to disk then you are safe, provided nothing goes wrong with your disk or system to destroy the information you have so carefully preserved. The worst thing would be if your computer failed and, as part of the repair, the engineers had to wipe off all the information from your hard disk. The only way you can safeguard your documents is to have *two* disks – one as your working disk and the second, containing exactly the same information, as a **back-up** for the first disk. This can also help if you accidentally delete any information or files from your working disk – you can restore them again from your back-up.

Remember, though, that your back-up disks need updating regularly, otherwise the information they carry will soon be out of date.

522

Obviously all the features of ordinary computer files also apply to back-up files in relation to ease of storage, retrieval, cost and security.

Did you know?

Some packages *automatically* back up the work you are doing every few minutes. This is a very useful feature as it means you don't have to remember to save your work regularly. If your package doesn't have this feature, then you should develop the habit of saving your work about every five minutes – in case anything goes wrong. There is nothing more frustrating than losing half an hour's work because somebody turned off the power by mistake when you were working!

Non-assessed activity

As a group, draw up a comparison chart summarising the information you have just been reading about the ways in which documents can be sent and stored. If only one master chart is compiled by everyone, photocopy it so that each person has his or her own copy. File this neatly for future reference.

Optional evidence assignment

*This activity can be carried out verbally in class **in a group** as a non-assessed activity to consolidate learning. Alternatively, if you do it **on your own**, it can count as supplementary evidence towards the following parts of the scheme.*

PC 4: Reference, correctly file and retrieve business documents

PC 5: Identify and evaluate ways to send and ways to store business documents

Range: Reference: alphabetically, by subject, number, date

Evaluate ways: ease of sending and storing, ease of finding and retrieving, cost, safety of documents, security of documents

Ways to send: special, delivery, post, electronic transmission (fax, electronic mail)

Ways to store: paper filing, computer files, computer back-up files.

Core skills: Communication, Information technology

Read the following case study and answer the questions which follow.

Case study

Louise, a new girl in your office, is driving everyone mad. She has been given the job of helping to set up a new database system and has to input customer names and addresses from the correspondence files. Louise hasn't much idea how the files were referenced and stored in the first place and spends ages looking for each one. Neither has she any idea how to put the files away when she has finished with them – they are at present in a huge heap on her desk.

Yesterday two other problems occurred. Louise was asked to print out six names and addresses urgently for a representative who was working from home. It took her most of the afternoon to retrieve the information required. Then, just before 5 pm, a computer fault occurred. The engineers arrived and announced that the hard disk had developed a fault and would probably have to be replaced before the computer was usable again. In the meantime they asked her to work on another machine.

This morning the representative rang in to say the information hadn't arrived. Your manager was furious when he found out that she had sent it by second-class post. He also went mad when he saw the number of files on her desk and told her if she didn't improve by the end of the week she'd be looking for a new job. After he left Louise burst into tears and confided that because she hadn't backed up any of her work she would have to start recreating the database from scratch on the new machine. You quite like her, and decide to take her to one side and see if you can help.

1 *Either* **write down** or explain **verbally** to your tutor (who can play the part of Louise):
   - the different methods of referencing documents
   - the reason why these different methods are used
   - the importance of correctly filing documents.

2 a State clearly a more appropriate method Louise could have used to send the information to the representative.
   b If the organisation for which you work has a range of modern systems installed, which method would you recommend she uses **now** to get the information to the rep quickly?

3 How should Louise have stored and retrieved the customer information on the database?

4 Write a list of hints and tips for Louise about:
   - how to create computer files

- how to create back-up files
- the safety of documents stored on computer
- the security of documents stored on computer.

Evidence assignment

At this point your tutor may wish you to continue work on the project which will prove to your verifiers that you understand this section of the element. If so, turn to page 526 and do Section 3 of the project. This covers the third evidence indicator for this element.

Revision test

True or false?

1 Floppy disks are very expensive.
2 Nobody uses typewriters in business these days.
3 Memos are used for internal business communication.
4 It is easy to make changes when you are word processing a document.
5 It is virtually as quick to send a fax to America as it is to Cardiff.

Fill in the blanks

6 Chronological filing means filing by _____ .
7 For a small fee, documents posted today will arrive by lunchtime tomorrow using the _____ _____ service
8 E-mail messages can be sent all over the world using the _____ system
9 To access a computer file you normally need to log in using your user ID and then key in a _____ .
10 All business letters are sent on _____ _____ paper.

Short answer questions

11 State **four** methods of sending a document.
12 State **four** ways of referencing a document.
13 State **five** ways in which documents can be processed.
14 State **six** components of a business letter.
15 State **two** advantages of making computer back-up files.

Write a short paragraph to show you clearly understand each of the following terms

16 Document format
17 Message form
18 Subject referencing
19 Electronic mail
20 Language

Evidence indicator project

Unit 4 Element 4.3

This project has been designed to cover all the evidence indicators related to Element 4.3. It is divided into three sections. Tutors may wish students to complete the sections at the appropriate points marked in the text. Alternatively, tutors may prefer their students to do the entire project at the end of the element.

Performance criteria: 1–5

Core skills: Communication
Application of number
Information technology

Section 1

The situations below all involve Mr Charles Dixon, Sales Manager of Bramley Products, Hightown. Prepare the documents he requires first in draft (using handwriting) and then produce a final version (using a typewriter or word processor). Bramley Products letter headed paper is included at the back of this book, together with a message form and a memo heading. Remember to work using photocopies – not the original documents in this book!

Make sure you complete this section of the project by the deadline date given to you by your tutor.

1   Students often contact the Sales department for information about the company if they are doing business studies projects. A standard information pack has been produced, which can be sent to all enquirers. Mr Dixon has asked you to send a letter to Jonathan Evans of 39 Highbury Walk, Hightown, HG3 9DM which:

   ■ thanks the student for his enquiry
   ■ explains that an information pack is enclosed
   ■ asks him to contact the company again if he requires any additional information.

2   Bramley Products makes a wide range of apple-based items, including a well-known apple drink. A letter of complaint has been received from a Mrs May Rickards of 2 Manor Road, Hightown, HS3 9KN. She bought a carton recently at Topwoods Superstore but the drink was very bitter. She has returned the carton. Mr Dixon has asked you to write to her:

   ■ thanking her for her letter
   ■ pointing out that the carton was past its 'use before' date when she bought it and the superstore should have removed it from the shelves
   ■ informing her that she should have returned the carton to the superstore
   ■ saying that as a gesture of goodwill Bramley Products is enclosing a voucher for £5 off her next purchase of their goods.

3   Mr Dixon has arranged to meet Mrs Sue Walker of Denton Packaging Ltd, 15 Station Road, Baxendale, BX3 8DK at 10 am next Tuesday. The arrangements were made over the phone but Mr Dixon said he would confirm the meeting in writing. Prepare the letter required.

4   Write a memo on behalf of Mr Dixon to the Human Resources Manager, Margaret Thompson. He has recently notified her of a vacancy for an administration assistant and wants to know when this will be advertised. The department has a backlog of work to clear and the vacancy needs filling as a matter of urgency.

5   Whilst he is out, you take a telephone call for Mr Dixon from Sue Walker. She wants to know if he can change the time of the appointment next week to 2 pm. Complete a message form for him. Her telephone number is 01437 474749.

6   Bramley Products is holding a Tasting Evening three weeks on Wednesday from 7 pm to 9 pm. Mr Dixon wants you to prepare an invitation to be sent out to local clubs and societies inviting people to the event. Two new products – Bramley Cider and Bramley Apple Sauce – will be launched at this event.

   Draft the invitation for Mr Dixon's approval.

7   Prepare a notice about the Tasting Evening to go on the staff notice board. Mention that staff and their friends/relatives are welcome to attend.

Make out an evaluation sheet giving your own evaluation of each document you have prepared in terms of:

   ■ quality of appearance
   ■ style
   ■ format
   ■ spelling
   ■ grammar.

Submit all your draft and final versions of each document to your tutor, together with your completed evaluation sheet.

Section 2

Your tutor has asked you to help prepare a one page information sheet on your course. This should contain:

- the title
- a brief description of the course content
- the entry requirement(s)
- how work is assessed on the course
- the courses to which you can progress on successful completion.

Put the reference OD/183 at the bottom of the document.

Make sure you complete this section of the project by the deadline date given to you by your tutor.

1   a   Draft out the leaflet in writing, paying particular attention to your spelling and grammar. Try to show how, in your opinion, the leaflet should be designed.

   b   Make a note of the time it takes you to produce the document.

   c   Check the content with your tutor and make any changes that are necessary as neatly as you can.

2   Prepare the leaflet using **one** of the following methods:

- using a typewriter
- using a word processor
- using a desktop publishing package.

Use any special effects you can to make the leaflet attractive to read. Proof-read your work carefully and correct any mistakes. Make sure you have a print-out of the work produced on the word processor. Again note the time it takes you to produce the final document.

3   Prepare to make 10 photocopies. At the moment you are about to make your copies you are informed that the reference **should** have been OD/102. Make the necessary change as neatly as you can and then make your copies. Make a note of

how long it takes you to make the change and make the copies.

4   Now make out a comparison chart for the **three** methods of processing documents you used. Make notes for each under the following headings:

- legibility
- time taken to produce
- ability to make changes
- storage.

5   Assume that typists and word processor operators employed in an organisation are paid £4.50 an hour. The DTP operator is paid £6 an hour and the person in the office who uses the photocopier is paid £5 an hour. From the time taken to produce each document estimate its cost, if the paper on each occasion costs 3p a sheet and photocopying costs 2p a page.

Enter your results on your comparison chart.

Section 3

Use **both** a paper-based filing system **and** a computer-based filing system over a period of one month. Note that your paper based system can be based on your portfolio or your work folder – provided that you have a good method of referencing and filing your assignments or notes. Your computer-based system can be based on the work you undertake in your IT or word processing lessons and the storage method you use.

Make a record that shows clearly how you have referenced, filed and retrieved **at least** 36 documents and 6 files.

Make sure you complete this section of the project by the deadline date given to you by your tutor.

Communication

The ability to communicate is probably the most important skill you will need in almost any job. If you aren't happy dealing with figures and need a calculator even for simple tasks, you may be wise to look for a job which has the minimum number of numerical tasks. If you don't particularly like using a computer, you could aim for a job where you are dealing mainly with people, e.g. on reception. But if you are hopeless at communicating, then you have little chance of getting a job at all! You simply can't sit at a desk all day, playing with papers and refusing to talk to anyone, to answer the phone or even write a simple note.

The ability to *communicate well* is important, not only at work but also in your private life. You will find it easier to talk to a wider variety of people on a range of different subjects. You will be able to write letters and other documents people can understand easily and to which they will respond. You will be better able to understand articles you read and programmes you watch. In fact, the benefits are enormous.

Communication and GNVQ

Your assessments in relation to Communication are mainly covered in a vocational context. This means that instead of simply dealing with the theoretical aspects of communication you will be assessed on your ability to use these skills in practical, work-related situations. Communication is a major part of most assignments and projects you produce for your mandatory and optional units.

However, before you can put your skills into practice you have to develop them! You may find that there are special lessons in your timetable, in which you learn and improve your Communication skills. This unit has been designed to:

■ introduce you to the basics of Communication skills
■ concentrate on the aspects of Communication on which you will be assessed
■ act as a reference guide if you forget anything
■ give you additional practice in areas where you are weak
■ improve your overall knowledge of Communication.

Note that there are no evidence indicator projects at the end of the unit because the evidence indicators will be achieved as part of your mandatory and optional unit assessments. However, some optional evidence assignments are included to give you additional opportunities to obtain evidence.

Did you know?

If you are very good at English – for instance, if you have achieved a good grade (A–C) in GCSE English Language, you can discuss with your tutor the possibility of undertaking your core skills to achieve higher than level 2 – the equivalent for Intermediate students. What you mustn't do is only cover Communication at level 1! However, given that the majority of students will be studying at the equivalent level, this unit concentrates on level 2 of the Core Skills scheme.

Communication level 2

There are **four** elements in the scheme. Bear in mind that the first number below refers to the **level** and the second to the **element**.

2.1   Take part in discussions
2.2   Produce written material
2.3   Use images
2.4   Read and respond to written materials

The sections in this unit are all designed to give you information and practice in each of these areas. There is also a section which gives you the basic rules of grammar, punctuation and spelling, together with some practical exercises for you to try.

At the end of the chapter is a Quick reference section, which contains a brief summary of the rules relating to various types of communication and which you can use as a memory aid.

Element 2.1 Take part in discussions

Discussions and verbal communication – speaking to other people

There are many occasions when it is necessary to take part in discussions with other people. These may be people you know, such as your tutor, parents or other members of your group, and people you don't know, such as visitors, other students or members of staff in school or college who are unfamiliar to you. They may be people who already have some knowledge of the topic under discussion or they may have no previous knowledge at all. You may be talking to one person, either in a face-to-face discussion or over the telephone. Alternatively you could be talking to a group of people.

In all these situations you have to learn how to cope. Why? Because when you are at work you will be expected to have the skills and confidence to talk to other employees in the company – some of whom you will know well and some of whom you won't. Some will be at a higher level than yourself and others will not be. You will be expected to talk to them about a variety of different matters. You will also be expected to be able to approach customers, visitors and other callers and speak to them so that you give a good impression – both of yourself and your company. Sometimes a person will arrive alone, at other times a group of people may call.

When you first start trying out your skills at talking to people – especially strangers – you may feel very nervous and shy. You may think you don't know what to say or how to talk to them. You may be frightened of making a fool of yourself and feel as if everyone is watching you. This feeling will go as you gain **confidence** – and the only way to do this is to **practise**. Once you feel happier about having the skills to cope, you will feel better about handling this type of situation.

Did you know?

Callers and visitors are often nervous too! The person you are approaching may be more apprehensive than you are! Believe it or not, a friendly smile and a pleasant greeting are often all that is needed to break the ice.

Figure C.1 A friendly smile and a pleasant greeting

The purpose of discussions

You may have a discussion with someone:

- to offer information
- to obtain information
- to exchange ideas.

The key facts to remember in relation to these are as follows.

1 If you are **offering** information, make sure you know what you are talking about! If you don't know the answer to a question, it is far better to be honest (and offer to find out) than to bluff and then be caught out!

2 If you are trying to **obtain** information, don't fire questions at the other person one after another. **Lead** him or her through the session by politely asking your questions in a sensible order. This implies you have done some preparation beforehand, even if only in your head! Be prepared to vary your approach and change your questions if the situation warrants it. Don't stick rigidly to what you planned to ask, and afterwards, don't forget to say 'thank you'!

3 If you are exchanging ideas with someone, this implies that you both have some thoughts on the matter. The key word in this is **exchange**. This means that not only do you have to talk, you also have to listen. The faults to avoid are:
- doing all the talking
- making no contribution to the discussion at all!

Try to identify which type of person you are most likely to be – someone who talks too much or someone who doesn't talk at all. Only very rarely can someone not make any useful contribution at all – usually two heads are better than one.

Skills you need to develop

Throughout this section there are several hints and tips to help you improve your ability to talk to people. You also need to develop certain other skills that are important when you are involved in discussions with other people.

1 Be flexible in your approach and prepared to adjust it to suit both the audience and the situation. Your ability to do this will improve with experience. As an example, if you find that your next visitor, Mrs Evans, is an elderly pensioner who is hard of hearing, you should hardly approach her as you would a young professional business person of 35! You should consider, for instance:
  ■ how to use language which would help her to understand, without using specialist terms she wouldn't know
  ■ how to express what you wanted to say in different ways – to help her to understand if there were difficulties
  ■ how to adjust your approach to be more or less formal according to the situation. Then, if Mrs Evans was quickly followed by the Managing Director you would know you should change your style a little!

2 Always look for confirmation that everyone understands what is going on, by checking key points and making sure that everyone has been listening and is clear about the situation. If people talk to you, and you do not understand what they mean, it is far more sensible to ask them to repeat it than to guess! Equally, if someone looks blank when you speak to them, the chances are they haven't understood you properly. However, they may find it difficult to ask you to explain – so check by careful questioning where things went wrong, and put them right!

3 Learn to move a discussion on, or take it forward purposefully if it is getting bogged down. This is a skill which will be much appreciated by other people present. Occasionally, in any discussion, situations arise when everyone starts going around in circles, for instance:
  ■ one person won't stop talking about his or her pet project
  ■ another keeps bringing up irrelevant information

  ■ no-one can make a decision on what to do.
At this point it is useful to stop, summarise what has happened so far and develop a plan of action to move on. Even if something has to be left over, this is better than the entire session grinding to a halt or getting nowhere.

Did you know?

Tutors are normally quite expert at moving things forward – for instance if someone keeps delaying everything in class. Watch the techniques your tutors use in this situation!

The importance of verbal communication skills

You will find that throughout your adult life, the way in which you speak is very important. People may even start to ignore you if you cannot make yourself understood, or if you let it be seen you are bored or irritated by what others are saying. Your voice is one of your most powerful weapons. You can inform, persuade, coax, instruct, demand – and you can gain all sorts of advantages in being able to use it well.

As with all skills, some people are more naturally gifted than others. If you don't think that speaking to people (other than your close friends or family) is one of your best assets, don't despair. You only need to grasp some basic points, practise a few skills and you'll soon feel your confidence grow as you see yourself beginning to improve.

By that stage you should be able to see why it is sometimes better to *say* something rather than write it down i.e:

■ it is direct – unlike the use of a letter or other form of written document
■ it is quick
■ it is normally much more informal than other forms of communication
■ there is instant feedback – you normally get an immediate response
■ it can be the most persuasive means of communication.

The following tips offer guidance on what you should be thinking about when you talk to people. There are also some practical exercises to be carried out, either individually or in a group.

Accuracy

Even when you are speaking to someone rather than writing to him or her, you still need to think through what you are saying before you say it. If you are talking to friends informally, you can correct yourself if you make a mistake (or someone may point it out to you pretty quickly). Even if you don't realise at the time that you have given incorrect information it may not matter – you can call your friend later to put it right.

However, if you are talking to someone more formally – at work, in a bank, in a doctor's surgery, etc. – you may not be able to correct yourself so easily, and the consequences may be more serious. Always put your brain into gear before you put your tongue into action!

Non-assessed activity

Work in pairs if possible. Think of **two** recent events you have attended – a party, a film, a pop concert, a sports event etc. Alternatively, select **two** television programmes you have watched recently.

1 **Without any preparation at all,** describe to your partner what happened at the first event. Let your partner do the same.
2 Then spend **two minutes** *mentally* working out what you are going to say about the second event – don't write anything down. Repeat the exercise. You should feel that you have given a more accurate (and more complete) account of the second event than the first.

Ambiguous or incomplete information

Remember that speech is instantaneous. You can re-read something you have written and alter any obvious errors without anyone else knowing anything about it. You can't do that when you are speaking, so try to avoid saying anything that is ambiguous or incomplete and therefore confusing, e.g:

- Can you come on the 2nd? (The 2nd of what?)
- Can you come on Monday? (Which Monday?)
- I want you to bring along the documents relating to the Robinson contract. (Suppose there are two clients named Robinson?)

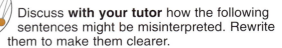

Non-assessed activity

Discuss **with your tutor** how the following sentences might be misinterpreted. Rewrite them to make them clearer.

- Would you ask Miss Lee whether Mrs Parkinson has finished with her file?
- Ask the caretaker about the radiator because it's cold.
- Please complete that application form in black ink.
- The group of students are not all there.
- If you've nothing on, why not come out with me?
- She watched the experiment taking down notes.
- The members of the meeting are listed on the notice board.
- If you let us know we shall arrange for you to look round the house as quickly as possible.
- This is the very last thing I want to do.
- The work needs doing badly.

Body language

Body language is often called **non verbal communication** (NVC) and is normally divided into:

- facial expressions
- eye contact
- gestures
- personal space.

One of the advantages of talking to people rather than writing to them is that you can immediately see their reactions. Remember that they are also forming an impression of how *you* are reacting to what *they* are saying.

Someone who smiles at you and nods would appear to like what you are saying. Someone who shrugs, stares out of the window or pointedly keeps looking at his or her watch may seem to be less impressed. Someone who keeps edging away from you might give you the same impression, but be careful to avoid making too many assumptions based on first impressions. The person who enters your **personal space** by standing very close to you might be indicating interest in what you are saying and feel relaxed in your company. The person who does not might be indicating the opposite. It could also be that the second person is very shy and therefore ill at ease, although he or she still agrees with what you are saying. The same is true if someone fails to make eye contact with you – don't necessarily assume that you are facing a shifty character!

Remember that we tend to mirror what another person is doing if we agree with what is being said.

Next time you are with a large group of people, especially when some are standing in pairs, watch their behaviour. You will often find that if one person crosses his or her legs the other will do the same, if one person is leaning against the bar, so is the other and so on. If you want to make use of body language for your own advantage, or to create a particular impression – nonchalance, earnestness, etc. – think about how you look as well as what you are going to say.

Non-assessed activity

As a group, discuss the body language you might use to show:

- confidence
- amusement
- agreement
- displeasure
- encouragement
- boredom.

Clarity

When you are speaking to someone it obviously helps if they can hear you properly – and without constantly asking you to repeat what you have said. Pitfalls to avoid include:

- speaking too quietly – no-one wants to listen to someone who shouts, but it can be just as difficult to follow someone who mumbles
- speaking too quickly – often someone who is nervous tends to speak quickly, so if you are in a situation new to you or in which you are slightly uncomfortable, make a conscious effort to slow down
- being too hesitant – saying 'er ... ' might give you a bit of thinking time but it can irritate your listener
- using abbreviations or jargon all the time – you know what you mean but your listener may not, and may not be bothered to find out
- having an accent which is so strong that even your best friends have difficulty in understanding you.

Did you know?

Research has shown that, at best, people can only take in about 70 per cent of what they hear. Don't reduce that percentage by giving them too much information in too short a space of time.

Non-assessed activity

Spot the deliberate errors in the following conversation.

What *should* the clerk have said?

Caller	Good morning. Could you let me know whether I can speak to Mr Friedrich please?
Clerk	LMF?
Caller	Sorry?
Clerk	Do you want to ... *(inaudible)*
Caller	I'm sorry but I just can't hear you.
Clerk	*(screams)* I said, do you want to speak to LMF?
Caller	Is LMF Mr Friedrich?
Clerk	Yes.
Caller	Well that's the person I want.
Clerk	Well, er, that's a bit, well um, it may be a bit ...
Caller	Sorry?
Clerk	*(very quickly)* I'll have to check with the R and D section to see if LMF is in an Ops Management meeting or whether he has stopped off at Comp Services to look at the new MIS system.
Caller	Well, perhaps I'll call back later.

Listening

When speaking with someone it is often easy to make the wrong assumption about what is being said and what is being understood.

Non-assessed activity

1 How many of the following have you either said (or secretly thought)?

- I can tell whether people are worth listening to as soon as they come through the door.
- He looked such a mess I couldn't be bothered listening to him.
- Sometimes I'm so busy that I have to listen to someone talking to me whilst I'm doing other things. It's OK – I'm used to doing two things at once.
- I'm frightened of looking a fool if I stop people too often to ask them to explain what they mean.
- I can tell what most people are going to say

almost immediately. In fact I often race ahead of them and finish off their sentences for them.

- Sometimes I pretend to listen when actually I'm miles away. No-one notices.
- When I listen to some people I'm amazed at my own cleverness – I often have to interrupt them to correct them on a few points.
- If I think people are talking nonsense, I've no hesitation in telling them so.

2 Discuss with your tutor why it might be dangerous to believe such statements. (Re-read the section on *Body language* for some assistance if you need to.)

Barriers to good communication

Communication is a two-way process and learning how to listen is just as important as learning how to talk. Assuming that you want to know what the other person is saying, remember the following points.

- Try to make certain that you are in surroundings that allow you to listen and to concentrate. It *is* possible to carry out a conversation at an airport, in a pub or in a busy office with people shouting to one another across the room, but it *isn't* easy. The more important the conversation, the more important it is that your surroundings are quiet and free from any distractions.
- Try not to interrupt (no matter how boring you find the conversation). The person who is talking will not become less boring and may possibly take even longer to come to the point.
- Don't pass the time by fiddling with paper clips on the desk, looking out of the window, looking up a telephone number or trying to sort out a few papers. You may miss an important point and you will probably irritate the speaker.
- Assess how you are feeling. It's not always possible to postpone an important conversation because you have a lot on your mind or are too tired to concentrate, but if it is, do so. Otherwise, simply be aware of your feelings and try to take them into account.
- Sometimes it is more difficult to take in information you don't really want to hear than information that is welcome to you. You might be much more ready to listen and understand if your tutor says that you can have a longer lunch hour, than you would if you were asked to stay an extra hour at the end of the afternoon! If, therefore, you are giving someone some unwanted information, you have to take extra care to make it clear.

Figure C.2 Barriers to good communication

Non-assessed activity

Can you repeat a message accurately? Read a passage from a newspaper *once* to your partner. Now ask your partner to repeat a summary of what you said to a second person and then the second to a third (conducting all these conversations out of the earshot of the others). Compare the summary at the beginning and at the end of the proceedings.

Tone

It's not what you say but the way that you say it … .

Even if you have something very important or interesting to say you are unlikely to be listened to if you are saying it in the wrong way. If you are asking a favour from someone, you are less likely to be successful if your manner is abrupt, than if you make the request pleasantly.

Always remember to whom you are speaking. Some tones of voice are rarely acceptable whatever the circumstances. No-one appreciates being bullied or ridiculed or made the subject of a series of sarcastic remarks. You may have to distinguish between talking to a nervous office junior, who wants everything explained in detail, and the managing director of a firm, who wants some information passed on quickly and efficiently. You may also use a slightly different tone of voice to a persistent and unwanted salesman from the one you would use to a valued client!

Non-assessed activity

As a group, discuss what tone of voice you think is likely to be used in the following situations.

- A mother is trying to prevent her child from running into road.
- A car salesman is trying to sell a car to a customer.
- A member of the Samaritans is taking a telephone call from a frightened and confused caller.
- A DJ is talking to an audience.
- A building society manager is talking to a first-time home buyer about a mortgage.

Telephoning

When you speak to someone over the telephone there are certain differences in the techniques you would use.

The use of body language or facial expressions becomes less important, although many telephone technique handbooks suggest you smile when answering the telephone because it affects your voice. Some books advise you to remain standing when making a difficult call or if you know you have a tendency to talk for too long – sheer weariness will make you put down the receiver!

However, you can't make your body language work for you as effectively over the telephone, so your tone of voice and what you actually say become even more important.

- Where possible be prepared. When making a telephone call, you have the initial advantage that you know what you want to say and, unlike most face-to-face conversations, you can write down a brief summary of at least your opening remarks.
- It is even more important in the case of a telephone conversation that you check that your listener really understands what you are saying. You won't be able to see an approving nod of the head or a puzzled expression.

Note: Making and receiving telephone calls is also dealt with in Element 3.3, page 362.

Non-assessed activity

Discuss **with your tutor** the ways in which you can check that a person at the other end of a telephone line has understood what you have said.

Optional evidence assignment

You work in a small firm of interior designers, which offers a service to the general public by:

- giving advice on all types of house decor
- recommending what types of fabrics, wallpapers and furnishings to use
- supplying the names and addresses of firms of suppliers.

There are four partners in the organisation, together with a receptionist/telephonist, an office manager and a part-time clerk.

As a group, decide who is to take the part of:

- the customer
- the receptionist
- the office manager
- the part-time clerk
- the four partners.

Act out the following situations. Discuss **with your tutor** your performance after each exercise. If you are brave enough, **as a group** award first, second and third prizes to your best performers!

Scene 1

Cast The customer

The receptionist

A valuable customer comes into the reception area and tells the receptionist that the chairs she has recently had re-upholstered are already showing wear and tear. The receptionist knows that the upholsterers reported that the previous damage was caused by the customer's cats. Try to explain this to the customer, a devoted pet lover, as tactfully as you can.

Scene 2

Cast The office manager

The part-time clerk

The office manager has to speak to the part-time clerk who, for the past two weeks has been coming in late. The clerk explains that this has been because the bus has either arrived late each day or not turned up at all.

Scene 3

Cast The part-time clerk

The receptionist

The part-time clerk is thinking about applying for a full-time job and discusses with the receptionist the advantages and disadvantages of working full-time.

Scene 4

Cast The four partners

There is a meeting of the partners to discuss:

■ whether to purchase a new database for keeping customer and supplier records – some partners are in favour, others think it too expensive

■ the bad debt situation – there are three outstanding accounts one for £150, one for £300 and one for £3000. The first two customers are new: the third has always paid his bills before. Various partners have different ideas about what to do.

Making a presentation

There are many occasions at school or college – and when you have actually started work – when you may be expected to stand up in front of a group of people and to talk to them. You may want to give them some information, to sell them something or to persuade them to do something for you. To do this, you have to sell yourself first.

You won't sell yourself if you:

■ don't know your subject matter
■ can't remember what you are going to say
■ repeat the same thing over and over again
■ speak so quietly that no-one can hear you or so quickly that no-one can understand you
■ use confusing technical jargon
■ give a mass of confusing and complicated facts
■ can't answer questions
■ look awful.

Remember that it is not unusual to feel nervous before you start to make a presentation. Almost everyone is, at the beginning. Look at the comments made below and decide whether or not you feel the same!

■ I'm far too frightened to stand up in public and say anything at all – even my name!
■ I'll make a complete fool of myself – I just know it.
■ What if my mind goes blank?
■ Suppose everyone laughs at me.

The problem is the fear of the unknown. All you need to do is to make one very small, very simple presentation and you'll realise that it's not as bad as you think.

However, you do need to be prepared – the better prepared you are, the more successful you will be and the more willing to try something more complicated. When making a presentation you have to:

■ **prepare** it
■ make sure that it is **well organised**
■ be able to **deliver** it well.

Preparation

■ For your first few presentations you will work as part of a group. Find out who is going to be in your group and try to get to know them, if you don't already. There will almost certainly be a mixture of personalities, so make use of it. The person with the outgoing personality can be the leader of the presentation, the quiet, thorough one can take charge of the research, etc, but be sure that *everyone* takes part in the actual presentation.

- Read the instructions carefully. Don't start the research for a topic before you know exactly what you want.
- Find out how long your presentation is expected to last. It will normally be between five and ten minutes. If you are not given a definite time, try to make it as brief as possible. After fifteen minutes, most people in an audience are beginning to fidget. After half an hour their concentration has almost completely disappeared.
- Find out about your audience. Do they know quite a bit about your topic? If so, you have to be very well prepared. Do they know nothing at all? If so, you will have to keep your presentation simple and not confuse them with too much complicated information, too much jargon or too many abbreviations.
- This might seem a chore but, in the early days at least, you should write down every word of what you want to say at the presentation. You can then either learn it off by heart – but still have your notes with you as a back up – or be sufficiently rehearsed to remember all the facts and the order in which you want to give them, even if you are not word perfect. Remember that if you are asked to give a presentation as part of your course assessment you will gain marks if you *don't* merely stand there and read your notes.
- *Whatever else you do,* memorise your introduction and your conclusion!
- You may find that you feel awkward clutching several sheets of paper and that you prefer to use small cards on which you have written key phrases as memory aids. Suppose, for instance, you were preparing a presentation on 'making a presentation'. Your key phrases would include *preparation, organisation* and *delivery* (each followed by a short list of points).
- Remember also that, however dynamic you may think you are, people will get bored just sitting and listening to you. Try to think of ways to illustrate your presentation – posters, charts, overhead projection transparencies, etc.

Organisation of your material

Speaking is the same as writing in many respects. You don't (or shouldn't) write down the first thing that comes into your head and then keep going. You plan an opening paragraph, the main body of the document and then a suitable closing paragraph. The same is true when you are making a presentation. *Plan* your talk so that you:

Figure C.3 Organisation is vital for a successful presentation

- introduce yourself and your team
- introduce what you are going to say
- expand on it, making one point at a time and illustrating each point with a visual aid or giving an example; make sure your audience knows when you move on to the next point
- summarise what you have said – put emphasis on the points you particularly want your audience to remember
- know when to hand over to the next member of the team.

Case study

Suppose you are asked to make a presentation to your group on the problems that have arisen over the student common room in your school or college. Your initial plan could look something like this.

Introduction

The problem – there have been complaints that the student common room is dirty and that there are not sufficient facilities for students.

Main points

1 Cleanliness

By 3 pm each afternoon every table in the common room is littered with empty coffee cups and cans and there are empty crisps packet, and food containers thrown all over the floor. Ash-trays are overflowing.

2 Facilities

There are ten tables and forty chairs. The chairs are dirty and tables stained. The drinks machine is always breaking down. There are few bins and the carpet is torn in one area. There are no lockers. The room looks unpleasant, there are no pictures or plants. No-one seems responsible for the upkeep.

Possible solutions

1 The Head could be approached to see whether:

- a cleaner could be employed for an extra two hours each afternoon to check on cleanliness
- the chairs could be cleaned and the tables repolished
- more bins could be provided
- the drinks machine could be replaced with a newer version – or at least that regular servicing of the existing machine could be arranged
- new lockers could be provided
- the carpet could be cleaned and repaired.

2 The student committee could be involved to:
- oversee the general cleanliness through the efforts of the student representatives and by the mounting of a publicity campaign
- check on the use of the lockers and possibly be responsible for the issuing and return of locker keys
- try to raise some money for plants, posters, etc. to brighten up the room.

Conclusion

There are two possibilities:

- a group representative could speak to the Head about the suggestions made
- a meeting of the student committee could be called to discuss the matter further.

Non-assessed activity

1 Write out the presentation in the above case study in full.

2 Make crib cards for the key phrases you will use when making the presentation.

3 **As a group,** discuss what visual aids or illustrations you could use during the presentation. Prepare **at least one** of them.
4 Ask for **two** volunteers to make the presentation to the rest of the group.
5 With your tutor, assess and discuss their performance and how this could be improved.

Organisation of yourself and your surroundings

Preparing your material is of major importance, but so is preparing yourself. Remember, you also need to prepare your surroundings.

Non-assessed activity

Read the following case study, then list what Shaheda has done wrong. Prepare a checklist of what she should have done.

Case study

Shaheda has to give a presentation to her tutors on the introduction of a new stock control system into a firm. She misses the bus and rushes in to college a few minutes before the presentation is due to take place. She has prepared her notes and crib cards but they are somewhere at the bottom of her bag and she keeps her tutors waiting as she searches for them. She has prepared an overhead projector transparency but, when she switches on the projector, she finds that the bulb has gone. She has forgotten to bring fixing materials for the poster she wants to display. She hasn't given a thought to what she looks like and has turned up wearing a sweatshirt and jeans. She hasn't had time to comb her hair.

Just as she is about to start her presentation she notices that one of the tutors is still standing up and that there are not enough chairs in the room. She also discovers that there is nowhere for her to prop up her notes.

She is so panic-stricken that she forgets to take two or three deep breaths to calm herself and launches straight into her presentation. It's a disaster!

Delivery

If you are well prepared, that's half the battle. The audience doesn't expect you to be a comedian – although a bit of humour does help. Remember one or two basic rules.

- Smile at the audience. Try to look confident even if you are not, but don't worry too much if you know you look nervous. Many people in your audience will sympathise and be on your side.
- If you have not been introduced already, introduce yourself (and the rest of your group), giving your name and the subject of your presentation.
- Make a deliberate effort to speak slowly. Nervous people tend to speak far too quickly and the audience loses track of what is being said.
- Make eye contact with your audience, i.e. look at them rather than at the floor or ceiling – but don't fix one person with a glassy stare and talk only to him or her.
- Be aware of body language (see page 530 for details). Try to avoid using irritating mannerisms – if you are not sure if you have any, ask a trusted friend for an honest opinion.
- Use short words and short sentences. Try to use sentence constructions such as, 'I think that this approach will benefit you,' rather than 'It is possible that this approach will be beneficial' – keep it simple.
- Try to show some enthusiasm – that always looks attractive.
- If you dry up, don't panic. Pause – don't worry that there is a silence – look at your notes and start again. Sometimes someone in the audience will help out with a question or a comment.
- Remember the value of a pause, particularly when you are moving from one point to another. Remember also to tell your audience that you are moving on to a new point.

Non-assessed activity

You will probably have listened to a number of people who bored or irritated you. You will also have half-listened to some people who couldn't manage to hold your interest after the first few minutes.

Colin is one of these people. He is a sales representative for a firm of office suppliers. He has come to give a presentation on the latest photocopier. List where you think he goes wrong and why he failed to make a sale!

Colin	Right, I want to talk to you this morning about our new photocopier – well, the point is that we have sold over 1000 of them since last year, 25 per cent up on our normal sales, 50 per cent up over our

rivals, best photocopier I've ever sold, 30 per cent better than any other photocopier ... (*long pause*) Er ... let me see – I seem to have lost my place ... (*mutters something*).

Manager	I'm sorry, but I can't hear you. Can you speak up please?
Colin	(*scratches his head*) The point is – well, what I mean to say is – this photocopier is worth buying.
Manager	Why?
Colin	(*mutters something at his feet – scratches his head*) Well the point is – it's the best on the market ... (*mutters again*).
Manager	I'm sorry, but I can't seem to hear the end of what you are saying.
Colin	Er ... do you want to look at some of the ... er ... brochures?
Manager	Perhaps that would be as well. Have you any price leaflets?
Colin	Er ... well the point is ... no, I've forgotten them – but I'll send them on to you.

Answering questions

Either during a presentation or at the end you may be expected to answer questions. If you know your topic well this should not be too much of a problem. If you are having difficulty in answering a question, remember to consider one (or more) of the following hints.

1 Ask the person to repeat the question to gain thinking time.
2 If you don't understand the question, say so and ask for it to be re-phrased e.g. 'I'm sorry but I don't know what you mean.'
3 Admit you don't know and say you will find out.
4 Ask for someone in your team to help. (Be ready to help out any other member of your team who seems to be struggling, but be careful not to interrupt too soon.)

Did you know?

Body language shows how you feel. Check that you and your team are not standing so far apart that the people in the audience think you are not speaking to each other, or that you are huddled in such a tight little group that they think you are too frightened to operate as individuals!

537

Types of question

You might also find it useful if you know the type of question you may be asked, and the purpose for asking it. Think about the following questions.

■ Won't this photocopier be very expensive to run?

That sort of question is a **concealed objection** question i.e. where the person asking the question may not be on your side. All you can do is to be factual and to remain pleasant. If the photocopier is going to be more expensive to run, say so, but try to point out the other advantages it may have – such as better quality and higher speeds.

■ Can this photocopier do double-sided pages, collate and staple?

This might be a **test** question, and the questioner may have some knowledge of the topic. If you don't know the answer, *don't* bluff. Say that you will find out whether or not it can and that you will get back to the questioner as quickly as possible.

■ Can you tell me if this type of photocopier is as good as the photocopier I saw at a recent exhibition I attended in New York?

This is a **display** question i.e. the person asking the question is merely trying to show off his own knowledge, or to let everyone know how important he is. Flatter him by being impressed with what he has to say.

■ What makes you think that we need a new photocopier?

The questioner here might be asking a **defensive** question. Perhaps she was responsible for choosing the last photocopier, and is worried in case you criticise that choice. Be careful not to do so.

Optional evidence assignment

Work in pairs. Research and prepare a short talk on a topic that you have discussed with your tutor. Topics you might like to consider include:

■ new developments in information technology
■ a piece of modern office equipment
■ health and safety at work
■ customer care
■ the rights of the consumer.

Time it to last for four minutes, talking for two minutes each.

1 Record your part of the talk on a cassette. Play it back and try to assess whether you need to improve any of the areas listed in the chart in Figure C.4. Write a paragraph about your conclusions.

Pitch

Pitch is the height or depth of your voice. Do you speak too loudly or too gently? Do you lower your voice at the end of each sentence, which may make it more difficult for the audience to hear you?

Pace

Pace is the rate at which you speak. Are you speaking too quickly? Does your subject matter affect you (e.g. if you are angry do you speak more quickly than if you are not)? Do nerves or embarrassment make you speak too quickly?

Pause

Are you pausing at the right places? Remember not to confuse pausing with hesitating!

Tone

Do you speak in a monotone (i.e. on one note) or do you vary the tone? Remember that varying your tone does help to keep your audience interested in what you are saying.

Emphasis

If you have a particularly important piece of information to give, do you place sufficient emphasis on it in order to attract the audience's attention?

Figure C.4 Notes on presentation

2 Deliver the talk to each other. Talk for **two minutes** whilst your partner listens, and then listen to your partner for two minutes. *Assess* each other by using the presentation assessment sheet in Figure C.5. Try to be honest but not brutal!

3 Deliver the same – or another – talk to the **whole group.** Ask them (or your tutor) to assess you, using the same form, and see if you get a better rating.

```
Name of presenter ....................................

Topic...........................................................

1     Delivery
Appearance/dress
Confidence
Mannerisms
Eye contact/body language
Pace/enthusiasm

2     Introduction
Did it create interest?
Was it clear?

3     Presentation
Was it clear?
Was it organised?
Was it suitable for the audience?
Was it the right length?

4     Illustrations/aids
Were notes used well?
Were the visual aids good?

5     Questions
Were the questions well handled?

6     Teamwork
Did the first person introduce the group?
Did each person hand over properly to the next
person?
Did the team support each other –
     verbally?
     non-verbally?
```

Figure C.5 Presentation assessment sheet

Element 2.2 – Produce written material

Even with the increased use of the telephone, there are still going to be many occasions on which you have to write down some information. If you are writing a note to a friend to remind him or her where to meet on Saturday night, it may not be so

important that you write clearly and grammatically, and that your spelling and punctuation are good. In a business situation it does matter. It is vitally important that you know in what form the information should be given – on a pre-printed form, in a letter or report or as the notes of a meeting.

Basic writing skills

This section includes a summary of the most common forms of written communication and the ways in which they should be presented. Examples are included, plus exercises to help you to practise creating these documents.

Firstly though, it is important that you **understand** the areas of the scheme you have to cover and that you have the basic skills for the job. Therefore, the section starts with *Using words in the right way,* which gives you some hints on basic spelling, punctuation, grammar and vocabulary. If you have excellent writing skills already, then you could omit this and move straight to page 549. However, it would be sensible to discuss this with your tutor first.

The key point to remember is that someone who communicates well in writing is able to carry out all the following tasks consistently well.

- **Writing a document that includes clear, accurate and relevant information and meets the main purpose of sending it in the first place.** If you are giving information then it all needs to be there! If you are asking for information, make your request clear – if you omit anything you'll have to write again. If you are giving an opinion or presenting an argument don't be **dogmatic** (look this word up if you don't know what it means!) **Suggest** rather than **dictate.**

- **Writing a document in the correct format.** This means knowing the range of documents that can be produced, their style and how to write them. As discussed in Element 4.3, **business letters** are sent to people outside the organisation, memos are sent to people inside. Sending your boss a written letter, therefore, may be rather novel but would certainly not be the right thing to do – unless you were resigning!

- **Using words – or vocabulary – to express meaning clearly, in terms appropriate for the audience.** You should not write to someone who is completely unfamiliar with a subject in the same style as you would to someone who is familiar with it. Remember that basic, simple sentences are almost always safer than long, elaborate ones. Never try to include words you are not familiar with in a vague desire to impress someone. Rather than impress, you'll look rather silly if you use words in the wrong way!

- **Spelling all the words used correctly, punctuating the document properly and using correct grammar.** If you have any doubts, don't skip the next few pages.

- **Creating a structured document that helps the reader to understand it easily and identify the main points and ideas.** You should find this book is structured in that way – by the use of headings, paragraphs, sentences, numbered and bulleted points, emboldening or italicisation of special words and so on.

Using words in the right way

It's pointless trying to manufacture a car if you don't know how to put all the parts together. The same is true when you produce a piece of writing. If you don't know which word to use, or how to spell it, or if you have difficulty in constructing a sentence, your image as an ambitious young executive will slip! Treat these pages as a reference section – you or your tutor will know if you have any particular difficulties. If you are in any doubt, try the short exercise at the beginning of each item.

Grammatical rules

Exercise 1

Spot the genuine mistake in each sentence. Give yourself two points for each correct answer.

1 Sending you the items today.
2 Details of the new product is to be found on page 2.
3 I think you and me should have a meeting.
4 What reason do you want this information for?
5 Neither the manager or his assistant had heard about the change in plans.
6 He promised to urgently deal with the matter.

Check page 646 for the correct answers. If you find all the mistakes, you can go on to page 544. If not – read on!

The difference between sentences and notes

A sentence has at least one verb, or 'doing' word. Notes are quicker to write, and are not usually in full sentences. The examples below show the verbs or 'doing' words in each sentence. If you're not sure what a verb is at this stage, it may be better for you to copy the style from another document. You'll probably find that eventually you are writing sentences automatically.

- Thinking of you = note form
- I *am* thinking of you = sentence form
- *Raining* outside = note form
- It *is* raining outside = sentence form
- *Wish* you were here = note form
- I *wish* you were here = sentence form

Matching up singular and plural words

Look back at sentence 2 in Exercise 1.

- Details of the new product is to be found on page 2.

This is what should have been written:

- Details of the new product **are** to be found on page 2.

The reason is that *details* (which is a plural word) are to be found on page 2, not the *product* (which is a singular word). Therefore the verb must be plural, i.e. **are**, and not singular, i.e. **is**.

If you have difficulty, try crossing out everything between the words you want to match up, e.g:

- The girl, who was with some friends, ... late.

Is it 'was' or 'were'? If you cross out 'who was with some friends' you are left with 'the girl ... late' and you can then see that the word you need is 'was'. (See also Element 4.3, page 498).

Pairs of words

Always put *neither* and *nor* together. Do the same with *either* and *or* e.g:

- Neither the girl nor her friend was aware of the problem.

- Either we go to the cinema or to the football match.

Do not mix *shall* and *should* or *will* and *would*. Use the same word throughout.

- I shall be pleased to come with you and shall get ready at once.
- He will be able to do the job this morning and will let you have the finished results this afternoon.

Note that if you want to use a combination of the words you *must* use 'shall' with 'will' and 'should' with 'would', e.g:

- I should be grateful if you would phone me tomorrow. Not: I shall be grateful if you would phone me tomorrow.

Remember also that you would normally use 'shall' or 'should' after 'I' or 'we' and 'will' or 'would' after 'you', 'he', 'she' or 'they'.

It is also easy to mix up 'who' and 'whom' and the grammatical rule is rather complicated. If you are unsure, find a way round it. For example if you want to write:

- This is the person who/whom has been selected for the job.

and don't know that the correct word in this case is 'who' you could say instead:

- This person has been selected for the job.

This avoids all sorts of difficulties!

The use of 'I' or 'me'

If sometimes you have difficulty in deciding whether to say 'you and I' or 'you and me' try changing it over to 'we' or 'us' e.g:

- You and I (i.e. we) must go to see the manager.

rather than:

- The manager wants to see you and me (i.e. us) after lunch.

Split words

Try not to separate 'to' from other words e.g. to go, to find, to decide, by putting another word in between, e.g:

- The manager had to decide *quickly* what to do.

rather than:

- The manager had to *quickly* decide what to do.

Sentence endings

Try not to end a sentence with 'to', 'of', 'with', 'about' or 'for'. Don't say:

- She is the person I gave the information to.

Say instead:

- She is the person to whom I gave the information.

Again if you find this difficult, think of a way around it, e.g:

- I gave the information to her.

Comparative and superlative

If you are comparing *two* things then add 'er'. If you are comparing more than two things add 'est':

- Frances walks faster than Bridget.
- He is the tallest of them all.

Note that in some cases you cannot use 'er' or 'est' and must use instead 'more' (for two things) and 'most' (for more than two):

- He is more handsome than his brother.
- She is the most attractive girl in the room.

Double negatives

Remember *not* to write:

- I'm not doing nothing! If you're not doing *nothing* you must be doing *something!*

Other common mistakes include:

- I can't hear nothing.
- I'm not going nowhere.

Who, which and that

You use 'who' when you are referring to a person. If you are referring to an object or thing you should use 'which' or 'that'. But what is the difference between them? Look at the two sentences below.

541

- The old house, **which** he bought for his mother, needs a fortune spending on it.
- That is the dog **that** bit him.

The rules regarding 'which' and 'that' are very complicated and are largely disregarded today. The main rule seems to be to use the word with which you are comfortable, and this, for most people today, is 'which' because it is more commonly used in conversation.

However, one rule you may wish to bear in mind is illustrated in the sentences above.

- If further information follows the phrase, especially if it can be separated from the rest of the sentence by commas, then the word to use is 'which'.
- If no separate information follows, then use 'that' instead.

In the 'house' sentence you were given more information, so 'which' was used. In the 'dog' sentence you were not. The phrase 'that bit him' is necessary for identifying the dog in question. See how this can be reversed.

- Here is the house that he bought.
- The dog which bit him last week now has to wear a muzzle.

Did you know?

'That' is also used:

- after all the following words – 'nothing', 'everything', 'anything', 'something' e.g.;
  Is there something that we can buy?

- after a superlative adjective, e.g:
  It was the smallest computer that the shop sold.

(See Element 4.3 for more about difficult points of grammar.)

Non-assessed activity

Re-test yourself by rewriting the following sentences and scoring 2 points for each correct answer. Your score should have improved. However, in case you want to check, the answers are on page 646.

1 He wants to see you and I.
2 The trainee forgot to carefully read the instructions.
3 She is someone I have always had difficulty with.
4 He never has no time for us.
5 Confirming our recent telephone conversation.
6 I shall be pleased if you would provide the information I need.

Easily confused words

Some words are very easy to confuse. For instance, it is a common error to mix up 'weather' as in 'What's the weather like today?' with 'whether' as in 'I don't know whether I shall be able to come.' Where you *know* that you are unsure, try to find another way of writing the sentence. For example, you may want to say that you agree with all the points made in a report except/accept, for one. The word you should use is 'except' but if you are any doubt you can always say instead:

- I disagree with only one item in the report.

To make sure you know some of the more commonly confused words try working through the following exercise.

Exercise 2

Complete the following sentences with the correct word.

To/too/two

Remember that 'two' = one + one, 'too' = above a certain standard e.g. too much, too big, etc.

- I have ... see you immediately.
- There are ... immediate improvements which can be made.
- It is far ... warm in here.

There/their

Remember that 'their' = ownership e.g. their hats, their opinions etc.

- Put the shopping over ... .
- ... is no reason for the delay.
- Where have they put ... belongings?

Past/passed

Remember 'pass' is changed to 'passed' in the past tense.

- He ... me in the corridor without speaking to me.
- In the ... he has been very helpful.
- He ... his examination and gained a distinction.

Of/off

If you are in doubt say the words out loud. Of sounds like ov, off like off.

- He is a man ... few words.
- Please keep ... the grass.

Remember, however, not to confuse 'of' with 'have'.

- I should **have** written last week. Not I should **of** written last week.

Whose/who's

(Remember that whose = ownership, who's = who is.)

- ... waving at you?
- ... coat have you borrowed?

Affect/effect

Remember that effect = a noun, e.g. the effect of the noise, the effects of the recession: affect = a verb, e.g: He affects me by his bad temper.

- What ... will these figures have on the overall position?
- Will it ... you at all?

Personal/personnel

Remember that 'personal' = about you, 'personnel' = people who work in an organisation.

- The ... manager was concerned about the changes made to the staff training programme.
- My ... view is that it is too risky.

Principle/principal

Remember that 'principle' = a noun meaning standard, 'principal' = an adjective meaning main or major or the head of a school or college.

- The ... talked to members of the students' union about the new identity card.
- I think the ... item on the agenda should be the possible redundancies in the warehouse.
- I agree with it in ... but need some more information before I can act.

Practice/practise

Remember that practice = noun, e.g. the practice, practise = verb, e.g. to practise.

- I think he must learn to ... what he preaches.
- The ... of using Ms rather than Mrs or Miss has increased over the past few years.

Check on page 646 to see if you have answered correctly.

 ### Did you know?

Some words are commonly misused. Remember:

- all right not alright
- thank you not thankyou.

Note also that a common mistake is to confuse e.g. meaning 'for example', which refers to general examples, and i.e. meaning 'that is', which refers to a specific instance. Compare the following two sentences.

- He talked about many different types of sales techniques e.g. direct sales, telephone sales, newspaper advertising.
- He made particular reference to what he thought was the most successful method, i.e. telephone sales.

Style

The type of language or words you use when writing to someone depends on:

- the subject matter
- the person to whom it is addressed.

If you are writing a postcard to a friend describing your holiday, you can use **informal** language. If you are sending a business letter to an important client, you have to be more **formal**. Your friend would be rather surprised if you wrote, 'I hope you will be interested in the following details about the holiday I have just spent in France. Please let me know if you require any further information.' The client would be even more surprised if you wrote 'Lots to tell you about your recent order. You're going to laugh when you hear it's going to be July before you get it!' Not only is the tone wrong in each case, so too is the use of vocabulary.

Although your vocabulary will increase with experience, you may find some of the following exercises useful, particularly if you know that you sometimes use the wrong word at the wrong time, or if you use the same words over and over again.

Exercise 3

1   Give a less formal alternative for each of the following words. Use a dictionary if necessary.

> manufactured
> terminate
> emancipate
> commencement
> ascend

2   Rewrite the following sentences replacing the words in italics with a single word from the list given. Again, use a dictionary, if necessary.

> incompetent
> reversed
> maintenance
> incessant
> obsolete
> momentary
> estimate

- She asked for an *idea of how much the work would cost.*
- The car *went backwards* into the wall.
- The noise from the engine was *going on all the time.*
- The relief from the pain was only *for a brief space of time.*

- I can't get spare parts for your television as it is now *out of production*.
- The supervisor found that the new employee was *not able or qualified to do the job*.
- The *care and upkeep* of the machinery is essential in our business.

3   Rewrite the following sentences using more formal vocabulary.
- Count me in when you're fixing up the trip to the match.
- If you can hang on for a week or two I'll be able to give you the info then.
- Thanks a lot for your help. You saved my life!

4   Rewrite the following extract from a police report in more **understandable** language.

> At the commencement of the evening I was proceeding along the thoroughfare when I observed a vagrant attempting to gain access to a stationary automobile. I enquired as to the reason for his actions and he struck me across my countenance with considerable force.

See page 646 for suggested answers.

Did you know?

Many people don't know how to use a dictionary or even what it contains. Remember you can use a dictionary:

- to check the meaning of a word
- to check its spelling
- to check how to pronounce it.

Many dictionaries also list the more common abbreviations and what they mean. They also give guidance on the pronunciation of words.

Another useful reference book is a **thesaurus** which gives you synonyms of words, i.e. words which have a similar or the same meaning.

Non-assessed activity

1   Look up the following words as quickly as possible and write down what they mean, in your own words.

damask	pedestal	truism
collage	impresario	ruminate

2   Look up the following words and, as well as writing down what they mean, try to work out how to pronounce them. Check with your tutor that you are able to pronounce each word correctly.

| debris | epoch | grimace |
| hyacinth | league | myopia |

3 Using a dictionary or thesaurus give an alternative word (a synonym) for each of the following words:

| minion | slaughter | intersect |
| apex | frivolous | notorious |

Punctuation

Exercise 4

Rewrite the following passage, using the correct punctuation and putting in capital letters where necessary. Check your answer on page 647. If you make more than two mistakes, work through the following pages dealing with the rules of punctuation.

> when we were little and had visitors to the house grandma didnt read to us instead we talked to the visitors and tried to make them play games like hide and seek with us one visitor uncle bernard was particularly good at this although sometimes he got bored and shouted im here the game then ended

The main punctuation marks

The most important punctuation marks are:

- full stops
- commas
- apostrophes.

Less frequently, you may have to use:

- question marks
- exclamation marks
- hyphens
- dashes.

You will also need to know where to put capital letters.

The easiest way for you to check whether or not you should use a full stop or a comma is to read the passage out loud. A slight pause normally indicates a comma and a longer pause, indicates a full stop.

Uses of the full stop

- to end a sentence
- after abbreviations e.g. B.A. (although nowadays abbreviations are often written without full stops e.g. BA)

Note the use of the question mark:

- Why are you here?

and the exclamation mark:

- He actually agreed!

Non-assessed activity

Read the following passage out loud and then rewrite it, adding full stops where necessary.

You may remember that I raised the matter of an exchange visit with colleagues working in a college in San Diego I have now received a request from them to send details of anyone interested in taking part in this exchange it may be necessary to have a meeting to discuss the matter further give me a ring if you are interested

See page 647 for a suggested answer.

Uses of the comma

Commas are used:

- to separate words or phrases in a list e.g:

  I bought some apples, pears and bananas.
  (Note that you need not use a comma before 'and' in a list.)

  Mohammed Naize, the Chief Purchasing Officer, gave the first presentation.

- to indicate that someone is being addressed, e.g:

  Miss Franks, will you give the panel some further information?

Non-assessed activity

Using the same procedure as for full stops, read the following sentences out loud and then rewrite them, adding commas where needed. Check your answers with those given on page 647.

- I got up late had no breakfast and ran all the way to the bus stop.
- I sent him to the shop to buy paint wallpaper and brushes.
- Fatima please answer the telephone.
- James and Richard the two best tennis players met in the final.

545

Uses of the apostrophe

Apostrophes are used:

- to show where a letter is missing, e.g.

  you'll = you will

  won't = will not

  I've = I have

- to show ownership, e.g:

  the student's book = the book of (belonging to) the student.

It is this second use that normally causes the problems. Try to remember the following steps:

- write down the name of the owner, e.g:

  the student (or the students)

- add an apostrophe at the end, e.g:

  the student' (or the students')

- add an 's' if there is only **one** owner, e.g:

  the student's book (i.e. the book belonging to **one** student) **but** not if there is more than one, e.g:

- the students' book (i.e. the book belonging to **more than one** student).

Note A few 'ownership' words never need an apostrophe, e.g:

his	ours	its
yours	theirs	mine
theirs	hers	

Some words **sound** alike but have different meanings e.g:

  its = belonging to it, e.g. its shape, its height
  it's = it is
  their = belonging to them, e.g. their books
  they're = they are
  your = belonging to you, e.g. your eyes
  you're = you are

Remember also the difference between whose (belonging to whom) and who's (who is).

Non-assessed activity

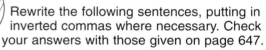

Rewrite the following passage, inserting apostrophes, where necessary. Check your answers with the ones given on page 647.

Dont worry, I know shell be here before long. In the meantime, can you try to borrow Franks calculator.

Yours is not working. Johns not in because hes gone to collect the Managing Directors car. Its also important for you to make certain that all the typists desks conform to the health and safety standards.

Uses of the inverted comma or quotation mark

Quotation marks are used:

- for direct speech (the actual words someone has said), e.g. She said, 'I like your hair.'
- for a quotation: He wrote, 'I do like to be beside the seaside.'
- for slang: The speaker admitted he wasn't 'with it' that morning as he had just returned from an overnight trip to London.

Non-assessed activity

Rewrite the following sentences, putting in inverted commas where necessary. Check your answers with those given on page 647.

- The chairman said, I welcome you to this meeting.
- Which television personality uses the catch phrase, Nice to see you, to see you, nice?
- I had never heard of the expression It's not over until the fat lady sings.

Uses of capital letters

Capital letters are used:

- at the beginning of sentences
- for proper nouns, e.g. Shelagh, Dundee

Remember not to use too many capital letters on other occasions – for words such as company, business or manager – unless they are connected to another proper noun. For example, you would write 'the bank' but 'National Westminster Bank'.

Non-assessed activity

Add capital letters to the following sentences. Check your answers with those given on page 647.

- there are many colleges in britain.
- she wants to attend bristol university.
- mary and danny went to nottingham to visit the firm and to see the personnel manager.

Spelling

Exercise 5

Rewrite the following paragraph, correcting all the spelling mistakes. Check your answer with the one given on page 647.

In buisness you must be good at accounts. You should be able to cheque figures accuratley and also to calclulate the correct amount each time. It is helpfull if you can remember to right clearly and to seperate one line of figures from another. Only competant mannagers are promoted.

Spelling tips

If you know your spelling is good, you can skip this section. If, on the other hand, you sometimes have difficulty, read on. You can't learn every word in the dictionary – but you **can** increase the number of words that you do know how to spell. Try to remember one or two hints.

- If you **know** you have trouble remembering how to spell a particular word, use the old trick of making each letter into a word and the words into a sentence. For example, if you always have difficulty with the word 'definite' you could remember it as:

  Did
  Eric
  find
  ice
  near
  Irene's
  toy
  engine?

  The sillier the better!

- Another method is to use the 'word within a word' technique e.g. be **lie** ve, ac **custom** ed, etc.
- If all else fails, use another word. If you can't remember how to spell 'conscientious', use 'hard-working'.

 ## Non-assessed activity

Think of silly sentences for the following commonly misspelled words.

separate	competent
address	occur

Some spelling rules

a In most words you would put 'i' before 'e', e.g. rel<u>ie</u>f except after 'c' e.g. rec<u>ei</u>ve.

Exceptions include s<u>ei</u>ze n<u>ei</u>ther <u>ei</u>ther financ<u>ie</u>r w<u>ei</u>rd spec<u>ie</u>s l<u>ei</u>sure.

b When a word ends in 'y' you should change it to 'i' if you want to add anything to it, e.g:

duty becomes dut i ful
beauty becomes beaut i ful
copy becomes cop i ed.

c If you add 'ing' to words ending in 'e' in many cases you drop the 'e', e.g.;

cease becomes ceas ing
make becomes mak ing.

d When 'full' is added to a word you do not need the second 'l', e.g. awful, plentiful.

e In most cases you can use either 'ise' or 'ize' at the end of a word but don't mix them up in the same piece of work.
I didn't recognize him. In fact, no-one recognized him. Not
I didn't recognize him. In fact, no-one recognised him.

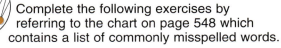 ## Non-assessed activity

Complete the following exercises by referring to the chart on page 548 which contains a list of commonly misspelled words.

1 Correct the mistakes in the following sentences.
   - Please make arrangments for the visit of the carreers officers who are very consientous and are looking forward to comming to the colledge.
   - The forein students are dissappointed because they are not going to have an end of term party.
   - I must reccomend you to try the new stationary – particularly the new envellopes.
   - In my opinnion the goverment have behaved unnreasonably.
   - Please list your prioritys when you have the opportunnity.
   - He wandered whether or not to say that he was suprised about the regretable incident.

2 **Work in pairs.** Make up one sentence using **at least one** word from each of the three columns in each section, e.g: one from A–D, one from E–I and so on. You can use as many other words as you want, for example:

547

Commonly misspelled words

A–D

accommodation	accustomed	acknowledge
actually	advertisement	advisers
already	apparently	arrangement
arrival	assistance	attention
attitude	awkward	because
behaviour	believe	busily
business	careers	college
colleague	coming	conscientious
decision	definite	disappointing

E–I

earnest	embarrassing	emergency
enthusiastic	excited	exercised
exhausted	experience	extraordinary
extremely	families	favourite
February	finally	finished
foreign	forty	frightened
government	honestly	immediately
immensely	information	intentions
interesting	interests	interrupted

J–Q

jealous	limit	liaison
loose	lose	luxury
meant	memories	mortgage
necessary	neighbour	nephew
niece	occasion	occasional
occasionally	opinion	opportunity
organisation	Parliament	patience
preferred	priority	priorities
probably	quality	quiet

R–Y

really	reassurance	receive
recognise	recommend	refer
referred	reference	regret
regrettable	restaurant	routine
scarcely	scheme	separate
similar	stationary	stationery
succeeded	successful	surprise
unconscious	unreasonably	unsuccessful
volunteered	whether	wondered

Figure C.6 Commonly misspelled words

Section A–D

The <u>accommodation</u> mentioned in the <u>advertisement</u> was <u>disappointing.</u>

Still in pairs, dictate the sentences to each other and check your answers.

Non-assessed activity

You work in the general office of a college. You are asked to look after a work experience trainee who has good keyboarding skills and who is very keen to help, but whose grammar, punctuation and spelling are poor. You realise that you will have to check anything he does before it leaves the office. One afternoon you are called into a meeting. When you get back to the office you find that the trainee has, on your instructions, completed the following piece of typing from an audio tape.

Draught

Information about the colege to be sent to job aplicants.

Their are ten departments in the colege each one of them provides a wide range of courses. In the Busness Studies department there are flurishing fowndation, intermediate and high level business and finnance courses with a wide variety of options there are also degree courses in business administration and law. The principle management courses are the diploma in management studies the certificate in management studies and the diploma in supervisery studies. Other courses cover marketing purchasing accountancey and personal management.

The departments examination results are good. It's general average has been over 85 per cent and in many cases above 90 per cent. Its' staff are well qualified and motivated and student welfare is regarded as of the utmost importance.

The senior staff of the department include the head, the deputies, and the divisional heads.

---

1 Read through the document and make the necessary corrections.

2 You note that the trainee seems to be very unsure about when to use commas and apostrophes.

Write or type out a short list of the rules relating to the use of each, so that the trainee can keep it beside him as a reminder when he next types out a document.

Written documents in business

The documents you need to know and be able to produce include:

- business letters
- memos
- invitations
- notices
- messages
- reports
- minutes or notes of a meeting
- summaries.

You also need to be able to complete a wide range of pre-printed forms, from telephone message forms to record cards and application forms.

The first five of these documents were covered in detail in Element 4.3, pages 484–493, as were telephone message forms. **If you are not sure about, or have not covered, any of these documents, turn back to page 482 and go through that section carefully with your tutor.** This section has been written on the basis that you are **already familiar** with these documents. It concentrates on **reports** and **minutes** or **notes** of meetings. It covers form-filling and gives you hints and tips on how to do this. Summaries are covered in this Core Skill, on pages 561–2.

Forms

During your working life you will probably have to complete many forms, both for internal use and for outside organisations. Possibly the most crucial form you will have to fill in is a job application form (see Element 2.4). There may also be occasions when you are asked to design a simple form yourself.

Completing forms

- Always read the form through first and identify any sections that must not be completed.
- Note the amount of space allowed for each entry so that you can adjust your writing to fit. If you have to include an explanation or comment in any area, draft it out first to find out if it will fit in the space available.
- Make a special note of the information to be provided in each space (a common mistake is to include the postcode in the space for the main address, when there is a separate space provided for it).
- Identify any special instructions, e.g. whether

block capitals are required, a special pen must be used or only certain sections completed.

- If you are worried about completing the form take a photocopy and practise first.
- Write clearly.
- Do not leave any blanks. If a section is not relevant then insert 'N/A' (for 'not applicable'). This shows the recipient that you did not miss out information accidentally.
- Check the form afterwards and find out whether you can date and sign it yourself or whether this must be done by your manager.

Non-assessed activity

1 Obtain a form for a driving licence from the post office. Complete it and ask your tutor to check your work.

2 You are applying for a job as a trainee accounts clerk. Complete the form which you will find at the back of the book, a copy of which is shown in Figure C.7. Ask your tutor to check it.

LANDSHIRE COUNTY COUNCIL　　　　　　　**FORM ESC/3**
JOB APPLICATION FORM

Application for the post of...

Please use block capitals for Sections 1, 4 and 8
1　Surname..
　　First name(s) ....
2　Date of birth..
3　Address ....
　　..
　　..
4　Present post...
　　..
5　Previous post ....
　　..
　　..
6　Education
　　(Please give details of secondary school/college/university attended –
　　together with starting and leaving dates)
　　..
　　..
　　..
7　Qualifications
　　(Please include dates, subjects and grades
　　..
　　..
　　..
　　..
8　Referees
　　(Please give the names and addresses of two persons to whom
　　reference can be made)
　　..
　　..
　　..
　　..
9　Signature..　　　Date..................

Figure C.7 Filling in a job application form

Designing forms

Always try to keep your form as simple as possible. Think about the information which is required and then choose suitable headings under which it could be recorded. Often a tabular layout is more appropriate than a questionnaire layout.

An example of a tabular layout is a mileage claim form (see Figure C.8). An example of a questionnaire layout is the driving licence application form you have just completed.

MILEAGE CLAIMS					
Month..					
Name	Miles at start of week	Miles at end of week	Total miles	Rate paid	Total payment due
		Total amount owing	£		

Figure C.8 A mileage claim form

Remember that if you are going to design a form to record information **yourself**, you will understand what you are trying to achieve. If other people will be using it, show it to **someone else** to see if he or she can understand it.

Always make sure that any **alternatives** are easy to follow, e.g. whether only one section or another needs to be completed.

Non-assessed activity

1   Suppose your boss is concerned that the photocopier in your office is being used too much and wants to monitor the numbers of copies taken over the next few weeks. He has asked you to design a form on which users must write their name, the date and time the copies were made, the number of pages copied and the quantity of copies made from each page. It will be your job to calculate and enter the total number of copies taken. Design a suitable form on which to record this information.

2   You are helping to organise your company's annual Christmas dinner dance. This will be held on the second Saturday in December at the Greenhill Hotel, Hightown, starting at 7.30 pm. Dinner will be served at 8 pm. There will be a disco starting at 9.30 pm. Transport is available for those who want it. There is no charge to staff, as this event is paid for by the company each year.

You have been asked to write a memo to all staff, informing them about the event and including a tear-off form that staff can complete to indicate if they will be attending, and whether they will require transport.

Did you know?

A tear-off form should be separated from the main text of a memo or letter by a series of hyphens which runs from *edge to edge* of the paper, *not* margin to margin. It is usual to put a heading on the form, so that you can remember what it is about when you get it back!

If there is any blank space this should come between the end of the memo or letter and the start of the form. The form itself should always end about an inch from the bottom of the paper, as shown in Figure C.9.

MEMORANDUM

TO   All sales staff
FROM   Sales Manager
DATE   18 November 199-

STAFF TRAINING DAY

This will be held on Tuesday, 28 November. The morning session will include a special section on consumer legislation and customer relations. In the afternoon there will be a demonstration of the range of new products which have been launched this year.

Refreshments will be provided in the morning and afternoon and lunch will be served at 12.30 pm.

Could you please confirm below whether you will require lunch and indicate if you will require a vegetarian meal.

- -

SALES TRAINING DAY

I will require lunch: Yes/No

Vegetarian meal requied: Yes/No

Signed   ....   Dated.................

Figure C.9 A memo with a tear-off slip

Reports

Reports are used:

- to present information on a particular topic after research has been carried out
- to give details of work carried out over a certain period with information on what still needs to be done
- to give an account of what actually happened at an event (e.g. a road accident report or a police report).

Reports vary considerably in length, complexity and the degree of formality required. Early in your career, you are only likely to be asked to produce short reports, probably of a relatively informal nature. Often common headings are used in a report and these are shown in Figure C.10.

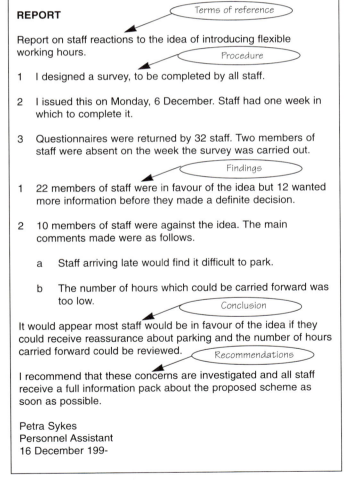

Figure C.10 A report form

Writing a report

- The **terms of reference** simply state what you have been asked to do.
- The **procedure** states the methods used to obtain your information.
- The **findings** are what you found out. These must be **facts**, not your own thoughts or opinions.
- The **conclusion** is a general statement summarising what you found.
- The **recommendations** are the actions you are suggesting, in view of your conclusion.

Non-assessed activity

There is a considerable difference between statements of fact and statements of opinion (i.e. personal views). In each of the following cases, can you state which is which?

1 a The car was black.
   b The driver was going too fast.
2 a The office is too cold in winter.
   b The office has only two small radiators.
3 a The quality of food served in the canteen is poor.
   b The canteen is unpopular with staff – only 10 out of 45 staff using it regularly.

Setting out a report

It is often easier to detail information using a list of numbered points. Because these may often have to be sub-divided, you need to use a system that will be consistent throughout your report. You have two options;

- a combination of letters and numbers, e.g.

    1 SALES DEPARTMENT
       a Staffing
          i   Full-time staff
          ii   Part-time staff

or

    a SALES DEPARTMENT
       1 Staffing
          a   Full-time staff
          b   Part-time staff

- a decimal numbering system, e.g:

    1 SALES DEPARTMENT
      1.1 Staffing
          1.1.1 Full-time staff
          1.1.2 Part-time staff
      1.2 Location

The decimal method may seem more complicated, but it has the advantage that in a long report you can divide your material into as many sections as you want with ease.

Whichever method you use, both the numbering system *and* the spacing must be consistent within your documents.

Non-assessed activity

Suppose your company is considering installing two payphones in the building, to reduce the number of private calls made on the company telephones. You were recently asked to prepare a brief report on this, including whether these should be cardphones and where they should be sited. You designed a questionnaire for staff, a summary of which is given below. From this summary prepare the report required.

```
        PAYPHONE QUESTIONNAIRE – SUMMARY

1a   Number of questionnaires issues: ......25..........................

1b   Number of questionnaires returned: ..22...............................

     Notes on difference: ...3.staff.absent...........................

2    Number in favour of idea of 2 payphones: 18

3    Number against (and main reason): 4
     May.be.charged.above.standard.rate..............
     May.be.queues.to.use.a.telephone........................

4    Ideas for siting phones:
     In.exit.foyer.to.car.park...............................
     On.main.admin.corridor............................
     Adjacent.to.canteen.................................

5a   Number in favour of cardphones: 15

5b   Number against (and main reason): 7
     Cannot.use.them.if.have.no.card.–.want.to.know.if....
     cards.will.be.sold.here...............
```

Figure C.11 A summary from a questionnaire

Did you know?

There are dozens of examples of written records in every company, including visit reports, customer complaints records, customer enquiry forms, filing records, log sheets and so on.

Make sure that any records for which you are responsible are neatly completed with accurate information and kept up to date.

Minutes or notes of a meeting

As you progress in your career you may become more involved in meetings, some of which may be quite formal. You will find that there are several documents relating to meetings.

- The **notice** says where and when it will be held. This information is often sent out in a brief memo.
- The **agenda** says what the meeting is about. It is usually a list of the points that are to be discussed.
- The **notes** or **minutes** are an account of what actually took place when the meeting was held. These are very important documents because:
  - they summarise the discussions
  - they highlight the action which has to be taken
  - they normally say who will undertake that job.

  They are then used as a source of reference, both by people who attended and people who should have attended but, for some reason, could not. People who have tasks to do, as a result of the meeting, can check their commitments on the minutes, as they will be expected to report back on the progress they have made at the next meeting.

Did you know?

Every meeting usually starts with a review of the last minutes. The purpose of this is to:

- check they were accurately written and typed
- check any developments that have taken place. This part of the meeting is known as **matters arising** because it covers anything which has arisen in relation to the topics discussed last time. This means that people would find out fairly early on in the meeting if you hadn't done what you promised to do!

Non-assessed activity

An **informal memo,** asking people to attend a meeting and including an agenda, is shown in Figure C.12. Check each item with your tutor if you are not sure what is meant.

M E M O

TO Members of the Safety Committee
FROM Mike Williams
DATE 20 May 199-

SAFETY COMMITTEE MEETING

The next meeting of the Safety Committee will take place in room B320 at 10 am on Tuesday, 4 June 199-. The agenda for the meeting is given below. Please make sure you bring with you relevant paperwork for your department relating to item 6.

AGENDA

1 Apologies for absence

2 Minutes of previous meeting

3 Matters arising from the minutes

4 Safety Officer's Report

5 Fire drill procedure

6 Accident figures for January - March

7 Any other business

8 Date and time of next meeting

Figure C.12 An informal memo about a meeting

Notes versus minutes

Minutes are always taken for formal meetings. They have a standard layout and style, explained below. Copies are always distributed to all the people who attended the meeting. Copies may also be sent to any other interested people. For instance, if you held a meeting of the students in your group, your tutor may be interested in receiving a copy of the minutes to see what took place.

Some meetings are held on a more informal basis and may be no more than a chat between a few people. However, if no record of the discussion is made, no-one will remember exactly what was said or what they promised to do. Even an informal discussion needs *some* written record – if only to remind those who attended what took place.

Handwritten notes are usually taken whilst the meeting takes place – otherwise the writer may have forgotten several key points afterwards.

Writing notes at a meeting

When taking notes at a meeting, make a clear heading for each part of the discussion and record the key points – in note form – underneath. You can then expand your notes later, either as an informal typed document or as proper minutes.

Start with one or two sharp pencils or good pens and a clean sheet of paper (preferably attached to a pad so that it is more difficult to lose!).

If an agenda has been circulated with a list of topics, use this as a guide because the topics should be discussed in the same order as they have been listed.

Often some people taking notes actually write them on the agenda itself and then expand them into minutes. This is an easy way to start as the agenda headings act as a guide.

Writing minutes

Minutes are usually set out with a clear list of headings which correspond to the agenda. If there was no agenda then you would have to make up your own headings.

The main heading at the top of the minutes should make it clear which meeting you are writing about. Busy people may receive different sets of minutes every day and need to be able to see which set belongs to which meeting.

The people who attended are listed, usually in alphabetical order. The name of the person who **chaired** or ran the meeting usually comes first.

Minutes are not a full account of everything anyone said, but are a summary of the **key points** which were discussed and what was agreed. When they are agreed as being correct they are signed by the chairperson and dated.

Non-assessed activity

The notes that were taken at the meeting of the Safety Committee are shown in Figure C.13. Figure C.14 shows the minutes which were prepared from them.

1 Note the layout of the minutes carefully. Why do you think an action column is included?

2 Minutes are written in the **past tense** and in the **third person**. The past tense is used because the meeting is now over. Writing in the third person means you don't say 'I' and 'you' but write about people by name.

    a Find some examples of the past tense and the third person in the minutes.

    b Check with your tutor that you clearly understand both of these terms.

3 Check carefully the way in which the notes have been expanded, the terms which have been used and the layout of the document.

M E M O

TO   Members of the Safety Committee
FROM   Mike Williams
DATE   20 May 199-

SAFETY COMMITTEE MEETING

The next meeting of the Safety Committee will take place in room B320 at 10 am on Tuesday, 4 June 199-. The agenda for the meeting is given below. Please make sure you bring with you relevant paperwork for your department relating to item 6.

AGENDA

1 Apologies for absence ✓   *Kevin Doughty*
                                 Corinne Fletcher

2 Minutes of previous meeting ✓ *OK*

3 Matters arising from the minutes *Peter - letter sent to St Johns about 1st aid courses. No reply yet.*
        ✓

4 Safety Officer's Report ✓ *v.gd. Fire doors -1st floor still being wedged open. Karen to see Sales Manager.*

5 Fire drill procedure *Mon 27/5. 'A'=2.5m 'B' = 4 min = too long. KA to investigate why*

6 Accident figures for January - March ✓ *v. low. 2 minor accidents only.*

7 Any other business ✓ *- Jane - staff struggling to complete new Acc. Report forms, Mike doing memo to explain how to do it.*

8 Date and time of next meeting ✓ *6/7 10 am B320.*

Figure C.13 Notes from the meeting, written on the agenda

MINUTES OF THE SAFETY COMMITTEE MEETING HELD TUESDAY, 4 JUNE 199-

<u>Present</u>

Mike Williams (Chair)
Katriona Abbott
Jane Knowles
Peter Salam
Karen Turner

KEY ISSUES DISCUSSED   ACTION

<u>Apologies for absence</u>

Apologies were received from Kevin Doughty and Corinne Fletcher.

<u>Minutes of previous meeting</u>

The minutes were accepted as an accurate record.

<u>Matters arising</u>

Peter confirmed that a letter had been written to the St John's Ambulance about First Aid courses and he was waiting for a reply.

<u>Safety Officer's report</u>

This was very favourable, the only criticism was that the fire doors were persistently wedged open on the first floor. Karen agreed to raise this matter with the Sales Manager whose staff occupy this area.   KT

<u>Fire drill procedure</u>

The last drill had been held on Monday, 27 May. 'A' block had been cleared in 2.5 minutes which was excellent. 'B' block had taken 4 minutes which was too long. Katriona Abbott agreed to investigate any possible causes for this delay and report back at the next meeting.   KA

<u>Accident figures for January - March</u>

These were excellent. Only two minor accidents had been reported during this period.

<u>Any other business</u>

Jane Knowles mentioned that some staff were having difficulty completing the new Accident Report form. Mike Williams agreed to issue an explanatory memo.   MW

<u>Date and time of next meeting</u>

10 am, Tuesday 6 July, B320.

Signed .... Dated ....

Figure C.14 The typed minutes

Optional evidence assignment

This assignment provides evidence for both Element 2.1 and Element 2.2 of Communication and can be cross-referenced to link with Consumers and Customers – Elements 3.3 and 3.4.

Your tutor wants your opinion of the service provided by your school or college library, and also wants to know if the rest of your group agree.

1   As a group, make a list of headings under which you can assess the library. These could include:

  ■ range of books
  ■ ordering system
  ■ attitude of library staff
  ■ quiet areas
  and so on.

2   Visit the library and check any aspects you are not sure about, then prepare a report which reflects your own opinion. Add any recommendations you feel you could suggest to improve the service provided.

3   **With your fellow students,** agree a joint meeting time when you can discuss the library facilities. Make out a short notice and agenda as a reminder to everyone, saying where and when the meeting will be held and listing the topics (i.e. the headings) which will be discussed. Remind everyone to bring a copy of their own reports to the meeting.

   As a group, choose the clearest and neatest report and make a copy for everyone.

4   Hold the meeting and discuss each issue. Try to reach agreement on the key points that need to be considered in each area, and what to recommend. Take notes at the meeting and expand them into minutes afterwards.

   Ask your tutor to choose the best set of minutes and give a copy to everyone.

5   Evaluate your own work against the 'model' documents you have received. If both *your* documents were chosen then you may have little work to do here! Write a memo to your tutor identifying where you think your weaknesses are and how you could improve on them in future.

Element 2.3 – Use images

'One picture is worth a thousand words'. Which of the following do you find more effective?

A pig

A wild or domesticated animal with broad snout and stout bristly body

A pig

Types of images

Even in business, some information is better displayed visually than in written form. There are several different types of image that can be used, including:

  ■ drawings
  ■ photographs
  ■ maps
  ■ sketches
  ■ models
  ■ tables
  ■ pie charts
  ■ pictograms
  ■ line graphs
  ■ bar charts.

You may be able to use images prepared by someone else, but you do need to take care not to infringe copyright law. This is especially true if you use a drawing, photograph, chart or graph that has appeared in a magazine or a newspaper. Talk to your tutor if you are going to copy something from another source.

If you have to create the image yourself, you need to know how to do this properly. Don't be too ambitious – a clever idea for a working model to accompany a presentation may not seem so bright when you are up for the fourth night in a row until 2 am, trying to get it to function properly! Therefore:

  ■ keep your images **simple**
  ■ use colour carefully and effectively
  ■ make sure any wording on a drawing or sketch is neat and easy to read
  ■ make sure any graphs or charts include an appropriate key
  ■ label diagrams, sketches and drawings so people know what they are
  ■ make sure the image you choose is appropriate for your audience, the situation and the purpose of the discussion.

Choosing suitable images

A suitable image clearly shows an illustration, without shocking or mystifying your audience. It must be an appropriate image for the situation.

555

You may be involved in:

- the preparation of written material such as a report
- a one-to-one discussion
- a group discussion.

When you are preparing written material, e.g. a report, check with the person who asked you to do it what type of images would be acceptable. Cut-outs from magazines, and photographs of the family cat, might have been acceptable in Year 8 at school but are not usually appropriate for professional business documents! Charts, graphs, tables and diagrams are usually welcomed, because they save the reader ploughing through many pages of explanation!

Remember, though, not to include an illustration and then either:

- ignore it in the text, or
- write five pages about it!

The following section on choice of illustrations provides some useful guidelines.

A **one-to-one discussion** may be informal – in which a quick sketch might suffice – or it may be formal. For instance, if you were making a presentation to your boss, you would probably be expected to have done some preparatory work. However, even the most demanding boss might be more than a little surprised if you led the way to the nearest lecture theatre and proceeded to give a computerised slide show!

In **group discussions**, you will need to produce an image everyone can see easily. One copy of a small chart is not usually sufficient. Either have it transferred onto an overhead transparency or enlarge it on the photocopier so you can put it on a wall.

Did you know?

Many computer packages – including graphics packages and spreadsheets – will create images for you (see the Core Skills unit on Information Technology). There are special presentation packages available on which you can prepare black and white overhead transparencies, hard copy handouts, speaker's notes or 35 mm slides with diagrams, graphs and clip-art images! However, it may be a little while before you need to use one of these for a formal presentation!

Creating tables

Compare the following two sets of information.

- The Annual Office Furniture Exhibition was held in the Haymarket Centre from 14 to 16 January. An official estimate of the number of visitors to the exhibition was 250 on Monday morning and 280 on Monday afternoon: 180 on Tuesday morning and 210 on Tuesday afternoon; 300 on Wednesday morning and 315 on Wednesday afternoon.

Number of visitors to Office Furniture Exhibition Haymarket Centre 14–16 January 199-

Monday		Tuesday		Wednesday	
am	pm	am	pm	am	pm
250	280	180	210	300	315

Figure C.15 A table is quick and easy to read

Non-assessed activity

Suppose you work in the office of Blackhurst School. One of your jobs is to sort out class timetables from information given to you by the Deputy Head. One note reads as follows.

Year 9 Blue Group: Monday's timetable: 9–10 English; 10–11 French; 11–12 Computer Studies; 12–1.30 Lunch; 1.30–2.30 Sports; 2.30–3.30 Careers

Year 9 Green Group: Monday's timetable: 9–10 French; 10–11 Computer Studies; 11–12 English; 12–1.30 Lunch; 1.30–2.30 Careers; 2.30–3.30 Sports

Display this information as a table.

Pie charts

A pie chart is always drawn as a circle cut into wedges, with each wedge showing the portion of the whole it represents. If, for instance, you want to show the percentage of students of different ages on one year of a business studies course, you could display the information in pie chart form, as in Figure C.16.

Number of students	Age range	Percentage
100	16–18	50
60	19–21	30
40	21+	20

The information could be presented as:

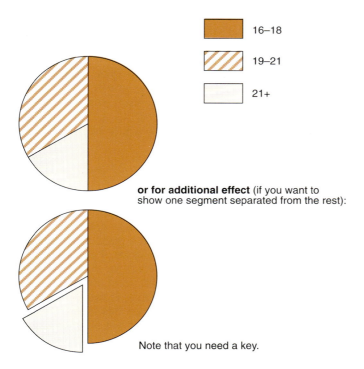

or for additional effect (if you want to show one segment separated from the rest):

Note that you need a key.

Figure C.16 Pie charts

How to do it

- Use this type of chart to give general information only – it is difficult to display detailed information in this way.
- As a start, mark your circle into quarters, each representing 25 per cent or one quarter, and adjust the wedges from there.
- Remember that the total of the percentages must equal 100.

Non-assessed activity

Suppose you have been asked to undertake a project about the media and have decided to analyse the time allocated to various television programmes during the course of one evening. Display the following information you have gathered together in the form of a pie chart.

Monday evening	BBC 1	5 pm – 10 pm
Comedy shows	25 per cent	
Chat show	15 per cent	
News	5 per cent	
Football	25 per cent	
Documentary	15 per cent	
Hospital drama	15 per cent	

Pictograms

Information can be displayed by means of picture graphs or diagrams called **pictograms.** The information can only be displayed in general form and pictograms are used simply for illustrative purposes in sales presentations, promotional material, etc, as in Figure C.17. You need a key to show what your first picture respresents.

Information about the gradual increase in numbers of children attending crèches over the past 20 years could be displayed as a pictogram *either* by one using one illustration and increasing its size:

The increase in the number of children attending the company crèche between 1972 and 1992

or by using an increasing number of illustrations:

The increase in the number of children attending the company crèche between 1972 and 1992

Figure C.17 Pictograms

Non-assessed activity

Suppose you work in a supermarket called Bestbuys. You have been asked to draw a pictogram to show the increase in sales of tinned cat food over the past four years. In 1989 10 000 tins were sold; in 1990 15 000; in 1991 20 000 and in 1992 25 000.

Line graphs

Line graphs are used to display more detailed information and to indicate trends. They may be composed of a single line, or they may show more than one line, in which case they are known as **multiline** graphs.

They are used for many kinds of statistical information, including:

- purchasing and sales figures
- price increases or decreases
- import and export figures

See the example in Figure C.18.

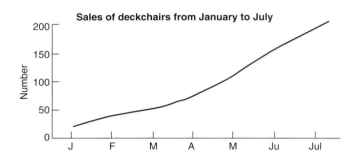

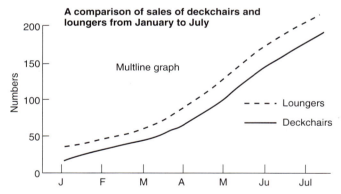

Figure C.18 Line graphs

How to do it

- The horizontal axis (line) goes across the page and is sometimes known as the x-axis. The vertical axis goes up the page and is sometimes known as the y-axis. Both must be labelled.
- Normally, the main variable, such as time, is shown on the horizontal axis, and the dependent

variable, such as number of sales, is shown on the vertical axis.
- It is also usual to have the lowest number at the foot of the vertical axis and to move upwards (see below).
- Choose the **scales** you are going to use, in terms of quantity (10s, 20s, 100s, or 1000s) and time (days, weeks, months, years). The scale must be big enough to allow important features of the data to be displayed effectively.
- Decide what colours or different types of line you are going to use for a multiline graph.
- Put in the dots in pencil and then join up the lines.
- For multiline graphs, include a **key** to indicate what each line represents.

Did you know?

You don't have to start your axis at zero! In fact, if you were dealing in very large quantities you could have a good argument for starting at a different point. For instance, if you were creating a profit line graph, and profits for that company always ranged between £30 million and £50 million, starting it at zero may not be sensible. However, be careful that no-one challenges you on this. Several people have argued that the Government often produces graphs (e.g. on unemployment) which start high and show a small range. Therefore a small reduction in the unemployment figures looks much greater!

Non-assessed activity

You work for a firm of opticians. As a publicity measure, you are asked to construct a line graph to indicate the general increase in sales of contact lenses over the past six months.

In July 30 people purchased them, in August 50, in September 60, in October 55, in November 65 and in December 70.

You are also asked to prepare a multiline graph to indicate the difference in the sales of contact lenses and of conventional glasses.

Sales of glasses were: July 40, August 40, September 50, October 60, November 65, December 75.

Bar charts

An alternative to a line graph is a bar chart, in which bars are used instead of continuous lines. The bars can be single or multiple (or compound) if you want to make comparisons (as in the case of a single line and multiline graph). The bars are normally vertical but can be horizontal. The rules of the construction are the same as those for line graphs. See the example in Figure C.19.

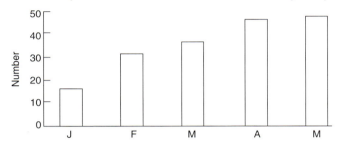

The number of enquiries made for information about the 'Adopt and animal' scheme at the local zoo for January to May

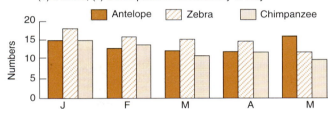

The number of applications received to adopt: (a) an antelope; (b) a zebra; (c) a chimpanzee from January to May

A **histogram** is a bar chart in which the areas of the bars represent the quantities

Figure C.19 Bar charts

Non-assessed activity

Your boss, the manager of Selectarecord, wants you to construct a bar chart to show the way in which the sales of compact discs have increased in comparison to a decrease in cassettes.

In 1989 sales of cassettes were 2500 and sales of compact discs 1500.

In 1990 sales of cassettes were 1750 and sales of compact discs 1850.

In 1992 sales of compact discs were 1650 and sales of compact discs 2000.

Diagrams, sketches and photographs

If you look through a magazine or newspaper article, or pick up a glossy brochure in a car salesroom or the reception area of a company, you will probably be more tempted to read what is written if the information given is illustrated with a diagram, a sketch or a photograph. This is particularly true if something is difficult to describe in words.

At work you don't have to be a gifted artist to make a rough sketch to illustrate something you have written, as you will generally be able to pass your outline to another member of staff, who is specifically employed to do any art work. However, if you need to sketch something, for example, when making a claim from an insurance company, you may have to rely solely on your own efforts!

Non-assessed activity

You are driving back from a college disco one evening at about 11 pm and stop at a set of traffic lights, ready to turn right from a side street, Ruskin Avenue, on to the main road, Brownside Street. Both streets are well lit. The traffic lights change and you move out. As you do so, however, a car on the main road comes through the lights at red (at least you think they were red – the other driver says they were amber) and hits your car. You were moving very slowly and not much damage was done to your car although the other car was badly damaged. No-one was hurt. A woman, Mrs Ellen Parker, waiting to cross the side street on your side of the road, has witnessed the accident and is prepared to say that the other driver did come through on the red light. The other driver is Anthony Williams. His car is a red Sierra 1990 registration, yours is a blue Fiesta 1987 registration.

You have to explain to your insurance company what happened. Write a paragraph giving your account of the incident and draw a sketch showing the position of both cars, indicating where any relevant witnesses were standing.

Give any other details you think may be relevant.

Optional evidence assignment

This assignment provides evidence for both Elements 2.2 and 2.3 of Communication and can be cross-referenced to link with Elements 1.2 and 3.1.

You are a college student on a Business Studies course. You are particularly interested in marketing and are therefore pleased when you are offered a part-time job in the college Marketing department during the summer holidays.

The Marketing department has several jobs to undertake in relation to promoting the college to visitors. It has been asked to:

- prepare materials for a visit by junior school children
- prepare a number of charts to be used in an audio visual presentation, about college developments, to the governors of the college
- consider suitable images for inclusion in the new college prospectus.

1 You have to illustrate a leaflet for junior school children which includes images showing:

- the percentage of students who study courses in Art, Business, Health and Social Care, Science and Humanities subjects. The figures are 15 per cent, 30 per cent, 18 per cent, 8 per cent and 29 per cent respectively.
- the growth in the number of 16/19-year-olds students at the college over the last five years. The figures are 5200, 6000, 6500, 8000, 9000.

Create images that would be suitable for the audience concerned.

2 Prepare the following charts for the college governors.

a a vertical bar chart to show the trends in the number of school-leavers in the district over the same period as the growth in student numbers.

Year 1	7 600
Year 2	8 400
Year 3	8 500
Year 4	10 000
Year 5	10 400

b a line graph to show the total number of students attending the college during the past twelve months.

September	8 900
October	11 000
November	10 900
December	10 500
January	12 000
February	11 590
March	11 580
April	11 000
May	10 800
June	9 800

3 Because the Principal sees you as representing the college customers, he asks you for your suggestions for the type of images to be included in the new prospectus. Write a memo giving your ideas.

Element 2.4 Read and respond to written materials

People read articles in newspapers, letters from business organisations and postcards from friends to **gain information.** However, there are two main possibilities (and a range of alternatives between the two extremes) in relation to what they do with the information they read.

- They can either ignore or discount it entirely.
- They can be very impressed by what they have read and start trying to convert everyone else!

There are valid – and less valid – reasons for ignoring or discounting information. The best reason for ignoring it is because you don't believe it. If someone sent you a postcard containing lots of gossip about a close friend, it would be sensible to throw it in the bin. Less valid reasons are that you find the information boring, or can't be bothered to read it properly, or because you don't understand it.

At the other extreme, if you are reading about a sensitive issue – such as animal rights, children starving in a poor country, or someone who has been punished for a crime they did not commit – you may be very influenced by what you read. In some cases you may be right to feel very strongly. However, it is always worth investigating the other side of the story. After all, what you have just read is the writer's own opinion. This is not necessarily the same as your opinion. Before you decide your own point of view it is important to try to find out all the facts you can. No-one is *always* right or *always* wrong, not even the Government, and certainly not newspaper reporters!

Non-assessed activity

Many articles have been written blaming computers and television for the fact that (they say) reading skills have declined in young people.

a Do you think this is true? Debate the issue in class and find out different people's views.
b Do a mini-survey in your class to find out:
  - how much (and what) people read
  - whether they read more than watch television or vice versa.

c If you had a friend whose reading skills were poor, what would you suggest they could do to improve them? Discuss your ideas with your tutor.

Did you know?

You should always **ask** if someone uses a word you have never heard before, or if you read a word and don't know the meaning. It is doubtful that *anyone* knows the meaning of every word in any language! Keep a dictionary close by and **use it.** Unless you understand what you read you are hardly in a position to respond to it.

Different ways of reading

We don't read information in only one way. There are **five** different ways in which you can read an article.

Skimming

Skimming means skipping through something quickly to see if there is anything of interest. If you are desperately trying to finish a novel as your train pulls into the station then you may skim read the last few pages – just to find out who ended up with whom!

Scanning

You scan when you are looking for a telephone number in a directory, a word in a dictionary or a book in the library, when you know the title. In other words, you program yourself to react to a certain word or words.

Light reading

This is reading for enjoyment, e.g. a magazine article or a novel. You are unlikely to remember much about it afterwards (like the names of the main characters) but it was fun at the time!

Reading for a purpose

You have a specific reason for reading something and are trying to concentrate. For instance, if you were mixing a dye to turn a white shirt blue – and were worried about doing it wrongly – you would read the instructions very carefully, line by line, and check anything you didn't understand.

Reading for study

This was how you should have read your notes for your end-tests and your GCSEs! You should have highlighted main points, made your own notes and gone back over key points time and time again until you knew them properly.

Did you know?

It is important to use the right method of reading for the purpose. If your boss wants you to read and then summarise an article in a newspaper, and you treat it as if it is a novel or skim read it, you are asking for trouble!

Extracting information

You may be asked to read an article – which may be all text, mainly images or a mixture of the two – to find the main points and then summarise them. This means you have to present the information in a shorter form. You may be asked to give a summary of this information, either verbally or in writing. Sometimes a list of points will be enough, but on other occasions you may be asked to provide a written summary in proper paragraphs.

Producing a summary

Two reasons why you may be asked to summarise information are:

- because you have written something that is too long
- to save your boss the trouble of reading a long and complicated document from beginning to end.

Did you know?

Examples of the type of information you may have to summarise include:

- an article from a newspaper for inclusion in a report or speech
- some information for use in a sales presentation
- a set of facts and figures which your boss has seen in a book or magazine
- some information for the staff.

Example

Main passage Ramblers' Associations in Berkshire, Buckinghamshire, Cheshire, Clwyd, Cornwall, Cumbria, Derbyshire, Hampshire, Hertfordshire, Kent, Lancashire, Leicestershire, Lothian, Northamptonshire, North Yorkshire, Nottinghamshire, Oxfordshire, Somerset, Suffolk and Warwickshire are all co-operating in protesting against the wilful blocking of tens of thousands of miles of Britain's footpaths and bridleways. In England and Wales, according to the Countryside Commission, the Government's countryside advisers, almost one fifth of the 140 000-mile network is impassable.

Final version Ramblers' Associations in many parts of the country are protesting about the blocking of many of Britain's footpaths and bridleways, 28 000 miles of which are now impassable according to the Countryside Commission.

How to do it

Skim read the document, don't try to take everything in at once. Read it more thoroughly. What you can do at this stage is to:

- cross out or underline unwanted words, e.g. Ramblers' Associations in <u>Berkshire, Buckinghamshire, Cheshire, Clwyd, Cornwall, Cumbria, Derbyshire, Hampshire, Hertfordshire, Kent, Lancashire, Leicestershire, Lothian, Northamptonshire, North Yorkshire, Nottinghamshire, Oxfordshire, Somerset, Suffolk and Warwickshire</u> are all co-operating in protesting against the wilful blocking of <u>tens of thousands of miles of</u> Britain's footpaths and bridleways. In England and Wales, according to the Countryside Commission, <u>the Government's countryside advisers</u>, almost one fifth of the 140 000 mile network is impassable.

- Where possible write over the top one word (or a reduced number) in place of several e.g. instead of the list of individual counties you could write 'in many parts of the country' or 'in most counties of the UK, etc.

- List the main points in note form – remember that you can leave out examples.

- At this stage your notes might read: Ramblers' Associations in a large number of counties protesting about the deliberate blocking of many of Britain's footpaths and bridleways.

  According to Countryside Commission almost 28 000 miles of network impassable.

- What you should then do is to check your list against the main document to make sure you haven't left out anything important.

- Finally, draft your summary from your notes and make sure this time that (unless otherwise agreed) you are writing in sentence and not note form (see *Using words in the right way* on page 540 for the difference if you are not sure).

Did you know?

Unless you want always to write in short sentences (and in many cases this is better than long and confused sentences) you could use conjunctions or joining words such as 'and', 'but', 'although' or 'because', to make what you have written read more smoothly. It is also very useful if you are asked to summarise a passage.

You may have written the following series of sentences.

Simply Red is protesting about the reduced royalty rates they are going to receive. Other groups are also protesting. The recording companies will not negotiate with them.

Although the passage is perfectly understandable, the use of one or two joining words will improve it.

Although Simply Red and other groups are protesting about the reduced royalty rate they are going to receive, the recording companies will not negotiate with them.

Non-assessed activity

 Try to improve the following passage by the use of some conjunctions – but don't go mad and try to turn it into one gigantic sentence!

Many children under five come from homes where English is not spoken. They do have some language skills. They probably have a well-developed first language. It could be Mandarin Chinese, Urdu or Bengali. It could be one of the many other languages used in the UK today.

Optional evidence assignment

This assignment provides evidence for both Elements 2.2 and 2.3 of Communication and can be cross-referenced to link with Elements 4.2 and 3.1.

You work for a local company which sells wine mainly by mail-order. Your boss, Tony Foulds, has asked you to undertake the following tasks.

1 Tony Foulds has a meeting with all the reps regarding sales figures tomorrow. Another member of staff produced a pictogram of wine sales for him recently, but he feels this is too childish to show to the sales staff.

   He has asked you to look at the pictogram and **in one paragraph** to summarise what it says and suggest reasons for the differences in sales in different months.

Figure C.20 A pictogram of wine sales

2 Tony Foulds is interested in introducing a staff appraisal system. He has glanced at the article in Figure C.21 but has not had time to study it properly. He has asked you to summarise it into about half its length. He is quite happy to accept a series of numbered points.

3 Tony Foulds is interested in finding out how he can rush parcels to customers who want wine in a hurry.
   a Visit your local post office and obtain any leaflets you can on express postal services. Ask at the counter for information if you can't find anything.
   b Look in your local *Yellow Pages* for information on private delivery companies. Summarise the information you obtain in a short report.

Staff appraisal

When you start work you may find that at the end of each year your supervisor will discuss your performance with you. This is known as staff appraisal. The objectives of staff appraisal are:

- to assess what you have done during the period in question – and how well you have done it
- to help you to improve in any areas where you are having difficulty
- to find out your additional training needs
.
If this appraisal is to be successful, however, certain elements must be present. Both you and your supervisor must look at it positively with a view to assessing what benefits can be gained from the exercise. The appraisal must therefore be designed to highlight your successes rather than concentrate on your failures.

Figure C.21 An article on staff appraisal

Quick reference section

How to lay out a letter, memo, notice, report

Letters	*Business address*
(Element 4.3)	Reference
	Date
	Recipient's name, status, address
	Salutation, i.e. Dear ....
	Heading
	Opening paragraph
	Main body of letter
	Closing paragraph
	Complimentary close, i.e. Yours ...
	Name of organisation
	Name of sender
	Status
	Enclosures
	Heading
Memos (Element 4.3)	Name of recipient
	Name of sender
	Date
	Heading
	Opening paragraph
	Main body of memo
	Closing paragraph
	Initials of sender
	Date

Notices
(Element 4.3)

Heading
Opening paragraph
Main body
Closing paragraph
Terms of reference

Reports
(pages 551–552)

Procedure
Findings
Conclusions
Recommendations
Signature and status of writer
Date
Heading

Minutes
(pages 552–554)

Those who attended
(alphabetical order, person who
chaired the meeting first)
Key items in order discussed and
action column
Signature of chairperson
Date signed

How to write grammatically

(pages 540–543 and Element 4.3)

- the difference between a sentence and a note
- how to match-up singular and plural words
- when to use neither/nor and either/or
- when to use shall/should and will/would
- when to use who/whom
- the use of you and I or you and me
- when not to split 'to' from another word
- how to avoid ending a sentence with 'to', 'of', 'with', 'about', 'for'
- when to end a word with 'er' or 'est'
- how to avoid using a double negative
- when to use 'which' and 'that'.

How to choose the right word

(page 543)

Check on the difference between

- to/too/two
- there/their

- past/passed
- of/off
- whose/who's
- affect/effect
- personal/personnel
- principle/principal
- practice/practise
- e.g. and i.e.

How to punctuate

(pages 545–546)

- the full stop
- the comma
- the apostrophe
- the inverted comma
- capital letters.

Images

(pages 555–559)

- tables
- pie charts
- pictograms
- line graphs
- bar charts
- diagrams
- sketches/photographs.

How to write a summary

(pages 561–562)

- Skim read the document.
- Read it more thoroughly.
- Cross out or underline unwanted words.
- Write over the top one word or a reduced number in place of several.
- List the main points in note form (this may be enough – check the format you have been asked to use).
- Check the list against the main passage.
- Draft the summary from the notes.
- Check grammar, punctuation, spelling.

Application of number

If you asked all the students on a GNVQ course which core skills topic they either most disliked or were most worried about, the chances are that 'Application of number' or 'the maths bit' would come out highest. Of course, those who are good at maths would probably put it a different way. They may tell you that 'the probability factor of people disliking numeracy is 0.75', or the 'ratio of those who dislike numeracy to those who dislike IT is 3 to 1', or that 'the mean percentage of GNVQ Business students who dislike numeracy is 65'.

Of course, if you gave up at maths about three weeks after you started school you won't have a clue what these people are talking about anyway, and will have even less interest in proving them right or wrong mathematically. You may say it's all to do with the tutor and leave it at that. In fact, it may be all you can do to count the number of students in your group, let alone play about with the figures.

However, the ability to manipulate figures is a very useful skill. Apart from anything else, it stops someone cheating you out of money you deserve or have earned. This is why it is considered so essential in business. It may be possible to find a job where the most you have to do in terms of numeracy is to count the number of times the phone rings before you answer it, but this is rare. Businesses tend to keep a great deal of information in numerical form – mainly to do with sales, income, costs, etc. – because they are extremely keen on making a profit at the end of the year and staying in business.

This unit has been designed to help you to use numeracy both to improve your employment prospects and to further your skills in your personal life. At least then, if you don't get a job, you'll know whether putting your last £10 on the National Lottery in a last-ditch attempt to become a teenage millionaire is a pretty good bet or the act of a desperate lunatic.

Application of number and GNVQ

Your **assessments** in relation to 'Application of number' are mainly covered in a vocational context. This means that you won't do peculiar sums linked to trying to fill a canal with water or digging holes in the road, which have little to do with business and even less, these days, to do with application of number. It means that you will be expected to use the numeracy skills you gain and apply them to business situations. You will find, therefore, that 'Application of number' is normally part of most assignments and projects you produce for your mandatory and optional units.

However, before you can put your skills into practice you have to obtain them! You may find that there are special lessons in your timetable, in which you learn and improve your numeracy skills. This unit has been designed to:

■ introduce you to the basic skills you need
■ concentrate on the aspects of 'Application of

Figure N.1 Application of number!

number' on which you will be assessed
- act as a reference guide if you forget anything
- give you additional practice in areas where you may be weak
- improve your overall skill at working with numbers.

Note that there are no evidence indicator projects at the end of the unit because the Evidence Indicators will be achieved as part of your mandatory and optional unit assessments. However, some optional evidence assignments are included to give you additional opportunities to obtain evidence.

Did you know?

If you are very good at Maths – for instance, if you have achieved a good grade (A–C) in GCSE Maths, discuss with your tutor the possibility of developing your core skills to achieve higher than level 2 – the equivalent for Intermediate students. What you mustn't do is only cover 'Application of number' at level 1! Given that the majority of students will be studying at the equivalent level, this unit concentrates on level 2 of the Core Skills scheme.

Application of number level 2

There are **three** elements in the scheme. The first number below refers to the **level** and the second to the **element.**

2.1 Collect and record data
2.2 Tackle problems
2.3 Interpret and present data

This unit gives you information and practice in each of these areas. For each element you are given information relating to the skills and the numerical operations you need to know, as well as examples of how to do them, and practice exercises. At the end of the unit is a quick reference guide which you can use if you forget anything.

Calculations you should be able to do at the start of your course

Start by giving yourself and your tutor some idea of where you are now. Theoretically, you should be able to do all these calculations in your head. Try them – then check your answers with a calculator.

1	22 + 10 =	2	14 + 28 =
3	52 – 21 =	4	94 – 56 =
5	7 × 10 =	6	6 × 9 =
7	30 ÷ 5 =	8	81 ÷ 9 =
9	31 + 62 =	10	71 + 19 =
11	65 – 8 =	12	82 – 11 =
13	8 × 5 =	14	2 × 6 =
15	49 ÷ 7 =	16	92 ÷ 2 =
17	11 + 5 =	18	18 + 53 =
19	37 – 15 =	20	42 – 31 =
21	3 × 9 =	22	5 × 4 =
23	18 ÷ 3 =	24	56 ÷ 8 =

If you have any problems, go back to see if you have made a fairly obvious, silly mistake. If you haven't a clue where you have gone wrong, have a word with your tutor.

Did you know?

1 Sometimes special words are used when working with numbers.

- To find the **difference** between two numbers subtract the smaller from the larger.
- To find the **product** of two numbers multiply one by the other.
- The **square** of a number is the result when you multiply a number by itself. So 2 squared is written as 2^2 and is $2 × 2$ (= 4), 5 squared is written as 5^2 and is $5 × 5$ (= 25) and so on.
- The **cube** of a number is the result when you multiply a number by itself *twice*. So 2^3 is $2 × 2 × 2 = 8$, $5^3 = 5 × 5 × 5 = 125$, and so on.

2 When you are adding or subtracting numbers on paper, make sure you line up the numbers – units under units, tens under tens, hundreds under hundreds. Decimal points must always be aligned one under the other – you can fill in any blank spaces on the right of the decimal point with noughts if this helps you.

```
  261.2
+ 324.0
-------
  585.2
```

3 Don't get confused if you are writing a long number which needs noughts inserting in the middle, e.g. three million four hundred and twelve. Think about how many digits are required. If the word 'million' is used you have at least *seven* digits to write and some of these may be noughts, e.g. if no 'thousands' are mentioned. The figure above has three noughts and is written as 3 000 412.

4 Figures that no one can read are of no use to anyone. It is not a good idea to write illegibly, in the hope that you can confuse your tutor about the answer you really meant. *Make sure you write clearly!*

What else should you be able to do now?

Calculators are very useful for working out difficult calculations. However, you do need to be able to do some of them in your head or on paper, in case you drop your calculator on the floor at a crucial moment. Try the following and see how you get on. Use a pen and paper if you want to.

If you have any problems, refer to the reference guide at the end of the unit to see where you went wrong.

1 State which of the following can be divided exactly by 3.
   9, 18, 20, 32, 66, 94
2 Add 314.32, 60, 4038.220 and 172.
3 Write down the answer to 64 ÷ 2.
4 What do you multiply by 7 to make 49?
5 Write eighteen thousand and three in figures.
6 What is the difference between 4 × 8 and 40?
7 What is 6^2?
8 Calculate 182.32 × 62.90.
9 Divide £189.20 by 215.
10 Solve 1624 ÷ 29.
11 Calculate 3 + 10 − 7.
12 Solve 22 ÷ 5 and give your answer as a decimal.

Figure N.2 Use a calculator when you can, to check!

Element 1 – Collect and record data

What is data?

Data are facts and figures that still have to be processed. If, during a boring lesson, you counted the number of students who passed the door of the classroom in 30 minutes, the number you would write down is data. When you process this data so that it has some meaning, you are dealing with information. If you discover that the frequency of students increased between 10.30 am and 10.45 am you can investigate this to find out why. If you find this increase was caused by the fact that it was break-time

for some groups, this is useful information. You could use it, for instance, to question why your group isn't having a break at the same time and so on.

In business a similar technique is used:

■ numerical data is gathered and processed
■ situations are represented or problems are tackled
■ the resulting information is interpreted and presented.

Did you know?

In a fire drill, people are always tempted to take the route they *normally* use to leave a building. Bearing in mind that people don't generally push open many fire exits on a routine journey out of the building, this can mean they would also ignore these exits in a real evacuation.

To establish if this is true in a particular building, data could be collected during a drill. (You could assess this for yourself in your next drill, if you get permission to collect the data!) You could also work out at which points in the building people need to be redirected. If the information showed that a problem existed, one solution could be to position fire marshals at main points where a change of direction is required by evacuees.

Deciding what data to collect

In the above example the data collected related to:

■ the number of people evacuating the building
■ the number of exits that were not used (or used by a very low number of people).

Unless you had collected all this data you would find it difficult to come to any worthwhile conclusion or use it to suggest any sensible solution. For instance:

■ if you didn't know the total number of people evacuating, you wouldn't know what percentage of people went wrong. In fact, it could be there was no-one in the building at all, at which point you'd look rather silly.
■ if you didn't know *how many* people left by *which* exit, you would hardly be in a position to claim people weren't using one.

Non-assessed activity

Suppose that your school or college refectory sells cans of Coca-Cola at 45p each. Last week they sold only four cans. They can't think why. You have tried telling the refectory manageress that the price is ridiculous, but she won't believe you. Your group has decided to lobby for the price to be lowered, but your tutor has suggested that you need some **evidence** to back up your recommendation and has suggested you undertake a data collection exercise.

As a group, decide exactly what data you would need to collect and why.

Data collection sheets

If you are collecting data you need to write something down. Even if you were only collecting data on the price of Coca-Cola in the local shops, the chances are you would have forgotten who sold it at what price, by the time you returned to your group. Therefore, it is sensible to design a **data collection sheet** on which the information can be recorded.

Always keep this simple. Don't risk confusing everyone by including irrelevant information. It doesn't matter that Mr and Mrs Ahmed only bought the local shop four weeks ago. What might matter, however, is the distance between the Ahmeds' shop and the school or college. Therefore you should only include facts which matter on your sheet.

Non-assessed activity

With the help of your tutor, draw up a suitable data collection sheet to record your 'Coke sales' information. Remember that you may need to find a few totals at some stage, so you should take this into account.

Reasons for collecting data

The reasons for the examples you have been given are obvious. In the first case you are trying to stop people being trapped in a fire and in the second you are trying to pay less for a popular drink. Improving health and safety and saving money are two excellent reasons for collecting data in business. So is trying to increase sales or improve quality. Your tutor may have other reasons for collecting data, e.g. to improve your success at end-tests or to reduce absenteeism.

It is usual to decide the **reason** *first,* because this determines the **type of data** you need. Quite often, data collected for one purpose is not suitable for another purpose. Although your attendance record is good for assessing absenteeism and *may* be useful for predicting end-test results, it is no good at all for working out how many students passed the course last year – for that a totally different set of data is required.

Non-assessed activity

1 Suggest reasons for companies collecting data on the following:

a the number of customers visiting a superstore each day of the week
b the number of mothers with small children who visit a superstore
c the number of products which couldn't be produced because a machine broke down
d the number of products coming off a production line which had to be rejected because they weren't fit to be used
e the amount of food on the shelves in a superstore which is not sold by its 'use-by' date
f the number of employees who leave the company within six months of starting work
g the price of competitors' products
h the number of customers who haven't paid their bills on time.

2 In **each** case, suggest other types of data that might be useful to give a more complete picture of the situation.

Sources of data

Once you have decided upon the data you need, you should think about how to find it. The two main sources are:

- written information
- people.

Written information

It is silly trying to find out data the hard way if you can obtain it the easy way. Sometimes the data you need has already been collected by someone else, which saves you a lot of time and trouble. The information may be available in newspapers, reference books, company files, advertising material and so on. Your school or college library staff will be very helpful in guiding you towards sources of information, provided you ask politely and are prepared to accept the fact that they are busy people and will expect you to do a fair amount of 'finding out' on your own!

Figure N.3 Know where to find the information

People

Before a general election numerous surveys are published about how people intend to vote. This type of information – which involves **current** opinions – can *only* be obtained by asking people *at the time.* There are certain points you should remember if you are asking people to help you.

- Ask politely and be prepared to accept a refusal. If you stand in a corridor with your data collection sheet, looking helpless, everyone will probably ignore you. If, on the other hand, you pin everyone against the wall as they pass you may find yourself being reported for being a nuisance! It is equally unacceptable to shout abuse after someone who ignores your request.
- Think carefully how to phrase the questions. This is dealt with in more detail on pages 570–1.
- People have short memories! Try to keep your questions relevant to their current behaviour. Don't ask them what they bought in a store three years ago!

If you don't ask the correct questions the data you collect will not be **valid.** That is, it will not be accurate or useful.

Non-assessed activity

Suppose that you have been asked to analyse the attendance record of the students in your group.

1 Where could you obtain this information already in written form?
2 Test the memories of your class! Ask each person, separately, how many half days they were not at school or college in the last month. Record your answers on a data collection sheet.
3 Compare this with the written record and analyse the result.
4 With your tutor's help (if necessary!) work out the percentage attendance of each person and produce a ranked chart, which shows the person with the highest attendance first, and so on.

Data collection procedures

You have just been involved in a data collection procedure which involved carrying out a very short survey with other members of your group. In the real world, the following data collection procedures are used:

- designing a questionnaire
- carrying out a survey
- undertaking an experiment.

Surveys

Have you ever wondered how the music industry decides which record is top of the charts each week? The chart is based on the number of records sold in the shops, but how are the numbers of sales calculated? There are thousands of shops in the country and it would be very difficult to get the information from each one.

The answer is that only a **selection** of shops is asked. This is called a survey and the selection is called a **sample.** It is important that the sample is **representative.** The shops chosen must be in different parts of the country and in small towns as well as cities.

The way in which the record chart is produced is an example of the use of **statistics.** Statistics involve:

- **collecting** data (collecting figures of record sales from selected shops)
- **analysing** the data to produce information (producing a list of best-selling records)
- **displaying** the results in tables, diagrams, graphs or charts (record charts are published in magazines).

Conducting a survey

The first step in conducting a survey is to decide exactly what you *want* to know. A supermarket manager may want to know how many customers use the shop at different times in the week. She can then plan when she will need extra part-time staff for busy periods at the check-outs.

The next step is to decide *how* the data could be collected. In the case of the supermarket the manager could have someone standing at the entrance making a note as people walk in. The data would then be collected purely by observation and may be recorded on a specially designed **data collection observation sheet.**

A sewing machine that is used to produce jeans occasionally develops a fault. There are two types of fault: sometimes the thread breaks and sometimes the needle falls out. The production supervisor asks the machine operator to record how often each fault happens so that she has information to give to the maintenance section. She produces the following data collection observation sheet.

Sewing Machine Fault Record Date	
Thread break	
Needle falling out	

Figure N.4 A data collection observation sheet

Did you know?

When carrying out this type of survey, a simple tally system is often used. The first four occasions are recorded as ////. When the fifth occurs it is recorded as ////. The sixth starts a new set //// /. It is an easy job to count up the groups of five.

Non-assessed activity

1 Design an observation sheet to count the number of vehicles passing in either direction on a road in an hour.
You need to distinguish between goods vehicles and private cars. Use your sheet and add up the results. It might be interesting if **two or three** of you carried out the survey independently, at the same time. Are your results the same? If not, can you find out why?
2 You have been asked to find out how many people eat meals in your school or college each day during a week. Discuss with your fellow students and your tutor how this information could be:
   a collected
   b analysed
   c displayed.

Did you know?

Surveys are often carried out to find information about people's attitudes or behaviour, e.g:

- Why do people prefer a certain brand of canned drink?
- Why is one night-club more popular than another?
- What kind of facilities would people like in a new sports centre?

It is easier to obtain this information in the form of **numerical** data (i.e. as numbers). This way the results are easier to analyse.

Questionnaires

Have you ever seen someone standing in a shopping centre with a clipboard talking to passers-by? They could be using a **questionnaire** to find out what people think about something. For example, they may be trying to find out people's reactions to a new product, or which way they intend to vote in a forthcoming election.

The rules for designing questionnaires are:

1 Think carefully about what you need to know. For instance, do you want facts or opinions?
2 Word your questions carefully. There are two types of question.

- A **closed** question invites a 'yes' or 'no' answer, e.g. 'Do you watch pop music programmes on television?'
- An **open** question asks for more general information, e.g. 'What do you think about sport on television?'

Questions can either yield **quantitative** information (i.e. a numerical answer) or **qualitative** information (i.e. an opinion). Quantitative information is much easier to analyse; in many cases computers are used (see point 7 below). Be careful how you phrase your questions so that you don't cause offence. For instance, don't ask people questions that they would prefer not to answer or would find embarrassing, such as questions about their earnings, weight, medical history or personal relationships.

3   A common mistake is to make the questionnaire too long. Keep to the **essential** points.

4   Carry out a **pilot** survey by getting a small number of people to fill in the questionnaire. Then check that they have understood the questions and reword any that were ambiguous.

5   Decide the number of people from whom you wish to obtain information (i.e. the size of your survey). If the organisers of a music festival wished to know people's opinions on various events, they would probably find out what was needed by asking 100 people at random. Different types of people would need to be questioned (e.g. different ages, male and female) to make sure that the results were not **biased** (i.e. slanted to give a false outcome).

6   Decide where you need to be to carry out your survey. There is little point in standing in a bus station, if you are doing a survey on cars! You may also want to consider the best time to do it. For instance, if you wanted to survey mothers with young children, you should stand in a shopping centre during mid-morning or afternoon, rather than during the lunchtime or late in the day when people are passing through on their way to or from work.

7   Analyse your questionnaires when they are returned. Draw a statistical diagram to analyse your result (see pages 556 and 559).

Did you know?

Questionnaires can be sent through the post or given to people to complete and return in their own time. This can be cheaper as more people can be surveyed more quickly. The problem is that usually only a few are returned.

An alternative method is the telephone survey. This is being used more frequently by many market research companies.

Non-assessed activity

As a group, decide where you would go and at what time, and the type of people you would ask, if you were carrying out a survey on each of the following:

1   How many people use taxis and how frequently
2   What people think of the local cinema
3   What people think of a new brand of paint
4   The favourite leisure activity of students in your school or college
5   The average amount of spending money given to young people in your area
6   Whether a new perfume would be popular.

Designing a questionnaire

The owner of a computer shop which sells games notices that many people who come into the shop leave without buying anything. She wonders if they intended to buy anything in the first place, if they were just curious to know what was the latest game on the market, or if they simply wanted to play on some of the computers. Perhaps they had been prepared to buy something but were unable to find what they wanted. She is aware that she does not stock a complete range of games for all machines. She also wonders whether she should rent games as well as sell them.

She designs the following questionnaire.

COMPUTER GAMES – CUSTOMER QUESTIONNAIRE

We are carrying out a survey to find out the kind of computer games people prefer. We would be grateful if you would help us by answering a few simple questions.

1   Do you own a computer games machine?   Yes ☐   No ☐
2   If so, what make is it? ....
3   Do you buy games?   Yes ☐   No ☐
4   Do you rent games?   Yes ☐   No ☐
5   When looking at the games in this shop, do you find what you need?   Always ☐   Sometimes ☐   Never ☐
6   If you have looked for something recently, and been unable to find it, please state the item(s) you were looking for:
....
7   Is there anything you think we could do to improve our service?
....

Figure N.5 A questionnaire set by the owner of a computer games shop

Non-assessed activity

Refer to the survey above.

1 Which questions are asking for quantitative information and which ones are asking for qualitative information?

2 Which are open and which are closed questions?

Using the questionnaire

At first the owner leaves the questionnaires next to the door for people to fill in and place in a box. After the first day she is disappointed with the number returned; several have been filled in incorrectly or are unreadable. She then decides to ask one of the assistants to stand by the door, ask people the questions and fill them in herself. This works much better and about 70 per cent of people co-operate.

When she analyses the completed questionnaires she discovers that:

1 About 83 per cent of people coming into the shop own games machines.
2 A games machine recently introduced on the market is not popular. The market leaders appear to be Sega and Nintendo.
3 About 92 per cent of people buy games.
4 Only 22 per cent rent games (although some of these also buy games).
5 Only 23 per cent always find the game they want, 54 per cent sometimes find it and 11 per cent say they never do.
6 Three or four games seem to be very popular – none of which she stocks.
7 Quite a few people think the shop is too cluttered with not enough space between the racks. Also people have to queue too long at the pay point.

Non-assessed activity

Overall the owner has received information that will help her improve the running of her shop if she takes note of the comments. She wonders about the 30 per cent of people who didn't answer the questionnaire and why some answered 'never' to question 5 but didn't answer question 6 at all.

1 What changes do you think she should make to the shop?
2 Why do you think some people refused to answer the questionnaire?
3 What explanation(s) can you offer for the fact that some answered 'never' to question 5 and then ignored question 6?

Conducting an experiment

Scientists would say that this is the most precise method, because facts are more **reliable** than opinions. What they mean is that you can find out how fast a car can travel more accurately by measuring it than by asking the owner! Therefore, organisations which produce motor reports find out the maximum speed and acceleration *not* by asking the manufacturers but by **testing** cars themselves. They then record the results and analyse them.

Non-assessed activity

1 Discuss with your tutor why the findings from measuring the performance of ten cars is likely to be more **reliable** than measuring the performance of one.

2 You have met two key ideas in relation to data collection – **validity** and **reliability.** Check with your tutor that you are sure you know what each of these terms means – and the difference between them.

Types of data and accuracy

You have one final aspect of data collection to consider before you start collecting it in earnest. This relates to the **type** of data you want or need, and the level of accuracy you require. For example you may need to collect:

- discrete or grouped data
- precise data or estimates.

You also need to consider which units of measurement to use and whether any special equipment is required. Finally, you need to decide the level of accuracy which is required.

Discrete and grouped data

Discrete data normally falls into specific categories or values. For instance, suppose you wanted to know how many women take size 4 shoes. In this case, both the number of women and 'size 4' are specific values. The number of children within a family is also an example of discrete data – you can only have whole numbers of children, not 3.5, for example. If you **group** data together, you can move away from the specific area and look at a range – for instance, the number of women who take sizes 4–6 shoes.

The type of data required will depend on who wants the survey and why it is required. For instance, if you were trying to find out the number of people who buy shower gel rather than bubble bath, you may not be interested in which make of shower gel people prefer. You would therefore group all the data on shower gel together. If, however, you were employed by a particular manufacturer of shower gel, it is likely that the separate figures would be required **as well** – i.e. how many people buy ours and how many people buy **each of the other makes.**

Precise data and estimates

Whilst you can be precise if you are trying to find out how many people visit a shop in an hour, it is rather more difficult to do this if you are finding out how many passengers pass through Heathrow Airport each hour, night and day, summer and winter. In this case you would **estimate** the numbers of people travelling at certain times, based on a range of information collected. In some surveys you can be precise, in others, an estimate is far more sensible.

People estimate all the time. You may say, 'She's twice the size of Susan' – but you haven't actually weighed or measured either of them! You need rather more accurate bearings to be able to make estimates in surveys, however. You could hardly judge the number of passengers passing through Heathrow by asking your friends or watching the place one Sunday afternoon. If you become skilled at estimating you can use this as a double check on whether the answer is reasonable. For instance, if you watch your friend spending money like water all week you may not like to ask how much he has managed to get through. You may estimate the amount instead. If you did decide to ask, there is a range of figures you would consider likely to be the truth – and outside this you would wonder who he was kidding – himself or you!

Estimates

1 A painter is told that a wall is 6.82 metres long by 3.2 metres high. He estimates the area by multiplying 7 metres by 3 metres to give 21 square metres. In both cases the figures of 7 and 3 are near enough to give him his answer.

The accuracy of this calculation can be checked by working it out with the exact figures.

6.82 m × 3.2 m = 21.82 m^2

2 A person in the Accounts department of a company that owns a fleet of lorries is asked for an estimate of the total fuel bill per month. The figures in his file show that the number of gallons of diesel fuel used is 2964 a month and that the price paid is £1.98 per gallon. The estimate he could give is:

3000 × 2 = £6000

The actual figure is:

2964 × £1.98 = £5868.72.

Did you know?

When Eurotunnel started building the Channel Tunnel they estimated it would cost £4.7 billion. In reality it has cost £8 billion!

Practise your skills

1 Best steak costs £7.89 per pound. How much do you think 7 oz will cost?
2 A man calls at a DIY shop and sees that the price of paint is £3.80 per tin and brushes are £2.20 each. He needs four tins of paint and one brush and he has £20. Can he afford them?
3 You are meeting your friend in half an hour. You still have to wash your hair (five minutes), dry it (eight minutes), get changed (ten minutes) and get there (five minutes). The phone rings in the middle and you spend five minutes talking. *Quickly* – can you still get there on time?

Non-assessed activity

Work out estimates for the following situations **in your head** and then check your answer using a calculator.

1 A supermarket manager is given a price of £3216 for a new checkout station. He needs 19 and he has a budget of £70 000 to spend on them. Can he afford them?
2 A production supervisor knows that a machine produces 72.5 litres of fluid per hour. One Friday the machine will be shut down early and it will only operate for four hours and ten minutes. How many litres will it produce?
3 A computer department works a five-day week for 49 weeks of the year. Each day 250 invoices are produced. Estimate the number produced each year.
4 Estimate the cost of 1542 pencils at 9p each and 189 files at £2.05 each.

Did you know?

When carrying out different types of calculation it is useful to estimate the result as a check. If you bought a chocolate bar for 19p and a drink for 29p the total is *about* 50p (20p + 30p). If you gave a £1 coin you should receive *approximately* 50p change.

Tolerance

You may have thought that **tolerance** means how laid-back your tutor is when you forget to hand in a piece of work on time, or how understanding your parents are if you arrive home an hour later than planned. In numeracy, however, tolerance means something different.

In terms of numbers, the degree of tolerance is the range on either side of a precise figure. Think back to the example about your friend spending money. Mentally, you may have thought he spent about £30. You may have decided that any figure between £25 or £35 could be acceptable. In other words, this is your tolerance limit, i.e. ±£5.

You therefore need to decide the **tolerances** to which you are working given the specific situation. If you estimate the speed of a car, it may be acceptable if your result is within ±5 mph. Outside this, your results may not be acceptable.

Generally, the broader or more general your survey the larger the tolerance. If you were working out data relating to world population a tolerance of ±10 per cent may be quite acceptable. If you were assessing data on the number of aeroplanes that crashed at an airport in a particular year, the aeroplane

manufacturers may not be very impressed if you had such a large tolerance factor built into your findings!

Did you know?

The police have to *estimate* the speed of a car that is coming towards them or passes them when they are stationary. They can only judge the speed more accurately if only they are behind or in front of the car – and even then there may be a marginal difference in the speedometer readings of their car and the 'speeding' car. The police therefore allow for this and are unlikely to stop anyone whom they 'clock' as doing 71 mph on a motorway. They are working within a certain tolerance. If someone flies past them at 94 mph, it would not be a sensible argument to suggest that they should adjust their tolerance levels!

Non-assessed activity

1 Can you estimate how many passengers use an airport in the course of a year if:

- one plane takes off or lands every two minutes between 1 April and 30 September and every five minutes the rest of the year
- the airport is only used for 16 hours a day
- each plane holds an average of 200 passengers?

2 Discuss **with your tutor** acceptable tolerance limits for the following surveys.
   a the number of workers injured by using a particular chemical
   b the number of babies born each year
   c the number of people who buy a particular newspaper
   d the number of students in your class who are up to date with their work!

Units of measurement

You probably know what is meant by this term. You should also have some idea of **sensible** units of measurement to use for different surveys. If you were estimating the distance from the Earth to the Sun you wouldn't use the same unit of measurement as that used to estimate the length of your classroom. Similarly, if you were estimating the amount of fuel used by a jumbo jet you would use different measures than you would for the amount of a medicine to take, and so on.

Units of measurement fall into the three different areas:

- unit of money (dollars, pounds, francs, etc.)
- units of physical dimensions, e.g:
  - length, breadth, height and distance – all connected to size
- units of another property, e.g:
  - time
  - temperature
  - capacity (related to liquids)
  - mass (similar to weight).

Did you know?

Some people get volume and mass muddled up. Don't make the same mistake. The volume of an object is the amount of space it takes up. The mass is the amount of material there is in the object, and is related to its weight. A bag of cotton wool or polystyrene would have a large volume but very little mass. If you think about it, you can see that it wouldn't weigh very much. A sack of gold ingots would be the opposite. So finding a treasure chest and running off with it quickly on foot is not usually an option!

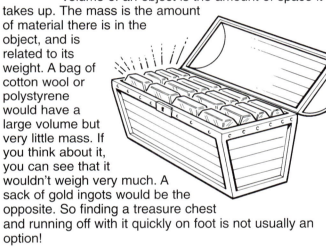

Systems of measurement

It is unfortunate that in many cases there are **two** systems of measurement. For instance, some petrol stations prominently display the price of petrol in gallons and some the price in litres. Your milkman sells milk in pints and the supermarket sells it in litres. Pubs still serve beer in pints! In the same way, some people buy vegetables in pounds, although they may be marked in kilograms – and most cars show speedometer markings in both miles per hour and kilometres per hour.

Why do we have different systems of measurement? The answer is that they were developed in different countries before international trading began. Today, the two main systems that survive are **metric** and **imperial.**

Did you know?

Fans of *Pulp Fiction* will know why John Travolta talked about buying a Royale with cheese in France. There is no metric equivalent for the quarter-pounder!

Measuring equipment

It seems fairly obvious to say that you should know which **type** of measurement you are going to use – and to take with you the appropriate equipment. Sometimes you may need more than one item. For instance, to measure **speed**, you need to measure both **distance travelled** and **time**. Therefore a stopwatch and measuring device would both be necessary.

Always make sure that:

- everyone carrying out the same survey is using the **same** unit of measurement
- everyone is well equipped!

Did you know?

If two people carried out a survey of milk sales and one brought back the information in litres and the other in pints, what would you do? The answer is not to panic and shout at both of them, but to use a conversion table! See below.

Units of money

In your private life, the only time you may even think about foreign currency is when you are going on holiday.

Nearly every country has its own type of currency. For example, if you went to the USA you would have to pay for things in dollars. If you travel abroad you need some of the local currency. For a small fee you can usually change British money into the type you need. The amount you get will be determined by the **exchange rate.** Exchange rates vary from day to day.

Calculating with exchange rates

Calculations involving exchange rates always involve the multiplication of decimal fractions. If you were going on holiday to Canada and had saved £400 for spending money, you would need it changed to Canadian dollars. The bank would quote you an exchange rate of, say, 2.18 dollars to the pound. How many dollars will you get in exchange for your £400?

Simply *multiply* your savings by the exchange rate, i.e:

400 × 2.18 = $872.

If the answer does not work out to a whole number, round it up or down. (You may like to note that banks usually round everything down!)

Did you know?

If you can't remember how to round decimal numbers, turn to page 582 to find out.

Practise your skills

Calculate how much you would receive in each of the examples below.

1   Austria – savings £260, rate 15.00 Schillings to the pound
2   France – savings £800, rate 7.43 francs to the pound
3   Germany – savings £460, rate 2.15 Marks to the pound
4   Spain – savings £500 – rate 195.0 pesetas to the pound
5   USA – savings £550 – rate 1.57 dollars to the pound
6   Portugal – savings £650 – rate 227.0 escudos to the pound

Did you know?

If you return from holiday abroad with any foreign money, you can change this back to British currency provided it is in notes and not coins. Obviously there is a charge for this (just as there is for changing your money in the first place). However, you can get a good idea of how much you have brought back if you **divide** the amount of Canadian money you have left by the current exchange rate, i.e.

160 Canadian dollars at 2.18 to the pound
= 160 ÷ 2.18 = £73.39.

Practise your skills

Calculate how much you would receive if you took the following amounts of foreign currency to the bank. Work out each answer to two decimal places for British currency.

1   26000 Belgian francs – exchange rate 43.90 to the British pound

2   100 Swiss francs – exchange rate 1.75 to the British pound
3   270 Norwegian krone – exchange rate 1.75 to the British pound
4   800 Danish krone – exchange rate 8.47 to the British pound

Units of physical dimensions

Did you know?

One metre is one ten millionth (what a fraction!) of the distance between the North Pole and the equator, on a line which travels through Paris.

Length, breadth, height, distance

You should already know that in the **metric** system

10 millimetres (mm)	= 1 centimetre (cm)
100 cm	= 1 metre (m)
1000 m	= 1 kilometre (km)

in the **imperial** system

12 inches (in)	= 1 foot (ft)
3 ft	= 1 yard (yd)
1760 yd	= 1 mile

Conversions

To be able to convert imperial to metric and vice versa you need to know equivalents. To two decimal places these are:

1 cm	= 0.39 in and	1 in	= 2.54 cm
1 m	= 1.09 yd and	1 yd	= 0.91 m
1 km	= 0.62 miles and	1 mile	= 1.61 km

1   The length of a corridor is known to be 25.20 yards. A carpet firm supplies in metric length. How many metres of carpet are needed?

1 yd = 0.91 m
25.20 yd = 25.20 × 0.91 m = 22.93 m

2   A sales representative has to drive from Paris to Nice. On his map it shows this is a journey of 934 km. He has no feel for the journey as he is used to miles. He also knows that he can average 55 mph. Tell him how far he has to drive and how long the journey is likely to take him.

1 km = 0.62 miles
934 km = 934 × 0.62 = 579.08 = 580 miles
580 ÷ 55 = 10.54 hours or 10 hours 32 minutes

Practise your skills

Convert the following.

1 18 in to centimetres
2 15.20 km to miles
3 2 ft 6 in to millimetres
4 240 cm to yards and also to feet.

Units of other properties

Time

Time is one unit of measurement that is universally accepted all over the world. An hour in Hong Kong is just the same as an hour in Britain. However, **the time of day** varies depending upon where you are in the world. For example, in America the time could be anything between five and eight hours **behind** the time in the UK. So if you decided to ring a friend in New York at 9 am UK time, you can work out for yourself the type of reception you would receive, bearing in mind that it would be five hours earlier in New York!

The situation is even more complicated because several countries change their times during the year to obtain maximum benefit from the hours of daylight available. In the UK, clocks are set forward one hour in spring and back one hour in the autumn. Many European countries have a similar system. In Australia, however, this occurs on different days in different states, causing a lot of confusion!

Calculating the differences

John Evans flies from London to New York on Monday. He leaves at 9 am UK time and the journey takes eight hours. However, New York is five hours behind London. On Wednesday he flies to New Orleans at mid-day. The flight takes three hours and New Orleans is one hour behind New York. On Saturday he flies to Los Angeles at 7 am. This journey takes four hours. Los Angeles is two hours behind New Orleans. On Sunday he returns to London, leaving at 6 pm. His flight takes ten hours.

At what time did he arrive in each city?

Note: *Before you read the answer why don't you try this problem yourself?*

1 He arrived in New York at 12 noon – i.e. plus eight hours and minus five hours
2 He arrived in New Orleans at 2 pm (+ 3 – 1)
3 He arrived in Los Angeles at 9 am (+ 4 – 2)
4 He arrived in London at 12 noon on **Monday** (+10 + 8).

Practise your skills

A man goes on a journey from his home. He takes 60 minutes to drive to the airport and checks in two hours before his plane leaves. He was due to arrive at his destination four-and-a-half hours later but the plane was delayed for 35 minutes. He spends 30 minutes waiting for his baggage and boarding the bus and his hotel is 20 minutes away. What time does he arrive at the hotel if he left the UK at 9 am and his destination is one hour ahead of British time?

Temperature

There are two main units for measuring temperature – Fahrenheit (°F) and Celsius (°C). The Celsius system is gradually becoming the more popular.

To convert from Fahrenheit to Celsius: subtract 32 and then multiply by $\frac{5}{9}$.

To convert from Celsius to Fahrenheit: multiply by $\frac{9}{5}$ and add 32.

To convert 86°F to Celsius:

$$(86 - 32) \times \frac{5}{9} = 54 \times \frac{5}{9} = \frac{270}{9} = 30°\text{C}$$

To convert 10°C to Fahrenheit:

$$\left(10 \times \frac{9}{5}\right) + 32 = \frac{90}{5} + 32 = 18 + 32 = 50°\text{F}$$

 ### Did you know?

Calculations in brackets must always be done first. Did you remember this from your school days?

Practise your skills

Convert the following. Give your answer to 2 decimal places.
1 Convert 15°F, 21°F, 47°F to °C
2 Convert 5°C, 21°C, 46°C to °F

Capacity

You should know that in the **metric** system:

1000 millilitres (ml) = 1 litre (l)

In the **imperial** system:

20 fluid ounces (fl oz) = 1 pint
8 pints = 1 gallon

Conversion

1 ml   = 0.09 fl oz   and   1 fl oz   = 10.99 ml
1 litre = 0.22 gallons and   1 gallon = 4.55 litre
1 litre = 1.76 pints   and   1 pint   = 0.57 litre

1   The instruction manual for a machine says that it needs filling with oil and that its capacity is 2.3 gallons. The oil is sold in litres. How many litres does it need?

1 gallon = 4.55 litre
2.3 gallons = 2.3 × 4.55 = 10.46 litres

2   Convert 10.74 ml to fluid ounces.

1 ml = 0.09 fl oz
10.74 ml = 0.09 × 10.74 = 0.97 fl oz

Practise your skills

Convert the following.

1   4.72 gallons to litres
2   21 litres to gallons
3   5.4 fl oz to ml
4   2.75 litre to fluid ounces
5   9 pints to litres

Weight or mass

You should know that in the **metric** system:

1000 grams (g) = 1 kilogram (kg) – sometimes called 'kilo'
1000 kg = 1 metric tonne (don't confuse this with 'ton' as used in the imperial system)

In the **imperial** system:

16 ounces (oz) = 1 pound (lb)
14 lb = 1 stone
8 stones = 1 hundredweight (cwt)
20 cwt = 1 ton

Note that stones are rarely used for measurement of weight these days.

Conversion

1 g = 0.035 oz and 1 oz = 28.35 g
1 kg = 2.21 lb and 1 lb = 0.45 kg
1 tonne = 0.98 tons and   1 ton = 1.016 tonnes

1   An old machine is to be moved and the removal firm needs to know the weight in kilograms. A label on the machine gives its weight as 265 lb.

1 lb = 0.45 kg
265 lb = 265 × 0.45 kg = 119.25 kg

2   Convert 5.5 ounces to grams.

1 oz = 28.35 g
5.5 oz = 5.5 × 28.35 g = 155.92 g

The answer to question 1 above is probably far more precise than the information required by a removal firm. What figure would have been near enough for their use?

Practise your skills

Convert the following.

1   280 g to pounds
2   5 tons to tonnes
3   7 lb to kilograms
4   2.20 oz to grams

Non-assessed activity

1   Convert 12 yards to metres.
2   Convert 2 metres to inches.
3   Convert 10 kilometres to miles.
4   Convert 5 ounces to grams.
5   Convert 8 pounds to kilograms.
6   Convert 2 fluid ounces to millilitres.
7   Convert 4 gallons to litres.
8   Convert 5 litres to pints.
9   You have been asked to take a parcel which weighs 25 lb to the post office. You know the post office charts for postage rates are given in kilograms. How many kilograms does your parcel weigh?
10 A business man is driving from Brussels to Frankfurt, a distance of 401 km. He wants to know the distance in miles.
11 You have to send a fax to your office in Rome. The manager there is visiting the UK in two weeks and will be driving from London to your Scottish office in Aberdeen. You know this is 543 miles. He wants the distance in kilometres. What distance will you fax?
12 Your friend sends you a postcard from holiday and says that the temperature is 40°C and he can't get

cool. What is the equivalent temperature in Fahrenheit?

13 A new machine is delivered and the instructions state that it must not be stored below 32°F. What is this in Celsius?

Did you know?

All units of measurement are based on some standard that can be checked – see, for example, where the metre came from on page 576. For temperature, 0°C or 32°F is the freezing point of water and 100°C or 212°F is the temperature at which water boils.

Conversions using tables, graphs and scales

Tables can be used to convert between metric and imperial units accurately. Graphs and scales can be used to obtain *reasonably* accurate results.

Tables

A conversion table gives a list of conversions from one type of system to another, as in Figure N. 6.

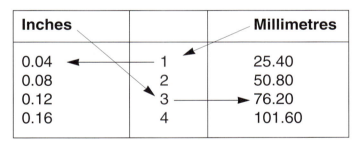

Inches		Millimetres
0.04	1	25.40
0.08	2	50.80
0.12	3	76.20
0.16	4	101.60

Figure N.6 Conversion of inches to millimetres

This may look complicated at first, but when you study it you will find that:

1 mm = 0.04 inch
3 inches = 76.20 mm

An easy way to use the table is to remember that you move diagonally downwards and then horizontally across – as shown on the chart.

Did you know?

Tables are not very useful since they only convert from whole numbers. If you wanted to know what 3.5 mm was in inches, you would have to *estimate*.

Estimating conversions

Sometimes it is useful to estimate a conversion between metric and imperial units. Some of these estimates are easier than others. A tonne is *almost* exactly the same as a ton. A yard is only slightly less than a metre.

For example, an office manager is told that the cost of cleaning carpets is 20p (£0.20) per square yard. He knows that the total floor area of his office is 420 square metres. He quickly estimates what the cleaning would cost him.

420 × 0.2 = £84

Since a metre is slightly more than a yard he estimates the cost at £100.

Non-assessed activity

Calculate the exact cost of the cleaning operation and work out the difference between this and the estimated figure given above.

Accuracy

The level of accuracy you require will depend upon the survey you are undertaking. You determine levels of accuracy every day in your own life. If you are running a bath you are not too concerned – within a few litres – how much water is in the bath. If you are measuring out hair dye or weighing the ingredients for a cake, the level of accuracy is more critical!

Remember that you should be equally comfortable with very large and very small numbers. On some occasions you may decide to work in whole numbers rather than decimals by rounding your answers. On other occasions, the decimal *difference* could be very important.

Non-assessed activity

Each of the following items of information was obtained as part of a survey.

a Write down **correctly** the number written here in words in figures – with millions as your maximum units of measurement.

b State the level of accuracy you think was required.

1 The pre-tax profits of Burmah Castrol were two hundred and forty three million pounds.

2 VAT is currently charged on these goods at seventeen point five per cent.

3 The sandwich industry in Britain is worth one point eight billion pounds.

4 Shami Ahmed, the former Burnley schoolboy who launched the Joe Bloggs clothing range, is worth fifty million pounds.

5 The average man's job now lasts six point four years compared with seven point nine years in 1975.

6 The internal bore of the hypodermic needles was nought point nought four millimetres.

Describing situations

When you have collected your data you will use it to describe the situations you find. For instance, if you report that the temperature was 70°F, you are describing a different situation than if the temperature was –5°C! You will not always be able to describe a situation using just whole numbers. When you start analysing data, the numbers can become very complicated. For instance, your boss would be rather surprised if you told him that 'the machine was out of production for 67 hours out of a total of 1340 hours'. Especially when he later realises that you could have simply said, 'The machine was out of production for five per cent of the time.'

To describe a situation properly you need to be able to use:

- fractions
- decimal fractions (normally just called decimals)
- percentages
- ratios
- negative numbers.

Fractions, decimals, percentages, ratios and negative numbers

All of these types of number are used to describe or analyse business situations. Quite often the same situation can be described using any one of these methods, e.g. if 100 g of baked beans contains 5 g of protein, this can be written in different ways.

- One-twentieth of a tin of baked beans is protein.
- Every gram of baked beans contains 0.05 g of protein.
- Five per cent of baked beans is protein.
- The *ratio* of protein to other ingredients in baked beans is 1:19.
- Of the content of a tin of baked beans, 95 per cent does not contain protein.

Sometimes one way of describing a situation is better than another. For example, which do you think sounds better?

- We've captured 50 per cent of the market.
- We've captured $\frac{1}{2}$ the market.
- We haven't captured half the market.

Most people would think the first option sounded best, and certainly it is the most commonly used. You need to know *all* the different methods so you can use the most appropriate in each situation and convert from one to another if necessary.

Fractions

In the business world fractions are not often used. For example, you would be very unlikely to say that $\frac{460}{1720}$ of the workforce is male (even if it is!). Normally a decimal figure or a percentage would be used since these are easier to understand at a glance (unless the fraction is a very common one, e.g. a half or a quarter). A further advantage is that decimal numbers can be entered on a calculator if you have to carry out another calculation – whereas fractions can't. It therefore helps if you know how to convert a fraction into a decimal in the first place.

Converting fractions to decimals

In fractions, the number on top is called the numerator and the one underneath the denominator, i.e.

$\frac{2}{5}$ numerator
denominator

To convert from fractions to decimals all you have to do is to divide the denominator into the numerator. Therefore $\frac{2}{5}$ as a decimal is:

$\frac{2}{5} = 2 \div 5 = 0.4$

The next step could be to convert from decimal figures into percentages (see page 583).

Practise your skills

Convert the following fractions into decimals:

1 $\frac{3}{4}$ 2 $\frac{7}{8}$ 3 $\frac{25}{7}$

4 $\frac{13}{7}$ 5 $\frac{8}{3}$ 6 $\frac{4}{8}$

Did you know?

If the numerator and the denominator of a fraction can both be divided by the same number, the fraction will 'cancel' to make it easier to work, with e.g. $\frac{80}{100}$ is really $\frac{4}{5}$ (both numbers can be divided by 20).

Working with fractions

- **Adding and subtracting:** You can only add or subtract fractions if their denominators are the same. You should already know this – if you don't know what to do, refer to the quick reference section on page 607.
- **Multiplying and dividing:** You should already know how to multiply fractions – to divide you simply turn the fraction upside down and multiply. (See quick reference section, page 608.)

Did you know?

If you are working with a whole number and fractions together you should put the whole number over '1' to make it easy to work with, e.g.

$$20 \times \frac{6}{7} = \frac{20}{1} \times \frac{6}{7} = \frac{120}{7}$$

You can tell if your answer is greater than 1 because the numerator will be larger than the denominator, as in the example above. Convert this by dividing the denominator into the numerator and writing any remainder as a fraction, e.g.

$$\frac{120}{7} = 17\frac{1}{7}$$

Practise your skills

Work out the following. Make sure you always check your answer to see if the fraction can be cancelled down.

1 $\frac{2}{3} + \frac{1}{4} =$ 2 $\frac{7}{8} - \frac{3}{8} =$ 3 $1\frac{5}{6} + 2\frac{8}{9} + 3\frac{2}{3} =$

4 $\frac{4}{5} - \frac{1}{4} =$ 5 $10\frac{1}{2} + 1\frac{1}{3} - 2\frac{1}{4} =$ 6 $\frac{1}{2} - \frac{2}{3} = \frac{3}{4} =$

7 $\frac{7}{20} - \frac{3}{10} =$ 8 $2\frac{5}{8} \div \frac{3}{10} =$

Did you know?

1 The word 'of' means 'multiply'. If you are asked to find $\frac{1}{2}$ of 240 then your 'sum' is

$$\frac{1}{2} \times \frac{240}{1} = \frac{240}{2} = 120$$

2 *Time* can be expressed as a fraction, e.g. $5\frac{1}{2}$ hours. In this case you must be careful to remember that you are dealing with a fraction of 60, i.e. $5\frac{1}{2}$ hours = 5 hours 30 minutes. Look back to page 576!

Non-assessed activity

Now try your skills at calculating with fractions.

1 At inspection on a production line, 105 products are checked and 15 are found to be faulty. What fraction of products is faulty?

2 A bank employee joins a pension scheme. He is told that his final pension will be $\frac{1}{60}$ of his best year's salary multiplied by the number of years he works for the bank. If he works there for 30 years, and his final year's salary is £40 000, what will his pension be?

3 A mechanic for a photocopying company is paid a basic wage of £3.60 an hour. He is paid time and a third for week-day overtime and time and a half for working on a Saturday. Last week he worked his basic 38 hour week, six hours overtime mid-week and four hours on Saturday. What was his wage?

4 Your boss is ordering new carpet for his office which is $7\frac{1}{2}$ metres long and $6\frac{1}{4}$ metres wide. How much carpet does he require?
   (**Note**: area = length × width)

5 A computer shop is reducing the prices of all printers by a third for a limited period. How much would you pay for a printer normally priced at £314.20?

6 Your boss is driving on the Continent next week. He knows that a kilometre is $\frac{5}{8}$ of a mile. He works out his journey on the map and it is 2336 kilometres. How far is this in miles?

7 A business person travels from her office in London to an office in New York. The total journey took her $10\frac{1}{2}$ hours. She spent $\frac{3}{4}$ of the time on the plane, $\frac{1}{8}$

of the time travelling by road and the remaining time waiting at airports.

a For how long was she on the plane?

b For how long was she travelling by road?

c What fraction of her journey was spent waiting at airports?

8 A businessman is told by his accountant that his van will depreciate (i.e. go down in value) by one quarter in the first year and a further one fifth *of the original price* for the next three years after that. The van costs £12 000 and the businessman keeps it for $2\frac{1}{2}$ years. How much is it worth when he sells it?

Did you know?

Sometimes fractions are used to give approximate information. For example if, out of £10 100 worth of stock in a food store, stock worth £957 is found to be past the sell-by date, someone might say 'One tenth of the stock will have to be thrown away.' In other words, $\frac{957}{10\,100}$ is near enough to $\frac{1000}{10\,000}$ to be able to call this $\frac{1}{10}$.

Sometimes people working in business only need to know approximate figures. If someone asked you how long it would take you to finish a task they wouldn't expect you to say 11 minutes and 20 seconds! It would be quite enough if you said 'about ten minutes'.

On other occasions complete accuracy is vital. Invoices must be calculated accurately or the business will lose money or upset its customers. You will naturally expect your pay to have been calculated accurately!

Decimals

The correct name for these is **decimal fractions**, since the numbers after the decimal point are 'less than a whole one', representing tenths, hundredths, and so on. As long as you *know* this, it is quite acceptable to *call* them 'decimals'.

There are two main uses for decimal figures. First of all, many things that need to be measured can't be described in whole numbers. For example, the length of a room would probably not be a whole number of metres. Equally, a 5 kg pack of potatoes is unlikely to weigh exactly 5 kg – it may be 5.02 kg or 5.03 kg.

The second main use of decimals in business is money. Two pounds and twenty pence is written as £2.20, five pounds and three pence as £5.03, and so on. In each case the amount in pence is a decimal.

Rounding decimals

Quite often a calculation will give an answer that has several numbers after the decimal point. For example:

£21.22 shared among five people is:
£21.22 ÷ 5 = £4.244 each.

For most purposes, two figures after the decimal point are accurate enough. In the above example you can't give someone 0.4 pence. Reducing the number of figures after the decimal point is called **rounding**.

The rule for rounding is as follows:

.5 and above – round *up*
.4 and below – round *down*
e.g. £3.48 ÷ 5 = 0.696 = 0.70 to 2 decimal places

If your answer contains several more decimal places than you need, then look at the figure to the right of the number you need. If it's 5 or more round up; 4 or less round down e.g:

£72.34<u>7</u>1 = £72.35 to 2 decimal places

Did you know?

When you deal with large amounts of money in business it is usual to omit the pence (i.e. to drop the decimals and round *up*). On VAT forms, for instance, the total amounts of purchases and sales are entered in whole numbers e.g. £12 542 *not* £12 541.83. In some cases figures might even be rounded to the nearest hundred or thousand. A company would not say it had sales of £253 251.60. What would it say?

Practise your skills

Round the following to two decimal places.

1 74.892
2 18.977
3 16.6558

Calculate the following and round your answers to two decimal places.

4 £142.68 ÷ 15
5 £63.70 ÷ 4
6 £27.42 ÷ 4

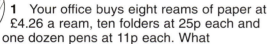

Non-assessed activity

1 Your office buys eight reams of paper at £4.26 a ream, ten folders at 25p each and one dozen pens at 11p each. What is the total cost of the stationery order?

2 Your boss is visiting America on business and wishes to change £200 into dollars. The exchange rate is currently $1.55 to the pound. How many dollars will he receive?

3 A solicitor is drawing up a will for a client who wants his total assets divided among his five children. His house is worth £115 000, he has £15 000 in a building society savings account and £38 000 worth of shares. His remaining assets are valued at £28 000. If the value of his assets remains unchanged, how much will each of his children receive?

4 A town hall employee is allowed to claim 38.4p a mile if he uses his own car for business. In one week he covers 240 miles. What will he claim?

5 Carpet tiles cost £12.54 each and 143 are required to cover the floor of reception. What is the total cost of covering the reception area?

6 You know that an inch equals 2.54 centimetres. What is the size, in centimetres, of:

a a $3\frac{1}{2}$" computer disk **b** a $5\frac{1}{4}$" computer disk?

7 A company charges 2.5p for photocopying. What is the cost of making 542 copies?

8 A paint company produces paint at the rate of 840.48 litres an hour. How much will be produced:
a in a single shift of eight hours
b in three days, assuming the company works two shifts a day
c each week from Monday to Friday? Note there is only one shift on a Friday.

Percentages

If the amount of income you spent on clothes was £23 out of every £100, you could say that you spend 23 per cent of your money on clothes. Percentages are used to compare one amount with another. For example, if a small shop makes a profit of £20 000 in one year on sales of £100 000, the profit on sales is 20 per cent. A supermarket selling a similar range of goods could make a profit of £1 000 000 on sales of £10 000 000. This would be a profit of 10 per cent. In this case the small shop makes twice as much profit on sales as the supermarket.

Did you know?

The situation described above is not unusual! However, before you start thinking all small shopkeepers must be millionaires – remember which shop makes more profit!

A percentage of a number

You may be asked to carry out a percentage calculation where you are given the percentage and asked to find the number, e.g. find 12 per cent of 340 or find 15 per cent of £60.

The easy way to do this is to remember that 12 per cent means 12 in every hundred (which is the same as $\frac{12}{100}$.)

Therefore 12 per cent of 340 = $\frac{12}{100} \times 340 = \frac{4080}{100} = 40.8\%$

15 per cent of £60 = $\frac{15}{100} \times 60 = \frac{900}{100} = 9\%$

On a calculator you can either press the per cent key (if it has one) or divide by 100.

Therefore on your machine simply enter the two numbers as a multiplication and press the per cent key.

Did you know?

If you have a fraction that will cancel down – such as that in the calculation above – it is always easier to do this *first* – then you are working with smaller numbers.

Practise your skills

Calculate the following to two decimal places.

1 16 per cent of 25
2 22 per cent of 1830
3 30 per cent of 180
4 62 per cent of £98.50
5 12 per cent of 110 kg
6 112 per cent of 80
7 168 per cent of £426
8 16 per cent of £93.24
9 74 per cent of 2354 kg
10 81 per cent of £12.30

A quantity as a percentage

Sometimes you may be given two numbers and asked to find one as a percentage of the other, e.g. what is 24 as a percentage of 400?

This is done by showing the two numbers as a fraction and then converting them to a percentage by multiplying by 100%, e.g.

$$\frac{24}{400} \times 100 = 6 \text{ per cent}$$

On a calculator you would enter the number you want to find as a percentage (24) press ÷, then enter the other number (400) and press the per cent key.

Practise your skills

Express the following as percentages. Round to two decimal places where necessary.

1 18 as a percentage of 60
2 40p as a percentage of £3.20
3 0.134 as a percentage of 5
4 135 as a percentage of 400
5 90 kg as a percentage of 2500 kg
6 £85 as a percentage of £50
7 950 as a percentage of 500
8 106 as a percentage of 108
9 12.5 as a percentage of 20.25
10 £36.40 as a percentage of £108.20

Did you know?

The phrase 'per cent' originates from the fact that another way of saying one hundred is to say a century (as with runs in cricket, years, etc.) or *centum*. Originally the phrase '23 per centum' was used; now it is shortened to 23 per cent or 23%.

Interest rates

When we invest money in a bank or building society we are paid **interest**. Similarly, if we borrow money we are charged interest. Knowing about percentages enables you to calculate the interest you will receive (or will be charged).

There are two types of interest – **simple interest** and **compound interest**. In this section we are only concerned with simple interest.

Suppose you have invested £500 in a building society and the current interest rate is 12 per cent. How much interest will you earn in a year? You can calculate this as follows.

Interest paid = 12 per cent of £500

$$\frac{12}{100} \times 500 = £60$$

Did you know?

Interest charged on loans by companies has to be clearly explained to the borrower. This is stated as the **annual percentage rate** (APR) charged on the loan. It is calculated by adding together the interest due on the outstanding loan and the administration charges.

The lower the APR, the cheaper the loan. Always make sure you look for the APR and ignore the monthly rate (which looks much cheaper) when calculating how much interest you would pay.

Non-assessed activity

1 There are 350 employees working in the offices of your company. 12 per cent work in purchasing, 24 per cent in office administration, 20 per cent in sales, 14 per cent in personnel, 18 per cent in accounts, 2 per cent in transport and 10 per cent in production. From these figures calculate the number of employees in each department.

2 A company gives discounts of 5 per cent, 8 per cent and $12\frac{1}{2}$ per cent to grade A, B and C customers respectively. How much discount will each of the following be allowed?

- C Jones – grade A – order £126
- J Roberts – grade B – order £230.10
- B Clements – grade C – order £414.50

3 A survey in your office regarding a proposed vending machine has shown that out of 80 people in the office, 33 want it to provide coffee, 21 prefer tea, 11 like orange juice and 8 consider hot chocolate their favourite. Five people don't mind and two said they wouldn't use it anyway as they dislike vending machines. Express all the preferences as percentages and round them to the nearest whole number so that you have a total of 100 per cent.

4 Your friend has £650 in the bank. How much would she receive in interest if the rate was:
a 8 per cent
b 11.5 per cent
c 12.75 per cent
d 13.75 per cent

5 You need to borrow £250. The following are the APR figures from the sources from which you could borrow. How much interest would you repay in one year in each case?
a Company A – APR 41.5 per cent
b Company B – APR 35 per cent
c Company C – APR 29.8 per cent
d Company D – APR 24.65 per cent

Value added tax (VAT)

Being able to calculate percentages is obviously essential in order to calculate VAT – currently charged at 17.5 per cent.

Did you know?

To calculate VAT quickly *without* a calculator, e.g. 17.5 per cent of £60, you should:

- find 10 per cent (divide by 10) = £6
- halve your answer (= 5 per cent) = £3
- halve your answer again (= 2.5 per cent) = £1.50
- add your answers together = £10.50

Adding on VAT

Organisations send accounts for the total of the goods or services plus VAT. Under normal circumstances you would calculate the amount of VAT and then add it. To find VAT using a calculator, simply enter the amount, press the × key and then enter the VAT amount followed by the percentage key. Then add the original amount, e.g.

£60 × 17.5 per cent = £10.50
£60 + £10.50 = £70.50.

Did you know?

1 On some calculators, if you want to calculate the total quickly, instead of pressing the × key, you can press the + key, so that the price including VAT of an item at £60 = 60 + 17.5 per cent = £70.50.

Test if this works on your calculator!

2 If it does, then the same short cut can also be used be used for finding an amount less a percentage. Simply press the – key instead, e.g. £30 – 10 per cent = £27.

Non-assessed activity

1 Quickly work out what the VAT is on the following amounts without using a calculator.
a £10   **b** £180
c £42   **d** £28

2 How much VAT would an organisation add to each of the following amounts?
a £420.40   **b** £18.80
c £116.80   **d** £25.58
e £610   **f** £85.25

3 Re-enter the figures above and calculate the total amount of each account.

VAT-inclusive accounts

In some cases the amount paid on an account is *inclusive* of VAT, e.g. petrol. If a petty cash voucher is submitted for a VAT inclusive item, the amount of VAT has to be calculated so that it can be recorded separately on the analysis sheet (see Financial Transactions, page 461).

Calculating VAT on inclusive accounts

Work this out by using the following formula:

$$\frac{\text{rate of VAT}}{\text{rate of VAT} + 100} \times \text{amount spent}$$

To see how this works, imagine a representative has spent £88 on petrol. VAT is 17.5 per cent.

$$\frac{17.5}{17.5 + 100} = \frac{17.5}{117.5} \times 88 = 13.106 = £13.11$$

You can cancel down the fraction $\frac{17.5}{117.5}$ to $\frac{7}{47}$ to make things easier.

Calculating the exclusive price

This is worked out *either* by subtracting the amount of VAT you have just calculated from the total paid (£88 – £13.11 = £74.89) *or* by using the following formula:

$$\frac{100}{\text{VAT rate} + 100} = \frac{100}{117.5} = \frac{40}{47} \times \text{amount paid}$$

This is a better system as it gives a double check on your first figure, as obviously the VAT plus the exclusive price must equal the total amount.

Changing VAT rates

The formula will operate even if VAT rates change – all you need to do is to substitute the new figures, so that if VAT went up to 20 per cent the formula to calculate the VAT would be:

$$\frac{\text{VAT rate}}{\text{VAT rate} + 100} = \frac{20}{100 + 20} = \frac{20}{120} = \frac{1}{6}$$

Non-assessed activity

1 Calculate the VAT and the exclusive price on each of these accounts to two decimal places.

a	£65.55	**b**	£97.75	**c**	£35.65
d	£17.63	**e**	£64.50	**f**	£22.60

2 Calculate the cancelled down formulae if VAT was lowered to:

    a 5 per cent   **b** 10 per cent   **c** 15 per cent.

Ratios

In the example on page 583, where the small shop was twice as profitable as the supermarket, it could be said that the profitability ratio is 2:1. If you were diluting concentrated orange squash, a ratio of one part squash to five parts water could be used – a ratio of 1:5. Usually ratios are expressed in whole numbers – but not always. You may, for instance, see the ratio 1.5 to 1 (which could also be expressed as 3:2).

Did you know?

1 You can cancel down ratios in the same way that you cancelled down fractions. Rather than say 24:12 it would be better to say 2:1.

2 Fractions, ratios and percentages are very similar. For example, if $\frac{3}{4}$ of the population drink mostly coffee and $\frac{1}{4}$ drink tea, this could also be written as:

coffee drinkers: total population = 3:4, *or*

75 per cent ($\frac{3}{4} \times 100$) of the population drink coffee.

Practise your skills

1 Convert $\frac{1}{5}$ into a ratio and a percentage.

2 25 per cent of a class drink Pepsi-Cola, the rest drink Coca-Cola.
    a What is the ratio of Coke to Pepsi drinkers?
    b What fraction of the class drink Pepsi?

3 The ratio of men to women attending a football match is 9:1. Express this as both a fraction and a percentage.

Non-assessed activity

1 A dye is made up in the ratio of 2:3:1 from white, navy blue and yellow colour. If 600 litres of dye are required, what quantity of each colour will be used?

2 Your company employs 72 men and 48 women. What is the ratio of men to women?

3 The ratio of the time taken to key in graphics on a computer to the time to print them out is 17:2. If it takes 2 hours 16 minutes to key in the data, how long will it take to print?

4   In a single day, 360 people visit a fast food restaurant but 216 arrive during the busy period between 5 pm and 7 pm. Work this out as a ratio in whole numbers. Then express it as a percentage and a fraction using an appropriate approximation.

Negative numbers

If you count the number of students in your group or the amount of money in your pocket you may come up with an amount such as 17 students or £1.35. These are obvious **positive** numbers. So how can a number be negative? Quite easily – especially where money is concerned!

Assume that you have £1.35 in your pocket but you owe your parents £5. How much money do you really have? The answer isn't nothing – it's worse! The correct answer is –£3.65, which is said as 'minus three pounds sixty-five'. This means that the second you receive any more money you have to take out £3.65 because you have to pay back the owed money. In other words, at the moment your wealth is a negative number!

The same can happen in a company. From various elements in this book, you will have seen that sometimes businesses make a loss and sometimes they make a profit. If they make a loss their accounts will show a negative amount, e.g. –£103 000. If, in the following year, they make a profit of £150 000 then, over the two years, they have only earned £47 000 because, just like you, they have to allow for the negative amount when they do their calculations.

Did you know?

Negative numbers can be found when measuring physical quantities. For example, 0°C is the freezing point of water. On a frosty winter morning the temperature could be – 4°C or even lower.

Non-assessed activity

How could negative figures apply in each of the following situations?

- A shop checks actual stock against its written records.
- An electricity bill is checked against forecast usage.
- A delivery of boxes of photocopier paper is less than the amount ordered.

Did you know?

You should be able to work with numbers of any size, negative as well as positive, no matter whether you have to add, subtract, multiply or divide. If you are still experiencing difficulty with any of these operations you **must** tell your tutor.

Optional evidence assignment

This assignment can be used to provide evidence for Element 2.1 of Application of number. It can also be cross-referenced with Element 3.1. Explain the importance of consumers and customers.

1   **With a small group of fellow students,** design and use a questionnaire for people in your class. The aim is to discover:

- what make of jeans people prefer
- how much they spend when they buy them
- how many pairs of jeans they own
- how many they buy each year
- what style they prefer (e.g. tight or easy fit, dark or pre-washed denim, zip or buttons, etc.)
- the most popular size of jeans

If possible, you also want to know the *reasons* for their preferences.

In your preparations, make decisions and write short notes on each of the following:

a   type of data required
b   units of measurement to be used
c   level of accuracy required
d   tolerances allowed.

2   Test your questionnaire on a small group of people. Compare the design of your questionnaire with that of other groups and decide which is the best, and why.

3   Make out a neat version of the best questionnaire (or combine your best efforts) and photocopy or duplicate it. Design a data collection sheet on which you can record your findings.

4   Now carry out your survey amongst fellow students within your school or college. Try to interview about 60 people.

5   Analyse your results. If you were a jean manufacturer whose sales have fallen recently, what information have you obtained and how could you use it to improve sales?

Element 2.2 Tackle problems

As we have seen, problems to be solved in a real business situation can involve:

- dealing with very large or very small numbers
- dealing with positive and negative numbers
- converting different units of measurements
- doing calculations that include fractions, decimals, percentages and ratios.

When you are trying to find answers to problems you may also have to 'play about' with your data or information. Suppose, for instance, you wanted to explain each of the following:

a how you reached a figure for actual stock that was different from recorded stock
b how you worked on a problem that involved part-time and full-time staff to reach one answer
c how you found the size of something
d how and why you found the average of something
e how you checked your calculations.

From the work you have covered already it would be difficult for you to do any of these – but there are simple techniques to help you. Let's look at these, one at a time.

Using formulae

Don't let the word 'formula' frighten you. (Incidentally, formulae – with an 'e' – is simply the plural of formula). A recipe book contains a formula for making pancakes. You wouldn't panic if you saw:

8 oz flour + 1 tps salt + 1 egg + 0.5 pints of milk especially if there was a picture of a pancake below it.

Neither do you panic if, in a restaurant, you see on your bill:

price of food + VAT = total price to pay

and yet these are both formulae! Formulae can often be written in words. Some other good examples are given in Element 4.2, e.g:

sales – cost of purchases = gross profit
gross profit – expenses = net profit.

Formulae are merely a simplified method of showing how a figure can be calculated. In the example above on stock, your formula might be

recorded stock – damaged stock = actual stock.

On some occasions a formula is expressed in symbols rather than words (probably because it is quicker to write). A formula is a set of words, figures or symbols giving a rule, or statement that can be used not once, but again and again in similar situations.

One of the most simple formulae is the one for the area of a rectangle or square:

area = length × breadth. It is written in symbols as follows:

$A = l \times b$ or $A = lb$

By substituting numbers for the letters you can find a value. The one above can always be used to calculate area. If a piece of paper measures 6 cm × 9 cm, by substituting the numbers in the formula, you find the answer, i.e.

$A = l \times b$ $A = 6 \times 9$ Area = 54 cm^2

Did you know?

If two letters are placed immediately next to each other, this means *multiply*. There is therefore no need to write $A = l \times b$ because $A = lb$ means the same thing!

Formulae and symbols

Symbols are just a way of shortening common words. So, for instance, you quite happily use C for Celsius or F for Fahrenheit. Rather than write out the conversion formula for temperature as

'take the temperature in Celsius, multiply by 9, then divide by 5 and add 32':

it is quicker to write:

$$F = \frac{9}{5}C + 32$$

The formula for converting from Celsius to Fahrenheit is a **standard** formula, it never varies. However, you could design a formula yourself for a particular occasion. For instance, look back at problem b) in the list above. How could you deal with information about part-time and full-time staff and express the answer as **one** figure? Easy. Simply decide how you are going to convert part-timers into full-timers. You could do this by finding out the average hours of one and the average hours of another. If, for instance, full-timers usually work 40 hours and part-timers usually work 20, then the formula is easy:

1 FT = 2 PT.

You could vary this as necessary, depending on the equivalencies you wanted to use.

Constructing a formula

You can make your own formula to help you when you are doing conversions. You should already know that 1″ = 2.5 cm from work you have done at school (otherwise see page 576). You could represent this in a formula by:

- representing inches by the letter x
- representing centimetres by the letter y.

Your formula would then be $2.5 \times y = x$, therefore $x = 2.5y$.

If a marketing department calculated the total cost of producing a booklet by adding together the cost of the copywriter at £25 per hour, a graphic designer who charged £50 per hour and a printer who charged £40 an hour, then they could construct a formula.

- Represent the copywriter by the letter x.
- Represent the designer by the letter y.
- Represent the printer by the letter z.
- Represent the total cost by the letter C.

Then the formula would be:

$C = 25x + 50y + 40z$.

If the booklet took four hours to write, three hours to illustrate and half an hour to print, the total cost would be calculated by the using the formula as follows:

$C = 25 \times 4 + 50 \times 3 + 40 \times 0.5$
$C = 100 + 150 + 20 = £270$

Transposing formulae

A formula can be **transposed** or rearranged to be used in a different way. The formula for the distance travelled on a journey is:

distance = average speed × time

$d = s \times t$

In this form d is the **subject** of the formula, i.e. the quantity that will be found by using the formula.

To make time the subject of the formula rearrange it as follows:

$d = s \times t$

$\dfrac{d}{s} = t$

Therefore $t = \dfrac{d}{s}$

So if a businessman plans to travel from London to Exeter by car, he can check the mileage from his road atlas to find that the distance is 200 miles. He thinks that, allowing for traffic hold-ups, he should be able to average 50 miles per hour. Hence the time taken should be:

$t = \dfrac{d}{s} = \dfrac{200}{50} = 4$ hours

589

Did you know

If you move something to the 'other side' of the equals sign (i.e. in the example above you moved 's'), then you must use the opposite sign on it.

In $d = s \times t$ there is a multiplication sign

If you move s to the other side of the equation you must change the sign to divide:

$d \div s = t$ or $t = \dfrac{d}{s}$

This is called **transposing** the formula.

Practise your skills

1 a The volume of a cube is calculated by multiplying length × breadth × height. Write this as a formula.
 b Use your formula to calculate the volume of a cupboard that measures 1.2 metres in length, 0.7 metres in breadth and is 1.9 metres high.
2 a Transpose the formula for area to make breadth the subject.
 b Use your formula to calculate the breadth of a rectangular field which has an area of 5400 m² and is 90 metres wide.

Non-assessed activity

1 A photocopier uses toner (a powder form of ink) at the rate of three grams for every 1000 copies. Express this as a formula and then calculate the amount of toner required to make 15 000 copies.

2 a The cost of decorating a room is calculated by adding together the number of tins of paint used, the number of rolls of wallpaper and the time spent by the decorator. Paint costs £5 a tin, wallpaper is £14 a roll and the decorator's time is charged at £30 an hour. Write a formula to represent these charges.
 b Use your formula to calculate the cost of decorating a room where three tins of paint and eight rolls of wallpaper are used and it takes 12 hours to complete.

3 The formula for calculating simple interest is

$I = \dfrac{PRT}{100}$

where P = the principal (i.e. amount borrowed)
   R = rate per cent
   T = time in years

a Use the formula to calculate the interest if £5000 is borrowed at a rate of twelve per cent over five years.
b Transpose the formula to make T the subject.

Using measurements

There isn't much point in taking measurements of an object if you don't know what to do with them afterwards. You need to be able to calculate perimeter (i.e. the distance round a square or rectangle), area and volume.

The shapes you may be working with are:

a a square
b a rectangle
c a triangle
d a cube
e a circle
f a cylinder.

There are other shapes, but this is enough for now! Incidentally, remember that many odd shapes are a combination of simple shapes. An L-shape, for instance, is simply two rectangles put together.

Two- and three-dimensional objects

You should already know that:

- **a two-dimensional object** is one which is flat, like the floor area of an office. It has two dimensions – width and length
- **a three-dimensional object** is one that has length, breadth and height – for example an office desk.

These are usually known as **2D** and **3D** objects.

Did you know?

In reality all *objects* have three dimensions. A piece of paper resting on a flat desk has the two dimensions of length and width *but* it also has thickness, which is the third dimension. However, it is sometimes useful to think of things in terms of two of the three dimensions. A company which manufactures glass for windows would probably measure output per machine in square metres per hour with a *standard* thickness (i.e. the one most commonly used).

When people refer to the 'fourth dimension' they are referring to **time.**

Two-dimensional objects

Areas and perimeters

Sometimes it is necessary to find the area of a two-dimensional shape. For example, a company that cuts grass on playing fields needs to know how many square metres there are in a particular field. Then they can estimate how long it will take to cut it.

In business, most shapes for which areas are needed are either **rectangular** (where the corners are 90° or right angles) or **circular.**

Shapes of objects

Some examples of regular shaped objects are:

- **rectangles** – desk tops, windows, doors
- **circles** – compact discs, wheels, waste bins

The **area** of a rectangle is found by multiplying the length by the width.

The **perimeter** of a rectangle is found by adding up the length of the four sides.

Squares and rectangles

A square and a rectangle are alike in some respects – a square is a special rectangle – but in a square the breadth and the width are the same and in a rectangle they are not.

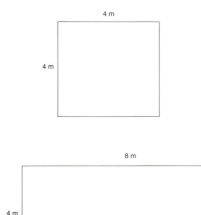

Figure N.7 Squares and rectangles

Because they are alike, you can use the same formula to find their perimeter and area. You can't find out volume because both are two-dimensional figures and don't have depth.

The formula for the perimeter of a rectangle is:

$$P = l + b + l + b = 2l + 2b$$

where l = length and b = breadth.

Because all the sides of a square are the same, the calculation is even easier – take the length of any side and multiply by four!

The formula for the area of both shapes is simply:

$$A = l \times b = lb$$

Areas are always expressed in **square units.** Therefore a football pitch measured in metres would have an area in square metres.

If you are calculating the area of a simple shape, don't forget that you may not need to be given every figure! If you are looking at a square you only need the length of one side to know the rest. In a rectangle, the opposite sides of the figure are always the same size.

1   An office is 22.1 m long by 18.6 m wide and the manager needs to know the area and the perimeter.

Area = length × width = 22.1 × 18.6 = 411.06 *square* metres

Perimeter = 2 × length + 2 × width = 2 × 22.1 + 2 × 18.6 = 44.2 + 37.2 = 81.4 metres

2   A kitchen is shaped as shown below. What is the floor area and the perimeter?

To work out the area, you need to divide the kitchen into rectangles, as shown by the dotted line. Then find the area of the two sections and add them together.

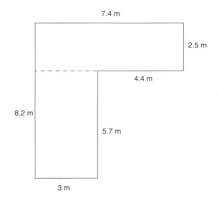

Figure N.8 An L-shaped kitchen

Area = 5.7 × 3 + 7.4 × 2.5 = 17.1 + 18.5 = 35.6 square metres

Another way to solve this is:

7.4 × 8.2 − 5.7 × 4.4 = 60.68 − 25.08 = 35.6 square metres

How has this been done? Check with your tutor if you don't understand.

Practise your skills

Work out the area and perimeter of the following shapes. Write down the formula first, then fill in the numbers and complete the calculations.

1 A rectangle 15.2 cm by 13.8 cm.
2 A square with sides of 2.9 m.
3 A circle with diameter of 2.3 m.
4 A kitchen worktop with the following shape:

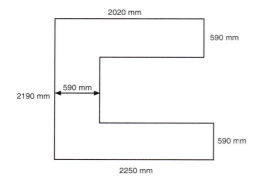

Figure N.9 A kitchen work-top

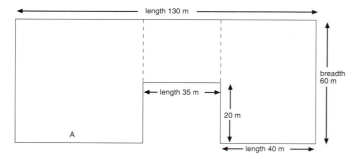

Figure N.10 A compound shape

Non-assessed activity

1 Write a formula for finding the perimeter of a square.

2 Look at diagram N.10.
  a What is the length of A?
  b Calculate the area of each shape.
  c Calculate the area of the whole diagram by adding the areas of all the shapes together.

Triangles

It is easy to work with right-angled triangles if you think of them as rectangles cut in half from top left to bottom right. If you therefore take **two** right-angled triangles, turn one upside down and stick them both together, you end up with a rectangle again.

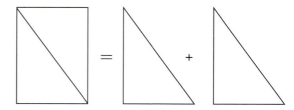

Figure N.11 Two right-angled triangles make a rectangle

Bearing in mind that you have divided the rectangle in two, this is reflected in the formula for finding the area of a triangle, i.e.

$$A = \frac{l \times b}{2} \ or \ \frac{1}{2} \text{base} \times \text{height}$$

This works for all triangles, as you can see if you study Figure N.12 carefully. A rectangle has been drawn round the triangle, and the two shaded areas are the same, in total, as the triangle. Ask your tutor for help if this isn't clear.

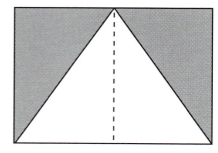

Figure N.12 Calculating the area of any triangle

Circles

Strange as it may seem, calculations with circles are very important. Suppose you worked for a printer who was producing circular badges for a charity event and who needed to know how much card to buy. You would find this very difficult if you couldn't work out the area of a circle! Another application of the area of a circle may become clearer when we move on to cylinders, which are very common.

If you study circles, you will find that the ratio of the circumference to the diameter is always about 3. This is true for all circles, and was first discovered by the ancient Greeks. They called this ratio π (pronounced pi), and worked out its value as close to 3.1416... .

This property of circles can be used to find the area. First, look at Figure N.13 to make sure that you know the difference between the radius, the diameter and the circumference of a circle!

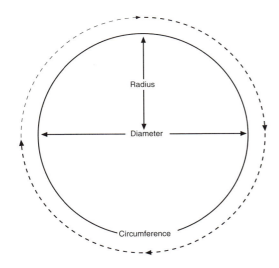

Figure N.13 Parts of a circle

The **radius** of a circle is the distance from the centre to the outside of the circle.

The **area** of a circle is found by the formula $A = \pi r^2$ where r is the radius.

The **perimeter** or **circumference** of a circle is found by the formula $C = 2\pi r$ or πd, where r is the radius or d is the diameter of the circle.

Remember that π is a constant number, and its value is usually taken as 3.14.

Did you know?

Pi is a number that never ends. Calculated to seven decimal places it is 3.1415927. Mathematicians have checked it using computers. The numbers after the decimal point go on endlessly without any pattern.

A useful approximation to π is $\frac{22}{7}$. Try working it out to see how close it is.

Did you know?

Mathematicians in history have been obsessed with finding a more exact value for pi. They decided that the level of accuracy used by the Greeks wasn't good enough. An Italian called Vieta calculated it to ten decimal places in the 1500s. However, the German mathematician van Ceulen went one better. He calculated pi to 35 decimal places and was so thrilled with his discovery he arranged to have it engraved on his tombstone. Pi to 14 places (which is quite enough for this book) is 3.14159265358979 which is far too many to remember. At this point, just be grateful that someone discovered how to round decimals!

Working with circles

An advertising agency wishes to produce a large metal disc, trimmed with blue ribbon around the edge, for a promotional display. The radius of the disc is 2.8 m. What area of sheet metal will they need and what length of ribbon?

Area = $\pi r^2 = 3.14 \times 2.8^2 = 3.14 \times 7.84$
= 2.462 square metres

Perimeter (for ribbon) = $2\pi r = 2 \times 3.14 \times 2.8$
= 17.58 metres

Non-assessed activity

A wall clock surround has the following shape, with a circular hole in the centre. Calculate the area of wood which it contains.

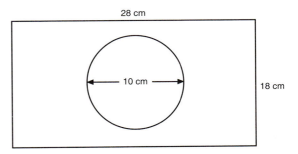

Figure N.14 The surround for a clock

Three-dimensional objects

Cubes and cuboids

A cube is a three-dimensional solid, and all of its faces are squares. A cuboid is like a cube, but all its faces are rectangles. This means that opposite faces are equal. Common examples are building bricks, books, boxes and briefcases. You may not be able to think of a sensible reason for finding the volume of a brick or a book, but there are several good reasons for calculating the volume of a box or a briefcase. Apart from anything else, given **two** boxes or briefcases you could find out which one would hold more.

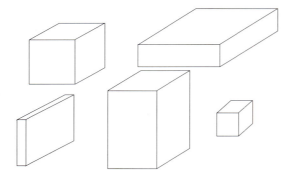

Figure N.15 Which are cubes and which are cuboids?

The formula for calculating volume is

$V = l \times b \times h$

If you know the area of one end, you just need to multiply by the length.

For a cube, the volume is $V = l^3$ (i.e. $l \times l \times l$, see page 566).

Did you know?

1 Volume is always expressed as **cubic units.** Therefore, a room measured in metres would have a volume in cubic metres.
2 The **surface area** of a 3D rectangular object is the sum of the area of the six surfaces. The formula is therefore:

$A = 2h \times l + 2h \times b + 2b \times l$

Don't forget: on a cube each surface is the same size! Therefore the formula simplifies to be $6l^2$

Working with volume

An engineer is responsible for installing an air-conditioning system in a large room. Once the system has been installed the room will be a 'clean' room because it will have filtered air blown into it at a constant temperature. He has to calculate the volume of the room to work out the size of air-conditioning plant to install. The room's floor is shaped as in Figure N.16 and the height of the room is 2.9 m.

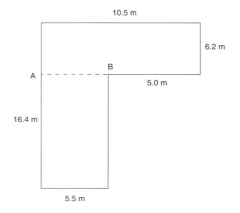

Figure N.16 The floor-shape of the room

The volume is found as follows.

1 Divide the floor area into two sections by drawing a line from A to B. This gives two rectangles, 10.5m × 6.2 m and 10.2 m × 5.5 m.
2 Use the formula given above to calculate the volume of each, i.e:

$V_1 = 10.5 \times 6.2 \times 2.9 = 188.79$ cubic metres (m³)
$V_2 = 10.2 \times 5.5 \times 2.9 = 162.69$ m³

3 Add the two figures together to find the total volume, i.e:

188.79 m³ + 162.69 m³ = 351.48 m³

Note that the engineer would not need such a precise figure and would probably use the figure of 350 cubic metres when working out his other calculations.

Practise your skills

A man wishes to lay concrete on his drive. It is shaped as in Figure N.17.

1 He wishes to make the concrete 140 mm thick. How many cubic metres of concrete does he need?

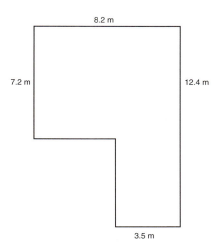

Figure N.17 The drive that is to be concreted

2 If the readymix concrete supplier will only deliver in quantities of half a cubic metre, how much should he order?

Non-assessed activity

1 A washing powder manufacturer supplies washing powder in boxes that are 12 cm wide, 26 cm long and 37 cm high. The average contents of a box takes up 10 484 cubic centimetres. What is the volume of space left at the top?

2 A rectangular heating oil storage tank for a company has internal dimensions of length 3.1 m, width 2.5 m and height 2.7 m. What volume of oil is in the tank when it is half full?

3 You have the choice between two briefcases in a shop. The first is 46 cm long × 35 cm wide × 14 cm deep. The second is 50 cm long × 40 cm wide × 10 cm deep.
  a What is the volume of each briefcase?
  b Which would you buy if you needed one to hold as much paper as possible?

Cylinders – and things

When is a cylinder not a cylinder? If you were asked how many cylinders you handle each day you would probable say 'none'. The chances are that you are wrong. For a start, most drinking mugs are cylindrical. So are tins of beans and cans of Coke. And if you visit a pub, you'll see people drinking out of them all the time – particularly if they are drinking pints of beer.

The volume of a cylinder is important for food and drink manufacturers, because the makers of beans and soft drinks need to know how much their cylinders will hold. It is equally important for beer drinkers who would be irate if they thought they weren't getting their money's worth.

To find the volume of a cylinder you need to think back to circles and area. A cylinder is like a stack of circles piled on top of one-another. Therefore, if you take the formula for the area of a circle and multiply by the length, you get the formula for the volume of a cylinder.

$$V = \pi r^2 \times \text{length}$$

As an interesting experiment in calculating volumes and using conversion factors for a purpose, you might like to try the experiment below – perhaps with the help of your tutor!

Non-assessed activity

Does a half-pint or pint glass really hold that amount?

a Start by measuring the bottom of the glass, then calculate the area of the base.
b Now measure the length (height) of the glass and work out the volume.
c If you have been working in centimetres you will have worked out the volume in cubic centimetres (cm^3). You now have to convert this to imperial measurements (i.e. pints!) You can estimate this in the following way.

- a litre = 1.76 pints
- 500 cm^3 = half a litre
- half a litre = 0.88 pints

If you are measuring a pint glass, therefore, your answer should come out at just under 600 cm^3 and if you are measuring a half-pint glass your answer should be just under 300 cm^3. Is it?

If it is not exactly right, can you suggest any reason why not?

Finding averages

Suppose, as the result of a survey asking how many hours the students in your group spent watching television last month, you are faced with a set of numbers. If you add all the numbers in the set together you find the total. The mathematical term for this is the 'sum of the values'. If you want to find the **average** of the set, then you divide this sum by the number of values in the set, or in our example, the number of students in your group.

The formula for this is given below.

$$\text{average} = \frac{\text{sum of the values}}{\text{number of values in the set}}$$

You may like to note that another name for this average is the **mean** or **arithmetic mean** (to give it its full name). If you are asked to find the mean, you do exactly the same calculation as you did when you found the average.

Therefore, three people aged 6, 9 and 21 have an average age of 12 (i.e. the mean is 12). All we have done is add the figures together and divide by the number of people.

The formula for finding the mean is:

$$\bar{x} = \frac{s}{n}$$

where

s is the **sum** of the items

n is the **number** of items and

$\bar{x}$ is the **mean** – a bar over any letter represents the **mean of a set of data.**

So in the case above, the formula is:

$$\bar{x} = \frac{6 + 9 + 21}{3} = \frac{36}{3} = 12$$

The **range** of a set of numbers is the difference between the highest and lowest values. In the question above, the range is 21 − 6 = 15.

Often, the **mean** and the **range** are the two most important things you will need to find out. Sometimes you get silly answers when you find the mean, such as finding that the number of cars owned by the average family is 1.4. At this point you need to be sensible when interpreting your data. You may need to use a different average, as follows.

Median and mode

There are two other 'averages' relating to a set of figures, which are the median and mode. The **median** is the middle number of set of numbers when they are arranged in order. So, for example, if the shoe sizes of 15 students in a class are:

11, 4, 9, 8, 8, 7, 5, 6, 7, 6, 9, 10, 9, 8, 7

these can be re-arranged in the following order:

4, 5, 6, 6, 7, 7, 7, **8**, 8, 8, 9, 9, 9, 10, 11

The median of these is number 8.

To find the median:

1 Rearrange the data into size order.
2 Count how many items of data there are in the set.
3 Divide this number by 2.
4 Use the answer to count along the set of data to find the median value.

The **mode** is the most common value in a range of data.

If the numbers of children in twelve families are:

1, 2, 4, 2, 1, 5, 2, 3, 3, 2, 4, 2

the most common value is 2. The mode of these numbers is, therefore, 2. If you look back at the example about shoe sizes, you will see that there are three modes in that set.

Sometimes data may be displayed in a frequency curve, as in Figure N.18, which shows the distribution of marks in an examination. The curve peaks at the most common value, where the mark is 63 per cent. This is the mode.

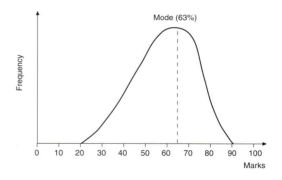

Figure N.18 Mathematics examination results

Did you know?

If you want to show off, next time someone tells you an average ask, 'Which average are you using?' As you have seen, there are three different types of average, and each can give a different impression. The Government and the trade unions will often argue with each other using different averages. For instance, the Government will state the 'average pay' in Britain using the mean figure. This will be fairly high, because it will include all the high earners in the country. The unions, on the other hand, will use the mode. This gives a lower figure because it is closer to what most people earn.

Non-assessed activity

1 Discuss **with your tutor** how using the mean, median and mode would give different figures for finding the average number of part-time hours worked each week by women in Britain.

2 There are ten people working in the sales office of a large company. The numbers of months each has worked for the company are given below.

85, 60, 18, 142, 56, 32, 128, 6, 4, 134

  a What is the mean or average time each person has worked for the firm? Give your answer in years and months.

  b What is the range?

  c Mean and range are both examples of *summarising* numbers. This means that they give some important information about a set of numbers. How useful do you think the information would be to the Personnel department? Why?

  d Why do you think the figures for analysis were given in months and not in years and months? Can you think of any other occasions when you may have to convert figures in this way?

Checking your answers

One final task in solving problems is the checking of your answers. One method of doing this was illustrated with the beer glass example, on page 595, when an **estimate** was used as a rationality check against the correct answer. A rationality check simply means using your common sense to see if the answer is likely to be correct.

As an example, think of an occasion when you have to work out a decimal figure, and you might enter it wrongly into your calculator. Assume you make 1342 photocopies on a machine where each copy costs 1.3p. At 1p a copy the cost would be £13.42. At 1.3p a copy the amount must be rather more – therefore a total of £17.45 is rationally correct.

If the cost had been incorrectly entered (e.g. as 1.3 instead of 0.013) the answer would have been £1744.60 – which is likely to make you the laughing stock of the office for a week.

The other method of checking the answer is to work out the calculation backwards. If you re-enter the

answer you got before rounding it (i.e. £17.446) and divide *this* figure by 0.013 (the cost) then you should get the number of copies as your answer.

Did you know?

An **approximation** is found when you deliberately use figures which have been rounded – to the nearest whole number, or to the nearest 10, or even to the nearest million! You can choose when to round. You might start with fairly accurate figures, and round the result, or start by rounding the figures before you work out the calculation. It would all depend on the information with which you were dealing, and the degree of accuracy you need. Remember, the earlier you round, the less accurate the result will be.

If you were talking about the number of people who use British banks, it would normally be rather silly to use a figure of 24 293 001. Generally, 24 million would be quite near enough. Similarly, if you were quoting percentages, it would be unnecessary to say that 85.7 per cent of the staff had voted to go on strike. 86 per cent (i.e. the rounded figure) would give the management all the information that was needed!

Optional evidence assignment

This assignment can be used to provide evidence for Element 2.2 of Application of number. It can also be cross-referenced with Element 4.2. Complete financial documents and explain financial records.

You work for a publishing company. Your boss, Sarah Taylor, is responsible for obtaining ideas for new books, liaising with authors and updating books that have been out for some time. She has asked you to undertake the following tasks and let her have your reply in a memo.

1 Sarah Taylor is visiting the Continent next week. She will be driving from Calais to Paris, then to Basle and Brussels before returning to Calais. Distances are as follows:

Calais to Paris – 276 km
Paris to Basle – 484 km
Basle to Brussels – 543 km
Brussels to Calais – 236 km

  a Sarah isn't used to kilometres and is too busy to work out how far she has to go. What is the total distance she will be covering in miles?

  b If she drives at an average speed of 40 mph, how long will it take her to do each stage of her journey?

c Petrol claims are allowed at 35.5p a mile. How much will her claim be for the total trip, assuming that *in addition* to the above she also drives 150 miles to Dover and back from your office?

d Sarah Taylor wants some French francs to take with her. At present the exchange rate is 8.04 francs to the pound. If you take £150 to the bank, how many francs do you estimate she will receive if the bank deducts £5 for changing the currency?

2 Sarah is updating an old recipe book and wants to show quantities in both the imperial and the metric systems. Below is given the recipe for damson jam. Convert all the quantities to metric quantities.

4 lb damsons
$4\frac{1}{2}$ lb granulated sugar
half a pint of water

3 A new book is priced to retail at £9.95. Sarah wants to cover production costs of £2 a book, distribution costs of 50p a book and has to allow for retailers to make 100 per cent profit. She also has to pay her authors 10 per cent in royalties.

a She estimates the book will sell 10 000 copies. How much do you *estimate* the company will gain in revenue?

b What do you *estimate* the book will sell at to the *retailers*?

c What are her *estimated* production, distribution and royalty costs when you add them together?

d How much profit do you *estimate* the company will make?

Element 2.3 Interpret and present data

You have now learned how to collect and analyse your data. The final step is learning how to present it so that it is accurate, effectively presented and makes sense to the reader.

One of the major decisions you have to make is *how* to present it. You could write a **report** that includes some calculations. In this case you would be expressing your information mainly in words and by the use of symbols. Or you could draw one or more diagrams to illustrate your findings, such as graphs, bar charts or pie charts.

The new areas you need to think about are as follows:

■ how to explain your data
■ how to use probability to describe situations
■ how to draw two-dimensional diagrams and how to represent three-dimensional objects in this way
■ how to construct statistical diagrams.

Explaining data

Explaining data does not necessarily mean writing about every piece of data you have collected! What it does mean is identifying the key features of your data and looking at how these relate both to each other and to the problem you are tackling.

This technique is actually the key to being able to negotiate. Identify the main facts, look at the relationships and keep to the point! If you wanted to persuade your parents to give you more spending money, then you *might* have some success if you found out how much other people received, identified when you last received an increase, worked out the cost of living and how much this has risen, and calculated if your parents could **afford** to give you an increase. This would all be very good, especially if you then produced a reasoned argument based on this information. Throwing in the facts that you washed up three times last week, tidied up your bedroom last February and didn't mean to forget your mother's birthday is irrelevant – and may even be damaging to your cause!

In this situation the way in which you present your findings should be by **reasoned argument.** Your parents might be a little shocked if you suddenly produced an overhead projector and gave them a slide show of bar charts and graphs showing average spending money for seventeen year olds, the lack of part-time jobs in your region, and so on. Yet in business this would be quite acceptable. Presentations and visual aids are often used as a means of explaining data.

Your parents may counter your arguments with one of their own – that if you continue looking for a part-time job you will probably find one in the next few weeks. At this point, you will have the advantage if you can argue about **probabilities** in a little more detail.

Using probability to describe situations

If you found out statistically that in every month, ten teenagers out of a hundred obtained a part-time job, then you could argue that the probability of you getting one is ten per cent. If you were being very clever you could use a probability scale and say that the probability factor is 0.1.

Probability is the likelihood of an event occurring. In real life you may think probability is nonsense. But think about it; the probability of the postman delivering a package to your house just as you step into the shower is probably very remote – but it seems to happen quite frequently. Conversely, as any driver will tell you, there are thousands of garages in Britain, therefore when they run low on petrol one should come into sight fairly soon. Yet when the needle moves onto red they regularly seem to be on the only road which hasn't a garage for miles.

Probabilities in business

In many situations in business, people have to estimate what may happen in the future. The Marketing Manager has to forecast sales, the Production Manager assesses the risk of a machine breaking down when accepting an urgent order. In other words, future situations often have an element of risk involved. People often have to assess the risk using numbers and this is **probability.**

An obvious example of probability is when someone tosses a coin. The chances of heads or tails is even, and this gives a probability factor of 0.5 heads, 0.5 tails (or 50 per cent each way) whenever a coin is tossed.

Did you know?

This can also be expressed as the ratio 50:50. You have probably heard this expression many times!

Using probabilities

Probability is expressed as a number between 0 and 1. The first, 0, is the certainty that something will not happen. The second, 1, is the certainty that something will happen.

Did you know?

It is quite difficult to think of events in the future where the probability is actually 0 or 1. These types of events are actually very rare – despite the fact that at times, you may think that the probability of your passing your course is 0! Most events have a probability somewhere between 0 and 1.

Assessing probabilities

In business, probabilities are assessed or estimated. For example, the Production Manager referred to

earlier may think that the probability of a machine breaking down is 0.1. In other words there is a one in ten chance that it will happen. He or she will make this assessment based on knowledge of the machine and its maintenance history.

Did you know?

It can be proved that a person travelling by car has a higher probability of being killed in an accident than someone making the same journey by plane. Why, then, do you think more people are afraid of travelling by plane than by car?

Calculating probabilities

The following are examples of events where probabilities are known.

1   A machine producing CDs is faulty and out of 1000 of a particular batch, 150 have faults resulting in poor sound quality. The probability of one disk taken at random from the batch being faulty is therefore

$$\frac{150}{1000} = 0.15$$

2   Records show that a photocopier breaks down once in every 20 working days. The probability of it breaking down on any particular day is:

$$\frac{1}{20} = 0.05$$

3   The police in a town keep records of how many times they are called out when burglar alarms are reported to be ringing. In a particular year they received 327 calls and 287 of them were, literally, false alarms. The probability of a false alarm is:

$$\frac{287}{327} \times 100 = 88 \text{ per cent (to the nearest whole number)}$$

Non-assessed activity

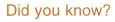

1   Imagine you have a faulty alarm clock that fails to wake you up on time one morning in every ten. What is the probability of your being late for class?

2   A newsagent calculates that the probability of selling a specialist magazine is 70 per cent. He buys 28 magazines. How many is he likely to have left unsold?

3   You and your friend have each bought a ticket for a raffle. A total of 2000 tickets have been sold and there are 20 prizes.

a What is the probability that *you* will win a prize?

b What is the probability that you *both* will win a prize?

The probability of winning the National Lottery

Since late in 1994, most of the nation has been fixated with the idea of winning the National Lottery. But what is the likelihood – or probability – of this happening?

The lottery operates on the following system. Six balls with numbers from 1 to 49 are drawn at random, so each has an equal chance of being picked. The probability of a particular set of numbers being selected is 1 in 13 983 816!

This is found in the following way.

$$\frac{49 \times 48 \times 47 \times 46 \times 45 \times 44}{6 \times 5 \times 4 \times 3 \times 2 \, (\times 1)}$$

The figures on the top line are the probabilities of a certain ball being chosen. So, for the first selection, the chances are 1 in 49. Once this ball has been removed, the probability for the next one is 1 in 48 and so on. The figures on the bottom line are needed because it doesn't matter in which order the balls are selected. If the order did matter, the probability would be one in 10 068 347 520! The chance of anyone winning the jackpot would be very remote!

Did you know?

It has been said that an easier way to visualise your chances of winning is to think of a row of 1p coins stretching from Manchester to Glasgow. To win you have to pick the **one** right coin! If you feel like it you could find out if this is true. Measure the diameter of a 1p coin, find out the distance from Manchester to Glasgow and see if the saying is a myth or quite accurate!

Non-assessed activity

Many people – and even newspapers – have been keeping a tally of the balls that have been selected so far and their frequency. Discuss with your tutor whether this is any use as an indicator of the next set of numbers.

Optional evidence assignment

This assignment can be used to provide evidence for Element 2.3 of Application of number. It can also be cross-referenced with Core Skills in Communication. (See pages 556–559)

You work for Eastern Insurance Brokers as a clerk in the general office. The manager, Tim Clark, has asked you to undertake several calculations for him and, in each case, to give him your answers in a short, typed memo.

1 Tim Clark has been looking at the types of insurance sold by the brokers for inclusion in an advertising brochure. He has calculated that

35 per cent is car insurance
27 per cent is household contents insurance
23 per cent is house buildings insurance
10 per cent is travel insurance
5 per cent is for miscellaneous insurance cover

He has asked you to design a pie chart, either by hand or on computer, to illustrate these figures. Make sure you have a clear key.

2 The brochure will be produced by an advertising company who charge £30 an hour for copy-writing, £60 an hour for artwork, £35 an hour for printing and £35 an hour for consultancy fees.

a construct a formula to show this

b Tim Clark has the choice of two styles of brochure. The first will have more text and fewer graphics and the second will be the reverse.

Type 1 will take six hours to write, two hours to illustrate, one hour to print. There will be three hours spent on consultancy.

Type 2 will take four hours to write, three-and-a-quarter hours to illustrate, one-and-a-half hours to print and two-and- three-quarter hours' consultancy will be required.

Use your formula to calculate the cost of each brochure.

3 Tim Clark regularly travels to London by train but grumbles because the train is often late. He has worked out that on the last 120 journeys the train has been late 45 times! He has been asked to attend a very important meeting next Monday and can't work out whether to travel down that morning or go the day before and stay overnight – which will cost him more. He knows that only if the train is punctual can he arrive at the meeting on time.

a What is the probability of his being punctual?

b What would you advise him to do?

4 On checking the files, Tim Clark has discovered that out of 251 drivers of high performance cars in the age group 18–25 years, 172 have at least one accident claim in a year. He has asked you to estimate the probability of a single driver putting in a claim.

Visual techniques

Just as you might have found it helpful to visualise the odds of winning the lottery by thinking about the pennies, so many people find it more useful to 'see' things than read words or figures. It is therefore useful to use visual methods of displaying information.

A **sketch** is a rough, incomplete or rapid drawing. It may be the first stage towards a finished drawing. The graphic designers who produced the artwork for this book started with sketches – but this would not have been satisfactory as the 'finished product'. You can make a quick sketch when you are short of time, when you only need a *rough* idea of what something looks like or when you want to convey this idea to someone else quickly.

Two-dimensional structures, which give the information required, are shown on page 591.

It is sometimes useful to sketch a 3D object. Place a paperback book on a table and look at it from above with one corner nearer to you. You can't see some of the edges, but they can be drawn in using dotted lines.

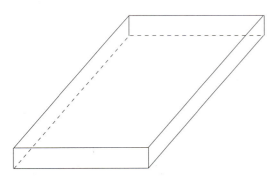

Figure N.19 You can't see all the edges, but you know they are there.

Did you know?

A two-dimensional figure can be shown in a plan of an area or in a drawing. Car handbooks, for instance, often show a drawing or diagram of a dashboard with appropriate labels.

A three-dimensional object can be represented on a piece of paper (i.e. in two dimensions) by drawing a sketch that indicates depth.

Practise your skills

Try sketching a rectangular box for yourself – say a packet of breakfast cereal. Hint – if you use paper with lines on it, you can use the printed lines for the horizontal lines of your sketch.

Can you find any other rectangular objects to sketch? What about the room you are in?

Did you know?

Because you are sketching on a flat piece of paper, you are working in **two dimensions**. You have therefore made **two-dimensional representations** of **three-dimensional** objects.

2D representations of 3D objects

Another way of showing three-dimensional objects on paper is to show **elevations**. An elevation is a picture of what an object looks like if you look at it from the front, side and above respectively. These are known as the **front**, **side** and **plan** elevations.

A box which is shaped as in Figure N.20 can be represented as in Figure N.21.

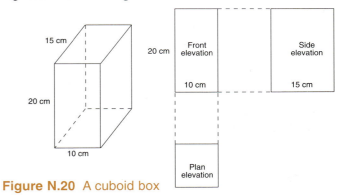

Figure N.20 A cuboid box

Figure N.21 Elevations of a box

Non-assessed activity

The elevations above have all been drawn to scale. Can you work out what the scale is?

Practise your skills

1 **Sketch** the three elevations of a table.
2 **Draw** the three elevations of a paperback book to scale.

Optional evidence assignment

This element provides evidence towards Element 2.3 of Application of number. It can also be cross-referenced with Core Skills in Communication and Element 3.2, Plan, design and produce promotional material.

You work for a local hospital, which has become a local trust hospital and undertakes a number of fund-raising activities to raise money to finance expansion, new equipment, and facilities for child patients and their parents. Your boss is Tom O'Brien, who is the appeals director.

The hospital has a spare area, off a main corridor on the ground floor, which has been allocated for use as a gift shop. The hospital joiners will construct a counter, and the display stands will be purchased from a local supplier. The diagram below gives an outline of the area together with the measurements.

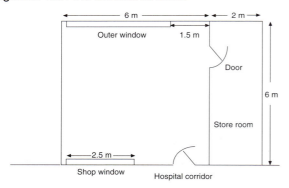

Figure N.22 Plan of the gift shop

1 Decide where you will put the main counter and display stands. Measure the amount of room you have available for the counter and, in a memo to Mr Marsh, the chief joiner, tell him:
  a the measurements of the counter
  b the volume of space it will occupy.

2 Obtain information on a range of display stands from a local supplier. Sketch the area of the shop *to scale* using a plan elevation to make sure there is enough room for the fixtures you want.

3 The window of the shop is rectangular and measures 2.5 metres across and 2 metres in depth. Tom O'Brien wants a special window display for the opening, which will feature red ribbon around the window and coloured circles, to represent balloons, across the top.
  a How much red ribbon will you need to cover the perimeter of the window?
  b If each circle has a radius of 150 centimetres, how many circles will you need to go across the window?
  c What will be the total area of the window covered by all the circles?

4 It has been decided that the shop should sell books, magazines, sweets, drinks, tapes, T-shirts and fluffy toys. Tom O'Brien wants a display stand near the window that features most, if not all, of these items so that people can easily see the goods sold even when the shop is closed.

He has asked you to make a sketch of the stand to show him how you think it should be set out. Note that this particular stand has four shelves but the heights of these are adjustable.

Working to scale

Another difference between a drawing and a sketch may be that some drawings are **to scale.** You may have seen scale models of cars in toy shops. Working to scale means that the lengths of the lines in the drawing are in the same proportion to each other as the lengths in the actual object. For example, if a box is 300 mm high, 400 mm long and 200 mm wide, it could be shown by a drawing which is 30 mm by 40 mm by 20 mm.

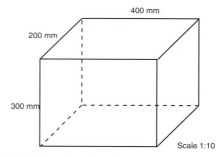

Figure N.23 A scale drawing of a box

There are two other points to note. Firstly the **actual** lengths of the box dimensions are shown on the diagram, not the scaled-down lengths. Also the 'scale

'1:10' means that the actual length of the lines of the drawing are all one tenth of the dimension of the box itself.

Did you know?

The expression 1:10 is a **ratio.** If you cannot remember what this means, check back to page 576.

Practise your skills

Find a box, such as a pack of breakfast cereals, measure its dimensions and draw it to a scale of 1:10. Show your finished drawing to your tutor.

Non-assessed activity

You work for a company which is ordering a reception desk and tables and chairs for a new reception area. Your reception area measures 9 metres by 10 metres and the layout is shown in Figure N.24.

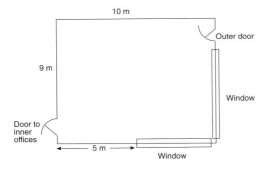

Figure N.24 An outline plan for the new reception area

Draw this area to scale on a piece of graph paper.

Using an office furniture catalogue, select some suitable furniture. Cut out some cardboard shapes, to scale, to represent the reception desk and the tables and chairs. Arrange these so that there is the maximum amount of seating without making the area congested.

Non-assessed activity

For the reception area above you created a **plan** elevation to make sure you had enough space for the furniture. Your boss wants to have an idea what the area would look like from the front and the side so that she can decide how to decorate the area and hang pictures. In other words, she wants to view the area from the customer's point of view.

Sketch the reception area you designed from both of these elevations.

Statistical diagrams

If a set of numbers can be converted into a picture the information is more interesting and people can interpret it (and remember it!) more easily. A common form of statistical diagram is a **histogram.** This is similar to a bar chart except that the areas of the bars represent the data (compare Figure N.25 with the bar chart in the Core Skills chapter on Communication, page 559).

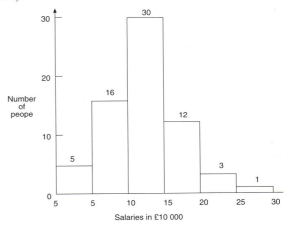

Figure N.25 A histogram showing the salaries of people working in a business

Figure N.25 shows the picture that might emerge if the salaries of 67 people working in a business were placed in bands of £5000. Guess which band the managing director comes in!

The y-axis (the 'number of people') is called the **frequency** and the x-axis (the bands of £5000) are called **class intervals.**

Optional evidence assignment

This assignment can be used to provide evidence towards Element 2.4 Application of number. It can also be cross-referenced with Core Skills in Communication as well as Elements 1.3 (Present results of investigation into employment) and 4.2 (Complete financial documents and explain financial recordings).

603

1 Draw a histogram to represent the information you were given on page 597 about the length of time ten people had worked for a company.

2 The owner of a shopfitting company is worried that he is receiving so many orders that he cannot complete work to customers' deadlines and is losing orders. He analyses the orders received over the past twelve months and discovers that the monthly work load in staff-hours is:

Jan	1682	July	1208
Feb	1428	August	1640
March	2039	September	1750
April	1938	October	2060
May	1518	November	1510
June	1200	December	1027

a Calculate the mean and the range.

b Draw a histogram to represent the information.

c The average number of hours worked by full-time employees is 40 and by part-time employees is 25.

   i If the owner wanted to employ only full-time workers *and* to have enough employees on the staff all year to cover the busiest times, how many people would he employ?

   ii If he paid each full-time employee an average of £300 a week, what would his total wage bill be each week? What would he pay in wages each year?

   iii Many employees can be hired on a casual basis (i.e. hired only when they are needed, to work on a part-time basis). The average part-time rate is £150 per week. If you owned the business, what would be your ratio of full-time to part-time employees *each month*? (Bear in mind that you will want some full-time workers at all times because they are more committed to working hard for the company.)

   iv On the figures you calculated above, what would be your total wage bill for the year? How much have you saved by using your staff more efficiently? You will need to compare your answer with that in point (ii) above.

Visual representations

Statistical information can be used to construct:

- pictograms
- bar charts
- pie charts
- line graphs.

Pictograms, charts and graphs are discussed in Core Skills – Communication, pages 557–9.

A final note

You have now covered all the main components of the numeracy scheme. Below is a quick reference section, so you can refresh your memory at any time. Remember that there is one good thing about numeracy. Once you've learned how to solve a problem or make a calculation, the **method** of doing it never changes – unlike the way of doing other things, such as using computers. For that reason, the huge benefit of working through this properly is that you should have improved your numeracy ability for life – and given up all hope of winning the National Lottery!

Application of number – quick reference section

This section contains a list in alphabetical order of all the calculations you should be able to do. It is designed to:

- help you, if you have any problems working out the calculations at the start of the unit
- act as a quick reference if you forget how to carry out the calculations you learned when you worked through the unit.

If you are asked to do a calculation in other sections of this book, and have some difficulty, try looking here. If you are still struggling, ask your tutor for help.

All measurements are given in the metric system. Use the conversion tables (under C in this section) if you need to convert to the imperial system.

Area

Area is the amount of space covered by a flat object and is measured in the number of centimetre squares or metre squares it takes up. This space is in **two dimensions**.

Rectangle – multiply the length by the width

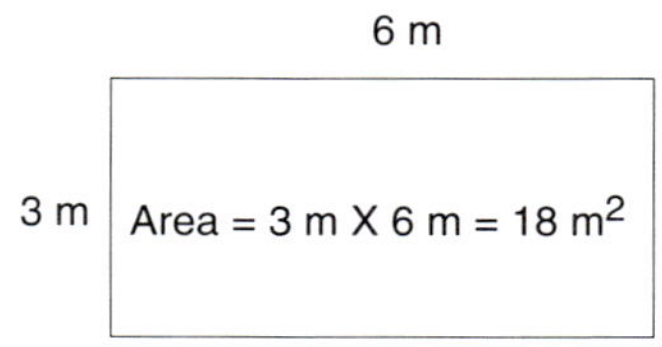

6 m

3 m | Area = 3 m X 6 m = 18 m^2

Figure N.26 The area of a rectangle

Square – even easier as length and width are the same

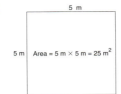

5 m

5 m | Area = 5 m × 5 m = 25 m²

Figure N.27 The area of a square

Circle – use the formula $A = \pi r^2$ where r is the radius (the distance between the centre and the circumference), π is very close to $\frac{22}{7}$, so if a circle has a radius of 14 metres, its area is $\frac{14}{1} \times \frac{22}{7} = 44$ m². If you use a calculator you can enter 14×3.14 instead, and you will get the answer 43.96 m².

Average

There are three types of average, and the most commonly used is the **mean**. It is found by adding together a set of figures and dividing by the number of figures in the set. If a bus was late on five consecutive days by 1, 3, 7, 4 and 0 minutes then the average time it is late is:

$$\frac{1+3+7+4+0}{5} = 3 \text{ minutes}$$

Calculators

If you have a calculator, it is worthwhile learning how to use it properly. A business calculator is easier to use than a scientific calculator for most of the calculations you need to carry out in business, and there are fewer functions to learn. However, only a scientific calculator will include π – although you can easily substitute the decimal figure 3.14.

A desktop calculator enables you to print out your calculations, which is useful for checking none has been missed or entered wrongly. The list can also be kept as a permanent record. These calculators normally have a date key which can also be used to enter the operator's number at the top of the print-out.

Check that on your calculator you know the following (if not, refer to the manual).

- There is a difference between the CE key and the C key. CE = clear last entry only, C = clear all the current calculation. On some pocket machines this is the same key. Pressing it *once* = CE and pressing it *twice* = C.
- You should always start a new calculation by pressing 'clear' first. This ensures that any previous calculations are no longer stored and will not affect your current work.
- On a desktop calculator, always end a calculation printout by turning up the paper a short distance, so you can tear off the printout without cutting off the last few lines.
- There is no need to enter zeros after a decimal point – therefore enter 48.50 as 48.5.
- If you are using a desktop calculator and carrying out calculations involving money, check that you are operating with two decimal places before you start.
- If you are entering money calculations in pence only, always start with the point.
- Learn how to use the memory function – it saves time entering and re-entering figures. On a calculator there are usually three or four memory keys:

M+ add to memory	MR recall memory
M– subtract memory	MC clear memory

If your machine only has three memory keys it is likely one is marked MRC and does the work of both MR and MC.

- Use M+ when you are entering columns of figures and want to add the *totals* of each column as well. Enter the column and then enter the total into memory by pressing M+. Press CE (C on some machines) so that the screen clears but the memory signal still shows. Enter the next column and press M+ when you have reached the total and so on. At the end press MR to see the total of all the figures you have entered into memory. Then press MC to clear the memory.
- Use M– if you want to *subtract* the total of one column from the total of another. Press M+ after the first column total (as above) and then M– after the second column.
- Use the memory whenever you want to carry out any numeric operation and keep the total for later use, e.g.

    47 small widgets @ £20 each + VAT
    62 large widgets @ £42 each + VAT

    Sub-total
    Less 10 per cent discount

    Total

A good test of whether you can use memory properly is whether you can input the exercise above with each line entered as one process and no figure having to be entered twice!

Circles

See Area and Perimeter, pages 604 and 609

Conversion tables

Length and distance

In the **metric** system
10 millimetres (mm) = 1 centimetre (cm)
100 cm = 1 metre (m)
1000 m = 1 kilometre (km)
In the **imperial** system
12 inches (in) = 1 foot (ft)
3 ft = 1 yard (yd)
1760 yd = 1 mile

Equivalents

1 cm	= 0.39 in	and	1 in	= 2.54 cm
1 m	= 1.09 yd	and	1 yd	= 0.91 m
1 km	= 0.62 miles	and	1 mile	= 1.61 km

Weight

In the **metric** system
1000 grams (g) = 1 kilogram (kg)
1000 kg = 1 metric tonne
In the **imperial** system
16 ounces (oz) = 1 pound (lb)
14 lb = 1 stone
8 stones = 1 hundredweight (cwt)
20 cwt = 1 ton

Equivalents

1 g	= 0.035 oz	and	1 oz	= 28.35 g
1 kg	= 2.21 lb	and	1 lb	= 0.45 kg
1 tonne	= 0.98 tons	and	1 ton	= 1.016 tonnes

Volume

In the **metric** system
1000 millilitres (ml) = 1 litre (l)
In the **imperial** system
20 fluid ounces (fl oz) = 1 pint
8 pints = 1 gallon

Equivalents

1 ml	= 0.09 fl oz	and	1 fl oz	= 10.99 ml
1 l	= 0.22 gallons	and	1 gallon	= 4.55 l
1 l	= 1.76 pints	and	1 pint	= 0.57 l

Cubes and cube roots

One meaning of the word 'cube' is a three-dimensional object where the length of each side is the same.

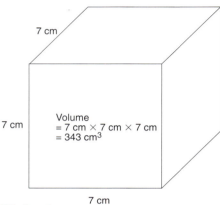

Figure N.28 A cube

The **volume** of a cube is found by multiplying the length × breadth × height (see also page 594). Therefore the answer is given in cubic metres or centimetres, e.g:

7 cm × 7 cm × 7 cm = 343 cubic centimetres (or 343 cm³).

The word cubed is used for any number which is multiplied by itself *twice*.

Therefore 5 **cubed** is $5 \times 5 \times 5$ and is written as 5^3.

The **cube root** of a number is the number that needs to be multiplied by itself twice to give the first number. For example, the cube root of 8 is 2 because $2 \times 2 \times 2$ (or 2^3) = 8.

Cylinders

Cylindrical objects can include glasses and tins and cans. To find the volume of a cylinder the formula to use is

$A = \pi r^2 \times \text{length}$

Decimals

A decimal is a way of writing a number, which may be made up of whole numbers and fractions, using place value including tenths, hundredths and so on. For example, if your class lasts for 1 hour, this is a whole number. If it lasts for $1\frac{1}{2}$ hours, this can be written as 1.5, which is a decimal. The decimal point simply means that the figures to the right are smaller than one. The first number to the right of the decimal is in tenths, the next in hundredths and so on. So 1.642 means:

$$1 + \frac{6}{10} + \frac{4}{100} + \frac{2}{1000}$$

For most business uses, figures are **rounded** to two decimal places.

Decimals are easier to use than fractions when adding and subtracting. To multiply and divide calculations where *both* numbers are decimals, most people use a calculator. Otherwise carry out the calculation as you would with a whole number, but:

- remember to include the decimal point (write a nought before it if necessary to help you remember)
- always make sure your decimal points are written under each other.

641.35	872.59	26.4
+ 579.83	− 624.84	× 4
1221.18	247.75	105.6

Remember that money is usually written in decimal form, e.g. £3.25.

Converting decimals to percentages

Convert decimals (or whole numbers) to percentages by multiplying by 100%, e.g. 0.342 as a percentage = $0.342 \times 100 = 34.2$ per cent.

Equations and formulae

Equations and formulae are very similar.

- In an equation letters are used to represent numbers to help you find the value of an 'unknown' figure.
- a formula is set of words or symbols that can be applied many times in similar situations.

As an example, $A = l \times b$ ($A = lb$) is an equation *and* a formula. Letters are used to represent the words area, length and breadth and, as a formula, it can be applied to find the area of a rectangle of any size.

Construct a formula by substituting letters for the items given.

Transpose a formula (or equation) to make a different quantity the subject. Remember to change the sign if you move a quantity to the other side of the equals sign (plus to minus, minus to plus, multiply to divide and divide to multiply). For example:

1. Find the value of x if $x + 3 = y$

   If $x + 3 = y$ then $x = y - 3$

2. If $26x = 3y$, find the value of x and y.

   $$x = \frac{3y}{26} \quad \text{and} \quad y = \frac{26x}{3}$$

Simplify a formula (or equation) by adding or subtracting **like terms** (e.g. all the xs or all the ys). Remember you cannot simplify **unlike terms**. For example:

Simplify $3x + 5y = 4x + 2y$
$\Rightarrow 5y - 2y = 4x - 3x$
$\Rightarrow 3y = x$

Fractions

Fractions, like decimals, are used when a number is less than a whole number. They are written as $\frac{1}{2}, \frac{1}{4}, \frac{1}{3}$. Common fractions, such as these, we use in everyday speech – such as 'just half a cup of coffee, please'. Sometimes fractions are more complicated, e.g. $\frac{1}{7}$ or $\frac{2}{9}$, and at other times whole numbers and fractions go together, e.g. $2\frac{1}{8}$ or $5\frac{2}{3}$.

Adding fractions

If there are whole numbers do these first. Then make sure all the fractions have the same denominator at the bottom. Do this by finding the lowest number all the **denominators** will go into (i.e. the **lowest common denominator**). Then multiply the numerator (top number) by the same number, i.e.

$8\frac{1}{6} + 1\frac{3}{4} =$

1. Whole numbers first: $8 + 1 = 9$
2. Find the lowest number both denominators will go into: answer = 12.
3. How many times does each denominator go into this figure? Answer: 6 goes into 12 twice and 4 goes into 12 three times.

4 Multiply each numerator by this figure, therefore

$$\frac{1 \times 2}{12} + \frac{3 \times 3}{12}$$

5 Write this as one sum and work it out, i.e.

$$\frac{2+9}{12} = \frac{11}{12}$$

6 Count back in any whole numbers. Final answer:

$$8\tfrac{1}{6} + 1\tfrac{3}{4} = 9\tfrac{11}{12}$$

Subtracting fractions

1 If the second fraction of the two is smaller than the first one, then do in the same way as addition, i.e.

- calculate whole numbers first
- find the lowest common denominator
- multiply the numerators
- carry out the subtraction
- cancel down your answer, if possible, e.g.

$$4\tfrac{2}{3} - 1\tfrac{1}{6} = 3\tfrac{4-1}{6} = 3\tfrac{3}{6} = 3\tfrac{1}{2}$$

2 If the second fraction is larger than the first then you need to change the fractions into **improper** fractions. In this case the numerator is greater than the denominator and the value is more than 1. After carrying out the subtraction you convert your answer back to whole numbers and fractions.

$$5\tfrac{1}{2} - 3\tfrac{3}{4} = \frac{11}{2} - \frac{15}{4} = \frac{22}{4} - \frac{15}{4} = \frac{22-15}{4} = \frac{7}{4} = 1\tfrac{3}{4}$$

Multiplication and division of fractions

1 Multiply fractions by multiplying the numerators together and then multiplying the denominators together. Then cancel down your answer (if possible), e.g:

$$\frac{5}{9} \times \frac{3}{8} \times \frac{3}{10} = \frac{45}{720} = \frac{5}{80} = \frac{1}{16}$$

2 Divide by turning the dividing fraction upside down and multiplying, e.g:

$$\frac{2}{3} \div \frac{7}{9} = \frac{2}{3} \times \frac{9}{7} = \frac{18}{21} = \frac{6}{7}$$

Remember – you can make life easier for yourself by cancelling down before you carry out the calculation, e.g.

$$\frac{2}{3} \div \frac{7}{9} = \frac{2}{3} \times \frac{9}{7} = \frac{2}{1} \times \frac{3}{7} = \frac{6}{7}$$

Converting fractions to decimals

Divide the numerator by the denominator, e.g:

$$\frac{3}{4} = 3 \div 4 = 0.75$$

Converting fractions to percentages

Multiply by 100, e.g. $\frac{1}{2} \times 100 = \frac{100}{2} = 50\%$

Mean

See under Average, page 605

Median

This is the middle number in a list of figures that have been collected as data. The numbers are listed in order starting with the lowest. The median is the centre value. If there is an even number of items in the set of data, the median is the mean of the two middle values.

Mode

This is the most frequent number in a set of figures.

Percentages

A percentage represents the number of parts out of one hundred. If eight faulty components were found in every batch of 100, then this could be written as eight per cent or 8%.

Converting fractions and decimals to percentages

Multiply by 100%, e.g. $\frac{1}{4} \times 100\% = \frac{100}{4}\% = 25\%$

or $0.20 \times 100 = 20\%$

Converting percentages to decimals and fractions

Simply divide by 100, e.g. 70 per cent as a fraction $= \frac{70}{100} = \frac{7}{10}$

or 53 per cent as a decimal $= \frac{53}{100} = 0.53$

Finding a percentage of a number

Multiply the number by the percentage and divide by 100 e.g. 25 per cent of £6 is therefore:

$$\frac{25}{100} \times £6 = £\frac{6}{4} = £1.50$$

Showing one quantity as a percentage of another

The relationship between two numbers, with one as a percentage of the other, is found by first showing the relationship as a fraction and then multiplying by 100%. So 30 as a percentage of 150 is therefore:

$\frac{30}{150} \times 100\% = \frac{1}{5} \times 100\% = \frac{100}{5} = 20\%$ or 20 per cent

Increasing and decreasing by percentages

Increase by first turning the number into a decimal, i.e. 15 per cent = 0.15 then *adding* 1. Therefore 1 + 0.15 = 1.15.
Then multiply.
If the price of an article is £12 without VAT and VAT is 17.5 per cent, the price including VAT is
£12 × 1.175 = £14.10

Decrease by turning the number into a decimal and *subtracting* from 1. For example, if a company offers 10 per cent discount on a price of £56, then
10 per cent = 0.10 and 1 − 0.10 = 0.9
£56 × 0.9 = £50.40.

Perimeter

The perimeter is the distance round a shape.

The perimeter of a rectangle is found by adding up the length of the four sides, e.g:

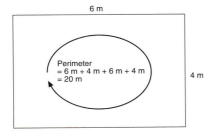

6 m

Perimeter
= 6 m + 4 m + 6 m + 4 m
= 20 m

4 m

Figure N.29 Perimeter of a rectangle

Perimeter = 6 + 4 + 6 + 4 = 20 m

The perimeter of a **circle** is found by using the formula $C = 2\pi r$.
Remember that $\pi = 3.14$ or $\frac{22}{7}$.

Therefore a circle with a radius (r) of 5 cm would have a perimeter of 2 × 3.14 × 5 = 31.4 cm.

Remember that the perimeter of a circle is more usually called its **circumference**.

Range

This is the difference between the smallest and largest numbers in a set of figures.

Ratio

A ratio is the proportion of one figure in relation to another. If there are 10 girls in a class and 15 boys then the ratio of girls to boys is 10:15 or 2:3.

Squares and square roots

The **square** of a number is the result when you multiply a number by itself.

Therefore 4 squared is 4 × 4 = 16. This is written as 4^2.

The **square root** of a number is the inverse of a square. A number's square root is the number which, multiplied by itself, gives the original number. The square root of 16 is therefore 4. This is usually written as $\sqrt{16} = 4$.

Volume

This is the space that something takes up, in three dimensions. The volume of a rectangular shape is found by multiplying length × width × height.

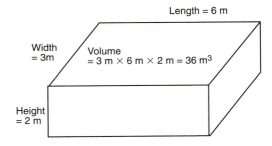

Length = 6 m

Width
= 3 m

Volume
= 3 m × 6 m × 2 m = 36 m³

Height
= 2 m

Figure N.30 The volume of a cuboid

Therefore the volume of the rectangular cuboid above is 6 × 2 × 3 = 36 cubic metres, written as 36 m³.

See also cubes, pages 606

Information technology

Using information technology (IT) equipment to prepare, process and present information offers great benefits to anyone who works in business today. Managers may have personal computers on their desks and probably take a laptops on business trips. Office staff at all levels and in all departments key in data and retrieve it as required. Filing may be undertaken electronically by the administration staff, personnel records may be kept on databases by human resources staff, accounts projections may be done on spreadsheet packages in the finance section, wages are probably paid through the payroll package, marketing leaflets can be created using desktop publishing and so on. These application programs are called *software*.

Without IT skills you are unlikely to be able to obtain a job in the business world. Business skills courses with the emphasis on IT are very popular with graduates who have taken degrees which do not contain this element. Their success in achieving jobs increases more than fourfold with good computer skills.

Skills in IT are extremely useful in other areas of life. If you study any course you can produce well-designed and attractive assignments and projects. You can do them quickly, because alterations are easy using a word-processing package. If you use a computer at home, even the letters you write to organisations to make requests (or complaints!) may receive more prompt attention because they look professional.

Information technology and GNVQ

You will find that your **assessments** in relation to IT are mainly covered in a vocational context. This means that you will not write or talk about using IT, but will use it in practical situations as part of the projects you will produce for your mandatory and optional units.

However, before you can use IT equipment you have to *learn* about it. You may do this in special lessons or in a workshop environment. This unit has been designed to:

- introduce you to the basics of computer systems and computer hardware
- develop your role in operating IT equipment
- give you the main facts you need in relation to computer software used in business
- act as a reference guide if you forget anything
- improve your overall knowledge of IT systems in business.

This unit has not been written to follow the exact Core Skills scheme in the same way as the main units and elements of this book. Instead, the information has been ordered so that you are first introduced to the basics of computer systems and then to your role as an operator in relation to the elements you need to cover. Information is given about the software used in business. Finally, at the end of the unit is a glossary of terms, which you can use as a quick reference guide.

Note that there are no evidence indicator projects because the Evidence Indicators will be achieved as part of your mandatory and optional unit assessments. However, some optional evidence assignments are included to give you additional opportunities to obtain evidence.

 ### Did you know?

If you have an aptitude for computers, you can discuss with your tutor the possibility of developing your core skills to achieve higher than level 2 – the equivalent for Intermediate students. What you must not do is only cover IT at level 1! Note that, given that the majority of students will be studying at the equivalent level, this unit concentrates on level 2 of the Core Skills scheme.

Information technology level 2

There are four elements in the scheme. The first number below refers to the **level** and the second to the **element**.

2.1   Prepare information
2.2   Process information
2.3   Present information
2.4   Evaluate the use of information technology

You will notice that the word 'information' occurs rather a lot! In the context of the scheme, information refers to 'text, graphics and numbers'. Quite simply this means that you must be able to use software that undertakes these operations, e.g:

- **text** – word processing, databases and desktop publishing
- **graphics** – drawing or painting software, graphics packages, desktop publishing, word-processing packages with a graphics element
- **numbers** – spreadsheet or accounts software or databases.

All the packages commonly used in business are explained later in this chapter (pages 631–641).

Information technology equipment and systems

Before you can understand the software you will be using, you will need to understand the **hardware.** This is the computer itself and any peripheral equipment. If you are already familiar with computer hardware and software you may like to skip this section and start at page 622, which concentrates on the role of the computer operator in business.

Computer hardware

The hardware of a computer system consists of:

- **input devices** – used to put the information into the system
- **the central processing unit** (CPU) – the 'brains' of the system which carries out all the instructions received (either from the operator or from the program)
- **storage devices** – used to save both data and programs
- **output devices** – used to display the end result.

The link between these can be seen in Figure IT.1.

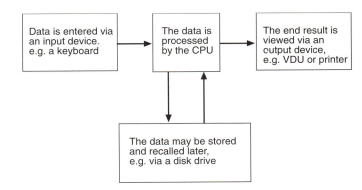

Figure IT.1 Links between input and output devices

Types of computer system

The type of equipment you will find in an office depends on whether the organisation has stand-alone micro-computers, a networked system or a mainframe computer.

Stand-alone system

The equipment will consist of at least:

- a keyboard
- a screen (called a visual display unit – VDU)
- a central processing unit (CPU)
- a disk drive
- a printer.

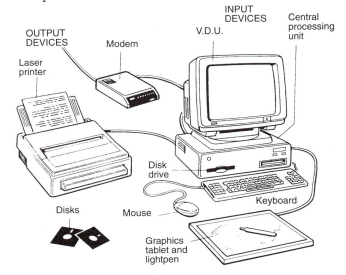

Figure IT.2 A stand-alone system

611

A 'stand-alone' system is self-contained and is not dependent on any other piece of equipment to operate it. It may be called a **workstation.** One advantage of a stand-alone system is that it is relatively easily transportable and can therefore be moved to different places (especially if it is really small, such as a laptop or notebook computer).

Although the system is 'stand-alone', there may be a telecommunications link between a workstation and other central computing facilities.

A networked system

In a network, some or all of the micro-computers are linked together, so that they have access to the same information. This may be in the form of:

- software programs, which are available on all or specified machines
- information useful to most or all of the staff (e.g. a customer address list).

If an organisation links its computers over a small (geographical) area this is known as a **local area network** (LAN). If the system covers a greater area this is referred to as a **wide area network** (WAN).

Users **log on** to a network, using their own user ID and a personal password. On most networks, users change their password regularly as a security precaution. Some users may have access to 'higher level' (i.e. more confidential) information than others (see page 628).

On some of the more sophisticated networks, more than just computers are linked. A wide variety of

Figure IT 3 Users have their own passwords and ID

office equipment can be incorporated into a network, including special fax machines, intelligent photocopiers and telex machines.

Did you know?

You will probably have read about Internet already. Internet is the International Network of Computers, over which computer enthusiasts communicate in 'cyberspace'.

Internet originated in the United States in the 1970s, as a means of linking computers in the military and defence area and between the universities. Today any computer user with a **modem,** telephone line and relevant software can gain access.

Any organisation can register as a **site** with its own address; a charge is made for access to the system. It is popular for sending E-mail and accessing databases all over the world. Video conferencing is also possible and, by adding an additional **gateway,** you can also send faxes. Internet is **interactive,** so, for example, you can read information on the holidays available from travel agents and make your booking at the same time!

The number of world-wide users is increasing rapidly and is forecast to be over 125 million by 1998/9.

Using a networked computer

All users of a network have to **log on** or **log in** to gain entry to the system, by keying in their user ID and their password. When they have finished working on the machine, they must **log off** or **log out** so that access has been officially ended. Computer staff can keep a record of the number of users. This can be useful for several reasons, including identifying main periods of use, whether the system is becoming overloaded and so on. It is important that every user follows the correct procedure for logging in and *never* switches off the computer without logging out of the system properly.

Did you know?

If you leave *any* computer switched on for a long period, with the same piece of text or graphics displayed on the VDU, it can create 'screen burn'. This means that the image will be 'burned on' to the screen and can be seen faintly, even when the computer is switched off. This is why many computers are designed automatically to blank the screen after a few minutes of non-use. Pressing any key on the keyboard restores the image to the screen.

Mainframe computers

A mainframe computer is capable of handling and processing a vast amount of information. These machines are leased or rented by large companies who have special computer departments and employ their own programmers and operators. Because these machines can be used by a number of people simultaneously, staff will each have on their desk a **terminal** – usually just a keyboard and a VDU – linked to the mainframe.

The **software** may have been individually written for the company by their own programmers and will probably include payroll, stock control and invoicing. In addition there may be some bought-in packages, e.g. spreadsheets and word processing. There will be a security system in operation so that confidential information is only available to specified staff.

A large mainframe computer will have a very large memory and a high processing speed. Despite this, much of the routine work (e.g. processing invoices) is done overnight so that the computer is not overloaded during the daytime. Many companies with mainframe computers operate a shift system so that computer staff are on duty 24 hours a day.

Did you know?

Executives who travel can take their computers with them if they own a **laptop** or **notebook** computer. This is a small, portable, self-contained unit incorporating a keyboard, floppy or hard disk drive and a screen. The smallest portable computers are known as **palm top** or **pen computers.** Palm tops can be held in the hand and the latest only measures 7″ by 4″! The drawback is that the keyboard becomes so small it is hard to use!

It is possible to communicate with the office via a portable computer and both download and receive information. This is done through a telephone line and a modem, which may be built in to the machine. The phone can even be a mobile phone.

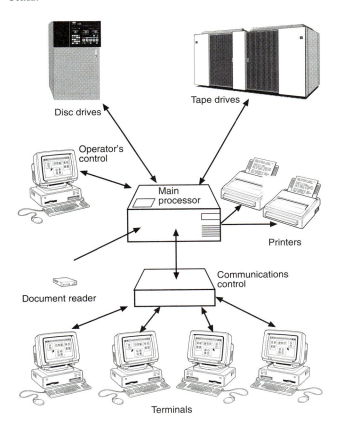

Figure IT.4 A mainframe computer set-up

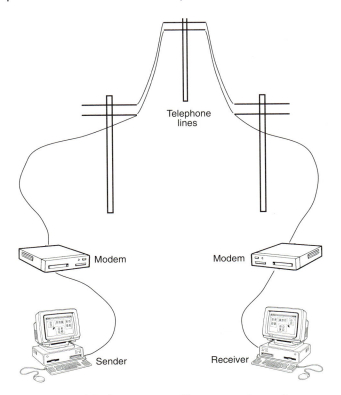

Figure IT.5 Modems connecting computers at a distance

Computers vary in the speed at which they can process an instruction. The faster they operate the more powerful they are and so the more they usually cost. Faster computers are usually required for more complex programs such as graphics, **computer-aided design** (CAD) and **computer-aided manufacturing** (CAM) packages. For character-based software, such as word processing, databases and spreadsheets, the processing speed is less important. However, if you use an applications package that is linked to a graphic operating system, such as Windows, you will find it much easier if you are operating a computer with a high-speed processor.

Memory

The amount of data that can be processed by a computer at any one time is determined by the size of its **memory.** The memory size is measured by the number of characters or **bytes** the computer can store at any one time.

The memory capacity of micro-computers is measured in kilobytes, abbreviated to Kb, or megabytes, abbreviated to Mb (kilo = 1000, mega = 1 000 000.). Therefore the older games computers with a 64K memory could hold approximately 64 000 characters in memory.

Most business micro-computers have a base memory size of 640K with optional extended memory of usually 4Mb or 8Mb. You will find computers on the market which, with the addition of extra memory cards, can have a capacity of 64Mb, or greater. This would be unnecessary additional expense if the computer was being used only to run business packages, but it might be required for sophisticated graphics packages or multimedia applications (see page 641).

The memory capacity of mainframe computers is measured in:

- megabytes (Mb)
- gigabytes (Gb – giga = 1000 million).

The storage memory capacity of the latest machines is being described in terms of terabytes (1000Gb)!

RAM

The proper term for a computer's working memory is **random access memory – RAM.** You can access any part of this data as you are working and replace it with something new if you want to. The RAM only operates on a temporary basis – when the computer is switched off any data held in RAM is lost. For this reason you need a **backing store**, usually a disk drive, so that data can be saved until it is next required.

ROM

Computers also have a **read only memory – ROM.** In this part of the memory you can read the information but cannot change it. When you switch on the computer it already 'knows' how to operate in a basic mode, because a systems program is always stored in ROM. You can therefore use this information, but cannot change or delete it. This basic program is different from the operating system (such as DOS) which is loaded into RAM every time the machine is started, usually from the hard disk.

Storage devices

Hard disks

Most computers today have hard disks installed. A hard disk is a non-removable disk positioned inside the computer, which can store a large number of programs and a large amount of data. This is where the operating system is stored.

Before a hard disk computer can be moved, the **read/write heads** must be parked to secure the disk and to avoid damage. This normally occurs automatically when you exit the system, but it may be an item on the menu that you need to select when you log out.

The size of the hard disk determines the amount of memory in your backing store (don't confuse this with RAM!). To give you some idea of computer development, in 1990 hard disks regularly had 40Mb capacity. Today 500Mb is common and 1Gb hard disks are not unusual.

Note: Computer hard disks are also covered in Element 4.3, page 519.

Floppy disks

These are available in two sizes – $5\frac{1}{4}$" and $3\frac{1}{2}$". The $5\frac{1}{4}$" size is now becoming obsolete, but you may still encounter it on some old machines. Disks may be single or double-sided and of single, double or high-density type. The storage capacity of the disk is determined by its type but, in general, all but double-sided, double or high density disks are becoming obsolete, and will only be encountered on older systems.

The $5\frac{1}{4}''$ disk has a vinyl jacket and a dust sleeve. The smaller disk has a hard plastic case with a metal cover which slides back when the disk is placed into the disk drive. This makes the $3\frac{1}{2}''$ physically more robust and durable.

All floppy disks have the ability to be **read/write protected** so that no information can be added to or deleted from the disk. This can protect your work and prevent anyone else from overwriting something important by accident. On a $5\frac{1}{4}''$ disk you must cover the read/write protect notch with a small piece of sticky paper (provided with the disk). On a $3\frac{1}{2}''$ disk there is a small plastic clip that can be slid into position.

Before you can use a floppy disk you must **format** it so that it is configured for use on your particular computer system. Remember that a disk formatted for one type of system may not work on another unless you reformat it – in which case you will lose all the records you have saved.

The care of floppy disks is discussed in Element 4.3, page 520.

Did you know?

Floppy disks are often used as back-up disks – as you may have already read in Element 4.3. Work stored on floppy disks or on the hard disk is transferred, for safety, to a further back-up disk, in case anything goes wrong with the original.

If you have a machine with a 500Mb hard disk, it would take no less than 400 diskettes to back-up the entire hard disk – and several hours of inserting/removing disks from the floppy drive! To overcome this problem, many computer users back-up their hard disk by using **tape streamers,** which use a special small tape cassette which slots into a 'letter box' in the front of the computer. They can automatically compress (or reduce) the data by half during the back-up process, so that all the data on the hard disk can be saved on a single tape. The whole process can be accomplished relatively quickly, but depends on the type of tape streamer being used and the amount of data being stored.

Optical disks

These are similar to music CDs and are gaining in popularity as they can store a vast amount of information, they are less likely to be damaged than magnetic disks, and data can be retrieved more quickly than from floppy disks. Different types of optical disks are used for different purposes.

- CD–ROM disks are used for large databases. The user can access the information but cannot erase or replace it.
- CD–WORM disks enable the user to write information to the disks but again it cannot be erased. They are mainly used with electronic filing systems. (Note – WORM stands for Write Once, Read Many times.)
- Erasable optical disks can be used as ordinary disks. Users can store and erase data as often as they wish. These are very expensive at present but as prices are falling they will probably become the 'floppy disk' of the future.

Did you know?

A wide range of encyclopaedias and dictionaries is available on CD-ROM, and CD-ROMs are used as archive storage for newspaper articles. These may be available in your school or college library. Through Internet you can even call up references from CD-ROMs held many miles away – such as the Folger Shakespeare Library in Washington.

The ability of CD-ROMs to store large quantities of information is having several effects. Some universities are putting their prospectus on CD-ROM and many publishers are setting up electronic publishing divisions. Even the National Gallery is not immune. In June 1995 it launched a portable audio CD-ROM guide. As visitors stand in front of a picture, they can key in a number and hear a detailed commentary on the work. Unlike a standard cassette guide, the CD-ROM gives visitors the ability to wander around the paintings in any order they choose. The gallery is now investigating producing different guides for students, young children and experts.

Care of hardware

1 Never switch a computer quickly off and on again.
2 Never move a computer without permission, without switching it off or without parking the heads on the hard disk first.

3 Never switch off a computer without logging out properly. Check whether your department leaves computers switched on during working hours.
4 Never try to take out a disk while the disk drive light is on.
5 Never leave a networked computer logged on when you have finished using it.
6 Never put food, drink or other liquids near a computer.
7 If your machine shows an unknown error message, check with your supervisor, tutor or user manual before pressing any keys – or you may make the problem worse.
8 The machines and the screens should be cleaned regularly but **only** by using the special products made for the job.

Did you know?

It is amazing how many people will stare at a computer that does not appear to be working without checking obvious causes! If your kettle did not work at home, presumably the first thing you would check is whether the appliance was plugged in! So start there. A basic checklist would be:

- check everything is plugged in
- check the equipment is switched on
- check there isn't a power cut
- check the power source by plugging in something else to the same socket
- check the connections (e.g. between VDU and computer and keyboard and computer)
- check the brightness control on the VDU (you'll look very silly if this is all that is wrong and you've called out a technician).

Non-assessed activity

1 Obtain a copy of a computer supplies catalogue.

a Compare the price of double-sided low-density disks with double-sided high-density disks.
b See if you can find any advertisements for tape streamers.

2 Either from advertisements about micro-computers *or* from a computer catalogue, compile a list of **four** different machines, in each case stating the price, processing speed and memory size. Can you find any correlation between this information, which perhaps would help you to choose the 'best buy' of the four machines you have listed?

Peripherals

This term is used to describe any item of equipment attached to or controlled by the computer and, strictly speaking, it includes the disk drive. However, the term is more usually used to describe the range of input and output devices that are external to the central processor unit and may be used by a computer operator, as well as communications devices, e.g. a **modem**. 'Modem' stands for **mo**dulator **dem**odulator.

Figure IT.6 A laptop computer

Input devices

In offices the main method of inputting data is by keyboard. However, in some organisations alternative methods may be preferred, sych as:

- **a bar code reader** – used to read the bar code on goods to input sales information into computerised electronic cash registers
- **touch sensitive screens** – used in organisations such as banks and hospitals, by personnel who are not trained typists, to input data: the operator simply touches the VDU screen at the required option
- **a mouse** – a small box moved around on a special mat next to the workstation, which changes the position of the cursor on the screen – essential with graphical operating systems such as 'Windows', and with graphics programs
- **a light pen** – used to wipe over bar codes and sometimes to produce graphics on screen by

'drawing', as with a normal pen, to create pictures and designs; often used with CAD programs

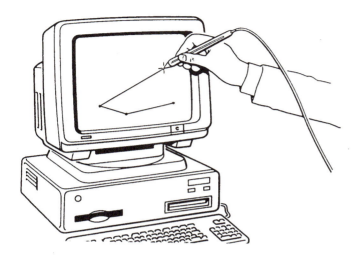

Figure IT.7 Using a light pen

- **a graphics tablet** – used extensively in CAD, as shapes can be drawn on them (with a special stylus)

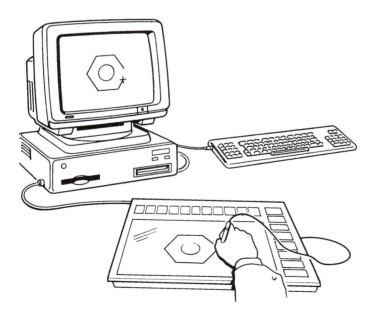

Figure IT.8 Graphics tablet

- **a digitiser** – used in conjunction with a special video camera to create sophisticated graphics on computer, by converting drawings, photographs and video stills to a format of digital impulses which can be displayed on the VDU screen

Video camera records the image

The digitiser, which is plugged into the back of the computer, converts the image to a form which the machine can read

Figure IT.9 Using a digitiser

- **a document reader or scanner** – a device that automatically reads text or graphics and puts it into a computer – may be a flatbed machine, or a hand-held device 'rolled' over the required information, and may be used with optical character recognition (OCR) software to interpret text images
- **a magnetic ink character reader** – used by banks automatically to identify cheques by the numbers on them, which are printed with special magnetic ink.

Output devices

The main output device is the printer. The two main types of printer are:

- **impact printers** (e.g. dot matrix, where direct contact is made with the paper)
- **non-impact printers** (e.g. ink jet or laser, where ink is placed on the paper by non-impact methods.

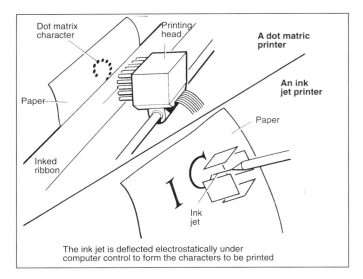

Figure IT.10 Printers

Other output devices include:

- **VDU screens**
- **plotters** – used to produce graphs, charts and a variety of other graphics. Colour can be used, although the number of colours is limited except on very expensive machines, and some can produce three-dimensional drawings.
- **computer output to microfilm (COM)** – output is automatically produced as microfiche, so that large amounts of information can be stored in a small area. The output can only be read by using special microfiche viewers such as those you might encounter in a public library.

Computer printers

The type of printer used in an office will depend on the type of output required. In-house documents such as payroll listings and account transactions do not need to be high quality, but do need to be produced quickly. A cheaper printer will therefore be quite suitable for this purpose.

Letters, memos and other business documents need to be printed on a good-quality printer so that customers gain a good impression of the organisation. Graphics and desktop publishing packages need a very high quality printer, especially if sophisticated shading or special text effects are required.

The main types of printer to be found in offices are:

- **dot matrix** – the cheapest type of printer. The image is formed by a series of dots placed on the paper by a platform of needles. Quality is only fair, but the printing is quite rapid. Quality can be improved by using the **near letter quality** (NLQ) function which means the printer goes over each character twice to improve the density.

- **ink-jet or bubble jet** – these spray tiny droplets of ink onto virtually any surface: paper, glass, plastic or metal. The quality is excellent and they are equally good for graphics and text. Desktop models are reasonably priced although the cost of replacing the ink cartridge can be quite high. They are relatively slow and the range of graphics and text sizes is limited.

- **laser printers** – these printers use laser beams to transfer the original image onto a drum, which then transfers it onto paper. Desktop models are now quite common in most offices, even though they are quite expensive. The copy quality is excellent both for text and graphics. A Postscript laser printer is one that can produce very sophisticated text and graphics using a special built-in processor. Such a machine is ideal for desktop publishing work, although it may be expensive.

Did you know?

Large 'smart' laser printers cost many thousands of pounds and are used mainly by computer centres and by newspaper publishers. Forms and headings can be memorised by the printer and printing is so rapid that hundreds of copies can be produced each minute.

Non-assessed activity

Note that although this activity is not assessed, the work you do can count as part of your evidence towards Element 4.3.

The chart below shows the advantages and disadvantages of different types of printers. Which would you buy if:

- you had to make long computer listings of product sales for company reps
- you had to produce quite sophisticated newsletters to send to clients
- you needed a relatively inexpensive colour printer
- you wanted a good-quality printer to produce business documents?

Type of printer	Advantages	Disadvantages
Dot matrix	Essential for impact printing onto multi-parts stationery (e.g. sets of invoices)	Only average quality print-out
	Inexpensive to buy and cheap to run	NLQ (near letter quality) available but still not very good quality and printing slow
	Highly reliable and lasts a long time	Most only suitable for use with continuous stationery
	Excellent for long print runs	Noisy in use
	Wide carriage versions available	
Ink Jet	Very good print quality	Cannot be used with multi-part stationery
	Can produce simple graphics/different fonts	Relatively slow unless in 'draft' mode
	Quiet in operation	
	Cheap to buy – including colour models	Not suitable for sophisticated DTP work
	Can print envelopes	Only top models suitable for long print runs
	Suitable for both A4 and A3 and wide paper – both cut sheet and continuous stationery	
Laser	Top quality documents produced	Normally only suitable with A4 cut-sheet paper
	Capable of printing sophisticated graphics	Not suitable for multi-part stationery
	Relatively fast	Expensive to buy – but prices are falling
	Quiet in operation	Highest running costs
	Capable of handling long print runs	

Figure IT.11 Pros and cons of different types of printers

Care of printers

1 First of all – and very important – find out how to stop the printer quickly if there is a problem. This usually means typing in a command on the computer or clicking on an item from the menu, *not* just pressing the 'off' switch! The command will vary from one computer program to another.

2 Make sure that the paper is properly loaded into the machine and correctly aligned. Continuous stationery should be positioned with the sprocket holes placed over the sprockets, to keep it in position. Single sheet paper should be fanned first. Make sure it is correctly aligned with the paper guides on your printer.

3 Only use the paper recommended for your printer. This is particularly important for laser printers, where the quality and weight of the paper can be vital.

4 *Never* block the area where your print-out emerges, or you may find you have reams of continuous stationery backing into the printer and jamming it.

5 On a printer for continuous stationery, use the TOF (top of form) or FF (form feed) button to turn up the paper automatically.

6 Remember that your printer *must* be **on line** before it will print. This is the first thing to check if, for any reason, nothing is happening.

7 Read your printer manual (or look at the chart in Figure IT.12) to find out:
   - how to rectify *simple* faults, e.g. a paper jam
   - how to change the ribbon, ink cartridge or laser cartridge

8 *Never* tamper with the printer if you are not sure what you are doing. Ask your tutor for help.

Did you know?

An alternative form of output is to send your message to someone else's computer by electronic mail (**E-mail**). If you are linked by a network, it is likely an E-mail system will be in use. E-mail is dealt with in Element 4.3, page 514.

Printer problems

Printer faults can have many causes. They range from simple problems, such as running out of paper, to more complex ones, such as incorrect computer-to-printer configurations (i.e. the computer and printer cannot communicate with one another).

To some extent the type of problem you may encounter will depend on the type of printer, ribbon or paper-feed system you are using. Every printer has its own operating manual which contains a 'troubleshooting' section. You should always refer to this if difficulties occur, so that you never, inadvertently, make the problem worse. The most common types of problems, and the action to take,

619

are given in the chart in Figure IT.12 – but this chart is no substitute for your own user manual!

Did you know?

If you use a set of computer manuals and reference materials regularly and can explain things from them to someone else, this can help to provide evidence for your Communication Core Skills – Element 2.4!

Fault	Probable cause	Action
No response to print command	No power to printer Printer not switched on Printer not connected to computer Printer 'off line' Wrong command given	Check plug lead Switch on Check printer lead Press 'on line' key Check software manual
Print is gibberish	Software and printer incompatible Printer lead faulty	Call supervisor Replace lead
Poor print quality	Ribbon needs changing Ribbon too near/far from paper **Ink jet/laser** – cartridge needs changing **Laser** – paper wrong specification/internal cleaning required	Replace ribbon Adjust ribbon setting Replace cartridge Check laser manual/arrange cleaning
Print wrong size	Printer 'remembering' earlier command	Clear memory by switching printer off and on again
Characters missing	**Laser** – wrong font selected	Check laser manual
Paper jam	**Document feed** – paper wrong specification/inserted wrongly **Tractor feed** – printed/unused sheets 'backing up' into printer **Ink jet/laser** – overfull in-tray/incorrect paper specification	Change paper and reinsert – check document feeder Stop printer. Use paper release to unjam. Clear area behind printer Remove paper from in-tray/change paper/check manual
Crooked print	**Tractor feed** – paper dislodged from sprocket holes **Ink jet/laser** – paper not inserted properly in paper tray	Stop printer. Realign paper properly on sprocket holes Remove paper, reset paper guides
Incorrect pitch/line spacing	Software over-riding printer settings	Check software

Figure IT.12 Printer problems and their solutions

Did you know?

If you are ever in a position where you cannot produce urgent documents by the specified deadline – because of printer problems or for any other reason – you must notify someone in authority immediately. Otherwise people may be standing by to receive them without knowing that they won't be available. Only if people know what is happening can they decide what emergency action to take.

Know your equipment

Using a keyboard

Keyboards vary from one computer to another, although most have the standard QWERTY layout, together with the following special keys. Find out where these are and learn how they work with each of the programs you use.

- **Function keys** will be either above or to the left of your character keys. There are usually up to 12 function keys, and each will have a special use for each program you use.
- **Backspace** deletes the character to the left of the cursor
- **Delete** deletes the character at the same position as the cursor
- **Cursor keys** are the four arrow keys that move the cursor up, down, to the left or right
- **Page Up and Page Down** are normally programmed by the software to move you forwards or backwards one page at a time
- **Home key** will either move your cursor to the beginning of the document or to the left of your screen
- **End key** will move your cursor either to the end of the document or the right of your screen
- **Esc key** usually enables you to escape from the option you have just chosen (useful if you choose the wrong one!)
- **Alt and Ctrl keys** usually have specific functions for the program you are using. You may like to note that holding down both Control and Alt together and pressing the Delete key will normally reset your computer. This can be useful to know if your screen 'freezes' for any reason, *but* you lose the job on which you were working.

Using a mouse

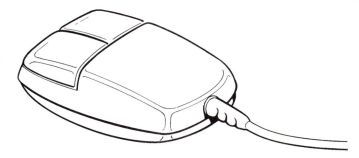

Figure IT.13 A typical two-button mouse

If possible, always use a special **mouse mat** to prevent dust and fluff being picked up from the desk and transferred to the rubber ball under the mouse. Roll the mouse over the surface of the mat smoothly – if you are about to fall off the edge of the desk, you can simply lift up the mouse and reposition it without moving your cursor on screen.

A mouse usually has two buttons, and clicking these will enable you to:

- select an option from a list on screen
- draw lines and shapes.

If you point to a specific option and then hold your button down, you may find you can **drag** an image or icon from one part of your page to another.

Two rules to note:

- make sure you know which button does what on the program you are using
- clean your mouse regularly by removing the detachable plate underneath and cleaning the little rubber ball.

Did you know?

Many programs requiring a mouse will only work if the mouse is connected *before you load the program.* If, therefore, nothing seems to work once you have switched on, switch off again, check your mouse is connected properly, and then try again.

Using a scanner

First rule – make sure the document you are scanning is clean, otherwise the scanner will interpret every dirty mark as a character and you will have to erase them all on screen! You will also have a much clearer, higher definition image if you make sure your original is black and white, rather than in colour. If necessary, photocopy it first.

A full-size document scanner usually takes a sheet of A4 paper and, provided you make sure it is straight when you insert it, there is little that can go wrong. A hand-held scanner is more tricky – it needs to be moved slowly and steadily down the image you are scanning. Remember that you can easily erase the image on screen and start again if you make a mess of it – the skill comes with plenty of practice!

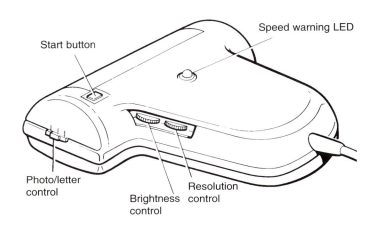

Speed warning LED

Start button

Photo/letter control

Brightness control

Resolution control

Figure IT.14 A hand-held scanner

Scanners are now being used in systems known as **document management.** This means scanning all documents and filing them *electronically* rather than in filing cabinets. Images of the documents are kept on magnetic or optical disk, so thousands can be held on a very small area. The aim is to reduce the amount of paper and the cost of the storage space it occupies.

Did you know?

The days of scanners, mice and keyboards may soon be over. Computer companies are busy developing speech-recognition technology. This allows computers to analyse, interpret and respond to human speech. At present, they are concentrating on developing computer recognition of basic commands such as 'save' or 'quit'. However, according to the designers, there is debate on the number of words a computer needs to recognise to 'undelete' data wiped by mistake – normally the first word spoken by an operator who makes a major error when entering data is *not* 'undelete'!

The role of the computer operator in business

A computer is simply a device that enables information to be processed quickly and easily. It has no in-built intelligence, but simply follows instructions. It is therefore almost impossible for it to go wrong on its own – if an error occurs it is because an operator made one! If you think of a computer as a rather clever slave, rather than having a life force of its own, you will realise that you must take responsibility for your own actions and cannot blame the computer.

To be able to operate a computer efficiently, you need to know how to use the equipment correctly and understand how the software is meant to operate, and the functions it can carry out. Failure to understand the first can result in expensive and time-consuming problems. Ignorance of the second can mean you waste hours of everyone's time, including your own. To be really effective, you must take a pride in your work, so that the documents you produce are of consistently high quality. You will gain a reputation for reliability and conscientiousness, which will pay dividends. You will be rewarded with progressively more difficult and challenging tasks – which will make your job more interesting and varied, as well as preparing you for a more senior position with more responsibility.

If you are using IT equipment, you will be involved in:

- preparing information
- processing information
- presenting information
- evaluating the use of IT.

These aspects of the job correspond to the elements you have to cover for your Core Skills. Each is considered in more detail below.

Preparing information

The term **source data** or **source information** is used for the original sources of information you are asked to input into a computer. This may be:

- an original document, such as keying in details on a database from a paper record, entering sales figures into a spreadsheet from a representative's report, or typing a memo on a word processor from notes you made yourself
- information developed during input – an example would be if you compose a document at the keyboard.

Your task as an operator would be to:

- know the package you are using
- input the information accurately
- input the information using the correct commands so that it is easy to edit
- correct errors as you notice them (otherwise they can become very difficult to find)
- save the work when it is complete with a clear label so that you can find it again when you want it.

As explained in Element 4.3, it is important that you use a sensible system of naming files and directories. It is also important that you save your work regularly – especially after you have made important or involved changes. You also need to make sure your work is copied to a back-up disk (see page 522).

Did you know?

If you are trying to redesign a document or use a command you are not sure about, it is sensible to make sure your document is **saved** *before* you start experimenting. Then, if anything goes wrong, you can recover the document in its previous form and you don't have to start again from the beginning!

Process information

There are many reasons why computer operators need to recall files and documents they have prepared earlier. A long document is unlikely to be completed in one sitting. Some files contain useful information and are used over and over again (e.g. customer records held on a database). Some contain information that can usefully be imported into another package and used a different way. A pie chart, for instance, produced on a spreadsheet could be included in a report produced on a word-processing package.

For this reason, storing information and then being able to find it again is important. Searching for information can be carried out by **name** (via a directory), through **key words** or through **key fields** in a database. This saves hunting through every document listed to find the one you want. Further information about searching is given in Element 4.3, page 520.

Often the information needs editing. This may mean:

- amending it (e.g. updating it with new facts and figures)
- moving it (e.g. because your boss wants to transpose the third and fourth paragraphs in a letter)
- reformatting it (changing the way it looks – see below)
- copying it (e.g. copying a paragraph from one letter into another – *without* retyping it!)
- deleting it (because it is no longer needed)
- inserting new text or figures (e.g. adding a row of figures to a spreadsheet)
- sorting it (e.g. changing the order of files or records).

Sometimes a major restructuring job will be required – the sequence of rows or columns in a spreadsheet may have to be changed, or pages of text in a word-processed document may have to be moved around with new headings and subheadings added.

When you are familiar with your computer system, and especially if you are using an **integrated** package, you may be expected to **import** text or graphics you have created using one package into a document you are creating in another. Examples would be:

- a graph created on a spreadsheet, which you want to include in a word-processed report
- a picture scanned into a graphics package, which you want to include in a desktop published newsletter
- customer name and address files entered in a database, which you want to mail-merge with a letter produced on a word-processing package to create a personalised mailshot.

Did you know?

Today many packages are **integrated.** This means that the components are designed to be compatible so that, for instance, a spreadsheet from one component of the package can be imported into a word-processed document. The most popular integrated packages for business are Microsoft

Office (which includes word-processing, spreadsheet, presentation graphics and mail package) and PerfectOffice (which incorporates word processing, spreadsheet, presentation package, E-mail and personal planners). Other 'add-ons' – such as databases – are also available.

Non-assessed activity

You can find out more about Microsoft products by telephoning 0345 002 000 or by writing to Microsoft Ltd, Microsoft Place, Winnersh, Wokingham, Berkshire RG11 5TP. Details of PerfectOffice are available by ringing 0800 177 277 or writing to Novell UK Ltd, Novell House, London Road, Bracknell, Berkshire RG12 2UY. Obtain details from both companies and decide which package you would buy if you had the choice.

Present information

A computer user in business needs to know enough about the packages available to choose the correct one for the task. You can't produce a newsletter on a spreadsheet package or an analysis of the sales accounts on a word-processing package! You should become familiar with the facilities and the limitations of the packages you are using – including their ability to do 'extra jobs'. For instance, can you produce two-column newsletters on your word processing package, or do you have to resort to a DTP package? Can you move charts you have created on your spreadsheet into a report?

You also need to consider the **best method** of presenting the information. Often a set of figures is better displayed in a table than discussed in a paragraph of text. If it is essential that **trends** are recognised quickly, a graph or bar chart may be more acceptable, and so on. The factors to consider include:

- who will read it (i.e. who is your audience?)
- why is it required?
- will the information be clearly presented?

Finally, you need to consider the **format** of your final documents. This is discussed in more detail below.

Did you know?

One of the most important considerations in formatting a document is **consistency.** All the margins, types of headings, paragraphs, etc. **must be the same** throughout one document.

Document format

This is the term used to decide what your document will look like. Document formats are covered in Element 4.3, page 494. The section below extends your knowledge of this area, particularly in relation to formatting documents using IT equipment.

Did you know?

If you want to set a format command that will apply *throughout* the document (e.g. margin width or justification) you usually need to have your cursor at the **beginning** of the document when you make the command. Otherwise you will find that only the text *after* the cursor position has been affected! This applies equally to **reformatting** – when you change the layout and appearance of your original document, e.g. by using different paragraphs, wider columns, a new style of heading, etc.

Hints and tips on document formats and production

1 Most office documents are printed on A4 paper, and many printers can only cope with this size of paper. You can always enlarge or reduce it later on a photocopier. However, for some work you may have a wider printer, for instance if you were operating with large spreadsheets that would not fit on A4 paper.

2 It should be relatively easy to decide whether **landscape** or **portrait** layout is more suitable. Unfortunately, only certain types of printer (e.g. ink jet and laser) will print out in landscape format. Use your common sense! If you are creating a table or poster that is wide but not deep, go for landscape. If it is deep and narrow, then stick to portrait.

3 A good guide for left-hand and right-hand margins is 1.5″ or 2″ each side. A document always looks better if your margins are equal. If, however, this would mean a small amount of text would be carried to another page, change your margins to 1″ each side. The wonderful thing about computers is that you can change your margins several times and compare the different effects.

4 The top and bottom margins determine the page length. They usually look better when they are equal. If you only have a small amount of text on a page you could go for wide top and bottom margins and double line spacing to make it look

more effective. You should **always** avoid:

- text being printed on the perforations of continuous stationery
- single words or lines being carried over to a second sheet of paper
- a broken table (i.e. split between two pages).

5 On virtually all packages, text or figures at the left side of the page will automatically be justified (i.e. start at the same point). Word processed documents can look much more professional if you set 'right justification' as well. The same applies if you are creating documents on a desktop publishing package. Look through some modern text books and see how they are laid out.

On a spreadsheet you can choose whether you want information in cells to be left or right justified – experiment to see which looks better (see page 635).

6 A **character set** is a particular group of characters. The keyboard holds one character set (usually ASCII codes, pronounced 'askey'). On some packages you have the opportunity to use other sets, which will include graphics or symbols not held on the standard set. For instance:

- other languages, e.g. Greek (ß), Hebrew (Π), Cyrillic (Я), in case you are writing to anyone in Greece, Israel or Russia and know enough to write in their language!
- mathematical and scientific signs, e.g. ÷, ×, ∴ and ≡
- other symbols not normally found on your keyboard, e.g. ‰, ✿, ✍ or ✳.

Check whether your printer will be able to print these out, even if you can select them in your program!

7 Fonts are the different typefaces and styles. You can choose different fonts in some word-processing packages and in all desktop publishing packages. However, for the widest range of fonts you need a Postscript laser printer.

This is an example of Times typeface

`This is an example of Courier typeface`

This is an example of Helvetica typeface

This is an example of Palatino typeface

Figure IT.15 Four different typefaces

Examples of fonts include

- Times
- Helvetica
- Courier
- Palatino

8 The size of your characters will also be determined by your printer. Again, if you have a Postscript laser printer you can vary these more. Size is given in points. Figure IT.16 shows examples of text in different point sizes:

This is 8 point

This is 12 point

This is 24 point

This is 34 point

Figure IT.16 Four different type sizes

9 On *some* word-processing packages and all desktop publishing packages, you can produce work in columns. This means the finished document looks something like a newspaper.
- From two to four columns is the best (three is often ideal). More than four means your text width is too narrow to be read easily.
- Drawing a vertical line between columns (only possible on a DTP package) makes the finished work look more professional.
- As a general rule it is always better to stick to equal columns and equal spaces between them.
- Most packages have *pre-set* column widths, which are standard size. Stick to these until you know what you are doing.

10 From Element 4.3 and Communication Core Skills, you should have learned the main typing conventions in relation to paragraphs. You should also *always* use headings if you are typing a long piece of continuous prose, as this makes your document much easier to read. Using numbered points and indenting text so that it is aligned throughout also makes the work look more attractive.

11 Producing tables and diagrams is much easier if you are working with a package, which almost does these automatically. On some word processing packages the 'outline' of a table can be produced automatically. You then simply readjust the column widths to fit in with your text, as in Figure IT.17.

MACHINE OUTPUT - LEEDS			
	January	**February**	**March**
Machine 1	29 738	48 379	19 728
Machine 2	20 389	22 038	19 361
Total	**50 127**	**70 417**	**39 089**

Figure IT.17 Producing tables automatically

Note that in Figure IT.17:
- the main heading has been typed in capitals, centred and emboldened for effect
- the headings and total lines have been emboldened to make them easier to read
- a space has been left after the 'thousands' column in the figures – to make the numbers clearer.

These effects are known as **text enhancement** and are achievable on most types of packages (see page 631).

Any tables or diagrams you produce should be:
- well-balanced
- easy to read
- clearly labelled
- well positioned
- pleasing to the eye.

Did you know?

If you can produce tables automatically, you can also draw boxes automatically! When you create a table you will be asked to say how many columns you want *down* the page and how many rows you want *across* the page. In the table above there four columns and five rows.

If you specify just one column and one row – you have a box!

You can usually alter the size of the box quite easily and type as much or as little text into it as you require.

Proof-reading

No matter what package you are using it is important that you check your work carefully. There is little point in knowing your program backwards and being expert at formatting if your work is full of mistakes! On word-processing packages you may find you have a spell check facility to help you – but this won't pick up keying-in errors if the word you have typed is still recognisable (see page 632).

There are some points you need to remember.

- Proof-reading from a screen is a **skill** that must be developed.
- Generally people find it harder to read 'word by word' from a screen than a piece of paper.
- Proof-reading on a computer may mean having to scroll backwards and forwards to check that you have spelled a word the same way every time.
- The process is even more difficult – and more important – when figures are involved. The reader will know when the word you have typed is wrong, because the sense of the sentence will give it away. No-one can tell if a figure is wrong just by reading a document – and yet this kind of mistake could be disastrous.

If you have problems then *always* take a **hard** (paper) copy of your work and proof-read this, perhaps with someone else's help as 'reader'. If necessary, you can then make any corrections before taking a final print-out.

Did you know?

On most packages a standard VDU cannot show all of an A4 page at once – it only shows the area you are working on. You therefore need to **scroll** from one part of your document to another, using the cursor arrow keys. On many packages there are special commands to enable you to move from one part of a document to another quickly – learn them and use them!

Information referencing

Information referencing means putting references on the page to enable both readers and creators to identify the document itself, and subsequent parts of it, quickly and easily.

The most obvious of these is a **page reference**. Think what would happen if the pages of this book were loose leaved and unnumbered, and you dropped them all over the floor! Indeed, you might already have experienced the frustration of opening a ring binder to find that the inner rings have become mis-aligned and half of your notes have come out. Trying to sort them out is little short of a nightmare.

Therefore, *always* number the pages of documents that have more than two sheets. In addition to pagination, many packages allow you to add the date and a title as a useful reference on all your documents. These can often be included on every page, simply by inserting a **header** or **footer** command (see page 632) in which the information is automatically placed at the head (top) or foot (bottom) of every page of information on your document.

Evaluate the use of information technology

There are two ways in which you can evaluate the use of IT. One is a very informal way, and one you may not even think about. Suppose you use a word-processing package with a very complicated mail merge feature. Mail merge is the feature that inserts names and addresses automatically in a pre-prepared document (see page 631). However, you have only four letters to send and the commands for mail merge are very complicated. Suppose you try mail merging but it takes ages – so that it would have been quicker to recall the letter, type in a name and address, print it, replace one name and address with the next, print again and so on. In this case, you have evaluated a method of operation and decided that mail merge is not appropriate when you are creating four or fewer letters. This does not mean that mail merge is rubbish! It simply means you need sufficient documents to make it worthwhile – your decision if you were creating 4000 documents may be rather different!

Other versions of this type of evaluation include:

- thinking of an easier or more effective method of processing a large amount of information
- thinking of a way to undertake a task using IT equipment which would save a lengthy manual operation.

The second method is more formal. You might be asked to try that particular word processing package and evaluate it for your supervisor. You may wish to report that mail merge is very complicated on that particular package and a different one may be a better buy for your organisation.

Whenever you are comparing one method of operation or type of package with another, think in terms of:

- speed – the more quickly you can do a job, the better
- ease of use – complicated operations are often ignored by users (think how many times people

ignore elaborate commands they can enter on a sophisticated telephone system or video recorder!)

- effort – the aim should be to reduce this as much as possible
- accuracy – don't substitute one method for another if the new way might cause more mistakes to be made.

Problems and IT equipment

Problems can occur in relation to:

- errors made by users (yours and everyone else's!)
- equipment faults
- loss of information.

A simple error on a computer system can cause havoc for users. A typical example would be an important document that wasn't saved on disk, or had been saved on the wrong disk or under the wrong name. The unfortunate person given the task of retrieving it may have to search for hours, possibly fruitlessly.

Equipment faults can have a variety of causes, from simple problems such as a lead becoming disconnected, to major difficulties with a hard drive or keyboard failure. Computer and printer faults have already been discussed on pages 616 and 620.

Loss of information can be caused by a mislabelled file (see above), a faulty floppy disk, a fault on a hard drive or even a computer virus (see page 522). The problem is usually remedied by preventing unauthorised access to the system (see *Security and IT*, below) and by regularly saving work and taking back-up copies (see Element 4.3, page 522).

Health and safety and IT

Another aspect of evaluation is in relation to health and safety. You obviously want to make sure you are working safely, that the equipment you are using is safe and that the information you are creating will also be kept safely. Pouring a hot cup of coffee over a floppy disk or your keyboard would obviously have repercussions for all three!

People who are asked to work on computers for the first time may be concerned about health and safety implications, such as:

- backache
- eye strain
- headaches and migraine
- RSI and tenosynovitis.

Backache is usually caused by poor seating, bad posture or sitting for hours on end at a computer. **Eye strain** can be caused by flickering screens, poor lighting, sunshine reflecting on a screen or by staring at a VDU for hours on end. **Headaches** and **migraine** often follow eye strain.

The abbreviation **RSI** stands for **repetitive strain injury.** This is caused by making many repetitive or awkward movements. A common form of this is tenosynovitis, sometimes called 'teno'. The tendon sheaths in the hand, wrist or arm become inflamed because of the action of constantly hitting keys to input data. The first symptoms are aching, tenderness or numbness of the hand, wrist or arm. The condition can become very painful and may result in a complete inability to grip objects.

Good workstation and keyboard design, and adequate rest breaks, can help to prevent RSI. Any workers who think they may have a problem should report it to their health and safety representative and see their doctor immediately.

Did you know?

In one legal battle, the Inland Revenue had to pay £79 000 to a former typist who is now registered as disabled because of RSI. In another case, BT had to pay £6000 to two former employees, plus court costs of about £100 000. Both the Inland Revenue and BT face at least another 150 claims.

Health and safety legislation

The design of workstations is covered by **the Health and Safety (Display Screen Equipment) Regulations.** The term **workstation** includes the display screen, keyboard, desk and chair, software and systems used, *in addition* to environmental factors such as lighting, noise and humidity. The design and position of workstations should take into account the fact that glare and light reflections from the screen can cause problems for a VDU operator.

Non-assessed activity

How many health and safety hazards can you spot in Figure IT.18?

Figure IT.18 How many health and safety hazards can you see?

Security and IT

Security systems exist for a number of reasons. These include the prevention of:

- accidental erasure of information on a disk – by the use of **write protection** notches
- accidental erasure of formula within a database (see page 633)
- unauthorised people using a computer network (see below).

In some computer installations very elaborate security procedures are set up to prevent access by unauthorised individuals to certain areas. These may include locked doors which will only respond to either a key code, a swipe card or even a voice or hand print!

However, most organisations use a system of user identification (IDs) and passwords to prevent or restrict access to important or confidential information, e.g:

- bank account information
- staff wages and salaries
- customer accounts
- the contents of electronic mailboxes.

Each user of a particular computer system will have his or her own ID. The computer will hold a set of authorities for that particular ID and may restrict or prevent access to certain files. For instance:

- Category A files may be unobtainable
- Category B files may be read only
- Category C files permit reading and amending.

A director of the company may have full access to all files. A junior employee may only be allowed to view category C files. A supervisor may be able to view some files and have full access to others, and so on.

In addition, each user will have his or her own password. This has to be used in conjunction with the user ID and enables the computer to check whether the person logging on is the genuine user. Needless to say, no-one should tell anyone else his or her password.

All passwords should be:

- changed frequently
- remembered – not written down
- original words rather than obvious ones.

As a final precaution, certain files may be made inaccessible unless an additional specific password is known. This may only be revealed to high-ranking people in the organisation or those in charge of, say, computer maintenance, who may need to be able to access system or operating files not available to anyone else.

Did you know?

A **hacker** is a person who illegally gains entry into a computer system by working out or bypassing the password. Six minutes after the Government joined Internet, a man from Edinburgh University hacked into the system used by the Office of Public Service and Science and redesigned some of the pages of information. The spokesman was grateful – he felt the new pages were an improvement!

Computers and the law

Data kept in a computer is covered by the **Data Protection Act 1984**, which gives legal rights to individuals regarding **personal** data held about them on computer. The requirements of this Act are covered in Element 4.3, page 522.

Under the provisions of the Act a person can find out information which is held on him or her by:

- referring to the **Data Protection Register** (a copy is held in all major libraries) which lists all holders of data
- writing to the holder and asking for a copy of the data held.

A holder *cannot* refuse to give the information unless the data is held for national security reasons. In addition, information on criminal, tax and social work records may also be withheld.

However, finding out information is not necessarily free! It can cost over £10 a time.

You should note that the Data Protection Act *only* covers information about *people* held on computer – with the exception of an organisation's own payroll. Exemptions include.

- information on companies or other topics, e.g. a book or car list
- all manual systems
- information held on personal computer systems for household use only.

Optional evidence assignment

If you undertake this assignment it can contribute to your evidence in the following areas

Element 2.2: Explain employee and employer rights and responsibilities (health and safety)

Element 4.3: Identify and evaluate ways to store business documents (computer files)

Core skills: Communication and Information technology

Suppose you are employed as an assistant in the Personnel department of Quantum Electronics. The personnel manager is Mrs Margery Stevens. The company employs several staff as VDU operators and has recently changed its policy in line with the EU directives. In future all operators will:

- receive free eye tests at regular periods
- have regular rest breaks away from the machine.

In addition the main office areas where VDUs are sited have been redecorated and new lighting and new workstations have been installed.

To make sure that all employees know why these measures have been taken, and that they understand other important aspects of working with VDUs and health and safety, Mrs Stevens has decided to hold a short training session for all VDU staff tomorrow

afternoon. She also wants to include a section on security of information.

She has asked you and your colleagues to undertake the following tasks, **in small groups.**

1 Carry out your own research on health and safety and IT equipment, both from the information provided and from that available in the library. Mrs Stevens has suggested that you might like to obtain additional information by contacting your local Health and Safety Executive (HSE) office. The address is in your phone book.
2 Find out the main requirements of the Data Protection Act. In addition, prepare notes explaining why a system of user IDs and passwords has been introduced for people logging into the computer system.
3 Prepare a short (**10-minute)** presentation to highlight the main aspects of both health and safety *and* security. Use visual aids such as overhead transparencies to make your main points.
4 Prepare a simple booklet, with a section on health and safety and a section on security, which can be given to all staff who attend the training session. If possible, create this on a desktop publishing package or integrated word-processing and graphics package so that you can include illustrations where these would be appropriate.

Computer software

Computer software is all the programs loaded into the computer to tell it what to do. There are two types of program used with micro-computers.

Systems programs

The operating system controls the computer's operation and tells it how to function. Whilst the most common is **DOS** (disk operating system), many people today use **Windows.** Not only is this more powerful than DOS, enabling the user to work on several tasks at once, it is also more 'user-friendly' as it relies on a system of **icons** (small pictures) and **drop-down menus** rather than keyed-in commands.

Applications programs

These are the actual business programs which can be loaded so that the computer can be used for a variety of business applications. Applications programs are

629

usually sold as a **package** comprising the software, a user manual and, sometimes, a tutorial disk or booklet. Sometimes, application programs are created by a user company's own programmers.

Did you know?

1 The small block on the screen where the colours are reversed and often flashing is the **cursor.** The cursor must be at the point at which you want to do something – whether this means choosing an option or changing some text.

2 Most packages are designed so that all the prompts are given to you on screen. Unfortunately, many people don't bother reading them, so all this effort by the programmer is wasted! If you're stuck, before you try to find help, **always read the screen.** It is very likely that the answer to your problem is on the screen waiting to be read!

Business application packages

In business a wide variety of software is used, all of which has different uses and functions.

- **Word-processing packages** are used for creating documents such as memos, letters and reports.
- **Database** packages are used for keeping records of customers and suppliers.
- **Spreadsheet** packages are used for carrying out calculations, including those which may be based on future plans, e.g. what will happen to our profit if we give all the staff a 5 per cent pay rise?
- **Graphics** packages may be used to create artwork for posters and adverts.
- **Desktop** publishing packages are used to create posters, newsletters and advertising material.
- **Accounting** packages are used for general book-keeping, producing invoices, calculating VAT returns and printing end-of-year financial documents (see Element 4.2, page 471).
- **Payroll** packages automatically calculate wages, and print pay slips and the other statutory returns required by companies.

At some time in your career you may be asked to use any of these types of software. If you work in a manufacturing organisation you may also see **CAD** (computer-aided design) or **CAM** (computer-aided manufacturing) in operation. At this stage in your career it is likely that you may be asked to use word

processing, database and spreadsheet packages together with some basic DTP or graphic packages.

User-friendly packages

Some programs are advertised as 'user-friendly' because they are supposed to be easy to learn and to use. This usually means that they will incorporate **menus** or **windows.** A menu simply gives you a list of choices, and you move the cursor to the option you want (or key in the letter to identify this option). A window operates on a similar basis. A range of options is shown across the top of your screen – when you select the one you want a menu drops down under this option giving you a range of choices.

Did you know?

On *any* package you *must* press the 'Enter' key (or click the correct mouse button) to select the option you want. The computer cannot know which choice you have made until you do this!

If you make the wrong choice by mistake, then (on most packages) pressing 'Esc' (or selecting this option with your mouse) will take you back to where you were before.

Common features

Features that are common to many different types of package include the following:

- **Status line(s)** – giving information on the piece of work you are creating.
- **A prompt line** – giving information on what you can do next.
- **An entry line** – usually identified by >. You enter your command immediately after this symbol.
- **A 'help' feature** – most packages offer a special 'Help' key. This will give you the assistance the programmer thought you might need if you are stuck at this part of the program.
- **Commands** – these vary considerably from one package to another. Learn the ones you need to use on a regular basis (make a note of them to start with, on a quick reminder sheet). You can look up the more obscure commands as and when you need them. The main commands you need to know are:
  - **retrieve** – how to recall information already stored on disk

- **save** – how to save information you have created on to disk

- **print** – how to print a hard copy of your work

- **quit** – how to close down the package when you have finished.

Did you know?

To use software or disks on a particular computer they must be **compatible** with the system you are using. You cannot take a disk you have used on an Apple Macintosh machine and use it on an IBM machine, although many Apple Macs can accept and produce DOS disks. In a similar way, you must make sure that any software you buy is compatible with the hardware system you are using.

Word-processing packages

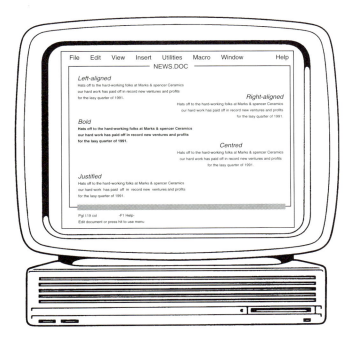

Figure IT.19 A word-processing package offers many features

Word-processing packages are used to produce letters, memos, reports and other business documents. They have removed much of the drudgery and repetitive work this used to involve. There is a variety of packages on the market, including WordPerfect,

Word, Wordstar, etc. If there is a number after the name of the program the *highest* number indicates the most up-to-date version of the software. While the packages are obviously not identical, the types of features to be found on a word-processing package are generally the same. It may only be the commands and the layout of your screen which are different. Therefore if you know one package well, this should help you to learn others quickly.

Did you know?

When you key text into a word-processing package, the text on your screen will automatically continue on to a new line whenever necessary. The only time you should press the Return or Enter key is to make a new paragraph.

Main features

- **Editing** – text can easily be inserted, deleted or amended in any document; there is never any need to retype whole pages just because some simple alterations need to be made.

- **Text enhancement** – text can be specially enhanced by using bold, underlining or other options. Some packages include special fonts – different styles, very large or very small, italic or other forms of typeface, such as a shadow effect. How effective these are will depend very much on the printer you are using.

- **Blocks** – chunks of text may be moved, copied, deleted or enhanced. The first step is to define the block by identifying where it starts and finishes. You then give the command for the operation you require.

- **Reformatting** – any aspect of the layout of a document can be changed at any time. You can alter the margins, change the style of headings (e.g. from blocked to centred), justify the right-hand margin, change paragraphs and number pages. The design can be changed as many times as necessary until the appearance is right.

- **Search (and replace)** – you can search for a particular word or phrase throughout any size of document. If you wish, you can replace this with another word or phrase either by choice (as you look through) or automatically.

- **Mail merge** – this is the way to produce personalised letters quickly and easily. You type in the letter and store it under one file name and then type in the 'variables' and store them under a different file name. Variables are those parts of the letter that are different for each recipient, e.g. name, address and possibly special details in the body of the letter, such as an interview time. When you give the computer special instructions, it will 'merge' the two files so that personalised letters are produced automatically.

■ **Printing** – the print screen will usually give a variety of options, such as choice of line spacing, margin settings, justification and so on. You may also be able to print out selected pages only or multiple copies, as required.

Did you know?

All WP systems have a directory showing all the documents stored on a particular disk. Good directory management is essential – particularly if you are using a hard disk – as hundreds of documents could be held on it at any one time. Directory management is discussed in Element 4.3, page 519.

Additional features

■ **Headers and footers** – these commands automatically put a space (and text if required) at the top and bottom of documents. If, for instance, you wanted to put the name of your organisation at the top of one or more pages, you would create a header with this information. If you wanted to put a special note at the bottom you would create a footer.

■ **Pagination** – this inserts page numbers automatically – an essential feature for a long document in case someone drops it on the floor and needs to sort it out again!

■ **Spell checks** – some packages will automatically check the spelling by comparing the words typed with those stored in their electronic dictionary. Highly technical words and proper nouns (e.g. place names) will probably not be in the dictionary, but can be added. Remember that words you have typed wrongly, but which are still correctly spelt, will be ignored by the spell check, e.g. form/from, now/know, kind/king, work/word. You still need to proof-read!

■ **Thesaurus** – an electronic thesaurus offers a list of words similar in meaning to the one at the cursor

position. This can be useful for improving the vocabulary of a document or by replacing repeated words. If you use a thesaurus do make sure you know the difference between a noun and a verb – otherwise you could replace a word with one that doesn't have the same meaning at all! For instance, 'object' (noun) is 'an article, a commodity or a thing', 'object' (verb) means 'to protest or dispute' – so be careful!

■ **Word count** – this may be included with the spell check. It can be useful if you have to complete a report or project of a certain length – as you can check the length as you go and add or delete words as required.

■ **Graphics** – this can involve actual graphics or, more usually in this context, tables and/or boxes (see page 625).

■ **Footnotes** – this option automatically numbers and places footnotes for you at any point in the text where they are required.

■ **Switch screens** – this option means you can work on two documents at once and simply 'toggle' between them, moving text as you wish.

Did you know?

The term WYSIWYG stands for 'what you see is what you get'. This is the term used for WP systems where you see the text on screen in the same way as it will look on the printed page.

Using a word-processing package

The only way you can become expert at word processing is to practise regularly. However, some basic pointers right at the beginning will help you to do well more quickly.

1 *Don't* 'hunt and peck' around the keyboard! Try to learn to key properly at the outset – it saves hours later.

2 Learn how to move around the screen easily and quickly (usually a combination of the arrow keys and special commands for larger jumps).

3 *Never* delete lots of text and retype it when all it needs is a quick deletion or insertion at a specific point!

4 Learn the commands you need to use regularly. These will usually include:

- **text commands** – bold, underscore
- **format commands** – changing margins, centering text, typing to a flush right margin, justification, inset/indented paragraphs, choosing size of paper
- **editing commands** – insert, delete, move/delete/copy blocks of text, search and replace, spell check and thesaurus
- **print commands** – number of copies, size of paper, line spacing, specific pages only.

Use the manual to look up any others you need when you want them.

5   Learn the functions you need for the job you do. For instance, if you regularly have to produce personalised letters, learn how to use the mail merge facility. If you have to type and store standard paragraphs then learn how to do this properly.

6   Develop a *sensible* and *logical* system of saving documents, so that you can access them easily (see page 519).

7   Set up directories for different types of documents (see page 519) – as you might store different types of files in a filing cabinet.

8   File your print-outs in the same way, using folders and files correctly labelled with the same names as your directories.

9   Learn the correct layout for business documents (see Core Skills in Communication). Then, when you go to work, check the layout you are required to use by your employer and stick to it – the one who pays the piper calls the tune!

Make sure that the documents you produce are correct and look professional so that they won't need altering by anyone else before they can be used.

10 Use your common sense and initiative. Don't expect to be told:
- to proof-read your typing
- to check your spelling
- to use the correct layout (or set it out as clearly and attractively as you can)
- to save an important document
- to keep the original document
- to keep confidential information to yourself
- to print out the correct number of copies.

You should do all this *automatically!*

Did you know?

If you are keying in confidential material and are interrupted, the best thing to do is to turn down the brightness on your VDU! If you are leaving your desk, save your work and clear your screen.

Optional evidence assignment

If you undertake this assignment it can contribute to your evidence in the following areas.

Element 4.3:   Compare the methods of processing business documents (typed and word processed)

Core skills: Communication and Information technology

Suppose you have recently started work for a local charity. Money is scarce in their offices and you notice that they are surrounded by several old typewriters. The manager, Mrs Thornhill, is 'anti-computer'. She thinks that:

- they are expensive
- they are limited – envelopes are still difficult to produce on a computer printer
- word-processors are useless for filling in forms
- they are no good at all if there is a power cut.

Your boss, Mark Short, doesn't agree and is desperate to buy a fairly cheap word processing system. He thinks the work could be done twice as quickly and the money would therefore be well spent.

He has asked for your help in trying to persuade Mrs Thornhill to buy a word processor.

1   List the advantages of using a word processor for standard documents such as letters, memos and reports.
2   Investigate **at least two** reasonably priced word-processing systems and printers and compare their main features. Write a paragraph stating which system you recommend and give your reasons.
3   Examine Mrs Thornhill's arguments carefully. Try to suggest a solution that will keep both Mrs Thornhill and Mr Sharp happy!
4   Produce a brief report for Mr Sharp summarising all your investigations. Use a word-processor to produce this and use text enhancement features so that your document(s) are themselves a good advertisement for using a word processor!

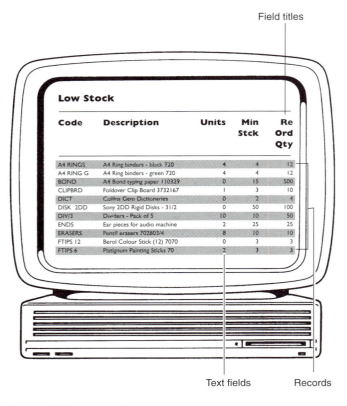

Field titles

Low Stock

Code	Description	Units	Min Stck	Re Ord Qty
A4 RINGS	A4 Ring binders - black 720	4	4	12
A4 RING G	A4 Ring binders - green 720	4	4	12
BOND	A4 Bond typing paper 110329	0	15	500
CLIPBRD	Foldover Clip Board 3732167	1	3	10
DICT	Collins Gem Dictionaries	0	2	4
DISK 2DD	Sony 2DD Rigid Disks - 31/2	0	50	100
DIV/3	Dividers - Pack of 5	10	10	50
ENDS	Ear pieces for audio machine	2	25	25
ERASERS	Pencil erasers 702803/4	8	10	10
FTIPS 12	Berol Colour Stick (12) 7070	0	3	3
FTIPS 6	Platignum Painting Sticks 70	2	3	3

Text fields   Records

Figure IT.20 A database on screen

Database packages

A database is an **electronic filing system** which not only stores and recalls information quickly and easily but can also sort it in various ways to suit the needs of the user.

You can keep a database for any topic on which you might normally keep paper records, e.g:

- a list of customers – names, addresses, telephone numbers, credit allowed etc.
- a list of cars in a fleet (e.g. for a hire car company) with model, year, registration number, date last serviced, etc.
- a list of books in a library with title, author, publisher, index number, year of publication, etc.
- a list of students in a college or school with name, address, course attended, work experience placements, etc.

The problem with manual filing is not in entering or keeping the records but rearranging them to find specific information. If your college or school kept student records on a card index system it would be very time-consuming to:

- sort through them all to find a specific student
- sort through them to make lists under different criteria, e.g.
  - all students aged under 18
  - all students who live more than 5 miles away
  - all female (or male) students
  - all students who did not complete their courses.

On a database system this can be done at the press of a key (or two!).

Main features

- **Form** – this is the 'card' on screen (similar to a paper record card) containing the information.
- **Field** – each area for completion with specific information is called a field.
- **Data** – this is the information to be entered in each field.
- **Record** – this is the name given to a completed form.
- **Editing** – the ability to change information in each field.
- **File** – the name of a specific system. In the system described above, the file name would probably be 'students'. When the database is completed the file will hold all the student records.

Additional features

- **Report** – this feature enables a report to be designed and printed so that information can be reordered and displayed in a number of different ways.
- **Search** – enables you to find a record very quickly by simply keying in a key piece of information and pressing enter. The required record will then be shown on screen in a matter of seconds.
- **Formula** – a formula can be entered to calculate amounts at certain points (see also the discussion of spreadsheets). For instance, if each college student could claim bus fares for every day he or she attended, the record may have three fields:
  - Name
  - Amount of fares
  - Days attended
  A formula could be entered to multiply the amount by the number of days attended, and only the result would appear on the report.
- **Essential data** – on many systems you can specify whether data *must* be entered in a field or not. On a student record the 'name' field would be 'essential data', but details of work experience would not.

In many organisations, designing reports is the job of a qualified computer technician. This is particularly the case if the package is difficult to operate or if complicated reports are required, e.g. those requiring formulae to be entered or those where the print-out has to be listed in a certain order, such as alphabetically.

Using database packages

1   Learn all the basic commands, e.g. load, save and print. Find out how to begin to design a blank form.
2   Think about the type of file you are going to create, the design of the records, and what fields you need.
3   Choose field names that cannot be misinterpreted by other users, and decide how much information needs to be inserted after each field name. This determines the lengths of your fields.
4   Create a record card on screen. Learn how to change and rearrange field names and field lengths and print out a copy of the blank form for reference.
5   Practise keying in data on several records. Learn how to edit records in case you make an error and how to save the latest version on disk.
6   Practise moving quickly from one record to another using the search command.
7   If you are operating an easy package you may be taught how to design a simple report. Think about the type of information users may want, and specify reports to give it to them.
8   Print out reports and check that the layout is 'user-friendly'.

Did you know?

1   Many database records are subject to the provisions of the **Data Protection Act** (see page 522). It would therefore be usual to have a security system in operation so that the records could not be accessed by unauthorised people (see page 628).
2   Computerised stock records are simply another version of a database – the cards have been specially designed to give details of stock held (see Figure IT.20).

Non-assessed activity

As a group, discuss the type of reports you would wish to see if you were operating a computerised stock record system.

Did you know?

An on-line database is one to which users subscribe to obtain information. Ceefax and Oracle, which you can access on your television, are examples. Another well-known example is Prestel. This is an interactive database, which means users can both request and transmit information. Your school or college library may have access to specialist databases – often known as databanks – e.g. LEXIS, which gives legal information, and DIALOG, which gives details of publications. You may have access to Campus 2000, an on-line database especially aimed at schools and colleges.

Non-assessed activity

Suppose that your organisation has many visitors from other parts of the UK and from abroad who are frequently entertained by your executives. You have been asked to create a database file on restaurants in your area.

1   Plan a suitable record card with field names and fields for information you think would be useful.
2   Decide which criteria you would use of sorting the cards to produce different reports. Produce a list for your computer technician.
3   Use your local Yellow Pages to make a list of **twelve** restaurants you think should be included.

Spreadsheet packages

Spreadsheet packages are used by company accountants or financial managers to assess how well the company is performing and/or how proposed changes will affect performance. They may also be used by sales, production and personnel staff if they are involved in making calculations or predictions based on numerical information.

A large 'sheet of paper' (which gives the spreadsheet its name) is ruled off into **columns** and **rows.** Headings can be given to both the columns and the rows. Figures can be added to show income, expenditure, sales, profit etc., either on a weekly or monthly basis.

Spreadsheets are particularly useful for 'what if' calculations. If you are involved in manual calculations you will know that problems occur when:

■   alterations have to be made to past figures
■   you want to try to predict the results of possible changes in the future.

635

This aspect of spreadsheets is discussed more fully in Element 4.2, page 474.

Did you know?

The spreadsheet on screen is usually known as a worksheet. You can design it to be 'user-friendly', by including effects such as underlining to separate headings from the data underneath, and to differentiate totals.

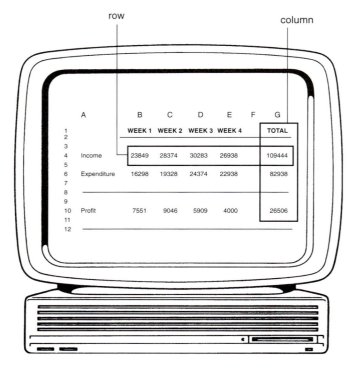

Figure IT.21 A spreadsheet package

Main features

- **Columns** – they always go *down* a spreadsheet and are identified by a letter – A, B, C, etc.
- **Rows** – they always go *across* a spreadsheet and have an identifying number – 1, 2, 3, etc.
- **Cells** – a cell is each square or box on the spreadsheet. The cell you are working on is called the **active cell**. Cells are always referred to by using the column letter first, e.g. A1, B5, W49, etc.
- **Entry line** – this is either immediately underneath or above your spreadsheet. It is the line on which you enter text, figures, formulae or commands. Pressing the 'enter' key moves the

data into the cell on which your cursor is positioned.

- **Figures** – they are entered by simply keying them in on the entry line and pressing enter. Figures can be either entered as whole numbers (called **integers**) or to a specified number of decimal places (2 decimal places if you are dealing in money).
- **Text** – on some packages this must be prefaced with a special sign so that the computer knows you are entering, say, a heading and not a set of figures for calculating.
- **Formulae** – a mathematical formula has to be entered at each point where a calculation has to take place. Normally these aren't visible on the spreadsheet.

Did you know?

Because a spreadsheet is so large, only a small part is shown on your screen at once. Therefore if you jump from cell A1 to cell W58 you are moving to a totally different part of the spreadsheet. There is usually a command to enable you to jump from one cell to another without scrolling, and it is well worth finding!

Non-assessed activity

Bearing in mind that some spreadsheets can have literally hundreds of columns and/or rows, **as a group** can you suggest how columns are identified after the letter 'Z' has been reached?

Additional features

- **Format** – this can include the type of numbers you are displaying (e.g. integer or decimal), column width, right- or left-justified text. You have the choice of changing the format of all the cells of a spreadsheet (i.e. a **global** command) or just one specific cell, row or column.
- **Erase** – this blanks a cell to remove the existing information.
- **Delete** – this removes a row or column.
- **Copy** – this copies an entry from one cell to another.
- **Insert** – this inserts a new row or column.
- **Protect** – this protects specific cells and formulae against erasure.
- **Locking** – this locks title cells in place (e.g. January, February, etc.) so that they continue to show on screen as the spreadsheet scrolls.

- **Graphics** – this spreadsheet packages are designed to enable you to print out your finished results in graphic form, e.g. by producing a bar chart, line graph or pie chart.
- **Recalculating** – spreadsheet packages recalculate the answer in every column or row automatically when you make an alteration to a figure. Whilst this is useful, it can be time-consuming if you have to wait for a large spreadsheet to be recalculated each time you make an entry. Therefore you have the option to turn recalculate 'off' whilst you make several entries. However, you must remember to turn it back on again or all your work will have been wasted!
- **Replicating** (see below) – once you have decided on your formula it would be time-consuming to enter it dozens of times. For instance, if you are trying to find the sum of 50 columns you wouldn't want to enter a 'sum' formula 50 times. If you use the replicate command this copies your command across all the other columns you specify.

Did you know?

You can print out a spreadsheet with *either* the figures *or* the formula showing. The latter option can be useful if you have entered a difficult formula and need to remember what it is!

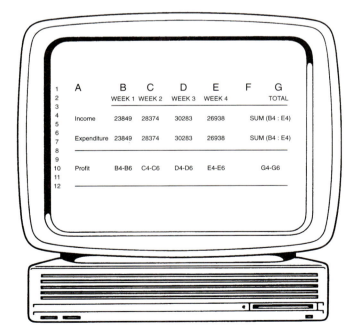

Figure IT.22 You can show figures or formulae

Using spreadsheet packages

1 Learn the basic commands (blank, edit and format) and how to enter figures and text.
2 Make sure you are aware of how to **load** a spreadsheet (from disk), **save** (to disk) and **print.** Learn how to clear the screen (which may be the command to **zap** the spreadsheet). If you are printing out a large spreadsheet on A4 paper you will need to know how to specify condensed (smaller) print.
3 Make sure you understand how to insert a formula. Simple formulae include add, subtract, multiply and divide. Remember that:
   - the answer will always be shown in the cell where the cursor is positioned
   - you can identify cells for inclusion in the formula or numbers, e.g. A1+C7 *or* A1+I8.
4 Understand the signs used for inserting formulae.
   - You can **add** by simply specifying cell names with a plus sign in between, e.g. A1+C3. However, this would be impractical for a large number of cells, so you need to find out how to enter a sum command for the package. This means the figures in any number of cells will be added together.
   - A subtraction is done by identifying the cells and inserting a subtraction sign, e.g. A1–B1.
   - Multiply is entered using the symbol *, e.g. B3*D7.
   - Divide is entered using the symbol /. Therefore D48/4 means divide the figure in cell D48 by 4.

Did you know?

When professional users insert the 'replicate' command, they never specify a basic range of cells but always add one on. Then if they need to insert an extra figure later the formula doesn't need to be altered!

Graphics and spreadsheets

Most spreadsheet packages will create a variety of graphics and charts, e.g. line graphs, bar charts and pie charts. The commands for creating these will vary from one package to another. Here are some tips to help.

- Decide on the type of graph or chart you want to produce.
- Work out:
   - the **headings** and **labels** which must be

included – each heading must appear somewhere in your spreadsheet; if it doesn't, then insert it in a blank cell, preferably one some distance from your main working area
  - identify the cells which you want to illustrate.

■ If you are creating a line graph or bar chart you need to know that the **vertical** axis is the *y*-**axis** and the **horizontal** axis is the *x*-**axis**, so that you can label them correctly.

■ Information that will be shown on the graph or chart is known as the **variables.** For instance, a bar chart with savings and expenditure has **two** variables, a bar chart for income, expenditure and profit has **three** variables, and so on. A pie chart can only have one variable or you would need more than one circle! You will need to know the range of cells in which each variable (set of information) is contained.

■ **Time labels** are only used on line graphs and bar charts. They refer to the time period the graph or chart is covering.

■ **Variable labels** are used to give a bar chart or line graph its **key** – otherwise no-one will understand what the lines or bars represent.

■ **Point labels** are the labels on a pie chart.

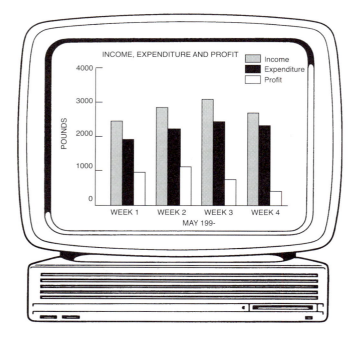

Figure IT.23 Graphs and graphics can be produced on computer spreadsheet programs

Graphics packages

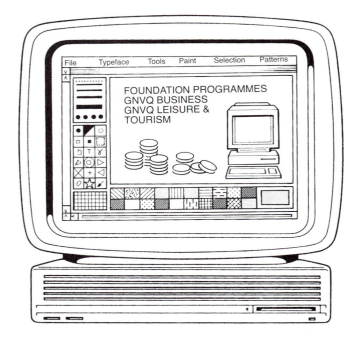

Figure IT.24 Graphics can be used to good advantage

Computer graphics can be used in business to create drawings, graphs and charts. They can be printed on paper, overhead transparencies or slides. Some packages are extremely sophisticated and can be used to create animation and even paintings – though an expensive colour printer would be required for the latter.

Virtually all require the use of a **mouse** to operate them. An alternative is to use a **graphics tablet** where the artist draws on a small area with an 'electronic pen'. Pointing to different options or, in some cases, just pressing harder, enables the artist to obtain different thicknesses of line, brush strokes and special effects.

Main features

■ **Pencil** – this is used to draw ordinary lines.
■ **Eraser** – to rub out mistakes!
■ **Spraycan** – to create a paint spray effect.
■ **Delete** – to remove lines or parts of an object.
■ **Copy** – replicates a drawing somewhere else.
■ **Move** – allows you to change the position of anything you have drawn.

- **Gridlock (snap to grid)** – enables you to position items precisely by aligning them to a predetermined set of points.
- **Toolbox** – may include different items, e.g. to enable you to cut out parts of your drawing.
- **Text** – enables you to add text to drawings.

Additional features

- **Rotate** – allows you to rotate a drawing to see it from different angles.
- **Zoom** – enables you to focus on a particular part of the drawing and enlarge it to allow you to make very precise changes.
- **Shapes** – gives a wide variety of shapes, e.g. squares, rectangles or circles, which can be positioned with the pointer.
- **Patterns** – enables you to fill in shapes with different patterns – or create some of your own.

Did you know?

1 Most of the graphics you see on television are produced on powerful computers, using sophisticated graphics packages. These may be animated to produce the movement you see on screen.

2 A **pixel** is a very small block of a drawing. The higher the resolution of your VDU the smaller (and the more numerous) are the pixels you have. You can therefore obtain greater detail in your drawing. If you zoom into a picture and enlarge it sufficiently, you normally see part of it pixel by pixel and you may be able to change each one of these separately.

Using graphics packages

1 Learn how to use the mouse – without it, drawing is impossible!

2 Find out how to load the program (and any files on disk), save and quit before you do anything else.

3 Play with the items in the toolbox or paintbox – see what effects you create. Don't be frightened to experiment – this is one case where you truly 'learn by doing'. You can always erase disasters, and if you select the wrong option then pressing 'Esc' (escape) will usually put you back to the beginning. Some of the facilities will not appear to be much use until you start to experiment, and seriously try to draw something.

4 Learn how to print out your work. The quality will be far higher if you have access to a laser printer.

Did you know?

Virtual reality (VR) is the name given to animated graphics that are so realistic the user feels as if he or she is are in the situation being portrayed. A headset contains stereo earphones for sound and the user either sits in a specially designed console or puts on a 'datasuit' so that all the movements of the body are electronically sensed.

Virtual reality systems are used for flight-test simulators, by architects and estate agents to 'walk' people through designs for buildings, and in computer arcade games. New applications include 'virtual' conferences (where you 'enter' a common computer-created environment to exchange information) and 'virtual' factories, where fashion designers and buyers can view and compare information on clothes worn by electronic models.

If you are tempted by the idea of having your own VR system, the price might put you off! The cost of a dedicated workstation is between £250 000 and £500 000 and programs start at about £6500!

Desktop publishing packages (DTP)

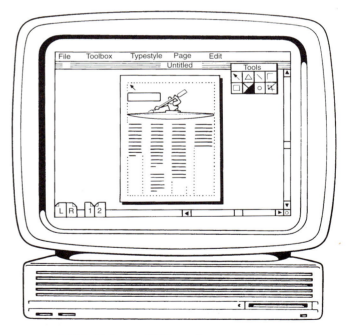

Figure IT.25 Using a DTP package

A desktop publishing package is neither a graphics package nor a word-processing package. It is one

639

that enables you to put together text and graphics to produce a variety of documents, e.g. notices, posters, reports, presentations, newspapers and even the pages of a book. However, DTP packages can also be used to design simple graphics, e.g. shaded boxes for title pages of a project. Complex graphics are created using other types of software and then 'imported' into the DTP package, where they are merged into one document, usually referred to as a **publication**.

Main features

- **Text** – this is usually input on a compatible word-processing package and then imported into the publication.
- **Fonts** – these are the different shapes and sizes of text characters. The variations you can achieve will depend on your printer, but there are many fonts from which you can choose (see page 624).
- **Graphics** – these are usually created by means of a drawing program or are input via a document scanner. All graphics should be 'clean' before they are scanned – otherwise it is time-consuming removing all the dirty marks that have also been scanned in.
- **Toolbox** – this will enable you to draw lines and shapes, shade them, and resize, cut or trim any graphics on your document.
- **Lines** – these can be drawn to any length, in a variety of thicknesses, and horizontally, vertically or at any angle.
- **Shades** – these can range from white through grey to black; some software offers full colour ranges, but you need a colour printer to take advantage of this.
- **Columns** – you can design your page to have columns if you wish (like a newspaper). To give them a professional look, draw vertical lines between them (as in your newspaper).

Additional features

- **Rulers** – these are guide lines which show on screen but not on your finished document. They enable you to align your text properly.
- **Guides** – these will enable you to position text and graphics more precisely.
- **Text wrap** – this will automatically wrap text around any drawings or graphics you import into your publication.

Did you know?

Clip-art is artwork, cartoons and designs that can be used without the usual reference to copyright considerations, provided you have paid for the clip-art feature. You can buy clip-art on disk and use it by importing it into your own document. You can resize it if you wish. At the back of this book are some examples of clip-art, which you can scan into your own computer, if you have a scanner, and use to enhance your own designs.

Using desktop publishing packages

1. Learn how to load the package, start a new publication and/or load a saved publication.

2. Learn how to use a mouse – essential for desktop publishing work.

3. Find out how to design your page, e.g. if you want columns of a certain number or width.

4. Find out how to import text you have produced on a word-processing package and how to adjust this to fit your columns.

5. Experiment with the different fonts and typefaces you have available to find out which you can use with your printer and which give the best effects.

6. Find out how to import or scan in graphics and how to size them. It is important that you keep the proportions of the image correct. If you alter the width but not the height – or vice versa – you will get a distorted picture!

7. Learn some of the basic rules about design, e.g. leaving white space for effect, not putting too much information on one page, and using margins effectively (see Element 3.2 page 330).

8. Don't be frightened to experiment. Some DTP packages are quite difficult to get used to – keep your ideas simple and straightforward to start with and you are more likely to be successful!

Did you know?

Hypermedia packages are now available which will store, retrieve and manipulate information in the form of text, graphics and **sound.** Today computers are commonplace in recording studios. They are linked to electronic instruments with a MIDI (musical instrument digital interface) socket e.g. a MIDI keyboard and the 'sound' is then transferred to the computer. Other effects can be added, e.g. rhythms via a drum machine, and laid down on separate tracks. A **sequencer** program is used to co-ordinate all the instruments and create the final product.

Multimedia is a merger of a number of technologies. You can watch television, play interactive games, see videos and even make telephone calls via your computer – when you are not using it for business applications or to play computer games or contact someone via Internet!

Accounting packages

This type of package is dealt with in full in Element 4.2, page 471.

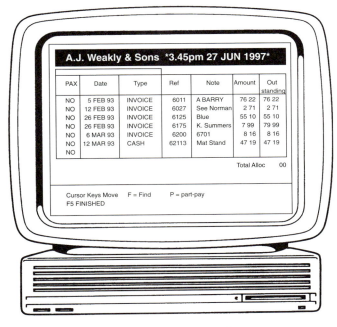

Figure IT.26 Using an accounts package

Payroll packages

These packages are very popular in many companies because they save hours of work, automatically calculating and producing wages documentation.

The package itself is actually a very sophisticated type of database that has been programmed with the latest National Insurance and income tax rates. If these change during the year, the suppliers of the package send an updated disk to their customers containing the new information. This is then loaded

Figure IT.27 Using a payroll package

into the computer and the rates are automatically revised.

Main features

Constant (i.e. unchanging) information about the company and the employees is entered. It is likely that *some* 'constant' details may change, e.g. an employee may move house, but generally the following items will remain unchanged for long periods.

- **Company details** – these include the name of the organisation, tax office reference, bank details, pay rates, etc.
- **Employee details** – the name and number of each employee, address, date of birth, NI number, tax code, rate of pay, bank details, union information, etc.

Variable data changes from one week or month to the next. It includes hours worked, overtime, holiday pay, sick pay and deductions. In a large organisation this may be entered on a daily basis.

Additional features

- **Payroll processing** – the system will automatically calculate the gross pay, deductions and net pay of each employee and print out the pay slip.

- **Cheque payments** – the package may print a list of cheques required or even print the actual cheques.
- **Credit transfers** – a list can be prepared of all personnel who will be paid direct through the banking system. This list can then be taken directly to the bank.
- **Year end process** – the package will produce P60s and P45s to meet Inland Revenue requirements, as well as providing a complete listing for the Inland Revenue.

Optional evidence assignment

If you undertake this assignment it can contribute to your evidence in the following areas.

Element 4.2: Identify and give examples of information technology which businesses use to record and monitor financial information (accounting software, spreadsheets)

Core skills: Communication and Information technology

Your brother owns his own business. He is a good salesman but has little knowledge of information technology. He employs two part-time staff and every week he moans about having to calculate their wages and keep his accounts. He has just found out that he will now have to register for VAT as his sales figures have risen above the minimum level for registration. This means even more accounts work, and he is becoming desperate.

He has also the chance of winning a large contract with a local organisation to supply goods to them over the next twelve months. However, they have asked him to attend a short presentation, during which he should bring charts showing his current sales figures to prove he runs a reliable business.

1. Write him a letter, using a word processor, telling him of the advantages of using a computer to do most of this work for him. Include details of one accounting package and one spreadsheet package that he could use in a small business. List their main features.
2. Enter his monthly sales figures for January to May on a spreadsheet (see Figure IT.28) and find the totals for each region and each month. Adjust column widths as necessary and rule off appropriately.

If you can, enter a formula to check that the total of the sales (horizontally) agrees with the total for each region when added together.

If you are able to produce graphs and charts on your package use the data to produce:

- a line graph, showing the performance of each region
- a bar chart, showing the sales per region per month
- a pie chart for just one month, showing the percentage of sales per region.

Sales by region						
	Jan	Feb	Mar	Apr	May	Total
South	8300	8966	9031	6890	7801	
Midlands	3898	4890	4881	3989	3991	
North	5897	5887	4789	5992	4118	
Scotland	3778	4283	4576	7503	3990	
Wales	5008	5882	5940	3082	4801	
N Ireland	3900	4800	5700	2890	4893	

Figure IT.28 Your brother's monthly sales figures

Quick reference section

The following is a list of IT terms you should know. Read them once and then check that *you* could write a definition for each one, which closely resembles that given below.

Note that words and phrases that are **highlighted in bold** in the explanations are those for which a separate definition is to be found elsewhere in the section.

Applications package A package containing a program designed to carry out a specific task for the benefit of the user, e.g. an accounts package or a word processing package, plus all the instructions and manuals for the program.

Backing store A device for storing programs and data, e.g. a disk drive.

Back-up copies Data copied on to floppy disks or a tape cartridge, for use if the original version develops a fault and becomes unreadable.

Bar code A pattern of bars and spaces, representing numbers, which can be read by a special computer scanner.

Bubble jet printer See *Ink jet printer*.

Buffer The part of memory that stores data temporarily, e.g. a printer buffer will hold documents until the printer is free to print them.

Bug An error in a program that causes it to fail or not to operate properly.

Byte The amount of computer memory required to store one character of data. A byte contains 8 bits. Computer memory is measured in bytes, e.g. **kilobytes** and **megabytes.**

CAD (computer-aided design) Using computers to create drawings for such purposes as engineering design and architecture. Designs may be two-dimensional, three-dimensional or even animated.

CAM (computer-aided manufacture) Using computers to help in the production of goods, e.g. by controlling robots or machines.

CD-ROM A compact disk that can be read but not written to (**read only memory**). The disk is manufactured with the data in place and this cannot be changed by the user.

Ceefax The BBC teletext service – a form of 'on-line' database.

CPU (central processing unit) The 'brain' of the computer, which processes information, carries out instructions and controls the peripherals.

Character set A set of symbols that can be recognised and used by the computer.

COM Computer output produced on microfilm or microfiche. This is often used with a mainframe computer

Computer graphics Pictures, photos, drawings and scanned images stored on computer or created by means of a **graphics package.**

Cursor The symbol on a screen showing the position where the next character will appear. It is usually a small flashing block, which may appear in reverse mode.

Database A program enabling the user to store, reorganise and extract data to give particular types of information.

Data communications The sending or receiving of data and information by telephone, fax or computer (e.g. electronic mail).

Data protection Safeguards for individuals to ensure that information about them held on computer is only used for specified purposes

Data security Measures taken to prevent data being lost or misused. e.g. user IDs, passwords and write-protect mechanisms on floppy disks.

Desktop publishing Packages which bring together text and graphics to produce newsletters, books, posters and other types of advertising material.

Digitiser A device enabling a video signal to be displayed on a computer.

Directory A list of file names under specific headings.

Disk A backing store for data.

Document reader An input device that recognises characters on preprinted documents.

DOS (disk operating system) The most common type of operating system for micro-computers

Dot matrix printer A printer that produces characters by making a pattern of small dots. The final result is not of the highest quality but is suitable for internal documents, e.g. payroll and accounts listings.

EPOS (electronic point of sale) Electronic cash registers that read bar codes via a scanner and automatically print itemised till receipts and adjust stock level records.

E-mail Electronic mail – messages are sent from one computer user to another, and stored in the user's personal mailbox.

File A collection of data in a computer's memory.

File access The ability to read or amend the data in a particular file.

Floppy disk A flexible and removable disk on which data is stored.

Font A set of printing characters of a particular design.

Format The layout and design of a document.

Gateway A computer linked to the Internet network.

Gigabyte Generally used to represent 1000 **megabytes.** More precisely, it is equal to 1024 megabytes.

Graphical user interface (GUI) The way in which a user communicates with the computer, i.e. by using a menu or clicking on an icon. The latter method involves the use of a **mouse.**

Graphics packages Programs enable drawings and paintings to be created on a computer.

643

Graphics tablet A device allowing drawings to be input to a computer by moving a stylus over a special pad.

Hacking Illegal access to a computer.

Hard disk A non-removable disk that can store large amounts of data.

Hardware The physical components of a computer system.

Hypermedia Software in which text, pictures and music may be linked to create a presentation.

Icon A small picture, used in a graphical user interface, which represents the function a user may wish to use.

Impact printer A printer that creates characters by hitting an inked ribbon, which transfers the image to the paper beneath.

Importing The practice of inserting text or graphics created in *one* package to a document created using *another*.

Ink jet printer A printer that creates graphics and text by spraying fine jets of ink onto paper.

Information referencing The generation of references – often as headers or footers – on a document, e.g. date, page, title.

Input device A device for entering data into a computer.

Joystick A vertical control stick that operates as an input device for computer games.

Justification The alignment of text to the left or right of a page.

Kilobyte A unit of computer memory, equal to 1024 bytes.

Laptop computer A portable micro-computer.

Laser printer A printer in which a high-quality image is formed by a laser beam.

Light pen An input device that can pinpoint certain locations on a computer screen.

LAN (local area network) A system linking computers over a small geographical area, e.g. between certain rooms or buildings.

Log off The process by which a network user exits the system.

Log on The process by which a network user identifies himself or herself to the system.

Mainframe computer A powerful computer with a very large data storage capacity.

Megabyte Memory equal to 1,024 kilobytes (sometimes used for 1 million bytes).

Memory The part of the computer in which programs and data are stored during operation.

Menu A list of options from which the user can choose.

MIDI (musical instrument digital interface) An interface enabling electronic musical instruments to be linked to a computer.

Modem A device allowing computer data to be transmitted over a telephone line.

Mouse An input device used to manipulate objects and select options on a computer screen.

Multimedia A combination system offering video/TV, sound systems, telephone, computer programs, etc.

Network A series of connected computers that share the same data and programs.

Notebook computer A small, portable computer.

OCR (optical character recognition) The means by which text can be recognised and input into a computer via a scanner.

On-line help Help given on screen by pressing a designated 'help' key.

Optical disks Laser disks that can store very large amounts of information.

Oracle The viewdata service provided by Independent Television.

Output device A device for displaying computer data and information.

Palmtop computer A tiny computer that can be held in the palm of a hand.

Password A secret code word confirming that a computer user is authorised for access.

Peripheral A device linked to or controlled by a computer.

Pixel A single dot on a computer screen.

Plotter An output device that draws pictures or diagrams, often in colour.

Prestel The viewdata service provided by British Telecom.

Publication A document produced on a desktop publishing system.

RAM (random access memory) Memory that can be read and changed by the user but from which data is lost when the computer is switched off.

ROM (read only memory) Memory that can only be read but cannot be changed, e.g. the basic operating system of the computer.

Reformatting Changing the design or format of a document, e.g. paragraph layout or column size.

Restructuring Radically changing the sequence of text in a document.

Root directory The top directory in a 'tree-and-branch' filing system.

Scanner A device that produces a digital image of a document for inputting and storing in a computer.

Scrolling Moving data on a VDU screen upwards or downwards to view lines at the top or bottom of the document.

Search A specific request for information by the user of a database or directory.

Search criteria Specific details to be searched for, e.g. gender and age details.

Smart card A plastic card that stores data. The data can be updated.

Software Computer programs.

Source information The origin of the data being input. This ranges from an original document to an idea in the mind of the operator.

Speech recognition The ability of a computer to respond to spoken commands.

Speech synthesis Computer generated speech (e.g. that used on telephone directory enquiries).

Spreadsheet A program enabling data to be input in rows and columns and to be subjected to calculations and analysis.

Systems program A program designed to enable the computer to operate.

Tape streamer A device that automatically compresses, transfers and stores a large amount of information onto tape. Used to back-up high capacity hard disks.

Touch screen A screen that enables the user to input data or initiate an action by touching certain parts of the screen.

Tree-and-branch filing A system where files are stored in directories. Main directories may be sub-divided into smaller directories, and so on.

User documentation Instructions and manuals provided with a computer program.

User ID The special name by which a computer system identifies a certain user.

Virtual reality Computer simulation where the participant perceives himself or herself as part of the simulated environment.

VDU (visual display unit) The screen on which computer data is displayed.

Virus Software that can transfer itself from one computer to another via floppy disk, and which can damage or destroy data.

Voice output *See Speech synthesis.*

WAN (wide area network) A network that connects computers over a wide geographical area.

Windows An operating system that controlled by pull-down menus. Windows 95 is the latest version.

Word-processor A program that allows for the manipulation, storage and retrieval of text.

Worksheet A spreadsheet currently being worked on.

WORM (write once read many times) Similar to a CD-ROM – but can be written to by means of a special device. Once the disk contains data it cannot be erased or replaced.

WYSIWYG (what you see is what you get) A program that shows documents in the same format as that in which they will be printed out.

Answers to Exercise 1 on page 540

1 I am sending you the items today.
2 Details of the new product are to be found on page 2.
3 I think you and I should have a meeting.
4 For what reason do you want this information? (or Why do you want this information?)
5 Neither the manager nor his assistant had heard about the change in plans.
6 He promised to deal urgently with the matter.

Answers to Non-assessed activity on page 542

1 He wants to see you and me.
2 The trainee forgot to read carefully the instructions (or to read the instructions carefully).
3 She is someone with whom I have always had difficulty (or – if you are stuck – I always find her difficult).
4 He never has any time for us.
5 I confirm our recent telephone conversation.
6 I should be pleased if you would provide the information I need (or I shall be pleased if you will provide the information I need).

Answers to Exercise 2 pages 542–3

To/too/two
- I have to see you immediately.
- There are two immediate improvements which can be made.
- It is far too warm in here.

There/their
- Put the shopping over there.
- There is no reason for the delay.
- Wher have they put their belongings?

Past/passed
- He passed me in the corridor without speaking to me.
- In the past he has been very helpful.
- He passed his examination and gained a distinction.

Of/off
- He is a man of few words.
- Please keep off the grass.

Whose/who's
- Who's waving at you?
- Whose coat have you borrowed?

Affect/effect
- What effect will these figures have on the overall position?
- Will it affect you at all?

Personal/personnel
- The personnel manager was concerned about the changes made to the staff training programme.
- My personal view is that it is too risky.

Practice/practise
- I think he must learn to practice what he preaches.
- The practice of using Ms rather than Mrs of Miss has increased over the past few years.

Answers to Exercise 3 on page 544

(Note that you may have slightly different answers to questions 3 and 4. Check with your tutor whether your answer is still correct.)

1
manufactured	made
terminate	end
emancipate	free
commencement	beginning
ascend	climb

2
- She asked for an estimate.
- The car reversed into the wall
- The noise from the engine was incessant
- The relief from the pain was only momentary.
- I can't get spare parts for your television as it is now obsolete.
- The supervisor found that the new employee was incompetent.
- The maintenance of the machinery is essential in our business.

3
- Can you include me when you are making arrangements for the trip to the match?
- If you can wait for a week or two I shall be able to give you the information them.
- Thank you for your help. It was most useful.

4
- 'At the beginning of the evening I was walking along the road when I saw a tramp trying to

break in to a parked car. I asked him what he was doing and he struck me hard across my face.

Answer to Exercise 4 on page 545

When we were little and had visitors to the house, grandma didn't read to us. Instead we talked to the visitors and tried to make them play games like 'hide and seek' with us. One visitor, Uncle Bernard, was particularly good at this although sometimes he got bored and shouted, 'I'm here'. The game then ended.

Answer to first Non-assessed activity on page 545

You may remember that I raised the matter of an exchange visit with colleagues working in a college in San Diego. I have now reveived a request from them to send details of anyone interested in taking part in this exchange. It may be necessary to have a meeting to discuss the matter further. Give me a ring if you are interested.

Answers to second Non-assessed activity on page 545

- I got up late, had no breakfast and ran all the way to the bus stop.
- I sent him to the shop to buy paint, wallpaper and brushes.
- Fatima, please answer the telephone.
- James and Richard, the two best tennis players, met in the final.

Answers to first Non-assessed activity on page 546

Don't worry, I know she'll be here before long. In the meantime, can you try to borrow Frank's calculator. Yours is not working. John's not in because he's gone to collect the Managing Director's car. Its also important for you to make certain that all the typists's desks conform to the health and safety standards.

Answers to second Non-assessed activity on page 546

- The chairman said, 'I welcome you to this meeting'.
- Which television personality uses the catch phrase, 'Nice to see you, to see you, nice'?
- I had never heard of the expression 'It's not over until the fat lady sings'.

Answers to third Non-assessed activity on page 546

- There are many colleges in Britain.
- She want to attend Bristol University.
- Many and Danny went to Nottingham to visit the firm and to see the Human Resources Manager.

Answer to Exercise 5 on page 547

In business you must be good at accounts. You should be able to check figures accurately and also to calulate the correct amount each time. It is helpful if you can remember to write clearly and to separate one line of figures from another. Only competent managers are promoted.

Blank documents for photocopying

QUALPRINT LTD.

22 CARNEI WAY
GLENDALE
NEWSHIRE
FE1 8CA

Tel: 01323 745612

ORDER

VAT Reg No 680/73842/88

To:

Date:

Order No:

Please supply

QUANTITY	DESCRIPTION	REF. NO.	UNIT PRICE

Delivery:

Signed:

QUALPRINT LTD.

Goods Received Note

Supplier

GRN No:
Date
Delivery Note No.:

ORDER NO.	QUANTITY	DESCRIPTION	REF NO.

Received by _____

QUALPRINT LTD.

22 CARNEI WAY
GLENDALE
NEWSHIRE
FE1 8CA

TEL: 01323 745612

VAT Reg No: 680/73842/88

INVOICE

To:

Deliver to:

Your order no.	Invoice date tax point	Invoice no.	Despatch date

Quantity	Description	Cat. no.	Unit price	Total price	VAT rate	VAT amount
			Delivery charge			
			Sub-total			
			VAT			
			Total amount due			

Terms:
E & OE

QUALPRINT LTD.

22 CARNEI WAY
GLENDALE
NEWSHIRE
FE1 8CA

TEL: 01323 745612

FAX: 01323 849783

VAT Reg No: 680/73842/88

DELIVERY NOTE

To:

Your order no.	Invoice date/tax point	Invoice no.	Despatch date

Quantity	Description	Cat No.

Received by _____   Date _____

QUALPRINT LTD.

22 CARNEI WAY
GLENDALE
NEWSHIRE
FE1 8CA

TEL: 01323 745612

FAX: 01323 849783

VAT Reg No: 680/73842/88

To:

CREDIT NOTE

Credit Note No.	Invoice no.	Date

Quantity	Description	Cat. no.	Unit price	Total price	VAT rate	VAT amount
			Delivery charge			
			Sub-total			
			VAT			
			Total amount due			

Terms:
E & OE

QUALPRINT LTD.

22 CARNEI WAY
GLENDALE
NEWSHIRE
FE1 8CA

TEL: 01323 745612

FAX: 01323 849783

VAT Reg No: 680/73842/88

STATEMENT

To:

Date

Account no.

Date	Details	Debit	Credit	Balance

REMITTANCE ADVICE

Please send this slip, together with your remittance, to

QUALPRINT LTD
22 Carnei Way
Glendale
Newshire
FE1 8CA

All cheques should be made payable to Qualprint Ltd

Invoice name and address:

Account No: Date:

Date of statement:

Amount owing:

Payment enclosed: ....

Cheque No.: ....

Your ref: ....

PAY ADVICE

		Pay period	
Emp no.	Employee name	Dept	Tax code

Pay and allowances			NI no		Method of payment
Hrs	Rate (£)	Amount (£)	Deductions		Total pay to date
			Item	Amt (£)	
					Tax to date
					NI to date
					Taxable pay to date
GROSS PAY			Total deductions		net pay

Date _____

✗ The Royal Midshire Bank plc

Date _____ 199____

16-13-99

Pay _____ only

ACCOUNT PAYEE

£

£ _____

265541

265541   16:13:99   12890635…

Date _____

✗ The Royal Midshire Bank plc

Date _____ 199____

16-13-99

Pay _____ only

ACCOUNT PAYEE

£

£ _____

265541

265541   16:13:99   12890635…

PETTY CASH VOUCHER   NO _____   Date _____

Name		Dept	

Purpose, attach all receipts & invoices	TOTAL incl. VAT	VAT	Net excl. VAT
The sum of in words as far to the left as possible	£	£	£

Approved by _____ date _____

Received by _____ date _____

QUALPRINT LTD.

22 CARNEI WAY
GLENDALE
NEWSHIRE
FE1 8CA

RECEIPT

No.

RECEIVED FROM _____

the sum of _____

_____ £

in payment of _____

_____

Received _____ Date _____

QUALPRINT LTD.

22 CARNEI WAY
GLENDALE
NEWSHIRE
FE1 8CA

RECEIPT

No.

RECEIVED FROM _____

the sum of _____

_____ £

in payment of _____

_____

Received _____ Date _____

659

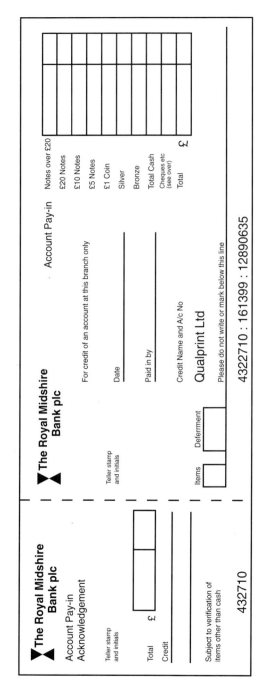

BRAMLEY PRODUCTS LTD

FALLOWFIELD LANE
HIGHTOWN
HG4 9GT

Tel: 01323 918279

Fax: 01323 246426

MESSAGE FORM

TO .... DEPT ....
DATE .... TIME ....

CALLER'S NAME ....
ORGANISATION ....
TEL NO .... **EXT NO** ....

Telephoned ☐
Returned your call ☐
Called to see you ☐
Left a message ☐

Please return call ☐
Please arrange appointment ☐

Message:
....
....
....
....
....

Taken by: .... Dept ....

MESSAGE FORM

TO .... DEPT ....
DATE .... TIME ....

CALLER'S NAME ....
ORGANISATION ....
TEL NO .... **EXT NO** ....

Telephoned ☐
Returned your call ☐
Called to see you ☐
Left a message ☐

Please return call ☐
Please arrange appointment ☐

Message:
....
....
....
....
....

Taken by: .... Dept ....

BRAMLEY PRODUCTS

M E M O

TO

FROM

DATE

SUBJECT

LANDSHIRE COUNTY COUNCIL JOB APPLICATION FORM	FORM ESC/3

Application for the post of...

Please use block capitals for Sections 1, 4 and 8

1   Surname..
      First name (s) ....
2   Date of birth...
3   Address ....
      ....
      ....

4   Present post ....
      ....

5   Previous post ....
      ....
      ....

6   Education
      (Please give details of secondary school/college/university attended –
      together with starting and leaving dates)
      ....
      ....
      ....

7   Qualifications
      (Please include dates, subjects and grades)
      ....
      ....
      ....
      ....

8   Referees
      (Please give the names and addresses of two persons to whom
      reference can be made)
      ....
      ....
      ....
      ....
      ....

9   Signature..   Date..............................

Computer Supplies

14 Waterside Road
HIGHTOWN
HG4 9DS

Tel: 01323 584798

VAT Reg No 930/493280/76

Fax: 01323 494955

To:

Date:

Date	Details	Debit	Credit	Balance

Index